SUNDERLAND
THE COMPLETE RECORD

SUNDERLAND
THE COMPLETE RECORD

MIKE GIBSON   ROB MASON   BARRY JACKSON

First published in Great Britain in 2012 by The Derby Books Publishing Company Limited, 3 The Parker Centre, Derby, DE21 4SZ.

© Rob Mason, Mike Gibson and Barry Jackson, 2012

All Rights Reserved. No part of this publication may be reproduced, stored in a retrieval system, or transmitted in any form, or by any means, electronic, mechanical, photocopying, recording or otherwise without the prior permission in writing of the copyright holders, nor be otherwise circulated in any form or binding or cover other than in which it is published and without a similar condition being imposed on the subsequent publisher.

ISBN 978-1-78091-021-5
Printed and bound by Oz Graf.

Contents

Foreword by Ellis Short, Chairman of SAFC	6
Foreword by Martin O'Neill, Manager of SAFC	7
Introduction	8
Acknowledgements	11
The Greatest Season	12
The History of Sunderland AFC	24
Wartime Fooball	109
Footballers of World War One	118
Footballers of World War Two	124
World War One Games	134
World War Two Games	136
Sunderland Stadia	144
For Us All	166
What's in A Name?	167
Sunderland Chairmen	168
James Allan	194
Sunderland Managers	196
Top Teams	234
The SAFC Badge	262
Matches to Remember	263
Match Programmes	298
Why are Sunderland called the Black Cats?	308
Season by Season	310
Summary of Sunderland's League Seasons	542
Sunderland Head to Head Records	548
Sunderland in the League 1890-2012	604
Sunderland in the FA Cup 1884-2012	607
Sunderland in the League Cup 1960-2012	609
Sunderland Games that have been abandoned	610
Landmarls in Sunderland AFC History	611
Sunderland's Pre-League Friendlies and Minor Cup Games	613
Sunderland's Friendlies, Testimonials and Minor Cups Since1890 (Exc. Wartime)	619
Sunderland's Christmas and New Year Games	636
Sunderland's Easter Games	640
Players with 200 first team Appearances	644
Sunderland Fastest Goals	645
Goalkeeping Records	646
Sunderland's Record Signings	648
Sunderland Debut Scorers	650
Top 10s and Sunderland Miscellany	652
Attendances	658
Players Sent Off For Sunderland	659
Sunderland Shirt Sponsorship	663
On Stage At Sunderland	664
Player Of The Year	667
Players On Loan To Sunderland	669
Sunderland Foreign Born Players	671
Most Capped Individual Players	673
Players Capped While With Sunderland	674
Career Records	688
Roll Of Honour	722

Foreword

Ellis Short, Chairman of SAFC

Over 13 decades of existence means that Sunderland AFC has a long and fascinating history. The journey stretches from the earliest days of a group of schoolteachers introducing the sport to the area, to the present day where the club are part of the most watched League in the world playing in a magnificent stadium in front of truly passionate fans.

This enormously detailed and meticulously researched official record of the club provides the definitive reference book covering every aspect of the club from 1879 to 2012. Every detail of every match is included along with an in depth narrative that gives every reader the opportunity to become an expert.

From the pioneers of the late 1870s through the good times and the bad, Sunderland's supporters have remained constantly behind the club. With such a magnificent history, in the modern era we are seeking to build on what has been achieved in the past. We have a passionate and accomplished manager in Martin O'Neill and are building what we hope will be an exciting side that will bring more good times and more exciting chapters for the future.

It is my privilege to be chairman of this great club and this Complete Record is befitting a club of Sunderland's stature. I trust you will enjoy it.

Best wishes
Ellis Short

FOREWORD

Martin O'Neill, Manager of SAFC

In football the most important game is the next one. You have to look forward and be constantly trying to improve. However, now in 2012 what has made football the world's most popular sport is a rich history that goes back to Victorian times. Since its formation way back in 1879, Sunderland has built a truly splendid story that includes many fabulous footballers, some wonderful games and the highs and lows of sporting endeavour covering times of glory and of frustration.

Some supporters who still come to watch Sunderland can tell of the great days of Charlie Hurley, Jim Montgomery and Johnny Crossan. More recently people talk with joy of Kevin Phillips and Niall Quinn and there are those still able to recall Len Shackleton, Trevor Ford and the players of the fifties. The careers of these and every one of the 900 plus players to have played in League or Cup for the club over the decades can be traced in fine detail in this Complete Record of Sunderland AFC.

It is a book for the football purist, the person interested in everything to do with the football club. Right from day one the history of the club is charted: every player, manager and chairman is covered as is every game including friendlies and wartime matches. Every international appearance by a player on Sunderland's books is included as is every individual and team record. Ultimately this is the book you will go to in order to settle any debate about anything to do with the club.

I am honoured to be the manager of Sunderland and to be charged with the task of doing all I can to help the next chapter of the club's history to be an enjoyable one.

All the best,
Martin O'Neill

INTRODUCTION

The Norfolk Hotel, Sunderland. The club was founded here in 1879 when the building was the British Day School.

When the first edition of 'Sunderland: The Complete Record' was published in 2005 our aim was to produce the definitive reference book on the club. We were delighted with the response as many supporters and journalists provided unstinting praise for the publication that quickly sold out and has since been sold for over four times its face value.

To commemorate the centenary of the club's finest ever season; when the Football League was won for a fifth time and combined with a first appearance in the FA Cup Final, we have once again burned much midnight oil in producing this greatly expanded second volume of The Complete Record. Amongst the new additions to this second edition are:

- A celebration of the 1912-13 season.
- A record of all known friendlies played by Sunderland.
- Head to Head records against every other club.
- Biographies of all Sunderland Chairmen.
- A chapter on wartime football along with appearances and fixtures.
- A team of the decade for each decade.
- A record of abandoned games.
- SAFC landmarks
- Christmas, Easter and New Year's Day games.
- Goalkeeping records.
- Substitute records.
- Quickest to 50 goals.
- Fastest goals.
- Shirt sponsorship.
- Players of the Year.
- On loan players.
- Foreign born players.

INTRODUCTION

Additionally all other chapters have been updated and expanded. A much more in depth history of match programmes is included – not least because the authors of this book all make significant contributions to Sunderland's official programme *Red and White*. Similarly the chapter on Sunderland stadia is considerably enlarged as a happy consequence of the original edition.

Since the first volume of *Sunderland: The Complete Record* ongoing work by the authors developed into a project to place blue plaques on the sites of all of Sunderland's former grounds as well as the building in which the club was formed in 1879. This project is now complete with all plaques in place and so far two guided tours of the sites have been taken by the authors in conjunction with English Heritage.

We wrote in the introduction to the first volume that, 'Every effort has been made to ensure that the facts in this book are correct. Past experience with other publications shows us that sometimes new information can emerge following publication.' This has proved to be the case, one example being greater detail provided in the club history chapter about the attendees of the inaugural meeting that formed the club in 1879.

We hope that the publication of this second edition will help yet more information about Sunderland AFC to come to light. The authors would be pleased to receive any such information in writing to:

SAFC Publications, The Stadium of Light, Sunderland SR5 1SU
or via email to redandwhite@safc.com

All of Sunderland's successful teams have been based on partnerships. Examples include the famous 'Roker triangle' of Cuggy, Mordue and Buchan who 100 years ago became the only trio of Sunderland players to play in the same international for England. While we cannot claim such recognition the three of us who have worked on this volume have certainly worked with the same sense of team-work. While each of us have had responsibilities for certain sections there has been great collaboration with all of 'The Stadium of Light triangle' helping each other out, offering feedback, support and suggestions along the way.

We hope that you enjoy the book, forgive us anything we may have made a mistake on in a book of so much data, and that like us you hope that indeed SAFC's record is not yet complete and that under Ellis Short and Martin O'Neill, to whom we are grateful for writing the Forewords, Sunderland still have great days ahead.

Rob Mason
Mike Gibson
Barry Jackson
August 2012.

Acknowledgements

Chris Gibson   (for data checking, proof reading and putting up with the all of the paperwork associated with the book)

Alan & Barbara Gibson   (for data checking, historical information and sparking the passion for Sunderland AFC)

Judith Jackson
Matthew Jackson
Barbara Mason
Andrew Smithson
Alan Candlish
Peter Holme
Eric Doig
Keith Gregson
Roy Berry
Hans de Roon
John Hendley
Bill Tate
Sunderland Central Library
Newcastle Central Library
Leeds City Library
Stoke-on-Trent City Library
Bury Library
Middlesbrough Library
National Football Museum Archives
Sunderland Echo
Newcastle Journal
Athletic News
Sporting Chronicle

THE GREATEST SEASON

Sunderland have enjoyed many great seasons. On a dozen occasions the club have topped the division they have been in, there have been three other promotions, two FA Cup wins and three other occasions when they have been finalists in a national Cup competition. Truly great teams have donned the stripes such as the all conquering team of the mid thirties, the Team of All The Talents who won the League three seasons out of four in the 1890s and of course Stokoe's Stars of 1973 who produced the most sensational of FA Cup triumphs. Surely though there can be no dispute that Sunderland's greatest ever season was that of 1912-13.

In re-issuing this updated and expanded volume of *Sunderland The Complete Record* we celebrate the centenary of that season when Sunderland combined winning the League title with reaching the FA Cup Final for the first time. Doing the 'double' of winning the League and the FA Cup in the same season has long been the holy grail of football clubs. The FA Cup – the creation of Sunderland born C.W. Alcock – is the world's oldest football competition, the first games having taken place on 11 November 1871. The world's oldest football League competition staged its opening fixtures on 8 September 1888. Preston North End were the first team to do the 'double' in the Football League's very first season and Aston Villa followed them in 1896-97 after which no side achieved the double until Bill Nicholson's 'Push and run' Tottenham side in 1960-61 – when even according to Spurs' own official history the nearest they came to being de-railed was at Roker Park in the Cup quarter-final. In that span of over half a century Sunderland came as close as any club to adding their name to the illustrious few to have been winners of both Cup and League in the same season.

Aston Villa were Sunderland's rivals in 1912-13, eventually the clubs denying each other the double as Sunderland pipped Villa in the League while Villa beat the Lads in the Cup Final. This wasn't the only time Villa had ended Sunderland's hopes of achieving the double. In both 1891-92 and 1894-95 Villa beat Sunderland in FA Cup semi-finals in seasons where the Lads won the League. Astonishingly between Villa's double of 1897 and Tottenham's of 1961 Villa were the team to thwart the aspirations of all three teams to win the League and reach the Cup Final in that period. As well as Sunderland in 1913, Newcastle United in 1905 and Manchester United in 1956 both also lost to Villa in the Cup Final in years when they were champions. Even when Tottenham did the double in 1961, it was Villa who carried off the newly created League Cup in the same season.

Sunderland went into the 1912-13 season having finished eighth, the previous season but third in two of the three years before that. The title had last been brought to Wearside a decade earlier in 1902 but in the Cup only in 1909 – when a home replay had been lost to Newcastle – had the Lads got as far as the quarter-finals since the semi-final appearance of 1895.

Sunderland's beaten FA Cup Final team of 1912-13.

Secretary-'manager' Bob Kyle was entering his eighth season and was yet to win a trophy. The League title had been won four times in the 15 seasons played as a League club before Kyle's appointment with three more of those seasons having seen Sunderland runners' up, still higher than Kyle's best finish of third.

Much is made of Sunderland's terrible start to what would be their greatest season but in fact they did well on the opening day, drawing away to Newcastle who had finished third the previous year when they had defeated Sunderland 3-1 on Tyneside. Debuting for Sunderland at St James' Park was centre-forward Jimmy Richardson, a player who would take a while to get going following an early season injury but would eventually end up with 17 goals from 27 appearances including the one that would mathematically seal the title. However it was Jackie Mordue who got Sunderland's goal, equalizing United's opener from Albert Shepherd.

From there though things went rapidly downhill with just one point gleaned from the next half dozen games. Two of these were against reigning champions Blackburn who twice stuck four goals past goalkeeper Walter Scott who was duly sacked after the second of these defeats after he missed training. The goalkeeper complained in the *Sunderland Echo* about the stick he had received from the crowd. The next home game saw another goalkeeper play his last game for the Lads, George Anderson at least helping earn a 2-2 draw with Spurs before a meagre attendance of 8,000.

A week later a 2-0 loss at Chelsea left Sunderland in 19th place out of 22 with just two points. A head start had been given to the rest of the League. Newcastle by this time had nine points with just one defeat – but would end the season in fourteenth place, 20 points behind Sunderland who would also knock them out of the Cup on their own turf. Villa, who would run Sunderland closest, had 10 points and on the day Sunderland lost at Chelsea, they thrashed eventual third placed 'Wednesday' 10-0 with centre-forward Harry Hampton netting five. Not officially known as Sheffield Wednesday until 3 August 1929, 'Wednesday' had won four and drawn one of their five games prior to their double-digit defeat at Villa, including beating champions Blackburn on the opening day. With just two points for a win in those days Sunderland looked to be in for a relegation battle rather than a charge for the Championship.

The club itself had been formed a third of a century earlier in October 1879 and the turning point of this greatest season coincided almost exactly with the anniversary of the club's formation. Local rivals Middlesbrough came to Roker just four places better off than Sunderland but the Teessiders were unbeaten in their last four games. Sunderland needed to tighten up defensively and a first clean sheet of the season was as valuable as the four goals put past Boro's goalkeeping captain and England international R.G. 'Tim' Williamson.

Following the opening 1-1 draw at Newcastle, Sunderland had conceded 17 goals in the six subsequent games and never less than two in a match. Beginning with this clean sheet against Boro only 32 more would be let in in the remaining 40 League and Cup games. In these 40 fixtures only a 3-1 reverse at West Brom would witness more than two goals leaked and of the six games where two were conceded only one of those games would be lost as the forwards found their shooting boots.

Like all clubs, over the years Sunderland have had failures as well as successes in the transfer market but rarely if ever can they have made such an effective double raid. The

THE GREATEST SEASON

Sunderland's FA Cup Final v Aston Villa in 1913. Lower half: Charlie Thompson (left) and 'keeper Joe Butler.

scouting system was evidently working magnificently as full-back Charlie Gladwin arrived from a Blackpool side that although it won three of the last five games he played prior to his move to the North East, would fall away badly after his departure and end up propping up the bottom of the two tier Football League. Similarly goalkeeper Joe Butler came from Glossop North End, then of the Second Division where they finished third from bottom in both the season of, and the season before, Butler's transfer to Sunderland.

This pair of astute purchases transformed Sunderland's season. Any successful team needs strong foundations and in goalie Butler and tough tackling Gladwin Sunderland established a rock on which to build. Butler's bow came in the game at Stamford Bridge with his home debut coinciding with Gladwin's first appearance in the hammering of Middlesbrough.

Beating Boro was the first of five successive wins which saw 19 goals scored and just three conceded, resulting in a swift climb to eleventh place. Added to that run of maximum points from five games was an additional win at Newcastle, who were beaten 1-0 at St James' in an Archibald Cup game in aid of Newcastle and Sunderland hospitals. George Holley scoring while Butler and Gladwin contributed to an additional clean sheet.

The winning run was punctuated at Hyde Road where George Wynn got the winner for Manchester City, where Sunderland would later return in the FA Cup. Next up was the first of the season's meetings with Aston Villa who remained in fine form. Starting with that 10-0 triumph over Wednesday the midlanders had remained unbeaten and had scored 30 goals in their last seven games. A crowd of 35,000 – the biggest for a home League game since a visit by Newcastle over three years earlier – saw first half goals by George Holley and Charlie Buchan put Sunderland in control and though Harry Hampton pulled one back after the break, a penalty from Jackie Mordue sealed a victory that lifted the Lads into the top ten for the first time that season and sparked Villa's poorest run of the campaign as they took only a single point from four games. All four of the goalscorers in the heavyweight meeting at Roker Park would play for England later in the season.

Sunderland's progress would be halted at Villa's near neighbours West Bromwich Albion the following Saturday where the aforementioned 3-1 defeat dropped Sunderland back into the bottom half of the table for the last time that season.

Charlie Buchan is Sunderland's all time record League goalscorer and in the next game became the first player to score five goals in a League match for Sunderland as he fired the Wearsiders to a 7-0 win over Liverpool, still managed by Sunderland's secretary-manager of the Team of All The Talents, Tom Watson. A week later, Merseysiders wanting to see the team who had slaughtered Liverpool had the chance to do so at Goodison Park where this time Everton were walloped 4-0 before a home win over Bolton saw the Final appearance for Wanderers of Tom Barber – who would go on to score the winning goal in the Cup Final for Villa against Sunderland later in the season.

Christmas Day saw Sunderland in Sheffield where a 2-1 win narrowed the gap with the 'Wednesday' dropping them from third to fifth and seeing Sunderland climb from ninth to a best yet seventh. Twenty-four hours later though the tables were turned as Wednesday goals from Davie McLean and Sam Kirkman defeated Sunderland and restored the clubs to their pre-Christmas positions. Still it was an improvement on a year earlier as on Boxing Day 1911, McLean had scored four and Kirkman two as Wednesday inflicted a record 8-0 defeat on Sunderland that has never been surpassed, The Owls being 7-0 up by half-time on that occasion.

Sunderland soon got over their first home defeat since the arrival of Butler and Gladwin. The pair had only ever tasted victory at Roker Park, Butler having played every game and Gladwin just missing a single match, the 7-0 win over Liverpool which had allowed Billy Troughear to make his 100th and last League appearance for the club. Just two days after the defeat by Wednesday there was the matter of Newcastle United being in town when the season's best home gate of 35,000 against Villa was matched.

Although the defeat of two days earlier had dropped Sunderland to ninth, the table was so tight that the Wearsiders were only three points adrift of the three teams level at the top of the table: Villa, WBA and Wednesday. By this stage Newcastle were eleventh. Sunderland were simply too good for the Magpies, winning 2-0 with both goals created by Richardson and scored by Holley while the crossbar prevented further embarrassment for the visitors as it denied Buchan, Mordue and Gladwin, the latter rattling it with a shot from outside the box as Sunderland ended 1912.

From a handsome New Year's Day win over Woolwich Arsenal, Sunderland would win every game bar two draws and one defeat in the League to the end of the season, meaning that from the win over Newcastle 32 out of 36 points were won.

Woolwich Arsenal meanwhile finished bottom of the League, no team ever having had fewer points, goals scored or wins other than in the first two seasons of the League when 16 fewer games were played. The Gunners never won promotion back to the top flight but were restored to it after the First World War when after finishing fifth in the last season before the League ceased for the war, they were added to the expanded top flight ahead of Barnsley and Wolves who had finished above the Londoners. Having benefitted from that stroke of fortune The Gunners have since surpassed Sunderland's long held record (1890-1958) of unbroken membership of the top flight.

No one was to surpass Sunderland's form in the run in to the end of the 1912-13 season however but after the Arsenal game attention turned to the FA Cup. Having been champions four times but never having got past the semi-final of the Cup, Wearsiders longed for the glamour of Cup success. While those 35,000 attendances against Villa and Newcastle had been the biggest in the League the previous Cup tie on Wearside had pulled in over 43,000. It was a more modest 12,000 though who saw lowly Second Division outfit Clapton Orient beaten 6-0 with four goals from Jimmy Richardson in the first round.

A replay was needed in the next round but rather than being due to the result of the game at Manchester City the re-arranged game was due to an abandonment following a pitch invasion at Hyde Road where Sunderland were leading 2-0 after which the FA ordered the tie to be re-staged at Roker. So it was that 60 years before City were beaten in the game voted the best ever at Roker Park in an FA Cup tie en route to the famous win of 1973, City came north and as in 1973 lost by a two goal margin.

Given a home draw against Southern League Swindon Town attention re-focussed on the League. Whereas the first win of the season had come against Middlesbrough on 12 October the return fixture at Ayresome Park four months later saw Sunderland go to the top of the table, for the first time since December 1910.

Victory over Swindon would take Sunderland into the quarter-final stage but the visit of the Southern Leaguers could not be a foregone conclusion. Swindon had been semi-finalists in two of the previous three seasons – the last non-League club to reach the last four. In 1910 they had lost to Newcastle after numbering top flight Spurs amongst their victims while in 1912 they had taken Barnsley to a replay at the semi-final stage after knocking out First Division Notts County and Everton.

With 4ft 10in referee Mr J. Talks of Lincoln in charge Sunderland made short work of The Robins, racing into a 2-0 lead within four minutes before going through 4-2 and the prospect of Newcastle in the next round. Highlight of the game was Charlie Gladwin's only goal for Sunderland – a free kick from 60 yards. Sunderland are not known to have scored a goal from greater distance.

So it was that a three game duel with the Magpies took place. As Sunderland progressed after a second replay it meant that including the charity game there were six Wear-Tyne derbies during the season with Sunderland remaining unbeaten. Not unusually for big games at the time Sunderland took the step of doubling admission charges and though people queued for well over three hours before the 3.30 kick off, the game attracted under 30,000 for what proved a dour goalless draw.

The replay had the same tied outcome but was a much better match. Level with four minutes to go Sunderland looked to have grabbed a winner when Buchan nodded home a Mordue corner. There was still time though for United to force extra-time. 1912-13 saw a change in the rules that meant defenders had to retreat 10 yards rather than six for a free kick and it was from a dead ball on the edge of the box that one of the Magpies all time greats, Colin Veitch, scored with the help of a deflection from Gladwin. That night Gladwin knocked a man off a tramcar after overhearing a suggestion that he'd been bribed to put through his own net.

With the sides still not separated after extra-time the respective secretaries tossed a coin for the right to stage a second replay, United's Frank Watt calling correctly, meaning that five days later the sides and spectators reconvened at St James' Park for Newcastle's fourth home game of the season against their local rivals.

The second replay took place on a Monday. 48 hours before Sunderland had played at Manchester United where they won 3-1, Buchan bagging a couple while Newcastle had lost 1-0 at home to Blackburn Rovers but had had the advantage of not having to travel. Despite Sunderland needing to maintain their challenge for the title, the pull of the Cup was indicated by the fact that the trip to Old Trafford; to face a side good enough to finish fourth, saw Jackie Mordue miss his only game of the season while captain Charlie Thomson and half-back Harry Low also missed the trip. In their places Jack Small made his only Sunderland appearance, Bobby Best played one of only three games he was selected for all season and Billy Cringan came in for one of 10 appearances he made in the campaign.

Thomson and Low had been selected for Scotland's game against Ireland in Dublin on the Saturday before the second replay but withdrew from the squad in Sunderland's cause. In Low's case he was never called up again and remained uncapped but Thomson was back in his international side as captain for their next game against England. Low's brother Wilf was a full international who played for Newcastle and was in opposition to him in the Cup ties. Sunderland may well have been without the influential George Holley as well as he was called up by England for their game with Wales on the day of the second replay but – sportingly supported by Newcastle – he was released from the England squad by the FA so he could line up for Sunderland. Without him England beat the Welsh 4-3 – Villa's Hampton notching the winner.

Languishing in mid table, Newcastle could devote all their energies to the Cup. It was little surprise that they lost at home to Blackburn as they fielded a second string side in order to keep their men fresh for the big Cup tie. Only goalkeeper Jimmy Lawrence and inside forward John McTavish played on the Saturday and against Sunderland.

Fresh legs were to no avail though as just as in the earlier League game at Sunderland when Richardson twice set up Holley, the same combination unhinged Newcastle as early as the eighth minute. The pair later linked to find the net again only for the 'goal' to be controversially disallowed for an alleged handball by Holley. Nonetheless the visitors doubled their advantage before the break. Having missed out on the possibility of a cap for his country Harry Low had the satisfaction of making a telling contribution. He was brought down in the box by Veitch (though some reports say the victim was winger Harry Martin) and Mordue duly converted.

Newcastle scrapped to get back into the game but found the Butler saw everything early as he offered Sunderland first class service in goal. With quarter of an hour to go Sunderland sealed the victory with one of the classic derby goals. Fed by Buchan, Mordue danced round the home defence before slotting the ball home. Newcastle had given it everything. They'd had home advantage for 210 of the 300 minutes of the tie, had nine men who hadn't played in the League fixtures two days before and had still been trounced on their own patch, only their second home Cup defeat in 17 years. In this greatest of seasons this was one of the greatest of days as Sunderland progressed to the semi-final of the Cup. Plenty of Sunderland supporters had travelled to the match after Bob Kyle had 'Match On' posters printed and paraded around Sunderland by sandwich board men to let people on snow bound Wearside know that the match was going ahead.

For all the importance of the Cup there was still a League title to win and now Sunderland had three games to play before the semi-final of the Cup where they were drawn to face Second Division Burnley at Sheffield United's Bramall Lane. Maximum points were accrued from those three games over the four days of Easter, the last of which was at Bramall Lane in the League.

Going into the semi five days later as table toppers Sunderland met stiff resistance from a Burnley side seeking their own double as they were en route to promotion. As in the quarter-final the first ninety minutes were goalless. Three days later the sides replayed at St Andrew's in Birmingham where despite Buchan heading Sunderland in front after only six minutes, the Lads trailed at half-time, Freeman and Boyle putting the Wearsiders in arrears. Having conceded a penalty in the first half Sunderland levelled through Mordue with one of their own before Holley took Sunderland to their first Cup Final with a late winner.

With the title race neck and neck Sunderland could not afford to bask in the glory of having reached the Cup Final. Only the League visits of Villa and Newcastle drew more to Roker Park than attended the next home game just three days later, when West Brom were defeated. While Sunderland were a point ahead of Cup Final opponents Villa at this stage, they were two behind League leaders Wednesday whose 6-0 win on the day Sunderland beat West Brom gave the Sheffield side a fourth successive win.

Sunderland though had a game in hand on the Owls after all of their Cup exertions and with the Cup Final 10 days away a 3-1 home win over mid table Everton took Sunderland to the top of the table where they would remain. Dominance over the Merseyside giants was confirmed the following Saturday when having completed the double over Everton, a 5-2 win at Anfield also ensured a double over Liverpool – a Buchan hat-trick giving him eight goals in two games against Liverpool who for the second time this season trailed 4-0 by half-time. Beating Everton and Liverpool home and away provided two of six League doubles during the season but of course it was the prospect of achieving the double of winning both League and Cup that occupied people's minds. The handsome win at Anfield was a seventh successive League victory as part of an unbeaten run of a dozen games in League and Cup going into the Cup Final.

Opponents Villa were in mixed form. Like Sunderland they were double chasers and had shown their commitment to winning the League by coming back from 2-0 down at half-time to win 3-2 at Bolton in the last game before the Final. Their form since the semi-final had been questionable though with just one point taken from their other two games including a home defeat by the Liverpool team Sunderland had just thrashed.

A squad of 13 players left for the Final at Crystal Palace from Monkwearmouth Station on the Friday, staying in Streatham at the Thrale Hall Hotel. The allowance of substitutes was more than half a century away but Sunderland had two spare players in addition to the accepted first choice side. Forward Walter Tinsley and half-back Billy Cringan. Neither had played in the Cup run where the same side had played all previous eight games bar at left-back where an injury to Albert Milton had seen Harry Ness replace him in the semi-final as we would do in the Final. Ness had the experience of having played in the 1910 Cup Final for Barnsley against Newcastle.

If it has always been the dream of footballers to win the Cup then perhaps Sunderland's first Cup Final was settled by two dreams. Famously Villa's Seaton Delaval born Clem Stephenson premonitiously dreamed that Tommy Barber would head the only goal of the game to win the Cup for Villa – which he duly did after Stephenson reportedly told Charlie Buchan of this during the first half. In years to come Sunderland half-back Frank Cuggy would reveal, to that great chronicler of north-east sport Arthur Appleton, that Walter Tinsley suffered a nightmare on the eve of the Final.

Having scored in all but one of the previous rounds, including a superb winner in the semi-final, crucially George Holley was not fit for the Final. The England forward had a damaged ankle and had missed the win over Liverpool. Tinsley had stood in for Holley at Anfield (and had scored against Albion a fortnight earlier when replacing Holley who was on international duty) but had a massive attack of nerves on Cup Final morning and according to Cuggy's conversation with Appleton, Tinsley had refused to play. A photograph of the Sunderland team taken on the morning of the Final wearing suits show Holley wearing football boots rather than shoes.

Holley had been constantly testing his ankle and attempted to play due to Tinsley's reluctance. Described as 'practically a non-entity' in reports of the game Holley clearly wasn't fit. Perhaps Cringan should have been selected instead just as debate still continues regarding whether Paul Hardyman should have played in the 1992 FA Cup Final or Colin West in the 1985 League Cup Final, both of which; like the 1913 Cup Final, were lost without Sunderland scoring.

Sunderland's 1912-13 Championship winning team. Back row, left to right: Butler, Cuggy, Ness, Richardson, Martin, Tinsley, Mordue. Front row: Cringan, Gladwin, Buchan, Thompson, Low, Holley, the latter in boots.

Tinsley's frame of mind would not have been helped by the size of the crowd. Reported variously as 120,081 or 121,919 what is certain is that it was a world record for a football match and in England has only ever been surpassed by the attendance for the first ever Wembley Cup Final of a decade later.

The 1913 FA Cup Final was the first Cup Final to be contested by the teams occupying the top two positions in the League. As yet the Championship was still in the balance and with Sunderland due to visit Villa Park in the League four days after the Cup Final both clubs still had the opportunity to do the double.

Key to the match was likely to be the contest between Sunderland captain and centre-half Charlie Thomson and Villa centre-forward and talisman Harry Hampton. Still Villa's record League goalscorer, Hampton had scored in every round including both goals in the Final the last time Villa had won the Cup eight years earlier. He had also scored Villa's goal at Roker Park earlier in the season and more recently – a fortnight before the Final – had scored the only goal of the game for England against Scotland at Stamford Bridge. The Scots were captained that day by Thomson – with Holley a teammate of Hampton's, as was Villa's Cup Final 'keeper Sam Hardy – the man who had deposed former Sunderland goalkeeper Ted Doig at Liverpool.

Hampton's goal that defeated Thomson's Scotland came from him charging Scottish 'keeper Brownlie into the net. This was perfectly legal then. Indeed in 1957 when Villa beat already crowned champions Manchester United in the Cup Final, United goalkeeper Ray Wood suffered a fractured jaw when charged by Villa's Peter McParland. With substitutes still not introduced Wood ended up as a passenger on the win while defender Jackie Blanchflower went in goal. A year earlier in 1956 Manchester City goalkeeper Bert Trautman famously played on in the Cup Final with a broken neck!

In the 1913 Final though it was Villa who had to do without their 'keeper for part of the game. Hampton certainly wasn't allowed to bully Sunderland 'keeper Butler. Charlie Thomson determined to keep Hampton quiet and the battle between the pair of them was ferocious. Up this point in history only five Sunderland players had ever been sent off, the most recent being Harry Low against Villa in 1911. The idea of being sent off in the Cup Final, the game's showpiece, was almost impossible. Thus it was that Thomson and Hampton proceeded to knock seven bells out of each other. At one point Thomson laid Hampton out, at another Hampton kicked Thomson heavily on the ground. While neither was dismissed the FA took a dim view of the battle and suspended both players and the referee, Mr Adams of Nottingham, for the opening month of the following season.

Tinsley wasn't the only player to be nervous. After only 15 minutes Gladwin conceded a penalty for felling Stephenson. The dead ball fell to Southwick born Charlie Wallace. It was only the second penalty kick in a Cup Final (Newcastle had had one in the 1910 FA Cup Final replay) but England international Wallace screwed his shot well wide against his home-town team. Distraught, Wallace locked himself in the toilet at half-time.

At the interval the game was still goalless, although for once escaping Thomson, Hampton had found the net only to be given offside. Sunderland had scored over 100 goals in League and Cup by the time of the Cup Final but had forgotten their shooting boots as chances came and went, even the great Buchan missing a good chance.

After half-time Villa 'keeper Hardy's left knee was injured in a collision with Sunderland winger Harry Martin. A four minute stoppage was followed by Hardy going off for over 10 minutes during which Sunderland's opponents were a man short and with half-back Jimmy Harrop in goal. The Wearsiders were unable to capitalize although twice the woodwork saved Villa, Martin coming agonisingly close with an effort that came back off the inside of the post in the closing stages.

Twelve minutes from time Stephenson's dream came true when Barber headed home. It came from a corner from Wallace who duly atoned for his penalty miss by firstly winning the flag kick from Ness and then picking out the onrushing Barber with a kick placed behind a bank of players close to the goal. Sadly, West Stanley born Barber would die in 1925 aged just 39 having contracted TB.

Despite defeat the Sunderland team attended a banquet in London that evening at The Trocadera. Losing the Cup Final was a huge disappointment but at least Sunderland had been in the Cup Final for the first time and that in itself was an achievement. More importantly the Lads were still top of the League with three games to go, starting of course at Villa the following Wednesday.

While Sunderland and Villa took part in the Cup Final, in Sheffield, Wednesday were beating West Brom to move behind Sunderland in second place but with just one game for them to play.

The gates were locked at Villa Park 45 minutes before kick off for the League showdown with Sunderland. An attendance of 59,740 was the second biggest attendance Sunderland had ever played in front of – beaten only by the previous weekend's Cup Final – and there were an estimated 30,000 locked out such was the clamour for the occasion.

Each side made one change from the Cup Final line-ups and both were significant. Hardy wasn't fit to play in goal for the Cup winners and was replaced by Brendel Anstey while for Sunderland Tinsley had conquered his nerves and duly replaced the injured Holley.

Just as Wallace had atoned for his penalty miss by setting up the winner in the Cup Final, so Tinsley went some way to making amends for his failure to play the previous Saturday when he gave Sunderland a first half lead. Villa managed to earn a draw through Harold Halse on his last appearance for the club but as the final whistle sounded Sunderland were in pole position to take the title.

With two games remaining Sunderland already had 50 points which was the most Villa could manage if they won their remaining fixtures. Wednesday could reach 51 points still but a win for Sunderland in their next match at Bolton would secure the title with a home game against Bradford City still to come.

While Villa won 3-2 at Newcastle where they were reportedly given 'a hearty round of applause', Wednesday lost at Everton. Bob Kyle's team took to the pitch at Bolton's Burnden Park knowing that victory would tie up the title regardless of results elsewhere. Sunderland took a tenth minute lead courtesy of a Mordue penalty after Low was brought down by Jones. Having opened the scoring Mordue went on to help quickly extend Sunderland's lead by creating a goal for Richardson and when Richardson made it 3-0 by the 24th minute the Lads looked odds on for the title.

Having conceded the early penalty Jones reduced the arrears just before half-time but his eventful afternoon ended early when he was carried off mid way through the second half leaving Bolton a man short. Seven days after losing the Cup Final, Sunderland had responded in magnificent fashion, earning a fighting draw at Villa and comfortably sealing the Championship at Bolton. Charlie Buchan's 30th goal of the season four days later was enough to end the season with a win over Bradford City and set a new record points tally for a title winning team – and that despite taking just two points from those first seven games.

Undoubtedly the team of 1912-13 deserve their own very special place in the history of SAFC. In the 133 years of the club so far the League title has been won six times and the FA Cup Final reached on four occasions. The class of 1912-13 achieved both in the same season. Four players – Buchan (30), Mordue (20), Holley (17) and Richardson (17) reached double figures in goals. Ten players played in all nine FA Cup ties and eight played in at least 30 of the 38 League games.

The famous 'Roker Triangle' of right-half, right-winger and inside-right Francis Cuggy, Jackie Mordue and Charlie Buchan all played in the same team for England during the season – the only time Sunderland have had three players in the same England team. George Holley also played for England during the season in an era when the three Home Internationals were the only games played by England in the season. Additionally Sunderland skipper Charlie Thomson captained Scotland and of course Harry Low turned down his only Scotland call up in order to play for Sunderland against Newcastle in the Cup. 1912-13 was also the season when Bob Kyle, Sunderland's longest serving 'manager' (1905-28) won what would prove to be his only trophy.

Sunderland had proved they were the best team in the country. Had European football existed how would the Lads have got on? Immediately after completing a hectic season the side departed for a seven match tour of Hungary, Austria and Germany, playing top clubs from those countries and an exhibition match against fellow tourists and 1912 champions Blackburn Rovers in Budapest. Sunderland won all seven of those games in the space of 16 days rattling up a goals tally of 39 for and five against.

The History of Sunderland AFC

The first edition of this book published in 2005 pointed out that only Liverpool, Manchester United, Arsenal, Everton and Aston Villa had been champions of England more times than Sunderland. As this updated and expanded volume is issued in 2012 that statement remains true. Manchester City and Chelsea could overtake Sunderland in the coming seasons. Mega rich Man City's triumph in 2012 means they have half Sunderland's total of six titles. Chelsea have been champions four times between 2005 and 2011 but still need to win the League again to equal The Wearsiders' tally of being six time champions. As far as the North East is concerned, no other club in the region has ever held as many titles as Sunderland since the Red and Whites became champions for the first time in 1892. In the 'Hotbed of Soccer' the Black Cats have always been top dogs.

Sunderland is the club of Raich Carter, Len Shackleton, Charlie Buchan, Charlie Hurley, Jimmy Montgomery and Niall Quinn: the club famed for the Roker Roar, for the biggest-ever crowd in the North-East, the club where Spurs' double-winning captain Danny Blanchflower was found after a game wandering the stands looking for the speakers he believed were hidden under the roof to amplify the crowd's noise, the club of whom Bob Stokoe said in the run-up to one of the game's most memorable Cup Finals, 'Until you've seen football on the north-east coast, you've never seen it.'

Sunderland's place as one of football's most illustrious clubs was established in the Football League's early days. The first club to join the League after the dozen Founder Members, Sunderland was the first club outside of the North West and Midlands to be allowed to join and was only then admitted after they agreed to pay the travelling expenses of every club that was concerned about making the long trek to Wearside.

Having beaten champions Preston North End 4–1, and thrashed League runners-up Aston Villa 7–2 in friendlies, Sunderland had proved that they had a side to stand comparison with the best the League had to offer and so, in 1890, Sunderland replaced Stoke for the third season of League football. The Wearsiders soon dominated the game. Champions in only their second season, they were the winners of the last-ever single-division Football League. A year later they were champions of the first-ever First Division, becoming the first club to score 100 League goals in a season (in just 30 games). Aston Villa prevented a hat-trick of title wins in the following season but runners-up Sunderland were champions for a third time in four seasons a year later. They were also crowned 'Champions of the World' after defeating Scottish champions Hearts 5–3 on their own Edinburgh turf in April 1895.

Having established itself as a footballing giant, Sunderland has never seen itself as anything less. A 'sleeping giant' for many years, yes, but always a giant. Indeed, until 1958

Sunderland proudly held the record of being the only club never to have played outside the top flight of English football – a record that no other club had been able to boast for over two decades, following the relegation of Aston Villa and Blackburn Rovers in Sunderland's sixth Championship-winning season of 1935–36.

Since that traumatic first relegation on goal average Sunderland have been the proverbial 'yo-yo' club, bouncing between divisions with never more than six successive seasons at the same level, a tally equalled in 2012-13 as the club prepared for a sixth successive season at the top table and looked to stay there long term. Despite the up and down nature of over half a century's football since the first ever relegation in 1958 the club's ability to impinge upon the national consciousness has never been lost. Only the Matthews' Final of 1953 rivals the FA Cup Final of Stokoe's Stars in 1973 for drama, excitement and sheer fame. The 1998 Play-off Final, when Sunderland scored TEN times and still lost (4–4 followed by a 7–6 penalty shoot-out defeat) is the stuff of legend and, following the 1997 move to the biggest new football ground built in England in the second half of the twentieth century, Sunderland's ability to pull in the third-highest average attendance in the country when not even playing top-level football (In 1998-99) proved once again that when it comes to footballing giants, Sunderland dwarf all but the greatest of clubs and stand comparison with even the mightiest. Should Sunderland ever experience a fraction of the success of Manchester United, Liverpool or Chelsea in the modern era, then only Manchester United could begin to compare with the power of the Black Cats!

BEGINNINGS (1879–1890)

Sunderland has always been proud of its Scottish heritage. Founded by a Scot, James Allan, the FA Cup winners of 1973, for instance, included four Scots, one of whom was captain and one of whom scored the only goal of the game. In 2001 Sunderland paid tribute to this Scottish ancestry with an away strip of 'Scotland' blue.

James Allan was an Ayrshire born schoolteacher working in Sunderland in the late 1870s at the Thomas Street Boys' School in Hendon. Allan had moved to Sunderland in 1877 and on a visit home two years later he brought back with him a round football. Already a member of the Sunderland rugby club, James Allan brought about Association Football in Sunderland by organising a meeting in the British Day School, a building still in use in 2012 as the Norfolk Hotel, (now a hostel) situated on the corner of Norfolk Street and Borough Road on the edge of Sunderland city centre and between the centre of Sunderland and the Hendon school in which he worked. The precise date of this meeting in October 1879 is not known but was in the middle of the month, the 16th or 17th although verification of an exact date is yet to be published.

Present at this inaugural meeting of the club were:
James Allan (elected vice-captain)
J. Anderson
Walter Charles Chappel, assistant at Hendon Board School
John Coates, assistant at Rectory Park

SUNDERLAND: THE COMPLETE RECORD

The 1883-84 team.

W. Elliott (Later Sunderland's first recorded goalscorer)
John Grayston (elected secretary)
James Jardine
Councillor J. Sewell, head of Wesleyan School, Robinson Street
Robert Singleton (elected as first captain), master at Grey School
Edward Gray Watson, master at Monkwearmouth National School

Schoolmaster Lynn Marr and his brothers were also formerly believed to have attended the inaugural meeting. However further research since the publication of the first Sunderland Complete Record casts doubt on this. Evidence for those claimed to have been at the inaugural meeting seems to all stem from a series of articles written by John Grayston in a six part series in the short lived *Sunderland Weekly News*. Grayston's series began in September 1931, some 52 years after the event he was recalling.

Tracking each person claimed to have attended in the 1881 Census casts doubt on Marr's attendance at the first meeting. Lynn is an unusual Christian name for a male and therefore relatively easy to research. The only person discovered on the Census is John Lynn Marr who was born in South Hylton on 23 September 1877 – meaning he would be just two years old when the football club's first meeting was held. He became Colonel Lynn Marr and died in 1931. The Grayston articles reference the late Colonel Lynn Marr. This person is the eldest son of James Marr (later Sir James Marr) who was a director of J.L. Thompson shipyards. His name 'Lynn' comes from the maiden name of his mother Mary Abigail Ann Lynn.

Grayston's fourth article of his series states an error of grammar in the original article which inferred Lynn Marr and his brothers were in the team. 'They were only bairns' stated Grayston. It still seems strange that a two-year-old Lynn Marr could have been brought to the club's inaugural meeting and John Grayston appears to have mixed memories from later when Sir James Marr invested in the club in the mid 1880s. James Marr was instrumental in obtaining jobs for the Scottish 'professionals' attracted to the club such as James Hunter. One of Grayston's articles states James Marr took a great interest and sat on the committee when it met. Sir James Marr died in 1932. The truth of whether Lynn Marr or any other member(s) of the Marr family attended the first ever meeting of the club may never be verified. Certainly as Sunderland historians, the authors of this book cast doubt upon the validity of the claim and will continue to search for evidence.

James Marr was born on 9 September 1854. Perhaps it was James Marr – who would have been 25 at the time – who attended the first meeting but it was a meeting of schoolteachers of which Marr was not, as far as records indicate. We are in the realms of conjecture here. The other children – apart from Lynn – born to James and Mary (born 12 March 1855) were Ellen; born in Monkwearmouth 'about 1879' according to the 1881 Census – and William, born on 4 October 1881. Further, James and Mary were married on 18 October 1876, so the first meeting of what became the football club would have taken place a day or two before their third wedding anniversary. Lynn Marr died of pneumonia aged 53. His obituary published in The Times on 3 September 1931 makes no mention of any connection with Sunderland AFC.

The FA Cup had first been competed for seven years prior to the meeting that formed what later became Sunderland AFC but the formation of the Football League was still nine years away. Twenty-five miles south of Sunderland a club had existed in Middlesbrough for three years, but there would be no football club in Newcastle for another two years after the formation of the Sunderland club, which was initially called the Sunderland and District Teachers' Association Football Club.

Financial crisis is not solely the preserve of clubs in the modern era and a year into its existence the Sunderland club dropped 'and District Teachers' from its title at a meeting on 16 October 1880 in order to make the club accessible to a wider range of people and preserve its very existence. Norwich City are called the Canaries, but Sunderland could have taken that nickname after the club's continued survival was supported by the raffle of a committee member's canary!

Alderman J. Potts became Sunderland's first President and the first competitive game was played on 13 November 1880 when Ferryhill from County Durham were the visitors in the Northumberland and District Challenge Cup. The match was played at Sunderland's first ground, the Blue House Field in Hendon, with the home line-up indicating that five of the team had attended the club's inaugural meeting a year earlier. Appropriately for a team whose ground was the Blue House Field, Sunderland wore blue. Red and white would not feature in the club's colours until 1885, and even then the colours now synonymous with Sunderland were not stripes but halves, in the style that Blackburn Rovers maintain. Sunderland wore blue shirts and knickerbockers with a white stripe on the knickerbockers in an age when players often also wore a tassled cap!

The first known game on 13 November 1880 was a second-round tie. Sunderland had received a bye in the first round. Ferryhill had eliminated Darlington Grammar School and their Cup run would continue as they beat Sunderland 1–0.

The Sunderland team that day was: Singleton, Taylor, Shirlaw, Gibbons, Anderson, Watson, Barron, Dove, Woodward, Chappel and Allan.

Fittingly Allan scored twice in Sunderland's first win, a 4-0 victory over Ovingham at the Blue House Field where W. Elliott is credited with the first recorded goal with Watson also on the mark.

A 1–1 draw with Burnopfield preceded a first-ever recorded away game, which took place on 18 December 1880 at Rowlands Gill, where Burnopfield were defeated 2–0 with founder James Allan scoring both of the goals.

Sunderland have been based on the north side of the River Wear since 1883–84, but the club's earliest years were spent on the south side of the town (Sunderland has been a city since 1992).

Valley Road Infants' School now occupies the site of the first ground, the Blue House Field, while the club's first headquarters was in the now demolished Norman Street. Two more games are known to have been played in the 1880–81 season. The win over Burnopfield took Sunderland though to the semi-final of the Northumberland and Durham Challenge Cup, which produced a heavy 5–0 defeat at the hands of the Rangers of Newcastle. This club had nothing to do with either of the clubs that later merged to become Newcastle United, but as the match was played at St James' Park, Sunderland can lay claim to having played there before the Magpies (as Everton played at Anfield before Liverpool FC). Original opponents Ferryhill were then faced in a return match, this time Sunderland battling for a 0–0 draw.

Annual rent of £10 a year meant that after a second season at the Blue House Field Sunderland sought pastures new. A pitch just up the road from the Blue House Field near 'The Cedars' in Sunderland is believed to have been briefly used by the club, but by the start of the 1882–83 campaign Sunderland were installed at what is still the centre of sporting activity on the south side of Sunderland, Ashbrooke Cricket Ground. Although Sunderland only played four games at Groves Field, Ashbrooke, one of that quartet saw Sunderland exceed what is commonly referred to as the club's record victory. An FA Cup first round 11–1 hammering of Fairfield is listed in every record book as Sunderland's biggest-ever victory, but Stanley Star went home on the wrong end of a 12–1 beating at Groves Field, Ashbrooke, in the first round of the Northumberland and Durham Challenge Cup in January 1883.

That 12–1 win set Sunderland on course for the club's first-ever Cup Final, which was lost 2–0 to Tyne at Brandling Park, Newcastle. With the split of the Northumberland and Durham FAs at the end of this season Sunderland would thereafter compete in the Durham Challenge Cup. As part of County Durham, until local government reorganisation created

THE HISTORY OF SUNDERLAND AFC

An 1886-87 team picture in halved shirts.

The oldest known picture in stripes 1887.

Tyne and Wear in 1974, Sunderland was traditionally 'County Durham's club', and to this day draws much of its support from the former Durham coalfield. With the Stadium of Light situated on what was once one of that coalfield's biggest pits, Wearmouth Colliery, a light still shines at Sunderland for the generations of pitmen and their families who made up the Roker Roar.

Sunderland moved north across the river in 1883. Although it would be another 15 years before the club set up home at what would become Roker Park, Roker was the site of a ground that was known as 'the Dolly Field'. This ground was also sometimes known by the street names, Horatio Street or Cooper Street, which ran alongside. The move north of the river began with an 8–1 win over Castle Eden and brought about the club's first trophy at the end of the first season there, the Durham Challenge Cup.

To this day Sunderland supporters are renowned for their passion and this evidently spilled over in the Cup Final against Darlington which was ordered to be replayed following complaints about supporters' behaviour. The original Cup Final was staged at the old cricket ground on Newcastle Road in Sunderland, where a crowd of 1,000–2,000 (the first recorded attendance figure for a Sunderland match) saw James Allan lead his team to a 4–3 win with goals from John McDonald, William Allan, Duncan Murdoch and John Grayston.

Illustrating that squad rotation is not a modern preserve, Sunderland 'rested' four key players, including captain James McMillan, for the solitary fixture before the replayed Final, maybe as a result suffering their first home defeat at the Dolly Field and only their second of the season. The move paid off though, as two of the rested quartet, McDonald and Joyce, got the goals in a 2–0 win in the replayed Final. This match was refereed by the President of the FA, Major Francis Marindin RE.

Marindin was the founder of the first-ever FA Cup finalists, the Royal Engineers, and refereed nine FA Cup Finals in his career. He had been brought in to replace the original referee, Mr Alfred Grundy of Whitburn, who was chairman of the Durham FA. However, it was Mr Grundy who got to present the trophy, all of eight months later, when the Durham FA had finally raised the funds to actually buy one!

After just one season at the Dolly Field the club was on the move again, this time to a ground half a dozen good goal kicks away from what would become the Fulwell End at Roker Park. This new home was at Abbs Field in Fulwell.

Sunderland would stay here for less than two seasons, but this spell witnessed the club colours change from blue to red and white, a 23–0 victory, entry into the FA Cup for the first time and the debut of a man who would play in Sunderland's first League game six years later and still be working for the club in the 1930s.

Birtley were beaten 2–1 in Sunderland's first home game at Abbs Field on 27 September 1884. That was a considerably better performance from the visitors than Castletown managed just before Christmas when, having arrived with just eight players, they borrowed three Sunderland Reserves and crashed to a 23–0 defeat, with James Allan plundering a dozen goals! This was the mid-point of a run of seven successive wins that followed a 3–1 defeat away to Redcar in the club's first-ever FA Cup game on 8 November 1884. Bulman, Harrison and Agar got the goals for the home side with Don McColl scoring Sunderland's first in the world's oldest Cup competition.

Right-winger McColl was at the centre of Sunderland's next defeat when he tried his hand in goal for the only time, and probably wished he hadn't, as visitors Port Glasgow inflicted a record 11–1 defeat. Painful though this was, a more important defeat followed later in the season at Feethams where they lost 3–0 to Darlington in the Durham Cup Final, the Quakers gaining revenge for the previous year.

Defences were tighter at the end of the season when a goalless draw marked the debut of goalkeeper William 'Stonewall' Kirkley. He would play in Sunderland's first-ever League game in 1890, go on to play for Sunderland Albion and return to stay involved with the club until the halcyon days of the 1930s when he ran the billiard room at Roker Park.

In 1885–86 Sunderland changed their colours to red and white. Initially the red and white kit consisted of halved shirts complete with white knickerbockers and socks. The famous stripes wouldn't appear until September 1887 when Darlington St Augustines (A side who would be the first ever Northern League champions in 1889-90) provided the opposition.

Redcar again accounted for Sunderland in the 1885-86 FA Cup, defeating the Wearsiders 3–0 in the zoned first round in what was the only 'competitive' fixture of the season. The club did not enter the Durham Challenge Cup in protest at having a complaint over the previous season's Final at Darlington rejected, in contrast to the sympathetic hearing given to the Quakers a year earlier.

That is not to say that the so-called friendly matches being played were not competitive. Unlike most modern tepid friendlies, in football's early days such games were 'Challenge Matches' and this was especially the case against sides from Scotland.

Port Glasgow returned on New Year's Day, when a sign of Sunderland's improvement (and a decent goalkeeper) was that the visitors could only win 2–1 before a crowd of 2,000. A day later 800 saw another Glasgow side; Linthouse, win by the same margin. The boot was on the other foot at the end of February when Sunderland travelled to Scotland for the first time and defeated Hearts 2–1.

Just over a month after that triumph Sunderland changed grounds again, moving to Newcastle Road, which would become the scene of fabulous success.

Beginning with a 3–1 win over rivals Darlington on 13 March 1886, the first full season at Newcastle Road brought Sunderland's first-ever home FA Cup tie, a 2–1 win over Newcastle West End. However, following a protest this game was declared void and Sunderland lost the replayed game on Tyneside 1–0.

As at the Dolly Field, Sunderland's first full season at Newcastle Road brought success in the Durham Challenge Cup, Darlington again being the runners-up.

Donning red and white stripes for the first time, Sunderland would enjoy an FA Cup run of their own the following season, beating Morpeth Harriers and Newcastle West End (who would later merge with Newcastle East End to become Newcastle United) before being eliminated despite beating Middlesbrough after a third-round replay. A record gate of 8,000 knew that a bye into the last 16 was the reward for the winners and roared Sunderland back from a 2–0 half-time deficit to a 4–2 win. Middlesbrough, however, protested that Sunderland's Scottish trio of Monaghan, Hastings and Richardson had played as professionals and they were reinstated in Sunderland's place, with the three players receiving three-month suspensions. Boro reached the quarter-finals – a performance they would not better for another 110 years!

The turn of the year into 1888 brought about a record defeat, visitors Cambuslang triumphing 11–0, but the season was still a success with the Durham Cup captured once again, and Bishop Auckland Church Institute being beaten 4–2 in the Final at Darlington, following which Scottish Cup winners Renton won a friendly 4–2 at Newcastle Road.

The Football League began in 1888–89. A dozen founder members, all from the North-West and the Midlands, competed. Preston North End became known as 'The Invincibles' as they were unbeaten and dropped only four points all season in taking the first title. However, they came a cropper on Wearside in a friendly late in the season as Sunderland thrashed them 4–1. Altogether in that first Football League season Sunderland won five, drew two and lost one against the Football League's founder clubs. Sunderland applied to join the Football League at the end of its first season but were turned down.

Three of the Renton players who had played in the friendly at Newcastle Road were signed in the summer of 1889. These included Johnny Campbell, who would become one of Sunderland's greatest goalscorers, as an already powerful Sunderland strengthened its squad. One of the most significant newcomers was not a player but the man who would become Sunderland's first and most successful 'manager', Tom Watson.

The strength of the team became more evident as Sunderland's record against League sides continued to impress. The one game lost against a League side had been a 10–1 hammering away to Bolton, but Sunderland returned there to win 3–2. In the FA Cup Sunderland travelled to Blackburn Rovers where a 4–2 defeat was suffered after extra-time. Rovers went on to win the Cup, scoring a further 17 goals with the only goal conceded, other than the two against Sunderland, coming in the Final, where they beat Sheffield Wednesday 6–1. Sunderland won their own piece of silverware, taking the Durham Challenge Cup for the fourth time.

However, what really set the football world talking was when Aston Villa – runners-up in the Football League's first season – came to Sunderland and were annihilated 7–2 on 5 April 1890. Less than a month later Sunderland became the first new club to join the Football League and would go on to dominate the game.

Local rivals Sunderland Albion and Newton Heath (later to become Manchester United) were among the other clubs seeking election, but with James Marr and former player Reverend J. Hindle representing Sunderland's case and overcoming geographical objections to their acceptance by offering to pay the travelling expenses to Wearside of every other club, Sunderland were admitted at a meeting in the Douglas Hotel, Manchester, on 2 May 1890, taking the place of Stoke.

The fall-out from the 1887 FA Cup tie with Middlesbrough caused a split at Sunderland with James Allan, by now retired from playing, leaving to form a new club. Allan felt that Sunderland had handled the situation with the FA poorly and on 13 March 1888 he held a meeting at the Empress Hotel to form a rival club south of the river. Taking six Sunderland players with him, including the suspended trio of Monaghan, Hastings and Richardson, he formed Sunderland Albion.

Playing their first match on 5 May, beating Shankhouse 3–0, Albion existed for four years, eventually becoming Sunderland Albion Football and Athletic Company Ltd. Based at the Waverley Hotel in Hendon, Albion used Sunderland's first pitch at the Blue House Field and became an organisation big enough to field four teams.

Over at Newcastle Road, the by now almost decade-old Sunderland were developing their ground and playing prestige friendlies in front of attendances of up to 14,000. There was no love lost between the two Wearside clubs and this was brought to a head when, within the space of a few days, they were paired together in both the FA Cup and the Durham Challenge Cup.

Sunderland had already knocked Elswick Rangers and Newcastle East End out of the FA Cup but not wanting to assist the embryonic Albion with the financial boost a local derby would provide, they withdrew from both competitions. James Marr argued that Cup football had now served its purpose in making football popular. Albion were furious but duly took their place in the next round, where they were beaten 3–1 by Grimsby Town.

Local pressure for the clubs to play each other led to a first meeting at Newcastle Road on 1 December 1888. On the day before the game James Allan wrote to Sunderland asking whether Albion members would be admitted free of charge and, in an indication of the distrust between the clubs, asked for details of how and where money and tickets would be collected and counted.

A record crowd of 18,000 squeezed into Newcastle Road to see Sunderland end Albion's 13-game unbeaten run. Seeking a rematch, a series of increasingly angry letters was exchanged throughout December between Sunderland secretary W.T. Wallace and Albion representative James Hartley. Four days before Christmas, for example, Hartley wrote: 'I am in receipt of your extremely discourteous note of the 20th and beg to repeat my offer: We will play you on March ninth on our own or neutral ground. I may say that I expect we can get the Ashbrooke ground on that date.'

W.T. Wallace's letter had read: 'I understood from you that February 16th was a clear date for you, however March ninth will do. I am surprised now to see you turn around when you agreed with me yourself to play the game at our ground as you had not accommodation for such a crowd that would in all probability be present. If you want to play us just say so and let us get a date fixed at once, or I expect in another day some fresh conditions will be added by you.'

The outcome of this spat was that Hartley rearranged an Albion game on 12 January to enable the rematch to take place quickly. When the sides lined up again at Newcastle Road on that date before 12,000 spectators the atmosphere was ugly and ended with James Allan, the founder of both clubs, requiring surgery to an eye injury after being stoned by Sunderland supporters.

Albion led the rematch 2–0 at half-time, only for Sunderland to fight back and level with goals from Peacock and Gibson before the game exploded in the 87th minute, when Breconridge scored a winner for Sunderland that Albion argued had gone over the bar, or 'crosspiece' in those far-off days before goal-nets were used. Albion's players stormed off in protest at the award of the goal and afterwards added to their protests by complaining that they had been stoned as they left, with James Allan, who had acted as Albion's umpire (assistant referee/linesman), being injured.

Albion secretary Thomas Jobling lodged a protest with the FA, writing, 'I beg to lodge a formal complaint as to the brutal conduct of the Sunderland supporters… Our players were openly threatened in the field, as was our umpire, and during the latter part of the game, mud was thrown at our players and umpire.'

A Committee of Inquiry was set up by the Durham FA, to whom the FA had referred the matter, and when this met at the Grand Hotel in Sunderland's Fawcett Street on 31 January Albion's case was dismissed.

This rumpus hadn't prevented Albion demanding another rematch on a neutral ground but Sunderland considered themselves to have seen off Albion both on and off the pitch, and it would be three years before the clubs met again. By then Albion would be in their death throes and Sunderland would be champions of England!

Ironically, given the circumstances of Albion's creation, they were removed from the FA Cup a year after the FA inquiry into their derby match as they had fielded ineligible players when they defeated Bootle. In 1891 they reached the second round, taking Nottingham Forest to two replays, and in 1892 they eliminated Birmingham St George's, only to be knocked out by Nottingham Forest again.

It was Easter Monday 1892 when the two Sunderland clubs met again, Sunderland winning easily 6–1. Nine days later Sunderland handed out another thrashing, winning 8–0 at Blue House Field. Albion folded in August 1892, leaving Sunderland in the clear to attract support from all of Wearside and beyond rather than developing into a two-team town.

The Team of All The Talents (1890–1898)

Legend has it that when Sunderland were elected to the Football League in 1890 they put a notice over the entrance to the ground which read: 'We have arrived and we are staying here'. Sunderland's place at the top table of English football was quickly established. Preston, who had won the Championship again in the only two seasons played before Sunderland were admitted, had six put past them in a pre-season fixture and, with the signings of Scots Hugh Wilson and Jimmy Millar, Sunderland had acquired two more players who would become all-time greats. A third would follow by the third League game in the form of goalkeeper Ted Doig, although his debut was to result in Sunderland's first-ever points also becoming the first ever to be deducted by the Football League.

Bill Kirkley had been with Sunderland for several years and had kept goal in the club's previous nine home FA Cup ties, but he leaked three at the Newcastle Road Ground as Burnley won Sunderland's inaugural League game 3–2. He then took the blame two days later for a 4–3 home defeat at the hands of Wolves after Sunderland had led 3–0.

Doig's signing from Arbroath was rushed through and he helped the team to a 4–0 win at West Brom in Sunderland's first-ever away League game, only for the club to be docked the points and fined £25 as the new goalkeeper hadn't been registered with the League for the required 14 days. Come the season's end that points deduction had cost Sunderland two

THE HISTORY OF SUNDERLAND AFC

1890-91 the first season in the Football League.

places in the table, with the Wearsiders finishing seventh, but the main excitement came from the FA Cup, in which Sunderland reached the semi-final stage.

En route to their first-ever Championship, Everton lost 1–0 at Sunderland in both the Cup and the League. Darwen were then dismissed. With three days left before the quarter-final Sunderland knew they could be facing a derby with Sunderland Albion, only for Nottingham Forest to beat Albion in a second-round second replay. Sunderland then prevented an all-Nottingham semi-final by chopping down Forest and going on to face Notts County at Bramall Lane, which also staged the replay as County won through.

It was a particularly busy time for right-back Tom Porteous – one of only two English regulars in the side – who between the two semi-finals made his international debut for England against Wales in the first international to be held at Sunderland. No other player would be capped while with Sunderland in the next five years, despite Sunderland winning three Championships! This was largely due to Scotland's policy of not selecting players with English clubs.

Sunderland were up and running, and although they had lost their first two home games, only one more home defeat would be suffered in the next five years.

The 1891–92 season would see Sunderland crowned champions in the last year of the single-tier Football League and reach the FA Cup semi-finals for a second successive year. Once again Bramall Lane staged the showpiece Cup game, with Sunderland disappointingly slumping 4–1 to Aston Villa, their heaviest defeat of the season.

Sunderland and silverware came together, however, in the League. Campbell and Millar scored five between them on the first day of the season, but the opening-day win was followed by three successive away defeats, which cast doubt on Sunderland's credentials.

Back on Wearside champions Everton were the first victims in a four-game winning run before a defeat at Blackburn preceded a club record 13 successive League victories. One more game was then lost before the club's first title was sealed with a resounding 6–1 home win over Blackburn, with Campbell helping himself to four goals.

Usually the team comprised 10 Scots and England international Porteous, a Tynesider who had learned his trade in Scotland with Hearts and Kilmarnock. Sunderland's style contrasted with the rest of the League. Whereas the prevailing style of the day focussed on individuals trying to dribble and shoot, Sunderland's Scots played more of a passing game and when it came off opponents were ripped apart.

Sunderland retained the title in 1892–93, thus becoming the first-ever winners of the First Division, as it was called after a second tier had been added. This season also saw Sunderland become the first-ever team to score 100 League goals in a season. This was 24 more than the second highest scorers and achieved in only 30 games. No other team managed a century of League goals in a season until the season was extended to 42 games after World War One. Over two seasons Sunderland had averaged just under three and a half goals a game, scoring 193 goals in 56 League games, and yet they also managed the League's tightest defence. Johnny Campbell alone averaged more than a goal a game over these back-to-back Championship-winning seasons. The seasonal tally of 42 away goals in 1892–93 remains a club record.

THE HISTORY OF SUNDERLAND AFC

1890-91 local rivals Sunderland Albion.

1890s The Team of All The Talents.

A total of only 19 different players featured in these two Championship-winning seasons (15 in each campaign), with Doig and Porteous ever-present in both seasons, and Auld, Campbell, Gibson, James Hannah and Wilson playing 50 or more of the 56 games with Millar managing 47.

Making the most of their popularity and success, Sunderland continued to play an incredible number of friendlies. In 1891–92 for instance, Sunderland played an astonishing 25 such fixtures, making 58 games in all, during which they rattled in a phenomenal 217 goals! Perhaps the title might have been retained again had friendlies not taken Sunderland's total number of fixtures to 68 in 1893–94.

Searching for a third successive Championship, Sunderland began the 1893–94 season sluggishly winning only one of the first six games and eventually had to settle for second place. Aston Villa wrestled away the title and also knocked Sunderland out of the Cup.

Normal service was resumed in 1894–95. Derby County were the visitors on the first day of the season and the referee turned up late. The game started without him and Sunderland took a 3–0 half-time lead. Punctuality might not have been his strong point, but when Mr Kirkham, the match official, arrived he wasn't happy with a stand-in taking the game and ordered the game to be restarted. Undaunted, Sunderland went on to rattle in another eight goals without reply.

Eleven goals had been scored but only eight recorded against Derby, but all 11 counted when a record win in major competitions was recorded against non-League Fairfield in the FA Cup. Jimmy Millar became the first player to score five in such a competitive game as an 11–1 scoreline was rattled up. Preston and Bolton were also knocked out of the Cup but once again Sunderland fell to Villa at the semi-final hurdle, going down 2–1 at Ewood Park, Blackburn.

Villa went on to lift the Cup, but had to be content with third place in the League as Sunderland were champions for the third time in four seasons, putting runners-up Everton in their place before 20,000 spectators packed into Newcastle Road on the last day of the season.

Sunderland's grip on the game loosened in 1895–96 when only fifth place could be managed, a smidgin behind Bolton Wanderers on goal average. Despite Campbell's 15 League goals, Sunderland's total of 52 was just one more than had been managed in home goals alone the season before. They fared no better in the FA Cup, going out in the second round to eventual winners Wednesday.

The summer of 1896 brought about big changes – and not for the better! The original club was wound up to enable Sunderland to become a limited liability company. John Potts Henderson became the club's first chairman and would become the driving force behind another change of ground, to Roker Park. Perhaps most significantly Tom Watson left to take over at Liverpool, leading the Merseysiders to their first two League Championships in 1901 and 1906. He was joined by Ted Doig for the second of these and the pair are now buried within 20 feet of each other in Anfield Cemetery in Liverpool.

Johnny Campbell's half-brother Robert (who had been in charge of the 'A' team) took over as manager at Sunderland. The new season began disastrously and it wasn't until the ninth game, when Tom Watson's Liverpool were the visitors, that a victory was achieved. Such bad runs were unheard of. Even half-brother Johnny's goals had dried up – it was the twelve game before he scored and he lost the season's top scorer mantle to Gillespie.

Despite rallying with a five-match unbeaten run at the end of the season, Sunderland found themselves second from bottom of the table. Fortunately they were not condemned to relegation but to a series of 'Test Matches.' These were similar to modern-day Play-offs but involved the bottom two of the First Division and top two of the Second.

The Test Matches began badly: Sunderland failed to score in the first two of the four games they played. Second Division champions Notts County beat Sunderland 1–0 at Trent Bridge and held the Wearsiders to a goalless draw at Newcastle Road. Everything hinged on a double header against Newton Heath (now Manchester United). The 'Team of All The Talents' had served Sunderland superbly but these were arguably their most important games.

A 1–1 draw was played out at Bank Street, Manchester, before Jimmy Gillespie became the hero with both goals in a 2–0 win that saved Sunderland's skin in the final game. A draw would not have been sufficient to avoid the drop. Gillespie, Campbell, Gow, Jimmy Hannah and Harvie all made their final appearances in that game.

The team was freshened up for the tenth and final year at Newcastle Road with Phil Bach, Sandy McAllister and Jimmy Leslie, all of whom would make their own footnotes in the club's history, among the newcomers.

A good start was made with four wins and a draw in the opening half-dozen games, but when only a solitary point was gleaned from the following five fixtures concerns began to surface. Thankfully a mid-season recovery saw only a single point dropped in 11 games and a creditable runners-up spot was registered, with 'Talents' survivors Doig and Wilson playing major roles in establishing the tightest defence in the country. Captain Hugh Wilson was awarded the takings from a 10,000 late-season crowd against Blackburn as a benefit match.

Roker Rising (1898–1914)

Throughout the final season at Newcastle Road, work had been going on at nearby Roker Park, which would become Sunderland's home for a year short of a century. 12 August was set as the new ground's opening day but the Marquis of Londonderry, who was due to open it, was unavailable that day when 14,000 people turned up for an 'Olympic Games' event. The modern Olympics had been revived two years earlier and this was the second 'Olympic' event staged by the club. Unlike the real Olympics, prize money was on offer, with a top prize of £20 for the 110 yards and £5 for the winner of a dribbling contest – perhaps an indication of the future value of athleticism over artistry!

In comparison Jimmy Leslie had cost Sunderland £40 from Clyde. He'd scored in the last game at Newcastle Road, got the first goal at Roker, would go on to get Sunderland's first goal against Newcastle United at the new ground and also notch the club's first goal of the 1900s. Not bad value for £40.

Tom Watson returned to Sunderland for the first-ever game at Roker Park as Liverpool's manager on 10 September 1898 before a crowd of over 30,000. Sunderland played in white shirts, as Liverpool were in red, with Leslie's big moment coming six minutes from time when he scored the only goal of the game. An identical scoreline was achieved 99 years later when Liverpool were invited to bring down the curtain at the stadium they'd opened.

Sunderland got off to a cracking start at Roker Park. It took visiting sides six games to score a goal, Everton's Laurie Bell scoring in a 2–1 Sunderland win, and it was December before Burnley became the first visitors to win, marking a double as they'd also won Sunderland's first League game at Newcastle Road.

Burnley winning was one thing, but defeat in the next home game was worse as it marked Newcastle United's first League visit to Sunderland, with the Magpies winning 3–2 on Christmas Eve. Sunderland further upset their supporters by raising prices. Away wins for both clubs were a feature of early League games between Sunderland and

THE GOLDEN PENNY.
MARCH 26, 1898.

NOTED FOOTBALL CLUBS.
XVIII.—SUNDERLAND.
Photographs by W. Church, Sunderland.

In many respects the career of the well-known Sunderland Club resembles that of the equally famous Preston North End organisation. Like the Prestonians, they were at one period of their history the cleverest Association combination in the world, and they were rightly dubbed "the team of all the talents." Then they declined just as North End did, and had last season to fight in the test matches for their very existence; but like their champion predecessors they conquered and retained their position in the League. This season they have so far proved themselves to be one of the finest combinations in the country, and it is quite within the range of possibility that they will again carry off the coveted League championship. In 1891-92, Sunderland for the first time won the championship of the League, and between that season and the one of 1895-96 they won the championship three times and were runners-up once.

Early History.
Unlike the majority of clubs whose careers we have already traced, the birth of the Sunderland organisation is of comparatively recent date. What really formed the nucleus of the present club was a team started some fifteen years ago by a number of schoolmasters and pupil teachers connected with the local schools for their own amusement. At that time there were only two or three clubs in the whole of Durham, which county was then federated with Northumberland for the purposes of controlling football in the two counties. As a consequence of the formation of numerous other clubs in the county, an independent body called the Durham Association was formed. In the meantime the team of teachers had developed into the Sunderland Club, which was one of the most powerful supporters of the new body. In 1887 several of the leading tradesmen in the town began to take an interest in the doings of the club, with the result that a strong committee was appointed to manage affairs. Mr. Robert Thompson was elected president, Mr. James Marr chairman of the committee, and Mr. Samuel Tyzack treasurer.

Outside Aid.
It was felt that the local talent at the disposal of the committee was not of the required strength, and it was decided to seek the aid of prominent players from over the border. Several capable men were imported and the club was steadily progressing towards fame. About this time there was a split in the club, and several gentlemen severed their connection and formed a rival organisation, which existed for a few seasons under the name of Sunderland Albion. In 1887-88 the Sunderland team, which was composed of Scotchmen and local players, was one of the strongest in that part of the North of England. Towards the latter end of the season, Mr. Tom Watson was secured as secretary. He had previously acted in the same capacity to the Newcastle West End and East End Clubs; and he now fills a similar position with Liverpool.

New Blood.
When Mr. Watson took over the secretarial duties the only players he retained were Kirtley

H. WILSON.

J. E. DOIG.

J. Moir.
J. Galbraith. H. Morgan. H. Wilson. R. McNeill.
P. Boyle. M. Ferguson. J. Leslie. A. McAllister. W. Williams (Trainer).
W. Dunlop. J. Hamilton. J. Hutton. J. Chalmers.
SUNDERLAND FOOTBALL TEAM, 1897-8.

THE HISTORY OF SUNDERLAND AFC

Newcastle and the red and whites duly won on Tyneside later in the campaign, which saw Sunderland finish in seventh position.

The season also saw England pay a second visit to Wearside and with Sunderland's Phil Bach in the side they made the most of it with a record 13–2 home win over Ireland. The cap cost Bach his place at Sunderland, who won away to Wednesday on the same day, and Bach moved on at the end of the season, later becoming a Director of Middlesbrough and an FA Councillor.

Two even more significant departures at the end of the first season at Roker Park were the second captain (John Auld had been the first) of the 'Team of All The Talents', Hugh 'Lalty' Wilson, to Bedminster (who later merged with Bristol City) and manager Robert Campbell to Bristol City. Campbell proved to be the only pre-World War Two Sunderland manager not to lift the Championship (excluding Bill Murray, who took over just before World War Two) although one runners-up position in a three-year transitional period, both on and off the pitch, was a record some later managers would have been more than pleased with.

Twenty-nine-year-old Alex Mackie succeeded Robert Campbell as manager. He was in charge for six seasons and based his team's game on a strong defence. Only 96 League goals were conceded in his first three seasons in charge, less than a goal a game, making the Sunderland defence the meanest in the country. Third in his first season, Sunderland were runners-up a year later and champions for a fourth time in 1902.

Sunderland had the opportunity to take the title in 1901 but lost out to Tom Watson's Liverpool, who took 21 points out of the last 24, starting with a 1–0 February win at Roker Park in a game that, had it been drawn, would have seen Sunderland take the title. Sunderland won 2–0 at Newcastle in the final game of the season but a 1–0 win at West Brom for Liverpool took the title to Anfield.

Ted Doig and Jimmy Millar, the latter having returned from Glasgow Rangers, each collected their fourth Championship medals in 1902. Sadly Millar would die of tuberculosis

1901-02
Champions

just five years later, aged 36, while captain Matthew Ferguson, who missed just four games in the Championship season, suffered an untimely death at the age of 29, just two months after the end of the season.

Sunderland went close to retaining their title in 1903, eventually finishing third on goal average, just a point behind champions Wednesday. The visit of Wednesday (they became Sheffield Wednesday in 1929) in March proved to be controversial. Sunderland supporters had been in trouble several times before for their partisanship, most notably in the clashes with Sunderland Albion, and Wearside fans took severe umbrage at the referee when Wednesday won 1–0 at Roker Park. The official was smuggled out of the ground and the supporters vented their anger by stoning the Sheffield team as they left.

As a punishment, Roker Park was closed for the last home game of the season. That game was a first League visit from Middlesbrough, which was arranged for St James' Park, a ground Sunderland then had to visit again for a final game of the season against Newcastle. Boro were beaten 2–1 but a 1–0 defeat against Newcastle cost the title.

Sunderland had been champions three times in four years a decade earlier, and with kinder fortune could have been champions three years running at the start of the century, but as it was they had to be content with one League win sandwiched between two very near misses.

1903–04 became a troubled season. On the pitch the team finished in sixth place in Ted Doig's last campaign before linking up with Tom Watson at Liverpool. Just as Doig was leaving after 14 years of distinguished service there was trouble at Roker Park concerning a financial dispute with full-back Andy McCombie.

A member of the 1902 Championship-winning side, McCombie was a Scotland international who had been given, or loaned, £100 by the club. McCombie believed the £100 had been a gift and was not at all happy to be asked to return it. Following a Benefit Match awarded to McCombie the club said that the £100 had been a loan. The consequence of this unpleasantness was that McCombie was sold to Newcastle and taken to court by Sunderland for the return of the £100. The court found in Sunderland's favour but, alarmed by these events, the FA investigated Sunderland's book-keeping and in October 1904 Sunderland were found guilty of making illegal payments to players.

Six directors, including chairman Sinclair Todd, were suspended for two and a half years, manager Alex Mackie was suspended for three months, and the club was fined £250. Mackie had earlier sold forward Alf Common to Sheffield United for £325, bought him back for £520 and in February 1905 sold him to Middlesbrough in the world's first £1,000 transfer fee. At the end of the season in which Sunderland finished fifth, Mackie moved to Middlesbrough himself where further financial problems followed him. McCombie went on to have considerable success with Newcastle, but put through his own goal on his first return to Wearside as a Magpie.

Once the dust had settled on Sunderland's punishment, good came out of it in the shape of F.W. Taylor and Bob Kyle. Frederick William Taylor was the only director not suspended after the McCombie affair. He took over as chairman, retaining the position until 1913, and stayed as a member of the Board until after the end of World War Two. He held numerous civic roles within the town and became known as 'Mr Sunderland.'

Taylor replaced manager Mackie with Robert Kyle, who in his reign from 1905 to 1928 set a record as Sunderland's longest-serving manager that is unlikely ever to be beaten. The trainer throughout the Bob Kyle era was Billy Williams, who had been with the club since the Newcastle Road era.

Taylor stuck with Kyle through three difficult seasons in which Sunderland finished fourteenth, tenth and 16th, in a division by now made up of 20 clubs. Only once previously had Sunderland finished lower than seventh and in over half of the seasons since joining the League in 1890 Sunderland had been in the top three.

The club was spending money. Roker Park was purchased at a cost of £10,000 in 1906 and Kyle was starting to assemble a promising team. Seaham-born George Holley and goalscoring winger Arthur Bridgett would become heroes for Sunderland and England. Any successful team needs a good goalkeeper and, having missed Doig's presence since his departure, Sunderland found their next great custodian in the shape of L.R. Roose, who signed at the start of 1908. Roose was soon followed by forward Jackie Mordue and Charlie Thomson, a Scottish centre-half as commanding in the team that would go close to the 'Double' in 1913 as Charlie Hurley would be in Sunderland's first-ever promotion season 51 years later.

The 1908–09 season saw Sunderland return to the top three. That season also brought one of the greatest days in Sunderland's history when arch-rivals Newcastle were slaughtered by nine goals to one at St James' Park. The Magpies won the Championship that season but Sunderland fielded five forwards, all of whom would play for England in their careers. Having been riled by seeing the home side equalise through a controversial penalty on the stroke of half-time, Sunderland regained the lead three minutes after the restart and then played amazing football, scoring seven times in an 18-minute spell before completing the scoring with 14 minutes still to play. The 9–1 scoreline remains Sunderland's biggest-ever away win and the joint record top-flight away win.

At the end of the season Sunderland undertook their first overseas tour, playing in Budapest, Vienna, Prague and Munich on an eight-game tour that brought seven wins and a defeat.

Kyle continued to assemble a team capable of bringing success back to Sunderland as the Lads finished eighth, third and eighth between 1910 and 1912.

The most important newcomer during this period was Charlie Buchan. Buchan started badly. He was a young man and the crowd got on his back as he initially struggled. Seventy-odd years later Sunderland failed to persevere with another young striker, Ally McCoist, who left to go on to become Rangers' record goalscorer. However, thanks especially to trainer Billy Williams, Buchan was persuaded to stay at Sunderland. He became one of England's finest-ever forwards and remains Sunderland's record League goalscorer.

Five of Buchan's 209 Sunderland League goals came in a 7–0 win over Liverpool in what proved to be Sunderland's greatest season of 1912–13. The campaign started well enough, with an opening day draw away to Newcastle, but only a single point was taken from the next six games and Sunderland found themselves bottom of the League. Kyle stiffened the defence with a new goalkeeper in Joe Butler after Walter Scott was sacked for 'palpable inefficiency'. Tough full-back Charlie Gladwin was also brought in and his debut coincided

The 1914-15 team.

with a first win of the season, 4–0 against Middlesbrough – that set Sunderland on a fabulous run of 25 wins in the last 31 games as the Championship was brought back to Roker Park.

Although this was the fifth time the League Championship trophy had been claimed, Sunderland had yet to reach an FA Cup Final, having been losing semi-finalists three times. Sunderland finally reached the Final in 1913. A Cup run of 10 games included an abandoned game at Manchester City (when with Sunderland leading 2–0 the overflowing crowd could be kept off the pitch no longer), a quarter-final tie with Newcastle that Sunderland won in a second replay on Tyneside and a semi-final against Burnley that also went to a replay.

The Cup Final at Crystal Palace paired Sunderland against Aston Villa, who like Sunderland were chasing the 'double' of League and Cup in the same season, a feat only Villa themselves in 1897 had achieved since Preston in the League's inaugural season and something no club would achieve again until Spurs in 1961.

Two crucial games against Villa, the Cup Final and a League game at Villa Park, hung on a player who would make only 10 appearances for Sunderland. Walter Tinsley was a 21-year-old from Derbyshire. Sunderland had won five of the six games Tinsley had played since making his debut a year earlier, including a 5–2 away win at Liverpool on the Saturday before the Final. The 21-year-old had scored twice in those games and was set to play as a replacement for George Holley, who had an ankle injury. Tinsley, though, suffered a bad attack of nerves on the morning of the Final, which was the first ever to be contested by the two teams at the top of the League. The game drew a crowd of over 120,000 – a figure only ever beaten in England by the first-ever Wembley FA Cup Final in 1923.

With Tinsley's mental strength not reflecting his birthplace of Ironville, the injured Holley was strapped up to play but was a mere passenger in the game, missing one good chance that he would normally have taken (only three players have ever scored more goals for Sunderland). Sunderland could have chosen travelling reserve Billy Cringan, a defender who went on to play for Scotland, but went for Holley instead and with substitutes still half a century away Sunderland suffered a handicap too hard to overcome. Villa won 1–0 despite Sunderland-born Charlie Wallace missing a penalty for them. Having sliced his 15th minute kick wide of the goal Wallace locked himself in a dressing room cubicle at half-time and was only persuaded to continue playing by the midlanders' chairman Frederick Rinder.

Wallace, from Southwick, was one of four north-easterners in the Villa team. Another of them, Clem Stephenson (whose brother Jim would play for Sunderland in the 1920s), told Charlie Buchan early in the game that he had dreamt that Newcastle-born Tommy Barber would score the game's only goal with a header for Villa. That dream came true when Barber headed past Butler in the 78th minute. Barber would die 12 years later of tuberculosis.

Late in the game Harry Martin hit the inside of the post for Sunderland, who missed inspirational skipper Thomson for a month through suspension at the start of the following season as a punishment for knocking out Villa's England centre-forward Harry Hampton – an offence for which in 1913 he was not sent off! Hampton too was suspended, for kicking Thomson when the Scot was on the ground.

Given the fierceness of the game and the size of the crowd, it is perhaps understandable that Walter Tinsley was so nervous. However, four days after Villa had lifted the Cup Tinsley took his place at Villa Park for a League game that was effectively a Championship decider. Tinsley for Holley was Sunderland's only change from the Final and before a crowd of almost 60,000 (An estimated 30,000 were locked out with the gates closed 45 minutes before kick off) Tinsley overcame his nerves to score Sunderland's goal and hit the woodwork no fewer than three times as the game finished 1–1, allowing Sunderland to wrap up the League with a comfortable win at Bolton three days later.

The following season Sunderland lost in a quarter-final FA Cup replay to eventual winners Burnley and a year later, before the cessation of football due to World War One, would go out at the first hurdle against Spurs. In the League almost identical records brought seventh and eighth place finishes before football closed down following a 5–0 home win over Spurs that featured a hat-trick from Buchan in April 1915.

By then the war had been underway for almost a year. Football had continued as 'an antidote to war', especially as initially the war had been expected to be over in a few months. However, with heavy losses in the trenches the game was halted and many footballers left for the fight, never to return. Goalkeepers L.R. Roose, Thomas Rowlandson and 1913 Championship-winning full-back Albert Milton were among those killed in action. For a fuller account of the war years see the Wartime football chapter later.

The 1919-20 team.

Not so Roaring Twenties (1915–28)

The 1920s was the only pre-World War Two decade in which Sunderland failed to win a trophy since its formation in 1879 (strictly speaking excluding the three months after its birth in the late 1870s). However, Sunderland did finish in the top four in half of the years of the decade.

Sunderland were one of eight teams, including Newcastle and Middlesbrough, to contest the 'Victory League' between January and April 1919 following the end of World War One in November 1918. Beginning with a 1–0 defeat away to Durham City – who joined the Football League two years later when the Third Division North and South were created – Sunderland won seven, drew two and lost five of their 14 fixtures.

The real thing got going again in August 1919. Charlie Buchan got the opener in the first League game since the war as Aston Villa were beaten. Buchan had scored Sunderland's last goal before the Football League was suspended during the war. He was Sunderland's top scorer in every season played between 1913 and 1924, and was the top flight's top scorer in 1923 with 30 League goals. Who knows how many more than his total of 222 he might have scored for Sunderland had it not been for the war, in which he won the Military Medal after serving with the Grenadier Guards and Sherwood Foresters.

Sunderland finished fifth at the end of the first post-war season but had to be content with 12th place for the following two years. It was again a transitional period for the Black Cats. The famous right-wing triangle of Jackie Mordue, Francis Cuggy and Charlie Buchan, who had played together for England before the war, was broken up with the departures of Mordue and Cuggy and manager Bob Kyle spent heavily in the transfer market. However, as in the 1950s and early 2000s, Sunderland found that spending money does not guarantee success.

Over £16,000 was spent in March 1922 to bring in four international players, including England full-back Warney Cresswell from South Shields for a new British record of £5,500. The previous day £5,250 had been paid for Scotland centre-half Michael Gilhooley from Hull City, while Gilhooley's countrymen, winger Alex Donaldson and centre-forward Jock Paterson, completed the quartet.

Paterson and Buchan, two of only six players to find the net in 1922–23 (two of the six scored just a single goal each) scored 55 League and Cup goals between them as Sunderland were runners-up to Liverpool. Five defeats in the last eight games, including the solitary home reverse of the season, cost Sunderland the title, which the Anfield outfit eventually won by a six-point margin.

It was a similar story of a Championship chance missed a year later. Five defeats in the last nine games left the League's leading scorers Sunderland in third place, four points short of the title which was claimed by Huddersfield, who pipped Cardiff on goal average. The title would have gone to Wales by virtue of goals scored had the modern-day goal difference system been in operation.

Sunderland had added Albert McInroy in goal – the only 'keeper to be capped by England while with Sunderland – but conceded 20 goals more than any of the other top four sides.

Forty-eight points were achieved in 1925 and 1926. In the first of those two years the tally was sufficient for a mere seventh position, while a year later it warranted third place behind Huddersfield, who achieved a third successive title. Over the two seasons only four games were lost at home but a combined total of 24 away defeats illustrated why Sunderland were not quite good enough to be champions.

Buchan failed to be the top scorer for the first time in 13 years in 1924–25, but it still came as a major shock when Sunderland agreed to sell him to Arsenal. Famously the Gunners failed to match manager Bob Kyle's £4,000 valuation and instead agreed to pay £2,000 plus £100 for every goal Charlie scored in his first season at Highbury. He cost them £100 more than Sunderland had asked by hitting 21.

As one great striker left another arrived. Dave Halliday cost £4,000 from Dundee in 1925 and in the worst of his four seasons with Sunderland he still scored more than any other Sunderland striker has ever managed in a season (excluding wartime football)!

Halliday began as he intended to continue. Ten goals in his first four games included two hat-tricks. Sunderland scored 20 times in those opening four matches and ended up scoring 32 more than the season before as forwards across the nation celebrated a change in the offside law that meant that only two opponents instead of three had to be between them and the goal for them to be on-side.

The record books were ripped up as Bobby Skinner broke the British seasonal scoring record with 53 for Dunfermline in 1925–26. A year later George Camsell hit 59 in 37 Second Division games for Middlesbrough. Camsell's record lasted only a season as Dixie Dean smashed 60 for Everton.

At Sunderland Halliday scored 42 in his first season, just one behind the First Division's leading scorer, Ted Harper of Blackburn. One day on which he didn't score was 10 April 1926 at Roker Park, in a game that featured three forwards who between them were Sunderland's top scorers in every year but one between 1913 and 1936. The day marked Charlie Buchan's return with Arsenal. Halliday was sensationally sent off along with Gunners goalie Dan Lewis, and the man to take advantage by scoring both of Sunderland's goals in a 2–1 win on his home debut was Bobby Gurney – the only man in the club's history to score more goals than Buchan!

The defeat effectively ended Arsenal's title hopes. It also probably cost Davie Halliday his chance to be the top flight's top scorer the following season, when he served a 14-day suspension for his misdemeanour. In all Halliday missed nine games during the season but still scored 35 goals in his 33 League games – just two behind Jimmy Trotter of the Wednesday. The Lads were the League's leading scorers but had to be content with third place once more.

It was the fourth year out of five that Sunderland had been in the top three, but there was a shock in store in 1927–28 when the club suffered its biggest relegation scare since the Test Matches of 1897. Halliday continued to rattle in the goals, hitting 33 in 38 League games plus another four in three Cup-ties, but Sunderland conceded more than they scored. The season began well enough with no defeats in the first five fixtures. Six successive defeats followed, however, and by the end of the campaign a record seven home defeats had been suffered. It would be over half a century before that record was surpassed.

1927–28 was the strangest of seasons. Only six points separated relegated Spurs and fourth-place Derby. Sunderland were one of seven teams who tied on 39 points and they finished 15th out of 22 teams, just one point ahead of Tottenham. With five games left, the Lads had 37 points, but four defeats in a row meant the last game of the season had to be won at Middlesbrough.

Boro also had 37 points going into the game, but a superior goal average meant that a draw would keep them above Sunderland, who needed to win to avoid the dreaded drop. As in the 1897 Test Matches this game marked the end of an era. Trainer Billy Williams had been with Sunderland since 1897 and in this, his last game, he played a crucial role.

The day after Arsenal had been trounced 5–1 in mid-March, manager Bob Kyle had announced he would leave at the end of the season, having been in charge since 1905. At the time of his announcement he couldn't have foreseen that the season would end so dramatically.

Goalkeeper Albert 'the Great' McInroy had missed the previous game through injury but had his fingers strapped up in an eel skin by Billy Williams. It was 45 years to the day before Jimmy Montgomery would provide the greatest save Wembley Stadium had ever witnessed and McInroy's double save from Boro's Carr and Bruce became just as legendary as Sunderland triumphed 3–0 with goals from Halliday, inevitably, and also David Wright

THE HISTORY OF SUNDERLAND AFC

(who had arrived in a double deal with Bill Murray, who would stay with the club until 1957) and Billy Death in his last game for the Lads.

In the stands watching Sunderland preserve the top-flight status they would keep for another 30 years were two people who would take Sunderland back to the very top: Johnny Cochrane and a 14-year-old supporter by the name of Horatio Stratton Carter.

COCHRANE AND CARTER (1928–39)

Johnny Cochrane had been manager of St Mirren since 1916 and had steered them to a first-ever Scottish Cup win over Celtic in 1926. At Sunderland he would emulate his achievement at St Mirren in taking the club to its first Cup win and also win the League. (To 2012 only Sir Alex Ferguson can equal Cochrane in managing FA Cup and Scottish Cup winning sides, in the latter's case with Manchester United and Aberdeen.) Carter wouldn't appear on the Sunderland scene for another couple of years but his role in winning both League and Cup would make him a pivotal member of those sides.

Frank Buckley of Wolves and George Jobey of Derby had been the Board's first two choices to succeed Bob Kyle, but Cochrane would go on to manage Sunderland for 11 years and build one of the club's greatest-ever teams. 'Major' Frank Buckley became a very famous manager at Molineux but never won a major honour, while Jobey had been a Cup-winner with Newcastle as a player but would eventually be suspended as a manager after being found guilty of financial irregularities spanning more than a decade.

1935-36 Sunderland are champions for the sixth time.

SUNDERLAND: THE COMPLETE RECORD

The 1937 team with the FA Cup.

Assisted by Andy Reid, who had followed him from St Mirren, Cochrane's first season saw Sunderland finish fourth, five points behind the Wednesday in their last season before officially adding 'Sheffield' to their name.

Dave Halliday set a club record for goals in a season. An ever-present in the 42-game season, he scored 43 goals to be the League's leading scorer. Halliday didn't even take the penalties and as Billy Clunas scored 10 from the spot that season, Halliday's record could have been even more astonishing.

What was also astonishing was that by the following November Sunderland had transferred Halliday, who like Buchan before him was sold to Arsenal. Another key departure was that of captain and centre-half Charlie Parker, who had been a stalwart throughout the 1920s and who left at the end of Cochrane's first campaign.

There were three main newcomers for the 1929–30 season. Forward Patsy Gallacher and centre-half Jock McDougall both debuted in September 1929, as did the new Main Grandstand, built by the renowned Archibald Leitch and featuring the famed criss-cross latticework on the front of the stand, still seen at Ibrox, Goodison Park and Fratton Park, but unique in its red and white at Roker and still preserved on display outside the Stadium of Light today.

A month after the new stand opened a record crowd of over 58,000 squeezed in to see Newcastle beaten but the season proved to be a tame one, the first of four consecutive mid-table finishes.

Cochrane went back to St Mirren in the summer to sign a player who would become one of the crowd's all-time favourites, winger Jimmy Connor. He was soon joined by another

Scot, Alex Hastings; who was signed from Stenhousemuir and would go on to captain Sunderland to the title. The pair made an inauspicious start. The 1930-31 season was nine games old before Sunderland won a game. High-scoring games were the norm, with 174 goals in Sunderland's 42 games and the top three of Arsenal, Villa and Sheffield Wednesday scoring 357 between them! Sunderland lost 7–2 at Sheffield Wednesday, beat Blackburn 8–2 after leading 7–0 at half-time, and in December had successive scores of 6–5 at home to Liverpool, 0–5 away to Chelsea, 6–1 at home to West Ham and 2–5 at home to Leicester on Christmas Day! It was certainly entertaining.

The FA Cup had brought little excitement since the Cup Final year of 1913. Much is made on Wearside of the club's two Cup-winning years of 1937 and 1973 being when the numbers were transposed. Similarly in 1931 when 13 was transposed Sunderland enjoyed their best run since 1913, only to lose at the semi-final stage.

The gates were closed at Roker with a record 63,016 inside for the fifth-round game with Sheffield United. That record crowd was soon broken, but one that still stands was set in the next round for the visit to St James's Park. That was St James's Park Exeter, not Newcastle, where Sunderland won a quarter-final replay in front of 20,984 before disappointingly losing 2–0 to Birmingham in the semi at Leeds. Jimmy Connor top-scored with six goals in the Cup run. It would be an injury en route to winning the Cup six years later that would end his career.

1931–32 started badly. Only three wins in the opening 18 games culminated in a 5-0 drubbing at Leicester (their biggest League win of the season) and a 4–1 home loss to Newcastle in November. Fortunately a strong late-season run saw the team climb to thirteenth. Nonetheless November 1931 was a key month for Sunderland as Horatio Stratton Carter – Raich – signed as a professional.

Arguably the best player ever to wear the stripes, Carter was Sunderland born but had failed in a trial with Leicester. He had been registered on amateur forms with Sunderland and was playing in the Northern League for Esh Winning when Clem Stephenson – veteran of the 1913 Cup Final dream when with Aston Villa and now managing Huddersfield – asked him to go for a trial. Johnny Cochrane was livid when he heard this and Carter was duly signed as a professional.

Carter had been born in the year of Sunderland's first Cup Final and would captain them to victory in their second, scoring the decisive goal, but it was to be another year before his debut at the age of 18 at Sheffield Wednesday.

Raich scored on his home debut in a 7–4 win over Bolton late in 1932. Bobby Gurney got four that day and the pair of them would become great pals. When the Championship was won in 1936 the pair were joint top scorers with 31 goals apiece and a year later, in the week before both scored in the Cup Final at Wembley, Gurney was Best Man at Carter's wedding.

Earlier in the same month as Carter's debut another piece of the jigsaw Cochrane was assembling was slotted into place. As in the 1913 side that won the League and got to the Cup Final, Sunderland's side that did the same in the thirties would also have a Scottish international defender called Charlie Thomson. They were not related but coincidentally played almost the same number of games; one playing 264 games for Sunderland and the other 263. The Thomson of the thirties, however, was more of a reader of the game, whereas the earlier Thomson was bigger, stronger and not one to take prisoners.

Leicester City were soon made to see the error of their ways in rejecting Carter when he scored both goals in a 2–1 win over them in his ninth game, as Sunderland recovered from their bad start to finish 1932–33 in twelve place.

Despite the lack of excitement in the season Sunderland registered a record attendance of 75,118 thanks to a dose of Cup fever. A thrilling quarter-final tie had been drawn 4–4 at Derby, but the huge gate for the replay would be disappointed as Sunderland lost 1–0. Indeed the following month the second-lowest accurate League gate of 3,911 turned up for a meaningless end-of-season game with Portsmouth on the afternoon that the Cup Final was broadcast live on the radio for the first time.

Sunderland had beaten Cup bogey team Aston Villa thanks to a Bobby Gurney hat-trick during their Cup run but when the clubs met again in 1933–34 Villa inflicted Sunderland's record FA Cup defeat of 7–2. There was an improvement in the League where the Lads climbed to sixth place. As was so often the case though, Sunderland did well at home but had a poor away record. Perhaps the perils of travelling great distances in those far off pre-motorway days took their toll. Only one game (the first) was lost at home, but a meagre two away wins was the worst performance since 1905–06.

Sunderland got their act together away from home in 1934–35, losing only three times on their travels and setting a club record. In those days of only two points for a win, a dozen draws on the road and half a dozen victories represented an excellent return. However, 12 goals were conceded in two games at Everton.

Christmas Day saw the Lads beaten 6–2 at Goodison, but revenge was swift with Sunderland winning 7–0 against the same opposition at home on Boxing Day. A month later Everton gave a better account of themselves in the Cup at Roker, drawing 1–1 to set up a classic replay which Sunderland lost 6–4 after extra-time.

Restored to the side for that Boxing Day bashing of Everton was 21-year-old goalkeeper Jimmy Thorpe. He would not miss another game until his tragic death three years later. A diabetic, he was injured in a match against Chelsea in which he was 'roughed up' in a goalmouth scramble and passed away in hospital five days later. His widow would receive his posthumous Championship medal. One consequence of these events was that the FA changed the rules to stop players raising their feet towards goalkeepers.

Thorpe kept a clean sheet at Arsenal before a never-surpassed Highbury crowd of 73,295 in March 1935 as Sunderland showed their worth as runners-up to the Gunners, who sealed a third successive Championship. In the spirit that marks them as a club of class and style, Arsenal invited the Sunderland players to their Championship Dinner. Sunderland attended with grace, but what they saw on the menu was their own Championship win, which was only a year away.

Arsenal's side was one of the best ever, including all-time greats such as Alex James, Cliff Bastin, Ted Drake, Joe Hulme and Eddie Hapgood. The Gunners began their defence of the title with a 3–1 win home win over Sunderland but by the time they came to Wearside for the last game of the calendar year Sunderland had lost just three more games, with an in-form Gurney having scored five in one match earlier in the month.

Oddly, Gurney didn't get on the scoresheet as Arsenal were beaten 5–4 in a game rivalled only by the FA Cup fifth round replay against Manchester City in 1973 as the greatest ever at Roker Park. Every other member of Sunderland's much-vaunted forward line of Davis, Carter, Gallacher and Connor scored, with Carter getting two. Arsenal had failed to beat Sunderland at Roker in any of the three title-winning seasons they had just enjoyed and this colossal victory in the battle of the giants set Sunderland up to become worthy champions for a sixth time.

Gurney hit four as Sunderland sealed the title with a 7–2 win away at Birmingham with three games to spare. Johnny Cochrane's Sunderland had done it in style. Conceding 74 goals was a record for a Championship-winning team but with the 109 rattled in at the other end Sunderland had scored 48 more than runners-up Arsenal, who had run out of ammunition in the League but still won the FA Cup.

Matt Middleton took over in goal following Jimmy Thorpe's death but after conceding six at Middlesbrough two months later he was replaced by teenager Johnny Mapson, who had been brought in from Reading. He would stay with the club until 1954 and join the ranks of the club's all-time greats.

A defence of the title was never on the cards as dreadful away form returned. Fifteen defeats on the road was the worst in the club's history and would remain so until 1965. Home form was identical to the Championship season with 17 wins, two draws and two defeats, the defeats ironically at the hands of the only two teams beaten away from home.

It was as well that Sunderland's Charity Shield game against Cup-winners Arsenal was staged at home. Goals from Gallacher and Carter gave Sunderland the trophy with a 2–1 win on 28 October 1936.

However, having avoided defeat in only six out of 21 away League games, Sunderland managed to stay unbeaten in six games away from Roker Park as the FA Cup was at long last brought to Wearside.

Second Division Southampton were defeated at the Dell in front of a record attendance before a visit to Luton Town, who would go on to be champions of the Third Division South that season. They were beaten in a Roker replay after Sunderland came back from two down to draw the first game. However, just as the Championship-winning season was marred by the death of Jimmy Thorpe, this Cup-winning campaign would be tinged with the sadness of the curtailment of the wonderful Jimmy Connor's career. Connor had scored in both games against the Hatters but was felled by an appalling tackle in the replay. Like Brian Clough in a later generation, Connor would fight back to play a few more games, but this was effectively the end of his career. Luton's goal at Roker came from Joe Payne, who had scored a record 10 goals in one game the previous season.

A comfortable 3–0 home win over Second Division Swansea sent Sunderland into the quarter-final against Wolves. An aggregate attendance of just under 170,000, including a Molineux record of 57,751, watched this tie, which was eventually settled in a second replay at Hillsborough. Wolves had attempted to settle it earlier with a bribe to goalkeeper Mapson. The teenager refused to take it, passing the offending note to manager Cochrane and keeping a clean sheet in the decisive third game, which Sunderland won 4–0.

Wolves looked to have won the first replay at Roker before a Wednesday afternoon crowd in excess of 61,000 when Galley opened the scoring with four minutes to go. It seemed to be a repeat of the quarter-final replay with Derby four years earlier as Sunderland's Cup curse continued, only for Gurney to somehow plunder an equaliser in the dying seconds. Both sides scored again in extra-time but a penalty from Charlie Thomson – who had set up Gurney's dramatic equaliser at Roker – and goals from the much vaunted front three of Carter, Gurney and Gallacher, gave Sunderland a handsome 4–0 win in the second replay at Hillsborough.

Third Division Millwall had beaten champions elect Manchester City in the quarter-finals and took an early lead against Sunderland through Dave Mangnall in the semi-final at Huddersfield, but Gurney and Gallacher turned things round to send Sunderland to Wembley for the first time.

Two days after the semi a much-changed team lost 6–0 at Grimsby and as Sunderland looked towards the Twin Towers of the old Wembley only one of the last five games was won, with Leeds particularly benefiting as they avoided the drop after beating Sunderland 3–0 on the last day of the League campaign.

The Cup Final opponents were Preston North End, who had finished three points and six places behind eighth-place Sunderland. Over half the players on the field were Scottish, Preston's seven including Bill Shankly.

For the fourth time in the Cup run Sunderland had to come from behind, Frank O'Donnell completing the personal achievement of scoring in every round by giving Proud Preston a half-time lead with his eleventh goal of that season's competition.

As ever Bobby Gurney was in the right place at the right time to score the equaliser six minutes into the second half when he flicked on Carter's header from an Eddie Burbanks corner. Carter and Burbanks went on to get onto the scoresheet themselves as finally the FA Cup was won by Sunderland. 'That is a nice wedding present for you' the Queen famously said to newlywed Raich Carter as he collected the trophy.

The team returned to Sunderland with the Cup to scenes of immense euphoria the following Monday. In those days North East pride took precedence over local rivalry, and the Mayor of Newcastle and a welcoming brass band greeted the team off the train on Tyneside before the onward journey to Monkwearmouth station. Here the team boarded a bus for a procession accompanied by horns blaring from ships on the Wear and thousands upon thousands of supporters acclaiming the returning heroes. No team had won the Championship more times than Sunderland, but this was the first time Cup glory had been felt after so many near misses.

Johnny Cochrane had built a team that over a period of 12 months had emptied the Highbury trophy cabinet of the only three senior pre-war club trophies. Seven of the team had been with Sunderland for five years or more and only two had been bought: Mapson (the youngest Cup Final 'keeper until Peter Shilton in 1969) after two League games for Reading and Scouser Jimmy Gorman, a strong full-back who had a tremendous Cup Final having been bought from Blackburn between the third and fourth rounds.

Sunderland fought doggedly to retain the Cup and reached the semi-final in 1938. As in the Cup-winning year the team finished eighth in the League with 44 points, although a lot more games were drawn both home and away. Having taken trophies away from Arsenal, Sunderland helped the Gunners to get the title back when a final day win over Wolves cost Wanderers the Championship by a single point. The Midlanders were still paying for trying to bribe Mapson in the Cup a year earlier.

Mapson didn't concede a goal on the way to the semis as Watford, Everton, Bradford Park Avenue and Spurs were all seen off by a single goal, with Mapson's performance at Goodison Park (Sunderland had let in six there in the Cup three years earlier) one of the finest performances ever produced by a Sunderland 'keeper. Carter hit the quarter-final winner at White Hart Lane as Spurs emulated their north London rivals in recording their record crowd (75,038) against Sunderland.

Huddersfield were the semi-final opponents at Blackburn. Former captain Alex Hastings for Sandy McNab at left-half – it had been a close decision between them in the '37 Final – was the only change from the team that won the Cup. As in so many semi-finals over the years though, Sunderland disappointed. Trailing to a goal from Beasley at half-time, further strikes from Barclay and McFadyen meant that Burbanks's late goal was a mere consolation. Huddersfield 'keeper Bob Hesford's son Iain would keep goal for Sunderland 50 years later.

1938–39 was to be the final full season before World War Two. It was to be the poorest for 30 years, with a joint record number of seven home defeats. The Cup offered little respite, Blackburn knocking the Lads out in a fifth-round second replay at Hillsborough in a game that ended Bobby Gurney's career.

Gurney was as good a servant as Sunderland ever had. In only the second minute of the second Blackburn replay he broke his leg in a collision with goalkeeper Barron. No substitutes were allowed and somehow Gurney continued until half-time. It was to be Sunderland's all-time top scorer's last-ever game. Ten man Sunderland hung on for a goalless draw in ninety minutes as they had in the first replay. Just before the end of extra-time Carter gave away a penalty when handling a goal-bound shot on the line. Rovers' centre-half Bob Pryde missed the target with his spot kick only for Billy Guest to score with a last-minute free-kick.

Two weeks later Johnny Cochrane resigned after a 3–0 defeat at Middlesbrough. He had been in charge for just under 10 years, having started by watching the final game of Bob Kyle's reign at the same ground. Cochrane's assistant George Crow saw Bill Robinson score four goals in a 5–2 win over Manchester United a day later, but three of his other four games in charge were lost before ex-player Bill Murray took over as manager.

Murray was the first former Sunderland player to become full-time manager of the club. He'd made over 300 appearances before finishing his playing days at St Mirren. Murray's reign as manager would last until 1957, meaning that excluding temporary appointments Sunderland had only three managers between 1905 and 1957. However, unlike Kyle and Cochrane, no silverware would come his, or Sunderland's, way and he wrapped up the 1938–39 season with a solitary win in his nine games in charge.

The 1939–40 season was abandoned after just three games. A promising opening day win over Derby was followed by a 2–1 defeat at Huddersfield and a 5–2 reverse at Arsenal, where Ted Drake scored four times, but a day later on 3 September 1939 Britain declared war on Germany. The era of Cochrane and Carter was consigned to history as one of the most terrible wars in history shook the world.

We'll Meet Again: Wartime Football 1939–45

Football struggled on during the war, Sunderland actually reaching four different Cup Finals. They won the West Riding FA Cup in 1943 having reached the Wartime Cup Final a year earlier and lost two more minor competitions towards the end of the war.

Cliff Whitelum scored 137 goals in 169 wartime games including a double hat-trick against Huddersfield at Roker Park in the first leg of the West Riding Cup Final, which Sunderland won 6–2 and thus scraped a 7–6 aggregate win after losing the second leg 4–1 away where Johnny Spuhler was Sunderland's scorer.

A 4–1 away defeat was also the result of the second leg of the 1942 Wartime Cup Final at Molineux against Wolves, but on this occasion Sunderland had no first-leg advantage, having drawn the initial game 2–2.

Oldham, both Bradford clubs – City and Park Avenue – and Grimsby were beaten en route to the 1942 War Cup Final. Carter scored in both legs for Sunderland and wartime guest Albert Stubbins also scored for the home side at Roker.

Wartime football was kept alive by the use of guest players, who would turn out for whatever club they were nearest to during the war. Albert Stubbins (hero of Liverpool, Newcastle and the cover of the Beatles 'Sergeant Pepper' LP) and Stan Mortensen (who would score a hat-trick for Blackpool in the 'Matthews Final' of 1953) were among those who briefly appeared for Sunderland, who drew on the services of Raich Carter, Jimmy Gorman, Alex Hastings, Eddie Burbanks, Johnny Spuhler, Jack Stelling, Len Duns and Johnny Mapson.

Having entered the North League in 1941 Raich Carter scored a hat-trick as Sheffield United were beaten 7–1 in Sunderland's opening game. Games tended to be played in pairs, home and away against the same club, as they had often been in the League during the early twenties.

Mapson was one of numerous Sunderland players who 'guested' for other teams during the war. In 1941 he played for his former club Reading against Brentford at Stamford Bridge in the London War Cup Final, helping them to a 3–2 win. Brentford came back to win this Cup a year later when the London War Cup-winners met the League War Cup-winners in a Cup-winners' Play-off at Stamford Bridge. Had Sunderland beaten Wolves they might have played in London during the war, but as it was Wolves drew with Brentford in the fixture.

Eddie Burbanks also played in a Cup Final as a guest. He played in both legs of the 1943 League North Cup Final for Blackpool against Sheffield Wednesday, scoring in the first leg and helping the Tangerines to a 4–3 aggregate win. Burbanks scored again in the Cup-winners' Play-off as Blackpool beat Arsenal 4–2 at Stamford Bridge in front of a huge wartime crowd of over 55,000.

Burbanks' understudy at Roker was Fred Bett and he too scored Cup Final goals. Guesting for Chester, Bett scored in both legs of the Division Three North Cup against Rotherham which Rotherham won 5–4 on aggregate, although these games took place after the war in 1946.

In 1944 and 1945 Sunderland also competed in a Tyne, Wear and Tees Cup but lost to Newcastle in the first year and 6–3 to Gateshead at St James' Park in the 1945 Final. Wallbanks (1) and Laidman (2) got Sunderland's goals. A further wartime Cup Final – the Durham Professional Cup – was lost 2–0 to Darlington in May 1945.

Roker Park suffered bomb damage in March and May 1943 and a policeman lost his life in the March raid. The area under the Roker End had been used as an air-raid shelter for local residents. Thankfully, unlike during World War One, no contracted players died during the conflict.

Football paled into insignificance during the war as millions lost their lives in one of the most horrific periods the world has known, but at least football's attempts to continue showed that people were determined to keep alive the good and enjoyable things in life.

A fuller account of SAFC during the war is provided in the Wartime football chapter later.

The Bank of England Club (1946–57)

Post-World War Two football resumed with the playing of the FA Cup in January 1946, the League not kicking off again until August of that year. In order to provide more games it was decided to play the Cup on a two-leg basis and Sunderland duly knocked Grimsby and Bury out on aggregate before losing to Birmingham, who had been beaten 1–0 at Roker in the first meeting. As a result of bomb damage to Roker Park, the Roker End was still closed to paying spectators at this point and 45,000 crammed into the other three sides of the ground for the Birmingham game. To relieve the crushing, many supporters ran across the pitch at half-time to stand in the 'closed' and potentially unsafe Roker End for the second half.

Pre-war players such as Mapson, Burbanks and Duns were still available to manager Bill Murray, who had waited seven years to start to build his own team after his brief spell in charge in 1939.

One player also on the pitch at Roker Park when the League restarted was Raich Carter, but he was in the opposition line up rather than Sunderland's. Carter had already won another FA Cup-winners' medal with Derby, for whom he had signed at the end of the war. Carter's wife had gone to stay with her family in Derby during the war after their home on Wearside suffered bomb damage. With his wife suffering from ill health and needing to stay with her parents Carter jumped at the chance to sign for Derby when Sunderland turned down his request for a 10-year contract given that he was by now 31.

Despite the loss of the maestro Carter, Sunderland would not be short of star names and in the coming decade became known as 'the Bank of England' club as a result of big spending in the transfer market, something Sunderland had done before, most notably in the twenties. The first big post-war signing was Willie Watson, who cost £8,000 from Huddersfield in April 1946. He would give great service as a wing-half over the next eight years and be capped by England at both football and cricket – something only Arthur Milton of Arsenal and Gloucestershire has achieved since.

Stanley-born centre-half Fred Hall arrived from Blackburn Rovers to take over as captain and Sunderland made a reasonable start with home wins over Derby and

The 1947-48 team.

Huddersfield and a draw at Arsenal before taking a hammering at Charlton. A moderate ninth place was achieved in a season in which unusually almost as many points were picked up away as were at home.

The FA Cup proved something of a disaster, with elimination at the first hurdle away to Chesterfield who finished just above Newcastle in the Second Division. Lower League opposition in the shape of Southampton knocked Sunderland out straight away the next year, but that was nothing compared to what was to follow in 1949 when non-League Yeovil Town humiliated Sunderland's stars, winning 2–1 on their infamous sloping pitch after extra-time.

By then Sunderland had begun to acquire a galaxy of stars, chief among them being the Clown Prince of Soccer, Len Shackleton, bought from Newcastle for a record fee of £20,050 in 1948. Shack's Valentine's Day debut had pitted him against Raich Carter at Derby's Baseball Ground, Carter massacring his old club by scoring four as the Rams tore Sunderland apart 5–1 for the second successive season.

Sunderland flirted with relegation as 1947–48 drew to a close. It was the first time for 20 years that the drop had come so close and as in 1928 a 3–0 win over Middlesbrough assured safety, though this time with a game to spare.

Despite the disaster at Yeovil, the 1948–49 campaign marked an improvement as Sunderland finished eighth. Only one defeat in the first nine games got Murray's men off to a good start. The sensational Cup defeat brought an instant response, with the £19,000 purchase of future England international Ivor Broadis from Carlisle. Broadis was actually Carlisle's player/manager, so he transferred himself to Sunderland! A further £9,000 purchased winger Tommy Wright from Partick Thistle a month later. If Bill Murray had been looking for a spirited response to the Yeovil defeat he was to be disappointed, as the following Saturday Broadis's debut, like Shackleton's, saw Sunderland ship five goals, this time without reply at Arsenal. There were then three successive defeats to endure, including one at Newcastle, before an encouraging 11-game unbeaten run – albeit including seven draws – closed the season.

The post-war football boom brought more than a million people through the turnstiles at Roker Park in 1949–50 when, Sunderland threw away the title. Champions Portsmouth edged out Wolves on goal average with Sunderland third, a point behind, having lost three late-season games in a row including one at home to Manchester City, who were destined for the drop! It was the only home defeat of the season and City's first away win. Full-back Jack Stelling scored a penalty but had another twice saved by Bert Trautmann. Neither of the top two had been able to beat Sunderland.

Pompey and Wolves had been given a head start, as Sunderland won only two of their opening eight games. However, a 13-game unbeaten spell in the League between the turn of the year and Easter Monday, when a third game in four days caught up with the team, had put Sunderland right into contention.

Centre-forward Dickie Davis was the First Division's top scorer with 25 goals including hat-tricks against Derby and Wolves, but crucially he missed those three late defeats while Willie Watson also missed the City game as he was on international duty. The Cup was again an embarrassment as after a healthy 6–0 thrashing of Huddersfield, Second Division champions Spurs beat the Wearsiders 5–1 in the capital.

Sunderland kept spending. Wales' international centre-forward Trevor Ford was bought for a British record £29,500 in October 1950, with another £9,000 going on Northern Ireland winger Billy Bingham to help supply the service. With Shackleton, Watson, Broadis, Davis and Wright to call upon, and pre-war Championship and Cup-winning winger Len Duns still getting an occasional game, Sunderland's firepower should have been enormous, but in 1951 even relegated Sheffield Wednesday scored more than Sunderland, who spent three seasons marooned in mid-table before their own flirtation with relegation.

Notoriously Shackleton and Ford, two of the finest forwards of the generation, did not get on at all. Sunderland had a set of individuals rather than a team. When they were in the mood they could be irresistible, such as when torturing reigning champions Arsenal to the tune of 7–1 in 1954. On other days good results were largely down to individuals producing match-winning performances of the sort Ford produced when smashing a home debut hat-trick.

Too often though the entertainment the big names were famous for had no end product and the fact is that in the four seasons from 1950–51 to 1953–54 the stars from the Bank of England side lost more games than they won.

During this spell they topped the table in January 1953 after beating eventual champions Arsenal but then went a dozen League games without a win and ended up ninth.

The Cup provided a similar tale of woe. After losing a quarter-final replay to Wolves in 1951, Stoke, Burnley and Doncaster ended Cup hopes in the next three years, during which time only Scunthorpe – after a replay – were beaten!

All through this period Sunderland kept pumping money into the transfer market, hoping it would cure the problems. Previous managers Cochrane and Kyle had built trophy-winning teams but the Bank of England era kept on rolling, with over £60,000 being spent in June 1953 on Billy Elliott (£26,000 from Burnley), 'keeper Jimmy Cowan (£16,000 from Morton) and Ray Daniel (£28,000 from Arsenal). Another £30,000 was spent during the season on Ken Chisholm and Ted Purdon (£15,000 each from Cardiff and Birmingham).

At last in 1954–55 the Bank of England side had something approaching a good season, although for the money invested fourth place and a Cup semi-final did not mean the jackpot had been hit.

Chelsea were the champions for the first time, finishing four points ahead of three sides including Sunderland. The Lads got off to a good start. By the time Newcastle were well beaten in a mid-October derby only a single defeat had been suffered in 12 games. Sunderland lost the fewest matches in the division but drew the most.

Burnley, Preston, Swansea and League runners-up Wolves were disposed of in the Cup to set up a first semi-final appearance since 1938. Manchester City were the opposition at Villa Park and there was much talk of the possibility of meeting Newcastle in the Final at Wembley, as the Magpies were due to face giant-killers York in the other semi. The double had already been done over Newcastle and hopes were high, but City put paid to Wearside ambitions just as they had five years earlier in the League. The semi-final was played on a mud-bath in torrential rain with City winning 1–0 and going on to meet Newcastle, who eventually disposed of York in a replay that was the only FA Cup semi-final ever staged at Roker Park.

There was more semi-final disappointment to come a year later. This time it was 3–0 at the hands of Birmingham City at Hillsborough, but not before holders Newcastle had been beaten on their own patch in the quarter-final, and this in a year when the Magpies had done the double over Sunderland and registered their biggest derby win (6–1 at Roker on Boxing Day and 3–1 at St James' a day later).

Goals flowed from the start of the season. In the opening two months a 3–0 win at Bolton represented the lowest number of goals scored in a game. Champions Chelsea were beaten 4–3, Huddersfield 4–1, Shack got two in a 3–1 win over Arsenal, Villa were beaten 5–1 and 4–1 while an opening day 3–1 reverse at Cardiff and a 7–3 defeat at Blackpool were the black spots. The generally good form continued with just one more defeat in the next seven games, and Sunderland topped the League before the wheels came off.

A floodlit friendly was lost at home to Moscow Dynamo before a crowd of over 55,000 and then League leaders Sunderland were slaughtered 8–2 at Luton. A spell of 10 games saw 34 goals conceded. The team ended up in ninth place having conceded 95 goals, 10 more than the next worst defence.

Any hopes that things would be better in 1956–57 were ended on the opening day when Luton enjoyed another field day against Sunderland, this time winning 6–2. Results were every bit as up and down as they had been throughout the fifties. 'Keeper Willie Fraser was replaced by John Bollands, who kept a clean sheet in the next game as Bolton were beaten 3–0. Newcastle then inflicted a 2–1 home defeat before Charlton were hammered 8–1. The

Addicks would concede 120 goals in all, in finishing bottom of the table, and Sunderland weren't much better off, finishing third from bottom when only two went down.

Sunderland had continued to brandish their chequebook. England left-winger Colin Grainger - the 'Singing winger' (he once appeared on the same bill as The Beatles!) had been signed from Sheffield United in February and another England international had arrived in November in the shape of deep-lying centre-forward Don Revie, who 16 years later would manage Leeds against Sunderland in the FA Cup Final.

Ever since Aston Villa and Blackburn Rovers had been relegated together in Sunderland's last Championship-winning year of 1936, Sunderland had boasted of being the only club to have only played in the top flight of English football. It was a fact worth boasting about. There had been close shaves with relegation, especially in the Test Matches of 1897 and the Tees–Wear showdown of 1928, but they had survived.

There was to be no such escape in 1957–58, when Sunderland's luck was out as they were relegated on goal average, having achieved the same number of points as Portsmouth and Newcastle, who escaped. However, with the defence leaking 97 goals while only just over half that amount were scored, the goal average was by far the worst of the clubs in trouble.

Sunderland's troubles were not confined to on the pitch. Just as the 1956–57 season drew to a close the Bank of England club was found guilty of making illegal payments. The club was fined £5,000, which was the biggest fine English football had ever seen. Chairman Ted Ditchburn and director W.S. Martin were permanently banned from football (this was rescinded five years later). Directors Stanley Ritson and L.W. Evans were banned indefinitely and other directors were severely censured.

Six players were named as receiving illegal payments. Sunderland were known to have handed over almost £5,500 in one pound notes to players. Sunderland's books showed that contractors had been paid over and above the going rate for various services and supplies. The contractors, who obviously wanted Sunderland to do well, had then returned the extra payments to the club in cash, which was then distributed in brown paper envelopes to the players who at that time were subject to the maximum wage of £15 a week.

Of the players named, Trevor Ford and Ken Chisholm had left the club. Ford had left in 1953, which gave some indication of how long the malpractice had been going on. Of the remaining quartet, Johnny Hannigan was out of the side but Willie Fraser, Billy Elliott and Ray Daniel were first-team regulars, although all three missed the final game of the season after being suspended. Sunderland were already narrowly safe from the drop so their omission from a 3–2 defeat at Portsmouth did not affect the temporarily preserved top-flight status.

The suspensions were lifted after the players (other than Ford who was playing overseas with PSV Eindhoven) admitted taking the illegal payments. Instead the players had to forfeit financial benefits due to them.

Manager Bill Murray was fined £200 and duly resigned along with trainer Bert Johnston. Murray had been with the club since 1927, barring a brief spell at the end of his playing days with St Mirren. It was a sad end for a loyal club servant.

Sunderland suffered for being the most high profile and most lavishly spending club in the country. They were made an example of. It was widely accepted that Sunderland were by no means the only club circumventing the restrictions of the maximum wage. Indeed Ken Chisholm, by now playing for Workington in the Third Division North, said that although he had received £750 in under-the-counter payments from Sunderland when he signed in 1953, he had received similar payments when he had moved between other clubs. Cliff Lloyd, the secretary of the Players' Union, set about collecting 1,000 signatures of professionals who admitted receiving extra payments. Ten more Sunderland players had been financially penalised for taking illegal Cup bonuses, although various punishments were later set aside after the Commission of the FA and Football League was found to have exceeded its powers when it was sued by five Sunderland players in late 1958. However, the damage had been done.

The scandal had come to light in January 1957 when, after receiving a letter from someone calling themselves simply 'Smith', the Football League asked to see Sunderland's books to investigate the allegations of financial irregularities. The maximum wage was abolished five years later but by then Sunderland had spent several seasons recovering in the Second Division.

BROWNED OFF (1957–72)

New chairman Colonel John Turnbull turned to Alan Brown to take over as manager. Brown would have two spells in charge at Sunderland. These would result in the club's first two relegations. The first relegation was perhaps inevitable, given the dire situation Brown inherited, and he did build a team to win promotion. In his second spell he created a youthful nucleus for success with an FA Youth Cup-winning team in 1969 that included Ritchie Pitt of the side that Bob Stokoe later propelled to FA Cup-winning glory. Fellow 1973 Cup heroes Bobby Kerr and Billy Hughes having been Youth Cup winners with Sunderland in 1967 (during Ian McColl's tenure as first team manager). Brown had a similar fate at Burnley, where the team he had built and led to successive First Division seventh place finishes would mature into a Championship-winning side three years after his departure from Turf Moor.

Brown had had a brief spell as a coach at Sheffield Wednesday before coming to Sunderland. He was a strict disciplinarian and moved Sunderland away from the Bank of England image to a team built on youth and honest endeavour. In later years Brian Clough, who played for him at Sunderland and became one of the all-time great managers, would name Brown as his major influence. Later Sunderland managers Martin O'Neill, Roy Keane, Alan Durban and Jimmy Adamson; along with Bobby Saxton who was assistant to Peter Reid and Frank Clark, assistant manager to Ken Knighton in the 1979-80 promotion season, all came under Clough's influence during their playing days thereby perpetuating the Brown influence on SAFC.

Just as Howard Wilkinson's first game in charge almost half a century later would also be Niall Quinn's last as a player, Alan Brown's first match as Sunderland manager coincided with Len Shackleton's final game as a player. 'Shack' eventually hung up his magical boots after an opening day defeat by Arsenal, who had famously rejected him as a youngster.

Youngsters, though, were to be the order of the day at Sunderland under Brown. The new manager quickly set about ridding Roker of established senior players on whom the club had lavished money throughout the decade, with only two losing semi-finals and a thrown away Championship back in 1950 to show for it.

Sunderland supporters had always loved a hero to idolise and Shackleton had been a great favourite. Since the days of John Campbell Sunderland had always had at least one star. Buchan, Halliday and Carter had carried the torch (with Gurney also a huge favourite) since Holley's era and, less than two months after the Clown Prince's final performance, a new star came to Wearside. This time, however, he was a little-known defender, and he would mark his first two games with 7–0 and 6–0 defeats.

Charlie Hurley was his name, to paraphrase the song that would in due course reverberate around Roker Park. Hurley would be voted 'Player of the Century' in the club's centenary year, would win more international caps than any other player while on Sunderland's books and only FA Cup-winning captain Bobby Moore would pip 'the King', as he was known by then, to the Footballer of the Year trophy when Charlie captained Sunderland back into the top flight in 1964. As Hurley prepared for a home debut – his new fans waiting to see a centre-half who had been part of a defence that had leaked 13 goals in his first two games – that success was a long way off.

In mid-March Sunderland were still without a win in 1958. Debutant South African centre-forward Don 'Rhino' Kichenbrand scored in a home draw with Sheffield Wednesday (who would accompany Sunderland to relegation this year and again in 1970) to end a run of four heavy defeats. A surprise 1–0 win at Spurs, where Don Revie got on the scoresheet, gave Sunderland a glimmer of hope which they built on with a good home win and away draw before going to Manchester United on Good Friday, just two months after the tragic Munich air disaster. An injury-time equaliser cost Sunderland a precious point and a day later they were hammered 6–1 at home by Birmingham before losing at home in the return to United two days later. It was a disastrous Easter and, after losing back in Manchester at City the following Saturday, Sunderland had two games to try and save themselves.

The biggest win of the season was equalled as Forest were beaten 3–0 at Roker and Kichenbrand took his tally to six goals in 10 games by scoring both in a 2–0 win at Portsmouth, but it was not enough. To stay up, Sunderland needed Leicester to drop a point. Leicester had the worst away record in the League but won 1–0 at Birmingham City and finished fifth from bottom. Second bottom Sunderland were level on points with Portsmouth and Newcastle but went down on goal average.

Leicester were managed by former Sunderland hero Dave Halliday, who in 1928–29 scored just 11 goals less than the paltry 54 Sunderland had scored all season. Sunderland's glory days were gone for the foreseeable future. Having been in the top flight since before even Ted Doig was signed, Sunderland were now a Second Division team. Even the town's *Football Echo* changed its colour from pink to blue in embarrassment.

Over 56,000 had been at Roker Park for the first game of the 1957–58 season. Around 40,000 fewer were at Sincil Bank to see Sunderland on the opening day of 1958–59, where Lincoln City opened Sunderland's fixture list. If Sunderland had felt like aristocrats of the game when arrogance cost them at Yeovil nine years earlier, they could afford no such delusions now. Lincoln were in the same division as Sunderland on merit and by the end of the game they were two points better off after humbling the Wearsiders 3–1.

By the end of October everyone in the Second Division was above Sunderland, who propped up the table with a pathetic eight points from 14 games. Six goals had been shipped at Fulham and Sheffield Wednesday, five at Swansea and four at Bristol City. The only away point from seven trips was from a goalless draw at Middlesbrough.

The team was undergoing considerable change. Teenage full-backs Len Ashurst and Cecil Irwin (Cec & Len, the Flowerpot Men as they became known) and left-half Jim McNab made their debuts together and would go on to play over 1,100 games between them. Irwin had to wait a year for his second appearance, while Ashurst would eventually play more games for the club than any other outfield player and become only the second player to go on and manage the club. All three would be stalwarts in the promotion year when it came.

On the way out were goalkeeper Willie Fraser, fellow Scottish international George Aitken and Don Revie, who had asked for a transfer at the start of the season after Brown had planned to build the team around him. Revie eventually departed after a dust up with 'Bomber Brown' at Rotherham.

As an old head among the youngsters Brown brought in Sunderland-born Ernie Taylor. Taylor had been Manchester United's first signing after Munich and had played in the Cup Final for United earlier in the year. His experience included winning the Cup with Blackpool and Newcastle and he had played for England on the day the Magical Magyars of Hungary famously won 6–3 to became the second overseas team to win on English soil – the Republic of Ireland having earlier beaten England at Everton.

A new goalkeeper also arrived in the shape of Peter Wakeham. He started with a rare clean sheet as a five-game unbeaten run began, but it was a false dawn and Sunderland ended up in 15th place. They had only finished as low as that eight times in the top division. Things got worse before they got better – they were 16th a year later.

After four terrible seasons things took a welcome upturn at the start of the sixties. A six-match unbeaten start included only two wins, but it was an improvement. The trouble was that by November the wins column still showed only two.

A first-ever League Cup tie was lost 4–3 at Brentford. Brown, however, had faith in his side and gave them a run of 10 games with an unchanged line-up, during which the team was unbeaten. By the time a change was needed due to injury the team was on a roll and, after taking so many beatings from Luton in recent years, this time the boot was on the other foot as the Hatters were hammered 7–1 with centre-forward Ian Lawther claiming a hat-trick.

A week later things got even better as Cup fever returned. Close to 60,000 packed into Roker for the eagerly awaited tie with old rivals Arsenal. Sunderland won 2–1, both goals being scored by Stan Anderson in his greatest match. Stan hailed from Horden and was the only player to survive Brown's purge of the Bank of England side. Unlike the big names of that team he had come through the ranks back in 1952, going on to play in both of the mid-fifties semi-finals. Second only to Len Ashurst in terms of games played as an outfield player for Sunderland, Anderson eventually won promotion in 1965. Sensationally that was with

Newcastle, Sunderland having sold him midway through their own promotion campaign the season before, after Martin Harvey had emerged in his place. Brown was never one for reputations!

Anderson, though, was at the top of his game in the 1961 Cup run, which took Sunderland to the quarter-finals. A comfortable 2–0 win at Liverpool, where Bill Shankly was in his first full season, set up what proved to be a tremendous tie at Norwich.

Norwich and Sunderland would develop something of a Cup tradition in the eighties and nineties. In 1961, like Sunderland, they were trying to climb out of the Second Division. A packed house at Carrow Road saw Sunderland put under enormous pressure, but there was no way past Hurley and it was 'the King' who duly thundered home the only goal of the game.

It was Hurley's third goal in eight weeks after previously playing over 100 without scoring. The difference was that as of Boxing Day 1960 when he scored against Sheffield United 'Charlie' had become the first centre-half in the game to go forward for corners. That had been skipper Stan Anderson's idea when the side were trailing and soon the sight of Hurley storming forward was as glorious as a ship being launched on the Wear. Soon of course other teams copied the tactic and now it is an accepted part of every game.

No team had come closer than the 1913 Sunderland side to doing the 'double' since the turn of the century and it was Second Division Sunderland that came closest to stopping Spurs from becoming the first side since 1897 to achieve the feat. Bill Nicholson's push and run side drew an all-ticket crowd of over 61,000 to Roker. Tottenham led at the interval through Cliff Jones, but pandemonium broke out five minutes after the restart when Willie McPheat equalised. The resultant pitch invasion gave Spurs a chance to regroup and the Londoners held on for a draw before showing their class by thumping Sunderland in the replay. The atmosphere was special at Roker, so much so that Spurs' legendary wing-half Danny Blanchflower was found after the game looking for loudspeakers he insisted must be there to amplify the crowd. Blanchflower had in fact just heard the Roker Roar in full voice.

It had been a good Cup run and although the team finished 11 points off a promotion place in sixth place, the season had brought excitement back to the supporters, who at last had cause for optimism that a serious promotion charge could be mounted the following season.

Sunderland again turned to the chequebook to buy success but this time it was to complement the nucleus of a team that was being assembled. The club record transfer fee was twice broken. £42,500 went to Clyde for their Scotland international inside-right George Herd, and then that was topped with the sensational £48,000 signing of goal machine Brian Clough from Middlesbrough. Clough had scored 204 goals in just 222 games for the Teessiders and would plunder 63 in 74 appearances for Sunderland before injury cruelly ended his playing career.

Clough duly scored on his debut, but Sunderland lost their first two matches, leaking seven goals in the process. A 2–1 midweek win over Stoke encouraged over 47,000 to Roker Park for Cloughie's first Saturday home game. He scored but visitors Liverpool trounced the Wearsiders 4–1 to dampen promotion hopes. The team soon clicked though, and by December Clough had already scored 20.

A run of seven successive late-season wins gave the Lads third place, but only two teams went up at that time and the Play-offs would not appear for another quarter of a century. The FA Cup had seen fourth-round elimination in a replay at Third Division Port Vale, but the new League Cup had provided a run to the quarter-finals, where Norwich took their revenge for the season before. The opening home game in the competition saw a Clough goal prove sufficient to eliminate Bolton while there was a hat-trick from Brian in the next round against Walsall. That match was significant for another reason as it marked the debut of Jimmy Montgomery.

Monty would wait five more months for a League debut, but would go on to play over 150 more competitive games for Sunderland than Len Ashurst or Ted Doig, the next highest Sunderland appearance makers. Montgomery would also make the greatest save ever seen at Wembley, but anyone who watched 'the Mighty Jim' regularly knew that his miraculous double save in the 1973 FA Cup Final wasn't even his best save of the Cup run – that was in the third round at Notts County to thwart Les Bradd.

For the time being, though, Wakeham would hold off the youngster's challenge and while Wakeham would be in goal at Roker on the day Sunderland finally won promotion, it was for the opposition, as Monty had made himself Sunderland's number one choice.

Sunderland had been a single point behind promoted Leyton Orient in 1962. They would miss out by an even closer margin in 1963 after adding international forwards George Mulhall and Johnny Crossan to the team. Again there was a good run in the League Cup, the old Cup bogey team Aston Villa ending their interest on aggregate at the semi-final stage. In the FA Cup Sunderland met non-League opposition for the first time since the Yeovil debacle in 1949. Gravesend and Northfleet held the Lads to a draw but, unlike in 1949, there was no immediate extra-time to face and five were put past the non-Leaguers in the replay before Sunderland bowed out in the fifth round.

It was the promotion campaign that caused most excitement…and disappointment. Clough had scored 28 goals in 28 games to put Sunderland on top of the table when he clashed with Bury goalkeeper Chris Harker on an icy Roker pitch on Boxing Day 1962. Despite Bury centre-half Bob Stokoe's claims to the referee that Cloughie was kidding, Clough couldn't stand up. He had ruptured his cruciate ligaments and the playing days of the quickest man to score 250 League goals in the history of football were over bar three games 18 months later as he bravely tried to resurrect his career.

Given the job of replacing the fastest goalscorer the game has ever known, teenager Nick Sharkey made a damn good go of it, joining the club's two highest-ever scorers, Bobby Gurney and Charlie Buchan, by becoming only the third Sunderland player to score five in a League game, a feat he achieved in the fifth League game after Clough's injury.

The big freeze of 1963, combined with Cup commitments, meant that only a single point was gleaned from three League games between Christmas and March, but the season ended strongly. Sunderland had lost only two in 16 going into the final fixture. Easter brought a double header with Stoke, who would go on to win the division. They held out for a goalless Good Friday draw in front of over 62,000 at Roker before winning 2–1 on Easter Monday, Sunderland having beaten Portsmouth in between. The last game of the season brought promotion rivals Chelsea to Wearside. Sunderland were four points ahead but Chelsea had another game to play. The only way Sunderland could not go up was if Chelsea beat them and went on to win their game in hand. It was a tough, dirty game, which Chelsea won with a goal fluked from a corner, the ball going in off Tommy Harmer's nether regions. It would be the final goal of Harmer's 14-year career. Inevitably Chelsea beat Portsmouth to leave Sunderland stranded in third place and still waiting for a return to the top flight.

Settled sides tend to bring success. Rarely can a team have made so few changes in a season as Sunderland did in 1963–64. Montgomery, Ashurst, Mulhall and Crossan were ever-presents. Hurley and right-winger Brian Usher missed one game, Herd and Irwin missed three, McNab five. At right-half Stan Anderson played the first 10 games then was replaced by Martin Harvey before his controversial move to Newcastle a month later. Nicky Sharkey got 18 goals in his 33 games, Crossan top-scoring with 22. The first choice 11 were named 25 times in the 32 games after Anderson was replaced.

Led by Hurley, the Lads were always on course to go up and eventually did as runners-up to Leeds. Monty kept 20 clean sheets. The goalkeeper was beaten only 13 times at home. This was the same as the year before, which meant that in Monty's first two full seasons Sunderland had conceded fewer goals at home than in any season since 1903. Away from home Monty was beaten just 24 times – and you had to go back to the 1902 Championship season (34 games) to better that! It wasn't as if Sunderland were based on defence either, as the 1996 promotion team would be; in fact they scored 10 goals more than Leeds, whom they took three points out of four from over Christmas.

Only one League defeat – away to Newcastle – was suffered after that and that was perhaps due to the fact that it came just a few days after a draining FA Cup quarter-final second replay with Cup holders Manchester United.

Reigning First Division champions Everton, in front of just under 63,000 at Roker, had been among the Cup victims before a sensational Cup marathon with Manchester United. Two goals from Crossan and another from Mulhall had Sunderland 3–1 up four minutes from time at Old Trafford. Monty was in the middle of a run where he conceded only one goal in nine League games, but he was beaten by Bobby Charlton and George Best in the last four minutes after being injured.

The gates at Roker Park were literally torn down for the replay. The official attendance of 46,727 is perhaps only half of the number inside the ground. Few there believed that the official record attendance of 75,118 hadn't been beaten. Sadly two people died at the game.

United escaped with another draw after Bobby Charlton equalised in the last minute of extra-time. The game took place three years to the day since Spurs had drawn another Cup quarter-final and, as with the Tottenham game, Sunderland were hit for five in the next match. Four years later Manchester United would become the first English team to win the European Cup. Their opponents then would be Benfica of Portugal. Sunderland put five past the team from the original Stadium of Light in a prestigious November friendly, Benfica having contested the three previous European Cup Finals, winning two of them.

Despite the glamour of such games, the one which mattered most was against fourth-placed Charlton Athletic in the last home game of the season. Needing a point to guarantee promotion, nothing was being taken for granted after the events of the previous campaign, even though there was another game to play. Sunderland added to supporters' nerves by going behind to an Eddie Firmani goal. Herd equalised just before half-time, but with former Sunderland 'keeper Peter Wakeham giving an inspired performance the Lads had to wait until the 89th minute to be sure, Johnny Crossan hitting the winner.

Promotion was won. Sunderland were back where they believed they belonged and the lap of honour with Charlie Hurley being chaired around the ground was undoubtedly the club's finest moment between the FA Cup wins of 1937 and 1973.

Three weeks before the eagerly awaited return to top-flight football Alan Brown shocked the club by resigning to take over at Sheffield Wednesday. He had coached at Hillsborough briefly before coming to Sunderland in the wake of financial wrongdoings and now the Owls wanted a wise old head after their own financial troubles.

The directors and trainers Arthur Wright and Jack Jones looked after the team until the 20th game of the season when George Hardwick was appointed manager. They had a brave decision to make at the start of the season. Monty was injured and they chose to play 15-year-old Derek Forster ahead of reserve 'keeper Derek Kirby. Forster remains, at 15 years and 185 days, Sunderland's youngest player and the youngest goalkeeper to play in the top flight. In goal for Leicester on Derek's debut day was none other than England's Gordon Banks. The game ended 3–3, but after losing the next two matches 4–1 and 3–1 Sunderland decided they couldn't wait for Monty's wrist to heal and invested £12,000 in Kilmarnock's Sandy McLaughlan.

McLaughlan was the 50th goalkeeper to play League football for Sunderland. The first and last of his 46 games came against West Brom. He performed competently in the first, a 2–2 draw, and kept his place for 11 games until Montgomery was fit. He then had three reasonable runs in the side until he conceded five at home to WBA on New Year's Day 1966, amid allegations that the Scot had celebrated Hogmanay a little too well the night before. Those allegations remained unproven, but he never played for Sunderland again.

By the time McLaughlan played his last game, Sunderland had appointed and dismissed George Hardwick as manager. The former England international, whose statue stands outside the ground of his former club Middlesbrough, lasted from November 1964 to the end of the season at Sunderland. Sunderland finished their first season back in the First Division in 15th place, having reverted to type with a good home record but a dreadful away one. It was December before a point was won on their travels, the first 10 away games yielding nothing.

Clough briefly attempted his comeback but there were few new faces, although young striker John O'Hare made a first appearance and would later sign for Clough three times. Northern Ireland international John Parke arrived for £30,000 from Hibs to stiffen the defence.

The second season after promotion is often a difficult one and, following the departure of George Hardwick, Sunderland turned to Ian McColl, who had just relinquished his post as Scotland's manager. McColl went back to Rangers, where he'd been a player, to invest a record £72,500 in 'Slim' Jim Baxter, one of the most skilful Scots of all time. Baxter was still on Sunderland's books two years later when he had his countrymen in raptures as he indulged in some 'keepy-uppy' against England at Wembley as he inspired Scotland to a 3–2 victory over World Champions England.

Baxter rarely produced his best form for Sunderland, despite scoring twice in a 4–1 win on his home debut. He was brilliant on his day… but his nights as 'Bacardi Jim' meant that those 'days' weren't delivered often enough. Centre-forward Neil Martin became another of McColl's men, £50,000 being paid to Hibs in October for a striker who became the first man to score 100 goals each side of the border, 46 in 99 in all competitions for Sunderland.

Home-grown forward Allan Gauden became the first player used as a substitute by Sunderland in a competitive game when he replaced Mike Hellawell at Aston Villa in September 1965. Hellawell – an England international at football and a county cricketer – had been Sunderland's first named substitute; without playing, on the first day twelve men were allowed.

During the summer of 1966 Roker Park hosted World Cup football. In preparation for the tournament a roof was put on the Fulwell End, which also had temporary benches installed. The Clock Stand also benefited from new seats. Italy beat Chile 2–0 but lost 1–0 to the USSR, the Soviets also beating Chile 2–1. Sunderland supporters still sing The Red Flag, and the USSR were certainly at home in Sunderland where, inspired by the great Lev Yashin, they also beat Hungary 2–1 in the quarter-final.

Only three points had separated Sunderland from a return to the Second Division and, despite England's success in the World Cup, the attendance boom that followed it wasn't true at Roker, where the average gate dropped by 3,000. With only two wins in the first 11 games this perhaps wasn't surprising. Sunderland stayed up thanks to 13 home wins – a figure not achieved since in the top flight. Away from home though, form was deplorable with only three wins and 30 defeats in the first two seasons after promotion.

Brown's belief in youth was showing signs of coming to fruition. Three times in four years the FA Youth Cup Final was reached and the trophy claimed twice. Four years after the second of those triumphs in 1969 the Youth Cup's big brother would be won at Wembley. Bobby Kerr would skipper that side. In 1966–67 he burst into the side as a teenager. Just 5ft 4in, the Scot took his tally to seven goals in 10 unbeaten games with a brace in a 3–0 derby win over Newcastle, only to have his leg broken a week later in a Cup tie against Leeds United. Despite breaking his leg a second time as he attempted a comeback, six years later 'the Little General' would be captaining Sunderland to victory against Leeds in the Cup Final.

There was bad blood between Sunderland and Leeds, who were managed by ex-Sunderland forward Don Revie. Four years earlier Willie McPheat had broken his leg against them and the 1964 promotion race had been closely fought, with Leeds pipping the Lads as both went up.

Sunderland had lashed a dozen goals past Brentford and Peterborough to reach the fifth round of the Cup where Leeds lay in wait, Kerr's leg being broken in the first game of a tie that ran to three matches. Two draws – the second before what remains Elland Road's record gate thanks to the red and white army – led to a second replay at Hull. A controversial last-minute penalty took Leeds through to the quarter-final as Herd and Mulhall were sent off for protesting over the decision, one that still rankles with Sunderland's players and supporters decades later and made the 1973 Cup Final even better on Wearside than the rest of the country could imagine.

Two days before the second replay with Leeds, youngster Colin Suggett made his debut at Stoke, joining fellow youth product Colin Todd in the team, Todd having made his debut as a substitute at Chelsea earlier in the season. Both would go on to become big favourites.

The summer of 1967 saw Sunderland travel across the Atlantic to play as the Vancouver Royal Canadians in a tournament that developed into the North American Soccer League. Twelve games were played from May to July against European and South American teams that were representing American and Canadian cities. Three wins, five draws and four defeats left Sunderland/Vancouver Royal Canadians in fifth place in their group of six. Back at home 15th place at the end of the following season equalled their best top-flight finish since promotion.

Alan Brown returned in February following the sacking of Ian McColl. Four successive defeats were a cause for concern, but there were to be only two more in the last 12 games. A strong end to the season included a final day win away to Manchester United shortly before they became the first English team to lift the European Cup.

England's 1966 World Cup hat-trick hero Geoff Hurst helped himself to an astonishing double hat-trick against Sunderland in October 1968 as an 8–0 defeat at West Ham equalled

Left: 1968

Below: 1969 FA Youth Cup winners.

the club's record defeat. Five more were conceded on each of two subsequent trips to London as Sunderland's away malaise continued to derail any progress. In the six seasons between the 1964 promotion and the relegation of 1970 only once were more than two away wins achieved.

Having brought Charlie Hurley to the club in 1957, Alan Brown gave 'the King' a free transfer in the summer of 1969. The close season also saw the departure of Colin Suggett, who had been top scorer for the previous two seasons, a fee close to six figures taking him to West Brom.

Sunderland had never had a top scorer with as few as the seven goals Gordon Harris scored in the 1969–70 season. Not surprisingly, this resulted in Sunderland being relegated for the second time in their long history and for the second time under Alan Brown. Sunderland failed to score at all in the first four fixtures and it was the eleventh game of the season before a win was achieved.

Left with home games against Everton and Liverpool to save themselves, Sunderland held newly crowned champions Everton to a goalless draw to stretch an unbeaten run to five games. Until 12 years earlier Sunderland supporters had believed that relegation was something that happened to other clubs. Managed by Bill Shankly, who had played against Sunderland for Preston at Wembley a third of a century earlier, the Anfield outfit had Hetton-born Bob Paisley as assistant manager. The visitors' celebrations were muted as full-back Chris Lawler almost apologetically scored the game's only goal four minutes from time. Eleven years later Paisley's Liverpool would 'surprisingly' lose the last game of the season at Anfield to Sunderland, who that time escaped the drop and returned to the dressing room to find Liverpool had reportedly left champagne in the visitors' dressing room. The ghosts of Tom Watson and Ted Doig hadn't forgotten where Liverpool's first successes originated.

Nonetheless, that 1981 escape was some way off and in 1970 Sunderland's tally of 26 points was the smallest since the 1897 flirtation with the drop. A dozen fewer games had been played in Victorian times, and the fact that no one was amused on Wearside was reflected in tiny attendances for Sunderland's participation in the post-league season Anglo-Italian Cup.

A second sojourn to the Second Division offered little hope when thirteenth place was the best Sunderland could manage. This was combined with depressing Cup exits at the hands of Lincoln and Orient, the latter to the tune of 3–0 at home when Sunderland, in unfamiliar all light blue kit (because of the FA Cup rule requiring both teams to change in the case of a colour clash), looked as far away from the club's glory days as Neil Armstrong did from the Earth when he became the first person on the moon at the start of the relegation season. This was at a time when matches had about as much atmosphere as Armstrong found on the lunar landscape.

Colin Todd was sold to Clough's Derby early in 1971 meaning that the Lads lost their best outfield player. Astonishingly, what was arguably Sunderland's greatest single day since the 9–1 win at Newcastle in 1908 was but two years away. Dick Malone from Ayr United and SAFC's first £100,000 signing, Dave Watson from Rotherham, arrived during the season, meaning that eight of the team who would win the Cup played during this depressing season. Only Horswill; still to make his way through the ranks, plus Guthrie and Halom were still to arrive, as was the man who would transform them from a team who could only finish level on points with Swindon and Oxford to a team who could beat the best in the land.

Brown's last full season brought a point a game away from home for the first time since the promotion season. Together with a decent home record fifth place was managed. Without ever threatening to win promotion there was at least a glimmer of encouragement and gates rose from the sub-10,000 who saw Bobby Park's career ended on the opening day of the season in torrential rain, to 39,000 who turned up on a Monday afternoon (a miners' strike meaning floodlights were banned) for a Cup replay with Cardiff. The Welshmen would go through after a second replay at Manchester City's Maine Road two afternoons later but 12 months on the same ground would see Stokoe's Stars come of age.

Sunderland were languishing in the bottom half of the division when the Board were finally browned off enough with 'the Bomber' to sack Alan Brown on 1 November 1972. Bank of England player Billy Elliott remained as a coach and as caretaker manager and he took the decision to switch Dave Watson from centre-forward to centre-half for a match at Carlisle. Watson was at fault for two goals in the opening quarter of an hour but would go on to win more caps for England than any player on Sunderland's books had ever done.

The new manager would be someone who had won the FA Cup as a player with Newcastle and had stood over the stricken Brian Clough almost exactly a decade earlier telling him to get up. That man was Bob Stokoe. A man who became known as 'the Messiah.' A man who literally put the sun back into Sunderland and whose statue now stands outside the Stadium of Light.

Seventies Success (1972–80)

Success and Sunderland had rarely been seen in the same sentence since the war, but within six months of Stokoe taking over the FA Cup was on the mantelpiece. Change was evident from Stokoe's first moment. When the team ran out for his first game the Lads were back in black shorts, eschewing the white ones Brown had introduced 12 years earlier.

Stokoe's inaugural programme notes said: 'I am no miracle worker, I make you only one promise, that I shall do absolutely everything in my power to put Sunderland where they belong – right at the top of the tree!' Eventual champions Burnley maintained their record of being red and white party-poopers by winning Stokoe's first match 1–0; they had won the first-ever League game at Sunderland and been the first visitors to ever win at Roker Park. Caretaker manager Elliott, however, had picked the side and Stokoe sent his selection out for the first time back at the scene of Sunderland's first relegation, Portsmouth.

With three minutes to go Pompey led 2–1, but two late goals that sparked a victory suggested Stokoe might have the Midas touch. The new manager then had a stroke of luck. Following a goalless home draw the weather intervened to postpone three matches, giving him valuable time to work with his players. When Brighton became first footers on Wearside they were walloped 4–0. A week later the fans following the Lads to Notts County

THE HISTORY OF SUNDERLAND AFC

The 1973 FA Cup winners.

for a third-round FA Cup tie included a young Gary Rowell, a man who would become Sunderland's record post-war scorer (since overtaken by Kevin Phillips) but who was skiving off youth team duty to secretly support the first team.

What became one of the most glorious Cup runs ever enjoyed by any club almost ended before it got going. Notts would go on to win promotion from the Third Division and with 10 minutes left led 1–0. Goalscorer Les Bradd must have thought he'd sewn the game up when another goalbound effort of his was miraculously saved by Montgomery, with what those there still rate as better than Monty's Wembley wonder save. A minute later Watson, who had been moved up front for the closing stages, headed the equalizer against his first club.

Gates had been down to 11,000, but over 30,000 saw Watson and Dennis Tueart seal a 2–0 win in the replay, which set up a home tie with Reading, by now managed by Charlie Hurley. Before the tie, Stokoe negotiated the transfers of two surplus-to-requirements Newcastle defenders from his old Tyneside teammate Joe Harvey. A cheque for £35,000 brought left-back Ron Guthrie and centre-back David Young to Wearside and both came straight into the team. Another new signing was ex-Celtic hero John 'Yogi' Hughes, the brother of Sunderland winger Billy, but 'Yogi' would be injured in what was his first and only match.

Reading 'keeper Steve Death played a 'blinder' to earn a replay, Tueart equalising for Sunderland, who had what looked a good goal from John Lathan disallowed late on. They were the last remaining Fourth Division side in the competition and Elm Park was bursting at the seams for the replay, but Sunderland were three up within half an hour and strode through 3–1.

The fifth round provided a trip to Manchester City, who had overcome League leaders and eventual champions Liverpool comprehensively in the fourth round. This was the fabulous City side of Colin Bell, Francis Lee, Mike Summerbee and Rodney Marsh. They had won four different trophies since Sunderland's win at their rivals United five years earlier on the day City had clinched the League title and they were expected to wipe the floor with the Wearsiders.

The 54,000 inside Maine Road included two huge banks of Sunderland supporters, whose cries of 'Ha'way the Lads' seemed to urge Sunderland on in stereo. The Cup-winning team was by now complete. Centre-forward Vic Halom had played for Stokoe earlier in his career and had been signed from Luton, while coach Arthur Cox had been recruited from Preston. A week earlier Halom had marked his home debut with a goal as Middlesbrough were crushed 4–0 on the first occasion that what would become the Cup Final team played together.

Tony Towers gave City the lead. (He would be sent off later in the game and later play for England after signing for Sunderland.) Monty had to be at his best as City fizzed in a series of well-hit shots to test him, but Sunderland were by now responding to Bob Stokoe and astonishingly took the lead. Mickey Horswill got them back into the game by reading a short kick from goalkeeper Joe Corrigan, intercepting it and blasting in the equalizer. Billy Hughes put Sunderland ahead midway through the second half with a goal that summed up the Cup run. It was a lightning fast raid on the City goal by Tueart, who provided the pass, and Hughes, who scored. These two wingers were the flair players in an exciting side. Both would become full internationals and three years later Tueart would score with a spectacular bicycle kick for City at Wembley against his home-town team Newcastle in the League Cup Final. Tueart later became a long serving City director.

City equalised when Monty, under pressure from Marsh, couldn't keep out a Summerbee corner, but the Lads were good value for the 2–2 draw, which set up one of Roker Park's greatest games. City were favourites for the FA Cup and Francis Lee had spoken to the press about how many goals he was going to score, but with an all-ticket crowd of almost 52,000 in full voice the Roker Roar swept City away.

Sunderland were irresistible. Watson and Monty provided the base for success. Ritchie Pitt, alongside Watson, let nothing pass, while Guthrie was solid at left-back and right-back Malone was always a threat with his marauding overlapping runs. In midfield the tigerish Horswill subdued one of the game's best playmakers in Colin Bell, just as he would negate Alan Ball in the semi-final and Johnny Giles at Wembley. The 'Little General' Bobby Kerr ran miles for the cause while Ian Porterfield stroked the ball around the park. There were willing targets for the midfield with Halom, a robust centre-forward who could hold the ball up, and dashing wingers Hughes and Tueart, whom defenders simply could not contain.

Three years earlier arguably the greatest-ever Brazil side had won the World Cup with captain Carlos Alberto scoring the pick of their four goals in the Final against Italy. Fourteen minutes into the City replay Sunderland scored an almost identical goal. Porterfield, Guthrie, Hughes, Horswill and Kerr moved the ball from left to right across the City box with Kerr teeing up Halom on the corner of the box, attacking the Fulwell End.

Halom caught the ball perfectly. It flew into the top right corner of Corrigan's net and, despite underdogs Sunderland going on to become the first Second Division team to win the FA Cup for over four decades, they might as well have given Sunderland the Cup there and then. The name Sunderland AFC was on the Cup and under 'the Messiah' nothing was going to stop the Lads.

Before half an hour was played Hughes had made it 2–0 and it would be Hughes, with his third goal of the tie, that completed Sunderland's passage. City had asserted their quality and pulled a goal back through Lee early in the second half, but with 12 minutes left Sunderland broke from a City corner and as in Manchester Tueart and Hughes combined for Hughes to find the net.

Quarter-final opponents were Luton Town, who hadn't conceded a goal in their Cup run. The Lads had beaten Luton en route to the 1937 Final and would do so again. Watson and Guthrie got the all-important goals from second-half Roker End corners as Sunderland won 2–0.

Wolves, Leeds and Chelsea or Arsenal joined Sunderland in the Monday lunchtime draw for the semi-final, which paired Sunderland with the Gunners once they had seen off Chelsea in a replay. Arsenal, going for a third successive Cup Final appearance, had become only the second side of the century to do the double two years earlier, and, being just a point behind League leaders Liverpool when they met Sunderland at Hillsborough, they had the double in their sights again.

Wearing all white and with the huge open Kop end given to Sunderland supporters, as well as plenty of Sunderland supporters evident in the Arsenal end, it was almost like a home game, especially as the neutrals were not neutral at all but new-found Sunderland supporters. Halom had several chances in the first half, punishing centre-half Jeff Blockley for one mistake to give Sunderland an interval lead. This was doubled in the 64th minute when a Kerr long throw was headed on by Tueart to Hughes, who's looping header found the net. Although Charlie George pulled one back for the Gunners with six minutes left, Sunderland had done enough to win on a day that ended with Bob Stokoe, arms aloft, taking the salute of Sunderland supporters who were in dreamland.

When red track-suited Stokoe and deadly serious Revie led the teams out at Wembley, Leeds were the most reviled team in the country. Their gamesmanship and rough-house play had not endeared them to the nation, despite the success they had enjoyed in recent years. They were Cup holders and had a European Final scheduled later in the month. Leeds's line-up boasted 10 full internationals, while for Sunderland only Ritchie Pitt had played at Wembley before – for a schoolboy international!

'So what!' was the attitude. To the rest of the country it was David v Goliath but on Wearside, Sunderland were the favourites. Sunderland had always considered themselves giants of the game and hadn't Arsenal and Manchester City already been slain? There was a point to prove against Leeds following the three-game Cup-tie of six years earlier, when Kerr's embryonic career had nearly been ended. Kerr was now the captain and notwithstanding his 5ft 4in frame he was a giant in all but height!

Ritchie Pitt clattered England striker Allan Clarke straight away. Leeds could mix it if they wanted; Sunderland weren't there to take prisoners and neither were they there to make up the numbers. Before the game TV audiences had seen Leeds reflect manager Revie's serious nature, while Billy Hughes' laughing box had caused uproar in the Sunderland interviews. Hughes had started the season on the transfer list under Bomber Brown, but Stokoe had freed the shackles and Stokoe's Stars were about to pass into legend.

The game turned on two moments. Ian Porterfield had been rejected by Leeds as a youngster and it was the Scot who scored the only goal of the game just after the half-hour mark from a corner. As the game wore on Leeds pressed more and more for an equalizer but when Monty produced the greatest save ever witnessed by the Twin Towers, Leeds must have known the Cup would have red and white ribbons. Montgomery went full length to thwart Trevor Cherry's diving header before miraculously bouncing up to block Peter Lorimer's close-range follow-up.

Twenty minutes later Stokoe's run to Montgomery greeted the final whistle. The only previous Cup win had been in 1937 and now in 1973 Sunderland were the country's favourites and the country's Cup holders.

Approximately a million people greeted the Lads' homecoming the following Tuesday when a coffin marked Leeds United RIP was paraded around Roker Park. 'Messiah' Stokoe had worked nothing short of a miracle. League games were played the night before and the night after the Cup homecoming, leaving Sunderland in sixth place having climbed the table alongside the Cup run. Promotion the following season was a must but being the Cup holders in the Second Division would prove to be a tough challenge.

Every club in the division of course saw their games with Cup holders Sunderland as their 'Cup Finals.' Sunderland were a big scalp to take and none of the first three home games were won, the last of these bringing a career-ending injury to Richie Pitt. The Cup-winning team had just nine games after the Final before it began to break up.

The Wembley win had brought European football to Sunderland. The adventure began in Hungary, where Vasas Budapest were beaten 2–0, Hughes and Tueart getting the goals, Tueart's a blistering solo run from inside his own half. Not for the first time Sunderland upset their fans by raising prices for a big game and when the second leg came round it was watched by the smallest crowd of the season so far. European games required higher-grade floodlights, which Sunderland had installed, but supporters were annoyed by doubled admission charges. Nonetheless a Tueart penalty completed the job and Sporting Lisbon were next up. Horswill and Kerr, with a hanging cross the 'keeper carried over the line, gave Sunderland a promising first-leg advantage, but disaster struck when Hector Yazalde, who would win the European Golden Boot that season, notched a late away goal for the Portuguese. Along with Fraguito, Yazalde would be on the mark in the return leg in Lisbon as Sunderland bowed out 3–2 on aggregate to Sporting, who would go on to reach the semi-finals.

Between the two games with Lisbon Sunderland had two more Cup games against high-flying Derby County. John Lathan had already scored twice in a thrilling 2–2 draw at the Baseball Ground. The replay was a pulsating affair, Tueart scoring and having a penalty saved by Colin Boulton as the tie ended level after extra-time. Sunderland won the toss to stage the second replay and two days later Roker staged its fourth home game in a week – Palace having visited in the League at the weekend. The second replay with Derby was comprehensively won 3–0 with a Halom hat-trick. Significantly Halom was being marked by England centre-half Roy McFarland, while in the same position for Sunderland Dave Watson was in imperious form. McFarland would hold his place for one more England game before Watson made his international debut, oddly enough back in Lisbon.

Sunderland's League Cup exploits were ended by Liverpool, while the defence of the FA Cup ended in early disappointment at home to Carlisle in a third-round replay. In the League three teams went up for the first time, but the Lads ended up sixth, as they had a year earlier. Sunderland would have gone up instead of Carlisle if a game they lost 1–0 at Carlisle four games from the end of the season had ended goalless. The only goal of that match had come from a penalty given for a foul clearly outside the box.

The season ended positively when the last home game saw two late goals end Blackpool's promotion dreams and already-promoted Luton were beaten in a seven-goal thriller on their own patch. Leeds invited Sunderland to be lambs to the slaughter in their skipper Billy Bremner's testimonial match at Elland Road. A crowd of over 50,000 saw Leeds presented with the Championship trophy before the game, which they saw as an opportunity to put Sunderland in their place. The champions dominated the game but still could not beat Montgomery, who earned Sunderland a goalless draw.

Freed from the pressures of being the Cup holders, hopes were high for the 1974–75 campaign. Tueart and Horswill had gone to Manchester City, with Towers coming to the North-East, but the acquisition of former Scotland and Newcastle captain Bobby Moncur was a masterstroke by Stokoe. Moncur coming to Sunderland would do what Stan Anderson had done going in the other direction a decade earlier. Another member of Newcastle's 1969 Fairs Cup-winning team had been signed in the shape of Sunderland-born Bryan 'Pop' Robson. The First Division's top scorer with West Ham just two years earlier, Pop would top-score for Sunderland.

The season began well, a 4–1 away win at Millwall being followed up by a 3–1 demolition of Southampton, Robson notching on his home debut. A defeat at WBA was considered no more than a blip when a Hughes hat-trick helped Sunderland defeat Bristol Rovers at the start of a 10-match unbeaten League run, punctured only by a League Cup exit at Third Division Preston, whose forward line consisted of Bobby Charlton, future England international Tony Morley and the man who would eventually partner Robson in Sunderland's promotion side of a year later, Mel Holden.

Promotion was lost on the season's last day, a 2–0 defeat at Villa enabling Norwich to join Villa and Manchester United in going up, with Sunderland fourth. Over 60,000 had seen Sunderland's thrilling BBC TV 'Match of the Season' defeat by 3–2 at Manchester United and a huge Wearside contingent meant there were only three thousand fewer at Villa Park. Had Sunderland not suffered the loss of the in-form Porterfield through a car crash before Christmas, promotion might not have been missed.

At last promotion would be won in 1975–76. Only Bristol City and Bristol Rovers took draws away from Roker, where the other 19 League games were won. There was home defeat though in the FA Cup, at the quarter-final stage, to Third Division Crystal Palace. The Londoners were managed by Malcolm Allison, who had tasted Cup defeat at Roker three years earlier with Manchester City, and captained by Ian Evans, who would become assistant manager at Sunderland under Mick McCarthy.

Over 50,000 spectators saw a young Peter Reid play for Bolton on the day promotion was clinched and the title followed in the next home game. Bottom-of-the-table Portsmouth sportingly formed a guard of honour to welcome the red and whites onto the pitch.

Bob Stokoe had taken the club back to the top flight, a prize to go with the sensational Cup triumph he had achieved. But by the time Sunderland were ready to strut their stuff in the top flight, only half of the Cup-winning team were still at the club.

The return to the First Division started well enough with three draws, but after 10 games the first win still hadn't been achieved and warning bells were sounding. A club record £200,000 was invested in striker Bob Lee from Leicester in October, and although Lee was much maligned by supporters, he did top-score.

More significantly, the same month saw a new goalkeeper signed: Barry Siddall from Bolton. Monty's reign was finally over, ending, as it had begun, in the League Cup. Montgomery would later win a European Cup-winner's medal as an unused substitute for Brian Clough's Nottingham Forest, but although he would later return to Sunderland as a player, a youth team coach and club ambassador, 'the Mighty Jim,' the club's record appearance maker, had played his last game.

Two days after Siddall's debut, Stokoe too called it a day. A 1–0 home defeat at the hands of Aston Villa left Sunderland bottom of the League and 'the Messiah' resigned due to ill-health. Like Montgomery, Stokoe would later return for a further spell.

Scot Ian McFarlane took over for a seven-game stint as caretaker manager, which brought two wins and a creditable 3–3 draw on a foggy night at Manchester United. 1973 FA Cup Final referee Ken Burns somehow managed not to abandon the game as Sunderland fought for a point.

McFarlane was dismissed upon the appointment of new manager Jimmy Adamson. Ashington-born Adamson was a disciple of Alan Brown, whom he'd played for at Burnley, and like his mentor Adamson turned to youth. His first four games were lost without a goal being scored. This would extend to 10 League games without a goal as the club tested the town's Latin motto of 'Nil Desperandum'.

Inspired by a trio of youngsters, Sunderland hit a spectacular run of form. Seaham-born Gary Rowell had been on the fringe of the first team for a while and would become only the second player since World War Two to top a century of goals. Playmaker Kevin Arnott and speedy defender Shaun Elliott made their bow in an FA Cup replay at Wrexham and would soon become regulars.

Mel Holden brought the goal drought to an end with a Friday-night winner over Bristol City and confidence came flooding back through the side. It was the first of nine wins and five draws in the next 16 games as, having been marooned at the foot of the table, Sunderland produced something akin to title-winning form in an effort to stay up. Sixteen goals were scored in three successive home wins after the Bristol City home game and Sunderland had won six in a row at home when Newcastle escaped with a 2–2 draw on Good Friday before Manchester United were beaten on Easter Monday, with a point gleaned at Leeds in between.

The last Saturday of the season saw Bobby Kerr come off the bench to inspire a late fight-back for a point at Norwich, meaning that if Sunderland could get a result at Everton the following Thursday they would have completed the greatest of escapes. Even if

Sunderland lost at Goodison, relegation would be avoided if either Coventry or Bristol City won their match against each other on the same night. Only defeat at Everton and a draw in the Coventry–Bristol game could send Sunderland down.

Having previously been relegated only twice, and with the club's centenary just two years away, it was unpalatable to be relegated again after only one year back in the top flight, but Everton, with nothing to play for, won 2–0. The game at Coventry had kicked off late due to crowd congestion, although the attendances at the two games were almost identical, the 36,000 on Merseyside including phenomenal backing for Sunderland. Rumours spread that Coventry were winning 3–1 and Sunderland were safe but the truth was that at Highfield Road, Sky Blues chairman Jimmy Hill had had Sunderland's final score put up on the electronic scoreboard and both sides spent the final 10 minutes playing uncontested keep-ball with the score at 2–2, safe in the knowledge that this would keep both of them up. The fact that Coventry were reprimanded by the Football League for this was of no consolation to Sunderland, who found themselves dumped back into the Second Division.

It would take three years to win promotion. It was a case of steady improvement, as sixth place became fourth and then second. As in the previous relegation years of 1958 and 1970 Sunderland started with an away defeat and at least three goals conceded. Nonetheless, over 31,000 loyal fans turned up for the first home game following the drop. They were rewarded with a 3–0 win but it would be mid-October before another win was celebrated. Form was up and down all season. Bristol Rovers, for instance, beaten 5–1 in November, returned two months later to win 1–0 at Roker in the FA Cup.

Few tears were spilt when Adamson left to succeed Jock Stein at Leeds in October 1978. Caretaker manager Dave Merrington had been among a sizeable ex-Burnley contingent that Adamson had brought to the club. He had eight games in charge, winning his last at home 5–0 before signing off with a draw at Cardiff prior to linking up with Adamson again.

Sunderland turned again to Billy Elliott, who had first signed for the club in 1953, had been trainer when the Cup was won and had acted as caretaker manager prior to Stokoe's arrival. Elliott inspired the team to within an ace of promotion, despite failing to win any of his first five League games in charge, to add to his four without a win in 1972.

There had been an exciting FA Cup win over Everton on a frosty floodlit night and a League win under Elliott over his former club Burnley sparked a tremendous run. Gary Rowell was the main man and sealed his lifetime popularity with a hat-trick in a 4–1 win at Newcastle.

Only a single League defeat had been suffered in 17 games as Sunderland studied the closing five fixtures, which included three at home. Sunderland would lose two of them 1–0, including one against bottom-of-the-table Blackburn. These defeats cost dearly, as Sunderland finished fourth, two points behind champions Palace and one behind Brighton and Stoke.

Elliott paid the price for not achieving promotion and was sacked, with first-team coach Ken Knighton promoted to manager. Knighton enjoyed instant success. As in the previous promotion season, Sunderland's only competitive home defeat came in the FA Cup. Of the 11 home games before Christmas only a single point was dropped, but only three draws were managed in 10 away games.

There was a notable away success in the League Cup at Newcastle, where Sunderland equalled the nine goals they had scored there in 1908! These included seven penalties in a 7–6 shoot out win after both legs of a second round tie finished two each.

Promotion was sealed with a 14-game unbeaten run that began with the debut of full-back Joe Hinnigan. He was one of several newcomers brought in by Knighton, the best of whom was goalkeeper Chris Turner, who would eventually oust Siddall as Sunderland's number one. The biggest disappointment was Argentinian international midfielder Claudio Marangoni, who arrived at a cost of £380,000 in December 1979, a month after the club's first £300,000 fee had brought the diminutive winger Stan Cummins from Boro. Marangoni made just 22 appearances before returning to South America.

Defeat to Cardiff had cost promotion a year earlier and Sunderland travelled to the Welsh capital hoping to seal promotion there in the penultimate match, only to be held to a draw in a game that saw stalwart centre-back Jeff Clarke stretchered off. He would be missing when promotion was won back on Wearside.

The gates were closed with thousands still outside for a Monday night meeting with West Ham. Two days earlier the Hammers had won the FA Cup at Wembley and goals from Cummins and Arnott ensured both clubs had something to celebrate.

It was the perfect way to commemorate the centenary season. An England XI had marked the occasion in November (the centenary was in fact in October) with a 2–0 win thanks to two Bob Latchford goals. Charlie Hurley was voted Player of the Century. Hurley had captained the first promotion team in 1964. Now it would be the turn of the class of 1980 to re-establish Sunderland in the top flight.

Roker's Last Stand (1980-1997)

Two games after promotion the top flight was fleetingly topped, with a John Hawley hat-trick at Manchester City sealing a 4–0 win after a shirt-sleeved crowd enjoyed a 3–1 opening day win over Everton. Dreams of doing well were soon punctured by Kevin Keegan's Southampton, who deflated a 41,000-plus gate by inflicting a home defeat, and although there were only two defeats in the next nine games the season gradually fell away.

Centre-back Sam Allardyce had been Ken Knighton's major summer signing to replace the injured Clarke. Needing firepower, the manager invested £180,000 in centre-forward Tom Ritchie from Bristol City in January 1981. Ritchie had a good record with Bristol but he was an ungainly and awkward player who had failed to score in his 11 games when Knighton, and his assistant Frank Clark, were sacked by chairman Tom Cowie, who had taken over from long-serving Keith Collings in 1980.

Knighton must have had mixed feelings when, five days after he was dismissed, Ritchie came good with a hat-trick in the first game under the caretaker-managership of former player Mick Docherty.

Docherty lost his second game 2–1, but seemed to have virtually secured top-flight status in the last home game against fellow strugglers Brighton until Roker was hushed as Gary Williams poached a dramatic last-minute winner for the visitors at the Fulwell End.

Sunderland in 1979-80.

There was still one game for Sunderland to save themselves… the trouble was it was away to Liverpool, who would end the season by beating Real Madrid in the European Cup Final!

Sensationally Sunderland emulated their 1968 feat of winning away to soon-to-be-crowned European Champions. In '68, Manchester United had a chance of winning the League on the day they lost to Sunderland but in '81 Liverpool were out of the Championship race and under the managership of Hetton-born Bob Paisley. Liverpool contrived to lose at Anfield to a Stan Cummins goal in front of Sunderland's traditional huge away support. Liverpool reputedly had champagne waiting for Sunderland in the dressing room but, with results elsewhere going favourably, the Wearsiders would have survived the drop regardless of their win on Merseyside.

Two years earlier Mick Docherty had scored the winner for Sunderland at Stoke in a top-of-the-table clash full of bad blood. The match had originally been postponed due to the Sunderland team being marooned in snowbound Sheffield, unable to complete their journey to the Potteries. City's manager Alan Durban was hugely critical of Sunderland and was also on record as saying he wasn't concerned with entertainment. This was the man Sunderland turned to as manager in the summer of 1981.

Durban had played for Clough at Derby and had therefore been influenced by a man whose mentor was Alan Brown. A decade and a half later Durban would become chief scout for Peter Reid at the Stadium of Light and be the guiding light behind Sunderland, signing the 'unknown' Kevin Phillips. His own signing of a young forward was a Scottish teenager by the name of Ally McCoist. Durban in fact paid more for McCoist in 1981 than Reid would initially pay for Phillips in 1997, but there was no doubt that 'Durbs' could spot a striker.

McCoist made an impact on his debut as a sub away to UEFA Cup holders Ipswich, but although the crowd loved him he only gave glimpses of the greatness he would go on to achieve when he returned north of the border. He went on to become Glasgow Rangers' all-time record goalscorer, most-capped player and manager. For Sunderland, however, Ally would only register nine goals in 65 games as the team struggled during his two years at the club.

Durban's first season saw the introduction of the three points for a win system but Sunderland could still only manage a mere 44 points as relegation was avoided by one place, a final day win over Manchester City saving Sunderland this time.

The average crowd dipped under 20,000 for the first time at top-flight level since the depression era of 1933–34. One of the reasons the fans were disillusioned was because of a departure from the club's traditional kit, a mainly all white shirt with red 'candy stripes' being accompanied by red shorts and socks. This le Coq Sportif outfit was quickly consigned to history after a couple of seasons and the club returned to more traditional garb.

Poor attendances and struggles in the lower reaches of the League characterised Durban's tenure, although there was a slow if unspectacular improvement. Nineteenth place in the Welshman's first season rose to 16th a year later and the Lads would end Durban's third campaign in thirteenth place. He wasn't around to see that, having been sacked following a 2–1 defeat at Manchester United, which extended a run of winless League games to seven.

Although supporters were reluctant to back Durban at the time, in later years it was generally agreed that he had been quietly assembling a promising team. Home-produced players Barry Venison and Nick Pickering partnered each other at full-back for England at Under-21 level, Pickering even winning a full cap on a tour of Australia in 1983. Midfielders Mark Proctor and especially Paul Bracewell were accomplished players, Wales international winger Leighton James injected some of the entertainment the crowd hadn't foreseen under Durban and Gary Rowell kept topping the scorers charts – a feat he achieved at least jointly in every year from 1977–78 to 1983–84, apart from the 1979–80 promotion season which he mostly missed through injury.

Pop Robson top-scored in that promotion year and it was Pop who acted as caretaker manager for a single game with Arsenal, which was drawn 2–2, before the manager's job was given to sixties full-back Len Ashurst.

Ashurst remains Sunderland's record holder for outfield appearances and he came back to Sunderland as manager in his sixth managerial position. His first game at the beginning of March resulted in a first League win of the year. It was one of five wins, as many defeats and three draws with which he brought the season to a close. The final table showed Sunderland eighth off bottom. Amazingly it was the club's highest League placing for over a quarter of a century, and yet, but for a final day win at Leicester and a combination of other results going in their favour, Sunderland could actually have been relegated!

THE HISTORY OF SUNDERLAND AFC

1980 promotion.

1982-83 Le Coq Sportif strip.

SUNDERLAND: THE COMPLETE RECORD

1984-85

Ashurst spent the summer shopping. He went back to his old club Cardiff for Gary Bennett who became one of the club's great servants and also signed Roger Wylde, who he'd had at Sheffield Wednesday, from Sporting Lisbon, Steve 'Chuck' Berry from Portsmouth and a pair of flying wingers in ex-Chelsea man Clive Walker and Howard Gayle from Liverpool. Former Middlesbrough striker David Hodgson soon followed Gayle from Anfield and former Wolves player Peter Daniel was recruited from Minnesota Kicks.

Two minutes into the new season Bennett marked his debut with a goal against England goalkeeper Peter Shilton as Southampton were beaten 3–1. Progress was made and by early November supporters were counting the League position from the top of the table rather than from the bottom for the first time since soon after promotion.

Midway though the season Ashurst signed Scottish striker and former £1 million man Ian Wallace from French club Brest and defender Reuben Agboola from Southampton. London-born Agboola would later become the first player outside the UK and Eire to be capped while with the club when he was called up by Nigeria.

The season, however, would end in disaster. A Wembley appearance in the club's first-ever League Cup Final ended in defeat to Norwich after a missed penalty and a deflected goal. Worse than that was that only one game in the dozen played after the Final was won and once again the club were relegated, this time along with their Cup Final conquerors.

Goalkeeper Chris Turner was the hero of the Cup run. In particular he was brilliant in the fourth-round tie with Spurs, keeping the Londoners at bay in a goalless home draw before capping an equally inspired performance with a late penalty save in the replay.

Manager Ashurst sprang a surprise in the Final, preferring Wallace to Colin West, who had scored three times having taken two penalties in the two-legged semi-final with Chelsea. However the Saturday before Wembley Wallace had scored in a League victory away to the Cup Final opponents in a game West missed and there weren't too many dissenting voices then. Former Chelsea man Walker scored twice in the second leg of the semi-final at Stamford Bridge but blotted his copybook by hitting the post with a penalty in the Final. West was the usual penalty taker and had scored from both of his semi-final spot kicks, albeit one from a rebound. Walker was an accomplished penalty taker though, four months to the day before his Wembley miss he'd scored two penalties as part of a first half hat-trick against Manchester United.

Having promised so much, the season ended with the sacking of Len Ashurst. Assistant manager Frank Burrows 'looked after the shop' for a few weeks in the close season until a new manager was appointed.

Whenever the Roker hot seat was vacant, local campaigns sprang up to 'Get Clough for Roker.' Sadly that never came to fruition, but when Tom Cowie announced that Gateshead-born former Southampton manager Lawrie McMenemy was the new man in charge the news was met with equal delight by the fans and McMenemy's bank manager, as news of his lucrative contract became known.

McMenemy's success with the Saints, combined with a high media profile, suggested that he'd quickly get Sunderland out of the Second Division. He did, but supporters wished he hadn't bothered, as the club went down to the Third Division for the only time in its history, 'Makem-enemy', as he was dubbed, did a moonlight flit when the writing was on the wall.

'Big Mac's' years with Southampton had been based on signing a veritable 'Dad's Army' of big-name players who were past their best but who could still do a job. He tried to recreate this at Sunderland by bringing in centre-forward Dave Swindlehurst from West Ham, forward Eric Gates from Ipswich, defender Frank Gray from Leeds and soon afterwards the pairing of Sunderland-born former Newcastle and Liverpool left-back Alan Kennedy and right-back George Burley from Ipswich.

McMenemy's men got off to a disastrous start. They failed to score in their first five matches, all of which were lost, starting with a 2–0 home defeat by a well-drilled Blackburn side managed by Bobby Saxton, who would surface at Sunderland just over a decade later as assistant manager to Peter Reid.

It wasn't just a shot-shy attack that supporters had to contend with under McMenemy. Traditionally a home of great goalkeepers, Sunderland had sold Turner to Manchester United. The first replacement was Jim 'Seamus' McDonagh, who lasted for only eight games, none of which were won and one of which saw him infamously question the size of the goal in a Full Members' Cup tie at Grimsby! Seamus would return to the club in 2011 as goalkeeping coach. Long-time Liverpool reserve Bob Bolder was brought in and played for six months until home-produced Cameron Duncan was given a solitary League game. Despite saving a penalty in a 1–1 draw he was discarded in favour of the on-loan Andy 'Officer' Dibble, who would help to save Sunderland.

The Lads had struggled all season and went into the last two games of the season needing to win them both to avoid relegation into the abyss of Third Division football. Dibble kept a pair of clean sheets to help achieve those results, leaving McMenemy to wave a white handkerchief of apology to the crowd as the players took a lap of honour (or perhaps relief) at having escaped the drop.

It was felt that, like the Titanic, McMenemy should never have left Southampton. Having come close to the iceberg in his first year at Sunderland, Lawrie's Lads continued to steam straight towards it in his second season. The club who had proudly played only top-flight football until 1958 found themselves cast down into the Third Division for the first and only time.

McMenemy's second term saw him bring in Steve Doyle from Huddersfield, goalkeeper Iain Hesford from Sheffield Wednesday and centre-half Steve Hetzke from Blackpool, but they fared no better in supporters' affections and when a 6–1 hammering was inflicted by Blackburn in the second away game the signs suggested that 1986–87 was going to be another dour campaign. Striker Dave Buchanan had been Leicester's youngest-ever player when he made his League debut on the same day as Gary Lineker for the Foxes. However, while Lineker's career headed ever onward and upward, Buchanan had slipped into non-League football and came to Sunderland via Blyth Spartans. He got off to a good start but then struggled along with the team.

Less than 9,000 turned up for an April meeting with Sheffield United, who won 2–1, meaning that only one point had been taken from six games. After the match much of the crowd besieged the car park, hurling abuse and stones at the club offices. McMenemy subsequently left in the middle of the night, packing up his belongings and heading south to leave Sunderland to pick up the pieces of an ill-starred reign.

New chairman Bob Murray had taken over the previous summer and he turned to 'the Messiah' Bob Stokoe in an attempt to rescue the situation. Sunderland were sixth from bottom of the table and in decline. Stokoe's first game brought an improved performance at Bradford but another defeat. The first home game ironically brought Leeds to Roker for Stokoe's return, but where Bob's goalkeeper had been a hero against Leeds at Wembley 14 years earlier, this time 'keeper Hesford would be beaten by a 40-yard shot from John Pearson, leaving Sunderland with an unsatisfactory point.

Stokoe procured two wins and a draw to leave Sunderland with the chance to stay up going into the final game at home to Barnsley, only for a missed penalty by Proctor to contribute to a 3–2 defeat that condemned Sunderland to the Play-offs.

As in the Test Matches of 90 years earlier, the Play-offs involved meeting teams aiming for promotion from the League below. Gillingham, who had finished fifth in Division Three, were Sunderland's opponents and won the first leg 3–2 in Kent, extending their lead with the first goal at Roker.

Sunderland fought back despite another missed Proctor penalty, but it needed a dramatic last-minute Gary Bennett header to take the game into extra-time. Each side scored once more, giving an aggregate score of 6–6, but despite identical score-lines of 3–2 over 90 minutes on each ground, Sunderland were relegated to the Third Division on the away goals rule by virtue of playing the extra-time at home! It could only happen to Sunderland.

Dropping into the Third Division was one of the darkest days in Sunderland's history. Bob Murray kept the club afloat with a substantial interest-free loan and pulled off a masterstroke by making Denis Smith his new manager. Former Stoke centre-half Smith knew the division, having managed York City. Sunderland paid 50% of a compensation package to his old club with Smith offering to pay the remaining £10,000 due at the end of the season out of his own pocket if he failed to win promotion for Sunderland.

Smith's money was safe. Sunderland finished nine points ahead of runners-up Brighton, thanks largely to Smith's signing of a new goalscoring hero from his former club, York. Marco Gabbiadini hit the post on his debut in a dismal home defeat to Chester, then went on to score twice in each of his next three games, setting Sunderland off on a run of six successive wins, which became a run of 15 victories in 19 games. Promotion was clinched at Port Vale and the title was won before just under 30,000 at home to Northampton.

Gabbiadini, his strike partner Gates, penalty specialist centre-back MacPhail and midfielder Paul 'Jack' Lemon all got into double figures. MacPhail had played for Smith at York and had been a summer signing from Bristol City. Along with full-back John Kay from Wimbledon, 'Monty' MacPhail had stiffened the back four for a combined outlay of a moderate £45,500.

The return to the Second Division marked a rare season in mid-table as, for the first time since being relegated from the top flight four years earlier, Sunderland at least held their own in the second tier.

1989–90 started and ended with games against Swindon Town, which resulted in promotion back to the First Division in the strangest of circumstances. Sunderland finished sixth in the League and enjoyed their first decent Cup run since 1985 when reaching the League Cup quarter-final with Coventry – a match that saw red cards for Gary Bennett and City's David Speedie, a pair who had clashed at the semi-final stage when Speedie was in Chelsea's colours five years earlier.

The real drama though came in the Play-offs, where Sunderland met Newcastle. Sunderland had had the better of both League games, which had ended as draws. The first leg of the Play-offs provided another draw, the Magpies celebrating a goalless game at Roker that erupted in the final minute as left-back Paul Hardyman was sent off for his follow up on Magpie 'keeper John Burridge, who had saved Hardyman's Fulwell End spot kick.

The 1990 team group.

Sunderland had won 10 away League games, a figure they had never bettered at this level of football and hadn't bettered at top-flight level since the 1912–13 team that came within one game of doing the double. Eric Gates gave Sunderland an early lead at Gallowgate and when Marco Gabbiadini made it two with four minutes left in front of the red and white army at the Leazes End, onto the pitch came thousands of Newcastle supporters in an attempt to get the game abandoned. Newcastle fans had invaded the pitch when they were losing before (en route to the 1974 FA Cup Final), but County Durham referee George Courtney took the players off the pitch and told them that even if they had to stay there until midnight they would be going back out to complete the fixture. Sunderland thus completed the club's most satisfying victory since the 1973 FA Cup Final.

Wembley beckoned for the Play-off Final. Recent red and white memories were dismal. Two years earlier a penalty shoot-out had been lost after a goalless draw with Wigan in the Mercantile Credit League Centenary Tournament and another penalty had been missed as the League Cup Final had been lost 1–0 in 1985. Play-off penalty heartbreak was another eight years away, but in 1990 Swindon played Sunderland off the park. 'Keeper Tony Norman had been a record signing 18 months earlier and brilliantly kept the score down to 1–0, Alan McLaughlin's goal – like Asa Hartford's in the 1985 League Cup Final – deflecting in off a Sunderland centre-back. Gary Bennett was the unlucky player as Norman was finally conquered.

All was not lost, however. Swindon were rumoured to have been involved in serious financial irregularities and on the day Sunderland opened a new club shop it was announced that Swindon would not be allowed to take their place in the top flight and Sunderland were to be promoted instead. Sunderland had suffered more than their share of bad luck in recent seasons, but this was undoubtedly a stroke of exceedingly good fortune. Just three years after dropping into the Third Division Sunderland were back in the top flight.

Glamour was the name of the game when Spurs showed up for the first home game. England had lost the World Cup semi-final only on penalties and Spurs' star names included top striker Gary Lineker and ex-Newcastle tearjerker Paul Gascoigne. Making his Sunderland debut was a man destined to be the 'Player of the Nineties' – Kevin Ball.

Bally had been signed from Portsmouth, but he had done badly in pre-season and had been left out of the opening game, which was lost 3–2 at Norwich. He was magnificent in a thrilling, if goalless, draw with Tottenham and would go on to earn legendary status, firstly as a centre-back and then as a midfield anchorman.

Despite a dramatic home win over Manchester United four days later, Gary Bennett hitting a sensational last-minute winner, Sunderland struggled and finally succumbed to relegation, although not without a fight. The 'Roker Roar on Tour' gave Manchester City their highest gate of the season on the final day when, managed by Peter Reid, City beat Sunderland 3–2 with two goals from Niall Quinn. It was a cruelly disappointing end to the campaign but one of those days that marked Sunderland's fans as exceptional. Which other team could take 14,000 fans to an away game when it was the avoidance of a third relegation in six seasons and not the pursuit of a trophy that was the prize? It was that

THE HISTORY OF SUNDERLAND AFC

sort of support that made Bob Stokoe tell the nation, 'Until you've seen football on the north-east coast you've never seen it' on the eve of the 1973 Cup Final when for the only time since before the second world war the red and white army had a major trophy to cheer.

There would be even more Sunderland fans on the road for the final trip of the following season, which was to Wembley for the FA Cup Final. By then Denis Smith had been replaced by former youth team coach Malcolm Crosby, Smith having dismissed his assistant Viv Busby shortly before his own departure.

Crosby took over at the turn of the year, just as the FA Cup third round was on the horizon. Although he couldn't arrest the League decline that saw Sunderland finish in 18th place, 'Crossa' steered the ship to the Cup Final, Chelsea being beaten thanks to a spectacularly dramatic last-minute replay winner by Gordon Armstrong in the quarter-final and Norwich being seen off at Hillsbrough in the semi.

Striker John Byrne scored in every round up to the Final but fluffed a gilt-edged chance against Liverpool under the Twin Towers. Second-half goals from Michael Thomas and Ian Rush (with the goal that made him the all-time top scorer in FA Cup Finals) earned Liverpool a 2–0 win, a week and a half after Crosby's caretaker-manager status had changed to manager.

Cup Final captain Paul Bracewell ended his second spell at SAFC by defecting to Newcastle during the summer. Entering Roker Park was ex-Coventry manager Terry Butcher. Butcher arrived as a player and became something of a cheerleader, 'conducting' the crowd after every victory. These, however, were few and far between, and Crosby was sacked at the start of February 1993, a week after being knocked out of the FA Cup against Sheffield Wednesday, the scene of the previous season's semi-final win.

Butcher took over as player-manager. A 1–0 home defeat was followed by five successive clean sheets as the defence tightened up, but the last three of those were goalless draws as the team continued to struggle.

A depressing end to the season saw tame defeats at Tranmere and Notts County and Butcher had his old Ipswich teammate Russell Osman to thank for Sunderland avoiding relegation to the old Third Division, although in this first season of the Premiership Sunderland were hanging on to survival in the new Division One. Sunderland would have been relegated if either Cambridge or Brentford had won. Cambridge lost at West Ham, who therefore secured their own promotion, while Brentford were hammered 4–1 at mid-table Bristol City, managed by Osman, the Robins thereby partially redeeming themselves for their part in the 1977 debacle at Coventry.

Bob Murray provided Butcher with more money to spend in the close season than any Sunderland manager had ever had and £2 million plus was invested in centre-back Andy Melville, midfielders Derek Ferguson and Ian Rodgerson, striker Phil Gray and 'keeper Alec Chamberlain. The season started disastrously, with three of the newcomers injured in a car crash and Derby inflicting a worst-ever first-day defeat of 5–0!

Sunderland were one place above the relegation zone when Butcher got the chop in late November, to be replaced by former Sunderland schoolboy player Mick Buxton.

Like Butcher and Crosby, Buxton had been at the club when the manager left. A day later former Roker assistant manager Frank Clark brought his Nottingham Forest team to Wearside to win 3–2, but Buxton brought about a quick improvement, three wins and a draw seeing out 1993 on a relative high, with Sunderland at least ending the season in mid-table.

The longest unbeaten start to a season since 1910 heralded the 1993–94 season, but there were six draws in that eight-game run. From November onwards Sunderland were in the bottom half of the table and 16 months after his appointment Buxton was sacked after a miserable Friday night defeat at Barnsley, a game that marked the debut of £600,000 centre-forward Brett Angell and the first and last appearance of Dominic Matteo. Matteo hadn't been registered properly following his loan move from Liverpool and Sunderland fortunately escaped with a fine rather than a points deduction.

This was just as well, as Sunderland were deep in trouble when Peter Reid was appointed with seven games to go and given the brief of keeping Sunderland up. Reid's appointment was a surprise. He had been out of work for a couple of years since leading Manchester City to two fifth-place top-flight finishes.

Local lad Craig Russell came off the bench to score a last-minute winner against Sheffield United in Reid's first game. The only defeat suffered in Reid's 'Magnificent Seven' was at his first club, promotion-bound Bolton. The key game saw a terrific winner from

1995-96

Martin Smith as relegation rivals Swindon were beaten at Roker. Relegation was avoided by one place, but there was a six-point cushion between Sunderland and the drop.

Reid recruited his old Everton colleague Paul Bracewell for his third spell at the club, bought John Mullin from Burnley and, a month into the season, splashed out a fee that eventually rose to £1 million for David Kelly from Wolves.

Despite losing the first game of the season at home, Reid steered Sunderland to the League title, meaning that the Football League Championship trophy came to Roker Park for the first time in 60 years.

Turning a team that had just avoided relegation into champions was a sign that Peter Reid was about to steer Sunderland into some of the club's best years for a generation. Even relegated Watford scored more than champions Sunderland, but the division's second-best defence conceded 15 more than the Wearsiders. Reid had caused consternation by dropping the reliable Chamberlain to bring in teenage loanee Shay Given, but Given kept nine clean sheets in his first 11 games and would be given his full Republic of Ireland debut by Mick McCarthy while on loan at Sunderland.

Runners-up Derby were comprehensively outplayed. Soon afterwards teenage sensation Michael Bridges left the bench to score two late goals past Sunderland's last promotion winning goalkeeper Tony Norman as a 2–1 deficit was turned into a 3–2 win over Huddersfield to seal a ninth successive victory.

Sunderland's first-ever season in the Premiership was to be the club's last at Roker Park. Since the dreadful Hillsborough Disaster in 1989 and the Taylor Report that followed it, chairman Bob Murray had looked to the future and recognised the need for Sunderland to move to a stadium fit for a new century, just as the club had done with the move to Roker Park in 1898.

Plans for a new stadium near the Nissan factory in Washington had been rejected and so, throughout the 99th and final season at Roker Park, a new home was springing up on the banks of the Wear.

Niall Quinn was signed for the new season and made an instant impression, scoring twice on his full debut in a 4–1 win at Nottingham Forest, but Sunderland failed to score in four of the first six games. The Championship-winning season had ended with Sunderland drawing a blank in five of the last six fixtures as the finishing line approached. It was clear that goalscoring in the top flight was going to be a problem and so it proved. With Quinn injured for much of the season no one scored more than four goals, three fewer than the previous lowest top scorer record, held by Gordon Harris in the 1970 relegation season. Sunderland went down with a record 40 points. It was a sad way to end the life of a ground which been home for almost a century.

Just two days after relegation was confirmed away to Wimbledon, Roker Park was filled for a farewell game against Liverpool. The Anfield club had been the first-ever visitors in 1898 and a John Mullin goal helped Sunderland to emulate their 1–0 victory in the ground's first game.

Before the match an emotional parade of former players was started by Eric Doig, the grandson of the 1890s 'keeper Ted, who carried a large framed picture of his grandad around the pitch. At the final whistle Player of the Century Charlie Hurley dug up the centre spot, which was to be replanted at the as yet unnamed new stadium.

A month later Roker Park's contents were auctioned off before the demolition men rolled in to turn the stadium into a housing estate. Roker Park had made its last stand. Sunderland's future would see the team move to a stadium that was light years ahead.

INTO THE LIGHT (1997–2012)

The move to the Stadium of Light heralded an exciting new era. Bob Murray and vice-chairman John Fickling had worked tirelessly behind the scenes to provide Sunderland with the stage on which stars could shine.

The club's grand new home was the biggest and best new stadium built in England in the second half of the twentieth century. Named the Sunderland Stadium of Light at midnight on the night before the opening match, the ground's moniker paid tribute to the miners who had hewn coal from beneath its surface for generations. Now, like a miners' cage rising from the depths into the light, it was to be the team's task to take Sunderland back to the top.

The ground was filled to its original 42,000 capacity for the curtain-raiser against Ajax of Amsterdam. A carnival atmosphere was created with a vast array of pre-match entertainment, climaxing with rock band Status Quo arriving by helicopter. More significantly the Bishop of Durham blessed the ground that everyone hoped would be one to bring good fortune to Sunderland.

Four new signings made their first home appearances, chief among them midfielder Lee Clark, signed from Newcastle, and a little-known striker plucked from Watford by the name of Kevin Phillips. The game finished goalless but Niall Quinn, Clark and Phillips were on the mark in the first competitive game against Manchester City, which coincidentally repeated the scoreline against the same club in the 1973 game that had been voted the best ever at Roker Park.

Five defeats in the first nine League games represented a disastrous start, culminating in the 'Nightmare at Elm Park' as Reading put four past Sunderland without reply, leaving Reid and Co. to run a gauntlet of abuse as they got on the team coach to return home. A midweek League Cup defeat at Middlesbrough preceded the visit of bottom-of-the-table Huddersfield. The mood threatened to become ugly as Sunderland struggled to win that game, but win it they did to begin a 17-game unbeaten run that propelled them into the promotion race.

The rest of the division had been given a head start, however, and although the 90 points the Lads ended up with would have been enough to gain automatic promotion in most seasons, the Play-offs beckoned as Middlesbrough edged out Sunderland by a point.

In contrast to the previous season at this level the team was full of flair. Free-scoring forwards Phillips and Quinn made Sunderland the country's top scorers. Sheffield United were excitingly beaten but the real drama was still ahead.

Charlton Athletic were the opponents at what would be Sunderland's final appearance at the old Wembley. Appearances in 1985, 1988 (League Centenary Tournament), 1990 and 1992 had not even yielded a goal, but Sunderland would score 10 times against Charlton and still lose! Kevin Phillips scored his 35th goal of the season, the best tally since Halliday's record set in 1928–29, but 'SuperKev' had to limp out of the action before the end of a sensational game that ended 4–4 after extra-time.

An unlucky 13 penalties found the back of the net without fail when Sunderland-born Michael Gray made the long walk from the halfway line. Gray's only previous penalty (in a League Cup tie at Liverpool) had been saved and his shot was comfortably stopped by 'keeper Sasa Ilic to condemn Sunderland to another season out of the top flight.

It remains to the eternal credit of that team that, far from slipping away the following year, as losing Play-off finalists so often do, Sunderland won promotion the next year with more points that any English team in history had ever achieved to that date.

A magnificent 105 points were racked up as Sunderland swept all before them. A mere three defeats in 46 games was another record for the nation, while 29 clean sheets was a club record, a mere 18 goals conceded away from home was the best since the 34-game season of 1900–01, and for the second successive season Sunderland were the country's leading scorers. All of this was achieved despite Phillips being missing for four months and Clark breaking his leg on the first day of the season!

Sunderland were back in the top flight. Ready for a second bash at the Premiership, the new season was anticipated with more optimism than any of the club's previous promotions. With the new stadium seen as a 'Black Catalyst' for success, the highest average gate for more than a third of a century and a set of players capable of more than holding their own, the 'Sleeping Giant' was finally shaking off its overlong slumber.

The team was based on partnerships. Phillips and Quinn were a match for the country's best, on the flanks full-back Chris Makin dovetailed with winger Nicky Summerbee on the right, while on the left Michael Gray and mercurial winger Allan Johnston were brilliant. Any combination of Ball, Clark and Alex Rae dominated the centre of the park, centre-backs Andy Melville and Paul Butler took no prisoners and in goal the Great Dane Thomas Sorensen was the latest in the fine tradition of Sunderland number ones. Back-up strikers Michael Bridges and Danny Dichio plundered a dozen goals each, and with Jody Craddock, Darren Williams and Darren Holloway to call upon, Reid had assembled a squad the public believed in.

The Lads came down to earth with a bump in London on the opening day of the season, however, as a classic Chelsea performance left Sunderland feeling fortunate to have lost by only 4–0. Four months later Sunderland were 4–0 up against the same side seven minutes before half-time! The Lads were playing the football the club's heritage of Carter, Buchan, Holley, Halliday and Shackleton were renowned for. Sunderland were simply sensational. The Magpies had been mauled in a downpour on their own patch and the next three away games were all won, with an aggregate score of 14–0!

Sunderland climbed as high as second in the Premiership, spent four successive months in the top four and, although things tailed off to a seventh-place finish, it was the best for 45 years, and in Kevin Phillips Sunderland had the country's top scorer and the first Englishman to win the European Golden Boot!

The North Stand of the Stadium of Light was extended, taking the capacity to 49,000, as the 2000–01 season started with a 1–0 win over Arsenal. Slovakian centre-back Stanislav Varga made one of the all-time great debuts, although he would never capture the same form after a serious injury in his second match, which coincided with the last of fellow centre-back Steve Bould's career. Arsenal legend Bould had enjoyed an Indian summer in Sunderland, helping the club to re-establish itself at the top. That same game at Manchester City marked the debut of Don Hutchison, another big signing, who added goalscoring quality to the midfield.

When Hutchison made his home debut he was one of £10 million worth of players making their bow along with record signing Emerson Thome from Chelsea and an Argentinian teenager, Julio Arca, destined to become a crowd favourite. Sunderland's spending in the transfer market was indicative of the brave new world of the TV-inspired riches of the world's richest League.

A steady start saw Sunderland in mid-table when they went to Newcastle in November. The black and whites had had the better of Wear–Tyne rivalry since Sunderland's 1992 FA Cup Final appearance, and had tried to excuse their home defeat the year before as being down to the weather, the pitch, the team selection of the manager they sacked after the game and anything else they could think of. Sunderland promptly handed out another 2–1 beating, a result rubber-stamped by Sorensen's wonderful late penalty save from Tyneside talisman Shearer.

'Cock o' the North' status set Sunderland off on a terrific run. Twelfth going into the derby, the Lads were second 10 games later and although they again tailed off to finish in seventh place, the feeling was that this was a better achievement than the same place a year earlier as the club had more than held its own in what was thought to be the traditionally 'difficult' second season.

In fact it would be the third and fourth seasons that were the difficult ones. Sunderland had had a glimpse of the glory years that had made the club great, but the following two years would be a slog that would end with the club relegated and in serious debt after attempting to spend millions in an effort to break into the highest echelons of the Premiership.

French and Swiss imports Lilian Laslandes and Bernt Haas were in the side that won the first two home games, but the season never took off after the exploits of recent campaigns. Mid-table until the end of January, Sunderland fell away to finish one place above the relegation trapdoor and could have gone down on the season's final day. As in the previous two years performances had declined towards the season's end, but that was nothing compared to what was in store.

Determined to make an impression on the Premiership, Sunderland invested over £20 million in the transfer market, breaking the club's transfer record for Norway striker Tore Andre Flo and paying substantial fees for a new right flank in Stephen Wright and Matt Piper, while striker Marcus Stewart, 'keeper Thomas Myhre and centre-back Phil Babb were also added to the squad.

Four points from the first three games was a reasonable start, but a trio of defeats without so much as a goal scored, including a woeful derby display, meant that the end of Peter Reid's seven-year reign was in sight. A home win over Aston Villa and the biggest away win since the 9–1 at St James' in 1908 when Cambridge were thrashed 7–0 in a record League Cup score couldn't paper over the cracks and Reid was sacked following a 3–1 defeat at Arsenal.

The 2004–05 Championship winning team.

Former Leeds boss Howard Wilkinson was the surprise choice as Reid's replacement with ex-Stoke manager Steve Cotterill as his assistant. Four games into their stewardship and still without a win, a 2–0 half-time deficit was transformed into a 3–2 League Cup win back at Highbury where Reid had fought his last battle. This was followed up with a solid home win over Spurs and a hard-won point at Anfield to offer some hope, which was rekindled despite a run of four defeats when Liverpool lost a League game on Wearside for the first time since 1958.

Already in the bottom three at Christmas, only a miserable and solitary point from a goalless home draw with Blackburn was achieved in the rest of the season as Sunderland went down with a pitiful 19 points, a Premiership low. Like Reid, Wilkinson's reign ended in the capital, a 1–0 defeat at Fulham proving to be the last of his 27 games.

Already doomed, Sunderland turned to former Republic of Ireland boss Mick McCarthy. McCarthy had led his country though troubled waters in the previous World Cup, in which they had been undefeated and eliminated only on penalties. Prior to that World Cup McCarthy had brought his side to Sunderland for a benefit match in honour of Niall Quinn, but by now Quinn had hung up his boots and come the end of the season almost all of Sunderland's top players would be jettisoned as the club cut costs and looked for a new start.

McCarthy made centre-back Gary Breen the rock on which his side would be built. Breen had won more caps under McCarthy than any other player and would become a lynchpin of the team, taking over the captaincy a year later.

A League Cup win was sandwiched between defeats in the opening two League games, meaning that when the field was taken for a live TV game at Preston, another defeat would see Sunderland enter the record books for equalling the game's longest run of consecutive defeats, which stood at 18.

The corner was turned with a 2–0 win, and as with the ending of the 10 games without a goal run in 1976–77 the shackles were cast off as confidence returned. Four games were won on the bounce and within a month even goalkeeper Mart Poom was scoring! The next 31 League games brought only five defeats, while a first serious Cup run since 1992 took the Lads to an FA Cup semi-final against Millwall in Manchester.

Millwall had been beaten in the semi-final when Sunderland first won the Cup in 1937, but the Lads' luck was out on this occasion. Deeper disappointment was to follow when again the Play-offs resulted in heartache. A two-legged tie with Crystal Palace finished level after the Londoners scored a controversial late equalizer before – as in 1998 – third-placed Sunderland fell victims to the lottery of a penalty shoot-out.

McCarthy decided to make a fresh start, transforming his squad in the summer with an influx of young, hungry players, mainly signed from lower League clubs or Premiership reserves.

Players such as Dean Whitehead and Liam Lawrence, from Oxford United and Mansfield Town, and Steve Caldwell and Stephen Elliott from the first-team fringes of Newcastle United and Manchester City, made an immediate impact during their first season at Sunderland. They blended with more experienced players such as Breen, Thomas Myhre, Marcus Stewart and Carl Robinson to become part of a squad good enough to win the Championship by a seven-point margin.

Promotion back to the Premiership as the club celebrated its 125th anniversary was impeccably timed. SAFC had been on a rollercoaster ride of ups and downs for half a century but this was a modern-day high celebrated with a Civic Parade through the city centre to the Stadium of Light.

Two years later promotion would be won again – but in 2007 the open topped bus was left in the garage as manager Roy Keane eschewed the thought of a parade for a club of Sunderland's size to celebrate promotion. It wasn't just a change of manager that the club had had in the intervening two years, the entire make up of the club was transformed following its sale by Bob Murray, the longest serving chairman Sunderland have ever had.

Following the 2005 promotion parade Sunderland prepared to return to the top flight they'd bowed out of with a record low points tally two years earlier with a clutch of signings that could at best be described as modest. Amongst them was a full-back acquired on a free transfer from a club relegated from the division Sunderland had just won. Nyron Nosworthy, ex of Gillingham was called upon sooner than expected. Former Liverpool right-back Stephen Wright was badly injured in the first game meaning that Nosworthy was thrown into the fray. The first ball that came to him was allowed to roll under his foot and out for a throw in. Moments later the Londoner produced an impressive mixture of tenacity and trickery to show that he had character. In a microcosm, Nosworthy's opening couple of minutes summed up the season that was to come.

Debutant goalkeeper Kelvin Davis patently got his angles all wrong to allow Addick Darren Bent to put Sunderland a goal down in only the tenth minute. Charlton would run out easy winners despite being reduced to 10 men, Bent scoring again in a 3-1 home defeat. There was at least a debut goal from Andy Gray – nephew of Frank from Lawrie McMenemy's ill-fated team of the late eighties. It was the only goal centre-forward Gray would score. His strike partner Jon Stead – the summer's most costly buy – took 30 games before he scored his only goal of the campaign.

The first five games were lost and though there was a brief and minor improvement in results that lifted the Lads to the dizzy heights of second from bottom, a heavy home defeat by Portsmouth in late October – when Davis was beaten by a shot hit from just short of Seaburn beach – plunged the team to the foot of the table where they became more and more marooned. Sunderland fell four points short of the record Premiership low points tally they had set in their previous top-flight season. A meagre 15 points were managed all season. After 19 home League fixtures they had failed to win any home games. Fortunately there was a 20th home fixture as the only Premier League fixture ever abandoned because of weather had occurred at the Stadium of Light. Sunderland had been trailing 1-0 to a Fulham side with a terrible away record when snow came to Sunderland's rescue – in April. So it was that on a Thursday night that 'extra' game finally saw Sunderland win at home. By then Mick McCarthy was long gone, losing his job after defeat at one of his former clubs, Manchester City.

Former captain Kevin Ball took over as caretaker manager and garnered a third of the season's meagre points tally in the 10 games he was in charge. Sunderland were so far adrift they could have doubled their points total and still been bottom. Clearly the players weren't good enough but to the great credit of those that played they never ever gave up. Losing week in week out at any level is dispiriting and teams of lesser commitment would have suffered some very heavy defeats. However the team that took only 15 points never lost a game by more than three goals as players such as Nosworthy, Breen, Danny Collins and Dean Whitehead refused to hoist the white flag. Goalkeeper Davis had a season to forget and it would have been easy for him to step aside. When he was left out after being sunk by Pompey he fought for his place, got back into the team quickly and like the rest of the side showed commendable character. Relegation when it was mathematically confirmed came at Old Trafford where Davis kept a rare clean sheet as a point was taken on a night when the title chasing home side went into the game with one eye on just how much they could improve their goal difference. Nonetheless as Sunderland left the pitch and the Premiership there were still as many points to play for as SAFC would win in the entire campaign.

By the time of the Easter visit to Manchester rumours were circulating that former player Niall Quinn was trying to put together a consortium to take over the club. Further rumours even surfaced that Quinn's former Republic of Ireland teammate Roy Keane could become Sunderland's new manager – despite the fall out that had embraced them – and Mick McCarthy – ahead of the 2002 World Cup, a tournament preceded by Keane's failure to turn out for the Republic in a Benefit Match for Quinn at Sunderland.

Takeover talks came to light during the close season. Quinn's ability to lead from the front off the pitch as well as he had on it, pulled together a group of mainly Irish businessman called The Drumaville Consortium. Sunderland based travel agent John Hays provided the group with a Wearside element, Hays becoming vice-chairman while the new chairman was Quinn himself.

Punctuated by a two and a half year spell when he stepped away from the chairmanship but remained on the board as the major shareholder at a time when he was looking to ensure the Stadium of Light would be built, Bob Murray spent a total of 17 years as the club chairman. No one else has ever served as many as 10 years. Along with his vice-chairman John Fickling, Bob Murray was a lifelong Sunderland supporter. Like many board members the pair took plenty of flak when things went badly and undoubtedly there were some extremely disappointing seasons while they were in charge. However there were some very good ones too and despite the 2006 relegation as they bowed out there could be no doubt that Sunderland AFC was in a much better state than when Murray first took over. At that time the club were heading for the Third Division in a crumbling stadium with a couple of shabby buildings and three pitches for a training ground.

As Niall Quinn took over the team plainly weren't good enough but the stadium and training ground were top class. The stage was set, what Sunderland needed was players. They needed a manager too and having placed coaches Kevin Richardson and Tim Carter in charge of pre-season training at Bath, Quinn pulled more strings than Pinocchio's handler as he tied up the Drumaville Consortium's commitment and searched for a charismatic manager to revitalise the red and whites.

The new dawn arrived at the unlikely setting of Forest Green Rovers, managed by ex-Sunderland man Gary Owers. Between that opening friendly and the closing stages of pre-season the new chairman realised that his ambition for a big name manager would have to be put on hold while he convinced people of his and the club's ambition and so Niall took the reins himself with Peter Reid's former coach Bobby Saxton alongside him to offer an old, experienced head.

Saxton had been the visiting Blackburn manager when Lawrie McMenemy's stint as Sunderland manager began with a run of five defeats. McMenemy's appointment had been the last time a new start at Roker had offered such hope of a new dawn. Quinn too though would begin with five defeats.

An opening day televised loss at Coventry was followed by successive home defeats before the Wearsiders visited the less than salubrious surroundings of Southend United's Roots Hall. There an injury time goal by Jon Stead – his second and last for the club – didn't even merit the word consolation as Sunderland were well beaten 3-1. Worse followed three days later at Bury.

Seven year's earlier Bury's Gigg Lane had been the venue as promotion was confirmed with a five goal showing in the 105 point season. That night Quinn had elatedly destroyed the Football League signage in the dressing room in a celebratory farewell to the lower Leagues. Now things couldn't get much lower. Bury were bottom of all four divisions but good enough to knock Sunderland out of the League Cup. Niall's new Spanish signing Arnau had been sent off three minutes into his full debut and the team relegated with a record low 15 points were now being beaten by everyone, including the 92nd best team in the country.

Bold as brass, Sunderland's new chairman bounded towards the waiting post match media to announce that by the following week Sunderland would have a world class figure installed as manager. Sure enough 24 hours after Quinn had signed off as manager on a winning note as a live TV audience saw West Brom beaten 2-0, Roy Keane breezed into the Stadium of Light to be appointed to his first managerial position.

The timing was immaculate. The transfer window was about to close and there was an international break to give the new manager a chance to begin to assess the squad he was inheriting. Keane hesitated about as much as he would going into a tackle – not at all. Six players were signed immediately including the new manager's veteran former Manchester United teammate Dwight Yorke.

Keane's first ever half-time team talk as a manager saw him speak to a side who were losing having conceded on the stroke of half-time at Derby. Soon though two goals in a minute in front of the travelling support transformed defeat into victory. Four days later a trip to Elland Road saw Sunderland's long time rivals Leeds played off their own park, two of Keane's signings scoring in a comprehensive 3-0 win.

Despite the next six games only producing four points and despite the team being 19th by mid October, the belief was that the 'magic carpet ride' – that had been spoken about when Niall Quinn assumed control of the club – was now under way.

Still in the bottom half at the turn of the year, things took off with the arrival on loan of Manchester United's young defender Jonny Evans. His League debut for the club saw him paired with erstwhile full-back Nosworthy, told to play centre back by Keane. It was a great partnership. Big, powerful and brave Nosworthy complemented by Evans's old head on young shoulders, calm, composed and able to read the game just as a Manchester United player operating in the Championship would be expected to. The pair walked away with the Player and Young Player of the Year awards as Sunderland walked away with the title.

Two games into the new defensive partnership over 6,000 travelling fans heralded a 4-2 away win at Sheffield Wednesday but Keane was livid. Two late goals conceded was sloppiness, the riot act was read – and 450 minutes were played before another goal was conceded. By this time Sunderland were fifth but no one was aiming for a Play-off position. Sunderland went top on Easter Monday – draw your own Biblical comparison – and finished the home programme with a pulsating 3-2 Friday night televised victory against Burnley. As Carlos Edwards' late screamer tested the strength of the net the TV cameras panned onto chairman Quinn and his wife Gillian. Niall rose from his seat like he had risen to head the derby winner in the Millennium year. Now as then a new dawn had arrived as the Sun was put back into Sunderland. Two days later promotion was mathematically guaranteed when challengers Derby lost at Crystal Palace leaving the lads to take the title with a 5-0 win at Luton on the final day as runners up Birmingham – managed by future Sunderland manager and former Keane teammate Steve Bruce – slipped up at Preston. Watching from the stands at Luton was Sunderland's first ever promotion winning captain Charlie Hurley – like Keane a son of Cork.

Having amassed a dreadful tally of a total of 34 points combined from the last two top flight campaigns Sunderland, backed by Drumaville, invested heavily in the transfer market, spending around twice as much on a goalkeeper than they had on the entire team following the previous promotion. Craig Gordon became Britain's costliest goalkeeper when joining from Hearts for a fee capable of reaching £9 million while further fees in the region of £5 million each were spent on striker Michael Chopra and midfielder Kieran Richardson, £3 million went on full-back Greg Halford, up to £2.5 million on defender Paul McShane, £1.5 million on midfielder Dickson Etuhu and £1 million on centre back

Russell Anderson. Before the transfer window closed another £7 million was lavished on centre-forward Kenwyne Jones with another seven-figure fee purchasing defender Danny Higginbotham.

There was an immediate return as Gordon kept an opening day clean sheet and Chopra notched an injury time winner to kick off with a win against Spurs. Another last minute goal earned a solid point at Birmingham thanks to some unorthodox work from another new signing, debutant Roy O'Donovan sitting on the Blues 'keeper as Stern John equalised.

Four defeats in a row urged caution but supporters had more to sadden them with the news that Ian Porterfield, the scorer of the winning goal in the FA Cup Final of 1973 had died. His Cup-winning colleagues attended the next home game. Fate decreed that it was against Reading, the only team beaten in the '73 Cup run that Porterfield had also played for. With the team running out to the tune of 'Z-Cars' that the boys of '73 used to emerge to, victory was achieved but it would be nine games until another win would be managed and even then it took an injury time winner to defeat a Derby team that would take away Sunderland's record of the lowest ever points tally, and this a week after the costliest goalkeeper in Britain had been beaten seven times at Everton.

The season carried on with the occasional win enough to keep Sunderland just above the relegation zone for most of the time before a late season run of three successive victories propelled the side away from any last day nerve shredding. Further mid season transfer activity brought Phil Bardsley, Andy Reid and Sweden international striker Rade Prica to the club as Sunderland ensured that the manager was backed to the hilt to prevent another immediate drop back into the Championship.

1973 team at Ian Porterfield tribute September 2007.

There had been times when supporters thought Sunderland had lost their chequebook but Keane continued to flourish it in the summer of 2008. Fears of 'second season syndrome' (where teams slide back after a promising first post promotion campaign) prompted Sunderland to keep buying. Three players including mercurial midfielder Steed Malbranque were bought from Spurs, and controversial Senegal international El-Hadji Diouf arrived along with a new back up 'keeper in Nick Colgan and promising midfielder in David Meyler. International strikers Djibril Cisse and David Healy were soon added, Cisse – like Chopra the year before – scoring a debut winner against Spurs.

Progress was slow but steady until the heights were hit in late October. Incredibly, rivals Newcastle United hadn't lost on Wearside for 28 long years although there had been some memorable wins for Sunderland on Tyneside in that period. Given the demand for a small number of tickets for away games though, an entire generation of supporters had never seen the Magpies beaten in the flesh. That changed in spectacular fashion when a stunning free kick from Kieran Richardson ensured victory that lifted the Lads into the top half of the table.

Just as a bad derby defeat would spark an impressive run under Steve Bruce two years later, the derby sparked a run of form this time. Bad form. Seven of the next eight games were lost and before the end of that run Keane was gone. The derby had been his last victory at the Stadium of Light. The end came following a 4-1 home defeat by Bolton Wanderers on a day when 'keeper Gordon played for the first time in six weeks though evidently some way off full fitness. He wouldn't play again for over two months.

Keane's assistant had been Tony Loughlan, someone he'd known and trusted since their days as apprentices at Nottingham Forest. Latterly he'd installed former Sunderland youth

The 2008-09 management team.

and reserve team coach Ricky Sbragia onto his coaching staff and it was Sbragia that Niall Quinn turned to to take over as manager. Highly regarded but low profile, Sbragia was a steady hand on the tiller. His side were well set up in his first game where only a last minute goal brought defeat at Manchester United but the players clicked into gear winning Sbragia's first home game by Sunderland's biggest top flight win in over 30 years as West Brom were beaten 4-0. A week later record book searchers had to go back to 1955 to find the last time Sunderland had scored four times in successive top tier home and away games after Hull were trounced 4-1.

Following this not untypical burst of form after the appointment of a new manager, results fell away. 18th when Keane left, Sbragia's side reached tenth after a goalless draw at Arsenal in February but only five points from the next 11 games left the club going into the final game of the season not safe from relegation and entertaining Champions League qualifiers Chelsea. Despite defeat there was celebration at the Stadium of Light as relegation was avoided leaving Sunderland as the only top-flight team in the North East as both Newcastle United and Middlesbrough were relegated.

Not only was it a time of managerial change at Sunderland where there were to be three managers in little more than half a season, behind the scenes Niall Quinn's on-going mission to establish the club at the top level had brought him to Ellis Short, an American of Irish descent. Reportedly Mr Short acquired a 30% stake in the club two months before the departure of Roy Keane, moved to increase his holding in SAFC just before Christmas and completed a 100% takeover from the Drumaville Consortium some three days after the final day of the season. His ambition for the club was illustrated by his continued financial backing and as time moved on his increasingly hands on role.

Having brought down the curtain at the Stadium of Light in 2008-09 Chelsea returned to raise it in the opening home game of the following season. Ricky Sbragia had stepped

2010-11 team with the plane to Portugal.

aside in the immediate aftermath of their previous visit to take over a scouting role. Replacing him in the hot seat was Steve Bruce. For all the big names that had managed Sunderland in the modern era Bruce was the first manager since 1985 to arrive having just been in charge of a top-flight club. It was to be hoped Bruce would be a more successful appointment than Lawrie McMenemy had been almost quarter of a century earlier.

Knowing Sunderland needed to buy goals, Bruce smashed the club's transfer record, lending his know-how and expertise to the deal that persuaded Spurs to broker a deal eventually worth £16.5m to bring Darren Bent north. Bent it had been who scored twice against Sunderland on the opening day of the awful 15 point season four years earlier. Soon nicknamed 'Dynamite', Bent had already helped claim three points taking just five minutes to bag what would be the only goal on the opening day at Bolton. He'd score against Chelsea as well and while the Londoners were too good for Sunderland once again, Bent was too good for just about everyone, netting 25 times in his first season to rekindle memories of Kevin Phillips.

Under Bruce Sunderland quickly looked the part. The manager returned to his old club Wigan to sign combative midfielder Lee Cattermole and partnered him with the captain of Albania, one Lorik Cana. Cana looked like he'd stepped off a Parisian catwalk and was a yellow card waiting to happen. He certainly had presence and could dominate midfield. After a second win in the first three games Bruce's side were sixth and would not drop lower than eighth until December.

Although Bent continued to find the back of the net, injuries; not least to Cattermole and later Cana, removed much of the power in the engine room although the promise of home grown youngster Jordan Henderson was one of several plusses. Eventually thirteenth place was managed, a rise of three places on the year before and the club's highest berth in nine seasons. Moreover following continued investment in the playing staff Sunderland were beginning to establish themselves in what was now the Barclays Premier League having negotiated a third successive season in the top tier and for the first time without a flirtation with relegation. Bruce's boys were never lower than fourteenth and people on Wearside were even seen to possess fingernails at the end of the season!

With Ellis Short continuing to financially back the manager Bruce continued to wheel and deal during the summer. Had it still been going 'Juke Box Jury' might have rated as many 'misses' as 'hits' though from the latest spending spree. The summer had seen the World Cup take place in South Africa. Having had success with South American signings at Wigan Bruce had already captured Paraguay midfielder Cristian Riveros before he headed off to the tournament to join his international teammate Paulo Da Silva who Bruce had already acquired. Argentina international right-back Marcos Angeleri was also signed as was former Newcastle centre back Titus Bramble who Bruce had rejuvenated at Wigan and young Belgian goalkeeper Simon Mignolet was a further arrival. The loan system was also utilised with the fabulous but fragile Ghana captain John Mensah brought back for a second season long loan while Egyptian Ahmed Elmohamady and two starlets from Manchester, Nedum Onuoha from City and Danny Welbeck from United, also arrived.

There had been a shock at the start of pre-season though when captain Cana beat a hasty exit and there was also a sale of striker Kenwyne Jones who Bruce had lost patience with due to lack of consistency. In the mood Jones was unplayable, but apparent moodiness was the problem, sometimes he simply didn't seem sufficiently motivated for the manager's liking.

Replacing Jones as the transfer window was about to close was a player whose ability to blow hot and cold would make Jones look as consistent as Kevin Phillips – Asamoah Gyan. Reported at the time as a club record fee the money eventually paid for Gyan was not as much as the final payment for Bent. Gyan had starred at the World Cup. His character in stepping up to score in a penalty shoot-out moments after missing a last minute game time spot kick that would have taken his country into the semi-final had captured the imagination of the world.

The striker came off the bench to score a spectacular goal that earned a point on his debut at Bruce's old club Wigan where for the second time in four appearances new captain Cattermole was sent off. By the end of October Sunderland had negotiated some tricky fixtures and sat handily placed in seventh position as they headed in confident mood to what was still known as St James' Park for the always eagerly anticipated derby match with Newcastle United. It was a Halloween horror show as the heaviest derby defeat in over half a century was endured, Bent's last minute goal raising barely a whimper from the stunned visiting fans who through their fingers had witnessed a 5-1 defeat.

When the end came for Bruce 13 months later – another derby defeat causing his undoing – there were claims that his Tyneside background counted against him. That was rubbish because there have been many 'black and whiters' who have succeeded at

2010-11.

Sunderland and equally plenty of 'red and whiters' who have become heroes at Newcastle. What was undoubtedly true is that the hammering hurt Bruce badly. Whereas there are those who have crossed the divide with heavy hearts – such as midfielder Lee Clark who chose a suit of feint black and white stripes to wear on the day he signed for Sunderland (an early sign of his doubtful sartorial elegance) – Bruce eschewed the easy option of a suit for his trip to Newcastle as Sunderland manager and proudly wore a Sunderland tracksuit. Further it was a mark of the man that as the goals went in against his side, as his ex Newcastle centre-half Bramble was sent off and as torrents of abuse were directed at him, he didn't run for the cover of his dug out but stood throughout in his technical area taking all the stick going.

Both manager and team had an enormous task to regain the trust of their shell-shocked supporters. Unlike Bruce who had taken stick for 90 minutes, fans now had to face it day in day out at work as people who had forgotten they even possessed black and white scarves miraculously all found them at the same time.

Gyan had been eased into English football but responded to his first League start with both goals as Stoke were beaten in the next match. Three days later he clinically finished again as a point was earned at Tottenham but the best was to come the following Saturday. Seven had been conceded on the previous season's visit to Chelsea who were in imperious form. Marauding England left-back Ashley Cole had done much to destroy Sunderland the year before when he had scored his club's goal of the season in their double winning year but Bruce detailed Kieran Richardson to nullify Cole as Sunderland produced an astonishing performance that stunned the nation as they didn't just beat Chelsea 3-0 they absolutely played them off the park.

Full-back Nedum Onuoha metamorphosed into Georgie Best as he waltzed around the home defence to score what would be Sunderland's goal of the season. Waltzing was much more of a stylish dance than Bolo Zenden managed later in trying to keep up with Gyan as he celebrated finishing off a slick move for his fourth goal in a week, before the icing on the cake came three minutes from time when Richardson hounded Cole into an error from which Welbeck had the pleasure of firing into an empty net. It was 14 days after the derby debacle. Zeroes to heroes? It was the best performance for a decade but only a big big win against Newcastle was going to begin to erase the memory of the derby.

Nonetheless the derby defeat had not derailed the team as it would the following season. By the time of the return fixture with the Magpies in mid January Sunderland were sixth and had remained either sixth or seventh since the week after the visit to Newcastle. As is so often the case in derby games the game was an anti-climax to the hyperbole. Sunderland failed to satisfy their supporters by winning and only the scrappiest of injury time goals by Gyan enabled the Lads to escape with a point. Worryingly Bent had looked out of sorts. It was to prove the England international's last game as he slapped in a transfer request and was swiftly sold to Aston Villa before the next match.

While a brace from the in form Kieran Richardson earned victory at Blackpool an awful run of form followed it, just a single point being gleaned from nine games when Sunderland's failure to score in over half of those highlighted the impact of Bent's sudden sale. Going behind at home to Wigan in the fifth from last game of the season, by which time the team had dropped to 15th, had people who had seen Sunderland turn a drama into a crisis too many times before nervously looking over their shoulders but a Jordan Henderson inspired fight-back brought the first of three victories from the final five fixtures. At half-time in the last of those Newcastle led 2-0 against West Brom but a fight-back by the Baggies earned a three all draw enabling Sunderland to finish just above their local rivals. Small consolation for the results of the season's two biggest games but it represented only Sunderland's third top 10 finish in 55 years.

Signs that Sunderland were beginning to be seen as a club capable of holding their own with the big boys were that unusually the Black Cats weren't among the clubs tipped for relegation at the start of the season and that established Premier League stars were prepared to move to the club, another sign of owner Ellis Short's ambition. Long serving Manchester United men John O'Shea and Wes Brown installed added experience to what had been a very young squad but there was ample investment in potential too with the expensive purchase of centre-forward Connor Wickham from Ipswich and South Korean starlet Ji Dong-won. Set piece specialist Seb Larsson along with fellow midfielders Craig Gardner and David Vaughan were snapped up from relegated sides and of a handful of other squad players brought in was a young winger from Northern Ireland who would prove to be a talisman for the second half of the campaign, James McClean.

The summer had also seen high profile departures, chief amongst them Jordan Henderson for a massive fee to Liverpool along with big names Steed Malbranque and Bolo Zenden. Even after the transfer window was ended striker Asamoah Gyan left for the Middle East where the transfer window was still open. Initially leaving for a hefty loan fee, Gyan's sale was completed the following summer. As with the sale of Bent in the previous transfer window though, it left Sunderland short of firepower, not least in the absence of long-term injury victim Fraizer Campbell who had been Bruce's first signing. Incoming on the striker front was Denmark international Nicklas Bendtner on loan from Arsenal.

Larsson lashed home a spectacular debut volley to gain an encouraging opening day point at Liverpool but all eyes were on the first home game which brought Newcastle to the Stadium of Light. Sunderland had a good first half but couldn't score and eventually

2011 v Hannover in Hameln.

lost by the only goal of the game. Coming on the back of the previous season's derby disasters this was a step too far for many. Under Steve Bruce Cup runs had failed to materialise and a tame shot-shy defeat at a Brighton team newly promoted into the Championship further deflated any new season optimism, especially as despite investment in the squad for one reason or another most of the new players weren't being picked.

By the end of November only two games had been won. At home to struggling Wigan, Bruce knew he needed three points against his former club. Desperate for them he substituted both full-backs as he pushed for a win. Almost inevitably the visitors hit Sunderland on the break, scoring a winner three minutes into injury time. The crowd turned on Bruce, derisively jeering him to the point where there was simply no way back. His sacking came four days later. It was a day short of a year since the Halloween derby but it was the most recent one from which he had never recovered.

Bruce's assistant Eric Black took charge of a defeat at lowly Wolves where the incumbent new manager Martin O'Neill watched from the stands. One of the most successful and highly respected managers in the game, O'Neill had been a strong possibility for the job as the first Sunderland manager after Niall Quinn took over. A Sunderland fan from boyhood, O'Neill arrived at the club less than two months after Quinn's tenure as chairman had drawn to a close as he moved to a new role as Director of International Development with Ellis Short stepping forward to take on the all important role as chairman. The Mighty Quinn would depart altogether two and a half months later.

By then Sunderland had risen from the relegation position they were in as the O'Neill era kicked off to the top half of the table and with an FA Cup quarter-final to look forward to. Such was the instant impact of Martin O'Neill. Just as Bob Stokoe's first win had seen two late goals turn defeat into victory so had O'Neill's. It was the first of 10 wins in his first 15 games.

The latter of the new manager's two tranches of 15 games though brought just two victories, a run that included an FA Cup quarter-final reverse against Everton. Nonetheless a final placing of thirteenth represented real improvement from the position he inherited. A lack of goals was the problem as no player reached double figures for the season as in exactly two thirds of the 45 games played the side failed to score more than a single goal.

As Sunderland headed into the centenary year of their most successful ever season – the 1912-13 campaign of League title and FA Cup Final – the Lads started a sixth successive season in the top flight. It is the first time that has been achieved since the spell following the first ever promotion in 1964. Should Sunderland stay in the Barclays Premier League then from 2013-14 they will enter what will be their second longest ever unbroken run in the top flight just as already in the young history of the Stadium of Light (opened in 1997) they have spent longer there than at any of their eight grounds bar Roker Park.

Under the leadership of Ellis Short and Martin O'Neill Sunderland are a club now with solid foundations, a club who after too many years looking longingly at the past can now look ambitiously to the future. This is the second version of *Sunderland: The Complete Record*. This record of course we hope will never be complete, there is always another game and another season to look forward to: another new signing, another Cup run, another generation of supporters. Sunderland is, always has been and always will be a very special club. Whenever a third volume of *Sunderland: The Complete Record* is published we hope the chapters yet to be written are happy ones.

WARTIME FOOTBALL

Appearances and goals scored in wartime games do not count in official records. Some players such as Norman Tapken, John Eves and Lewis Wheatman only appeared in wartime fixtures but could proudly point to the fact that they had donned the red and white stripes and represented the club.

With many players serving overseas, football kept going and while in general – and for pretty obvious reasons – crowds were nowhere near what they would be in peacetime, whenever Roker Park and other grounds around the country continued to stage football, it allowed a little normality and light relief in the most troubled of times.

As the game strove to continue to provide entertainment through top class sport, wartime football threw up the phenomenon of 'Guest Players'. This was where players could turn out for clubs other than the one they were contracted to. Hence during World War Two Newcastle hero Jackie Milburn played for Sunderland, as did Albert Stubbins, a man given a second lease of fame a generation later when he popped up on the cover of The Beatles *Sergeant Pepper's Lonely Hearts Club Band* LP. Equally, Sunderland players 'guested' for other clubs. These included Raich Carter for Derby who he subsequently signed for after the war, Johnny Mapson who played in the 1941 London War Cup for Reading who beat Brentford in front of 9,000 at Stamford Bridge, Fred Bett who scored in both legs of the Final of the Division Three Cup for Chester against Rotherham in 1945–46 (before the resumption of the post-war Football League) and Bill Robinson who helped Charlton to win the Football League South Cup at Wembley in April 1944 where 85,000 saw The Addicks beat Chelsea 3–1. Robinson officially joined Charlton after the war and helped them to win the FA Cup in 1947.

Like Carter, Eddie Burbanks had scored for Sunderland in the 1937 FA Cup Final. Six years to the day later Burbanks would also score in a Wartime Cup Final. Guesting for Blackpool he netted in the 1942–43 League North Cup Final first leg as Sheffield Wednesday drew 2–2 at Bloomfield Road in front of 28,000. Burbanks helped The Tangerines triumph, playing as they won the second leg 2–1 at Hillsborough where almost 43,000 were in attendance.

Burbanks also featured in further success for Blackpool, scoring in a 4–2 win over Arsenal on 15 May 1943 in a North v South Cup winners' Play-off in front of over 55,000 at Stamford Bridge.

Since Sunderland's entry into the Football League in 1890 to the publication of this book in 2012, no one has scored more than five goals in one peacetime match for the club. During World War Two, however, Cliff Whitelum didn't just score six goals in one game – he did it in a Cup Final! Whitelum's double hat-trick came in the Final of the West Riding FA Combined Counties Cup at Roker Park on 1 May 1943 – the same day that Burbanks was playing in the first leg of the Blackpool v Sheffield Wednesday Final.

Despite Whitelum's half dozen goals another was needed. Huddersfield fought back from their 6–2 first leg deficit to win the second leg 4–1, Johnny Spuhler's goal edging Sunderland to a 7–6 aggregate win.

Beyond the goals and the glory of the game though were the guns and the gore of the wars themselves. Over 75 million people were killed in the killing fields of the two World Wars. While here we concern ourselves with football during the war years, never let it be forgotten that millions lost their lives in appalling circumstances and millions more suffered the heartache of losing not games of football but those closest to them. Indeed Roker Park itself was bombed more than once and a policeman, Special Constable Lancelot Slawther, lost his life in July 1943.

This wasn't the only time Roker Park was hit by the Luftwaffe. On the night of 15 May 1943 – just a fortnight after Whitelum's goalscoring record – a bomb came through the roof of the Main Stand and left a crater on the pitch.

While never forgetting that for all the passion surrounding football the game matters not a jot compared to the horrors endured across the globe in two World Wars, from a Sunderland point of view it is true that the club were in golden periods shortly before both World Wars and endured barren years after them.

World War One began in July 1914. Having been champions and Cup finalists one year before the outbreak of World War One it would take Sunderland 17 seasons following the resumption of football to win a trophy. Prior to World War One the longest the club had gone without silverware since entering the Football League was 11 years.

Bomb damaged Main Stand at Roker Park.

WARTIME FOOTBALL

In the three years before World War Two, which the UK entered on 3 September 1939, Sunderland had won the League, the FA Cup and the Charity Shield. Following the war it would take 27 seasons to win what is to date Sunderland's only major post-war trophy.

Despite the outbreak of war in 1914 the 1914–15 season not only started, it was completed. There were 153 goals in Sunderland's 38 League fixtures, The Wearsiders' 81 goals making them second top scorers in the country as eighth place was reached leaving The Lads five points behind champions Everton. Unfortunately the 72 goals leaked were more than second and third bottom Chelsea and Manchester United.

Charlie Buchan and George Philip each scored over 20 goals and both were on the mark – Buchan with a hat-trick – as that season's Cup conquerors Spurs were hammered 5–0 at Roker Park on 24 April 1915. That was to be the club's last 'official' game until 30 August 1919 when Buchan started where he left off – scoring the club's first post-war goal, having netted their last before the Football League was brought to a halt.

Also on the mark was Barney Travers – who had been a Prisoner of War – as Aston Villa were beaten 2–1 before 35,000 at Roker some nine and a half months after the Great War's Armistice Day. New Delaval born Clem Stephenson (who had played against Sunderland in the 1913 FA Cup Final having famously correctly predicted Villa would win 1–0 with a header from Tommy Barber having had a dream that turned out to be true) notched Villa's goal on this occasion.

In the four years and three months between the 'consecutive' League victories football initially ground almost to a complete standstill.

While there were more serious matters to concern people, financially the club was close to ruin. An Extraordinary General Meeting was held in the Palatine Hotel (latterly known as the Mowbray Hotel) in Sunderland on 11 May 1915. The chairman of Sunderland

Barney Travers (kneeling on the left in the front row) as a Prisoner of War in Germany.

Football Club Ltd, Mr Sam Wilson, revealed to the directors and shareholders present that the previous season's accounts had resulted in a loss of £8,000, gate receipts having dropped by £11,000 compared to the previous season with the average attendance halving from 22,000 in 1913–14. The team had finished just one place lower (eighth compared to seventh). Evidently the appetite for football had declined with the war occupying people's minds. It wasn't just at Sunderland that gates halved. The same was true elsewhere. At Villa for example, 40,000 watched Sunderland in January but only 12,000 attended the same fixture in September.

Boosted by their pre-war success, Sunderland had invested in a new stand at Roker Park. The initial proposed cost of £6,250 had more than doubled to £13,000 but the club had only been able to pay off £10,000.

A summary of the club's debts in May 1915 showed that as well as being in debt by £3,000 for the new stand, the club required a further £1,330 to guarantee that it remained in business until September and a further £1,350 would then be required to keep the club operating until September of the following year although it was accepted that in all likelihood no football would be played in that time. The plan was to review the situation ahead of what could be the 1916–17 season depending on whether the war would be over by then.

The directors of the football club made it clear at the May 1915 meeting that they were willing to pay £2,680 of the £5,680 that the club needed. It was decided, as a first step, to release £3,300 of unissued capital in the hope that tradesmen and members of the public would buy shares in the club. There was a real possibility that the club would be wound up with the *Sunderland Echo* reporting: '…if the townspeople and public support the club to this extent, then the directors will in all probability take responsibility to meet any liabilities in excess of this amount. However, failing a favourable response to the appeal there will, in all possibility, be no alternative but to voluntarily wind up the club.'

Ten days after the meeting a letter appeared in the *Sunderland Echo* from Councillor Walter Raine who would become chairman of SAFC between 1930 and 1938. The letter had been originally sent to Sunderland's secretary-manager Bob Kyle who subsequently forwarded it to the local paper to be published as an open letter. Councillor Raine argued that in buying shares people would in fact be making a gift to the football club as at this time the shares were unsaleable. Instead the councillor promoted the idea that the club should seek guarantors who would be named on a Lloyd's Policy Form for a £7,000 guarantee to the club. Raine argued that if the existing directors would cover £3,000 worth of this guarantee then other people could step forward to guarantee a set amount and that he would be willing to be such a guarantor.

Among the footballing heroes of the club's history, perhaps Raine deserves his contribution to SAFC to be noted a century on. Continuing his optimistic theme he wrote; '…as you know I have been an ardent supporter of the Club for some time and do not wish to see it disbanded. One or two good seasons after the War will easily liquidate the guarantee.'

Unlike so many who perished in the conflict of World War One, SAFC survived its hardships. The most prominent of the people who stepped forward to be guarantors of the club was one of its first heroes.

John Auld played in Sunderland's first ever League match in 1890. It was one of 115 League and Cup games the Scottish international played as he captained the team to its first two titles. He went on to appear briefly in the third League winning season prior to becoming the first man to move between Sunderland and Newcastle United where he later became a director. Thanks to Councillor Walter Raine, John Auld and his fellow guarantors, and in no small part to Bob Kyle – the club's longest serving 'manager' from 1905 to 1928 – who did so much to hold the club together, SAFC survived the financial fall out of the war and would move on to happier times.

On 12 December 1919, three and a half months into the first post World War One Football League season, with Sunderland sitting third in the table and having just pulled in a record crowd of 47,148 for a comfortable home win over Newcastle Bob Kyle wrote to John Auld. The letter read: 'Dear Johnny, I have much pleasure in reporting that the Directors are now in a position to cancel the guarantee which you so kindly gave in 1915 to enable them to carry on the club during the period of the war and to return your guarantee duly cancelled. The Directors wish to thank you for the generous support given them at a time when the existence of the club was in jeopardy and but for which they would not have been able to carry on. Please acknowledge. I am, dear Sir, Yours faithfully, Robert Kyle.'

From the Extraordinary General Meeting of May 1915 only three games are known to have been played by Sunderland until five days before Christmas in 1918. All of these were played at St James' Park against Newcastle United although sometimes Sunderland players would get a game as 'Guests' elsewhere, Billy Hogg for example scoring for Hartlepool against a 21st Durham Light Infantry XI in February 1916 in a game to raise money for the families of DLI members who were Prisoners of War.

On Tyneside on 6 May 1916, 3,299 assembled for a Tyne-Wear derby played in aid of military charities. The war was coming into a significant period. The only full-scale naval battle of the war – The battle of Jutland – began at the end of the month while the battle of the Somme commenced at the beginning of July.

While this was Sunderland's solitary game of the '1915–16 season' it was Newcastle's fifth. In the previous month they had played home and away to Blackburn Rovers, had visited South Shields in November and met a Combined English and Southern League XI at Brough Park in September. Also in 1916 Sunderland's Walker-born England international Francis Cuggy helped to organise a charity match at Wallsend between his own XI and a side organised by Newcastle United's Bill McCracken. These two legendary players organised another such charity match in 1919, 15,000 attending St James' Park on 24 May where McCracken's XI won 1–0.

Sunderland's 1916 side at St James' included William Cooke who was a 'guest' player from Sheffield United and goalkeeper James Boe whose only peacetime game for the club saw him concede seven goals but it was a very strong side especially the forward line which comprised of four England internationals in Jackie Mordue, Charlie Buchan, George Holley and Harry Martin along with centre-forward Bobby Best who had scored a hat-trick against the Magpies at St James' on Christmas Day 1914.

Seaham lad George Holley also had a hat-trick for Sunderland at Newcastle to his name. He'd scored three in the record 9–1 win at St James' in 1908 and gave Sunderland a first half

Letter dated 16 December 1919 from SAFC to 1890s captain of The Team of All The Talents John Auld, thanking him for being a Guarantor of the club during World War One.

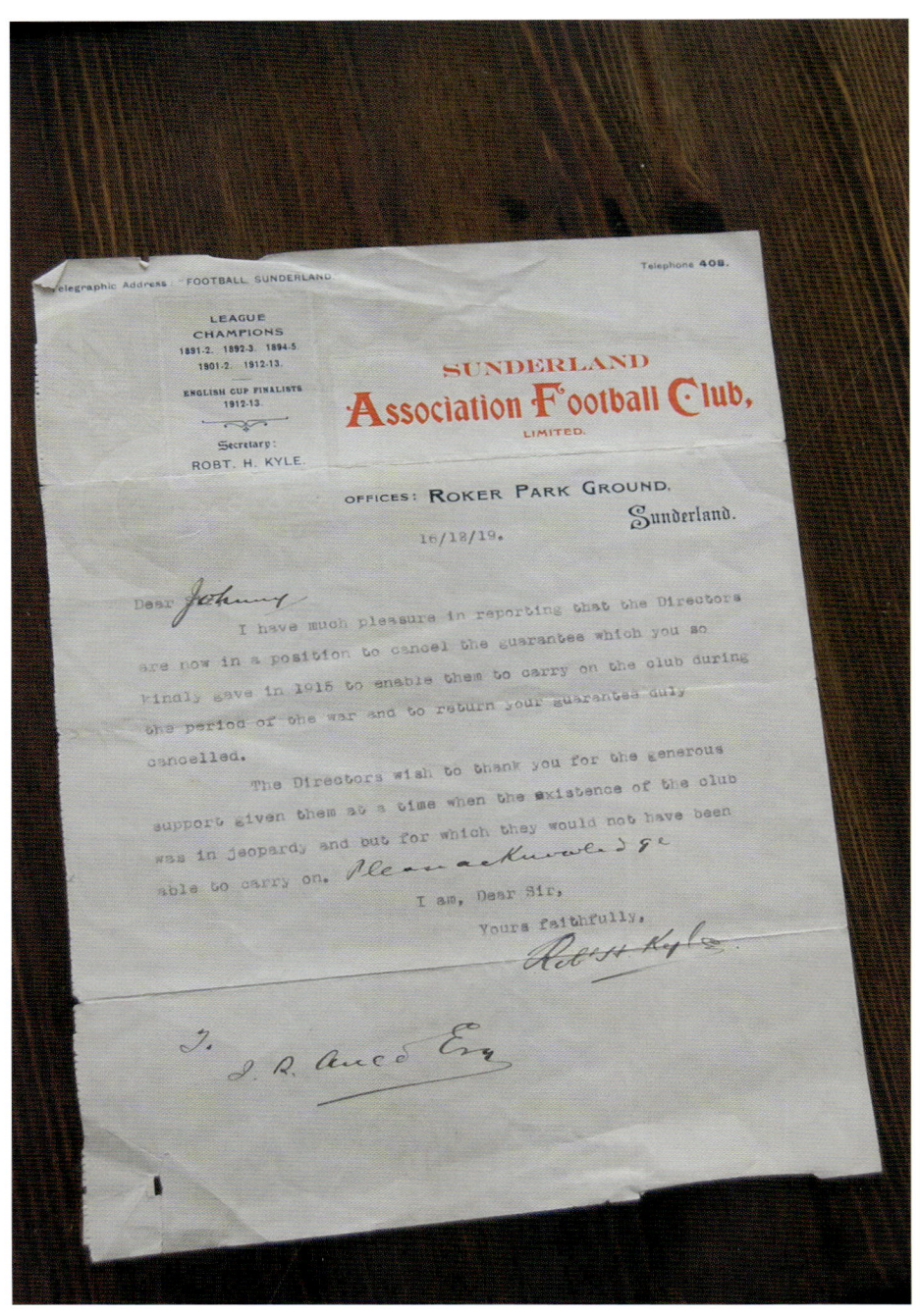

WARTIME FOOTBALL

lead on this occasion. The home side drew level after half-time, their goal coming from Wilf Low, the brother of Sunderland's Harry Low who also played in the game.

Newcastle's Low was a Scottish international. Sunderland's Low chose to play for Sunderland rather than Scotland when he was selected by his country but on a date that clashed with a crucial Cup quarter-final second replay with the Magpies in 1913. Harry was never given another chance by Scotland and even more sadly he would die in 1920, aged just 38.

Two days short of two years after the 1916 meeting, a Sunderland side again took to the pitch at St James'. An estimated 6,000 watched a game played in aid of the National Football War Fund. Once more the Low brothers lined up against each other. Sunderland won the game 3–1, Buchan bagging a brace and Holley the other with Tom Philipson scoring Newcastle's consolation. While it is always great to win a derby match, at this time it was a coming together to enjoy a rare game and celebrate friendship in sport. If anyone wanted an enemy, the real one was only too evident on the continent.

Sunderland were next in action on 31 August 1918, once again at Newcastle. Holley kept up his record, scoring for the third successive game – over three years. Holley was joined on the scoresheet by Harry Williams and Harry Leonard who got two as the Wearsiders triumphed 4–0. Once again the fixture was in aid of the National Football War Fund, 5,000 attending.

Two months and 11 days later it was triumph for the whole country as World War One officially ended. The eleventh day of the eleventh month 1918 finally concluding the war that was meant to end all wars.

What a Christmas it must have been in 1918. Times were hard, many had lost loved ones but the war was over. Better times were ahead and indeed the decade just around the corner would become known as the Roaring Twenties. As normality began to return the footballing giants of County Durham and Northumberland staged a double header – yes football would return to Roker Park.

Five days before Christmas Sunderland once again travelled across the Tyne where an estimated gate of 19,000 saw Newcastle win the match 4–0, one of their scorers being the great Steve Bloomer 'guesting' for the Magpies at the age of almost 45. Joining the man whose statue today sits splendidly next to the bench at Derby County's Pride Park were Clarke and E. Cooper who got two. Sunderland's side in the game; played in aid of the Comrades of the Great War Fund, once again included George Holley and Harry Low.

After Sunderland's series of trips to Newcastle the Tynesiders came to Roker on Boxing Day 1918. A first half goal from George Philip gave the red and whites a win. As the New Year of 1919 was seen in, the Hogmanay toast would have been one of optimism and Philip had given Sunderland supporters a win to end a year where even beating Newcastle wasn't the biggest victory. That had been won on the killing fields rather than the football field.

Even losing 3–1 at home to Middlesbrough on New Year's Day couldn't dampen enthusiasm. Football was returning and suddenly Roker Park had staged two games in five days. Boro came back less than three weeks later and were beaten 2–0, Barney Travers and Bertie Hobson getting the goals.

Moreover the latter win over Boro was a competitive game. A Victory League had been set up in a meeting at the Grand Hotel on Bridge Street in Sunderland on 6 December 1918. Joining SAFC at this meeting were representatives of Durham City, Newcastle United, Scotswood, South Shields and Middlesbrough who all agreed to participate following a proposal by Boro's John French which was seconded by Sunderland's Bob Kyle. Invitations were extended to Hartlepools United who accepted and Darlington FC. The Quakers were unable to raise a team and had their place snapped up by Darlington Forge Albion who Sunderland beat 1–0 away but lost to at home! The Darlington outfit also managed to beat Newcastle United 2–0 at St James' Park and 3–0 at home.

Between Boro's two January visits defeat had been tasted by a single goal away to Durham City in the first of what would be 14 Victory League fixtures. Sunderland won eight, drew two and lost four of these Victory League games.

Football was re-surfacing after the war. A meeting of the Football League, the powerful Southern League, the Scottish League and the Irish League had been held at the Winter Gardens in Blackpool on 3 July 1915, just a couple of months after Sunderland's pivotal EGM. At this 1915 meeting of the Leagues, which followed vehement criticism in the press of players receiving payment for football while their contemporaries were being killed in battle, it had been decreed that only amateur football would be allowed and that any games played would be friendlies. The FA formally announced this on 19 July 1915.

In fact payment for playing continued in Scotland where a 20 team League completed full seasons in 1915–16 and 1916–17, Celtic winning both times. In 1917–18 and 1918–19 an 18 team Scottish League saw Celtic win in 1919 after Rangers had punctuated their run.

While football in the North East largely ground to almost a complete halt, elsewhere in England football managed to carry on. In Lancashire 'Principal' and 'Subsidary' Leagues consisting of 14 and then 16 teams ran right through the war with Manchester City, Liverpool, Stoke and Everton finishing top of the main League. There was also a Midland 'Principal' League of 14 rising to 16 clubs along with three six club regional Midland Subsidiary Leagues, Nottingham Forest and Leeds each twice winning the 'Principal' Leagues between 1915 and 1919.

In London 'Prinicipal' and 'Supplementary' Leagues saw up to 14 clubs involved. Chelsea, twice, and West Ham won these competitions with Brentford coming out on top in a 'London Combination' in 1918–19. In 1915–16 there was even a South Western League consisting of the Bristol clubs, Swindon, Southampton, Portsmouth, and the Welsh pair of Cardiff City and Newport County, Pompey coming out on top.

In the North East though, apart from the occasional charity match – once a year in Sunderland's case – it wasn't until the 1919 Northern Victory League that football could occupy people.

Middlesbrough emerged as winners of the Victory League, Sunderland born George Elliott powering them home with 20 goals in 14 games. Appropriately for the literary minded he got one in 'Middle March' against Sunderland who were runners' up.

Boro lost just three and drew one of their 14 games but lost both home and away to Sunderland. The Wearsiders also took part in the Durham Senior Cup, defeating South

Shields in a replay and hammering Felling Colliery 8–1 in the semi-final although no record has been discovered of the Final.

A total of 22 fixtures were played between New Year's Day and the end of the season, the 1918–19 season ending with a 3–2 home win over Newcastle in a fixture played in aid of the Footballers' National War Fund. Jackie Mordue netted twice in front of a gate of 16,000 with Keenleyside scoring Sunderland's other goal and A. Hagen grabbing both of the Tynesiders' efforts.

In football terms London did well out of the war. The post-war First Division was extended from 20 clubs to 22. While Spurs – who had finished bottom in the last season before the League closed down due to the war – were duly relegated but won immediate promotion, second bottom Chelsea were allowed to stay in the top flight and finished third in the opening post-war campaign. Derby and Preston were promoted having been the top two in the 1914–15 Second Division but who were the other team to make up the new 22 strong top flight?

Barnsley and Wolves had finished third and fourth but it was Arsenal who had finished fifth on the same points as Birmingham and Hull who were given the final First Division place. The Gunners did not win through via Play-offs – there weren't any.

The Official History of Arsenal by Phil Soar and Martin Tyler offers this account of how Arsenal chairman and Conservative MP Sir Henry Norris talked the powers that be – including his close friend and League President John McKenna – into allowing Arsenal to take up a place in the top flight without having won promotion: 'It was at this point that Henry Norris set out on the single most outrageous enterprise ever to be conceived in the history of English football…there is still no convincing explanation of how Norris achieved his object and it is almost inconceivable that any other individual, before or since, could have carried it off at all. Norris's aim, very simply, was to talk The Arsenal back into the First Division.'

Norris succeeded despite Arsenal having debts of £60,000 (compared to the £3,000 Sunderland had needed to raise from Guarantors to stay afloat) and had been relegated in 1913 with the lowest points, goals and number of wins ever recorded, records that were never beaten until two points for a win was ended more than seven decades later.

To date (2012) Arsenal have never been relegated and in the process now have the longest unbroken membership of the top flight, usurping Sunderland's record from 1890 to 1958.

Footballers of World War One

George Anderson
Served in Royal Artillery.
Goalkeeper who made 10 pre-war appearances for Sunderland.

Alex Barrie
Glasgow-born Corporal in Highland Light Infantry second Battalion.
Played 71 games between 1902 and 1907.

Bobby Best
Third Durham Light Infantry.
Scored a hat-trick away to Newcastle for Sunderland on Christmas Day 1914 among a total of 25 goals in 97 games either side of the war.

James Boe
Served in the army in World War One.
Goalkeeper who conceded seven on his only peacetime appearance.

Archie Brown
Served in Marines in World War One.
Played six games beginning in January 1922.

Charlie Buchan
Gained Military Medal having been commissioned in the Sherwood Foresters before serving in the Grenadier Guards.
Sunderland's all time record League goalscorer with 209.

Ted Clack
Gained Military Medal in 1917 (see also World War Two).
Made nine post-war appearances for Sunderland.

Stephen Coglin
Served in the Sherwood Foresters and fifth Battalion of Notts and Derby Regiment.
Scored nine goals in 20 games in the mid-1920s.

Tim Coleman
Served in the 17th Battalion of the Middlesex Regiment and was once posted as 'Missing'. As 904 Private of B company Coleman received the Military Medal for bravery on 21 October 1918.
England international with 21 goals in 32 games for Sunderland before the war.

Bob Coverdale
Served in Durham Light Infantry.
Played as a 'guest' for Hull City during World War One and played four games in 1914–15 and 18 after the war.

Warney Cresswell
Served in Royal Artillery before becoming a gym instructor.
England international who played 190 games for Sunderland in the 1920s after signing for a national record transfer fee. Went on to win the League and Cup with Everton.

Charles Arthur Crossley
Was a stoker on a submarine destroyer during World War One.
Debuted just before World War One and scored 17 goals in 46 peacetime games.

John Curtis
Served in Royal Field Artillery.
Solitary Sunderland appearance in 1906 but played for several clubs including Brentford during the war.

William Farquahar
Army Dental Engineer.
Had retired from playing in 1907 after 198 appearances for Sunderland.

Michael Gilhooley
Fife born, served in Highland Light Infantry in France.
Scottish international for whom Sunderland broke the transfer record to sign him in 1922.

James Hindmarsh
Won the Military Medal.
Made one appearance for Sunderland in 1905 but went on to greater things at Manchester City and as manager of Newport.

Bert Hobson
Won the Military medal having joined the army in May 1915.
Played 172 peacetime games between 1913 and 1922 plus 12 1919 Victory League games having 'guested' for Stoke and Wolves during the war.

Jack Huggins
Killed in action when a private in the first/eighth Battalion of the Durham Light Infantry.
A scoring debut against Manchester United in 1906 was one of two goals in 14 first-team appearances.

Joe Kasher
Served as a Petty Officer in a Naval Division in World War One during which time he was taken Prisoner of War.
Was the club's oldest surviving player up to his death in 1992 a week before what would have been his 98th birthday. Played 90 first-team games.

Bob Kelly
Served in Royal Field Artillery.
England international who Sunderland smashed the transfer record for in December 1925.

Josiah Kelsall
Stationed in India where he was a Lance Corporal in World War One.
Played one League game, for Sunderland against Sheffield Wednesday in April 1914.

Joseph Lane
Served in Egypt with the Hertfordshire Yeomanry in World War One.
Played in Budapest before the war and coached Barcelona after it. Two appearances for Sunderland in 1913.

George Livingstone
A member of the Royal Army Medical Corps in Africa during World War One.
Scottish international who played in Cup Finals in England and Scotland with Celtic and Manchester City and scored a dozen goals in 31 games for Sunderland in 1900–01.

Harry Low
Served in the navy in World War One.
Played 228 games either side of the war including the 1913 FA Cup Final in a season where he helped win the League.

Sandy McAllister
Died in World War One in Italy as a result of Bright's Disease. A Private in the tenth Battalion of Northumberland Fusiliers.
Played 222 games for Sunderland including the first ever match at Roker Park in 1898. Championship winner at Sunderland in 1902.

Andrew McCreadie
Served in Royal Scots Fusiliers then 10th Battalion of Scottish King's Liverpool Regiment.
Member of The Team of All The Talents, winning a League title with Sunderland in 1895 to add to three trophies won with Rangers and two Scottish caps.

Isaac Martin

Served in Royal Engineers and in a munitions factory.
Nicknamed 'Pompey' following a spell with Portsmouth who he joined after 16 appearances for Sunderland.

Albert Milton

Killed in action on 12 October 1917. Served as a Bombardier in the Royal Field Artillery. Won a Championship medal with Sunderland in 1913.

Name:	MILTON, ALBERT
Initials:	A
Nationality:	United Kingdom
Rank:	Bombardier
Regiment/Service:	Royal Field Artillery
Unit Text:	"B" Bty. 64th Bde.
Age:	31
Date of Death:	11/10/1917
Service No:	151944
Additional information:	Son of John and Emily Milton, of 38, Kimberworth Park Rd., Bradgate, Rotherham; husband of Agnes Milton, of 6, Stansfield St., Roker, Sunderland.
Casualty Type:	Commonwealth War Dead
Grave/Memorial Reference:	Panel 4 to 6 and 162.
Memorial:	TYNE COT MEMORIAL

John Morrison

Served in the RAF during World War One where he was a bomber pilot.
Played once for Sunderland after the war, was an Oxford 'triple Blue' in soccer, cricket and golf and once scored 233 runs for Somerset v the MCC.

Bill Murray

Just as he gave long service to SAFC as both player and manager, Bill Murray served as an under age enlistee with the Gordon Highlanders in World War One and was then a captain in the Army Welfare Service in World War Two.
Played over 300 games for Sunderland and won a Championship medal in 1936 and was Sunderland's manager from 1939 to 1957.

Thomas Naisby

Served in Royal Garrison Artillery in World War One.
Had two spells as a goalkeeper with his home-town team Sunderland.

Harry Ness

Lance Corporal in the Black Watch.
101 Sunderland appearances in a spell interrupted by the war. Won the League with Sunderland and played in two FA Cup Finals for Barnsley and Sunderland in 1910 and 1913.

Richard Parker
Served in Northumberland Fusiliers.
Scored twice in six Sunderland appearances but set seasonal scoring records at Millwall and Norwich. Represented The Football League against The Army in 1927.

Jock Paterson
Served in 61st Division and was reported to be wounded five times with the Black Watch.
Scottish international who was second top scorer as Sunderland were runners up in 1923.

Geoffrey Power
Served with Lancashire Fusiliers.
Made 10 post-war appearances for his home-town team Sunderland.

James Raine
Major in ninth Battalion of Durham Light Infantry.
England Amateur international who also represented The Football League.

Ephraim Rhodes
Served in Royal Fusiliers. Rejected from joining up four times and spent the war in the Army Pay Corps and Records Office during which he remained player-manager of Brentford, making over 100 wartime appearances for The Bees.
Penalty taking full-back who played over 100 times for Sunderland between 1902 and 1908.

Ray Robinson
Served as a Corporal in the Tank Corps.
Played for Grimsby Town as a wartime 'guest' and was transferred from Newcastle to Sunderland in 1920.

Leigh Richmond Roose
Killed in action and gained the Military Medal. Incorrectly recorded as L.R. Rouse in army records but served in Royal Army Medical Corps and then the ninth Battalion Welsh Fusiliers.
Injured against Newcastle on his 99th and last game for Sunderland in 1910.

Thomas Rowlandson
Killed in action. Gained Military Medal while serving as Captain in fourth Battalion of Yorkshire Regiment.
Played a dozen games as Sunderland's goalkeeper between 1 April 1904 and 1 April 1905.

Leslie Scott
Served in third Battalion of Durham Light Infantry.
Goalkeeper who played 95 League and Cup games between 1911 and 1922.

John Small
Served in Royal Army Medical Corps.
Only first-team appearance was in a 3–1 away win over Manchester United on 15 March 1913.

James Stephenson
Served in Royal Field Artillery.
All of his 22 first-team appearances were in the 1921–22 campaign.

Thomas Stewart
Served in Coldstream Guards.
Made five first-team appearances in January and February 1905.

Tom Thompson
Injured in a crash while in the RAF.
Played five wartime games and represented the club at reserve level after the war, moving on to Gillingham, Guildford and then to Spain with Real Murcia in 1924.

Barney Travers
Prisoner of War in Germany from August 1915 until the end of World War One. Served in Durham Light Infantry.
A scoring debut in the first post World War One game was the first of 28 goals in 63 games until January 1921. Later banned for life after being caught up in an attempted match fixing scandal when a Fulham player.

Thomas Urwin
Served in India and Egypt with the Royal Field Artillery.
Sunderland's oldest ever player, he was 39 years and 76 days old when he made his 55th and final appearance in 1935.

Isaac Webb
Served in Yorkshire Regiment as a catering orderly, believed to be around the time of World War One.
Goalkeeper who made 24 appearances in the first decade of the 20th century.

Reg Wilkinson
Served with King's Royal Rifle Corps.
Played twice in the early 1920s.

Bob Young
Gained Military Medal while serving in Durham Light Infantry.
Played 56 times either side of World War One.

Footballers of World War Two

George Ainsley
Served in the RAF in World War Two.
Played four times for Sunderland in the 1930s.

Richard Bell
Served in Essex Regiment Territorials and Royal Artillery in World War Two.
His solitary first-team opportunity came in the last League game before the 1937 FA Cup Final.

Ivor Broadis
Served as an Officer and Bomber pilot during World War Two.
England international who transferred himself to Sunderland when player-manager of Carlisle in 1949.

Eddie Burbanks
Served in the RAF in India in World War Two.
Scored in the 1937 FA Cup Final.

Raich Carter
Served in the RAF in Loughborough in World War Two.
England legend who was joint top scorer in the 1936 Championship win and scored in the 1937 FA Cup Final as he skippered Sunderland to the trophy.

Ken Chisholm
A pilot for the RAF in World War Two after training in the USA.
Scored 37 goals in 86 games for Sunderland in the 1950s.

Ted Clack
Veteran of Dunkirk in World War Two having won Military Medal in World War One.
Winger who played nine times in the early 1920s.

Dickie Davis
Served in the RAF in World War Two.
Top scorer in the First Division with Sunderland in 1949–50.

FOOTBALLERS OF WORLD WAR TWO

Billy Elliott
Served in the Royal Navy in World War Two on frigates hunting U-Boats.
Tough 1950s England international who later became trainer to the 1973 FA Cup winners and had two spells as caretaker manager.

John Finlay
Served in World War Two.
On the club's books either side of World War Two but his single first-team official game was a 5–0 defeat at Charlton in the first post World War Two League defeat.

Trevor Ford
Served in Royal Artillery. His Sergeant Major converted him from a full-back to a centre-forward.
Fearsome early 1950s forward who scored 70 goals in 117 games.

Patsy Gallacher
Served in the RAF in World War Two.
Legend of the 1930s who scored the winner in the 1937 FA Cup semi-final.

Fred Hall
Served in the RAF in World War Two
Centre-half who played over 200 post-war games for the club.

Davie Halliday
Relinquished his job as Aberdeen manager to serve the war effort.
165 goals in 175 games for Sunderland including a seasonal record of 43 in 1928–29.

Arthur Hudgell
Served in the RAF in World War Two.
Left-back who played 275 post-war games.

Bert Johnston
Served in the RAF in World War Two.
Scottish international who was a member of the 1937 FA Cup winning team.

John Lynas
Prisoner of War in Thailand during World War Two.
Played 10 times beginning in 1929.

Tommy McLain
Pilot in the RAF in Ceylon (now Sri Lanka) in World War Two.
Wing-half who played 73 post-war games for Sunderland.

Bill Murray
Captain in the Army Welfare Service (see also World War One).
From 1927 to 1957 served Sunderland as player and manager with just a two year break.

Ken Oliver
Pilot in the RAF in Ceylon (now Sri Lanka) in World War Two.
Played briefly for Sunderland after the war but spent most of his career with Derby and Exeter.

Harry Poulter
Served in the Atlantic Fleet of the Royal Navy.
Centre-forward who made three appearances in the early 1930s, all in the FA Cup, scoring twice.

Tommy Reynolds
Pilot in the RAF in Ceylon (now Sri Lanka) in World War Two.
Winger who played 172 times for Sunderland after the war.

Robert Robinson
Served in the army in World War Two.
Goalkeeper who played 33 times for Sunderland and five times for Newcastle after the war.

Percy Saunders
Killed in action – memorial in Singapore Cemetery. Served in Army Ordnance Corps.
Scored six times in 26 games during the 1930s – and had the military middle name Kitchener.

Ernie Taylor
Served in Submarine service in World War Two.
At 5ft 4in this England international had been a Cup winner with Newcastle and Blackpool and came to Sunderland in the late 1950s from Manchester United.

James Temple
Served in World War Two.
Scored a dozen goals in 34 games in the early 1930s.

Robert Thomson
Served in American Eagle squadron of RAF in the Middle East during World War Two.
Scottish international who won the French League with Racing Club de Paris in 1936 as Sunderland were winning the English title. Also played for Marseille after making 22 appearances for Sunderland in the 1920s.

Harry Thompson
Served in RAF in World War Two.
Registered with Sunderland until after the war but all 14 of his first-team games were in the 1938–39 season.

William Walsh
Served in Royal Artillery.
Played 105 times having joined the club during World War Two.

Ken Walshaw
Member of Durham Light Infantry training staff.
His only two peacetime appearances came in the FA Cup in the first post-war season, including a scoring debut.

Willie Watson
Served in the army and played alongside Matt Busby, Tom Finney, Tommy Lawton and Joe Mercer in army football.
Represented England at both football and cricket.

Cliff Whitelum
Served in Royal Artillery.
Scored six goals in a wartime Cup Final and added 19 goals in 50 peacetime games.

Arthur Wright
Served in Royal Engineers.
Played 281 games either side of World War Two before coaching the club.

Benny Yorston
Army Physical Training Corps.
Averaged exactly a goal per two games in 52 early 1930s appearances.

The inter-war years saw Sunderland's top flight membership remain unbroken, indeed by the outbreak of World War Two Sunderland were the last remaining club to have only ever played at the top level. Finishing a disappointing 16th out of 22 in 1938–39 was the lowest inter-war placing and only the sixth time in 21 inter-war seasons Sunderland finished outside the top half of the table. In the mid 1920s the Lads had finished in the top three in four years out of five while they had been champions in 1936, runners-up in 1935 and Cup winners in 1937.

The 1939–40 season kicked off on 26 August with 21,859 seeing Raich Carter score twice in a 3–0 win over Derby County. Carter stands two goals behind Kevin Phillips in the all time list of SAFC top scorers (Phillips is sixth highest) but would be higher had not these goals against Derby and another four days later against Huddersfield not been expunged from the records due to the League programme being cancelled due to the outbreak of war. Carter's next official Football League appearance would be for Derby rather than against them.

2 September 1939 saw Sunderland sunk by four Ted Drake goals in a 5–2 defeat at the hands of Arsenal at Highbury. This was the third and last game played of the 1939–40 campaign. The embryonic League table showed Sunderland 15th in a 22 team division where Blackpool, who were due to be the next visitors to Roker, were the only team to boast a 100 per cent record.

Carter was one of six members of the Sunderland side defeated at Highbury who would never play an official game for the club again. Fellow FA Cup winners Bert Johnston, Alex Hall and Jimmy Gorman also bowed out as did John Smeaton and Bill Robinson.

Following the closure of the League programme Sunderland did not play during the winter of 1939–40. On the cancelled fixture list the Lads should have been due to entertain Aston Villa on the Good Friday of 22 March 1940. However, Sunderland did play a game that Easter, visiting South Shields. Sunderland won the game 8–2 in front of a crowd of 6,700. In goal was Barney Bircham, the brother of Clive who played on the wing for Sunderland in the late fifties. Barney was aged just 15 years and 204 days old thereby making him just 19 days older than Derek Forster was when he set the record that still stands in 2012 as both the youngest top flight player and the youngest goalkeeper in any division, when he debuted on the opening day of the 1964–65 season.

Whereas in World War One football was slow in shutting down, perhaps in World War Two it was too quick to do so. Having quickly halted the 1939–40 season, by around Easter it was decided that as Great Britain had not so far been extensively bombed (the first air raid had been in October 1939 but up to this point such raids were relatively rare compared to later in the war) that a competition could be set up to re-start competitive football. The resulting tournament was the League War Cup.

Sunderland played five games including two 'home' fixtures that were staged at St James' Park due to Roker Park being closed.

A 1–1 'home' draw with Darlington on 20 April watched by 6,023 preceded a 3–2 victory away to the same opponents a week later. Similarly an away win at Leeds followed a 'home' goalless draw on Tyneside (attendance 11,226) against the men from Elland Road before the Lads bowed out of the competition at Blackburn where they went down 3–2 on 18 May. Rovers went on to reach the Final on 8 June, West Ham beating them 1–0 at Wembley in front of over 42,000.

On 30 March and 13 April 1940 the Wearsiders also played a couple of away games at their temporary 'home' ground of St James' Park. Friendlies against Newcastle United were won 2–0 and lost 3–2. Both games were in aid of The Journal and North Mail War Fund. The first attracted a gate of 15,000 to see Sunderland win with a brace from William Scott while a fortnight later an Albert Stubbins hat-trick overcame a Charlie Thomson penalty and a goal from Cliff Whitelum in front of 8,666. In between these derbies Sunderland lost 4–2 at Hartlepool on 6 April.

1939–40 saw players start to appear as 'guests' for other clubs. Len Duns for instance scored twice in seven games for Newcastle while Patsy Gallacher also made an appearance for the Magpies whose goalkeeper at the time was Tom Swinburne, whose son Trevor would keep goal for Sunderland in the 1970s as Jimmy Montgomery's understudy.

Bert Johnston and Alex Hastings 'guested' for Hartlepool against Darlington at the Victoria Ground on 7 October 1939. It was the first of eight wartime appearances Hastings would make in Hartlepool colours while Johnston would play 20 times and go on to 'guest' in over 120 games for Lincoln City. Raich Carter also later appeared for 'Pools, as he did for Derby, Cardiff, Nottingham Forest, Notts County, Huddersfield and York.

A 'North League' was set up in 1940–41 but minus Sunderland. However, a total of 70 Football League clubs participated, including 36 from the north.

Sunderland did play quite regularly in 1940–41 though. In September an Army XI were beaten 4–0. Four days before Christmas there was a 3–1 defeat away to Newcastle watched by 3,226 while on Christmas Day there was a goal fest as Sunderland Police were beaten 11–5! This was a record score for any game ever played at Roker Park.

Sunderland entered the Durham War Cup, beating South Shields ex-Schoolboys, Murton CW and Eppleton CW only to lose 2–1 in the Final at home to Chopwell Colliery on 17 May. However between the semi-final victory over Eppleton there had been 4–3 friendly wins away to Newcastle (With Len Duns of Sunderland 'Guesting' for Newcastle – he scored six goals in 12 games for NUFC in 1940–41)) and Middlesbrough while the season ended with a tenth game as the Durham Light Infantry were beaten 3–2 on 24 May.

1941–42 saw Sunderland join The North League. This comprised of: Sunderland, Newcastle United, Gateshead, Middlesbrough York City, Leeds United, Bradford Park Avenue, Bradford City, Huddersfield Town and Sheffield United.

Following a 12–1 win over the Reserves in a public practice match a week earlier, it was The Blades who were the first visitors to Roker, Sunderland celebrating with a handsome 7–1 victory on 30 August 1941 with Raich Carter getting a hat-trick, and Cliff Whitelum a brace. Whitelum would top score for Sunderland with 13 goals in 14 North League games while Carter would average a goal a game from his 10 appearances.

The win over Sheffield United was the first of nine wins, four draws and five defeats from a fixture list that gave Sunderland back to back fixtures against each other club in a competition structured on a geographical basis designed to reduce non essential travel. To qualify for the second stage teams had to finish in the top half of 32 clubs, Sunderland just managing this by reaching thirteenth place. The League ended on Christmas Day with a 3–1 home defeat at the hands of Gateshead.

In the second stage Sunderland finished tenth out of 38 teams with Blackpool finishing top. These days working out how some Leagues are structured can be bizarre but nowhere on the globe can there be a stranger system in place than determined Manchester United as the champions of 1941–42. All games played by clubs between the day after Boxing Day and 30 May, including friendlies, were taken into account in establishing an 'average points total' where clubs had to play at least 18 games to qualify. With mathematical precision cricket's Duckworth-Lewis system would be proud of it was decreed that Sunderland were tenth with 25 points from 22 games (two points for a win then) equating to 26.13 points over a '23 game' season. Winners Manchester United's average was 33.89.

However, not for the first time Sunderland were more interested in Cup football. The Lads had embarked on a massive 20 game Cup run that culminated with a two-legged War Cup Final with Wolves.

After progressing through home and away games with five of their North League opponents Boro were met in a Friendly before two legged ties with Oldham Athletic, both Bradford Clubs (thereby again meeting Park Avenue who had already been played in the Cup) and Grimsby Town (the Mariners' home leg being played at Scunthorpe) in order for Sunderland to reach the Final. Three goals had been needed in the last 12 minutes of the second leg against Bradford City to progress.

Wolves held Sunderland to a two all draw at Roker in the first leg of the Final on 23 May when Carter and Guest Albert Stubbins got Sunderland's goals with Dennis Westcott netting both for the men from Molineux. Seven days later Carter scored in the return leg but Wolves were worthy winners, cruising to a 4–1 (6–3 aggregate) triumph with Westcott, Frank Broome 'guesting' from Aston Villa and two goal Jack Rowley 'Guesting' from Manchester United on the mark.

In February 2012 supporters taking anything up to nine hours to return from Stoke in a sudden snowstorm thought they'd had a difficult journey but it was nothing compared to what was endured on the way to the 1942 second leg at Molineux. The *Sunderland Echo* on 1 June 1942 records: 'Sunderland supporters on their way to Wolverhampton for the Cup Final had the experience of being under machine gun fire from the air in the early hours of Saturday morning. Between 60 and 70 Wearsiders were passengers on a train which, it is thought, was the target of the guns of a Nazi 'hit and run' raider which swooped on the station of a North East town…bullets were heard splattering on the station roof and on the track. No one was injured and the train continued its journey.'

The attack was at Newcastle station but it wasn't possible for the *Echo* to clarify this at the time due to wartime censorship.

Sunderland would reach a Cup Final the following year too, this time coming out on top with Cliff Whitelum scoring an incredible six goals in the first leg of the Final.

Once again Raich Carter was Sunderland's talisman with Whitelum and Johnny Spuhler – who scored four goals in 36 peacetime appearances being the main marksmen. Spuhler has a modern link to the Stadium of Light with Foundation of Light Chief Executive Lesley Spuhler at one point marrying into the family.

Following a 4–2 win away to Newcastle in a pre-season friendly consisting of two 40 minute halves, the season began with Carter, Whitelum and R.G. Ramsay getting the goals in a 4–3 away defeat at the hands of Bradford City in the second season of the North League. With fixtures again organised on a two by two basis whereby clubs routinely faced each other home and away before moving on to new opponents, The Lads got their home programme off to a winning start seven days later beating The Bantams 3–1, this time Spuhler and George Robinson joining Whitelum among the goals.

There were goals aplenty with entertaining play to win football highlighted by just three draws from the 18 fixtures. Having scored in a Cup Final for Sunderland (where he worked in the shipyards as a draughtsman) the year before, Albert Stubbins returned to Roker in Newcastle colours and scored four in a 5–3 win for the Magpies while the biggest win saw Johnny Spuhler get a hat-trick at Ayresome Park in a 7–2 win over Middlesbrough – for whom he'd go on to play 241 times after the war. Seven days later though Boro gained revenge with a 4–0 Christmas Day beating of Sunderland at Roker where the home line up showed 10 changes to the side who had won on Teesside, only full-back Jimmy Gorman playing both matches.

There was method in Sunderland fielding what was effectively a reserve team on Christmas Day. Twenty-four hours later most of the regulars returned for the first Cup tie of the season as once again seven goals were wracked-up. Gateshead were the team on the receiving end in the League North Cup. There were even more goals when the sides met again a week later with Gateshead coming out on top, but by the more even 5–4. These were the first of 10 games in the qualifying rounds of this competition, Sunderland winning only two of the remaining eight but at least they were a 7–0 thrashing of Boro and a 3–2 win over Newcastle.

Between ending their League North Cup fixtures at the end of February and embarking on the Combined Counties West Riding FA Cup on 20 March, Sunderland played Gateshead home and away, each side winning their away game.

Middlesbrough must have been sick of the sight of Sunderland. Having twice put seven past the Teessiders that season Sunderland walloped them 8–0 in the opening game of the West Riding Cup campaign, Whitelum getting his second hat-trick against them in four months while Spuhler took his personal tally against his future employers to five in his last two games. Boro won the return 1–0 but the boot was on the other foot in the next round as Sunderland had to retrieve a 5–2 deficit against Bradford City. Progress was made with five different scorers seeing the Lads to a 5–1 win and preventing a Bradford showdown in the next round where the club that Len Shackleton and Billy Elliott came to prominence with – Bradford Park Avenue – were beaten 3–2 on aggregate to propel Sunderland into the Final.

Six years to the day since Sunderland had won the FA Cup for the first time, 1937 FA Cup winners Raich Carter and Jimmy Gorman lined up along with Alex Hastings who had missed the big day at Wembley through injury. In 1943 rather than the 93,500 that had seen the lads beat Preston, this time 6,500 were at Roker Park to see the club who Preston beat as they won the Cup themselves a year later: Huddersfield Town. Moreover, those 6,500 saw something very special; Nick Sharkey, Bobby Gurney, Charlie Buchan and Jimmy Millar are the only men to have ever scored five goals in a game for Sunderland in peacetime but in this Wartime Cup Final Cliff Whitelum went one better.

The scorer of 130 goals in 167 wartime appearances (all but 41 of those games being for Sunderland) Whitelum scored all six goals as Sunderland romped home 6–2 in the first leg of the Final. There was no such thing as a foregone conclusion in football in this era, however, and Huddersfield made Sunderland sweat for the trophy in the second leg at Leeds Road where Sunderland were grateful for Johnny Spuhler's goal in order to edge home on aggregate after going down 4–1.

For all the footballing ups and downs, the war continued apace, Sunderland's Cup win coming just a week before the Dambusters Raid of Squadron 617 which utilised the famous 'bouncing bomb' devised by Barnes Wallace who drew on Bishopwearmouth born engineer William Halcrow's extensive knowledge of dam construction.

When football resumed for the 1943–44 North League season, Whitelum began with nine goals in his first three games. Scoring four in a 7–1 opening day home win over Leeds, he bagged a hat-trick in a 5–1 away win against the same team a week later before grabbing two in a 3–0 home victory over Hartlepool. Spuhler remained in fine form too, notching seven in his first four games.

Gorman and Hastings were still playing regularly but after playing in three of the first four games, Carter didn't appear again until the week before Christmas. Raich marked his return with two goals in a 6–1 win over Boro but was on the wrong end of a 4–0 Christmas Day defeat at Ayresome as the North League programme concluded with a fifth defeat to add to three draws and 10 wins.

Having won a Cup the season before and reached a Cup Final the year earlier, in 1943–44 the qualifying rounds of the League North Cup saw Sunderland concede four or more goals in eight of the 10 fixtures! Goalkeeper John Farey was beaten seven times on his solitary appearance for the club in a 7–4 defeat at Gateshead, Darlington inflicted 5–1 thrashings both home and away while Gateshead and Hartlepool both scored four times in wins at Roker. Four were also conceded away to both Newcastle and Middlesbrough – though Boro were beaten 5–4 with Stan Mortensen on the mark in his only 'guest' appearance for Sunderland nine years before his hat-trick for Blackpool in the FA Cup Final that despite the South Shields born marksman's three goals became known as 'The Matthews' Final'.

Boro must have been gluttons for punishment. Sunderland had lost six in a row before completing their Cup qualifying games with two victories against them but with the Cup qualification games completed by the end of February, Sunderland played seven friendlies, four of them being against the men from Teesside. Boro at least had the consolation of winning the last of these after a draw and two Sunderland victories.

Finally Sunderland participated in a Tyne-Wear-Tees Cup, playing Newcastle twice but going down 0–3 at home and 2–5 at Newcastle.

As in 1942–43, final positions were based on average points scored in the second half of the season. With 11 defeats in the 19 games played in this period Sunderland ended in 45th position out of 50.

There was better in 1944–45. An opening home goalless draw with Boro preceded five wins in a row including 5–1 victories over Boro, Leeds and away to Newcastle where that man Whitelum got another hat-trick in front of 29,000 (he'd get another against them in the Cup later in the season). That bright start continued as Sunderland ended with a dozen wins and only two defeats from 18 games, placing them third behind Huddersfield and Derby in a 'table' of 54 northern clubs.

The second half of the season fell away again, Sunderland being placed 31st out of 60 clubs this time, having lost 13 of 25 games played as once again averages were assessed.

Once more the League War Cup failed to see Sunderland at their best with five defeats and a draw out of 10 games preceding seven further fixtures in March and April after elimination was confirmed. Of these the highlight was a 3–0 away win at Newcastle.

Sunderland would have two further games at St James' Park shipping 11 goals in two defeats but despite that stark statistic gloom was conspicuous by its absence. Firstly a 6–3 defeat at the home of Newcastle United was not against them but Gateshead in the Final of the Tyne-Wear-Tees Cup while a 5–0 defeat at the hands of Newcastle on 9 May 1945 was despite the defeat a Victory game celebrating the end at last of World War Two in Europe, Germany having surrendered two days earlier.

By the day after the first home game of the 1945–46 season the war came to a complete end with the surrender of Japan on 2 September – six years to the day after the final 'expunged' pre-war League game away to Arsenal. The Football League had quickly pulled the plug on League fixtures and would take until 1946–47 to resume an official League programme. However, 1945–46 saw a Northern Professional League up and running, the 1 September game being a 1–0 home win over Sheffield Wednesday a week after losing 6–3 away to the same opponents where hat-tricks from Jackie Robinson and Alf Rogers did for the Lads.

Back to back League games were the norm and this was also the case in the FA Cup. While the 1945–46 season 'league' games do not count in official records as the season was not an official Football League season, the FA Cup from 1945–46 does indeed count as post-war rather than wartime football. Consequently Raich Carter – who scored Sunderland's first two goals of the season at Hillsborough – is not considered to have played official post-war football for Sunderland. He turned out in seven 'league games' the last on 15 December away to Manchester United (at City's Maine Road as United's Old Trafford was still to be repaired following bomb damage) but had departed for Derby – who he had 'guested' for during the war – before the official FA Cup games took place.

For the only season in its history the FA Cup was played on a two-leg basis but this cost Sunderland. Having won both legs of their first tie with Grimsby, Bury were beaten in the first game of the next stage (although the second leg brought defeat. In any other season a fifth round 1–0 home win over Birmingham would have taken the Lads into the quarter-final but a 3–1 second leg defeat brought elimination.

Derby County were the first post-war Cup winners and with Raich Carter in their ranks for what would be his League debut for his new club who else should be Sunderland's first post-war League visitors but Derby who were beaten 3–2 with 1937 Cup Final goalscorer Eddie Burbanks and wartime goal machine Cliff Whitelum, who got two, getting the goals.

With the resumption of League football and with it competitive fixtures every week football returned to normal after the war. Wartime appearances, goals and results do not count in official records and thus wartime football is a much neglected part of sporting history. That is understandable given the dire state of the nation – indeed the world – at that time but thankfully weekly football was a positive sign that things were beginning to recover from the most dreadful man made destruction ever wrought upon the planet.

World War One Games

Season	Date	Opponents	Venue	Result	Comments
1915–16	May 6	Newcastle United	A	D 1–1	in aid of Military Charities
1917–18	May 4	Newcastle United	A	W 3–1	in aid of National Football War Fund
1918–19	Aug 31	Newcastle United	A	W 4–0	in aid of National Football War Fund
	Dec 21	Newcastle United	A	L 0–4	in aid of Comrades of the Great War Fund
	Dec 26	Newcastle United	H	W 1–0	
	Jan 1	Middlesbrough	H	L 1–3	
	Jan 11	Durham City	A	L 0–1	Victory League
	Jan 18	Middlesbrough	H	W 2–0	Victory League
	Jan 25	Newcastle United	A	L 3–4	Victory League
	Feb 1	South Shields	H	D 3–3	Victory League
	Feb 8	Darlington	A	W 1–0	Victory League
	Feb 15	Hartlepool United	H	W 5–2	Victory League
	Feb 22	Scotswood	A	D 2–2	Victory League
	Mar 15	Middlesbrough	A	L 1–2	Victory League
	Mar 22	Newcastle United	H	W 2–1	Victory League
	Mar 29	South Shields	A	D 1-1	Durham Senior Cup tie
	Apr 2	South Shields	H	W 4–1	Durham Senior Cup tie replay
	Apr 5	Darlington	H	L 0–2	Victory League
	Apr 12	Hartlepool United	A	W 2–0	Victory League
	Apr 18	Bradford City	H	W 2–1	
	Apr 19	Felling Colliery	H	W 8–1	Durham Senior Cup semi-final
	Apr 21	South Shields	A	L 1–3	Victory League
	Apr 22	Durham City	H	W 2–0	Victory League
	Apr 26	Third Lanark	H	L 2-3	
	Apr 30	Scotswood	H	W 6–1	Victory League
	May 3	Crook	Feethams	W 8-0	Durham Senior Cup Final
	May 17	Newcastle United	H	W 3–2	in aid of Footballers' National War Fund

Sunderland – The War Years
World War One

Bold = Guest	1916–19	
	Apps	Gls
Batey / Batty	2	
Baverstock, John	7	
Best, Robert	17	3
Boe, James	1	
Bowran	2	
Britton	1	
Buchan, Charles Murray	13	8
Charlton, Edward	4	

Bold = Guest

	1916–19	
	Apps	Gls
Cook, William	1	
Cook, John	1	
Cooper	1	
Coverdale, William Robert	2	
Crossley, Charles Arthur	1	2
Cuggy, Francis	17	
Hafekost, Charles Henry	3	
Hobson, Herbert Bertie	13	1
Holley, George	14	6
Hopkins, William	6	
Hugall, James Cockburn	10	
Hunter, George	1	
Johnson	2	
Johnston	1	
Kasher, Joseph William Robinson	1	
Keenleyside	1	1
Leonard, Henry Droxford	2	2
Leslie	1	
Little	1	1
Low, Henry Forbes	11	
Martin, Henry	2	
Mordue, John	15	8
Ness, Harry Marshall	1	
Newton	1	
Parker, Richard	3	3
Philip, George	1	1
Poole, John Smith	1	
Rodgerson, Ralph	5	
Scott, Leslie	1	
Seed, James Marshall	1	
Sherwin, Harry	9	
Smith, N	1	
Thompson	5	
Travers, Bernard	10	5
Turnbull	1	
Watson	1	
Williams, Harry	5	1
Williamson, John Robert	1	
Wilson	6	1
Wood	3	
Young, Robert Thornton	9	
Young, E	1	

World War Two Games

Season	Date	Opponents	Venue	Result	Comments
1939–40	Mar 22	South Shields	A	W 8-2	
	30	Newcastle United	A	L 0-2	In aid of the 'Chronicle War Relief Fund
	Apr 6	Hartlepools United	A	L 2-4	
	13	Newcastle United	A	L 2-3	
	20	Darlington	St James' Park	D 1–1	League War Cup first round (home tie but Roker Park closed)
	27	Darlington	A	W 3–2	League War Cup first round
	May 4	Leeds United	St James' Park	D 0–0	League War Cup second round (home tie but Roker Park closed)
	May 11	Leeds United	A	W 1–0	League War Cup second round
	18	Blackburn Rovers	A	L 2–3	League War Cup third round
1940–41	Sep 14	Army XI	H	W 4–0	
	Dec 21	Newcastle United	A	L 1–3	
	Dec 25	Sunderland Police	H	W 11–5	
	Jan 25	South Shields ex-Schoolboys	H	W 3–2	Durham War Cup first round
	Feb 15	Murton Colliery Welfare	H	W 2–1	Durham War Cup second round
	Mar 8	Eppleton Colliery Welfare	H	W 2–1	Durham War Cup semi-final
	Apr 14	Newcastle United	A	W 4–3	
	May 10	Middlesbrough	A	W 4–3	
	17	Chopwell Colliery	H	L 1–2	Durham War Cup Final
	24	Durham Light Infantry	H	W 3–2	
1941–42	Aug 30	Sheffield United	H	W 7–1	North League
	Sep 6	Sheffield United	A	W 1–0	North League
	13	Bradford Park Ave	H	L 1–2	North League
	20	Bradford Park Ave	A	D 2–2	North League
	27	Leeds United	A	W 2–1	North League
	Oct 4	Leeds United	H	H 6–1	North League
	11	Middlesbrough	H	D 4–4	North League
	18	Middlesbrough	A	D 2–2	North League
	25	Newcastle U	A	D 1–1	North League
	Nov 1	Newcastle U	H	W 3–2	North League
	8	Bradford City	H	W 5–1	North League
	15	Bradford City	A	L 2–4	North League
	22	Huddersfield Town	A	L 0–1	North League
	29	Huddersfield Town	H	W 5–0	North League
	Dec 6	York City	H	W 4–2	North League
	13	York City	A	W 4–1	North League
	20	Gateshead	A	L 0–2	North League
	25	Gateshead	H	L 1–3	North League
	Dec 27	Middlesbrough	H	W 6–0	League War Cup (Qualifying game)
	Jan 3	Middlesbrough	A	L 0–3	League War Cup (Qualifying game)
	10	Newcastle United	H	D 2–2	League War Cup (Qualifying game)

WORLD WAR TWO GAMES

Season	Date		Opponents	Venue	Result		Comments
		17	Newcastle United	A	L	1–2	League War Cup (Qualifying game)
		31	Gateshead	A	W	2–1	League War Cup (Qualifying game)
	Feb	14	York City	H	W	8–3	League War Cup (Qualifying game)
		21	Bradford Park Ave	A	L	0–3	League War Cup (Qualifying game)
		28	Bradford Park Ave	H	W	4–2	League War Cup (Qualifying game)
	Mar	14	York City	A	D	2–2	League War Cup (Qualifying game)
		21	Gateshead	H	W	5–1	League War Cup (Qualifying game)
		28	Middlesbrough	H	L	1–2	
	Apr	4	Oldham Athletic	A	D	1–1	League War Cup first round first leg
		6	Oldham Athletic	H	W	5–2	League War Cup first round second leg
		11	Bradford City	H	D	2–2	League War Cup second round first leg
		18	Bradford City	A	W	6–4	League War Cup second round second leg
		25	Bradford Park Ave	H	W	1–0	League War Cup third round first leg
	May	2	Bradford Park Ave	A	D	2–2	League War Cup third round second leg
		9	Grimsby Town	H	D	0–0	League War Cup semi-final first leg
		16	Grimsby Town	A	W	3–2	League War Cup semi-final second leg
		23	Wolverhampton Wanderers	H	D	2–2	League War Cup Final first leg
		25	Newcastle United	A	D	2–2	
		30	Wolverhampton Wanderers	A	L	1–4	League War Cup Final second leg
1942–43	Aug	15	Newcastle United	A	W	4–2	
		29	Bradford City	A	L	3–4	North League
	Sep	5	Bradford City	H	W	3–1	North League
		12	York City	H	D	0–0	North League
		19	York City	A	W	3–0	North League
		26	Huddersfield Town	H	L	1–3	North League
	Oct	3	Huddersfield Town	A	D	2–2	North League
		10	Bradford Park Ave	A	L	2–4	North League
		17	Bradford Park Ave	H	W	2–1	North League
		24	Leeds United	A	W	2–1	North League
		31	Leeds United	H	W	4–1	North League
	Nov	7	Middlesbrough	H	W	4–1	North League
		14	Middlesbrough	A	W	4–3	North League
		21	Gateshead	H	L	3–4	North League
		28	Gateshead	A	L	0–1	North League
	Dec	5	Newcastle United	H	L	3–5	North League
		12	Newcastle United	A	D	3–3	North League
		19	Middlesbrough	A	W	7–2	North League
		25	Middlesbrough	H	L	0–4	North League
		26	Gateshead	H	W	7–1	League North Cup (Qualifying game)
	Jan	2	Gateshead	A	L	4–5	League North Cup (Qualifying game)
		9	Middlesbrough	A	L	1–4	League North Cup (Qualifying game)
		16	Middlesbrough	H	W	7–0	League North Cup (Qualifying game)
		23	York City	A	L	0–4	League North Cup (Qualifying game)
		30	York City	H	L	4–5	League North Cup (Qualifying game)
	Feb	6	Newcastle United	H	D	3–3	League North Cup (Qualifying game)
		13	Newcastle United	A	W	3–2	League North Cup (Qualifying game)
		20	Bradford Park Ave	H	D	1–1	League North Cup (Qualifying game)
		27	Bradford Park Ave	A	D	1–1	League North Cup (Qualifying game)
	Mar	6	Gateshead	H	L	1–2	

SUNDERLAND: THE COMPLETE RECORD

Season	Date		Opponents	Venue	Result	Comments
		13	Gateshead	A	W 2–1	North League Second Championship
		20	Middlesbrough	H	W 8–0	West Riding FA Cup first round first leg
		27	Middlesbrough	A	L 0–1	West Riding FA Cup first round second leg
	Apr	3	Bradford City	A	L 2–3	West Riding FA Cup quarter-final first leg
		10	Bradford City	H	W 5–1	West Riding FA Cup quarter-final second leg
		17	Bradford Park Ave	A	W 1–0	West Riding FA Cup semi-final first leg
		24	Bradford Park Ave	H	D 2–2	West Riding FA Cup semi-final second leg
		28	Durham Light Infantry	H	L 2–7	in aid of charity
	May	1	Huddersfield Town	H	W 6–2	West Riding FA Cup Final first leg
		8	Huddersfield Town	A	L 1–4	West Riding FA Cup Final second leg
1943–44	Aug	28	Leeds United	H	W 7–1	North League
	Sep	4	Leeds United	A	W 5–1	North League
		11	Hartlepool United	A	W 3–0	North League
		18	Hartlepool United	H	W 3–0	North League
		25	Huddersfield Town	A	L 0–4	North League
	Oct	2	Huddersfield Town	H	W 3–2	North League
		9	Darlington	A	W 2–1	North League
		16	Darlington	H	W 4–2	North League
		23	Bradford Park Ave	H	D 1–1	North League
		30	Bradford Park Ave	A	D 0–0	North League
	Nov	6	Newcastle United	H	W 4–2	North League
		13	Newcastle United	A	L 1–3	North League
		20	Gateshead	A	W 3–2	North League
		27	Gateshead	H	L 2–3	North League
	Dec	4	Hartlepool United	H	L 1–2	North League
		11	Hartlepool United	A	D 1–1	North League
		18	Middlesbrough	H	W 6–1	North League
		25	Middlesbrough	A	L 0–4	North League
		27	Newcastle United	A	L 2–4	League North Cup (Qualifying game)
	Jan	1	Newcastle United	H	W 3–0	League North Cup (Qualifying game)
		8	Darlington	A	L 1–5	League NorthCup (Qualifying game)
		15	Darlington	H	L 1–5	League NorthCup (Qualifying game)
		22	Hartlepool United	H	L 3–4	League NorthCup (Qualifying game)
		29	Hartlepool United	A	L 2–4	League NorthCup (Qualifying game)
	Feb	5	Gateshead	A	L 4–7	League North Cup (Qualifying game)
		12	Gateshead	H	L 1–4	League North Cup (Qualifying game)
		19	Middlesbrough	A	W 3–0	League North Cup (Qualifying game)
		26	Middlesbrough	A	W 5–4	League North Cup (Qualifying game)
	Mar	4	Middlesbrough	H	W 4–1	North League Second Championship
		11	Middlesbrough	A	W 3–2	North League Second Championship
		18	Hartlepool United	H	W 3–0	North League Second Championship
		25	Hartlepool United	A	L 1–2	North League Second Championship
	Apr	10	Gateshead	H	D 1–1	North League Second Championship
		15	Newcastle United	H	L 0–3	Tyne Wear Tees Cup semi-final first Leg
		33	Newcastle United	A	L 2–5	Tyne Wear Tees Cup semi-final second Leg
		29	Middlesbrough	H	D 3–3	North League Second Championship
	May	6	Middlesbrough	A	L 2–4	North League Second Championship
1944–45	Aug	26	Middlesbrough	H	D 0–0	North League
	Sep	2	Middlesbrough	A	W 5–1	North League
		9	Leeds United	A	W 1–0	North League

138

Season	Date		Opponents	Venue	Result	Comments
		16	Leeds United	H	W 5–1	North League
		23	Newcastle United	H	W 2–0	North League
		30	Newcastle United	A	W 5–1	North League
	Oct	7	Bradford City	A	D 1–1	North League
		14	Bradford City	H	W 2–1	North League
		21	Hartlepool United	A	W 6–2	North League
		28	Hartlepool United	H	W 4–2	North League
	Nov	4	Huddersfield Town	A	L 0–3	North League
		11	Huddersfield Town	H	D 2–2	North League
		18	York City	A	W 5–3	North League
		25	York City	H	D 3–3	North League
	Dec	2	Darlington	A	W 3–1	North League
		9	Darlington	H	W 6–2	North League
		16	Gateshead	H	W 2–1	North League
		23	Gateshead	A	L 0–1	North League
		26	Newcastle United	A	L 1–3	League North Cup (Qualifying game)
		30	Newcastle United	H	W 4–3	League North Cup (Qualifying game)
	Jan	6	Darlington	H	D 1–1	League North Cup (Qualifying game)
		13	Darlington	A	L 2–3	League North Cup (Qualifying game)
		20	Middlesbrough	H	W 4–3	League North Cup (Qualifying game)
	Feb	3	Gateshead	A	L 1–2	League North Cup (Qualifying game)
		10	Gateshead	H	W 3–0	League North Cup (Qualifying game)
		17	Hartlepool United	H	W 6–2	League North Cup (Qualifying game)
		24	Hartlepool United	A	L 1–3	League North Cup (Qualifying game)
	Mar	3	Gateshead	H	L 0–2	North League Second Championship
		10	Darlington	H	L 1–5	North League Second Championship
		17	Middlesbrough	H	L 1–2	League North Cup (Qualifying game)
		24	Gateshead	H	D 2–2	North League Second Championship
	Mar	31	Gateshead	A	L 2–4	North League Second Championship
	Apr	2	Newcastle United	A	W 3–0	North League Second Championship
		7	York City	H	D 0–0	North League Second Championship
		14	York City	A	L 2–4	North League Second Championship
		21	Hartlepool United	H	W 5–0	Tyne Wear Tees Cup
		28	Hartlepool United	A	W 2–0	Tyne Wear Tees Cup
	May	5	York City	A	L 1–2	Tyne Wear Tees Cup
		9	Newcastle United	A	L 0–5	to celebrate WW2 Victory
		12	York City	H	W 6–1	Tyne Wear Tees Cup
		19	Huddersfield Town	A	L 0–1	Tyne Wear Tees Cup semi-final first leg
		21	Huddersfield Town	H	W 2–0	Tyne Wear Tees Cup semi-final second leg
		26	Gateshead	St James' Park	L 3–6	Tyne Wear Tees Cup Final
1945–46	Aug	25	Sheffield Wednesday	A	L 3–6	North League
	Sep	1	Sheffield Wednesday	H	W 1–0	North League
		8	Huddersfield Town	H	L 0–2	North League
		13	Sheffield United	A	L 0–4	North League
		15	Huddersfield Town	A	L 1–4	North League
		22	Chesterfield	A	L 0–3	North League
		29	Chesterfield	H	L 0–5	North League
	Oct	6	Barnsley	H	W 1–0	North League
		13	Barnsley	A	L 2–4	North League
		17	Stoke City	H	W 4–2	North League

Season	Date	Opponents	Venue	Result	Comments
	20	Everton	A	L 0–4	North League
	27	Everton	H	L 0–4	North League
	Nov 3	Bolton Wanderers	H	W 1–0	North League
	10	Bolton Wanderers	A	W 2–1	North League
	17	Preston North End	A	D 1–1	North League
	24	Preston North End	H	L 0–1	North League
	Dec 1	Leeds United	A	L 2–3	North League
	8	Leeds United	H	W 5–1	North League
	15	Manchester United	A	L 1–2	North League
	22	Manchester United	H	W 4–2	North League
	25	Burnley	H	D 1–1	North League
	26	Burnley	A	W 3–2	North League
	29	Sheffield United	H	L 1–2	North League
	Jan 1	Middlesbrough	A	L 0–1	North League
	19	Stoke City	A	D 0–0	North League
	Feb 2	Grimsby Town	H	W 2–0	North League
	16	Blackpool	A	L 0–4	North League
	23	Liverpool	A	D 2–2	North League
	Mar 2	Liverpool	H	L 0–2	North League
	9	Bury	H	W 2–1	North League
	13	Blackpool	H	W 3–1	North League
	16	Bury	A	L 0–3	North League
	23	Blackburn Rovers	A	L 1–2	North League
	26	Grimsby Town	A	L 1–4	North League
	Mar 30	Blackburn Rovers	H	D 2–2	North League
	Apr 6	Bradford Park Ave	H	W 1–0	North League
	13	Bradford Park Ave	A	L 0–1	North League
	17	Gateshead	H	W 3–0	Durham Senior Professional Cup semi-final
	19	Manchester City	A	W 2–0	North League
	20	Newcastle United	H	W 1–0	North League
	22	Manchester City	H	W 4–0	North League
	Apr 29	Newcastle United	A	L 1–4	North League
	May 4	Middlesbrough	H	L 0–1	North League
	8	Darlington	H	L 0–2	Durham Senior Professional Cup Final

Sunderland – The War Years
World War Two

Bold = Guest

		1939-40		1940-41		1941-42		1942-43		1943-44		1944-45		1945-46		Total	
		Apps	Gls	Apps	Gls	Apps	Gls	Apps	Gls	Apps	Gls	Apps	Gls	Apps	Gls	Apps	Gls
Ainsley	George Edward							1								1	0
Allan	T.A.					1		1	4	2						5	3
Anderson	D.							1								1	0
Anderson	James													1		1	0
Bell	Henry D									7	2	16	3			23	5
Bell	Joseph									20	3	5	1			25	4
Bett	Frederick													4		4	0
Bircham	Bernard	1		1				21		13		26		3		65	0
Borthwick	Matthew					1										1	0
Boyd	Jack							1		1				4		6	0
Boyes	Walter							3	1							3	1
Bradwell	S			1		8	1	18	1	15						42	3
Breen	C.							1								1	0
Brown	Cyril									9	5	22	4	31	9		
Buglass		1	2													1	2
Burbanks	William Edwin	2						1				14	1	34	6	51	7
Burns	Oliver H.					1										1	0
Cairns	William H.													1	1	1	1
Carter	Horatio Stratton	3	2	1	1	27	23	24	15	5	2	3	3	7	4	70	50
Clark	J.					1		10		23						34	0
Collins	G. E.									17	4					17	4
Coupland	J.							1								1	0
Cunningham	Laurence									1						1	0
Curzon	William Alfred					1		1								2	0
Davie	John													8	5	8	5
Dawes	T.							1								1	0
Dawson	Thomas									1	1					1	1
Dinsdale														1		1	0
Dixon	John T.											1				1	0
Dryden	John G.							1								1	0
Dunn	E.													15	2	15	2
Duns	Leonard			1	4	3	1	1		3	1			17	3	25	9
Ellison	Samuel Walter									1		1		10	4	12	4
Elms	Charles F.									1						1	0
Eves	John R.			1		28		26		24		34		11		124	0
Farey	John A.									1						1	0
Fleck	John S.											9		14		23	0
Forde	Stephen													2		2	0
Fraser	N.							1								1	0
Freeman	A.									1						1	0
Gallacher	Hughie Kilpatrick			1												1	0
Gorman	James	3		2		29	1	36		27		28	1	1		126	2
Gray	A. E.													3		3	0
Green	J. H.							1								1	0
Gurney	Robert	2	2	2	2	8	2									12	6
Hall	A. Webster	1														1	0
Hall	J. L									1						1	0

SUNDERLAND: THE COMPLETE RECORD

		1939-40		1940-41		1941-42		1942-43		1943-44		1944-45		1945-46		Total	
		Apps	Gls	Apps	Gls	Apps	Gls	Apps	Gls	Apps	Gls	Apps	Gls	Apps	Gls	Apps	Gls
Hamill	George											1				1	0
Harrison	J. Y.									2						2	0
Harvey														1		1	0
Hastings	A. Cockburn	3	2			26	1	25	5	26	3	22		8		112	9
Heslop					1											1	0
Hetherington	Henry											2	1	4	1	6	2
Hewison	William J.	1		1		16		21								39	0
Heywood	Albert Edward	2		1		39		4				17		8		71	0
Hindmarsh	Eddie									19						19	0
Hodges	Cyril L.									6	3					6	3
Horton	L.											3	2			3	2
Housam	Arthur			1		38		4		9		14	1	41	1	107	2
Humble	Douglas													3	1	3	1
Ireland	E.					6	1					1				7	1
Irwin	J.									1	2					1	2
Jameson	John W.											1				1	0
Jenkins	Thomas F.									1						1	0
Johnston	Robert	1												2		3	0
Johnston	T.							1								1	0
Jones	John Edward													23		23	0
Jones	S.											1				1	0
Kearney	Sydney F.							1								1	0
Kilgallon	J.									1						1	0
Laidman	Frederick							17		22	5	28	10			67	15
Laurie	John S.													1		1	0
Lilley	John											6				6	0
Lloyd	William Stanley					2		7	3	1		2				12	3
Lockie	A. James	2		2		26	1	19	1	34		42		36		161	2
Lown		1	2													1	2
McArdle														1		1	0
McCormack	Cecil							4								4	0
McGuire	J. E.											1				1	0
McMahon	Hugh			1		27	7			2						30	7
Maguire				1												1	0
Mapson	John													33		33	0
Mather	Harry									5						5	0
Merry	Thomas A.											1	1			1	1
Milburn	John											2				2	0
Milsom	D.					2	1	2		3	1	3	1			10	3
Mortensen	Stanley Harding									1	1					1	1
Nicholson	William Edward							7								7	0
Potts	Henry J.							17	8	6	3	1				24	11
Purvis	Bartholomew													1		1	0
Ramsay	R.G.					3		2	1							5	1
Reay	Thomas									2	1	1	1			3	2
Richardson				1												1	0
Robb	Norman									1	1					1	1
Robinson	George Henry					31	8	25	6							56	14
Robinson	J. S.									1						1	0
Robinson	William					1		5		3				3	1	12	1
Rodgerson	Ralph	1				21		1								23	0
Scotson	Reginald	1								5				4		10	0
Scott	William R.											1				1	0
Short	John D.							1								1	0
Slack	Thomas					1	1									1	1

WORLD WAR TWO GAMES

		1939-40		1940-41		1941-42		1942-43		1943-44		1944-45		1945-46		Total	
		Apps	Gls	Apps	Gls	Apps	Gls	Apps	Gls	Apps	Gls	Apps	Gls	Apps	Gls	Apps	Gls
Smallwood	Frederick					1		17	8							18	8
Spuhler	John Oswald	3			2	35	16	35	22	36	23	36	18	6	1	153	80
Stelling	J. G. Surtees											24		41		65	0
Stokoe	Dennis									1						1	0
Stubbins	Albert					4	2									4	2
Tapken	**Norman**							2								2	0
Taylor	John W. R.															0	0
Thomson	Charles	3	2													3	2
Thompson	George H.									1						1	0
Thompson	Harry	1				4	1	1						2		8	1
Thompson	Raymond													6		6	0
Tulip	Henry									1		1				2	0
Tuttle	Ernest H.							4	1							4	1
Wallbanks	**Harold**											37	2	4		41	2
Wallbanks	**James**											2				2	0
Waller	**Herbert**													3		3	0
Walsh	William					3		1		1						5	0
Walshaw	Kenneth									3	1	25	10	9	1	37	12
Watson	William													2		2	0
Wensley	Laurence							1		16	6					17	6
Wharton	**Guy**													1		1	0
Wheatman	Lewis					7		4		4						15	0
White	Thomas											9	1	19	9	28	10
Whitelum	Clifford	3	2			29	26	33	31	27	25	36	42	41	11	169	137
Williams	**George**									1						1	0
Willingham	C. Kenneth													16		16	0
Wright	A. W. Tempest					3	4	1	1	2	1			7		13	6

143

Sunderland Stadia

Since the publication of the original Sunderland AFC Complete Record in 2005 on-going research has revealed new information concerning Sunderland's former grounds, in particular the precise location of Abbs Field which Sunderland called home from 1884 to 1886. Subsequent to the publication of the earlier version of this book tours of the former grounds have been held as part of the English Heritage local history projects, led by the authors of the Complete Record.

With the support of then chairman Niall Quinn, Sunderland City Council and vital funding from Sunderland AFC Supporters' Association, club historian Rob Mason subsequently organized the siting of blue plaques to mark the club's former grounds. While the places where players formed the history of the club now have other uses, their parts in the city's footballing heritage are now identified so that current and future generations realise how near to their area of Sunderland the Lads once used to play. Thanks of course remain due to the property owners who willingly gave their permission for the siting of the plaques.

The BBC 1 TV local history programme '*Inside Out*' broadcast a 15 minute film covering the Blue Plaques Project. Their siting was also seen around the world in a TV feature produced by Premier League Productions which provides material for the 200+ countries outside of the UK which take TV coverage of the Barclays Premier League.

The Stadium of Light is Sunderland's eighth home ground. Mirroring Roker Park in that the club moved into it shortly before the dawn of a new century, the Stadium of Light will surely go on to emulate Roker in that Sunderland will spend many years on the banks of the Wear, just as Roker Park proved to be the club's home for 99 years. Long-term residence was the case in the 20th century, but in its infancy Sunderland had six home grounds in less than two decades!

Modern-day supporters are used to fabulous facilities in all-seater stadia covered on all four sides, with extensive catering, toilet and first aid facilities, concourse televisions, glossy match programmes, electronic scoreboards and a PA that blasts out stirring entrance music. However, back in 1879 when Sunderland were formed a roped-off field was as much as could be expected.

Sunderland's home grounds:

The Blue House Field 1879–1882
The club's first football ground was in Hendon at the Blue House Field, near to the current Blue House pub. Having been founded by Scots-born Hendon schoolteacher James Allan, and initially named Sunderland and District Teachers' Association Football Club, Sunderland's first recorded home game came on 13 November 1880 when Ferryhill left the Blue House as 1–0 victors.

The ground was on the site of what is now Commercial Road, but with an annual rent of £10 Sunderland – who had dropped the 'and District Teachers' from their title in October 1880 – moved to a new home.

Sunderland would return to the Blue House Field, as an away side, after James Allan left the club and set up the rival Sunderland Albion outfit. For a spell Albion tried to become Wearside's premier club and they built a stand at the Blue House Field, around which they also created a cycle track, but following Sunderland's election to the Football League in 1890 Albion's claim to be Sunderland's top club sank without trace and the outfit founded in 1888 ceased in 1892. Appropriately, given that Sunderland's first ground was the Blue House Field, the club's original strip was blue. Sunderland didn't wear red and white stripes until 1886. Blue shirts and knickerbockers with a white stripe on the knickerbockers, along with a tassled cap, was the original attire!

Pleasingly in 2012 Sunderland's original ground is once again a football pitch. It is the only one of the club's former grounds to still be a football pitch although there is five-a-side football played at Ashbrooke. The site of the pitch where club founder James Allan and his

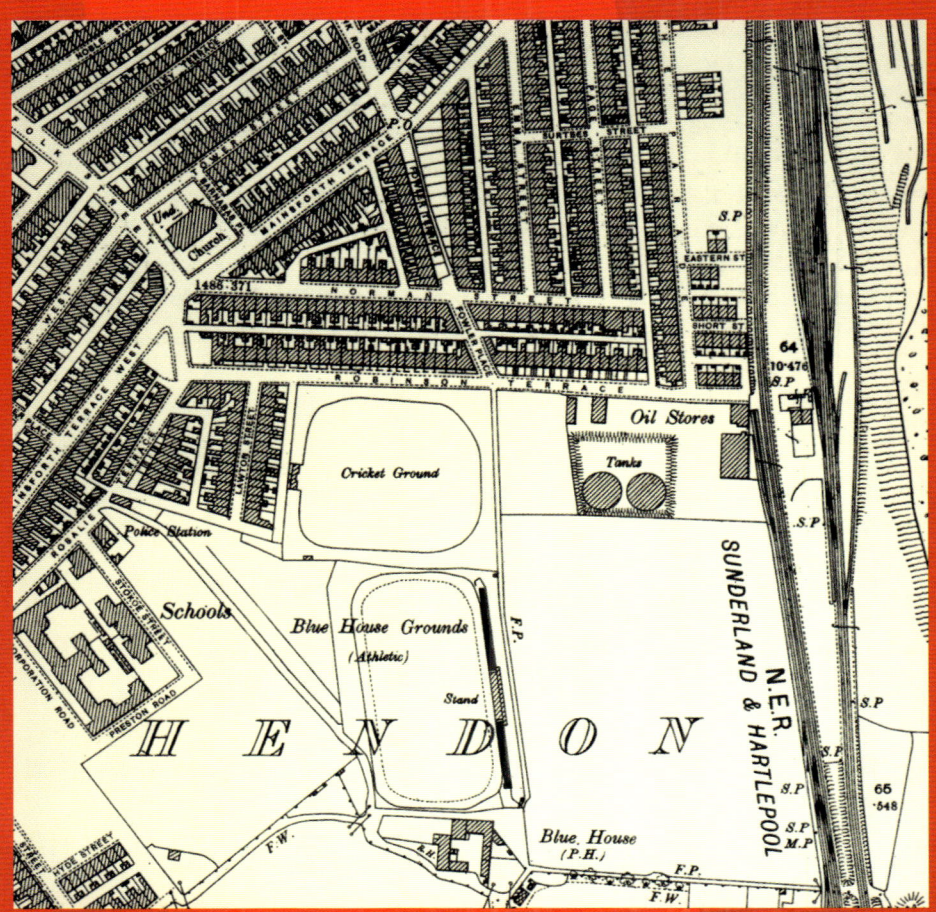

team first played is now the home ground of Valley Road Community Primary School. 'We found a map of where the pitch originally was and have laid our pitch out in what we believe is exactly the same place with the centre spot right where the original one was' said deputy head and Sunderland supporter George Stobbart.

Adjacent to the pitch is the Raich Carter Centre, a modern sports facility that includes all weather football pitches and is named after arguably Sunderland's finest ever footballer, Horatio Stratton Carter. He was born in 1913 near where the club had played its first games and attended the old Hendon Board School which stood on the site of the modern Valley Road Community Primary School.

Sunderland Cricket Club had previously played at The Blue House Field. They were resident there from 1850 until 1864. Prior to the club, which became known as Sunderland Cricket Club, playing at The Blue House Field it had been home to Hendon Terrace Cricket Club. Maps of the period around the 1890s – after Sunderland left of course – indicate four sports pitches in the area. Research by Lynn Pearson for the English Heritage publication 'Played in *Tyne and Wear*' purports that the Blue House Fields were used for various sports from around 1845 until circa 1914.

It is known from '*The History of The Sunderland Cricket and Rugby Football Club 1808-1963*' that shortly after 1860 a wooden hut was erected at the site and that this was later known as the pavilion and was improved and painted while a mast was placed on a grass plot and graced by a flag presented by John. T. French. As a tail-end batsman French once helped Sunderland to a famous draw against the all-powerful side of the time, Stockton, by striking a final over ball that knocked out All England bowler Jonathan Joy! Whether the pavilion or flagpole were still in evidence when Sunderland began playing football at the ground 15 years after the cricket club left for a ground in Holmeside is not verified.

A Sunderland team is last known to have played at the Blue House site in 1903 when a reserve team played a game there

The Cedars 1881

It is believed that Sunderland played briefly on a ground near The Cedars in 1881 between moving from the original Blue House Field site and setting up home in Ashbrooke. They may actually have used several local fields and one such site where Manila Street now stands has been marked with a blue plaque, near The Victoria Gardens Pub. Like the previous pitch the venue was more a roped-off field than a stadium of any sort.

Groves Field, Ashbrooke 1882–83

Sunderland's last ground on the south side of the Wear witnessed only four recorded games in the year Sunderland called it home. Since crossing the river in 1883 the club has never returned to the

SUNDERLAND STADIA

Groves Field, Ashbrooke, SAFC's home in 1882–83. This was the last of the grounds south of the river.

side on which it was formed, although a potential site at Ryhope was one of those mooted prior to the move from Roker Park to the Stadium of Light.

The Ashbrooke Cricket and Rugby Ground now occupies the Groves Field site. The first known Sunderland game there took place on 4 November 1882, when North Eastern were beaten 2–1. Perhaps Sunderland should have stayed there, as a 100 per-cent record in the ground's quartet of fixtures included a mammoth 12–1 win over Stanley Star – not the only result from the club's early years to exceed the official club record win of 11–1, which stands as it came in a major competitive (FA Cup) match. The dozen goals smacked in against Stanley Star came in the Northumberland and Durham Challenge Cup.

Five years after Sunderland left the Ashbrooke Ground it staged Sunderland Albion's first-ever game, which saw them go down 3–0 to Shankhouse Black Watch. It was the only game Albion were to play there as they then made the Blue House Field their home.

Ashbrooke is a major sporting venue which is Wearside's home of cricket and rugby as well as having bowls, squash, tennis and five-a-side football while it also has a gym and provides a base for hockey and the Sunderland Strollers running club. The Ashbrooke Sports Ground opened in 1887, some four years after Sunderland AFC's final game there when the ground was known as Groves Field.

Additionally Ashbrooke hosts a hugely popular annual fireworks display and successful music event known as the Split Festival. In its long history, which like SAFC's continues to this day, it has hosted many major sporting events, for instance attracting 20,678 people to the opening day of a cricket match between Durham and Australia in June 1926.

Horatio Street, Roker 1883–84

Known as 'the Dolly Field' and sometimes as Cooper Street or Horatio Street, Sunderland's first ground after crossing the Wear was known by various names, just as West Ham and QPR's grounds still are. To most people the Hammers play at Upton Park, but many locals insist they play at the Boleyn Ground, while a visit to QPR sees you at Loftus Road, South Africa Road or Rangers' Stadium, depending on who you talk to.

THE DOLLY FIELD, HORATIO STREET
In 1883-84 this was Sunderland A.F.C.'s fourth ground. Appley Terrace and Givens Street now stand on the pitch which ran along Cooper Street. The Club won its first trophy here and used The Wolsey as its changing rooms.

The Wolseley. Used as changing rooms when the club played at the 'Dolly Field'.

Situated near a claypit and brickworks, the Horatio Street pitch was regularly heavy to play on and gained the nickname the Dolly Field or Clay-Dolly Field. With Horatio Street running down one side of the pitch and Cooper Street along another, both locations were used to describe the ground, which itself was built over in later years by what became Givens Street and Appley Terrace.

While playing at Horatio Street the players used the nearby Wolseley Pub as changing rooms and that pub, just five minutes from the Stadium of Light, still stands, although thankfully these days the players change at the ground. Had Sunderland played at their present site a century ago, perhaps the Colliery Tavern would have been in demand as a changing room!

An 8–1 win marked Sunderland's inaugural match at Horatio Street, Castle Eden being the visitors on 29 September 1883. The new ground saw Sunderland win the club's first trophy, although it didn't host the Final. However, by the time the Durham Challenge Cup was actually awarded Sunderland had moved again – the Durham FA not having had enough money to pay for its new trophy at the time of the Final!

Sunderland spent only one year at Horatio Street. Although various names were referred to for this ground perhaps Horatio Street was most apt given that in the years to come Horatio 'Raich' Carter would become arguably the greatest ever to play for the Lads, having been born spitting distance from the club's first-ever ground in Hendon.

Abbs Field, Fulwell 1884–86

Situated opposite the top of Side Cliff Road on Fulwell Road where Prengarth Avenue stands now, Abbs Field is the furthest north of Sunderland's homes. Significantly it was also the first to be completely enclosed, meaning that an entrance charge could be made to spectators, therefore enabling the club to boost its finances for the challenges ahead as football's popularity grew. The foundation of the Football League was only four years away and just two years after that Sunderland would become the first club to join the Founder Members.

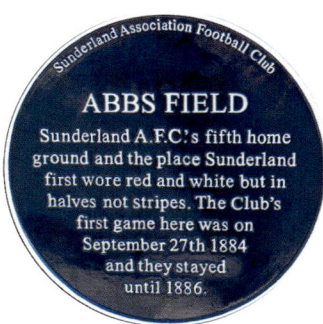

ABBS FIELD
Sunderland A.F.C.'s fifth home ground and the place Sunderland first wore red and white but in halves not stripes. The Club's first game here was on September 27th 1884 and they stayed until 1886.

Birtley were beaten 2–1 in Sunderland's first game there on 27 September 1884. Despite a good record at Abbs Field, which was also used by St Bede's FC, Sunderland's nomadic existence continued after the initial rent for the ground rose 500 per-cent from £2 10s to £15 at the start of their second season. The club was on the move again in March 1886, two months before the season ended, after crowds grew to as large as 3,500.

Abbs Field is where Sunderland changed from their original colours of blue to red and white for the first time, although at this stage the Lads played in red and white halves (like Blackburn Rovers in style if not colour) rather than stripes. Interesting to note that Sunderland never wore red and white at half of their eight home grounds and indeed would only wear stripes at the three they played at after leaving Abbs Field. The change to red and white was heralded by a club record win of 23-0 over Castletown soon after the change of colours.

As with The Cedars, The Dolly Field and Roker Park, Abbs Field now has houses built on it.

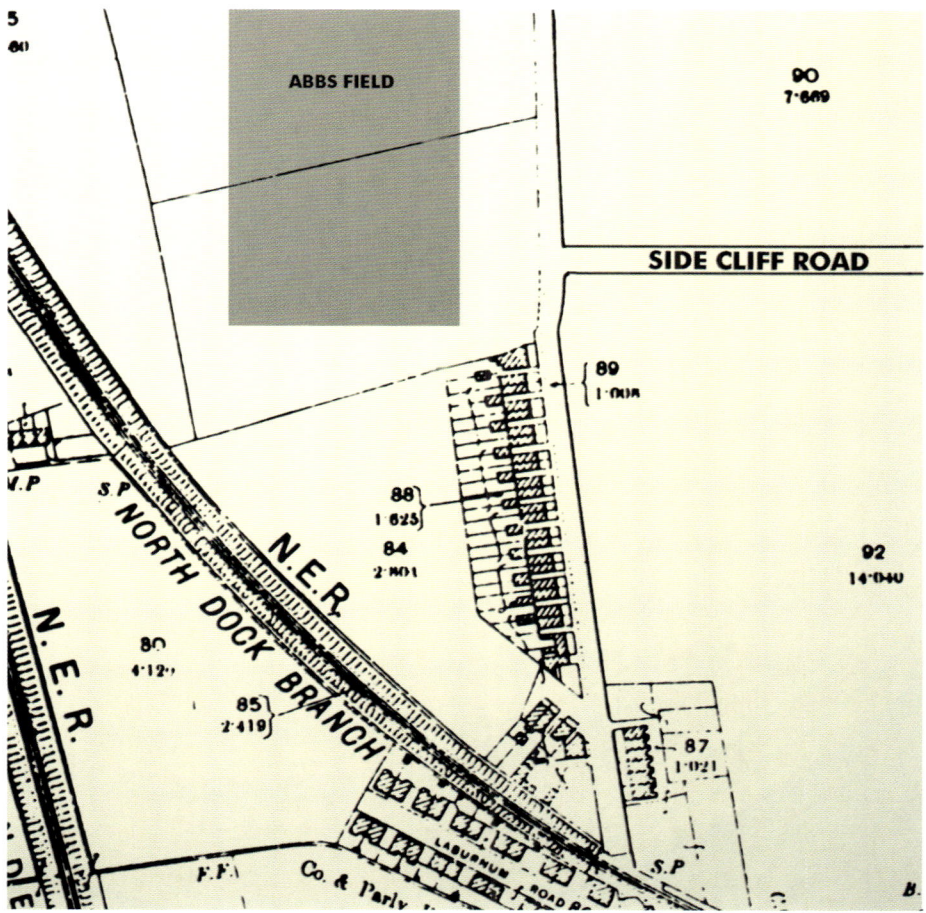

SUNDERLAND: THE COMPLETE RECORD

Newcastle Road 1886–1898

Sunderland's move to Newcastle Road was to herald one of the club's most successful periods. A dozen years were spent at the ground, which was nearer to the Stadium of Light than any of Sunderland's other homes. The spell brought the beginning of League football to the North East, three Championships courtesy of 'The Team of All The Talents' and the new strip of red and white stripes that has since become synonymous with Sunderland.

Renowned as the best ground in the region, just as the Stadium of Light is now, Newcastle Road attracted crowds of up to 22,000 and remains immortalised in the world's oldest and biggest oil painting of a football match. This work of art by Thomas M.M. Hemy adorns the main entrance to the Stadium of Light and shows a January 1895 meeting with Aston Villa.

Sunderland had staged the 1884 Durham FA Challenge Cup Final at Newcastle Road when a bigger ground was needed and Sunderland's Cup Final opponents Darlington were coincidentally the first visitors to the ground once Sunderland had made it their home. A crowd of a thousand turned up to see Sunderland win 3–1 and a week later club founder James Allan claimed a hat-trick against visitors Birtley.

Rent at the new ground cost £15, as it had at Abbs Field, but the new venue was far superior and so Sunderland moved in mid-season. In fact an unexpected bonus was received when the Thompson sisters, the owners of the ground, refunded £3 15s of the rent as a token of their appreciation of how well the property had been cared for.

The close season saw the pitch let for grazing while work went on to build a club house. Tents served as changing rooms with a house in nearby Ellerslie Terrace used for this purpose in later years. At the same time that the club moved to Newcastle Road the venue

SUNDERLAND STADIA

for club meetings moved from Thomas Street School to Whitburn Street Workman's Hall, which in itself marked the changing power structure at the club. Originally founded by schoolteachers, it was now the money men of the shipyards who were taking over as the club adopted an increasingly professional approach to the game.

The 24 September 1887 saw Sunderland wear red and white stripes for the first time, Arnie Davison bagging the first goal in the new strip as the Lads beat Darlington St Augustine's 1-0 at Newcastle Road.

Fencing surrounded the ground, allowing an admittance charge to be made, and the ground soon boasted a Grandstand and Press Gallery – evidence itself of increasing interest in the team.

As the club progressed the facilities at the Newcastle Road ground were developed. The venue hosted Sunderland's first-ever League game on 13 September 1890 when Burnley triumphed 3–2. Sunderland in fact lost the first two home games, but from then on lost only once at home in the next six astonishing years as 'The Team of All The Talents' established Sunderland as the most successful club in the game.

Seventh place in the club's first season in the League was followed by three Championships in the next four seasons, with a runners-up spot in the odd year out. Newcastle Road was impregnable as Sunderland took the 1891–92 title with a 100 per cent home record, while a year later the title was retained as Sunderland became the first club to score 100 League goals in a season – and that in only 30 games!

In 1896 the Newcastle Road ground was described in the club's Share Prospectus as, '…one of the best and most comfortable in the country and can, with ease, accommodate 18,000 spectators'. The ground's status was nationally recognised in 1891 when England played a full international there, beating Wales 4–1. Sunderland's Tom Porteous played for England and therefore became the first player to be capped while with the club.

With the ground now leased on an annual rent that had risen to £30 in the time the club

The site of the Newcastle Road ground, home of the Team of All The Talents 1886–98. Note the old pitch markings.

were based at Newcastle Road, Sunderland looked for another new home that they could own and develop. Newcastle Road had played a vital part in the still embryonic history of Sunderland but the next step was to Roker Park.

Roker Park 1898–1997
Having had six grounds in less than 20 years, the move to Roker Park was to be for just a year short of a century. During that time the ground would hold a record crowd of 75,118, host a World Cup quarter-final, three other World Cup Finals games, three full England internationals, an FA Cup semi-final replay, two FA Amateur Cup Finals and, most importantly, become a focal point in the minds of the people of Sunderland, the Durham coalfields and beyond. As history was being made from the Boer War, through two World Wars, the Roaring Twenties and Swinging Sixties, right up to almost the very end of the 20th century, generations upon generations of North East folk made their fortnightly pilgrimage to Roker Park.

They returned home to spread stories of great players, great games and most of all the greatness of the 'Roker Roar': a roar that made Sunderland as world famous as its one-time claim to be the biggest shipbuilding town on the planet. Ships and shouts signified Sunderland and the noise of the people of the North East throatily roaring on Charlie Buchan, Raich Carter, Len Shackleton, Charlie Hurley and Jimmy Montgomery would travel like the ships that left the Wear.

People living miles away from Roker Park would know how many goals Sunderland had

The main stand and Fulwell End at Roker Park. Sunderland v Leeds, 1997.

SUNDERLAND STADIA

The main stand at Roker Park is taken down.

The demolition of Roker Park.

Houses on the estate built on the site of the Roker End.

The concrete canyons of The Roker End.

scored by the number of huge cheers they counted and the sound of Sunderland supporting voices would spread news of the legends to be seen at Roker wherever they went. In Buenos Aires, for instance, a club calling itself Sunderland has been in existence since the turn of the 20th century, having been inspired by the tales of a Sunderland supporter working on the railway there.

Football support is so often territorial, people expressing their pride in supporting their team from their home. 'To follow Sunderland is your birth-right', as former SAFC chairman Bob Murray said.

Sunderland supporters have often taken pride in their team, not least during the Depression of the 1930s when unemployment hit the North East hard, but the Lads won the Championship in '36 and the FA Cup at long last in '37 to give people something to delight in. Cup-winning goalkeeper Johnny Mapson couldn't believe it was true that kids really didn't have shoes to wear when he arrived in Sunderland to sign for the Lads, but through the darkest of times the pride people took in the club brought necessary distraction and consolation.

Equally there have been occasions when the team has disappointed – a series of relegations from 1958 for instance – but when times have been hard Sunderland's supporters have stuck with the club and it remains a fact that the club's pride in its supporters mirrors the backing the fans provide. Roker Park's lifespan had come full circle by the time the club moved to the Stadium of Light. A final Roker capacity of 22,657 was smaller than the 30,000-plus who watched the inaugural match there against Liverpool on 10 September 1898. At its peak over 75,000 had made up the official record crowd, with many believing that figure was exceeded for a Cup tie with Manchester United in 1964 when fans pulled down the gates to gain admittance on a night when players struggled to reach the ground and some estimates claim as many as 100,000 were shoehorned in.

The ground was bought by the club in 1905, having originally been leased from a Mr Tennant. The original grandstand seated between two and three thousand people, but by 1929 a 10,000-seater stand replaced it at a cost of £25,000. Designed by the renowned architect Archibald Leitch, the stand resembled those of Ibrox, Goodison and Fratton Park, but stood out as Leitch's trademark criss-cross latticework was often painted red and white rather than blue and white as at the other venues. Preserved pieces of this latticework still adorn the surroundings of the Stadium of Light.

Opposite this Main Stand stood the Clock Stand. This was rebuilt seven years after the Main Stand and remained largely unchanged until 1966.

In living memory the ends at Roker Park were called the Roker and Fulwell Ends, but when the ground opened these were the South and North Ends – just as the ends at the Stadium of Light were originally named.

The Roker (South) End was significantly expanded at a cost of £20,000 in 1912, a move that lifted the ground's capacity to 50,000 and provided that end of the ground with a most distinctive underbelly of concrete that Simon Inglis in his definitive study, *The Football Grounds of England and Wales* described as, '…a dark, cavernous web of beams' adding, 'Truly there was never terracing like it, nor ever will be again.'

Holding 23,000, the Roker End held more than the entire ground did in its final years,

SUNDERLAND STADIA

The Main Stand at Roker Park.

Roker Park was hemmed in by houses.

the Roker End itself being slashed to virtually a third of its former size for safety reasons in 1982.

Hosting 1966 World Cup games brought significant improvements, including new club offices. The Clock Stand gained new seats and a TV gantry, while the Fuwell End gained a roof, which only added to the noise generated by the fans who gathered at that end. 'The Fulwell' attracted the chanters, who from the sixties onwards made this the most colourful part of Roker Park.

Having become only the second top-flight ground to have floodlights in 1952, Sunderland installed a completely new system following the 1973 FA Cup triumph to cope with the increased demands of televised evening matches and European competitions.

Those new lights proved to be the last significant addition to Roker Park, excluding later safety work. A quarter of a century later the ground had become a relic of the past. Its decline symbolised the club's slide to becoming a 'sleeping giant.' The cobwebs of former glories at a once proud ground enveloped a stagnant Sunderland. The great expectations of those who made Roker roar could not begin to be realised until the club literally saw the light and moved to its current home, ready to embrace a new century, just as the club had when first moving to Roker Park.

The Sunderland Stadium of Light
When England staged the World Cup in 1966 Roker Park was held in such high esteem that, despite being out on a limb geographically, it was awarded a quarter-final in addition to staging three group games. England's bid to stage the 2006 World Cup failed, but had the tournament come to England Roker Park would not have been worth considering, given its decline and out-dated stature.

Nonetheless, Sunderland would still have been expected to stage a major game, potentially a semi-final, at their new home. The Sunderland Stadium of Light was presented by the FA in their campaign literature and presentations as one of England's major stadia. Although England's bid to hold the World Cup in 2018 proved to be a dismal failure had England been awarded the tournament, once again Sunderland would have been a host ground. Backed by the football clubs of Middlesbrough, Hartlepool, Darlington and Carlisle, Sunderland's name was the first to be announced when the names of the successful grounds were revealed as the English bid confirmed its candidate cities.

The construction of the Stadium of Light.

SUNDERLAND STADIA

The construction of the Stadium of Light.

Sunderland and Ajax line up for the first game at the Stadium of Light in 1997.

The game finished 0–0. The teams changed strips at half-time.

Driven by the vision of chairman Bob Murray and supported by vice-chairman John Fickling, Sunderland responded to the Taylor Report, which followed the tragic events at Hillsborough in 1989, by showing the ambition to build the biggest and best football stadium in the country since World War Two.

A 119-acre site next to the Nissan car factory at Washington, but still within the boundaries of Sunderland, was considered, and an alternative site at Ryhope was also put forward. However, eventually a site less than half a mile from Roker Park was decided upon.

One of the biggest pits in Durham, Wearmouth Colliery, had stood on the site of what is now the Sunderland Stadium of Light. It was the coalfield's oldest pit, dating back to 1826. On 9 February 1995, SAFC let it be known that the site of the former pit was now the preferred place for a new ground.

Given that coalminers and shipyard workers had long provided the backbone of Sunderland's support, the decision to build the club's new home on the site of the former colliery and alongside the banks of the River Wear was a fitting way of celebrating the integral partnership between the club and its vast support. This fact has since been further highlighted by the works of public art that now surround the stadium, such as a huge Davy lamp, a pit wheel, and statues dedicated to fans and 1973 FA Cup winning manager Bob Stokoe.

Planning permission, initially for a 34,000-seater stadium, was granted by the Tyne and Wear Development Corporation in November 1995, but it quickly became apparent that with the 'sleeping giant' of SAFC stirring, demand would outstrip such a capacity and so a 42,000-seater stadium was planned. In fact Sunderland did so well at their new home once it opened in 1997 that within three years the capacity had to be increased to 49,000 with the construction of an extra tier on the North Stand.

The Stadium of Light was built by Ballast Wiltshier plc, part of Ballast Needham NV. The Tyne and Wear Development Corporation and English Partnerships cleared the site in readiness for construction to commence on 15 May 1996. A key part of the development was to excavate a giant bowl for the laying of the 68 x 105m pitch, which is below ground level. Admiring the Stadium of Light from outside it is a magnificent landmark on the Sunderland skyline, but inside it appears to be even bigger because ground level is actually at the top of the first tier of the seating deck.

The stadium was built as a continuous bowl rather than as four separate stands. The main stand (West) had a second 'Premier Concourse' tier, which was subsequently extended with the expansion of the North Stand. Should the stadium require further

expansion in future it will be possible to further extend the South and East stands in the same manner.

Once the ground was opened (see the 'Into the Light' section of the history chapter) it soon became renowned as one of the country's finest arenas. England staged their first full international on Wearside for almost half a century in October 1999, beating Belgium 2–1 in a friendly that included Sunderland's Kevin Phillips winning his second cap. The national side returned three and a half years later for a crucial Euro 2004 qualifying game against Turkey that England won 2–0. The ground was also called upon to stage numerous junior international fixtures including the European Under-16 Final between Spain and France.

Already Sunderland have spent longer at the Stadium of Light than at any of their other grounds bar Roker Park. The opening of Roker Park in 1898 gave Sunderland a ground fit for a new century and, in moving to the Stadium of Light three years before the turn of the millennium, Sunderland again prepared themselves for the dawn of a new age.

Left: Archibald Leitch latticework ready for restoration after the demolition of Roker Park. Right: Part of the Archibald Leitch latticework from the Main Stand at Roker Park. It is now situated in the car park at the Stadium of Light.

SUNDERLAND: THE COMPLETE RECORD

Above: The Fans' Statue.

SUNDERLAND STADIA

SUNDERLAND: THE COMPLETE RECORD

The Stokoe Statue.

The Murray Gates at the Stadium of Light.

FOR US ALL

The Stadium of Light was the biggest and best football ground built in England in the second half of the 20th century. One of the major additions to the stadium since its opening in 1997 has been a distinctive pair of ornate wrought-iron gates which stand either side of the main entrance at the West Stand. Although not officially named so, these have become popularly known as 'The Murray Gates' as they were sponsored by the family of chairman Bob Murray.

Stone pillars at each gate are topped by a pair of flames, which honour the memory of past supporters. The gates bear the words 'Into the Light' and 'For Us All', which aptly illustrate how the club believes its supporters are an integral part of SAFC.

Former Chairman Bob Murray CBE, now Sir Bob Murray CBE.

WHAT'S IN A NAME?
WHY IS THE GROUND CALLED THE STADIUM OF LIGHT?

Unlike the home of the Portuguese club Benfica, whose home is officially called the Estadio do Sport Lisboa e Benfica, but is commonly known as the Stadium of Light, the name of the Sunderland Stadium of Light carries its own meaning and significance. Benfica's ground takes the nickname 'Stadium of Light' because it is situated in the Lisbon district of Luz (meaning light). Similarly, Derby County's stadium is called Pride Park because Pride is the name of the place in which the stadium is situated. If the same applied at Sunderland the stadium could be called the Stadium of Monkwearmouth.

The city of Sunderland has its own place in the history of the development of light. The inventor of the incandescent electric lamp, Joseph Wilson Swan, was a native of Sunderland and the miners' safety lamp known as the Davy lamp was invented by Sir Humphry Davy at a pit in the Durham coalfield. A monument of a Davy lamp shines permanently outside the stadium, welcoming all who visit, while the Murray Gates outside the imposing West Stand carry burning beacons at their pinnacle.

Miners at Wearmouth Colliery, and throughout the mining industry, carried Davy lamps with them as part of their everyday working lives, to provide light in the darkness and a vital aid to safety. Reflecting this tradition the name of the stadium allows the image to shine forever in memory of those who worked in the mining industry and along the river as part of Sunderland's proud shipbuilding history.

The Sunderland Stadium of Light reflects the desire of the club and its supporters to be in the limelight, and like a torch it illuminates the way forward.

Sunderland Chairmen

	Name	Born	Died	Years
1	John Potts Henderson	Q4 1863 (Sunderland)	Late Feb 1927 (Sunderland) aged 63	July 1896 – Sept 1903
2	Sinclair Todd	Q2 1857 (Sunderland)	Q3 1920 (Sunderland)	Sept 1903 – Oct 1904
3	Frederick William Taylor	Q4 1871 (Sunderland)	Q2 1947 (aged 76)	Oct 1904 – 1913 (retired as director in 1946)
4	Samuel Wilson	?	? Still alive 1930	1913 – 1921
5	William Henry Bell	c1866	Q1 1930 (aged 64)	1921 – 1930
6	Sir Walter Raine	Q2 1874 (Sunderland)	19/12/1938 (aged 64)	1930 – 1938
7	Duncan White	Q4 1886 (Sunderland)	29/11/1940 (aged 54)	1938 – 29 Nov 1940
8	Col. Joseph Merriman Prior	07/04/1875 (Sunderland)	08/10/1949	Dec 1940 – 8 Oct 1949
9	Edward William Ditchburn	Q1 1888 (Sunderland)	15/9/1964	Oct 1949 – 6 April 1957
10	Col. John Turnbull	?	28/01/1970	April 1957 – 1958
11	Stanley Ritson	Q2 1889 (Sunderland)	17/8/1971	1958 – 1960
12	Sidney Stirling Collings	Q2 1903 (Gateshead)	15/5/1976	1960 – Sept 1969
13	Jack Parker	?	5/5/1971	10 Sept 1969 – 5 May 1971
14	Keith Irwing Collings	Q2 1934 (Sunderland)	25/10/2009 (aged 75)	5 May 1971 – 25 June 1980
15	Sir Tom Cowie	09/09/1922	18/01/2012	26 June 1980 – 13 Aug 1986
16	Sir Robert Sydney Murray	03/08/1946		14 Aug 1986 – 26 Nov 1993
and				June 1996 – 3 July 2006
17	John Robson Featherstone	26/4/1933		8 Dec 1993 – June 1996
18	Niall John Quinn	06/10/1966		3 July 2006 – 3 Oct 2011
19	Ellis Short	06/10/1960		3 Oct 2011 –

Q = Quarter, e.g. Q1 means sometime in January to March.

** Ascertaining verified information on exact dates regarding chairmen has sometimes proved much more difficult than with players. Where precise information is unknown it is indicated in the table above. Perhaps in time some of these dates will come to light.

*** James Marr is not included in the above list of club chairman but preceded any of these as chairman of the Management Committee, a position he held before the role of chairman of the club was created. A biography of James Marr is included along with biographies of all club chairmen.

SUNDERLAND CHAIRMEN

Founded in 1879, the club was initially run by a committee. Alderman Potts was the club's first President. He was subsequently one of the club members to leave and follow founder James Allan in forming the rival Sunderland Albion club.

In March 1886 Mr J. Cooke was the President at a half yearly meeting in Monkwearmouth Workmen's Hall. One of Sunderland's leading shipbuilders Robert Thompson J.P. was appointed President of the club in 1887 at which point James Marr, also a leading shipbuilder, became chairman of the Management Committee. Robert Thompson remained President until submitting his resignation at the AGM at the Queens Hotel in Fawcett Street on 2 August 1894 when Councillor J.P. Henderson was unanimously elected after Samuel Tyzack had declined an invitation to stand for the position.

August 1887-July 1896

JAMES MARR

Manager inherited:
Appointments: W. Wallace (Secretary), Tom Watson (first manager)
Honours: 1892, 1893 and 1895 League Champions

James Marr was born on 9 September 1854 in Byker, Newcastle upon Tyne. Like many of his time he worked in the shipyards from an early age. In 1876 he joined J.L. Thompson and Sons; a shipbuilding company instrumental in propelling Sunderland AFC to become one of the most powerful football clubs in the land. It was J.L. Thompson and Sons who are believed to have provided employment to Sunderland's first Scottish import James Hunter.

Marr worked with club treasurer Samuel Tyzack of Monkwearmouth Ironworks – who took over from club founder James Allan at the club's annual meeting on 3 May 1888 – to make sure that Sunderland recruited many of the best players from Scotland. Although excluded from the Football League which began in the 1888-89 season Sunderland welcomed six of the newly formed Football League's 12 teams to Newcastle Road, beating five of them and only being held by Wolves although the Wearsiders were hammered out of sight to the tune of 10-1 in the one away game they played to a Football League side in the first season of that competition. Bolton Wanderers inflicted that defeat 10 days before Christmas in 1888. Having won only three of their 13 Football League games up to that point. The Trotters clearly drew inspiration and won their next three in a row.

Their Lancashire neighbours Preston North End earned the nickname of 'The Invincibles' after winning the first ever Football League season without defeat and adding the FA Cup for good measure to become the first 'double' winners. They did lose that season though: going down 4-1 to Sunderland at Newcastle Road on 29 April 1889.

Sunderland impressed again in the second season of the Football League, winning six and drawing three of a dozen friendlies against sides from the League. Additionally although losing 4-2 away to eventual FA Cup winners Blackburn Rovers defeat had only come in extra-time, Sunderland having drawn in 90 minutes but with no replay played.

Having demonstrated their playing strength Sunderland's application to join the Football League saw James Marr be one of two Sunderland representatives, along with the Reverend Robinson Hindle of Eppleton Village who attended a meeting at The Douglas Hotel in Manchester on 2 May 1890 when Sunderland were admitted to the Football League. In replacing Stoke Sunderland became the first club admitted after the dozen Founder Members.

The Founder Members were all from the North West or Midlands and saw Sunderland as geographically out on a limb, Marr and Hindle having to offer to pay the travelling expenses of all other clubs in order to gain support.

Just before J.P. Henderson became the first club chairman of SAFC, Marr joined J.L.Thompson's board of directors and two years later established the Sunderland Forge and Engineering Company with Robert Thompson – this company later becoming the starting point of Horatio Stratton Carter's career. Upon the death of Robert Thompson in 1908, Marr was appointed as chairman of J.L. Thompson's, a position he held until his death in 1932. James Marr was knighted on May twelve 1919 at the time being chairman of J.L. Thompson & Sons Ltd, Sir James Laing & Sons Ltd, Sunderland Forge & Engineering Company and The Silver Line (Shipowners).

1895-1903

JOHN POTTS HENDERSON

Manager inherited: Tom Watson
Appointments: Robert Campbell and Alex Mackie
Honours: 1902 League Champions.

Although the Club was formed in 1879, John Potts Henderson became the first chairman of the club as a Limited Company following a special meeting held on 9 July 1896 at the Assembly Rooms in Fawcett Street.

With 'The Team of All The Talents' having won the League Championship for the third time in four seasons in 1895 interest was booming and J.P. Henderson was the man who led the club to a new ground fit for a new century.

Ninety nine years later Bob (later Sir Bob) Murray would emulate him in

J.P. Henderson – seventh from right, back row. This is at the first match at Roker Park.

ensuring the club was equipped for the demands of a new age by having the foresight and drive to provide the club with a new home fit for a new age. (Co-incidentally in JP Henderson's time as chairman one of Sunderland's vice presidents was a Robert Murray).

J.P. Henderson's obtained what was farmland from a Mr 'Tushy' Tennant and set about creating the Roker Park ground with which Sunderland and its supporters (via the 'Roker Roar') became synonymous.

Henderson had first become involved with the Club in 1892, as a guarantor of funds, just two years after Sunderland had joined the Football League and a year after becoming Councillor for Bridge Ward in Sunderland. At this point he was elected onto the committee that ran the Club becoming vice-chairman and later succeeding Robert Thompson as Club President in August 1894.

When share capital of £5,000 was issued the Club became a Limited Company in August 1896, J.P. Henderson's brother James also became a director along with Robert and C.E. Thompson along with future chairman Samuel Wilson. The Henderson brothers' father was Councillor James Henderson. He had a wine and spirit business, which included a Bridge Street hostelry called 'The Bells" which was adjacent to the old Sunderland Echo offices where the Echo 24 building now stands. If you know the area you'll know that the building overlooks the River Wear, J. P. Henderson's father having also been the man who set up the Corporation Steam Ferry.

John Henderson followed his father in trading in alcohol. He had been educated at school in Gainford and in addition to his interests in SAFC he also was a member of Sunderland Rovers Rugby Club and set up the Monkwearmouth Parish Church Football Club.

The Hendersons' business appears to have got into trouble after J.P. Henderson's time as chairman of SAFC had ended. Trading under the name of James Henderson & Sons, the firm of Wines & Spirits Merchants and Licensed Victuallers with branches throughout County Durham at: Sunderland, Fulwell, South Shields Bishop Auckland, West Hartlepool, Hartlepool, New Shildon, Seaton Carew and Stockton on Tees apparently became bankrupt in April 1908 with the *London Gazette* of 13 January 1911 offering advice to creditors. Similarly a report in the Edinburgh Gazette of 1 October 1907 reports the dissolving on 30 June 1907 of a brewers called Bass Crest of Alloa and elsewhere that listed the Henderson brothers along with John Fitzgerald, George Bell and Henry Taylor as partners.

While Roker Park is long gone, turned now into housing, J.P. Henderson's impact on the area remains. When seeking permission to build the football ground in the late 19th century Henderson commissioned architects plans for the streets that still stand between Fulwell Road and what became Roker Park.

1903-1904

SINCLAIR TODD

Manager inherited: Alex Mackie
Appointments: None
Honours: None.

Sunderland's second chairman since the club became a Limited Company held the post for just a single season and received a silver cigar box as a token of thanks for his service to SAFC. Champions two years earlier, The Lads had finished third the year before Todd's time as chairman but a falling away to sixth place and Cup exit at the first hurdle made for a disappointing season. The season saw the departure of several of the old guard including Sandy McAllister and especially James Millar and Ted Doig, the only two men in history to win four Championship medals on Wearside.

Todd was suspended from football for two and a half years, along with six of his directors, after the club were found guilty by the FA of making illegal payments during his chairmanship. Read more about this in the earlier club history chapter RE the gift to Andy McCombie.

The 1841 Census records Scots born pair David and Jane Sinclair living at Queen Street, Bishopwearmouth. Their daughter Elizabeth married Henry Todd whose son was Sinclair Todd. In later years he became a cabinetmaker and had an upholstery business in Holmeside in Sunderland. From Census records it is known that in 1881 he was living in Alice Street in Sunderland (Near where the Park Lane interchange is now) with a wife and young daughter while working as a cabinetmaker. Further, the 1911 Census reveals him to have two daughters and two sons and be living at 2 Thornhill Park – opposite where Argyle House School is now.

As with William Henry Bell who would join the board in 1908 and later become chairman, Todd was a member of the Ashbrooke Cricket and Rugby Club.

1904-1913

FREDERICK WILLIAM TAYLOR

Manager inherited: Alex Mackie
Appointments: Fred Dale (Caretaker), Bob Kyle
Honours: 1913 League Champions and FA Cup finalists.

F.W. Taylor first served on the Board at SAFC in 1897 prior to the move from the Newcastle Road Ground to Roker Park. He left the Board a year after the move to Roker but returned in 1903, succeeding Sinclair Todd as chairman in October 1904 when Taylor was the only member of the Board not to be suspended following the McCombie affair. As he took over the club was in disarray with Sinclair Todd and the rest of the board banned from the game for two and a half years and manager Alex Mackie suspended for three months.

On the pitch the team were doing well at the time. New chairman Taylor appointed former Sunderland player Fred Dale as caretaker manager the day before a Bonfire night trip to Woolwich Arsenal where fireworks were lacking in a goalless game. However a comfortable home win a week later took Sunderland to the top of the table although the Lads would eventually finish fifth with McCombie – transferred for a record £700 earlier in the year prior to Taylor taking the chair – a regular in the Magpies' side which became champions for the first time.

Alex Mackie left his position at Sunderland at the end of the season, Taylor's appointment Bob Kyle becoming Sunderland's longest serving manager although in those days the role was still called secretary and indeed was much more administrative than the manager's role commonly is today.

Four years into his chairmanship, Taylor made a key purchase for the club, buying the land on which Roker Park was situated, Sir Theodore Doxford (the shipbuilder) was reportedly amongst those providing the funds.

Frederick William Taylor was certainly a busy man. He had also become a town councillor for East Ward in 1904 and from 1906-10 would be an elected committee member at the Sunderland Cricket and Rugby Football Club at Ashbrooke where, before injury ended his playing days, he captained the second team at rugby and occasionally is believed to have turned out for the firsts.

Stepping down from the chairmanship in 1913, the year when Sunderland were the champions and Cup finalists, F.W. Taylor appears to have sold the last of his shares to Duncan White (chairman from 1938-40) on 25 June 1935. Taylor though remained on the Board until his retirement as a director in 1946. He died a year later at the age of 76.

During his time as a director of the club, Taylor simultaneously held many other positions of influence. Between 1917 and 1922 he was a River Wear Commission member and served as an FA Councillor. In 1925 he commenced a decade long stint as chairman of the Watch Committee resuming that role for a further three years between 1938 and '41 after a three year gap. In 1927 he became Alderman for the Hendon Ward in the town, being mentioned in the London Gazette in August of that year. He also had a two-year term as Sunderland's Deputy Mayor.

In addition to a considerable amount of public service and sporting interests F.W. Taylor was an enthusiastic breeder of dogs and birds. He became President of the Sunderland Canine Society, reportedly owning as many as 80 bulldogs at once although those numbers were surpassed by the aviary containing over 400 birds that he had in Backhouse Park, not far from Ashbrooke, in the year the football club won the FA Cup in 1937. Having been chairman at the time of the club's first FA Cup Final in 1913 he was still a director when the Cup was finally won almost quarter of a century later.

A religious man, he was a key figure in the building of Grangetown Methodist Church, apparently in memory of his mother. Cambridge educated he rose to become the senior partner in the Colliery Agents and Coal Exporters John Taylor & Son, a firm started by his grandfather.

In 1881 F.W. Taylor was living at 9 Park Place East, by 1901 he was resident at 14 Thornhill Gardens and in 1911, by which time he was a ship broker in addition to being a coal exporter, he lived at Cresswell Villa.

During his time as chairman F.W. Taylor once famously took over as a linesman. The game was an FA Cup tie against

Gainsborough Trinity on 3 February 1906 at Roker Park. Referee J.T. Howcroft of Bolton (who refereed the 1920 FA Cup Final) took the full force of a ball struck by Sunderland's Jimmy Gemmell in the first half of the match and was unable to continue. Senior linesman Mr Morton took the whistle and the two clubs' secretaries tossed a coin to decide which club would provide an official to run the line. Sunderland's Bob Kyle called correctly and thus F.W. Taylor took over.

By half-time Sunderland were trailing to a Dixon goal with the Lads leaving it until the 83rd minute before equalising through Alex Barrie. Taylor's role in the tie didn't end with the final whistle however as he offered the cash strapped then Second Division opponents £300 to play the replay at Roker Park. Consequently Sunderland progressed comfortably to the next round although at a cost as the replay gate receipts fell £56 short of the fee accepted by Gainsborough. Ultimately though Sunderland were thumped 5-0 by Woolwich Arsenal in the next round.

In keeping with his reputation as a man known simply as 'Mr. Sunderland' F.W. Taylor had the first vehicle registration number in Sunderland: BR1 being the number plate on his single cylinder car, one of the first in the country.

1913-1921

SAMUEL WILSON

Manager inherited: Bob Kyle
Appointments: None
Honours: None

Samuel Wilson became chairman in 1913 having been on the board since investing in the new share capital issues in 1896. He was a landowner and senior partner in the timber merchants J. & W. Wilson and Sons Ltd. His brother Frank had two spells as Premier of Western Australia between July 1910 and October 1911 and again between July 1916 and June of the following year.

Pictured as part of the team line up on the occasion of the opening of Roker Park in 1898, his appreciation of the history of the club he was connected with for over four decades is indicated by him being the person who bought Thomas Marie Madawaska Hemy's painting of the match between Sunderland and Aston Villa at the Newcastle Road ground from January 1895. Wilson presented this painting to the Club on December fourth 1930 and while it hasn't always been in the club's possession it has dominated the entrance foyer of the Stadium of Light since the ground's opening in 1997 having previously hung above the main staircase in Roker Park. Samuel Wilson can be seen on the painting. He is the gentleman on the left of the front row in the little box just behind the goal.

Like Sir Tom Cowie who was chairman of SAFC in the 1980s, Samuel Wilson was an enthusiast of game shooting. He owned 13,000 acres in Sutherlandshire where he also participated in deer stalking and salmon fishing.

As chairman, Wilson's main success was to see the club survive beyond World War One. As football on Wearside came to a halt during the Great War (See Wartime football chapter) the Board had to seek guarantors to ensure the long-term continuation of SAFC. Of Wilson's nine years at the helm only four seasons of football were played but his biggest victory came away from the pitch.

SUNDERLAND CHAIRMEN

1921-1930

WILLIAM HENRY BELL

Manager inherited: Bob Kyle
Appointments: Johnny Cochrane
Honours: None

William Henry Bell gave 22 years of service to SAFC, nine of them as chairman until his death in 1930 at the age of 64. However if football was his first love it seems it was of the rugby code. Long associated with Sunderland rugby club at Ashbrooke (SAFC's home ground in 1883-84), Bell represented 'The North' at rugby in 1890 and is known to have been 'reserve' for England at least once as well as reportedly playing brilliantly against the first Maori visitors as a guest for West Hartlepool.

According to '*The History of The Sunderland Cricket & Rugby Football Club*' Bell was 'powerfully built and a fearless tackler he was equally at home as full-back or centre three-quarter' apparently playing regularly in both positions in 18 appearances at county level between 1884 and 1892. A long-standing rugby player for Sunderland for many years Bell enjoyed the prestigious role of captain from 1890 to 1892.

Coming to Association Football as an administrator later, Bell's sporting prowess wasn't limited to rugger. In 1890 he won the Charles Lilburn Challenge Cup at tennis.

William Bell was a long standing member of the rugby, tennis and cricket committees at Ashbrooke as well as serving on the governing board as both an elected member (1889-1906) and trustee (1906-1929). After hanging up his rugby boots he became President of the County Union from 1895 to 1900, becoming County Durham's representative for the Rugby Football Union.

W.H. Bell back row, second from right. Picture courtesy of Ashbrooke Archives.

Away from the sporting world and administration centres William Henry Bell married the daughter of the Sunderland shipbuilder James Elliott Thompson, Kathleen Isobel Thompson. Professionally, Bell was a lawyer, becoming Senior Partner at Bells Solicitors based in Sunniside in Sunderland having become a solicitor following his education at Durham School. His clients included the Northumberland and Durham Dairy Farmers Association and the Sunderland Licenced Victuallers Association. While chairman of SAFC he became President of the Sunderland Law Society in 1928.

Bell first became involved with SAFC in 1908 as a director and was vice-chairman to Samuel Wilson in 1913-14. Succeeding Wilson as chairman in 1921 no honours came to Roker Park during his time in charge although the twenties saw Sunderland have a more than decent side, being in the top three for four seasons out of five in the middle of the decade.

An indication of his rugby background came in 1924 as during his chairmanship Roker Park was used to stage a rugby game against the touring New Zealand All Blacks who beat County Durham 43-7.

1930-1938

SIR WALTER RAINE

Manager inherited: Johnny Cochrane
Appointments: None
Honours: 1936 League Champions and Charity Shield winners. 1937 FA Cup winners.

Sir Walter Raine became chairman of the Club a year after ceasing to be the town's Unionist MP, a position he had held for seven years, and three years after receiving his knighthood. He remained chairman until his death at the age of 64 on December 19th 1938. His eight year tenure had witnessed the club's most golden age since before the First World War. The era of Raich Carter, Bobby Gurney and Jimmy Connor had secured a sixth League Championship in 1936 with the Charity Shield to go with it. The pinnacle though was a first FA Cup triumph at Sunderland's first ever Wembley appearance in 1937.

Raine was born at 2 Beechwood Street, Bishopwearmouth in 1874. According to the 1881 Census he was the eldest of four children living with his parents Elizabeth and John. His father was a Coal and Iron Merchant and Walter joined his business as a 16-year-old in 1890 after being educated at Barnard Castle.

In 1902 he became a town councillor for Park Ward and gave many years public service, at one time being vice-chairman of the Sunderland Chamber of Commerce and also being an active member of the Methodist Church. From November 1920 until November 1922 he was Mayor of Sunderland relinquishing the role just as he was elected as the town's MP.

Only a month prior to ceasing to be an MP, Sir Walter's wife Rosa (nèe Barnes) passed away. They had married in 1899. In September 1930 he married for a second time, Violet Evans becoming Lady Raine. In 1936 she was presented with a wristwatch by the famous footballing architect Archibald Leitch on the occasion of the opening of The Clock Stand at Roker Park.

Interestingly, one of the River Wear ferries, first established by the father of SAFC's first chairman J.P. Henderson, was named Sir Walter Raine, probably due to him being a member of the River Wear Commission.

Since Raine's period as chairman only one major trophy has been won by the club. Johnny Cochrane, the manager of the team in the halcyon days of the thirties, resigned less than three months after Sir Walter Raine's death.

1938-40

DUNCAN WHITE

Manager inherited: Johnny Cochrane
Appointments: George Crow (Caretaker), Bill Murray
Honours: None.

Chairman as World War Two started, Duncan White had been educated in Germany. Although chairman of the Sunderland Master Builders' Association after assuming control of his father's building and contracting business, White did not enjoy the opportunity of building the club as he died in the second year of his chairmanship of SAFC.

A player at local level himself in his youth, Duncan White's claim to fame as a footballer was in once scoring five goals in a Wearside League match against Seaham White Star when representing Southwick.

After his death on 29 November 1940 his shareholding passed to his widow Gertrude White whose address was listed as Flat 3, St Peterborough House, St Peterborough Place, London W2. The shares, which included £5,500 original issue shares bought on 18 May 1933 and a further £3,500 worth bought from F.W. Taylor and a Mr Young in June 1935 were sold by Gertrude White in June 1945 and September 1947.

1940-1949

COLONEL JOSEPH PRIOR

Manager inherited: Bill Murray
Appointments: None
Honours: League War Cup finalists 1942, West Riding FA Cup (Combined Counties) winners 1943.

On becoming a director of SAFC in 1919 just after the First World War Joseph Merriman Prior was already known as Colonel Prior after serving with the Northumberland Yeomanry in South Africa. Colonel Prior had also been second in command of the Tyneside Irish during World War One.

After over two decades on the Board at Sunderland, Colonel Prior succeeded Duncan White following White's death in 1940 and remained in charge throughout the rest of the Second World War and into the post war era until his own death of a

heart attack at his home at Tunstall Lodge on 8 October 1949, a day when Sunderland drew with Blackpool at Roker Park. As chairman Prior was evidently well connected, not least as area representative of the Football Association.

Perhaps his greatest scoop had been to oversee the signing of Len Shackleton from Newcastle United. Shack's transfer on Valentine's Day 1948 had been by sealed bid, Sunderland taking the 'Clown Prince of Soccer' from their rivals for a record fee of £20,050 having been tipped off that the highest bid was twenty grand.

Born on 7 April 1875, before the foundation of the football club, Joseph was the son of John and Mary Ann Prior who lived at 14 York Street, Sunderland. Christened on 23 May 1875 at St Peter's Church in Monkwearmouth he would serve as a chorister at the church which 74 years later would hold his funeral service five days after his death.

In his business life, Prior took over from his father in the haulage business that his dad had founded. Colonel Prior married twice, firstly Mary Ann Wishart and secondly Jen Taylor. With his first wife he had two daughters: Sheila and Marion.

A racehorse owner, Colonel Prior was known to be jovial and popular so perhaps it is appropriate that today there is a pub called The Colonel Prior at Moorside in Sunderland.

1949-1957

EDWARD WILLIAM DITCHBURN OBE

Manager inherited: Bill Murray
Appointments: None
Honours: None

Bill Ditchburn – often known in formal business circles as Edward – had the ignominy of being banned from football for life bringing his tenure as SAFC chairman to a premature close. A Freemason and former Mayor (from 1934) of Sunderland, Ditchburn was banned from football by the FA on 6 April 1957 when the club were found guilty of breaching FA rules by sanctioning illegal payments.

Chairman Ditchburn and director W.S. (Bill) Martin were suspended permanently from football. A further two Board members; Stan Ritson and L.W. Evans were also banned indefinitely – Lawrence Evans receiving news of his ban when he was still in bed on the morning of his birthday. The other directors of the period: John Reed, an accountant, and three future chairmen in Colonel John Turnbull, Syd Collings and Jack Parker, were all severely censured for failing to report their suspicions to the FA. Collings was on holiday in France when he learned the news from a newspaper report. At the time he had only recently been elected to the FA Council.

SAFC were further punished by a fine of £5,000, the biggest fine ever imposed on a club up that point. The previous highest fine was £750 to Newcastle United in 1924 for fielding weakened teams in the League while they concentrated on the Cup.

Manager Bill Murray was fined £200 for making 'under the counter payments' and many players were punished, in most cases by forfeiting benefits.

Backed by the Players' Union campaigning for the abolition of the Maximum Wage the rumpus caused by the 1957 investigation into Sunderland's financial affairs rumbled on until 1962. The case was finally heard in the High Court in April of that year when bans were lifted and fines returned as a host of errors in procedure in the original case were found proven.

Chairman Bill Ditchburn and director Bill Martin had their own day in court in June 1962 even though they had already agreed an out of court financial settlement with the FA, not that either of them were in need of the £650 compensation. 'I have fought many battles in my life but winning this case has given me greater satisfaction than anything else. All I want now is to get back into football' declared Ditchburn in the *Daily Mail* following his triumph.

Evidently supporters would have welcomed him back. In 1960, by which time Sunderland had finished in the bottom half of the Second Division in both of their first two seasons at this level and had had two more chairmen since Ditchburn's departure, 30,000 people (almost 7,000 more than 1959-60's average attendance) had signed a petition calling for his return.

Apparently Bill Ditchburn drove his Rolls Royce straight from the 1962 hearing to Roker Park which he had not visited since he was banned five years earlier. Former colleague and now chairman Syd Collings however resisted his offer to return to the board and Ditchburn's wish to be re-instated was never fulfilled. Bill Martin on the other hand made no such attempt at a Roker return, commenting: 'I was so disgusted by the treachery that I never made the slightest effort to get back on the board.'

Bill Ditchburn's son John Mushens Ditchburn, known as Jack, was vice-chairman of SAFC when the FA Cup was lifted in 1973. By this time Syd Collings' son Keith was chairman. Jack Ditchburn was a solicitor in the firm Bretherton, Ditchburn & Nelson of John Street in Sunderland and died on 5 November 1980.

A case can be made to argue that only in 2012 are Sunderland finally recovering from the disaster that befell the club during Bill Ditchburn's era. When the aforementioned punishments were handed out in 1957, the Club's proud boast was that Sunderland were the only club to have only ever played at the top level. The first club elected to the one tier Football League in 1890 (The 12 Founder Members had kicked off in 1888), Sunderland had never been relegated and since 1936, when both Blackburn Rovers and Aston Villa went down, had spent over two decades as the club with this unique claim to sit at football's top table.

Left in turmoil by the events of the scandal of 1957, Sunderland were relegated for the first time in 1958. Since then the club have never spent more than six successive seasons at any level (to the publication of this book in 2012). To equal the run broken in 1958, Sunderland would need to stay in the Barclays Premier League until 2074, which puts the run ended in the fifties into some perspective.

So how did Ditchburn's Sunderland get into such a pickle? The chances are that even before Ditchburn assumed control in 1949, having been on the board since 1930, the club were 'bending the rules' to attract the best players in the land. Whereas in the modern game footballers are paid astronomical amounts of money, back in the fifties player wages were as earthbound as the human race – the first manned spaceflight not occurring until 1961 – in the fifties players were bound by a maximum wage of £15 per week, despite the fact that they were star performers attracting bumper crowds. The Wearsiders brought the star names of the sport to the North East not because they liked the Cat and Dog Stairs at Roker beach or even Jacky White's

Market but because they were 'well looked after.'

In other words some of Sunderland's players had their 'maximum wage' supplemented by illegal payments and it was being found guilty of this that Sunderland were punished. Typical of the high life Bill Ditchburn tried to provide for the footballers of the fifties was the lavish tour of the USA and Canada in 1955, on which he and director Stan Ritson accompanied the team. The post-season trip included visits to New York's Radio City Music Hall, the Empire State Building and Belmont Race Track.

Awarded the OBE in 1946 following service as Director of Fighting Vehicles Production, Bill Ditchburn had been Mayor of Sunderland and was director of the family businesses which included 'Dependable Products' and Ditchburns Limited, the latter being a furniture factory which began life in Villiers Street. By the fifties the business was reputedly one of the top three furniture businesses in the country.

It was in 49 Villiers Street that in 1888 Edward William Ditchburn was born. Bill Ditchburn was 76 when he passed away in September 1964. His loyal friend Bill Martin saying of him: 'He had red and white eyes.' A players' man who made an emotional speech to the team in the dressing room on his departure, Bill Ditchburn saw to it that Sunderland bought the biggest stars in the game, earning the club the nickname 'The Bank of England Club.' Clearly top stars didn't come to the North East for less than a bit more than the going rate; Ditchburn also regularly fixed up new signings with a part time job or commercial interest to supplement their official footballing income.

Echoing Niall Quinn's attempts half a century later to persuade people to come to the match rather than relying on broadcasts, Ditchburn also had an issue with the broadcasting of games potentially keeping people away from the turnstiles. In Ditchburn's case he banned radio commentaries from Roker Park.

Bill Ditchburn, who lived in Barnard House, Ledbury Road, Sunderland was described in *The Daily Express* by Bob Pennington as: "This bow-tied, wing-collared little man [who] looks like a character from Dickens. His approach to football is a strange mixture of business tycoon's 'Money talks' and the naïve enthusiasm of a soccer bobbysoxer." That 'strange mixture' was also noted when he often went to get fish and chips in his pink and mauve Rolls-Royce.

Sunderland suffered, as did Bill Ditchburn himself, as a consequence of the illegal payments Sunderland were found guilty of. However it should be said in Ditchburn's defence that he remained popular with supporters and that while the 'Bank of England' team ultimately failed to deliver trophies to Sunderland, the chairman and his board in that era showed real and consistent ambition to take Sunderland to the very top.

1957-1958

COLONEL JOHN TURNBULL

Manager inherited:
Appointments: Alan Brown
Honours: None

Colonel John Turnbull was an Estate Agent and Auctioneer who had been President of the Agricultural Valuers' Association, the Northumberland and Durham Auctioneers and Estate Agents Institute and Chester-le-Street Cricket Club. His address was given as Mains House, Chester-le-Street when he was appointed Deputy Lieutenant of County Durham on 9 January 1926, one of seven people to be appointed to the title of Deputy Lieutenant on that day. In 1950 his address was 'Springfield' Chester-le-Street.'

Colonel Turnbull was an Honorary Colonel of the Durham Light Infantry Eighth Battalion, a position he succeeded his uncle in, having been commissioned in 1910.

A keen local cricketer and rugby player, Colonel Turnbull was listed as holding 104 shares in SAFC in 1932-33 and had been on the board during the illegal payments scandal of 1957 after which he briefly held the position of chairman during a period of transition. He died on 28 January 1970.

1958-1960

STANLEY RITSON OBE FRCS JP

Manager inherited: Alan Brown
Appointments: None
Honours: None

Stanley Ritson OBE was a renowned surgeon who reputedly carried out more operations in his lengthy career than there are seats in the Stadium of Light.

Listed as holding 81 shares in the club in 1932-33 (This had risen to 353 by the end of the 1970-71 season) he had joined the board of SAFC in 1941 when he was in his early fifties but was banned 'Sine Die' (Indefinitely) by the Football League following the illegal payments scandal that rocked football and punished Sunderland in 1957. Following the lifting of Ritson's ban the following year he took over as chairman of the club for a two year spell during Sunderland's first sojourn into the Second Division.

Born in Sunderland in 1889, he became a Batchelor of Medicine, being educated at King's College, London where he qualified in 1911. Having held clinical and teaching positions in London he returned to the North East becoming medical officer and surgeon at Sherburn Hospital in Durham after the First World War, during which he had served in Egypt as a captain in the Royal Army Medical Corps being invalided out of the army and reputedly being given just six months to live. He did however live until 1977 when he died after a fall.

Ritson held his position at Sherburn Hospital until the unit closed just as the National Health Service started in 1948. In 1921 Stan Ritson had taken up a role at Monkwearmouth Hospital where he later spent quarter of a century as Honorary Surgeon. He also spent 20 years as Honorary Surgeon to SAFC which in itself was only half the four decades service he gave as Chief Consultant Surgeon to Durham Police. Respected as a General Surgeon, Stan was also renowned for performing thyroid gland operations.

He was also known as a big believer in exercise and would regularly walk from Newcastle to his homes in Grange Crescent Sunderland and later Hart Terrace, South Bents on Sunderland sea front.

Following his resignation as SAFC chairman, Stan Ritson became a Vice President of the club, holding the position until his death early in 1977. He was awarded the OBE in 1973.

1960-1969

SYDNEY STIRLING COLLINGS

Manager inherited: Alan Brown
Appointments: George Hardwick, Ian McColl, Alan Brown.
Honours: Promotion 1964, FA Youth Cup winners 1967 and 1969, finalists 1966.

Perhaps it was his experience as chairman of the International Select Committee on which he served from 1963 to '66 that led Syd Collings to believe that the directors could pick the Sunderland team which they did under his chairmanship for the first 19 League and three League Cup games following promotion in 1964. In Syd Collings' era the England international team were picked by a group of selectors across the country. Collings Senior (His son Keith would be chairman of Sunderland from 1971 to 1980) certainly had an influence that benefitted Sunderland.

Stan Anderson credited Collings with helping him become the only man capped by England during the sixties, his two caps won in 1962 came under Sir Alf Ramsay's predecessor as England manager, Walter Winterbottom, despite Anderson having been told he'd never represent his county again after being sent off in a 'B' international against Bulgaria in 1957.

Syd Collings' influence also played a significant role in 1966 World Cup Finals games being played at Sunderland. Roker Park staged a quarter-final and three group games. Speaking to SAFC's official club magazine '*Legion of Light*' in 2007 Syd Collings' son Keith explained: 'I think Newcastle were having a bit of trouble with the council at the time and it rather crossed them out. That left ourselves and Middlesbrough to form a group which we did, and of course we undertook numerous improvements to Roker Park at that time. In 1966 my father was the top man at Wembley during the World Cup because the chairman of the FA died only a couple of months beforehand so my father had all the introductions to do before the games.'

Syd Collings then takes credit for making Wearside the 1966 World Cup's north-east centre point. Also in his 'plus' column is the fact that having become chairman when the Lads were in the Second Division for the first time in their history, he secured promotion and at the time of his departure in 1968 the club had been back in the top flight for three seasons and possessed a world class star in Jim Baxter, bought for a club record fee, so undoubtedly the team were in a better

Sunderland Chairman Syd Collings introduces England captain Bobby Moore to the Queen before the 1966 World Cup Final.

place when his reign as chairman ended than when it began.

On the other hand the alternative view is that Collings Senior missed a great opportunity to build on the superb promotion team of 1964. Momentum was lost when manager Alan Brown was allowed to leave over a money dispute. Failing to appoint a manager the directors picked the Sunderland team for the opening 19 League games back in the top flight. While coaches Arthur Wright and Jack Jones took training and apparently captain Charlie Hurley essentially ran things on a day to day basis, nonetheless the directors officially selected the side.

When Sunderland won the last of these 19 games on the eve of George Hardwick's appointment as manager, it was only the second League win of the directors' almost half season in charge, leaving the Lads in 20th position (out of 22). Perhaps such a record supported former star Len Shackleton's claim as to the average director's knowledge of football given that 'Shack' had infamously left a blank page in his 1955 published autobiography under this heading. Certainly Collings senior was displeased at Shack describing him as a 'laundryman' in one of his newspaper columns. The Collings' family business was in laundry.

Born in 1903 in Gateshead, Sydney Stirling Collings later had three addresses in Whitburn. He joined the board at SAFC in 1947 when he was invited to replace Dr. I.G. Modlin and became a member of the FA Council in 1950, becoming chairman of the FA Youth International Committee two years later. He was on the board during the illegal payments scandal in 1957, becoming chairman three years later.

In 1962 he was appointed to the FA Challenge Cup Committee, joining the Football League Management Committee the following year and then becoming chairman of the full England International Selection Committee.

Having stepped down as chairman of Sunderland AFC in September 1969 he became vice chairman. Upon the appointment of his son Keith as chairman in 1981 he handed over the role of vice chairman to Jack Ditchburn, the son of Bill Ditchburn who had been chairman while Syd was on the board in the fifties. Collings senior remained on the board until February 1976 when he resigned at the AGM and was unanimously appointed as the first President of the club since the Marquess of Londonderry. It was to be a short-lived Presidency as Syd Collings passed away just three months later.

1969-1971

JACK PARKER

Manager inherited: Alan Brown
Appointments: None
Honours: None

Jack Parker was a local businessman, builder and contractor. As a shareholder since January 1948 he replaced Sir Myers Wayman on the board following a goalless home draw with Portsmouth in November 1950. A lifelong supporter of the club, he began watching matches from behind the goal, and was particularly respected by the SAFC Supporters' Association who he gave great encouragement to when they formed in 1965. Indeed he was a 'hands on' chairman who tried to assist with scouting duties despite his lack of a professional background in the game.

Along with his passion for football, Parker raced pigeons, owning many lofts in Hendon, the home of the club's original ground. He also enjoyed angling.

Despite the relegation suffered in 1970 one major contribution completed during his time at the top was the opening of the club training centre at Washington, at the time thought to be one of the best in the land.

Talking of Jack Parker in 2007, his successor as chairman, Keith Collings, who was a director under Parker said, 'Jack Parker I had a lot of time for. He was an honest Sunderland supporter and businessman. He went though a very worrying time and his health deteriorated because of it. I did have difficulties with Jack but I supported him. The difficulties were that I wanted [manager] Alan Brown to go but Jack wanted to keep him.'

Jack Parker died suddenly in May 1971 while still SAFC chairman. On 30 September of that year the club renamed an area of Roker Park as 'The Jack Parker Lounge' in his honour.

1971-1980

KEITH IRWING COLLINGS

Manager inherited: Alan Brown
Appointments: Billy Elliott (caretaker), Bob Stokoe, Ian MacFarlane (caretaker), Jimmy Adamson, Dave Merrington (caretaker), Billy Elliott (caretaker, second spell), Ken Knighton.
Honours: 1973 FA Cup winners, 1976 Second Division champions. Promotion 1980.

Keith Collings was chairman from 13 May 1971 to 26 June 1980 but was a Board member from 1965 when he joined at the age of 31 – four days before the dismissal of manager George Hardwick – to September 1983. The son of the previous chairman but one, Syd Collings, Keith took over as chairman following the sudden death of Jack Parker, explaining: 'Sometimes you're lucky and sometimes you aren't. Ted Evans joined the board at the same time as I did. He was slightly younger than me but the rest of the directors were pretty elderly. When Jack died quite suddenly, there was this great big age gap. Jack Ditchburn who was the only one in between became my vice chairman. He supported me and that's how I became chairman – it was decided unanimously across the board…Coming in as a young chairman I listened to the older directors who were Stanley Ritson and Jack Cooke. They were in their seventies and I think I listened to them too much.'

Up to 2012 only Bob Murray had served Sunderland longer as chairman than Keith Collings who oversaw the glorious FA Cup triumph of 1973 and the only ever presentation of the old Second Division trophy three years later.

'I brought in the idea of individual directors having specific responsibilities once I became chairman' Keith Collings explained in an interview in 2007.

Like many a former chairman, Keith Collings was a member at Ashbrooke, going on a rugby tour of Sweden in the summer of 1954 as a forward in a team that scored 317 points in winning all five of its games. His brother Derek was a fellow forward on the tour. Keith was also involved in the development of Squash at Ashbrooke and was a regular member of their side that won 12 of the 20 matches played in their inaugural season on 1960-61 and for a time lived at The Grove that is adjacent to Ashbrooke Sports Ground. He also lived in Boldon, Whitburn and at the time of his death Tudhoe Village near Spennymoor.

His main business interests during his time as chairman of the club was in laundries. His company owned the Central Laundry on Fulwell Road, not far from Roker Park and adjacent to what had been

Keith Collings (centre) at the presentation of the 1976 Division Two trophy to Tony Towers by Lord Westwood.

Abbs Field, the club's home ground from 1884-86. Further laundries were owned in Grimsby and in Leeds, city of course of Sunderland's Wembley opponents in the Cup-winning year. As the laundry business declined in the seventies, Collings diversified with a car repair firm, Clark's Coachbuilders.

Including caretakers, seven people managed Sunderland during Keith Collings' nine years as chairman and while Bob Stokoe's Cup success earned legendary status, Keith Collings was one of two Sunderland chairman, along with Tom Cowie to decline the opportunity to have Brian Clough as manager. He also came close to installing Bobby Robson and Don Revie at Roker: 'Bobby came to my house and met my directors. Bobby is a decent man,' said Collings in 2007. 'He said he'd join Sunderland. I shook his hand and asked: "Do you want me to ring your chairman?" He said, "No I'll have a word with him on Monday". When he called me next, he said, "I'm sorry but my chairman won't release me and I'm not prepared to do the dirty on him…" As regards the other two – I was asked for things I shouldn't have been asked for. Brian Clough was very bitter when he didn't get the job. To be honest I don't think I could have worked with him.'

Collings resigned as chairman following the securing of promotion in 1980. Again in *Legion of Light*, he explained his reason for stepping down: "There were clear indications that Tom Cowie wanted to be chairman and it was clear that the board was split right down the centre. It went to a situation where there were six of us there and it was split right down the middle. I'm certain that the one board member who wasn't there would have voted for me but I had too much pride as chairman and I did not want to stay in with half the board against me so I used my casting vote to put Tom Cowie in the chair."

Keith Collings remained on the board for three years under Cowie before his resignation brought the end of almost three decades of Collings family boardroom involvement (although the Collings family never owned more than 20% of the shares). 'Tom Cowie asked me to stay on as vice chairman. It was about that time that there was a battle for the shares and Barry Batey got involved. The unfortunate situation for me was that I did not want to join Barry Batey but I was not happy with the way Tom Cowie was running the club…There was a terrible atmosphere at the club as there were two sides and I was in between.'

Keith Collings died on 25 October 2009, aged 75.

1980-1986

SIR TOM COWIE OBE

Manager inherited: Ken Knighton
Appointments: Mick Docherty (Caretaker), Alan Durban, Bryan 'Pop' Robson (Caretaker), Len Ashurst, Lawrie McMenemy
Honours: League Cup finalists 1985

Sir Tom Cowie was a hugely successful Sunderland born businessman. Having begun his career with a motorcycle shop in Hylton Road in Sunderland, Cowie certainly knew how to make money becoming a major motor magnate. 'I got into contract hire and had about 50,000 cars out on contract hire and we made good money…There was a lot of profit

and I bought out other companies. I can say that we had the biggest fleet in the country.'

Sir Tom's company had turnover of £934m in 1994, the year after he left it. The company continues today under the name Arriva. Sir Tom was also chairman of Leeds based Aurora Property Developments, also ran shooting companies and for many years was a significant donor to the Conservative Party before finding disagreement with Prime Minister David Cameron over education policy after which Sir Tom withdrew his financial support.

On becoming chairman in June 1980 just after promotion had been won to the top flight, Sir Tom recalled his first thoughts: 'The directors of the club had been there for years and I came in with new ideas to try and change things. The first thing that passed my mind when I became chairman of the club was that the management throughout the club wasn't very good. They were all nice guys but they'd been there for yonks. There was the Ditchburn family and the Collings family so I thought to myself: 'Well I don't think I can do any worse than this."

By his own admission however, Cowie was to find football more difficult to be successful in than business: 'One always wanted to have success. I'm a bad loser and don't like losing at all. Everything I've done in business I've found different to football.'

Sir Tom was a lifelong supporter of the club, recalling: 'I started going to the match when I was nine or 10. My father used to sit me on the railings at The Roker End.' Half a century later Cowies became the first shirt sponsor of the club, the Lads shirts first being emblazoned with the word COWIES in October 1983 for a visit of Manchester United.

Stepping aside from the club in 1986 with the team struggling under McMenemy – a manager universally acknowledged as an exciting appointment when he arrived but an unmitigated failure at Sunderland – Sir Tom remained a supporter but mainly restricted his support to following the club on television and through the newspapers. Being chairman of SAFC didn't completely put him off football however as he later became chairman of Crook Town.

In later years Sir Tom became a benefactor to several worthy causes including the University of Sunderland which renamed its St Peter's campus after him in September 2002 three years before he opened a Business and Enterprise Centre at Thornhill School in Sunderland. Sir Tom also endowed a hospice in Lanchester near where he lived at Broadwood Hall for many years as well as assisting a woodland project in Consett.

He died on 18 January 2012 aged 89. A memorial service was held at Sunderland Minster on 26 April 2012 when one of his former managers Len Ashurst was amongst those paying tribute.

1986-1993 and 1996-2006

SIR ROBERT SYDNEY MURRAY CBE

Managers inherited: Lawrie McMenemy (Chairman's first spell) & Peter Reid (Chairman's second spell)
Appointments: Bob Stokoe (Stokoe's second spell), Denis Smith, Malcolm Crosby, Mick Buxton, Terry Butcher, Howard Wilkinson, Mick McCarthy, Kevin Ball (Caretaker).

Honours: Division Three 1987-88, Promotion to Division One 1989-90, Championship 1998-99, Championship 2004-05.

Bob Murray – since 2010 Sir Bob Murray CBE – is by far the club's longest serving chairman. His vision in building the Stadium of Light despite traditionalists' wishes to stay at Roker Park, meant that Sunderland obtained the biggest football stadium built in England in the second half of the twentieth century rather than being left with the problems that in 2012 clubs such as Liverpool, Everton and Spurs find themselves wrestling with, i.e. wanting to move from or massively redevelop their traditional homes but so far being unable to do so.

That Sir Bob succeeded in enabling Sunderland to have a stadium fit for a new century for a fraction of the cost now mooted for new stadia is to his credit, as is the extension of it under his chairmanship in addition to the provision of first class training facilities at the Academy of Light.

Small wonder that the FA subsequently benefited from his expertise in rescuing the much delayed and way over budget rebuilding of Wembley Stadium and subsequently appointed him Project Director of the £100m England training base St George's Park which opened on time and on budget in 2012.

Robert Sydney Murray was born in Consett, County Durham on 3 August 1946. A Certified Accountant, he excelled in the business world with his kitchen and bathroom manufacturing company Spring Ram. He has since had numerous other business interests and divides his time between Jersey and mainland England.

In 1996 he floated SAFC on the Stock Exchange and later in 2006, two decades after taking on the chairmanship – agreed to sell the club, the sale to the Drumaville Consortium led by Niall Quinn being completed on 3 July 2006 for a reported fee of £10 million of which £5.7 million apparently went to Murray, an amount considered by many to be a bargain price but with Murray and his vice-chairman John Fickling – another diehard Sunderland supporter – anxious to pass on the baton of responsibility for the club to someone they had belief in. Murray and Fickling's faith in the club heritage was further highlighted by measures they included in the sale agreement concerning such things as ensuring the club's strip would always remain red and white stripes.

A self-made millionaire from humble beginnings Bob Murray always strove to connect the football club with the fans. In the face of ever rising prices in the game he sought to make football affordable while his commitment to the club's Foundation saw this charity arm of the club grow into the biggest and most successful in the country. After leaving the board Murray maintained his commitment to the Foundation and in 2012 remained as its Honorary Life President. Sunderland University's library on Chester Road is named the Murray Library in his honour.

1993-1996

JOHN ROBSON FEATHERSTONE

Manager inherited: Vacant position.
Appointments: Mick Buxton and Peter Reid
Honours: Championship 1995-96

John Featherstone stepped in as chairman for a two and a half year spell midway through Bob Murray's two lengthy stints as SAFC chairman. Standing down on the day of manager Terry Butcher's dismissal, Murray remained on the Board as major shareholder until resuming as chairman once promotion to the new Premier League was won for the first time.

Featherstone is a Sunderland born Chartered Accountant and Recruitment Specialist, being chairman of Hoggett Bowers plc which he sold in 1986. He also had business interests in the British Virgin Islands and had 20 years as a non-executive director of the firm who built the Emirates and Olympic stadia in London, and roofed Wimbledon. However with regard to Sunderland's move from Roker Park to The Stadium of Light in 1997 he stated: 'I never had anything to do with the stadium'.

John Featherstone first joined the Board in the summer of 1990 having been introduced to Bob Murray by his solicitor Martin Shaw. Featherstone explains how he ended up becoming chairman following Murray stepping aside on 26 November 1993.

'There were three of us on the Board with Bob Murray: Graham Wood as vice-chairman, John Wood and myself. None of us really wanted the job as chairman because none of us really had the money. I mean I'm comfortable but not as wealthy as a chairman might be. There was a lot of discussion. We had a Board meeting that went on for about eight hours until I finally decided to take on the job of chairman…I took the chairmanship because I thought I could do a good job. My aim was to bring in new money and I approached so many people.'

Born on 26 April 1933 in Croft Avenue on Chester Road, Sunderland, John Featherstone attended Bede School and remembers seeing Sunderland play at the age of six, just before World War Two broke out. Later residing at Grange Park

Avenue, just off Newcastle Road, Featherstone lived near star players Len Shackleton, Willie Watson and Ted Purdon, 'Shack' sometimes joining in with John's schoolboy kick-a-bouts while his father was friendly with SAFC director Jack Cooke who provided Featherstone senior and junior with tickets for big Cup ties. Cooke was still a Vice President of the club in the late 1970s.

Like several previous chairmen, Featherstone was an active member at Ashbrooke, playing rugby for them and says, 'I always say the most successful years at the football club have been when they have had a chairman with Ashbrooke connections.'

After relinquishing the chairman's role in June 1996 and stepping down from the board along with Graham and John Wood, Featherstone accepted a position as 'associate director' until the club left Roker Park in 1997 but says: 'The new title didn't really mean anything. We got a seat in the Directors' Box but we didn't go to Board meetings. We were considered to be friends of the club but we no longer had any influence.'

In 2012 John Featherstone was still supporting the Lads, attending matches as a Black Cats Bar season card holder and travelling from his Yorkshire home with his friend, the former Rotherham United centre-forward Brian Sawyer.

2005-2011

NIALL QUINN, Honorary MBE

Manager inherited: (Caretaker) Kevin Ball
Appointments: Kevin Richardson / Tim Carter (temporarily in charge during the opening pre season games in 2006), himself – Niall Quinn, Roy Keane, Ricky Sbragia, Steve Bruce.
Honours: Championship 2006-07

There is a lot of rivalry between Cork and Dublin. Cork born Charlie Hurley was Sunderland's Player of the Century from the club's first 100 years. When the bi-centenary comes around in 2079, Dubliner Niall Quinn must be considered as a candidate for Sunderland's most important person of the second century regardless of what happens between now and 2079.

Having scored twice against Sunderland for Manchester City to relegate the Lads in 1991, Quinn became Sunderland's record purchase when he signed for Peter Reid – his City manager from that day in 1991 – at the start of the last ever season at Roker Park. Debuting as a substitute in Sunderland's first ever game in the recently created Premiership, Quinn duly scored twice on his full debut as the Lads recorded their first ever win in the newly re-named top flight. Following the move to the Stadium of Light Niall notched both the first goal and the first

SUNDERLAND CHAIRMEN

Three Sunderland chairmen, left to right: Niall Quinn, Ellis Short and (slightly behind) Sir Bob Murray CBE.

hat-trick at the stadium before going on to form a lethal partnership with fellow striker Kevin Phillips. As Phillips became Europe's top scorer it was Quinn who provided most of the ammunition as well as scoring a healthy 14 goals himself as Superkev claimed the European 'Golden Shoe.' In the 1998 Play-off Final, Niall also became the only man (to date – 2012) to score twice in a game at Wembley for Sunderland. He also converted a penalty in the ultimately unsuccessful shoot out before then showing his strength of character in being a leading light in helping the club get over the potentially psychologically damaging impact of the nature of such a loss.

Having enjoyed an 'Indian Summer' to an impressive playing career, Quinn emulated Len Shackleton in retiring after one game under a new manager. 'Shack' had bowed out after one game under Alan Brown in 1957, while Quinn hung up his boots after one match under Howard Wilkinson in 2002, coincidentally in both Shackleton and Quinn's cases after 1-0 Wearside defeats to London opposition.

Altogether Quinn scored 69 goals in 220 games for Sunderland to add to the 20 goals in 94 games for his first club Arsenal and 78 goals in 244 appearances for Manchester City. At international level, when he retired from the Republic of Ireland side he was his country's all time record goalscorer with 21 goals from his 92 games including playing in the 1990 and 2002 World Cups and 1988 European Championships; injury prevented his participation in the 1994 World Cup. For club and country combined he totalled 188 goals in 650 games. Combining club and country again Quinn enjoyed a Benefit Match on 14 May 2002 at the Stadium of Light when he played part of the match in the red and white of Sunderland and part in the green and white of the Republic of Ireland. The proceeds of this game were split between childrens' hospitals in Sunderland and Dublin with the money for gifts to players instead diverted to a charity helping street children in India. The Niall Quinn Childrens' Centre is now part of the main hospital in Sunderland.

A talented all round sportsman, Quinn's father and uncles played hurling for

Tipperary, the county of his parents' birth. As a youngster Niall played Gaelic football for Robert Emmets GAC in Dublin and took part in the 1983 All Ireland Minor Hurling Championship Final and before becoming a professional soccer player in England had the opportunity to take up Australian Rules football.

Having seen Sunderland set a record low Premier League points tally in the season of his retirement, and then break their own unwanted record three years later, Quinn assembled a consortium of mainly Irish businessmen to buy the club and re-invigorate it. This Drumaville Consortium had Sunderland based John Hays of Hays Travel as vice-chairman with Niall taking over as chairman.

Having inherited a side with Quinn's old teammate Kevin Ball in temporary charge, the Drumaville Consortium sought to appoint either Martin O'Neill or Roy Keane as manager. Initially unable to do so, after a brief spell with coaches Kevin Richardson and Tim Carter in charge, chairman Quinn took on the manager's role himself beginning the morning after a friendly against Shelbourne in his home city.

Taking charge of the final pre-season friendly, a win at Carlisle United, Quinn's stint as manager began badly with four successive League defeats followed by League Cup dismissal at Bury, then propping up the entire Football League and coincidentally the scene of Quinn's celebratory destruction of Football League signs after Sunderland sealed promotion to the top flight at the same ground in 1999. Post match he announced that by the following week Sunderland would have a world class figure installed as manager and sure enough 24 hours after Quinn the manager signed off with a 2-0 win over West Brom, Roy Keane was appointed to his first managerial position.

With Drumaville providing financial backing Sunderland won the Championship with Quinn now able to focus on his preferred role as chairman. Under his stewardship the club connected with the fans, not least through an incident when en route back from a game at Cardiff, Sunderland supporters were harshly ejected from an Easyjet flight about to depart from Bristol on which Quinn was travelling, Niall subsequently organizing and paying for taxis for all from Bristol to Wearside.

Touring the region with his appointed chief executive Steve Walton, Quinn railed against the watching of illegal broadcasts of games from pubs, urging fans to attend in person. He also threw himself into the championing of the club's charity arm, then called the SAFC Foundation.

The team having finished 15th, 16th, thirteenth and tenth in the top flight, Quinn relinquished the role of chairman on 3 October 2011 taking on a role as Director of International Development before leaving the club altogether on 20 February 2012 with the club in the top half of the Barclays Premier League and having just beaten his first club Arsenal to reach the FA Cup quarter-final.

Amidst much clamour from fans to name a stand in honour of Quinn's contribution the club recognized Niall's modesty in not going that far but, given his legendary liking for Guinness, came up with the appropriate solution of renaming the stadium's sports bar as Quinn's with Niall himself visiting to drink the first pint.

Niall Quinn's autobiography, penned by Tom Humphries, was published in 2002 and nominated for the William Hill Sports Book of the Year award.

2011-

ELLIS SHORT

Manager inherited: Steve Bruce
Appointments: Martin O'Neill
Honours:

Ellis Short, an American with Irish roots, took over as chairman three days before his 51st birthday. Born on 6 October 1960 in Independence, Missouri, USA, Mr Short had become involved with Sunderland in September 2008 when, after meeting his predecessor as chairman, Niall Quinn, he invested in a 30 per cent stake in the club thereby becoming the majority shareholder while the Drumaville Consortium were in control. By 27 May of the following year Ellis Short had gained 100 per cent of the club and in so doing became the first ever sole owner of Sunderland AFC.

His considerable wealth allowed him to provide Sunderland with the financial backing to build on its place in the top flight with sustained guarantees that enabled the club to stop the cycle of promotion followed by almost immediate relegation. In 2012 SAFC go into the centenary of their most successful ever season equalling a sixth successive top flight campaign for the first time since the six years following their first ever promotion in 1964. Continued membership of the top flight from 2013-14 onwards would see Sunderland embarking on the second longest unbroken top flight run in their history.

Having attended Missouri University of Science and Technology, in Rolla, between 1979 and 83, Ellis Short gained experience at General Electric prior to forming a business partnership with John Grayken at Lone Star Funds, a private equity firm located in Dallas, Texas. As the senior executive with responsibility for operations in Asia he was the brains behind a takeover of the South Korean Korea Exchange Bank in 2003. Now retired from Lone Star, he maintains the position of President.

Based in London, the USA, including Hawaii, and also the owner of Skibo Castle – the venue for the wedding of Madonna and Guy Ritchie – in Scotland, Ellis Short enjoys golf and cycling amongst his many interests.

Often to be seen at the Academy of Light enjoying Under 18 games as well as regularly attending first team matches at home and away, once he became chairman, Ellis Short assumed a more public role than he had previously done as owner. A regular chairman's column in the club's match programme '*Red and White*' saw him increasingly reveal his passion for Sunderland and its supporters.

JAMES ALLAN

James Allan was the founder of what is now Sunderland AFC. He was a schoolteacher who was born in Ayrshire on 9 October 1857. In 1879 he organised a meeting at the British Day School (now the Norfolk Hotel) in Sunderland to set up a football team which was initially called the Sunderland and District Teachers' Association Football Club.

Allan had graduated from Glasgow University and moved to Sunderland in 1877. He taught at the Thomas Street Boys' School in Hendon. Football had become popular in Scotland before it did in the North East (Scotland had met England in the first-ever international match in 1872) and Allan returned from one trip home with footballs with which to introduce the locals to the game.

At the inaugural meeting of the club Allan took the post of vice-captain, with Robert Singleton becoming captain and John Grayston secretary.

Allan played in Sunderland's first-ever game, which was lost 1–0, but scored twice in the next match, which was won 4–0. He was a left-winger who once scored an amazing 12 goals in a single match against Castletown in a 23–0 win!

Sadly he later fell out with the club following controversy surrounding a Cup tie with Middlesbrough in 1887. Allan left to form a rival club called Sunderland Albion. In the short lived history of Albion, passions ran deep in games between the local rivals and on one occasion Allan was stoned at a game at Sunderland's home ground of Newcastle Road and required eye surgery.

Despite the feud that developed between him and the club he formed, James Allan's unique role in the history of what quickly became one of England's greatest football clubs deserves to be recognised. Without him no doubt someone else would have introduced football to Wearside, but whether the club would have grown in the way it did, or as well as it did, is something that can only be guessed at.

James Allan passed away on 18 October 1911, almost 32 years to the day after he was responsible for bringing the club into being. Having sadly fallen out with the powers that be at Sunderland following his departure to set up the short lived rival Sunderland Albion, there was no known contact between the Allan family and SAFC until 2009 when James Allan's Great Grandson Ray O'Donnell contacted the club historian following an article about James Allan in the Legion of Light magazine. As a result of renewed contact the Allan family were invited to the Stadium of Light for a match in 2009 on the 130th anniversary of the founding of the club. Niall Quinn made a presentation to Mr O'Donnell and his children (Allan's Great Great grandchildren) on the pitch at what was the first ever Sunderland match attended by the club founder's descendants.

Above: Niall Quinn with James Allan's family. Opposite, bottom left: Letter signed by James Allan, then of Sunderland Albion, to Sunderland, dated 30 November 1888.

Sunderland Managers

Sunderland Managers – first team games = League, FA Cup, League Cup, Play-offs, European Cup-Winners' Cup, Charity Shield, Sheriff of London's Shield and Minor Cups (Anglo-Scottish, Texico, Anglo-Italian, Freight Rover, Simod, Zenith Data Systems and Full Members)

No	Manager	From	To	Played	Won	Drawn	Lost
42	Martin O'Neill	2011		30	12	9	9
41	Eric Black	2011	2011	1	0	0	1
40	Steve Bruce	2009	2011	98	29	27	42
39	Ricky Sbragia	2008	2009	26	6	7	13
38	Roy Keane	2006	2008	100	43	16	41
37	Niall Quinn	2006	2006	6	1	0	5
36	Tim Carter	2006	2006	0	0	0	0
35	Kevin Richardson	2006	2006	0	0	0	0
34	Kevin Ball	2006	2006	10	1	2	7
33	Mick McCarthy	2003	2006	147	63	25	59
32	Howard Wilkinson	2002	2003	27	5	7	15
31	Peter Reid	1995	2002	353	160	93	100
30	Mick Buxton	1993	1995	76	25	24	27
29	Terry Butcher	1993	1993	45	14	8	23
28	Bobby Ferguson	1993	1993	0	0	0	0
27	Malcolm Crosby	1991	1993	60	21	15	24
26	Denis Smith	1987	1991	238	92	63	83
	Bob Stokoe (2nd spell)	1987	1987	9	3	2	4
25	Lawrie McMenemy	1985	1987	90	28	22	40
24	Frank Burrows	1985	1985	0	0	0	0
23	Len Ashurst	1984	1985	66	21	16	29
22	Bryan Robson	1984	1984	1	0	1	0
21	Alan Durban	1981	1984	130	37	40	53
20	Mick Docherty	1981	1981	4	2	0	2
19	Ken Knighton	1979	1981	94	35	24	35
	Billy Elliott (2nd spell)	1978	1979	26	14	7	5
18	Dave Merrington	1978	1978	8	4	2	2
17	Jimmy Adamson	1976	1978	88	29	28	31
16	Ian McFarlane	1976	1976	7	2	1	4
15	Bob Stokoe	1972	1976	197	92	49	56
14	Billy Elliott	1972	1972	4	0	2	2
	Alan Brown (2nd spell)	1968	1972	218	62	68	88
13	Ian McColl	1965	1968	125	40	27	58

SUNDERLAND MANAGERS

No	Manager	From	To	Played	Won	Drawn	Lost
12	George Hardwick	1964	1965	28	13	3	12
	Directors in charge	1964	1964	19	4	6	9
11	Alan Brown	1957	1964	332	138	88	106
10	Bill Scott	1957	1957	0	0	0	0
9	Bill Murray	1939	1957	510	185	140	185
8	George Crow	1939	1939	4	2	0	2
7	Johnny Cochrane	1928	1939	500	212	122	166
6	Bob Kyle	1905	1928	817	371	155	291
5	Fred Dale	1904	1905	15	7	2	6
4	Alex Mackie	1899	1905	200	98	44	58
3	Alex Watson	1899	1899	0	0	0	0
2	Robert Campbell	1896	1899	103	41	22	40
1	Tom Watson	1889	1896	191	119	28	44
	Club secretaries in charge	1884	1889	9	5	1	3
Totals				5012	2036	1196	1780

To end 2011-12

Best Win %

No	All games	Games	Win %
1	Tom Watson	191	62.3
2	Alex Mackie	200	49
3	Bob Stokoe	206	46.1
4	Bob Kyle	817	45.4
5	Peter Reid	353	45.3
6	Roy Keane	100	43
7	Mick McCarthy	147	42.9
8	Johnny Cochrane	499	42.5
9	Robert Campbell	103	39.8
10	Denis Smith	237	38.4
11	Alan Brown	550	36.4
12	Bill Murray	510	36.3
13	Ian McColl	125	32
14	Alan Durban	130	28.5

qual: 100 games

No	Top flight games	Games	Win %
1	Tom Watson	168	63.1
2	Alex Mackie	189	50.3
3	Bob Kyle	758	45.5
4	Johnny Cochrane	449	41.6
5	Robert Campbell	94	40.4
6	Bill Murray	471	35.2
7	Peter Reid	161	32.9
8	Roy Keane	53	28.3
9	Steve Bruce	89	28.1
10	Alan Durban	112	27.7
11	Len Ashurst	55	27.3
12	Alan Brown	100	23

qual: 50 games

3 June 1889 to 17 August 1896

Thomas Watson

Born: Byker, Newcastle, 8 April 1859
Died: Liverpool, 6 May 1915

Tom Watson was Sunderland's first manager and he proved to be one of the club's most successful as he steered the 'The Team of All The Talents' to three League titles in the 1890s. From a low point in the summer of 1888 when many of the playing staff left to join rivals Sunderland Albion, John Grayston, one of the club's original players who remained loyal, told the committee that he knew the man who could reverse the club's fortunes. Watson was currently out of work after enjoying success with the Newcastle United precursors, Newcastle West End and East End and he eagerly accepted the forthcoming job offer for a salary of 35 shillings a week and a house to live in. With treasurer, Samuel Tyzack, he made several trips to Scotland to secure the services of talented players such as Johnny Campbell, David Hannah and John Harvie and the team won 34 of their 47 games in Watson's first season in charge.

After election to the Football League in 1890, Watson further strengthened the team with the signings of Hugh Wilson, Jimmy Millar and Ted Doig. The semi-final of the FA Cup was reached in their first season and in 1891-92 they were confirmed as champions, with two games to go, when they beat Blackburn Rovers 6-1. They won all 13 home games, averaging slightly better than 4-1 and their 13 successive League wins remains a club record. The Championship was retained with 100 goals scored and an 11 point margin and the club finished runners-up in 1893-94 before lifting the title again the following season. They reached the FA Cup semi-finals in 1892 and 1895, the latter run including the club's record FA Cup victory, 11-1 over Fairfield. During his time with Sunderland Watson lived just round the corner from the Newcastle Road ground in Warwick Street and also owned a tobacconist's shop opposite Monkwearmouth station.

On 25 July 1896, he accepted a higher pay offer, £300 per annum, to manage Liverpool and left Sunderland three weeks later. Watson went on to manage two more League title-winning teams in 1901 and 1906 with his new club. He was popular with the players, many of whom attended his funeral when he died in office in 1915. He is buried in Anfield Cemetery, less 6 metres away from legendary Sunderland goalkeeper Teddy Doig.

17 August 1896 to 1 May 1899

Robert Campbell

Born: Cardross, Dumbartonshire 1864/65
Died: Canada, September 1945

Robert Campbell, arrived on Wearside in December 1889, shortly after his younger

SUNDERLAND MANAGERS

half-brother Johnny, who was a mainstay of the 'Talents'. He worked as a storekeeper at J.L. Thompson's ship-yard and lodged with Johnny at Tom Watson's home. He helped with training at the club before becoming secretary of the 'A' team. After taking over from Watson, Campbell piloted the team through a series of Test Matches to preserve their First Division status after they had finished second bottom. The famous old team was in decline and only Doig and Wilson were retained to be joined by new players such as Sandy McAllister, Phil Bach and Colin McLatchie.

The strict training of Billy Williams, who had replaced Tommy Dodds as trainer, helped Campbell mould a well disciplined team who finished runners-up the following season, 1897-98, and conceded the fewest goals, despite lacking the brilliance of the 'Talents'.

Following Sunderland's first season at Roker Park in 1898-99 Campbell moved on to Bristol City. He had accepted the job in late March 1899 but remained Sunderland manager until the end of the season. The club's directors tried to stop him leaving, stating that he still had time to run on his three year contract but Campbell insisted that it had only been a verbal agreement and was not binding.

Bristol City were elected to the Football League under his leadership and he also managed Bradford City and Clapton Orient before returning to Scotland.

He lectured on football and passed away in Canada having travelled there to be with his son.

1 May 1899 to August 1899

(no first team games)

Alexander Watson

(caretaker)

Born: Patterdale Q3 1864
Died: Sunderland 12 July 1931

Alex Watson was in temporary charge through the summer of 1899 and stayed on as secretary until he received an 18 months suspension following the Andrew McCombie affair (see below).

He was a school-teacher prior to, during and after his time at the club and also secretary-manager for Birmingham 1908-10. He later wrote a column for the *Sunderland Echo* in the 1927-28 season and died in the St Andrew's church choir vestry in 1931, aged 67.

August 1899 to June 1905

Alex Mackie

Born: Auchterless, Banffshire 1870

An administrator who never played professional football, Alex Mackie was associated with several Scottish clubs before securing the sought-after job as

Sunderland manager. Sunderland finished in the top three in each of the next four seasons and went close to three consecutive titles. They were denied by a late run by Tom Watson's Liverpool in 1900-01, won their fourth Championship in 1902-03 and then finished a point behind Sheffield Wednesday in 1902-03.

Mackie's playing recruits included forwards Jimmy Gemmell and Billy Hogg but it was the defence, strengthened by the arrival of Jimmy Watson, that won the title, ensuring that a single goal was enough for victory on eight occasions.

His last two seasons were clouded by the results of an FA investigation which followed the claim by Scottish international Andy McCombie that Sunderland had made him a gift of £100 to start a business. The club said it was a loan but when the books were examined irregularities were found. Mackie was suspended for three months and Fred Dale, a former Sunderland player, took over as manager for this period.

When Mackie returned he sold Alf Common to Middlesbrough for £1,000, the first four figure transfer fee in football history and shortly afterwards he followed the player to Ayresome Park, becoming their secretary-manager in June 1905. He was suspended for a second time after investigations into illegal payments and, disillusioned with the game, he left football in June 1906 to become a publican.

4 November 1904 to 31 January 1905

Fred Hetherington Dale
(caretaker)
Born: Sunderland, Q3 1864
Died: Sunderland, 30 July 1927

Fred Dale's temporary appointment was highlighted by a 3-1 win over eventual champions Newcastle United and a 1-0 away win at runners-up Everton.

He had played at half-back for Sunderland in the pre-League days, making his debut against Wearmouth in April 1885 and appearing in the club's second ever FA Cup tie in the following October. He had joined the club from Monkwearmouth Working Men's Hall and was captain of the side in the 1887-88 season.

After retiring from playing he became a foreman plater and then yardsman at

William Pickersgill & Sons shipyard and also recommended local players to the club.

1 August 1905 to 5 May 1928

Robert Hugh Kyle

Born: Belfast 16 December 1870
Died: Sunderland 17 February 1941

Bob Kyle played as a goalkeeper for Belfast Distillery and was later the club's secretary. He was the successful applicant, ahead of Fred Dale, to replace Alex Mackie and began a 23 year period as manager during which the club won one Championship but missed out on further honours despite Kyle spending large amounts of money on players.

His start was shaky as Sunderland's once secure defence struggled for three seasons until the arrival of goalkeeper Leigh Richmond Roose and seasoned Scottish international centre-half Charlie Thomson in 1908. The attack was strengthened with the signing of Jackie Mordue and Arthur Brown, the latter for a then world record fee of £1,600. Sunderland finished third in 1908-09 and 1910-11 and enjoyed their record away win, 9-1 at Newcastle in December 1908 but title success proved elusive. Kyle did the club a great service by first acquiring 19-year-old Charlie Buchan from Leyton in 1911 and then persuading him to stay after he became unsettled. Buchan went onto become one of Sunderland's all time great players.

Sunderland started the 1912-13 season badly but Kyle bolstered the defence with new signings Joe Butler in goal and Charlie Gladwin at right-back and the Championship was clinched with 25 wins in 31 games after no wins in the first seven. Charlie Buchan scored 32 goals. Eventual runners-up Aston Villa denied Sunderland the double by winning the FA Cup Final 1-0 at Crystal Palace.

After the war Kyle had to rebuild the team and the British record transfer fee was broken twice when Michael Gilhooley signed from Hull City for £5,250 and a further £5,500 secured the services of another international Warney Cresswell three days later. Gilhooley was unfortunate with injuries but with Cresswell forming an effective defensive duo with Ernie England and Charlie Buchan combining well up front with another big money signing Jock Paterson, Sunderland finished second to Liverpool in 1922-23. They finished in the top three in three out of the next four seasons. Buchan left for Arsenal and England international Bob Kelly was bought from Burnley for another record fee. The prolific goalscorer David Halliday

proved to be one of Kyle's most inspired signings.

However, with Sunderland struggling to avoid relegation, Kyle announced his retirement on 15 March 1928. New manager Johnny Cochrane watched from the stands on the last day of the season as trainer Billy Williams guided the team to a win at Middlesbrough that preserved their First Division status and relegated their Teesside rivals.

5 May 1928 to 3 March 1939

John Cochrane

Born: Paisley, 1891
Died: London, 19 December 1961

Johnny Cochrane was only Sunderland's third choice as replacement for Bob Kyle behind George Jobey and Major Frank Buckley but during his 11 years as manager he brought the League Championship and FA Cup to Wearside, becoming the first manager to achieve Cup success in England and Scotland. He also took Sunderland to two FA Cup semi-finals, in 1931 and 1938.

Born in Paisley, Cochrane was a player and later secretary at St Johnstone before managing St Mirren for 12 years, leading them to Scottish Cup success in 1926. He brought the club's trainer, Andy Reid, with him to Sunderland, to replace the retired Billy Williams. Cochrane quickly boosted the team with Scottish internationals Adam McLean and Tommy McInally and with David Halliday scoring a club record 43 goals, there was an immediate improvement and a fourth place finish in 1928-29.

Cochrane gradually developed a team capable of challenging for the title. He brought on local talents like Bobby Gurney and Raich Carter and successfully combined them with fine Scottish imports such as Alex Hastings, Jimmy Connor, Alex Hall, Patsy Gallacher and Charlie Thomson. His greatest skill was developing the young players he had acquired for just the basic signing-on fee of £10 whereas his big money purchases such as Evelyn Morrison (£6,500 from Falkirk) often didn't work out. However, he enjoyed considerable success in transferring players for substantial fees, notably Les McDowall who was sold to Manchester City for £8,000.

Second place was achieved in 1934-35, followed by the League Championship in 1935-36 and then the FA Cup in 1936-37, along with the Charity Shield, as Cochrane presided over a great period in the club's history. His teams were usually entertaining with the emphasis on attack, particularly during the title-winning season when 109 goals were scored and 74 conceded, the most ever scored against the First Division champions. The club's strength in depth at half-back enabled a formidable front-line to flourish and though their League form dipped over the next three seasons, the FA Cup, which had proved so elusive over the years, finally came to Wearside for the first time when Preston North End were defeated 3-1 at Wembley on 1 May 1937.

Cochrane's laid back style of management was popular with his players and it came as a surprise when he announced his resignation on 3 March 1939. He became manager of Reading but resigned after only 14 days in charge. Afterwards he retired from football management and lived in Hendon, London.

3 March to 24 March 1939

George Crow (caretaker)

Born: Sunderland, 22 September 1899
Died: Sunderland, 25 September 1972

Crow was Johnny Cochrane's assistant for nine years before taking over as caretaker manager and secretary when Cochrane resigned. He remained as Sunderland's first full-time secretary after Bill Murray took over as manager and delayed his

retirement by one year to October 1966 to organise World Cup games at Roker Park.

He won two and lost two of the four matches Sunderland played under his direction in 1939.

24 March 1939 to 26 June 1957

William Murray

Born: Aberdeen, 10 March 1900
Died: 15 December 1961

Bill Murray's length of service to Sunderland amounted to 28 years as a player and manager. Born in Aberdeen, he

Bill Murray signs Ivor Broadis

was studying to become an engineer when he was approached by several clubs. He abandoned his engineering plans as his football career blossomed as a stylish full-back, firstly with Cowdenbeath and then with Sunderland whom he joined in April 1927. He won a Championship medal in 1936 but had left for St Mirren before the FA Cup win.

He returned to take over as manager from Johnny Cochrane and after the War despite missing out on the signing of Tommy Lawton, he constructed a stylish team that went close to the title in 1949-50, finishing third. The outstanding Len Shackleton had been signed by Murray in 1948 to join consistent performers such as Willie Watson, Tommy Wright and Fred Hall.

Chairman Bill Ditchburn gave Murray licence to spend freely and this lead to the club's label as the 'Bank of England club'. Of the big money signings, Trevor Ford and Billy Elliott made most impression and fourth place (joint-second) and an FA Cup semi-final was achieved in 1954-55. Stan Anderson, Billy Bingham and Charlie Fleming proved to be excellent Murray signings but after a second FA Cup semi-final appearance in 1956 a steady decline began which saw the club finish third bottom in 1956-57.

Following an inquiry into illegal payments to players, Bill Murray resigned in June 1957, a sad end to his lengthy tenure, with coach Bill Scott taking over while Sunderland recovered from the scandal and searched for a new manager. He died just four years later, four days before the passing of Johnny Cochrane.

26 June 1957 to 30 July 1957
(no first team games)

William (Bill) Scott
(caretaker)

Born: Willington Quay, 1893

Scott played for South Shields as an amateur either side of serving as a Royal Navy gym instructor and petty officer in World War One. He was a trainer at Preston North End when they lost to the Lads in the FA Cup Final in 1937 and when they won it themselves a year later. He later became secretary and returned to manage the club 1949-53 after a spell at Blackburn Rovers as manager and scout. He joined Sunderland on 7 August 1954 and had various coaching roles, including assistant manager in 1960, until leaving the club on 30 June 1969. He was also youth team manager prior to Brian Clough's appointment in the role and continued to work with Clough afterwards.

30 July 1957 to 31 July 1964

Alan Winston Brown

Born: Corbridge, 26 August 1914
Died: Barnstaple, 8 March 1996

Alan Brown signs Nick Sharkey

Corbridge-born Alan Brown was appointed before the start of the 1957-58 season but unfortunately he couldn't arrest the club's decline which culminated in Sunderland's first ever relegation. His ability to find and develop young players gradually paid off, however, as he managed Sunderland back to the top flight in 1963-64.

Brown had begun his playing days with Huddersfield Town, a club for whom his cousin, Austen Campbell, also played. He was a dominant defender, particularly at Burnley, with whom he won promotion to the First Division and an FA Cup runners-up medal in consecutive seasons. His first managerial appointment was also at Burnley where his youth development skills and attention to detail on the pitch soon made an impression.

After three years at Turf Moor and a brief spell as Sheffield Wednesday coach he took over at Sunderland and immediately attempted to build a new side. As a tracksuit manager, he led from the front on the training ground he acquired for the club and with the help of Charlie Ferguson, the outstanding talent scout he had brought with him from Burnley, he began to bring in new players.

However even the arrival of the incomparable Charlie Hurley failed to stave off the drop in 1958 as Sunderland leaked 97 goals, the most in their history.

Undeterred, Brown overcame a bad start to the next season which threatened another relegation. He blooded youngsters Jimmy McNab, Len Ashurst, Cecil Irwin and Martin Harvey as he gradually built a promotion-winning side. He was heavily involved in the setting up of the North Regional League for Football League reserve sides, organised recruitment staff and had five Sunderland teams playing at various levels.

Brown supplemented his youngsters with sound investments such as George Herd and Brian Clough before the 1961-62 season. Johnny Crossan and George Mulhall followed a year later but promotion was twice narrowly missed before second place was secured in 1963-64. Jimmy Montgomery, given his debut by Brown in 1961, was ever-present in goal but the founder of this promising young team did not stay.

He resigned in July 1964 and took over as Sheffield Wednesday manager, taking them to the FA Cup Final in 1966.

Following his resignation there was a period of four months when the vacant Sunderland manager's post was linked with several names, notably Chelsea's Tommy Docherty and Northampton's Dave Bowen. The club were also keen on Burnley's Jimmy Adamson, who was still playing at the time and Burnley's subsequent complaint about Sunderland's approach led to a League inquiry in October which cleared the club of any wrongdoing.

The Directors', under the chairmanship of Syd Collings, picked the team for the first 16 League games of the season winning only twice. All eight away games under their control were lost and while the Lads were unbeaten at home, six of the eight games there were drawn. Under the team selection of the Directors there were also two home wins followed by an away defeat in the League Cup.

14 November 1964 to 1 May 1965

George Francis Moutrey Hardwick

Born: Saltburn, 2 February 1920
Died: 19 April 2004

Sunderland returned to First Division football without a manager and it was not until November that George Hardwick was appointed for the rest of the season.

His grandfather, Frank, played for Middlesbrough Ironopolis in 1890 and 'Gentleman George' was one of the classiest defenders in the period just after World War Two, earning 13 England caps, captaining the side on each occasion. He was player-manager at Oldham 1950-56 and coached at PSV Eindhoven and Middlesbrough before working as a supervisor to a North East oil company. He resigned from this post to join Sunderland though he did not sign a contract, stating that he wanted to be judged on results.

The club was precariously placed at third bottom when he took over but impressive home form and the consistent goal-scoring of Nick Sharkey, another Alan Brown youth product, led to a safe mid-table berth. Despite his worthy efforts, Hardwick was dismissed at the end of the season. He went on to manage Gateshead from 1968-70 and then left football to become chairman of a structural steelwork company.

21 May 1965 to 8 February 1968

John Miller (Ian) McColl

Born: Alexandria, Dumbartonshire 7 June 1928
Died: Glasgow, 25 October 2008

Ian McColl was Scotland's team manager before joining Sunderland but despite considerable investment in the transfer market he was unable to lift the team beyond the lower reaches of the First Division.

McColl qualified as an engineer from Glasgow Technical College but also developed into one of Scotland's finest right-halves, making over 400 post-war appearances for Rangers and earning 14 caps. He became Scotland manager in 1960 but had to share team selection and tactical input with the Scottish FA. He won 17 of his 28 internationals in charge.

Despite benefiting from the ongoing production line of young talent set up by Alan Brown, McColl struggled to inspire the team and average home gates dropped by 9,000 during his time in charge. He paid large fees for former Ibrox teammate Jim Baxter and forward Neil Martin from Hibs and gave debuts to Colin Todd, Bobby

SUNDERLAND MANAGERS

Kerr, Billy Hughes and Colin Suggett but the club finished 19th and 17th in his two full seasons in charge.

Sunderland's board sanctioned McColl's big money signings of Geoff Butler and Gordon Harris in January 1968, only to promptly sack him the following month with the club, once again, precariously placed in the League. On 8 February 1968, McColl announced to the press that he had been relieved of his duties and Alan Brown was to be his successor so it seems the board had chosen a manager before the incumbent had left office.

9 February 1968 to 1 November 1972

Alan Winston Brown
second spell

Having returned from Sheffield Wednesday to manage Sunderland for a second time Alan Brown succeeded in steadying the ship and the club finished in 15th place in 1967-68. However there was no improvement in 1968-69 and relegation came the following season. The youth set up remained strong, with the Youth Cup coming to Wearside for the second time in three years in 1969, but financial needs led to the sale of two of the finest products, Colin Suggett and Colin Todd. Brown signed Dave Watson and Dick Malone but the first season back in Division Two was a poor one. Fifth place was achieved in 1971-72 but when the club posted only four wins in the opening 19 games of 1972-73, Brown was sacked. Ultimately his commitment to the development of younger players was thought by some to be at the expense of dealing with the more complex problems of established professionals. However he had laid the groundwork for the 1973 phenomenon.

He went on to coach in Norway and finally assisted at Plymouth Argyle and his influence on other managers lived on for a further generation not least through Brian Clough, Lawrie McMenemy and Peter Reid's assistant Bobby Saxton who worked with 'Der Bomber' as he was nicknamed at Plymouth.

1 November to 29 November 1972

William (Billy) Henry Elliott
(caretaker)

Born: Bradford, 20 March 1925
Died: Sunderland, 21 January 2008

Billy Elliott made his reputation as a fast determined left-winger but also played at left-half and left-back for Bradford Park Avenue, Burnley and Sunderland. He won five England caps in the early 1950s, scoring three goals. After playing, he became coach to the Libyan national team and was employed at home and abroad in a variety of other coaching and scouting roles before returning to Sunderland in a coaching capacity in January 1968.

Following the sacking of Alan Brown, Elliott took over as caretaker manager for four matches before the appointment of Bob Stokoe. During this spell he switched centre-forward Dave Watson to centre-half, the position in which he went on to become Sunderland's most capped England international. Elliott stayed on as coach until June 1973 and coached Norwegian club Brann between 1974 and 1978 later returning to Sunderland for a further spell in temporary charge of the team.

29 November 1972 to 18 October 1976

Robert (Bob) Stokoe

Born: Mickley, nr Gateshead, 21 September 1930
Died: Hartlepool, 1 February 2004

Bob Stokoe spent 14 years playing for Newcastle United, initially as a centre-forward then as centre-half, winning an FA Cup winners medal in 1955. He moved to Bury as player-manager and was on the Roker Park pitch on the fateful Boxing Day in 1962 when Brian Clough's career was effectively finished by injury. He took Bury to the semi-finals of the League Cup and also signed the young Colin Bell in 1963.

Financial restraints contributed to his resignation and he took over at Charlton Athletic. They struggled against relegation under him and he angered the fans by selling Billy Bonds to West Ham United. He was sacked in September 1967 and went on the manage Rochdale, Carlisle United and Blackpool, producing an upturn in each club's fortunes before moving on.

The revival that Stokoe sparked on Wearside was quite astonishing and unprecedented in the club's history. He made a few shrewd signings but essentially turned an under-performing Second Division team into a side capable of beating three of the top sides in England on the way to securing Sunderland's

second ever FA Cup Final win. In doing so he became one of the few managers to play for and manage an FA Cup winning team and earned the nickname 'The Messiah' on Wearside. In honour of the achievement Stokoe was given the status of freeman of the Borough of Sunderland, along with the whole of the Sunderland team, on 21 January 1974.

Stokoe's endeavours to gain promotion to follow up the Cup win were handicapped by the sale of influential players such as Dennis Tueart and Dave Watson but gradually his new signings, particularly Bob Moncur, Bryan Robson, Tony Towers and Jeff Clarke, proved their worth and the Second Division title was won for the first time in the club's history in 1975-76.

A nine game winless start to the first season back in Division One saw Stokoe resign, a decision he later regretted.

He returned to management a year later and had second spells at Bury, Blackpool and Rochdale but he only found success on returning to Carlisle in September 1980. He led the Cumbrians to promotion to the Second Division in 1981-82 but he resigned following their relegation in May 1986. Stokoe returned to Sunderland briefly for a second spell as caretaker manager just over a decade later.

18 October to 30 November 1976

Ian MacFarlane
(caretaker)

Born: Lanark, 26 January 1933

Ian MacFarlane had a limited playing career as a full-back with Aberdeen, Leicester City and Chelsea. He coached at

Sunderland (July – October 1969) then had a brief spell at Newcastle United before managing Carlisle United (1970-72). He then worked as assistant manager at Middlesbrough and Manchester City before Bob Stokoe appointed him as his assistant on 11 March 1976; three days after the resignation of FA Cup winning assistant manager Arthur Cox. Took over as caretaker manager in October when Stokoe resigned. During his seven match tenure Sunderland won their first two League matches of the season but MacFarlane was immediately dismissed by new manager Jimmy Adamson.

He was assistant manager-coach at Leicester City from 1977-1982, Yeovil Town manager in 1984 and later became chief scout at Leeds United in 1990.

30 November 1976 to 25 October 1978

James (Jimmy) Adamson

Born: Ashington, 4 April 1929
Died: Burnley, 8 November 2011

Jimmy Adamson was a miner when he signed for Burnley as a professional in January 1947. He developed into one of the finest wing-halves in the country, was ever-present in Burnley's Championship winning side in 1960 and voted Footballer of the Year in 1961-62. He had also qualified as an FA coach in 1957 and was coach to the England World Cup side in Chile in 1962. After Walter Winterbottom's retirement as England manager, Adamson was offered the job but he turned it down due to lack of experience. Instead he became coach at Turf Moor after retiring from playing in 1964. He took over as manager in 1970 and had a short spell at Sparta Rotterdam before joining Sunderland.

He experienced the worst start of any Sunderland manager up to then with the first seven League games lost without a goal scored. In response Adamson blooded youth products Shaun Elliott and Kevin Arnott and gave another, Gary Rowell, a regular berth. He also made two shrewd signings in Colin Waldron and Mick Docherty. The subsequent dramatic resurgence in form was top six standard but not quite enough to avoid relegation.

There was a hangover after the heroic attempt to avoid the drop and only one of the first 12 games back in Division Two was won. Although there was a recovery to a final placing of sixth, crowds dwindled and there was little immediate improvement in 1978-79. However, the club had lost just one League game in eight when Adamson resigned to become manager of Leeds United. He had declined to sign a contract during his time at Sunderland and had struggled to live with the widespread call from the fans for Brian Clough to become manager.

He left Leeds in 1980 and spent the rest of his life in Burnley, without any more involvement in the professional game.

25 October 1978 to 11 December 1978

David (Dave) Robert Merrington
(caretaker)

Born: Barley Mow, nr Chester-le-Street, 26 January 1945

Merrington played at centre-half for Burnley from 1964-70 before becoming reserve team coach at Turf Moor. When Jimmy Adamson became Sunderland manager he recruited Merrington, his former colleague from Burnley, as his assistant to replace Ian MacFarlane. When Adamson left for Leeds, Merrington took temporary charge of the team and under him they enjoyed their best winning margin

SUNDERLAND MANAGERS

in a game for 21 months, 5-0 over Bristol Rovers. He declined an offer to take the post permanently and after the appointment of Billy Elliott in December 1979, he left to join Adamson at Leeds United.

Later he worked in the probation service and then as youth team coach at Southampton from 1984-1991. He served as assistant manager to Ian Branfoot (later to become Academy Director at Sunderland) and Alan Ball at the Dell between 1991 and 1995 and was in charge for the 1995-96 season. He went on to scout for Wolves, became assistant manager at Walsall in 2001-02 and was a lay preacher in his spare time.

13 December 1978 to 24 May 1979

William (Billy) Henry Elliott
second spell (caretaker)

After intense speculation about who would be the next manager, the club recruited Billy Elliott from his coaching post in Norway. He was given the job, on a caretaker basis, until the end of the season after Brian Clough, Lawrie McMenemy and Bobby Robson resisted Sunderland's overtures.

Elliott took on the role with enthusiasm and determination and despite a poor start, took the club to the brink of promotion. The team's points per game, during Elliott's 23 games in charge, was equivalent to a title winning total for the season, so the poor start to 1978-79 had ultimately cost promotion. Despite being denied the services of top scorer Gary Rowell for the latter part of the season, Elliott inspired Sunderland to their record unbeaten away run of 14 games and many considered he was unfortunate to be sacked at the end of the season despite supporters organising a petition to have him installed as manager.

He moved onto Darlington, who he managed through troubled times until June 1983.

7 June 1979 to 13 April 1981

Kenneth (Ken) Knighton

Born: Barnsley, 20 February 1944

Knighton started his working life as a trainee miner before signing for Wolves under Stan Cullis who influenced his later management style. He gave good midfield service to Oldham Athletic, Preston North End, Blackburn Rovers, Hull City and Sheffield Wednesday.

On retiring in 1976 he became youth team coach at Hillsborough, who were managed at the time by Len Ashurst. Sunderland appointed him onto the coaching staff in July 1978 and he graduated to chief coach by the start of 1978-79.

At 35 years of age, he was the youngest Sunderland manager since Robert Campbell and he was immediately

Ken Knighton (centre) with assistant manager Frank Clark (with moustache) and coach Peter Eustace. Sunderland Echo

successful in firstly prising Frank Clark away from Brian Clough at Nottingham Forest to become his assistant and then piloting a successful promotion campaign which accelerated after Christmas with the positive input of new arrivals Stan Cummins, Chris Turner and Joe Hinnigan. A 14 game unbeaten run sealed second place and a return to the top flight.

However Knighton struggled to gain the full confidence of new chairman Tom Cowie and when, belatedly, funds were released for necessary team strengthening the following season, his purchases failed to spark and he and assistant Frank Clark lost their jobs in April 1981 with the club in 17th place.

Knighton briefly scouted for Manchester United before taking over the manager's job at Orient in October 1981. He was sacked in May 1983 and later managed non-League teams Dagenham Town and Trowbridge Town.

13 April 1981 to 12 June 1981

Michael (Mick) Docherty
(caretaker)

Born: Preston, 29 October 1950

Docherty began as apprentice with his father Tommy's club Chelsea in 1966 but soon moved to Burnley where he developed quickly to make his League debut as a full-back at 18. A brief spell at Manchester City preceded his move to Sunderland in December 1976 where he linked up with his former manager Jimmy Adamson. Appointed as club captain in 1978, he moved into midfield, notching some vital goals, the first of his career.

A chronic knee injury finally caused his retirement in September 1979, Sunderland staging a Testimonial Match for him against his father's side QPR. With his playing days at an end Mick joined the coaching staff and when Ken Knighton was sacked Docherty was appointed to oversee the remaining four matches of the season, top flight survival being ensured with a last day win at Liverpool.

He became Hartlepool United's manager in June 1983 but one win in 23 games led to his sacking in December. Spells as coach at Wolves and assistant manager at Blackpool, Burnley and Hull City came before a coaching post at Rochdale led to another caretaker manager appointment and finally the permanent manager's job at Spotland from January 1995 to May 1996. He later coached at Huddersfield Town and Burnley.

12 June 1981 to 1 March 1984

William Alan (Alan) Durban

Born: Port Talbot, 7 July 1941

Alan Durban was a skilful inside forward and midfielder with Cardiff City, Derby County and Shrewsbury Town but it was at the Baseball Ground, under Brian Clough, that his career peaked and he won a Championship medal and 27 caps for Wales. After 10 years at Derby he moved to Shrewsbury in September 1973 and soon became their player-manager.

He steered the Shrews from the Fourth to the Second Division and moved on to manage Stoke City in February 1978 and took them up to Division One the following season. In 1979-80 he gave debuts to Lee Chapman and Paul Bracewell, later to have contrasting fortunes at Sunderland with Durban, while his squad included future Roker manager Denis Smith and his assistant Viv Busby. His tactics in preserving the Potters' top flight status were critcised as being overly negative by some, not least by then Sunderland manager Ken Knighton.

Despite a rather dour image as a manager, Durban's ability to fashion successful teams from modest means proved attractive to Sunderland chairman Tom Cowie and he attracted him to

Alan Durban with new signing Ally McCoist.

Wearside in June 1981. Durban was low key in his opening comments, offering only slow improvement and this proved to the case with relegation only narrowly avoided in his first season. A shocking start, including eight consecutive games without a goal, was followed by a recovery on a par with 1976-77 which was initiated by Durban selecting young striker Colin West ahead of his expensive signing Ally McCoist to partner Gary Rowell. Over the last 10 games, six were won and the goals tally almost doubled.

There was a slight improvement in 1982-83 with Sunderland often proving difficult to beat and 1983-84 saw further improvement in the solidity of the team if not the flair. However results were modest and Durban was sacked in March 1984. He stated that he had not had a working relationship with the chairman for several months and cited 'elements within the club' that were hindering progress.

He returned to his first club, Cardiff City as manager but the club sank from Second Division to Fourth in consecutive seasons. In May 1986 he left football to manage an indoor tennis club in Telford. He had previously played tennis to county standard and once competed in the All England Tennis Championship at Wimbledon. Following a spell scouting for Derby County he returned to Sunderland as chief scout in June 1995 and was instrumental in bringing Kevin Phillips to Sunderland. He left to become assistant manager back at Stoke City in September 1997, was caretaker manager for a short spell in 1998 and later he acted as a mentor to academy players. He also had a spell as a regional scout for Norwich City.

1 March 1984 to 5 March 1984

Bryan Stanley (Pop) Robson
(caretaker)

Born: Sunderland, 11 November 1945

Bryan Robson was one of the outstanding goalscorers of his era with almost 300 goals in nearly 700 appearances for Newcastle United, West Ham United, Sunderland, Chelsea and Carlisle United. After his second spell at Sunderland ended in March 1981, he had spells as player-coach at Carlisle and Chelsea before returning to Sunderland in the same role in July 1983.

He took charge of the team for one match, a 2-2 home draw with Arsenal, after Alan Durban's departure and reverted to his coaching role after the arrival of Len Ashurst. Uniquely in Sunderland's history, his brief management stint was followed by his last goal for the club at the age of 38, in his last game before returning to Carlisle United.

There he became assistant to Bob Stokoe and briefly managed the club from August to October 1985. He resigned to allow Stokoe to take over again, happier in the role of coach. His playing career continued into his forties with non-League Gateshead and Newcastle Blue Star. His coaching career took in stints at Manchester United, Leeds United and Hartlepool United and he has had three spells with Sunderland, most recently as chief scout.

5 March 1984 to 24 May 1985

Len Ashurst

Born: Liverpool 10 March 1939

Len Ashurst made more appearances for Sunderland than any other outfield player and was first choice left-back for 12 years between 1958 and 1970. However his return as manager proved unsuccessful despite his extensive rebuilding of the team.

Ashurst's first managerial appointment was at Hartlepool United in March 1971 and he had spells at Gillingham, Sheffield Wednesday, Newport County and Cardiff City before turning down a three year contract at Ninian Park to take over at Sunderland without a contract and without money for team strengthening.

Having turned down an earlier opportunity to return in 1979 he now said, 'I am confident that in 15 months time my record here will justify a contract being offered and I intend to give supporters value for money.' Through the summer of 1984 he brought in nine new players, including future captain Gary Bennett from his old club Cardiff, raising the necessary finance with the sales of Paul Bracewell and Lee Chapman.

Initial results the following season were promising with the club in seventh place by November but while momentum was sustained in the League Cup with a first Final contested, League form declined

Len Ashurst (right) leads Sunderland out at Wembley for the 1985 League (Milk) Cup Final.

sharply and though Ashurst was given a contract at the end of 1984, there were only three League victories in the New Year and relegation was confirmed with defeat in the penultimate match of the season. Chairman Tom Cowie gave Ashurst the dreaded vote of confidence three weeks before sacking him.

Ashurst went on to coach the national teams of Kuwait and Qatar and was assistant manager at Blackpool before a second, two-year spell managing Cardiff City. Brief periods at non-League Weymouth and Weston-super-Mare sandwiched another sojourn abroad in 1996, to coach the Malaysian national team.

In 1998 he became involved with the FA Premier League department overseeing the development of the Academy systems throughout the country and on 30 July 2005 he celebrated 50 years since his start in the professional game. In 2004 Len returned to the North East, retiring to Whitburn, but continuing his role as a Premier League match delegate.

24 May to 11 July 1985
(no first team games)

Frank Burrows
(caretaker)

Born: Larkhall, 30 January 1944

Frank Burrows was a solid defender for Raith Rovers, Scunthorpe United, Swindon Town, where he won a League Cup winners medal, and Mansfield Town.

He moved into coaching and management with Swindon, Portsmouth and Southampton before joining Sunderland in the summer of 1984 as Len Ashurst's assistant. Following Ashurst's sacking a year later he acted as caretaker manager through the close season.

After leaving Sunderland he experienced more than 20 years in coaching and management with Cardiff City, Portsmouth, Swansea City, West Bromwich Albion, Nottingham Forest and Leicester City.

11 July 1985 to 16 April 1987

Lawrence (Lawrie) McMenemy

Born: Saltwell Park, Gateshead 26 July 1936

Lawrie McMenemy's much heralded arrival at Sunderland failed to produce the anticipated revival of the club's fortunes. By the time of his departure Sunderland were heading for Division Three, for the first time in their history.

McMenemy was a junior at Newcastle United but played most of his football at Gateshead until injury finished his career at the age of 25. He stayed on as trainer coach until joining Bishop Auckland in 1964 and managed them to the Northern League title and third round of the FA Cup. He spent two years as coach at Sheffield Wednesday, under Alan Brown, and became manager of Doncaster Rovers in 1968 who he led to the Fourth Division title in his first season. Following relegation in 1971 he was sacked but was soon appointed at Grimsby Town and repeated his first season title success in 1971-72.

He moved to Southampton as assistant manager in July 1973 and took over from Ted Bates in December. This time he suffered relegation in his first season but

SUNDERLAND MANAGERS

Lawrie McMenemy and Lew Chatterley.

there was a shock FA Cup Final win over Manchester United in 1976 before promotion was eventually achieved in 1977-78. McMenemy established Southampton as a leading First Division side using senior players whose careers he revived and extended.

By 1985 he was ready for a fresh challenge and secured the Sunderland post ahead of Ian Porterfield, Mick Buxton and Arthur Cox. He ignored the young players that had broken into the first team the previous season and selected his own experienced imports. However the first five games were lost without Sunderland scoring and there was only marginal improvement throughout the season with relegation only avoided with a last day win.

After a brief spell in the top six in 1986-87 only four wins were managed in 23 games before the Sheffield United home game on 11 April 1987. Roker's lowest crowd for 34 years witnessed another defeat before demonstrations outside the ground confirmed that patience with the highly paid manager had run out. His departure was announced five days later. His son, Chris, was on Sunderland's coaching staff from 1985 to 1988.

Despite his failure he became one of the few ex-Sunderland managers to secure a high profile job after leaving Wearside when he was appointed as assistant to England manager Graham Taylor in July 1990. He returned to Southampton to become a director in December 1993 and also served as general manager for three years. He was later Northern Ireland manager from February 1998 until December 1999.

16 April to 30 May 1987

Robert (Bob) Stokoe
second spell (caretaker)

Chairman Bob Murray turned to former hero Bob Stokoe to steer Sunderland to safety in their last seven games but the club finished third bottom and were forced into the Play-Offs. Defeat over two legs meant Third Division football for the first time in Sunderland's history. Stokoe confirmed after the decisive home leg with Gillingham that he did not want to be considered for the manager's job the following season.

Though his management career was over, Stokoe stayed in the game as a scout for Chelsea and then Swindon Town.

30 May 1987 to 30 December 1991

Denis Smith

Born: Stoke, 19 November 1947

Denis Smith lifted Sunderland from the lowest place in their history, secured a Division Three title and brought top flight football back to Wearside only for Sunderland to be relegated again after just one season.

Smith was an uncompromising central defender with a Stoke City side that enjoyed considerable success in the early 1970s highlighted by a League Cup Final win in 1972. After 16 years in the Potteries he moved to York City in March 1982 and became their player-manager three months later. He led York to the Fourth Division title in 1983-84, their first major trophy, and they also reached the FA Cup Fifth Round in each of the following two seasons.

Bob Murray paid £20,000 compensation to York when Smith joined Sunderland and the new manager promised to pay more, out of his own pocket, if he failed to win promotion in his first season. In contrast to Lawrie McMenemy's reported £200,000 salary, Smith signed up for less than his £45,000 salary at York declaring that he was very happy at York but 'How can you turn down a club like Sunderland?' His former Stoke teammate Viv Busby followed him from York as his assistant.

Smith made a pair of astute early buys in defenders John Kay and John MacPhail and went back to his former club for young striker Marco Gabbiadini. The team played in an attractive style, scoring on average two goals per game, to win the title with Smith drawing improved performances out of many of the players he had inherited.

A season of consolidation back in Division Two followed and then a promotion after defeat in the 1989-90 Play-Off Final when victors Swindon were punished for financial irregularities. Relegation on the last day of the 1990-91 season capped a year-long struggle. Smith chose to stay on rather than accepting an offer to manage his former club Stoke City but despite breaking the club transfer record to bring in striker Don Goodman to replace record sale Gabbiadini, results were poor. The last game of 1991 was lost decisively at lowly Oxford United and Smith's sacking followed two days later.

In March 1992 he took over at Bristol City and shortly afterwards he returned to Sunderland with his new team, receiving a good reception from the Roker crowd. He was sacked in January 1993 and was appointed at Oxford United eight months later, where his initial four years spell was followed by two years at West Bromwich Albion before another short period back at Oxford. In October 2000 he relinquished his managerial duties but stayed on in an advisory capacity until becoming manager of Wrexham in October 2001 where he stayed for six years. He is one of only a few managers to clock up 1,000 games in the role.

30 December 1991 (permanently 29 April 1992) to 1 February 1993

Malcolm Crosby

Born: South Shields, 4 July 1954

A life-long Sunderland supporter, Malcolm Crosby led Sunderland to the FA Cup Final but continuing poor League form led to his dismissal only nine months later.

The majority of Crosby's playing career was at Aldershot where he spent nine years before joining York City in November

1981. He amassed almost 500 first team appearances as a midfielder and featured in Aldershot's promotion in 1972-73 and York's Fourth Division title success in 1983-84.

After retiring in 1986, he spent two years coaching in Kuwait before his former boss at York, Denis Smith, took him to Sunderland as youth team coach in July 1988. He graduated to reserve team coach in 1989 and Smith's dismissal of Viv Busby at the end of 1991 ensured that Crosby was next in line to take over when Smith was sacked.

While the board deliberated over Neil Warnock and Don Mackay, amongst others, as potential successors, Crosby enjoyed the best start of any Sunderland manager, caretaker or otherwise. His first four games were won and he earned the January 1992 manager-of-the-month award. The glory of a run to the FA Cup Final resulted in him being offered the manager's job once Second Division status was secured with two games to spare. Only three of the last 18 League games were won and Liverpool denied Sunderland a third FA Cup Final victory.

The departure of Cup Final captain Paul Bracewell to Newcastle United was a blow and Sunderland never got into the top half of the table during the following campaign. A home defeat to Watford in February 1993 saw Sunderland in the same position (17th) as they were when Crosby first took over and he was dismissed with his assistant Bobby Ferguson taking over as caretaker.

After a short spell coaching Gateshead, Crosby joined Denis Smith at Oxford United and once again filled a caretaker role when Smith left for West Bromwich Albion in December 1997.

Crosby followed Smith to the Hawthorns in February 1998 and returned to a coaching role which he continued at Derby County in 1999. He served as assistant manager at Swindon Town from 2000 to 2004 and also scouted for the England team prior to the Euro 2000 Finals. 'Crossa' returned to the North East in 2004 as reserve team manager at Middlesbrough and remained there until 2009. He has since managed at Northampton Town and is now Head of Youth Development at Oxford United.

1 February to 5 February 1993

(no first team games)

Robert Burnitt (Bobby) Ferguson

(caretaker)

Born: Newcastle-upon-Tyne, 8 January 1938

Ferguson played full-back for Newcastle United, Derby County, Cardiff City, Barry Town and Newport County between 1955 and 1971, acting as player-manager for the latter two clubs. He was the coach of the Ipswich Town youth team that won the FA Youth Cup twice and progressed to become reserve, first team coach and finally manager 1982-87. Further managerial and coaching appointments followed in Kuwait, Birmingham City, Colchester United and Coventry City before he became first team coach at Sunderland in June 1992. Terry Butcher took him as his assistant in February 1993 after he had overseen affairs for the few days since Malcolm Crosby's dismissal. He stayed until 18 May 1993 and later scouted for the club.

5 February to 26 November 1993

Terence (Terry) Ian Butcher

Born: Singapore, 28 December 1958

Terry Butcher was signed as a player by Malcolm Crosby but six months later replaced him as manager. Playing performances during his time in charge were poor and relegation was barely avoided at the end of his first season. No improvement was forthcoming despite considerable investment in players and his tenure ended with five straight defeats and the club languishing in 20th place.

Butcher was a commanding and competitive central defender who played in three World Cup Finals tournaments for England and captained them to the semi-final against Germany in 1990. The majority of his club career was at Ipswich Town where he enjoyed UEFA Cup success in 1981 and two Division One runners-up positions. He was a major influence in Bobby Robson's attractive team and after he joined Rangers in 1986 he was instrumental as they became the dominant team in Scotland, winning both the Premier Division and League Cup three times.

In November 1990 he returned to England to become player-manager at Coventry City but was sacked following his refusal to take a pay-cut after playing only a handful of first team games. Long-term knee problems had taken their toll but he accepted the offer of a playing comeback from Sunderland and signed on a free transfer in August 1992.

Butcher was chosen as Sunderland manager instead of Dave Bassett and Steve Coppell who had both declined the job and he was assisted by Bobby Ferguson, who had helped him in his early Ipswich career. He continued playing, becoming the first Sunderland manager to do so, and missed only one of the remaining matches. His forthright manner and cheer-leading ritual on the pitch were not enough however and only results elsewhere kept Sunderland up after a dismal defeat at Notts County in their last game.

Despite being given a record amount of money to invest in the summer, Sunderland slumped to their heaviest ever opening day of the season defeat (5-0 at Derby County) although Butcher wasn't

helped by some of his buys being injured in a pre-season car crash. The only highlight at the start of 1993-94 was a 4-2 aggregate win over Premiership side Leeds United in the League Cup as most of Butcher's two million pounds plus worth of signings failed to spark. His sacking came just three months into the season, six days after a 2-0 home defeat to Southend United.

Butcher returned to Scotland to become a hotelier in Stirlingshire and also coached at Raith Rovers and Dundee United. In October 2001 he became assistant manager at Motherwell and took the permanent post in April 2002. He later managed Sydney FC and Brentford and assisted George Burley with Scotland before enjoying considerable success in charge of Inverness Caledonian Thistle.

26 November 1993 to 29 March 1995

Michael James (Mick) Buxton

Born: Corbridge, 29 May 1943

Mick Buxton initially did well at Sunderland in lifting the club from the relegation zone into the top half of Division Two. However he could not sustain the momentum and at the time of his departure the club were in 20th place, the same position as when he took over.

As a player, Buxton had few first team opportunities as a full-back during his eight years at Burnley. He faired little better at Halifax Town but began his coaching career at the Shay before moving on to Southend United, Watford, Barnsley and Mansfield Town and then Huddersfield Town in 1978. Here he gained his first managerial post and was an instant success leading the team to the Fourth Division title in 1979-80 with 101 goals scored. Promotion to Division Two followed in 1982-83 and three comfortable mid-table finishes preceded a poor start to 1986-87 which led to Buxton's sacking in December 1986. He took over at Fourth Division Scunthorpe United in April 1987 and they reached the Play-Offs in 1988 and 1989, only to miss out on promotion each time. Crowd discontent contributed to his sacking in February 1991 and he returned to coaching with Wimbledon and then the England Under-21 squad.

He had just completed a short spell back at Huddersfield when Terry Butcher offered him the job as reserve team coach at Sunderland and he arrived in July 1993.

Buxton described the day of his appointment as Sunderland manager as 'the worst day of my life' due to the sympathy he had for Butcher and his assistant, former Sunderland captain Ian Atkins, adding that Sunderland were the only club he would have come back into management for.

He was given the job initially until the

end of the 1993-94 season and Buxton ignored the continual speculation linking the club with Dave Bassett to quickly improve results on the field. The team became more cohesive with Buxton drawing improved performances from Butcher's signings Phil Gray, Andy Melville and Alec Chamberlain and showing confidence in younger players Craig Russell and Martin Smith. Darius Kubicki proved to be an excellent signing along with Steve Agnew and Martin Scott the following season. However despite the longest unbeaten start to a season for 80 years, performances declined through 1993-94 and a run of only 12 goals in 20 games led to the transfer deadline day signing of £700,000 striker Brett Angel.

Buxton was sacked six days later after a dismal defeat at Barnsley. In June 1995 he was appointed manager of the Zimbabwe national team but the deal fell through before he actually started the job. He managed Scunthorpe United between March 1996 and February 1997 and coached the Chinese national team in the late 1990s. Upon his return to England he was employed by the Premier League to monitor the quality of Academy football.

29 March 1995 (permanently 22 May 1995) to 7 October 2002

Peter Reid

Born: Huyton, Liverpool 20 June 1956

Peter Reid enjoyed immediate success at Sunderland with the Division One title, a feat that was repeated in fine style three seasons later. Under his leadership the club

then achieved their highest top flight finish for 45 years in 1999-00, matching the seventh place the following season. Unfortunately the momentum could not be sustained and Reid departed shortly after the start of the disastrous 2002-03 campaign.

As a player, Reid was a tenacious ball-winning midfielder who overcame serious injuries to amass 535 League appearances and earn 13 England caps. He joined Bolton Wanderers in 1971 and missed only four games in three and a half years before a broken leg and knee injuries threatened his career. Subsequently he moved to Everton for a modest fee in 1982 but then became a major contributor to the Toffees outstanding success in winning two League Championships, the FA Cup and European Cup Winners Cup. He appeared in three successive FA Cup Finals and was voted Players' Player of the Year in 1985 when he played a total of 60 games. Three of his international caps came in the 1986 World Cup Finals in Mexico.

His last two years at Goodison were spent as player-coach before a short spell as a player at QPR in 1989. This was followed by a return to his previous role at Manchester City under his former Everton boss Howard Kendall. In November 1990 he succeeded Kendall to become player-manager at Maine Road, guided the team to two fifth place finishes and stayed until August 1993 when he was sacked after a disagreement with chairman Peter Swales. He signed Niall Quinn from Arsenal and saw him score twice to relegate Sunderland in 1991, describing the visiting support as 'absolutely unbelievable'. The atmosphere of a full Roker Park had also left an impression on him as a Bolton player during Sunderland's promotion-clinching match of 1976.

Marking time before a return to management, Reid played for Southampton, Notts County and Bury before accepting the challenge of keeping Sunderland up in 1994-95. Three wins and three draws in the seven games confirmed safety and during 1995-96 Reid gradually moulded the squad he inherited into a promotion- winning outfit. Paul Bracewell was re-signed as assistant-manager and player and a solid workmanlike team secured the title on the back of nine straight wins in the New Year.

Reid signed Niall Quinn for a club record £1.3m but he was injured early on and goals proved elusive. However survival was still possible until the last day defeat at Wimbledon. The forty points gained would have been enough for safety in most seasons. Initial struggles the following season saw Reid's job under threat but a 17 match unbeaten run and the blossoming of new striker Kevin Phillips fuelled a strong promotion challenge that came to an unfortunate end in the Play-Off Final.

There was no hang-over in 1998-99 as the title was won in style with a record points total. Reid made the required improvements in defence by signing goalkeeper Thomas Sorensen and centre back Paul Butler. Reid's preferred 4-4-2 formation saw wingers Alan Johnston and Nicky Summerbee provide the service for forwards Phillips and Quinn. A club record 19 League games unbeaten was achieved and promotion was secured with four games to spare.

The club enjoyed a successful return to the Premiership and were close to European qualification. The high-point of Reid's reign was second place in January 2001 but only 14 more wins followed in the next 62 League games. The lack of goals led to an increasingly desperate search for a striker and when finally Reid paid a club record fee for Tore Andre Flo and Marcus Stewart in August 2002 he had only five more weeks in office before his sacking. The less heralded signings generally proved more successful and contributed hugely to Reid's legacy from 1997 to 2001 of providing some of the most exciting football on Wearside in the last 50 years.

In March 2003 he took over at Leeds United as caretaker manager and steered them to Premiership safety. However he was less successful in the permanent post and was sacked in November 2003. He became manager at Coventry City in May 2004 but was sacked after only eight months in charge and became a regular television pundit for the BBC.

10 October 2002 to 10 March 2003

Howard Wilkinson

Born: Sheffield, 13 November 1943

Howard Wilkinson's appointment as Sunderland manager was a major surprise as neither he nor his assistant Steve

SUNDERLAND MANAGERS

Cotterill had been mentioned in speculation following Peter Reid's dismissal three days earlier. Their stewardship proved to be a disaster with only two Premiership victories achieved in 20 games and the pair

were sacked with the team rooted to the bottom of the table and heading for relegation.

Wilkinson had been a player for Sheffield United, Sheffield Wednesday and Brighton & Hove Albion before beginning his managerial career at Boston United in 1970. He gained a degree in physical education at Sheffield University and was a teacher for a spell. Prior to becoming England's Under-21 coach in November 1982 he had been a FA regional coach in Sheffield and manager of England's semi-professional team. He combined the Under-21 post with managing Notts County for one season in the top flight.

In June 1983 he took over at Sheffield Wednesday and they were promoted in his first season. He established them in Division One, with a best finish of fifth, before moving to Leeds United in October 1988. From 21st place when he took over, they won the title the following season and first place in 1991-92 meant Wilkinson stands as the last Englishman to guide a team to top flight success. Leeds struggled the following season and Wilkinson was sacked in September 1996.

He became FA technical director in January 1997 and was integral in the development of the National Football Centre at Burton. His reputation as a dour devotee of direct football concerned many observers when he arrived at Sunderland but he had an eager young assistant in Steve Cotterill, who had enjoyed great success at Cheltenham Town, and they were among only 12 coaches in Britain to hold the UEFA pro-licence, the highest football qualification in Europe. While with the FA, Wilkinson twice took temporary charge of the full England team (verses France 1998 and Finland 2000) and thus became the second former international manager to take the reigns at Sunderland, after Ian McColl.

He promised a brand of management that was 'as modern and forward-thinking as any in the world', but the effect was negligible. After the highlight of beating Liverpool on Wearside for the first time in 44 years, a Boxing Day defeat to Leeds United began a desperate decline. Only one point was gained from 10 games in the New Year with poor performances from the established players and the expensive imports alike.

The Board acted decisively and dismissed Wilkinson and Cotterill five months after their appointment. Wilkinson served the shortest period of any Sunderland manager, excluding caretakers.

In March 2004 he became head coach

of Shanghai Shenua and served a short spell as first team coach at Leicester City the following October.

12 March 2003 to 6 March 2006

Michael Joseph (Mick) McCarthy

Born: Barnsley, 7 February 1959

Mick McCarthy inherited a team that were certainties for relegation and suffered the worst start of any Sunderland manager with 11 successive League defeats punctuated only by a League Cup win at Mansfield after 10 League games in charge over two seasons. From such adversity he rebuilt the team into promotion contenders and FA Cup semi-finalists within one season before going on to convincingly win the newly named Championship and with it promotion to the Premiership in his second full season.

McCarthy made several shrewd signings to further improve the squad

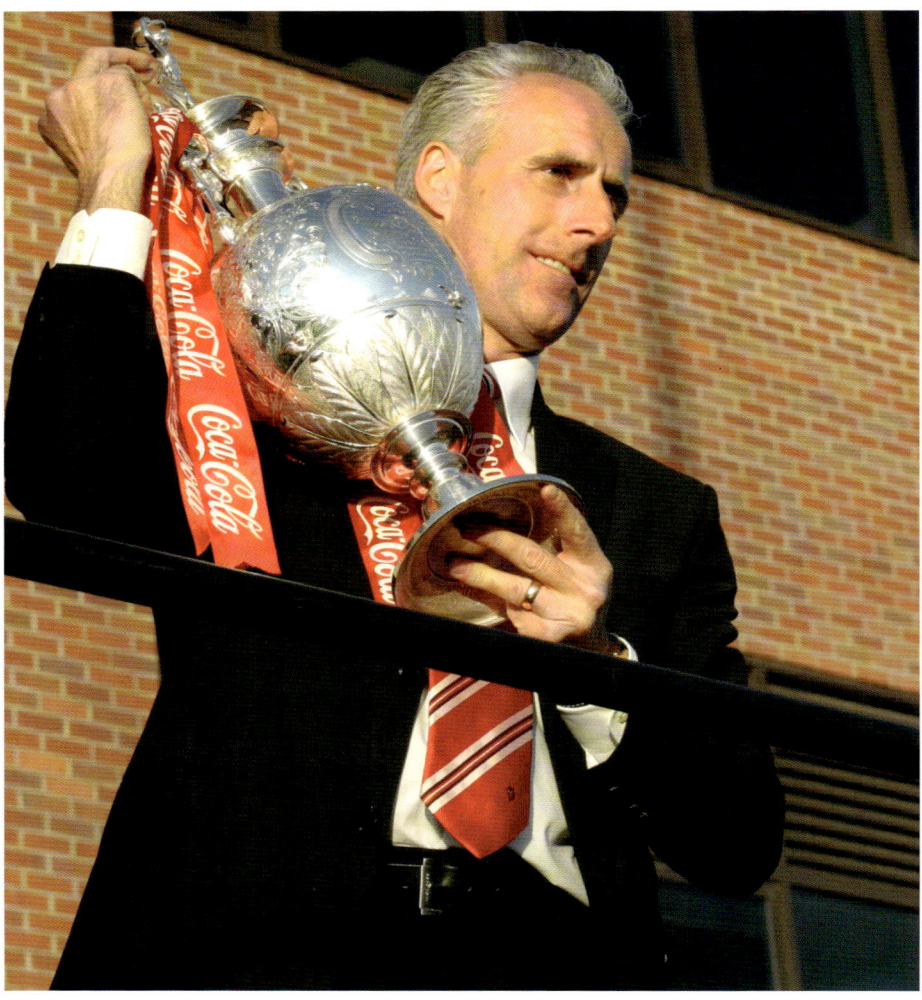

SUNDERLAND MANAGERS

after going to close to success in 2003-04 and winning the title a year later completed a remarkable return to the top flight. Unfortunately the necessary team strengthening was not forthcoming and McCarthy was sacked three quarters of the way through the worst season in the club's history.

In his playing days McCarthy was a dominant centre-back for Barnsley, Manchester City, Celtic, Olympic Lyonnais and Millwall, winning 57 caps for the Republic of Ireland.

His first managerial experience was as player-manager, then manager at Millwall, between 1992 and 1996. He was on the end of two six goal hammerings at Roker Park with Millwall as player and manager. A Play-Off finish in 1994 and first position in December 1995 were high points before he left to manage the Republic of Ireland national team in February 1996.

Mick took over an ageing squad from Jack Charlton but maintained their competitiveness while rebuilding the team. Under his guidance they climbed from 54th to thirteenth in the FIFA world rankings, reached the Play-Offs for France 98 and Euro 2000 and qualified ahead of Holland for the 2002 Finals. With a trio of Sunderland players (Niall Quinn, Kevin Kilbane and Jason McAteer) Ireland were unbeaten through the group stage and were unlucky to lose to Spain on penalties in the Second Round. At the time of his resignation, just four months later, he was Europe's longest serving coach.

Four months after leaving Sunderland McCarthy took over at Wolves, leading them back into the top flight in his second season. He finally recorded his first top flight win in charge of a team at the SOL at his 16th attempt in May 2011 but was sacked in February 2012 with the club struggling at the foot of the table.

6 March 2006 to 9 May 2006

Kevin Anthony Ball
(caretaker)

Born: Hastings, 12 November 1964

Rejected as a youngster with Coventry City, Ball showed the determination that would characterise his whole career by establishing himself firstly with Portsmouth and then at Sunderland, initially as a centre-half then as a ball-winning midfielder with natural leadership skills. He became one of the club's finest ever captains and led the Lads to Championship titles in 1996 and 1999 before finishing his playing career at Burnley and Fulham.

Bally returned to the club on 10 February 2003 as coach and then became assistant academy manager. When Mick McCarthy left he took over as caretaker manager for the last 10 games during which time the team won its only home game of the season.

He expressed an interest in taking the manager's position on a full-time basis but incoming chairman Niall Quinn had his eyes set on Roy Keane for the job. Despite speculation linking him with other managerial vacancies, he remained at Sunderland, working under the new regime in his previous post.

On 4 July 2012 Martin O'Neill appointed him as senior professional development coach.

9 May to 24 July 2006

(No competitive first team games)

Kevin Richardson

Born: Newcastle-upon-Tyne, 4 December 1962

Timothy Douglas (Tim) Carter

Born: Bristol, 5 October 1967
Died: Manchester, 19 June 2008
(caretakers)

Kevin Richardson played over 500 games as a versatile mid-fielder between 1980 and 2000 and won two top flight title medals with Everton, where he was a teammate of Paul Bracewell and Peter Reid and Arsenal, where he played with Niall Quinn. He captained Aston Villa to a League Cup Final victory in 1994 and won his only England cap in the same year.

After retirement he was youth team coach at Sunderland from August 2000 until the following autumn and returned to the club in October 2004 as reserve team coach after a spell as assistant manager at Stockport County. He became first team coach under Niall Quinn and was retained in the role until Neil Bailey's arrival in January 2007. He stayed on the coaching staff until December 2007 and then had a period of coaching at Newcastle United either side of helping Steve Staunton manage Darlington.

Tim Carter was a goalkeeper who signed for Sunderland from Bristol Rovers on Christmas Eve 1987 and spent five years at the club making 50 appearances as Tony Norman's under-study. He played for eight other clubs, notably Millwall, before becoming a goal-keeping coach. Working with Mart Poom led to him helping the Estonia national team on a part-time basis and he coached Sunderland's first team (2005-07) and academy (2007-08) goalkeepers.

Richardson and Carter took charge of the first team during for the first three per-season friendlies in the summer of 2005 and handed over to Niall Quinn with an exemplary record of played three won three with seven goals scored and none conceded.

25 July to 28 August 2006

Niall John Quinn

Born: Dublin, 6 October 1966

Niall Quinn followed a superb six years as a player for the Lads with an equally effective spell off the pitch, firstly as a stand-in manager and then as chairman, helping the club recover from a demoralising relegation in 2006 to become an established top flight club six years later.

He began his playing career as an awkward, gangling striker with Arsenal but by the time he joined Sunderland from Manchester City in 1996 he was one the most effective target-men in the game. His Wearside career was initially stalled by injury but took off in partnership with Kevin Phillips as the pair's goals fuelled a record-breaking Championship title in 1999. Their form continued to flourish in the top flight until injury took its toll and he retired in November 2002.

His benefit match was at the SOL on 14 May 2002 between Sunderland and the Republic of Ireland for whom he made 91 appearances and scored 21 goals between 1985 and 2002. In an unprecedented move, Quinn donated the £1 million proceeds from the game to charity.

His five years as Sunderland chairman began on 3 July 2006 when he headed the Drumaville consortium which took over the club and he combined this with the manager's role for a month prior to the appointment of Roy Keane. He signed off with a win after the club's poor form had continued into the new season.

On standing down as chairman he worked as director of international development until 20 February 2012.

28 August 2006 to 4 December 2008

Roy Maurice Keane

Born: Cork, 10 August 1971

Roy Keane was Niall Quinn's vision of a 'World Class figure' and he enjoyed immediate success, fashioning a side that won 26 of his first 41 games in charge to seal a title-winning return to the top-flight at the first time of asking. He brought in many new players notably David Connolly and Carlos Edwards and successfully converted Nyron Nosworthy to centre-back. His signings in the top flight were generally less successful and although the club avoided relegation

they were third bottom the following December when Keane abruptly resigned after a home defeat to Bolton Wanderers.

As a player, Keane was a world-class midfield power-house who was nurtured and developed by Brian Clough at Nottingham Forest and matured under Sir Alex Ferguson at Manchester United. He signed for United for £3.75 million in July 1993 and won seven titles and four FA Cup-winners medals before finishing his career at Celtic. He was capped 67 times by the Republic of Ireland and famously came home early from the 2002 World Cup Finals in Japan after a fall-out with Ireland manager Mick McCarthy.

His experiences with Clough and Ferguson undoubtedly shaped his managerial style and his ultra-competitive outlook sometimes served to intimidate, rather than stimulate, his charges.

He managed Ipswich Town between April 2009 and January 2011 and recruited several players who had been with him at Sunderland.

4 December 2008 (permanently 27 December 2008) to 24 May 2009

Richard (Ricky) Sbragia

Born: Glasgow, 26 May 1956

Ricky Sbragia was a somewhat reluctant manager, perhaps in the mould of Malcolm Crosby, who picked up the pieces after Roy Keane's sudden departure and fulfilled his brief of keeping the club in the top flight. The team hit four goals in his second and third matches in charge but this good form fell away alarmingly and a final total of 36 points meant the club stayed up partly due to the failings of others, notably Newcastle United.

SUNDERLAND MANAGERS

Sbragia had 11 years as a player, notably at York City 1982-87, under Denis Smith, when he formed an effective centre-back pairing with future Sunderland pivot John MacPhail. He moved into coaching with York City and was youth team and reserve coach at Sunderland between October 1994 and November 2002. He then coached at Manchester United and Bolton Wanderers before returning to the Sunderland coaching staff in November 2007.

After stepping down as manager, Sbragia was offered a 'job for life' by chairman Niall Quinn and he became chief scout, a role he retained until April 2011. In August 2011 he was appointed head coach of the Scotland national under-17 team.

3 June 2009 to 30 November 2011

Stephen Roger (Steve) Bruce

Born: Corbridge, 31 December 1960

Steve Bruce was a sensible choice as a steady hand to consolidate Sunderland's position in the top flight and this he achieved. However he had never managed a team beyond the middle reaches of the top flight and his tactical limitations combined with the loss of key players led to his dismissal rather than his Newcastle origins which had not hindered the career of a certain Bob Stokoe on Wearside.

Bruce was only one of three Sunderland managers to start with an away victory and the team started 2009-10 well with five wins lifting them to seventh place after the first nine games. Record signing Darren Bent scored freely and the new central midfield pairing of Lee Cattermole and Lorik Cana functioned well initially. A mid-season slump hindered progress but the Lads still finished thirteenth, their highest position for nine years. There was a slight improvement in points and position (tenth) the following season thanks in part to Bent's new expensive strike partner Asamoah Gyan. However Bruce was unfortunate that both Bent and Gyan left

the club abruptly and the consequent lack of goals contributed to his eventual dismissal despite the arrival of good signings such as Sebastian Larsson and Stephan Sessegnon.

He had been a whole-hearted and consistent central defender during an almost 20 year playing career with Gillingham, Norwich City, Manchester United, Birmingham City and Sheffield United. He was a League Cup Final winner with Norwich when they beat Sunderland in 1985, won three Premier League titles at Old Trafford and finally called time on his playing days when given the run-around by Michael Bridges when the Lads won 4-0 at Sheffield in November 1998.

Player-manager with the Blades, he moved onto Huddersfield Town, Wigan Athletic, Crystal Palace and spent his longest managerial spell of six years at Birmingham City (2001-07). Prior to joining Sunderland he had been back at Wigan for two years.

On 8 June 2012 he was appointed manager of Hull City.

30 November 2011 to 3 December 2011

Eric Black
(caretaker)

Born: Bellshill, 1 October 1963

Eric Black was a consistent striker in Aberdeen's successful side of the early 1980s under Sir Alex Ferguson. He scored in the Dons' 1983 European Cup Winners' Cup Final win over Real Madrid and picked up three Scottish title medals. He won the French Cup with Metz before his career was curtailed by injury at 27.

He moved into coaching with the Scottish national U18s and Celtic and then managed Motherwell in 2001-02 with Terry Butcher as his assistant. He had a short spell as Coventry City manager in early 2004 before linking up with Steve Bruce as his assistant in July 2004 and following him to Wigan Athletic and Sunderland.

He had one game as caretaker manager of Birmingham City in November 2007 following Bruce's departure and he took charge in similar circumstances for Sunderland four years later with the Lads losing 2-1 at Wolves with Martin O'Neill watching from the stands.

Appointed 3 December 2011

Martin Hugh Michael O'Neill

Born: Kilrea, 1 March 1952

Martin O'Neill was hired by Ellis Short with the club precariously placed in the top flight, but within two months the man from Kilrea had fashioned nine wins from 13 games, the best start by any Sunderland manager, and the Lads had reached eighth position in the League and secured a fifth round FA Cup place.

O'Neill's 10 year playing career as an attacking midfielder with Nottingham Forest embraced the club's renaissance under Brian Clough and earned him top flight title and European Cup Winner's medals. He also played for Norwich City, Manchester City and Notts County after starting his career with Derry City and then Lisburn Distillery.

He began in management with Grantham Town in 1987 and after a short spell at Shepshed Charterhouse he spent five years at the helm of Wycombe Wanderers, steering them into the Football League for the first time, before leaving for Norwich City. Differences with the chairman meant his stay was brief and he took over at Leicester City in December 1995. Immediate promotion alongside the Lads the following May heralded a five year stint with the Foxes which brought four top 10 finishes and two League Cup wins, the second of which, in 2000, saw Sunderland beaten over two legs at the semi-final stage. Three months later he took over at Celtic, staying for five seasons, and helping the club regain supremacy over Rangers and become competitive in Europe, reaching the UEFA Cup Final in 2003.

Following a period out of the game for family reasons O'Neill became manager of Aston Villa in August 2006 and took them to three consecutive sixth place finishes and a League Cup Final in 2010. He resigned just prior to the start of the 2010-11 season and was linked with the England manager's job just after taking over at Sunderland, having previously been interviewed for the post in 2008.

Top Teams

These are the Sunderland teams considered by the authors to be the best line-ups in each decade or era since Sunderland entered the League in 1890. Beyond the obvious choices, the players have been selected primarily on numbers of appearances in the period concerned but occasionally the player's individual ability and impact has prompted their inclusion. This may well prompt some discussion and differences of opinion! The teams are set up in the style of the day so there are five forwards (no's 7 to 11) up until the 1960s and subs only in the later selections. Six players feature twice but are only profiled once; Jimmy Millar, George Holley, Charlie Buchan, Len Shackleton, Jim Montgomery and Kevin Phillips.

1890s

1	Ted Doig
2	Tom Porteous
3	Don Gow
4	Hugh Wilson
5	Johnny Auld
6	Willie Gibson
7	Jim Gillespie
8	David Hannah
9	Johnny Campbell
10	Jimmy Millar
11	James Hannah

Ted Doig (1890-1904)

Considered one of the greatest goalkeepers of all time and the club's highest appearance maker, if friendlies included. Holds the club records of four Championship medals (shared with Jimmy Millar), the longest period without conceding a goal (806 mins) and the most ever-present seasons (seven). Missed only 15 of the 472 League, Cup and Play-off games played during his 14 years at the club.

Tom Porteous (1889-94)

Signed from Kilmarnock yet the only English-born regular in the first two Championship-winning seasons, in which he played every game. The first Sunderland player to be capped by England when he appeared in the first full international staged in Sunderland.

Don Gow (1891-92 & 1893-97)

Leading Scottish amateur sprinter who played mainly at left-back and won a Championship medal in his first season at the club. Captained Scotland when barely 20 years old and was one of the first Scots to play for the Football League. Two spells on Wearside and also for Rangers.

Hugh 'Lalty' Wilson (1890-99)

Exceptional half-back who captained the Team of All The Talents. The only player to appear in the club's first ever League game and also their first game at Roker Park. Converted the first ever penalty awarded to Sunderland and the effectiveness of his one-handed throw-in led them being deemed illegal. The first outfield player to be capped by Scotland while with the club.

Johnny Auld (1889-96)

Reliable Scottish centre-half who captained the Lads in their first ever League season. His signing terms included the club setting him up in business and he gave six years excellent service before becoming the first player to move from Sunderland to Newcastle where he later became a director.

Willie Gibson (1888-94 & 1895-96)

Ever-present during the 1892-93 Championship-winning season, this stout Scot from Ayrshire joined the club in the pre-league years and played for Rangers in between two spells on Wearside, each transfer to and from Glasgow involving an exchange with Andrew McCreadie. Also played left-back and recorded the first League goal by a Sunderland full-back.

Jim Gillespie (1890-91 & 1892-97)

The first player to score twice on his League debut for the club and had a spell with rivals Sunderland Albion before returning to score 12 goals from the right-wing in the title winning season of 1892-93, including a spell of seven goals in six games. Returned to his native Scotland after achieving a half-century of goals in five full seasons.

David Hannah (1889-94)

One of the three pre-league signings from the famous Renton FC (others were Johnny Campbell and John Harvie). Born in Northern Ireland and versatile enough to play on both wings in addition to his usual inside-forward birth. Two titles with Sunderland and one with Liverpool before spells with Dundee and Woolwich Arsenal and a return to Renton completed his career.

Johnny Campbell (1889-97)

Fifth top scorer in the club's history with 154 goals at a strike-rate only bettered by Halliday and Clough. Scored Sunderland's first home and away League hat-tricks and first FA Cup goal as a League club. Top scorer in the Football League in the club's first three Championship-winning seasons. Died aged only 36 in 1906, just eight months before his forward partner Millar – in the 148 games they played together they scored 209 goals.

Jimmy 'Jamie' Millar (1890-96 & 1900-04)

His haul of four top flight Championship medals with Sunderland can only be matched by Ted Doig and his skilful inside-forward play brought him a century of goals including five in one match (one of only four players to achieve this for the Lads). Had two spells on Wearside and also Rangers where he won two more titles.

James 'Blood' Hannah (1891-97)

This Glaswegian with the mystery nickname switched wings for the arrival of Jim Gillespie but also played at inside-forward in his six years with the club. Scored four in one game playing on the left-wing and added two Championship titles to his Scottish Cup medal earned with Third Lanark.

1900s

1	**Dick Roose**
2	**Dusty Rhodes**
3	**Jimmy Watson**
4	**William Farquhar**
5	**Sandy McAllister**
6	**Dicky Jackson**
7	**Billy Hogg**
8	**George Holley**
9	**Jimmy Gemmell**
10	**Jimmy Millar**
11	**Arthur Bridgett**

Note: Ted Doig made the most appearances of any goalkeeper in the 1900s and is excluded only because of the unique influence of Dick Roose. Matthew Ferguson's career straddled the turn of the century otherwise he would also be a strong contender along with Tommy Tait for Farquhar's half-back slot. Andy McCombie just missed out at right-back on appearances.

Dick Roose (1908-11)

Remarkable character and brilliant goalkeeper whose signing ended the club's long search for a successor to Doig. His habit of bouncing the ball up to the halfway line led to a rule change and his tendency to play sweeper was innovative at the time. A winner in his first two visits to Newcastle including the 9-1, a broken wrist at St James' ended his Sunderland career.

Dusty Rhodes (1902-08)

Middlesbrough-born defender who initially played at left-back but switched to right-back after Andy McCombie's controversial transfer and gave solid service, scoring one of his five goals in his last appearance and netting two penalties in the club's joint highest scoring draw against Liverpool.

Jimmy Watson (1900-1907)

'Daddy Long Legs' was an integral part of the best defence in the League during 1900-01 and also during the following title-winning season. Capped with Doig and full-back partner Andy McCombie in April 1903 – the only occasion three Sunderland players have played together for Scotland.

William Farquhar (1898-1907)

The beneficiary of Matthew Ferguson's tragically early demise from pneumonia in 1902 when he took over his position at half-back for the next four seasons after being previously used most frequently as a centre or inside-forward.

Sandy McAllister (1896-1904)

Arrived from Kilmarnock as the age of the 'Talents' was coming to an end. Debuted in the relegation averting Test Match victory in April 1897 and became a mainstay of the defence with his three ever-present seasons being the highest ever number for an outfield player and included the inaugural season at Roker Park and the title-winning season 1901-02.

Dicky Jackson (1898-1905)

Capable left-half and occasional left-back who signed from Middlesbrough and once established missed only five games in four years. A mainstay in the half-back line of the title-winning side in 1902-03 alongside McAllister and Ferguson and awarded a joint benefit with Billy Hogg in December 1904.

Billy Hogg (1899-1909)

Sunderland-born winger or centre-forward best known for his hat-trick in the 9-1 triumph at Newcastle in December 1908. One of Alex Mackie's first and best signings in 1899, his skill and speed belied his stature and he was joint top scorer in the title-winning season of 1901-02. Served as a coach at the club 1927-34.

George Holley (1904-19)

Charlie Buchan described being frequently 'spellbound' by the talent of this supreme ball artist from Seaham Harbour who apparently put four of Buchan's famous five goals against Liverpool 'on a plate'. A creator and a scorer from inside or centre-forward, he recorded 11 hat-tricks including one in the 9-1 derby win and scored eight goals for England, a club best.

Jimmy Gemmell (1900-07 & 1910-12)

Versatile Glaswegian who usually played centre or inside forward but also on occasion appeared in the backs. Linked effectively with Bridgett and was joint top scorer on two occasions – with Hogg in the title-winning side and with Millar and Joe Hewitt the following season.

Jimmy Millar (1890-90 & 1900-04)
See 1880s

Arthur Bridgett (1903-12)

Outstanding England international who is the most prolific winger to have played for the club. Pacy and direct, he top scored in consecutive seasons 1905-07 when the combined efforts of the various centre-forwards used could not match his tally of 44 goals. Scored in a club record nine successive matches in 1907.

1910-15

1	Joe Butler
2	Charlie Gladwin
3	Albert Milton
4	Frank Cuggy
5	Charlie Thomson
6	Harry Low
7	Jackie Mordue
8	Charlie Buchan
9	Jimmy Richardson
10	George Holley
11	Harry Martin

Joe Butler (1912-14)

A key signing, along with Gladwin, after a poor start to the 1912-13 season and 100 years later he retains the fewest goals conceded per game record for Sunderland goalkeepers who have played 50 top flight matches. One of only three Sunderland goalkeepers to win a top flight title-winner's medal.

Charlie Gladwin (1912-15)

Signed from Blackpool, this physically powerful full-back stiffened a shaky defence and provided a catalyst for the team's run of 25 wins in 31 games which took the Lads from 19th position in October 1912 to the top of the table by the following April.

Albert Milton (1908-14)

Yorkshire-man who became integral part of the famous 1912-13 team five years after making his debut with Jackie Mordue. The club won that game, 3-0 at Middlesbrough, and won their first five games with Milton at left-back including the historic 9-1 win at Newcastle.

Frank Cuggy (1909-21)

Tenacious right-half whose superb link-up play with Mordue and Buchan was an outstanding feature of the 1912-13 side. He was described by Buchan as 'the nearest thing to perpetual motion I ever saw'. World War One interrupted his career at its peak after he had earned an England cap.

Charlie Thomson (1908-15)

Gave seven years sterling service despite being almost 30 years old when signed from Hearts. Immense presence at centre-half especially when captaining the 1912-13 side, flanked by Cuggy and Low. The first Sunderland player to score for Scotland.

Harry Low (1907-19)

Mainly a left-half this gifted and versatile Aberdonian played in almost every position for the club, once registering a hat-trick as centre-forward. One of five debutants on September second 1907 and missed only one game in the 1912-13 title-winning campaign.

Jackie Mordue (1908-20)

Formed the flank of the famous right-wing triangle with Cuggy and Charlie Buchan that started 120 games for the Lads either side of World War One and featured in 40 of the 47 games played in 1912-13 when they also played together once for England. Scored in the record 9-1 win at Newcastle and added two more in the FA Cup second replay at St James in March 1913.

Charlie Buchan (1911-25)

Legendary inside-forward who hailed from London and became Sunderland's leading League goalscorer and sole top scorer on a club record seven occasions. During 1912-13 he became the first player to score five in a League game for the club and was top scorer in the country in 1922-23.

Jimmy Richardson (1912-14)

Prolific goalscorer, particularly in the FA Cup, in his short spell with the club, Richardson's wife could apparently not settle on Wearside hence his early return to Scotland. He scored four times in successive FA Cup first round matches and scored the goals that secured the club's fifth Championship title at Bolton on 26 April 1913.

George Holley (1904-19)
See 1900s

Harry Martin (1912-22)

Gained his place on the left-wing on Good Friday 1912 when Bridgett stood-down on religious grounds and then missed only one of the next 74 games. Long-striding with an excellent cross, he was ever-present during 1912-13 and was capped with Cuggy a year later.

1920s

1	**Albert McInroy**
2	**Warney Cresswell**
3	**Ernie England**
4	**Billy Clunas**
5	**Charlie Parker**
6	**Arthur Andrews**
7	**Bobby Marshall**
8	**Charlie Buchan**
9	**David Halliday**
10	**Arthur Hawes**
11	**Bill Ellis**

Note: Marshall played rarely on the right-wing but is included due to the lack of other outstanding contenders and his considerable success in the inside and centre-forward positions.

Albert McInroy (1923-30)

Manager Bob Kyle, fearing he would miss out on this Lancastrian goalkeeper, secured his signature in the toilets of the Grand Hotel in Manchester and he with McInroy went on to become one of the club's finest custodians and the only one to be capped by England while with Sunderland.

Warney Cresswell (1921-27)

The 'Prince of full-backs' whose classy, composed play on the right was a perfect complement to the no-nonsense style of Ernie England on the left. Signed for a British record fee of £5,500 from his native South Shields and later became the club's record sale.

Ernie England (1919-30)

Right-footer from Derbyshire but second only to Len Ashurst for appearances at left-back for the Lads. Most appearances without a goal for an outfielder for the club but gave sterling service in defence and was a master of the sliding tackle.

Billy Clunas (1923-31)

Dominant Scottish right-half who was a vital cog in the team that finished third three years out of four in the mid-1920s. His prowess from the spot helped him to the first double figures goal tally by a defender in the club's history and his best of 12 in 1928-29 was not surpassed for 59 years.

Charlie Parker (1920-29)

Born in Seaham Harbour six years after George Holley and signed for a big fee at a similar age to Charlie Thomson when also an established centre-half. Played at right-half initially but starred in the centre and later captained the team to successive third place finishes.

Arthur Andrews (1922-31)

Played on the left of the reliable half-back line of the mid 1920s with Parker and Billy Clunas. Sunderland-born, he made an immediate impact on replacing Jack Poole and was a consistent performer for seven seasons before the arrival of Alex Hastings.

Bobby Marshall (1920-28)

Inside-forward later turned centre-half from Nottingham who was versatile enough to appear in this line up on the right-wing, Sunderland's problem position in the 1920s. Top scored in 1924-25 playing at inside or centre-forward and notched 20 two seasons later from 34 games at inside-right.

Charlie Buchan (1912-25)
See 1910-15

David Halliday (1925-29)

Powerful centre-forward with a deadly left-foot and holder of Sunderland's individual scoring record for one season with 43 goals in 1928-29. Opened with 10 in his first four matches and his tally of 153 came at almost one per game. Recorded a club record 15 hat-tricks or four goal games and was said to be disappointed not to play with Buchan who left three months after he signed.

Arthur 'Tricky' Hawes (1921-27)

His two goal scoring debut coincided with stand-in centre-forward John Mitton scoring three and this native of Norfolk, signed from South Shields, progressed to an England trial match in 1925 when teammate Albert McInroy was in opposition. Played at inside-forward, opposite Buchan, usually holding a handkerchief.

Bill Ellis (1919-27)

Brummie left-winger who understudied then replaced Harry Martin and was a reliable supplier to Buchan and Jock Paterson in his first full season 1922-23 when the Lads finished second. Forged an effective partnership with Arthur Hawes and his speed and craft later provided many of David Halliday's goals.

1930s

1	**Jimmy Thorpe**
2	**Bill Murray**
3	**Alex Hall**
4	**Charlie Thomson**
5	**Bert Johnston**
6	**Alex Hastings**
7	**Bert Davis**
8	**Raich Carter**
9	**Bobby Gurney**
10	**Patsy Gallacher**
11	**Jimmy Connor**

Note: Jock McDougall and Harold Shaw were both just edged out by Johnston and Hall, the former by virtue of his involvement in the FA Cup winning side and the latter by slightly more appearances in the decade. Eddie Burbanks, scorer of the third Wembley goal in 1937 misses out due to Connor's brilliance.

Jimmy Thorpe (1930-36)

Jarrow-born goalkeeper and at the time of his debut at 17 the youngest player to appear for the Lads. Vied with the Middletons, Bob and Matt, for a regular place but had made 52 consecutive appearances when he tragically died five days after being injured against Chelsea during the 1935-36 title-winning season.

Bill Murray (1927-37)

Worthy successor to Warney Cresswell and the first former player to become full-time manager, giving the club a total of almost 30 years' service. Regular right-back for nine seasons, earning a League Championship winning medal in his last season.

Alex Hall (1929-39)

Initially understudied his fellow Scot, Bill Murray on the right but finally earned a regular place at left-back when aged 26 following injury to Harold Shaw in the first game of the Championship-winning season. One of six players to appear in every game of the 1937 FA Cup winning run.

Charlie Thomson (1931-40)

Uncannily similar in all but stature to the 1908-15 version and one of several excellent halfbacks signed from Scottish junior football in the early 1930s. Holds the club record for most consecutive appearances, the run only broken during the latter stages of the FA Cup run of 1937 when he was amongst several players rested.

Bert Johnston (1929-40)

Falkirk-born centre-half who had to be patient for a regular place until the departures of Jock MacDougall and Jimmy Clark but was an FA Cup winner in 1937. No senior goals until guesting in World War Two with four in three games for Hartlepools. Trainer for Sunderland 1951-57.

Alex Hastings (1930-46)

The last Sunderland captain to be presented with the 'top division' title winning trophy and a fine servant to the club at half-back where he had stiff competition from Sandy McNab who took his place for the 1937 FA Cup Final.

Bert Davis (1932-36)

Yorkshire man signed to fill the problem right-wing position and he was a regular for three years, becoming the first player for over 30 years to record consecutive ever-present seasons. Useful goalscorer, contributing 10 to the title-winning season before losing his place to the up and coming Len Duns.

Raich Carter (1931-45)

Sunderland-born and among the greatest players in the history of the game. An inside-forward with supreme passing and scoring ability with either foot who in 1933 swapped positions with Patsy Gallacher to great effect. Shared 62 goals with Gurney in the title winning season and recieved the FA Cup as captain at Wembley a year later.

Bobby Gurney (1925-46)

Thirteen goals in his first two reserve games heralded the start of an outstanding career for the Boy Gurney from County Durham. Top scorer for seven seasons at his peak between 1929-37, he holds the club all-time goal-scoring record, passing Buchan's total on Christmas Eve 1937 after signing professional two months before Buchan's departure.

Patsy Gallacher (1927-38)

Often used at inside-right early in his career, this talented forward in the best Scottish tradition blossomed on the left in the mid-1930s and was considered to be the best since Holley in that role. At his peak he notched 40 goals in 77 games in consecutive seasons 1934-36 and created many goals for Gurney and Raich Carter. His semi-final winning header took the Lads to Wembley in 1937.

Jimmy Connor (1930-39)

One of the most popular players in the club's history and the 1930s were lit up by his dazzling displays on the left wing and his powerful shooting. He and Charlie Thomson were the only ever-presents in the Championship-winning side and he won the most caps of all the 1930s Wearside Scots.

1946-50

1. Johnny Mapson
2. Jack Stelling
3. Arthur Hudgell
4. Willie Watson
5. Fred Hall
6. Arthur Wright
7. Len Duns
8. Ivor Broadis
9. Dickie Davis
10. Len Shackleton
11. Tommy Reynolds

Johnny Mapson (1936-54)

Signed to replace Jimmy Thorpe and after a confident debut at 18 years of age played in 140 of the next 144 games including the FA Cup Final win, achieved on the eve of his 20th birthday. Positionally sound, his post-war career included a major contribution to the Lads' title near miss in 1949-50.

Jack Stelling (1944-58)

Reliable right-back from Washington who was the regular partner of Arthur Hudgell in the immediate post-war seasons. He was ever-present during 1949-50 and had his twice taken penalty at home to Manchester City gone in the Lads would probably have been champions.

Arthur Hudgell (1947-57)

The first Londoner of note to sign since Buchan and the first of the post-war big money imports. Gave unsung service, usually at left-back and was first choice for five years.

Willie Watson (1946-54)

Converted from inside-forward to international class half-back and the only Sunderland player to have been selected for an England World Cup Finals squad in 1950. All of his four England caps were earned at Sunderland, literally in the case of his last, against Wales at Roker Park. He also won 14 of his 23 England cricket caps while on Wearside.

Fred Hall (1946-55)

Returned to his roots as a 29-year-old and captained the side in the early post-war years He was an intimidating physical presence at centre-half and recovered well from serious injuries to be ever-present during 1951-52.

Arthur Wright (1934-55)

Tremendous servant to the club firstly as a progressive left-half who debuted at 18 before World War Two and on retirement served as a trainer until he was 50. Possessed a fierce shot and formed an effective half-back line with Fred Hall and Willie Watson.

Len Duns (1933-52)

Arguably the best outside-right since Mordue and a title-winning medal at the age of 19 in his first season was followed with an FA Cup medal a year later. Created a goal for Carter within 10 minutes of his first game and two goals on his home debut were a prelude to an impressive haul of 21 in the Cup winning season.

Ivor Broadis (1949-51)

Notable post World War Two inside-forward whose potential in combination with Shackleton and Ford did not materialise but one of four players in double figures for goals in 1949-50 and one of his two hat-tricks the following season came in a memorable 5-3 win at Old Trafford.

Dickie Davis (1939-54)

Birmingham-born centre or inside-forward with the distinction of being the top flight's leading scorer in 1949-50, a feat not matched by a Sunderland player for another half century. Unfortunate to then lose his central position to Trevor Ford but continued to score regularly despite limited appearances.

Len Shackleton (1948-57)

Truly inspired ball-artist whose sublime skills at inside-forward didn't always fit into the team pattern but enthralled the big post-war crowds. Hailed from Bradford but signed from Newcastle and his post-war goal tally remained the highest for almost 27 years.

Tommy 'Tich' Reynolds (1946-54)

Winger from Felling who made an inauspicious start on the right but eventually gave good service on the left as Eddie Burbanks' successor. One of three ever-presents when the Lads just missed out on the title in 1949-50.

1950s

1. Willie Fraser
2. Jack Hedley
3. Joe McDonald
4. Stan Anderson
5. Ray Daniel
6. George Aitken
7. Billy Bingham
8. Charlie Fleming
9. Trevor Ford
10. Len Shackleton
11. Billy Elliott

Note: Tommy Wright would be substitute if they existed in the 1950s – his exclusion from the 11 is only due to the wealth of attacking talent available at the time.

Willie Fraser (1954-58)

Australian-born Scot, signed from Airdrie in 1954 and whose capable handling immediately improved the club's defensive performances. He was first choice, playing in both losing FA Cup semi-finals, during his first two full seasons and earned both his Scottish caps while on Wearside.

Jack Hedley (1950-59)

Solid full-back who played on either flank in his first four seasons and then exclusively on the right after the arrival of Joe MacDonald. The only ever-present in a settled side that finished fourth in 1954-55 and one of the 10 players to play in both of the consecutive FA Cup semi-final defeats.

Joe McDonald (1954-58)

Another Scot who was one of several signings that helped the club to avoid relegation in 1954. Part of a settled back division that performed well during the following campaign and only missed a handful of games in his first three seasons.

Stan Anderson (1952-64)

Exceptional wing-half and a rare local product who played alongside all the expensive 1950s players (except Broadis) but was the only established regular to play beyond the first season after relegation. Missed only three games out of 153 between February 1958 and September 1961 and starred in the 1961 FA Cup run.

Ray Daniel (1953-57)

Highly regarded Welsh international centre-half who was signed from Arsenal as part of a 1953 summer spending spree but enjoyed mixed fortunes on Wearside as the club's defence faltered. His best season was 1954-55 in combination with Fraser, MacDonald and Hedley and his 40 yard strike that won an FA Cup replay a year later proved his occasional usefulness as a forward.

George Aitken (1951-59)

A product of the successful post-war East Fife club, alongside Charlie Fleming and became a competitive yet constructive half-back who mainly played on the left for the Lads. Switched to centre-half to good effect as relegation was temporarily averted in 1957.

Billy Bingham (1950-58)

The first player to appear in the World Cup Finals while with Sunderland and played in every Northern Ireland game during his eight years on the right wing for the Lads. With Tommy Wright earning Scottish recognition the Lads had the first choice right-wingers for two of the home nations on their books in the early 1950s.

Charlie 'Cannonball' Fleming (1955-58)

Also known as 'Legs' due to a distinctive galloping gait. Endeared himself to the club's faithful with his first two goals coming at Newcastle, including an injury time winner. Quickest to 50 goals since David Halliday and third best post World War Two strike-rate. Died aged 70 on the eve of the first League game at the Stadium of Light.

Trevor Ford (1950-53)

Fearsome, battering-ram of a centre-forward with an excellent goals per game ratio that belies the fact that his time on Wearside was not considered his best. The only Sunderland player to score double figures of goals in internationals which came in just 13 games for Wales.

Len Shackleton (1948-57)
See 1946-50

Billy Elliott (1953-59)

Tough, uncompromising Yorkshireman signed at the peak of the club's 'Bank of England' spending in June 1953. Fast and direct, he was used on the left wing initially and later switched to left-half and left-back. Caretaker manager on two occasions and trainer of the 1973 FA Cup winning team.

1960s

1	Jim Montgomery
2	Cec Irwin
3	Len Ashurst
4	Martin Harvey
5	Charlie Hurley
6	Jimmy McNab
7	George Herd
8	Jim Baxter
9	Brian Clough
10	Johnny Crossan
11	George Mulhall
12	Colin Todd

Note: honourable mentions to centre-forwards Nick Sharkey and Neil Martin, both overshadowed by Clough.

Jim Montgomery (1958-77 & 1980-82)

Top of the all-time appearance list for the Lads and surely the finest goalkeeper not to be capped by England. Debuted at 17 and released prematurely at 33, his 1973 Wembley exploits provided just a glimpse to the wider public of his outstanding ability, regularly witnessed by Sunderland supporters.

Cec Irwin (1958-72)

Sunderland's youngest debutant at 16 when he took his bow with fellow youngsters Len Ashurst (19) and Jimmy McNab (18) in the first season after relegation. First choice during the 1963-64 promotion campaign and was a fine early example of the more forward thinking full-back.

Len Ashurst (1957-71)

Liverpudlian who holds the record for the most outfield appearances for the club. Thoroughly committed left-back who immediately established himself as a fixture in the side and missed just four games out of 220 between April 1960 and November 1964. Managed the club in 1984-85.

Martin Harvey (1957-73)

Understudied Anderson for four years before taking his place during the promotion season and dovetailed smoothly with Hurley and McNab at half-back. Also played left-back and remains the club's most capped Northern Ireland international.

Charlie Hurley (1957-69)

One of the all-time greats and Sunderland's most capped international. Dominant presence at centre-half and also the club's highest scoring defender. He endured the trauma of relegation and led the club back to the top flight in 1964. Voted 'Player of the Century' in the club's centenary year by supporters a decade after his departure in 1969.

Jimmy McNab (1956-67)

Another of Alan Brown's successful youthful introductions, this stylish Scot was a fixture at left-half for six seasons and was a key member of the side that earned the club's first ever promotion in 1964. Between them, the youthful debutants, McNab, Irwin and Ashurst, amassed 1,133 first team appearances for the Lads.

George Herd (1961-70)

Signed at his peak as Scottish International inside-right who could also play on the wing. An instant success, he was crucial to the promotion season, providing a personal best of 16 goals and numerous assists. Scored the first goal by a Sunderland substitute at Blackpool in Jan 1967 and two spells as youth team coach.

Jim Baxter (1965-67)

World class player blessed with such talent that he was, in the words of Billy Hughes, 'too clever for the rest of us'. Unforgettable when on song in his favoured left-half position, his Wearside form only sporadically touched the heights but he remained the club's most capped Scottish international for over 40 years.

Brian Clough (1961-64)

Already a goal per game striker when signed from Middlesbrough, his 34 goals in his first season was a post-war record and included five hat-tricks. He had actually improved his average, which ultimately was second only to David Halliday, when cruelly struck down by injury on Boxing Day 1962.

Johnny Crossan (1962-65)

The first player with European Cup experience signed by the club and the Derry man quickly became a crowd favourite, creating and scoring goals from inside-left. He was one of four ever-presents and top-scored with 27 goals in League and FA Cup during the successful promotion campaign .

George Mulhall (1962-69)

Stirling-born outside-left who reeled off 114 consecutive League appearances from his debut which included every game of the 1963-64 promotion season. Direct in style and an eye for goal shown by his half century haul.

Colin Todd (1964-71)

Half-back from Chester-le-Street who matured into one of England's finest central defenders and commanded the biggest fee for a defender at the time when he left the club to rejoin his former youth team coach Brian Clough at Derby. League ever-present in 1967-68, the season after his first team debut at 17.

1970s

1	**Jim Montgomery**
2	**Dick Malone**
3	**Joe Bolton**
4	**Dave Watson**
5	**Jeff Clarke**
6	**Ian Porterfield**
7	**Bobby Kerr**
8	**Billy Hughes**
9	**Vic Halom**
10	**Bryan Robson**
11	**Dennis Tueart**
12	**Kevin Arnott**

Note: Shaun Elliott and Gary Rowell made the majority of their appearances in the 1980s so miss out here. Barry Siddall, Ritchie Pitt and Tony Towers are other potential number 12s.

Jim Montgomery (1958-77 & 1980-82)
See 1960s

Dick Malone (1970-77)

'Super Dick' was Ayrshire born and was a fixture at right-back in the early 70s. He succeeded Irwin and showed similar attacking inclinations with storming, if ungainly, forward runs and accurate crossing. An effective defender, he saw off Leeds' main threat Eddie Gray in the 1973 FA Cup Final.

Joe Bolton (1970-81)

Accurately described as a 'rugged, strong-tackling defender' and a formidable barrier to opposition right-wingers in the 70s. Youth team product from Birtley who possessed a fierce shot that brought him nine goals from left-back, a record for a Sunderland full-back.

Dave Watson (1970-75)

Bought as a virtually unknown centre-forward, for the club's first £100,000 fee, he was converted by Billy Elliott into an international class centre-half and remains the club's most capped Englishman. Dominant in the air and man-of-the-match in the 1973 FA Cup Final.

Jeff Clarke (1975-82)

Yorkshire-born centre-half who arrived as part of the Dave Watson sale and matured alongside Bob Moncur in the 1975-76 title-winning side before forming an excellent partnership with Shaun Elliott that underpinned another promotion success in 1980.

Ian Porterfield (1967-77)

Elegant midfielder who strongly favoured the left-side but a rare strike with his right foot was responsible for one of the most famous goals in the club's history at Wembley in 1973. Made 227 appearances in the 1970s despite first team exile in 1969-70 and serious injury in 1974.

Bobby Kerr (1963-79)

The 'Little General' captained the 1973 FA Cup winning side and recovered from twice breaking his leg to become a virtual ever-present in midfield, missing just two matches between 1972-76. Joint top scorer in 1970-71, he and Gordon Armstrong are the only two midfielders in the last 40 years to score 50 goals for the Lads.

Billy Hughes (1965-77)

Direct and versatile Scottish forward who could play centrally or wide and top scored in 1972-73 when his personal best of 19 goals included the decisive second in the FA Cup semi-final. The following season he scored the club's first ever goal in a European tie.

Vic Halom (1973-76)

Strong and aggressive centre-forward who played with a smile. He was the third and final player signed by Bob Stokoe who made the FA Cup Final squad and scored a magnificent Fifth Round replay goal against Manchester City.

Bryan 'Pop' Robson (1974-76, 1979-81 & 1983-84)

Classy forward and superb finisher who was top scorer in each of his three full seasons at his home-town club when the Lads were twice promoted. In 1983-84 he was caretaker manager for one game and also set the current record for the oldest player to score a first team goal for the Lads. Later he had three spells on the backroom staff.

Dennis Tueart (1966-74)

Exciting, two-footed left-winger with excellent shooting ability who played in the Youth Cup winning team of 1967 and was a shining light in the struggling team of the late 1960s. 138 of his 214 appearances came between 1971-74 when he scored an impressive and often spectacular 44 goals.

Kevin Arnott (1974-82)

Gateshead midfielder whose introduction as an 18-year-old in January 1977, along with Elliott and Mick Docherty coincided with a remarkable upturn in the club's fortunes . His ability on the ball and eye for a pass peaked during the 1979-80 promotion season when one of his eight goals was the first in the decisive last home game.

1980s

1	**Chris Turner**
2	**Barry Venison**
3	**Nick Pickering**
4	**Gary Bennett**
5	**Shaun Elliott**
6	**Gordon Armstrong**
7	**Gary Owers**
8	**Gary Rowell**
9	**Eric Gates**
10	**Marco Gabbiadini**
11	**Stan Cummins**
12	**Gordon Chisholm**

Note: Mark Proctor, Mick Buckley and Ian Atkins are other substitute contenders.

Chris Turner (1979-85)

Brave and agile Sheffield-born goalkeeper who initially competed with Barry Siddall for his place but was undisputed number one from 1982-85 and ever-present in two consecutive seasons. Excelled in a struggling team in 1984-85 and saved four out of six penalties faced including a brilliant full-length effort at Tottenham in a League Cup replay.

Barry Vension (1979-86)

The youngest ever player to score a top-flight goal for the Lads when he volleyed a superb winner at Man City two months after his debut at 17 in Oct 1981. Better known for his effective displays at right-back where he was a regular between 1983-85 and from where he captained the team at Wembley in 1985.

Nick Pickering (1979-86)

Energetic left-footer who debuted in midfield at 18, in Alan Durban's first game as manager, and starred in the late season recovery that kept the Lads in the top flight. Capped by England at left-back before becoming a regular number three for the club in 1983-84.

Gary Bennett (1984-95)

A loyal and steadying influence during turbulent times and made more appearances at centre-half than any other player in the club's history. His tally of 25 goals is second only to Charlie Hurley's total for a defender and included many memorable strikes including the fastest debut goal since World War Two. Three Wembley visits with the club and a title-winning captain in 1987-88.

Shaun Elliott (1974-86)

Outstanding central defender whose speed and anticipation complemented the aerial strength of especially Jeff Clarke and later Rob Hindmarch and Gordon Chisholm. Won an England 'B' cap for his excellent form during the promotion season of 1979-80 when he switched to midfield for the run-in.

Gordon Armstrong (1983-96)

Made his bow at centre-half but made his name as a goal-scoring centre or left-sided midfielder. His dramatic winner in the 1992 FA Cup replay win over Chelsea highlighted his aerial prowess and his durability was shown by his missing just one game out of 113 played in two seasons 1988-90.

Gary Owers (1985-94)

Athletic and competitive right-sided midfielder or full-back who won a title-winning medal in his first season, having debuted in the club's first ever third tier League game. Contributed nine goals towards the 1989-90 promotion campaign and his solitary top flight goal was the prelude to Benno's famous winner against Man United.

Gary Rowell (1972-84)

Only the second player to score 100 post World War Two goals for the Lads and at his peak touted for England as a goal-scoring midfielder in the mould of Martin Peters. Also played up front and top scorer in six out of seven seasons 1977-84 with a best return of 21 in 1978-79. Career tally of 48 top flight goals was the highest since Charlie Fleming.

Eric Gates (1985-90)

Ferryhill born striker who, alongside Marco Gabbiadini, formed one of the most cohesive and potent strike partnership for the club prior to Quinn and Phillips. The pair shared 42 goals during the promotion season 1987-88 and two years later both scored at Newcastle in the Play-offs in their penultimate match together.

Marco Gabbiadini (1987-91)

Made his mark during the darkest period in the club's recent history and quickly developed into one of the most exciting players of modern times. Strength and speed allied to powerful finishing saw him record six goals in three games following his debut and he became the first player since the days of Carter and Gurney to finish top scorer in four consecutive seasons.

Stan Cummins (1979-83 & 1984-85)

A diminutive live-wire on the left-wing who boosted the club's promotion effort after signing in late 1979 and often lifted a struggling team back in the top flight with inspired moments of individual skill. Ever-present in 1980-81 and contributed 10 goals.

Gordon Chisholm (1977-85)

One of six players to debut for the club in the Anglo-Scottish Cup and marked his debut season with a stunning volley to open a goal account that later included several useful Cup goals. Robust and under-rated Glaswegian centre-half who started his career in mdifield.

1990s

1	**Tony Norman**
2	**Dariusz Kubicki**
3	**Michael Gray**
4	**Andy Melville**
5	**Richard Ord**
6	**Paul Bracewell**
7	**Nicky Summerbee**
8	**Kevin Ball**
9	**Niall Quinn**
10	**Kevin Phillips**
11	**Allan Johnston**

Subs (2)
John Kay, Alex Rae

Note: Michael Bridges, the club's most used and highest scoring substitute, misses out due to the appearance count of Kay and Rae.

Tony Norman (1988-95)

Arrived as a record signing involving his predecessor Iain Hesford and became first choice goalkeeper, ahead of Tim Carter, for four years before sharing the role with Alec Chamberlain. Consistent and technically sound with his five penalty saves being the best tally since Monty and gave stand-out performances in the 1990 Play-off Final and 1992 FA Cup run.

Dariusz Kubicki (1994-97)

Polish-born and polished performer at right-back where he was secure in defence and a willing over-lapping runner as seen in March 1996 when Michael Bridges headed in his inch-perfect cross to seal a dramatic win over Huddersfield. Ever-present from signing until controversially dropped 3½ years and 124 games later.

Michael Gray (1990-2004)

Sunderland-born left-back or wing who missed the vital penalty at Wembley in 1998 but drew on the great character shown earlier in his career when left out of the side to perform magnificently in partnership with Allan Johnston as the Lads stormed to promotion in 1999. Capped by England and has the twin club records of most Premier League (170) and most SOL appearances (125).

Andy Melville (1993-99)

The club's most capped Welsh international and a sound performer at centre-half. Part of a defence that conceded the third fewest goals in 1994-95, despite the team finishing 20th, and improved to finish top on both counts the following season when he partnered Richard Ord. Played alongside Paul Butler in 1998-99 when the club record of lowest average goals conceded in a season was set.

Richard Ord (1986-98)

Dickie from Murton was a young debutant in the Lads' biggest win for 31 years and his enthusiastic, yet cultured, play from centre or left-back made him a cult hero with a song recorded in his honour. Key member of the miserly defence that underpinned the 1995-96 title winning campaign.

Paul Bracewell (1983-84, 1989-92 & 1995-97)

An accomplished holding midfielder whose three spells at the club encompassed pivotal roles firstly in Alan Durban's promising side and then the promotion teams assembled by Denis Smith and Peter Reid. Also served as Reid's assistant manager and captained the side at Wembley in 1992.

Nicky Summerbee (1997-2001)

Purveyor of old-fashioned wing play who was a chief provider for the 108 goal 1998-99 promotion campaign and then enjoyed a good half-season as the Lads climbed to third place in the top tier. goalscorer in extra-time at Wembley in 1998 and arguably the club's best right-winger since Bingham.

Kevin Ball (1990-99)

Courage and commitment were the bywords for the Hastings-born central-defender turned ball-winning midfielder. One of the club's finest ever captains who led the side to promotion in 1996 and 1999 and has since become an invaluable member of the backroom staff, taking over as reserve team coach in July 2012.

Niall Quinn (1996-2002)

Uniquely player, coach, manager and chairman and hugely influential figure since firstly impressing as a first-class target man with supreme heading ability and deft ball skills. At its peak his lethal partnership with Kevin Phillips yielded 128 League goals in three seasons and later his off the field efforts were integral to the stabilising of the club following relegation in 2006.

Kevin Phillips (1997-2003)

Sunderland's highest post World War Two scorer in League and FA Cup and one of only five players to score 30 goals in the top flight since the fixtures were reduced to 38 in 1995. Quick, incisive and perfectly in tune with Quinn, he also holds the post World War Two seasonal record with 35 goals in 1997-98. Under used by England after winning the first of eight England caps with Michael Gray.

Allan Johnston (1997-99)

Primarily right-footed, 'Magic' was a skilful left-winger who excelled during the first two seasons at the SOL, combining effectively with Michael Gray. A useful goalscorer, he netted the last League goal at Roker Park, was one of four players in double figures in 1997-98 and is the only Sunderland player to have two goals for Scotland to his credit.

John Kay (1987-96)

Of the 16 players to play in the top three tiers for the club he and John MacPhail have the most appearances in the lowest League, being the only ever-presents in 1987-88. Locally-born, fiercely competitive right-back and a Denis Smith bargain signing to rival Gabbiadini and MacPhail.

Alex Rae (1996-2001)

Stop-start Sunderland career but at his best a combative attacking central midfielder whose form peaked in late 2001 when partnered with Darren Williams or Gavin McCann as the Lads won eight games from 10 to move to second in the table. Scored twice in the biggest Sunderland win at the SOL in September 1998.

2000s

1	**Thomas Sorensen**
2	**Darren Williams**
3	**George McCartney**
4	**Jody Craddock**
5	**Danny Collins**
6	**Dean Whitehead**
7	**Steed Malbranque**
8	**Gavin McCann**
9	**Darren Bent**
10	**Kevin Phillips**
11	**Julio Arca**

Subs (3)
Stefan Schwarz, Claudio Reyna, Marcus Stewart

Note: Don Hutchison, Phil Bardsley and Kieran Richardson are other substitute contenders.

Thomas Sorensen (1998-2003)

Danish international with the lowest average goals conceded of all goalkeepers to have played 100+ games for the club. Excellent handling and shot-stopping ability with a club record of 29 clean sheets in his debut season 1998-99 and the best of four penalty saves assuring his Wearside immortality in November 2000.

Darren Williams (1996-2004)

Middlesbrough-born utility player who enjoyed his best spells in the centre of a young back-four, unchanged for 15 unbeaten games in 1997-98, and as a central midfielder or right-back during early 2000-01 when the Lads lost only once in 16 games.

George McCartney (1997-2006 & 2008-12)

Youth team product who firmly established himself in 2003-04 with 42 consecutive starts, initially in the centre then at left-back where he excelled behind Arca in the following title season. Goalless in 203 first team games but scored on his Northern Ireland debut just seven games into his club career.

Jody Craddock (1997-2003)

Talented centre-half who first impressed during the Lads revival during 1997-98 when he played 30 consecutive games mainly alongside Darren Holloway, Michael Gray and Darren Williams. Formed a solid partnership with Emerson Thome in 2000-01 and has more top flight appearances (108) than any other Sunderland centre-half in the last 30 years.

Danny Collins (2004-09)

Reliable and determined left-sided centre-back or left-back whose form blossomed under Roy Keane and was a key member of the 2006-07 title winning campaign. His popularity was later rewarded by consecutive SAFCSA player-of-the-season awards and he is the only player to have made his debut for Wales while with the club.

Dean Whitehead (2004-09)

One of several astute signings from the lower Leagues that engineered the club's return to the top flight in 2005. Industrious midfielder and occasional right-back who missed just four games out of 137 between August 2004 and May 2007. Captained the side 2007-09 after taking over from Steven Caldwell.

Steed Malbranque (2008-11)

Gifted Frenchman with adhesive close control who provided a touch of class in the Lads' midfield, either playing centrally or on either flank. Linked effectively with compatriot Djibril Cisse in his first season and later provided opportunities for his former Spurs teammate Darren Bent.

Gavin McCann (1998-2003)

Competitive midfielder who was a regular during the Lads' fine spells of top-flight form in early 1999-00 and mid 2000-01. Best known for his work-rate and tackling but scored the occasional brilliant goal such as at Arsenal in Dec 2000 and against Blackburn in February 2003.

Darren Bent (2009-11)

Predatory goalscorer whose excellent chance conversion rate brought him 25 goals in his first season – the highest return and first top flight hat-trick since Phillips in 1999-2000 and five consecutive top flight scoring games for first time in over 40 years. Sixth best strike-rate for top flight matches in club's history and the first Sunderland player to score for England in nearly 56 years.

Kevin Phillips (1997-03)

See 1990s

Julio Arca (2000-06)

Wonderfully talented Argentine and one of the most popular players in recent decades. Technically superb at left-back or midfield and scorer of probably the finest goal scored by a Sunderland full-back at Bradford in August 2003. Scored nine goals in the title-winning campaign of 2004-05.

Stefan Schwarz (1999-2003)

Added international experience to the Lads midfield when signing aged 30 for a then club record fee following promotion in 1999. Allied crisp passing to decisive tackling and the occasional superb goal but injuries limited his appearances.

Claudio Reyna (2001-03)

United States international midfielder who was one of five Sunderland players to appear in the 2002 World Cup Finals. Signed for a club record equalling fee of £4.5 million and he brought composure to a struggling team. Scored two superb goals in a vital win over Leicester but his stay at the club was curtailed by injury.

Marcus Stewart (2002-05)

Recovered from difficult start in 2002-03 to finish top League goalscorer in the following two seasons. Whole-hearted striker who formed effective partnerships with Kevin Kyle and Stephen Elliott and in 2004-05 became just the second player in 38 years to record two hat-tricks in one season.

THE SAFC BADGE

Sunderland's club badge is headed by a colliery winding gear wheel, which acknowledges that the Stadium of Light stands on what was once Wearmouth Colliery. This also acknowledges the role mining has played in the lives of the people of the North-East, from where Sunderland draws its support. A replica colliery wheel also stands outside the West Stand of the stadium.

The central shield of the crest is split into quarters. Two of these show the red and white stripes that are synonymous with Sunderland. The remaining quarters feature two important landmarks. In the top left quarter Penshaw Monument signifies that Sunderland's support is drawn from beyond the centre of Sunderland. Visible from a considerable distance, Penshaw Monument is also a sign to travellers that they are nearly home.

In the remaining quarter is a silhouette of part of the Wearmouth Bridge; as synonymous with Sunderland as red and white stripes. Beneath it flows the River Wear on its journey from Upper Weardale to the North Sea. Supporters from the club's heartlands of support in County Durham also follow the path of the river to watch their team.

The Stadium of Light is but a few decent goal kicks away from Wearmouth Bridge, which links both sides of Sunderland: the south side where the club was born and the north side where it has resided for the vast majority of its history.

Two black lions at the sides of the crest also feature on the City of Sunderland's coat of arms and provide a reference to the tradition of mutual support between two great institutions.

The club motto – unveiled with this badge in 1997 – is 'Consectatio Excellentiae' which translates from the Latin as 'In Pursuit of Excellence.'

Matches to Remember

16 April 1892
Sunderland 6 Blackburn Rovers 1

Football League
This was the game in which Sunderland sealed their first League Championship. It was the fourth season of The Football League and Sunderland's second as members. Slaughtering glamour outfit Blackburn who had won the FA Cup in the previous two years was a fine way to seal the title. Winning their first national honour began a period of dominance by the Lads who would be champions twice more and runners up once in the next three seasons. Additionally this victory completed a 100% home record that to date no other side have ever matched – Sunderland's point at Manchester City in 2011-12 protecting their own record as mega rich City swept all but Sunderland before them. Moreover 48 hours after this stunning victory in 1892 Sunderland scored another six goals in a 'Friendly' against bitter local rivals Sunderland Albion. It was the death knell for Albion, hammered by Sunderland who were now champions of the Football League they had dreamed of joining themselves.

It was the last season of the single tier Football League. A Second Division was formed at a meeting in The Queen's hotel in Sunderland during the summer and in retaining their title the following season the Wearsiders became not only the last ever winners of the single tier Football League but also the first ever winners of Division One. It was another 6-1 win in September of that season – duly inflicting Aston Villa's record home Football League defeat – that caused Villa chairman William McGregor – the founder of the Football League no less – to say that Sunderland had a talented man in every position giving rise to the epithet 'The Team of All The Talents' Indeed they were and the win over Blackburn to bring the title to the North East for the first time (Only Preston and Everton had previously been champions) established Sunderland as the dominant force in the country. From that day on Sunderland have also held more League titles to their name than any other club in the North East meaning that in what has become known as 'The Hotbed of Soccer' the Black Cats have always been top dogs.

Still the club's fourth top goalscorer of all time – with 24 more goals than Kevin Phillips and in 20 fewer appearances – Johnny Campbell was the hero of the day with four goals, the opener coming after a mere eight minutes when he converted a cross from John Smith who thus marked his final appearance for the Lads.

Rovers – for whom centre-forward James Cockshutt made his solitary appearance in this match-made a fight of it equalising when Coomb Hall headed past Ted Doig (who had played one game for Blackburn in a 9-1 win over Notts County in 1889) but Jimmy Millar (who three years later would become the first man to score five goals in one game for the club) immediately restored the lead after being set up by Hugh Wilson. Although some contemporary reports credit David Hannah with Sunderland's third goal it was officially given to Campbell who added to his haul after the break with two more goals both coming from corners he headed past Blackburn 'keeper Herbie Arthur. Two minutes from time Jimmy 'Blood' Hannah (no relation to David) completed the scoring with Sunderland's sixth goal. It could have been worse for the visitors to Newcastle Road as Sunderland had hit the woodwork four times!

Sunderland: Doig, Porteous, Gow, Wilson, Gibson, Murray, Hannah J., Smith, Campbell, Millar, Hannah D.
Blackburn Rovers: Arthur, McKeown, Forbes, Almond, Dewar, Stringfellow, Walton, Campbell, Cockshutt, Hall, Chippendale.
Referee: Mr R.H. Lythgoe, (Liverpool)
Attendance: 10,000

26 April 1897

Sunderland 2 Newton Heath 0

Test Match (Play-off)
Modern-day Play-offs were introduced in 1987, but in the early days of the game a similar series of fixtures called 'Test Matches' existed from 1893 to 1898. The only time Sunderland were involved in these was in 1897, when the teams at the bottom of the First Division 'played off' in a series of games against those at the top of the Second. This was the last of Sunderland's four matches. A draw and a defeat had been registered against Notts County, while the first game at Newton Heath, who became known as Manchester United five years later, had been drawn 1–1. This was a game Sunderland needed to win!

Prior to the game a trumpeter livened up the crowd by playing *The Campbells Are Coming*. This was in honour of forward Johnny Campbell, one of a quintet of The Team of All The Talents playing his final game for Sunderland. However, it was another Scot, James Gillespie, who marked his final appearance by becoming the hero with both goals in a vital victory that meant Sunderland survived their first skirmish with relegation.

Sunderland won the toss and kicked off at 6pm, attacking the west goal. They had the best of the opening encounters, Harvie twice going close. After 15 minutes, Wilson passed the ball to Morgan and his cross was headed in by Gillespie to put Sunderland into the lead. Following the goal the pace continued to be fast and exciting, Jenkyns shooting narrowly wide for the Heathens.

Immediately after the interval Barrett saved well from Morgan as Sunderland looked to extend their lead. As the match wore on the 8,000 crowd were on tenterhooks as the game remained finely balanced until Gillespie scored his 54th and final goal for the club. When the final whistle blew the crowd came onto the pitch and chaired the victorious players off the ground. After three League titles earlier in the decade this was the first time supporters had experienced the sheer relief of avoiding the drop.

Sunderland: Doig, McNeill, Gow, Ferguson, McAllister, H. Wilson, J. Gillespie, Harvie, Morgan, Hannah, Campbell.
Newton Heath: Barrett, Doughty, Errentz, Draycott, Jenkyns, McNaught, Bryant, Donaldson, Boyd, M. Gillespie, Cassidy.
Referee: T. Helme (Farnsworth)
Attendance: 8,000

---

5 December 1908
Newcastle United 1 Sunderland 9

Division 1

The football result of all football results. Newcastle United 1, Sunderland 9. It cannot be said too many times. Sunderland supporters never tire of hearing it. In the history of the game it has only once been equalled as the record away win in the top flight of English football (by Wolves at Cardiff in 1955).

What makes the result even more astonishing is that Newcastle went on to win the Championship in this season. Sunderland played the football of the gods, scoring eight goals in 28 second-half minutes, the Magpies having equalised with a penalty on the stroke of half-time. There were hat-tricks for George Holley and Billy Hogg, two members of a five-man Sunderland forward line who all won England caps during their careers. Hogg opened the scoring in the eighth minute, dribbling from the halfway line before shooting past Jimmy Lawrence. The equaliser, which proved to be a mere consolation for the Magpies, came from a hotly disputed penalty decision of handball against centre-half Charlie Thomson, which home debutant and England cap Albert Shepherd converted past the celebrated L.R. Roose in the Sunderland goal.

Perhaps it was the feeling of injustice over that decision that fired Sunderland up even more in the second half. Just three minutes after the restart George Holley restored the lead after a breathtaking run by left-winger Arthur Bridgett. Ten minutes later it was 3–1 when Hogg got his second goal as Sunderland's domination became total.

Within another 10 minutes Holley had become the first to reach his hat-trick, helping himself to goals in the 63rd and 67th minutes, the latter from a Jackie Mordue cross.

Back at Roker Park, the crowd watching Sunderland Reserves cheered each of these goals as they were announced on the hand-operated scoreboard. However, when within another four minutes two more goals were credited to Sunderland, the crowd on Wearside threatened the scoreboard operator, believing he was making it up. But it was true. Within four minutes of Holley making the scoreline 5–1, Bridgett had scored twice with blistering shots from outside the penalty area.

Amazingly Sunderland scored twice more in the next five minutes before 'declaring' at 9–1 with 14 minutes still to play. Mordue added his name to the scoresheet in the 73rd minute before Hogg completed the second hat-trick of the game. Newcastle later knocked Sunderland out of the FA Cup, but a League double was completed when United were defeated 3–1 at Roker Park late in the season, in which Sunderland finished third.

There have been many great games between the old rivals from the Wear and the Tyne but none to match this – a match that must rank as the black and whites' blackest day but one of the red and whites' greatest.

Newcastle United: Lawrence, Whitson, Pudan, Liddell, Veitch, Willis, Duncan, Higgins, Shepherd, Wilson, Gosnell.
Sunderland: Roose, Forster, Milton, Daykin, Thomson, Low, Mordue, Hogg, Brown, Holley, Bridgett.
Referee: A.E. Farrant (Bristol)
Attendance: 56,000

5 May 1928

Middlesbrough 0 Sunderland 3

Division 1

Most Sunderland supporters would trade 10 wins over Middlesbrough for one over Newcastle, as the Wear-Tyne rivalry is felt more deeply than that with the Tees, but this was undoubtedly the most important Middlesbrough v Sunderland match ever played.

It was the last match of the season and the losers were certain to be relegated. A draw would be enough to keep the home side up and condemn Sunderland, who had never been out of the top flight.

An astonishingly tight table saw only two points separate the bottom 11 teams in the First Division. The North East duo were two of four locked at the bottom on 37 points. Sunderland had thrown away a 2–0 lead to lose 3–2 the previous Saturday at home to another team now also on 37 points, Sheffield Wednesday. Goalkeeper Paddy Bell had taken the blame for that crucial defeat so first choice Albert McInroy was patched and strapped up to take his place, though he was far from fully fit.

Long-serving manager Bob Kyle had already resigned and so, with the new manager-in-waiting Johnny Cochrane watching in the Ayresome Park stands, the task of supervising the Sunderland team fell to trainer Billy Williams, a servant of the club since 1897. Williams made major changes to the team from the previous week but was handicapped by the absence through injury of centre-forward Bobby Gurney.

On a baking hot day, Boro battered Sunderland but could find no way past Albert 'the Great' McInroy. The game took place 45 years to the day before Sunderland's famous 1973 FA Cup Final triumph over Leeds, which featured Jimmy Montgomery's miraculous 'double' save. Here McInroy made a double save just as spectacular to push Jacky Carr's effort onto the post and then spin back to thwart Bobby Bruce's follow up. Soaking up pressure at one end, Sunderland had stung Boro with a sucker punch of a goal on the break, taking the lead in the thirteenth minute through David Wright, who made the most of an isolated attack.

The Teessiders continued to bombard Sunderland in the second half but two goals in five minutes sent the Boro back down to the Second Division they had won the year before. Dave Halliday and then Wright with his second on the hour mark let Sunderland breathe easily, the win taking the Lads above Boro and the unfortunate Spurs, who were without a game, having completed their fixtures earlier, and were therefore powerless to prevent the drop as a series of results conspired against them.

Sunderland finished in 15th place (out of 22), one of seven teams on 39 points, only five behind fourth-placed Derby County. It was the end of an era as Cochrane took over in the summer. Sunderland's side of the mid-twenties had achieved nothing like the success of The Team of All The Talents of the 1890s, although they had been in the top three in four out of the previous five seasons. Like the Talents, though, the team of the twenties had ended the era by heroically avoiding relegation and Sunderland's proud record of only playing top-flight football would survive for another three full decades.

Middlesbrough: Mathieson, Jarvis, Smith, Miller, Ferguson, Peacock, Pease, J. Carr, Camsell, Bruce, Williams.
Sunderland: McInroy, Murray, England, Clunas, Allan, Andrews, Robinson, Wright, Halliday, Hargreaves, Death.
Referee: T.G. Bryan (Willenhall)
Attendance: 41,997

8 March 1933

Sunderland 0 Derby County 1 (aet)

FA Cup sixth-round replay
This game is famous for its attendance. The crowd of 75,118 is 7,000 higher than the second greatest attendance ever recorded at a game in the North-East, although it is commonly believed that Sunderland exceeded it in 1964 for a game against Manchester United. That game officially had a crowd of only 46,727, but tens of thousands poured in without paying after gates were pulled down.

In both 1933 and 1964 the reason for these astonishing crowds was the traditional magic of the FA Cup: both of these games were quarter-final replays. Sunderland had drawn 4–4 at Derby to set up this replay and three decades later went into the Manchester United replay on the back of a dramatic 3–3 draw at Old Trafford.

A nostalgic view of thirties football is to envisage fluent, attacking football played in a traditionally sporting manner. Rubbish! This was as ugly a game as you might see in the modern era on a bad day. Rough house tactics were applied by both teams, with Sunderland

The record crowd at Roker Park, for a match v Derby in 1933.

centre-forward Bobby Gurney, who had scored twice in the first game at County's Baseball Ground, led off in agony at one point after being smashed into by Derby's Jack Barker.

Substitutes, of course, were so far off that they were not introduced until after that Manchester United tie over 30 years later, so Gurney, being the wholehearted hero he always was, came back on to attempt to make up the numbers, but he was little more than a passenger in a game that eventually went to extra-time.

Earlier in the game Gurney had thought he'd put Sunderland into the lead, the referee Mr Gould signalling a goal when Gurney found the back of the net midway through the first half, only for a late offside flag to cut short the crowd's celebrations.

Right-winger Bert Davis missed Sunderland's best chance, lifting a shot over the bar after good work by the left-wing combination of Jimmy Connor and Raich Carter. Playing at inside-left, Carter too passed up a good chance as Sunderland had the better of the first half as they attacked the Roker End.

Spurred on by ex-Durham City player Sammy Crooks, Derby came into the game more after half-time but the match remained a scrappy affair with many stoppages, sometimes caused by the squashed crowd keeping the ball in protest at others blocking their view.

The massive attendance had been pressed up close to the touchlines since the start of the game, the police doing their best to keep the pitch free of spectators. Such was the crowd that the game had kicked off 15 minutes early because of fears of people being crushed.

Sunderland pressed for a late winner, with Gallacher bringing a good save out of 'keeper Kirby and Derby surviving an almighty scramble in their penalty area, but the game was finally settled in extra-time with the only goal of the game coming from visiting inside-left Peter Ramage. Derby lost out to Manchester City in the semi-final and had to wait until the first post-World War Two Cup Final to win the trophy for the first time, when Raich Carter won his second Cup-winner's medal to add to the one he won with Sunderland in 1937.

Sunderland: Thorpe, Murray, Shaw, Thomson, McDougall, Edgar, Davis, Gallacher, Gurney, Carter, Connor.
Derby County: Kirby, Cooper, Collin, Nicholas, Barker, Keen, Crooks, Fabian, Bowers, Ramage, Duncan.
Referee: G.T. Gould
Attendance: 75,118

30 January 1935
Everton 6 Sunderland 4 (aet)

FA Cup fourth-round replay

Sunderland and Everton had already shared 15 goals in two League games on Christmas Day and Boxing Day. Sunderland had led the table for most of the first half of the season, but suffered a first away defeat of the season when they were walloped 6–2 at Goodison on Christmas Day. Revenge was swiftly extracted with a 7–0 home win over the same opposition 24 hours later.

Paired together a month later in the Cup, the original tie at Roker proved to be a scrappy game. Raich Carter gave Sunderland the lead, only for Nat Cunliffe to equalise late on when Everton were briefly down to 10 men due to the legendary Dixie Dean being off the field changing a pair of torn shorts. Of the 13 goals Everton scored against Sunderland in 1934–35 Dean scored just one, failing to get on the scoresheet in this 10-goal thriller.

Jackie Coulter was the home hero with a hat-trick. The Irishman had Everton two goals up in the opening half hour. Connor hit the bar for Sunderland between Coulter's first two goals but the Wearsiders were rewarded when Connor's 40th-minute cross was converted by Bert Davis.

The score remained 2–1 until Alex Stevenson looked to have wrapped things up for the Toffees with a third goal 15 minutes from time, only for Connor to quickly pull one back. Sunderland pressed hard for an equaliser and, with just seconds to go, Bobby Gurney scored a goal that ranks among the finest of the 228 he scored in the Sunderland colours he wore with such pride. Gurney gave home 'keeper Ted Sagar no chance with an acrobatic overhead kick to take the pulsating tie into extra-time.

Coulter completed his hat-trick but Sunderland were level again when, with a move that reversed the roles from the team's first goal, Connor powered home a cross from Davis. Sunderland were on top at this stage with the score at 4–4 and for a split second looked to have gone ahead when Gallacher beat Sagar only to have the tightest of offside decisions given against him. Had that goal stood the Lads might have gone through to the next round, but it was Everton who marched on thanks to two late goals from winger Albert Geldard.

Everton: Sagar, Cook, Jones, Britten, Gee, J. Thomson, Geldard, Cunliffe, Dean, Stevenson, Coulter.
Sunderland: Thorpe, Murray, Hall, C. Thomson, Johnston, Hastings, Davis, Carter, Gurney, Gallacher, Connor.
Referee: E. Pinkston (Birmingham)
Attendance: 59,213

28 December 1935

Sunderland 5 Arsenal 4

Division 1

The 1973 FA Cup fifth-round replay with Manchester City took the accolade of Roker Park's 'greatest ever match' when Roker Park closed in 1997, but had more people who saw this match been alive to vote there is every chance that this classic game, between two great sides of one of football's finest decades, would have been duly recognised as an even greater game!

Arsenal were defending champions, having won the Championship for the past three seasons. Sunderland had been runners-up the season before and this year would take the title away from Highbury at long last. At the start of the game Sunderland were top of the table, five points ahead of the second-placed Gunners.

Both sides included some of the greatest players of the era: Raich Carter, Jimmy Connor and Bobby Gurney for the Wearsiders, Cliff Bastin, Ted Drake and Eddie Hapgood for the Gunners.

Over 58,000 were squeezed into Roker Park on the Saturday between Christmas and New Year on a wet and wild day that made the pitch fast and the football fierce rather than fluent.

Modern-day supporters recall the 1999 match with Chelsea where Sunderland raced into a 4–0 lead. It was 4–1 at half-time against Arsenal in 1935, but Sunderland still needed to score again after the Gunners blasted back in the second half.

Right-winger Bert Davis made the early running, giving Sunderland the lead in the seventh minute and setting up the second for Patsy Gallacher 10 minutes later, the visitors having had a goal from Pat Beasley disallowed in between. Arsenal, however, halved the deficit midway through the first half with a Cliff Bastin penalty.

Carter and Gurney would be joint top scorers with 31 goals each in that Championship-winning season and the pair of great pals combined 10 minutes before the break when Carter netted with a low drive after good work from Gurney. Carter scored again on the stroke of half-time, beating Frank Moss with a penalty conceded by Herbie Roberts.

Arsenal were not reigning champions for nothing and fought back. Five minutes after the restart Sandy McNab scored an own goal in trying to prevent an inevitable goal from Drake, who a fortnight earlier had scored a record seven goals in a First Division match against Villa.

MATCHES TO REMEMBER

Raich Carter and Eddie Hapgood shake hands at the start of the match.

Sunderland had to lift themselves once more after Ray Bowden headed home a Roberts cross to pull the score back to 4–3. Left-winger Jimmy Connor swapped positions with inside-left Patsy Gallacher, the latter having taken a knock and therefore been consigned to making up the numbers on the wing. Sunderland made a virtue of this though, Connor soon dovetailing with fellow inside-forward Carter, and the pair combined for Connor to score Sunderland's fifth goal and take the game away from the visitors. Connor's goal was the goal of the game. Starting on the halfway line, he beat two players, traded passes with Carter and struck an unstoppable shot from well outside the penalty area.

To their credit Arsenal kept fighting and gave themselves a chance with Bowden's second goal of the match, albeit with the help of a hefty deflection off Clark, with a quarter of an hour to go. However, Johnny Cochrane's side ran out worthy winners in a nine-goal thriller, and come the end of the season lifted the League Championship trophy for the first time in 23 years.

Sunderland: Thorpe, Morrison, Hall, Thomson, Clark, McNab, Davis, Carter, Gurney, Gallacher, Connor.
Arsenal: Moss, Male, Hapgood, Crayston, Roberts, Copping, Rodgers, Bowden, Drake, Bastin, Beasley.
Referee: H.E. Hull (Stockport)
Attendance: 58,773

13 April 1936
Birmingham 2 Sunderland 7

Division 1

Bobby Gurney is Sunderland's record goalscorer and this was one of his finest days. Gurney scored four times as the Lads won magnificently to secure the First Division title.

Mid-table Birmingham had lost 2–1 at Sunderland four days earlier on what was Good Friday. On the Saturday both teams had been defeated, Sunderland at Bolton and Blues at Huddersfield. When the sides lined up at St Andrews on Easter Monday for their third fixture of the weekend, both were missing a couple of regular players due to the demands of the Easter programme.

Gurney got the game's first goal after 14 minutes. Raich Carter was the creator and the Sunderland skipper restored the lead (with Sunderland's 100th League goal of the season) after good work by Connor nine minutes from half-time, Joe Loughran having levelled for the Blues, who equalised again through Albert Clarke four minutes from the break.

In for the injured Gallacher, Cecil Hornby headed home a Connor cross to give Sunderland a 3–2 half-time lead. That scoreline indicated a close game, but in fact Sunderland had had much the better of it, only to concede a couple of sloppy goals. The

The 1936 Championship-winning team, presented with the trophy after the next game v Huddersfield.

second half, however, saw Sunderland much more focussed in what became an exhibition worthy of new champions.

Gurney got the first of a second-half hat-trick when dribbling around 'keeper Frank Clack. Carter raced in to knock the ball into the back of the net, but it was Gurney's 55th-minute goal. Eight minutes later Carter slid through a ball for Gurney to smack home to complete his hat-trick and with a further 12 minutes gone Gurney again found the back of the net, glancing home a Davis corner to make it 6–2.

For all the glory of Gurney and Carter, it was perhaps fitting that the final goal on the day the Championship was won should be scored by left-winger Jimmy Connor, whose brilliance had set up so many goals and whose career would be halted by injury the following season. Connor it was who made it a magnificent seven in the closing stages after Carter again shredded the home defence. Sunderland were the champions of English football for the sixth and so far last time.

Birmingham: Clack, Barkas, Steele, Stoker, Sykes, Loughran, Jennings, Divine, Clarke, Harris, Morris.
Sunderland: Mapson, Morrison, Hall, Thomson, Johnston, McNab, Davis, Hornby, Gurney, Carter, Connor.
Referee: C. Booth (Heywood)
Attendance: 21,693

---

1 May 1937

Sunderland 3 Preston North End 1

FA Cup Final
Had a sending off been automatic for a 'professional foul' in 1937, Sunderland might well have found themselves a man down as well as a goal down to Preston North End on the club's first-ever trip to Wembley Stadium.

Moments after Scottish international Frank O'Donnell had given the Lancastrians a 38th-minute lead, the same player was through again when Sunderland centre-half Bert Johnston unceremoniously launched into him in a manner Joe Bolton would have been proud of four decades later. Johnston received a stern ticking off from referee Mr Rudd of London, but all Preston got was a free-kick that came to nothing.

Several key decisions went against Sunderland later in the game, including a strong penalty appeal, but the denial of the opportunity for the lethal O'Donnell to double North End's advantage was the turning point on what proved to be the day when Sunderland finally won the FA Cup. O'Donnell's goal took his FA Cup tally for the season to 11 and made him only the fourth player in the history of the competition to score in every round.

As so often happens with Cup Finals, the match was scrappy. Nerves played their part and neither team was allowed to settle on the ball as the fouls mounted up and the play became more and more disjointed.

Raich Carter is presented with the FA Cup in 1937.

The 1937 FA Cup Final.

The opening goal of the game saw Johnny Mapson, in the Sunderland goal, beaten after good work from brothers Hugh and Frank O'Donnell, the latter converting the former's cross to give Preston a half-time lead that could so easily have been doubled.

Bobby Gurney put Sunderland's best chance of the first half over the bar, and although he found the back of the net before half-time, he was clearly offside. Gurney, though, was a player who would always come back for more. Six minutes after the restart he scored Sunderland's equaliser. It was the Lads' first-ever goal beneath the Twin Towers, it was scored at the same end that Ian Porterfield scored at in 1973 and, as with Porterfield's goal, it came from a corner. Eddie Burbanks's flag kick was met by Gurney's well-timed leap, the centre-forward guiding the ball into the far corner of Mickey Burns's net. Leeholme (County Durham) born Burns had been on Newcastle's books and reserve for the Magpies at the 1932 Final.

The goal calmed nerves and Sunderland began to play. Passes started to find their targets. Where two touches had been needed before, the confidence flooding into the side meant that one-touch football started to tear Preston apart, despite the efforts of their stalwart right-half, Bill Shankly, who in years to come would become the legendary manager of Liverpool.

Carter fluffed a great chance, Preston survived a clear penalty appeal for handball, Carter drove narrowly wide and Gallacher was felled in the box without reward, but the goal that was evidently coming duly arrived 20 minutes after Gurney's equaliser.

Renowned as Sunderland's highest-ever goalscorer, Bobby Gurney's endless endeavour also created many goals for his colleagues. Such was the case in the 1937 Cup Final. Having drifted out to the left wing, Gurney gained possession, cut inside and crossed to Raich Carter – at whose wedding he had served as Best Man earlier in the week. Carter made no mistake, tucking his shot beyond Burns to put the Lads ahead.

Preston fought to get back into the match but this was a fine Sunderland side on one of their greatest days and they made sure of taking the trophy home with a third goal from winger Burbanks, who capitalised on a piercing pass from Gallacher.

Champions of England six times, Sunderland had never won the FA Cup and many believed the club was cursed, never to succeed in the tournament, but now the game's most glamorous trophy had finally been captured by a club for whom the magic of the FA Cup has always been special.

Sunderland: Mapson, Gorman, Hall, Thomson, Johnston, McNab, Duns, Carter, Gurney, Gallacher, Burbanks.
Preston North End: Burns, Gallimore, Beattie, Shankly, Tremelling, Milne, Dougal, Beresford, F. O'Donnell, Fagan, H. O'Donnell.
Referee: R.G. Rudd (London)
Attendance: 93,495

■ SUNDERLAND: THE COMPLETE RECORD

Sunderland v Arsenal. Len Shackleton, the 'Clown Prince of Soccer', is in action for the Lads.

12 September 1953

Sunderland 7 Arsenal 1

Division 1

Seven minutes before half-time Sunderland were losing this game, but seven goals in less than 50 minutes of play was reminiscent of the famous day in 1908 when Sunderland scored eight times in 28 minutes away to Newcastle.

Sunderland had lavished so much money on their side that they were known as 'the Bank of England team'. This match marked the goalscoring home debut of £26,000 England international Billy Elliott, while centre-forward Trevor Ford got a hat-trick, Tommy Wright a couple and 'Shack' ensured his name was among the scorers against the club that had notoriously rejected 'the Clown Prince of Soccer' as a youngster.

The Bank of England team were often overdrawn, not putting in as much as they should, but when they were in the mood this team full of big names could really turn it on. One win, a draw and four defeats – two involving the conceding of five goals, including a 5–4 loss to Manchester City in the previous home game – had preceded this early season fixture, but nonetheless the gates were closed at Roker Park with close to 60,000 inside.

Arsenal went one up halfway through the first half, Doug Lishman heading home a rebound from the crossbar. Sunderland were back on level terms seven minutes before half-time. Shackleton and Ford were two of the game's biggest names, but didn't gel, owing to Shackleton's wish to entertain first clashing with Ford's committed 'play to win' attitude. On this occasion though, the pair combined well for Ford to equalise and within five minutes Sunderland were ahead though home debutant Elliott after great play from Stan Anderson, Billy Bingham and Trevor Ford.

Sunderland's passing football wore the Gunners down in the second half, but the Lads had to wait for another goal. However, once it arrived the floodgates opened, two in two minutes from Shackleton and Ford signalling the start of five goals in half an hour, with Tommy Wright helping himself to two in four minutes in the game's final quarter and Ford sealing his hat-trick when converting a Billy Bingham cross three minutes from time.

It would be Sunderland's biggest win of the season. Arsenal were the reigning champions but were also on the receiving end of a 4–1 home defeat in the reverse fixture four months later when Ted Purdon scored after only 10 seconds! It was Purdon's away debut, having been signed to replace the transferred Ford, and he quickly matched Ford's feat with a well taken hat-trick.

Sunderland: Cowan, Hedley, Hudgell, Anderson, Daniel, Snell, Bingham, T. Wright, Ford, Shackleton, Elliott.
Arsenal: Swindin, Barnes, Evans, Forbes, Dodgin, Mercer, Logie, Lishman, Milton, Holton, Roper.
Referee: H. Webb (Leeds).
Attendance: 59,784

3 March 1956
Newcastle United 0 Sunderland 2

FA Cup sixth round

Cup-holders Newcastle had already done the double over Sunderland in the League, comprehensively enjoying their biggest ever derby win by 6–1 at Roker Park on Boxing Day, but this didn't stop Sunderland having an estimated 16,000 supporters in an all-ticket crowd at St James'. Both teams wore away kits, as was the norm in those days when a colour clash occurred in the Cup, although both teams had worn their traditional stripes in the earlier League fixture at the same ground.

The programme from the 1956 Tyne-Wear FA Cup quarter-final.

Sunderland's side included Bill Holden, along with the celebrated big names of the Bank of England era such as Ray Daniel, Billy Bingham, Billy Elliott and former Newcastle star Len Shackleton. Holden was an England 'B' cap who had scored at Newcastle on his Sunderland debut earlier in the season. He would score both goals in this game, meaning that three of the seven goals he scored for the club came away to Newcastle.

It was Shack, however, who finally unlocked the home defence with a second-half centre that enabled Holden to break the stalemate of a typically hard-fought derby, where fluent football had been at a premium.

With future Sunderland Cup-winning manager Bob Stokoe in their defence, the Magpies pressed for an equaliser, leaving themselves open at the back. Holden raced through to add a late second goal and put Sunderland into the semi-final for a second successive year.

Had Sunderland won their semi a year earlier, they would have faced Newcastle in the Final, United having won a semi-final replay at Roker Park against York. As it was, Newcastle lifted the FA Cup in 1955. In 2012 they were still waiting for another domestic trophy after Sunderland ended their reign as holders.

Newcastle United: Simpson, Batty, McMichael, Stokoe, Paterson, Scoular, Milburn, Davies, Keeble, Curry, Mitchell.
Sunderland: Fraser, Hedley, McDonald, Anderson, Daniel, Aitken, Bingham, Fleming, Holden, Elliott, Shackleton.
Referee: R.H. Mann (Worcester)
Attendance: 61,474

4 March 1961

Sunderland 1 Tottenham Hotspur 1

FA Cup quarter-final

Spurs were en route to becoming the first club to win the 'double' in the 20th century, Sunderland having gone as close as any club in 1913. In 1961, however, Sunderland were very much the underdogs and were just emerging from the trauma of a first-ever relegation three years earlier.

Two goals from Stan Anderson had beaten Arsenal in the third round, since when Sunderland had eliminated fellow Second Division sides Liverpool and Norwich. The great Spurs 'push and run' team of Bill Nicholson was the country's

Crowds queue for tickets for the 1961 FA Cup match with Spurs.

MATCHES TO REMEMBER

A pitch invasion gave Spurs the chance to recover after Willie McPheat's equaliser.

finest, and the quarter-final at Roker was the only FA Cup game Spurs would not win at the first attempt.

It looked plain sailing for Spurs when, after nine minutes, a corner was only partially cleared and Cliff Jones headed them into the lead. The same player went close to doubling the visitors' advantage before half-time, beating 'keeper Peter Wakeham to the ball but seeing full-back Colin Nelson clear off the line. Sunderland had another escape when Bobby Smith saw a shot come back off the post, but it wasn't all one-way traffic and Sunderland were well in the game with nippy Scottish winger John Dillon having probably his best game for the club. Red and white to the core, Dillon was still making regular trips from Scotland to cheer on Sunderland over half a century later. Even more importantly he was still making weekly trips across Glasgow to visit Willie McPheat, who while a million miles from the best of health was able to still count on his former teammate.

Five minutes after half-time Sunderland were level thanks to McPheat, who had been brought back after recovering from injury at the expense of John Goodchild, despite the latter's hat-trick in the previous match at Leeds (it was Goodchild's only game of the season!).

A huge Cup tie was always likely to result in the Roker Roar being at its best. This match heard the Roker Roar at its loudest, but the crowd unintentionally worked against Sunderland as well as for them, with a pitch invasion after McPheat's close range equaliser giving Spurs time to compose themselves before the restart.

Sunderland piled on the pressure, forcing a series of free-kicks and corners, with Charlie Hurley a constant threat to the visitors' defence at set pieces. Tottenham were seriously rocked at Roker but escaped with a draw and demonstrated their class with a scintillating display in the replay that saw them win convincingly 5–0. For Sunderland, though, the Cup run had brought excitement back to the club following a disappointing period.

Sunderland: Wakeham, Nelson, Ashurst, Anderson, Hurley, McNab, Hooper, Fogarty, Lawther, McPheat, Dillon.
Tottenham Hotspur: Brown, Baker, Henry, Blanchflower, Norman, Mackay, White, Allen, Jones, Smith, Dyson.
Referee: A. Murdoch (Sheffield)
Attendance: 61,326

---

4 March 1964
Sunderland 2   Manchester United 2 (aet)

FA Cup sixth-round replay
Three years to the day after the great Cup-tie with Tottenham, an equally big FA Cup quarter-final took place under the lights at Roker Park. This was a replay with Cup holders Manchester United, the sides having drawn 3–3 at Old Trafford when United pulled back two late goals after an injury restricted Jimmy Montgomery.

Although the official attendance for this match was only 46,727, estimates of the actual size of the crowd suggest that more than twice that number were inside the ground, with the record gate of 75,118 being exceeded. Fearful that they weren't going to get in, fans had torn down the gates at the Roker End and thousands had poured into the stadium. Such were the crowds that Sunderland's players, who had spent the day at the Roker Hotel on the seafront, struggled to make it up to the ground.

Len Ashurst and Denis Law in the epic three-game 1964 Sunderland v Manchester United FA Cup quarter-final.

Sunderland were top of the Second Division at the time and full of confidence, having won nine and drawn one of the 10 games leading up to the United tie. Sunderland gave as good as they got against a star-studded United team. Charlie Hurley came close to breaking the deadlock with a trademark header from a Brian Usher corner, only to see his effort just clear the bar, while at the other end Monty had to be at his best to whip the ball away from Georgie Best as he tried to latch onto a through ball from Bobby Charlton.

Three minutes before half-time Sunderland opened the scoring with as good a goal as any of the 62 Nicky Sharkey scored for the Lads, the diminutive Scottish goal-poacher arching his back balletically in producing a brilliant scissor-kick from outside the box.

Inspired and roared on by the huge crowd, Sunderland had United on the back foot early in the second half, but the second goal would not come and the visitors levelled after 62 minutes when Denis Law needed no second invitation to despatch a close-range half chance.

Sunderland swept back at United, left-back Len Ashurst in particular supplementing the attack at every opportunity and backing up winger George Mulhall, who along with Sharkey, George Herd and Johnny Crossan threatened to score a winner.

Although they had sporadic chances of their own, United were fortunate not to concede again until the 91st minute, but by then the game was into extra-time and there was nearly half an hour in which to equalise. Sunderland's second goal was an own goal by Maurice Setters, who beat his 'keeper in trying to cut out a Sharkey cross before Herd could apply the finishing touch. Denis Law hit the bar late on for the Red Devils but Sunderland just could not quite hang on to the lead, Bobby Charlton levelling two minutes from the end of extra-time.

United had not led in either game but would run out convincing 5–1 winners in the second replay at Huddersfield, only to go out at the semi-final stage as Sunderland went on to seal promotion.

Sunderland: Montgomery, Irwin, Ashurst, Harvey, Hurley, Elliott, Usher, G. Herd, Sharkey, Crossan, Mulhall.
Manchester United: Gaskell, Brennan, Dunne, Crerand, Foulkes, Setters, Chisnall, Law, D. Herd, Charlton, Best.
Referee: E. Crawford (Doncaster)
Attendance: 46,727

---

27 February 1973

Sunderland 3 Manchester City 1

FA Cup fifth-round replay
Voted the greatest game ever seen at Roker Park when the ground closed after 99 years, this pulsating Cup replay included one of the best goals Sunderland have ever scored.

Centre-forward Vic Halom was playing his first home Cup-tie following his transfer from Luton Town (whom Sunderland would entertain in the next round) a month earlier.

Vic Halom scores one of Sunderland's greatest-ever goals.

Halom hit home an unstoppable shot to finish a flowing move that had seen Stokoe's Stars shift the ball around the edge of the penalty area in a manner akin to Brazil's fourth goal in the previous World Cup Final against Italy, when Carlos Alberto applied the finishing touch.

Manchester City boasted an array of top players, including Colin Bell, Franny Lee and Rodney Marsh. City were still licking their wounds from being held 2–2 in Manchester the previous Saturday and Lee in particular had claimed that City's class would show through in the replay. But they didn't get a chance to shine. Like their Mancunian counterparts almost a decade earlier, and Danny Blanchflower's Spurs in 1961, they were about to be hit by the 'Roker Roar.'

City were simply blown away. Sunderland opened the scoring in the 15th minute. Porterfield twice, Guthrie, Hughes and Kerr combined to create a chance for Halom, who caught the ball as sweetly as any of his career and a split second later it nestled in the back of the Fulwell End net. Three minutes later City's giant goalkeeper Joe Corrigan went full length to deny Halom a second but Sunderland were rampant and doubled their lead before the half-hour mark through Billy Hughes, who capitalised on a Bobby Kerr throw-in and fired in a telling shot. Hughes would go on to score from a throw-in in the semi-final as well.

The visitors made a fight of it after the break and halved the deficit eight minutes into the second half through Lee. Bell, Marsh and Tony Towers, who would later join Sunderland, all threatened, but the Lads weathered the storm and killed City off with a third goal 12 minutes from time. Like the opening goal it was a result of good teamwork. Porterfield, Malone and Halom combined to set up Dennis Tueart, and when Corrigan failed to hold his shot Hughes was first on the scene to force the ball over the line and cue pandemonium in the stands as the 'impossible dream' started to become a reality.

Sunderland: Montgomery, Malone, Guthrie, Horswill, Watson, Pitt, Kerr, Hughes, Halom, Porterfield, Tueart. Sub. Chambers (unused).
Manchester City: Corrigan, Book, Donachie, Doyle, Booth, Jeffries, Mellor, Bell, Marsh, Lee, Towers.
Referee: R. Tinkler (Boston)
Attendance: 51,782

MATCHES TO REMEMBER

5 May 1973

Sunderland 1 Leeds United 0

FA Cup Final

Cup Finals come and go. There are several major ones annually, including European competitions. Liverpool's 2005 European Cup Final win was sensational, albeit unsatisfactorily decided on penalties; the 1953 FA Cup 'Matthews' Final was another classic, but the 1973 FA Cup Final matches any of them for drama and had one extra ingredient the others were missing, despite having only a single goal compared to the high-scoring matches that normally pass into legend.

Sunderland beating Leeds United was probably the biggest Cup Final upset of all time. Sunderland fans baulked at the media's 'David v Goliath' tagline because in the eyes of Sunderland followers Sunderland will always be much bigger than Leeds United, without taking anything away from the Yorkshire giants. Undeniably, though, at the time of the 1973 FA Cup Final, Leeds were one of the most powerful teams in Europe, while Sunderland were in the second tier of English football.

Led by 'the Messiah' Bob Stokoe, Sunderland had already beaten Cup favourites Manchester City and prevented Arsenal reaching a third successive Final. While hardly anyone outside of Wearside believed Sunderland had any chance of beating the Cup holders Leeds, those that did tip Sunderland weren't bad judges: Bill Shankly, Brian Clough and Bob Wilson, the goalkeeper of the vanquished Gunners.

If ever a team had its 'name on the Cup', it was Sunderland. The euphoria sweeping the town had everyone convinced that Sunderland would beat Leeds. Recent history between the clubs included a closely fought promotion race in 1964 when both went up, with Leeds as champions, and a 1967 fifth-round Cup-tie that had gone to two bitterly contested replays. Sunderland's Cup Final captain, the smallest ever, Bobby Kerr, had broken his leg as a teenager in the 1967 tie. Had Sunderland not lost a fourth-round second replay to

Monty dives to parry Trevor Cherry's far-post header…

…and miraculously manages to deflect Peter Lorimer's follow-up onto the bar.

Cardiff in 1972 they would have met Leeds at the fifth-round stage, but destiny was not to be denied and so Sunderland met Leeds under the Twin Towers at Wembley on a day that began with rain but ended with Sunderland bringing sunshine to all of the footballing world, beating a team almost universally disliked because of their notorious foul play and gamesmanship.

Managed by former Sunderland player Don Revie, Leeds were supremely confident but Sunderland tore into them. United's Bremner and Giles were used to dominating games but ginger terrier Mick Horswill nullified Giles as he had Alan Ball and Colin Bell in the wins over Arsenal and Manchester City, and the entire Sunderland team showed absolutely no respect for their big-name opponents, being more concerned with making their own names pass into legend. Leeds's trump card was meant to be winger Eddie Gray. He had been predicted to torture right-back Dick Malone, but Stokoe detailed Kerr to support Malone and the ploy worked so well that Gray was substituted.

Bobby Kerr, 1973.

MATCHES TO REMEMBER

Bob Stokoe and Jimmy Montgomery celebrate at the final whistle.

With FA Cup in hand and a supporter's hat on his head, manager Bob Stokoe is ecstatic.

The only goal of the game came after 31 minutes. Kerr floated in a high ball that United 'keeper Harvey chose to put behind for a corner under pressure. From Billy Hughes's corner Vic Halom and Man of the Match Dave Watson drew the attention of the Leeds defence and the ball came to Ian Porterfield. Rejected by Leeds as a youngster, Porterfield controlled the ball and, using his right foot, scored high into the net.

Leeds had an hour to make their class count, but to win games you have to score goals and there was no way Jimmy Montgomery was going to be beaten. Monty's Cup Final double save from Trevor Cherry and Peter Lorimer is commonly accepted as Wembley's greatest-ever save. Commentators went wild about it and still do. For those people who watched Monty regularly in that era, however, it was just typical Monty. Spectacular reaction saves were what Monty was all about, but thankfully 'the Mighty Jim' chose perhaps the club's greatest-ever day to show the world what a great goalkeeper he was.

It was Monty that the red track-suited Bob Stokoe ran gleefully towards at the final whistle. There were tears of joy on the terraces and in thousands of Wearside homes, where people had watched the game on new colour TVs bought for the occasion. Sunderland had won the Cup. Not any Cup, THE Cup. When people talk about the magic of the Cup, this was its most special trick.

Sunderland: Montgomery, Malone, Guthrie, Horswill, Watson, Pitt, Kerr, Hughes, Halom, Porterfield, Tueart. Sub. Young (unused).
Leeds United: Harvey, Reaney, Cherry, Bremner, Madeley, Hunter, Lorimer, Clarke, Jones, Giles, Gray (Yorath).
Referee: K. Burns (Stourbridge)
Attendance: 100,000

---

5 December 1984
Tottenham Hotspur 1   Sunderland 2

League (Milk) Cup fourth-round replay
Despite being smaller than most goalkeepers at 5ft 10in, Chris Turner deserves his place on the list of great goalkeepers who have served Sunderland. The run to the 1985 League (Milk) Cup Final was overwhelmingly inspired by Turner.

Brilliant against Forest in the third round, he would be superb at Watford in the quarter-final and tremendous in both legs of the semi-final, as well as in the Final in front of 100,000 against Norwich at Wembley. Spurs must have cursed him for ending their run in the competition. An excellent Cup side at the time, Tottenham were the UEFA Cup holders but could find no way past Turner in the original tie at Roker, which finished goalless despite constant pressure from the visitors. Many thought Tottenham would turn Sunderland over in the replay at White Hart Lane, as they had after the epic FA Cup game at Roker in 1961. England internationals Graham Roberts and Clive Allen had been sent off at Sunderland earlier in the season in a League game which they had lost 1–0, so there was a feeling that Spurs had a point to prove. When Roberts put them ahead with a fifth-minute penalty it looked as if the Lads were in for a long night, but Spurs were in for a shock.

Sunderland equalised halfway through the first half through ex-Chelsea winger Clive Walker, who made the most of excellent approach work from former Liverpool pair David Hodgson and Howard Gayle. Straight after half-time Hodgson and Gayle combined again to open up a shooting chance for centre-half Gordon Chisholm, who had conceded the early penalty. 'Chis' would go on to see Norwich's Cup Final winner deflect in off him, but on this occasion the Scot benefited when his effort clipped Spurs's Paul Miller to wrong-foot England 'keeper Ray Clemence and nestle in the back of the net.

MATCHES TO REMEMBER

Although it was not yet Christmas, Spurs had scored four or more goals on eight occasions already and were fourth in the table with Glenn Hoddle as their kingpin. Try as they might though, they could find no way past the elastic Turner. Then, with 10 minutes left, Spurs were given their second penalty of the night when Shaun Elliott handled a cross from Chris Hughton. Up stepped Roberts, possessor of one of the hardest shots in the game. He drilled his effort low into the corner, only for Turner to miraculously reach it. This was not just a penalty save, it was one of the greatest penalty saves. Having long since thrown the kitchen sink at Sunderland, Spurs threw absolutely everything at the Lads in the closing stages, but a resolute defence with Turner impregnable behind them held out for a famous victory.

Tottenham Hotspur: Clemence, Stevens, Hughton, Roberts, Miller, Perryman, Chiedozie, Falco, Allen (Mabbutt), Hoddle, Hazard.
Sunderland: Turner, Venison, Daniel, Bennett, Chisholm, Elliott, Berry, Gayle, Hodgson (West), Proctor, Walker.
Referee: B. Stevens (Gloucestershire)
Attendance: 25,835

17 May 1987

Sunderland 4 Gillingham 3

(aet – Gillingham won on away goals)

Play-off semi-final

Penalties: so often the bane of Sunderland supporters' lives. Two years before this game Clive Walker missed one in the League Cup Final at Wembley. Less than a year after this fateful day the Lads would lose in a penalty shoot-out at Wembley to Wigan, although that was nothing compared to the Wembley shoot-out defeat to Charlton in the Play-off Final of 1998 or the Play-off semi-final defeat on penalties at the hands of Crystal Palace in 2004.

This Play-off game didn't go to a penalty shoot-out, but penalties effectively settled it. Had Mark Proctor not missed from the spot in the final League game against Barnsley, when Sunderland threw away a 2–0 lead to lose 3–2, the Lads wouldn't have been in the

Gary Bennett scores against Gillingham in 1987.

newly created Play-off system, which at that time pitted the team finishing third from bottom of the second level (Now 'Championship' in 2012) of English football with those finishing third, fourth and fifth in the old Division Three.

Thus it was that Sunderland were pitted against Gillingham for the first time since facing them in the FA Cup in 1908, when the Gills were known as New Brompton. The Kent side had finished fifth in Division Three and faced Sunderland, with the winners due to meet the victors of the other Play-off semi-final between Swindon Town and Wigan Athletic over two legs. Play-off Finals were yet to move to Wembley.

Proctor had partly atoned for his error by scoring twice, including a penalty, in the first leg at the Priestfield Stadium, where a Tony Cascarino hat-trick had given Gillingham a 3–2 advantage.

Proctor, however, would crucially miss from the spot at Roker, while Gillingham scored from a penalty of their own, albeit courtesy of a follow-up tucked away by Cascarino after Trevor Quow was first to the ball when Sunderland 'keeper Iain Hesford parried Howard Pritchard's penalty.

Pritchard had opened the scoring, extending the visitors' aggregate lead to 4–2 in only the third minute, but goals from Eric Gates in the 17th and 22nd minutes had Sunderland level with three-quarters of the game to go. Proctor then had the chance to put Sunderland ahead, only to fluff his 33rd-minute spot kick, Phil Kite saving. Then came Cascarino's goal after 52 minutes and as the clock ticked down the gaping chasm of the Third Division spread its unwelcoming arms to beckon Sunderland, Sunderland, one of the greatest clubs in the history of the Football League, to a level where they would be merely 'Associate Members.'

Just when all seemed lost, captain Gary Bennett, playing on despite injury, and pushed up front from his normal central defensive position, rose at the Fulwell End to score two minutes from time to throw Sunderland a lifeline and take the game into extra-time. It was a Hurley-esque header, but ultimately a forlorn one, just as Benno's header at Manchester City three years later would be, when Sunderland suffered their third relegation in six seasons.

Away goals counting double was always meant to encourage attacking football. Sunderland suffered from having to play an extra 30 minutes at home, thereby giving Gillingham the opportunity to have an extra half-hour to score to take advantage of the away goals rule after identical scorelines at each ground.

Just as Sunderland had conceded a goal three minutes into the game, they did so again three minutes into extra-time, nemesis Cascarino scoring his fifth goal of the tie. Sunderland needed to score twice more but could only manage one, Keith Bertschin's diving header winning the game 4–3 but losing the tie 6–6 through the extra away goal.

So it was that having been the first club outside the dozen Founder Members to join the League, and until 1958 the only club to have only played at the highest level, Sunderland, once 'The Team of All The Talents', now found themselves demoted to Division Three and the long-suffering supporters had the added trauma of coping with the taunts of several hundred Newcastle fans, who had congregated in the Clock Stand Paddock to see Sunderland sink.

This game was Bob Stokoe's last in charge of Sunderland. The 'Messiah' had tried to come up with another miracle after taking over the reins following the sudden departure of the man responsible for the debacle, Lawrie McMenemy. Thanks to Denis Smith, who was soon to be installed as the new manager, those Newcastle fans wouldn't be quite so keen on the Play-offs just three years later!

Sunderland: Hesford, Lemon, Kennedy (Corner), Doyle, Gray, Bennett, Armstrong, Proctor, Bertschin, Swindlehurst, Gates.
Gillingham: Kite, Haylock, Pearce, Berry, Quow, Greenhall, Pritchard, Weatherley (Shearer), Smith, Elsey, Cascarino.
Referee: M. Peck (Kendal)
Attendance: 25,470

16 May 1990

Newcastle United 0 Sunderland 2

Division Two Play off semi-final (Aggregate score 0-2)
Watching from behind the Leazes End goal, which was the Sunderland supporters were, members of the red and white army were looking at the old Gallowgate End where at the back there was a scoreboard with yellowish letters. It counted down the minutes of the match. Normally in a derby when Sunderland are winning time seems to go by very slowly but on this night the minutes rolled by inexorably. From the moment Eric Gates put Sunderland ahead in the thirteenth minute, the Wearsiders seemed to have an air of superiority that exuded a calmness that was the polar opposite of the atmosphere of most derbies, let alone in this one, perhaps the most important derby game of them all.

The prize for the winners was a place at Wembley and with it the chance to be promoted into the top flight. As it happened Sunderland lost at Wembley yet were still promoted when victors Swindon Town were punished for being found guilty of financial irregularities.

Sunderland had already been punished in this Play-off semi-final as they were without suspended left-back Paul Hardyman. He had been sent off in the first leg of the semi-final three days earlier for his follow up on United 'keeper John Burridge who had saved Hardyman's injury time penalty as the Roker leg of the tie finished goalless. Sunderland supporters allow themselves wry smiles at the tendency of the Magpies to crow about their triumphs before they have actually achieved them. Never was this truer than in the 72 hours between the two legs of the 1990 Play-off. Having emerged from Roker with a draw the black and whiters thought they were nailed on to see off Sunderland at St James'. This reckoned without the fact that Sunderland had had the better of all three derbies played so far that season, all of which had been draws. It also ignored the reality that only in their solitary campaign in the third tier had Sunderland won more away games in a season than since the glorious 1912-13 campaign. In that year they'd been within one win of doing the double and Sunderland's current away form was such that they had won six of the last seven games on the road.

Newcastle came at Sunderland as expected, Mark McGhee hitting the post though as Sunderland 'keeper Tony Norman remarked: 'I know this sounds funny, but when he hit it I thought 'That's not in''. Newcastle were caught napping from an early throw in. Gabbiadini knocked Kay's throw on to the ever-willing Gary Owers and from his cross Eric Gates showed his predator's eye by gobbling up the chance. Owers then went close himself, bringing a good save out of Burridge who later kept the home side in the game with another outstanding save from Gabbiadini.

Going for their second promotion in three years since the low point of 1997, the red and white renaissance had been powered by the 'G-Force' – Gates and Gabbiadini. Eric Gates was the veteran England international who saw passes a move ahead of everyone else and had the ability to execute them, Marco Gabbiadini was the speed merchant with the power to punish opponents. The pair operated on exactly the same wavelength and four minutes from time they combined as they had done so often for Marco to make it 2-0.

For many supporters the result of this game is the most important since the 1973 FA Cup Final. A year after Stokoe's Stars brought the FA Cup back to the North East, Newcastle reached the Cup Final after they came back in a game against Nottingham Forest after their fans invaded the pitch when they were losing. Unable to take defeat, many Newcastle fans tried the same tactic against Sunderland and poured onto the playing surface forcing the teams off. They reckoned without Spennymoor's finest – World Cup referee George Courtney – who assured the teams that even if they were there until midnight and he had to have the ground cleared, the final four minutes would be played and he would not consider an abandonment.

After an 18 minute hiatus on a night of 66 arrests, the final moments were played out in an eerie atmosphere akin to the second leg of the Milk Cup Final at Chelsea five years earlier. Now as then, Sunderland had won a crucial game in the most hostile of home arenas. It was a well deserved victory and the yellow letters of the scoreboard spelled it out as the Tyneside hordes slunk out of the ground and the Wearside legions knew they had just witnessed a legendary night.

Newcastle United: Burridge, Scott, Stimson, Aitken, Anderson, Bradshaw (Dillon 45), Brock, Askew (O'Brien 77), Quinn, McGhee, Kristensen.
Sunderland: Norman, Kay, Agboola, Bennett, MacPhail, Owers, Bracewell, Armstrong, Gates, Gabbiadini, Hawke. Unused subs: Brady, Hauser.
Referee: Mr G. Courtney (Spennymoor)
Attendance: 32,199

MATCHES TO REMEMBER

Niall Quinn celebrates the first of his two goals in a game that finished 4–4 before the Lads lost on penalties despite another 'goal' from Niall in the penalty shoot-out.

25 May 1998

Sunderland 4 Charlton Athletic 4

(Charlton won 7–6 on penalties)

'New' Division One Play-off Final

For footballing drama, many neutrals place this game among the peaks of Wembley Stadium's rich history. In inimitable fashion, Sunderland scored 10 times and still lost in the Pay-off Final, which because of its Premiership promotion prize, by now made it the most financially important game in club football worldwide.

Having narrowly missed out on automatic promotion after an exhilarating first season at the Stadium of Light, a pulsating Play-off semi-final victory over Sheffield United sent Sunderland to Wembley for what would be the last time before the demolition of the Twin Towers.

Sunderland-born Charlton striker Clive Mendonca would break Wearside hearts with a hat-trick, while Sunderland striker Kevin Phillips had to go off through injury after beating Brian Clough's post-war record for goals in a season with his 35th, and Sunderland's 100th, of the season.

Mendonca put the Londoners ahead midway through the first half, and the scoreline stayed that way until the 50th minute, when Niall Quinn brought Sunderland level against a side with nine successive clean sheets behind them. Eight minutes later the Lads took the lead for the first time through talisman Phillips. The lead lasted for 13 minutes until Mendonca struck again, but in a rollercoaster match Quinn restored Sunderland's advantage within two minutes.

Substitute Danny Dichio fluffed a great chance to make it 4–2 to Sunderland, but the outcome of the match turned on two goalkeepers. Sunderland's French 'keeper Lionel Perez had become a cult figure at Sunderland and had been the hero of the semi-final. However, with the club five minutes from the Premiership, he left his line to come for a corner, got nowhere near the ball, and was stranded as Addicks defender Richard Rufus headed home his first goal in 185 games.

Extra-time beckoned for Sunderland for the first time ever in a major Final. Nine minutes into it Nicky Summerbee scored to put Sunderland 4–3 up, but before the half-time whistle sounded Mendonca completed his hat-trick to make the final score 4–4 and take the game to penalties.

Charlton went first and scored all seven of the spot kicks they took. Six times Sunderland refused to let the pressure get to them, but when left-back Michael Gray stepped forward for his home town club, 'keeper Sasa Ilic easily saved his tame shot to win the game. Denied a return to the Premiership and condemned to another season outside of the top flight of English football, the defeat on penalties was a massive disappointment and yet for a game of such drama this was, in a cruel way, a fitting end.

Sunderland bounced back with a record 105-point promotion season a year later with Gray recovering from his spot-kick trauma to earn three full England caps.

Penalty shoot-out: Mendonca (1–0), Summerbee (1–1), Brown (2–1), Johnston (2–2), K. Jones (3–2), Ball (3–3), Kinsella (4–3), Makin (4–4), Bowen (5–4), Rae (5–5), Robinson (6–5), Quinn (6–6), Newton (7–6) and Gray (7–6).
Sunderland: Perez, Holloway (Makin), Gray, Clark (Rae), Craddock, Williams, Summerbee, Ball, Quinn, Phillips (Dichio), Johnston.
Charlton Athletic: Ilic, Mills (Robinson), Bowen, K. Jones, Rufus, Youds, Newton, Kinsella, Bright (Brown), Mendonca, Heaney (S. Jones).
Referee: E.K. Wolstenholme (Blackburn)
Attendance: 77,739

4 December 1999

Sunderland 4 Chelsea 1

Premiership

More than any other game, this match summed up the excitement of the early years at the Stadium of Light. Playing to packed houses, Peter Reid's team rose as high as second in the table, eventually finishing seventh: the club's highest top-flight finish for over 40 years.

Chelsea had hammered Sunderland 4–0 on the opening day of the season, a result that had been kind to Sunderland given the Londoners' dominance. By this stage, half a season later, Sunderland were taking the Premiership by storm, with Kevin Phillips and Niall Quinn the most feared partnership in the land.

MATCHES TO REMEMBER

Phillips getting the third goal against Chelsea.

Although missing four players, Sunderland had a point to prove. They were one up within a minute and 4–0 up seven minutes before half-time. Punch drunk Chelsea had been struck by a whirlwind of attacking football, with Sunderland's front two bagging a couple of goals each in what became the Wearsiders' biggest top-flight home win since the week after the club's joint record 8–0 defeat 17 years earlier.

Frenchman Eric Roy pulled the strings in midfield. Just 44 seconds into the game Roy wrong-footed the visitors' defence to tee up the opening goal for Quinn. Sunderland's dazzling first-half play included the greatest goal yet seen at the two and a half-year-old stadium, Phillips firing home a spectacular shot from fully 30 yards.

Chelsea centre-back Marcel Desailly had won a World Cup-winner's medal with France a year earlier, but he simply could not deal with the Mighty Quinn, whose dominance led to two more Sunderland goals in a three-minute spell that had supporters in ecstasy. Dutch 'keeper Ed De Goey parried a Quinn shot that Phillips followed up to net, then Quinn volleyed home the fourth goal.

Uruguayan Gustavo Poyet pulled a goal back for Chelsea in the second half but few visiting fans were there to see it, many of them having left at half-time, their pre-match taunts of '4–0' having stuck in their throats!

Sunderland: Sorensen, Makin, Gray, Thirlwell, Craddock, Williams, Summerbee (Holloway), Schwarz, Quinn, Phillips, Roy. Unused subs: Marriott, T. Butler, Oster, Reddy.
Chelsea: De Goey, Lambourde, Babayaro, Morris, Hogh, Desailly (Terry), Harley (Goldbaek), Poyet, Flo, Zola, Wise (Wolleaston).
Referee: S. Dunn (Bristol)
Attendance: 41,199

23 April 2005
Sunderland 2 Leicester City 1

Championship

Denied promotion a year earlier; after a controversial last-minute equaliser in a Play-off semi-final eventually lost on penalties to Crystal Palace, Mick McCarthy's reshaped Sunderland stormed to the Championship title, winning it with two games to spare.

An experienced Leicester side contributed to an excellent match, won in fine style by a team bristling with belief. A series of injuries to 'keepers meant that teenager Ben Alnwick was making his debut and the rookie goalie needed to call on all his self-belief when his first touch in senior football was to pick the ball out of the back of his net. Racing onto a ball from Danny Tiatto, overlapping full-back Alan Maybury put the visitors ahead with a deliciously curling effort that left Alnwick with no chance.

Alnwick instantly added his name to the list of Wearside goalkeeping heroes with two brilliant saves to deny Connolly and De Vries before top scorer Marcus Stewart brought the Lads level when coolly finishing off a measured pass from Chris Brown.

Played at a high tempo, the game entertainingly swung from end to end, but it was Sunderland who claimed what proved to be the winner on the hour mark. Steve Caldwell had headed the winner in the reverse fixture in the Midlands earlier in the season, but the Foxes failed to pick up the centre-back at a Lawrence corner and the Scotland international gloriously found the back of the net.

The game that sealed promotion in 2005. Steve Caldwell headed the winning goal in the 2–1 win over Leicester.

MATCHES TO REMEMBER

Steve Caldwell celebrates his winning goal.

Leicester pushed forward for an equaliser, but could find no way past a resolute defence and an accomplished young goalkeeper. At the final whistle promotion to the Premiership was still not a mathematical certainty; Sunderland needed Ipswich to fail to win at Leeds. Once news had come through of Ipswich's draw at Elland Road, celebrations began in earnest at the Stadium of Light. This was the first time promotion had been won in a home game for quarter of a century, and the lap of honour which followed was one of pure emotion, not least as seen in the eyes of manager Mick McCarthy, whose team went on to seal the title with a win at West Ham six days later.

Sunderland: Alnwick, Wright, Arca, Robinson, Breen, Caldwell, Lawrence, Whitehead, Brown (Deane), Stewart (Elliott), Welsh (D. Collins).
Leicester City: Walker, Kenton, McCarthy, Dublin, Maybury, Hughes, Gudjonsson (Williams), Nalis (Stearman), Tiatto, De Vries (Moore), Connolly.
Referee: Mr M. Jones (Ellesmere Port)
Attendance: 34,815

14 November 2010

Chelsea 0 Sunderland 3

Barclays Premier League
This was Sunderland's best ever result against a side who were reigning double champions. Chelsea were in imperious form. The Londoners had not conceded a League goal at home for over seven months (and that in a game they won 7-1), when Sunderland scored their first of what was a comprehensive victory it was 916 minutes playing time since Stamford Bridge had been breached, and Chelsea had netted 39 goals at home in the League since they had last conceded there. If they were shocked when Sunderland scored they were simply stunned by the final whistle – as was the whole country.

The result was no fluke. Sunderland simply clicked. Even without top scorer Darren Bent the lads produced easily their best performance during manager Steve Bruce's time in charge. His worst day had come just a fortnight earlier. On that occasion Halloween horror had been endured with the heaviest derby defeat in half a century. Since then a home win over Stoke and a creditable draw at Spurs had been very welcome but had not even begun to heal the wound from the derby. Nothing would do that until Newcastle are next really trounced. However this performance and result was at the other end of the scale, the best of times rather than the worst.

On Sunderland's previous trip to Chelsea, seven goals had been conceded with marauding England left-back Ashley Cole exploiting more space than Neil Armstrong and taking 'one giant leap' of his own as he scored what proved to be Chelsea's 'Goal of the Season' in their double winning year.

This time Cole production was stopped effectively. Just as in the 1973 FA Cup Final when Kerr and Malone doubling up on Eddie Gray was the game's most telling tactical move, this time detailing the speedy Kieran Richardson to play on the right wing and track Cole worked like a dream. So well indeed that Sunderland right-back Nedum Onuoha found time to saunter forward and waltz through the home defence to score what would be another 'Goal of the Season' in this fixture, only this time for Sunderland.

The goal came in first half injury time but in no way was against the run of play as Sunderland had surprised Chelsea by taking the game to them. Six minutes after the re-start the lead was doubled as the visitors' free flowing football was rewarded with Asamoah Gyan's fourth goal in a week. The Ghanaian celebrated with a trademark dance though former Chelsea man Bolo Zenden's attempt to join in undid much of the ex-Barcelona and Marseille Dutchman's uber-cool exterior. If anything that moment added to what was a joyous performance and the result was completed when Richardson's relentless hounding of Cole forced the England full-back into a mis-judged back pass that the effervescent Danny Welbeck gleefully latched onto to join Onouha in claiming his first goal for the club.

It was Chelsea's heaviest home defeat in the League for eight years, the first time they'd lost a home League game to a side outside the 'big four' in 15 years and the heaviest home

League defeat since being taken over by their mega-rich owner Roman Abramovich. For Sunderland it was the first away win over reigning champions since a Gary Rowell goal at Liverpool in 1983 and the end of a run of 11 successive defeats against the Blues. It wasn't a Cup Final or a game that won a League or avoided relegation but it was just one of those too rare days when everything goes right. To produce this performance against the highest calibre opposition in the aftermath of the recent derby debacle illustrated football's unerring capacity to conjure up the finest unscripted drama and Sunderland's ability to be the lead character.

Chelsea: Cech, Bosingwa, Ferreira, Ivanovic, Cole, Mikel, Ramires (McEachran 46), Zhirkov (Kakutu 44), Anelka, Drogba, Malouda (Kalou 58). Unused subs: Turnbull, Van Aanholt, Bruma, Sala.
Sunderland: Gordon, Onuoha, Bardsley, Turner, Bramble, Richardson, Henderson, Cattermole (Riveros 90+3), Zenden, Gyan (Malbranque 83), Welbeck (Elmohamady 89).
Unused subs: Mignolet, Angeleri, Da Silva, Adams.
Referee: Mr C. Foy
Attendance: 41,072

Match Programmes

Match programmes are a curiously British obsession. In the UK for many people having a programme from a game is as important as attending the fixture itself whereas overseas there is often no such thing as a match programme, or if there is it is a much smaller publication than we are used to in Britain and if produced at all it is usually done so in small numbers. In recent years clubs in Germany, the Netherlands and Italy for example have developed their match programmes but even the best of them lag a long way behind what is typical in England where even non League issues can run to 100 pages, be packed with information and be professionally produced.

In 2011 a Sunderland programme from a game against Sunderland Albion on 1 December 1888 was sold for over £5,000 indicating the collectability of match programmes. This four page issue from 1888 is the oldest known existing Sunderland programme. A note in this programme from 1888 indicates that programmes had been issued for the two previous seasons although none of these are known to survive.

Rarity is the name of the game as with any collection so while many a supporter has a 1973 FA Cup final programme locked away, anyone with a mint condition programme from the 1992 Sunderland v Liverpool FA Cup final, complete with the poster and key ring given away with it, will find it is worth much more than the 1973 issue against Leeds.

As far back as 1901 Sunderland issued an official programme called *Roker Football Chat*, consisting of 16 pages, half of which were adverts and half packed with informative pages.

By the 1920s Sunderland's programme was called the *Sunderland News and Record* and 'did what it said on the tin'. A 20 page publication costing tuppence provided good reading albeit mainly in the form of snippets of information along with a syndicated lengthy topical discussion piece under the name of the legendary Derby, Middlesbrough and England player Steve Bloomer.

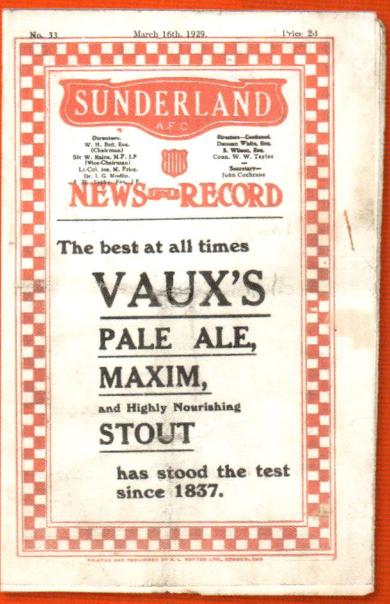

1928-29 v Bury

In the 1930s a name change to, the *Sunderland News and Official Programme* was accompanied by covers adorned with the black cat. In the FA Cup winning season of 1936-37 for instance the programme cost half the price of a 1920s programme – at just a penny perhaps an indication of the hard times people lived in during that decade of the depression. All the covers of the season were the same with the masthead of the programme accompanied by an advert for Sunderland based Vaux breweries. Teams were given inside the front cover but while there were occasional photographs, other than listing the first team and reserve fixtures and a brief introduction to the game there was little to read apart from a lengthy syndicated article on a general topic such as long or short passing.

During World War Two a single sheet four-page programme costing one old penny was produced. Due to paper rationing this size continued until 1947 when the Sunderland AFC official programme increased to 16 pages at two old pence. It featured a picture of the Wearmouth bridge on the cover. Now part of the club badge, an image of the bridge was restored to the cover in 2012.

The programme remained the same size during the fifties when photographs became more prominent and the cover developed into a style where half of the page was red and white stripes with an aerial football shaped photo of Roker Park. In the days before the Fulwell End was roofed this amply illustrated how much bigger the Roker End was.

For the start of the 1963-64 season; the club's first ever promotion campaign, a small pocket sized programme was introduced. At 16 pages this was four more than the previous year but was accompanied by a 50% price hike from fourpence to sixpence.

1938-39 v Everton   1939-40 v Leeds United

This small format continued for three and a half seasons until suddenly in January 1967 the programme doubled in page size with another 50% price rise to nine old pence. The reason for this radical mid season change was so the club could introduce *The Football League Review*. The latter was a 16 page official journal of The Football League. By the time Sunderland took the decision to increase the size of the programme's pages to facilitate the inclusion of *The Football League Review* the national publication was already up to issue 25.

The plus points of the FL Review were that it was professionally put together, included plenty of interesting articles and began to introduce colour. The minuses were that the content was not about Sunderland or the day's visitors except for the occasional item, if you had two games in a week or went to away games you got more than one copy of the same insert as the FL Review was carried by most clubs and also the change resulted in a mid season price rise.

Now featuring a red and white top half picture of the new main entrance to Roker Park, still with the red and white stripes incorporated, and a black and white recent action photograph on the bottom half, the cover design remained basically unchanged until 1969-70. For what proved to be a relegation season a larger page size was brought in with a price increase to a shilling (5 new pence) and a name change that was to remain from 1969 until the closure of Roker Park in 1997: a goalless draw with Coventry heralded the birth of *The Roker Review*.

The first issue began with chairman Syd Collings penning an article entitled, 'Our new magazine…a closer link' in which he stated: 'I would like you to regard this as your own magazine and another closer link between the club and

1958-59 v Fulham

1963-64 v Bristol City

MATCH PROGRAMMES

supporters.' 16 pages of Sunderland information were offered including a range of bright new features – manager Alan Brown began a column from the second issue – with the expected teams returning to the front cover as they had during World War two.

The next change came two seasons later when the page size returned to almost exactly what it had been in 1968-69. Strangely having had Volume one and two of *The Roker Review* this page size alteration co-incided with a re-start of the numbering sequence: hence both seasons 1969-70 and 1971-72 are listed as Volume one of the *Roker Review* and equally both seasons 1970-71 and 1972-73 are Volume two!

Whereas in previous decades often the cover, size and price had barely changed in most years, the seventies began an era where the look of the programme was re-vamped on an annual basis.

The Cup winning season of 1972-73 had a distinctive look with a white masthead above an all red cover containing a football shaped black and white photo. The first home FA Cup issue was a four page replay issue v Notts County with a slightly different cover than usual and a penny off the normal 6p price for what was usually 16 pages. For the fourth round with Reading a grey cover made it stand out but for the games in the fifth and sixth rounds normal red and white covers were employed. For the final game of the season – four days after the Cup Final when QPR were faced in a re-arranged fixture – an out of date programme from the original date five weeks earlier was used. Added to it was a four page wraparound cover with the FA Cup on the front and full page pictures from the Cup final inside. Presciently the original issue from 2 April had Cup final goalscorer Ian Porterfield on the cover.

1966-67 v Peterborough

1972-73 v Manchester City

301

The following season's covers made an excellent collection of black and white photo's from the Cup final, an increase to 24 pages being accompanied by a price rise to 10p, twice what it had been two seasons before. As with so many Sunderland programmes through the years there was little in the way of reading material for what is after all the official publication and voice of the club.

The mid seventies saw full colour photographs introduced into the club programme and from 1976 a two season spell saw a landscape page format used. This was followed by two years of large page size programmes, the biggest ever used by the club other than for one off brochure style issues for special matches such as Testimonials or the games that closed and opened Roker Park and The Stadium of Light.

The first full season in the 1980s saw the *Roker Review* still essentially consisting of 16 pages but with a nationally produced 20 page insert that was in a word: awful. Whereas the *Football League Review* that had once been issued with the programme was clearly for the football minded, the *Programme Plus* insert produced by London based Sportopia Promotions Ltd was little more than a glossy way of justifying the price which by now was 30p. Lots of articles on foreign football, cars, music and other sports might well have been interesting in a magazine bought in a newsagents but for people coming to Roker Park to see Sunderland and buying Sunderland's programme it was Joe Bolton, Kevin Arnott and co they wanted to read about not hatchback cars, Hurricane Higgins or the history of Whitbread beer!

By 1984 a square – and often poorly printed – 24 page programme was introduced and while it was better than many previous SAFC programmes

1976-77 v Manchester United

MATCH PROGRAMMES

supporters who travelled away knew it lagged a long way behind the best publications in the country.

1985 brought a return to Second Division football and a 10p price rise to 50p but a much improved 32 page programme that won Sunderland's first Programme of the Season award, taking the Second Division prize.

Current programme editor Rob Mason first became involved from 1986-87 and has remained so ever since. Along the way Rob's co-authors of this and the original Complete Record – Mike Gibson and Barry Jackson – have become involved as long standing contributors to the programme along with a host of other Sunderland enthusiasts.

The Roker Review retained the same size, shape and price until 1990 by which time the Lads had suffered relegation to the Third Division but risen again to the First. The return to the top flight in 1990 brought another makeover to the programme which increased in page size if not number (32) but doubled in cost to £1.

1993-94 brought a significant if not instantly apparent change. Responsibility for the design of the programme switched to Polar Print Group of Leicester and while that company has since gone out of business, programme editor Rob Mason has kept faith with the people who design the programme ever since. The former creative director of Polar now has his own business called Ignition Publications who still produce the multi award winning Sunderland programme.

April '94 brought an additional four pages as a precursor to another price rise to £1.30 in the summer. A year later the programme rose to £1.50 but reverted to 32 pages until the last seven issues of a Championship winning season when a big game with promotion rivals Derby County coincided with a jump to 48 pages.

1984-85 v Tottenham Hotspur

Sunderland's first season in the Premiership in 1996-97 saw the team relegated but the programme runner up in the top flight Programme of the Year awards, by this time the sixth season an award or at least a high placing had been received by a match programme making strenuous efforts to provide Sunderland supporters with a top class publication. The season also saw the closure of Roker Park with special issues produced for both the final League game and Farewell match against Liverpool who had been the ground's first visiting team 99 years earlier.

Following another special issue for the opening game at the Stadium of Light against Ajax the programme stayed the same size as the previous season's League issues albeit with a 20p price hike but more significantly the first name change since 1969. No longer at Roker Park, the *Roker Review* became *Red 'n' White Review* which it remained for five years, staying the same size, albeit with a rise to £2 in 1999-2000.

2002-03 brought big changes. The word 'Review' was dropped from the name leaving the programme as *Red and White*, a name it holds to this day and which it is hoped simply sums up what it is – red and white through and through just like the people who buy it. Buying it saw a steep price rise to £2.50 but an increase of 16 pages taking it to 64 and with the addition of what proved to be a very popular addition of free specially produced SAFC stickers to accompany a sticker album given away with the programme's sister publication *Legion of Light*, the club's official magazine which had come into being following the move to the Stadium of Light.

Sadly, what was a popular programme accompanied a dismal season when the team were relegated with a record low 19 points. At a time of cost cutting and redundancies at the club the programme took a hit of reducing back to 48 pages in 2003-04 (the club magazine *Legion of Light* simultaneously dropping from 10 issues a season to four) while the price remained at £2.50. Replacing the stickers though was an additional eight page pull out poster supplement called *Game On*, aimed at the younger supporters. Unlike previous programme supplements such as *Programme Plus* or *The Football League Review*, *Game On* was produced by the same people producing the rest of the programme and was geared entirely to Sunderland supporters.

While the programme supplement – like the previous season's stickers – was a one year project, *Red and White* was restored to 64 pages for the 2004-05 season just as the team restored itself to the top flight by winning the Championship. The

2001-02 v West Ham

MATCH PROGRAMMES

final issue of the season when promotion was already won saw a laminated cover added taking the programme to a biggest ever 68 pages and a price increase to £3.

Despite rising costs, an increase to 84 pages, plus in 2012-13 an additional young person's supplement along with the introduction of 'Perfect bound' issues from 2009 *Red and White* has remained unchanged in price ever since, the longest spell without a price increase in over half a century.

2009 saw *Red and White* also experiment with digital versions which enabled people to get an exact copy of the programme on their computer on the day of the game. Consequently for the subscriber from Australia to Alaska they could have the programme at their fingertips while the game was going on and they listened to the commentary on the club website safc.com rather than having to wait for the programme to arrive in the post several days later. Since 2011-12 supporters have been able to obtain *Red and White* on their mobile devices such as ipads.

2011-12 brought in a revolution in programme technology with the introduction of a 'QR' code. This enabled people with smart phones to scan the back cover of the programme and 25 minutes before kick off actually be able to see the teams named for that day's game. No need now for team changes to be written onto the programme!

There is no doubt that the world of football programmes has come a long way since the glorified team sheets of the Victorian era. Just as the Stadium of Light is a world away from the Newcastle Road ground that pre-dated Roker Park and is where Sunderland are first known to have issued such a thing as a match programme, the modern day '*Red and White*' is a world away from the issue of 1888. And yet, both the stadium and the programme fulfill the same functions they did in the game's early years. Things change and things stay the same. Now as in 1888. Sunderland are synonymous with red and white and the Sunderland match programme tries hard to live up to that heritage while always trying to read the game and be one step ahead.

AWARDS

Over the years some awards bodies have been short lived, The Northern Programme Club in its present form has been making awards since 2007-08 while Sunderland entered the Soccer Club Swap Shop awards for the first time in 2010-11. The Programme Monthly magazine awards have been running for many years and are something of an institution in the programme collecting world.

Since 1985-86 Sunderland's match programme has received 18 Programme of the Year awards, seven runners' up spots and 14 other awards.

2011-12

Programme Monthly magazine 'Programme of the Year'
Soccer Club Swap Shop 'Programme of the Year'
Northern Programme Club – Third place

2010-11
Northern Programme Club: Editor of the Year

Northern Programme Club 'Programme of the Year' runner up

Northern Programme Club Premier League 'Best Value' award.

Soccer Club Swap Shop, 'Programme of the Year'

Programme Monthly magazine 'Programme of the Year' runner up

Programme Monthly magazine 'Best Read in the Premier League' award

2009-10
Programme Monthly magazine 'Programme of the Year'

Northern Programme Club 'National Programme of the Year and Premier League Programme of the Year'

Northern Programme Club: Third in Most Improved category.

2008-09
Northern Programme Club 'National Programme of the Year and Premier League Programme of the Year'

Programme Monthly 'Best Read in the Premier League'

2007-08
Northern Programme Club 'National Programme of the Year and Premier League Programme of the Year' runner up

Northern Programme Club Merit Award for Continued Excellence

Programme Monthly 'Best Read in the Premier League'

Programme Monthly 'Premier League Programme of the Year' runner up

2006-07
Programme Monthly 'Best Read in the Premier League'

Programme Monthly 'Programme of the Year' runner up

2005-06
Programme Monthly commendation for 'Continued Excellence'

2004-05
Commercial and Marketing Managers' Association 'Programme of the Year'

Programme Monthly 'Merit Award'

Programme Monthly 'Championship Programme of the Year' third place.

2001-02
Special award for Niall Quinn Benefit Match programme

1999-2000
Programme Monthly 'Programme of the Year'

1998-99
CMMA D1 Programme of the Year runner up

1997-98
CMMA D1 Programme of the Year

Programme Monthly Championship 'Programme of the Year'

1996-97
Programme Monthly Programme of the Year runner up

1992-93
CMMA awards, fifth in D1

MATCH PROGRAMMES

1989-90
City of London School D2 Programme of the Year

1988-89
City of London School D2 Joint Programme of the Year

Northern Programme Club D2 Programme of the Year

1987-88
CMMA / FLESA D3 Programme of the Year

City of London School Joint D3 Programme of the Year

1985-86
Programme Monthly, Championship 'Programme of the Year'

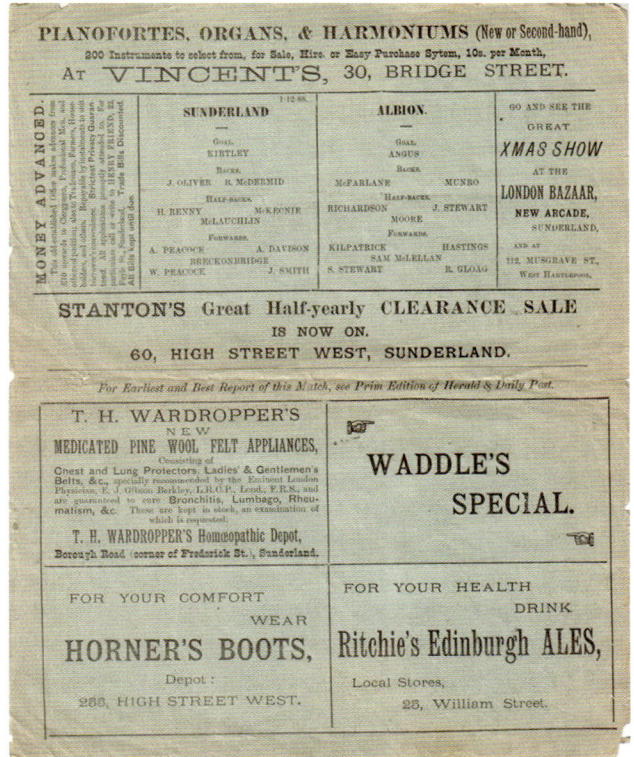

Sunderland's oldest known programme from a game against Sunderland Albion in 1888.

WHY ARE SUNDERLAND CALLED THE BLACK CATS?

It is over 200 years since Sunderland first became linked with black cats and over 100 years since the football club is first known to have adopted the black cat as its mascot, although it was not until 2000 that the Black Cats officially became Sunderland AFC's nickname.

In 1805, 74 years before the foundation of the football club, the south of the two piers of Sunderland harbour at Roker housed a gun battery known as the John Paul Jones Battery. This was during a time of American raids on England. John Paul Jones was the name of the adventurer behind these raids. One night in 1805 a soldier from the Sunderland Loyal Volunteers heard such loud and piercing wailing he thought it was the devil! Closer investigation showed the source of the noise to be a black cat and from then on the battery was known as the Black Cat Battery.

Black cats are of course widely associated with good luck and, shortly after the club's move to Roker Park in 1898, Sunderland are known to have used the black cat as a lucky mascot. The chairman of the club, F.W. Taylor, was pictured in a cartoon with a black cat sitting on a football in 1905. Team photographs from as far back as 1908 sometimes include black cats and at Sunderland's first appearance in the FA Cup Final in 1913, many supporters are known to have sported black cats on tie pins accompanying their red and white ribbons. It was also reported that at Sunderland railway station a large black cat made of cardboard was placed over the station entrance as a sign of good luck on the day of the final.

Sunderland's match programmes of the 1930s often pictured a black cat on the cover and it was common for people to bring black cats to the match, often releasing them to run across the pitch. Black cat imagery was prominent again in 1937 when Sunderland reached the FA Cup Final for a second time, this time bringing the longed-for Cup back to Wearside after half a dozen League Championships. A 12-year-old supporter called Billy Morris was reported to have kept a black kitten, wearing red and white ribbons, in his pocket throughout the game on Sunderland's first trip to Wembley.

In 1965 when Sunderland AFC Supporters' Association was founded, a black cat was used as its emblem and has remained so ever since, often featuring in the name of associated supporters' publications.

In 1999 the club included the traditional black cat emblem on the sleeve of its shirts, only to be reprimanded by the Premiership for using an additional image other than the club badge, sponsor name and kit manufacturer.

Sunderland's modern-day matchday mascots are black cats: Samson (named after one of former club sponsor Vaux breweries' beers) and Delilah. The club badge adopted

This black cat had an unhappy tale to tell at the 1985 League (Milk) Cup Final at Wembley.

following the 1997 move to the Stadium of Light shows two black lions – the head of the cat family – one at either side of the club crest.

In 2000 the club held a vote among supporters to decide upon a new official nickname. Other suggestions were: the Miners, the SoLs, the Light Brigade and the Mackems (a word originally used as a derogatory description of Wearside accents by those on the Tyne, but often adopted with pride by younger Wearsiders). The Black Cats was a clear winner and was adopted as Sunderland AFC's official nickname.

1884-90

Sunderland's Pre-League FA Cup Games

Did you know that?

One of Sunderland's earliest players, Duncan Bell Murdoch, emigrated to Hawaii in 1891 and became a financial auditor for a pineapple plantation then later a magistrate for a district court.

1884-85

Date	Round	Venue	Opponents	Result	FT	HT	Scorers	Attendance
Nov 8	R1	A	Redcar	L	1-3	0-3	McColl	

Appearances
Goals

1885-86

Date	Round	Venue	Opponents	Result	FT	HT	Scorers	Attendance
Oct 24	R1	A	Redcar	L	0-3	0-1		

Appearances
Goals

1886-87

Date	Round	Venue	Opponents	Result	FT	HT	Scorers	Attendance
Nov 13	R1	A	Newcastle West End	L	0-1	0-0		4,000

Appearances
Goals

Newcastle successfully protested after Sunderland won the first game 2-1 after extra time on 30 October and then won the replay 1-0

1887-88

Date	Round	Venue	Opponents	Result	FT	HT	Scorers	Attendance
Oct 22	R1	A	Morpeth Harriers	W	3-2	1-2	Monaghan (2), Stewart	
Nov 5	R2	H	Newcastle West End	W	3-1*	0-1	Stewart (2), Halliday	7,000
26	R3	A	Middlesbrough	D	2-2	2-0	Gloag (2)	5,000
Dec 3	R3r	H	Middlesbrough	W	4-2	0-2	Halliday, Stewart, Davison, Monaghan	10,000

* after extra-time

Appearances
Goals

The first game against Morpeth was won by Sunderland at home but a replay was ordered after a dispute (Ford had played but was not registered in time). Sunderland were disqualified, after an appeal by Middlesbrough, for fielding 3 professionals (Hastings, Monaghan and Richardson) in the competition

1888-89

Sunderland received a bye in the first qualifying round

Date	Round	Venue	Opponents	Result	FT	HT	Scorers	Attendance
Oct 27	R2Q	H	Elswick Rangers	W	5-3	3-3	A. Peacock (2), Breconridge (3)	5,000
Nov 17	R3Q	H	Newcastle East End	W	2-0	0-0	Davison, Peacock	5,000
Dec 8	R4Q	A	Sunderland Albion*					

*Sunderland scratched after deciding not to play Sunderland Albion

Appearances
Goals

1889-90

Date	Round	Venue	Opponents	Result	FT	HT	Scorers	Attendance
Jan 18	R1	A	Blackburn Rovers	L	2-4*	1-0	Hannah, Scott	9,000

*after extra-time

Appearances
Goals

Kirkley, J.	Hall, J.	Elliott, J.	Thompson	Allan, W.	Burlinson, W.	McColl, D.	McDonald, J.	Grayston, J.	McMillan, J.	Allan, J.
1	2	3	4	5	6	7	8	9	10	11
1	1	1	1	1	1	1	1	1	1	1
					1					

Kirkley, J.	Inglis, J.	Hunter, J.	McMillan, J.	Dale, F.	Marshall, W.	Murdoch, D.	Erskine, W.	McDonald, J.	Allan, J.	Logan, D.
1	2	3	4	5	6	7	8	9	10	11
1	1	1	1	1	1	1	1	1	1	1

Kirkley, W.	Elliott, J.	Oliver, J.	McMillan, J.	Smart, J.	Dale, F.	Erskine, W.	Rooney, P.	Smith, R.	Lord, P.	Davison, A.
1	2	3	4	5	6	7	8	9	10	11
1	1	1	1	1	1	1	1	1	1	1

Kirkley, W.	Hastings, A.	Oliver, J.	Richardson, J.	Stewart, S.	Dale, F.	Allan, J.	Rooney, P.	Smith, R.	Davison, A.	Monaghan, G.	Halliday, T.	Ford, P.	Gloag, R.
1	2	3	4	5	6	7	8	9	10	11			
1	9	3	6	7	4		8	11	10	2	5		
1	11	2	5	8	4		7	10	6	3	9		
1		2	4	8	6		9	7	11	5	3	10	
4	3	4	4	4	4	1	3	4	4	3	3	2	
			4			1	3	2		2			

Kirkley, W.	Archbold, R.	McDermid, R.	Remmie, H.	McLauchlan, H.	Gibson, W.	Davison, A.	Brady, A.	Breconridge, J.	Peacock, A.	Peacock, W.	Oliver, J.	Ford, P.	Spain, J.	Jobling, J.
1	2	3	4	5	6	7	8	9	10	11				
1		8		5	4	7		9	10		2	3	6	11
2	1	2	1	2	2	2	1	2	2	1	1	1	1	
						1	3	3						

Kirkley, W.	Porteous, T.	Oliver, J.	Stevenson, J.	Auld, J.	Gibson, W.	Harvie, J.	Smith, J.	Campbell, J.	Hannah, D.	Scott, J.
1	2	3	4	5	6	7	8	9	10	11
1	1	1	1	1	1	1	1	1	1	1
									1	1

1890-91

The Football League

Ground: Newcastle Road

Manager: Tom Watson

League Table

	P	W	D	L	F	A	Pts
Everton	22	14	1	7	63	29	29
Preston NE	22	12	3	7	44	23	27
Notts Co	22	11	4	7	52	35	26
Wolverhampton W	22	12	2	8	39	50	26
Bolton W	22	12	1	9	47	34	25
Blackburn R	22	11	2	9	52	43	24
SUNDERLAND *	22	10	5	7	51	31	23
Burnley	22	9	3	10	52	63	21
Aston Villa	22	7	4	11	45	58	18
Accrington S	22	6	4	12	28	50	16
Derby Co	22	7	1	14	47	81	15
WBA	22	5	2	15	34	57	12

*Sunderland deducted two points for unapproved registration

FA Cup Winners: Blackburn Rovers

Did you know that?

When Sunderland were elected to the Football League in 1890 a banner was erected above the entrance to the Newcastle Road ground which read "We have arrived and we are staying here". Sunderland remained in the top flight until 1958; a record (68 years) only since bettered by Arsenal.

Match 1: Wilson, Spence and Millar made debuts
Match 2: Gillespie debut and Kirkley last game
Match 3: Doig made debut
Match 4: Murray made debut
Match 12: Spence last game

Match No.	Date	Round	Venue	Opponents	Result	FT	HT	Pos.	Scorers	Attendance
1	Sep 13		H	Burnley	L	2-3	2-3		Spence, Campbell	5,000
2	15		H	Wolverhampton W.	L	3-4	3-0	10	Gillespie (2), Scott	5,000
3	20		A	West Bromwich Albion	W*	4-0	2-0	6	Scott, Millar (2), Campbell	8,557
4	27		A	Burnley	D	3-3	3-2	7	Harvie, Scott, Spence	10,000
5	Oct 11		A	Blackburn Rovers	L	2-3	1-2	9	Millar, Campbell	10,000
6	18		H	Accrington	D	2-2	2-1	9	Millar (2)	4,000
7	25		A	Bolton Wanderers	W	5-2	1-2	11	Campbell (4), Millar	4,000
8	Nov 1		H	Blackburn Rovers	W	3-1	1-1	10	Campbell (2), Millar	14,000
9	8		H	West Bromwich Albion	D	1-1	0-0	11	Scott	6,000
10	15		A	Everton	L	0-1	0-1	11		12,000
11	22		A	Accrington	L	1-4	0-3	11	Campbell	1,000
12	Dec 15		A	Notts County	L	1-2	0-0	12	Wilson	8,000
13	20		H	Everton	W	1-0	0-0	10	Hannah	8,000
14	26		A	Aston Villa	D	0-0	0-0	10		6,000
15	27		A	Wolverhampton W.	W	3-0	1-0	9	Scott, Auld, Millar	8,000
16	Jan 10		H	Aston Villa	W	5-1	3-1	8	Campbell (3), Hannah (2)	6,000
18	24		H	Notts County	W	4-0	0-0	8	Campbell, Millar (3)	6,000
20	Feb 7		A	Derby County	L	1-3	1-2	8	Scott	4,000
21	10		H	Bolton Wanderers	W	2-0	1-0	6	Scott (2)	6,000
23	21		A	Preston North End	D	0-0	0-0	6		15,000
26	Mar 14		H	Preston North End	W	3-0	2-0	6	Ross, N. o.g., Campbell, Millar	6,000
27	21		H	Derby County	W	5-1	3-0	7	Smith, Campbell, Hannah, Wilson, Millar	3,000

* = 2 Points deducted and fined £50 for fielding Doig as an ineligible player.

Appearances
Goals

FA Cup

17	Jan 17	R1	H	Everton	W	1-0	1-0		Campbell	21,000
19	31	R2	A	Darwen	W	2-0	0-0		Scott (2)	5,000
22	Feb 14	R3	H	Nottingham Forest	W	4-0	1-0		Millar (2), Campbell (2)	19,000
24	28	S	N*	Notts County	D	3-3	2-2		Smith, Harvie, Campbell	25,000
25	Mar 11	Sr	N*	Notts County	L	0-2	0-2			16,000

* at Bramall Lane

Appearances
Goals

	Kirkley	Porteous	Oliver	Wilson	Auld	Gibson	Spence	Millar	Campbell	Scott	Hannah	Harvie	Gillespie	Doig	Murray	Smith	
1	2	3	4	5	6	7	8	9	10	11							1
1	2	3	4	5		6		9	10	11	7	8					2
	2	3	4	5		6	8	9	10	11	7		1				3
	2		4	5		6	8	9	10	11	7		1	3			4
	2		6	5	4		8	9	10	11	7		1	3			5
	2		6	5	4		8		10	11	7	9	1	3			6
	2	3	6	5			8	9	10	11	7		1	4			7
	2	3	6	5			8	9	10	11	7		1	4			8
	2	3	6	5			8	9	10	11	7		1	4			9
	2	3	4	5			8	9	10	11	7		1	6			10
	2	3		5	4		8	9	10	11	7		1	6			11
	2	3	4		5		8	10	11	7			1	6	9		12
	2	3	4	5				9	10	11	7		1	6	8		13
	2	3	4	5				9	10	11	7		1	6	8		14
	2	3	4	5			8	9	10	11	7		1	6			15
	2	3	4	5				9	10	11	7		1	6	8		16
	2	3	4	5			8	9	10	11			1	6	7		18
	2	3	4		5		8	9	10	11			1	6	7		20
	2	3	4	5			8	9	10	11			1	6	7		21
	2	3	4		5		8	9	10	11			1	6	7		23
	2	3	4		5		8	9	10	11			1	6	7		26
	2	3	4		5		8	9	10	11			1	6	7		27
2	22	19	21	17	8	5	17	21	22	22	15	2	20	19	10		
		2	1		2		13	16	8	4	1	2		1			

	Kirkley	Porteous	Oliver	Wilson	Auld	Gibson	Spence	Millar	Campbell	Scott	Hannah	Harvie	Gillespie	Doig	Murray	Smith	
	2	3	4	5				9	10	11	7		1	6	8		17
	2	3	4	5			8	9	10	11			1	6	7		19
	2	3	4	5			8	9	10	11			1	6	7		22
	2	3	4		6			9	10	11	7		1	5	8		24
	2	3	4	5			8	9	10	11			1	6	7		25
	5	5	5	4	1		3	5	5	5	2		5	5	5		
							2	4	2		1				1		

Right-back Tom Porteous became Sunderland's first international player when he was capped by England against Wales on 7 March 1891. The match, played at Newcastle Road, ended 4-1 to England.

1891-92

The Football League

Ground: Newcastle Road
Manager: Tom Watson

League Table

	P	W	D	L	F	A	Pts
SUNDERLAND	26	21	0	5	93	36	42
Preston NE	26	18	1	7	61	31	37
Bolton W	26	17	2	7	51	37	36
Aston Villa	26	15	0	11	89	56	30
Everton	26	12	4	10	49	49	28
Wolverhampton W	26	11	4	11	59	46	26
Burnley	26	11	4	11	49	45	26
Notts Co	26	11	4	11	55	51	26
Blackburn R	26	10	6	10	58	65	26
Derby Co	26	10	4	12	46	52	24
Accrington S	26	8	4	14	40	78	20
WBA	26	6	6	14	51	58	18
Stoke	26	5	4	17	38	61	14
Darwen	26	4	3	19	38	112	11

FA Cup Winners:
West Bromwich Albion

Did you know that?

Darwen scored after 2 minutes of their home game against Sunderland on St George's Day 1892 however the "Team of all the Talents" hit back with seven unanswered goals (and two further were disallowed) to win 7-1.

Match 2: Logan made debut
Match 3: Gow made debut
Match 5: Jimmy Hannah made debut
Match 6: Logan last game
Match 14: Oliver last game
Match 29: Smith last game and crowned League champions
Match 31: Murray last game

Match No.	Date		Round	Venue	Opponents	Result	FT	HT	Pos.	Scorers	Attendance
1	Sep	5		H	Wolverhampton W.	W	5-2	2-2		Campbell (2), Millar (3)	7,000
2		12		A	Preston North End	L	1-3	1-1	5	Millar	7,000
3		19		A	Bolton Wanderers	L	3-4	2-4	8	Campbell, Millar, Wilson (pen)	9,000
4		28		A	Aston Villa	L	3-5	1-3	14	Campbell (2), Wilson	10,000
5	Oct	3		H	Everton	W	2-1	1-1	10	Campbell, Scott	8,000
6		17		A	West Bromwich Albion	W	5-2	1-2	10	Millar, Scott (2), Campbell (2)	5,500
7		24		H	West Bromwich Albion	W	4-0	1-0	6	Campbell (2), J. Hannah, Wilson (pen)	7,000
8		31		H	Accrington	W	4-1	3-0	5	J. Hannah (2), Campbell, Scott	6,000
9	Nov	7		A	Blackburn Rovers	L	1-3	1-1	5	Arthur o.g.	18,000
10		14		H	Derby County	W	7-1	5-1	4	J. Hannah, Scott, Campbell (4), Millar	5,000
11		21		H	Burnley	W	2-1	1-1	4	Wilson (pen), Smith	5,000
12		28		A	Stoke	W	3-1	2-0	4	Campbell, Scott (2)	1,500
13	Dec	5		H	Notts County	W	4-0	3-0	4	J. Hannah (2), Campbell (pen), Wilson	5,000
14		12		H	Darwen	W	7-0	3-0	3	Millar (3), Wilson, D. Hannah, Campbell (2)	4,000
15		25		A	Everton	W	4-0	3-0	3	Campbell, D. Hannah, J. Hannah, Auld	16,000
16		26		A	Wolverhampton W.	W	3-1	2-1	3	Campbell, J. Hannah, Wilson	17,000
22	Mar	1		H	Bolton Wanderers	W	4-1	1-1	3	Millar, J. Hannah (2), Scott	5,000
23		5		A	Accrington	W	5-3	3-0	3	Millar (2), Scott, J. Hannah, McLellan o.g.	2,000
24		12		H	Preston North End	W	4-1	2-1	2	Auld (2), Campbell, D. Hannah	12,000
25		19		A	Derby County	W	1-0	0-0	2	Auld	8,000
26		26		H	Aston Villa	W	2-1	0-0	1	Wilson, J. Hannah	17,000
27	Apr	2		H	Stoke	W	4-1	2-1	1	Campbell (2), J. Hannah (2)	5,000
28		9		A	Notts County	L	0-1	0-0	1		10,000
29		16		H	Blackburn Rovers	W	6-1	3-1	1	Campbell (4), J. Hannah, Millar	10,000
30		23		A	Darwen	W	7-1	4-1	1	Scott, J. Hannah (2), Campbell (3), Wilson	4,000
31		30		A	Burnley	W	2-1	0-0	1	Campbell, Millar	10,000

Appearances
Goals

FA Cup

17	Jan	23	R1	H	Notts County	W	4-0	4-0		J. Hannah, Campbell (2), Smith	12,000
18	Feb	6	R2	A	Accrington	W	3-1	0-1		Campbell (3)	8,000
19		13	R3	A	Stoke	D	2-2 (aet)	2-2		Campbell, Millar	9,000
20		20	R3r	H	Stoke	W	4-0	2-0		Campbell, Millar, D. Hannah, J. Hannah	9,000
21		27	S	N*	Aston Villa	L	1-4	1-1		Scott	28,000

* at Bramall Lane

Appearances
Goals

MARCH 12, 1892. THE ILLUSTRATED SPORTING AND DRAMATIC NEWS.

Porteous (captain), right back. H. Wilson, right half-back. E. Doig, goal. J. Dalton, centre half. W. Gibson, left half-back. J. Murray, left back. T. Norris, referee. S. Tyzack, J. Hannah, D. Hannah, J. Campbell, J. Miller, J. Scott, T. Watson, hon. treasurer. outside right forward. inside right forward. centre forward. inside left forward. outside left forward. secretary.

FOOTBALL TEAMS No. 40 — SUNDERLAND.

Doig	Oliver	Porteous	Gibson	Auld	Murray	Smith	Milliar	Campbell	Hannah D.	Scott	Logan	Gow	Wilson	Hannah J.		
1	2	3	4	5	6	7	8	9	10	11						1
1	2	3	4	5	6		8	9	10	11	7					2
1		2		5	6	7	8	9	10	11		3	4			3
1		2		5	6	7	8	9	10	11		3	4			4
1		2	4	5	6	7		9	10	11		3		8		5
1		2	6	5	3		8	9			11	10	4	7		6
1		2	6	5		7	10	9		11		3	4	8		7
1		2	6	5	3	7	10	9		11			4	8		8
1		2	6	5	3	7	10	9		11			4	8		9
1		2	6	5	3	7	10	9		11			4	8		10
1		2	6	5	3	7	10	9		11			4	8		11
1		2		5	4	7	10	9		11		3	6	8		12
1		2	6	5	4		10	9	8			3	11	7		13
1	3	2		5	6		10	9	8	11			4	7		14
1		2		5	6		10	9	8	11		3	4	7		15
1		2		5	6	10		9	8	11		3	4	7		16
1		2	6	5			9	10		8	11	3	4	7		22
1			6	5	2	9	10		8	11		3	4	7		23
1		2	6	5			10	9	8	11		3	4	7		24
1		2	6	5	4		10	9	8	11		3		7		25
1		2	6	5	4		10	9		11		3	8	7		26
1		2	6	5			10	9	8	11		3	4	7		27
1		2	5		4		10	9	8	11		3	6	7		28
1		2	5		4	8	10	9		11		3	6	7		29
1		2	6	5	3		10	9	8	11			4	7		30
1		2	6	5	3		10	9	8	11			4	7		31
26	3	25	20	24	22	14	24	24	18	24	2	16	22	22		
			4		1	15	32	3	10			9	17			

Doig	Oliver	Porteous	Gibson	Auld	Murray	Smith	Milliar	Campbell	Hannah D.	Scott	Logan	Gow	Wilson	Hannah J.		
1		2	6	5	4	8		9	11	10		3		7		17
1		2	6	5	4		10	9	8	11		3		7		18
1		2		5	6	7	10	9	8	11		3	4			19
1		2		5	6		10	9	8	11		3	4	7		20
1		2		5	6		10	9	8	11		3	4	7		21
5		5	2	5	5	2	4	5	5	5		5	4	4		
						1	2	7	1	1			2			

Campbell scored 32 League goals in 24 appearances and seven FA Cup goals in five appearances. This included four hat-tricks.

315

1892-93

Division One

Ground: Newcastle Road

Manager: Tom Watson

League Table

	P	W	D	L	F	A	Pts
SUNDERLAND	30	22	4	4	100	36	48
Preston NE	30	17	3	10	57	39	37
Everton	30	16	4	10	74	51	36
Aston Villa	30	16	3	11	73	62	35
Bolton W	30	13	6	11	56	55	32
Burnley	30	13	4	13	51	44	30
Stoke	30	12	5	13	58	48	29
WBA	30	12	5	13	58	69	29
Blackburn R	30	8	13	9	47	56	29
Nottingham F	30	10	8	12	48	52	28
Wolverhampton W	30	12	4	14	47	68	28
Sheffield W	30	12	3	15	55	65	27
Derby Co	30	9	9	12	52	64	27
Notts Co	30	10	4	16	53	61	24
Accrington S	30	6	11	13	57	81	23
Newton Heath	30	6	6	18	50	85	18

FA Cup Winners: Wolverhampton Wanderers

Did you know that?

William McGregor, chairman of Aston Villa, dubbed Sunderland the "Team of all the Talents" following their 6-1 victory at Perry Barr on 17 September 1892. He came into their dressing room after the game to congratulate them and to make this statement.

Match 1: Smellie made debut
Match 22: Dunlop made debut
Match 25: John Gillespie made debut
Match 29: Smellie last game
Match 30: Crowned League champions
Match 32: John Gillespie last game

Match No.	Date		Round	Venue	Opponents	Result	FT	HT	Pos.	Scorers	Attendance
1	Sep	3		A	Accrington	W	6-0	3-0	1	Campbell (3), Millar, Scott, D. Hannah	4,000
2		10		H	Notts County	D	2-2	1-2	5	Campbell, Wilson	6,000
3		17		A	Aston Villa	W	6-1	3-1	3	Wilson, Campbell (2), J. Hannah (2), Harvie	15,000
4		24		H	Blackburn Rovers	W	5-0	2-0	2	Harvie, J. Hannah, Campbell (2), Millar	8,000
5	Oct	1		H	Stoke	W	3-1	2-1	2	Campbell, J. Hannah (2)	10,000
6		8		A	Everton	W	4-1	3-0	2	Gillespie (2), Wilson, Millar	16,000
7		15		H	Accrington	W	4-2	2-0	2	Millar, Campbell (2, 1 pen), Gibson	5,000
8		22		H	West Bromwich Albion	W	8-1	2-1	2	Wilson, Campbell (2), Millar (3), Gibson, Scott	5,000
9		29		A	Sheffield Wed.	L	2-3	2-2	2	Campbell, Scott	20,000
10	Nov	5		H	Burnley	W	2-0	2-0	2	Campbell, Scott	6,000
11		19		H	Nottingham Forest	W	1-0	1-0	2	Campbell	5,000
12		26		A	Notts County	L	1-3	1-1	2	J. Hannah	6,000
13	Dec	3		A	Nottingham Forest	W	5-0	3-0	2	Gillespie, Campbell (3), Wilson	8,000
14		17		H	Preston North End	W	2-0	0-0	2	Campbell, J. Hannah	20,000
15		24		A	West Bromwich Albion	W	3-1	3-1	1	J. Hannah, D. Hannah, Campbell	8,000
16		26		A	Wolverhampton W.	L	0-2	0-0	2		15,000
17	Jan	2		H	Wolverhampton W.	W	5-2	4-1	1	J. Hannah (4), Millar	3,000
18		3		H	Everton	W	4-3	3-0	1	Millar (2), Jardine o.g., Gillespie	5,000
19		7		A	Preston North End	W	2-1	2-1	1	Gillespie (2)	14,000
20		14		H	Aston Villa	W	6-0	2-0	1	Campbell (2), Gillespie (2), D. Hannah, J. Hannah	7,000
22		28		H	Sheffield Wed.	W	4-2	2-0	1	Gillespie, J. Hannah (2), Millar	8,000
24	Feb	14		H	Bolton Wanderers	D	3-3	0-2	1	D. Hannah, J. Hannah, Gibson	6,000
26	Mar	4		A	Newton Heath	W	5-0	4-0	1	Campbell (2), Jas. Gillespie, Harvie, Scott	15,000
27		11		H	Derby County	W	3-1	2-1	1	Campbell (2), Jas. Gillespie	6,000
28		18		A	Stoke	W	1-0	1-0	1	Wilson	10,000
29		31		A	Blackburn Rovers	D	2-2	1-1	1	J. Hannah, Gillespie	12,000
30	Apr	1		A	Bolton Wanderers	L	1-2	0-2	1	Campbell	13,000
31		4		H	Newton Heath	W	6-0	1-0	1	J. Hannah, Campbell, Millar (2), Wilson	8,000
32		8		A	Derby County	D	1-1	1-1	1	J. Hannah	8,000
33		15		A	Burnley	W	3-2	3-0	1	Harvie (2), Wilson	10,000

Appearances
Goals

FA Cup

21	Jan	21	R1	H	Royal Arsenal	W	6-0	5-0		D. Hannah, Campbell (2), Millar (3)	3,000
23	Feb	4	R2	A	Sheffield United	W	3-1	3-0		Millar (2), Campbell	14,769
25		18	R3	A	Blackburn Rovers	L	0-3	0-1			20,000

Appearances
Goals

Doig	Porteous	Smellie	Wilson	Auld	Gibson	Hannah, J.	Hannah, D.	Campbell	Millar	Scott	Gillespie, Jas.	Harvie	Dunlop	Gillespie, John	
1	2	3	4	5	6	7	8	9	10	11					1
1	2	3	4	5	6	7	8	9	10		11				2
1	2	3	4	5	6	11	10	9		7	8				3
1	2	3	4	5	6	11		9	10	7	8				4
1	2	3	4	5	6	11		9	10	7	8				5
1	2	3	4	5	6	11		9	10	7	8				6
1	2	3	4	5	6	11	7	9	10		8				7
1	2	3	4	5	6	7		9	10	11	8				8
1	2	3	4	5	6	7		9	10	11	8				9
1	2	3	4	5	6	10		9		11	7	8			10
1	2	3	4	5	6	7	10	9		11	8				11
1	2	3	4	5	6	7	10		11	9	8				12
1	2	3	4	5	6	11	10	9		7	8				13
1	2	3	4	5	6	11	10	9		7	8				14
1	2	3	4	5	6	11	10	9		7	8				15
1	2	3	4	5	6	11	10			7	8				16
1	2	3	4	5	6	11	10	9		7	8				17
1	2	3	4	5	6	11	10		9	7	8				18
1	2	3	4	5	6	11	10	9	8	7					19
1	2	3	4	5	6	11	10	9	8		7				20
1	2	3	4		6	11	10	9	8		7		5		22
1	2	3	4	5	6	11	10	9	8		7				24
1	2			5	6			9	10	11	7	8	4	3	26
1	2		4	5	6			9	10	11	7	8		3	27
1	2		4	5	6	11	8	9	10		7			3	28
1	2	3	4	5	6	11	8	9	10		7				29
1	2		4		6	11	8	9	10		7	5		3	30
1	2		4	5	3	7		9	10	11		8	6		31
1	2		4		6	11	8	9	10		7		5	3	32
1	2		4	5	3	7		9	10	11		8	6		33
30	30	23	29	27	30	28	20	27	22	10	23	21	5	5	
		8		3	19	4	30	13	5	12	5				

1	2	3	4	5	6	11	10	9	8		7				21
1	2	3	4	5	6	11	10	9	8		7				23
1	3		4	5	6	8	10	9		11	7		2		25
3	3	2	3	3	3	3	3	2	1	3		1			
						1	3	5							

John Harvie preferred his surname to be spelled 'Harvey'.

1893-94

Division One

Ground: Newcastle Road

Manager: Tom Watson

League Table

	P	W	D	L	F	A	Pts
Aston Villa	30	19	6	5	84	42	44
SUNDERLAND	30	17	4	9	72	44	38
Derby Co	30	16	4	10	73	62	36
Blackburn R	30	16	2	12	69	53	34
Burnley	30	15	4	11	61	51	34
Everton	30	15	3	12	90	57	33
Nottingham F	30	14	4	12	57	48	32
WBA	30	14	4	12	66	59	32
Wolverhampton W	30	14	3	13	52	63	31
Sheffield U	30	13	5	12	47	61	31
Stoke	30	13	3	14	65	79	29
Sheffield W	30	9	8	13	48	57	26
Bolton W	30	10	4	16	38	52	24
Preston NE	30	10	3	17	44	56	23
Darwen	30	7	5	18	37	83	19
Newton Heath	30	6	2	22	36	72	14

FA Cup Winners: Notts County

Did you know that?

The FA Cup 2nd round tie at home to Aston Villa on 10 February 1894 produced record receipts for the Newcastle Road ground; £960.

Match 1: Walker and Dalton made debuts
Match 2: Meechan made debut
Match 5: Porteous last game
Match 6: Walker last game
Match 8: Dalton last game
Match 20: Matthew Scott only game
Match 24: Hyslop made debut

Match No.	Date		Round	Venue	Opponents	Result	FT	HT	Pos.	Scorers	Attendance
1	Sep	2		A	Sheffield Wed.	D	2-2	2-1	8	J. Hannah (2)	20,000
2		9		H	Aston Villa	D	1-1	0-1	10	Millar	10,000
3		16		A	Preston North End	W	2-1	1-1	6	J. Hannah, Gillespie	12,000
4		23		H	Sheffield Wed.	D	1-1	1-0	7	Millar	3,000
5		30		A	Everton	L	1-7	1-5	12	Gillespie	30,000
6	Oct	7		A	Sheffield United	L	0-1	0-1	14		12,000
7		14		H	Stoke	W	4-0	2-0	11	Millar (2), D. Hannah, Campbell	6,000
8		21		A	Blackburn Rovers	L	3-4	3-2	13	Campbell (2), Millar	10,000
9		28		H	Derby County	W	5-0	5-0	10	D. Hannah, Gibson, Millar, Auld, Gillespie	5,000
10	Nov	4		H	Wolverhampton W.	W	6-0	3-0	6	D. Hannah (2), Millar (3), Scott	8,000
11		11		A	Aston Villa	L	1-2	0-0	7	Millar	14,100
12		25		H	West Bromwich Albion	W	2-1	1-0	7	Campbell (2)	6,000
13	Dec	2		A	Burnley	L	0-1	0-0	11		9,500
14		6		H	Newton Heath	W	4-1	3-0	7	Millar (2), Campbell (2)	5,000
15		9		H	Blackburn Rovers	L	2-3	1-2	9	Campbell, D. Hannah	10,000
16		16		H	Burnley	D	2-2	2-1	9	Campbell, Millar	7,000
17		23		A	West Bromwich Albion	W	3-2	1-1	8	Millar, Campbell, J. Hannah	3,000
18		30		H	Bolton Wanderers	W	2-1	1-0	7	Harvie, Gillespie	7,000
19	Jan	1		H	Preston North End	W	6-3	3-0	7	Campbell (2), J. Hannah (2), Millar, Gillespie	11,000
20		6		A	Wolverhampton W.	L	1-2	0-0	8	Campbell	5,000
21		13		A	Nottingham Forest	W	2-1	0-1	7	Wilson, Harvie	10,000
22		20		H	Sheffield United	W	4-1	2-0	8	Millar, Campbell (2), Gow	8,000
24	Feb	6		H	Everton	W	1-0	1-0	4	Gillespie	10,000
27	Mar	3		A	Newton Heath	W	4-2	3-1	3	J. Hannah (2), Campbell (2)	8,000
28		7		A	Derby County	W	4-1	2-0	2	Millar (2), D. Hannah, Campbell	3,000
29		17		H	Nottingham Forest	W	2-0	1-0	2	Hyslop, Millar	8,000
30		24		A	Stoke	L	0-2	0-1	2		10,000
31		27		H	Darwen	W	4-0	3-0	2	Wilson, Gibson, Shaw o.g., Gillespie	3,000
32	Apr	7		A	Darwen	W	3-0	2-0	2	Gillespie, Hyslop (2)	5,000
33		23		A	Bolton Wanderers	L	0-2	0-1	2		6,000

Appearances
Goals

FA Cup

23	Jan	27	R1	H	Accrington	W	3-0	1-0		Gillespie, Wilson, J. Hannah	4,000
25	Feb	10	R2	H	Aston Villa	D	2-2(aet)	2-0		Harvie, Wilson	15,956
26		21	R2r	A	Aston Villa	L	1-3	0-2		J. Hannah	25,000

Appearances
Goals

Doig	Porteous	Walker	Wilson	Dalton	Gibson	Gillespie	Hannah, D.	Campbell	Millar	Hannah, J.	Meechan	Auld	Dunlop	Harvie	Scott, J.	Gow	Scott, M.	Hyslop	
1	2	3	4	5	6	7	8	9	10	11									1
1		2	4		6	7	8	9	10	11	3	5							2
1		2	6			7		9	10	11	3	5	4	8					3
1		2	6			7		9	10	11	3	5	4	8					4
1	2	3	6			5	7	9	10	11			4	8					5
1		2	6		3	7	10	9	8	11		5	4						6
1			6	2	3		10	9	8			5	4	7	11				7
1		6		2	3		8	9	10			5	4	7	11				8
1		6			3	7	10	9			2	5	4	8	11				9
1		6			3	10		9	7	2	5	4	8	11					10
1		6			3		10	8	9		2	5	4	7	11				11
1			6	7	10	9			2	5	4	8	11	3					12
1		6				7		9	10		2	5	4	8	11	3			13
1		6			3	7	6	9	10			5	4	8	11	2			14
1					6	7	11	9	10		2	5	4	8		3			15
1		6				10	9	8		2	5	4	7	11	3				16
1		6				7		9	10	11	2	5	4	8		3			17
1		6				7		9	10	11	2	5	4	8		3			18
1		6				7		9	10	11	2	5	4	8		3			19
		6			3	7		9	10	11	2	5	4	8		2	1		20
1		6				7		9	10	11	2	5	4	8		3			21
1		6				7	8	9	10	11	2	5	4			3			22
1		6				7		9	10		2	5	4	8		3	11		24
1		4		3			6	9	8	11	2	5		7			10		27
1		6			3	7	10	9	8	11		5	4			2			28
1		6				7	8		9	11	2	5	4			3	10		29
1		6				7	10	9		11	2	5	4	8		3			30
1		6		5	7			9	11	2		4	8			3	10		31
1		6		4	7			9	11	2	5		8			3	10		32
1		6				7		9		11	2	5	4	8		3	10		33
29	2	6	27	3	17	24	17	25	27	20	22	27	26	24	9	18	1	6	
		2			2	8	6	18	19	8		1		2	1	1		3	

Doig	Porteous	Walker	Wilson	Dalton	Gibson	Gillespie	Hannah, D.	Campbell	Millar	Hannah, J.	Meechan	Auld	Dunlop	Harvie	Scott, J.	Gow	Scott, M.	Hyslop	
1		6				7		9	10	11	2	5	4	8		3			23
1		6				7		9	10	11	2	5	4	8		3			25
1		6				7		9	10	11	2	5	4	8		3			26
3		3			3	3		3	3	3	3	3	3	3		3			
		2			1			2				1							

Jimmy Hannah

Hannah is one of only two players to have been signed from Sunderland Albion (2 January 1891). He collected one Scotland cap in his career, in 1889 while playing for Renton. Jimmy was not related to David Hannah who regularly partnered him on the left wing.

1894-95

Division One

Ground: Newcastle Road

Manager: Tom Watson

League Table

	P	W	D	L	F	A	Pts
SUNDERLAND	30	21	5	4	80	37	47
Everton	30	18	6	6	82	50	42
Aston Villa	30	17	5	8	82	43	39
Preston NE	30	15	5	10	62	46	35
Blackburn R	30	11	10	9	59	49	32
Sheffield U	30	14	4	12	57	55	32
Nottingham F	30	13	5	12	50	56	31
Sheffield W	30	12	4	14	50	55	28
Burnley	30	11	4	15	44	56	26
Bolton W	30	9	7	14	61	62	25
Wolverhampton W	30	9	7	14	43	63	25
Small Heath	30	9	7	14	50	74	25
WBA	30	10	4	16	51	66	24
Stoke	30	9	6	15	50	67	24
Derby Co	30	7	9	14	45	68	23
Liverpool	30	7	8	15	51	70	22

FA Cup Winners: Aston Villa

Did you know that?

Sunderland's game against Derby County on 1 September 1894 consisted of three 45 minutes 'halves'. The referee, Mr Kirkham, was late so an alternative referee officiated. Sunderland were winning 3-0 at the interval by the time Mr Kirkham arrived and decided to restart the game at 0-0. Sunderland scored another three goals without reply in the 'second' first half and eventually won 8-0. Apparently The Rams played the first 90 minutes against a strong wind and visibly tired in the final half.

Match 1: McCreadie and Johnston made debuts
Match 2: McNeill made debut
Match 5: David Hannah last game
Match 21: Hyslop last game
Match 24; Auld last game
Match 29: Goodchild only game and Meechan last game
Match 34: Crowned League champions

Match No.	Date		Round	Venue	Opponents	Result	FT	HT	Pos.	Scorers	Attendance
1	Sep	1		H	Derby County	W	8-0	3-0	1	J. Hannah, Gillespie (2), Millar (2), Campbell, Hyslop (2)	9,000
2		8		H	Burnley	W	3-0	1-0	2	Hyslop (3)	6,000
3		15		A	Aston Villa	W	2-1	1-1	2	Campbell, J. Hannah	20,000
4		22		H	West Bromwich Albion	W	3-0	2-0	2	Campbell, Gillespie (2)	8,000
5		29		A	Bolton Wanderers	L	1-4	0-1	3	Campbell	11,000
6	Oct	6		H	Stoke	W	3-1	2-0	2	Clare o.g., Hyslop, Millar	6,000
7		13		A	Derby County	W	2-1	1-1	2	Hyslop, Campbell (pen)	8,000
8		27		A	Everton	D	2-2	2-0	4	Millar (2)	30,000
9	Nov	3		H	Wolverhampton W.	W	2-0	0-0	3	Campbell, Millar	8,000
10		10		A	Blackburn Rovers	D	1-1	1-0	2	McCreadie	16,000
11		17		H	Bolton Wanderers	W	4-0	2-0	2	J. Hannah (2), Campbell, Gillespie	9,000
12		24		H	Liverpool	W	3-2	0-2	2	J. Hannah, Campbell, Gillespie	8,000
13	Dec	8		H	Small Heath	W	7-1	3-0	3	Gillespie (2), Campbell, Millar, Wilson (2), McCreadie	6,000
14		15		H	Blackburn Rovers	W	3-2	2-1	2	Campbell, Gillespie (2)	8,000
15		26		A	West Bromwich Albion	W	2-0	0-0	3	Meechan, Wilson	12,000
16		27		A	Nottingham Forest	L	1-2	1-1	3	Campbell	7,000
17		29		A	Preston North End	L	0-1	0-1	3		3,000
18	Jan	1		H	Preston North End	W	2-0	0-0	1	Campbell, J. Hannah	10,000
19		2		A	Aston Villa	D	4-4	2-3	1	Gillespie (2), J. Hannah, Millar	12,000
20		5		H	Nottingham Forest	D	2-2	1-2	1	Millar, Campbell	6,000
21		12		A	Wolverhampton W.	W	4-1	1-0	1	J. Hannah, Millar, Campbell (2)	10,000
22		26		A	Stoke	W	5-2	3-0	1	J. Hannah, McCreadie, Millar, Campbell (2)	8,000
24	Feb	9		A	Small Heath	D	1-1	1-0	1	J. Hannah	10,000
26		23		H	Sheffield United	W	2-0	2-0	1	McCreadie, Campbell	7,000
27		26		H	Sheffield Wed.	W	3-1	1-0	1	McCreadie, Campbell, Johnston	6,000
29	Mar	9		A	Sheffield United	L	0-4	0-2	1		8,000
31		23		A	Sheffield Wed.	W	2-1	1-0	1	Dunlop, Campbell	5,000
32		25		A	Liverpool	W	3-2	1-1	1	Campbell, Wilson, Millar	18,000
33	Apr	13		A	Burnley	W	3-0	1-0	1	McCreadie, Gillespie (2)	8,000
34		20		H	Everton	W	2-1	1-0	1	McCreadie, J. Hannah	20,000

Appearances
Goals

FA Cup

23	Feb	2	R1	H	Fairfield	W	11-1	6-1		Millar (5), J. Hannah (3), Gillespie, McCreadie, Scott	1,500
25		16	R2	H	Preston North End	W	2-0	2-0		Campbell (2)	15,000
28	Mar	2	R3	H	Bolton Wanderers	W	2-1	0-1		Wilson (2)	14,000
30		16	S	N*	Aston Villa	L	1-2	1-0		Millar	15,000

* at Ewood Park

Appearances
Goals

	Doig	Meechan	Gow	Wilson	McCreadie	Johnstone	Gillespie	Millar	Campbell	Hyslop	Hannah, J.	McNeill	Auld	Harvie	Scott	Hannah, D.	Dunlop	Goodchild	
1	1	2	3	4	5	6	7	8	9	10	11								1
2	1	2			4	6			9	10	7	3	5	8	11				2
3	1	2		4	5	6	7	8	9	10	11	3							3
4	1	2		4	5	6	7	8	9	10	11	3							4
5	1	2		4	5	6	7	8	9		11	3		10					5
6	1	2		4	5	6	7	8	9	10	11	3							6
7	1	2		4	5	6	7	8	9	10	11	3							7
8	1	2		4	5	6	7	8	9	10	11	3							8
9	1	2		4	5	6	7	10	9			3	8	11					9
10	1	2		4	5	6	7	8	9	10	11	3							10
11	1	2	6	5	3	7	8	9	10	11				4					11
12	1	2	6	5	3	7	8	9	10	11				4					12
13	1	2	6	5	3	7	8	9	10			11							13
14	1	2	6	5	3	7	8	9	10			11		4					14
15	1	2	6	5	3	7	8	9	10			11		4					15
16	1		6	5	3	7	10	9		2		8	11	4					16
17	1		6	5		7	8	9	3	10	2		11	4					17
18	1			4	3	7	8	9	10	2	5		11	6					18
19	1	2		5	6	7	8	9	10	3			11	4					19
20	1		6	3	7	8	9		11	2	5		10	4					20
21	1		6	5	3	7	8	9	10	11	2			4					21
22	1		6	5	3	7	8	9	10	2		11		4					22
24	1		6		3	7	8	9	10	2	5	11		4					24
26	1	2		4	5	6	7	8	9	10	3		11						26
27	1	2	3	6	5	11	7	8	9	10				4					27
29	1	2	3	10	5	6		8	9	11				4	7				29
31	1		3	4		6		8	9	11	2		7	10	5				31
32	1		3	4		6		8	9	11	2		7	10	5				32
33	1		3	4	5	6	7	8	9	11	2		10						33
34	1		3		5	6	7	10	9	11	2		8		4				34
	30	19	7	25	27	29	26	29	30	12	28	22	4	6	16	1	18	1	
		1		4	7	1	14	12	21	7	11				1				
23	1		6	5	3	7	8	9		11	2		10	4					23
25	1	2		4		6	7	10	9		3	8	11	5					25
28	1	2		6	5	11	7	8	9	10	3			4					28
30	1		3	4	5	6		10	9	7	2	8	11						30
	4	2	1	4	3	4	3	4	4	3	4	2	3	3					
			2	1		1	6	2		3			1						

Jimmy Millar scored five goals v Fairfield.

1895-96

Division One

Ground: Newcastle Road
Manager: Tom Watson

League Table

	P	W	D	L	F	A	Pts
Aston Villa	30	20	5	5	78	45	45
Derby Co	30	17	7	6	68	35	41
Everton	30	16	7	7	66	43	39
Bolton W	30	16	5	9	49	37	37
SUNDERLAND	30	15	7	8	52	41	37
Stoke	30	15	0	15	56	47	30
Sheffield W	30	12	5	13	44	53	29
Blackburn R	30	12	5	13	40	50	29
Preston NE	30	11	6	13	44	48	28
Burnley	30	10	7	13	48	44	27
Bury	30	12	3	15	50	54	27
Sheffield U	30	10	6	14	40	50	26
Nottingham F	30	11	3	16	42	57	25
Wolverhampton W	30	10	1	19	61	65	21
Small Heath	30	8	4	18	39	79	20
WBA	30	6	7	17	30	59	19

FA Cup Winners: Sheffield Wednesday

Did you know that?

Hugh Wilson became the first Sunderland player to be sent off in a League game, v Stoke, 14 March 1896. The offence was insulting the referee, Mr Kingscott of Derby.

Match 2: Cowan made debut
Match 3: Thompson and McKenzie made debuts
Match 5: McKenzie last game
Match 9: Hartley made debut
Match 21: Scott last game
Match 24: McCreadie last game
Match 31: Thompson last game
Match 32: Tom Watson last as Sunderland manager and Gibson last game

Match No.	Date		Round	Venue	Opponents	Result	FT	HT	Pos.	Scorers	Attendance
1	Sep	2		H	Preston North End	W	4-1	1-0		Gillespie (2), Johnston, Wilson	3,000
2		7		H	Blackburn Rovers	W	2-1	1-1	2	Hannah, Cowan	10,000
3		9		A	Burnley	D	0-0	0-0	1		9,000
4		14		A	Derby County	L	0-2	0-0	2		10,000
5		21		H	Wolverhampton W.	D	2-2	1-0	4	McKenzie, Hannah	8,000
6		28		H	Bury	D	0-0	0-0	4		7,000
7	Oct	5		A	Aston Villa	L	1-2	0-0	9	Hannah	20,000
8		7		A	Sheffield United	W	2-1	0-1	3	McCreadie, Campbell	5,000
9		19		A	Sheffield Wed.	L	0-3	0-2	9		14,000
10		26		A	Blackburn Rovers	W	4-2	2-0	5	Johnston, Harvie, Gillespie, Campbell	8,000
11	Nov	2		H	Derby County	D	2-2	1-0	7	Campbell, Harvie	8,000
12		9		H	Aston Villa	W	2-1	1-0	5	Campbell, Millar	17,000
13		16		A	Everton	L	0-1	0-0	7		15,000
14		23		H	Bolton Wanderers	W	1-0	1-0	6	Gillespie	5,000
15	Dec	14		H	Small Heath	W	2-1	1-0	7	Campbell, Hannah	3,000
16		21		A	Bolton Wanderers	L	0-1	0-1	8		7,000
17		26		A	West Bromwich Albion	D	1-1	1-1	7	Millar	15,124
18		27		A	Wolverhampton W.	W	3-1	1-1	5	Scott, Campbell (2)	8,000
19	Jan	4		A	Preston North End	L	1-4	1-2	6	Gibson	11,000
20		11		H	Sheffield United	D	1-1	1-0	6	Harvie	3,000
21		18		A	Nottingham Forest	L	1-3	0-0	6	Harvie	15,000
22		25		H	West Bromwich Albion	W	7-1	3-0	6	Millar (3), Gillespie, Hannah, Campbell (2)	3,000
24	Feb	8		H	Nottingham Forest	D	1-1	1-1	5	Campbell	3,000
26		18		H	Burnley	W	3-1	1-1	4	Cowan (2), Millar	4,000
27		22		H	Everton	W	3-0	2-0	4	Campbell, Wilson, Gillespie	7,000
28	Mar	7		H	Sheffield Wed.	W	2-1	1-0	4	Cowan, Hannah	6,000
29		14		H	Stoke	L	0-5	0-3	4		8,000
30		28		H	Stoke	W	4-1	2-0	4	Cowan, Millar, Campbell (2)	3,000
31	Apr	3		A	Bury	W	2-1	1-0	4	Campbell (2)	15,000
32		11		A	Small Heath	W	1-0	1-0	5	Millar	8,000

Appearances
Goals

FA Cup

| 23 | Feb | 1 | R1 | H | Preston North End | W | 4-1 | 1-0 | | Millar (2), Campbell (2) | 13,755 |
| 25 | | 15 | R2 | A | Sheffield Wed. | L | 1-2 | 0-2 | | Millar | 22,000 |

Appearances
Goals

	Doig	McNeill	Gow	Wilson	McCreadie	Johnston	Gillespie	Millar	Campbell	Hannah	Scott	Cowan	Thompson	Dunlop	McKenzie	Gibson	Harvie	Hartley	
1	2	3	4	5	6	7	8	9	10	11									1
1	2	3	4	5	6	7		9	10	11	8								2
	2	3	4	5		7	8	9		11		1	6	10					3
1	2	3	8	5	6	7		9	10	11		4							4
1	2	3	6	5		7		9		11		8		4	10				5
1		3	4	5	6	7		9	11	10	8			2					6
1		2	4	5	6	7		9	10	11	8			3					7
1		2	4	5	10	7		9		11		6		3	8				8
1		2	4	5		7		10	11			6		3	8	9			9
1		2	4	5	6	7		9	10	11				3	8				10
1		2	4		6	7		9	10	11		5		3	8				11
1		2	4	5	6	7	8	9	10	11				3					12
1		2	4	5	6	7	8	9	10	11				3					13
1		2	4			7	8	9	11			6		3		10			14
1		2	4	5	3	7	8	9	11			6			10				15
1	3	2	4		6		8	9	7	11		5			10				16
1	3	2	4		6	7	8	9	11			5			10				17
1	3	2	4		6	7	10	9		11		5			8				18
1	2	3			6	7	10	9	11			4	5	8					19
1	2	3			6	4	9	10	11	8		5			7				20
1	2	3			6		10	9	7	11		4	5	8					21
1	2	3	4		6	7	10	9	11			5		8					22
1		2		5	6	7	10	9	11			4	3	8					24
1	2	3	4		6		11	10		8		5			7	9			26
1	2	3	4		6	7	10	9	11			5		8					27
1		2	4		6		10	9	11	7		5	3	8					28
1	2	3	4		6	7	10	9	11			5		8					29
1	2	3			6	7	10	9	11	8		4	5						30
	2	3			6	7	10	9	11		1	4		5	8				31
1	2	3			6	7	10	9	11			8	4	5					32
28	18	30	23	15	26	25	21	30	26	15	9	2	23	2	16	16	5		
	2	1	2	6	8	15	6	1	5			1	1	4					

1	2	3	4		6	7	10	9	11			5		8					23
1	2	3	4		6	7	10	9	11			5		8					25
2	2	2	2		2	2	2	2	2			2		2					
							3	2											

Hugh Wilson
Captain of the 'Team of All The Talents.

1896-97

Division One

Ground: Newcastle Road
Manager: Robert Campbell

League Table

	P	W	D	L	F	A	Pts
Aston Villa	30	21	5	4	73	38	47
Sheffield U	30	13	10	7	42	29	36
Derby Co	30	16	4	10	70	50	36
Preston NE	30	11	12	7	55	40	34
Liverpool	30	12	9	9	46	38	33
Sheffield W	30	10	11	9	42	37	31
Everton	30	14	3	13	62	57	31
Bolton W	30	12	6	12	40	43	30
Bury	30	10	10	10	39	44	30
Wolverhampton W	30	11	6	13	45	41	28
Nottingham F	30	9	8	13	44	49	26
WBA	30	10	6	14	33	56	26
Stoke	30	11	3	16	48	59	25
Blackburn R	30	11	3	16	35	62	25
SUNDERLAND	30	7	9	14	34	47	23
Burnley	30	6	7	17	43	61	19

FA Cup Winners: Aston Villa

Did you know that?

The Sunderland goalscorer at Burnley on Monday 7 September 1896 will probably always remain a mystery as no contemporary match reports give his name. This is the only uncredited goal in Sunderland's League history.

Incidentally, on their return the Sunderland team missed their train connection at York by 15 minutes and had to spend the night in a hotel.

Match 1: Robert Campbell first as Sunderland manager and Longair, Ferguson & Hamilton debuts
Match 6: Joe Wilson made debut
Match 7: Hartley and Joe Wilson last games
Match 8: R. Johnston made debut and Harry Johnston last game
Match 11: Longair last game
Match 14: Hartness made debut
Match 15: Hartness last game
Match 16: Boyle made debut
Match 18: Morgan made debut
Match 26: McAllister made debut
Match 28: McIntosh made debut
Match 32: Knowles only game and Hamilton & R. Johnston last games
Match 34: Cowan last game
Match 36: Campbell, Gillespie, Gow, Hannah and Harvie last games

Match No.	Date		Round	Venue	Opponents	Result	FT	HT	Pos.	Scorers	Attendance
1	Sep	1		H	Bury	L	0-1	0-1			4,000
2		5		H	Bolton Wanderers	D	1-1	1-1	14	Hannah	6,000
3		7		A	Burnley	D	1-1	1-1	9	Unknown Scorer	9,000
4		12		A	Preston North End	L	3-5	2-1	15	Gillespie, Hartley, Hannah	10,000
5		19		A	Sheffield United	L	0-3	0-1	16		7,000
6		26		A	Bolton Wanderers	L	0-1	0-0	16		9,000
7	Oct	3		H	Wolverhampton W.	L	0-3	0-1	16		7,000
8		10		A	Sheffield Wed.	D	0-0	0-0	16		8,000
9		17		H	Liverpool	W	4-3	3-0	15	Hannah (2), Hamilton (2)	6,000
10		24		A	Wolverhampton W.	W	1-0	1-0	12	Dunlop	5,000
11	Nov	7		A	Liverpool	L	0-3	0-1	15		9,000
12		21		A	Nottingham Forest	L	1-2	1-0	16	Campbell	7,000
13		28		A	West Bromwich Albion	L	0-1	0-0	16		4,000
14	Dec	5		H	Sheffield Wed.	D	0-0	0-0	15		2,000
15		12		H	Everton	D	1-1	1-0	15	Hannah	12,000
16		19		H	Blackburn Rovers	L	0-1	0-0	15		2,000
17		25		A	Blackburn Rovers	W	2-1	1-0	15	Gillespie, Cowan	12,000
18		26		A	Everton	L	2-5	1-2	15	Morgan, Gillespie	35,000
19	Jan	1		H	Preston North End	D	1-1	1-0	16	Hannah	10,000
20		2		H	Derby County	L	1-2	0-1	16	Morgan	7,000
21		9		H	Aston Villa	W	4-2	1-1	15	Gillespie (2), R. Johnston, Morgan	10,000
22		16		A	Aston Villa	L	1-2	0-0	15	Gillespie	15,000
23		23		A	Derby County	L	0-1	0-1	16		6,000
26	Feb	20		H	Stoke	W	4-1	1-1	15	Gillespie (2), Morgan, Campbell	4,000
27		27		H	Sheffield United	L	0-1	0-1	15		4,000
28	Mar	2		H	Burnley	D	1-1	0-1	15	Campbell	3,000
29		6		H	West Bromwich Albion	W	2-1	2-0	14	Wilson, Morgan	3,000
30		13		H	Nottingham Forest	D	2-2	1-1	14	Morgan, Hannah	4,000
31	Apr	3		A	Stoke	W	1-0	0-0		Cowan	5,000
32		16		A	Bury	D	1-1	0-0	15	Campbell	8,000

Appearances
Goals

Test Matches

33	Apr	17		A	Notts County	L	0-1	0-0			7,000
34		19		H	Notts County	D	0-0	0-0			10,000
35		24		A	Newton Heath	D	1-1	1-1		Morgan	18,000
36		26		H	Newton Heath	W	2-0	1-0		Gillespie (2)	8,000

Appearances
Goals

FA Cup

24	Jan	30	R1	A	Burnley	W	1-0	1-0		Morgan	8,000
25	Feb	13	R2	H	Nottingham Forest	L	1-3	1-2		Harvie	17,000

Appearances
Goals

	Doig	McNeill	Gow	Dunlop	Longair	Wilson, H.	Gillespie	Ferguson	Campbell	Hannah	Hamilton	Johnston, H.	Hartley	Harvie	Wilson, J.	Johnston, R.	Cowan	Harness	Boyle	Morgan	McAllister	McIntosh	Knowles	
	1	2	3	4	5	6	7	8	9	10	11													1
	1	2	3	5		8	7	6	9	10		4	11											2
	1		2	5		6		4	9	7	11	3	10	8										3
	1		2	5		6	7	4	9	10		3	11	8										4
	1	2		5		6	7	4	9	11		3	10	8										5
	1	2	3	5		6	7	4	9	11			10	8										6
	1	2	3	5		6	7	4	9	11			10	8										7
	1	2	3	5			7	4	9	10	6		8	11										8
	1	2	3	5		6	7	4	9	10	11		8											9
	1	2	3	5		6	7	4	9	10	11		8											10
	1	2	3	6	5		7	4	9	10	11		8											11
	1	2	3	5		6	7	4	9	11			8		10									12
	1	2	3	5		6	7	4	9	10			8	11										13
	1	2	3	5		6	7	4	9	10				11		8								14
	1	2	3	5		6	7	4	9	10				11		8								15
	1		3	5		6	7	4	9	10				11	8		2							16
	1	2	3	5		6	7	4	11	10		9		8										17
	1	2	3	5		6	7	4	10	11				8			9							18
	1	2	3	5		6	7	4	10	11				8			9							19
	1	2		5		6	7	4	10			8		11			3	9						20
	1	2	3	5		6	7	4		11				8	10			9						21
	1	2	3	5		6	7	4	8		11				10			9						22
	1	2	3	5		6	7	4	8	11					10			9						23
	1	2	3			6	7	4	9	11		8						10	5					26
	1	2	3	5		6	7	4	8	11					10			9						27
	1	2	3	5		6	7	4	8	11								10	9					28
	1	2	3	5		6	7	4	9	11				8				10						29
	1	2	3		5	7	4	9	11					8	6	10								30
	1	2	3			7	4	5	10					11	8		6	9						31
	1			6	7	4	9	11	8				10		2		5		3					32
	30	26	27	26	2	27	29	30	29	28	7	5	6	13	2	12	8	2	5	12	2	1	1	
			1		1	8			4	7	2		1			1	2			6				

	Doig	McNeill	Gow	Dunlop	Longair	Wilson, H.	Gillespie	Ferguson	Campbell	Hannah	Hamilton	Johnston, H.	Hartley	Harvie	Wilson, J.	Johnston, R.	Cowan	Harness	Boyle	Morgan	McAllister	McIntosh	Knowles	
	1	2	3			5	7	4	9	11				8			6	10						33
	1	2	3			5	7	4	9	11				8			6	10						34
	1	2	3			5	7	4	9	11		8					6	10						35
	1	2	3			6	7	4	11	10				8				9	5					36
	4	4	4			4	4	4	4	4		2		2			3	4	1					
						2												1						

	Doig	McNeill	Gow	Dunlop	Longair	Wilson, H.	Gillespie	Ferguson	Campbell	Hannah	Hamilton	Johnston, H.	Hartley	Harvie	Wilson, J.	Johnston, R.	Cowan	Harness	Boyle	Morgan	McAllister	McIntosh	Knowles	
	1	2	3	5		6	7	4	9			8	11					10						24
	1	2	3	5		6	7	4	9			8	11					10						25
	2	2	2	2		2	2	2	2			2	2					2						
												1						1						

James Gillespie

His goals in the last test match kept Sunderland in Division One. Test matches were used to determine promotion and relegation issues up until 1898. He became only the second player to be signed from Sunderland Albion (summer 1892 after spending one season away from Newcastle Road).

1897-98

Division One

Ground: Newcastle Road

Manager: Robert Campbell

League Table

	P	W	D	L	F	A	Pts
Sheffield U	30	17	8	5	56	31	42
SUNDERLAND	30	16	5	9	43	30	37
Wolverhampton W	30	14	7	9	57	41	35
Everton	30	13	9	8	48	39	35
Sheffield W	30	15	3	12	51	42	33
Aston Villa	30	14	5	11	61	51	33
WBA	30	11	10	9	44	45	32
Nottingham F	30	11	9	10	47	49	31
Liverpool	30	11	6	13	48	45	28
Derby Co	30	11	6	13	57	61	28
Bolton W	30	11	4	15	28	41	26
Preston NE	30	8	8	14	35	43	24
Notts Co	30	8	8	14	36	46	24
Bury	30	8	8	14	39	51	24
Blackburn R	30	7	10	13	39	54	24
Stoke	30	8	8	14	35	55	24

FA Cup Winners: Nottingham Forest

Did you know that?

James Chalmers scored the final goal at Sunderland's Newcastle Road Ground in the game v Nottingham Forest on 23 April 1898.

Match 1: Bach, Bradshaw, Brown, Chalmers and Leslie made debuts
Match 10: McIntosh last game
Match 15: Bradshaw last game and Lavery only game
Match 23: Saxton made debut and Haining only game
Match 25: Galbraith made debut
Match 27: Benefit game for Wilson.
Match 30: Lee made debut and Galbraith last game
Match 31: Prince made debut and Lee last game

Match No.	Date		Round	Venue	Opponents	Result	FT	HT	Pos.	Scorers	Attendance
1	Sep	4		A	Sheffield Wed.	W	1-0	0-0		Morgan	5,000
2		11		H	Wolverhampton W.	W	3-2	1-1	3	Wilson, Brown, Morgan	15,000
3		18		A	Preston North End	L	0-2	0-1	6		10,000
4		25		H	Sheffield Wed.	W	1-0	1-0	5	Ferguson	12,000
5	Oct	2		A	Nottingham Forest	D	1-1	1-0	3	Morgan	10,000
6		9		H	Derby County	W	2-1	2-0	3	Bradshaw, Chalmers	10,000
7		16		H	West Bromwich Albion	L	0-2	0-1	4		8,000
8		23		H	Aston Villa	D	0-0	0-0	4		22,000
9		30		A	Bolton Wanderers	L	0-1	0-0	6		12,000
10	Nov	13		A	Wolverhampton W.	L	2-4	2-2	10	Morgan, Wilson	3,000
11		27		A	Aston Villa	L	3-4	2-1	12	Chalmers, Morgan, Brown	15,000
12	Dec	4		H	Stoke	W	4-0	2-0	11	Leslie, Dunlop, Morgan, Bradshaw	5,000
13		11		A	Derby County	D	2-2	1-1	10	Leslie, Brown	5,000
14		18		H	Everton	D	0-0	0-0	10		8,000
15		25		A	Blackburn Rovers	L	1-2	0-0	12	Brown	20,000
16		27		A	Liverpool	W	2-0	0-0	10	Brown, Cleghorn o.g.	20,000
17	Jan	1		H	Preston North End	W	1-0	1-0	7	Wilson	18,000
18		3		H	Notts County	W	2-0	2-0	7	Leslie, Brown	3,000
19		8		A	Stoke	W	1-0	1-0	5	Wilson	12,000
20		15		H	Bury	W	2-1	2-0	3	Wilson, Chalmers	6,000
21		22		H	Liverpool	W	1-0	0-0	2	Leslie	9,000
22	Feb	5		A	Notts County	W	1-0	1-0	2	Saxton	10,000
23		19		A	West Bromwich Albion	D	2-2	1-2	2	Wilson, Brown	5,000
24		22		H	Bolton Wanderers	W	2-0	2-0	2	Wilson, Leslie	6,000
25	Mar	5		H	Sheffield United	W	3-1	1-1	2	Howell o.g., Wilson, Leslie	20,000
26		12		H	Blackburn Rovers	W	2-1	1-0	2	Dunlop, Leslie	10,000
27	Apr	2		A	Sheffield United	L	0-1	0-0	2		20,000
28		8		A	Bury	L	0-1	0-1	2		12,000
29		11		A	Everton	L	0-2	0-2	2		20,000
30		23		H	Nottingham Forest	W	4-0	4-0	2	Chalmers (2), Brown, Leslie	13,000

Appearances
Goals

FA Cup

22	Jan	29	R1	H	Sheffield Wed.	L	0-1	0-0			17,893

Appearances
Goals

	Doig	Boyle	Bach	Ferguson	McAlister	Wilson	Bradshaw	Leslie	Brown	Morgan	Chalmers	McNeill	Dunlop	McIntosh	Lavery	Haining	Saxton	Galbraith	Lee	Prince	
1	1	2	3	4	5	6	7	8	9	10	11										1
2	1		2	4	5	6	7	8	9	10	11	3									2
3	1		2	4		6	7	8	9	10	11	3	5								3
4	1	2		8	5	6	7	9		10	11	3	4								4
5	1	2		8	5	6	7	9		10	11	3	4								5
6	1	2		8	5	6	7	9		10	11	3	4								6
7	1	2		8	5	6	7	9		10	11	3	4								7
8	1	3	2	8	5	6	7	9		10	11		4								8
9	1	3	2	4	5	6	7	9	8	10	11										9
10	1	3	2	8	5	6		7		10	11		4	9							10
11	1		2	4	5		7	8	9	10	11	3	6								11
12	1		2	4		6	7	8	9	10	11	3	5								12
13	1	3	2	4		6	7	8	9	10	11		5								13
14	1	3	2	4	5	6	7	8	9	10	11										14
15	1	3	2			6	7	8	9	10			5		11						15
16	1	3	2	4	5	10		8	9	7	11		6								16
17	1	3	2	4	5	10		8	9	7	11		6								17
18	1		2	4	5	10		8	9	7	11	3	6								18
19	1	3	2	4	5	10		8	9	7	11		6								19
20	1	3		4	5	10		8	9	7	11	2	6								20
21	1	3		4	5	10		8	9	7	11	2	6								21
23	1	3	4		5	10			9	8		2	6		7	11					23
24	1	3	2	4	5	10		8	9	7			6			11					24
25	1	3	2	4	5	10		8	9				6			11	7				25
26	1	3	2	4	5	10		8	9	7			6			11					26
27	1	3		4	5	10		8	9	7		2	6			11					27
28	1	3		4	5	10		8	9	7		2	6			11					28
29	1	3			5	4		8	9	7	10	2	6								29
30	1		3	2	5			8	9		10		4			11	7	6			30
31	1		2	5	3			8	9	7	11		4				6	10			31
	30	23	20	28	26	28	14	29	24	28	23	15	26	1	1	8	2	2	1		
			1		8	2	8	8	6	5		2				1					

	Doig	Boyle	Bach	Ferguson	McAlister	Wilson	Bradshaw	Leslie	Brown	Morgan	Chalmers	McNeill	Dunlop	McIntosh	Lavery	Haining	Saxton	Galbraith	Lee	Prince	
22	1	3	2	4	5	10		8	9	7	11		6								22
	1	1	1	1	1	1		1	1	1	1		1								

James Chalmers
Scorer of Sunderland's last League goal at Newcastle Road.

1898-99

Division One

Ground: Roker Park

Manager: Robert Campbell

League Table

	P	W	D	L	F	A	Pts
Aston Villa	34	19	7	8	76	40	45
Liverpool	34	19	5	10	49	33	43
Burnley	34	15	9	10	45	47	39
Everton	34	15	8	11	48	41	38
Notts Co	34	12	13	9	47	51	37
Blackburn R	34	14	8	12	60	52	36
SUNDERLAND	34	15	6	13	41	41	36
Wolverhampton W	34	14	7	13	54	48	35
Derby Co	34	12	11	11	62	57	35
Bury	34	14	7	13	48	49	35
Nottingham F	34	11	11	12	42	42	33
Stoke	34	13	7	14	47	52	33
Newcastle U	34	11	8	15	49	48	30
WBA	34	12	6	16	42	57	30
Preston NE	34	10	9	15	44	47	29
Sheffield U	34	9	11	14	45	51	29
Bolton W	34	9	7	18	37	51	25
Sheffield W	34	8	8	18	32	61	24

FA Cup Winners: Sheffield United

Did you know that?

Roker Park staged its first international on 18 February 1899. The game, against Ireland, ended in a record 13-2 win for England.

Match 1: Raisbeck and Crawford made debuts
Match 4: Chalmers last game
Match 6: Benefit game for Doig and he received £150.
Match 9: Boyle last game
Match 10: McLatchie made debut
Match 15: Dunlop last game
Match 16: Jackson made debut
Match 18: Saxton last game
Match 21: Morgan last game
Match 22: Brown last game
Match 26: Farquhar and McCombie made debuts
Match 30: Simpson made debut and Bach last game
Match 31: Fotheringham and Pallister both played their only games
Match 33: Naisby made debut and Harker only game
Match 34; Simpson last game
Match 35: Hugh Wilson last game
Match 36: Robert Campbell last game as Sunderland manager

Match No.	Date		Round	Venue	Opponents	Result	FT	HT	Pos.	Scorers	Attendance
1	Sep	3		A	Preston North End	W	3-2	0-1		Chalmers, Leslie, Morgan	8,000
2		10		H	Liverpool	W	1-0	0-0	3	Leslie	30,000
3		17		A	Nottingham Forest	D	1-1	1-0	2	Wilson	12,000
4		24		H	Bolton Wanderers	D	0-0	0-0	4		12,000
5	Oct	1		A	Derby County	L	2-4	1-2	10	Wilson, Dunlop	6,000
6		8		H	West Bromwich Albion	W	2-0	0-0	6	Leslie (2)	17,000
7		15		A	Blackburn Rovers	L	2-3	1-2	7	Crawford, Leslie	15,000
8		22		H	Sheffield Wed.	W	2-0	1-0	6	Saxton, Wilson	12,000
9		29		H	Bury	W	3-0	1-0	4	Wilson (3)	10,000
10	Nov	5		A	Wolverhampton W.	L	0-2	0-1	6		5,000
11		12		H	Everton	W	2-1	0-0	4	Crawford, Morgan	17,000
12		19		A	Notts County	L	2-5	1-2	6	Morgan, McLatchie	16,000
13		26		H	Stoke	W	2-0	0-0	6	Dunlop, McLatchie	6,000
14	Dec	3		A	Aston Villa	L	0-2	0-1	7		25,000
15		10		H	Burnley	L	0-1	0-1	8		8,000
16		17		A	Sheffield United	L	0-2	0-0	9		10,000
17		24		H	Newcastle United	L	2-3	1-2	14	Leslie, Raisbeck	30,000
18		31		H	Preston North End	W	1-0	1-0	12	Morgan (pen)	10,000
19	Jan	2		H	Derby County	W	1-0	1-0	11	Morgan (pen)	18,000
20		7		A	Liverpool	D	0-0	0-0	9		20,000
21		14		H	Nottingham Forest	D	1-1	1-1	9	Brown	9,000
22		21		A	Bolton Wanderers	L	1-6	0-3	10	Leslie	1,500
24	Feb	4		A	West Bromwich Albion	L	0-1	0-1	11		5,000
26		18		A	Sheffield Wed.	W	1-0	1-0	11	Raisbeck	12,000
27	Mar	4		H	Wolverhampton W.	W	3-0	1-0	9	McLatchie, Farquhar, Fulton	9,000
28		11		A	Everton	D	0-0	0-0	9		17,000
29		18		H	Notts County	D	1-1	1-0	8	Farquhar	6,000
30		25		A	Stoke	L	0-1	0-1	9		4,000
31		31		A	Bury	W	2-1	1-1	8	McLatchie, Simpson	5,000
32	Apr	1		H	Aston Villa	W	4-2	3-1	7	McCombie, Farquhar (2), McLatchie	20,000
33		3		H	Blackburn Rovers	L	0-1	0-0	7		15,000
34		8		A	Burnley	L	0-1	0-0	9		6,000
35		22		A	Newcastle United	W	1-0	0-0	10	McLatchie	22,000
36		29		H	Sheffield United	W	1-0	1-0	7	Leslie	6,000

Appearances
Goals

FA Cup

| 23 | Jan | 28 | R1 | A | Bristol City | W | 4-2 | 3-2 | | Leslie, Crawford, Fulton, Wilson | 16,945 |
| 25 | Feb | 11 | R2 | A | Tottenham Hotspur | L | 1-2 | 0-1 | | Fulton | 12,371 |

Appearances
Goals

Doig	Ferguson	McNeill	Raisbeck	McAllister	Dunlop	Crawford	Leslie	Morgan	Wilson	Chalmers	Bach	Saxton	Brown	Boyle	McLatchie	Fulton	Jackson	McCombie	Farquhar	Simpson	Fotheringham	Pallister	Naisby	Harker		
1	2	3	4	5	6	7	8	9	10	11																1
1	4	3		5		7	8	9	6	10	2	11														2
1	4	3		5		7	8	9	6		2	11	10													3
1	4	3		5	6		8	7	10	11	2		9													4
1	4	3	10	5	6	7	8		9		2	11														5
1	4	3		5	6	7	8	9	10		2	11														6
1	4	3	9	5	6	7	8		10		2	11														7
1	4	3	9	5	6	7		8	10		2	11														8
1	4		9	5	6	7	8		10		2	11	3													9
1	4	3	9	5	6	7	8				2	11			10											10
1	4	3	9	5	6	7		8			2	11			10											11
1	4	3	9	5	6	7		8			2		11		11											12
1	4	3		5	6	7	10				2		9		11	8										13
1	4	3		5	6	7	8	9	10		2				11											14
1	4	3		5	6	7		8			2	11	9		10											15
1	4	3	9	5		7	10		8		2				11		6									16
1	4	3	9	5		7	8		10		2				11		6									17
1	4	3		5		7	8	9	6		2	11			10											18
1	4	3	6	5		7	8	10			2		9		11											19
1	4	3	6	5		7	8	10			2		9		11											20
1	4	3	6	5			8	10	7		2		9		11											21
1	4	3	6	5		7	8		10		2				11											22
1	4	3	6	5		7	8		10		2				11	9										24
1		3	6	5		7	10		4						11	9		2	8							26
1		3	6	5		7	10		4						11	9		2	8							27
1		3	6	5		7	10		4						11	9		2	8							28
1		3	6	5		7	10		4	2					11	9			8							29
1	6	3		5		7			4	2					11	9		10	8							30
1			6	5		7	8								11	9		3		10	2	4				31
1		3	6	5		7	8		4						11	10		2	9							32
		3	6	5		7			4						11	10		2	9			1	8			33
		3	6	5		7	8								11	10		2	9	4		1				34
1		3	6	5		7	8		4						11	10		2	9							35
1	4	3	6	5		7	8								11	10		2	9							36
32	25	32	25	34	13	32	28	13	25	3	24	11	9	1	25	13	2	9	10	3	1	1	2	1		
		2		2	2	8	5	6	1		1	1			6	1			1	4	1					

Doig	Ferguson	McNeill	Raisbeck	McAllister	Dunlop	Crawford	Leslie	Morgan	Wilson	Chalmers	Bach	Saxton	Brown	Boyle	McLatchie	Fulton	Jackson	McCombie	Farquhar	Simpson	Fotheringham	Pallister	Naisby	Harker		
1	4	3	6	5		7	8		10		2				11	9										23
1	4	3	6	5		7	8		10		2				11	9										25
2	2	2	2	2		2	2		2		2				2	2										
						1	1		1							2										

James Leslie

Scorer of penultimate goal at Newcastle Road and first goal at Roker Park.

329

1899-1900

Division One

Ground: Roker Park

Manager: Alex Mackie

League Table

	P	W	D	L	F	A	Pts
Aston Villa	34	22	6	6	77	35	50
Sheffield U	34	18	12	4	63	33	48
SUNDERLAND	34	19	3	12	50	35	41
Wolverhampton W	34	15	9	10	48	37	39
Newcastle U	34	13	10	11	53	43	36
Derby Co	34	14	8	12	45	43	36
Manchester C	34	13	8	13	50	44	34
Nottingham F	34	13	8	13	56	55	34
Stoke	34	13	8	13	37	45	34
Liverpool	34	14	5	15	49	45	33
Everton	34	13	7	14	47	49	33
Bury	34	13	6	15	40	44	32
WBA	34	11	8	15	43	51	30
Blackburn R	34	13	4	17	49	61	30
Notts Co	34	9	11	14	46	60	29
Preston NE	34	12	4	18	38	48	28
Burnley	34	11	5	18	34	54	27
Glossop NE	34	4	10	20	31	74	18

FA Cup Winners: Bury

Did you know that?

Sunderland probably played in front of their lowest First Division crowd on Monday 26 March 1900. This match at Stoke was rearranged from 17 March and was played following at least 3 hours of heavy snow fall. Press reports of the time state the crowd to range from a few hundred to a thousand.

Match 1: Alex Mackie first as Sunderland manager
Match 3: Becton made debut
Match 6: Robert Hogg made debut
Match 10: Benefit for club captain McNeill and he received £200.
Match 13: Billy Hogg made debut
Match 19: Becton last game
Match 26: Watson made debut
Match 33: Crawford last game
Match 37: Fulton last game

Match No.	Date		Round	Venue	Opponents	Result	FT	HT	Pos.	Scorers	Attendance
1	Sep	2		H	Aston Villa	L	0-1	0-1			27,000
2		9		A	Liverpool	W	2-0	2-0	9	McLatchie, Farquhar	20,000
3		16		H	Burnley	W	2-1	0-0	7	Farquhar, Becton	12,000
4		23		A	Preston North End	W	1-0	0-0	5	Raisbeck	7,000
5		30		H	Nottingham Forest	W	1-0	0-0	2	McLatchie	5,000
6	Oct	2		A	Sheffield United	D	2-2	2-1	2	R. Hogg, Becton	10,000
7		7		A	Glossop North End	W	2-0	2-0	2	McLatchie, Becton	7,000
8		14		H	Stoke	W	3-0	1-0	2	R. Hogg, Crawford, McLatchie	12,000
9		28		A	West Bromwich Albion	L	0-1	0-0	3		6,117
10	Nov	4		H	Everton	W	1-0	0-0	3	McLatchie	20,000
11		11		A	Blackburn Rovers	W	2-1	1-0	2	Becton, R. Hogg	5,000
12		25		A	Bury	L	0-2	0-1	3		5,000
13	Dec	2		H	Notts County	W	5-0	2-0	3	Raisbeck, McLatchie, R. Hogg, W. Hogg, Crawford	10,000
14		9		A	Manchester City	L	1-2	1-0	3	Becton	18,000
15		16		H	Sheffield United	D	1-1	0-1	3	McLatchie	25,000
16		23		A	Newcastle United	W	4-2	1-2	3	R. Hogg (3), McLatchie	19,129
17		26		A	Wolverhampton W.	L	0-1	0-0	3		14,000
18		30		A	Aston Villa	L	2-4	0-2	4	Farquhar, Leslie	20,000
19	Jan	1		H	Wolverhampton W.	L	1-2	1-2	5	Leslie	18,000
20		6		H	Liverpool	W	1-0	0-0	4	Raisbeck	3,000
21		13		A	Burnley	L	1-3	1-2	4	W. Hogg	5,000
22		20		H	Preston North End	W	1-0	1-0	4	Fulton	6,000
26	Feb	24		H	Glossop North End	D	0-0	0-0	5		6,000
27	Mar	3		A	West Bromwich Albion	W	3-1	1-0	4	McLatchie (2), Ferguson	10,490
28		10		A	Everton	L	0-1	0-1	5		20,000
29		21		H	Derby County	W	2-0	2-0	4	McLatchie, R. Hogg	3,000
30		24		A	Derby County	L	0-2	0-1	4		5,000
31		26		A	Stoke	W	2-1	0-0	4	Leslie (2)	1,000
32		31		H	Bury	W	1-0	1-0	4	W. Hogg	11,000
33	Apr	7		A	Notts County	L	1-3	1-3	4	Leslie	5,000
34		14		H	Manchester City	W	3-1	1-1	3	Leslie, Farquhar, R. Hogg	4,000
35		16		H	Blackburn Rovers	W	1-0	0-0	3	W. Hogg	6,000
36		17		A	Nottingham Forest	W	3-1	2-0	3	Farquhar, W. Hogg (2)	5,000
37		28		H	Newcastle United	L	1-2	1-2	3	Fulton	22,000

Appearances
Goals

FA Cup

Match No.	Date		Round	Venue	Opponents	Result	FT	HT	Pos.	Scorers	Attendance
23	Jan	27	R1	A	Derby County	D	2-2	1-0		Fulton, Leslie	15,000
24		31	R1r	H	Derby County	W	3-0	1-0		W. Hogg, R. Hogg (2)	6,000
25	Feb	10	R2	A	Nottingham Forest	L	0-3	0-1			12,000

Appearances
Goals

Doig	McCombie	McNeill	Ferguson	McAllister	Raisbeck	Crawford	Leslie	Farquhar	Fulton	McLatchie	Becton	Hogg R.	Jackson	Hogg W.	Watson	Prince	
1	2	3	4	5	6	7	8	9	10	11							1
1	2	3	4	5	6	7	8	9	10	11							2
1	2	3	4	5	6	7	8	9		11	10						3
1	2	3	4	5	6	7	8	9		11	10						4
1	2	3	4	5	6	7	8	9		11	10						5
1	2	3	4	5	6	7		8		11	10	9					6
1	2	3	4	5			7	8		11	10	9	6				7
1	2	3	4	5	6	7	8			11	10	9					8
1	2	3		5	4	7	8		10	11		9	6				9
1	2	3		5	4	7		8		11	10	9	6				10
1	2	3		5	4	7		8		11	10	9	6				11
1	2		4	5	6	7		8		11	10	9	3				12
1	2	3	4	5	6	7				11	10	9		8			13
1	2	3	4	5	6	7	8			11	10	9					14
1	2	3	4	5	6	7	8	10		11		9					15
1	2	3	4	5	6		8			11	10	9		7			16
1	2	3	4	5	6		8			11	10	9		7			17
1	2	3	6	5	4		8	9		11	10			7			18
1	2	3		5	4		8	9		11	10		6	7			19
1	2		4	5	6	7	8		10	11			3	9			20
1	2		4	5	6	7	8		10	11			3	9			21
1	2	3	4	5			8		10	11		9	6	7			22
1	2		4	5	6	7	8	10				9			3	11	26
1	2	3	4	5	6	7	8		10	11		9					27
1	2	3	4	5	6	7	8		10	11		9					28
1	2	3		5	4		8		10	11		9	6	7			29
1	2	3		5	4		8		10	11		9	6	7			30
1	2	3		5	4	8	10	9		11			6	7			31
1	2		4	5	6	8	10			11				7	3		32
1	2		4	5	6	8	10	9		11				7	3		33
1	2	3	4	5			10	8		11		9	6	7			34
1	2	3	4	5	6		10	8		11		9		7			35
1	2	3	4	5				8	6	10	11	9		7			36
1	2	3	4	5	6		8		10	11		9		7			37
34	34	28	27	34	30	23	29	18	13	33	15	20	13	19	3	1	
		1			3	2	6	5	2	11	5	9		6			

1	2	3	4	5	6		8		10	11		9		7			23
1	2	3	4	5	6		8		10	11		9		7			24
1	2	3	4	5	6		8		10	11		9		7			25
3	3	3	3	3	3		3		3	3		3		3			
							1		1			2		1			

Robert Hogg

Scorer of first League hat-trick by a Sunderland player against Newcastle United (23 December 1899).

331

1900-01

Division One

Ground: Roker Park

Manager: Alex Mackie

League Table

	P	W	D	L	F	A	Pts
Liverpool	34	19	7	8	59	35	45
SUNDERLAND	34	15	13	6	57	26	43
Notts Co	34	18	4	12	54	46	40
Nottingham F	34	16	7	11	53	36	39
Bury	34	16	7	11	53	37	39
Newcastle U	34	14	10	10	42	37	38
Everton	34	16	5	13	55	42	37
Sheffield W	34	13	10	11	52	42	36
Blackburn R	34	12	9	13	39	47	33
Bolton W	34	13	7	14	39	55	33
Manchester C	34	13	6	15	48	58	32
Derby Co	34	12	7	15	55	42	31
Wolverhampton W	34	9	13	12	39	55	31
Sheffield U	34	12	7	15	35	52	31
Aston Villa	34	10	10	14	45	51	30
Stoke	34	11	5	18	46	57	27
Preston NE	34	9	7	18	49	75	25
WBA	34	7	8	19	35	62	22

FA Cup Winners: Tottenham Hotspur

Did you know that?

Sunderland's home games against Sheffield United (FA Cup) on 26 January and Liverpool (League) on 2 February were both postponed due to the Football Association's decision to postpone all football matches scheduled to be played between the death of Queen Victoria and her funeral.

Match 1: Livingstone made debut and McNeill last game
Match 3: Common made debut
Match 15: Gemmell made debut
Match 29: Raisbeck and Prince last games
Match 32: Leslie last game
Match 35: Livingstone last game

Match No.	Date		Round	Venue	Opponents	Result	FT	HT	Pos.	Scorers	Attendance
1	Sep	1		A	Notts County	D	2-2	2-1		Millar, Ferguson	10,000
2		8		H	Preston North End	W	3-1	1-1	7	Raisbeck, Leslie, Livingstone	12,000
3		15		A	Wolverhampton W.	D	2-2	0-2	6	Livingstone, W. Hogg	7,000
4		22		H	Aston Villa	D	0-0	0-0	8		31,613
5		29		A	Liverpool	W	2-1	1-0	6	Millar, W. Hogg	20,000
6	Oct	6		H	Newcastle United	D	1-1	0-1	7	Livingstone	28,688
7		13		A	Sheffield United	L	0-2	0-2	8		8,000
8		20		H	Manchester City	W	3-0	1-0	7	McLatchie, Livingstone (2)	20,000
9		27		A	Bury	D	0-0	0-0	7		8,000
10	Nov	3		H	Nottingham Forest	L	0-1	0-1	7		13,000
11		10		A	Blackburn Rovers	W	1-0	0-0	6	McLatchie	4,000
12		17		H	Stoke	W	6-1	2-1	4	McLatchie, Common, W. Hogg (2), Livingstone, Raisbeck	6,000
13		24		A	West Bromwich Albion	L	0-1	0-0	8		10,045
14	Dec	1		H	Everton	W	2-0	1-0	5	McLatchie, Common	8,000
15		8		H	Sheffield Wed.	W	1-0	1-0	4	Ferguson (pen)	6,000
16		25		A	Manchester City	D	1-1	1-1	6	R. Hogg	25,000
17		26		A	Derby County	D	1-1	0-0	7	McLatchie	18,000
18		29		H	Notts County	D	1-1	1-1	6	Livingstone	8,000
19	Jan	1		H	Derby County	W	2-1	0-0	4	Millar, Livingstone	20,000
20		2		A	Bolton Wanderers	D	0-0	0-0	3		16,000
21		5		A	Preston North End	D	1-1	1-0	3	Raisbeck	6,000
22		12		H	Wolverhampton W.	W	7-2	2-1	2	Livingstone (2), Millar (3), McLatchie, W. Hogg	8,000
23		19		A	Aston Villa	D	2-2	1-1	2	R. Hogg, Millar	10,000
25	Feb	16		H	Sheffield United	W	3-0	1-0	2	McLatchie (2), W. Hogg	11,841
26		23		H	Liverpool	L	0-1	0-0	2		11,249
27	Mar	2		H	Bury	W	4-1	2-1	2	Millar (2), Common, Jackson	11,574
28		9		A	Nottingham Forest	D	0-0	0-0	2		7,000
29		16		H	Blackburn Rovers	W	2-0	2-0	1	R. Hogg, McCombie	10,000
30		23		A	Stoke	D	0-0	0-0	1		9,000
31		30		H	West Bromwich Albion	W	3-0	3-0	1	W. Hogg (2), Leslie	10,500
32	Apr	6		A	Everton	L	0-1	0-1	1		30,000
33		8		H	Bolton Wanderers	W	5-1	3-0	2	Livingstone (2), Common, McLatchie (2)	10,000
34		13		A	Sheffield Wed.	L	0-1	0-0	2		14,000
35		24		A	Newcastle United	W	2-0	1-0	2	W. Hogg, R. Hogg	18,694

Appearances
Goals

FA Cup

24	Feb	9	R1	H	Sheffield United	L	1-2	1-1		McLatchie	25,787

Appearances
Goals

	Doig	McCombie	McNeill	Ferguson	McAllister	Raisbeck	Hogg W.	Leslie	Millar	Livingstone	McLatchie	Watson	Jackson	Common	Farquhar	Hogg R.	Gemmell	Prince	
1	1	2	3	4	5	6	7	8	9	10	11								1
2	1	2		4	5	6	7	8	9	10	11	3							2
3	1	2		4	5		7		9	10	11	3	6	8					3
4	1	2		4	5	6	7		8	10	11	3		9					4
5	1	2		4	5		7		9	10	11	3		8	6				5
6	1	2		4	5		7		9	10	11	3		8	6				6
7	1	2		4	5	6	7		9	10	11		3	8					7
8	1	2		4	5		7		8	10	11	3		6	9				8
9	1	2		4	5		7		8	10	11	3		6	9				9
10	1	2		4	5		7	10	8	11		3		6	9				10
11	1	2		4	5		7		8	10	11	3	6	9					11
12	1	2		4	5	6	7		9	10	11	3		8					12
13	1	2		4	5	6	7		9	10	11	3		8					13
14	1	2		4	5	6	7		9	10	11	3		8					14
15	1	2		4	5		7		8	10	11	3	6			9			15
16	1	2		4	5		7		9	10	11	3		6	8				16
17	1	2		4	5	6			9	10	11	3		8					17
18	1	2		4	5	6	7			10	11	3		9	8				18
19	1	2		4	5		7		9	10	11	3	6		8				19
20	1	2		4	5		7		9	10	11	3	6	8					20
21	1	2			5	6	7		9	10	11	3			4	8			21
22	1	2				6	7		9	10	11	3	5		4	8			22
23	1	2			5		7		9	10	11	3	6		4	8			23
24	1	2			5	4	7			10	11	3	6		9	8			24
25	1	2	4	5			7			10	11	3	6		8	9			25
26	1	2			5	4	7		9		11	3	6	8			10		26
27	1	2			5	4	7		9			3	6	8			10	11	27
28	1	2			5	4	7		9			3	6	8			10	11	28
29	1	2			5	4	7		9			3	6	8			10	11	29
30	1	2		4	5		7	8	9	10	11	3	6						30
31	1	2		4	5		7	8	9	10	11	3	6						31
32	1	2		4	5		7	8	9	10	11	3	6						32
33	1		2	5						10	11	3	6	8	4		9		33
34	1	2		4	5		7		9		11	3		8	6	10			34
35	1	2		4	5		7		9	10	11	3	6		8				35
	34	33	1	27	33	14	34	6	30	30	31	32	19	14	15	16	3	2	
		1		2		3	9	2	9	12	10		1	4		4			

	Doig	McCombie	McNeill	Ferguson	McAllister	Raisbeck	Hogg W.	Leslie	Millar	Livingstone	McLatchie	Watson	Jackson	Common	Farquhar	Hogg R.	Gemmell	Prince	
	1	2		4	5		7		9	10	11	3		6	8				24
	1	1		1	1		1		1	1	1	1		1	1				
											1								

Sandy McAllister

Sandy only missed one game out of 181 played by Sunderland during the period 27 December 1897 to 17 January 1903 inclusive. The game was the 7-2 home win over Wolverhampton Wanderers on 12 January 1901.

1901-02

Division One

Ground: Roker Park
Manager: Alex Mackie

League Table

	P	W	D	L	F	A	Pts
SUNDERLAND	34	19	6	9	50	35	44
Everton	34	17	7	10	53	35	41
Newcastle U	34	14	9	11	48	34	37
Blackburn R	34	15	6	13	52	48	36
Nottingham F	34	13	9	12	43	43	35
Derby Co	34	13	9	12	39	41	35
Bury	34	13	8	13	44	38	34
Aston Villa	34	13	8	13	42	40	34
Sheffield W	34	13	8	13	48	52	34
Sheffield U	34	13	7	14	53	48	33
Liverpool	34	10	12	12	42	38	32
Bolton W	34	12	8	14	51	56	32
Notts Co	34	14	4	16	51	57	32
Wolverhampton W	34	13	6	15	46	57	32
Grimsby T	34	13	6	15	44	60	32
Stoke	34	11	9	14	45	55	31
Small Heath	34	11	8	15	47	45	30
Manchester C	34	11	6	17	42	58	28

FA Cup Winners: Sheffield United

Did you know that?

Teddy Doig kept goal for a club record 806 minutes without conceding a goal. The run started with Spencer scoring for Notts County after 3 minutes (21 December 1901) and ended with Orr scoring for Newcastle United after 89 minutes (12 February 1902).

Match 6: Mearns made debut
Match 11: Prior made debut
Match 12: Craggs made debut
Match 29: Murray made debut
Match 32: Mearns last game
Match 34: Ferguson last game, Gibson only game & crowned League champions
Match 35: Prior last game

Match No.	Date	Round	Venue	Opponents	Result	FT	HT	Pos.	Scorers	Attendance
1	Sep 2		H	Sheffield United	W	3-1	1-1		R. Hogg, Common (2)	14,271
2	7		H	Manchester City	W	1-0	1-0	2	W. Hogg	20,000
3	14		A	Wolverhampton W.	L	2-4	1-4	4	Millar, R. Hogg	6,000
4	21		H	Liverpool	D	1-1	1-1	5	Jackson	15,000
5	28		A	Newcastle United	W	1-0	1-0	2	Gemmell	23,330
6	Oct 5		H	Aston Villa	W	1-0	0-0	2	R. Hogg	10,000
7	12		A	Sheffield United	W	1-0	0-0	1	Gemmell	12,000
8	19		H	Nottingham Forest	W	4-0	1-0	1	Millar (3), Jackson	10,000
9	26		A	Bury	L	0-1	0-0	1		14,000
10	Nov 2		H	Blackburn Rovers	W	3-2	2-0	1	W. Hogg, Millar, McCombie	12,000
11	9		A	Stoke	L	0-3	0-1	1		10,000
12	16		H	Everton	L	2-4	1-1	2	Gemmell, McLatchie	13,200
13	23		A	Grimsby Town	D	3-3	2-2	2	W. Hogg, Gemmell (2)	5,000
14	30		A	Small Heath	W	3-2	0-1	2	Millar, McLatchie, W. Hogg	18,000
15	Dec 14		A	Sheffield Wed.	D	1-1	0-0	2	R. Hogg	2,000
16	21		H	Notts County	W	2-1	0-1	2	W. Hogg, Gemmell	7,249
17	26		A	Liverpool	W	1-0	0-0	2	McLatchie	30,000
18	28		A	Bolton Wanderers	D	0-0	0-0	1		4,000
19	Jan 1		H	Derby County	W	1-0	1-0	1	Jackson	21,000
20	4		A	Manchester City	W	3-0	1-0	1	W. Hogg (2), Gemmell	14,000
21	11		H	Wolverhampton W.	W	2-0	0-0	1	W. Hogg (2)	13,019
23	Feb 1		A	Aston Villa	W	1-0	1-0	1	McLatchie	23,000
25	15		A	Nottingham Forest	L	1-2	0-2	1	R. Hogg	14,000
26	Mar 1		A	Blackburn Rovers	W	1-0	1-0	1	Gemmell	27,000
27	8		H	Stoke	W	2-0	1-0	1	Craggs, Gemmell	8,000
28	15		A	Everton	L	0-2	0-2	1		20,000
29	22		H	Grimsby Town	W	3-1	0-0	1	McAllister, Craggs, Murray	10,000
30	29		H	Small Heath	D	1-1	1-0	1	Hewitt	8,600
31	31		H	Newcastle United	D	0-0	0-0	1		34,819
32	Apr 5		A	Derby County	L	0-1	0-1	1		2,000
33	12		H	Sheffield Wed.	L	1-2	0-1	1	Murray	9,300
34	16		H	Bury	W	3-0	1-0	1	Millar (3)	10,000
35	19		A	Notts County	L	0-2	0-1	1		10,000
36	26		H	Bolton Wanderers	W	2-1	1-0	1	Gemmell, W. Hogg	8,000

Appearances
Goals

FA Cup

22	Jan 25	R1	A	Sheffield Wed.	W	1-0	1-0		Millar	30,096
24	Feb 12	R2	A	Newcastle United	L	0-1	0-0			19,700

Appearances
Goals

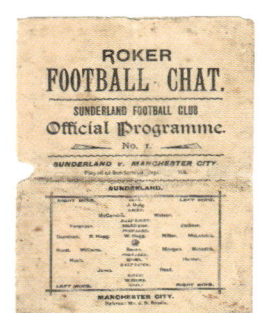

	Doig	McCombie	Watson	Ferguson	McAllister	Jackson	Common	Hogg, R.	Gemmell	Millar	McLatchie	Hogg, W.	Farquhar	Mearns	Prior	Craggs	Hewitt	Murray	Gibson	
1	1	2	3	4	5	6	7	8	9	10	11									1
2	1	2	3	4	5	6	7	8			10	11	9							2
3	1	2	3		5	6	8	10		9	11	7	4							3
4	1	2	3		5	6	7	8	9	10	11		4							4
5	1	2	3	4	5	6		8	10	9	11	7								5
6		2	3	4	5	6		8	10	9	11	7		1						6
7	1	2	3	4	5	6		8	10	9	11	7								7
8	1	2	3	4	5	6		8	10	9	11	7								8
9	1	2	3	4	5	6		8	10	9	11	7								9
10	1	2	3	4	5	6		8	10	9	11	7								10
11	1	2	3	4	5	6		8	10		11	7			9					11
12	1	2	3	4	5	6		8	10	9	11					7				12
13	1	2	3	4	5	6		8	10		11	7			9					13
14	1	2	3	4	5	6		8	10	9	11	7								14
15	1	2	3	4	5	6		8	10	9	11	7								15
16	1	2	3	4	5	6		8	10	9	11	7								16
17	1	2	3	4	5			8	10	9	11	7	6							17
18	1	2	3	4	5	6		8	10	9	11	7								18
19	1	2	3	4	5	6		8	10	9	11	7								19
20	1	2	3	4	5	6			10	9	11	7		8						20
21	1	2	3		5	6			10	9	11	7	4	8						21
23	1	2		4	5	3	8	10	9	11	7	6								23
25	1	2	3	4	5			8	10	9	11	7	6							25
26	1	2	3	4	5	6			10	9	11	7				8				26
27	1	2	3	4	5	6		8	10	9	11			7						27
28	1	2	3	4	5	6		8	10	9		7			11					28
29	1		3	2	5	6		8	10	9		4		7	11					29
30	1		3	4	5	2			10	9		7	6		8	11				30
31	1		3	4	5	2	8		9			7	6		11	10				31
32			3	4	5	2	8	10	9			6	1		7	11				32
33	1		3	4	5	2	8	10	9			7	6			11				33
34	1		3	4	5	6		8	10	9						11	2			34
35	1		3		5	2		10	9			7	4	8		6	11			35
36	1		3		5	2		8	10	9			7	4		6	11			36
	32	26	33	29	34	32	4	29	31	32	25	28	13	2	5	6	5	7	1	
		1			1	3	2	5	10	9	4	10			2	1	2			

	Doig	McCombie	Watson	Ferguson	McAllister	Jackson	Common	Hogg, R.	Gemmell	Millar	McLatchie	Hogg, W.	Farquhar	Mearns	Prior	Craggs	Hewitt	Murray	Gibson	
22	1	2	3	4	5	6		8	10	9	11	7								22
24	1	2	3	4	5	6		8	10	9	11	7								24
	2	2	2	2	2		2	2	2	2	2									
										1										

Matthew Ferguson who died of pleuropneumonia on 12 June 1902 while captain of Sunderland.

1902-03

Division One

Ground: Roker Park
Manager: Alex Mackie

League Table

	P	W	D	L	F	A	Pts
Sheffield W	34	19	4	11	54	36	42
Aston Villa	34	19	3	12	61	40	41
SUNDERLAND	34	16	9	9	51	36	41
Sheffield U	34	17	5	12	58	44	39
Liverpool	34	17	4	13	68	49	38
Stoke	34	15	7	12	46	38	37
WBA	34	16	4	14	54	53	36
Bury	34	16	3	15	54	43	35
Derby Co	34	16	3	15	50	47	35
Nottingham F	34	14	7	13	49	47	35
Wolverhampton W	34	14	5	15	48	57	33
Everton	34	13	6	15	45	47	32
Middlesbrough	34	14	4	16	41	50	32
Newcastle U	34	14	4	16	41	51	32
Notts Co	34	12	7	15	41	49	31
Blackburn R	34	12	5	17	44	63	29
Grimsby T	34	8	9	17	43	62	25
Bolton W	34	8	3	23	37	73	19

FA Cup Winners: Bury

Did you know that?

Sunderland's first home League game against Middlesbrough was played at St James' Park. Roker Park had been closed by the FA for one game as punishment following crowd disturbances after the game against Sheffield Wednesday on 21 March 1903.

Match 1: Maxwell made debut
Match 7: Rhodes made debut
Match 8: Robert Hogg and McLatchie last games
Match 9: Willis made debut and Murray last game
Match 10: Barrie, Buckle and Robinson made debuts
Match 13: Harper made debut
Match 20: Maxwell last game
Match 21: Bridgett made debut
Match 31: Lindsay made debut and Annan only game
Match 35: Harper last game

Match No.	Date		Round	Venue	Opponents	Result	FT	HT	Pos.	Scorers	Attendance
1	Sep	1		H	Nottingham Forest	L	0-1	0-0			15,000
2		6		A	Wolverhampton W.	D	3-3	2-2	11	Gemmell, Maxwell (2)	5,000
3		13		H	Liverpool	W	2-1	1-0	7	Millar, Jackson	20,000
4		20		A	Sheffield United	L	0-1	0-0	12		16,000
5		27		H	Grimsby Town	W	5-1	2-0	9	W. Hogg (2), McLatchie (2), Millar	9,000
6	Oct	4		A	Aston Villa	W	1-0	0-0	8	Jackson	15,000
7		18		A	Bury	L	1-3	1-1	13	W. Hogg	13,000
8		25		H	Blackburn Rovers	D	2-2	1-1	12	Jackson, Farquhar	9,158
9	Nov	1		A	Derby County	L	2-5	1-2	14	Farquhar, Murray	10,000
10		8		H	Stoke	D	1-1	0-0	14	W. Hogg	7,000
11		15		H	Everton	W	2-1	1-1	11	Robinson, McAllister	12,000
12		22		A	Sheffield Wed.	L	0-1	0-1	12		12,500
13		29		H	West Bromwich Albion	D	0-0	0-0	14		10,457
14	Dec	6		A	Notts County	D	0-0	0-0	11		10,000
15		13		H	Bolton Wanderers	W	3-1	0-0	10	McCombie (pen), Gemmell (2)	7,500
16		20		A	Middlesbrough	W	1-0	1-0	9	Gemmell	15,000
17		25		A	Blackburn Rovers	W	2-0	1-0	8	W. Hogg, Gemmell	20,000
18		27		H	Newcastle United	D	0-0	0-0	8		24,000
19	Jan	1		H	Derby County	W	2-0	2-0	8	Gemmell, Harper	20,000
20		3		H	Wolverhampton W.	W	3-0	1-0	6	Millar, Maxwell, McCombie (pen)	10,000
21		17		H	Sheffield United	D	0-0	0-0	6		12,500
22		24		A	Grimsby Town	W	4-2	1-1	3	Gemmell, Hewitt, Bridgett, Barrie	5,000
23		31		H	Aston Villa	W	1-0	1-0	3	Millar	19,374
25	Feb	14		H	Bury	W	3-1	3-1	3	McAllister (2), Hewitt	13,000
27	Mar	14		A	Everton	W	3-0	1-0	3	Millar, Hewitt (2)	15,000
28		21		H	Sheffield Wed.	L	0-1	0-0	3		22,000
29		28		A	West Bromwich Albion	W	3-0	0-0	2	Robinson (2), Millar	10,517
30		30		A	Liverpool	D	1-1	1-0	2	Bridgett	3,000
31	Apr	4		H	Notts County	W	2-1	2-0	2	W. Hogg, Hewitt	11,000
32		10		H	Stoke	D	0-0	0-0	2		25,000
33		11		A	Bolton Wanderers	L	0-2	0-0	2		12,000
34		13		A	Nottingham Forest	L	2-5	0-4	2	Hewitt, Robinson	15,000
35		18		H*	Middlesbrough	W	2-1	1-0	2	Hewitt, Millar	26,000
36		25		A	Newcastle United	L	0-1	0-0	3		26,562

* at St. James' Park

Appearances
Goals

FA Cup

| 24 | Feb | 7 | R1 | A | Aston Villa | L | 1-4 | 0-1 | | Bridgett | 47,150 |

Appearances
Goals

Sheriff of London's Shield (forerunner of Charity Shield)

| 26 | Feb | 28 | | N* | Corinthians | W | 3-0 | 0-0 | | Millar (2), Hewitt | 5,000 |

* at White Hart Lane

Appearances
Goals

Doig	McCombie	Watson	Farquhar	McAllister	Jackson	Hogg. W.	Gemmell	Millar	Maxwell	McLatchie	Hogg. R.	Rhodes	Hewitt	Willis	Murray	Barrie	Robinson	Buckle	Harper	Bridgett	Lindsay	Annan	
1	2	3	4	5	6	7	8	9	10	11													1
1	2	3	4	5	6	7	8	9	10	11													2
1	2	3	4	5	6	7	8	9	10	11													3
1	2	3	4	5	6	7		9	10	11	8												4
1	2	3	4	5	6	7	10	9	8	11													5
1	2	3	4	5	6	7	10	9	8	11													6
1	2		4	5	6	7	10	9		11		3	8										7
1	2	3	4	5	6	7	10	9		11	8												8
1	2	3	9	5	6	7	10						8	4	11								9
1	2	3		5	6	7		9		10				4	8	11							10
1	2	3	4	5	6	7	10	9		11					8								11
1	2	3	4	5	6	7	10	9		11					8								12
1	2	3	4	5	6	7	9			11					8		10						13
1	2	3	4	5	6		9	7		11					8		10						14
1	2	3	4	5	6		9	7		11					8		10						15
1	2	3	4	5	6	7	9	8		11							10						16
1	2	3	4	5	6	7	9	8		11							10						17
1	2	3	4	5	6	7	9	8		11							10						18
1	2	3	4	5	6	7	9	8		11							10						19
1	2	3	4	5	6	7		9	8	11							10						20
1	2	3	4	5	6	7	9	8									10	11					21
1	2	3	4		6	7	9			10				5	8			11					22
1	2	3	4	5	6	7	9	8		10								11					23
1	2	3	4	5	6	7	9	8		10								11					25
1	2	3	4	5	6	7		9		10					8			11					27
1	2	3	4	5	6		10	9		7					8			11					28
1	2	3	4	5	6	7		9		10					8			11					29
1	2	3	4	5	6	7		9		10					8			11					30
			4	5	6	7		9		10		3			8			11	1	2			31
1	2	3	4	5	6	7		9		10					8			11					32
1	2	3	4	5	6	7		9		10					8			11					33
1	2		4	5	6	7		9		3					8			11					34
1	2			4	5	6	7		9		3	10					8	11					35
1		2	4		6	7		9				3	10		5	8		11					36
33	32	30	33	32	34	31	22	31	7	8	2	5	26	1	1	3	16	1	10	14	1	1	
	2		2	3	3	6	7	7	3	2			7		1	1	4		1	2			

1	2	3	4	5	6	7	9	8									10	11					24
1	1	1	1	1	1	1	1	1									1	1					
																		1					

1	2	3	4	5	6	7		9					10			8		11					26
1	1	1	1	1	1	1		1					1			1		1					
								2					1										

Photo of Ephraim Rhodes. Rhodes made his debut during this season and although a left back was pushed up to assist the forward line in the final game of the season to try and get an equaliser. This action was unusual during Edwardian times and was heavily criticised in the match reports of the game.

1903-04

Division One

Ground: Roker Park
Manager: Alex Mackie

League Table

	P	W	D	L	F	A	Pts
Sheffield W	34	20	7	7	48	28	47
Manchester C	34	19	6	9	71	45	44
Everton	34	19	5	10	59	32	43
Newcastle U	34	18	6	10	58	45	42
Aston Villa	34	17	7	10	70	48	41
SUNDERLAND	34	17	5	12	63	49	39
Sheffield U	34	15	8	11	62	57	38
Wolverhampton W	34	14	8	12	44	66	36
Nottingham F	34	11	9	14	57	57	31
Middlesbrough	34	9	12	13	46	47	30
Small Heath	34	11	8	15	39	52	30
Bury	34	7	15	12	40	53	29
Notts Co	34	12	5	17	37	61	29
Derby Co	34	9	10	15	58	60	28
Blackburn R	34	11	6	17	48	60	28
Stoke	34	10	7	17	54	57	27
Liverpool	34	9	8	17	49	62	26
WBA	34	7	10	17	36	60	24

FA Cup Winners: Manchester City

Did you know that?

The oldest known film footage of Sunderland is a few minutes long showing the game at Roker Park on 9 January 1904 against Middlesbrough. It was recorded by the renowned film makers Mitchell and Kenyon.

Match 5: Lindsay last game
Match 9: James Watson (junior) made debut
Match 10: Hewitt last game
Match 16: Fullarton made debut and Robinson last game
Match 21: Benefit game for McCombie
Match 23: McCombie last game
Match 26: Yorke made debut
Match 27: Yorke last game
Match 28: Bertram only game
Match 31: Millar last game
Match 32: Rowlandson and Wardle made debuts
Match 33: Doig last game
Match 35: McAllister last game

Match No.	Date		Round	Venue	Opponents	Result	FT	HT	Pos.	Scorers	Attendance
1	Sep	1		H	Notts County	W	4-1	2-1		Bridgett, Craggs, Robinson, Hogg	10,000
2		5		H	Aston Villa	W	6-1	4-1	1	Robinson, Bridgett, Gemmell, Hogg (2), Craggs	20,000
3		12		A	Middlesbrough	W	3-2	0-1	1	Robinson, Hogg, Gemmell	30,000
4		19		H	Liverpool	W	2-1	1-0	2	Gemmell (2)	17,000
5		26		A	Bury	L	1-3	0-2	4	Hogg	15,000
6	Oct	3		H	Blackburn Rovers	W	2-0	0-0	3	Bridgett, Hewitt	8,000
7		10		A	Nottingham Forest	L	0-3	0-0	4		13,000
8		17		H	Sheffield Wed.	L	0-1	0-0	6		15,000
9		24		A	Wolverhampton W.	L	1-2	0-2	5	Hogg	10,000
10		31		A	West Bromwich Albion	D	1-1	1-0	7	Craggs	10,128
11	Nov	7		H	Small Heath	W	3-1	2-1	5	Gemmell (2), Craggs	9,000
12		14		A	Everton	W	1-0	1-0	5	Hogg	15,000
13		21		H	Stoke	W	3-0	2-0	4	Hogg, Buckle, Craggs	10,000
14		28		A	Derby County	L	2-7	0-2	5	Morris o.g., Hogg	5,000
15	Dec	5		H	Manchester City	D	1-1	0-1	5	Buckle	12,000
16		12		A	Notts County	L	1-2	1-1	8	Buckle	6,000
17		19		H	Sheffield United	W	2-1	1-0	5	Buckle, Bridgett	15,000
18		26		A	Newcastle United	W	3-1	2-0	5	Buckle (2), Bridgett	28,397
19	Jan	1		H	Newcastle United	D	1-1	0-0	5	McCombie (pen)	37,000
20		2		A	Aston Villa	L	0-2	0-1	7		30,000
21		9		H	Middlesbrough	W	3-1	2-0	6	Gemmell (2), Hogg	14,000
22		16		A	Liverpool	L	1-2	1-1	7	Buckle	20,000
23		23		H	Bury	W	6-0	0-0	7	Craggs (2), Hogg (2), Gemmell, Millar	10,000
24		30		A	Blackburn Rovers	W	3-1	2-0	6	Bridgett, Buckle, Craggs	8,000
26	Feb	13		A	Sheffield Wed.	D	0-0	0-0	6		10,000
27		27		H	West Bromwich Albion	D	1-1	0-0	5	Gemmell	5,632
28	Mar	5		A	Small Heath	L	1-2	0-1	5	Craggs	12,000
29		12		H	Everton	W	2-0	2-0	4	Kitchen o.g., Craggs	12,000
30		19		A	Stoke	L	1-3	0-2	5	Millar	10,000
31		26		H	Derby County	L	0-3	0-1	6		8,000
32	Apr	1		H	Wolverhampton W.	W	2-1	1-0	5	Buckle, Wardle	12,000
33		2		A	Manchester City	L	1-2	1-1	7	Bridgett	13,000
34		4		H	Nottingham Forest	W	3-1	1-0	6	Bridgett, Craggs, Hogg	9,000
35		16		A	Sheffield United	W	2-1	1-1	6	Bridgett (2)	15,000

Appearances
Goals

FA Cup

25	Feb	6	R1	A	Manchester City	L	2-3	1-2		Buckle, Craggs	23,000

Appearances
Goals

	Doig	McCombie	Watson J (Snr)	Farquhar	McAllister	Jackson	Craggs	Robinson	Hogg	Gemmell	Bridgett	Lindsay	Hewitt	Millar	Rhodes	Watson J (Jnr)	Barrie	Buckle	Fullarton	Yorke	Bertram	Rowlandson	Wardle	
1	1	2	3	4	5	6	7	8	9	10	11													1
2	1	2	3	4	5	6	7	8	9	10	11													2
3	1	2	3	4	5	6	7	8	9	10	11													3
4		2	3	4	5	6	7	8	9	10	11	1												4
5		2	3	4	5	6	7	8	9	10	11	1												5
6	1	2	3	4	5	6	7		9	10	11													6
7	1	2	3	4	5	6	7			10	11	8	9											7
8	1	2		4	5	6	7	8	9		11	10		3										8
9	1	2		6	5		7	8	9		11	10		3	4									9
10	1	2		4		6	7		9	3	8	10												10
11	1	2		4		6	7		9	10	8			3		5	11							11
12	1	2	3	4		6	7		9	10	8					5	11							12
13	1	2	3	4		6	7		9	10	8					5	11							13
14	1	2	3	4		6	7		9	10	8					5	11							14
15	1	2	3	4	5	6	7		9	10	8						11							15
16	1	2	3	4		6	7	8	9	10							11	5						16
17	1	2	3	4		6	7		9	10	8					5	11							17
18	1	2	3	4	5	6	7		9	10	8						11							18
19	1	2	3	4	5	6	7		9	10	8						11							19
20	1	2	3	4	5	6	7		9	10	8						11							20
21	1	2	3	4		6	7		9	10	8					5	11							21
22	1	2		4		6	7		9	10	8			3		5	11							22
23	1	2	3	4		6	7		9	10	11		8			5								23
24	1		3	4		6	7		9	10	8			2		5	11							24
26	1		3	4		6	8		7	10				2		5	11	9						26
27	1		3	4		6	7		9	10	11			2		5		8						27
28	1		3	4			7		9	10	8			2			11	5	6					28
29	1		3			6	7		9	10	11			8	2	4	5							29
30	1		3			6	7		9	10	11			8	2	4	5							30
31	1		3			6	7		9	10	11			8	2	4	5							31
32		3	4			6	7		9		8			2		5	11			1	10			32
33	1	3	4			6	7		9	10	8			2		5	11							33
34		3	4	5		6	7		9		8			2			11			1	10			34
35		3	4	5	6	7		9		8			2			11				1	10			35
	29	23	29	31	15	32	34	8	33	29	32	2	5	5	15	4	17	20	2	2	1	3	3	
		1				11	3	13	10	10		1	2				9				1			
25	1		2	4		6	7		9	10	8			3		5	11							25
	1		1	1		1	1		1	1	1			1		1	1							
							1									1								

Teddy Doig

Doig played his 457th, and last, first team game for Sunderland on 2 April 1904 at Manchester City. This total remained a record until beaten by Len Ashurst (458 inc. substitute appearances) and then Jim Montgomery (627).

1904-05

Division One

Ground: Roker Park

Manager: Alex Mackie & Fred Dale

League Table

	P	W	D	L	F	A	Pts
Newcastle U	34	23	2	9	72	33	48
Everton	34	21	5	8	63	36	47
Manchester C	34	20	6	8	66	37	46
Aston Villa	34	19	4	11	63	43	42
SUNDERLAND	34	16	8	10	60	44	40
Sheffield U	34	19	2	13	64	56	40
Small Heath	34	17	5	12	54	38	39
Preston NE	34	13	10	11	42	37	36
Sheffield W	34	14	5	15	61	57	33
Woolwich A	34	12	9	13	36	40	33
Derby Co	34	12	8	14	37	48	32
Stoke	34	13	4	17	40	58	30
Blackburn R	34	11	5	18	40	51	27
Wolverhampton W	34	11	4	19	47	73	26
Middlesbrough	34	9	8	17	36	56	26
Nottingham F	34	9	7	18	40	61	25
Bury	34	10	4	20	47	67	24
Notts Co	34	5	8	21	36	69	18

FA Cup Winners: Aston Villa

Did you know that?

Between June 1903 and January 1905 Sunderland had two players called James Watson on their books. Both were Scottish born defenders. As such the older one, born in Larkhall in 1877, was identified as 'senior' and the other, born in Inverness in 1883, identified as 'junior'.

Match 1: Lewis made debut
Match 4: Lewis last game
Match 6: McCallum made debut & Wardle last game
Match 8: Whitbourn made debut & Craggs last game
Match 9: Watkins made debut
Match 11: Fred Dale first game as caretaker manager
Match 12: McCallum last game
Match 13: Brown made debut
Match 15: Whitbourn last game
Match 16: Webb made debut
Match 19: Holley made debut
Match 20: Benefit for Hogg & Jackson and J. Watson (junior) last game
Match 21: Stewart made debut
Match 25: Fred Dale last game as caretaker manager
Match 27: Stewart and Common last games
Match 30: Watkins last game
Match 31: Thompson made debut
Match 32: Thompson last game
Match 33: Daykin made debut and Rowlandson last game
Match 35: Jackson last game
Match 36: Alex Mackie last as Sunderland manager

Match No.	Date		Round	Venue	Opponents	Result	FT	HT	Pos.	Scorers	Attendance
1	Sep	1		A	Preston North End	L	1-3	0-2		Bridgett	15,000
2		5		H	Notts County	W	5-0	2-0	4	Bridgett (2), Common (2), Buckle	8,000
3		10		H	Middlesbrough	D	1-1	0-0	7	Buckle	16,000
4		17		A	Wolverhampton W.	L	0-1	0-1	9		8,000
5		24		H	Bury	W	2-1	2-0	8	Farquhar, Gemmell	7,000
6	Oct	1		A	Aston Villa	D	2-2	1-2	8	Jackson, Wardle	30,000
7		8		H	Blackburn Rovers	W	2-1	0-1	4	Hogg, Crompton o.g.	15,000
8		15		A	Nottingham Forest	W	3-2	2-1	4	Farquhar (2), Common	10,000
9		22		H	Sheffield Wed.	W	3-0	2-0	2	Watkins (2), Hogg	27,000
10		29		H	Stoke	W	3-1	2-1	2	Bridgett, Watkins (2)	10,000
11	Nov	5		A	Woolwich Arsenal	D	0-0	0-0	2		30,000
12		12		H	Derby County	W	3-0	2-0	1	Hogg (pen), Jackson, Common	16,000
13		19		A	Everton	W	1-0	0-0	1	Bridgett	25,000
14		26		H	Small Heath	L	1-4	1-2	1	Common	15,000
15	Dec	3		A	Manchester City	L	2-5	0-4	3	Watkins, Hogg	27,000
16		17		A	Sheffield United	L	0-1	0-1	8		17,000
17		24		H	Newcastle United	W	3-1	2-1	4	McCombie o.g., Buckle, Jackson	25,000
18		26		A	Blackburn Rovers	L	1-2	0-1	6	Rhodes (pen)	15,000
19		27		A	Sheffield Wed.	D	1-1	1-0	5	Holley	30,000
20		31		H	Preston North End	W	3-2	3-0	4	Holley, Bridgett (2)	16,000
21	Jan	2		H	Nottingham Forest	W	1-0	1-0	4	Gemmell	15,000
22		7		A	Middlesbrough	W	3-1	2-0	3	Common, Holley, Gemmell	14,000
23		14		H	Wolverhampton W.	W	3-0	2-0	2	Watkins, Farquhar, Bridgett	9,000
24		21		A	Bury	L	0-1	0-1	3		8,000
25		28		H	Aston Villa	L	2-3	2-1	4	Watkins, Holley	15,000
28	Feb	25		A	Stoke	W	3-1	2-1	6	Fullarton, Watkins (2)	4,000
29	Mar	4		H	Woolwich Arsenal	D	1-1	0-1	5	Gemmell	12,000
30		11		A	Derby County	L	0-1	0-1	7		5,000
31		18		H	Everton	L	2-3	2-0	7	Holley, Hogg	18,000
32		25		A	Small Heath	D	1-1	1-0	7	Hogg	12,000
33	Apr	1		H	Manchester City	D	0-0	0-0	7		8,000
34		8		A	Notts County	D	2-2	0-0	7	Hogg, Holley	2,000
35		22		A	Newcastle United	W	3-1	2-1	7	Holley (2), Buckle	30,000
36		24		H	Sheffield United	W	2-1	1-0	5	Holley, Gemmell	14,000

Appearances
Goals

FA Cup

| 26 | Feb | 4 | R1 | H | Wolverhampton W. | D | 1-1 | 1-0 | | Common | 14,000 |
| 27 | | 8 | R1r | A | Wolverhampton W. | L | 0-1 | 0-0 | | | 15,000 |

Appearances
Goals

	Lewis	Rhodes	Watson J. (Snr)	Farquhar	Barrie	Jackson	Buckle	Common	Hogg	Gemmell	Bridgett	Fullarton	Rowlandson	McCallum	Wardle	Craggs	Whitbourn	Watkins	Brown	Webb	Holley	Watson J. (Jnr)	Stewart	Thompson	Willis	Daykin	
1	2	3	4	5	6	7	8	9	10	11																	1
1	2	3	4		6	11	8	7	9	10	5																2
1	2	3	4		6	11	8	7	9	10	5																3
1	2	3	4		6	11	8	7	9	10	5																4
	2	3	4		6	11	8	7	9	10	5	1															5
	2		4		6		8	7	9	11	5	1	3	10													6
	2	3	4		6		8	7	9	10	5	1			11												7
	2	3	9	4	6		8	7	10		5				11	1											8
	2	3	4		6		8	7	10	11	5	1			9												9
	2	3	4		6		8	7	10	11	5	1			9												10
		3	4		6		8	7	10	11	5		2		9		1										11
		3	4		6		8	7	10	11	5	1	2		9												12
	2	3	4		6		8		10	11	5	1			9	7											13
	2	3	4		6		8		10	11	5	1			9	7											14
	2	3	4		6		8	7	10	11	5			1	9												15
	2	3	4		6		8	7	10	11	5				9		1										16
	2	3	4		6	11	9	7	10	8	5						1										17
	2	3	4		6	11	9	7	10	8	5						1										18
	2	3	4	5	6	11		7	9	10							1	8									19
		3	4		6			7	10	11	5				9		1	8	2								20
		3		4	6			7	10	11	5				9		1	8	2								21
	2	3	4		6		9	7	10	11	5						1	8									22
		3	4		6			7	10	11	5				9		1	8	2								23
		4	6	3		8	7	9	11	5							1	10	2								24
	2	3	4	5	6			7	10	11					9		1	8									25
	2	3	4		6		7	10	11	5					9		1	8									28
	2	3	4		6			7	10	11	5				9		1	8									29
	2	3	4	5	6			9	10	11					8	7	1										30
	2	3	4	5	6			9	10	11							1	8		7							31
	2	3	4	5		11		9		10							1	8		7	6						32
	2		4	5		11		9	10			1				7		8			6	3					33
	2		4	5		11		9		10						7	1	8			6	3					34
	2	3		5	6	11		7	9	10							1	8		4							35
	2	3	4	5		11		7	9	10							1	8		6							36
4	28	30	32	13	30	13	20	32	32	32	24	9	3	1	2	3	15	5	18	15	1	3	2	5	2		
	1		4		3	4	6	7	5	8	1			1			9		9								

		3	4		6		9	7	10	11	5						1	8		2							26
		3	4		6	11	8	7		10	5				9		1			2							27
		2	2		2	1	2	2	1	2	2				1		2	1		2							
						1																					

Andy McCombie

A payment of £100 to McCombie in 1903 was deemed by the FA to be a gift. As a result Sunderland Football Club were found guilty of paying players illegal bonuses. By this time McCombie had moved to Newcastle United. However, Sunderland manager Alex Mackie was suspended in October 1904 for a period of three months. Former Sunderland player (pre-League days) Fred Dale took over during this period (4 November 1904 to 31 January 1905). Six directors were also banned from football for 2½ years.

1905-06

Division One

Ground: Roker Park

Manager: Robert Kyle

League Table

	P	W	D	L	F	A	Pts
Liverpool	38	23	5	10	79	46	51
Preston NE	38	17	13	8	54	39	47
Sheffield W	38	18	8	12	63	52	44
Newcastle U	38	18	7	13	74	48	43
Manchester C	38	19	5	14	73	54	43
Bolton W	38	17	7	14	81	67	41
Birmingham	38	17	7	14	65	59	41
Aston Villa	38	17	6	15	72	56	40
Blackburn R	38	16	8	14	54	52	40
Stoke	38	16	7	15	54	55	39
Everton	38	15	7	16	70	66	37
Woolwich A	38	15	7	16	62	64	37
Sheffield U	38	15	6	17	57	62	36
SUNDERLAND	38	15	5	18	61	70	35
Derby Co	38	14	7	17	39	58	35
Notts Co	38	11	12	15	55	71	34
Bury	38	11	10	17	57	74	32
Middlesbrough	38	10	11	17	56	71	31
Nottingham F	38	13	5	20	58	79	31
Wolverhampton W	38	8	7	23	58	99	23

FA Cup Winners: Everton

Did you know that?

The FA Cup 2nd round replay between Sunderland and Gainsborough Trinity was played at Roker Park instead of Gainsborough. Sunderland had a poor away record and the Trinitarians accepted £300 to switch the tie. In consideration of this Sunderland received all of the gate receipts for the replay. They won the tie but lost money as the gate receipts were only £244.

Match 1: Robert Kyle first game as Sunderland manager
Match 3: Benefit game for Watson & Kelly only game
Match 5: Hindmarsh only game
Match 8: McKenzie made debut and Fullarton last game
Match 9: McConnell and O'Donnell made debuts
Match 12: Bell made debut
Match 14: Brebner made debut
Match 19: Brebner last game
Match 21: Joseph Shaw made debut & Buckle last game
Match 28: Edgar made debut
Match 30: Tomlin made debut
Match 33: Benefit game for Farquhar
Match 36: McKenzie last game
Match 37: John Shaw only game
Match 38: Webb last game
Match 39: McIntosh made debut & O'Donnell last game
Match 40: Edgar last game
Match 42: Tomlin last game

Match No.	Date		Round	Venue	Opponents	Result	FT	HT	Pos.	Scorers	Attendance
1	Sep	2		H	Newcastle United	W	3-2	1-1		Bridgett (2), Gemmell	30,000
2		9		A	Aston Villa	L	1-2	0-0	11	Bridgett	26,000
3		16		H	Liverpool	L	1-2	1-1	14	Bridgett	16,000
4		23		A	Sheffield United	L	1-4	1-3	18	Gemmell	15,000
5		30		H	Notts County	L	1-3	0-1	19	Brown	7,000
6	Oct	7		A	Stoke	L	0-1	0-1	20		6,000
7		14		H	Bolton Wanderers	D	3-3	1-2	19	Buckle, Hogg (2)	5,000
8		21		A	Woolwich Arsenal	L	0-2	0-1	19		13,000
9		28		H	Blackburn Rovers	W	3-0	0-0	18	Farquhar, O'Donnell, Hogg	10,000
10	Nov	4		A	Wolverhampton W.	L	2-5	0-2	19	Bridgett, Rhodes (pen)	2,000
11		11		A	Birmingham	L	0-3	0-2	19		14,000
12		18		H	Everton	W	2-1	1-1	18	Holley, McKenzie	12,000
13		25		A	Derby County	L	0-1	0-1	19		4,000
14	Dec	2		H	Sheffield Wed.	W	2-0	2-0	18	Bridgett (pen), Gemmell	12,000
15		9		A	Nottingham Forest	W	2-1	1-1	16	Holley, Gemmell	7,000
16		16		H	Manchester City	W	2-0	1-0	16	Gemmell, Bridgett	12,000
17		23		A	Bury	L	1-3	0-1	16	Holley	2,000
18		25		A	Preston North End	D	1-1	1-1	17	Bridgett	12,000
19		27		A	Notts County	L	1-4	0-0	17	Holley	8,000
20		30		A	Newcastle United	D	1-1	1-1	17	Hogg	56,000
21	Jan	1		H	Middlesbrough	W	2-1	2-0	16	Shaw, Holley	24,000
23		20		A	Liverpool	L	0-2	0-2	18		12,000
24		27		H	Sheffield United	W	2-0	0-0	16	Shaw, Bridgett	11,000
27	Feb	10		H	Stoke	W	1-0	1-0	16	Shaw	10,000
28		17		A	Bolton Wanderers	L	2-6	1-2	17	Holley, Bridgett	15,000
30		28		H	Aston Villa	W	2-0	0-0	16	Shaw, Gemmell	7,000
31	Mar	3		A	Blackburn Rovers	W	3-0	2-0	15	Bridgett, Willis, Hogg	10,000
32		10		H	Wolverhampton W.	W	7-2	4-1	14	O'Donnell, Bridgett (2), Hogg (2), Willis, Gemmell	14,000
33		17		A	Birmingham	W	3-1	1-0	13	Bridgett, O'Donnell, Shaw	15,000
34		24		A	Everton	L	1-3	1-1	14	Shaw	10,000
35		31		H	Derby County	W	2-0	1-0	14	Shaw, O'Donnell	14,000
36	Apr	7		A	Sheffield Wed.	D	3-3	2-1	13	Shaw, Burton o.g., Tomlin	6,000
37		13		A	Middlesbrough	L	1-2	1-1	14	Jos. Shaw	24,000
38		14		H	Nottingham Forest	L	0-1	0-0	15		12,000
39		16		H	Preston North End	W	2-0	0-0	14	Bridgett, O'Donnell	13,000
40		21		A	Manchester City	L	1-5	0-2	14	Bridgett	2,000
41		25		H	Woolwich Arsenal	W	2-2	0-0	14	McIntosh, Bridgett	8,000
42		28		H	Bury	L	0-3	0-0	14		16,000

Appearances
Goals

FA Cup

Match	Date		Round	Venue	Opponents	Result	FT	HT	Scorers	Attendance
22	Jan	13	R1	H	Notts County	W	1-0	0-0	Shaw	18,280
25	Feb	3	R2	H	Gainsborough Trinity	D	1-1	0-1	Barrie	10,000
26		7	R2r	H	Gainsborough Trinity	W	3-0	2-0	Bridgett, Brown, Holley	8,250
29		24	R3	A	Woolwich Arsenal	L	0-5	0-2		30,000

Appearances
Goals

	Naisby	Rhodes	Watson	Farquhar	Barrie	Willis	Hogg	Holley	Gemmell	Bridgett	Buckle	Kelly	Fullarton	Daykin	Brown	Hindmarsh	McKenzie	McConnell	O'Donnell	Webb	Bell	Brebner	Shaw, Joseph	Edgar	Tomlin	Shaw, John	McIntosh	
1	2	3	4	5	6	7	8	9	10	11																		1
1	2	3	4	5	6	7	8	9	10	11																		2
1	2	3	4	5		7	8	9	10	11	6																	3
1	2	3	4	6		7	8	9	10	11	5																	4
1	2		4	6		9	8			11		5	3	7	10													5
1	2	3	4			7	8	9	10	11	5	6																6
1	2	3				7	8	9	10	11	5																	7
1	2	3	4	6		7	8	10		11	5			9														8
1	2	3	4	5		7		9	10	11					6	8												9
1	2		4	5		7		3	10	11					9	6	8											10
	2	3	4	5		7		10	11						9	6	8	1										11
	3		4	5	6		10		11				7		9		8	1	2									12
1	3		4	5	6		8		10	11			7		9				2									13
	3	4	5	6		10	9	11				7				8	2	1									14
1		3	4	5	6		10	9	11				7				8		2									15
1		3	4	5	6		10	9	11				7				8	2										16
1	2	3	4	5	6		10	9	11				7				8											17
1		3	4	5	6	7	10	9	11								8		2									18
		3	4	5	6	7	10	9	11								8		2	1								19
1		3	4	5	6	7	10	9	11								8		2									20
1		3	4		6		8		10	11			7			5			2		9							21
1		3	4	5	6	7	10								8				2		9							23
1		3		5	6	7	10	8	11							4			2		9							24
1		3		5	6		10	8	11				7			4			2		9							27
1	3		4	5	6		10	8	11						9				2			7						28
1	2	3	4		6	7		10	11								8				9	5						30
1	2	3	4		6	7		10	11								8				9	5						31
1	2	3	4		6	7		10	11								8				9	5						32
1	2	3	4		6	7		10	11								8				9	5						33
1	2	3	4		6	7		10	11								8				9	5						34
1	2	3	4		6	7		10	11								8				9	5						35
	2	3			6	7			11							10	4	8	1		9	5						36
1	2	3	4		6	7			11								8				9	5	10					37
	2	3	10		6	7			11								4	8	1		9	5						38
1		3	4		6	7			11								8		2		9	5	10					39
1		3	4		6			8	11										2		9	7	5	10				40
1		3	4		6			8	11				7						2		9		5	10				41
1		3	4		6			8	11				7						2		9		5	10				42
32	24	33	35	23	29	26	22	29	38	10	1	5	2	11	1	8	8	21	4	17	2	17	2	13	1	4		
	1		1		2	7	6	7	17	1			1		1		5		9		1	1						

1		3	4	5	6	7		10	11								8		2		9							22
1		3	4	5	6	7	10	8	11										2		9							25
1		3	4	5	6		10	8	11				7						2		9							26
1		3		5	6		10	8	11				7			4			2		9							29
4		3	4	4	4	2	3	4	4				2			1	1		4		4							
				1			1		1				1						1									

Arthur Bridgett

Bridgett was the top goalscorer in this and the following season with 18 and 26 League and FA Cup goals respectively. His tally of 348 appearances for Sunderland could have been more had he not refused to play on religious days because of his active involvement with the Brotherhood Movement.

343

1906-07

Division One

Ground: Roker Park

Manager: Robert Kyle

League Table

	P	W	D	L	F	A	Pts
Newcastle U	38	22	7	9	74	46	51
Bristol C	38	20	8	10	66	47	48
Everton	38	20	5	13	70	46	45
Sheffield U	38	17	11	10	57	55	45
Aston Villa	38	19	6	13	78	52	44
Bolton W	38	18	8	12	59	47	44
Woolwich A	38	20	4	14	66	59	44
Manchester U	38	17	8	13	53	56	42
Birmingham	38	15	8	15	52	52	38
SUNDERLAND	38	14	9	15	65	66	37
Middlesbrough	38	15	6	17	56	63	36
Blackburn R	38	14	7	17	56	59	35
Sheffield W	38	12	11	15	49	60	35
Preston NE	38	14	7	17	44	57	35
Liverpool	38	13	7	18	64	65	33
Bury	38	13	6	19	58	68	32
Manchester C	38	10	12	16	53	77	32
Notts Co	38	8	15	15	46	50	31
Derby Co	38	9	9	20	41	59	27
Stoke	38	8	10	20	41	64	26

FA Cup Winners:
Sheffield Wednesday

Did you know that?

The 5-5 draw with Liverpool on 19 January 1907 is the highest scoring draw of any Sunderland home game. During this game Ephraim Rhodes became the first Sunderland player to score two penalties in a game.

Match 1: Tait and Hall made debuts
Match 2: McGhie made debut
Match 3: Ward made debut
Match 7: Law only game
Match 8: Huggins made debut
Match 11: Hall last game
Match 14: Hurdman made debut
Match 15: Curtis only game
Match 17: Raine made debut
Match 25: Forster made debut
Match 27: Metcalf only game
Match 30: Benefit game for Gemmell & Naisby last game
Match 35: Watson last game
Match 37: Barrie and Shaw last games
Match 40: Brown last game
Match 41: Carmichael only game
Match 42: Willis last game
Match 43: Farquhar last game

Match No.	Date	Round	Venue	Opponents	Result	FT	HT	Pos.	Scorers	Attendance
1	Sep 1		A	Newcastle United	L	2-4	0-1		Bridgett (2)	56,875
2	8		H	Aston Villa	W	2-1	1-1	13	Shaw, Hogg	24,000
3	15		A	Liverpool	W	2-1	0-1	10	Bridgett, Hogg	18,000
4	22		H	Bristol City	D	3-3	1-1	11	Hogg, Bridgett, Shaw	23,000
5	29		A	Notts County	D	0-0	0-0	11		20,000
6	Oct 6		H	Sheffield United	L	1-2	1-2	13	Bridgett (pen)	20,000
7	13		A	Bolton Wanderers	L	0-1	0-0	14		20,000
8	20		H	Manchester United	W	4-1	2-0	10	Huggins, Bridgett (2), Hogg	16,000
9	27		A	Stoke	D	2-2	2-2	9	Bridgett (2)	5,000
10	Nov 3		H	Blackburn Rovers	W	1-0	1-0	9	Bridgett	12,000
11	10		H	Derby County	L	0-2	0-0	12		12,000
12	17		A	Birmingham	L	0-2	0-1	13		10,000
13	24		H	Everton	W	1-0	0-0	12	Gemmell	18,000
14	Dec 1		A	Woolwich Arsenal	W	1-0	0-0	10	Gemmell	20,000
15	8		H	Sheffield Wed.	D	1-1	1-1	10	Shaw	18,000
16	15		A	Bury	W	3-2	1-1	8	Shaw, Tait, Bridgett	8,000
17	22		H	Manchester City	D	1-1	0-1	10	Shaw	5,000
18	25		A	Middlesbrough	L	1-2	0-1	12	Gemmell	17,000
19	Jan 5		A	Aston Villa	D	2-2	0-2	12	Bridgett (2)	30,000
21	19		H	Liverpool	D	5-5	1-4	13	Bridgett, Rhodes (2 pens), Hurdman (2)	20,000
22	26		A	Bristol City	D	1-1	1-1	14	Holley	15,000
25	Feb 9		A	Sheffield United	L	2-3	0-0	15	McIntosh, Huggins	10,000
26	13		H	Preston North End	W	1-0	0-0	14	Bridgett	5,000
27	16		H	Bolton Wanderers	L	1-2	1-1	14	Hogg	19,000
30	Mar 2		H	Stoke	W	3-1	1-1	16	McIntosh, Holley, Bridgett	10,000
31	9		A	Blackburn Rovers	L	1-2	0-2	15	McIntosh	6,000
32	16		A	Derby County	D	1-1	1-0	14	McIntosh	4,000
33	20		H	Newcastle United	W	2-0	0-0	11	Hogg, Holley	31,000
34	23		H	Birmingham	W	4-1	1-0	9	Raine (2), Bridgett, Hogg	18,000
35	25		A	Manchester United	L	0-2	0-1	10		10,000
36	29		A	Preston North End	L	0-2	0-1	11		10,000
37	30		A	Everton	L	1-4	0-2	11	Bridgett	12,000
38	Apr 1		H	Middlesbrough	W	4-2	2-0	11	Hogg, Bridgett (2), Holley	26,000
39	6		H	Woolwich Arsenal	L	2-3	0-1	11	Bridgett, Holley	12,000
40	13		A	Sheffield Wed.	L	1-2	1-2	11	Bridgett	3,000
41	20		H	Bury	L	3-5	1-2	12	Raine (2), Bridgett (pen)	3,000
42	24		H	Notts County	W	3-1	2-1	11	Hurdman, Farquhar, Bridgett	3,000
43	27		A	Manchester City	W	3-2	1-1	10	Raine, Bridgett, Gemmell	10,000

Appearances
Goals

FA Cup

20	Jan 12	R1	H	Leicester Fosse	W	4-1	3-0		Bridgett, McIntosh (2), Raine	21,336
23	Feb 2	R2	A	Luton Town	D	0-0	0-0			10,333
24	6	R2r	H	Luton Town	W	1-0	0-0		McIntosh	20,000
28	23	R3	A	Sheffield Wed.	D	0-0	0-0			36,324
29	27	R3r	H	Sheffield Wed.	L	0-1	0-0			35,856

Appearances
Goals

344

	Naisby	Rhodes	Watson	Tait	Barrie	Willis	Hogg	Gemmell	Shaw	Hall	Bridgett	McGhie	Ward	McConnell	McIntosh	Law	Brown	Huggins	Daykin	Hurdman	Curtis	Raine	Holley	Forster	Metcalf	Bell	Carmichael	Farquhar	
1	2	3	4	5	6	7	8	9	10	11																			1
1	2	3	4		6	7	8	9	10	11	5																		2
	2	3	4			7	8	9	10	11	5	1	6																3
	2	3	4			7	8	9	10	11	5	1	6																4
	2	3	4			7	9		10	11	5	1	6	8															5
	2	3	4		6	7	8	9	10	11	5	1																	6
	2	3	4		6	7	8	9	10		5	1			11														7
	2	3	4			8	10			9	5	1	6			7	11												8
	2	3	4			8	10			9	5	1	6			7	11												9
	2	3	4			8	10			9	5	1	6			7	11												10
	2	3	4			8			10	9	5	1	6			7	11												11
	2	3	4	5		8		9		11		1	6	10		7													12
	2	3	4	5		7	8	9		10		1	6				11												13
	2		4	5		8	10	9		11		1	6						3	7									14
	2	3	4	5		8	10	9		11		1	6					7											15
	2	3	4	5		8	10	9		11		1	6					7											16
	2	3	4	5		8	10	9		11		1	6								7								17
	2	3	4	5		8	10	9		11		1	6								7								18
	2	3	4			8	9			10	5	1	6				11		7										19
	2	3	4				10			11	5	1	6	9						7		8							21
	2		4				8			11	5	1	6	9					3			7	10						22
	2						8			10	5	1	6	9			11	3	7					4					25
	2		4		6	7	8			11	5	1		9					3				10						26
		2	4				8			11		1		9					3	7			10	6	5				27
1			4				8			11	5		6	9					3			7	10	2					30
			4				8			11	5	1	6	9					3			7	10			2			31
	2		4			8	10			11	5	1	6	9					3			7							32
	2		4			8				11	5	1	6	9					3			7	10						33
	2		4			8	5			11		1	6	9					3			7	10						34
	2	3	4		6	8	5			11		1		9								7	10						35
	2		4	5	6	8	10			11		1		9	7		3												36
	2		4	5	6	8	10	9		11		1			7									3					37
	2		4		6	8				11	5	1		9	7		3					10							38
	2		4		6	8				11	5	1		9	7		3					10							39
	2		4		6	8				11	5	1		9	7		3					10							40
	2		4		6					11	5	1		9			3					7	10		8				41
	2			6		8				11	5	1					3	9				7	10			4			42
	2		4				8			11	5	1		9			3					7	10			6			43
3	35	21	36	10	13	30	30	14	8	37	25	35	23	19	1	10	7	17	7	1	12	15	4	1	1	1	2		
	2		1			8	4	5		25				4			2		3		5	5				1			
	2	3	4			10				11	5	1	6	9							7	8							20
	2	3	4				8			11	5	1	6	9							7	10							23
	2	3	4			8	10			11	5	1	6	9							7								24
	2		4			7	8			11	5	1	6	9					3				10						28
		3	4			7	8			11	5	1	6	9					2				10						29
	4	4	5			3	5			5	5	5	5	5					2			3	4						
								1					3						1										

James Gemmell

Glaswegian Gemmell played 227 League and FA Cup games for Sunderland in two spells between 1900 and 1912 scoring 46 goals in the process. He left in May 1907 to join Stoke but returned to Sunderland from Leeds City on 30 May 1910.

1907-08

Division One

Ground: Roker Park
Manager: Robert Kyle

League Table

	P	W	D	L	F	A	Pts
Manchester U	38	23	6	9	81	48	52
Aston Villa	38	17	9	12	77	59	43
Manchester C	38	16	11	11	62	54	43
Newcastle U	38	15	12	11	65	54	42
Sheffield W	38	19	4	15	73	64	42
Middlesbrough	38	17	7	14	54	45	41
Bury	38	14	11	13	58	61	39
Liverpool	38	16	6	16	68	61	38
Nottingham F	38	13	11	14	59	62	37
Bristol C	38	12	12	14	58	61	36
Everton	38	15	6	17	58	64	36
Preston NE	38	12	12	14	47	53	36
Chelsea	38	14	8	16	53	62	36
Blackburn R*	38	12	12	14	51	63	36
Woolwich A*	38	12	12	14	51	63	36
SUNDERLAND	38	16	3	19	78	75	35
Sheffield U	38	12	11	15	52	58	35
Notts Co	38	13	8	17	39	51	34
Bolton W	38	14	5	19	52	58	33
Birmingham	38	9	12	17	40	60	30

*Woolwich Arsenal & Blackburn Rovers finished in equal 14th place

FA Cup Winners:
Wolverhampton Wanderers

Did you know that?

Injured Sunderland keeper Dick Roose became the first player to be replaced by a substitute in an international match when Dai Davies, of Bolton Wanderers, came on for him; Wales v England at Wrexham on 16 March 1908.

Match 1: Bonthron, Jarvie, Low and Raybould made debuts and Brown only game
Match 3: Allen and Morley made debuts
Match 8: Montgomery made debut
Match 15: Bell last game
Match 16: Foster made debut
Match 17: Morley last game
Match 19: Allen last game
Match 20: Thompson made debut
Match 25: Roose made debut, Bonthron last game & Grey only game
Match 26: Benefit game for Rhodes & McGhie last game
Match 27: Benefit game for Bridgett
Match 28: Raine and Foster last games
Match 29: Rhodes last game
Match 30: Marples made debut & McConnell last game
Match 31: Ward last game
Match 35: Huggins last game
Match 37: Hurdman last game
Match 39: Marples and Raybould last games

Match No.	Date		Round	Venue	Opponents	Result	FT	HT	Pos.	Scorers	Attendance
1	Sep	2		H	Manchester City	L	2-5	0-3		Holley, Bridgett	20000
2		7		H	Notts County	W	4-3	2-1	12	Raybould, Bridgett, Low, Bonthron	20000
3		9		A	Aston Villa	L	0-1	0-1	13		18000
4		14		A	Manchester City	D	0-0	0-0	14		30000
5		21		H	Preston North End	W	4-1	3-0	10	Morley, McIntosh, Raybould, Bridgett	20000
6		28		A	Bury	L	1-2	1-2	14	Raine	15000
7	Oct	5		H	Aston Villa	W	3-0	2-0	10	Holley, McIntosh, Bridgett	25000
8		12		A	Liverpool	L	0-1	0-1	12		20000
9		19		H	Middlesbrough	D	0-0	0-0	8		25000
10		26		A	Sheffield United	L	3-5	1-2	14	Raybould (2), McIntosh	7000
11	Nov	2		H	Chelsea	W	3-0	2-0	11	Bridgett (pen), Raybould (2)	12000
12		9		A	Nottingham Forest	L	1-4	1-2	14	Raybould	5000
13		16		H	Manchester United	L	1-2	0-0	14	Raybould	20882
14		23		A	Blackburn Rovers	L	2-4	0-2	18	Raybould (2)	2000
15		30		H	Bolton Wanderers	L	1-2	0-1	18	Holley	10000
16	Dec	7		A	Birmingham	W	2-0	0-0	18	Foster, Holley	10000
17		14		H	Everton	L	1-2	1-2	19	Holley	12000
18		21		H	Newcastle United	L	2-4	2-3	19	Hogg, Bridgett	30000
19		25		H	Bristol City	D	3-3	2-3	19	Hogg, Holley, Bridgett (pen)	15000
20		26		A	Sheffield Wed.	W	3-2	2-1	17	Thompson (2), Bridgett	20000
21		28		A	Woolwich Arsenal	L	0-4	0-2	20		5000
22	Jan	1		H	Woolwich Arsenal	W	5-2	1-1	18	Holley, Hogg, Foster (2), Thompson	22000
23		4		A	Notts County	L	0-4	0-1	19		5000
25		18		A	Preston North End	L	2-3	1-1	20	Thompson, Bridgett	5000
26		25		H	Bury	W	6-2	3-1	20	Holley (2), Bridgett, Hogg (2), McIntosh	12000
27	Feb	8		H	Liverpool	W	1-0	0-0	18	Bridgett	30000
28		15		A	Middlesbrough	L	1-3	0-3	20	Holley	25000
29		22		H	Sheffield United	W	4-1	2-0	17	Holley (2), Rhodes, Bridgett	7000
30		29		A	Chelsea	L	1-2	1-0	18	Holley	32000
31	Mar	7		H	Nottingham Forest	W	7-2	4-1	18	Holley (3), Hogg, Thompson (2), Bridgett	12000
32		14		A	Manchester United	L	0-3	0-2	18		12000
33		21		H	Blackburn Rovers	W	4-0	2-0	17	Holley (3), Hogg	10000
34		28		A	Bolton Wanderers	W	3-2	1-1	16	Holley (2), Jarvie	18000
35	Apr	4		H	Birmingham	W	1-0	0-0	14	Hogg (pen)	15000
36		11		A	Everton	W	3-0	2-0	12	Raybould (2), Holley	12000
37		17		H	Sheffield Wed.	L	1-2	0-1	13	Bridgett	30200
38		18		A	Newcastle United	W	3-1	1-0	11	Holley, Low, Bridgett	50000
39		20		A	Bristol City	L	0-3	0-1	16		19500

Appearances
Goals

FA Cup

24	Jan	11	R1	A	New Brompton	L	1-3	1-1		Holley	13,765

Appearances
Goals

	Ward	Bonthron	Daykin	Tait	Jarvie	Low	Raine	Brown	Raybould	Holley	Bridgett	McGhie	Allen	McIntosh	Morley	Foster	Huggins	Hogg	Montgomery	Bell	McConnell	Foster	Rhodes	Thompson	Roose	Grey	Marples	Hurdman	
1	1	2	3	4	5	6	7	8	9	10	11																		1
2	1	2	3	4	6	8	7		9	10	11	5																	2
3		2	3	4		6			10	8	11	5	1	7	9														3
4		2	3			6	7		9	10	11	5	1		8	4													4
5		2	3			6			9	10	11	5	1	7	8	4													5
6		2	3			6	7		9	10	11	5	1		8	4													6
7		2	3	4		6	7		8	10	5	1		9		11													7
8		2	3	4	6				9		5	1	7		11	8	10												8
9		2	3	4	6		7		10		5	1		9	11	8													9
10		2	3	4	6		7	10	8		5	1		9	11														10
11		2	3	4	6		7	10	8	11	5	1		9															11
12		2	3	4	6		7	10	8	11	5	1		9															12
13	1	2	3	4	5	6	7		9	10	11					8													13
14	1	2	3	4	5	6	7		10		11			9		8													14
15	1	2		4	5	6	7		10	11	9					8	3												15
16	1	2	3	4					10		5		7			11	8			6	9								16
17	1	2	3	4					10		5		7			11	8			6	9								17
18	1	2	3	4		5			10	8	11						7			6	9								18
19		2		4	6	5			10	8	11		1				7				9	3							19
20	1			4	6	5			10		11				9	3	7						2	8					20
21	1	2		4	6	5			10		11				9		7						3	8					21
22	1	2	3	4		6			10	11	5						7		9		8								22
23	1		3	4		6			10	11	5						8				9	2	7						23
25		2			4				10	11						3	8			6	9		7	1	5				25
26					4				10	11	5			9	3		8			6		2	7	1					26
27				4		5			10	11				9	3		8			6		2	7	1					27
28				4		5	7		10	11					3					6	9	2	8	1					28
29			4	6	5			9	10	11					3		8					2	7	1					29
30				6	5			9	10						3		8	11	4				7	1		2			30
31	1		4	6	5			9	10	11					3		8						7			2			31
32			4	6	5			9	10	11					3		8						7	1		2			32
33			4	6	5			9	10	11					3		8						7	1		2			33
34			4	6	5			9	10	11					3		8						7	1		2			34
35			4	6	5			9	10						3	11	8						7	1		2			35
36			4	6	5			9	10	11					3		8						7	1		2			36
37			4	6	5			9	10	11					3		8						1		2	7			37
38			4	6	5			9	10	11				7	3		8						1		2				38
39			4	6	5			9	10	11				7	3		8						1		2				39
	13	22	21	30	24	31	13	1	27	35	31	16	11	5	16	19	7	27	2	1	8	8	8	16	14	1	10	1	
		1			1	2	1		12	23	15			1	4		8			3	1	6							

	1	2		4	6	5			9	10	11			8	3		7												24
	1	1		1	1	1			1	1	1			1	1		1												
										1																			

Harry Low

Harry Low made his debut at the start of this season having signed from his native Aberdeen. He went on to play over 200 games for Sunderland before retiring in May 1919. His retirement was short-lived as he died suddenly just over a year later aged only 38. Sunderland AFC staged a benefit game on 6 April 1921 with the proceeds going to his widow.

1908-09

Division One

Ground: Roker Park
Manager: Robert Kyle

League Table

	P	W	D	L	F	A	Pts
Newcastle U	38	24	5	9	65	41	53
Everton	38	18	10	10	82	57	46
SUNDERLAND	38	21	2	15	78	63	44
Blackburn R	38	14	13	11	61	50	41
Sheffield W	38	17	6	15	67	61	40
Woolwich A	38	14	10	14	52	49	38
Aston Villa	38	14	10	14	58	56	38
Bristol C	38	13	12	13	45	58	38
Middlesbrough	38	14	9	15	59	53	37
Preston NE	38	13	11	14	48	44	37
Chelsea	38	14	9	15	56	61	37
Sheffield U	38	14	9	15	51	59	37
Manchester U	38	15	7	16	58	68	37
Nottingham F	38	14	8	16	66	57	36
Notts Co	38	14	8	16	51	48	36
Liverpool	38	15	6	17	57	65	36
Bury	38	14	8	16	63	77	36
Bradford C	38	12	10	16	47	47	34
Manchester C	38	15	4	19	67	69	34
Leicester C	38	8	9	21	54	102	25

FA Cup Winners: Manchester Utd

Did you know that?

Sunderland set the following records when they beat Newcastle 9-1 on 5 December 1908:

- Highest away win by any team in Division 1.

- Quickest time for a team to score 8 goals (during a 28 minute period in the second half).

Match 1: Agnew, Thomson, Clark & Brown made debuts
Match 3: Milton and Mordue made debuts
Match 9: McIntosh last game
Match 16: Daykin last game
Match 20: Kelly last game
Match 28: Allan made debut
Match 34: Martin made debut and Hope only game
Match 35: Johnston only game
Match 42: Hogg last game
Match 43: Montgomery last game & Hastings only game

Match No.	Date		Round	Venue	Opponents	Result	FT	HT	Pos.	Scorers	Attendance
1	Sep	1		A	Manchester City	L	0-1	0-1			25,000
2		5		A	Bury	L	2-4	1-3	18	Brown, Holley	10,000
3		9		A	Middlesbrough	W	3-0	1-0	10	Mordue, Holley, Bridgett	18,000
4		12		H	Sheffield United	W	3-1	1-1	6	Holley (2), Thomson	25,000
5		19		A	Aston Villa	L	0-2	0-1	10		26,000
6		26		H	Nottingham Forest	W	2-1	2-1	8	Holley (2, 1 pen)	18,000
7	Oct	3		H	Sheffield Wed.	W	4-2	2-1	6	Hogg, Brown, Mordue, Holley	28,000
8		10		A	Chelsea	L	0-2	0-0	8		35,000
9		17		H	Blackburn Rovers	L	0-1	0-1	10		6,000
10		24		A	Bradford City	W	2-0	1-0	9	Brown, Mordue	20,000
11		31		H	Manchester United	W	6-1	3-1	6	Brown (2), Holley (2), Bridgett (2)	30,000
12	Nov	7		A	Everton	L	0-4	0-1	10		20,000
13		14		H	Leicester Fosse	W	3-1	1-0	7	Holley, Bridgett, Mordue	8,000
14		21		A	Woolwich Arsenal	W	4-0	1-0	6	Hogg (3), Bridgett	14,000
15		28		H	Notts County	L	0-1	0-1	6		10,000
16	Dec	5		A	Newcastle United	W	9-1	1-1	5	Hogg (3), Holley (3), Bridgett (2), Mordue	56,000
17		12		H	Bristol City	L	0-2	0-1	5		10,000
18		19		A	Preston North End	L	0-1	0-0	7		10,000
19		26		H	Middlesbrough	W	2-0	1-0	8	Low, Holley	20,000
20	Jan	1		H	Liverpool	L	1-4	0-1	9	Hogg	20,000
21		2		H	Bury	W	3-1	1-1	7	Low, Bridgett, Brown	4,000
22		9		A	Sheffield United	W	2-0	1-1	5	Hogg, Thomson	14,000
24		23		H	Aston Villa	W	4-3	2-1	5	Thompson (3), Brown	15,000
25		30		A	Nottingham Forest	L	0-4	0-3	6		9,000
27	Feb	13		H	Chelsea	L	1-2	1-1	7	Holley	18,000
29		27		H	Bradford City	W	2-1	1-1	6	Brown, Montgomery	10,000
32	Mar	13		H	Everton	W	2-0	0-0	6	Brown (2)	8,000
33		15		A	Manchester United	D	2-2	2-1	5	Montgomery, Brown	10,000
34		20		A	Leicester Fosse	L	3-4	2-1	6	Clark, Bridgett, Jarvie	12,000
35		22		A	Blackburn Rovers	L	1-8	1-3	7	Clark	5,000
36		27		H	Woolwich Arsenal	W	1-0	1-0	6	Bridgett	7,500
37		29		A	Sheffield Wed.	W	5-2	2-2	3	Brown (2), Mordue (2), Bridgett	6,000
38	Apr	3		A	Notts County	D	0-0	0-0	3		10,000
39		9		H	Manchester City	W	2-0	1-0	3	Brown, Holley	16,000
40		10		H	Newcastle United	W	3-1	0-1	3	Brown (2), Holley	27,493
41		12		A	Liverpool	L	0-3	0-1	3		15,000
42		17		A	Bristol City	W	4-2	0-2	3	Holley (2), Brown (2)	7,000
43		24		H	Preston North End	W	2-1	1-0	3	Thompson (2)	5,000

Appearances
Goals

FA Cup

Match No.	Date		Round	Venue	Opponents	Result	FT	HT		Scorers	Attendance
23	Jan	16	R1	A	Sheffield United	W	3-2	0-1		Thomson, Hogg, Brown	23,575
26	Feb	6	R2	A	Preston North End	W	2-1	0-1		Thomson, Bridgett	21,000
28		20	R3	A	Bradford City	W	1-0	1-0		Holley	40,000
30	Mar	6	R4	A	Newcastle United	D	2-2	2-2		Mordue, Brown	53,353
31		10	R4r	H	Newcastle United	L	0-3	0-1			27,512

Appearances
Goals

	Roose	Agnew	Forster	Daykin	Thomson	Low	Clark	Hogg	Brown	Holley	Bridgett	Tait	Milton	Mordue	Thompson	McIntosh	Jarvie	Montgomery	Kelly	Allan	Martin	Hope	Johnston	Hastings	
	1	2	3	4	5	6	7	8	9	10	11														1
	1	2	3		5	6	7	8	9	10	11	4													2
	1	2			5	6	7		9	8	10	4	3	11											3
	1	2			5	6	7		9	8	10	4	3	11											4
	1	2	3		5	6	7		9	8	10	4		11											5
	1	2			5	6			9	8	10	4	3	11	7										6
	1	2			5	6		8	9	10	11	4	3	7											7
	1	2	3		5	6		8	9	10	11	4			7										8
	1	2	3		5	6			9	10	11	4		7	8										9
	1	2	3		5	6		8	9	10	11			7		4									10
	1	2	3		5	4		8	9	10	11			7		6									11
	1	2	3		5	4		8	9	10	11			7		6									12
	1	2	3		5	4		8	9	10	11			7		6									13
	1	2	3	4	5	6		8	9	10	11			7											14
	1	2	3	4	5	6		8	9	10	11			7											15
	1		2	4	5	6		8	9	10	11		3	7											16
	1		3		5			8	9	10	11	4		7		6	2								17
	1	2			5	6		8	9	10	11	4	3	7											18
	1	2			5	6		8	9	10	11	4	3	7											19
	1	2			5	6		8	9	10	11	4		7				3							20
	1		3		2	5		8	9	10	11	4		7		6									21
	1	2			5			7	9	8	10	4	3	11		6									22
	1		2		5				9	8	10	4	3	11	7	6									24
	1				5	2		8	9		11	4	3		7	6	10								25
	1	3			2	5		8	9	10		4		11	7	6									27
	1	2			5	4	7	9	8				3	11		6	10								29
	1				5	8			9	10	11	4	3	7		6									32
		2			5	8		9				4	3	11	7	6	10	1							33
		2		5		7			9			3	11			6	10	1	4	8					34
		3		5		7		9		8			11			6	10	1	4		2				35
	1	2	3	5	8	7		9		10	4		11			6									36
	1	2	3			5	7		9		11	4		10		6	8								37
	1	2	3	5	8	7		9			4			11		6	10								38
	1	2	3	5		7		9	8	11				10		6									39
	1			5		7		9	8	11	4	3	10			6									40
	1	2		5	7			9	8	11	4	3	10			6									41
	1	2		5	7		8	9	10	11	4	3				6									42
	1	3			5			9		11	4		7	8		6	10				2				43
	35	19	33	4	36	31	12	21	37	30	34	27	17	33	7	1	23	9	1	3	2	1	1	1	
					2	2	2	9	18	19	11		7	5		1	2								
	1	2			5		7	9	8	10	4	3	11			6									23
	1	3			2	5	7	9	8	10	4		11			6									26
			3	5	4		7	9	8	10		2	11			6		1							28
	1	2			5	6	7	9	8	10	4	3	11												30
	1	2			5	3	7	9	8	10	4		11			6									31
	4		5		5	4	5	5	5	5	4	3	5			4			1						
				2			1	2	1	1			1												

Billy Hogg

Scored a hat-trick in Sunderland's 9-1 victory at St James' Park. This was his last League game against Newcastle United. In total he scored 84 goals for Sunderland in 303 first team appearances in the 10 years he was at Roker Park. He returned in 1927 and spent seven years on the coaching staff.

1909-10

Division One

Ground: Roker Park

Manager: Robert Kyle

League Table

	P	W	D	L	F	A	Pts
Aston Villa	38	23	7	8	84	42	53
Liverpool	38	21	6	11	78	57	48
Blackburn R	38	18	9	11	73	55	45
Newcastle U	38	19	7	12	70	56	45
Manchester U	38	19	7	12	69	61	45
Sheffield U	38	16	10	12	62	41	42
Bradford C	38	17	8	13	64	47	42
SUNDERLAND	38	18	5	15	66	51	41
Notts Co	38	15	10	13	67	59	40
Everton	38	16	8	14	51	56	40
Sheffield W	38	15	9	14	60	63	39
Preston NE	38	15	5	18	52	58	35
Bury	38	12	9	17	62	66	33
Nottingham F	38	11	11	16	54	72	33
Tottenham H	38	11	10	17	53	69	32
Bristol C	38	12	8	18	45	60	32
Middlesbrough	38	11	9	18	56	73	31
Woolwich A	38	11	9	18	37	67	31
Chelsea	38	11	7	20	47	70	29
Bolton W	38	9	6	23	44	71	24

FA Cup Winners: Newcastle Utd

Did you know that?

Play was stopped for at least 15 minutes during the first half of the Sunderland v Newcastle United derby game on 18 September 1909 because of a pitch invasion from the Fulwell End. Two police horses were used to drive the crowd back and during this charge one of the horses was stabbed. The police chief constable offered a £5 reward if someone named the offender.

Match 10: Logan made debut
Match 11: Troughear made debut
Match 17: Benefit game for Holley (he was guaranteed £500)
Match 21: Agnew last game
Match 25: Logan last game
Match 26: Cuggy made debut
Match 28: Thompson last game
Match 33: Gibson made debut
Match 36: Gibson last game
Match 37: Hall made debut
Match 39: Healey made debut
Match 40: Clark last game
Match 41: Read made debut and Brown last game

Match No.	Date		Round	Venue	Opponents	Result	FT	HT	Pos.	Scorers	Attendance
1	Sep	1		H	Tottenham Hotspur	W	3-1	2-0		Holley (2), Brown	10,000
2		4		H	Preston North End	W	2-1	1-1	3	Holley, Brown	10,000
3		11		A	Notts County	D	1-1	1-0	5	Bridgett	5,000
4		18		H	Newcastle United	L	0-2	0-1	10		41,000
5		25		A	Liverpool	W	4-1	1-0	7	Holley, Mordue, Thompson (2)	25,000
6	Oct	2		H	Aston Villa	D	1-1	0-0	8	Thompson	20,000
7		9		A	Sheffield United	L	0-3	0-0	10		17,000
8		16		H	Woolwich Arsenal	W	6-2	2-0	9	Bridgett, Holley (3), Thompson, Mordue	6,000
9		23		A	Bolton Wanderers	L	1-2	1-1	9	Brown	3,000
10		30		H	Chelsea	W	4-0	0-0	9	Holley (3), Mordue	8,000
11	Nov	6		A	Blackburn Rovers	D	0-0	0-0	10		25,000
12		13		H	Nottingham Forest	W	2-1	2-1	8	Maltby o.g., Holley	10,000
13		20		A	Middlesbrough	L	2-3	1-1	10	Mordue, Holley	18,000
14		27		A	Everton	L	1-2	0-1	11	Bridgett	15,000
15	Dec	4		H	Manchester United	W	3-0	1-0	11	Low, Holley (2)	14,000
16		11		A	Bradford City	L	1-3	0-2	11	Low	15,000
17		18		H	Sheffield Wed.	W	2-0	1-0	10	Low (2)	5,000
18		25		A	Bury	W	1-0	1-0	8	Clark	10,000
19		27		H	Bury	L	2-3	2-1	9	Holley, Mordue	17,000
20		28		A	Bristol City	W	3-2	1-0	7	Holley, Low (2)	12,000
21	Jan	1		H	Bristol City	W	4-0	0-0	7	Bridgett, Mordue (2), Low	18,000
22		8		A	Preston North End	L	0-1	0-1	8		6,000
24		22		H	Notts County	L	0-3	0-1	9		5,000
26	Feb	12		A	Aston Villa	L	2-3	1-1	10	Bridgett, Low	25,000
28		26		A	Woolwich Arsenal	W	2-1	0-1	9	Low (2)	8,000
29	Mar	5		H	Bolton Wanderers	W	3-0	2-0	9	Mordue (2), Holley	5,000
30		12		A	Chelsea	W	4-1	1-1	8	Bridgett, Low (2), Holley	15,000
31		16		H	Sheffield United	W	1-0	1-0	7	Holley	8,000
32		19		H	Blackburn Rovers	D	0-0	0-0	7		14,000
33		25		A	Tottenham Hotspur	L	1-5	0-2	9	Mordue	35,000
34		26		A	Nottingham Forest	W	3-1	1-0	7	Low (2), Mordue	8,000
35		28		H	Liverpool	W	2-1	2-1	6	Clark, Holley	20,000
36	Apr	2		H	Middlesbrough	D	2-2	2-1	5	Mordue (2)	12,000
37		9		H	Everton	L	0-1	0-0	9		2,000
38		13		A	Newcastle United	L	0-1	0-0	9		40,000
39		16		A	Manchester United	L	0-2	0-1	9		10,000
40		23		H	Bradford City	W	3-0	1-0	7	Healey, Bridgett (2)	5,000
41		30		A	Sheffield Wed.	L	0-1	0-0	8		5,000

Appearances
Goals

FA Cup

Match No.	Date		Round	Venue	Opponents	Result	FT	HT	Pos.	Scorers	Attendance
23	Jan	15	R1	H	Leeds City	W	1-0	0-0		Holley	10,100
25	Feb	5	R2	H	Bradford Park Avenue	W	3-1	3-1		Low (2), Bridgett	16,800
27		19	R3	A	Everton	L	0-2	0-0			40,000

Appearances
Goals

	Roose	Forster	Milton	Tait	Thomson	Jarvie	Thompson	Holley	Brown	Mordue	Bridgett	Agnew	Clark	Logan	Troughear	Low	Martin	Allan	Cuggy	Gibson	Hall	Healey	Read	
1	2	3	4	5	6	7	8	9	10	11														1
1	2	3	4	5	6	7	8	9	10	11														2
1	2	3	4	5	6	7	8	9	10	11														3
1	2	3	4	5	6	7	8	9	10	11														4
1	2	3	4	5	6	7	8	9	10	11														5
1	2		4	5	6	7	8	9	10	11	3													6
1	2		4	5	6	8		9	10	11	3	7												7
1	4	3		5	6	7	10	9	8	11	2													8
1		3	4	5	6	7	10	9	8	11	2													9
1		3	4	5	6		9		11	10	2	7	8											10
1		3	4	5	6		8	9	11	10		7	2											11
1		3	4	5	6		8	9	11	10		7	2											12
1	8	3	4	5	6			10	11	9		7	2											13
1		3	4	5	6		9		11	10		7	2	8										14
1		3	4	5	6		9		11	10		7	2	8										15
1		3	4	5	6		9		11	10		7	2	8										16
1		3	4	5	6		9		11	10		7	2	8										17
1			4	5			9		11	10	3	7	2	8	6									18
			4	5			9		11	10	3	7	2	8	6	1								19
			4	5	6		9		11	10	3	7	2	8		1								20
1	6		4	5			9		11	10	3	7	2	8										21
1	6	3	4	5			9		11	10		7	2	8										22
1	6	3	4	5			9		11	10		7	2	8										24
	3		4		6	7		11	10			8	2	9			1	5						26
1		3	4	5	6	7		11	10			8	2	9										28
	3			5	6		10	7	11			8	2	9			1	4						29
	3		4	5	6		10	7	11			8	2	9			1							30
	3		4	5	6		10	7	11			8	2	9			1							31
1	3		4	5	6		10	7	11			8	2	9										32
1	3		4	5	6		10	7				8	2	9					11					33
1	6	3	4	5			10	7	11			8	2	9										34
1		3	4	5	6		10	7	11			8	2	9										35
1		3	4		6		10	7				8	2	9		5			11					36
1	6	3	4	5				7	11			8	2	9						10				37
1	3		4	5	6		10	7	11			8	2	9										38
1	3			5	6		10	7	11			9	2	4				8						39
	2	3	4	5	6			10	7	11		9						8						40
1	2	3	4		6		10	9	8	11				5							7			41
1	24	24	35	35	31	11	33	13	38	36	9	29	1	26	24	2	7	3	2	1	2	1		
				4	20	3	13	8		2		14			1									

	Roose	Forster	Milton	Tait	Thomson	Jarvie	Thompson	Holley	Brown	Mordue	Bridgett	Agnew	Clark	Logan	Troughear	Low	Martin	Allan	Cuggy	Gibson	Hall	Healey	Read	
1	6	3	4	5			9		11	10		7	2	8										23
		3	4	5	6			11	10		7	8	2	9										25
1	3		4	5	6		10	7	11			8	2	9										27
	2	2	3	3	2		2		3	3		3	1	3	3									
							1			1				2										

Charlie Thomson

Centre-half Charles Bellany Thomson was an unmistakable figure in pre-WW1 football with his large bushy moustache. He captained both Sunderland and his native Scotland. It was later during his captaincy that Sunderland came closest to achieving the League and Cup double (1912-13).

1910-11

Division One

Ground: Roker Park
Manager: Robert Kyle

League Table

	P	W	D	L	F	A	Pts
Manchester U	38	22	8	8	72	40	52
Aston Villa	38	22	7	9	69	41	51
SUNDERLAND	38	15	15	8	67	48	45
Everton	38	19	7	12	50	36	45
Bradford C	38	20	5	13	51	42	45
Sheffield W	38	17	8	13	47	48	42
Oldham A	38	16	9	13	44	41	41
Newcastle U	38	15	10	13	61	43	40
Sheffield U	38	15	8	15	49	43	38
Woolwich A	38	13	12	13	41	49	38
Notts Co	38	14	10	14	37	45	38
Blackburn R	38	13	11	14	62	54	37
Liverpool	38	15	7	16	53	53	37
Preston NE	38	12	11	15	40	49	35
Tottenham H	38	13	6	19	52	63	32
Middlesbrough	38	11	10	17	49	63	32
Manchester C	38	9	13	16	43	58	31
Bury	38	9	11	18	43	71	29
Bristol C	38	11	5	22	43	66	27
Nottingham F	38	9	7	22	55	75	25

FA Cup Winners: Bradford City

Did you know that?

Tim Coleman played the first half of his last game for Sunderland, at Preston North End on 15 April 1911, wearing a false moustache. He confused the referee by removing it at half time such that the official delayed the restart until he was sure that a new player had not come on.

Match 1: Coleman made debut
Match 7: Carr only game
Match 9: Cowell made debut
Match 13: Roose last game
Match 14: Cringan made debut
Match 17: Main made debut
Match 18: Main last game
Match 24: Hodkin made debut
Match 25: Hodkin and Cowell last games
Match 27: Allan last game
Match 28: Worrall made debut
Match 29: Read last game
Match 33: Buchan made debut
Match 36: Arthur made debut
Match 37: Coleman last game
Match 39: Worrall last game

Match No.	Date		Round	Venue	Opponents	Result	FT	HT	Pos.	Scorers	Attendance
1	Sep	1		H	Newcastle United	W	2-1	1-0		Holley, Coleman	30,000
2		3		A	Sheffield United	W	2-1	0-0	1	Holley, Coleman	18,000
3		10		H	Aston Villa	W	3-2	1-0	1	Coleman, Tait, Gemmell	30,000
4		17		H	Oldham Athletic	W	2-1	1-0	1	Holley, Coleman	25,000
5		24		A	Woolwich Arsenal	D	0-0	0-0			16,000
6	Oct	1		H	Bradford City	D	1-1	1-1	1	Bridgett	30,000
7		8		A	Blackburn Rovers	W	1-0	1-0	1	Bridgett	18,000
8		15		H	Nottingham Forest	D	2-2	1-1	2	Holley (2)	18,000
9		22		A	Manchester City	D	3-3	2-1	2	Coleman (2), Cowell	25,000
10		29		H	Everton	W	4-0	2-0	1	Mordue (2), Holley, Coleman	16,000
11	Nov	5		A	Sheffield Wed.	D	1-1	0-1	1	Holley	15,000
12		12		H	Bristol City	W	3-1	2-0	1	Coleman (2), Cowell	13,000
13		19		A	Newcastle United	D	1-1	1-1	1	Coleman	57,416
14		26		H	Tottenham Hotspur	W	4-0	2-0	1	Mordue, Coleman (2), Bridgett	8,000
15	Dec	3		A	Middlesbrough	L	0-1	0-1	1		27,980
16		10		H	Preston North End	D	1-1	1-0	2	Bridgett	12,000
17		17		A	Notts County	D	1-1	0-1	1	Hall	10,000
18		24		H	Manchester United	L	1-2	0-1	4	Low	24,000
19		26		A	Liverpool	W	2-1	1-0	3	Coleman (2)	35,000
20		31		H	Sheffield United	L	0-2	0-2	4		15,000
21	Jan	2		H	Liverpool	W	4-0	4-0	2	Holley, Mordue, Coleman, Cowell	12,000
22		7		A	Aston Villa	L	1-2	1-2	4	Cowell	18,000
24		21		A	Oldham Athletic	L	1-2	1-0	5	Coleman	8,000
25		28		H	Woolwich Arsenal	D	2-2	0-2	5	Bridgett, Cowell	12,000
26	Feb	4		H	Bury	W	4-1	1-1	3	Holley (4)	8,000
27		11		H	Blackburn Rovers	D	2-2	2-1	4	Holley, Coleman	12,000
28		18		A	Nottingham Forest	W	3-1	1-0	4	Coleman, Holley, Low	9,000
29		25		H	Manchester City	W	4-0	1-0	3	Read (2), Bridgett, Coleman	10,000
30	Mar	4		A	Everton	D	2-2	1-2	3	Bridgett, Mordue	15,000
31		11		H	Sheffield Wed.	L	1-2	1-2	3	Mordue	12,000
32		18		A	Bristol City	D	1-1	0-1	3	Coleman	7,000
33	Apr	1		A	Tottenham Hotspur	D	1-1	1-1	3	Low	25,000
34		8		H	Middlesbrough	W	3-1	2-1	3	Low (3)	15,000
35		11		A	Bradford City	L	0-3	0-2	4		6,000
36		14		A	Bury	D	0-0	0-0	4		17,000
37		15		A	Preston North End	W	2-0	0-0	3	Coleman, Low	7,000
38		22		H	Notts County	D	1-1	1-1	3	Buchan	10,000
39		29		A	Manchester United	L	1-5	1-3	3	Low	12,000

Appearances
Goals

FA Cup

| 23 | Jan | 14 | R1 | A | Norwich City | L | 1-3 | 0-2 | | Bridgett | 11,333 |

Appearances
Goals

	Roose	Troughear	Milton	Tait	Thomson	Low	Mordue	Coleman	Holley	Gemmell	Bridgett	Allan	Forster	Carr	Cowell	Cringan	Cuggy	Jarvie	Main	Hall	Hodkin	Read	Worrall	Buchan	Arthur	Martin	
1	1	2	3	4	5	6	7	8	9	10	11																1
2	1	2	3	4	5	6	7	8	9	10	11																2
3	1	2	3	4	5	6	7	8	9	10	11																3
4		2	3	4	5	6	7	8	9	10	11	1															4
5	1	2	3	4	5	6	7	8	9	10	11																5
6	1	2	3	4	5	6	7		9	8	10	11															6
7	1	2		4	5	6	7	8		10	11		3	9													7
8	1	2		4	5	6	7	8	9	10	11		3														8
9	1	2		4	5	6	7	8	10		11		3	9													9
10	1	2		4	5	6	7	8	10		11		3	9													10
11	1	2		4	5	6	7	8	10		11		3	9													11
12	1	2		4	5	6	7	8		10	11		3	9													12
13	1	2		4	5	6	7	8	10		11		3	9													13
14		2			5	6	7	8	10		11	1	3	9	4												14
15		2		4	5	6	7	8	10		11	1	3	9													15
16		2		4		6	7	8		10	11	1	3	9		5											16
17		2		4			7	8			11	1	3			5	6	9	10								17
18		2		4	5	6	7	8	10		11	1	3					9									18
19		2		4	5	6	7	8	10		11	1	3	9													19
20		2		4	5	6	7	8		10	11	1	3	9													20
21		2	3	4	5	6	7	8	10		11	1		9													21
22		2	3	4	5	6	7	8	10		11	1		9													22
24		2	3		5		7	8	10		11	1		9		6			4								24
25		2	3		5	6	7	8			11	1		9				10	4								25
26		2	3	4	5	6	7	8	9	10	11	1															26
27			3	4	5	6		8	9	10	11	1	2							7							27
28		2	3	4	5	9		8	10		11					6				7	1						28
29		2	3	4	5	9		8	10		11					6				7	1						29
30		2	3	4	5	9	7	8	10		11					6					1						30
31		2	3	4	5	9	7	8	10		11					6					1						31
32		2	3	4		9	7	8		10	11				5	6					1						32
33		2	3	4	5	9	7			10	11					6					1	8					33
34		2	3	4	5	9	7			10	11					6					1	8					34
35		2	3	4	5	9	7			10	11					6					1	8					35
36		2	3	4	5	9	7		10							6					1	8	11				36
37		2	3	4	5	9	7	8	10		11										1			6			37
38		2	3	4	5	9	7		10		11					6					1	8					38
39		2	3	4	5	9	7		10		11										1	8		6			39
	12	37	24	35	35	36	35	32	25	20	37	14	15	14	1	14	1	3	12	2	2	3	12	6	1	2	
		1			8	6	21	14	1	7				5			1		2			1					

	Roose	Troughear	Milton	Tait	Thomson	Low	Mordue	Coleman	Holley	Gemmell	Bridgett	Allan	Forster	Carr	Cowell	Cringan	Cuggy	Jarvie	Main	Hall	Hodkin	Read	Worrall	Buchan	Arthur	Martin	
23		2		4	5	6	7	8	9	10	11	1	3														23
	1		1	1	1	1	1	1	1	1	1	1	1														
										1																	

Leigh Richmond Roose

Dick Roose broke his wrist in his 99th, and last, game for Sunderland, at Newcastle on 19 November 1910, Bridgett took over in goal for the last 15 minutes. During his career he was famous for bouncing the ball right out to the halfway line on occasions. As a result of this the rules were changed in summer 1912 to restrict goalkeepers to handling the ball only while inside their penalty area.

353

1911-12

Division One

Ground: Roker Park
Manager: Robert Kyle

League Table

	P	W	D	L	F	A	Pts
Blackburn R	38	20	9	9	60	43	49
Everton	38	20	6	12	46	42	46
Newcastle U	38	18	8	12	64	50	44
Bolton W	38	20	3	15	54	43	43
Sheffield W	38	16	9	13	69	49	41
Aston Villa	38	17	7	14	76	63	41
Middlesbrough	38	16	8	14	56	45	40
SUNDERLAND	38	14	11	13	58	51	39
WBA	38	15	9	14	43	47	39
Woolwich A	38	15	8	15	55	59	38
Bradford C	38	15	8	15	46	50	38
Tottenham H	38	14	9	15	53	53	37
Manchester U	38	13	11	14	45	60	37
Sheffield U	38	13	10	15	63	56	36
Manchester C	38	13	9	16	56	58	35
Notts Co	38	14	7	17	46	63	35
Liverpool	38	12	10	16	49	55	34
Oldham A	38	12	10	16	46	54	34
Preston NE	38	13	7	18	40	57	33
Bury	38	6	9	23	32	59	21

FA Cup Winners: Barnsley

Did you know that?

Former Sunderland amateur goalkeeper Ronald Brebner won an Olympic gold medal in Stockholm when Great Britain beat Denmark 4-2 in the football final on 4 July 1912.

Match 1: Scott made debut
Match 7: Best made debut & Healey last game
Match 10: Ness and Payne made debuts
Match 11: Payne last game
Match 13: Kirby only game
Match 16: Young made debut
Match 20: Forster last game
Match 21: Anderson made debut & Jarvie last game
Match 30: McCulloch only game
Match 34: Arthur last game
Match 36: Tinsley made debut & Gemmell last game
Match 37: Bridgett and Young last games
Match 38: Harry Martin made debut & Tait last game
Match 42: George Martin last game

Match No.	Date		Round	Venue	Opponents	Result	FT	HT	Pos.	Scorers	Attendance
1	Sep	2		H	Middlesbrough	W	1-0	1-0		Holley	28,000
2		6		H	Blackburn Rovers	W	3-0	2-0	3	Holley (2), Bridgett	20,000
3		9		A	Notts County	L	1-3	1-2	6	Holley	18,000
4		16		H	Tottenham Hotspur	D	1-1	1-1	5	Holley	16,000
5		23		A	Manchester United	D	2-2	1-0	6	Buchan, Mordue	15,000
6		30		H	Liverpool	L	1-2	0-0	7	Mordue (pen)	10,000
7	Oct	7		A	Aston Villa	W	3-1	0-1	5	Holley (2), Best	28,000
8		14		H	Newcastle United	L	1-2	0-1	11	Holley	31,000
9		21		A	Sheffield United	W	2-1	0-0	7	Holley (2)	10,000
10		28		H	Oldham Athletic	W	4-2	3-0	3	Gemmell (2), Bridgett, Mordue	10,000
11	Nov	4		A	Bolton Wanderers	L	0-3	0-2	8		20,000
12		11		H	Bradford City	D	1-1	1-1	7	Buchan	10,000
13		18		A	Woolwich Arsenal	L	0-3	0-2	11		4,000
14		25		H	Manchester City	D	1-1	1-0	9	Bridgett	4,000
15	Dec	2		A	Everton	L	0-1	0-0	12		20,000
16		9		H	West Bromwich Albion	W	3-2	2-2	11	Holley, Mordue (pen), Young	10,000
17		16		H	Preston North End	W	3-0	1-0	10	Holley (2), Mordue	10,000
18		23		A	Blackburn Rovers	D	2-2	1-0	11	Bridgett, Buchan	14,219
19		25		A	Bury	W	2-0	1-0	8	Buchan, Mordue (pen)	10,000
20		26		A	Sheffield Wed.	L	0-8	0-7	11		29,995
21		30		A	Middlesbrough	D	3-3	1-1	11	Holley (2), Young	18,750
22	Jan	1		H	Sheffield Wed.	D	0-0	0-0	9		15,000
23		6		H	Notts County	W	5-0	0-0	5	Holley (2), Buchan, Mordue (2, 1 pen)	10,000
25		20		A	Tottenham Hotspur	D	0-0	0-0	5		17,000
26		27		H	Manchester United	W	5-0	1-0	4	Holley (4), Buchan	12,000
29	Feb	10		H	Aston Villa	D	2-2	0-1	4	Low (2)	12,000
30		17		A	Newcastle United	L	1-3	0-1	5	Low (pen)	45,000
32		28		H	Sheffield United	D	0-0	0-0	5		5,000
33	Mar	2		A	Oldham Athletic	D	0-0	0-0	5		8,000
34		9		H	Bolton Wanderers	L	0-1	0-1	7		10,000
35		16		A	Bradford City	L	1-2	0-0	11	Low	14,000
36		23		H	Woolwich Arsenal	W	1-0	0-0	10	Low	6,000
37		30		A	Manchester City	L	0-2	0-1	10		20,000
38	Apr	5		A	Liverpool	L	1-2	1-0	11	H. Martin	40,000
39		6		H	Everton	W	4-0	0-0	8	Holley (3), H. Martin	8,000
40		8		H	Bury	W	1-0	1-0	7	Holley	4,000
41		13		A	West Bromwich Albion	L	0-1	0-1	8		20,151
42		20		A	Preston North End	W	3-0	2-0	8	Buchan, Mordue, Cuggy	7,000

Appearances
Goals

FA Cup

24	Jan	13	R1	H	Plymouth Argyle	W	3-1	2-1		Mordue (2, 1 pen), Bridgett	28,317
27	Feb	3	R2	A	Crystal Palace	D	0-0	0-0			20,000
28		7	R2r	H	Crystal Palace	W 1-0 (aet)	0-0			Low	34,100
31		24	R3	H	West Bromwich Albion	L	1-2	0-2		Bridgett	43,383

Appearances
Goals

	Scott	Troughear	Milton	Tait	Thomson	Martin I.G.	Mordue	Buchan	Holley	Gemmell	Bridgett	Cringan	Best	Healey	Cuggy	Ness	Jarvie	Payne	Hall	Kirby	Forster	Young	Anderson	Low	McCulloch	Arthur	Tinsley	Martin H.	
1	2	3	4	5	6	7	8	9	10	11																			1
1	2	3	4	5	6	7	8	9	10	11																			2
1	2	3	4	5	6	7	8	9	10	11																			3
1	2	3	4	5	6	7	8	9	10	11																			4
1	2	3	4	5	6	7	8	9	10	11																			5
1	2	3	4	5	6	7	8	9	10	11																			6
1	2	3	4	5				11		9	10		6	7	8													7
1	2	3	4	5				11	8	9	10		6	7														8
1	2	3	4					11		9	10	8	6	7		5												9
1	2		4	5				11		8	9		7				3	6	10									10
1	2		4	5				11		9	8		7				3	6	10									11
1	2	3	4	5	6	11	8				9		7							10								12
1	2	3	4	5			11			8	10		7		6						9							13
1	2	3	4	5		10	8	9		11		7	6															14
1	2	3		5		7	8	9	10	11			6						4									15
1	2	3		5		7	8	10		11			6						4	9								16
1	2	3	4			7	8	10		11			5						6	9								17
1	2	3		5		7	8	10		11			4						6	9								18
1	2	3		5		7	8	10		11			4						6	9								19
1		3	6	5		7	8	10		11			4						2	9								20
	2	3				7	8	10		11	4		5		6					9	1							21
1	2	3				7	8	10	4	11	6		5							9								22
1	2	3		5		7	8	10		11	4		6							9								23
1		3		5		7	8	10		11	6		4	2						9								25
1				5		7	8	10		11	6		4	2						9								26
1	2	3		5	6		8		10	11		7	4							9								29
1	2	3		5	6			11			7		4				10			9	8							30
	2	3		5		7	8	10	11	6			4						9	1								32
	2	3				7	8	10		11	6		4						9	1	5							33
	2	3		5		7	8	10			6		4						1	9		11						34
		3		5			8	10		11	6		4	2					9	1	7							35
		3	4			7			8	11	6		5	2					1	9		10						36
		3	4			7	8	10		11	6		5	2					9	1								37
		3	4			7	8	10					5	2		9			1	6			11					38
1	2			5		7	8	10			6		4	3		9							11					39
1	2			5		7	8	10			6		4	3		9							11					40
1	2			5		7	8	10			6		4	3		9							11					41
1	2			5	6	7	8	10					4	3		9							11					42
30	31	32	19	30	10	35	31	32	16	29	17	10	1	27	12	3	2	7	1	6	13	8	8	1	1	1	5	
						9	7	25	2	4		1		1							2		5				2	

1	2	3		5		7	8	10		11	6		4							9								24
1	2	3		5		7	8	10		11	6		4						9									27
1	2	3		5		7	8	10		11	6		4							9								28
1	2	3		5		7	8	10		11	6		4						9									31
4	4	4		4		4	4	4		4	4		4						2	2								
							2			2										1								

Seaham born George Holley was top scorer with 25 League goals. He was top, or joint top, scorer in five other seasons; 1904-05, 1907-08, 1908-09, 1909-10 and 1913-14. He is Sunderland's leading goalscorer for England with seven goals in 10 appearances (1909-13).

1912-13

Division One

Ground: Roker Park
Manager: Robert Kyle

League Table

	P	W	D	L	F	A	Pts
SUNDERLAND	38	25	4	9	86	43	54
Aston Villa	38	19	12	7	86	52	50
Sheffield W	38	21	7	10	75	55	49
Manchester U	38	19	8	11	69	43	46
Blackburn R	38	16	13	9	79	43	45
Manchester C	38	18	8	12	53	37	44
Derby Co	38	17	8	13	69	66	42
Bolton W	38	16	10	12	62	63	42
Oldham A	38	14	14	10	50	55	42
WBA	38	13	12	13	57	50	38
Everton	38	15	7	16	48	54	37
Liverpool	38	16	5	17	61	71	37
Bradford C	38	12	11	15	50	60	35
Newcastle U	38	13	8	17	47	47	34
Sheffield U	38	14	6	18	56	70	34
Middlesbrough	38	11	10	17	55	69	32
Tottenham H	38	12	6	20	45	72	30
Chelsea	38	11	6	21	51	73	28
Notts Co	38	7	9	22	28	56	23
Woolwich A	38	3	12	23	26	74	18

FA Cup Winners: Aston Villa

Did you know that?

An elaborate scheme to blow up at least one of the stands at Crystal Palace on the day before the Sunderland versus Aston Villa FA Cup final was foiled. The scheme, devised by the Suffragette Movement, was discovered by the police just 12 days before the final.

Match 1: Richardson made debut
Match 4: Conner made debut & Scott last game
Match 6: Anderson last game
Match 7: Butler made debut
Match 8: Gladwin made debut
Match 16: Troughear last game
Match 34: Small only game
Match 38: Hobson made debut & Hall last game
Match 46: Crowned League champions

Match No.	Date	Round	Venue	Opponents	Result	FT	HT	Pos.	Scorers	Attendance
1	Sep 7		A	Newcastle United	D	1-1	0-1		Mordue	54,200
2	9		A	Blackburn Rovers	L	0-4	0-2	14		17,821
3	14		H	Derby County	L	0-2	0-1	18		12,000
4	18		H	Blackburn Rovers	L	2-4	0-3	19	Mordue, Buchan	15,000
5	21		A	Oldham Athletic	L	0-3	0-1	19		16,000
6	28		H	Tottenham Hotspur	D	2-2	1-1	17	Hall, Mordue	8,000
7	Oct 5		A	Chelsea	L	0-2	0-1	19		25,000
8	12		H	Middlesbrough	W	4-0	2-0	17	Hall, Holley, Low, Mordue	20,000
9	19		A	Woolwich Arsenal	W	3-1	1-0	17	Mordue (2, 1pen), Holley	10,000
10	26		H	Notts County	W	4-0	4-0	14	Hall, Martin, Buchan (2)	12,000
11	Nov 2		A	Bradford City	W	5-1	2-0	12	Buchan, Holley (3), Low	22,000
12	9		H	Manchester United	W	3-1	1-1	11	Mordue (pen), Tinsley, Hall	20,000
13	16		A	Manchester City	L	0-1	0-1	12		16,000
14	23		H	Aston Villa	W	3-1	2-0	10	Holley, Buchan, Mordue (pen)	35,000
15	30		A	West Bromwich Albion	L	1-3	0-2	12	Holley	13,529
16	Dec 7		H	Liverpool	W	7-0	4-0	10	Buchan (5), Martin, Mordue	14,000
17	14		A	Everton	W	4-0	2-0	10	Richardson (2), Buchan, Mordue	25,000
18	21		H	Bolton Wanderers	W	2-1	0-0	9	Buchan, Mordue (pen)	18,000
19	25		A	Sheffield Wed.	W	2-1	1-1	7	Mordue (pen), Holley	37,000
20	26		H	Sheffield Wed.	L	0-2	0-2	9		12,000
21	28		H	Newcastle United	W	2-0	1-0	7	Holley (2)	35,000
22	Jan 1		H	Woolwich Arsenal	W	4-1	1-0	5	Buchan, Cuggy, Mordue, Richardson	22,000
24	18		H	Oldham Athletic	D	1-1	0-1	7	Buchan	12,000
25	25		A	Tottenham Hotspur	W	2-1	2-1	4	Martin, Low	31,000
27	Feb 8		H	Chelsea	W	4-0	2-0	3	Buchan (2), Richardson, Low	12,000
28	15		A	Middlesbrough	W	2-0	0-0	2	Martin, Richardson	13,992
30	26		A	Derby County	W	3-0	3-0	1	Hall (2, 1 pen), Martin	6,000
31	Mar 1		A	Notts County	L	1-2	1-1	2	Hall	15,000
34	15		A	Manchester United	W	3-1	1-1	2	Richardson, Buchan (2)	25,000
36	21		H	Sheffield United	W	1-0	0-0	2	Thomson	26,000
37	22		H	Manchester City	W	1-0	1-0	1	Buchan	20,000
38	24		A	Sheffield United	W	3-1	0-1	1	Buchan (2), Holley	25,000
41	Apr 5		H	West Bromwich Albion	W	3-1	2-0	2	Mordue (pen), Buchan, Tinsley	33,700
42	9		H	Everton	W	3-1	1-1	1	Buchan, Richardson, Holley	12,000
43	12		A	Liverpool	W	5-2	4-0	1	Buchan (3), Richardson (2)	28,000
45	23		A	Aston Villa	D	1-1	1-0	1	Tinsley	59,740
46	26		A	Bolton Wanderers	W	3-1	3-1	1	Mordue (pen), Richardson (2)	14,000
47	30		H	Bradford City	W	1-0	0-0	1	Buchan	15,000

Appearances
Goals

FA Cup

Match No.	Date	Round	Venue	Opponents	Result	FT	HT	Scorers	Attendance
23	Jan 11	R1	H	Clapton Orient	W	6-0	3-0	Richardson (4), Mordue, Holley	12,895
26	Feb 5	R2	H	Manchester City	W	2-0	0-0	Mordue, Holley	27,974
29	22	R3	H	Swindon Town	W	4-2	3-0	Buchan, Richardson (2), Gladwin	24,865
32	Mar 8	R4	H	Newcastle United	D	0-0	0-0		29,111
33	12	R4r	A	Newcastle United	D	2-2 (aet)	1-1	Holley, Buchan	56,717
35	17	R4r2	A	Newcastle United	W	3-0	2-0	Holley, Mordue (2, 1 pen)	49,354
39	29	S	N*	Burnley	D	0-0	0-0		33,656
40	Apr 2	Sr	N‡	Burnley	W	3-2	1-2	Buchan, Mordue (pen), Holley	30,000
44	19	F	N°	Aston Villa	L	0-1	0-0		120,081

N* at Bramall Lane
N‡ at St. Andrews
N° at Crystal Palace

Appearances
Goals

	Scott	Troughear	Ness	Cuggy	Thomson	Low	Mordue	Buchan	Richardson	Holley	Martin	Conner	Anderson	Milton	Cringan	Hall	Butler	Gladwin	Tinsley	Best	Small	Hobson	
1	1	2	3	4	5	6	7	8	9	10	11												1
2	1	2	3	4	5	6	7	8	9	10	11												2
3	1	2	3	4	5	6	7	8	9	10	11												3
4	1	2	3	4	5	6	7	8		10	11	9											4
5		2	4	5	10	7	8			11	9	1	3	6									5
6		2	4	5	6	7	8		10	11		1	3		9								6
7	2			5	4	7	8		10	11			3	6	9	1							7
8			4	5	6	7	8		10	11			3		9	1	2						8
9			4	5	6	7	8		10	11			3		9	1	2						9
10			4	5	6	7	8		10	11			3		9	1	2						10
11			4	5	6	7	8		10	11			3		9	1	2						11
12			4	5	6	7	8			11			3		9	1	2	10					12
13			4	5	6	7	8		10	11			3		9	1	2						13
14				5	6	7	8		10	11			3	4	9	1	2						14
15				5	6	7	8		10	11			3	4	9	1	2						15
16		2	4	5	6	7	8		10	11			3		9	1							16
17			4	5	6	7	8	9	10	11			3			1	2						17
18			4	5	6	7	8		10	11			3		9	1	2						18
19			4	5	6	7	8		10	11			3		9	1	2						19
20			4	5	6	7	8		10	11			3		9	1	2						20
21			4	5	6	7	8	9	10	11			3			1	2						21
22		3	4	5	6	7	8	9		11						1	2	10					22
24			4	5	6	7	8	9	10	11			3			1	2						24
25			4	5	6	7	8		10	11			3		9	1	2						25
27			4	5	6	7	8	9		11			3		10	1	2						27
28				5	6			9	8	11			3	4	10	1	2		7				28
30			4		5	7	8		10	11			3	6	9	1	2						30
31				5	6				8	11			3	4	9	1	2	10	7				31
34		5				8	9	10	11				3	6		1	2		7	4			34
36			4	5	6	7	8	9	10	11			3			1	2						36
37			4	5	6	7	8	9	10	11			3			1	2						37
38		3	4	5	6	7	8		10	11					9	1			2				38
41		3	4		5	7	8	9		11				6		1	2	10					41
42			4	5	6	7	8	9	10	11			3			1			2				42
43		3		5	6	7	8	9		11				4		1		10	2				43
45		3	4	5	6	7	8	9		11						1	2	10					45
46		3	4	5	6	7	8	9		11						1	2	10					46
47		3	4	5	6	7	8	9	10	11						1	2						47
	4	6	13	32	35	37	35	36	18	30	38	2	2	27	10	20	32	27	7	3	1	3	
			1		1	4	15	27	11	12	5				7			3					

	Scott	Troughear	Ness	Cuggy	Thomson	Low	Mordue	Buchan	Richardson	Holley	Martin	Conner	Anderson	Milton	Cringan	Hall	Butler	Gladwin	Tinsley	Best	Small	Hobson	
23			4	5	6	7	8	9	10	11			3			1	2						23
26			4	5	6	7	8	9	10	11			3			1	2						26
29			4	5	6	7	8	9	10	11			3			1	2						29
32			4	5	6	7	8	9	10	11			3			1	2						32
33			4	5	6	7	8	9	10	11			3			1	2						33
35			4	5	6	7	8	9	10	11			3			1	2						35
39			4	5	6	7	8	9	10	11			3			1	2						39
40		3	4	5	6	7	8	9	10	11						1	2						40
44		3	4	5	6	7	8	9	10	11						1	2						44
		2	9	9	9	9	9	9	9	9			7			9	9						
					5	3	6	5									1						

Charlie Buchan scored five goals at home to Liverpool in a 7-0 win and a hat-trick in the return fixture in a 5-2 win. Unsurprisingly, he was also the season's top scorer with 30 League and FA Cup goals.

1913-14

Division One

Ground: Roker Park
Manager: Robert Kyle

League Table

	P	W	D	L	F	A	Pts
Blackburn R	38	20	11	7	78	42	51
Aston Villa	38	19	6	13	65	50	44
Middlesbrough	38	19	5	14	77	60	43
Oldham A	38	17	9	12	55	45	43
WBA	38	15	13	10	46	42	43
Bolton W	38	16	10	12	65	52	42
SUNDERLAND	38	17	6	15	63	52	40
Chelsea	38	16	7	15	46	55	39
Bradford C	38	12	14	12	40	40	38
Sheffield U	38	16	5	17	63	60	37
Newcastle U	38	13	11	14	39	48	37
Burnley	38	12	12	14	61	53	36
Manchester C	38	14	8	16	51	53	36
Manchester U	38	15	6	17	52	62	36
Everton	38	12	11	15	46	55	35
Liverpool	38	14	7	17	46	62	35
Tottenham H	38	12	10	16	50	62	34
Sheffield W	38	13	8	17	53	70	34
Preston NE	38	12	6	20	52	69	30
Derby Co	38	8	11	19	55	71	27

FA Cup Winners: Burnley

Did you know that?

The Football Association suspended Sunderland's captain Charlie Thomson for the first month of the 1913-14 season as a result of incidents that occurred during the previous year's FA Cup final. Aston Villa centre forward, Harry Hampton, and the match referee, Mr Adams, received the same punishment.

Match 4: Hopkins made debut
Match 5: Lane made debut
Match 8: Tinsley last game
Match 9: Lane last game
Match 21: Waugh only game
Match 28: Moore made debut
Match 29: Benefit game for Thomson (he was guaranteed £500)
Match 31: Richardson last game
Match 33: Conner last game
Match 34: Sherwin and Crossley made debuts & benefit game for Milton (he was guaranteed £500)
Match 38: Butler last game
Match 39: Scott made debut & Kelsall only game
Match 41: Milton last game
Match 42: Benefit game for Mordue (he was guaranteed £500)

Match No.	Date		Round	Venue	Opponents	Result	FT	HT	Pos.	Scorers	Attendance
1	Sep	1		A	Preston North End	D	2-2	2-1		Martin, Buchan	16,000
2		6		H	Newcastle United	L	1-2	1-1	14	Holley	40,000
3		8		A	Manchester United	L	1-3	1-1	14	Buchan	22,000
4		13		A	Liverpool	W	3-1	1-0	9	Buchan, Richardson (2)	20,000
5		20		H	Aston Villa	W	2-0	0-0	8	Holley (2)	25,000
6		27		A	Middlesbrough	W	4-3	0-1	5	Buchan, Holley (2), Richardson	26,972
7	Oct	4		H	Sheffield United	L	1-2	0-1	8	Buchan	20,000
8		11		A	Derby County	D	1-1	0-0	7	Cuggy	12,000
9		18		H	Manchester City	D	0-0	0-0	9		20,000
10		25		A	Bradford City	W	2-0	0-0	6	Richardson, Best (pen)	20,000
11	Nov	1		H	Blackburn Rovers	W	2-1	2-0	6	Richardson, Buchan	40,000
12		8		A	Tottenham Hotspur	W	4-1	2-0	4	Best (pen), Cringan, Richardson, Buchan	36,000
13		15		A	Everton	W	5-1	2-1	4	Best (3, 1 pen), Buchan (2)	25,000
14		22		H	West Bromwich Albion	D	0-0	0-0	3		29,700
15		29		A	Sheffield Wed.	L	1-2	1-1	5	Mordue	25,000
16	Dec	6		H	Bolton Wanderers	W	3-2	1-2	3	Holley (3)	17,000
17		13		A	Chelsea	D	1-1	0-1	3	Richardson	30,000
18		20		H	Oldham Athletic	W	2-0	1-0	3	Best, Low	25,000
19		25		A	Burnley	W	1-0	0-0	2	Cuggy	25,000
20		26		H	Burnley	D	1-1	0-1	2	Holley	35,000
21		27		A	Newcastle United	L	1-2	0-0	2	Buchan	50,000
22	Jan	1		H	Preston North End	W	3-1	1-1	2	Richardson, Martin, Best (pen)	30,000
23		3		H	Liverpool	L	1-2	0-1	2	Richardson	15,000
25		17		A	Aston Villa	L	0-5	0-4	2		32,000
26		24		H	Middlesbrough	W	4-2	0-1	2	Conner (2), Holley, Mordue	25,000
28	Feb	7		A	Sheffield United	L	0-1	0-0	2		22,151
29		14		H	Derby County	W	1-0	0-0	2	Best	15,000
31		28		H	Bradford City	L	0-1	0-0	3		15,000
34	Mar	14		H	Tottenham Hotspur	W	2-0	1-0	4	Crossley, Buchan	10,000
35		18		A	Manchester City	L	1-3	0-1	4	Mordue (pen)	20,000
36		21		H	Everton	W	5-2	3-0	4	Buchan, Holley (3), Crossley	8,000
37		23		A	Blackburn Rovers	L	1-3	0-1	4	Buchan	10,000
38		28		A	West Bromwich Albion	L	1-2	0-2	5	Mordue (pen)	23,366
39	Apr	4		H	Sheffield Wed.	L	0-1	0-1	6		12,000
40		10		H	Manchester United	W	2-0	1-0	4	Best, Holley	20,000
41		11		A	Bolton Wanderers	L	1-2	1-0	4	Cringan	27,243
42		18		H	Chelsea	W	2-0	2-0	7	Buchan, Holley	15,000
43		25		A	Oldham Athletic	L	1-2	0-1	7	Cringan	14,000

Appearances
Goals

FA Cup

Match No.	Date		Round	Venue	Opponents	Result	FT	HT	Pos.	Scorers	Attendance
24	Jan	10	R1	H	Chatham Town	W	9-0	5-0		Best (2), Buchan, Thomson, Richardson (4), Mordue	10,000
27		31	R2	H	Plymouth Argyle	W	2-1	0-0		Mordue (pen), Conner	37,132
30	Feb	21	R3	H	Preston North End	W	2-0	1-0		Buchan, Conner	34,448
32	Mar	7	R4	H	Burnley	D	0-0	0-0			34,581
33		11	R4r	A	Burnley	L	1-2	0-1		Conner	49,734

Appearances
Goals

	Butler	Gladwin	Ness	Cringan	Cuggy	Low	Mordue	Buchan	Richardson	Holley	Martin	Best	Hopkins	Lane	Tinsley	Thomson	Hobson	Waugh	Connor	Moore	Sherwin	Crossley	Scott	Kelsall	Milton	
1	2	3	4	5	6	7	8	9	10	11																1
1	2	3	4	5	6		8	9	10	11	7															2
1	2	3	4	5	6		8	9	10	11	7															3
1	2	3	6	4			8	9	10	11	7	5														4
1	2	3	6	4			8		11		7	5	9	10												5
1	2	3	6	4			8	9	10	11	7	5														6
1	2	3		4	6		8	9	10	11	7			5												7
1		3		4	6		8		9	11	7		10	5	2											8
1		3	6	4			8		10	11	7		9	5	2											9
1		3	6	4			8	9	10	11	7			5	2											10
1		3	6	4			8	9	10	11	7			5	2											11
1		3	6	4			8	9	10	11	7			5	2											12
1		3	6	4		7	8		10	11	9			5	2											13
1		3	6	4		7	8		10	11	9			5	2											14
1		3	6	4		7	8		10	11	9			5	2											15
1		3	6	4		7	8	9	10	11				5	2											16
1		3	6	4		7	8	9	10	11				5	2											17
1		3		4	6		8	9	10	11	7			5	2											18
1		3		4	6		8	9	10	11	7			5	2											19
1		3	6	4	9		8		10	11	7			5	2											20
1		3	6	4			8		10	11	7			5	2	9										21
1		3		4	6		8	9	10	11	7			5	2											22
1		3		4	6	11	8	9	10		7			5	2											23
1		3		4	6		8	9	10	11	7			5	2											25
1		3		4	6	7	8		10	11				5	2	9										26
1		3		4	6	7			10	11				5	2	9	8									28
1		3			6	11	8		10		7	4		5	2	9										29
1		3		4	6	7	8	9	10	11				5	2											31
1		3			6	7	9			11		5			2			10	4	8						34
1		3	4		6	7	9			11		5			2			10		8						35
1		3	6			7	9		10		11			5	2				4	8						36
1		3	6			7	9		10		11			5	2				4	8						37
1		3	6			7	9		10	11	8			5	2				4							38
	3		6	4	5	7	8		10	11					2						1	9				39
	3		4		6	7	8		10	11	9			5	2						1					40
		9	4	6	2	7			10	11				5	2				8	1		3				41
	3		9	4	6	7	8		10	11				5	2					1						42
	3		9	4	6	7	8		10	11				5	2					1						43
33	11	33	26	31	22	21	36	17	36	33	26	6	2	29	31	1	3	3	4	5	5	1	1			
		3	2		1	4	14	9	15	2	9				2			2								

	Butler	Gladwin	Ness	Cringan	Cuggy	Low	Mordue	Buchan	Richardson	Holley	Martin	Best	Hopkins	Lane	Tinsley	Thomson	Hobson	Waugh	Connor	Moore	Sherwin	Crossley	Scott	Kelsall	Milton	
1		3		4	6	11	8	9	10		7			5	2											24
1		3		4	6	7	8		10	11				5	2	9										27
1		3		4	6	7	8		10	11				5	2	9										30
1		3		4	6	7	8		10	11				5	2	9										32
1		3		4	6	7	8		10	11				5	2	9										33
5		5		5	5	5	5	1	5	4	1			5	5	4										
				2	2	4			2					1		3										

James Richardson

Richardson only played two seasons for Sunderland yet is the only Sunderland player to score four goals in an FA Cup tie on two occasions. In total he scored 30 League and FA Cup goals in only 45 appearances.

1914-15

Division One

Ground: Roker Park
Manager: Robert Kyle

League Table

	P	W	D	L	F	A	Pts
Everton	38	19	8	11	76	47	46
Oldham A	38	17	11	10	70	56	45
Blackburn R	38	18	7	13	83	61	43
Burnley	38	18	7	13	61	47	43
Manchester C	38	15	13	10	49	39	43
Sheffield U	38	15	13	10	49	41	43
Sheffield W	38	15	13	10	61	54	43
SUNDERLAND	38	18	5	15	81	72	41
Bradford PA	38	17	7	14	69	65	41
WBA	38	15	10	13	49	43	40
Bradford C	38	13	14	11	55	49	40
Middlesbrough	38	13	12	13	62	74	38
Liverpool	38	14	9	15	65	75	37
Aston Villa	38	13	11	14	62	72	37
Newcastle U	38	11	10	17	46	48	32
Notts Co	38	9	13	16	41	57	31
Bolton W	38	11	8	19	68	84	30
Manchester U	38	9	12	17	46	62	30
Chelsea	38	8	13	17	51	65	29
Tottenham H	38	8	12	18	57	90	28

FA Cup Winners: Sheffield United

Did you know that?

Bobby Best is the only Sunderland player to score a hat-trick on Christmas Day; a feat he achieved at St James' Park in 1914.

Match 1: Philip made debut
Match 8: Coverdale made debut
Match 9: Williamson made debut
Match 13: Boe only game
Match 27: Gladwin last game
Match 29: Williamson last game
Match 31: Cringan last game
Match 32: Hopkins last game
Match 36: Holley last game
Match 37: Young made debut
Match 39: Thomson, Low and Philip last games

Match No.	Date		Round	Venue	Opponents	Result	FT	HT	Pos.	Scorers	Attendance
1	Sep	2		H	Sheffield United	W	3-2	2-1		Buchan, Martin, Holley	12,000
2		5		A	Aston Villa	W	3-1	1-1	5	Buchan, Philip (2)	12,000
3		12		H	Liverpool	D	2-2	1-1	3	Mordue (pen), Buchan	15,000
4		19		A	Bradford P.A.	L	1-2	0-2	7	Philip	20,000
5		26		H	Oldham Athletic	L	1-2	0-2	9	Mordue (pen)	12,000
6	Oct	3		A	Manchester United	L	0-3	0-1	16		20,000
7		10		H	Bolton Wanderers	W	4-3	3-2	13	Buchan, Philip, Moore (2)	18,000
8		17		A	Blackburn Rovers	L	1-3	0-1	15	Philip	15,000
9		24		H	Notts County	W	3-1	1-0	12	Philip (3)	10,000
10		31		A	Manchester City	L	0-2	0-1	13		8,000
11	Nov	7		A	Sheffield Wed.	W	2-1	2-1	12	Buchan (2)	22,000
12		14		H	West Bromwich Albion	L	1-2	0-2	13	Philip	10,000
13		21		A	Everton	L	1-7	0-5	15	Buchan	15,000
14		28		H	Chelsea	W	2-1	1-0	11	Best, Crossley	8,000
15	Dec	5		A	Bradford City	L	1-3	0-0	13	Buchan	6,000
16		12		H	Burnley	W	2-1	2-0	13	Buchan, Best	2,000
17		19		A	Tottenham Hotspur	W	6-0	2-0	11	Philip (2), Best (2), Buchan, Martin	5,000
18		25		A	Newcastle United	W	5-2	2-0	10	Best (3), Buchan, Philip	40,000
19		26		H	Newcastle United	L	2-4	2-2	10	Mordue, Buchan	20,000
20	Jan	1		A	Middlesbrough	W	3-2	1-1	11	Martin (2), Best	12,000
21		2		H	Aston Villa	W	4-0	2-0	8	Martin, Philip, Buchan, Mordue	15,000
23		16		A	Liverpool	L	1-2	1-0	10	Philip	16,648
24		23		H	Bradford P.A.	D	3-3	1-1	10	Buchan, Martin, Mordue	7,000
25	Feb	1		A	Oldham Athletic	W	5-4	2-1	8	Buchan (2), Philip (2), Moore	3,235
26		6		H	Manchester United	W	1-0	1-0	7	Mordue (pen)	5,000
27		20		H	Blackburn Rovers	W	5-1	3-0	6	Mordue, Philip (2), Buchan, Moore	6,000
28		27		A	Notts County	L	1-2	1-1	8	Holley	10,000
29	Mar	6		A	Manchester City	L	0-2	0-1	8		20,000
30		10		H	Bolton Wanderers	D	1-1	0-0	8	Buchan	5,000
31		13		H	Sheffield Wed.	W	3-1	1-0	7	Mordue (pen), Philip (2)	12,000
32		20		A	West Bromwich Albion	W	2-1	1-0	6	Mordue (2)	10,227
33	Apr	2		H	Middlesbrough	W	4-1	2-0	6	Buchan (2), Crossley, Philip	16,000
34		3		A	Chelsea	L	0-3	0-1	7		20,000
35		5		A	Sheffield United	D	1-1	0-1	7	Crossley	25,000
36		6		H	Everton	L	0-3	0-2	8		10,000
37		10		H	Bradford City	D	1-1	0-0	8	Crossley	10,000
38		17		A	Burnley	L	1-2	0-1	9	Crossley	10,000
39		24		H	Tottenham Hotspur	W	5-0	4-0	8	Buchan (3), Crossley, Philip	10,000

Appearances
Goals

FA Cup

| 22 | Jan | 9 | R1 | A | Tottenham Hotspur | | L | 1-2 | 0-0 | | Mordue (pen) | 17,000 |

Appearances
Goals

Scott	Gladwin	Hobson	Cuggy	Thomson	Low	Mordue	Buchan	Philip	Holley	Martin	Moore	Crossley	Ness	Cingan	Best	Coverdale	Williamson	Boe	Sherwin	Hopkins	Young	
1	2	3	4	5	6	7	8	9	10	11												1
1	2	3	4	5	6	7	8	9		11	10											2
1	2	3	4	5	6	7	8	9		11	10											3
1	2	3	4	5	6	7	8	9		11		10										4
1	2		4	5	10	7	8	9				3	6	11								5
1	2	3	4	5	10	7	8	9		11			6									6
1	2	3	4	5		7	8	9		11	10		6									7
1	2	3	4	5	6	7	8	9			10			11								8
1	2		4	5		7	8	9		11	10		6		3							9
1		2	4	5		7	8	9		11	10		3	6								10
1	2	3	4	5		7	8	9		11	10		6									11
1	2	3	4	5		7	8	9		11	10		6									12
	2	3	4	5		7	8	9		11	10		6			1						13
1	2			5		7	8			11		10	3	6	9		4					14
1	2			5		7	8	9		11		10	3	6			4					15
1		2	4	5		7	8	10		11			3	6	9							16
1		2	4	5		7	8	10		11			3	6	9							17
1		2	4	5		7	8	10		11			3	6	9							18
1		2	4	5		7	8	10		11			3	6	9							19
1			4	5		7	8	10		11			3	6	9		2					20
1			4			7	8	10		11			3	6	9		2		5			21
1		2	4	5		7	8	9		11		10	3					6				23
1		2	4	5		7	8	9	10	11			3	6								24
1	2		4			7	8	9		11	10		3			6			5			25
1	2			5		7	8	9	10	11			3	4		6						26
1	2		4	5		7	8	10		11	9		3	6								27
1			4	5		7	8	9	10	11			3	6			2					28
1			4	5		7	8	9	10	11			3	6			2					29
1		2		5		7	8	9		11		10	3	6				4				30
1		2		5		7	8	9		11		10	3	6					4			31
1		2		5	6	7		10					8	3		9	11		4			32
1		2	4	5	6	7	8	9		11			10	3								33
1		2	4	5	6	7	8	9		11			10	3								34
1		2	4	5		7	8	9	6	11			10	3								35
1	2			5	6	7	8	9	4	11			10	3								36
1		2	4	5	6	7	8	9		11		10								3		37
1		2	4	5	6	7	8	9		11			10	3								38
1		2	4	5	6	7	8	9		11			10	3								39
37	16	28	31	36	14	38	37	37	7	35	11	14	26	23	9	4	5	1	4	4	1	
							10	23	22	2	6	4	6		8							

1		2	4	5		7	8	10		11			3	6	9							22
1		1	1	1		1	1	1		1			1	1	1							
								1														

James Boe played only one game as goalkeeper for Sunderland. It is not documented whether this was because he let in seven goals on his debut at Everton, 21 November 1914. Incidentally he appeared as a stand in linesman at the next game, Sunderland v Chelsea on 28 November 1914.

1919-20

Division One

Ground: Roker Park
Manager: Robert Kyle

League Table

	P	W	D	L	F	A	Pts
WBA	42	28	4	10	104	47	60
Burnley	42	21	9	12	65	59	51
Chelsea	42	22	5	15	56	51	49
Liverpool	42	19	10	13	59	44	48
SUNDERLAND	42	22	4	16	72	59	48
Bolton W	42	19	9	14	72	65	47
Manchester C	42	18	9	15	71	62	45
Newcastle U	42	17	9	16	44	39	43
Aston Villa	42	18	6	18	75	73	42
Arsenal	42	15	12	15	56	58	42
Bradford PA	42	15	12	15	60	63	42
Manchester U	42	13	14	15	54	50	40
Middlesbrough	42	15	10	17	61	65	40
Sheffield U	42	16	8	18	59	69	40
Bradford C	42	14	11	17	54	63	39
Everton	42	12	14	16	69	68	38
Oldham A	42	15	8	19	49	52	38
Derby Co	42	13	12	17	47	57	38
Preston NE	42	14	10	18	57	73	38
Blackburn R	42	13	11	18	64	77	37
Notts Co	42	12	12	18	56	74	36
Sheffield W	42	7	9	26	28	64	23

FA Cup Winners: Aston Villa

Did you know that?

Sunderland released inside forward Jimmy Seed after deciding that he would never recover enough to play top class football after being gassed during WW1. He went on to score almost 100 League goals for Spurs and Sheffield Wednesday and gain five England Caps. Seed had been signed by the Black Cats from Whitburn in April 1914 but never made a first team competitive appearance.

Match 1: Poole, Parker and Travers made debuts
Match 3: Allen made debut
Match 6: Kasher made debut
Match 12: Parker last game
Match 13: Ness last game
Match 19: Morrison only game
Match 21: Haggan made debut
Match 22: England made debut
Match 24: Haggan last game
Match 34: Ellis made debut
Match 36: Mordue last game
Match 37: Benefit game for Buchan
Match 38: Allen last game
Match 41: Crossley last game
Match 42: Dempster made debut
Match 43: Johnson, Page and Shore made debuts
Match 44: Turner only game
Match 45: Cooke made debut
Match 46: Benefit game for R.H. Kyle (for 15 years as manager), Ardley only game & Johnson and Page last games

Match No.	Date		Round	Venue	Opponents	Result	FT	HT	Pos.	Scorers	Attendance
1	Aug	30		H	Aston Villa	W	2-1	2-0		Buchan, Travers	35,000
2	Sep	1		A	Chelsea	L	0-2	0-2	12		35,000
3		6		A	Aston Villa	W	3-0	2-0	8	Travers, Buchan, Parker	40,000
4		10		H	Chelsea	W	3-2	1-2	4	Buchan (2), Parker	35,000
5		13		H	Arsenal	D	1-1	0-0	5	Buchan	35,000
6		20		A	Arsenal	L	2-3	2-1	9	Buchan (2)	42,000
7		27		H	Everton	L	2-3	1-1	13	Best, Buchan	20,000
8	Oct	4		A	Everton	W	3-1	1-1	9	Buchan (2), Travers	20,000
9		11		H	Bradford City	W	2-0	0-0	8	Best, Travers	25,000
10		18		A	Bradford City	L	0-2	0-1	9		20,000
11		25		H	Bolton Wanderers	W	2-0	1-0	7	Mordue (pen), Travers	20,000
12	Nov	1		A	Bolton Wanderers	L	0-1	0-0	7		25,000
13		8		H	Notts County	W	3-1	1-0	6	Travers (3)	15,000
14		15		A	Notts County	D	2-2	2-2	5	Best, Martin	12,000
15		22		H	Newcastle United	W	2-0	1-0	5	Buchan (2)	47,148
16		29		A	Newcastle United	W	3-2	2-0	4	Mordue, Travers (2)	61,761
17	Dec	6		H	Sheffield Wed.	W	2-1	1-1	3	Travers, Crossley	20,000
18		13		A	Sheffield Wed.	W	2-0	2-0	3	Martin, Mordue	25,000
19		20		H	Manchester City	W	2-1	1-1	3	Crossley (2)	22,000
20		25		A	Liverpool	L	2-3	1-1	3	Mordue (pen), Buchan	27,794
21		26		A	West Bromwich Albion	L	0-4	0-1	3		43,529
22		27		A	Manchester City	L	0-1	0-1	4		30,000
23	Jan	1		H	West Bromwich Albion	W	4-1	2-1	4	Crossley, Travers (3)	32,500
24		3		A	Derby County	L	1-3	1-1	5	Crossley	14,000
26		17		H	Derby County	W	2-1	1-0	5	Buchan, Mordue (pen)	20,000
27		24		H	Oldham Athletic	W	3-0	0-0	3	Crossley, Travers (2)	20,000
30	Feb	7		H	Manchester United	W	3-0	2-0	2	Mordue (2, 1 pen), Moore	30,000
31		14		A	Manchester United	L	0-2	0-0	3		58,661
33		28		A	Sheffield United	L	1-3	0-1	5	Buchan	30,000
34	Mar	6		A	Middlesbrough	W	2-0	1-0	3	Buchan, Crossley	21,581
35		8		A	Oldham Athletic	L	1-2	0-1	4	Buchan	7,441
36		13		H	Middlesbrough	D	1-1	0-0	4	Travers	30,000
37		17		H	Sheffield United	W	3-2	1-0	3	Crossley, Travers, Buchan	12,000
38		20		A	Burnley	L	1-2	1-1	5	Travers	22,500
39		27		H	Burnley	W	3-0	1-0	3	Best, Buchan (2)	30,000
40	Apr	2		A	Blackburn Rovers	L	0-3	0-1	5		38,388
41		3		A	Preston North End	L	2-5	0-3	5	Crossley, Travers	22,000
42		5		H	Blackburn Rovers	W	2-0	1-0	5	Moore (2)	25,000
43		10		H	Preston North End	W	1-0	0-0	4	Shore	10,000
44		17		A	Bradford P.A.	D	2-2	1-2	4	Buchan, Moore	14,000
45		24		H	Bradford P.A.	W	2-0	0-0	5	Buchan, Cooke	18,000
46	May	1		H	Liverpool	L	0-1	0-1	5		30,000

Appearances
Goals

FA Cup

Match No.	Date		Round	Venue	Opponents	Result	FT	HT	Pos.	Scorers	Attendance
25	Jan	14	R1	H	Hull City	W	6-2	2-1		Buchan (4), Travers (2)	35,586
28		31	R2	A	Burnley	D	1-1	0-0		Travers	33,227
29	Feb	4	R2r	H	Burnley	W	2-0	2-0		Buchan, Poole	49,618
32		21	R3	A	Aston Villa	L	0-1	0-1			31,784

Appearances
Goals

	Scott	Hobson	Ness	Cuggy	Sherwin	Poole	Mordue	Buchan	Parker	Travers	Martin	Allen	Crossley	Kasher	Best	Coverdale	Young	Moore	Morrison	Haggan	England	Ellis	Dempster	Johnson	Page	Shore	Turner	Cooke	Ardley	
1	2	3	4	5	6	7	8	9	10	11																				1
1	2	3	4	5	6	7	8	9	10	11																				2
	2	3	4	5	6	7	8	9	10	11	1																			3
	2	3	4	5	6	7	8	9	10	11	1																			4
	2	3	4	5	6	7	8		9	11	1	10																		5
	2	3		4	6	7	8		9	11	1	10	5																	6
	2	3	4	5	6	7	8		10		1			9	11															7
	2		4	5	6	10	8		9	11	1		7		3															8
	2		4		6	10			9	11	1	8	5	7	3															9
	2		4		6	10	8		9	11	1		5	7	3															10
	2		4	5	6	7	8	9	10		1			11	3															11
	2	3	4	5	6		8	9	10	11	1			7																12
	2	3	4		6			9	11	1	8	5	7			10														13
1	2		4		6			9	11			8	5	7	3	10														14
	2		4		6	10	8		9	11	1		5	7	3															15
	2		4		6	7	8		9	11	1	10	5		3															16
	2		4		6	7	8		9	11	1	10	5		3															17
1	2		4		6	7	8		9	11		10	5		3															18
1	2		4		6	7	8		9			10	5	11			3													19
1	2		4		6	7	8		9			10	5	11	3															20
1	2		4		5	7			9			8		11	3	10	6													21
1			4		6				9	11		8	5	7	3	10		2												22
1	2		4		6	7	8		9	11		10	5		3															23
	2			6		8			9	11	1	10	5	7	3		4													24
	2		4		6	7	8		9	11	1		5		3	10														26
1	2		4		5	7	8		9	11		10			6	3														27
1	2		4		6	7	8		9	11			5		3	10														30
1	2		4		6	7	8		9	11		10	5		3															31
1	2		4		6	7	8		9			10	5		3															33
1	2			5	6	7	8		9			10			4	3					11									34
1	2				6	7	8		9			10	5		4	3					11									35
	2			5	6	7	8		9		1	10			4	3					11									36
	2			5	6		8		9	11	1	10		7	4					3										37
	2			5	6		8		9	11	1			7	4		10			3										38
1	2			5	6		8		9			10		7	4	3					11									39
1	2		4	5	6		8		9	11		10		7		3														40
1	2		4		5		8		9	11		10		7	6			3												41
	2		4		6		8		9	11			5	7		10		3	1											42
			4		6				9	11			5			10		2	1	3	7	8								43
	2		4		6		8		9	11			5			10		3	1				7							44
	2		4		6		8		9	11			5						1	3	7			10						45
	2		6				8		9	11			5			10			1	3	7				4					46
18	40	9	34	16	41	27	36	6	42	33	19	24	24	20	9	24	11	1	2	7	4	5	3	3	1	1	1	1		
						7	22	2	20	2		9		4		4				1		1								

	Scott	Hobson	Ness	Cuggy	Sherwin	Poole	Mordue	Buchan	Parker	Travers	Martin	Allen	Crossley	Kasher	Best	Coverdale	Young	Moore	Morrison	Haggan	England	Ellis	Dempster	Johnson	Page	Shore	Turner	Cooke	Ardley	
	2		4		6	7	8		9	11	1	10	5		3															25
1	2		4		5	7	8		9	11		10			6	3														28
	2		4		6	7	8		9	11		10	5		3															29
1	2		4		6	10	8		9	11			5	7	3															32
3	4		4		4	4	4		4	4	1	3	3	1	1	4														
				1		5			3																					

Jackie Mordue

England international, Mordue, played his 294th, and final game, for Sunderland during this season. He scored 81 goals of which at least 25 were penalties.

1920-21

Division One

Ground: Roker Park
Manager: Robert Kyle

League Table

	P	W	D	L	F	A	Pts
Burnley	42	23	13	6	79	36	59
Manchester C	42	24	6	12	70	50	54
Bolton W	42	19	14	9	77	53	52
Liverpool	42	18	15	9	63	35	51
Newcastle U	42	20	10	12	66	45	50
Tottenham H	42	19	9	14	70	48	47
Everton	42	17	13	12	66	55	47
Middlesbrough	42	17	12	13	53	53	46
Arsenal	42	15	14	13	59	63	44
Aston Villa	42	18	7	17	63	70	43
Blackburn R	42	13	15	14	57	59	41
SUNDERLAND	42	14	13	15	57	60	41
Manchester U	42	15	10	17	64	68	40
WBA	42	13	14	15	54	58	40
Bradford C	42	12	15	15	61	63	39
Preston NE	42	15	9	18	61	65	39
Huddersfield T	42	15	9	18	42	49	39
Chelsea	42	13	13	16	48	58	39
Oldham A	42	9	15	18	49	86	33
Sheffield U	42	6	18	18	42	68	30
Derby Co	42	5	16	21	32	58	26
Bradford PA	42	8	8	26	43	76	24

FA Cup Winners: Tottenham Hotspur

Did you know that?

Charlie Buchan became the first Sunderland player to captain England when he led them to a goalless draw against Wales in Cardiff on 14 March 1921.

Match 1: Robinson made debut
Match 5: Johnston made debut
Match 7: Foster made debut
Match 8: George made debut
Match 10: George last game
Match 11: Mitton, Parker & Marshall made debuts
Match 12: Gilhespy made debut & Watson only game
Match 13: Coverdale last game
Match 15: Gibson made debut
Match 23: Sherwin and Travers last games
Match 24: Power made debut
Match 32: Williams only game & Cuggy last game
Match 36: Marsden made debut & Johnston last game
Match 37: Gregory only game & Gilhespy last game
Match 38: Cooke last game
Match 39: Shore last game
Match 40: Robinson last game
Match 41: Foster last game
Match 43: Power last game

Match No.	Date	Round	Venue	Opponents	Result	FT	HT	Pos.	Scorers	Attendance
1	Aug 28		A	Sheffield United	D	1-1	0-1		Buchan	30,000
2	Sep 1		H	Bradford P.A.	W	5-1	1-0	4	Robinson, Travers, Buchan (2), Martin	38,000
3	4		H	Sheffield United	W	3-1	2-0	3	Travers (2), Robinson	25,000
4	8		A	Bradford P.A.	D	1-1	0-1	2	Buchan	15,000
5	11		A	Blackburn Rovers	L	0-2	0-1	5		35,000
6	18		H	Blackburn Rovers	W	2-0	1-0	4	Buchan (2)	35,000
7	25		A	Huddersfield Town	D	0-0	0-0	6		40,000
8	Oct 2		H	Huddersfield Town	W	2-1	1-0	5	Travers, Buchan	45,000
9	9		A	Newcastle United	L	1-6	0-2	7	Buchan	58,016
10	16		H	Newcastle United	L	0-2	0-0	10		38,000
11	23		A	Bradford City	D	2-2	1-0	10	Best, Marshall	20,000
12	30		H	Bradford City	D	0-0	0-0	8		25,000
13	Nov 6		A	Middlesbrough	L	0-2	0-0	14		34,000
14	13		H	Middlesbrough	L	1-2	0-0	16	Travers	35,000
15	20		A	Everton	D	1-1	1-1	15	Cooke	35,000
16	27		H	Everton	L	0-2	0-1	16		25,000
17	Dec 4		A	West Bromwich Albion	L	1-4	0-2	17	Buchan	23,726
18	11		H	West Bromwich Albion	W	3-0	2-0	15	Buchan (2), Cooke	15,000
19	18		H	Manchester City	W	1-0	1-0	14	Cooke	18,000
20	25		A	Bolton Wanderers	L	2-6	0-1	16	Buchan, Moore	39,521
21	27		H	Bolton Wanderers	D	0-0	0-0	15		45,000
22	Jan 1		A	Manchester City	L	1-3	0-1	17	Parker	35,000
24	15		A	Liverpool	D	0-0	0-0	17		36,249
25	22		H	Liverpool	W	2-1	1-0	16	Buchan (2)	18,000
26	29		A	Arsenal	W	2-1	0-0	13	Buchan (2)	40,000
27	Feb 5		H	Arsenal	W	5-1	2-0	11	Moore (2), Buchan (2), Marshall	30,000
28	12		A	Aston Villa	W	5-1	2-1	9	Thompson o.g., Marshall (2), Buchan (2)	40,000
29	23		H	Aston Villa	L	0-1	0-0	10		35,000
30	26		A	Manchester United	L	0-3	0-2	11		40,000
31	Mar 5		H	Manchester United	L	2-3	0-2	13	Marshall, Buchan	25,000
32	12		A	Chelsea	L	1-3	1-0	16	Gilhespy	35,000
33	19		H	Chelsea	W	1-0	0-0	14	Buchan	20,000
34	25		H	Derby County	W	3-0	2-0	13	Parker, Buchan, Marshall	20,000
35	26		H	Tottenham Hotspur	L	0-1	0-0	12		35,000
36	28		A	Derby County	W	1-0	0-0	10	Buchan	16,000
37	Apr 2		A	Tottenham Hotspur	D	0-0	0-0	10		35,000
38	9		H	Oldham Athletic	D	1-1	1-0	12	Cooke (pen)	9,000
39	16		A	Oldham Athletic	L	1-2	0-0	14	Mitton	16,328
40	23		H	Preston North End	D	2-2	2-1	12	Buchan, Parker	10,000
41	30		A	Preston North End	D	1-1	0-1	13	Martin	20,000
42	May 2		H	Burnley	W	1-0	1-0	11	Buchan	20,000
43	7		A	Burnley	D	2-2	2-1	12	Buchan, Marshall	22,000

Appearances
Goals

FA Cup

23	Jan 8	R1	H	Cardiff City	L	0-1	0-1			41,923

Appearances
Goals

Scott	Hobson	England	Cuggy	Kasher	Poole	Robinson	Buchan	Travers	Moore	Martin	Coverdale	Johnston	Foster	George	Best	Shore	Cooke	Mitton	Parker	Marshall	Watson	Gillespy	Young	Gibson	Dempster	Sherwin	Ellis	Power	Williams	Marsden	Gregory	
1	2	3	4	5	6	7	8	9	10	11																						1
1	2	3		5	6	7	8	9	10	11	4																					2
1	2	3		5	6	7	8	9	10	11	4																					3
1	2	3		5	6	7	8	9	10	11	4																					4
1	2			5	6	7	8	9	10	11	4	3																				5
1	2	3		5	6	7	8	9	10	11	4																					6
1	2	3		5	6		8	9	10	11	4		7																			7
1	2	3		5	6		8	9	10	11			7	4																		8
1	2	3	4	5	6		8	9		11			7	10																		9
1	2	3		5	6		8	9		11			4	7		10																10
1	2	3			6	7				11				9	10		4	5	8													11
1		3			6		8			11	10			9			4	5		2	7											12
1	2	3			6		8			11	10			7			4	5														13
1		2			6		8	9		11				7		10	4	5			3											14
1		3			6		8	9		11				7		10	4	5				2										15
1		2			6		8	9		11				7		10	4	5			3											16
1		2			6		8	9		11						10	4	5			7	3										17
	2						8		10	11						9	6	4			7	3	1	5								18
	2						8		10	11						9	6	4			7	3	1	5								19
	2						8	7	10	11						9	6	4				3	1	5								20
	2						8		10	11			7			9	6	4				3	1	5								21
	2		5				8		10	11			7			9	6	4				3	1									22
	2		5				9			11							6	4	10			3	1		7	8						24
	2		5	6			9			11							4		10			3	1		7	8						25
	2	3	5				9			11							6	4	10	7		1				8						26
	2	3	5				9		10								6	4	8	7		1			11							27
	2	3	5				9		10								6	4	8	7		1			11							28
	2	3	5				9		10				7				6	4	8	11		1										29
	2	3	5	6			9			11								4	10	7		1			8							30
	2	3	5	6			9			11								4	10	7		1			8							31
	2	3	9	5	6			8		11								4		7		1				10						32
	2	3		5			9		10							8	6	4		7		1			11							33
	2	3		5			9		10	11							6	4	8	7		1										34
	2	3		5			9			11			7				6	4	8			1	10									35
	2			4			9			11	3						6	5		7		1			8	10						36
	2	3		5			9			11							6	4	8	7		1					10					37
	2	3		5		7	9			11						10	6	4	8			1										38
	2	3			4	7	9			11					8		6	5	10			1										39
	2	3		5		7	9			11							6	4	10			1			8							40
	2	3		5	6					11		7		9				4	10			1			8							41
	2	3			6		9			11				7			4	5	10			1			8							42
	2	3			6		9			11				7			4	5	10			1			8							43
17	36	34	3	27	26	10	39	16	19	38	8	2	5	2	13	∠	11	28	31	18	1	15	10	1	25	4	6	10	1	1	1	
						2	27	5	3	2					1		4	1	3	7		1										

Scott	Hobson	England	Cuggy	Kasher	Poole	Robinson	Buchan	Travers	Moore	Martin	Coverdale	Johnston	Foster	George	Best	Shore	Cooke	Mitton	Parker	Marshall	Watson	Gillespy	Young	Gibson	Dempster	Sherwin	Ellis	Power	Williams	Marsden	Gregory	
	2						8	9	10	11			7				6	4				3	1	5								23
1							1	1	1	1			1				1	1				1	1	1								

Francis Cuggy

Cuggy played his final game for Sunderland during this season. He formed part of the famous Cuggy, Buchan, Mordue triangle that worked so effectively for Sunderland. His appearances for both Sunderland (187) and England (2) were curtailed by the First World War.

1921-22

Division One

Ground: Roker Park

Manager: Robert Kyle

League Table

	P	W	D	L	F	A	Pts
Liverpool	42	22	13	7	63	36	57
Tottenham H	42	21	9	12	65	39	51
Burnley	42	22	5	15	72	54	49
Cardiff C	42	19	10	13	61	53	48
Aston Villa	42	22	3	17	74	55	47
Bolton W	42	20	7	15	68	59	47
Newcastle U	42	18	10	14	59	45	46
Middlesbrough	42	16	14	12	79	69	46
Chelsea	42	17	12	13	40	43	46
Manchester C	42	18	9	15	65	70	45
Sheffield U	42	15	10	17	59	54	40
SUNDERLAND	42	16	8	18	60	62	40
WBA	42	15	10	17	51	63	40
Huddersfield T	42	15	9	18	53	54	39
Blackburn R	42	13	12	17	54	57	38
Preston NE	42	13	12	17	42	65	38
Arsenal	42	15	7	20	47	56	37
Birmingham	42	15	7	20	48	60	37
Oldham A	42	13	11	18	38	50	37
Everton	42	12	12	18	57	55	36
Bradford C	42	11	10	21	48	72	32
Manchester U	42	8	12	22	41	73	28

FA Cup Winners: Huddersfield Town

Did you know that?

The British transfer record was broken on 3 March 1922 when Sunderland signed full back Warneford Cresswell from Second Division South Shields for £5,500. He is also the last player that Sunderland signed from South Shields.

Match 1: Stephenson and Stannard made debuts
Match 8: Black made debut
Match 9: Yorke only game and Black last game
Match 17: Clack made debut
Match 20: Hawes made debut
Match 23: Moore last game
Match 24: Hunter made debut
Match 25: Ferguson made debut & Dempster last game
Match 26: Harper and Staley made debuts & Gibson and Best last games
Match 27: Brown made debut
Match 32: Hobson and Brown last games
Match 33: Cresswell, Gilhooley and Paterson made debuts
Match 34: Stephenson last game
Match 37: Donaldson made debut
Match 43: Scott and Martin last games

Match No.	Date		Round	Venue	Opponents	Result	FT	HT	Pos.	Scorers	Attendance
1	Aug	27		H	Liverpool	W	3-0	2-0		Buchan (2), Martin	40,000
2		31		H	Burnley	W	3-2	0-1	2	Buchan (2), Marshall	30,000
3	Sep	3		A	Liverpool	L	1-2	0-1	7	Buchan	41,693
4		5		A	Burnley	L	0-2	0-1	11		30,000
5		10		H	Huddersfield Town	D	2-2	2-1	10	Buchan (2)	25,000
6		17		A	Huddersfield Town	W	2-1	2-0	8	Stannard (2)	15,000
7		24		H	Birmingham	W	2-1	0-1	5	Buchan (2)	30,000
8	Oct	1		A	Birmingham	L	0-1	0-0	9		30,000
9		8		H	Arsenal	W	1-0	1-0	6	Buchan	30,000
10		15		A	Arsenal	W	2-1	1-0	5	Buchan (2)	40,000
11		22		H	Blackburn Rovers	W	3-1	1-0	3	Marshall, Martin, Parker	10,000
12		29		A	Blackburn Rovers	W	2-1	1-0	3	Stephenson, Marshall	18,000
13	Nov	5		H	Oldham Athletic	W	5-1	1-1	2	Marshall (2), Buchan (2), Parker	20,000
14		12		A	Oldham Athletic	L	0-3	0-1	3		12,000
15		19		A	Newcastle United	D	2-2	0-2	3	Buchan, Marshall	46,000
16		26		H	Newcastle United	D	0-0	0-0	3		49,483
17	Dec	3		A	Cardiff City	L	0-2	0-1	4		30,000
18		10		H	Cardiff City	W	4-1	3-1	3	Mitton (2), Buchan, Martin	18,000
19		17		A	West Bromwich Albion	L	1-2	0-1	6	Mitton	18,251
20		24		H	West Bromwich Albion	W	5-0	1-0	3	Hawes (2), Mitton (3)	10,552
21		26		H	Everton	L	1-2	0-1	6	Mitton	38,000
22		31		A	Manchester City	L	0-3	0-0	6		25,000
23	Jan	2		A	Everton	L	0-3	0-1	8		45,000
26		14		H	Manchester City	L	2-3	1-3	10	Buchan, Martin (pen)	10,000
27		21		H	Manchester United	W	2-1	0-1	9	Buchan, Brown	8,000
28		28		A	Manchester United	L	1-3	1-2	10	Stephenson	18,000
29	Feb	4		H	Aston Villa	L	1-4	1-2	11	Ellis (pen)	6,000
30		11		A	Aston Villa	L	0-2	0-0	11		30,000
31		18		H	Middlesbrough	D	1-1	0-1	12	Buchan	20,000
32		25		A	Middlesbrough	L	0-3	0-0	12		35,000
33	Mar	4		H	Sheffield United	W	1-0	1-0	11	Buchan	35,000
34		11		A	Tottenham Hotspur	L	0-1	0-1	11		41,003
35		18		A	Bradford City	D	0-0	0-0	11		25,000
36		25		H	Bradford City	D	0-0	0-0	11		20,000
37	Apr	1		A	Preston North End	D	1-1	1-0	13	Parker	19,945
38		5		H	Tottenham Hotspur	W	2-0	1-0	11	Hawes, Paterson	37,000
39		8		H	Preston North End	W	1-0	0-0	11	Buchan	18,000
40		14		H	Bolton Wanderers	W	6-2	4-2	10	Parker, Paterson (3), Hawes, Ellis	15,000
41		15		A	Chelsea	L	0-1	0-1	11		40,000
42		17		A	Bolton Wanderers	D	1-1	0-1	11	Hawes	30,000
43		22		H	Chelsea	L	1-2	0-0	11	Ellis (pen)	9,000
44		29		A	Sheffield United	L	1-4	1-1	12	Paterson	22,500

Appearances
Goals

FA Cup

	Date		Round	Venue	Opponents	Result	FT	HT		Scorers	Attendance
24	Jan	7	R1	H	Liverpool	D	1-1	0-1		Stannard	28,684
25		11	R1r	A	Liverpool	L	0-5	0-1			46,000

Appearances
Goals

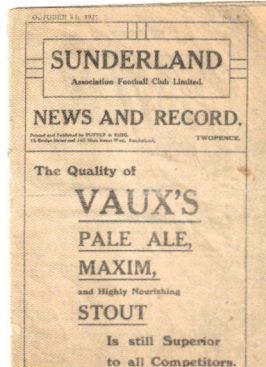

	Dempster	Hobson	England	Parker	Kasher	Poole	Stephenson	Buchan	Stannard	Marshall	Martin	Mitton	Moore	Scott	Best	Black	Young	Yorke	Ellis	Clack	Gibson	Hawes	Harper	Staley	Brown	Hunter	Cresswell	Gillooley	Paterson	Donaldson	Ferguson	
1	1	2	3	4	5	6	7	8	9	10	11																					1
2	1	2	3	4	5	6	7	8	9	10	11																					2
3		2	3	4	5	6	7	8	9	10	11																					3
4	1	2	3		5	6	7	8	9		11	4	10																			4
5		2	3	4	5	6		8	9	10	11			1	7																	5
6		2	3	4	5	6		8	9	10	11			1	7																	6
7		2	3	4	5	6		8	9	10	11			1	7																	7
8		2	3	4	5	6			9	10	11			1	7	8																8
9			4	5	6		9			10	11			1	7	8	2	3														9
10		2		4	5	6	8	9		10	11			1	7		3															10
11		2		4	5	6	8	9		10	11			1	7		3															11
12		2	3	4	5	6	8	9		10	11			1	7																	12
13		2	3	4	5	6	7	8	9	10				1					11													13
14		2	3	4	5	6	7	8		10		9		1					11													14
15		2	3	4	5	6	8	9		10	11			1	7																	15
16		2	3		5	6	8	9		10	11	4		1	7																	16
17	1	2	3	4		6		8	9	10	11	5							7													17
18	1		3	4	5	6		8		10	11	9			7					2												18
19	1		3	4	5	6	7	8		10	11	9								2												19
20	1	2		4	5	6	7	8			11	9				3					10											20
21	1	2	3	4	5	6	7	8			11	9									10											21
22		2	3	4	5	6	7	8			11	9		1							10											22
23	1	2	3	4	5	6	7	9					8							11	10											23
26			3	4		6		8			11	5			7						2	10	1	9								26
27			2	4		6	7	8			11	5				3					10	1		9								27
28			2	4	5	6	10	8								3	11	7		1				9								28
29			2	4	5	6		8								3	11	7			10	1		9								29
30			2		5	6		8				4				3	11	7			10	1		9								30
31		2	3	5		6	10	8			11	4						7				1		9								31
32		2	3	5			7	8			11	6									10	1		9	4							32
33			3	4				8				6								11	10	1			7	2	5	9				33
34			3	4		8					11	6						7			10	1				2	5	9				34
35			3	4				8			11	6						7			10	1				2	5	9				35
36			3	4				8			11	6						7			10	1				2	5	9				36
37			3	4	5			8			11	6									10	1				2		9	7			37
38			3	4	5			8			11	6									10	1				2		9	7			38
39			3	4	5			8			11	6									10	1				2		9	7			39
40			3	4	5			8				6								11	10	1				2		9	7			40
41			3	4		5		8				6								11	10	1				2		9	7			41
42			3	4	5			8				6								11	10	1				2		9	7			42
43			3	4		5		8			11	6	1								10					2		9	7			43
44			3	4	5	6		8												11	10	1				2		9	7			44
	10	22	38	39	31	32	21	40	10	18	31	25	2	14	12	2	8	1	11	8	3	21	18	1	6	2	12	4	12	8		
				4			2	21	2	6	4	7								3		5			1			5				

24	1	2	3		5	6		8	9						7					11		10			4							24
25	1		3		6	7	8			9							11	2	10			4				5						25
	2	1	2	1	2	1	2	1		1			1			1	2	1	2			2			2	1						
								1																								

Warney Cresswell

Cresswell, nicknamed 'Prince of Full-backs', was capped five times for England while at Sunderland. He was sold to Everton for £7,000 on 3 February 1927 after 190 first team appearances.

1922-23

Division One

Ground: Roker Park
Manager: Robert Kyle

League Table

	P	W	D	L	F	A	Pts
Liverpool	42	26	8	8	70	31	60
SUNDERLAND	42	22	10	10	72	54	54
Huddersfield T	42	21	11	10	60	32	53
Newcastle U	42	18	12	12	45	37	48
Everton	42	20	7	15	63	59	47
Aston Villa	42	18	10	14	64	51	46
WBA	42	17	11	14	58	49	45
Manchester C	42	17	11	14	50	49	45
Cardiff C	42	18	7	17	73	59	43
Sheffield U	42	16	10	16	68	64	42
Arsenal	42	16	10	16	61	62	42
Tottenham H	42	17	7	18	50	50	41
Bolton W	42	14	12	16	50	58	40
Blackburn R	42	14	12	16	47	62	40
Burnley	42	16	6	20	58	59	38
Preston NE	42	13	11	18	60	64	37
Birmingham	42	13	11	18	41	57	37
Middlesbrough	42	13	10	19	57	63	36
Chelsea	42	9	18	15	45	53	36
Nottingham F	42	13	8	21	41	70	34
Stoke	42	10	10	22	47	67	30
Oldham A	42	10	10	22	35	65	30

FA Cup Winners: Bolton Wanderers

Did you know that?

Albert McInroy was twice signed by Sunderland. The first occasion was inside a toilet in a Manchester hotel only minutes after his contract with Leyland Motors had expired, 7 May 1923. Bob Kyle, the Sunderland manager, had taken him there to prevent any other club from signing him. The second time was on a free transfer from Leeds United in June 1934.

Match 1: Robson made debut
Match 4: Kasher last game
Match 5: Oakley made debut & Whipp only game
Match 18: Andrews made debut
Match 27: Hunter last game
Match 34: Clack last game
Match 35: Prior and Wagstaffe made debuts
Match 39: Harper last game
Match 41: Jackson made debut & Donaldson last game
Match 42: Wagstaffe last game
Match 43: Stewart only game

Match No.	Date	Round	Venue	Opponents	Result	FT	HT	Pos.	Scorers	Attendance
1	Aug 26		A	Nottingham Forest	L	0-1	0-1			25,000
2	30		H	Liverpool	W	1-0	0-0	10	Paterson	28,000
3	Sep 2		H	Nottingham Forest	D	0-0	0-0	11		25,000
4	6		A	Liverpool	L	1-5	1-3	18	Buchan	29,243
5	9		A	Bolton Wanderers	D	1-1	0-0	17	Ellis	30,000
6	16		H	Bolton Wanderers	W	5-1	3-1	11	Buchan (4), Hawes	30,000
7	23		A	Blackburn Rovers	D	0-0	0-0	12		20,000
8	30		H	Blackburn Rovers	W	4-3	3-1	8	Buchan (2), Hawes, Paterson	25,000
9	Oct 7		A	Cardiff City	W	4-2	2-1	6	Hawes, Paterson (2), Buchan	35,000
10	14		H	Cardiff City	W	2-1	0-0	4	Keenor o.g., Paterson	25,000
11	21		A	Chelsea	W	3-1	3-0	2	Buchan (2), Paterson	38,000
12	28		H	Chelsea	D	1-1	1-1	2	Buchan	25,000
13	Nov 4		A	Newcastle United	L	1-2	0-1	4	Buchan	60,000
14	11		H	Newcastle United	W	2-0	0-0	2	Paterson, Hawes	47,000
15	18		H	Arsenal	D	3-3	1-0	2	Ellis (pen), Parker, Paterson	16,000
16	25		A	Arsenal	W	3-2	3-1	2	Hawes, Paterson, Donaldson	30,000
17	Dec 2		H	Everton	W	3-1	0-1	2	Paterson (2), Buchan	25,000
18	9		A	Everton	D	1-1	0-1	2	Buchan	30,000
19	16		H	West Bromwich Albion	W	3-2	1-2	2	Buchan (2), Paterson	10,000
20	23		A	West Bromwich Albion	D	1-1	1-0	2	Hawes	23,092
21	26		A	Stoke	W	2-1	1-0	2	Paterson, Hawes	35,878
22	30		H	Birmingham	W	5-3	3-1	2	Barton o.g., Hawes, Buchan, Paterson (2)	16,000
23	Jan 1		H	Stoke	W	2-0	2-0	2	Paterson, Hawes	30,000
24	6		A	Birmingham	W	2-1	1-0	2	Paterson (2)	25,000
26	20		H	Huddersfield Town	D	1-1	1-1	2	Hawes	30,000
27	27		A	Huddersfield Town	W	1-0	0-0	2	Buchan	30,135
29	Feb 10		H	Middlesbrough	W	2-1	0-1	2	Ellis (pen), Paterson	12,000
30	17		A	Oldham Athletic	D	0-0	0-0	2		13,953
31	24		H	Oldham Athletic	W	2-0	0-0	2	Buchan, Hawes	20,000
32	Mar 3		A	Sheffield United	L	1-3	1-1	2	Hawes	44,500
33	17		H	Preston North End	D	2-2	2-0	2	Buchan (2)	35,000
34	24		A	Preston North End	L	0-2	0-0	2		19,708
35	30		H	Manchester City	W	2-0	0-0	2	Allen o.g., Buchan	35,000
36	31		H	Tottenham Hotspur	W	2-0	1-0	2	Buchan, Paterson	18,000
37	Apr 2		A	Manchester City	L	0-1	0-1	2		32,000
38	7		A	Tottenham Hotspur	W	1-0	0-0	2	Paterson	23,571
39	11		H	Sheffield United	L	3-5	3-4	2	Buchan (3)	27,500
40	14		H	Burnley	W	3-1	2-1	2	Ellis, Paterson, Buchan	20,000
41	18		A	Middlesbrough	L	0-2	0-1	2		20,000
42	21		A	Burnley	L	0-2	0-2	2		12,000
43	28		H	Aston Villa	W	2-0	0-0	2	Buchan (2)	10,000
44	May 5		A	Aston Villa	L	0-1	0-1	2		20,000

Appearances
Goals

FA Cup

25	Jan 13	R1	H	Burnley	W	3-1	1-0		Paterson (3)	41,581
28	Feb 3	R2	A	West Bromwich Albion	L	1-2	1-1		Buchan	56,474

Appearances
Goals

	Robson	Cresswell	England	Parker	Kasher	Mitton	Donaldson	Buchan	Paterson	Marshall	Ellis	Hawes	Oakley	Poole	Whipp	Hunter	Ferguson	Andrews	Harper	Gillooley	Young	Clack	Prior	Wagstaffe	Jackson	Stewart	Stannard	
1	2	3	4	5	6	7	8	9	10	11																		1
1	2	3	4	5	6	7	8	9	10		11																	2
1	2	3	4	5	6	7	8	9	10	11																		3
1	2	3	4	5	6	7	8	9	10	11																		4
1		3	5		4	7	9	10		11		2	6	8														5
1	2	3	5		4	7	8	9		11	10		6															6
1	2	3	5		4	7	8	9		11	10		6															7
1	2	3	5		4	7	8	9		11	10		6															8
1	2	3	5			7	8	9		11	10		6	4														9
1	2	3	5			7	8	9		11	10		6	4														10
1	2	3	5			7	8	9		11	10		6	4														11
1	2	3	5			7	8	9		11	10		6	4														12
1	2	3	5			7	8	9		11	10		6	4														13
1	2	3	5			7	8	9		11	10		6	4														14
1	2	3	5			7	8	9		11	10		6		4													15
1	2	3	5			7	8	9		11	10		6		4													16
1	2	3	5			7	8	9		11	10		6		4													17
1	2	3				7	8	9		11	10		5		4	6												18
1	2	3	5			7	8	9		11	10		6		4													19
1	2	3	5			7	8	9		11	10		6		4													20
1	2	3	5			7	8	9		11	10		6		4													21
1	2	3	5			7	8	9		11	10		6		4													22
1	2	3	5			7	8	9		11	10		6	4														23
1	2	3	5			7	8	9		11	10		6		4													24
1	2	3	5			7	8	9		11	10		6		4													26
1	2	3	5			7	8	9		11	10		6	4														27
	2	3	4			7	8	9		11	10					6	1	5										29
		2	4			7		9	8	11	10		6				1	5	3									30
	2	3	4			7	8	9		11	10		6				1	5										31
	2	3	4			7	8	9		11	10		6				1	5										32
1	2	3	4			7	8	9		11	10		6					5										33
	2	3	5				8	9		11	10		6			4	1		7									34
	2	3	5	4			8		10	11			6				1		7	9								35
	2	3	5	4			8	9	10		11		6				1		7									36
	2	3	5	4			8	9	10		11		6				1		7									37
	2	3	5	4		7	8	9		11	10		6				1											38
	2	3	5	4		7	8	9		11	10		6				1											39
1	2	3	5	4		7	8	9		11	10		6															40
1	2	3				7	8	9		11	10		6		4						5							41
1	2	3		4			8			11	10		6					5			7	9						42
1		3	5				8		10		11		6		4						7			2	9			43
1		3	5	4			8	9		11	10		6					2			7							44
32	38	42	39	4	16	35	41	39	9	38	37	1	37	1	8	13	2	10	6	2	1	6	2	1	1	1		
			1				1	30	21		4	12																

	Robson	Cresswell	England	Parker	Kasher	Mitton	Donaldson	Buchan	Paterson	Marshall	Ellis	Hawes	Oakley	Poole	Whipp	Hunter	Ferguson	Andrews	Harper	Gillooley	Young	Clack	Prior	Wagstaffe	Jackson	Stewart	Stannard	
1	2	3	5			7	8	9		11	10		6		4													25
1	2	3	5			7	8	9		11	10		6		4													28
2	2	2	2			2	2	2		2	2		2		2													
								1	3																			

Joe Kasher

Centre-half Joe Kasher made his final appearance for Sunderland during this season. When he died on 8 January 1992, just short of his 98th birthday, he was the oldest surviving professional footballer in England.

369

1923-24

Division One

Ground: Roker Park
Manager: Robert Kyle

League Table

	P	W	D	L	F	A	Pts
Huddersfield T	42	23	11	8	60	33	57
Cardiff C	42	22	13	7	61	34	57
SUNDERLAND	42	22	9	11	71	54	53
Bolton W	42	18	14	10	68	34	50
Sheffield U	42	19	12	11	69	49	50
Aston Villa	42	18	13	11	52	37	49
Everton	42	18	13	11	62	53	49
Blackburn R	42	17	11	14	54	50	45
Newcastle U	42	17	10	15	60	54	44
Notts Co	42	14	14	14	44	49	42
Manchester C	42	15	12	15	54	71	42
Liverpool	42	15	11	16	49	48	41
West Ham U	42	13	15	14	40	43	41
Birmingham	42	13	13	16	41	49	39
Tottenham H	42	12	14	16	50	56	38
WBA	42	12	14	16	51	62	38
Burnley	42	12	12	18	55	60	36
Preston NE	42	12	10	20	52	67	34
Arsenal	42	12	9	21	40	63	33
Nottingham F	42	10	12	20	42	64	32
Chelsea	42	9	14	19	31	53	32
Middlesbrough	42	7	8	27	37	60	22

FA Cup Winners: Newcastle United

Did you know that?

Sunderland headed the top flight for nine games towards the end of this season. This is their longest continuous run of games at the top without winning the League title.

Match 1: Wilkinson made debut
Match 2: Wilkinson last game
Match 4: Stoneham made debut
Match 6: Stannard last game
Match 7: Robson last game
Match 8: McInroy made debut
Match 11: Scott made debut
Match 12: Scott last game
Match 13: Marsden last game
Match 15: Jackson last game
Match 17: Mitton last game
Match 18: Clunas made debut
Match 19: Grimshaw made debut
Match 27: Hogg made debut
Match 28: Ditchburn made debut
Match 39: Rogers made debut & Poole last game
Match 42: Gilhooley last game

Match No.	Date	Round	Venue	Opponents	Result	FT	HT	Pos.	Scorers	Attendance
1	Aug 25		H	West Ham United	D	0-0	0-0			35,000
2	27		A	Cardiff City	L	1-2	1-2	16	Paterson	30,000
3	Sep 1		A	West Ham United	W	1-0	0-0	11	Paterson	25,000
4	5		H	Cardiff City	L	0-3	0-2	17		30,000
5	8		A	Birmingham	W	2-0	1-0	12	Ellis, Paterson	25,000
6	15		H	Birmingham	D	1-1	1-1	12	Buchan	25,000
7	22		A	Manchester City	L	1-4	0-2	18	Marsden	33,952
8	29		H	Manchester City	W	5-2	3-1	14	Buchan (3), Marshall, Prior	15,000
9	Oct 6		H	Bolton Wanderers	D	2-2	1-1	13	Hawes, Buchan	30,000
10	13		A	Bolton Wanderers	L	0-1	0-0	16		25,000
11	17		H	Chelsea	W	2-0	1-0	10	Buchan, Hawes	20,000
12	20		H	Tottenham Hotspur	W	1-0	0-0	9	Buchan (pen)	20,000
13	27		A	Tottenham Hotspur	D	1-1	1-1	8	Marsden	24,840
14	Nov 3		H	Preston North End	W	2-1	1-0	7	Marshall, Buchan	15,000
15	10		A	Preston North End	W	2-1	0-0	5	Marshall, Buchan	25,000
16	17		H	Blackburn Rovers	W	5-1	1-1	5	Hawes, Ellis (pen), Buchan (3)	20,000
17	24		A	Blackburn Rovers	L	2-3	1-1	6	Buchan (2)	15,000
18	Dec 1		H	Huddersfield Town	W	2-1	1-0	4	Marshall, Buchan	29,000
19	8		A	Huddersfield Town	L	2-3	1-2	8	Ellis (pen), Buchan	20,000
20	15		H	Newcastle United	W	3-2	2-2	6	Hawes (2), Paterson	45,000
21	22		A	Newcastle United	W	2-0	1-0	5	Paterson (2)	50,000
22	26		A	Everton	W	3-2	1-2	5	Hawes, Paterson, Buchan	45,000
23	29		H	Notts County	D	1-1	0-0	5	Paterson	18,000
24	Jan 1		H	Everton	W	3-0	2-0	3	Hawes (2), Ellis	20,000
25	5		A	Notts County	W	2-1	1-1	3	Paterson, Ferguson	16,000
27	19		H	Sheffield United	D	2-2	2-1	3	Hogg, Buchan	25,000
28	26		A	Sheffield United	D	1-1	0-0	3	Hogg	25,000
29	Feb 9		A	Aston Villa	W	1-0	1-0	2	Buchan	40,000
30	13		H	Aston Villa	W	2-0	1-0	2	Hawes, Marshall	12,000
31	16		H	Liverpool	D	0-0	0-0	2		20,000
32	Mar 1		H	Nottingham Forest	W	1-0	1-0	2	Hogg	16,000
33	8		A	Nottingham Forest	W	2-1	0-0	1	Hogg (2)	12,000
34	15		A	Burnley	W	3-0	2-0	1	Marshall, Hawes, Hogg	14,000
35	19		A	Liverpool	L	2-4	2-2	1	Hogg (2)	20,395
36	22		H	Burnley	L	0-1	0-1	1		20,000
37	29		A	Middlesbrough	W	3-1	2-0	1	Marshall, Buchan (2)	20,000
38	Apr 5		H	Middlesbrough	W	3-2	0-1	1	Freeman o.g., Buchan, Poole	14,473
39	12		A	Arsenal	L	0-2	0-1	1		18,000
40	18		H	West Bromwich Albion	W	2-0	1-0	1	Buchan, Hawes	13,000
41	19		H	Arsenal	D	1-1	0-0	1	Buchan	20,000
42	21		A	West Bromwich Albion	L	1-3	0-1	2	Grimshaw	12,033
43	26		A	Chelsea	L	1-4	0-1	3	Buchan	24,000

Appearances
Goals

FA Cup

| 26 | Jan 12 | R1 | A | Oldham Athletic | L | 1-2 | 0-2 | | Buchan | 24,726 |

Appearances
Goals

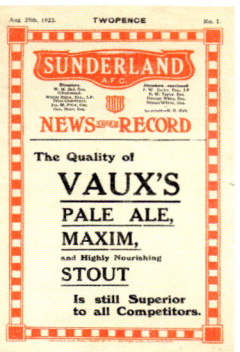

	Robson	Cresswell	England	Wilkinson	Parker	Poole	Marshall	Buchan	Paterson	Hawes	Ellis	Prior	Young	Ferguson	Mitton	Stoneham	Gilhooley	Andrews	Stannard	Marsden	McIlroy	Jackson	Scott	Clunas	Grimshaw	Oakley	Hogg	Ditchburn	Rogers	
1	2	3	4	5	6	7	8	9	10	11																				1
1	2	3	4	5	6		8	9	10	11	7																			2
1	2				6		8	9	10	11	7	3	4	5																3
	2	3			6		8	9	10	11	7		4		1	5														4
1	2	3					8	10		11	7		4		5	6	9													5
1	2	3					8	10		11	7		4		5	6	9													6
1	2						8	9		11	7	3	4		5	6		10												7
	2				8	9		10	11	7	3	4			6				1	5										8
	2						8	9		10	11	7	3	4		6			1	5										9
	2	3					8	9	10		11	7		4		6			1	5										10
	2	3		5			8	9		10	11			4		6			1		7									11
	2	3		5			8	9	11	10				4		6			1		7									12
	2	3		5			8	9	7	11				4		6		10	1											13
	2	3					8	9		10	11	7		4		6			1	5										14
	2	3					8	9		10	11	7		4		6			1	5										15
	2	3		5			8	9		10	11	7		4		6			1											16
	2	3		5			8	9		10	11	7		4		6			1											17
	2	3		5			8	9		10	11	7				6			1		4									18
	2	3		5			8	9		10	11					6			1		4	7								19
		3		5			8	9	10	11						6			1		4	7	2							20
	2	3		5			8	9	10	11						6			1		4	7								21
	2	3		5			8	9	10	11						6			1		4	7								22
	2	3		5			8	9	10	11				6					1		4	7								23
	2	3		5			8	9	10	11				6					1		4	7								24
	2	3		5			8	9	10	11				6					1		4	7								25
	2	3		5			8	10		11				6					1		4	7		9						27
	2	3					8			10	11			6					1		4	7		9	5					28
		3		5			8	9	10	11				6					1		4	7	2							29
		3		5			8	9		10	11			6					1			7	2		4					30
		3		5			8	9		10	11			6		5			1			7	2		4					31
	2	3						8		10	11			5					6		1	4	7		9					32
	2	3			6	10	8			11					5				1			7		9	4					33
		3					8			10	11				5	6			1		4	7	2	9						34
	2	3					8		10	11		5				6			1		4	7		9						35
	2	3					8	7	10	11					5	6			1		4			9						36
		3		5	9	8		10	11	7				6					1		4		2							37
		3		5	9	8		10	11					6					1		4	7	2							38
		3		5	6	9		10	11			4							1			7	2			8				39
	2	3		5			8	9		10	11			6					1		4	7								40
	2	3		5			8	9		10	11					6			1		4	7								41
		3				10	8			11				5	6				1		4	7	2	9						42
		3		5			8	9	10	11						6			1		4	7	2							43
6	32	38	2	22	8	26	39	18	35	40	15	4	17	10	1	9	28	2	2	35	5	2	21	22	10	8	4	1		
					1	7	25	9	11	4	1		1				2					1		8						
	2	3		5			8	9	10	11			6						1		4	7								26
1	1		1			1	1	1	1		1								1		1	1								
						1																								

Michael Gilhooley

After signing for a British transfer record £5,250 he only made 19 appearances; due to a broken leg (v Bradford City 25 March 1922) that reduced his mobility.

371

1924-25

Division One

Ground: Roker Park
Manager: Robert Kyle

League Table

	P	W	D	L	F	A	Pts
Huddersfield T	42	21	16	5	69	28	58
WBA	42	23	10	9	58	34	56
Bolton W	42	22	11	9	76	34	55
Liverpool	42	20	10	12	63	55	50
Bury	42	17	15	10	54	51	49
Newcastle U	42	16	16	10	61	42	48
SUNDERLAND	42	19	10	13	64	51	48
Birmingham	42	17	12	13	49	53	46
Notts Co	42	16	13	13	42	31	45
Manchester C	42	17	9	16	76	68	43
Cardiff C	42	16	11	15	56	51	43
Tottenham H	42	15	12	15	52	43	42
West Ham U	42	15	12	15	62	60	42
Sheffield U	42	13	13	16	55	63	39
Aston Villa	42	13	13	16	58	71	39
Blackburn R	42	11	13	18	53	66	35
Everton	42	12	11	19	40	60	35
Leeds U	42	11	12	19	46	59	34
Burnley	42	11	12	19	46	75	34
Arsenal	42	14	5	23	46	58	33
Preston NE	42	10	6	26	37	74	26
Nottingham F	42	6	12	24	29	65	24

FA Cup Winners:
Sheffield Wednesday

Did you know that?

Sunderland sold their record League scorer Charlie Buchan to Arsenal on 2 July 1925 for the unusual fee of £2,000 plus £100 for every goal he scored in the following season. He scored 21 times for Arsenal making the fee £4,100.

Match 2: Fall made debut
Match 4: Paterson last game
Match 7: Death made debut
Match 11: Coglin made debut
Match 18: Ferguson last game
Match 21: Hogg last game
Match 30: Young last game
Match 34: Rogers last game
Match 36: Scott made debut
Match 37: Scott last game
Match 43: Coxford made debut
Match 44: Fall last game
Match 45: Buchan last game

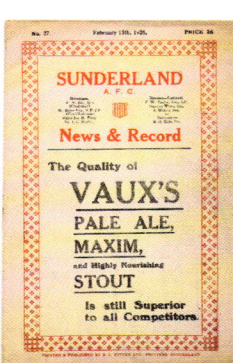

Match No.	Date	Round	Venue	Opponents	Result	FT	HT	Pos.	Scorers	Attendance
1	Aug 30		A	Leeds United	D	1-1	1-1		Paterson	33,722
2	Sep 3		H	Preston North End	W	2-0	1-0	5	Clunas, Buchan	35,000
3	6		H	Birmingham	W	4-0	1-0	3	Ellis, Buchan, Hawes, Paterson	30,000
4	13		A	West Bromwich Albion	L	1-2	0-1	7	Hawes	24,166
5	20		H	Tottenham Hotspur	W	4-1	2-0	6	Marshall, Buchan, Hawes (2)	30,000
6	27		A	Bolton Wanderers	W	2-1	2-0	5	Buchan, Marshall	30,000
7	29		A	Burnley	W	2-1	1-1	2	Clunas (pen), Marshall	10,000
8	Oct 4		H	Notts County	L	0-1	0-1	4		25,000
9	11		A	Everton	W	3-0	1-0	3	Marshall, Buchan, Death	37,000
10	18		H	Newcastle United	D	1-1	1-1	4	Marshall	55,642
11	25		A	Liverpool	L	1-3	0-3	5	Parker	40,886
12	Nov 1		H	Nottingham Forest	W	3-1	2-0	4	Buchan (2), Ellis	18,000
13	8		A	Bury	L	0-3	0-1	5		30,000
14	15		H	Manchester City	W	3-2	1-0	4	Parker, Marshall, Ellis	20,000
15	20		A	Preston North End	W	2-1	2-0	2	Marshall (2)	10,760
16	22		A	Arsenal	D	0-0	0-0	2		35,000
17	29		H	Aston Villa	D	1-1	1-1	2	Parker	22,000
18	Dec 6		A	Huddersfield Town	L	0-4	0-0	5		15,000
19	13		H	Blackburn Rovers	W	1-0	0-0	3	Marshall	12,000
20	20		A	West Ham United	L	1-4	1-2	4	Death	20,000
21	25		H	Sheffield United	L	0-1	0-1	8		21,500
22	26		A	Sheffield United	L	1-2	0-1	8	Rogers	44,500
23	27		H	Leeds United	W	2-1	2-1	7	Hawes (2)	18,000
24	Jan 1		H	Cardiff City	W	1-0	1-0	4	Hawes	18,000
25	3		A	Birmingham	L	1-2	1-1	4	Marshall	25,000
27	17		H	West Bromwich Albion	W	3-0	2-0	5	Death, Hawes, Rogers	33,000
28	24		A	Tottenham Hotspur	L	0-1	0-0	7		26,696
31	Feb 7		H	Notts County	L	1-4	1-3	8	Marshall	16,000
32	11		H	Bolton Wanderers	W	1-0	1-0	8	Marshall	6,000
33	14		H	Everton	W	4-2	2-1	7	Buchan (2), Ellis, Marshall	10,000
34	21		A	Newcastle United	L	0-2	0-0	7		52,000
35	28		H	Liverpool	W	3-0	1-0	6	Buchan, Ellis, Clunas (pen)	18,000
36	Mar 7		A	Nottingham Forest	D	1-1	0-0	7	Marshall	8,000
37	14		H	Bury	D	1-1	0-1	6	Marshall	10,000
38	21		A	Manchester City	W	3-1	1-1	7	Marshall (2), Ellis	30,000
39	28		H	Arsenal	W	2-0	1-0	6	Hawes, Buchan	18,000
40	Apr 4		A	Aston Villa	W	4-1	2-1	6	Marshall, Andrews, Hawes, Clunas (pen)	20,000
41	11		H	Huddersfield Town	D	1-1	0-1	6	Hawes	35,000
42	13		A	Cardiff City	L	0-2	0-1	7		25,000
43	18		A	Blackburn Rovers	W	1-1	1-1	6	Buchan	8,000
44	25		H	West Ham United	D	1-1	0-0	6	Ellis	10,000
45	May 2		H	Burnley	D	1-1	0-1	7	Grimshaw	7,000

Appearances
Goals

FA Cup

26	Jan 10	R1	A	Bury	W	3-0	2-0		Clunas, Rogers, Buchan	24,872
29	31	R2	H	Everton	D	0-0	0-0			45,852
30	Feb 4	R2r	A	Everton	L	1-2	1-1		Marshall	50,000

Appearances
Goals

	McInroy	Cresswell	England	Clunas	Parker	Andrews	Grimshaw	Buchan	Paterson	Hawes	Ellis	Fall	Marshall	Death	Ferguson	Coglin	Prior	Young	Hogg	Oakley	Rogers	Ditchburn	Scott	Stoneham	Coxford	
1	1	2	3	4	5	6	7	8	9	10	11															1
2	1	2	3	4	5		7	8	9	10	11	6														2
3	1	2	3	4	5		7	8	9	10	11	6														3
4	1	2	3	4	5		7	8	9	10	11	6														4
5	1	2	3	4	5	6	7	9		10	11		8													5
6	1	2	3	4	5	6	7	9		10	11		8													6
7	1	2	3	4	5	6	7	9		10			8	11												7
8	1	2	3	4	5	6	7	9		10	11		8													8
9	1	2	3	4	5	6	7	9		10			8	11												9
10	1	2	3	4	5	6	7	9		10			8	11												10
11	1	2	3		5	6	7	9		11			8		4	10										11
12	1	2	3	4	5	6		9		10	11		8				7									12
13	1	2		4	5	6		9		10	11		8				7	3								13
14	1	2	3	4	5	6	7	9		10	11		8													14
15	1	2	3	4	5	6	7	8		10			9	11												15
16	1	2	3	4	5	6	7	8		10			9	11												16
17	1	2	3	4	5	6	7	8		10	11		9													17
18	1	2	3	4			6	7	8	10	11		9		5											18
19	1	2	3	4	5	6	7	8		10	11		9													19
20	1	2	3	4	5	6	7	8		10			9	11												20
21	1	2	3	4	5	6	7	8					10	11				9								21
22	1		3	4	5	6		8					10	11		7			2	9						22
23	1		3	4	5	6		8	10					11		7			2	9						23
24	1		3	4	5	6		8		10	11					7			2	9						24
25	1	2	3	4	5	6		8		10			9	11		7										25
27	1		3	4	5	6	7	8		10				11					2	9						27
28	1	2	3	4		6	7			10			8	11						9	5					28
31	1	3		4	5	6		8			10		9	11		7			2							31
32	1	2		4	5	6		8			10		9	11		7		3								32
33	1	2		4	5	6		8			10		9	11		7		3								33
34	1	2		4	5	6					10		8	11		7		3	9							34
35	1	2		4	5	6		8		10	11		9			7		3								35
36	1	2		4	5	6				10	11		9			7		3				8				36
37	1	2		4	5	6				10	11		9			7		3				8				37
38	1	2		4	5	6	7	8		10	11		9					3								38
39	1	2		4	5	6	7	8		10	11		9					3								39
40	1	2		4	5	6				10	11		9					3								40
41	1	2	3	4	5	6	7	8		10	11		9													41
42	1	2	3	4	5	6	7	8		10	11		9													42
43		2		4	5	6	7	8			11		9		10			3				1	6			43
44	1	2		4	5	6	7	8		11	10	9						3								44
45	1	2		4	5	6	7	8		10			9	11				3								45
	41	38	28	41	40	38	29	38	4	34	28	4	35	17	2	2	13	1	1	17	6	1	2	1	1	
			4	3	1	1	12	2	11	7			18	3						2						

	McInroy	Cresswell	England	Clunas	Parker	Andrews	Grimshaw	Buchan	Paterson	Hawes	Ellis	Fall	Marshall	Death	Ferguson	Coglin	Prior	Young	Hogg	Oakley	Rogers	Ditchburn	Scott	Stoneham	Coxford	
26	1		3	4	5	6	7	8		10	11								2	9						26
29	1		3	4	5	6	7	8		10	11								2	9						29
30	1			4	5	6	7	8		10	11		9			3			2							30
	3		2	3	3	3	3	3		3	3		1			1			3	2						
				1				1					1							1						

Bobby Marshall – Top scorer for the season.

373

1925-26

Division One

Ground: Roker Park

Manager: Robert Kyle

League Table

	P	W	D	L	F	A	Pts
Huddersfield T	42	23	11	8	92	60	57
Arsenal	42	22	8	12	87	63	52
SUNDERLAND	42	21	6	15	96	80	48
Bury	42	20	7	15	85	77	47
Sheffield U	42	19	8	15	102	82	46
Aston Villa	42	16	12	14	86	76	44
Liverpool	42	14	16	12	70	63	44
Bolton W	42	17	10	15	75	76	44
Manchester U	42	19	6	17	66	73	44
Newcastle U	42	16	10	16	84	75	42
Everton	42	12	18	12	72	70	42
Blackburn R	42	15	11	16	91	80	41
WBA	42	16	8	18	79	78	40
Birmingham	42	16	8	18	66	81	40
Tottenham H	42	15	9	18	66	79	39
Cardiff C	42	16	7	19	61	76	39
Leicester C	42	14	10	18	70	80	38
West Ham U	42	15	7	20	63	76	37
Leeds U	42	14	8	20	64	76	36
Burnley	42	13	10	19	85	108	36
Manchester C	42	12	11	19	89	100	35
Notts Co	42	13	7	22	54	74	33

FA Cup Winners: Bolton Wanderers

Did you know that?

Bobby Gurney scored nine goals on his debut for Sunderland Reserves in a 14-0 win against Hartlepool Reserves on 5 September 1925.

Match 1: Halliday made debut
Match 4: Ramsay made debut
Match 7: Heyes made debut
Match 11: Ditchburn last game
Match 12: McGorian made debut
Match 15: Henderson made debut
Match 19: Heyes last game
Match 20: Kelly made debut
Match 39: Lloyd made debut
Match 41: Gurney made debut
Match 42: Stoneham last game
Match 43: Pegg only game

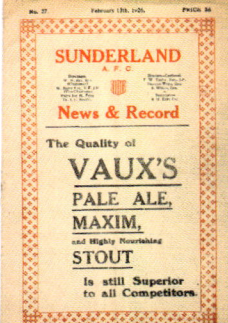

Match No.	Date	Round	Venue	Opponents	Result	FT	HT	Pos.	Scorers	Attendance
1	Aug 29		H	Birmingham	W	3-1	1-0		Halliday (2), Grimshaw	27,215
2	Sep 2		H	Blackburn Rovers	W	6-2	2-2	2	Coglin, Halliday (2), Ellis (2), Clunas (pen)	19,701
3	5		A	West Bromwich Albion	W	5-2	2-1	1	Halliday (3), Coglin, Ellis	16,110
4	12		H	Sheffield United	W	6-1	4-0	3	Halliday (3), Ellis, Ramsay, Grimshaw	35,247
5	21		A	Blackburn Rovers	L	0-3	0-1	6		16,682
6	23		A	Cardiff City	W	1-0	1-0	2	Clunas	18,316
7	26		H	Tottenham Hotspur	W	3-0	1-0	2	Halliday (2), Grimshaw	30,700
8	Oct 3		A	Manchester City	L	1-4	0-1	2	Ellis	39,461
9	5		A	Aston Villa	L	2-4	0-2	2	Halliday, Coglin	18,593
10	10		H	Everton	W	7-3	2-2	2	Clunas (pen), Parker, Marshall (2), Halliday (2), Ramsay	26,755
11	14		H	Bury	W	1-0	1-0	1	Ellis	14,434
12	17		A	Newcastle United	D	0-0	0-0	1		51,604
13	24		H	Bolton Wanderers	W	2-1	0-1	1	Haworth o.g., Prior	23,516
14	28		A	Bury	D	2-2	1-2	1	Halliday (2)	11,748
15	31		A	Liverpool	D	2-2	0-2	1	Halliday, McNab o.g.	34,838
16	Nov 7		H	Burnley	D	2-2	2-1	1	Halliday, Marshall	9,366
17	14		A	Leicester City	L	1-4	1-2	1	Halliday	22,706
18	21		H	West Ham United	W	4-1	1-0	2	Marshall (2), Prior, Clunas (pen)	17,667
19	28		A	Arsenal	L	0-2	0-1	2		44,870
20	Dec 5		H	Manchester United	W	2-1	0-0	2	Halliday (2)	25,507
21	12		A	Notts County	L	0-2	0-2	2		20,583
22	19		H	Aston Villa	W	3-2	1-1	2	Clunas (2, 1 pen), Halliday	14,707
23	26		A	Huddersfield Town	D	1-1	1-1	2	Halliday	27,136
24	Jan 1		H	Leeds United	L	1-3	0-0	2	Clunas (pen)	29,527
25	2		A	Birmingham	L	1-2	0-1	3	Kelly	22,433
27	16		H	West Bromwich Albion	W	4-0	3-0	2	Kelly, Death, Halliday (2)	20,352
28	20		H	Huddersfield Town	W	4-1	2-1	2	Prior (2), Death, Halliday	27,833
29	23		A	Sheffield United	L	1-4	1-1	2	Prior	25,700
31	Feb 6		A	Tottenham Hotspur	W	2-0	0-0	2	Kelly, Halliday	31,434
32	13		H	Manchester City	W	5-3	2-0	2	Halliday (2), Ellis, Clunas (pen), Kelly	25,284
35	27		H	Newcastle United	D	2-2	1-1	2	Halliday, Death	34,902
36	Mar 13		H	Liverpool	W	3-2	2-2	2	Halliday (2), Prior	19,944
37	17		A	Everton	L	1-2	1-2	3	Marshall	16,313
38	20		A	Burnley	L	2-5	1-3	3	Kelly, Clunas (pen)	25,077
39	27		H	Leicester City	W	3-0	1-0	3	Halliday, Kelly, Prior	13,185
40	31		H	Cardiff City	W	1-3	1-2	3	Kelly	4,315
41	Apr 3		A	West Ham United	L	2-3	2-2	3	Gurney, Prior	21,942
42	6		A	Leeds United	W	2-0	2-0	3	Halliday (2)	27,345
43	7		A	Bolton Wanderers	L	2-3	0-2	3	Halliday (2)	12,076
44	10		H	Arsenal	W	2-1	0-1	3	Gurney (2)	20,990
45	21		A	Manchester United	L	1-5	0-2	3	Death	10,913
46	24		H	Notts County	W	3-1	2-1	3	Death, Gurney, McGorian	8,262

Appearances
Goals

FA Cup

26	Jan 9	R3	H	Boston	W	8-1	2-0		Kelly (3), Halliday (3), Marshall (2)	24,864
30	30	R4	A	Sheffield United	W	2-1	0-0		Prior, Kelly	62,041
33	Feb 20	R5	H	Manchester United	D	3-3	2-1		Marshall, Death (2)	50,500
34	24	R5r	A	Manchester United	L	1-2	0-2		Halliday	58,661

Appearances
Goals

	McInroy	Cresswell	England	Clunas	Parker	Coxford	Grimshaw	Marshall	Halliday	Coglin	Ellis	Andrews	Ramsay	Oakley	Heyes	Prior	Ditchburn	McGorian	Death	Stoneham	Hawes	Henderson	Kelly	Lloyd	Gurney	Pegg
1	1	2	3	4	5	6	7	8	9	10	11															
2	1	2	3	4	5	6	7	8	9	10	11															
3	1	2	3	4	5	6	7	8	9	10	11															
4	1	2	3	4	5		7	8	9		11	6	10													
5	1	2	3	4			7	8	9		11	6	10													
6	1	2		4	5		7	8	9		11	6	10	3												
7	1	2	3	4	5		7		9		11	6	10		8											
8	1	2		4	5			8	9	10	11	6		3		7										
9	1	2		4	5			8	9	10	11	6		3		7										
10	1	2	3	4	5			8	9		11	6	10			7										
11	1	2	3		5			8	9		11	6	10			7	4									
12	1	2	3		5			8	9			6	10			7	4	11								
13	1	2		4	5			10	9		11	6		3	8	7										
14		2	3		5			8	9		11	6				7	4		1	10						
15		2	3			6		8	9		11					7	4		1	10	5					
16	1	2	3	4	5	6		8	9		11					7				10						
17	1	2	3	4	5			8	9		11	6				7				10						
18	1	2	3	4	5			8	9		11	6	10			7										
19	1	2	3	4					9			6			8	7		11		10	5					
20	1	2	3	4	5			10	9		11	6				7						8				
21	1	2	3	4				10	9		11	6				7				5		8				
22		2	3	4				5	9		11	10				7	6		1			8				
23		2	3	4				5	9			10				7	6	11	1			8				
24		2	3	4			7	5	9		11	10					6		1			8				
25		2	3	4				5	9		11	6				7			1	10		8				
27		2	3	4	5			10	9			6				7		11	1			8				
28		2	3	4	5			10	9			6				7		11	1			8				
29		2	3	4	5				9	10		6				7		11	1			8				
31	1	2	3	4	5			10	9			6				7		11				8				
32	1	2	3	4	5			10	9		7	6						11				8				
35	1	2	3	4	5			10	9							7	6	11				8				
36	1	2	3	4	5			10	9							7		11				8				
37	1	2	3	4	5	6		10	9							7		11				8				
38	1	2	3	4	5			10	9		6					7		11				8				
39	1	2		4				10	9		6					7		11		5		8	3			
40	1	2		4		6		10	9							7		11		5		8	3			
41			3	4				5	9			2		7			6	11	1		8			10		
42			3	4			7	5	9		11	2					6		1		8			10		
43	1		3	4			7	5	9			2					6				8			10	11	
44	1		3	4	5		7		9			2					6	11			8			10		
45	1		3	4	5		7		9			2					6	11			8			10		
46	1	2	3	4	5		7		9								6	11			8			10		
	31	37	36	38	30	7	13	36	42	6	24	28	8	9	3	28	1	13	18	11	6	5	23	2	6	1
			9	1		3	6	38	3	7		2				8		1	5				7		4	
26		2	3		5			10	9		11	6				7	4		1			8				
30	1	2	3	4	5			10	9			6				7		11				8				
33	1	2	3	4	5			10	9			6				7		11				8				
34	1	2	3	4	5			10	9							7	6	11				8				
	3	4	4	3	4			4	4		1	3				4	2	3	1			4				
								3	4			1						2				4				

Bobby Gurney

– goalscorer on both his reserve and first team debuts

– nine goals on his debut for the reserves

– the opening goal at West Ham United on his first team debut on 3 April 1926. This was the first of over 200 goals he was to score for Sunderland in the next 13 years.

1926-27

Division One

Ground: Roker Park

Manager: Robert Kyle

League Table

	P	W	D	L	F	A	Pts
Newcastle U	42	25	6	11	96	58	56
Huddersfield T	42	17	17	8	76	60	51
SUNDERLAND	42	21	7	14	98	70	49
Bolton W	42	19	10	13	84	62	48
Burnley	42	19	9	14	91	80	47
West Ham U	42	19	8	15	86	70	46
Leicester C	42	17	12	13	85	70	46
Sheffield U	42	17	10	15	74	86	44
Liverpool	42	18	7	17	69	61	43
Aston Villa	42	18	7	17	81	83	43
Arsenal	42	17	9	16	77	86	43
Derby Co	42	17	7	18	86	73	41
Tottenham H	42	16	9	17	76	78	41
Cardiff C	42	16	9	17	55	65	41
Manchester U	42	13	14	15	52	64	40
Sheffield W	42	15	9	18	75	92	39
Birmingham	42	17	4	21	64	73	38
Blackburn R	42	15	8	19	77	96	38
Bury	42	12	12	18	68	77	36
Everton	42	12	10	20	64	90	34
Leeds U	42	11	8	23	69	88	30
WBA	42	11	8	23	65	86	30

FA Cup Winners: Cardiff City

Did you know that?

Frank and Warney Cresswell became the first brothers to play together in a League game for Sunderland when they appeared against Huddersfield Town on 14 September 1926.

Match 5: Frank Cresswell made debut
Match 6: Prior last game
Match 18: Coxford last game
Match 25: Bartley made debut
Match 27: Coglin last game
Match 28: Warney Cresswell last game
Match 29: Kelly last game
Match 32: Lloyd last game
Match 33: Grimshaw last game
Match 34: Wilks made debut
Match 36: Bell made debut
Match 40: Hawes last game

Match No.	Date	Round	Venue	Opponents	Result	FT	HT	Pos.	Scorers	Attendance
1	Aug 28		A	West Bromwich Albion	L	0-3	0-2			24,945
2	Sep 4		H	Bury	W	3-0	0-0	14	Prior, Ellis, Gurney	16,238
3	8		H	Huddersfield Town	D	1-1	0-1	14	Gurney	27,739
4	11		A	Birmingham	L	0-2	0-1	19		28,035
5	14		A	Huddersfield Town	D	0-0	0-0	16		15,090
6	18		H	Tottenham Hotspur	W	3-2	1-1	14	Marshall (2), Gurney	17,459
7	20		A	Blackburn Rovers	W	2-0	0-0	7	Ellis, Kelly	24,464
8	25		A	West Ham United	W	2-1	0-1	4	Gurney, Coglin	20,778
9	Oct 2		H	Sheffield Wed.	W	4-1	2-0	1	Marshall (2), Coglin, Ellis	16,211
10	6		H	Burnley	W	7-1	3-0	1	Halliday (3), Coglin (3), Kelly	19,550
11	9		A	Leicester City	L	1-2	0-2	1	Halliday	27,585
12	12		A	Burnley	L	2-4	0-2	2	Death (2)	14,590
13	16		H	Aston Villa	D	1-1	1-1	3	Henderson	17,155
14	23		A	Cardiff City	L	0-3	0-2	6		15,870
15	30		H	Newcastle United	W	2-0	1-0	2	Halliday, Death	31,152
16	Nov 6		A	Leeds United	D	2-2	1-1	4	Marshall, Halliday	15,667
17	13		H	Liverpool	W	2-1	1-1	2	Marshall, Halliday	9,186
18	20		A	Arsenal	W	3-2	1-2	1	Ellis, Halliday, Marshall	20,087
19	27		H	Sheffield United	W	3-0	1-0	1	Marshall, Kelly (2)	16,063
20	Dec 4		A	Derby County	L	2-4	0-2	2	Marshall, Halliday	18,927
21	11		H	Manchester United	W	6-0	0-0	1	Halliday (4), Gurney, Clunas (pen)	15,385
22	18		A	Bolton Wanderers	D	2-2	0-1	1	Halliday, Clunas	24,232
23	25		A	Everton	L	4-5	3-3	3	Halliday (2), Clunas (pen), Ellis	37,500
24	27		H	Everton	W	3-2	2-2	3	Halliday, Marshall, Gurney	32,574
25	Jan 1		H	Blackburn Rovers	W	2-5	2-3	3	Marshall, Halliday (pen)	25,212
27	15		A	West Bromwich Albion	W	4-1	3-0	3	Halliday (3), Coglin	16,413
28	29		H	Leicester City	W	3-0	1-0	4	Gurney, Halliday (2)	11,009
29	Feb 5		A	Tottenham Hotspur	W	2-0	2-0	3	Marshall (2)	32,506
30	12		H	West Ham United	L	2-3	0-3	4	Halliday (2)	17,038
31	16		H	Birmingham	W	4-1	2-0	2	Ramsay (2), Bartley, Grimshaw	10,525
32	19		A	Sheffield Wed.	L	1-4	1-2	3	Halliday	24,581
33	Mar 5		A	Aston Villa	L	1-3	0-2	3	Ramsay	33,847
34	12		H	Cardiff City	D	2-2	2-0	3	Ramsay, Clunas (pen)	17,194
35	19		A	Newcastle United	L	0-1	0-1	5		67,067
36	26		H	Leeds United	W	6-2	2-0	3	Ramsay (3), Halliday (3)	12,288
37	30		A	Bury	W	2-1	1-0	3	Halliday, Ramsay	8,125
38	Apr 2		A	Liverpool	W	2-1	1-1	3	Halliday (2)	20,086
39	9		H	Arsenal	W	5-1	2-0	2	Marshall (3), Halliday (2)	23,168
40	16		A	Sheffield United	L	0-2	0-1	3		24,184
41	19		H	Bolton Wanderers	W	6-2	4-1	3	Marshall (3), Halliday (2), Clunas (pen)	14,316
42	23		H	Derby County	L	1-2	0-1	3	Halliday	15,064
43	30		A	Manchester United	D	0-0	0-0	3		17,300

Appearances
Goals

FA Cup

Match No.	Date	Round	Venue	Opponents	Result	FT	HT	Scorers	Attendance
26	Jan 8	R3	A	Leeds United	L	2-3	2-2	Marshall, Halliday	31,000

Appearances
Goals

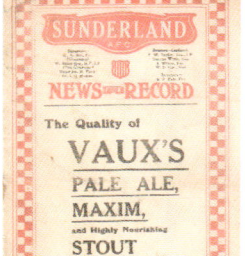

	McInroy	Cresswell, W.	England	Clunas	Parker	Andrews	Grimshaw	Kelly	Halliday	Hawes	Death	Marshall	Prior	Gurney	Ellis	Cresswell, F.	Henderson	Coglin	McGorian	Coxford	Oakley	Lloyd	Bartley	Ramsay	Wilks	Bell	
1	2	3	4	5	6	7	8	9	10	11																	1
1	2	3	4		6		8		10		5	7	9	11													2
1	2	3	4		6		8		10		5	7	9	11													3
1	2	3		4	6		8		10		5	7	9	11													4
1	2	3	4		6		8				5	7	9	11	10												5
1	2	3	4		6				8	7	9	11				5	10										6
1	2	3			6		7				8		9	11	10	5		4									7
1	2	3			6		7				8		9	11		5	10	4									8
1	2	3	4		6		7				8		9	11		5	10										9
1	2	3	4		6		7	9			8			11		5	10										10
1	2	3			6		7	9		11	8					5	10										11
1	2	3	4		6		7	9		11	8					5	10										12
1	2	3	4		6		7	9		11	8					5	10										13
1	2	3	4		6		7			11	8	9				5	10										14
1	2	3			6	7	8	9		11		10				5		4									15
1	2	3	4	5	6		7	9		11	8	10															16
1	2	3	4	5			7	9			8			11	10			6									17
1	2	3	4	5			7	9			8			11			10	6									18
1	2	3	4	5	6		7	9			8			11			10										19
1	2	3	4	5	6		7	9			8			11			10										20
1	2	3	4		6		7	9			8			11		5											21
1	2	3	4		6		7	9			8		10	11		5											22
1		3	4		6		7	9			8		10	11		5				2							23
1		3	4		6		7	9			8		10	11		5				2							24
1	2		4	5			7	9	10		8			11							3	6					25
1	2	3			6		7	9			8		10			5	11	4									26
1	2	3	4		6		7	9			8		10	11		5											27
1		3	4	5	6		7	9			8		10	11					2								28
1		3	4			7		9			8		10	11		5		6		2							29
1		3	4	5		7		9				8	11							2		6	10				30
1		3	4	5		7		9		10		8	11							2	6						31
1		3	4	5	6	7		9				8	11							2		10					32
1		3	4	5	6			9					8	11						2		10	7				33
1		3	4	5	6			9			8			11						2		10	7				34
		3	4	5	6			9			8			11						2		10	7	1			35
		3	4	5	6			9			8			11						2		10	7	1			36
		3	4	5	6			9		11	8									2		10	7	1			37
		3	4	5	6			9			8			11						2		10	7	1			38
		3	4	5	6			9			8			11						2		10	7	1			39
		3	4	5	6			9	10		8									2			7	1			40
		3	4	5	6			9			8			11	10					2			7	1			41
		3	4	5	6			9			8			11						2		10	7	1			42
		3	4	5	6			9		11	8				10					2			7	1			43
4	25	41	37	22	36	6	27	33	6	9	37	5	23	32	5	17	12	5	2	16	2	3	9	10	8		
		6			1	4	36		3	19	1	7	5		1	6				1	8						

	2	3	4		6		7	9			8		10	11		5											26
1	1	1	1		1		1	1			1		1	1		1											
							1				1																

Albert McInroy

Lancashire born Albert McInroy is the only Sunderland goalkeeper to have gained a full cap for England. His sole appearance was a 3-3 draw against Ireland at Anfield on 26 October 1926.

1927-28

Division One

Ground: Roker Park

Manager: Robert Kyle

League Table

	P	W	D	L	F	A	Pts
Everton	42	20	13	9	102	66	53
Huddersfield T	42	22	7	13	91	68	51
Leicester C	42	18	12	12	96	72	48
Derby Co	42	17	10	15	96	83	44
Bury	42	20	4	18	80	80	44
Cardiff C	42	17	10	15	70	80	44
Bolton W	42	16	11	15	81	66	43
Aston Villa	42	17	9	16	78	73	43
Newcastle U	42	15	13	14	79	81	43
Arsenal	42	13	15	14	82	86	41
Birmingham	42	13	15	14	70	75	41
Blackburn R	42	16	9	17	66	78	41
Sheffield U	42	15	10	17	79	86	40
Sheffield W	42	13	13	16	81	78	39
SUNDERLAND	42	15	9	18	74	76	39
Liverpool	42	13	13	16	84	87	39
West Ham U	42	14	11	17	81	88	39
Manchester U	42	16	7	19	72	80	39
Burnley	42	16	7	19	82	98	39
Portsmouth	42	16	7	19	66	90	39
Tottenham H	42	15	8	19	74	86	38
Middlesbrough	42	11	15	16	81	88	37

FA Cup Winners: Cardiff City

Did you know that?

If Sunderland had lost the final game of the season they would have suffered relegation for the first time. Instead it was opponents Middlesbrough who went down.

Match 1: Allan and Wright made debuts & Lilley only game
Match 2: Murray, Thomson and Hargreaves made debuts
Match 4: Whelan made debut
Match 11: Wood made debut & Ellis last game
Match 28: Marshall and Ramsay last games
Match 29: Dowsey made debut
Match 42: McGorian last game
Match 43: Thomson last game
Match 45: Robinson made debut, Death last game & Robert Kyle last game as Sunderland manager

Match No.	Date	Round	Venue	Opponents	Result	FT	HT	Pos.	Scorers	Attendance
1	Aug 27		H	Portsmouth	D	3-3	1-3		Marshall, Halliday, Moffatt o.g.	35,106
2	Sep 1		A	West Ham United	W	4-2	2-2	5	Halliday (2), Marshall, Wright	19,037
3	3		A	Leicester City	D	3-3	1-2	7	Ellis, Halliday (2)	28,977
4	7		H	Birmingham	W	4-2	4-0	4	Halliday, Clunas, Wilks, Marshall	23,007
5	10		H	Liverpool	W	2-1	2-1	1	Hargreaves, Halliday	29,479
6	17		A	Arsenal	L	1-2	1-1	6	Halliday	45,561
7	24		H	Burnley	L	2-3	1-3	8	Halliday, Somerville o.g.	22,420
8	Oct 1		A	Bury	L	3-5	3-3	12	Halliday (3)	10,233
9	8		H	Sheffield United	L	0-1	0-0	13		18,854
10	15		A	Aston Villa	L	2-4	2-2	17	Wright, Clunas	38,116
11	22		A	Tottenham Hotspur	L	1-3	0-0	18	Ellis (pen)	19,039
12	29		H	Huddersfield Town	W	3-0	2-0	17	Cresswell, Ramsay, Wright	22,070
13	Nov 5		A	Newcastle United	L	1-3	1-1	19	Marshall	44,780
14	12		H	Manchester United	W	4-1	2-1	17	Halliday (3), Marshall	13,319
15	19		A	Everton	W	1-0	1-0	16	Hargreaves	35,993
16	26		H	Bolton Wanderers	D	1-1	0-0	15	Halliday	20,406
17	Dec 3		A	Blackburn Rovers	D	0-0	0-0	15		16,175
18	10		H	Cardiff City	L	0-2	0-2	16		16,450
19	17		A	Sheffield Wed.	D	0-0	0-0	16		19,755
20	24		H	Middlesbrough	W	1-0	0-0	13	Ramsay	23,633
21	26		A	Birmingham	D	1-1	1-0	14		20,120
22	Jan 2		H	West Ham United	W	3-2	3-1	15	Halliday (2), Hargreaves	27,542
23	7		A	Leicester City	D	2-2	2-1	16	Halliday, Ramsay	20,770
26	21		A	Liverpool	W	5-2	3-2	11	Hargreaves, Halliday (2), Riley o.g., Marshall	28,243
28	Feb 4		A	Burnley	L	0-3	0-1	14		11,442
29	11		H	Bury	W	1-0	1-0	10	Clunas	13,586
30	18		A	Portsmouth	W	5-3	1-1	8	Halliday (4), Dowsey	23,955
31	25		H	Aston Villa	L	2-3	2-3	11	Hargreaves (2)	29,444
32	Mar 10		A	Huddersfield Town	L	2-4	1-1	15	Halliday, Hargreaves	17,497
33	14		H	Arsenal	W	5-1	2-0	9	Gurney (3), Halliday, Wilks	9,478
34	17		H	Newcastle United	D	1-1	1-1	9	Halliday	40,071
35	28		A	Tottenham Hotspur	D	0-0	0-0	11		9,244
36	31		H	Everton	L	0-2	0-0	15		15,407
37	Apr 6		H	Derby County	L	0-1	0-0	17		27,431
38	7		A	Bolton Wanderers	W	2-1	2-0	12	Halliday (2)	18,064
39	9		A	Derby County	L	0-1	0-1	16		24,226
40	14		H	Blackburn Rovers	W	1-0	0-0	12	Halliday	12,577
41	16		A	Sheffield United	L	1-5	1-2	12	Wright	8,545
42	21		A	Cardiff City	L	1-3	1-2	16	Hargreaves	10,268
43	25		A	Manchester United	L	1-2	1-1	18	Halliday	9,545
44	28		H	Sheffield Wed.	L	2-3	2-2	19	Halliday (2)	19,339
45	May 5		A	Middlesbrough	W	3-0	1-0	15	Wright, Halliday, Death	41,997

Appearances
Goals

FA Cup

Match No.	Date	Round	Venue	Opponents	Result	FT	HT	Pos.	Scorers	Attendance
24	Jan 14	R3	H	Northampton Town	D	3-3	3-2		Wright, Hargreaves, Halliday	25,454
25	19	R3r	A	Northampton Town	W	3-0	0-0		Halliday (2), Clunas (pen)	21,140
27	28	R4	H	Manchester City	L	1-2	0-1		Halliday	38,650

Appearances
Goals

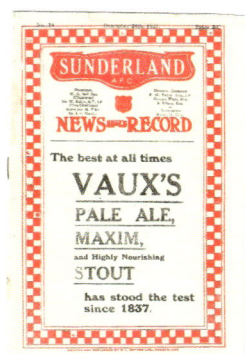

378

	McInroy	Oakley	Lilley	Clunas	Allan	Andrews	Wilks	Marshall	Halliday	Wright	Ellis	Murray	Thomson	Hargreaves	Whelan	England	McGorian	Parker	Wood	Bell	Ramsay	Cresswell	Bartley	Henderson	Death	Dowsey	Gurney	Robinson	
1	2	3	4	5	6	7	8	9	10	11																			1
1			4	5	6	7	8	9	10		2	3	11																2
1			4	5	6	7	8	9	10	11	2	3																	3
1	3		4	5		7	8	9	10	11	2			6															4
1	3		4	5	6	7	8	9	10		2		11																5
	3		4	5	6	7	8	9	10		2		11					1											6
	3		4	5		7	8	9	10		2		11	6				1											7
1	3		4	5	6	7	8	9	10	11	2																		8
1	3		4	5	6	7	8	9	10	11	2																		9
	3		4	5	6	7	8	9	10	11	2																		10
1					6	7		9	10	11	2			3	4	5	8												11
			5	6	7			9			2		11	3		4		1	8	10									12
			5	6	7	8	9		10		2		11	3		4		1											13
			5		7	8	9		10		2		11	3		4		1			6								14
		4			7	8	9		10		2		11	3		5		1			6								15
		4			7	8	9		10		2		11	3		5		1			6								16
			5		7	8	9				2		11	3		4		1		10	6								17
						8	9				2		11	3		4		1		10	6	5	7						18
		4		6	7	8	9	10			2		11	3				1				5							19
1		4		6	7		9	10			2		11	3					8			5							20
1		4		6	7		9	10			2		11	3					8			5							21
1		4		6	7		9	10			2		11	3					8			5							22
1		4		6	7		9	10			2		11	3					8			5							23
1		4		6	7	8	9				2	3	11						10			5							26
1		4		6	7	8	9				2	3							10			5	11						28
1		4			7		9				2	3	11			10					6	5		8					29
1		4			7		9	10			2	3	11								6	5		8					30
1		4			7		9	10			2	3	11								6	5		8					31
		4	5		7		9	10			2	3	11	6				1						8					32
1		4			7		9	10			2	3	11	6		5								8					33
1		4			7		9	10			2	3	11	6		5								8					34
1		4			7		9	10			2	3	11	6		5								8					35
1		4			7		9				2	3	11	6		5	10							8					36
1		4		6	7						2	3							10		5	11	8	9					37
1		4		6	7		9				2	3							10		5	11	8						38
1		4		6	7		9				2	3							10		5	11	8						39
1		4	5	6	7		9	10			2	3									11		8						40
1		4		6	7		9				2	3							11		5		8	10					41
1			5	6	7			10			2	3	11		4						9	8							42
1		4	5	6	7		9	10			2	3							11			8							43
		8	5	6	7		9				2		11	3		4	1					10							44
1		4	5	6			9	8			2		10	3							11		7						45
30	8	1	35	20	27	40	19	38	32	7	41	19	28	7	15	2	13	3	12	7	7	8	15	9	9	9	1		
		3			2	6	35	5	2			8						4	1			1	1	3					
1			4		6	7	8	9	10		2	11		3					5										24
1			4		6	7	8	9			2	3	11					10	5										25
1			4		6	7	8	9			2	3	11			10			5										27
3		3		3	3	3	3	1			2	3	3	1		1		1	3										
		1				4	1					1																	

Photo of Billy Death taken at Sunderland Centenary dinner in 1979. He made his last appearance for Sunderland in the relegation decider at Middlesbrough on 5 May 1928.

1928-29

Division One

Ground: Roker Park

Manager: John Cochrane

League Table

	P	W	D	L	F	A	Pts
Sheffield W	42	21	10	11	86	62	52
Leicester C	42	21	9	12	96	67	51
Aston Villa	42	23	4	15	98	81	50
SUNDERLAND	42	20	7	15	93	75	47
Liverpool	42	17	12	13	90	64	46
Derby Co	42	18	10	14	86	71	46
Blackburn R	42	17	11	14	72	63	45
Manchester C	42	18	9	15	95	86	45
Arsenal	42	16	13	13	77	72	45
Newcastle U	42	19	6	17	70	72	44
Sheffield U	42	15	11	16	86	85	41
Manchester U	42	14	13	15	66	76	41
Leeds U	42	16	9	17	71	84	41
Bolton W	42	14	12	16	73	80	40
Birmingham	42	15	10	17	68	77	40
Huddersfield T	42	14	11	17	70	61	39
West Ham U	42	15	9	18	86	96	39
Everton	42	17	4	21	63	75	38
Burnley	42	15	8	19	81	103	38
Portsmouth	42	15	6	21	56	80	36
Bury	42	12	7	23	62	99	31
Cardiff C	42	8	13	21	43	59	29

FA Cup Winners: Bolton Wanderers

Did you know that?

This is the first season in which accurate attendance figures showed more than half a million people attended Sunderland's home League games (529,107).

Match 1: Lynas and McInally made debuts, Cresswell last game & John Cochrane first as Sunderland manager
Match 2: Wallace and McLean made debuts
Match 6: Wallace last game
Match 8: Dowsey last game
Match 9: McKay made debut
Match 24: Morris made debut
Match 26: Hargreaves last game
Match 31: Henderson last game
Match 40: Parker last game
Match 41: Wilks last game
Match 42: Lynas last game
Match 43: Hall made debut

Match No.	Date		Round	Venue	Opponents	Result	FT	HT	Pos.	Scorers	Attendance
1	Aug	25		A	Burnley	L	1-3	0-1		Halliday	21,448
2		29		H	Blackburn Rovers	W	3-1	2-1	9	McLean, Jones o.g., Whyte o.g.	28,979
3	Sep	1		H	Derby County	W	4-0	2-0	3	Halliday (3), McInally	37,133
4		8		A	Sheffield Wed.	L	1-2	0-1	8	Clunas (pen)	25,716
5		15		H	Bolton Wanderers	W	4-0	3-0	8	Clunas (pen), Halliday (2), Lynas	29,617
6		17		A	Blackburn Rovers	L	0-2	0-2	10		20,270
7		22		A	Portsmouth	L	0-4	0-3	15		25,345
8		29		H	Birmingham	L	3-4	2-2	16	Clunas (pen), Halliday, McInally	26,986
9	Oct	6		A	Manchester City	L	3-5	2-3	18	McKay (2), Halliday	39,152
10		13		H	Huddersfield Town	W	4-1	3-1	17	Halliday, Clunas (2, 1 pen), Hargreaves	33,783
11		20		A	Cardiff City	W	1-0	1-0	13	Hargreaves	15,361
12		27		H	Newcastle United	W	5-2	3-1	11	McKay (2), Halliday (2), Hargreaves	50,519
13	Nov	3		A	Bury	W	3-1	1-1	9	McKay, Halliday (2)	13,099
14		10		H	Aston Villa	L	1-3	1-2	10	McKay	21,250
15		17		A	Leicester City	L	0-1	0-1	13		24,178
16		24		H	Manchester United	W	5-1	2-1	9	McLean, Halliday (3), Clunas (pen)	15,932
17	Dec	1		A	Leeds United	W	3-0	0-0	8	Clunas (2 pens), Halliday	30,082
18		8		H	Liverpool	W	2-1	1-0	7	Halliday, McKay	20,851
19		15		A	West Ham United	D	3-3	0-2	6	McInally, Halliday (2)	16,206
20		22		H	Sheffield United	D	4-4	4-2	5	Halliday (4, 1 pen)	18,899
21		25		A	Everton	D	0-0	0-0	5		37,583
22		26		A	Arsenal	D	1-1	1-1	5	Halliday	15,747
23		29		H	Burnley	W	2-1	1-0	4	Halliday, McKay	23,678
24	Jan	1		H	Arsenal	W	5-1	2-1	3	McKay (2), Halliday (2), Robinson	32,843
25		5		A	Derby County	D	0-0	0-0	3		12,488
27		19		H	Sheffield Wed.	W	4-3	3-2	3	Halliday (2), McKay, Robinson	36,475
28	Feb	2		H	Portsmouth	W	5-0	2-0	2	Robinson (2), Halliday (2), McKay	23,156
29		9		A	Birmingham	L	0-1	0-1	3		17,022
30		16		H	Manchester City	W	3-1	1-0	3	Halliday, Clunas (2 pens)	11,752
31		20		A	Bolton Wanderers	D	2-2	1-0	2	Clunas, Halliday	11,315
32		23		A	Huddersfield Town	W	2-1	0-0	2	Halliday, McLean	13,258
33	Mar	2		H	Cardiff City	W	1-0	1-0	2	Clunas (pen)	21,546
34		9		A	Newcastle United	L	3-4	2-2	2	Robinson, McKay, McLean	65,838
35		16		H	Bury	W	3-1	0-0	2	McLean, Robinson, McKay	18,118
36		25		A	Aston Villa	L	1-3	1-1	2	Halliday	8,573
37		29		H	Everton	D	2-2	2-2	2	Halliday (2)	33,066
38		30		H	Leicester City	L	1-2	0-0	2	McLean	22,847
39	Apr	6		A	Manchester United	L	0-3	0-3	5		27,772
40		13		H	Leeds United	W	2-1	1-1	4	Wright, McLean	12,208
41		20		A	Liverpool	L	2-5	1-2	5	Halliday (2)	24,425
42		27		H	West Ham United	W	4-1	2-0	4	Halliday (3), McKay	9,469
43	May	4		A	Sheffield United	L	0-4	0-1	4		11,849

Appearances
Goals

FA Cup

| 26 | Jan | 12 | R3 | A | West Ham United | L | 0-1 | 0-0 | | | 35,000 |

Appearances
Goals

	McInroy	Murray	England	Clunas	Allan	Andrews	Lynas	McInally	Halliday	Cresswell	Hargreaves	Wallace	McLean	Henderson	Dowsey	Wood	Bartley	Oakley	Parker	McKay	Wilks	Robinson	Morris	Wright	Bell	Whelan	Hall	
1	2	3	4	5	6	7	8	9	10	11																		1
1	2	3	4	5	6	7	10	9			8	11																2
1	2	3	4	5	6	7	10	9			8	11																3
1	2	3	4	5	6	7	10	9			8	11																4
1	2	3	4		6	7	10	9			8	11	5															5
1	2	3	4		6	7	10	9			8	11	5															6
1	2	3	4		6	7		9			11	5	8	10														7
1	2	3	4	5		7	10	9			11		8	6														8
1		3	4			7		9	11		10			6	2	5	8											9
1	2	3	4				10	9	11		7			6		5	8											10
1	2	3	4	6			10	9	11		7					5	8											11
1	2	3	4		6		10	9	11		7					5	8											12
1	2	3	4		6		10	9	11		7					5	8											13
1	2	3	4		6		10	9	11		7					5	8											14
1	2	3	4	6			10	9			11	5				8	7											15
1		3	4	5	6		10	9			11				2	8	7											16
1		3	4	5	6		10	9			11				2	8	7											17
1		3	4	5	6		10	9			11				2	8	7											18
1		3	4	5	6		10	9			11				2	8	7											19
1		3		5	6		10	9			11				2	4	8	7										20
1		3	4	5	6		10	9			11				2	8	7											21
1	3		4		6		10	9			11	5			2	8	7											22
1		3	4	5	6		10	9			11				2	8	7											23
1	2	3		5	6		10	9			11					8	7	4										24
1	2	3		6			10	9			11	5				8	7	4										25
1	2	3	4	5	6		10	9			11					8	7											27
1	2	3	4		6		10	9			11					8	7											28
1	2	3	4	5	6		10	9			11					8	7											29
1	2	3	4		6			9			11	5				8	7		10									30
1	2	3	4		6			9			11	5				8	7		10									31
	3		4	5	6						11				2	8	7		10	1								32
1		3	4	5	6		10	9			11					8	7				1							33
1	2	3	4	5	6		10	9			11					8	7											34
	2	3	4	5				9			11			6		8	7		10	1								35
	2	3	4	5	6			9			11					8	7		10	1								36
1	2	3	4	5	6			9			11					8	7		10									37
1	2	3		5	6		10	9			11					8	7	4	10									38
1	2	3	4		6			9			11				5	10	7		8									39
1	2	3	4					11			10				5	8		7	9		6							40
1		3	4	5	6			9			11					2	8	7		10								41
1	2	3		5	6	7	10	9			11					8		4										42
1		3	7	5	6		10	9								8		4	11			2						43
8	32	40	37	29	34	10	31	42	1	7	5	40	8	2	1	4	11	9	34	2	24	5	10	4	1	1		
			12				1	3	43		3	7					15		6		1							

	McInroy	Murray	England	Clunas	Allan	Andrews	Lynas	McInally	Halliday	Cresswell	Hargreaves	Wallace	McLean	Henderson	Dowsey	Wood	Bartley	Oakley	Parker	McKay	Wilks	Robinson	Morris	Wright	Bell	Whelan	Hall	
	2	3	4	5	6		10	9		11						8	7											26
	1	1	1	1	1		1	1		1						1	1											

David Halliday scored record number of goals for Sunderland in a season (43).

1929-30

Division One

Ground: Roker Park

Manager: John Cochrane

League Table

	P	W	D	L	F	A	Pts
Sheffield W	42	26	8	8	105	57	60
Derby Co	42	21	8	13	90	82	50
Manchester C	42	19	9	14	91	81	47
Aston Villa	42	21	5	16	92	83	47
Leeds U	42	20	6	16	79	63	46
Blackburn R	42	19	7	16	99	93	45
West Ham U	42	19	5	18	86	79	43
Leicester C	42	17	9	16	86	90	43
SUNDERLAND	42	18	7	17	76	80	43
Huddersfield T	42	17	9	16	63	69	43
Birmingham	42	16	9	17	67	62	41
Liverpool	42	16	9	17	63	79	41
Portsmouth	42	15	10	17	66	62	40
Arsenal	42	14	11	17	78	66	39
Bolton W	42	15	9	18	74	74	39
Middlesbrough	42	16	6	20	82	84	38
Manchester U	42	15	8	19	67	88	38
Grimsby T	42	15	7	20	73	89	37
Newcastle U	42	15	7	20	71	92	37
Sheffield U	42	15	6	21	91	96	36
Burnley	42	14	8	20	79	97	36
Everton	42	12	11	19	80	92	35

FA Cup Winners: Arsenal

Did you know that?

Roker Park's new Grandstand was officially opened before the home game against Manchester City on 7 September 1929. This 10,000 capacity stand, designed by Archibald Leitch and famous for its iron latticework, had cost £35,000 to construct.

Match 1: Lawley made debut
Match 2: McDougall made debut
Match 4: McPhee and Gunson made debuts & McGregor only game
Match 5: Gallacher made debut
Match 6: McInroy and McInally last games
Match 7: McPhee last game
Match 8: Bartley last game
Match 10: Eden made debut
Match 11: Halliday last game
Match 14: McNestry made debut
Match 15: Wilkins and Morrison made debuts
Match 16: Wilkins last game
Match 17: McNestry last game
Match 18: Robert Robinson made debut & Wright last game
Match 29: Urwin made debut
Match 30: England last game
Match 31: Oakley and Gunson last games
Match 32: Shaw made debut
Match 46: Allan last game

Match No.	Date		Round	Venue	Opponents	Result	FT	HT	Pos.	Scorers	Attendance
1	Aug	31		A	Derby County	L	0-3	0-2			13,938
2	Sep	7		H	Manchester City	W	5-2	5-0	13	Halliday (3), McMullen o.g., McKay	33,869
3		10		A	Burnley	L	0-2	0-0	15		19,691
4		14		A	Portsmouth	D	1-1	0-0	18	Halliday	20,157
5		21		H	Arsenal	L	0-1	0-0	21		34,804
6		28		A	Aston Villa	L	1-2	1-1	21	McLean	41,919
7	Oct	2		H	Everton	D	2-2	2-2	21	McLean, Gurney	19,333
8		5		H	Leeds United	L	1-4	1-1	21	Gurney	23,503
9		12		A	Sheffield Wed.	D	1-1	0-1	21	Wood	23,158
10		19		H	Newcastle United	W	1-0	1-0	20	Gunson	58,519
11		26		A	Sheffield United	L	2-4	1-3	22	Gunson, McKay	19,025
12	Nov	2		H	Huddersfield Town	W	1-0	1-0	20	Clunas (pen)	18,712
13		9		A	Middlesbrough	L	0-3	0-1	22		29,953
14		16		H	Leicester City	W	2-1	1-1	20	Clunas, Gunson	16,732
15		23		A	Grimsby Town	W	1-0	0-0	19	Gunson	10,640
16		30		H	Manchester United	L	2-4	1-1	22	Gunson, Morrison	11,508
17	Dec	7		A	West Ham United	D	1-1	0-0	21	Wright	16,456
18		14		H	Liverpool	L	1-2	1-3	22	Morrison (2)	21,396
19		21		A	Birmingham	L	1-3	0-2	22	Gunson	16,327
20		25		A	Blackburn Rovers	L	3-5	3-3	22	Gunson (2), Gallacher	19,704
21		26		H	Blackburn Rovers	W	3-1	1-1	21	McLean, Wood, Gunson	25,109
22		28		H	Derby County	W	3-1	1-0	19	Morrison, Wood, McDougall	23,667
23	Jan	1		H	Burnley	D	3-3	1-2	19	Wood, Morrsion, Gunson	28,615
24		4		A	Manchester City	D	2-2	1-0	19	Gurney, McLean	37,258
26		18		A	Portsmouth	D	1-1	1-1	19	Wood	26,100
28	Feb	1		H	Aston Villa	W	4-1	1-0	19	Gunson, Clunas (2, 1 pen), Wood	8,909
29		8		A	Leeds United	L	0-5	0-3	20		22,377
32		22		A	Newcastle United	L	0-3	0-1	20		49,304
33	Mar	1		H	Sheffield United	W	3-2	1-2	20	McLean, Gurney, Clunas	17,713
34		8		A	Huddersfield Town	W	2-0	1-0	18	Eden (2)	19,601
35		15		H	Middlesbrough	W	3-2	1-1	19	Ashman o.g., Gurney, Eden	32,874
36		22		A	Leicester City	W	2-1	1-1	16	Eden, McLean	16,979
37		29		H	Grimsby Town	W	2-0	1-0	15	Gallacher, McLean	23,842
38	Apr	5		A	Manchester United	L	1-2	0-0	16	Gurney	13,230
39		12		H	West Ham United	W	4-2	3-2	15	Eden, Gurney (2), Urwin	20,459
40		18		A	Bolton Wanderers	L	0-3	0-0	16		16,333
41		19		A	Liverpool	W	6-0	2-0	14	Gurney (4), Lawley, Wood	22,799
42		21		H	Bolton Wanderers	W	4-1	4-1	13	Gallacher (2), Gurney, Clunas (pen)	28,072
43		26		H	Birmingham	W	2-0	0-0	10	Wood, Clunas (pen)	15,486
44		28		A	Arsenal	W	1-0	1-0	8	Gurney	31,259
45		30		H	Sheffield Wed.	L	2-4	1-1	9	Gurney, Eden	26,259
46	May	3		A	Everton	L	1-4	1-2	9	Clunas	51,133

Appearance
Goal

FA Cup

Match No.	Date		Round	Venue	Opponents	Result	FT	HT		Scorers	Attendance
25	Jan	11	R3	A	Coventry City	W	2-1	1-0		Gallacher, Gurney	31,67
27		25	R4	H	Cardiff City	W	2-1	1-0		Gurney, McLean	49,62
30	Feb	15	R5	H	Nottingham Forest	D	2-2	2-0		McLean, Gunson	39,82
31		19	R5r	A	Nottingham Forest	L	1-3	1-0		Eden	31,10

Appearance
Goal

	McInroy	Murray	England	Clunas	Allan	Andrews	Lawley	McKay	Halliday	Wright	McLean	McDougall	McInally	Morris	Bartley	McPhee	McGregor	Gurney	Gunson	Whelan	Gallacher	Bell	Wood	Eden	Oakley	McNestry	Wilkins	Morrison	Robinson, R.	Urwin	Shaw	
1	1	2	3	4	5	6	7	8	9	10	11																					1
2	1	2	3	4		6	7	8	9		11	5	10																			2
3	1	2	3	4		6	7	8	9		11	5	10																			3
4	1	2	3					9			5			4	6	7	8	10	11													4
5	1	2	3					9	8			5	10	4		7				6	11											5
6	1	2	3					8	9		11	5	10	4	6	7																6
7		2	3					8	10		11	5		4	6	7		9			1											7
8		2	3					10	9	7	11	5		4	6			8			1											8
9		2	3	4	6		7	8	9		11	5									1	10										9
10		2	3	4	6			8	9			5							11		1	10	7									10
11		2	3	4	6			8	9			5							11		1	10	7									11
12		2	3	4	6				8			5						9	11		1	10	7									12
13			3	4	6				8			5						9	11		1	10	7	2								13
14			3	4	6		8		9			5							11		1	10		2	7							14
15				4	6				10			5							11		1			2	7	8	9					15
16				4	6				10			5							11		1			2	7	8	9					16
17			3		6		8		10		5			4					11		1			2	7		9					17
18			3			6	8		10	7	5			4					11					2			9	1				18
19		2	3	4		6				7	5								11		10	1	8				9					19
20		2	3	4		6				7	5								11		10	1	8				9					20
21			3	4		6				7	5								11		10		8	2			9	1				21
22			3	4		6				7	5								11		10		8	2			9	1				22
23			3	4		6				7	5								11		10		8				9	1				23
24				4	6			8		7	5							9	11	3	10			2				1				24
26		2		4	6					7	5								11	3	10	8					9	1				26
28		3		4	5	6												9	11		10	8	7	2				1				28
29		3		4	5	6												9	11		10	8		2			1	7				29
32		2		4		6	8				11	5									1	10				9			7	3		32
33		2		4		6					11	5						9			10		7					1	8	3		33
34		2		4		6					11	5						9			10		7					1	8	3		34
35		2		4		6					11	5						9			10		7					1	8	3		35
36		2		4		6					11	5						9			10		7					1	8	3		36
37		2		4		6					11	5						9			10		7					1	8	3		37
38		2		4		6					11	5						9			10		7					1	8	3		38
39		2		4		6					11	5						9				10	7					1	8	3		39
40		2		4		6					11	5						9			10		7					1	8	3		40
41		2		4		6	11					5						9				10	7					1		3		41
42		2		4		6	11					5						9			10	8	7					1		3		42
43		2		4		6	11					5						9			10	8	7					1		3		43
44		2		4		6	11					5						9			10	8	7					1		3		44
45		2		4	5	6					11							9			10		7					1	8	3		45
46		2		4	5	6	11											9			10		7					1	8	3		46
	38	17	35	14	28	9	14	11	10	25	37	4	7	4	4	1	22	19	3	22	14	20	19	12	4	2	11	22	13	15		
		8			1	2	4		7	1							15	11		4		8	6				5		1			

	McInroy	Murray	England	Clunas	Allan	Andrews	Lawley	McKay	Halliday	Wright	McLean	McDougall	McInally	Morris	Bartley	McPhee	McGregor	Gurney	Gunson	Whelan	Gallacher	Bell	Wood	Eden	Oakley	McNestry	Wilkins	Morrison	Robinson, R.	Urwin	Shaw	
25		3	4		6		8			7	5							9	11		10			2			1					25
27	3		4		6					7	5							9	11		10	8		2			1					27
30	2	3	4	5	6					8								9	11		10		7				1					30
31	3		5		6					8		4						11	10			7	2		9	1						31
	3	2	4	1	4		1			4	2	1						3	4		4	1	2	3		1	4					
										2								2	1		1		1									

Ernie England holds the record of most outfield appearances for Sunderland without scoring a goal (352).

1930-31

Division One

Ground: Roker Park

Manager: John Cochrane

League Table

	P	W	D	L	F	A	Pts
Arsenal	42	28	10	4	127	59	66
Aston Villa	42	25	9	8	128	78	59
Sheffield W	42	22	8	12	102	75	52
Portsmouth	42	18	13	11	84	67	49
Huddersfield T	42	18	12	12	81	65	48
Derby Co	42	18	10	14	94	79	46
Middlesbrough	42	19	8	15	98	90	46
Manchester C	42	18	10	14	75	70	46
Liverpool	42	15	12	15	86	85	42
Blackburn R	42	17	8	17	83	84	42
SUNDERLAND	42	16	9	17	89	85	41
Chelsea	42	15	10	17	64	67	40
Grimsby T	42	17	5	20	82	87	39
Bolton W	42	15	9	18	68	81	39
Sheffield U	42	14	10	18	78	84	38
Leicester C	42	16	6	20	80	95	38
Newcastle U	42	15	6	21	78	87	36
West Ham U	42	14	8	20	79	94	36
Birmingham	42	13	10	19	55	70	36
Blackpool	42	11	10	21	71	125	32
Leeds U	42	12	7	23	68	81	31
Manchester U	42	7	8	27	53	115	22

FA Cup Winners: West Bromwich Albion

Did you know that?

The most goals scored by Sunderland in the first half of a game is seven, Sunderland v Blackburn Rovers, 4 February 1931, half time score 7-0.

Match 1: Connor made debut
Match 3: Hastings made debut
Match 7: McLean last game
Match 8: Lawley last game
Match 9: Leonard made debut
Match 11: McKay last game
Match 12: Thorpe made debut
Match 14: Bell and Clunas last games
Match 15: Middleton made debut
Match 21: Robert Robinson last game
Match 26: Keeton made debut
Match 30: Devine made debut
Match 44: Andrews and Wood last games
Match 46: Morrison last game
Match 48: Johnston made debut
Match 49: Whelan and George Robinson last games

Match No.	Date	Round	Venue	Opponents	Result	FT	HT	Pos.	Scorers	Attendance
1	Aug 30		H	Manchester City	D	3-3	0-2		Urwin, McDougall, Gurney	32,892
2	Sep 3		A	Sheffield United	D	3-3	1-1	8	Wood, Gurney, Gibson o.g.	15,239
3	6		A	Portsmouth	D	1-1	1-1	9	Wood	23,270
4	10		H	Derby County	L	1-3	1-2	14	Gurney	23,805
5	13		H	Arsenal	L	1-4	1-2	18	Morrison	26,525
6	17		A	Derby County	L	1-4	0-1	21	Gurney	8,911
7	20		A	Blackburn Rovers	L	0-3	0-2	21		18,081
8	27		H	Blackpool	L	2-4	1-3	21	Gurney, Morrison	20,087
9	Oct 4		A	Leeds United	W	3-0	1-0	20	Leonard, Connor, Gurney	16,378
10	11		H	Aston Villa	D	1-1	0-1	21	Leonard	34,847
11	18		A	Middlesbrough	L	0-1	0-0	21		30,307
12	25		H	Huddersfield Town	W	4-2	1-1	20	Urwin (3), Gurney	27,554
13	Nov 1		A	Sheffield Wed.	L	2-7	2-3	21	Gurney, Connor	19,299
14	8		H	Grimsby Town	W	3-2	1-1	19	Gurney, Connor (2)	21,225
15	15		A	Bolton Wanderers	D	2-2	2-1	20	Gurney, Connor	10,835
16	22		H	Newcastle United	W	5-0	2-0	16	Eden (2), Connor (2), Gurney	24,120
17	29		A	Manchester United	D	1-1	0-0	16	Gurney	10,971
18	Dec 6		H	Liverpool	W	6-5	4-3	16	Leonard, Connor, Gurney (3), Lucas o.g.	22,616
19	13		A	Chelsea	L	0-5	0-3	16		31,295
20	20		H	West Ham United	W	6-1	2-1	16	Leonard (3), Eden, Connor, Gurney	20,846
21	25		H	Leicester City	L	2-5	0-2	16	Gurney, Leonard	32,618
22	26		A	Leicester City	D	1-1	1-1	16	Gallacher	23,108
23	27		A	Manchester City	L	0-2	0-1	17		28,696
24	Jan 3		H	Portsmouth	D	0-0	0-0	17		24,100
26	17		A	Arsenal	W	3-1	0-1	16	Gurney (2), Eden	35,975
29	31		A	Blackpool	L	1-3	1-1	16	Eden	7,310
30	Feb 4		H	Blackburn Rovers	W	8-2	7-0	16	Leonard (3), Gurney, Eden (3), Devine	10,635
31	7		H	Leeds United	W	4-0	2-0	16	Leonard (2), Gurney, Eden	25,765
33	18		A	Aston Villa	L	2-4	1-4	15	Leonard (2)	10,875
34	21		H	Middlesbrough	D	1-1	1-1	16	Leonard	31,183
37	Mar 7		H	Sheffield Wed.	W	5-1	3-1	14	Gurney (3), Andrews, Eden	14,987
39	16		A	Huddersfield Town	L	0-2	0-0	15		4,091
40	21		H	Bolton Wanderers	W	3-1	2-0	14	Gurney (2), Connor	17,143
41	24		A	Grimsby Town	L	1-2	0-1	14	Gallacher	9,396
42	28		A	Newcastle United	L	0-2	0-0	17		33,419
43	Apr 3		H	Birmingham	W	1-0	0-0	15	Wood	18,180
44	4		A	Manchester United	L	1-2	1-2	15	Leonard	13,590
45	6		A	Birmingham	L	0-1	0-0	16		11,207
46	11		H	Liverpool	W	4-2	1-0	15	Leonard, Gurney (2), Connor	19,122
47	18		H	Chelsea	W	2-0	2-0	13	Gurney, Robinson	8,854
48	25		A	West Ham United	W	3-0	2-0	11	Devine, Keeton, Gurney	10,111
49	May 2		H	Sheffield United	W	2-1	1-1	11	Gurney, Robinson	10,734

Appearances
Goals

FA Cup

Match No.	Date	Round	Venue	Opponents	Result	FT	HT	Pos.	Scorers	Attendance
25	Jan 10	R3	H	Southampton	W	2-0	1-0		Eden, Urwin	35,37
27	24	R4	A	Bolton Wanderers	D	1-1	0-0		Leonard	36,60
28	28	R4r	H	Bolton Wanderers	W	3-1	1-1		Connor (2), Leonard	46,90
32	Feb 14	R5	H	Sheffield United	W	2-1	1-1		Connor, Gurney	63,01
35	28	R6	H	Exeter City	D	1-1	1-0		Connor	51,64
36	Mar 4	R6r	A	Exeter City	W	4-2	2-1		Connor (2), Eden, Gurney	20,98
38	14	S	N*	Birmingham	L	0-2	0-1			43,57

* at Elland Road

Appearances
Goals

	Robinson, R.	Murray	Shaw	Clunas	McDougall	Andrews	Eden	Urwin	Gurney	Gallacher	Connor	Wood	Morris	Hastings	Bell	Morrison	McLean	Lawley	Leonard	McKay	Thorpe	Robinson, G.	Middleton	Whelan	Hall	Keeton	Devine	Johnston	
1	2	3	4	5	6	7	8	9	10	11																			1
1	2	3	4	5	6	7	8	9		11	10																		2
1	2	3		5		7	10	9		11	8	4	6																3
	2	3		5		7	10	9		11	8	4	6	1															4
	2	3	4	5		7	8		10	11			6	1	9														5
1	2	3	4	5			7	9	8	11			6			10													6
1	2	3	4	5			7		8	11			6		9	10													7
1	2	3	4	5				8	10	11			6		9		7												8
1	2	3	4	5		7	8	9		11			6			10													9
1	2	3	4	5		7	8	9		11			6			10													10
1	2	3	4	5			7	9		11			6			10	8												11
	2	3	4	5			8	9		11			6			10		1	7										12
1	2	3	4	5	6		8	9		11						10			7										13
	2	3	4	5			8	9		11			6	1		10			7										14
	2	3		5		7	8	9		11	4		6			10		1											15
	2	3		5		7	8	9		11		4	6			10		1											16
		3		5		7	8	9		11		4	6			10		1	2										17
	2	3		5		7	8	9		11		4	6			10		1											18
	2	3		5		7	8	9		11		4	6			10		1											19
1	2	3		5		7	8	9		11		4	6			10													20
1	2	3		5		7	8	9		11		4	6			10													21
	2	3		5		7		9	8	11		4	6			10		1											22
		3		5		7	8	9		11		4				10		1			6	2							23
	2	3		5		7	8	9		11		4	6			10		1											24
	2	3		5		7		9	10	11		4	6					1		8									26
		3		5		7		9	8	11		4	6			10		1		2									29
	2	3		5		7		9		11		4	6			10		1					8						30
	2	3		5	6	7		9		11		4	6			10		1					8						31
	2	3		5		7		9		11		4	6			10		1					8						33
			5			7		9		11		4	6			10		1	3	2	8								34
	3		5	6	7	8	9		11				4					1		2		10							37
		3		5		7	8	9		11		6	4					1		2		10							39
	2	3		5			7	8	9	10	11		6	4				1											40
	2	3		5			7	10	9	11				4		6		1				8							41
	2	3		5		7	8	9		11		4	6					1				10							42
	2	3		5	6	7				11	9	4				10		1				8							43
	2	3			6	7	4			11	9	5				10		1				8							44
		3	5			11	9	7			4							1	6	2		8							45
		3	5				9		11		4			7		10		1	6	2		8							46
		3	5				9		11		4					10		7	1	6	2	8							47
		3					9		11		4							7	1	6	2	8	10	5					48
		3	5				9		11		4							7	1	6	2	8	10						49
2	32	40	12	40	7	30	29	38	11	40	6	28	30	3	4	2	1	26	1	4	6	23	8	10	6	12	1		
			1		1	11	4	30	2	11	3					2		17		2			1	2					

	2	3		5		7	8	9		11		4	6			10		1											25
	2	3		5		7	8	9		11		4	6			10		1											27
	2	3		5		7	8	9		11		4	6			10		1											28
	2	3		5		7		9		11		4	6			10		1				8							32
		3		5		7		9		11		4	6			10		1		2		8							35
		3		5	6	7		9		11		4				10		1		2		8							36
	2	3		5	6	7		9		11		4				10		1				8							38
	5	7		7	2	7	3	7		7		5	7			7		7		2		4							
				2	1	2		6				2						2											

Billy Clunas

Sunderland's record penalty scorer with at least 30 successful spot kicks; hence his nickname of 'The Penalty King'.

385

1931-32

Division One

Ground: Roker Park
Manager: John Cochrane

League Table

	P	W	D	L	F	A	Pts
Everton	42	26	4	12	116	64	56
Arsenal	42	22	10	10	90	48	54
Sheffield W	42	22	6	14	96	82	50
Huddersfield T	42	19	10	13	80	63	48
Aston Villa	42	19	8	15	104	72	46
WBA	42	20	6	16	77	55	46
Sheffield U	42	20	6	16	80	75	46
Portsmouth	42	19	7	16	62	62	45
Birmingham	42	18	8	16	78	67	44
Liverpool	42	19	6	17	81	93	44
Newcastle U	42	18	6	18	80	87	42
Chelsea	42	16	8	18	69	73	40
SUNDERLAND	42	15	10	17	67	73	40
Manchester C	42	13	12	17	83	73	38
Derby Co	42	14	10	18	71	75	38
Blackburn R	42	16	6	20	89	95	38
Bolton W	42	17	4	21	72	80	38
Middlesbrough	42	15	8	19	64	89	38
Leicester C	42	15	7	20	74	94	37
Blackpool	42	12	9	21	65	102	33
Grimsby T	42	13	6	23	67	98	32
West Ham U	42	12	7	23	62	107	31

FA Cup Winners: Newcastle United

Did you know that?

Hendon born Horatio Stratton Carter fulfilled a boyhood dream when he signed professional forms with Sunderland on 12 November 1931. His starting wage was £3 per week.

Match 4: Welsby made debut
Match 9: Temple made debut
Match 10: Thomson made debut
Match 14: Vinall made debut
Match 17: Keeton last game
Match 21: Laird made debut
Match 23: Laird last game
Match 25: Poulter made debut & Wallace only game
Match 27: Bedford made debut & Morris last game
Match 28: Poulter last game
Match 30: Yorston made debut
Match 34: Leonard last game
Match 38: Edgar made debut
Match 40: Eden last game
Match 41: Welsby last game
Match 46: Bedford last game

Match No.	Date	Round	Venue	Opponents	Result	FT	HT	Pos.	Scorers	Attendance
1	Aug 29		A	Manchester City	D	1-1	0-0		Gallacher	31,294
2	Sep 2		H	West Bromwich Albion	W	2-1	2-0	6	Devine, Connor	16,981
3	5		H	Everton	L	2-3	1-2	11	Eden, Gurney	28,474
4	7		A	West Bromwich Albion	L	0-1	0-1	12		24,906
5	12		A	Arsenal	L	0-2	0-0	18		22,926
6	16		H	Birmingham	L	2-3	0-2	19	Gurney, Connor	20,376
7	19		H	Blackpool	W	4-0	2-0	16	Gallacher, Gurney (2), Welsby	14,901
8	23		A	Birmingham	D	0-0	0-0	13		9,761
9	26		A	Sheffield United	D	1-1	0-1	13	Temple	22,259
10	Oct 3		H	Blackburn Rovers	D	2-2	2-0	13	Gurney, Connor (pen)	20,566
11	10		A	Portsmouth	D	0-0	0-0	12		21,044
12	17		H	Chelsea	W	2-1	2-1	12	Temple, Connor	17,294
13	24		A	Huddersfield Town	L	1-4	1-3	14	Devine	11,071
14	31		H	Middlesbrough	D	0-0	0-0	14		28,387
15	Nov 7		A	Bolton Wanderers	L	1-3	1-1	14	Vinall	14,928
16	14		H	Liverpool	L	1-3	1-2	17	Gurney	17,646
17	21		A	Leicester City	L	0-5	0-2	17		14,098
18	28		H	Newcastle United	L	1-4	0-3	19	Devine	34,195
19	Dec 5		A	Grimsby Town	W	3-1	1-1	19	Gurney, Gallacher (2)	8,962
20	12		H	Sheffield Wed.	W	3-1	1-1	17	Gurney (3)	21,818
21	19		A	West Ham United	D	2-2	1-1	16	Gurney (2)	6,505
22	26		A	Derby County	L	1-3	0-2	20	Vinall	23,257
23	Jan 1		H	Derby County	D	0-0	0-0	20		23,086
24	2		H	Manchester City	L	2-5	1-4	20	Gallacher (2)	19,689
27	16		A	Everton	L	2-4	1-2	20	Leonard, Shaw (pen)	29,491
30	30		A	Blackpool	L	2-3	2-0	20	O'Donnell o.g., Yorston	14,547
32	Feb 6		H	Sheffield United	W	1-0	0-0	20	Yorston	23,294
33	13		A	Blackburn Rovers	L	2-5	1-2	20	Yorston (2)	10,934
34	20		H	Portsmouth	W	5-1	1-0	20	Bedford, Yorston (2), Temple, Leonard	24,894
35	Mar 2		A	Chelsea	D	2-2	1-1	20	Temple, Yorston	20,087
36	5		H	Huddersfield Town	L	1-3	0-1	20	Temple	29,549
37	12		A	Middlesbrough	W	1-0	1-0	19	Yorston	21,551
38	19		H	Bolton Wanderers	W	3-0	2-0	19	Gallacher, Yorston, Connor	21,765
39	25		H	Aston Villa	D	1-1	1-0	19	Gallacher	44,866
40	26		A	Liverpool	W	2-1	0-1	19	Eden, Gurney	22,512
41	28		A	Aston Villa	L	0-2	0-2	19		25,401
42	Apr 2		H	Leicester City	W	4-1	1-0	18	Temple, Gurney, Shaw (pen), Devine	16,390
43	6		H	Arsenal	W	2-0	1-0	15	Gallacher, Devine	30,443
44	9		A	Newcastle United	W	2-1	1-0	15	Yorston, Gallacher	43,599
45	16		H	Grimsby Town	W	2-0	2-0	14	Gurney, Gallacher	17,614
46	23		A	Sheffield Wed.	L	2-3	1-2	15	Temple, Bedford	7,908
47	30		H	West Ham United	W	2-0	2-0	13	Yorston (2)	13,528

Appearances
Goals

FA Cup

Match No.	Date	Round	Venue	Opponents	Result	FT	HT	Scorers	Attendance
25	Jan 9	R3	H	Southampton	D	0-0	0-0		28,931
26	13	R3r	A	Southampton	W	4-2	3-0	Vinall, Poulter (2), Shaw (pen)	22,927
28	23	R4	H	Stoke City	D	1-1	0-1	McDougall	43,700
29	28	R4r	A	Stoke City	D	1-1(aet)	0-1	Gallacher	30,575
31	Feb 1	R4r2	N*	Stoke City	L	1-2	0-0	Gallacher	7,470

* at Maine Road

Appearances
Goals

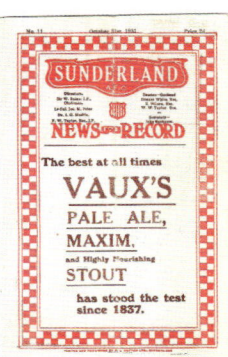

	Middleton	Murray	Shaw	Morris	McDougall	Hastings	Eden	Gallacher	Gurney	Devine	Connor	Keeton	Welsby	Johnston	Urwin	Temple	Vinall	Thomson	Thorpe	Hall	Leonard	Laird	Bedford	Yorston	Edgar	Wallace	Poulter	
1	2	3	4	5	6	7	8	9	10	11																		1
1	2	3	4	5	6	7	8	9	10	11																		2
1	2	3	4	5	6	7		9	10	11	8																	3
1	2	3	4	5	6		10	9		11	8	7																4
1	2	3	4	5	6	7	8	9	10	11																		5
1	2	3	4	5	6	7	8	9	10	11																		6
1	2	3	4	5	6	7	8	9	10		11																	7
1	2	3	4		6	7		9	10	11		5	8															8
1	2	3	6	5	4		10	9		11			8	7														9
1	2	3	6	5				9		11	8		10	7	4													10
1	2	3	6	5	4				10	11	9		8	7														11
1	2	3	4	5	6			9	10	11	8			7														12
1	2	3	4	5	6		8	9	10	11				7														13
1	2	3	4	5	6			7	10	11			8			9												14
1	2	3	4	5	6		8	7	10	11						9												15
1	2	3	4	5	6	7		8	10	11						9												16
	4	3		5		7		8	6	11	10					9	1	2										17
3	5	4			10	8	6	11				7				9	1	2										18
	2	3		5	4	8	9	6	11							7	1		10									19
	2	3		5	4	8	9	6	11							7	1		10									20
	2	3		5	4	8		9	6	11						7	1			10								21
	2	3		5	4	8	9	6		11						7	1		10									22
	2	3		5	4	8		6		11						7	1		10	9								23
	2	3	4	5		7	8		6	11				9			10	1										24
		3	6	5	4					11				7		10	1	2	9		8							27
	2	3		5	4			6		11				7			1		10		8	9						30
	2	3			4	8		6		11		5		7			1		10			9						32
	2	3			4			6		11		5		7	8	1			10			9						33
	2	3			4			6		11		5		7			1		10		8	9						34
	2	3			4		10	6		11		5		7			1				8	9						35
	2	3			4		10	6		11		5		7			1				8	9						36
1	2	3		5	4	10	8	6		11				7								9						37
1	2	3		5	4	10	8			11				7								9	6					38
1	2	3		5	4	10	8			11				7								9	6					39
1	2	3		5		7	11	8								4	10					9	6					40
	3				4						11	5		7		10		2			8	9	6					41
1	2	3		5	4		11	8	10					7								9	6					42
1	2	3		5	4		11	8	10					7								9	6					43
1	2	3		5	4		11	8	10					7								9	6					44
1	2	3		5	4		10	8	6	11				7								9						45
1	2	3		5	4		10		6	11				7							8	9						46
1	2	3		5	4		10	8	6	11				7								9						47
27	40	42	19	34	37	11	29	30	34	36	6	3	7	22	2	15	15	4	9	2	7	17	7					
		2				2	11	15	5	5		1		7		2			2		2	12						

	Middleton	Murray	Shaw	Morris	McDougall	Hastings	Eden	Gallacher	Gurney	Devine	Connor	Keeton	Welsby	Johnston	Urwin	Temple	Vinall	Thomson	Thorpe	Hall	Leonard	Laird	Bedford	Yorston	Edgar	Wallace	Poulter	
	2	3			4	7	8		6	11						10	1						5	9				25
		3		5	4		8		6	11			7			10	1	2						9				26
	2	3		5	4		8		6	11						10	1							9				28
	2	3		5	4		10		6	11			8	9		7	1											29
		3			4	7	10		6	11		5	8			9	1	2										31
3	5		3	5	2	5		5	5			1	2	3		5	5	2					1	3				
	1		1		2									1				2										

Benny Yorston

Benny scored 12 goals in 17 games after signing from Aberdeen on 23 January 1932. This included seven in his first eight games and signficantly helped Sunderland avoid a first ever relegation.

387

1932-33

Division One

Ground: Roker Park

Manager: John Cochrane

League Table

	P	W	D	L	F	A	Pts
Arsenal	42	25	8	9	118	61	58
Aston Villa	42	23	8	11	92	67	54
Sheffield W	42	21	9	12	80	68	51
WBA	42	20	9	13	83	70	49
Newcastle U	42	22	5	15	71	63	49
Huddersfield T	42	18	11	13	66	53	47
Derby Co	42	15	14	13	76	69	44
Leeds U	42	15	14	13	59	62	44
Portsmouth	42	18	7	17	74	76	43
Sheffield U	42	17	9	16	74	80	43
Everton	42	16	9	17	81	74	41
SUNDERLAND	42	15	10	17	63	80	40
Birmingham	42	14	11	17	57	57	39
Liverpool	42	14	11	17	79	84	39
Blackburn R	42	14	10	18	76	102	38
Manchester C	42	16	5	21	68	71	37
Middlesbrough	42	14	9	19	63	73	37
Chelsea	42	14	7	21	63	73	35
Leicester C	42	11	13	18	75	89	35
Wolverhampton W	42	13	9	20	80	96	35
Bolton W	42	12	9	21	78	92	33
Blackpool	42	14	5	23	69	85	33

FA Cup Winners: Everton

Did you know that?

Roker Park witnessed its highest aggregate score in a competitive game; 11 goals in a 7-4 win over Bolton Wanderers on 29 October 1932. This equalled the 6-5 win over Liverpool two years earlier.

Match 1: Davis made debut
Match 2: McNab made debut
Match 3: Vinall last game
Match 4: Ives made debut
Match 5: Beach made debut
Match 10: Carter made debut & Beach last game
Match 36: Gibson made debut
Match 38: Thorley made debut
Match 39: Robert Middleton and Temple last games
Match 45: Devine last game
Match 47: Ainsley made debut & Gibson last game

Match No.	Date	Round	Venue	Opponents	Result	FT	HT	Pos.	Scorers	Attendance
1	Aug 27		H	Manchester City	W	3-2	1-0		Yorston, Cowan o.g., Gurney	27,056
2	29		A	Aston Villa	L	0-1	0-1	7		23,802
3	Sep 3		A	Arsenal	L	1-6	0-3	18	Davis	28,896
4	7		H	Aston Villa	D	1-1	0-1	16	Temple	22,214
5	10		H	Everton	W	3-1	1-1	9	Temple, Gurney, Gallacher	23,005
6	17		A	Blackpool	L	1-3	0-0	15	Temple	18,234
7	24		H	Derby County	L	0-2	0-0	18		19,120
8	Oct 1		A	Blackburn Rovers	W	3-1	0-1	13	Gallacher (3)	10,545
9	8		H	Leeds United	D	0-0	0-0	15		9,651
10	15		A	Sheffield Wed.	L	1-3	0-2	15	Yorston	11,385
11	22		A	Middlesbrough	W	2-1	1-1	15	Connor, Yorston	14,491
12	29		H	Bolton Wanderers	W	7-4	6-2	11	Connor, Gurney (4), Carter, Temple	10,182
13	Nov 5		A	Huddersfield Town	L	1-2	0-2	12	Temple	13,253
14	12		H	Sheffield United	D	2-2	2-2	12	Carter, Davis	12,222
15	19		A	Wolverhampton W.	W	2-0	2-0	11	Gurney (2)	18,390
16	26		H	Newcastle United	L	0-2	0-1	13		38,401
17	Dec 3		A	Liverpool	D	3-3	2-2	12	Connor (2), Carter	18,568
18	10		H	Leicester City	W	2-1	1-0	11	Carter (2)	9,225
19	17		A	Portsmouth	W	3-1	3-0	10	Thomson, Gurney (2)	14,917
20	24		H	Chelsea	W	2-1	2-1	9	Yorston, Davis	21,494
21	26		A	West Bromwich Albion	L	1-5	0-2	9	Yorston	26,175
22	31		A	Manchester City	W	4-2	3-2	10	Gurney (2), Connor, Gallacher	24,036
23	Jan 2		H	West Bromwich Albion	D	2-2	2-2	8	Gurney, Davis	28,095
24	7		H	Arsenal	W	3-2	1-2	8	Gallacher (2), Carter	36,707
26	21		A	Everton	L	1-6	0-4	9	Connor	23,173
28	Feb 1		H	Blackpool	D	1-1	0-0	9	McDougall	19,873
29	4		A	Derby County	L	0-3	0-0	10		15,213
30	11		H	Blackburn Rovers	W	4-2	0-2	9	Davis (3), Gurney	15,939
32	22		A	Leeds United	W	3-2	1-2	9	Yorston (2), Gallacher	7,971
33	25		H	Sheffield Wed.	L	1-2	1-2	9	Gallacher	10,074
36	Mar 11		A	Bolton Wanderers	D	0-0	0-0	9		10,353
37	18		H	Huddersfield Town	L	1-2	1-1	10	Davis	14,494
38	22		H	Middlesbrough	D	0-0	0-0	9		9,005
39	25		A	Sheffield United	L	0-3	0-2	11		14,062
40	Apr 1		H	Wolverhampton W.	L	0-1	0-1	12		8,273
41	8		A	Newcastle United	W	1-0	1-0	11	Gurney	35,613
42	14		H	Birmingham	W	1-0	0-0	9	Connor	14,658
43	15		H	Liverpool	D	0-0	0-0	10		8,725
44	17		A	Birmingham	L	0-2	0-1	10		12,596
45	22		A	Leicester City	L	2-4	0-2	12	Gallacher, Gurney	13,466
46	29		H	Portsmouth	L	0-3	0-2	12		3,911
47	May 6		A	Chelsea	D	1-1	0-0	12	Gibson	22,322

Appearances
Goals

FA Cup

25	Jan 14	R3	A	Hull City	W	2-0	0-0		Gurney, Connor	22,566
27	28	R4	A	Aston Villa	W	3-0	1-0		Gurney (3)	53,686
31	Feb 18	R5	A	Blackpool	W	1-0	0-0		Gurney	46,950
34	Mar 4	R6	A	Derby County	D	4-4	3-3		Connor, Davis, Gurney (2)	34,218
35	8	R6r	H	Derby County	L	0-1(aet)	0-0			75,118

Appearances
Goals

	Middleton	Murray	Shaw	Hastings	McDougall	Devine	Davis	Gurney	Yorston	Gallacher	Connor	Edgar	McNab	Vinall	Ives	Temple	Johnston	Thorpe	Thomson	Beach	Carter	Hall	Gibson	Thorley	Ainsley	
1	2	3	4	5	6	7	8	9	10	11																1
1	2	3	4	5		7	9		10	11	6	8														2
1	2	3	4	5	6	7	9		10	11			8													3
1	2		4	5	10	8	9			11		6			3	7										4
1	2		4	5	10	8	9			11		6			3	7										5
1	2		4	5	10	8	9			11		6			3	7										6
1	2	3	4		10	8	9			11		6			7	5										7
	2	3		5	10		9			11		6				7		1	4	8						8
	2	3	4	5	6	7		9	10	11								1		8						9
	2	3		5	6	7			9		11							1	4	8	10					10
	2	3		5			8	9		11	6			7				1	4		10					11
	2	3		5			9		8	11	6			7				1	4		10					12
	2	3		5			9		8	11	6			7				1	4		10					13
	2	3		5	6	7	9		8	11								1	4		10					14
	2	3		5	6	7	9		8	11								1	4		10					15
	2	3		5	6	7	9		8	11								1	4		10					16
		3	6	5		7	9		8	11								1	4		10	2				17
		3	6	5		7	9		8	11								1	4		10	2				18
		3	6	5		7	9		8	11								1	4		10	2				19
		3	6	5		7		9	8	11								1	4		10	2				20
		3	6	5		7		9	8	11								1	4		10	2				21
		3	6			7	9		8	11							5	1	4		10	2				22
		3	6			7	9		8	11							5	1	4		10	2				23
	2	3	6	5		7	9		8	11								1	4		10					24
	2		6		10	7		9	8	11				3			5	1	4							26
	2	3	6	5		8	7			9		11						1	4		10					28
	2	3				8	7		9		11	6					5	1	4		10					29
	2	3		5			7	9	8			11	6					1	4		10					30
		3			10	7		9	8	11	6						5	1	4			2				32
	2	3		5		7	9		8	11	6							1	4		10					33
	3	4	5	10	7		8		11	6								1				2	9			36
	2	3		5		7		9	8	11	6							1	4		10					37
1		3	8	5		7		9	10		6								4			2		11		38
1	2	3		5	10			9	8		6	4			7									11		39
	2	3	8	5		7		9	11		6							1	4		10					40
	2	3		5	10	7	9		8	11	6							1	4							41
	2	3		5	10	7	9		8	11	6							1	4							42
	2	3	6			7	9	8	11		5							1	4		10					43
	2	3	6		10	7	9		8		5							1	4			11				44
	2	3	6	5	10	7	9			11		8						1	4							45
	2	3				7	9	8	11		6						5	1	4		10					46
		3	6	5		7				11								1	4		10	2	9		8	47
9	31	38	25	33	22	37	28	18	35	30	24	2	1	4	9	7	33	32	3	24	11	2	3	1	
			1		8	16	7	10	7					5			1		6		1				

	2	3	6	5		7	9		8	11								1	4		10					25
	2	3	6	5		7	9		8	11								1	4		10					27
	2	3		5		7	9		8	11	6							1	4		10					31
	2	3		5		7	9		8	11	6							1	4		10					34
	2	3		5		7	9		8	11	6							1	4		10					35
	5	5	2	5		5	5		5	5	3							5	5		5					
					1	7			2																	

Jimmy Connor

Reputedly the most skillful left-winger ever to play for Sunderland. He had an excellent record for Sunderland in FA Cup games scoring 13 times in 29 appearances.

1933-34

Division One

Ground: Roker Park
Manager: John Cochrane

League Table

	P	W	D	L	F	A	Pts
Arsenal	42	25	9	8	75	47	59
Huddersfield T	42	23	10	9	90	61	56
Tottenham H	42	21	7	14	79	56	49
Derby Co	42	17	11	14	68	54	45
Manchester C	42	17	11	14	65	72	45
SUNDERLAND	42	16	12	14	81	56	44
WBA	42	17	10	15	78	70	44
Blackburn R	42	18	7	17	74	81	43
Leeds U	42	17	8	17	75	66	42
Portsmouth	42	15	12	15	52	55	42
Sheffield W	42	16	9	17	62	67	41
Stoke C	42	15	11	16	58	71	41
Aston Villa	42	14	12	16	78	75	40
Everton	42	12	16	14	62	63	40
Wolverhampton W	42	14	12	16	74	86	40
Middlesbrough	42	16	7	19	68	80	39
Leicester C	42	14	11	17	59	74	39
Liverpool	42	14	10	18	79	87	38
Chelsea	42	14	8	20	67	69	36
Birmingham	42	12	12	18	54	56	36
Newcastle U	42	10	14	18	68	77	34
Sheffield U	42	12	7	23	58	101	31

FA Cup Winners: Manchester City

Did you know that?

The attendance at the home game against Manchester City on Wednesday 11 April 1934 was the lowest accurately recorded for a League game at Roker Park – 3,841.

Match 26: Matt Middleton made debut
Match 28: McDougall and Yorston last games
Match 42: Foreman made debut & Ainsley last game
Match 43: Foreman last game
Match 44: Ives last game

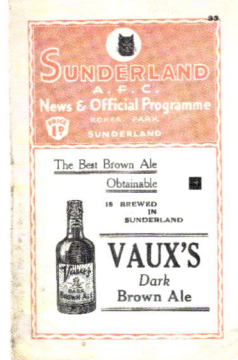

Match No.	Date		Round	Venue	Opponents	Result	FT	HT	Pos.	Scorers	Attendance
1	Aug	26		A	Huddersfield Town	L	1-2	1-1		Yorston	11,346
2		30		H	Portsmouth	L	0-2	0-0	20		20,123
3	Sep	2		H	Stoke City	W	4-1	3-1	13	Yorston (3), Davis	14,639
4		6		A	Portsmouth	D	0-0	0-0	14		18,674
5		9		A	Wolverhampton W.	W	6-1	3-1	7	Shaw o.g., Davis, Connor, Gurney (2), Gallacher	32,839
6		16		H	Sheffield United	W	5-0	3-0	3	Connor, Gallacher (2), Gurney, Davis	22,752
7		23		A	Aston Villa	L	1-2	0-1	7	Gurney	39,137
8		30		H	Leicester City	W	2-1	1-1	5	Davis, Yorston	21,083
9	Oct	7		A	Tottenham Hotspur	L	1-3	0-1	11	Gurney	44,235
10		14		H	Liverpool	W	4-1	2-0	4	Gallacher (3), Yorston	25,321
11		21		A	Newcastle United	L	1-2	1-1	9	McDougall	43,439
12		28		H	Leeds United	W	4-2	3-2	5	Carter (2), Gurney, Davis	14,578
13	Nov	4		A	Manchester City	L	1-4	1-2	9	Davis	29,177
14		11		A	West Bromwich Albion	D	2-2	2-1	9	Gurney (2)	18,013
15		18		A	Birmingham	D	1-1	0-0	10	Gallacher	15,277
16		25		H	Sheffield Wed.	W	4-0	2-0	8	Gurney (2), Carter, Davis	14,638
17	Dec	2		A	Middlesbrough	W	4-0	3-0	7	Gallacher (3), Carter	28,915
18		9		H	Arsenal	W	3-0	2-0	6	Gallacher, Gurney (2)	35,166
19		16		A	Everton	L	0-1	0-0	7		21,728
20		23		H	Derby County	D	0-0	0-0	7		24,794
21		26		A	Chelsea	L	0-4	0-3	10		12,820
22		30		H	Huddersfield Town	D	1-1	1-0	9	Gurney	19,557
23	Jan	1		H	Chelsea	D	0-0	0-0	9		13,890
24		6		A	Stoke City	L	0-3	0-2	12		16,316
27		20		H	Wolverhampton W.	D	3-3	0-2	12	Gurney, Carter, Connor	18,833
29		29		A	Sheffield United	L	0-2	0-2	12		8,054
30	Feb	3		H	Aston Villa	W	5-1	3-1	11	Carter (2), Gallacher (2), Davis	15,582
31		10		A	Leicester City	D	0-0	0-0	11		18,919
32		21		H	Tottenham Hotspur	W	6-0	5-0	9	Gurney (2), Connor, Carter (3)	16,105
33		24		A	Liverpool	D	1-1	1-0	9	Carter	20,120
34	Mar	3		H	Newcastle United	W	2-0	1-0	5	Davis, Shaw (pen)	31,776
35		10		A	Leeds United	L	1-3	0-2	9	McNab	7,333
36		17		A	Derby County	D	0-0	0-0	9		13,713
37		24		A	West Bromwich Albion	L	5-6	3-4	9	Gurney (3), Carter, Shaw	11,869
38		30		H	Blackburn Rovers	W	3-0	0-0	7	Carter (2), McNab	20,626
39		31		H	Birmingham	W	4-1	2-0	5	Gallacher, Davis, Gurney, Carter	14,158
40	Apr	2		A	Blackburn Rovers	D	0-0	0-0	5		13,860
41		7		A	Sheffield Wed.	L	0-2	0-2	8		11,799
42		11		H	Manchester City	D	0-0	0-0	7		3,841
43		14		H	Middlesbrough	W	2-0	0-0	5	McNab, Gallacher	12,204
44		21		A	Arsenal	L	1-2	0-2	7	Carter	37,783
45		28		H	Everton	W	3-2	1-1	6	Carter, Gurney, Gallacher	5,976

Appearances
Goals

FA Cup

25	Jan	13	R3	H	Middlesbrough	D	1-1	0-1		Carter	43,600
26		17	R3r	A	Middlesbrough	W	2-1	1-1		Gurney, Yorston	40,822
28		27	R4	A	Aston Villa	L	2-7	1-4		Carter, Hastings	57,265

Appearances
Goals

#	Thorpe	Murray	Shaw	Thomson	McDougall	Hastings	Davis	Gallacher	Yorston	Carter	Connor	McNab	Edgar	Ainsley	Gurney	Hall	Johnston	Middleton	Ives	Foreman	#
1	1	2	3	4	5	6	7	8	9	10	11										1
2	1	2	3		5		7	10			11	4	6	8	9						2
3	1	2	3		5		7	10	8		11	4	6		9						3
4	1	2	3		5		7	10	8		11	4	6		9						4
5	1	2			5		7	10	8		11	4	6		9	3					5
6	1	2	3		5		7	10	8		11	4	6		9						6
7	1	2	3		5		7	10	8		11	4	6		9						7
8	1	2	3		5		7	10	8		11	4	6		9						8
9	1	2	3		5		7	10			11	4	6		9						9
10	1	2	3		5		7	10	8		11	4	6		9						10
11	1	2	3		5		7	10		8	11	4	6		9						11
12	1	2	3	6	5		7	10		8	11	4			9						12
13	1	2	3	6	5		7	10		8	11	4			9						13
14	1	2	3	6	5		7	10		8	11	4			9						14
15	1	2	3	6	5		7	10		8	11	4			9						15
16	1	2	3	8	5	6	7			10	11	4			9						16
17	1	2	3		5	6	7	10		8	11	4			9						17
18	1	2	3		5	6	7	10		8	11	4			9						18
19	1		3		5	6	7	10		8	11	4			9	2					19
20	1	2	3		5	6	7	10		8	11	4			9						20
21	1	2	3		5	6	7	10	8		11	4			9						21
22	1	2	3		5	6	7		8	10	11	4			9						22
23	1	2	3			6	7		8	10	11	4			9	5					23
24	1	2	3			6	7	10			11	4		8	9	5					24
27		2	3		5	6	7		8	10	11	4			9		1				27
29			8			6	7			10	11	4			9	2	5	1	3		29
30		2	3	4		6	7	10		8	11				9		5	1			30
31		2	3	4		6	7	10		8	11				9		5	1			31
32		2	3	4		6	7	10		8	11				9		5				32
33			3	4		6	7	10		8	11				9	2	5	1			33
34		2	3	4		6	7	10		8	11				9		5	1			34
35		2	3	4		6	7			8	11	10			9		5	1			35
36		2	3	4		6	7			8	11	10			9		5	1			36
37		2	3	4		6	7			8	11	10			9		5	1			37
38		2		4		6	7	11		8		10			9		5	1	3		38
39		2		4		6	7	10		8		11			9		5	1	3		39
40				4		6	7	10		8	11				9	2	5	1	3		40
41				4			7	10		8	11	6			9	2	5	1	3		41
42		2		4		6	7				10	8			9		5	1	3	11	42
43		2		4		6	8	10			11				9		5	1	3	7	43
44		2		4		6	7	10		8	11				9		5	1	3		44
45		2	3	4		6	7	10		8	11				9		5	1			45
	24	37	33	23	23	27	42	32	14	29	38	32	11	3	41	6	19	18	8	2	
		2		1			10	16	6	17	4	3			21						
25	1	2	3		5	6	7		8	10	11	4			9						25
26		2	3		5	6	7		8	10	11	4			9		1				26
28		2	3		5	6	7		8	10	11	4			9		1				28
	1	3	3	3	3	3	3		3	3	3	3			3		2				
					1		1	2		1	3	3			1						

Bill Murray

Bill's career at Sunderland Football Club totalled 28 years as player then manager. He came to Roker Park from Cowdenbeath on 4 May 1927 and stayed until 12 January 1937 making 328 appearances. He then rejoined the club as manager on 24 March 1939 and remained in that position until 26 June 1957.

1934-35

Division One

Ground: Roker Park

Manager: John Cochrane

League Table

	P	W	D	L	F	A	Pts
Arsenal	42	23	12	7	115	46	58
SUNDERLAND	42	19	16	7	90	51	54
Sheffield W	42	18	13	11	70	64	49
Manchester C	42	20	8	14	82	67	48
Grimsby T	42	17	11	14	78	60	45
Derby Co	42	18	9	15	81	66	45
Liverpool	42	19	7	16	85	88	45
Everton	42	16	12	14	89	88	44
WBA	42	17	10	15	83	83	44
Stoke C	42	18	6	18	71	70	42
Preston NE	42	15	12	15	62	67	42
Chelsea	42	16	9	17	73	82	41
Aston Villa	42	14	13	15	74	88	41
Portsmouth	42	15	10	17	71	72	40
Blackburn R	42	14	11	17	66	78	39
Huddersfield T	42	14	10	18	76	71	38
Wolverhampton W	42	15	8	19	88	94	38
Leeds U	42	13	12	17	75	92	38
Birmingham	42	13	10	19	63	81	36
Middlesbrough	42	10	14	18	70	90	34
Leicester C	42	12	9	21	61	86	33
Tottenham H	42	10	10	22	54	93	30

FA Cup Winners:
Sheffield Wednesday

Did you know that?

Arthur Wright signed for Sunderland on 26 September 1934 as an apprentice. He retired from playing at the end of 1954-55 season but remained with the club as a coach until June 1969. This makes him the club's longest serving player.

Match 11: Edgar and Thorley last games
Match 16: McDowall made debut
Match 18: Goddard made debut
Match 29: Clark made debut
Match 43: Urwin last game
Match 44: Burbanks made debut

Match No.	Date		Round	Venue	Opponents	Result	FT	HT	Pos.	Scorers	Attendance
1	Aug	25		H	Huddersfield Town	W	4-1	3-1		Gallacher (2), Gurney, Davis	29,846
2		28		A	Grimsby Town	D	0-0	0-0	2		15,604
3	Sep	1		A	Wolverhampton W.	W	2-1	1-1	1	Gallacher, Carter	29,525
4		5		H	Grimsby Town	W	3-0	3-0	1	Connor, Gurney, Gallacher	27,753
5		8		H	Chelsea	W	4-0	2-0	1	Gallacher (3), Carter	33,592
6		15		A	Aston Villa	D	1-1	0-1	1	Allen o.g.	45,138
7		22		H	Derby County	L	1-4	1-1	3	Nicholas o.g.	25,945
8		29		A	Leicester City	W	2-0	1-0	2	Gurney, Davis	16,002
9	Oct	6		H	Middlesbrough	D	1-1	0-1	2	Davis	34,829
10		13		H	Tottenham Hotspur	L	1-2	1-1	3	Connor	28,204
11		20		A	Blackburn Rovers	D	0-0	0-0	3		14,034
12		27		H	Arsenal	W	2-1	0-1	3	Carter (2)	43,744
13	Nov	3		A	Stoke City	W	3-0	3-0	2	Gurney (3)	27,738
14		10		H	Manchester City	W	3-2	2-2	1	Gallacher, Gurney (2)	14,725
15		17		A	Leeds United	W	4-2	1-0	1	Gallacher, Carter, Connor, Gurney	24,141
16		24		H	West Bromwich Albion	L	0-1	0-1	1		30,128
17	Dec	1		A	Sheffield Wed.	D	2-2	0-1	1	Thomson, Davis	22,880
18		8		H	Birmingham	W	5-1	3-1	1	Gurney (3), Gallacher, Connor	22,002
19		15		A	Portsmouth	W	4-2	3-1	1	Gallacher (2), Davis, Gurney	16,348
20		22		H	Liverpool	L	2-3	2-1	1	Gallacher, Gurney	24,317
21		25		H	Everton	L	2-6	2-4	2	Gurney, Connor	37,931
22		26		A	Everton	W	7-0	3-0	1	Gurney (2), Connor (2), Gallacher (2), Thomson	35,271
23		29		A	Huddersfield Town	W	3-0	1-0	1	Gallacher (2), Connor	23,923
24	Jan	5		H	Wolverhampton W.	D	0-0	0-0	1		26,150
26		19		A	Chelsea	D	2-2	0-1	2	Goddard, Gurney	37,096
29	Feb	2		A	Derby County	L	1-3	0-1	3	Carter	24,181
30		6		H	Aston Villa	D	3-3	2-2	2	Gurney, Carter (2)	14,904
31		9		H	Leicester City	W	2-0	0-0	2	Gurney, Carter	18,048
32		16		A	Middlesbrough	D	0-0	0-0	2		17,416
33		23		A	Tottenham Hotspur	D	1-1	0-1	2	Gurney	44,886
34	Mar	2		H	Blackburn Rovers	W	3-0	1-0	2	Gurney (2), Davis	17,898
35		9		A	Arsenal	D	0-0	0-0	2		73,295
36		16		H	Stoke City	W	4-1	2-0	2	Davis (pen), Gurney, Connor, Gallacher	22,063
37		30		H	Leeds United	W	3-0	1-0	2	Hall, Gurney (2)	19,118
38	Apr	6		A	West Bromwich Albion	D	1-1	1-0	2	Gallacher	24,462
39		10		A	Manchester City	L	0-1	0-0	2		23,262
40		13		H	Sheffield Wed.	D	2-2	1-2	2	Gurney, Carter	22,900
41		19		H	Preston North End	W	3-1	0-1	2	Davis (2), Gurney	32,170
42		20		A	Birmingham	D	2-2	1-2	2	Gallacher, Gurney	21,841
43		22		A	Preston North End	D	1-1	0-0	2	Goddard	26,163
44		27		H	Portsmouth	W	4-1	1-0	2	Goddard, Burbanks, Carter, Davis	9,361
45	May	5		A	Liverpool	D	2-2	0-1	2	Gurney, Goddard	14,357

Appearances
Goals

FA Cup

25	Jan	12	R3	H	Fulham	W	3-2	2-1		Gurney (3)	40,100
27		26	R4	H	Everton	D	1-1	1-0		Carter	45,199
28		30	R4r	A	Everton	L	4-6 (aet)	1-2		Davis, Connor (2), Gurney	59,213

Appearances
Goals

	Middleton	Murray	Shaw	Thomson	Johnston	Hastings	Davis	Carter	Gurney	Gallacher	Connor	McNab	Hall	Edgar	Thorley	McDowall	Goddard	Thorpe	Clark	Urwin	Burbanks	
1	1	2	3	4	5	6	7	8	9	10	11											1
2	1	2	3	4	5	6	7	8	9	10	11											2
3	1	2	3	4	5	6	7	8	9	10	11											3
4	1	2	3	4	5	6	7	8	9	10	11											4
5	1	2	3	4	5	6	7	8	9	10	11											5
6	1	2	3	4	5	6	7	8	9	10	11											6
7	1	2	3	4	5	6	7	8	9	10	11											7
8	1	2	3	4	5		7	8	9	10	11	6										8
9	1	2	3	4	5		7	8	9	10	11	6										9
10	1	2	3	4	5		7	8	9	10	11	6										10
11	1	2		4	5		7	8	9		10	3	6	11								11
12	1	2		4	5	6	7	8	9	10	11	3										12
13	1	2		4	5	6	7	8	9	10	11	3										13
14	1	2		4	5	6	7	8	9	10	11	3										14
15	1	2		4	5	6	7	8	9	10	11	3										15
16	1	2		4	5		7	8	9	10	11	3		6								16
17	1	2		4	5	6	7	8	9	10	11	3										17
18	1	2		4	5	6	7		9	10	11	3				8						18
19	1	2		4	5	6	7		9	10	11	3				8						19
20	1	2		4	5	6			9	10	11	3				8						20
21	1	2		4	5	6	7	8	9	10	11	3										21
22			3	4	5		7	8	9	10	11	6	2			1						22
23			3	4	5		7	8	9	10	11	6	2			1						23
24			3	4	5	6	7	8	9	10		11	2			1						24
26		2	3	4	5		7	10	9		11	6				8	1					26
29			3	4			7	8		10	11	6	2			9	1	5				29
30		2	3	4		6	7	10	9		11					8	1	5				30
31			3	4			7	10	9		11	6	2			8	1	5				31
32		2	3	4	5	6	7	8	9	10	11					1						32
33		2	3	4	5	6	7	8	9	10	11					1						33
34		2		4	5	6	7	8	9	10	11	3				1						34
35		2		4	5	6	7	8	9	10	11	3				1						35
36		2		4	5	6	7	8	9	10	11	3				1						36
37		2		4	5	6	7	8	9	10	11	3				1						37
38			3	4	5	6	7			10	11	8	2			9	1					38
39			3	4	5	6	7	8	9	10	11		2				1					39
40			3	4	5	6	7	8	9	10	11		2				1					40
41			3	4	5	6	7	8	9	10	11		2				1					41
42			3	4	5	6	7	8	9	10	11		2				1					42
43		2		4	5	6	7	8	9			3				10	1		11			43
44		2	3	4	5	6	7	10	9							8	1		11			44
45		2	3	4		6	7	10	9							8	1	5	11			45
	21	32	26	42	38	32	42	38	40	35	37	11	26	1	1	11	21	4	1	2		
						2		10	11	30	20	9		1		4			1			

	Middleton	Murray	Shaw	Thomson	Johnston	Hastings	Davis	Carter	Gurney	Gallacher	Connor	McNab	Hall	Edgar	Thorley	McDowall	Goddard	Thorpe	Clark	Urwin	Burbanks	
25			3	4	5		7	8	9	10	11	6	2			1						25
27		2	3	4	5	6	7	8	9	10	11					1						27
28		2		4	5	6	7	8	9	10	11	3				1						28
		2	2	3	3	2	3	3	3	3	3	1	2			3						
							1	1	4		2											

Thomas Urwin

Urwin is the only player to have received a benefit from Middlesbrough, Newcastle United and Sunderland. He became Sunderland's oldest player when he played at Preston on 22 April 1935 aged 39 years and 76 days (his first game since February 1932).

1935-36

Division One

Ground: Roker Park

Manager: John Cochrane

League Table

	P	W	D	L	F	A	Pts
SUNDERLAND	42	25	6	11	109	74	56
Derby Co	42	18	12	12	61	52	48
Huddersfield T	42	18	12	12	59	56	48
Stoke C	42	20	7	15	57	57	47
Brentford	42	17	12	13	81	60	46
Arsenal	42	15	15	12	78	48	45
Preston NE	42	18	8	16	67	64	44
Chelsea	42	15	13	14	65	72	43
Manchester C	42	17	8	17	68	60	42
Portsmouth	42	17	8	17	54	67	42
Leeds U	42	15	11	16	66	64	41
Birmingham	42	15	11	16	61	63	41
Bolton W	42	14	13	15	67	76	41
Middlesbrough	42	15	10	17	84	70	40
Wolverhampton W	42	15	10	17	77	76	40
Everton	42	13	13	16	89	89	39
Grimsby T	42	17	5	20	65	73	39
WBA	42	16	6	20	89	88	38
Liverpool	42	13	12	17	60	64	38
Sheffield W	42	13	12	17	63	77	38
Aston Villa	42	13	9	20	81	110	35
Blackburn R	42	12	9	21	55	96	33

FA Cup Winners: Arsenal

Did you know that?

Sunderland headed the top flight of English football from 9 November 1935 until the end of the season. This consecutive run of 29 games (168 days) at the top is the longest in the club's history.

Match 1: Shaw last game
Match 12: Goddard last game
Match 13: Duns made debut
Match 14: Morrison made debut
Match 28: Thorpe last game
Match 31: Hornby made debut
Match 38: Mapson made debut
Match 40: Murray last game
Match 41: Crowned League champions
Match 42: Rodgerson made debut
Match 44: Russell made debut & Morrison last game

Match No.	Date	Round	Venue	Opponents	Result	FT	HT	Pos.	Scorers	Attendance
1	Aug 31		A	Arsenal	L	1-3	1-2		Gurney	66,428
2	Sep 4		A	West Bromwich Albion	W	3-1	1-1	10	Gallacher (2), Carter	24,396
3	7		H	Manchester City	W	2-0	1-0	7	Bray o.g., Gurney	38,224
4	11		H	West Bromwich Albion	W	6-1	4-0	4	Carter (4), Gallacher, Davis	35,276
5	14		A	Stoke City	W	2-0	0-0	2	Davis, Gallacher	34,516
6	16		A	Aston Villa	D	2-2	1-1	2	Carter, Gurney	24,717
7	21		H	Blackburn Rovers	W	7-2	3-1	2	Davis, Gallacher (3), Carter, Gurney (2)	29,704
8	28		A	Chelsea	L	1-3	1-1	4	Gallacher	61,051
9	Oct 5		H	Liverpool	W	2-0	1-0	2	Goddard, Carter	30,114
10	12		A	Grimsby Town	L	0-4	0-1	3		11,751
11	19		A	Wolverhampton W.	W	4-3	3-1	3	Carter (2), Davis, Connor	29,006
12	26		H	Sheffield Wed.	W	5-1	2-0	1	Thomson, Gallacher, Davis, Carter (2, 1 pen)	32,890
13	Nov 2		A	Portsmouth	D	2-2	1-2	2	Carter (2)	22,709
14	9		H	Preston North End	W	4-2	1-2	1	Carter, Duns (2), Gurney	16,739
15	16		A	Brentford	W	5-1	2-1	1	Gurney (2), Duns, Carter, Gallacher	24,720
16	23		H	Middlesbrough	W	2-1	0-1	1	Carter (2, 1 pen)	58,902
17	30		A	Everton	W	3-0	2-0	1	Carter, Connor, Gurney	39,366
18	Dec 7		H	Bolton Wanderers	W	7-2	3-1	1	Carter, Gurney (5), Gallacher	27,375
19	14		A	Huddersfield Town	L	0-1	0-0	1		30,690
20	21		H	Derby County	W	3-1	2-0	1	Carter (2, 1 pen), Gurney	33,665
21	26		H	Leeds United	W	2-1	0-1	1	Gurney (2)	25,296
22	28		H	Arsenal	W	5-4	4-1	1	Davis, Gallacher, Carter (2, 1 pen), Connor	58,773
23	Jan 1		H	Aston Villa	L	1-3	0-1	1	Gallacher	34,476
24	4		A	Manchester City	W	1-0	0-0	1	Carter	48,732
27	18		A	Stoke City	W	1-0	1-0	1	McNab	16,946
28	Feb 1		H	Chelsea	D	3-3	2-1	1	Gurney (2), Gallacher	23,755
29	8		A	Liverpool	W	3-0	3-0	1	Gurney (2), Gallacher	33,332
30	15		A	Blackburn Rovers	D	1-1	0-1	1	Gurney	18,628
31	19		H	Grimsby Town	W	3-1	2-1	1	Gurney, Davis (2)	12,108
32	22		H	Wolverhampton W.	W	3-1	2-1	1	Carter (2), Davis	26,461
33	29		A	Preston North End	L	2-3	1-1	1	Gallacher, Gurney	18,718
34	Mar 7		H	Everton	D	3-3	3-0	1	Duns, Gurney, Carter	23,268
35	14		A	Sheffield Wed.	D	0-0	0-0	1		31,787
36	21		H	Brentford	L	1-3	0-1	1	Duns	26,348
37	28		A	Middlesbrough	L	0-6	0-2	1		29,990
38	Apr 4		H	Portsmouth	W	5-0	2-0	1	Gallacher, Carter (pen), Gurney, Connor (2)	19,101
39	10		H	Birmingham	W	2-1	1-1	1	Gallacher (2)	40,660
40	11		A	Bolton Wanderers	L	1-2	1-1	1	Carter	32,306
41	13		A	Birmingham	W	7-2	3-2	1	Gurney (4), Carter, Hornby, Connor	21,693
42	18		H	Huddersfield Town	W	4-3	2-1	1	Hornby, Gurney, Davis, Connor	27,859
43	22		A	Leeds United	L	0-3	0-0	1		16,682
44	25		A	Derby County	L	0-4	0-3	1		15,712

Appearances
Goals

FA Cup

| 25 | Jan 11 | R3 | H | Port Vale | D | 2-2 | 0-1 | | Connor, Gallacher | 29,270 |
| 26 | 13 | R3r | A | Port Vale | L | 0-2 | 0-2 | | | 16,677 |

Appearances
Goals

Thorpe	Murray	Shaw	Thomson	Johnston	Hastings	Davis	Carter	Gurney	Gallacher	Connor	Hall	Clark	Goddard	Duns	Morrison	McNab	Middleton	Hornby	Mapson	Rodgerson	McDowall	Russell	
1	2	3	4	5	6	7	8	9	10	11													1
1	2		4		6	7	8	9	10	11	3	5											2
1	2		4		6	7	8	9	10	11	3	5											3
1	2		4		6	7	8	9	10	11	3	5											4
1	2		4		6	7	8	9	10	11	3	5											5
1	2		4		6	7	8	9	10	11	3	5											6
1	2		4		6	7	8	9	10	11	3	5											7
1	2		4		6	7	8	9	10	11	3	5											8
1	2		4		6	7	8		10	11	3	5	9										9
1	2		4		6	7	8	9	10	11	3	5											10
1	2		4		6	7	8		10	11	3	5	9										11
1	2		4		6	7	8		10	11	3	5	9										12
1	2		4		6		8	9	10	11	3	5		7									13
1			4		6		8	9	10	11	3	5		7	2								14
1			4		6		8	9	10	11	3	5		7	2								15
1			4		6		8	9	10	11	3	5		7	2								16
1			4		6		8	9	10	11	3	5		7	2								17
1			4		6		8	9	10	11	3	5		7	2								18
1			4				8	9	10	11	3	5		7	2	6							19
1			4			7	8	9	10	11	3	5			2	6							20
1			4			7	8	9	10	11	3	5			2	6							21
1			4			7	8	9	10	11	3	5			2	6							22
1			4			7	8	9	10	11	3	5			2	6							23
1			4		6	7	8	9		11	3	5			2	10							24
1	2		4	5	6		8	9		11	3			7		10							27
1	2		4	5	6	7	8	9	10	11	3												28
			4		6	7	8	9	10	11	3	5			2		1						29
			4	5	6	7	8	9	10	11	3				2		1						30
			4		6	7	8	9	10	11	3				2		1	5					31
			4			7	8	9	10	11	3				2	6	1	5					32
			4		6		8	9	10	11	3			7	2		1	5					33
			4				8	9	10	11	3			7	2		1	5					34
	2		4	5	6		8	9	10	11	3			7			1						35
	2		4		6			9	10	11	3	5		7			1	8					36
	2		4	5	6	7	8	9	10	11	3						1						37
	2		4		6		8	9	10	11	3	5		7				1					38
	2		4		6		8	9	10	11	3	5		7				1					39
	2		4	5			8	9	10	11	3			7		6		1					40
			4	5		7	10	9		11	3				2	6			8	1			41
			4	5		7	10	9		11					2	6			8	1	3		42
			4	5				9	10	11				7	2	6			8	1	3		43
			4					9		11			5		7	2	10			1	3	6	8	44
26	21	1	42	10	31	25	39	39	37	42	38	28	3	17	21	13	9	8	7	3	1	1	
			1			10	31	31	19	7				1	5			1		2			

1			4	5	6		8	9	10	11	3			7	2								25
1			4			5	7	8	9	10	11	3			2	6							26
2		2	1	2	1	2	2	2	2	2		1	2	1									
								1	1														

Jimmy Thorpe who died after after injuries sustained in Sunderland v Chelsea game on 1 February 1936. His Championship medal was given to his widow.

395

1936-37

Division One

Ground: Roker Park

Manager: John Cochrane

League Table

	P	W	D	L	F	A	Pts
Manchester C	42	22	13	7	107	61	57
Charlton A	42	21	12	9	58	49	54
Arsenal	42	18	16	8	80	49	52
Derby Co	42	21	7	14	96	90	49
Wolverhampton W	42	21	5	16	84	67	47
Brentford	42	18	10	14	82	78	46
Middlesbrough	42	19	8	15	74	71	46
SUNDERLAND	42	19	6	17	89	87	44
Portsmouth	42	17	10	15	62	66	44
Stoke C	42	15	12	15	72	57	42
Birmingham	42	13	15	14	64	60	41
Grimsby T	42	17	7	18	86	81	41
Chelsea	42	14	13	15	52	55	41
Preston NE	42	14	13	15	56	67	41
Huddersfield T	42	12	15	15	62	64	39
WBA	42	16	6	20	77	98	38
Everton	42	14	9	19	81	78	37
Liverpool	42	12	11	19	62	84	35
Leeds U	42	15	4	23	60	80	34
Bolton W	42	10	14	18	43	66	34
Manchester U	42	10	12	20	55	78	32
Sheffield W	42	9	12	21	53	69	30

FA Cup Winners: Sunderland

Did you know that?

Just before the 1913 FA Cup Final Sunderland captain Charlie Thomson reputedly asked a gypsy if his team would win. Her reply was that Sunderland would never win the Cup until a Scottish lassie sits upon the throne of England. Sunderland won the Cup for the first time in 1937; 11 days after the coronation of Scottish born Queen Elizabeth, the current Queen's mother.

Match 1: Collin made debut
Match 4: Davis last game
Match 6: Feenan made debut
Match 25: Wylie made debut
Match 28: Gorman made debut
Match 39: Saunders made debut
Match 44: Spuhler made debut
Match 47: Hornby last game
Match 48: Lockie made debut & Wylie last game
Match 49: Collin last game
Match 50: Clark last game
Match 51: Bell only game

Match No.	Date		Round	Venue	Opponents	Result	FT	HT	Pos.	Scorers	Attendance
1	Aug	29		A	Sheffield Wed.	L	0-2	0-0			25,436
2	Sep	2		H	Derby County	W	3-2	3-0	14	Gallacher, Carter (2)	42,731
3		5		H	Preston North End	W	3-0	2-0	6	Connor, Gurney, Carter	31,383
4		9		A	Derby County	L	0-3	0-1	11		29,783
5		12		A	Arsenal	L	1-4	1-3	19	Thomson	56,820
6		19		H	Brentford	W	4-1	1-0	17	Duns (2), Gallacher, Gurney	37,407
7		26		A	Bolton Wanderers	D	1-1	0-0	15	Gurney	28,453
8	Oct	3		H	Everton	W	3-1	2-0	9	Gallacher, Carter, Gurney	36,697
9		10		A	Huddersfield Town	L	1-2	1-1	13	Duns	26,531
10		17		A	Middlesbrough	D	5-5	4-3	14	Duns (2), Gurney, Connor, Carter	36,030
11		24		H	West Bromwich Albion	W	1-0	1-0	9	Carter (pen)	24,503
13		31		A	Manchester City	W	4-2	1-1	7	Gurney (2), Carter, McNab	39,444
14	Nov	7		A	Portsmouth	W	3-2	2-0	3	Burbanks, Duns, Carter	34,401
15		14		A	Chelsea	W	3-1	0-0	2	Gurney, Burbanks, Duns	48,901
16		21		H	Stoke City	W	3-0	3-0	1	Gurney (2), Carter (pen)	33,665
17		28		A	Charlton Athletic	L	1-3	0-0	2	Carter (pen)	38,519
18	Dec	5		H	Grimsby Town	W	5-1	3-0	1	Gurney, Connor, Duns, Carter (2)	25,040
19		12		A	Liverpool	L	0-4	0-1	3		27,269
20		19		H	Leeds United	W	2-1	1-1	1	Gallacher, McDougall o.g.	23,633
21		25		A	Birmingham	L	0-2	0-0	3		37,191
22		26		H	Sheffield Wed.	W	2-1	0-0	3	Gurney, Carter (pen)	48,786
23		28		H	Birmingham	W	4-0	2-0	2	Carter (2), Trigg o.g., Duns	17,306
24	Jan	1		A	Manchester United	L	1-2	0-2	3	Carter	46,257
25		2		A	Preston North End	L	0-2	0-1	4		20,360
26		9		H	Arsenal	D	1-1	0-0	4	Duns	54,694
28		23		A	Brentford	D	3-3	2-2	4	Duns, Carter, Gurney	29,389
31	Feb	6		A	Everton	L	0-3	0-2	9		41,147
32		10		H	Bolton Wanderers	W	3-0	2-0	4	Gurney, Carter (2)	10,975
33		13		H	Huddersfield Town	W	3-2	2-2	4	Wylie, Carter, Duns	23,336
35		24		H	Middlesbrough	W	4-1	2-1	3	Carter (3), Gallacher	32,309
36		27		A	West Bromwich Albion	L	4-6	2-1	5	Burbanks, Carter, Gurney, Duns	25,387
39	Mar	13		A	Portsmouth	L	2-3	0-1	8	Duns, Wylie	20,870
41		20		H	Chelsea	L	2-3	2-1	9	Gurney (2)	21,825
42		26		H	Wolverhampton W.	W	6-2	6-2	8	Gallacher (3), Burbanks, Carter, Gurney	35,218
43		27		A	Stoke City	L	3-5	0-3	8	McNab, Gurney, Duns (pen)	29,376
44		29		A	Wolverhampton W.	D	1-1	0-0	8	Saunders	36,267
45	Apr	3		H	Charlton Athletic	W	1-0	0-0	8	Gallacher	26,203
47		12		A	Grimsby Town	L	0-6	0-2	8		8,306
48		14		H	Manchester City	L	1-3	1-0	9	Wylie	14,827
49		17		H	Liverpool	W	4-2	2-1	9	Gurney (2), Duns, Burbanks	14,255
50		21		H	Manchester United	D	1-1	1-1	8	Carter	12,876
51		24		A	Leeds United	L	0-3	0-2	8		22,324

Appearances
Goals

FA Cup

27	Jan	16	R3	A	Southampton	W	3-2	2-0		Gurney, Hornby, Gallacher	30,380
29		30	R4	A	Luton Town	D	2-2	0-2		Connor, Gurney	20,134
30	Feb	3	R4r	H	Luton Town	W	3-1	2-1		Duns, Connor, Carter	53,200
34		20	R5	H	Swansea Town	W	3-0	0-0		Gurney, Duns, Caldwell o.g.	48,500
37	Mar	6	R6	A	Wolverhampton W.	D	1-1	0-1		Duns	57,751
38		10	R6r	H	Wolverhampton W.	D	2-2(aet)	0-0		Gurney, Duns	61,796
40		15	R6r2	N*	Wolverhampton W.	W	4-0	3-0		Gurney, Carter, Gallacher, Thomson (pen)	48,960
46	Apr	10	S	N‡	Millwall	W	2-1	1-1		Gurney, Gallacher	62,813
52	May	1	F	N°	Preston North End	W	3-1	0-1		Gurney, Carter, Burbanks	93,495

N* at Hillsborough.   N‡ at Leeds Rd.   N° at Wembley.

Appearances
Goals

Charity Shield

| 12 | Oct | 28 | | H | Arsenal | W | 2-1 | 0-0 | | Burbanks, Carter | 11,500 |

Appearances
Goals

	Mapson	Hall	Collin	Thomson	Johnston	Hastings	Davis	Carter	Gurney	Gallacher	Connor	McNab	Duns	Feenan	Clark	McDowall	Burbanks	Hornby	Wylie	Gorman	Saunders	Middleton	Spuhler	Russell	Lockie	Rodgerson	Bell	
1	2	3	4	5	6	7	8	9	10	11																		1
	2	3	4	5		7	8	9	10	11	6																	2
1	2	3	4	5		7	8	9	10	11	6																	3
1	2	3	4	5	6	7	8	9	10	11																		4
1	2	3	4	5	6		8	9	10	11		7																5
1		3	4		6		8	9	10	11		7	2	5														6
1	2	3	4		6		8	9	10	11		7		5														7
1	2	3	4	5	6		8	9	10	11		7																8
1		3	4	5			8	9	10	11		7	2		6													9
1		3	4	5			8	9	10	11	6	7	2															10
1	2	3	4	5			8	9	10		6	7				11												11
1	2	3	4	5			8	9	10		6	7				11												13
1	2	3	4	5			8	9	10		6	7				11												14
1	2	3	4	5	6		8	9	10			7				11												15
1	2	3	4	5	6		8	9	10			7				11												16
1	2	3	4		6		8	9	10	11		7		5														17
1	2	3	4		6		8	9	10	11		7		5														18
1	2	3	4		6		8	9		11	10	7		5														19
1	2	3	4		6		8	9	10	11		7		5														20
1	2	3	4		6		8	9	10			7		5		11												21
1	2	3	4		6		8	9	10			7		5		11												22
1	2	3	4		6		8	9	10	11		7		5														23
1	2	3	4		6		8	9	10	11		7		5														24
1	2	3	4		6		8	9		11		7		5			10											25
1	2	3	4		6		8	9	10	11		7		5														26
1		3		4	5		8	9	10	11	6	7					2											28
1	2	3	4	5			10				6	7				11	8	9										31
1	3		4	5			8	9	10		6	7				11	2											32
1	3		4	5			8	9			6	7				11	10	2										33
1	3		4				8	9	10		6	7		5		11	2											35
1	3		4				8	9	10		6	7		5		11	2											36
1		3	4		6			9				7		5		11	10	2	8									39
1	3		4	5			8	9	10		6	7				11	2											41
1	3			6			8	9	10			7		5	4	11	2											42
1	3		4	5				9			6	7				11	8		2	10								43
		3			6		8							2	5	4	11		9		10	1	7					44
1	3		4	5			8	9	10		6	7				11		2										45
1		3									7	2	5	6	11	4	9		10		8							47
1	3		4								7			6	11		9	2	10		8	5						48
1		3	4		6						7			6	11		2	8			5							49
1			4				8	9	10		6		5		11		2		7			3						50
1	3		4	5			8	9	10		6	7					2						11					51
41	33	31	39	21	21	4	37	38	33	19	18	36	5	17	7	22	4	7	14	6	1	2	2	1	1			
		1					26	21	9	3	2	16			5		3		1									

	Mapson	Hall	Collin	Thomson	Johnston	Hastings	Davis	Carter	Gurney	Gallacher	Connor	McNab	Duns	Feenan	Clark	McDowall	Burbanks	Hornby	Wylie	Gorman	Saunders	Middleton	Spuhler	Russell	Lockie	Rodgerson	Bell	
1	2	3	4	5			9	10	11	6	7				8													27
1	3		4	5			8	9	10	11	6	7				2												29
1	3		4	5			8	9	10	11	6	7				2												30
1	3		4				8	9	10		6	7	5			11	2											34
1	3		4	5			8	9	10		6	7				11	2											37
1	3		4	5			8	9	10		6	7				11	2											38
1	3		4	5			8	9	10		6	7				11	2											40
1	3		4	5	6		8	9	10			7				11	2											46
1	3		4	5			8	9	10		6	7				11	2											52
9	9	1	9	8	1		8	9	9	3	8	9	1		1	6	8											
		1					3	6	3	2		5				1	1											

	Mapson	Hall	Collin	Thomson	Johnston	Hastings	Davis	Carter	Gurney	Gallacher	Connor	McNab	Duns	Feenan	Clark	McDowall	Burbanks	Hornby	Wylie	Gorman	Saunders	Middleton	Spuhler	Russell	Lockie	Rodgerson	Bell	
1	2	3	4	5			8	9	10		6	7				11												12
1	1	1	1	1			1	1	1		1	1				1												
											1																	

Raich Carter, Sunderland's first FA Cup winning captain, holding the FA Cup.

397

1937-38

Division One

Ground: Roker Park

Manager: John Cochrane

League Table

	P	W	D	L	F	A	Pts
Arsenal	42	21	10	11	77	44	52
Wolverhampton W	42	20	11	11	72	49	51
Preston NE	42	16	17	9	64	44	49
Charlton A	42	16	14	12	65	51	46
Middlesbrough	42	19	8	15	72	65	46
Brentford	42	18	9	15	69	59	45
Bolton W	42	15	15	12	64	60	45
SUNDERLAND	42	14	16	12	55	57	44
Leeds U	42	14	15	13	64	69	43
Chelsea	42	14	13	15	65	65	41
Liverpool	42	15	11	16	65	71	41
Blackpool	42	16	8	18	61	66	40
Derby Co	42	15	10	17	66	87	40
Everton	42	16	7	19	79	75	39
Huddersfield T	42	17	5	20	55	68	39
Leicester C	42	14	11	17	54	75	39
Stoke C	42	13	12	17	58	59	38
Birmingham	42	10	18	14	58	62	38
Portsmouth	42	13	12	17	62	68	38
Grimsby T	42	13	12	17	51	68	38
Manchester C	42	14	8	20	80	77	36
WBA	42	14	8	20	74	91	36

FA Cup Winners: Preston North End

Did you know that?

Sunderland were 3-0 up after 30 minutes at Leeds United on 4 December 1937, however, they lost 4-3.

Match 2: Robinson made debut
Match 6: Russell last game
Match 14: Rowell only game
Match 16: McMahon made debut
Match 19: Gaughran made debut
Match 20: Gaughran last game
Match 33: McNab last game
Match 34: Curran only game
Match 37: Bett made debut & McDowall last game
Match 44: Wright made debut
Match 47: Housam made debut

Match No.	Date		Round	Venue	Opponents	Result	FT	HT	Pos.	Scorers	Attendance
1	Aug	28		H	Middlesbrough	W	3-1	2-1		Gurney (2), Saunders	56,717
2		30		A	Leicester City	L	0-4	0-3	10		23,906
3	Sep	4		A	Derby County	D	2-2	2-1	14	Saunders (pen), Hastings	21,816
4		8		H	Leicester City	W	1-0	1-0	7	Duns	23,635
5		11		H	Manchester City	W	3-1	2-1	5	Saunders, Carter, Burbanks	32,617
6		15		A	Wolverhampton W.	L	0-4	0-1	9		25,198
7		18		A	Arsenal	L	1-4	1-4	15	Gurney	65,635
8		25		H	Blackpool	W	2-1	0-1	12	Burbanks, Gallacher	31,356
9	Oct	2		A	Brentford	L	0-4	0-2	15		35,584
10		9		H	Bolton Wanderers	W	3-1	0-0	12	Duns, Gallacher, Gurney	29,932
11		16		H	Birmingham	W	1-0	0-0	9	Carter	24,615
12		23		A	West Bromwich Albion	W	6-1	2-0	5	Carter (3), Gurney, Saunders, Spuhler	27,713
13		30		H	Liverpool	L	2-3	2-2	8	Carter, Gallacher	25,217
15	Nov	6		A	Chelsea	D	0-0	0-0	9		50,554
16		13		H	Grimsby Town	D	2-2	2-1	8	Gallacher, Gurney	23,171
17		20		A	Stoke City	D	0-0	0-0	7		31,799
18		27		H	Charlton Athletic	D	1-1	1-1	9	Burbanks	24,870
19	Dec	4		A	Leeds United	L	3-4	3-1	11	Saunders, Carter, Duns	15,349
20		11		H	Portsmouth	L	0-2	0-0	11		9,327
21		18		A	Preston North End	D	0-0	0-0	10		18,296
22		25		H	Huddersfield Town	W	2-1	1-0	10	Carter, Gurney	30,730
23		27		A	Huddersfield Town	D	1-1	0-0	9	Hastings	13,198
24	Jan	1		A	Middlesbrough	L	1-2	1-0	11	Gurney	45,854
26		15		H	Derby County	W	2-0	0-0	9	Thomson, Duns	16,088
28		29		H	Arsenal	D	1-1	1-0	8	Gallacher	42,638
29	Feb	2		A	Manchester City	D	1-1	1-0	8		23,644
30		5		A	Blackpool	D	0-0	0-0	8		16,682
32		16		H	Brentford	W	1-0	1-0	8	Burbanks	18,970
33		19		A	Bolton Wanderers	D	1-1	0-1	8	McMahon	23,943
34		26		A	Birmingham	D	2-2	0-2	9	Thomson, Spuhler	25,960
36	Mar	9		H	West Bromwich Albion	W	3-0	1-0	9	Gallacher, Carter, Sandford o.g.	15,011
37		12		A	Liverpool	L	0-4	0-2	9		26,616
38		19		H	Chelsea	D	1-1	0-1	9	Gurney	19,327
40		29		A	Grimsby Town	W	2-0	1-0	8	Gallacher, Robinson	11,393
41	Apr	2		H	Stoke City	D	1-1	0-1	8	Carter	15,848
42		9		A	Charlton Athletic	L	1-2	1-1	8	Robinson	27,702
43		15		A	Everton	D	3-3	2-2	8	Carter, Burbanks (2)	40,010
44		16		H	Leeds United	D	0-0	0-0	8		21,450
45		18		H	Everton	W	2-0	2-0	8	Robinson, Carter	22,332
46		23		A	Portsmouth	L	0-1	0-0	9		26,140
47	May	4		H	Preston North End	L	0-2	0-1	9		22,307
48		7		H	Wolverhampton W.	W	1-0	1-0	8	Carter	21,622

Appearances
Goals

FA Cup

25	Jan	8	R3	H	Watford	W	1-0	1-0		Duns	35,713
27		22	R4	A	Everton	W	1-0	1-0		Gurney	68,158
31	Feb	12	R5	H	Bradford P.A.	W	1-0	0-0		Duns	59,806
35	Mar	5	R6	A	Tottenham Hotspur	W	1-0	0-0		Carter	75,038
39		26	S	N*	Huddersfield Town	L	1-3	0-1		Burbanks	47,904

N* at Ewood Park

Appearances
Goals

Charity Shield

| 14 | Nov | 3 | | A | Manchester City | L | 0-2 | 0-0 | | | 16,000 |

Appearances
Goals

	Mapson	Gorman	Hall	Thomson	Johnston	McNab	Duns	Carter	Gurney	Saunders	Burbanks	Robinson	Hastings	Russell	Middleton	Feenan	Spuhler	Gallacher	McMahon	Lockie	McDowall	Gaughran	Curran	Bett	Wright	Housam	Connor	Rowell	
1	1	2	3	4	5	6	7	8	9	10	11																		1
2	1	2	3	4	5	6	7	8		10	11	9																	2
3	1	2	3	4	5	6	7	8		10	11		9																3
4	1	2	3	4	5	6	7	8		10	11		9																4
5	1	2	3	4	5	6		8	9	10	11			7															5
6	1	2	3	4	5	6		8	9	10	11		7																6
7		2		4	5			8	9	10	11		6		1	3	7												7
8	1	2	3	4	5			8	9		11		6					7	10										8
9	1	2	3	4	5	6		8	9		11							7	10										9
10	1	2	3	4	5		7	8	9		11		6						10										10
11	1	2	3	4	5		7	8	9		11		6						10										11
12	1	2	3	4	5			8	9	10			6					7	11										12
13	1	2	3	4	5			8	9	10			6					7	11										13
15	1	2		4	5	10		8	9				6			3	7		11										15
16	1	2		4	5	10		8	9				6			3		7	11										16
17	1	2		4				8	9				6			3	7	10	11	5									17
18	1	2			4			8	9		11		6			3		10	7	5									18
19	1	2	3			4	7	8		10	11	6									5	9							19
20	1	2		4	5	6	7	8		10	11			3								9							20
21	1	2	3	4	5	6	7	8	9		11								10										21
22	1	2	3	4	5	6	7	8	9		11								10										22
23	1	2	3	4	5	6	7	8			11	9							10										23
24	1	2	3	4	5	6	7	8	9		11								10										24
26	1	2	3	4	5	6	7	8	9		11								10										26
28	1		3	4	5	6	7	8	9		11				2				10										28
29	1		3	4				8	9			6			2	7	10	11		5									29
30	1		3	4		6		8			11	9			2	7	10			5									30
32	1	2	3	4	5	8	7		9		11	6																	32
33	1	2	3	4	5	8			9			6				7	10	11											33
34	1	2	3	4	5					9	6					7	10	11			8								34
36	1	2	3	4	5		7	8	9		11	6						10											36
37	1		3	4				8			11	9	6		2	7				5		10							37
38	1	2	3	4	5		7	8	9		11	6							10										38
40	1		3	4				8			11	9	6		2	7	10			5									40
41	1	2	3	4	5			8			11	9	6			7	10												41
42	1	2	3		4			8		6	11	9				7	10			5									42
43	1	2	3	4	5			8		6	11	9				7	10												43
44	1		3		4			8	9		11				2	7	10			5					6				44
45	1		3	4				8		10	11	9	6		2	7				5									45
46	1	4	3					8			11	9	6		2	7	10			5									46
47	1		3					8		10		9	6		2	7				5				4	11				47
48	1	2	3					8	9		11		6			7	10			5				4					48
	41	34	36	35	31	21	17	39	26	15	33	10	28	2	1	15	21	30	6	9	4	2	1	1	1	2	1		
		2				4	13	9	5	6	3	2				2	7	1											

	Mapson	Gorman	Hall	Thomson	Johnston	McNab	Duns	Carter	Gurney	Saunders	Burbanks	Robinson	Hastings	Russell	Middleton	Feenan	Spuhler	Gallacher	McMahon	Lockie	McDowall	Gaughran	Curran	Bett	Wright	Housam	Connor	Rowell	
25	1	2	3	4	5	6	7	8	9		11								10										25
27	1		3	4	5	6	7	8	9		11			2					10										27
31	1	2	3	4			7	8	9		11	6							10	5									31
35	1	2	3	4	5		7	8	9		11	6							10										35
39	1	2	3	4	5		7	8	9		11	6							10										39
	5	4	5	5	4	2	5	5	5		5	3		1			5		1										
								2	1		1																		

	Mapson	Gorman	Hall	Thomson	Johnston	McNab	Duns	Carter	Gurney	Saunders	Burbanks	Robinson	Hastings	Russell	Middleton	Feenan	Spuhler	Gallacher	McMahon	Lockie	McDowall	Gaughran	Curran	Bett	Wright	Housam	Connor	Rowell	
14	1	2	3	4	5			8	9			6						7	10						11				14
	1	1	1	1				1	1			1					1	1							1				

Charlie Thomson

Charles Morgan Thomson's career with Sunderland was remarkably similar to his pre-WW1 namesake; both won a Division One Championship medal, played in an FA Cup Final and were capped by Scotland.

He made 263 first team appearances scoring eight goals compared with Charles Bellany Thomson's 264 and six goals.

1938-39

Division One

Ground: Roker Park

Managers: John Cochrane, George Crow & Bill Murray

League Table

	P	W	D	L	F	A	Pts
Everton	42	27	5	10	88	52	59
Wolverhampton W	42	22	11	9	88	39	55
Charlton A	42	22	6	14	75	59	50
Middlesbrough	42	20	9	13	93	74	49
Arsenal	42	19	9	14	55	41	47
Derby Co	42	19	8	15	66	55	46
Stoke C	42	17	12	13	71	68	46
Bolton W	42	15	15	12	67	58	45
Preston NE	42	16	12	14	63	59	44
Grimsby T	42	16	11	15	61	69	43
Liverpool	42	14	14	14	62	63	42
Aston Villa	42	16	9	17	71	60	41
Leeds U	42	16	9	17	59	67	41
Manchester U	42	11	16	15	57	65	38
Blackpool	42	12	14	16	56	68	38
SUNDERLAND	42	13	12	17	54	67	38
Portsmouth	42	12	13	17	47	70	37
Brentford	42	14	8	20	53	74	36
Huddersfield T	42	12	11	19	58	64	35
Chelsea	42	12	9	21	64	80	33
Birmingham	42	12	8	22	62	84	32
Leicester C	42	9	11	22	48	82	29

FA Cup Winners: Portsmouth

Did you know that?

Bobby Gurney broke his ankle in the second minute of the fifth round FA Cup second replay against Blackburn Rovers at Hillsborough on 20 February 1939. This was to be his final appearance for The Lads.

Match 7: Smeaton made debut
Match 15: Gallacher last game
Match 16: Bolton made debut
Match 19: Thompson made debut
Match 21: Spuhler last game
Match 27: Whitelum made debut
Match 31: Connor last game
Match 33: Gurney last game
Match 34: John Cochrane last as Sunderland manager
Match 35: Rodgerson last game & George Crow first as caretaker manager
Match 38: George Crow last as caretaker manager
Match 39: Bill Murray first game as Sunderland manager
Match 40: Heywood made debut
Match 41: Gorman last game
Match 42: Saunders and Spuhler last games
Match 43: Heywood last game
Match 44: McMahon and Robinson last games
Match 45: Bett last game
Match 46: Thomson, Bolton and Johnston last games
Match 47: Middleton, Hall, Carter, Smeaton and Feenan last games

Matches

Match No.	Date	Round	Venue	Opponents	Result	FT	HT	Pos.	Scorers	Attendance
1	Aug 27		A	Birmingham	W	2-1	0-0		Gurney, Carter	32,117
2	Sep 3		H	Grimsby Town	D	1-1	1-1	9	Duns	23,318
3	7		H	Wolverhampton W.	D	1-1	0-0	10	Robinson	20,551
4	10		A	Derby County	L	0-1	0-0	14		19,377
5	14		A	Huddersfield Town	W	1-0	0-0	7	Robinson	9,724
6	17		H	Blackpool	L	1-2	1-2	11	Carter (pen)	26,295
7	24		A	Brentford	W	3-2	0-2	8	Connor, Carter (2, 1 pen)	26,128
8	Oct 1		H	Arsenal	D	0-0	0-0	9		51,042
9	8		A	Portsmouth	L	1-2	1-1	9	Duns	24,789
10	15		A	Leicester City	W	2-0	1-0	7	Spuhler, Smeaton	17,208
11	22		H	Middlesbrough	L	1-2	0-1	11	Smeaton	39,440
12	29		A	Manchester United	W	1-0	0-0	8	Carter	33,565
13	Nov 5		H	Stoke City	W	3-0	2-0	8	Carter, Gallacher (2)	22,956
14	12		A	Chelsea	L	0-4	0-2	9		37,103
15	19		H	Preston North End	L	1-2	1-1	10	Gurney	20,184
16	26		A	Charlton Athletic	L	0-3	0-2	14		28,707
17	Dec 3		H	Bolton Wanderers	D	2-2	1-1	14	Connor, Lockie	17,815
18	10		A	Leeds United	D	3-3	2-2	12	Carter (2), Smeaton	20,853
19	17		H	Liverpool	L	2-3	1-1	14	Bolton, Duns	15,309
20	24		A	Birmingham	W	1-0	1-0	12	Spuhler	14,555
21	26		H	Aston Villa	L	1-5	1-1	15	Carter	38,612
22	27		A	Aston Villa	D	1-1	1-0	14	Gurney	61,221
23	31		A	Grimsby Town	W	3-1	3-1	12	Carter (2, 1 pen), Thompson	11,565
25	Jan 14		H	Derby County	W	1-0	1-0	10	Burbanks	25,822
27	25		A	Blackpool	D	1-1	0-1	10	Housam	13,237
28	28		H	Brentford	D	1-1	1-0	11	Burbanks	19,591
29	Feb 4		A	Arsenal	L	0-2	0-1	12		45,875
32	18		H	Leicester City	W	2-0	2-0	12	Carter, Smeaton	15,631
34	25		A	Middlesbrough	L	0-3	0-1	14		23,882
35	Mar 4		H	Manchester United	W	5-2	1-0	11	Duns, Robinson (4)	11,078
36	11		A	Stoke City	L	1-3	1-2	15	Duns	17,902
37	15		H	Portsmouth	L	0-2	0-1	15		9,768
38	18		H	Chelsea	W	3-2	3-1	13	Robinson (2), Carter	10,954
39	25		A	Preston North End	L	1-2	0-1	14	Robinson	17,130
40	Apr 1		H	Charlton Athletic	D	1-1	0-0	14	Burbanks	14,458
41	7		H	Everton	L	1-2	1-2	15	Duns	40,521
42	8		A	Bolton Wanderers	L	1-2	1-1	15	Robinson	22,692
43	10		A	Everton	L	2-6	1-2	16	Housam, Duns	46,016
44	15		H	Leeds United	W	2-1	0-0	15	Robinson, Duns	10,913
45	22		A	Liverpool	D	1-1	0-0	15	Carter	15,607
46	29		H	Huddersfield Town	D	0-0	0-0	14		7,729
47	May 6		A	Wolverhampton W.	D	0-0	0-0	16		24,832

Appearances
Goals

FA Cup

Match No.	Date	Round	Venue	Opponents	Result	FT	HT	Scorers	Attendance
24	Jan 7	R3	H	Plymouth Argyle	W	3-0	3-0	Clark o.g., Gorman, Carter	26,000
26	21	R4	A	Middlesbrough	W	2-0	2-0	Carter, Smeaton	50,891
30	Feb 11	R5	H	Blackburn Rovers	D	1-1	0-0	Hastings	52,637
31	16	R5r	A	Blackburn Rovers	D	0-0 (aet)	0-0		47,248
33	20	R5r2	N*	Blackburn Rovers	L	0-1 (aet)	0-0		30,217

* at Hillsborough

Appearances
Goals

	Mapson	Gorman	Hall	Thomson	Lockie	Wright	Duns	Carter	Gurney	Gallacher	Burbanks	Johnston	Robinson	Hastings	Spuhler	Sneaton	Connor	Saunders	Bolton	McMahon	Bett	Middleton	Feenan	Housam	Thompson	Whitelum	Rodgerson	Heywood	
1	1	2	3	4	5	6	7	8	9	10	11																		1
2	1	2	3	4	5	6	7	8	9	10	11																		2
3	1	2	3	4		6	7	8		10	11	5	9																3
4	1	2	3	4		6	7	8		10	11	5	9																4
5	1	2	3			6	7	8		10	11	5	9	4															5
6	1	2	3	4		6	7	8		10	11		9	5															6
7	1	2	3	4	5		7	8					6	9	10	11													7
8	1	2	3	4	5		7	8					6	9	10	11													8
9	1	2	3		5	6	7	8					4	9	10	11													9
10	1	2	3		5	6	7	8					4	9	10	11													10
11	1	2	3		5	6	7	8					4	9	10	11													11
12	1	2	3	4	5	6		8	9					7	10	11													12
13	1	2	3	4	5			8	9	10	11		6	7															13
14	1	2	3	4	5			8	9	10	11			7			6												14
15	1	2	3	4	5	6		8	9	10	11			7															15
16	1	2	3	4	5		10		7				6					8	9	11									16
17	1	2	3	4	5		7	8					6			11		9	10										17
18			3		5			8					6	7	10	11		9			1	2	4						18
19		2	3		5		7	10					6			11		9			1		4	8					19
20	1	2	3					8				5	6	7		11		9					4	10					20
21	1	2	3					8				5	6	7		11		9					4	10					21
22	1	2	3	4	5		7		9		11		6		10									8					22
23	1	2	3		5		7	8			11		6		10								4	9					23
25	1	2	3		5		7	8			11		6		10								4	9					25
27	1	2	3	7	5						11		6		10								4	8	9				27
28	1	2	3	7	5			8			11				10	6							4	9					28
29	1	2	3		5		7	8			11		6		10								4	9					29
32	1	2	3	4			7	8	9		11	5	6		10														32
34	1		3				7	8			11	5	6		10							2	4	9					34
35	1	2		4			7	8			11	5	9	6	10										3				35
36		2	3	4			7	8			11	5	9	6	10					1									36
37		2	3	4			7	8			11	5	9	6	10					1									37
38		2	3		5		7	8			11		9	6	10					1			4						38
39		2	3		5		7	8			11		9	6	10					1			4						39
40		2	3		5		7	8			11		9	6	10								4			1			40
41		2	3		5		7	8			11		9	6	10								4			1			41
42			3		5		7				11		9		10	6						2	4	8		1			42
43			3		5		7	8			11		9	6	10							2	4			1			43
44			3		5		7	8					9	6	10				11			2	4						44
45	1		3	4		6	7	8			5			10			9		11			2							45
46	1		3	4			7	8			11	5	6	10			9					2							46
47			3		5		7	8			11		6	10							1	2	4		9				47
	31	34	41	22	29	12	32	39	8	9	29	12	14	31	12	28	11	5	8	2	2	7	8	18	11	2	1	4	
				1			8	14	3	2	3		11		2	4	2		1				2	1					

	Mapson	Gorman	Hall	Thomson	Lockie	Wright	Duns	Carter	Gurney	Gallacher	Burbanks	Johnston	Robinson	Hastings	Spuhler	Sneaton	Connor	Saunders	Bolton	McMahon	Bett	Middleton	Feenan	Housam	Thompson	Whitelum	Rodgerson	Heywood	
24	1	2	3		5		7	8			11		6		10								4	9					24
26	1	2	3		5		7	8			11		6		10								4	9					26
30	1	2	3		5		7	8			11		6		10								4	9					30
31	1	2	3		5		7	8	9				6		10	11							4						31
33	1	2	3				7	8	9		11	5	6		10								4						33
	5	5	5		4		5	5	2		4	1	5		5	1							5	3					
		1					2				1		1																

Patsy Gallacher

Gallacher was sold to Stoke City on 29 November 1938 for £5,500.

In total he made 309 first team appearances, scoring 107 goals. He scored on his only appearance for Scotland, v Ireland in Belfast on 20 October 1934. (Jimmy Connor was also in that Scotland line up).

1939-40

Division One

Ground: Roker Park

Manager: Bill Murray

League Table

	P	W	D	L	F	A	Pts
Blackpool	3	3	0	0	5	2	6
Sheffield U	3	2	1	0	3	1	5
Arsenal	3	2	1	0	8	4	5
Liverpool	3	2	0	1	6	3	4
Everton	3	1	2	0	5	4	4
Bolton W	3	2	0	1	6	5	4
Derby Co	3	2	0	1	3	3	4
Charlton A	3	2	0	1	3	4	4
Stoke C	3	1	1	1	7	4	3
Manchester U	3	1	1	1	5	3	3
Brentford	3	1	1	1	3	3	3
Chelsea	3	1	1	1	4	4	3
Grimsby T	3	1	1	1	2	4	3
Aston Villa	3	1	0	2	3	3	2
SUNDERLAND	3	1	0	2	6	7	2
Wolves	3	0	2	1	3	4	2
Huddersfield T	3	1	0	2	2	3	2
Portsmouth	3	1	0	2	3	5	2
Preston NE	3	0	2	1	0	2	2
Blackburn R	3	0	1	2	3	5	1
Middlesbrough	3	0	1	2	3	8	1
Leeds U	3	0	1	2	0	2	1

Did you know that?

The Football League was abandoned at the outbreak of WW2. This is the fixture list that should have been played. All results from this season were expunged from the record books.

These appearances and goals are not included in any players' career records in this book.

LEAGUE WAR CUP.
Second Round Tie,
Saturday, 4th May, 1940.

Sunderland
v.
Leeds United
Kick-off 3-15 p.m.

ST. JAMES'S PARK,
NEWCASTLE UPON TYNE.

Official Programme - One Penny.

Match No.	Date	Round	Venue	Opponents	Result	FT	HT	Pos.	Scorers	Attendance
1	Aug 26		H	Derby County	W	3-0	2-0	8	Hastings, Carter (2)	21,859
2	30		H	Huddersfield Town	L	1-2	1-1		Carter	16,315
3	Sep 2		A	Arsenal	L	2-5	0-2	15	Hastings, Burbanks	17,141
4	6		A	Charlton Athletic				All matches cancelled due to World War Two		
5	9		H	Blackpool						
6	16		A	Brentford						
7	23		H	Blackburn Rovers						
8	30		A	Portsmouth						
9	Oct 7		H	Everton						
10	14		H	Grimsby Town						
11	21		A	Manchester United						
12	28		H	Stoke City						
13	Nov 4		A	Middlesbrough						
14	11		H	Chelsea						
15	18		A	Sheffield United						
16	25		H	Preston North End						
17	Dec 2		A	Leeds United						
18	9		H	Liverpool						
19	16		A	Bolton Wanderers						
20	23		A	Derby County						
21	25		H	Wolverhampton W.						
22	26		A	Wolverhampton W.						
23	30		H	Arsenal						
24	Jan 6		A	Blackpool						
25	20		H	Brentford						
26	27		A	Blackburn Rovers						
27	Feb 3		H	Portsmouth						
28	10		A	Everton						
29	17		A	Grimsby Town						
30	24		H	Manchester United						
31	Mar 2		A	Stoke City						
32	9		H	Middlesbrough						
33	16		A	Chelsea						
34	22		H	Aston Villa						
35	23		H	Sheffield United						
36	25		A	Aston Villa						
37	30		A	Preston North End						
38	Apr 6		H	Leeds United						
39	13		A	Liverpool						
40	20		H	Bolton Wanderers						
41	27		H	Charlton Athletic						
42	May 4		A	Huddersfield Town						

Appearances
Goals

Mapson	Gorman	Hall	Housam	Lockie	Hastings	Duns	Carter	Robinson	Sneaton	Burbanks	Johnston
1	2	3	4	5	6	7	8	9	10	11	
1	2	3	4	5	6	7	8	9	10	11	
1	2	3	4		6	7	8	9	10	11	5

3	3	3	3	2	3	3	3	3	3	3	1
				2		3				1	

Right: Eddie Burbanks – scorer of Sunderland's last goal before WW2 cut short the season. He went on to play a further 46 League and seven FA Cup ties for Sunderland after the war.

Left: Len Duns was almost 24 years old when WW2 broke out. Although he played on for six League seasons after 1945 the war robbed him of his prime playing days.

1945-46

FA Cup

Ground: Roker Park

Manager: Bill Murray

FA Cup Winners: Derby County

Did you know that?

The crowd of 44,820 for the FA Cup 5th Round 1st leg game against Birmingham City was packed into only three sides of Roker Park. The Roker End was still closed due to bomb damage. At half time thousands of fans ran across the pitch to stand in the potentially unsafe but much less crowded Roker End.

Match 1: Stelling, Jones, Willingham, White and Brown made debuts
Match 4: Walshaw made debut
Match 5: Hastings last game
Match 6: Lockie, Brown and Walshaw last games

Match No.	Date		Round	Venue	Opponents	Result	FT	HT	Pos.	Scorers	Attendance
1	Jan	5	R3/L1	A	Grimsby Town	W	3-1	2-1		Brown, Hastings, Housam	12,050
2		9	R3/L2	H	Grimsby Town	W	2-1	2-1		Whitelum, Hastings	19,500
3		26	R4/L1	H	Bury	W	3-1	1-0		Brown (2), Duns	29,003
4		29	R4/L2	A	Bury	L	4-5(aet)	2-3		White, Walshaw, Brown, Burbanks	11,236
5	Feb	9	R5/L1	H	Birmingham City	W	1-0	0-0		Duns	44,820
6		13	R5/L2	A	Birmingham City	L	1-3	0-0		Brown	38,000

Appearances
Goals

Alex Hastings

Alex played regularly for Sunderland from his late teens and was soon appointed club captain. He retired at the end of this season having made over 300 first team competitive appearances. In 1965 Alex emigrated to Australia, later becoming president of the South Australian Soccer Federation. He was awarded the British Empire Medal in 1981.

Mapson	Stelling	Jones	Willingham	Lockie	Housam	Whitelum	White	Brown	Hastings	Duns	Burbanks	Walshaw																	
1	2	3	4	5	6	7	8	9	10	11																			1
1	2	3	4	5	6	8		9	10	7	11																		2
1	2	3	4	5	6			9	10	7	11																		3
1	2	3	4	5	6	7	8	9			11	10																	4
1	2	3	4	5	6	8		9	10	7	11																		5
1	2	3	4	5	6	7	8	9			11	10																	6
6	6	6	6	6	6	3	6	4	4	5	2																		
				1	1	1	5	2	2	1																			

1946-47

Division One

Ground: Roker Park
Manager: Bill Murray

League Table

	P	W	D	L	F	A	Pts
Liverpool	42	25	7	10	84	52	57
Manchester U	42	22	12	8	95	54	56
Wolverhampton W	42	25	6	11	98	56	56
Stoke C	42	24	7	11	90	53	55
Blackpool	42	22	6	14	71	70	50
Sheffield U	42	21	7	14	89	75	49
Preston NE	42	18	11	13	76	74	47
Aston Villa	42	18	9	15	67	53	45
SUNDERLAND	42	18	8	16	65	66	44
Everton	42	17	9	16	62	67	43
Middlesbrough	42	17	8	17	73	68	42
Portsmouth	42	16	9	17	66	60	41
Arsenal	42	16	9	17	72	70	41
Derby Co	42	18	5	19	73	79	41
Chelsea	42	16	7	19	69	84	39
Grimsby T	42	13	12	17	61	82	38
Blackburn R	42	14	8	20	45	53	36
Bolton W	42	13	8	21	57	69	34
Charlton A	42	11	12	19	57	71	34
Huddersfield T	42	13	7	22	53	79	33
Brentford	42	9	7	26	45	88	25
Leeds U	42	6	6	30	45	90	18

FA Cup Winners: Derby County

Did you know that?

The final game of this season was delayed until 24 May due to severe winter weather in January and February. This is the latest date Sunderland have played a League game (equalled in 2008-09 v Chelsea).

- Match 1: Hall, Lloyd and Watson made debuts
- Match 4: Walsh and Reynolds made debuts, White last game & Finlay only game
- Match 9: McLain made debut
- Match 11: Robinson made debut
- Match 18: Davis made debut
- Match 24: Willingham last game
- Match 26: Scotson and Ellison made debuts
- Match 27: Hudgell made debut
- Match 28: Ellison last game
- Match 35: Lindsay only game
- Match 41: Jones last game

Matches

Match No.	Date	Round	Venue	Opponents	Result	FT	HT	Pos.	Scorers	Attendance
1	Aug 31		H	Derby County	W	3-2	2-1		Burbanks (pen), Whitelum (2)	48,466
2	Sep 4		H	Huddersfield Town	W	3-0	1-0	2	Whitelum (2), Lloyd	37,595
3	7		A	Arsenal	D	2-2	2-1	4	White, Burbanks	53,377
4	11		A	Charlton Athletic	L	0-5	0-3	6		27,425
5	14		H	Blackpool	W	3-2	2-1	3	Whitelum (2), Lloyd	40,653
6	21		A	Brentford	W	3-0	1-0	3	Whitelum (2), Burbanks	33,766
7	25		A	Huddersfield Town	D	0-0	0-0	3		15,551
8	28		H	Blackburn Rovers	W	1-0	0-0	3	Duns	43,611
9	Oct 5		A	Portsmouth	L	1-4	0-2	3	Lloyd	33,502
10	12		H	Everton	W	4-1	2-0	3	Lloyd, Whitelum, Burbanks, Duns	40,830
11	19		H	Grimsby Town	L	1-2	0-2	5	Robinson	42,763
12	26		Maine Rd	Manchester United	W	3-0	1-0	4	Whitelum (3)	48,566
13	Nov 2		H	Stoke City	L	0-1	0-1	6		57,188
14	9		A	Middlesbrough	W	3-1	2-0	5	Whitelum, Duns, Robinson	40,219
15	16		H	Chelsea	L	1-2	0-1	7	Whitelum	41,297
16	23		A	Sheffield United	L	2-4	1-1	8	Robinson, Watson (pen)	30,017
17	30		H	Preston North End	L	0-2	0-2	10		31,621
18	Dec 7		A	Leeds United	D	1-1	1-0	10	Robinson	25,784
19	14		H	Liverpool	L	1-4	1-2	10	Davis	33,291
20	21		A	Bolton Wanderers	W	1-0	0-0	10	Whitelum	19,757
21	25		H	Wolverhampton W.	L	0-1	0-0	10		37,068
22	26		A	Wolverhampton W.	L	1-2	0-0	10	Whitelum	53,834
23	28		A	Derby County	L	1-5	0-1	12	Robinson	30,911
24	Jan 4		H	Arsenal	L	1-4	0-2	14	Whitelum	36,812
26	18		A	Blackpool	W	5-0	1-0	10	Robinson (4), Reynolds	20,049
27	Feb 1		A	Blackburn Rovers	W	2-1	1-1	10	Wright, Watson	24,194
28	8		H	Portsmouth	D	0-0	0-0	10		20,401
29	15		A	Everton	L	2-4	2-1	11	Robinson, Reynolds	39,658
30	Mar 1		A	Manchester United	D	1-1	0-0	12	Robinson	25,038
31	15		H	Middlesbrough	W	1-0	0-0	12	Davis	39,521
32	22		A	Chelsea	L	1-2	1-2	13	Robinson	45,415
33	29		H	Sheffield United	W	2-1	1-0	12	Wright (pen), Duns	20,119
34	Apr 4		H	Aston Villa	W	4-1	3-1	10	Watson (2), Robinson, Burbanks	53,796
35	5		A	Preston North End	D	2-2	1-0	9	Robinson (2)	19,650
36	8		A	Aston Villa	L	0-4	0-3	12		30,686
37	12		H	Leeds United	W	1-0	1-0	12	Watson	30,429
38	19		A	Liverpool	L	0-1	0-1	12		41,589
39	26		H	Bolton Wanderers	W	3-1	0-0	10	Reynolds, Robinson, Davis	19,359
40	May 3		A	Charlton Athletic	D	1-1	0-1	10	Duns	21,323
41	10		A	Grimsby Town	W	2-1	1-0	10	Robinson, Burbanks (pen)	12,777
42	17		A	Stoke City	D	0-0	0-0	10		28,709
43	24		H	Brentford	W	2-1	1-1	9	Davis, Burbanks	20,160

Appearances
Goals

FA Cup

Match No.	Date	Round	Venue	Opponents	Result	FT	HT	Pos.	Scorers	Attendance
25	Jan 11	R3	A	Chesterfield	L	1-2	1-1		Robinson	27,500

Appearances
Goals

#	Mapson	Stelling	Jones	Willingham	Hall	Housam	Duns	Lloyd	Whitelum	Watson	Burbanks	White	Walsh	Wright	Reynolds	Finlay	McLain	Robinson	Davis	Scotson	Ellison	Hudgell	Lindsay
1	1	2	3	4	5	6	7	8	9	10	11												
2	1	2	3	4	5	6	7	8	9	10	11												
3	1	2	3	4	5	6	7		9	10	11	8											
4	1	2		4		5			9		11	10	3	6	7	8							
5	1	2	3	4	5	6	7	8	9	10	11												
6	1	2	3	4	5	6	7	8	9	10	11												
7	1	2	3	4	5	6	7	8	9	10	11												
8	1	2	3	4	5	6	7	8	9	10	11												
9	1	2	3	4	5	6	7	8	9		11						10						
10	1	2	3	4	5	6	7	8	9	10	11												
11	1	2	3	4	5	6	7		9	10	11							8					
12	1	2	3	4	5	6	7	8	9	10	11												
13	1	2	3	4	5	6	7	8	9	10	11												
14	1	2	3		5	4	7		9	10	11		6					8					
15	1	2	3		5	4		7	9	10	11		6					8					
16	1	2	3		5	4	7		9	10	11		6					8					
17	1	2	3		5	4			9	10	11		6										
18	1	2	3		5	4			7	10			6	11				8	9				
19	1	2			5	4			7	10		3	6	11				8	9				
20	1	2	3		5	4	7	10	9				6	11				8					
21	1	2			5	4	7	10	9		11		6					8					
22	1	2	3		5	4	7	10	9		11				6			8					
23	1	2			5	4	7		9	10	11		3		6			8					
24	1	2	3	4	5		6	7	10	9	11							8					
25	1	2	3		5				9	10			6	11				8		4	7		
26	1	2			5				9	10			6					8		4	7		
27	1	2			5				9	10			6	11				8		4	7	3	
28	1	2							9	10			5	6	11			8		4	7	3	
29	1	2					7	10					5	6	11			8	9	4		3	
30	1	2					7		9	10	11		5	6				8		4		3	
31	1	2				4	7			10	11		5	6				8	9			3	
32	1	2				4	7			10	11		5	6				8	9			3	
33	1		3			4	7	10	9		11		5	6				8				2	
34	1	2				4	7		9	10	11		5	6				8				3	
35	1						7		9	10			5	6	11		4	8				3	2
36	1	2				4	7		9	10	11		5					6	8			3	
37	1	2				4	7			10	11		5					6	8	9		3	
38	1	2					7			10			5	6	11		4	8	9			3	
39	1	2					7			10			5	6	11		4	8	9			3	
40	1	2					7			10	11		5	6			4	8	9			3	
41	1	2	3			4	7	10			11		5					6	8	9			
42	1	2				4	7	10			11		5					6	8	9		3	
43	1	2				4	7	10			11		5					6	8	9		3	
	42	40	24	14	25	33	33	19	34	32	32	2	18	23	11	1	12	30	12	5	3	16	1
					5	4	17	5	7	1			2	3				17	4				

#	Mapson	Stelling	Jones	Willingham	Hall	Housam	Duns	Lloyd	Whitelum	Watson	Burbanks	White	Walsh	Wright	Reynolds	Finlay	McLain	Robinson	Davis	Scotson	Ellison	Hudgell	Lindsay
25	1	2	3		5	4		7	10	11			6					8	9				
	1	1	1		1	1		1	1	1			1	1				1					

Willie Watson – England international at both football (4 caps) and cricket (23 tests).

Made his first of 223 appearances for Sunderland in the opening game of the season.

1947-48

Division One

Ground: Roker Park
Manager: Bill Murray

League Table

	P	W	D	L	F	A	Pts
Arsenal	42	23	13	6	81	32	59
Manchester U	42	19	14	9	81	48	52
Burnley	42	20	12	10	56	43	52
Derby Co	42	19	12	11	77	57	50
Wolverhampton W	42	19	9	14	83	70	47
Aston Villa	42	19	9	14	65	57	47
Preston NE	42	20	7	15	67	68	47
Portsmouth	42	19	7	16	68	50	45
Blackpool	42	17	10	15	57	41	44
Manchester C	42	15	12	15	52	47	42
Liverpool	42	16	10	16	65	61	42
Sheffield U	42	16	10	16	65	70	42
Charlton A	42	17	6	19	57	66	40
Everton	42	17	6	19	52	66	40
Stoke C	42	14	10	18	41	55	38
Middlesbrough	42	14	9	19	71	73	37
Bolton W	42	16	5	21	46	58	37
Chelsea	42	14	9	19	53	71	37
Huddersfield T	42	12	12	18	51	60	36
SUNDERLAND	42	13	10	19	56	67	36
Blackburn R	42	11	10	21	54	72	32
Grimsby T	42	8	6	28	45	111	22

FA Cup Winners: Manchester United

Did you know that?

Ron Turnbull became the highest scoring debutant for Sunderland when he scored all four goals in a 4-1 win at home to Portsmouth, 29 November 1947

Match 2: Housam last game
Match 3: Quinn made debut
Match 4: Robert Robinson made debut
Match 6: Hetherington made debut
Match 7: Hetherington and Whitelum last games
Match 13: Lloyd last game
Match 14: Oliver made debut
Match 19: Turnbull made debut
Match 28: Quinn last game
Match 29: Bee made debut
Match 30: Shackleton made debut
Match 34: Bee and Burbanks last games
Match 35: Ramsden and McGuigan made debuts

Match No.	Date	Round	Venue	Opponents	Result	FT	HT	Pos.	Scorers	Attendance
1	Aug 23		A	Arsenal	L	1-3	0-0		Lloyd	58,184
2	27		H	Aston Villa	D	0-0	0-0	17		42,253
3	30		H	Grimsby Town	W	4-2	2-0	13	J. Robinson (2), Whitelum, Burbanks	35,937
4	Sep 1		A	Aston Villa	L	0-2	0-1	14		31,271
5	6		A	Manchester City	L	0-3	0-1	18		55,172
6	10		A	Chelsea	D	1-1	0-1	17	Reynolds	30,085
7	13		H	Blackburn Rovers	L	0-1	0-0	18		36,039
8	17		H	Chelsea	L	2-3	1-1	19	Davis (2)	31,444
9	20		A	Blackpool	W	1-0	1-0	19	Scotson	25,343
10	27		H	Derby County	D	1-1	0-1	19	Duns	54,792
11	Oct 4		A	Huddersfield Town	D	2-2	2-0	19	Reynolds (2)	24,928
12	11		A	Sheffield United	L	2-3	2-0	19	Davis, Reynolds	40,614
13	18		H	Manchester United	W	1-0	0-0	17	Duns	37,148
14	25		A	Preston North End	D	2-2	1-1	19	Davis, Reynolds	31,595
15	Nov 1		H	Stoke City	W	1-0	1-0	17	Oliver	36,734
16	8		A	Bolton Wanderers	L	1-3	0-2	19	Duns	26,729
17	15		H	Liverpool	W	5-1	2-1	16	Davis (2), Watson, Quinn (2)	37,258
18	22		A	Burnley	L	0-4	0-1	18		21,939
19	29		H	Portsmouth	W	4-1	2-0	14	Turnbull (4)	39,581
20	Dec 6		A	Middlesbrough	D	2-2	2-2	14	Turnbull, Burbanks	45,145
21	13		H	Charlton Athletic	L	0-1	0-1	17		41,602
22	20		H	Arsenal	D	1-1	0-0	17	Davis	58,397
23	25		H	Everton	W	2-0	1-0	13	Reynolds, Turnbull	40,925
24	26		A	Everton	L	0-3	0-2	15		47,828
25	Jan 3		A	Grimsby Town	W	2-1	1-1	15	Burbanks, Turnbull	15,882
27	17		H	Manchester City	L	0-1	0-0	17		36,958
28	24		H	Bolton Wanderers	L	1-2	0-1	17	Wright (pen)	24,326
29	31		A	Blackburn Rovers	L	3-4	2-1	17	J. Robinson (2), Watson	23,749
30	Feb 14		A	Derby County	L	1-5	0-4	18	Turnbull	35,180
31	21		H	Huddersfield Town	W	2-0	0-0	15	Bee, Shackleton	33,416
32	28		H	Sheffield United	D	1-1	0-1	15	Shackleton	48,415
33	Mar 6		Maine Rd	Manchester United	L	1-3	0-1	15	Reynolds	56,384
34	13		H	Preston North End	L	0-2	0-2	20		45,920
35	20		A	Stoke City	L	1-3	0-1	21	Davis	26,757
36	26		H	Wolverhampton W.	W	2-1	2-1	20	Duns, Davis	59,840
37	29		A	Wolverhampton W.	L	1-2	1-1	21	Shackleton	33,840
38	Apr 6		A	Liverpool	D	0-0	0-0	20		49,687
39	10		H	Burnley	W	2-0	1-0	20	Shackleton, J. Robinson	47,003
40	12		H	Blackpool	W	1-0	0-0	19	Davis	61,084
41	17		A	Portsmouth	D	2-2	2-2	19	Wright, Davis	29,807
42	24		H	Middlesbrough	W	3-0	1-0	18	Wright, Davis, J. Robinson	51,581
43	May 1		A	Charlton Athletic	L	0-1	0-1	20		28,787

Appearances
Goals

FA Cup

26	Jan 10	R3	A	Southampton	L	0-1	0-0			24,288

Appearances
Goals

408

	Mapson	Stelling	Hudgell	Housam	Hall	Wright	Durns	Robinson, J.	Whitelum	Lloyd	Burbanks	McLain	Quinn	Robinson, R.	Hetherington	Watson	Reynolds	Walsh	Scotson	Davis	Oliver	Turnbull	Bee	Shackleton	Ramsden	McGuigan	
1	2	3	4	5	6	7	8	9	10	11																	1
1	2	3	4	5	6	7	8	9	10	11																	2
1	2	3		5	6	7	8	9		11	4	10															3
	2	3		5	6	7	8	9		11	4	10	1														4
1	2	3		5	6	7	8	9		11	4	10															5
1	2	3		5	6		8	9			4			7	10	11											6
1	2	3		5	6		8	9			4			7	10	11											7
1	2			5	6	7	8							10	11	3	4	9									8
1	2			5	6	7	10		8						11	3	4	9									9
1	2	3		5	6	7			8					10	11		4	9									10
1	2	3			6	7	8							10	11	5	4	9									11
1	2	3			6	7	8							10	11	5	4	9									12
1	2	3		5	6	7		8			4			10	11			9									13
1	2	3		5	6	7					4			10	11			8	9								14
1	2	3		5	6	7								10	11		4	8	9								15
1	2	3		5	6	7				11	4			10				8	9								16
1	2	3		5	6	7				11	4	10		9				8									17
1	2	3		5	6	7				11	4			9				8									18
1	2	3		5	6	7				11	4			10				8	9								19
1	2	3		5	6	7				11	4			10				8	9								20
1	2	3		5	6	7				11	4			10				8	9								21
1	2	3		5	6	7					4			10	11			8	9								22
1	2	3		5	6	7					4			10	11			8	9								23
1	2	3		5	6	7					4			10	11			8	9								24
1	2	3		5	10	7	8			11	6						4		9								25
1	2	3		5	6	7	8							10	11	4			9								27
1	2	3		5	6	7					10			8	11	4			9								28
1	2	3		5	6	7	8							11			4		9	10							29
1	2	3		5	6	7	8							11			4		9	10							30
1	2	3		5	6	7					4			11					9	8	10						31
1	2	3		5		7					4			11		6			9	8	10						32
1	2	3		5						7	4			11		6			9	8	10						33
1	2	3			6	7				11	4				5				9	10	8						34
1		3		5			8				4			11			9	6			10	2	7				35
1		3		5	6	7	8							11		4	9				10	2					36
1	2	3		5	6	7	8							11		4	9				10						37
1	2	3		5	6	7	8							11		4	9				10						38
1	2	3		5	6	7	8							11		4	9				10						39
1	2	3		5	6	7	8							11		4	9				10						40
1	2	3		5	6	7	8							11		4	9				10						41
1	2	3		5	6	7	8							11		4	9				10						42
1	2	3		5	6	7								11		4	9	8			10						43
41	40	40	2	39	39	38	23	7	5	14	22	6	1	2	22	27	8	18	26	4	16	5	14	2	1		
				3	4	6	1	1	3		2			2	7		1	12	1	8	1	4					

	Mapson	Stelling	Hudgell	Housam	Hall	Wright	Durns	Robinson, J.	Whitelum	Lloyd	Burbanks	McLain	Quinn	Robinson, R.	Hetherington	Watson	Reynolds	Walsh	Scotson	Davis	Oliver	Turnbull	Bee	Shackleton	Ramsden	McGuigan	
1	2	3		5	6	7				11	4			10				8	9								26
1	1	1		1	1	1				1	1			1				1	1								

Jack Stelling – he was married on the morning of 20 December 1947 then left the reception to play for Sunderland against Arsenal in the afternoon.

1948-49

Division One

Ground: Roker Park

Manager: Bill Murray

League Table

	P	W	D	L	F	A	Pts
Portsmouth	42	25	8	9	84	42	58
Manchester U	42	21	11	10	77	44	53
Derby Co	42	22	9	11	74	55	53
Newcastle U	42	20	12	10	70	56	52
Arsenal	42	18	13	11	74	44	49
Wolverhampton W	42	17	12	13	79	66	46
Manchester C	42	15	15	12	47	51	45
SUNDERLAND	42	13	17	12	49	58	43
Charlton A	42	15	12	15	63	67	42
Aston Villa	42	16	10	16	60	76	42
Stoke C	42	16	9	17	66	68	41
Liverpool	42	13	14	15	53	43	40
Chelsea	42	12	14	16	69	68	38
Bolton W	42	14	10	18	59	68	38
Burnley	42	12	14	16	43	50	38
Blackpool	42	11	16	15	54	67	38
Birmingham C	42	11	15	16	36	38	37
Everton	42	13	11	18	41	63	37
Middlesbrough	42	11	12	19	46	57	34
Huddersfield T	42	12	10	20	40	69	34
Preston NE	42	11	11	20	62	75	33
Sheffield U	42	11	11	20	57	78	33

FA Cup Winners: Wolverhampton Wanderers

Did you know that?

Sunderland lost to non-League Yeovil Town in the FA Cup 4th Round after extra-time. The Football Association had decided that to limit excess travelling and loss of work days (industrial productivity was very important so soon after WW2) extra-time would be played in Cup ties to first try and avoid a replay.

Match 15: McGuigan last game
Match 20: Dougall made debut
Match 22: Dougall last game
Match 29: Ramsden last game
Match 30: Broadis made debut
Match 33: Tommy Wright made debut & Oliver last game
Match 39: Kirtley made debut
Match 42: Jackie Robinson last game
Match 44: Turnbull last game

Match No.	Date	Round	Venue	Opponents	Result	FT	HT	Pos.	Scorers	Attendance
1	Aug 21		H	Bolton Wanderers	W	2-0	2-0		Davis (2)	47,854
2	25		A	Wolverhampton W.	W	1-0	1-0	2	Davis	41,072
3	28		A	Liverpool	L	0-4	0-1	6		52,253
4	Sep 1		H	Wolverhampton W.	D	3-3	1-1	7	Davis, W. Wright o.g., A. Wright (pen)	46,121
5	4		H	Blackpool	D	2-2	1-1	8	Shackleton (2)	48,750
6	6		A	Sheffield United	W	5-2	2-0	4	J. Robinson (2), Duns, Davis, McGuigan	25,702
7	11		A	Derby County	D	2-2	1-0	6	Shackleton, Reynolds	29,991
8	15		H	Sheffield United	W	2-0	0-0	4	Shackleton, J. Robinson	42,624
9	18		H	Arsenal	D	1-1	1-0	4	Davis	64,436
10	25		A	Huddersfield Town	L	0-2	0-2	8		23,035
11	Oct 2		H	Manchester United	W	2-1	1-0	5	Davis, Reynolds	54,419
12	9		H	Newcastle United	D	1-1	1-1	5	Shackleton	51,399
13	16		A	Portsmouth	L	0-3	0-3	9		35,205
14	23		H	Manchester City	W	3-0	1-0	6	Turnbull, J. Robinson (2)	46,979
15	30		A	Charlton Athletic	L	0-4	0-2	8		40,427
16	Nov 6		H	Stoke City	D	1-1	1-1	8	Watson	41,871
17	13		A	Burnley	L	1-3	1-1	11	J. Robinson	18,939
18	20		H	Preston North End	D	0-0	0-0	11		37,683
19	27		A	Everton	L	0-1	0-0	13		38,170
20	Dec 4		H	Chelsea	W	3-0	1-0	11	J. Robinson, Shackleton (2)	38,934
21	11		A	Birmingham City	D	0-0	0-0	10		28,249
22	18		A	Bolton Wanderers	L	1-4	1-1	11	Turnbull	24,309
23	25		H	Middlesbrough	W	1-0	1-0	11	Turnbull	43,692
24	27		A	Middlesbrough	D	0-0	0-0	11		43,455
25	Jan 1		H	Liverpool	L	0-2	0-1	11		43,109
27	15		A	Blackpool	D	3-3	0-2	11	J. Robinson, Reynolds, Shackleton	18,917
28	22		H	Derby County	W	2-1	2-1	10	Turnbull (2)	52,033
30	Feb 5		A	Arsenal	L	0-5	0-2	10		53,742
31	19		H	Huddersfield Town	L	0-1	0-1	14		42,719
32	Mar 5		A	Newcastle United	L	1-2	1-0	15	Turnbull	58,250
33	12		H	Portsmouth	L	1-4	1-3	15	Broadis	57,229
34	19		A	Preston North End	W	3-1	1-1	15	Davis (3)	34,195
35	26		H	Everton	D	1-1	1-0	15	Turnbull	36,226
36	Apr 2		A	Stoke City	D	0-0	0-0	16		22,505
37	9		H	Burnley	D	0-0	0-0	16		34,410
38	15		H	Aston Villa	D	0-0	0-0	12		51,374
39	16		A	Manchester City	D	1-1	1-1	13	A. Wright	34,461
40	19		A	Aston Villa	D	1-1	0-1	14	A. Wright	46,476
41	21		Maine Rd	Manchester United	W	2-1	2-1	10	Broadis, J. Robinson	33,437
42	23		H	Charlton Athletic	W	1-0	1-0	9	T. Wright	39,755
43	30		A	Chelsea	W	1-0	1-0	9	Turnbull	32,003
44	May 7		H	Birmingham City	D	1-1	0-0	8	Stelling (pen)	28,007

Appearances
Goals

FA Cup

Match No.	Date	Round	Venue	Opponents	Result	FT	HT	Pos.	Scorers	Attendance
26	Jan 8	R3	A	Crewe Alexandra	W	2-0	0-0		Turnbull (2)	15,550
29	29	R4	A	Yeovil Town	L	1-2 (aet)	0-1		J. Robinson	17,123

Appearances
Goals

	Mapson	Stelling	Hudgell	Scotson	Hall	Wright, A.	Duns	Robinson, J.	Davis	Shackleton	Reynolds	Turnbull	Robinson, R.	McGuigan	Watson	McLain	Ramsden	Dougall	Oliver	Broadis	Walsh	Wright, T.	Kirtley	
1	1	2	3	4	5	6	7	8	9	10	11													1
2	1	2	3	4	5	6	7	8	9	10	11													2
3	1	2	3	4	5	6	7	8	9	10	11													3
4	1	2	3	4	5	6	7		9	10	11	8												4
5	1	2	3	4	5	6	7	8	9	10	11													5
6		2	3	4	5	6	7	8	9	10			1	11										6
7		2	3	4	5	6	7	8	9	10	11		1											7
8	1	2	3	4	5	6	7	8	9	10	11													8
9	1	2	3	4	5	6	7	8	9	10	11													9
10	1	2	3	4	5	6			8	9		11	7		10									10
11	1	2	3		5	6		8	9	10	11	7			4									11
12	1	2	3		5	6		8	9	10	11				4	7								12
13		2	3		5	6	7	8	9	10	11		1		4									13
14	1		2	4	5	6	7	8		10		9			11	3								14
15	1		2	4	5	6	7	8		10		9		11		3								15
16		2	3	4	5	6	7		8	10		9	1		11									16
17	1		2	4	5	6	7	10	8			9			11	3								17
18	1		2	4	5	6	7	10		8		9			11	3								18
19	1		2	4	5	6			8	9	10	11			7	3								19
20	1		2		5	6		8		10	11	9			4	3	7							20
21	1		2		5	6		8		10	11	9			4	3	7							21
22	1		2		5	6		8		10	11	9			4	3	7							22
23	1	2	3		5	6	7	8		10	11	9			4									23
24	1	2	3			6	7	8		10	11	9			4		5							24
25	1	2			5	6		8		10	11	9			4	3								25
27	1	2			5	6	7	8		10	11	9			4	3								27
28	1	2	3			6	7	8		10	11	9			4		5							28
30	1	2	3			6		8		10	11	9			4		5	7						30
31	1	2	3			6	7		9	10	11				4			8	5					31
32	1	2	3			6	7			10	11	9			4			8	5					32
33	1	2	3			6				10	11	9			4	5		8		7				33
34	1	2	3	4	5	6			9	10					11			8		7				34
35	1	2	3	4	5	6				10		9			11			8		7				35
36	1	2	3	4	5	6			9	10					11			8		7				36
37	1	2	3	4	5	6		9		10					11			8		7				37
38	1	2	3		5	6				10	11	9			4			8		7				38
39		2	3		5	6				10	11	9	1		4					7	8			39
40		2	3		5	6		9	10	11			1		4			8		7				40
41		2	3		5	6		8		10	11		1		4			9		7				41
42		2	3		5	6		8		10	11		1		4			9		7				42
43		2	3	4	5	6					11	9	1					8		7	10			43
44		2	3	4	5	6				10	11	9	1							7	8			44
	32	33	41	22	36	42	22	29	20	39	32	24	10	2	30	1	10	3	4	13	2	12	3	
		1				3	1	9	10	8	3	8			1	1		2		1				

	Mapson	Stelling	Hudgell	Scotson	Hall	Wright, A.	Duns	Robinson, J.	Davis	Shackleton	Reynolds	Turnbull	Robinson, R.	McGuigan	Watson	McLain	Ramsden	Dougall	Oliver	Broadis	Walsh	Wright, T.	Kirtley	
26	1	2	3		5	6	7	8		10	11	9			4									26
29	1	2			5	6	7	8		10	11	9			4	3								29
	2	2	1		2	2	2	2		2	2	2			2	1								
						1					2													

Arthur Wright

— ever present during 1948-49.

Arthur joined his only club, Sunderland, straight from Castletown School in 1934. He went on to make 281 appearances before retiring to become Sunderland trainer in May 1955, a position he held until 1969 when his 35 years continuous spell at Roker Park ended.

1949-50

Division One

Ground: Roker Park
Manager: Bill Murray

League Table

	P	W	D	L	F	A	Pts
Portsmouth	42	22	9	11	74	38	53
Wolverhampton W	42	20	13	9	76	49	53
SUNDERLAND	42	21	10	11	83	62	52
Manchester U	42	18	14	10	69	44	50
Newcastle U	42	19	12	11	77	55	50
Arsenal	42	19	11	12	79	55	49
Blackpool	42	17	15	10	46	35	49
Liverpool	42	17	14	11	64	54	48
Middlesbrough	42	20	7	15	59	48	47
Burnley	42	16	13	13	40	40	45
Derby Co	42	17	10	15	69	61	44
Aston Villa	42	15	12	15	61	61	42
Chelsea	42	12	16	14	58	65	40
WBA	42	14	12	16	47	53	40
Huddersfield T	42	14	9	19	52	73	37
Bolton W	42	10	14	18	45	59	34
Fulham	42	10	14	18	41	54	34
Everton	42	10	14	18	42	66	34
Stoke C	42	11	12	19	45	75	34
Charlton A	42	13	6	23	53	65	32
Manchester C	42	8	13	21	36	68	29
Birmingham C	42	7	14	21	31	67	28

FA Cup Winners: Arsenal

Did you know that?

The Sunderland v Newcastle United game on 4 March 1950 was witnessed by a Roker Park record League attendance of 68,004 with record gate receipts for a League game of £93,568.

Match 9: Craig only game
Match 23: Case made debut
Match 37: Wood only game

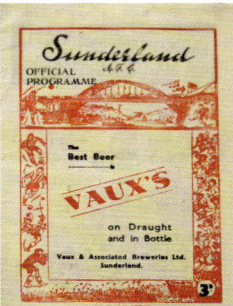

Match results

Match No.	Date	Round	Venue	Opponents	Result	FT	HT	Pos.	Scorers	Attendance
1	Aug 20		A	Liverpool	L	2-4	1-2		Davis, Broadis	49,811
2	23		A	Burnley	D	2-2	2-2	13	Davis, Shackleton	35,599
3	27		H	Arsenal	W	4-2	2-2	9	Shackleton (2), Broadis, T. Wright	56,504
4	31		H	Burnley	W	2-1	1-1	8	Shackleton, Stelling (pen)	53,032
5	Sep 3		A	Bolton Wanderers	L	1-2	1-1	11	Shackleton	32,092
6	7		A	Chelsea	L	1-3	1-2	16	Reynolds	40,061
7	10		H	Birmingham City	D	1-1	0-1	15	Shackleton	48,552
8	17		A	Derby County	L	2-3	2-0	19	Stelling (pen), Davis	31,796
9	24		H	West Bromwich Albion	W	2-1	1-1	15	Broadis, Davis	50,896
10	Oct 1		A	Manchester United	W	3-1	3-0	11	Carey o.g., Davis, Shackleton	51,240
11	8		H	Blackpool	D	1-1	1-0	13	A. Wright	64,889
12	15		A	Newcastle United	D	2-2	2-1	12	T. Wright, Davis	57,999
13	22		H	Fulham	W	2-0	1-0	9	Davis, Stelling (pen)	46,253
14	29		A	Manchester City	L	1-2	1-2	10	T. Wright	37,182
15	Nov 5		H	Charlton Athletic	W	2-1	0-0	9	Davis (2)	40,503
16	12		A	Aston Villa	L	0-2	0-2	12		42,160
17	19		H	Wolverhampton W.	W	3-1	2-0	9	T. Wright, Broadis, Reynolds	51,487
18	26		A	Portsmouth	D	2-2	0-2	8	Davis, Broadis	36,035
19	Dec 3		H	Huddersfield Town	D	1-1	0-1	8	Davis	33,951
20	10		A	Everton	W	2-0	2-0	8	T. Wright, Davis	33,329
21	17		H	Liverpool	W	3-2	2-2	8	T. Wright, Shackleton, Kirtley	46,515
22	24		A	Arsenal	L	0-5	0-1	9		43,249
23	26		H	Stoke City	W	3-0	0-0	8	Shackleton, Case (2)	50,246
24	27		A	Stoke City	L	1-2	1-0	9	Watson	41,685
25	31		H	Bolton Wanderers	W	2-0	0-0	9	Shackleton, Davis	38,135
26	Jan 7	R3	H	Huddersfield Town	W	6-0	4-0		Davis (2), Broadis (2), Shackleton(2)	55,097
27	14		A	Birmingham City	W	2-1	1-1	9	Shackleton, Davis	32,095
28	21		H	Derby County	W	6-1	3-0	7	Davis (3), Broadis, T. Wright, Shackleton	62,413
29	28	R4	A	Tottenham Hotspur	L	1-5	1-2		Davis	66,246
30	Feb 4		A	West Bromwich Albion	W	2-0	0-0	5	T. Wright, Broadis	36,101
31	18		H	Manchester United	D	2-2	1-1	4	Davis, Reynolds	63,251
32	25		A	Blackpool	W	1-0	1-0	3	Shackleton	21,317
33	Mar 4		H	Newcastle United	D	2-2	1-2	3	Shackleton, Broadis	68,004
34	11		A	Wolverhampton W.	W	3-1	1-0	4	Davis (3)	44,318
35	18		H	Portsmouth	D	1-1	1-1	4	Davis	44,591
36	25		A	Charlton Athletic	D	2-2	0-1	3	Stelling (pen), Davis	33,286
37	Apr 1		H	Aston Villa	W	2-1	1-0	4	Broadis (2)	36,293
38	7		H	Middlesbrough	W	2-0	0-0	3	Broadis (2)	62,487
39	8		A	Fulham	W	3-0	1-0	1	Reynolds, Duns, T. Wright	39,545
40	10		A	Middlesbrough	L	0-2	0-1	2		44,260
41	15		H	Manchester City	L	1-2	0-0	3	Stelling (pen)	40,404
42	22		A	Huddersfield Town	L	1-3	1-2	5	Reynolds	31,439
43	29		H	Everton	W	4-2	2-0	4	Duns, T. Wright (3)	23,519
44	May 6		H	Chelsea	W	4-1	1-1	3	Davis (2), Broadis, T. Wright	21,567

FA Cup

Match No.	Date	Round	Venue	Opponents	Result	FT	HT	Scorers	Attendance
26	Jan 7	R3	H	Huddersfield Town	W	6-0	4-0	Davis (2), Broadis (2), Shackleton(2)	55,097
29	28	R4	A	Tottenham Hotspur	L	1-5	1-2	Davis	66,246

	Robinson, R.	Stelling	Hudgell	Scotson	Hall	Wright, A.	Wright, T.	Broadis	Davis	Shackleton	Reynolds	Mapson	Watson	Craig	Walsh	Kirtley	McLain	Case	Wood	Duns	
1		2	3	4	5	6	7	8	9	10	11										1
2	1	2	3	4	5	6	7	8	9	10	11										2
3		2	3	4	5	6	7	8	9	10	11	1									3
4		2	3	4	5	6	7	8	9	10	11	1									4
5		2	3	4	5	6	7	8	9	10	11	1									5
6		2	3		5	6	7	8	9	10	11	1	4								6
7		2	3		5	6	7	8	9	10	11	1	4								7
8		2	3		5	6	7	8	9	10	11	1	4								8
9		2			5	6	7	8	9	10	11	1	4	3							9
10		2	3		5	6	7	8	9	10	11	1	4								10
11		2	3		5	6	7	8	9	10	11	1	4								11
12		2	3			6	7	8	9		11	1	4		5	10					12
13		2	3	6			7	8	9	10	11	1	4		5						13
14		2	3		6	7	8		9	10	11	1	4		5						14
15		2	3			7	8	9	10	11	1	4		5	6						15
16		2	3			7	8	9	10	11	1	4		5	6						16
17		2	3		6	7	8	9	10	11	1	4		5							17
18		2	3		6	7	8	9	10	11	1			5	4						18
19		2	3	4		7	8	9	10	11	1			5	6						19
20		2	3	4	6	7	8	9	10	11	1			5							20
21		2	3		6	7		9	10	11	1	4		5	8						21
22		2	3		6	7	8	9	10	11	1	4		5							22
23		2	3		6	7	8		10	11	1	4		5		9					23
24		2	3		6	7	8		10	11	1	4		5		9					24
25		2	3		6	7	8	9	10	11	1	4		5							25
27		2	3			7	8	9	10	11	1	4		5	6						27
28		2	3			7	8	9	10	11	1	4		5	6						28
30		2	3		6	7		9		10	11	1	4		5	8					30
31		2	3		6	7	8	9	10	11	1	4		5							31
32		2	3		6	7	8	9	10	11	1	4		5							32
33		2	3		6	7		9	10	11	1	4		5							33
34		2	3	5	6	7	8	9	10	11	1	4									34
35		2	3	5	6	7	8	9	10	11	1	4									35
36		2	3		6	7	8	9	10	11	1	4		5							36
37		2		4		6	7	8	9	10	11	1		5			3				37
38		2	3		6	7	8	9	10	11	1	4		5							38
39		2	3		6	9	8		10	11	1	4		5				7			39
40		2	3		6	9	8		10	11	1	4		5				7			40
41		2	3	4	6	7	9		10	11	1			5	8						41
42		2	3		6	7	8		10	11	1	4		5		9					42
43		2	3	6		9	8		10	11	1	4		5				7			43
44		2	3		6	7	8	9		11	1	4		5	10						44
	2	42	40	11	13	35	42	41	34	40	42	40	32	1	29	5	6	3	1	3	
		5			1	13	13	25	14	5		1			1		2		2		

26		2	3			7	8	9	10	11	1	4		5		6					26
29		2	3			7	8	9	10	11	1	4		5		6					29
	2	2				2	2	2	2	2	2	2		2		2					
							2	3	2												

Dickie Davis – Division One leading scorer with 25 goals.

1950-51

Division One

Ground: Roker Park

Manager: Bill Murray

League Table

	P	W	D	L	F	A	Pts
Tottenham H	42	25	10	7	82	44	60
Manchester U	42	24	8	10	74	40	56
Blackpool	42	20	10	12	79	53	50
Newcastle U	42	18	13	11	62	53	49
Arsenal	42	19	9	14	73	56	47
Middlesbrough	42	18	11	13	76	65	47
Portsmouth	42	16	15	11	71	68	47
Bolton W	42	19	7	16	64	61	45
Liverpool	42	16	11	15	53	59	43
Burnley	42	14	14	14	48	43	42
Derby Co	42	16	8	18	81	75	40
SUNDERLAND	42	12	16	14	63	73	40
Stoke C	42	13	14	15	50	59	40
Wolverh'pton W	42	15	8	19	74	61	38
Aston Villa	42	12	13	17	66	68	37
WBA	42	13	11	18	53	61	37
Charlton A	42	14	9	19	63	80	37
Fulham	42	13	11	18	52	68	37
Huddersfield T	42	15	6	21	64	92	36
Chelsea	42	12	8	22	53	65	32
Sheffield W	42	12	8	22	64	83	32
Everton	42	12	8	22	48	86	32

FA Cup Winners: Newcastle United

Did you know that?

In June 1950 Willie Watson became the first, and so far only, Sunderland player to be named in an England World Cup squad. Watson travelled to Brazil with the squad but did not make an appearance during the tournament.

Match 3: Hedley made debut
Match 4: Case last game & Agnew only game
Match 5: Smith made debut
Match 6: Scotson last game
Match 14: Cunning made debut
Match 16: Cunning last game
Match 19: Bingham made debut

Match No.	Date		Round	Venue	Opponents	Result	FT	HT	Pos.	Scorers	Attendance
1	Aug	19		H	Derby County	W	1-0	1-0		Shackleton	52,452
2		21		A	Aston Villa	L	1-3	1-2	7	Davis	37,143
3		26		A	Liverpool	L	0-4	0-3	20		52,080
4		30		H	Aston Villa	D	3-3	2-1	18	Duns, T. Wright, Broadis	40,893
5	Sep	2		H	Fulham	L	0-1	0-0	20		43,080
6		6		A	Wolverhampton W.	L	1-2	1-1	21	T. Wright	38,163
7		9		A	Bolton Wanderers	W	2-1	0-0	18	Broadis, Shackleton	30,745
8		16		H	Blackpool	L	0-2	0-0	20		56,204
9		23		A	Tottenham Hotspur	D	1-1	0-1	19	Broadis	59,190
10		30		H	Charlton Athletic	W	4-2	2-0	19	Broadis (3), Stelling (pen)	26,340
11	Oct	7		H	Huddersfield Town	D	0-0	0-0	19		33,571
12		14		A	Middlesbrough	D	1-1	1-0	19	Davis	52,764
13		21		H	Burnley	D	1-1	1-1	19	Stelling (pen)	38,982
14		28		A	Chelsea	L	0-3	0-0	19		51,315
15	Nov	4		H	Sheffield Wed.	W	5-1	2-1	16	Shackleton, T. Wright, Ford (3)	48,939
16		11		A	Arsenal	L	1-5	1-1	18	Davis	68,682
17		18		H	Portsmouth	D	0-0	0-0	17		46,111
18		25		A	Everton	L	1-3	1-3	19	Broadis	46,060
19	Dec	2		H	Stoke City	D	1-1	0-1	19	Kirtley	36,037
20		9		A	West Bromwich Albion	L	1-3	0-0	19	Ford	26,666
21		16		A	Derby County	L	5-6	2-3	19	Davis (2), Ford (2), T. Wright	15,952
22		23		H	Liverpool	W	2-1	1-1	17	Watson, Davis	30,150
23		25		H	Manchester United	W	2-1	1-1	16	T. Wright (2)	41,215
24		26		A	Manchester United	W	5-3	4-2	15	Bingham, Broadis (3), Davis	37,024
25		30		A	Fulham	D	1-1	0-0	15	Davis	33,615
26	Jan	6	R3	H	Coventry City	W	2-0	0-0		T. Wright, A. Wright	36,983
27		13		H	Bolton Wanderers	L	1-2	1-2	15	T. Wright	47,197
28		20		A	Blackpool	D	2-2	1-1	15	Ford, Davis	22,797
29		27	R4	H	Southampton	W	2-0	1-0		Davis (2)	61,314
30	Feb	3		H	Tottenham Hotspur	D	0-0	0-0	15		56,817
31		10	R5	H	Norwich City	W	3-1	1-0		Davis, Watson, T. Wright	65,125
32		17		A	Charlton Athletic	L	0-3	0-3	17		24,627
33		24	R6	H	Wolverhampton W.	D	1-1	1-1		Davis	62,373
34		28	R6r	A	Wolverhampton W.	L	1-3	0-1		Ford	54,243
35	Mar	3		H	Middlesbrough	W	2-1	1-0	17	Kirtley, Ford	57,958
36		7		A	Huddersfield Town	W	4-3	2-1	15	T. Wright (2, 1 pen), Shackleton, Bingham	11,537
37		10		A	Burnley	D	1-1	1-0	15	Ford	25,065
38		17		H	Chelsea	D	1-1	1-1	15	Ford	24,270
39		23		A	Newcastle United	D	2-2	1-1	15	T. Wright, Ford	62,173
40		24		A	Sheffield Wed.	L	0-3	0-1	15		48,488
41		26		H	Newcastle United	W	2-1	2-1	15	Kirtley, Ford	55,159
42		31		H	Arsenal	L	0-2	0-0	15		31,505
43	Apr	7		A	Portsmouth	D	0-0	0-0	16		30,264
44		14		H	Everton	W	4-0	3-0	14	Shackleton, Kirtley, Ford, Bingham	27,283
45		21		A	Stoke City	W	4-2	1-1	13	Ford (2), Shackleton, Bingham	23,398
46		28		H	West Bromwich Albion	D	1-1	1-0	12	Ford	17,727
47	May	5		H	Wolverhampton W.	D	0-0	0-0	12		23,198

	Mapson	Stelling	Hudgell	Scotson	Walsh	Wright, A.	Duns	Broadis	Davis	Shackleton	Reynolds	Wright, T.	Hedley	Agnew	Case	McLain	Smith	Watson	Kirtley	Cumming	Ford	Bingham	Hall	
1	2	3	4	5	6	7	8	9	10	11														1
1	2	3	4	5	6		8	9	10	11	7													2
1		3	4	5	6		8	9	10	11	7	2												3
		3	4	5	6	11	8		10		7	2	1	9										4
1		3		5	6		8		10	11	7	2		4	9									5
1		3	2	5	6	7	8		10	11	9			4										6
1	2	3		5	6		8	9	10	11	7			4										7
1	2	3		5	6		8	9	10	11	7			4										8
1	2			5	6		8	9	10	11	7	3		4										9
1	2	3		5	6	7	8		10	11	9			4										10
1	2	3		5	6	7	8			11	9		4			10								11
1	2	3		5	6	7	10	9		8				4		11								12
1	2	3		5	6	7	10	9		11	8			4										13
1	2	3		5			10	8			7		6	4		11	9							14
1	2	3		5	6			8	10		7			4		11	9							15
1	2	3		5			10	8			7			4		11	9							16
1	2	3		5	6			8	9		11	7		4			9							17
1	2	3		5	6		8		10	11	7			4			9							18
1	2	3		5	6	11			10					4	8		9	7						19
1	2	3		5	6			10					4		11	8	9	7						20
1		2		5	6			10			7	3		4		11	8	9						21
1		3		5	6			10			7	2		4		11	8	9						22
1		3		5	6			10			7	2		4		11	8	9						23
1		3		5	6	10	9			8	2		4		11			7						24
1		3		5	6	10	9			8	2		4		11			7						25
1		3		5	6			10	11		8	2		4			9	7	5					27
1		3	4	6			8	10			7	2				11		9	5					28
1		3		5	6	11		8	10		7	2		4				9	5					30
1		3	4			10	8	11			7	2		6				9	5					32
1	2	3		6				10	11	7				4	8			9	5					35
1	2	3		6			9	10	11	8				4				7	5					36
1	2	3		6				10	11	8				4				9	7	5				37
1	2	3		6				10	11	8				4				9	7	5				38
1		3		6				10	11	7	2			4	8			9		5				39
1		3		6				10	11	7	2			4	8			9		5				40
1		3		6				10	11	7	2			4	8			9		5				41
1		3		6				10	11	7	2			4	8			9		5				42
1	2	3		6			8	10	11					4				9	7	5				43
1		3		6				10	11		2			4				9	7	5				44
1		3		6				10	11		2		4		8			9	7	5				45
1		3		6				10	11		2		4		8			9	7	5				46
1		3		6				10	11		2		4		8			9	7	5				47
1	21	41	5	32	37	9	20	24	30	26	34	21	1	1	17	1	28	15	4	26	13	15		
	2			1	10	9	6		10						1	4		16	4					

		3		5	6	11	10	8			7	2				4		9						26
		3		5	6	11		8	10		7	2		4				9						29
		3		5	6			8	10		7	2		4		11		9						31
		3		5	6		10	8	11		7	2		4				9						33
		3		5	6		10	8	11		7	2		4				9						34
5		5	5	2	3	5	4		5	5	5		3	3		5								
				1			4			2				1		1								

Trevor Ford had an eventful home debut v Sheffield Wednesday, 4 November 1950. He scored a hat-trick, accidentally broke the opposing centre-half's jaw and split one of the goal posts as he and Wednesday's goalkeeper collided with it.

1951-52

Division One

Ground: Roker Park

Manager: Bill Murray

League Table

	P	W	D	L	F	A	Pts
Manchester U	42	23	11	8	95	52	57
Tottenham H	42	22	9	11	76	51	53
Arsenal	42	21	11	10	80	61	53
Portsmouth	42	20	8	14	68	58	48
Bolton W	42	19	10	13	65	61	48
Aston Villa	42	19	9	14	79	70	47
Preston NE	42	17	12	13	74	54	46
Newcastle U	42	18	9	15	98	73	45
Blackpool	42	18	9	15	64	64	45
Charlton A	42	17	10	15	68	63	44
Liverpool	42	12	19	11	57	61	43
SUNDERLAND	42	15	12	15	70	61	42
WBA	42	14	13	15	74	77	41
Burnley	42	15	10	17	56	63	40
Manchester C	42	13	13	16	58	61	39
Wolverh'pton W	42	12	14	16	73	73	38
Derby Co	42	15	7	20	63	80	37
Middlesbrough	42	15	6	21	64	88	36
Chelsea	42	14	8	20	52	72	36
Stoke C	42	12	7	23	49	88	31
Huddersfield T	42	10	8	24	49	82	28
Fulham	42	8	11	23	58	77	27

FA Cup Winners: Newcastle United

Did you know that?

McLain and Hudgell scored own-goals in the 3-1 home defeat by Aston Villa on 5 September 1951. This was the first time Sunderland had scored two own-goals in a game at Roker Park.

Match 5: Broadis last game
Match 12: McSeveney made debut
Match 16: McLain last game
Match 17: Aitken made debut
Match 36: Marston made debut
Match 37: Duns last game
Match 44: Robinson last game

Match No.	Date		Round	Venue	Opponents	Result	FT	HT	Pos.	Scorers	Attendance
1	Aug	18		A	Derby County	W	4-3	1-2		Shackleton, McLain, Bingham, Ford	24,676
2		25		H	Manchester City	W	3-0	2-0	3	Shackleton (3, 1 pen)	45,396
3		27		A	Aston Villa	L	1-2	0-2	7	Shackleton	42,295
4	Sep	1		A	Arsenal	L	0-3	0-2	15		66,137
5		5		H	Aston Villa	L	1-3	1-2	16	Shackleton	44,107
6		8		H	Blackpool	L	1-3	1-0	18	Shackleton	55,163
7		15		A	Liverpool	D	2-2	0-2	19	Shackleton, Davis	37,381
8		22		H	Portsmouth	W	3-1	2-0	14	Shackleton, Kirtley, Bingham	45,389
9		29		A	Chelsea	L	1-2	0-2	16	Kirtley	49,762
10	Oct	6		A	Bolton Wanderers	D	1-1	1-1	18	A. Wright	43,887
11		13		H	Stoke City	L	0-1	0-0	19		41,806
12		20		A	Manchester United	W	1-0	0-0	17	Davis	42,707
13		27		H	Tottenham Hotspur	L	0-1	0-1	18		50,513
14	Nov	3		A	Preston North End	L	2-4	1-3	20	Kirtley, Ford	28,488
15		10		H	Burnley	D	0-0	0-0	20		33,139
16		17		A	Charlton Athletic	L	1-2	0-1	20	Kirtley	22,853
17		24		H	Fulham	D	2-2	1-1	19	Shackleton (2)	34,014
18	Dec	1		A	Middlesbrough	W	2-0	1-0	18	Watson, A. Wright	36,629
19		8		H	West Bromwich Albion	D	3-3	1-2	19	Shackleton, Ford, Bingham	26,774
20		15		H	Derby County	W	3-0	1-0	18	McSeveney, Bingham, Ford	36,131
21		22		A	Manchester City	L	1-3	0-1	18	Ford	28,626
22		25		H	Newcastle United	L	1-4	0-2	18	Ford	52,274
23		26		A	Newcastle United	D	2-2	1-0	18	Bingham, Ford	63,665
24		29		H	Arsenal	W	4-1	0-0	18	Shackleton, Ford (2), Bingham	47,045
25	Jan	1		H	Wolverhampton W.	D	1-1	0-1	17	Shackleton	35,172
26		5		A	Blackpool	L	0-3	0-1	19		22,252
29		19		H	Liverpool	W	3-0	2-0	17	Shackleton (2), Davis	33,549
30		26		A	Portsmouth	W	2-0	1-0	15	Ford, Shackleton	33,613
31	Feb	9		H	Chelsea	W	4-1	3-0	16	Shackleton, Ford (3)	37,298
32		16		H	Bolton Wanderers	L	0-2	0-1	17		43,397
33		23		A	Wolverhampton W.	W	3-0	1-0	15	Ford (2), Bingham	37,546
34	Mar	1		A	Stoke City	D	1-1	1-0	15	Kirtley	24,218
35		8		H	Manchester United	L	1-2	1-0	15	Ford (pen)	48,078
36		15		A	Tottenham Hotspur	L	0-2	0-1	16		51,745
37		22		H	Preston North End	D	0-0	0-0	16		34,147
38		29		A	Burnley	W	1-0	1-0	15	Davis	11,618
39	Apr	5		A	Charlton Athletic	D	1-1	1-1	15	Ford	21,206
40		11		H	Huddersfield Town	W	7-1	3-1	15	Shackleton (2), Davis (2), Ford, Gallogly o.g., McSeveney	34,640
41		12		A	Fulham	W	1-0	0-0	12	Shackleton	29,622
42		15		A	Huddersfield Town	D	2-2	0-1	12	Ford (2)	32,961
43		19		H	Middlesbrough	W	3-1	0-1	12	T. Wright, Shackleton, Ford	37,670
44		26		A	West Bromwich Albion	D	1-1	1-0	12	Ford	30,997

Appearances
Goals

FA Cup

27	Jan	12	R3	H	Stoke City	D	0-0	0-0			45,100
28		14	R3r	A	Stoke City	L	1-3	1-2		McSeveney	31,841

Appearances
Goals

	Mapson	Hedley	Hudgell	McLain	Hall	Wright, A.	Bingham	Broadis	Ford	Shackleton	Duns	Robinson	Reynolds	Watson	Kirtley	Stelling	Davis	McSeveney	Aitken	Marston	Wright, T.	
1	2	3	4	5	6	7	8	9	10	11												1
1	2	3	4	5	6	7	8	9	10	11												2
	2	3	4	5	6	7	8	9	10	11	1											3
	2	3	4	5	6	7	8	9	10		1	11										4
	2	3	4	5	6	7	8	9	10		1	11										5
1	2	3		5	6	7		9	10			11	4	8								6
1		3	6	5		7			10			11	4	8	2	9						7
1		3		5	6	7		9	10			11	4	8	2							8
1		3		5	6	7			10			11	4	8	2							9
1		3	4	5	6			9	10	7		11		8	2							10
1		3	4	5	6	7		9	10			11	8	2								11
1		3		5	6	7			10			4	8	2	9	11						12
1		3		5	6	7			10			4	8	2	9	11						13
1		3		5	6	7		9	10			4	8	2		11						14
1		3		5	6			9	10	7		4		2	8	11						15
1		3	4	5	6			9	10	7	1		8	2		11						16
	3			5		7		9	10		1	4	8	2		11	6					17
	3			5	6	7		9	10		1	4	8	2		11						18
	3			5	6			9	10		1	4	8	2		11						19
	3			5				9	10		1	4	8	2		11	6					20
	3			5		7		9	10		1	4	8	2		11						21
	3			5		7		9	10		1	4	8	2		11	6					22
	2	3		5	10	7		9	8		1	4				11	6					23
	2	3		5		7		9	10		1	4	8			11	6					24
	2	3		5		7		9	10		1	4	8			11	6					25
	2	3		5		7		9	10		1	4	8			11	6					26
1		3		5	6	7		9	10			11		2	8		4					29
1		3		5	6	7		9	10			11		2	8		4					30
1		3		5	6			9	10			11		2	8		4					31
1		3		5	6	7		9	10			11		2	8		4					32
1		3		5	6	7		9	10			11	8	2			4					33
1	3			5	6	7		9	10			11	8	2			4					34
1	3			5	6	7		9	10			11	8	2			4					35
1	3			5				9	10	7		4				8	11	6	2			36
	3			5				9	10	7	1	4				8	11	6	2			37
1	3			5		7						4				8	11	6	2			38
1	3			5		7		9	10			4				8	11	6	2			39
1	3			5		7		9	10			4				8	11	6	2			40
1	3			5		7		9	10			4				8		6	2	11		41
	3			5		7		9	10		1	4	8				6	2	11			42
	3			5				9	10		1	11	4	8	2		6		7			43
	3			5	6	7		9			1	11	4	10	2				8			44
24	26	26	9	42	26	36	5	39	41	8	18	8	36	25	25	14	20	23	7	4		
			1		2	7		22	22				1	5		6	2			1		

	2	3		5		7		9	10	1		4	8			11	6					27
	2	3		5		7		9	10	1		4	8			11	6					28
	2	2	2	2	2	2		2	2	2		2	2			2	2					
										1												

Len Shackleton

Shackleton's best goals haul in a season while at Sunderland ending up joint top scorer with Trevor Ford.

417

1952-53

Division One

Ground: Roker Park
Manager: Bill Murray

League Table

	P	W	D	L	F	A	Pts
Arsenal	42	21	12	9	97	64	54
Preston NE	42	21	12	9	85	60	54
Wolverh'pton W	42	19	13	10	86	63	51
WBA	42	21	8	13	66	60	50
Charlton A	42	19	11	12	77	63	49
Burnley	42	18	12	12	67	52	48
Blackpool	42	19	9	14	71	70	47
Manchester U	42	18	10	14	69	72	46
SUNDERLAND	42	15	13	14	68	82	43
Tottenham H	42	15	11	16	78	69	41
Aston Villa	42	14	13	15	63	61	41
Cardiff C	42	14	12	16	54	46	40
Middlesbrough	42	14	11	17	70	77	39
Bolton W	42	15	9	18	61	69	39
Portsmouth	42	14	10	18	74	83	38
Newcastle U	42	14	9	19	59	70	37
Liverpool	42	14	8	20	61	82	36
Sheffield W	42	12	11	19	62	72	35
Chelsea	42	12	11	19	56	66	35
Manchester C	42	14	7	21	72	87	35
Stoke C	42	12	10	20	53	66	34
Derby Co	42	11	10	21	59	74	32

FA Cup Winners: Blackpool

Did you know that?

Sunderland played their first floodlit game at Roker Park on 10 December 1952, a 5-3 victory in a friendly against Dundee. The four floodlight towers only had 12 lamps on each of them.

Match 1: Threadgold made debut
Match 4: Toseland made debut
Match 10: Anderson made debut
Match 12: Snell made debut
Match 18: Toseland last game
Match 21: Marston last game
Match 37: Mapson last game
Match 38: Fairley made debut & Smith last game
Match 39: Fairley last game
Match 42: Reynolds last game
Match 43: Kemp made debut
Match 45: Threadgold and Walsh last games

Match No.	Date	Round	Venue	Opponents	Result	FT	HT	Pos.	Scorers	Attendance
1	Aug 23		H	Charlton Athletic	W	2-1	1-0		T. Wright, Shackleton	49,110
2	30		A	Arsenal	W	2-1	2-0	5	Bingham, Ford	56,873
3	Sep 1		A	Aston Villa	L	0-3	0-0	10		37,240
4	6		H	Derby County	W	2-1	2-1	8	Toseland, Ford (pen)	40,881
5	10		A	Newcastle United	D	2-2	1-0	8	Watson, T. Wright	60,728
6	13		A	Blackpool	L	0-2	0-1	12		35,350
7	17		H	Newcastle United	L	0-2	0-1	14		59,665
8	20		H	Chelsea	W	2-1	1-1	8	Ford, Kirtley	40,388
9	27		A	Manchester United	W	1-0	1-0	8	Ford	30,771
10	Oct 4		H	Portsmouth	D	1-1	1-0	8	Ford (pen)	45,144
11	11		H	West Bromwich Albion	W	1-0	1-0	7	Barlow o.g.	40,756
12	18		A	Middlesbrough	W	2-1	0-0	4	Davis, Kirtley	38,305
13	25		H	Liverpool	W	3-1	2-0	2	Kirtley, Ford (2)	50,545
14	Nov 1		A	Manchester City	W	5-2	3-2	2	Ford (4, 1 pen), Kirtley	33,210
15	8		H	Stoke City	D	1-1	1-1	2	Ford	43,441
16	15		A	Preston North End	L	2-3	1-3	3	Davis, Kirtley	28,693
17	22		H	Burnley	W	2-1	1-0	2	Watson, T. Wright	40,225
18	29		A	Tottenham Hotspur	D	2-2	2-0	2	Ford (2, 1 pen)	45,980
19	Dec 6		H	Sheffield Wed.	W	2-1	0-1	2	Shackleton, Kirtley	49,854
20	13		A	Cardiff City	L	1-4	0-2	2	Ford	42,518
21	20		A	Charlton Athletic	L	1-3	0-1	5	Bingham	14,548
22	26		A	Wolverhampton W.	D	1-1	1-1	6	Bingham	51,419
23	27		H	Wolverhampton W.	W	5-2	3-0	3	Davis (2), Bingham (2), Kirtley	41,493
24	Jan 1		H	Aston Villa	D	2-2	1-1	3	Ford, A. Wright	41,821
25	3		H	Arsenal	W	3-1	2-1	1	Ford (pen), Shackleton, Bingham	54,912
28	17		A	Derby County	L	1-3	0-2	2	Watson	21,506
29	24		H	Blackpool	D	1-1	0-0	2	T. Wright	53,653
31	Feb 7		A	Chelsea	L	2-3	2-2	6	T. Wright (2)	40,720
32	18		H	Manchester United	D	2-2	0-1	6	Chilton o.g., Watson	24,263
33	21		A	Portsmouth	L	2-5	1-2	6	Smith (2)	29,669
34	28		A	West Bromwich Albion	D	1-1	1-1	7	Shackleton	31,686
35	Mar 7		H	Middlesbrough	D	1-1	0-1	8	Aitken	38,237
36	14		A	Liverpool	L	0-2	0-2	8		40,409
37	21		H	Manchester City	D	3-3	2-2	8	Davis (2), Shackleton	26,270
38	25		A	Stoke City	L	0-3	0-2	9		19,622
39	Apr 3		A	Bolton Wanderers	L	0-5	0-1	9		34,862
40	4		H	Preston North End	D	2-2	1-1	9	Ford, McSeveney	29,793
41	6		H	Bolton Wanderers	W	2-0	1-0	9	T. Wright (2)	32,227
42	11		A	Burnley	L	1-5	0-1	9	T. Wright	21,252
43	18		H	Tottenham Hotspur	D	1-1	0-1	9	Walsh	24,953
44	25		A	Sheffield Wed.	L	0-4	0-2	10		44,481
45	27		H	Cardiff City	W	4-2	1-1	9	Ford (2), Shackleton, Kirtley	7,469

Appearances
Goals

FA Cup

26	Jan 10	R3	H	Scunthorpe United	D	1-1	0-0		Ford	56,507
27	15	R3r	A	Scunthorpe United	W	2-1	1-0		T. Wright, Ford	21,624
30	31	R4	A	Burnley	L	0-2	0-2			53,231

Appearances
Goals

	Threadgold	Stelling	Hedley	Aitken	Hall	Wright A.	Bingham	Wright T.	Ford	Shackleton	Reynolds	Kirtley	Toseland	Watson	Mapson	Marston	Hudgell	Anderson	Snell	Davis	McSeveney	Smith	Walsh	Fairley	Kemp	
1		2	3	4	5	6	7	8	9	10	11															1
2	1	2	3	4	5	6	7	8	9	10	11															2
3	1	2	3	4	5	6	7	8	9	10	11															3
4	1	2	3	4	5	6	7	8	9		10	11														4
5	1	2	3	4	5	6		7	9	8			11	10												5
6				4	5	6		7	9			8	11	10	1	2	3									6
7	1	2	3	4	5	6	7	8	9		11			10												7
8	1	2		4	5	6		7	9		11	8		10			3									8
9	1	2	3		5	6		7	9	10	11	8		4												9
10	1	2	3		5	6		7	9	10		8	11				4									10
11	1	2	3	4	5	6		7	9	10	11			8												11
12	1	2			5		7			10	11	8		4		3		6	9							12
13	1	2		6	5			7	9	10	11	8		4		3										13
14	1	2		6	5			7	9	10	11	8		4		3										14
15	1	2		6	5			7	9	10	11	8		4		3										15
16	1	2		6	5			7		10	11	8		4		3			9							16
17	1	2		4	5	6		7	9			8	11	10		3										17
18	1	2		4	5	6		7	9			8	11	10		3										18
19	1	2		4	5	6	7	9			10	11	5			3										19
20	1		2	4	5	6		7	9	10	11			8		3										20
21	1		2	4	5	6	7	10	9			11	8				3									21
22		2	3	5		6	7		9			11	10		4	1			8							22
23			2	5		6	7		9			11	8		1		3	4	10							23
24			2	5		6	7		9			11	10		1		3	4	8							24
25	1		2	5		6	7		9	10			8	4		3				11						25
28	1	2		6	5			7		10			8	11		3	4		9							28
29	1	2		6	5			7		10			8	11		3	4		9							29
31	1		2	5		6	7	11				8		10		3	4		9							31
32	1	2		6	5	10	7	11		8				4		3			9							32
33	1		2	4	5	6		7		10		8		11		3				9						33
34	1	2	3	6				7		10			8	11			4			9	5					34
35	1	2	3	6				7		10			8	11			4			9	5					35
36	1	2		4		6		7	9	10	11	8				3				5						36
37		2	3	4		6		7	9	10				1					8	11	5					37
38		2	3		6	7			10	11								4	8		9	5	1			38
39		2	3	4		6		7	9	10	11	8									5	1				39
40	1	2	3		5	6	7	8	9	10				4				11								40
41	1	2	3		5	6	7	8	9	10				4				11								41
42	1	2	3		5	6	7	8	9	10	11			4												42
43	1	2	3	4		6			9	10		8						11		5		7				43
44	1	2	3	4		6		7	9	10		8						11		5						44
45	1	2	3	4		6	7	11	9	10		8								5						45
	35	34	28	35	28	33	19	35	31	31	22	29	6	25	5	20	9	2	11	6	4	9	2	1		
			1			1	6	9	20	6		8	1	4			6	1	2	1						

	Threadgold	Stelling	Hedley	Aitken	Hall	Wright A.	Bingham	Wright T.	Ford	Shackleton	Reynolds	Kirtley	Toseland	Watson	Mapson	Marston	Hudgell	Anderson	Snell	Davis	McSeveney	Smith	Walsh	Fairley	Kemp	
26	1		2	4	5	6	7		9	10			8			3				11						26
27	1		2	4	5	6	7	11	9	10			8			3										27
30	1	2		6	5			7		10			8	11		3	4		9							30
	3	1	2	3	3	2	2	2	2	3			3	1		3	1		1	1						
							1	2																		

Johnny Mapson played his 384th, and final, first team game for Sunderland during this season. He is the last goalkeeper to play for any full England national team while on Sunderland's books, albeit in a Wartime International against Wales on 26 April 1941.

419

1953-54

Division One

Ground: Roker Park
Manager: Bill Murray

League Table

	P	W	D	L	F	A	Pts
Wolver'pton W	42	25	7	10	96	56	57
WBA	42	22	9	11	86	63	53
Huddersfield T	42	20	11	11	78	61	51
Manchester U	42	18	12	12	73	58	48
Bolton W	42	18	12	12	75	60	48
Blackpool	42	19	10	13	80	69	48
Burnley	42	21	4	17	78	67	46
Chelsea	42	16	12	14	74	68	44
Charlton A	42	19	6	17	75	77	44
Cardiff C	42	18	8	16	51	71	44
Preston NE	42	19	5	18	87	58	43
Arsenal	42	15	13	14	75	73	43
Aston Villa	42	16	9	17	70	68	41
Portsmouth	42	14	11	17	81	89	39
Newcastle U	42	14	10	18	72	77	38
Tottenham H	42	16	5	21	65	76	37
Manchester C	42	14	9	19	62	77	37
SUNDERLAND	**42**	**14**	**8**	**20**	**81**	**89**	**36**
Sheffield W	42	15	6	21	70	91	36
Sheffield U	42	11	11	20	69	90	33
Middlesbrough	42	10	10	22	60	91	30
Liverpool	42	9	10	23	68	97	28

FA Cup Winners: West Bromwich Albion

Did you know that?

Ted Purdon scored after only 10 seconds of the match at Arsenal on 23 January 1954. This is believed to be the fastest goal in Sunderland's history.

Match 1: Cowan, Daniel and Elliott made debuts
Match 9: McNeill made debut
Match 14: Sheppeard made debut
Match 16: Watson last game
Match 17: Ford last game
Match 19: Davis last game
Match 20: McNeill last game
Match 25: Chisholm made debut
Match 28: Purdon made debut
Match 35: Fraser made debut
Match 37: Cowan last game
Match 40: McDonald made debut

Match Results

Match No.	Date	Round	Venue	Opponents	Result	FT	HT	Pos.	Scorers	Attendance
1	Aug 19		A	Charlton Athletic	L	3-5	1-3		T. Wright, Ford (2, 1 pen)	49,742
2	22		A	Newcastle United	L	1-2	1-1	20	Shackleton	58,516
3	26		H	Wolverhampton W.	W	3-2	2-0	17	Shackleton, T. Wright, Ford	57,135
4	29		H	Manchester City	L	4-5	1-3	18	Shackleton, T. Wright, A. Wright, Branagan o.g.	49,434
5	31		A	Wolverhampton W.	L	1-3	1-1	18	T. Wright	41,442
6	Sep 5		A	Cardiff City	D	1-1	0-0	19	T. Wright	42,002
7	12		H	Arsenal	W	7-1	2-1	17	Ford (3), Elliott, Shackleton, T. Wright (2)	59,784
8	14		A	Aston Villa	L	1-3	0-1	17	T. Wright	35,722
9	19		A	Portsmouth	L	1-4	1-2	21	T. Wright	38,873
10	26		H	Blackpool	W	3-2	1-2	18	Ford (2), Daniel	60,998
11	Oct 3		A	Chelsea	D	2-2	1-0	19	T. Wright, Kemp	56,685
12	10		A	Manchester United	L	0-1	0-0	20		36,482
13	17		H	Bolton Wanderers	L	1-2	0-1	22	Bingham	45,358
14	24		A	Preston North End	L	2-6	0-0	22	T. Wright (2)	34,466
15	31		H	Tottenham Hotspur	W	4-3	1-2	22	T. Wright, Elliott, Ford, Bingham	38,345
16	Nov 7		A	West Bromwich Albion	L	0-2	0-0	22		37,553
17	14		H	Liverpool	W	3-2	1-2	20	Aitken, Elliott (2)	36,537
18	21		A	Sheffield Wed.	D	2-2	1-0	18	T. Wright, Davis	37,446
19	28		H	Middlesbrough	L	0-2	0-1	21		41,538
20	Dec 5		A	Burnley	L	1-5	1-2	22	Shackleton	27,839
21	12		H	Charlton Athletic	W	2-1	2-0	21	Shackleton (2)	29,652
22	19		H	Newcastle United	D	1-1	0-0	20	Anderson	49,822
23	25		H	Huddersfield Town	D	1-1	1-1	20	Hall	36,751
24	26		A	Huddersfield Town	L	1-2	0-1	21	Shackleton	40,898
25	Jan 1		H	Aston Villa	W	2-0	1-0	20	Chisholm, Shackleton	44,337
26	2		A	Manchester City	L	1-2	1-0	21	T. Wright	23,742
28	16		H	Cardiff City	W	5-0	3-0	20	T. Wright (2), Shackleton, Purdon (2)	40,629
29	23		A	Arsenal	W	4-1	1-1	18	Purdon (3), T. Wright	60,218
30	Feb 6		H	Portsmouth	W	3-1	1-1	19	Elliott, Shackleton, Purdon	45,935
31	13		A	Blackpool	L	0-3	0-2	19		23,058
32	20		H	Chelsea	L	1-2	1-2	18	Willemse o.g.	45,755
33	27		H	Manchester United	L	0-2	0-1	19		38,400
34	Mar 6		A	Bolton Wanderers	L	1-3	0-2	19	Shackleton	26,379
35	20		A	Tottenham Hotspur	W	3-0	2-0	19	Chisholm, Shackleton, Purdon	39,393
36	31		H	West Bromwich Albion	W	2-1	1-0	19	Elliott, Purdon	26,632
37	Apr 3		A	Liverpool	L	3-4	1-1	19	Shackleton, Chisholm, Purdon	30,417
38	7		H	Preston North End	D	2-2	1-2	19	Chisholm, Elliott	36,143
39	10		H	Sheffield Wed.	L	2-4	0-3	19	Elliott, Anderson	36,982
40	16		H	Sheffield United	D	2-2	0-1	19	Bingham, Anderson (pen)	49,419
41	17		A	Middlesbrough	D	0-0	0-0	19		38,762
42	19		A	Sheffield United	W	3-1	0-0	19	Purdon (2), Elliott (pen)	31,387
43	24		H	Burnley	W	2-1	2-1	18	Chisholm (2)	28,014

Appearances
Goals

FA Cup

| 27 | Jan 9 | R3 | H | Doncaster Rovers | L | 0-2 | 0-2 | | | 49,435 |

Appearances
Goals

	Cowan	Stelling	Hedley	Aitken	Daniel	Wright A.	Wright T.	Kirtley	Ford	Shackleton	Elliott	McSeveney	Hudgell	Anderson	Bingham	Snell	McNeill	Davis	Watson	Kemp	Sheppeard	Hall	Chisholm	Purdon	Fraser	McDonald	
1	2	3	4	5	6	7	8	9	10	11																	1
1	2	3	4	5	6	7	8	9	10		11																2
1	2	3	4	5	6	7	8	9	10		11																3
1	2	3	4	5	6	7	8	9	10		11																4
1		2		5	6	9	8		10		11	3	4	7													5
1		2		5		8		9	10		11	3	4	7	6												6
1		2		5		8		9	10	11		3	4	7	6												7
1		2		5		8		9	10	11		3	4	7	6												8
		2	6	5		8			10	11		3	4	7		1	9										9
1		2	6	5		8		9		11		3	4	7					10								10
1		2	6	5		8		9		11		3	4						10	7							11
1	2		5			9			8	11		3	4	7	6				10								12
1	2		6	5		8			10	11		3	4	7					9								13
1	2		6	5		7	8	9		11		3							4	10							14
	2		6	5		8	10	9		11		3	4	7		1											15
		6			9	10		8	11			3	4	7		1		2		5							16
		6	5			8		9	10	11		3	4	7		1				2							17
		6	5		8				10	11		3	4	7		1	9			2							18
			4	5	6	8			10	11		3		7		1	9			2							19
	2		6	5		9	8		10	11		3	4	7		1											20
1		2	6	9		7	8		10	11		3	4							5							21
1		2	6	9		7	8		10	11		3	4							5							22
1		2	6	9		7	8		10	11		3	4							5							23
1			6	5		9	8		10	11		3	4	7						2							24
1		2	6	9		7			8	11		3	4							5	10						25
1		2	6	9		7			8	11		3	4							3	10						26
1		2	5		6	7			8	11		3	4								10	9					28
1		2	5		6	7			8	11		3	4								10	9					29
1		2	5		6	7			8	11		3	4								10	9					30
1		2	5		6	7			8	11		3	4								10	9					31
1		2	5		6	7			8	11		3	4								10	9					32
1		2			6				8	11		3	4	7						5	10	9					33
1		2		5	6				8	11		3	4	7							10	9					34
		2		5	6	7			8	11		3	4								10	9	1				35
1	2	3	5		6	7			8	11			4								10	9					36
1	2	3		5	6	7			8	11			4								10	9					37
	2	3	6			7			8	11			4						5	10	9	1					38
	2	3	6			7			8	11			4						5	10	9	1					39
	2		5		6				8	10	11		4	7						9		1	3				40
	2		5		6				8	11			4	7						10	9	1	3				41
	2		4		6	8			7	11									5	10	9	1	3				42
	2	3	4		6	7			8	11									5	10	9	1					43
8	17	29	34	27	20	38	13	12	38	37	6	30	34	19	4	7	3	6	1	15	17	16	7	3			
			1	1	1	18		9	14	9		3	3			1			1		1	6	11				

	2	6	5		9	10		8	11			3	4	7													27
	1	1	1			1	1		1	1			1	1													

Fred Hall scored his only goal for Sunderland in 224 appearances on Christmas Day 1953. He only made another 10 appearances following this game, his centre-half spot being taken by Welsh International Ray Daniel.

421

1954-55

Division One

Ground: Roker Park

Manager: Bill Murray

League Table

	P	W	D	L	F	A	Pts
Chelsea	42	20	12	10	81	57	52
Wolverh'pton W	42	19	10	13	89	70	48
Portsmouth	42	18	12	12	74	62	48
SUNDERLAND	42	15	18	9	64	54	48
Manchester U	42	20	7	15	84	74	47
Aston Villa	42	20	7	15	72	73	47
Manchester C	42	18	10	14	76	69	46
Newcastle U	42	17	9	16	89	77	43
Arsenal	42	17	9	16	69	63	43
Burnley	42	17	9	16	51	48	43
Everton	42	16	10	16	62	68	42
Huddersfield T	42	14	13	15	63	68	41
Sheffield U	42	17	7	18	70	86	41
Preston NE	42	16	8	18	83	64	40
Charlton A	42	15	10	17	76	75	40
Tottenham H	42	16	8	18	72	73	40
WBA	42	16	8	18	76	96	40
Bolton W	42	13	13	16	62	69	39
Blackpool	42	14	10	18	60	64	38
Cardiff C	42	13	11	18	62	76	37
Leicester C	42	12	11	19	74	86	35
Sheffield W	42	8	10	24	63	100	26

FA Cup Winners: Newcastle United

Did you know that?

The Black Cats started their season in front of the club's highest home opening game attendance. The game against West Bromwich Albion attracted 56,827 even though 'The Bank of England Club', as Sunderland were referred to by the press, had not bought anyone during the close season.

Match 1: Dodds made debut
Match 7: Evans only game
Match 8: Hall last game
Match 11: Tommy Wright last game
Match 17: Bone made debut & Snell last game
Match 20: McSeveney last game
Match 31: Fleming made debut
Match 32: Wood only game
Match 39: Arthur Wright last game
Match 42: Kirtley last game
Match 43: Morrison made debut

Match No.	Date	Round	Venue	Opponents	Result	FT	HT	Pos.	Scorers	Attendance
1	Aug 21		H	West Bromwich Albion	W	4-2	1-0		Anderson (pen), Chisholm, Purdon (2)	56,827
2	23		A	Aston Villa	D	2-2	1-1	3	Parkes o.g., Chisholm	32,983
3	28		A	Tottenham Hotspur	W	1-0	1-0	3	Purdon	53,646
4	Sep 1		H	Aston Villa	D	0-0	0-0	3		50,562
5	4		H	Sheffield Wed.	W	2-0	0-0	2	Chisholm, Shackleton	52,112
6	8		A	Wolverhampton W.	L	0-2	0-1	6		39,048
7	11		A	Portsmouth	D	2-2	0-1	7	Shackleton, Anderson (pen)	33,512
8	15		H	Wolverhampton W.	D	0-0	0-0	6		46,463
9	18		H	Blackpool	W	2-0	0-0	4	Chisholm (2)	51,556
10	25		A	Charlton Athletic	W	3-1	1-1	2	Shackleton, Bingham	28,615
11	Oct 2		H	Bolton Wanderers	D	1-1	1-0	3	Purdon	50,486
12	9		H	Newcastle United	W	4-2	2-0	1	Purdon, Bingham (2), Chisholm	66,654
13	16		A	Everton	L	0-1	0-0	3		61,189
14	23		H	Sheffield United	D	2-2	1-2	3	Chisholm, Furniss o.g.	39,936
15	30		A	Arsenal	W	3-1	2-0	2	Chisholm, Bingham, Anderson (pen)	65,423
16	Nov 6		H	Chelsea	D	3-3	2-2	2	Snell, Shackleton, Purdon	42,416
17	13		A	Leicester City	D	1-1	1-1	3	Purdon	39,509
18	20		H	Burnley	D	2-2	1-0	2	Purdon, Chisholm	42,305
19	27		A	Preston North End	L	1-3	0-1	3	Purdon	28,353
20	Dec 4		H	Manchester City	W	3-2	2-0	2	Shackleton (2), Chisholm	33,733
21	11		A	Cardiff City	W	1-0	0-0	2	Purdon	32,098
22	18		A	West Bromwich Albion	D	2-2	2-1	2	Purdon (2)	27,828
23	25		H	Huddersfield Town	D	1-1	0-1	2	Chisholm	39,900
24	27		A	Huddersfield Town	D	1-1	1-1	1	Bingham	47,450
25	Jan 1		H	Tottenham Hotspur	D	1-1	1-0	1	Chisholm	49,884
27	15		A	Sheffield Wed.	W	2-1	1-0	1	Bingham (2)	16,275
28	22		H	Portsmouth	D	2-2	0-0	2	Shackleton, Aitken	38,603
31	Feb 5		H	Blackpool	D	0-0	2-1	1		21,899
32	12		A	Charlton Athletic	L	1-2	0-2	2	Shackleton	43,148
35	26		A	Newcastle United	W	2-1	1-0	2	Fleming (2)	62,835
36	Mar 2		A	Bolton Wanderers	L	0-3	0-1	2		17,190
37	5		H	Cardiff City	D	1-1	0-1	2	Fleming	41,096
39	14		A	Sheffield United	L	0-1	0-1	3		14,806
40	19		H	Arsenal	L	0-1	0-1	4		40,279
42	29		A	Chelsea	L	1-2	0-2	6	Fleming	33,203
43	Apr 2		H	Leicester City	D	1-1	1-1	6	Chisholm	30,495
44	8		H	Manchester United	W	4-3	1-2	5	Chisholm (3), Anderson	43,882
45	9		A	Manchester City	L	0-1	0-0	5		60,61
46	11		A	Manchester United	D	2-2	2-1	6	Chisholm, Bingham	37,87
47	16		H	Preston North End	W	2-1	1-1	5	Purdon (2)	22,60
48	23		A	Burnley	W	1-0	1-0	4	Fleming	19,22
49	30		H	Everton	W	3-0	1-0	4	Chisholm, Fleming, Bingham	20,98

Appearances
Goal

FA Cup

26	Jan 8	R3	H	Burnley	W	1-0	0-0		Elliott	50,10
29	29	R4	A	Preston North End	D	3-3	2-1		Purdon, Chisholm, Shackleton	38,81
30	Feb 2	R4r	H	Preston North End	W	2-0	0-0		Chisholm (2)	57,43
33	19	R5	A	Swansea Town	D	2-2	1-0		Chisholm, Fleming	28,48
34	23	R5r	H	Swansea Town	W	1-0	0-0		Fleming	39,67
38	Mar 12	R6	H	Wolverhampton W.	W	2-0	0-0		Purdon (2)	54,85
41	26	S	N*	Manchester City	L	0-1	0-0			58,48

* at Villa Park

Appearances
Goal

	Dodds	Hedley	McDonald	Anderson	Daniel	Aitken	Wright, T.	Shackleton	Purdon	Chisholm	Elliott	Fraser	Bingham	Kirtley	Wright, A.	McSeveney	Hall	Evans	Hudgell	Snell	Bone	Fleming	Wood	Kemp	Morrison	
1	2	3	4	5	6	7	8	9	10	11																1
	2	3	4	5	6	7	8	9	10	11	1															2
	2	3	4	5	6		8	9	10	11	1	7														3
	2	3	4	5	6		8	9		11	1	7	10													4
	2	3	4		5		8	9	10	11	1	7		6												5
	2	3	4	5			8	9	10	6	1	7			11											6
	2	3	4		6		8	9		11	1	7		5	10											7
	2	3	4	9	6	8		10		11	1	7		5												8
	2	3	4	5	6	8		9	10	11	1	7														9
	2	3	4	5	6		8	9	10	11	1	7														10
	2	3	4	5	6	7	8	9		11	1		10													11
	2	3	4	5	6		8	9	10	11	1	7														12
1	2		4	5			8	9	10	11		7					3	6								13
	2	3	4	5	6			9	10	11	1	7	8													14
	2	3	4	5	6		8	9	10	11	1	7														15
	2	3	4	5			8	9	10	11	1	7						6								16
	2	3	4				8	9	10	11	1	7						6	5							17
	2	3	4	5	6		8	9	10	11	1	7														18
	2	3	4	5	6		8	9	10		1	7		11												19
	2	3	4	5	6		8	9	10		1	7		11												20
	2	3	4	5	6		8	9	10	11	1	7														21
	2	3	4	5	6		8	9	10	11	1	7														22
	2	3	4	5	6		8	9	10	11	1	7														23
	2	3	4	5	6		8	9	10	11	1	7														24
	2	3	4	5	6		8	9	10	11	1	7														25
	2	3	4	5	6		8	9	10	11	1	7														27
	2	3	4	5	6		8	9	10	11	1	7														28
	2	3	4	5	6				10	11	1	7	8							9						31
	2	3	4	5			8			10	1	7								9	6					32
	2	3	4	5	6			9	10	11	1									8	7					35
	2	3	4	5	6		8		10	11	1									9	7					36
	2	3	4	5	6			9	10	11	1	7								8						37
	2	3	4	5				9	10	11	1		6							8	7					39
	2	3	4	5	6			9	10	11	1	7								8						40
	2	3	4	5	6		8		10	11	1		7							9						42
1	2	3		5	6		8		10	11		7								9			4			43
	2	3	4	5	6		8	9	10	11	1	7														44
1	2	3	4		6		8	9	10	11		7							5							45
	2	3	4	5	6		8		10	11	1	7								9						46
	2	3	4	5	6		8	9		11	1	7								10						47
	2	3	4	5	6			9	10	11	1	7								8						48
	2	3	4	5	6			9	10	11	1	7								8						49
4	42	41	41	38	36	5	32	36	37	40	38	35	5	2	3	2	1	1	3	2	13	1	3	1		
			4		1		8	14	18			10							1		6					
	2	3	4	5	6		8	9	10	11	1	7														26
	2	3	4	5	6		8	9	10	11	1	7														29
	2	3	4	5	6		8	9	10	11	1	7														30
	2	3	4	5	6		8		10	11	1	7								9						33
	2	3	4	5	6		8		10	11	1	7								9						34
	2	3	4	5	6			9	10	11	1	7								8						38
	2	3	4	5	6		10	9		11	1	7								8						41
	7	7	7	7		6	5	6	7	7	7									4						
							1	3	4	1										2						

Billy Elliott

Billy was one of a number of expensive players signed in the mid 1950's earning Sunderland the nickname of 'The Bank of England Club'. Elliott went on to play 212 games for Sunderland, was coach of the 1973 FA Cup winning side and managed the club on two occasions in the 1972-73 and 1978-79.

423

1955-56

Division One

Ground: Roker Park
Manager: Bill Murray

League Table

	P	W	D	L	F	A	Pts
Manchester U	42	25	10	7	83	51	60
Blackpool	42	20	9	13	86	62	49
Wolverh'pton W	42	20	9	13	89	65	49
Manchester C	42	18	10	14	82	69	46
Arsenal	42	18	10	14	60	61	46
Birmingham C	42	18	9	15	75	57	45
Burnley	42	18	8	16	64	54	44
Bolton W	42	18	7	17	71	58	43
SUNDERLAND	42	17	9	16	80	95	43
Luton T	42	17	8	17	66	64	42
Newcastle U	42	17	7	18	85	70	41
Portsmouth	42	16	9	17	78	85	41
WBA	42	18	5	19	58	70	41
Charlton A	42	17	6	19	75	81	40
Everton	42	15	10	17	55	69	40
Chelsea	42	14	11	17	64	77	39
Cardiff C	42	15	9	18	55	69	39
Tottenham H	42	15	7	20	61	71	37
Preston NE	42	14	8	20	73	72	36
Aston Villa	42	11	13	18	52	69	35
Huddersfield T	42	14	7	21	54	83	35
Sheffield U	42	12	9	21	63	77	33

FA Cup Winners: Manchester City

Did you know that?

The first floodlit League game at Roker Park was played on 21 March 1956. The game, against Preston North End, kicked off at 7.15pm and ended in a 2-2 draw.

Match 10: Hannigan made debut
Match 18: Dodds last game
Match 21: Weddle made debut
Match 23: Holden made debut
Match 40: Bolton made debut
Match 47: Bollands made debut & Chisholm last game
Match 48: Stelling last game
Match 49: Holden last game

Match No.	Date		Round	Venue	Opponents	Result	FT	HT	Pos.	Scorers	Attendance
1	Aug	20		A	Cardiff City	L	1-3	0-0		Fleming	36,098
2		24		H	Aston Villa	W	5-1	1-0	5	Purdon, Fleming, Bingham (2), Chisholm	33,761
3		27		H	Huddersfield Town	W	4-1	1-0	3	Chisholm (2), Fleming, Elliott	42,369
4		29		A	Aston Villa	W	4-1	1-0	2	Bingham (2), Purdon, Shackleton	28,276
5	Sep	3		A	Blackpool	L	3-7	1-2	6	Shackleton, Purdon, Chisholm	34,546
6		10		H	Chelsea	W	4-3	1-3	6	Fleming (2), Chisholm (2)	45,240
7		17		A	Bolton Wanderers	W	3-0	1-0	3	Shackleton, Fleming, Chisholm	33,178
8		24		H	Arsenal	W	3-1	2-1	3	Fotheringham o.g., Shackleton (2)	55,397
9	Oct	1		A	Portsmouth	L	1-2	1-1	5	Chisholm	38,396
10		8		A	Birmingham City	W	2-1	1-1	4	Fleming (2)	37,946
11		15		H	West Bromwich Albion	W	2-1	1-1	2	Fleming (2)	47,094
12		22		A	Tottenham Hotspur	W	3-2	1-0	1	Fleming, Shackleton, Purdon	36,396
13		29		H	Everton	D	0-0	0-0	2		45,978
14	Nov	5		A	Preston North End	D	2-2	1-1	2	Hannigan, Purdon	27,688
15		12		H	Burnley	D	4-4	2-3	1	Fleming (2, 1 pen), Elliott, Chisholm	39,787
16		19		A	Luton Town	L	2-8	0-4	5	Purdon (2)	25,802
17		26		H	Charlton Athletic	W	3-2	2-0	4	Elliott, Fleming (2)	36,536
18	Dec	3		A	Manchester United	L	1-2	0-0	5	Purdon	40,150
19		10		H	Sheffield United	W	3-2	3-0	3	Fleming (2), Elliott	24,290
20		17		H	Cardiff City	D	1-1	1-1	4	Elliott	29,823
21		24		A	Huddersfield Town	L	0-4	0-1	5		21,803
22		26		H	Newcastle United	L	1-6	0-4	6	Fleming	55,723
23		27		A	Newcastle United	L	1-3	1-0	10	Holden	61,058
24		31		H	Blackpool	D	0-0	0-0	8		41,626
25	Jan	2		H	Wolverhampton W.	D	1-1	0-1	6	Fleming	48,246
27		14		A	Chelsea	W	3-2	2-1	4	Fleming, Shackleton, Elliott	43,999
28		21		H	Bolton Wanderers	D	0-0	0-0	4		38,871
31	Feb	4		A	Arsenal	L	1-3	0-1	7	Bingham	38,780
32		11		A	Portsmouth	W	4-2	3-1	4	Daniel (pen), Fleming (2), Bingham	29,761
35		25		A	West Bromwich Albion	L	0-3	0-2	8		23,495
37	Mar	7		H	Luton Town	L	1-2	0-1	10	Fleming	21,317
38		10		A	Everton	W	2-1	1-1	5	Holden (2)	49,183
40		21		H	Preston North End	D	2-2	0-1	7	Fleming, Elliott	20,438
41		24		A	Burnley	L	0-4	0-0	11		23,782
42		30		H	Manchester City	L	0-3	0-1	13		40,394
43		31		H	Tottenham Hotspur	W	3-2	1-1	9	Holden, Fleming (2)	22,311
44	Apr	2		A	Manchester City	L	2-4	2-1	13	Kemp, Fleming	40,915
45		7		A	Charlton Athletic	L	1-2	0-1	15	Hannigan	19,057
46		14		H	Manchester United	D	2-2	2-1	14	Anderson (pen), Elliott	19,855
47		18		H	Birmingham City	W	1-0	0-0	10	Holden	14,824
48		21		A	Sheffield United	W	3-2	2-0	8	Purdon (2), Anderson	26,341
49		28		A	Wolverhampton W.	L	1-3	1-1	9	Fleming	29,511

Appearances
Goals

FA Cup

Match No.	Date		Round	Venue	Opponents	Result	FT	HT	Pos.	Scorers	Attendance
26	Jan	7	R3	H	Norwich City	W	4-2	1-2		Fleming (3), Elliott	46,380
29		28	R4	A	York City	D	0-0	0-0			22,000
30	Feb	1	R4r	H	York City	W	2-1	1-0		Anderson, Fleming	43,928
33		18	R5	A	Sheffield United	D	0-0	0-0			51,516
34		22	R5r	H	Sheffield United	W	1-0 (aet)	0-0		Daniel	39,888
36	Mar	3	R6	A	Newcastle United	W	2-0	0-0		Holden (2)	61,474
39		17	S	N*	Birmingham City	L	0-3	0-1			65,103

* at Hillsborough

Appearances
Goals

	Fraser	Hedley	McDonald	Anderson	Bone	Aitken	Bingham	Fleming	Purdon	Chisholm	Elliott	Daniel	Shackleton	Stelling	Hudgell	Morrison	Hannigan	Dodds	Weddle	Kemp	Holden	Bolton	Bollands	
1	2	3	4	5	6	7	8	9	10	11														1
1	2	3	4		6	7	8	9	10	11	5													2
1	2	3	4		6	7	8	9	10	11	5													3
1	2	3	4		6	7	8	9	10		5	11												4
1	2	3	4		6	7	8	9	10		5	11												5
1			4		6	7	8	9	10		5	11	2	3										6
1	2	3	4		6	7	8	9	10		5	11												7
1	2	3	4		6	7	8	9	10		5	11												8
1	2	3			6	7	8	9	10		5	11		4										9
1	2		4		6		8	9	10		5	11	3		7									10
1	2	3	4		6	7	8	9	10		5	11												11
1	2	3	4		6	7	8	9	10		5	11												12
1	2	3	4		6	7	8	9	10		5	11												13
1		3	4		6	7	8	9		10	5		2		11									14
1	2	3	4		6	7	8	9	10	11	5													15
1	2	3	4		6	7	8	9	10		5	11												16
1		2	3	4	6		8	9	10	11	5				7	1								17
	2	3	4		6	7	8	9	10	11	5					1								18
1	2	3	4		6		8	9		11	5	10			7									19
1	2	3	4		6		8	9	10	11	5				7									20
1	2	3			6	7	8			11	5	10					9							21
1	2	3	4		6		8	9	10	11	5	7												22
1	2	3	4		6		8			10	5	11							7	9				23
1	2	3	4		6		8		10		5	11							7	9				24
1	2	3	4		6		8	11	10		5								7	9				25
1	2	3	4	5	6		8			10		11							7	9				27
1	2	3	4	5	6		8			10		11							7	9				28
1	2	3	4		6	7		9		10	5	11								8				31
1	2	3			6	7	8			10	5	11		4						9				32
1	2	3	4		6	7	8			10	5	11								9				35
1	2	3			6	7	8			10	5	11		4						9				37
1	2	3	4		6	7			10	8	5	11								9				38
1	2	3			6		8			10	5	11							7	9	4			40
1		3	4		6	7	8			11	5	10	2							9				41
1	2	3	4			5	7	8	10	6	9	11												42
1	2	3	4	5	6		8			10		11							7	9				43
1	2	3	4	5			8			10					11				7	9	6			44
1			4	5	6		8			10			2	3	11				7	9				45
1		3	4	5	6		8			10		11	2						7	9				46
	3	4			6	7	8		10	11	5	2								9		1		47
1		3	8		6	7		9		10	5		2		4					11				48
		2			6	7	8	9		10	5			3	4					11		1		49
38	34	39	37	7	41	27	39	25	24	29	35	28	7	4	5	7	2	1	10	19	2	2		
			2			6	28	10	9	8	1	7			2				1	5				

1	2	3	4		6		9	11	10	8	5								7					26
1	2	3	4		6	7	9		10	8	5	11												29
1	2	3	4		6	7	8			10	5	11								9				30
1	2	3	4		6	7	8			10	5	11								9				33
1	2	3	4		6	7	8			10	5	11								9				34
1	2	3	4		6	7	8			10	5	11								9				36
1	2	3	4		6	7	8			10	5	11								9				39
7	7	7	7		7	6	7	1	2	7	7	6							1	5				
			1			4			1	1										2				

Charlie Fleming – top scorer in his first full season with Sunderland. He was nicknamed 'Cannonball' due to the ferocity of his shooting. His first goals for Sunderland were a brace at St James' Park in a 2-1 victory on 26 February 1955. He died, aged 70, on the eve of the first League game played at the Stadium of Light.

425

1956-57

Division One

Ground: Roker Park
Manager: Bill Murray

League Table

	P	W	D	L	F	A	Pts
Manchester U	42	28	8	6	103	54	64
Tottenham H	42	22	12	8	104	56	56
Preston NE	42	23	10	9	84	56	56
Blackpool	42	22	9	11	93	65	53
Arsenal	42	21	8	13	85	69	50
Wolverh'pton W	42	20	8	14	94	70	48
Burnley	42	18	10	14	56	50	46
Leeds U	42	15	14	13	72	63	44
Bolton W	42	16	12	14	65	65	44
Aston Villa	42	14	15	13	65	55	43
WBA	42	14	14	14	59	61	42
Birmingham C*	42	15	9	18	69	69	39
Chelsea*	42	13	13	16	73	73	39
Sheffield W	42	16	6	20	82	88	38
Everton	42	14	10	18	61	79	38
Luton T	42	14	9	19	58	76	37
Newcastle U	42	14	8	20	67	87	36
Manchester C	42	13	9	20	78	88	35
Portsmouth	42	10	13	19	62	92	33
SUNDERLAND	42	12	8	22	67	88	32
Cardiff C	42	10	9	23	53	88	29
Charlton A	42	9	4	29	62	120	22

*Birmingham City & Chelsea finished in equal 12th position

FA Cup Winners: Aston Villa

Did you know that?

Season tickets were first introduced for the Clockstand at the start of the 1956-57 season.

Match 7: Chilton made debut
Match 11: Bone last game
Match 14: Bolton last game
Match 15: Morrison last game
Match 16: Maltby made debut
Match 17: Hope and Revie made debuts & Weddle last game
Match 23: Purdon last game
Match 27: Kemp last game
Match 31: Grainger made debut
Match 36: Clark made debut
Match 43: Daniel last game
Match 44: Routledge made debut, Hudgell and Clark last games & Bill Murray last game as Sunderland manager

Match No.	Date		Round	Venue	Opponents	Result	FT	HT	Pos.	Scorers	Attendance
1	Aug	18		A	Luton Town	L	2-6	0-1		Bingham, Purdon	23,049
2		22		H	Bolton Wanderers	W	3-0	1-0	14	Elliott (2), Fleming	33,307
3		25		H	Newcastle United	L	1-2	0-1	17	Shackleton	51,032
4	Sep	1		H	Charlton Athletic	W	8-1	4-0	14	Shackleton (2), Hannigan (3), Daniel (pen), Anderson, Fleming	36,509
5		5		A	Bolton Wanderers	L	1-2	1-1	16	Fleming	33,786
6		8		A	Manchester City	L	1-3	0-1	17	Daniel (pen)	35,753
7		12		A	Wolverhampton W.	D	2-2	1-1	18	Fleming (2)	42,382
8		15		H	Blackpool	W	5-2	2-2	13	Fleming (2), Bingham, Anderson, Purdon	45,914
9		22		A	Everton	L	1-2	1-0	16	Fleming	41,595
10		29		H	Tottenham Hotspur	L	0-2	0-0	18		41,657
11	Oct	6		A	Sheffield Wed.	L	2-3	1-1	19	Elliott, Fleming (pen)	32,248
12		13		H	Manchester United	L	1-3	1-1	19	Purdon	49,487
13		20		A	West Bromwich Albion	L	0-2	0-1	21		22,948
14		27		H	Portsmouth	D	3-3	2-0	21	McDonald, Fleming, Purdon	29,781
15	Nov	3		A	Preston North End	L	0-6	0-5	21		26,021
16		10		H	Chelsea	L	1-3	0-1	21	Shackleton	27,182
17		17		A	Cardiff City	L	0-1	0-0	21		20,017
18		24		H	Birmingham City	L	0-1	0-0	22		33,807
19	Dec	1		A	Arsenal	D	1-1	0-1	22	Shackleton	36,442
20		8		H	Burnley	W	2-1	2-1	21	Fleming (2)	29,588
21		15		H	Luton Town	W	1-0	0-0	21	Fleming	28,473
22		22		A	Newcastle United	L	2-6	1-3	21	Fleming (2)	29,727
23		25		H	Aston Villa	W	1-0	0-0	20	Bingham	18,543
24		29		A	Charlton Athletic	L	2-3	1-3	20	Shackleton, Anderson	24,536
25	Jan	1		H	Wolverhampton W.	L	2-3	0-3	20	Anderson, Hannigan	28,396
27		12		H	Manchester City	D	1-1	0-1	20	Fleming	34,119
28		19		A	Blackpool	W	2-1	2-1	20	Fleming (2)	18,702
30	Feb	2		H	Everton	D	1-1	0-1	20	Bingham	31,463
31		9		A	Tottenham Hotspur	L	2-5	0-0	20	Shackleton, Fleming	52,104
32		16		H	Sheffield Wed.	W	5-2	2-2	20	Daniel (pen), Fleming (2), Revie, Shackleton	44,135
33	Mar	9		A	Burnley	L	0-2	0-0	20		21,982
34		13		H	West Bromwich Albion	L	1-4	0-1	21	Revie	26,336
35		16		H	Preston North End	D	0-0	0-0	20		37,907
36		23		A	Chelsea	W	2-0	1-0	19	Daniel, Fleming	36,160
37		30		H	Cardiff City	D	1-1	1-0	19	Bingham	40,100
38	Apr	6		A	Birmingham City	W	2-1	1-1	20	Fleming, Anderson	24,548
39		8		A	Aston Villa	D	2-2	1-1	20	Fleming, Hannigan	8,930
40		13		H	Arsenal	W	1-0	1-0	19	Anderson	34,749
41		19		H	Leeds United	W	2-0	1-0	18	Anderson, Fleming	56,551
42		20		A	Manchester United	L	0-4	0-1	19		58,725
43		22		A	Leeds United	L	1-3	0-0	19	Grainger	29,328
44	May	1		A	Portsmouth	L	2-3	1-2	20	Hope (2)	20,253

Appearances
Goals

FA Cup

| 26 | Jan | 5 | R3 | H | Queens Park Rangers | W | 4-0 | 3-0 | | Elliott, Hannigan (2), Fleming | 30,557 |
| 29 | | 26 | R4 | A | West Bromwich Albion | L | 2-4 | 0-2 | | Fleming, Bingham | 42,010 |

Appearances
Goals

#	Fraser	Hedley	McDonald	Anderson	Daniel	Aitken	Bingham	Fleming	Purdon	Elliott	Shackleton	Bollands	Morrison	Hannigan	Chilton	Bone	Bolton	Maltby	Hope	Weddle	Revie	Kemp	Grainger	Clark	Routledge	Hudgell	#
1	1	2	3	4	5	6	7	8	9	10	11																1
2		2	3	8	5	6			9		11	10	1			4	7										2
3		2	3	8	5	6			9		11	10	1			4	7										3
4		2	3	8	5	6			9		11	10	1			4	7										4
5		2	3	8	5	6			9		11	10	1			4	7										5
6		2	3	8	5	6			9		11	10	1			4	7										6
7		2		8	5	6	7	10	9				1	4	11	3											7
8		2	3	8	5	6	7	10	9				1	4	11												8
9		2	3	8	5	6	7	10	9				1	4	11												9
10		2	3			6		8	9	11	10		1	4	7		5										10
11		2	3			6		8	9	11	10		1	4	7		5										11
12		2	3		5	6	7	10	9		8		1	4	11												12
13		2		4		6	7	8	9	10	11		1	6		3											13
14		2	3	8	5	6			10	9	11		1		7			4									14
15		2	3	8	5	6			9	10	11		1	4	7												15
16		2	3	4	5	6	7	9			10	1		11				8									16
17		2		4	5	6					11	3	1		7			8	9	10							17
18		2	11	4	5	6		9			3		1		7			8		10							18
19		2	3	4	5	6	7		9	11	10	1						8									19
20		2	3	4	5	6	7	9			11	10	1					8									20
21		2	3	4	5	6	7	9			11	10	1					8									21
22		2	3	4	5	6	7	9			11	10	1								8						22
23		2	3	4	5	6	7	9	11	10			1					8									23
24	1	2	3	4	5	6	7	9			11	10						8									24
25		2	3	4	5	6		9			10		1	11				8			7						25
26		2	3	4	5	6		9			10	8	1	11							7						26
27		2	3	4	5	6	7	9			10	8	1	11													27
28		2	3	4	5	6	7	9			10	8	1	11													28
29		2		4	5	6	7	9			3	8	1	10							11						29
30	2		4	5	6	7	9			3	10	1						8			11						30
31		2	3	4	5	6	7	9			10		1					8			11						31
32		2		4	5	6	7	9			3	10	1					8			11						32
33		2	3		9	5	7	8			6	10	1					4			11						33
34		2	3		9	5	7	8			6		1					4			11	10					34
35		2	3		9	5	7	8			6		1					4			11	10					35
36		2	3	8	9	5	7	10			6	11	1					4									36
37		2	3	8	5			9			6		1		7			4			11	10					37
38		2	3	8	9	5	7	10			6		1					4			11						38
39		2	3	8			5	7	9		6		1					4			11	10					39
40		2	3	8			5	7	9		6	10	1					4			11						40
41	1	2	3	8	5			7	9		6							4			11	10					41
42		2		6		5		9				7						8	4		11	10	1	3			42
43	3	42	35	36	36	40	27	40	13	36	26	38	13	22	2	2	1	1	9	1	16	2	13	6	1	1	43
			1	7	4		5	25	4	3	8			5					2		2		1				
26		2	3	4	5	6		9			10	8	1		11						7						26
29		2	3	4	5	6	7	9			10	8	1		11												29
		2	2	2	2	1	2		2	2	2		2								1						
				1	2		1			2																	

Full-backs Arthur Hudgell & Jack Hedley.

Hedley was ever present during this season where as his long time partner, Hudgell, made only one appearance, his 275th, and final one, for Sunderland on 1 May 1957. He retired five days later becoming one of Sunderland's coaches.

1957-58

Division One

Ground: Roker Park
Manager: Alan Brown

League Table

	P	W	D	L	F	A	Pts
Wolverh'pton W	42	28	8	6	103	47	64
Preston NE	42	26	7	9	100	51	59
Tottenham H	42	21	9	12	93	77	51
WBA	42	18	14	10	92	70	50
Manchester C	42	22	5	15	104	100	49
Burnley	42	21	5	16	80	74	47
Blackpool	42	19	6	17	80	67	44
Luton T	42	19	6	17	69	63	44
Manchester U	42	16	11	15	85	75	43
Nottingham F	42	16	10	16	69	63	42
Chelsea	42	15	12	15	83	79	42
Arsenal	42	16	7	19	73	85	39
Birmingham C	42	14	11	17	76	89	39
Aston Villa	42	16	7	19	73	86	39
Bolton W	42	14	10	18	65	87	38
Everton	42	13	11	18	65	75	37
Leeds U	42	14	9	19	51	63	37
Leicester C	42	14	5	23	91	112	33
Newcastle U	42	12	8	22	73	81	32
Portsmouth	42	12	8	22	73	88	32
SUNDERLAND	42	10	12	20	54	97	32
Sheffield W	42	12	7	23	69	92	31

FA Cup Winners: Nottingham Forest

Did you know that?

Sunderland's relegation ended 68 years continuous membership of the highest division. Since 1936 they had been the only team that had solely played in the top flight of English football.

Match 1: Shackleton's last game & Alan Brown first game as Sunderland manager
Match 3: Graham made debut
Match 4: Goodchild made debut
Match 12: Hurley and Spence made debuts
Match 13: Routledge, Graham and Chilton last games
Match 17: Fogarty made debut
Match 19: Reed made debut
Match 21: Spence last game
Match 22: Godbold made debut
Match 28: Reed last game
Match 29: Fleming last game
Match 31: McDonald last game
Match 33: Pearce made debut & Bingham last game
Match 34: Whitelaw made debut & Hannigan last game
Match 35: Kichenbrand made debut
Match 44: Relegation confirmed

Match No.	Date		Round	Venue	Opponents	Result	FT	HT	Pos.	Scorers	Attendance
1	Aug	24		H	Arsenal	L	0-1	0-1			56,493
2		28		A	Leicester City	L	1-4	1-1	19	Grainger	34,164
3		31		A	Wolverhampton W.	L	0-5	0-1	22		38,645
4	Sep	4		H	Leicester City	W	3-2	2-1	21	O'Neill (2), Goodchild	39,629
5		7		H	Aston Villa	D	1-1	1-0	20	O'Neill	43,901
6		11		A	Bolton Wanderers	D	2-2	2-1	18	Goodchild, Bingham	17,647
7		14		A	Everton	L	1-3	1-0	20	Revie	47,119
8		18		H	Bolton Wanderers	L	1-2	0-1	21	Revie	30,021
9		21		H	Newcastle United	W	2-0	1-0	19	Revie, Grainger	45,718
10		25		A	Leeds United	L	1-2	1-1	19	O'Neill	17,600
11		28		H	Luton Town	W	3-0	2-0	17	Fleming (2), O'Neill	36,724
12	Oct	5		A	Blackpool	L	0-7	0-4	20		33,172
13		12		A	Burnley	L	0-6	0-2	20		22,868
14		19		H	Preston North End	D	0-0	0-0	20		34,676
15		26		A	Sheffield Wed.	D	3-3	0-0	20	O'Neill, Grainger, Spence	21,168
16	Nov	2		H	Tottenham Hotspur	D	1-1	0-1	20	Bingham	36,091
17		9		A	Birmingham City	W	3-2	2-1	18	Revie (2), Bingham	25,315
18		16		H	Chelsea	D	2-2	2-2	16	Fogarty, Bingham	32,678
19		23		A	West Bromwich Albion	L	0-3	0-2	17		32,522
20		30		H	Manchester City	W	2-1	2-0	16	Revie, Anderson	35,442
21	Dec	7		A	Nottingham Forest	L	0-2	0-1	18		24,262
22		14		H	Portsmouth	D	1-1	1-1	17	Maltby	25,920
23		21		A	Arsenal	L	0-3	0-3	19		28,156
24		26		H	Leeds United	W	2-1	1-1	18	Revie, Godbold	34,875
25		28		H	Wolverhampton W.	L	0-2	0-1	19		46,479
26	Jan	11		A	Aston Villa	L	2-5	2-5	21	Grainger, Fleming	22,645
29		18		H	Everton	D	1-1	1-0	20	Revie	26,507
30	Feb	1		H	Newcastle United	D	2-2	0-2	20	Elliott (pen), O'Neill	47,739
31		8		A	Luton Town	L	1-7	0-2	21	Fogarty	15,932
32		15		H	Blackpool	L	1-4	1-3	21	O'Neill	28,127
33		22		H	Burnley	L	2-3	0-2	21	O'Neill, Hannigan	30,595
34	Mar	1		A	Preston North End	L	0-3	0-1	22		23,974
35		8		H	Sheffield Wed.	D	3-3	1-2	22	O'Neill (2), Kichenbrand	22,549
36		15		A	Tottenham Hotspur	W	1-0	1-0	22	Revie	40,751
37		22		H	West Bromwich Albion	W	2-0	0-0	20	O'Neill, Kichenbrand	38,323
38		29		A	Chelsea	D	0-0	0-0	21		32,929
39	Apr	4		A	Manchester United	D	2-2	1-1	19	Revie, O'Neill	47,421
40		5		H	Birmingham City	L	1-6	0-4	20	Revie	34,184
41		7		H	Manchester United	L	1-2	1-1	20	Fogarty	51,328
42		12		A	Manchester City	L	1-3	1-1	22	Kichenbrand	31,166
43		19		H	Nottingham Forest	W	3-0	2-0	21	Revie, Kichenbrand, Elliott (pen)	28,753
44		26		A	Portsmouth	W	2-0	1-0	21	Kichenbrand (2)	22,545

Appearances
Goals

FA Cup

| 26 | Jan | 4 | R3 | H | Everton | D | 2-2 | 1-1 | | Bingham, Fogarty | 34,602 |
| 27 | | 8 | R3r | A | Everton | L | 1-3 (aet) | 1-1 | | Fleming | 56,952 |

Appearances
Goals

	Bollands	Hedley	McDonald	Anderson	Aitken	Elliott	Bingham	Revie	Fleming	Shackleton	Grainger	Maltby	Graham	O'Neill	Goodchild	Fraser	Hurley	Hannigan	Spence	Routledge	Chilton	Fogarty	Reed	Godbold	Pearce	Whitelaw	Kitchenbrand	
1	1	2	3	4	5	6	7	8	9	10	11																	1
2	1	2	3	4	5	6	7	8	9		11	10																2
3	1		3	4	5	6	7	8			11	9	2	10														3
4	1		3	4	5	6	7	8	9				2	10	11													4
5	1	2	3	4	5	6	7	8	9					10	11													5
6	1	2	3	4	5	6	7	8	9					10	11													6
7	1	2	3	4	5	6	7	8	9					10	11													7
8		2	3	4	5	6	7	8	9		11			10		1												8
9		2	3	4	5	6	7	8	9		11			10		1												9
10		2	3	4	5	6	7	8	9		11			10		1												10
11		2	3	4	5	6	7	8	9		11			10		1												11
12		2	3	4		6		8			11			10		1	5	7	9									12
13				4		6	7	8	9			2	10	11		1	5			3								13
14		2	3	4		6	7	8			11			10		1	5		9									14
15		2		4	6	3	7	8			11			10		1	5		9									15
16		2		4	6	3	7	8	9		11			10		1	5											16
17		2		4	6	3	7	8			11			9		1	5				10							17
18		2		4	6	3	7	8			11			9		1	5				10							18
19		2		4	5	3	7	8			11			9		1					10	6						19
20		2		4	6	3	7	8								1	5		9		10							20
21			2	8	6	3	7				11					1	5		9		10	4						21
22		2		4	6	3	7	8				9				1	5				10		11					22
23			2	4		3	7		9	8						1	5				10	6	11					23
24		2			6	3	7	8				9				1	5				10	4	11					24
25		2		4	6	3	7	8				9				1	5				10		11					25
28			2		6	3	7	9	8		11					1	5				10	4						28
29		2		4	6	3	7	9	8		11					1	5				10							29
30		2	3	4		6	7	9			11		10			1	5				8							30
31		2	3	4		6	7	9					10			1	5				8		11					31
32		2			6	3	7	4			11	8	10			1	5	9										32
33		2	6			3	7	8			11		10			1	5	9					4					33
34		2		4	5	3					11		10			1		7			8			6	9			34
35		2		4	5	3					11		8	1							7			6	10	9		35
36		2		4	5	3		8			11		10	1							7			6		9		36
37		2		4	5	3		8			11		10	1							7			6		9		37
38		2		4	5	3		8			11		10	1							7			6		9		38
39		2		4	5	3		8			11		10	1							7			6		9		39
40		2		4	5	3		8					10	11	1						7			6		9		40
41		2		4	5	3		8					10	11	1						7			6		9		41
42	1	2		4		3		8			11		10				5				7			6		9		42
43		2		4		3		8			11		10			1	5				7			6		9		43
44		2		4		3		8			11		10			1	5				7			6		9		44
	8	35	19	39	32	42	30	39	15	1	30	6	3	32	7	33	22	4	5	1	24	5	5	12	2	10		
			1		2	4	12	3			4	1		13	2		1	1			3		1			6		

26		2	4		3	7	9	8								1	5				10	6	11					26
27		2	4		3	7	9	8		11						1	5				10	6						27
	2	2		2	2	2	2	1			2	2				2	2	1										
						1		1									1											

Billy Bingham was capped 56 times by Northern Ireland (33 while with Sunderland including appearances in 1958 World Cup finals).

1958-59

Division Two

Ground: Roker Park
Manager: Alan Brown

League Table

	P	W	D	L	F	A	Pts
Sheffield W	42	28	6	8	106	48	62
Fulham	42	27	6	9	96	61	60
Sheffield U	42	23	7	12	82	48	53
Liverpool	42	24	5	13	87	62	53
Stoke C	42	21	7	14	72	58	49
Bristol R	42	18	12	12	80	64	48
Derby Co	42	20	8	14	74	71	48
Charlton A	42	18	7	17	92	90	43
Cardiff	42	18	7	17	65	65	43
Bristol C	42	17	7	18	74	70	41
Swansea T	42	16	9	17	79	81	41
Brighton & HA	42	15	11	16	74	90	41
Middlesbrough	42	15	10	17	87	71	40
Huddersfield T	42	16	8	18	62	55	40
SUNDERLAND	42	16	8	18	64	75	40
Ipswich T	42	17	6	19	62	77	40
Leyton O	42	14	8	20	71	78	36
Scunthorpe U	42	12	9	21	55	84	33
Lincoln C	42	11	7	24	63	93	29
Rotherham U	42	10	9	23	42	82	29
Grimsby T	42	9	10	23	62	90	28
Barnsley	42	10	7	25	55	91	27

Division 1 Champions:
Wolverhampton W. 61 pts

FA Cup Winners: Nottingham Forest

Did you know that?

On 30 March Sunderland suffered their worst League defeat outside of the top flight; 6-0 at Leyton Orient.

Match 1: Bircham made debut
Match 4: Aitken last game
Match 8: Willie Fraser last game
Match 9: Irwin, Ashurst and McNab made debuts
Match 13: Hedley and Whitelaw last games
Match 14: Nelson made debut
Match 15: Wakeham made debut
Match 18: Revie last game
Match 21: Taylor made debut & Elliott last game
Match 32: Robson and John Fraser made debuts

Match No.	Date		Round	Venue	Opponents	Result	FT	HT	Pos.	Scorers	Attendance
1	Aug	23		A	Lincoln City	L	1-3	0-1		Grainger	17,386
2		27		H	Fulham	L	1-2	0-0	19	Bircham	37,772
3		30		H	Liverpool	W	2-1	0-1	17	Pearce, Kichenbrand	36,168
4	Sep	3		A	Fulham	L	2-6	2-1	19	Kichenbrand, O'Neill	26,393
5		6		H	Stoke City	W	3-1	2-0	14	O'Neill (2), Kichenbrand	31,894
6		10		H	Sheffield Wed.	D	3-3	1-2	14	Kichenbrand (2), Elliott (pen)	33,684
7		13		A	Swansea Town	L	0-5	0-2	19		22,696
8		17		A	Sheffield Wed.	L	0-6	0-2	19		30,398
9		20		H	Ipswich Town	L	0-2	0-2	21		26,970
10		27		A	Bristol Rovers	L	1-2	1-0	22	Kichenbrand	24,602
11	Oct	4		H	Derby County	W	3-0	2-0	22	Anderson (2), Kichenbrand	23,049
12		11		A	Middlesbrough	D	0-0	0-0	21		37,223
13		18		H	Charlton Athletic	L	0-3	0-1	22		29,835
14		25		A	Bristol City	L	1-4	1-2	22	Grainger	25,510
15	Nov	1		H	Grimsby Town	W	1-0	0-0	22	Kichenbrand	23,045
16		8		A	Huddersfield Town	D	1-1	0-1	21	Kichenbrand	20,301
17		15		H	Barnsley	D	2-2	2-1	21	Anderson (pen), Goodchild	24,390
18		22		A	Rotherham United	W	4-0	1-0	19	Kichenbrand (3), Revie	8,801
19		29		H	Sheffield United	W	4-1	4-1	18	Goodchild (3), Grainger	23,553
20	Dec	6		A	Brighton & H.A.	L	0-2	0-1	18		21,396
21		13		H	Cardiff City	L	0-2	0-1	20		30,097
22		20		H	Lincoln City	W	2-0	1-0	18	Kichenbrand, Maltby	20,178
23		26		A	Scunthorpe United	L	2-3	0-2	19	Kichenbrand, Nelson	14,509
24		27		H	Scunthorpe United	W	3-1	1-0	16	Taylor, Anderson, Maltby	27,550
25	Jan	1		H	Leyton Orient	W	4-0	0-0	14	Kichenbrand, Goodchild (2), Pearce	33,040
26		3		A	Liverpool	L	1-3	1-1	16	Goodchild	36,953
28		31		H	Swansea Town	W	2-1	1-1	13	Taylor (2, 1 pen)	28,595
29	Feb	7		A	Ipswich Town	W	2-0	1-0	13	Goodchild (2)	16,745
30		14		H	Bristol Rovers	W	3-1	1-1	11	Goodchild, Bircham, Watling o.g.	24,188
31		21		A	Derby County	L	0-2	0-1	13		24,227
32		28		H	Huddersfield Town	W	1-0	1-0	11	Kichenbrand	27,264
33	Mar	7		A	Charlton Athletic	L	2-3	0-2	13	Goodchild, Kichenbrand	17,818
34		14		H	Bristol City	W	3-1	0-1	11	Taylor (2), Goodchild	24,049
35		21		A	Grimsby Town	D	1-1	0-1	12	Kichenbrand	10,533
36		28		H	Middlesbrough	D	0-0	0-0	12		45,954
37		30		A	Leyton Orient	L	0-6	0-3	14		15,648
38	Apr	4		H	Barnsley	W	2-0	0-0	14	Goodchild, Fraser	10,274
39		6		A	Stoke City	D	0-0	0-0	12		7,513
40		11		H	Rotherham United	D	1-1	1-0	13	Taylor	19,920
41		18		A	Sheffield United	L	1-3	0-2	14	Goodchild	14,390
42		22		A	Cardiff City	L	1-2	0-1	14	Goodchild	10,734
43		25		H	Brighton & H.A.	W	4-1	1-0	15	Kichenbrand (3), Goodchild	12,024

Appearances
Goals

FA Cup

| 27 | Jan 10 | R3 | A | Everton | L | 0-4 | 0-2 | | | 57,788 |

Appearances
Goals

	Fraser, W.	Hedley	Elliott	Anderson	Aitken	Pearce	Bircham	Fogarty	Kitchenbrand	O'Neill	Grainger	Whitelaw	Hurley	Revie	Goodchild	Bollands	Irwin	Ashurst	McNab	Nelson	Maltby	Wakeham	Godbold	Taylor	Robson	Fraser, J.	
1	2	3	4	5	6	7	8	9	10	11																	1
1	2	3	4	5	6	7	8	9	10	11																	2
1	2	3	4	5	6	7		9	10	11	8																3
1	2	3	4	5	6	7		9	10	11	8																4
1	2	3	4		6	7		9	10	11		5	8														5
1	2	3	4		6	7		9	10	11		5	8														6
1	2	3	4		6	7			8	11		5	9	10													7
1	2	3	4		6	7		9	10	11		5	8														8
			4		8	7		9	10	11		5			1	2	3	6									9
	2		8		6	7		9		11		5	10		1		3	4									10
	2		8		6	7		9		11		5	10		1		3	4									11
	2		8		6	7		9		11		5	10		1		3	4									12
	2		8		6	7			11	9		5	10		1		3	4									13
			8		6	7		9	10	11		5			1		3	4	2								14
		10			6	7		9		11		5					3	4	2	8	1						15
		10			6	7		9		11		5		8			3	4	2		1						16
		10			6	7		9				5		8			3	4	2		1	11					17
					6	7		9		11		5	10				3	4	2	8	1						18
			4		6			9	10	11		5		8			3		2	7	1						19
			4		6		7	9	10	11		5		8			3		2		1						20
		3	4		6			9		11		5		8					2	7	1	10					21
			4		6			9		11		5		8			3		2	7	1	10					22
			4		6			9		11		5		8			3		2	7	1	10					23
			4		6			9		11		5		8			3		2	7	1	10					24
			4		6	7		9		11		5		8			3		2		1	10					25
			4		6	7		9		11		5		8			3		2		1	10					26
			4		6			9		11		5		8			3		2		1	10					28
			4		6	7		9		11		5		8			3		2		1	10					29
			4		6	7		9		11		5		8			3		2		1	10					30
			4		6	7		9		11		5		8			3		2		1	10					31
			4		6			9		11				8			3		2		1	10	5	7			32
			4		6			9						8			3		2		1	11	10	5	7		33
			4		6			9				5		8			3		2		1	11	10		7		34
			4		6			9				5		8			3		2		1	11	10		7		35
			4		6	7		9				5		8			3		2		1	11	10				36
			4		6	7		9				5		8			3		2		1	11	10				37
			4		6			9		11		5		8			3		2		1		10		7		38
			4		6			9		11				8			3		2		1		10	5	7		39
			4		6			9		11		5		8			3		2		1		10		7		40
			4		6			9		11		5		8			3		2		1		10		7		41
			4		6			9		11		5		8			3		2		1		10		7		42
			4		6			9		11		5		8			3		2		1		10		7		43
8	12	9	41	4	42	26	3	40	12	36	3	35	9	27	6	1	33	10	29	7	28	6	22	3	10		
		1	4		2	2		21	3	3		1	16				1	2			6		1				

| | | | 4 | | 6 | | | 9 | | 11 | | 5 | | 8 | | | 3 | | 2 | 7 | 1 | | 10 | | | | 27 |
| | | | 1 | | 1 | | | 1 | | 1 | | 1 | | 1 | | | 1 | | 1 | 1 | 1 | | 1 | | | | |

Jimmy McNab, Cecil Irwin and Len Ashurst – all made their debuts at home to Ipswich Town on 20 September 1958. They went on to make over 1,100 first team appearances between them. Irwin still holds the record of being Sunderland's youngest defender at 16 years 166 days.

1959-60

Division Two

Ground: Roker Park
Manager: Alan Brown

League Table

	P	W	D	L	F	A	Pts
Aston Villa	42	25	9	8	89	43	59
Cardiff C	42	23	12	7	90	62	58
Liverpool	42	20	10	12	90	66	50
Sheffield U	42	19	12	11	68	51	50
Middlesbrough	42	19	10	13	90	64	48
Huddersfield T	42	19	9	14	73	52	47
Charlton A	42	17	13	12	90	87	47
Rotherham U	42	17	13	12	61	60	47
Bristol R	42	18	11	13	72	78	47
Leyton O	42	15	14	13	76	61	44
Ipswich T	42	19	6	17	78	68	44
Swansea T	42	15	10	17	82	84	40
Lincoln C	42	16	7	19	75	78	39
Brighton & HA	42	13	12	17	67	76	38
Scunthorpe U	42	13	10	19	57	71	36
SUNDERLAND	42	12	12	18	52	65	36
Stoke C	42	14	7	21	66	83	35
Derby Co	42	14	7	21	61	77	35
Plymouth A	42	13	9	20	61	89	35
Portsmouth	42	10	12	20	59	77	32
Hull C	42	10	10	22	48	76	30
Bristol C	42	11	5	26	60	97	27

Division 1 Champions:
Burnley 55 pts

FA Cup Winners:
Wolverhampton Wanderers

Did you know that?

Alan O'Neill is the only player to score for Sunderland under two different surnames; Hope (1957) and his stepfather's surname O'Neill (1957-60).

Match 3: Kichenbrand last game
Match 4: Lawther made debut
Match 9: Bollands last game
Match 10: Robson last game
Match 12: Bircham last game
Match 14: Harvey made debut
Match 17: Fraser last game
Match 18: Davison made debut
Match 25: Godbold last game
Match 29: Jones made debut
Match 39: Sharkey made debut
Match 42: Jones last game
Match 44: Grainger last game

Match No.	Date		Round	Venue	Opponents	Result	FT	HT	Pos.	Scorers	Attendance
1	Aug	22		A	Stoke City	L	1-3	0-1		Kichenbrand	20,728
2		26		H	Aston Villa	W	1-0	1-0	13	Pearce	29,860
3		29		H	Brighton & H.A.	D	0-0	0-0	14		28,482
4		31		A	Aston Villa	L	0-3	0-2	15		32,891
5	Sep	5		A	Swansea Town	W	2-1	1-1	12	Griffiths o.g., Lawther	16,001
6		7		A	Sheffield United	W	2-1	1-0	7	Fogarty (2)	21,459
7		12		H	Bristol Rovers	D	2-2	1-0	9	Fogarty, Grainger	29,968
8		16		H	Sheffield United	W	5-1	2-0	7	Taylor (2), Fogarty, Lawther, Grainger	27,451
9		19		A	Ipswich Town	L	1-6	0-4	11	Fogarty	14,941
10		26		H	Huddersfield Town	D	0-0	0-0	12		31,655
11	Oct	3		A	Leyton Orient	D	1-1	1-1	12	Fogarty	16,235
12		10		A	Middlesbrough	D	1-1	0-1	12	Fogarty	47,297
13		17		H	Derby County	W	3-1	1-0	7	Lawther (2), Grainger	27,307
14		24		A	Plymouth Argyle	D	0-0	0-0	9		21,990
15		31		H	Liverpool	D	1-1	1-0	7	Fogarty	30,208
16	Nov	7		A	Charlton Athletic	L	1-3	1-1	10	Anderson	17,480
17		14		H	Bristol City	W	3-2	1-1	7	Grainger, Fogarty (2)	21,025
18		21		A	Scunthorpe United	L	1-3	1-1	10	Lawther	11,822
19		28		H	Rotherham United	L	1-2	0-1	12	Grainger	26,909
20	Dec	5		A	Cardiff City	L	1-2	1-1	12	Lawther	20,016
21		12		H	Hull City	L	1-3	0-1	14	Lawther	17,695
22		19		H	Stoke City	L	0-2	0-1	16		12,221
23		26		H	Lincoln City	L	2-4	2-2	16	O'Neill (2)	23,848
24		28		A	Lincoln City	D	0-0	0-0	16		16,483
25	Jan	2		A	Brighton & H.A.	L	1-2	1-0	17	Lawther	10,628
28		16		H	Swansea Town	W	4-0	2-0	16	Lawther (3), Anderson	13,501
29		23		A	Bristol Rovers	L	1-3	0-3	17	Grainger	17,883
30	Feb	6		H	Ipswich Town	L	0-1	0-0	17		18,636
31		13		A	Huddersfield Town	D	1-1	0-1	17	Lawther	9,648
32		20		H	Leyton Orient	L	1-4	1-3	18	Pearce	16,981
33		27		A	Middlesbrough	D	2-2	1-1	18	Taylor, O'Neill	37,059
34	Mar	5		A	Derby County	W	1-0	1-0	16	Lawther	16,716
35		12		H	Plymouth Argyle	W	4-0	2-0	16	Lawther, O'Neill (3)	16,783
36		19		A	Rotherham United	L	0-1	0-0	16		8,867
37		26		H	Charlton Athletic	L	1-3	0-1	16	Hewie o.g.	11,944
38	Apr	2		A	Bristol City	L	0-1	0-1	20		13,437
39		9		A	Scunthorpe United	W	1-0	1-0	18	Fogarty	16,952
40		15		H	Portsmouth	W	2-0	1-0	16	Lawther (2)	20,299
41		16		A	Hull City	D	0-0	0-0	16		9,744
42		18		A	Portsmouth	W	2-1	1-1	15	Taylor, Lawther	16,151
43		23		H	Cardiff City	D	1-1	1-1	15	Fogarty	20,663
44		30		A	Liverpool	L	0-3	0-1	16		25,916

Appearances
Goals

FA Cup

26	Jan	9	R3	H	Blackburn Rovers	D	1-1	0-0		Lawther	34,129
27		13	R3r	A	Blackburn Rovers	L	1-4	0-2		O'Neill	27,600

Appearances
Goals

	Wakeham	Nelson	Ashurst	Anderson	Hurley	Pearce	Fraser	Goodchild	Kichenbrand	Taylor	Grainger	Bollands	McNab	Lawther	O'Neill A.	Fogarty	Irwin	Robson	Bircham	Maltby	Harvey	Davison	Godbold	Jones	Sharkey	
1	2	3	4	5	6	7	8	9	10	11																1
1	2	3	4	5	6	7	8	9	10	11																2
	2	3	4	5		7	8	9	10	11	1	6														3
	2	3	4	5		7		8	11	1	6	9	10													4
	2	3	4	5		7		8	11	1	6	9	10													5
	2	3	4	5		7		10	11	1	6	9		8												6
	3	4	5		7			10	11	1	6	9		8	2											7
	2	3	4	5		7		10	11	1	6	9		8												8
	2	3	4			7		10	11	1	6	9		8		5										9
1	2	3	4			7		10	11		6	9		8		5										10
1	2	3	4	5				10	11		6	9		8			7									11
1	2	3	4	5				10	11		6	9		8			7									12
1		3	4	5				10	11		6	9		8	2		7									13
1	2	3	5			7			11		6	9	10	8				4								14
1		3	4	5		7		10	11		6	9		8	2											15
1		3	4	5		7		10	11		6	9		8	2											16
1	2	3	4	5		7		10	11		6	9		8												17
1	2	3	4	5				10	11		6	9		8						7						18
1	2	3	4	5				10	11		6	9		8						7						19
1	2	3	4	5				10	11		6	9		8						7						20
1	2	3	4	5				10	11		6	9		8						7						21
1	2	3	4	5		7		10	11		6	9		8												22
1		3	5						11		6	9	10	8	2			4	7							23
1		3	4	5				8	11		6	9	10	7	2											24
1		3		5				8			6	9	10	7	2			4		11						25
1	2	3	4	5				8	11		6	9	10	7												28
1	2		4	5				8	11		6	9	10	7							3					29
1	2	3	4	5		10		8	11		6	9		7												30
1	2		8	5	6		10		11			9		7				4			3					31
1	2		8	5	6		10		11			9		7				4			3					32
1	2		4	5				10	11		6	9	8	7							3					33
1	2		4	5				10	11		6	9	8	7							3					34
1	2		4	5				8	11		6	9	10	7							3					35
1	2		4	5				8	11		6	9	10	7							3					36
1	2		4	5				10	11		6	9		8						7		3				37
1	2		4	5				10	11		6	9		8						7		3				38
1	2	3	4	5				10	11		6			8						7			9			39
1	2	3	4	5				10	11		6	9		8						7						40
1	2	3	4	5	6			10	11			9		8			7									41
1	2		4	5	6			10	11			9		8			7					3				42
1	2	3	4	5					11		6	9	10	8			7									43
1	2	3	4	5					11		6	9	10	8			7									44
35	35	32	41	38	6	12	9	3	36	41	7	36	38	14	37	7	2	2	5	5	9	1	10	1		
		2		2				1	4	6			17	6	12											

	Wakeham	Nelson	Ashurst	Anderson	Hurley	Pearce	Fraser	Goodchild	Kichenbrand	Taylor	Grainger	Bollands	McNab	Lawther	O'Neill A.	Fogarty	Irwin	Robson	Bircham	Maltby	Harvey	Davison	Godbold	Jones	Sharkey	
1	2	3	4	5				8	11		6	9	10	7												26
1	2	3	4	5				8	11		6	9	10	7												27
2	2	2	2	2				2	2		2	2	2	2												
													1	1												

Stan Anderson – the first person to captain Sunderland, Newcastle United and Middlesbrough during his career. This was the second of three successive seasons that he played in all bar one of the games.

1960-61

Division Two
Ground: Roker Park
Manager: Alan Brown

League Table

	P	W	D	L	F	A	Pts
Ipswich T	42	26	7	9	100	55	59
Sheffield U	42	26	6	10	81	51	58
Liverpool	42	21	10	11	87	58	52
Norwich C	42	20	9	13	70	53	49
Middlesbrough	42	18	12	12	83	74	48
SUNDERLAND	42	17	13	12	75	60	47
Swansea T	42	18	11	13	77	73	47
Southampton	42	18	8	16	84	81	44
Scunthorpe U	42	14	15	13	69	64	43
Charlton A	42	16	11	15	97	91	43
Plymouth A	42	17	8	17	81	82	42
Derby Co	42	15	10	17	80	80	40
Luton T	42	15	9	18	71	79	39
Leeds U	42	14	10	18	75	83	38
Rotherham U	42	12	13	17	65	64	37
Brighton & HA	42	14	9	19	61	75	37
Bristol R	42	15	7	20	73	92	37
Stoke C	42	12	12	18	51	59	36
Leyton O	42	14	8	20	55	78	36
Huddersfield T	42	13	9	20	62	71	35
Portsmouth	42	11	11	20	64	91	33
Lincoln C	42	8	8	26	48	95	24

Division 1 Champions: Tottenham Hotspur 66 pts
FA Cup Winners: Tottenham Hotspur
League Cup Winners: Aston Villa

Did you know that?

Danny Blanchflower, Tottenham's captain, reckoned that the loudest noise he heard in his football career was when Willie McPheat scored against them in the FA Cup 6th round at Roker Park on 4 March 1961.

Match 1: Overfield made debut
Match 9: Maltby last game
Match 10: Dillon made debut & Alan O'Neill last game
Match 11: Hooper made debut
Match 12: McPheat made debut
Match 14: Taylor last game
Match 35: Goodchild last game
Match 43: Rooks made debut & Pearce last game
Match 47: Lawther last game
Match 48: Herd made debut & Hird only game

Match No.	Date	Round	Venue	Opponents	Result	FT	HT	Pos.	Scorers	Attendance
1	Aug 20		H	Swansea Town	W	2-1	1-0		O'Neill, Fogarty	26,435
2	22		A	Stoke City	D	0-0	0-0	1		14,691
3	27		A	Luton Town	D	3-3	2-2	6	McNab, Lawther, O'Neill	17,632
4	31		H	Stoke City	W	4-0	3-0	3	Taylor, O'Neill, Lawther (2)	19,007
5	Sep 3		H	Lincoln City	D	2-2	1-1	3	Lawther, Fogarty	26,512
6	7		A	Charlton Athletic	D	2-2	0-2	6	Lawther (2)	7,698
7	10		A	Portsmouth	L	1-2	0-1	7	Anderson	16,387
8	14		H	Charlton Athletic	D	2-2	1-0	4	Lawther, Maltby	18,289
9	17		H	Huddersfield Town	L	1-2	0-0	9	Fogarty	21,336
10	24		A	Middlesbrough	L	0-1	0-0	11		27,458
11	Oct 1		A	Plymouth Argyle	L	0-1	0-1	14		23,464
12	8		H	Leeds United	L	2-3	0-2	18	McPheat, Lawther	22,296
13	15		A	Southampton	L	2-3	0-2	19	Hooper, Fogarty	20,188
14	22		H	Rotherham United	D	1-1	0-1	18	Lawther	19,240
15	29		A	Liverpool	D	1-1	0-0	18	Lawther	30,612
16	Nov 5		H	Bristol Rovers	W	2-0	1-0	16	Hooper, Lawther	17,942
17	12		A	Derby County	D	1-1	1-1	15	Lawther	21,608
18	19		H	Leyton Orient	W	4-1	0-0	10	Anderson, Lawther (2), Fogarty	16,815
19	26		A	Scunthorpe United	D	3-3	2-1	10	McPheat, Hooper, Overfield	9,156
20	Dec 3		H	Ipswich Town	W	2-0	0-0	9	McPheat (2)	21,251
21	10		A	Brighton & Hove Albion	W	2-1	1-0	9	Lawther, Fogarty	13,803
22	17		A	Swansea Town	D	3-3	1-3	9	Hooper (2), Lawther	7,922
23	26		H	Sheffield United	D	1-1	0-1	8	Hurley	46,099
24	27		A	Sheffield United	W	1-0	1-0	8	McPheat	28,525
25	31		H	Luton Town	W	7-1	1-0	7	Lawther (3), Davison, Hurley, McPheat, McNab	28,695
26	Jan 14		A	Lincoln City	W	2-1	1-1	6	Lawther, Anderson	9,012
27	21		A	Portsmouth	W	4-1	1-1	5	Fogarty, Lawther (2), Dillon	31,062
28	Feb 4		A	Huddersfield Town	L	2-4	0-2	7	Fogarty, Ashurst	16,341
29	11		H	Middlesbrough	W	2-0	2-0	7	Hooper, McPheat	53,254
30	22		H	Plymouth Argyle	W	2-1	0-0	6	McNab (2)	34,333
31	25		A	Leeds United	W	4-2	4-1	5	Lawther, Goodchild (3)	15,136
32	Mar 11		A	Rotherham United	D	0-0	0-0	6		10,588
33	18		H	Brighton & Hove Albion	W	2-1	0-1	4	Lawther, McPheat	26,782
34	25		A	Bristol Rovers	L	0-1	0-1	6		15,265
35	31		H	Norwich City	L	0-3	0-1	7		33,690
36	Apr 1		H	Scunthorpe United	W	2-0	1-0	6	Fogarty, McPheat	18,242
37	3		A	Norwich City	L	0-3	0-2	6		22,574
38	8		A	Leyton Orient	W	1-0	0-0	6	Sharkey	12,765
39	15		H	Derby County	L	1-2	1-1	6	McPheat	21,122
40	17		H	Southampton	W	3-1	2-0	6	McPheat, Sharkey (2)	14,635
41	22		A	Ipswich Town	L	0-4	0-2	6		21,115
42	29		H	Liverpool	D	1-1	1-0	6	Sharkey	30,040

Appearances
Goals

FA Cup

27	Jan 7	R3	H	Arsenal	W	2-1	0-1		Anderson (2)	58,575
30	28	R4	A	Liverpool	W	2-0	2-0		Hooper, Lawther	46,485
33	Feb 18	R5	A	Norwich City	W	1-0	0-0		Hurley	42,000
36	Mar 4	R6	H	Tottenham Hotspur	D	1-1	0-1		McPheat	61,326
37	8	R6r	A	Tottenham Hotspur	L	0-5	0-3			64,797

Appearances
Goals

League Cup

15	Oct 26	R2	A	Brentford	L	3-4	3-1		Lawther, McPheat, Fogarty	10,400

Appearances
Goals

	Wakeham	Nelson	Ashurst	Anderson	Hurley	McNab	Fogarty	Taylor	Lawther	O'Neill, A.	Overfield	Davison	Maltby	Harvey	Dillon	Hooper	McPheat	Goodchild	Irwin	Rooks	Pearce	Sharkey	Hird	Herd	
1	1	2	3	4	5	6	7	8	9	10	11														1
2	1	2	3	4	5	6		8	9	10	11	7													2
3	1	2	3	4	5	6	7	8	9	10	11														3
4	1	2	3	4	5	6	7	8	9	10	11														4
5	1	2	3	4	5	6	7	8	9	10	11														5
6	1	2	3	4	5	6	10		9		11	7	8												6
7	1	2	3	4	5	6	7	8	9	10	11														7
8	1	2	3	4	5	6	10		9		11	7	8												8
9	1	2	3	4	5	6	10		9		11	7	8												9
10	1	2	3		5	6	7	8	9	10				4	11										10
11	1	2	3	4	5	6	8	10	9						11	7									11
12	1	2	3	4	5	6	8		9						11	7	10								12
13	1	2	3	4	5	6	8	10	9			7			11										13
14	1	2	3	4	5	6	8	10	9		11					7									14
16	1	2	3	4	5	6	8		9		11					7	10								16
17	1	2	3	4	5	6	8		9		11					7	10								17
18	1	2	3	4	5	6	8		9		11					7	10								18
19	1	2	3	4	5	6	8		9		11					7	10								19
20	1	2	3	4	5	6	8		9		11					7	10								20
21	1	2	3	4	5	6	8		9		11					7	10								21
22	1	2	3	4	5	6	8		9		11					7	10								22
23	1	2	3	4	5	6	8		9		11					7	10								23
24	1	2	3	4	5	6	8		9		11					7	10								24
25	1	2	3	4	5	6	8		9		11					7	10								25
26	1	2	3	4	5	6	8		9		11	7					10								26
28	1	2	3	4	5	6	8		9						11	7	10								28
29	1	2	3	4	5	6	8		9						11	7	10								29
31	1	2	3	10	5	6	8		9					4	11	7									31
32	1	2	3	4	5	6	8		9						11	7	10								32
34	1	2	3	4	5	6	8		9						11	7	10								34
35	1	2	3	4	5	6	8		9						11	7		10							35
38	1	2	3	6	5		8		9		11	7		4			10								38
39	1	2	3	4	5	6	8		9						11	7	10								39
40	1	2	3	4	5	6	8		9						11	7	10								40
41	1	2	3	5		6	8		9					4	11	7	10								41
42	1	3		5		6	8		9		11			4		7	10		3						42
43	1	3		4			8								11	7	10	3	5	6	9				43
44	1	2	3	4		6	8								11	7	10		5		9				44
45	1	2	3	4		6	8					7				11	10		5		9				45
46	1	2	3	4		6	8					7				11	10		5		9				46
47	1	2	3	4		6	8		9			7				11	10		5						47
48		2	3	4	5	6	10				11	7							9	1	8				48
	41	42	40	41	35	40	41	10	37	7	24	11	3	5	17	26	26	1	2	5	1	5	1	1	
		1	3	2	4	9	1	24	3	1	1		1	6	11	3			4						

	Wakeham	Nelson	Ashurst	Anderson	Hurley	McNab	Fogarty	Taylor	Lawther	O'Neill, A.	Overfield	Davison	Maltby	Harvey	Dillon	Hooper	McPheat	Goodchild	Irwin	Rooks	Pearce	Sharkey	Hird	Herd	
27	1	2	3	4	5	6	8		9		11					7	10								27
30	1	2	3	4	5	6	8		9						11	7	10								30
33	1	2	3	4	5	6	8		9						11	7	10								33
36	1	2	3	4	5	6	8		9						11	7	10								36
37	1	2	3	6	5		8		9					4	11	7	10								37
	5	5	5	5	5	4	5		5		1			1	4	5	5								
		2	1			1								1	1										

	Wakeham	Nelson	Ashurst	Anderson	Hurley	McNab	Fogarty	Taylor	Lawther	O'Neill, A.	Overfield	Davison	Maltby	Harvey	Dillon	Hooper	McPheat	Goodchild	Irwin	Rooks	Pearce	Sharkey	Hird	Herd	
15	1	2	3	4	5	6	8		9						11	7	10								15
	1	1	1	1	1	1	1		1						1	1	1								
					1		1																		

George Herd.

George Herd made his debut in the last game of the season shortly after joining from Clyde. He went on to play over 300 games for the club before joining the coaching staff in May 1969.

1961-62

Division Two

Ground: Roker Park
Manager: Alan Brown

League Table

	P	W	D	L	F	A	Pts
Liverpool	42	27	8	7	99	43	62
Leyton O	42	22	10	10	69	40	54
SUNDERLAND	42	22	9	11	85	50	53
Scunthorpe U	42	21	7	14	86	71	49
Plymouth A	42	19	8	15	75	75	46
Southampton	42	18	9	15	77	62	45
Huddersfield T	42	16	12	14	67	59	44
Stoke C	42	17	8	17	55	57	42
Rotherham U	42	16	9	17	70	76	41
Preston NE	42	15	10	17	55	57	40
Newcastle U	42	15	9	18	64	58	39
Middlesbrough	42	16	7	19	76	72	39
Luton T	42	17	5	20	69	71	39
Walsall	42	14	11	17	70	75	39
Charlton A	42	15	9	18	69	75	39
Derby Co	42	14	11	17	68	75	39
Norwich C	42	14	11	17	61	70	39
Bury	42	17	5	20	52	76	39
Leeds U	42	12	12	18	50	61	36
Swansea T	42	12	12	18	61	83	36
Bristol R	42	13	7	22	53	81	33
Brighton & HA	42	10	11	21	42	86	31

Division 1 Champions: Ipswich Town 56 pts
FA Cup Winners: Tottenham Hotspur
League Cup Winners: Norwich City

Did you know that?

Sunderland received a bye in the 4th Round of the League Cup in 1961-62.

The Sunderland v Charlton Athletic game scheduled for 30 December 1961 was the first home game to be postponed since Christmas Day 1925.

Match 1: Clough made debut
Match 14: Montgomery made debut
Match 16: Dillon last game
Match 31: James O'Neill made debut
Match 43: James O'Neill last game
Match 45: Wakeham last game

Match No.	Date		Round	Venue	Opponents	Result	FT	HT	Pos.	Scorers	Attendance
1	Aug	19		A	Walsall	L	3-4	2-2		Clough, Herd, Hooper (pen)	18,420
2		23		A	Liverpool	L	0-3	0-0	21		48,963
3		26		H	Stoke City	W	2-1	0-1	17	Fogarty (2)	34,183
4		30		H	Liverpool	L	1-4	1-2	20	Clough	47,261
5	Sep	2		A	Bristol Rovers	W	3-2	2-0	17	McPheat, Fogarty, Sykes o.g.	12,214
6		9		H	Leeds United	W	2-1	2-0	15	Clough (2)	30,737
8		16		A	Norwich City	L	1-3	0-0	18	McPheat	21,910
9		19		A	Bury	L	2-3	1-0	19	Clough, McNab	17,095
10		23		H	Scunthorpe United	W	4-0	3-0	17	Herd (2), Fogarty (2)	35,112
12		27		H	Bury	W	3-0	2-0	10	Clough (3)	39,893
13		30		A	Brighton & Hove Albion	D	1-1	1-0	12	Hurley	17,070
15	Oct	7		A	Derby County	D	1-1	0-0	11	Hurley	16,452
16		14		H	Leyton Orient	W	2-1	1-1	8	Clough (2)	36,780
17		21		A	Preston North End	W	1-0	0-0	4	Hurley	17,973
18		28		H	Plymouth Argyle	W	5-0	3-0	3	Hooper (2, 1 pen), Clough (3)	30,023
19	Nov	4		A	Huddersfield Town	D	0-0	0-0	3		19,017
20		11		H	Middlesbrough	W	2-1	2-0	3	Hooper, Herd	48,428
22		18		A	Southampton	L	0-2	0-1	6		16,690
23		25		H	Luton Town	D	2-2	1-0	5	Hooper (pen), Clough	32,763
24	Dec	2		A	Newcastle United	D	2-2	0-1	5	Clough (2)	53,991
25		9		H	Swansea Town	W	7-2	2-1	3	Fogarty (3), Clough (3), Hooper	27,560
26		16		H	Walsall	W	3-0	0-0	3	Overfield (2), Clough	30,690
27		23		A	Stoke City	L	0-1	0-0	3		25,273
28		26		A	Charlton Athletic	L	0-2	0-1	4		18,342
31	Jan	13		H	Bristol Rovers	W	6-1	2-1	5	Hooper (pen), O'Neill (2), McNab, Bumpstead o.g., McPheat	32,650
32		20		A	Leeds United	L	0-1	0-1	7		17,763
35	Feb	3		H	Norwich City	W	2-0	1-0	5	O'Neill, McPheat	26,643
37		10		A	Scunthorpe United	L	1-3	1-2	7	Overfield	11,656
38		17		H	Brighton & Hove Albion	D	0-0	0-0	6		22,575
39		24		H	Derby County	W	2-1	2-0	7	Hurley, Herd	22,143
40	Mar	3		A	Leyton Orient	D	1-1	1-0	8	McPheat	19,972
41		14		H	Charlton Athletic	W	4-1	1-0	7	Herd (2), O'Neill, Anderson	21,706
42		17		A	Plymouth Argyle	L	2-3	2-1	7	O'Neill (2)	16,726
43		21		H	Preston North End	D	0-0	0-0	6		21,714
44		24		H	Huddersfield Town	W	3-1	2-0	5	Clough (3)	26,412
45		31		A	Middlesbrough	W	1-0	1-0	4	Clough	35,666
46	Apr	7		H	Southampton	W	3-0	1-0	5	Clough, Herd, Hooper	28,865
47		14		A	Luton Town	W	2-1	0-1	3	Overfield, Harvey	9,571
48		21		H	Newcastle United	W	3-0	1-0	3	Herd (2), McPheat	57,666
49		23		H	Rotherham United	W	4-0	1-0	3	Hooper, Hurley, McPheat, Clough	38,903
50		24		A	Rotherham United	W	3-0	0-0	2	Clough (2), Hurley	8,674
51		28		A	Swansea Town	D	1-1	1-0	3	Clough	18,071

Appearances
Goals

FA Cup

29	Jan	6	R3	A	Southampton	D	2-2	1-1		Hooper (pen), Anderson	22,248
30		10	R3r	H	Southampton	W	3-0	1-0		McPheat, Herd (2)	58,527
33		27	R4	H	Port Vale	D	0-0	0-0			48,468
34		31	R4r	A	Port Vale	L	1-3	0-1		McPheat	28,206

Appearances
Goals

League Cup

7	Sep	13	R1	A	Bolton Wanderers	D	1-1	1-1		Fogarty	13,175
11		25	R1r	H	Bolton Wanderers	W	1-0	1-0		Clough	19,557
14	Oct	4	R2	H	Walsall	W	5-2	1-1		Clough (3), McNab, Hill o.g.	29,558
21	Nov	15	R3	H	Hull City	W	2-1	0-1		Herd, Hooper	15,969
36	Feb	7	R5	H	Norwich City	L	1-4	0-2		Clough	17,813

Appearances
Goals

	Wakeham	Nelson	Ashurst	Anderson	Hurley	McNab	Hooper	Herd	Clough	Fogarty	Overfield	McPheat	Rooks	Harvey	Sharkey	Irwin	Davison	Dillon	O'Neill, J.	Montgomery	
1	2	3	4	5	6	7	8	9	10	11											1
1	2	3	4	5	6	7		9	8	11	10										2
1	2	3	4		6	7		9	8	11	10	5									3
1	2	3	4		6	7		9	8	11	10	5									4
1	2	3	4	5	6	7		9	8	11	10										5
1	2	3	4	5	6	7		9	8	11	10										6
1	2	3		5	6	7		8	11	10		4	9								8
1	2	3	4	5	6	7		9	8	11	10										9
1		3	4	5	6		8	9	10	11			2	7							10
1		3	4	5	6	7	8	9	10	11			2								12
1		3	4	5	6	7	8	9	10	11			2								13
1		3	4	5	6	7	8	9	10	11			2								15
1		3	4	5	6	7	8	9	10				2	11							16
1		3	4	5	6		7	9	8	11	10		2								17
1		3	4		6	7	8	9		11	10	5	2								18
1		3	4	5	6	7	8	9	10	11			2								19
1		3	4	5	6	7	8	9	10	11			2								20
1		3	4	5	6	7	8	9	10	11			2								22
1		3	4	5	6	7	8	9	10	11			2								23
1		3	4	5	6	7	8	9	10	11			2								24
1		3	4	5	6	7	8	9	10	11			2								25
1		3	4	5	6	7	8	9	10	11			2								26
1		3			6	7		9	8	11	10	5	4		2						27
1		3			6	7		9	8	11	10	5	4		2						28
1		3	4	5	6	7	8			11	10			2		9					31
1		3	4	5	6		8	9		11	10			2	7						32
1		3	4	5	6	11	8				10			2	7	9					35
1	2	3	4	5	6			8	9					7							37
1		3	4	5	6	7	8	9		11	10		2								38
		3	4	5	6		8			11	10			2	7		9	1			39
		3	4		6		8			11	10	5		2	7		9	1			40
		3	4	5	6		8			11	10	5		2	7		9	1			41
		3	4		6		8			11	10	5		2	7		9	1			42
		3	4	5	6		8			11	10			2	7		9	1			43
		3	4	5	6	7	8	9		11	10			2				1			44
1		3	4	5	6	7	8	9		11	10			2							45
		3	4	5	6	7	8	9		11	10			2				1			46
		3			6	7	8	9		11	10	5	4	2				1			47
		3	4	5	6	7	8	9		11	10			2				1			48
		3	4	5	6	7	8	9		11	10			2				1			49
		3	4	5	6	7		9	8	11	10			2				1			50
		3	4	5	6	7	8	9		11	10			2				1			51
30	9	42	38	33	42	33	32	34	24	40	29	9	4	1	33	9	1	7	12		
		1	6	2	9	10	29	8	4	7		1				6					

	Wakeham	Nelson	Ashurst	Anderson	Hurley	McNab	Hooper	Herd	Clough	Fogarty	Overfield	McPheat	Rooks	Harvey	Sharkey	Irwin	Davison	Dillon	O'Neill, J.	Montgomery	
1		3	4	5	6	7	8	9		11	10			2							29
1		3	4	5	6		8	9		11	10			2	7						30
1		3	4	5	6	7	8	9		11	10			2							33
1		3	4	5	6	7	8	9		11	10			2							34
4		4	4	4	4	3	4	4		4	4			4	1						
			1			1	2				2										

	Wakeham	Nelson	Ashurst	Anderson	Hurley	McNab	Hooper	Herd	Clough	Fogarty	Overfield	McPheat	Rooks	Harvey	Sharkey	Irwin	Davison	Dillon	O'Neill, J.	Montgomery	
1	2	3			5	6	7		9	8	11	10	4								7
1	2	3	4	5	6	7		9	8	11	10										11
		3	4	5	6	7	8	9		11	10		2			1					14
1		3	4	5	6	7	8	9	10	11			2								21
1		3	4	5	6	11	8	9			10			2	7						36
4	2	5	4	5	5	5	3	5	3	4	4			3	1			1			
			1	1	1	5	1														

Brian Clough – scorer of five hat-tricks during his first season with Sunderland.

437

1962-63

Division Two

Ground: Roker Park
Manager: Alan Brown

League Table

	P	W	D	L	F	A	Pts
Stoke C	42	20	13	9	73	50	53
Chelsea	42	24	4	14	81	42	52
SUNDERLAND	42	20	12	10	84	55	52
Middlesbrough	42	20	9	13	86	85	49
Leeds U	42	19	10	13	79	53	48
Huddersfield T	42	17	14	11	63	50	48
Newcastle U	42	18	11	13	79	59	47
Bury	42	18	11	13	51	47	47
Scunthorpe U	42	16	12	14	57	59	44
Cardiff C	42	18	7	17	83	73	43
Southampton	42	17	8	17	72	67	42
Plymouth A	42	15	12	15	76	73	42
Norwich C	42	17	8	17	80	79	42
Rotherham U	42	17	6	19	67	74	40
Swansea T	42	15	9	18	51	72	39
Portsmouth	42	13	11	18	63	79	37
Preston NE	42	13	11	18	59	74	37
Derby Co	42	12	12	18	61	72	36
Grimsby T	42	11	13	18	55	66	35
Charlton A	42	13	5	24	62	94	31
Walsall	42	11	9	22	53	89	31
Luton T	42	11	7	24	61	84	29

Division 1 Champions: Everton 61 pts

FA Cup Winners: Manchester United

League Cup Winners: Birmingham City

Did you know that?

Sunderland reached the two legged semi-final of the League Cup for the first time in 1962-63. These two games had a record 101 days between them due to the snow, ice and associated fixture backlog suffered by most of England that winter.

Match 1: Clarke made debut
Match 3: McPheat last game
Match 4: Overfield last game
Match 5: Mitchinson made debut
Match 8: Mulhall made debut
Match 10: Kiernan made debut
Match 11: Kiernan last game
Match 18: Crossan made debut
Match 20: Clarke last game
Match 42: Kerr made debut
Match 48: Hooper last game
Match 53: Davison last game

Match No.	Date	Round	Venue	Opponents	Result	FT	HT	Pos.	Scorers	Attendance
1	Aug 18		H	Middlesbrough	W	3-1	1-0		Clough (2), Hurley	48,106
2	22		H	Charlton Athletic	W	1-0	0-0	2	McPheat	37,028
3	25		A	Leeds United	L	0-1	0-0	6		17,755
4	28		A	Charlton Athletic	D	2-2	1-0	5	McNab, Clough	17,055
5	Sep 1		H	Swansea Town	W	3-1	2-1	7	Clough (2), Anderson	36,982
6	5		H	Rotherham United	W	2-0	0-0	2	Clough, Fogarty	38,172
7	8		A	Chelsea	L	0-1	0-1	4		32,901
8	11		A	Rotherham United	L	2-4	0-1	6	Fogarty (2)	13,064
9	15		H	Luton Town	W	3-1	0-0	7	Clough (2), Fogarty	36,399
10	22		A	Southampton	W	4-2	1-1	4	Clough (3), Mulhall	18,535
12	29		H	Scunthorpe United	D	0-0	0-0	7		43,230
13	Oct 6		H	Derby County	W	3-0	2-0	4	Clough (2), Young o.g.	35,340
14	13		A	Newcastle United	D	1-1	1-1	3	Clough	62,321
16	20		H	Walsall	W	5-0	2-0	2	Davison (2), Anderson, Clough, Mulhall	36,750
17	27		A	Norwich City	L	2-4	2-1	4	Clough, Hurley	23,439
18	Nov 3		H	Grimsby Town	W	6-2	3-0	3	Davison (2), Clough (3), Herd	43,087
19	10		A	Plymouth Argyle	D	1-1	0-0	3	Clough	18,561
21	17		H	Preston North End	W	2-1	1-1	3	Davison, Hurley	29,976
23	24		A	Portsmouth	L	1-3	0-0	5	Nelson	15,000
24	Dec 1		H	Cardiff City	W	2-1	1-0	4	Davison, Clough	37,603
26	8		A	Huddersfield Town	W	3-0	0-0	2	Clough (2), Mulhall	21,260
27	15		A	Middlesbrough	D	3-3	3-3	2	Mulhall, Clough, Herd	43,509
28	22		H	Leeds United	W	2-1	1-0	2	Mulhall, Hurley	40,252
29	26		H	Bury	L	0-1	0-0	2		42,407
30	29		A	Bury	L	0-3	0-0	3		17,329
35	Feb 23		A	Derby County	D	2-2	0-2	2	Crossan, Anderson	15,460
36	Mar 2		H	Newcastle United	D	0-0	0-0	2		62,420
37	9		A	Walsall	W	3-2	2-2	2	Crossan (3)	7,234
38	20		H	Norwich City	W	7-1	3-0	2	Sharkey (5), Anderson, Crossan	42,393
39	23		A	Grimsby Town	W	2-1	1-0	1	Herd, Hurley	12,332
41	30		H	Plymouth Argyle	D	1-1	1-1	1	Crossan	31,276
42	Apr 6		A	Preston North End	D	1-1	0-1	2	Davison	14,015
43	12		H	Stoke City	D	0-0	0-0	3		62,138
44	13		H	Portsmouth	W	1-0	1-0	3	Hooper	35,356
45	15		A	Stoke City	L	1-2	1-1	3	Kerr	42,394
46	20		A	Cardiff City	L	2-5	0-4	3	Kerr, Edwards o.g.	12,293
48	27		H	Huddersfield Town	D	1-1	0-0	3	Mulhall	37,098
49	30		A	Scunthorpe United	D	1-1	0-0	3	Crossan	9,090
50	May 4		H	Southampton	W	4-0	2-0	3	Crossan (3), Davison	34,612
51	11		A	Swansea Town	W	4-3	3-2	2	Davison, Crossan (2), Herd	8,567
52	13		A	Luton Town	W	3-0	1-0	1	Sharkey (2), Mulhall	16,419
53	18		H	Chelsea	L	0-1	0-1	3		47,918

Appearances
Goals

FA Cup

31	Jan 5	R3	A	Preston North End	W	4-1	1-1		Sharkey (2), Fogarty, Davison	25,917
33	Feb 12	R4	A	Gravesend & Northfleet	D	1-1	1-0		Mulhall	12,032
34	18	R4r	H	Gravesend & Northfleet	W	5-2	4-0		Mulhall, Crossan (2), Fogarty, Sharkey	29,659
40	Mar 25	R5	A	Coventry City	L	1-2	1-0		Crossan	40,487

Appearances
Goals

League Cup

11	Sep 24	R2	H	Oldham Athletic	W	7-1	2-1		Clough (2), Fogarty (2), Kiernan (2), Mulhall	15,742
15	Oct 18	R3	H	Scunthorpe United	W	2-0	1-0		Rooks, Mulhall	18,154
20	Nov 14	R4	A	Portsmouth	D	0-0	0-0			13,411
22	21	R4r	H	Portsmouth	W	2-1	1-1		McNab, Herd	14,484
25	Dec 5	R5	H	Blackburn Rovers	W	3-2	2-1		Clough (2), McNab	24,727
32	Jan 12	S1L	H	Aston Villa	L	1-3	0-2		Sharkey	33,237
47	Apr 23	S2L	A	Aston Villa	D	0-0	0-0			22,102

Appearances
Goals

Montgomery	Irwin	Ashurst	Anderson	Hurley	McNab	Hooper	Herd	Clough	McPheat	Clarke	Davison	Fogarty	Overfield	Rooks	Mitchinson	Mulhall	Kiernan	Nelson	Harvey	Crossan	Sharkey	Kerr	
1	2	3	4	5	6	7	8	9	10	11													1
1	2	3	4	5	6		8	9	10	11	7												2
1	2	3	4	5	6	7	8	9	10			11											3
1	2	3	4	5	6		8	9			7	10	11										4
1	2	3	4		6		8	9		11	7			5	10								5
1	2	3	4	5	6	7	8	9		11		10											6
1	2	3	4	5	6		8	9			7	11		10									7
1	2	3	4	5	6		8	9			7	10			11								8
1	2	3	4	5	6		8	9			7	10			11								9
1	2	3	4				8	9			7	10	5		11	6							10
1	2	3	4	5	6		8	9			7	10			11								12
1		3	4	5	6		8	9			7	10			11	2							13
1		3	4		6		8	9			7	10	5		11	2							14
1		3	4		6		8	9			7	10	5		11	2							16
1		3	4	5	6		8	9			7	10			11	2							17
1		3		5	6		8	9			7				11	2	4	10					18
1		3		5	6		8	9			7				11	2	4	10					19
1		3	4	5	6		8	9			7				11	2		10					21
1		3	4	5	6			9			7	8			11	2		10					23
1		3	4	5	6		8	9			7				11	2	4	10					24
1		3		5	6		8	9			7				11	2		10					26
1		3		5	6		8	9			7	10			11	2	4						27
		3	4	5	6	7	8	9				10			11	2							28
1		3		5	6		8	9			7	10			11	2	4						29
1		3	4	5	6		8				7				11	2		10	9				30
1		3	4	5	6		7					8			11	2		10	9				35
1		3	4	5	6		7					8			11	2		10	9				36
1		3	4	5	6		8				7				11	2		10	9				37
1		3	4	5	6		8				7				11	2		10	9				38
1		3		5	6		8				7				11	2	4	10	9				39
1	2		4	5	6						7	8			11	3		10	9				41
1	2		4	5	6		8				7				11	3		10		9			42
1	2	3	4	5	6		8				7				11			10		9			43
1	2	3	4	5	6	7	8								11			10		9			44
1	2	3	6	5			7					8			11		4	10		9			45
1	2	3	6	5			8				7				11		4	10		9			46
1	2	3	4	5	6	7	8								11			10		9			48
1		3		5	6		8				7				11	2	4	10		9			49
1		3	4	5	6		8				7				11	2		10		9			50
1		3	4	5	6		8				7				11	2		10	9				51
1		3	4	5	6		8				7				11	2		10	9				52
1		3	4	5	6		8				7				11	2		10	9				53
42	18	40	35	38	39	6	40	24	3	4	33	20	1	4	2	35	1	26	9	24	10	8	
		4	5	1	1		4	24	1		9	4				7		1		12	7	2	

1		3	4	5	6						7	8			11	2		10	9				31
1		3		5	6		7					8			11	2	4	10	9				33
1		3		5	6		7					8			11	2	4	10	9				34
1		3	4	5	6		8				7				11	2		10	9				40
4		4	2	4	4		3				2	3			4	4	2	4	4				
											1	2			2			3	3				

1	2	3	4	5			8	9			7	10			11	6							11
1		3			6		8	9			7	10	5		11	2	4						15
1		3	4	5	6			9		11	7	8			2			10					20
1		3	4	5	6		8				7				11	2		10	9				22
1		3		5	6	7	8	9				10			11	2	4						25
1		3	4	5	6						7	8			11	2		10	9				32
1		3	6	5							7	8			11	2	4	10	9				47
7	1	7	5	6	5	1	4	4		1	6	6	1		6	1	6	3	4	3			
			2		1		4				2		1		2	2			1				

Nick Sharkey equalled Sunderland's goalscoring record with five goals v Norwich City, 20 March 1963.

439

1963-64

Division Two

Ground: Roker Park
Manager: Alan Brown

League Table

	P	W	D	L	F	A	Pts
Leeds U	42	24	15	3	71	34	63
SUNDERLAND	42	25	11	6	81	37	61
Preston NE	42	23	10	9	79	54	56
Charlton A	42	19	10	13	76	70	48
Southampton	42	19	9	14	100	73	47
Manchester C	42	18	10	14	84	66	46
Rotherham U	42	19	7	16	90	78	45
Newcastle U	42	20	5	17	74	69	45
Portsmouth	42	16	11	15	79	70	43
Middlesbrough	42	15	11	16	67	52	41
Northampton T	42	16	9	17	58	60	41
Huddersfield T	42	15	10	17	57	64	40
Derby Co	42	14	11	17	56	67	39
Swindon T	42	14	10	18	57	69	38
Cardiff C	42	14	10	18	56	81	38
Leyton O	42	13	10	19	54	72	36
Norwich C	42	11	13	18	64	80	35
Bury	42	13	9	20	57	73	35
Swansea T	42	12	9	21	63	74	33
Plymouth A	42	8	16	18	45	67	32
Grimsby T	42	9	14	19	47	75	32
Scunthorpe U	42	10	10	22	52	82	30

Division 1 Champions:
Liverpool 57 pts

Division 2 Champions:
Leeds United 63 pts
Sunderland (2nd) 61 pts

FA Cup Winners: West Ham United

League Cup Winners: Leicester City

Did you know that?

The crowd for the FA Cup 6th round replay at home to Manchester United on 4 March was estimated to be 70,000. The gates were shut long before kick off but thousands surged in to the ground when the gates at the Roker End were forced open.

Match 1: Usher made debut
Match 9: Fogarty last game
Match 11: Anderson last game
Match 22: Kerr last game
Match 36: Elliott made debut
Match 48: Promotion confirmed
Match 49: Alan Brown last game as Sunderland manager

Match Results

Match No.	Date	Round	Venue	Opponents	Result	FT	HT	Pos.	Scorers	Attendance
1	Aug 24		A	Huddersfield Town	W	2-0	1-0		Kerr, Mulhall	20,894
2	28		H	Portsmouth	W	3-0	1-0	2	Mulhall (2), Crossan	40,300
3	31		H	Northampton Town	L	0-2	0-2	5		39,201
4	Sep 4		A	Portsmouth	W	4-2	3-1	4	Crossan (2), Kerr, Dickinson o.g.	16,520
5	7		A	Bury	W	1-0	1-0	3	Usher	11,901
6	9		A	Scunthorpe United	D	1-1	1-0	3	Kerr	10,489
7	14		H	Manchester City	W	2-0	1-0	2	Crossan, Fogarty	39,298
8	18		H	Scunthorpe United	W	1-0	1-0	2	Crossan	36,128
9	21		A	Swindon Town	L	0-1	0-1	2		26,273
10	25									
11	28		H	Cardiff City	D	3-3	2-3	2	Sharkey (2), Hurley	37,287
12	Oct 2		A	Plymouth Argyle	D	1-1	1-0	2	Herd	13,609
13	5		A	Norwich City	W	3-2	0-0	2	Hurley, McNab, Crossan	19,694
14	9		H	Newcastle United	W	2-1	1-1	2	Ashurst, Herd	56,903
15	16		A	Derby County	W	3-0	1-0	3	Sharkey (2), Herd	20,305
16	19		H	Plymouth Argyle	W	1-0	0-0	1	Hurley	36,787
17	26		A	Middlesbrough	L	0-2	0-1	3		43,905
18	Nov 2		H	Grimsby Town	W	3-0	2-0	1	Crossan (2), Herd	29,004
19	9		A	Preston North End	D	1-1	0-0	2	Herd	26,579
20	16		H	Leyton Orient	W	4-1	3-1	1	Hurley, Mulhall, Crossan, Herd	35,004
21	23		A	Swansea Town	W	2-1	0-0	1	Hurley, Sharkey	10,880
22	30		H	Southampton	L	1-2	1-0	2	Crossan	34,998
23	Dec 7		A	Charlton Athletic	D	0-0	0-0	2		29,819
24	14		H	Huddersfield Town	W	3-2	1-2	2	Sharkey, Herd, Crossan (pen)	27,417
25	21		A	Northampton Town	L	1-5	0-3	2	Herd	12,130
26	26		A	Leeds United	D	1-1	0-0	2	Mulhall	41,167
27	28		H	Leeds United	W	2-0	2-0	2	Herd, Sharkey	55,046
29	Jan 11		H	Bury	W	4-1	2-1	2	Crossan (2), Herd, Sharkey	36,962
30	18		A	Manchester City	W	3-0	2-0	2	Crossan (2, 1 pen), Mulhall	31,136
32	Feb 1		H	Swindon Town	W	6-0	2-0	1	Sharkey (3), Crossan (2), Usher	41,334
33	8		A	Cardiff City	W	2-0	0-0	1	Mulhall, Sharkey	15,600
35	19		H	Norwich City	D	0-0	0-0	1		44,514
36	22		H	Derby County	W	3-0	2-0	1	Sharkey, Usher, Waller o.g.	43,945
39	Mar 7		H	Middlesbrough	D	0-0	0-0	1		46,855
41	14		A	Newcastle United	L	0-1	0-1	2		27,341
42	21		H	Preston North End	W	4-0	4-0	2	Crossan, Mulhall, Sharkey (2)	35,420
43	27		A	Rotherham United	W	2-0	0-0	2	Herd (2)	56,675
44	30		A	Rotherham United	D	2-2	0-2	2	Crossan (2)	21,641
45	Apr 4		H	Swansea Town	W	1-0	1-0	2	Usher	42,505
46	6		A	Leyton Orient	W	5-2	1-1	2	Bishop o.g., McNab, Crossan, Mulhall, Sharkey	16,133
47	11		A	Southampton	D	0-0	0-0	2		21,944
48	18		H	Charlton Athletic	W	2-1	1-1	2	Herd, Crossan	50,827
49	25		A	Grimsby Town	D	2-2	0-1	2	Sharkey, Usher	16,442

Appearances
Goals

FA Cup

Match No.	Date	Round	Venue	Opponents	Result	FT	HT		Scorers	Attendance
28	Jan 4	R3	H	Northampton Town	W	2-0	0-0		Usher, Crossan	40,683
31	25	R4	A	Bristol City	W	6-1	3-1		Herd (2), Hurley, Sharkey, Crossan (2)	46,201
34	Feb 15	R5	H	Everton	W	3-1	3-0		McNab, Hurley, Meagan o.g.	62,851
37	29	R6	A	Manchester United	D	3-3	1-0		Mulhall, Crossan (2, 1 pen)	61,700
38	Mar 4	R6r	H	Manchester United	D	2-2 (aet)	1-0		Sharkey, Setters o.g.	46,727
40	9	R6r2	N*	Manchester United	L	1-5	0-0		Sharkey	54,952

* at Leeds Road.

Appearances
Goals

League Cup

Match No.	Date	Round	Venue	Opponents	Result	FT	HT		Scorers	Attendance
10	Sep 25	R2	A	Swansea Town	L	1-3	1-1		Herd	8,697

Appearances
Goals

	Montgomery	Irwin	Ashurst	Anderson	Hurley	McNab	Usher	Herd	Kerr	Crossan	Mulhall	Fogarty	Sharkey	Harvey	Mitchinson	Elliott	Nelson	Rooks	
	1	2	3	4	5	6	7	8	9	10	11								1
	1	2	3	4	5	6	7	8	9	10	11								2
	1	2	3	4	5	6	7	8	9	10	11								3
	1	2	3	4	5	6	7	8	9	10	11								4
	1	2	3	4	5	6	7	8	9	10	11								5
	1	2	3	4	5	6	7	8	9	10	11								6
	1	2	3	4	5	6	7		9	10	11	8							7
	1	2	3	4	5	6	7		9	10	11	8							8
	1	2	3	4	5	6	7		9	10	11	8							9
	1	2	3	4	5	6	7	8		10	11		9						11
	1	2	3		5	6	7	8		10	11		9	4					12
	1	2	3		5	6	7	8		10	11		9	4					13
	1	2	3		5	6	7	8		10	11		9	4					14
	1	2	3		5	6	7	8		10	11		9	4					15
	1	2	3		5	6	7	8		10	11		9	4					16
	1	2	3		5	6	7	8		10	11		9	4					17
	1	2	3		5	6	7	8		10	11		9	4					18
	1	2	3		5	6	7	8		10	11		9	4					19
	1	2	3		5	6		8		10	11		9	4	7				20
	1	2	3		5	6	7	8		10	11		9	4					21
	1	2	3			6	7	8	5	10	11		9	4					22
	1	2	3		5	6	7	8		10	11		9	4					23
	1	2	3		5	6	7	8		10	11		9	4					24
	1	2	3		5	6	7	8		10	11		9	4					25
	1	2	3		5	6	7	8		10	11		9	4					26
	1	2	3		5	6	7	8		10	11		9	4					27
	1	2	3		5	6	7	8		10	11		9	4					29
	1	2	3		5	6	7	8		10	11		9	4					30
	1	2	3		5	6	7	8		10	11		9	4					32
	1	2	3		5	6	7	8		10	11		9	4					33
	1	2	3		5	6	7	8		10	11		9	4					35
	1	2	3		5		7	8		10	11		9	4		6			36
	1	2	3		5		7	8		10	11		9	4		6			39
	1		3		5		7	8		10	11		9	4		6	2		41
	1		3		5		7	8		10	11		9	4		6	2		42
	1		3		5		7	8		10	11		9	4		6	2		43
	1	2	3		5	6	7	8		10	11		9	4					44
	1	2	3		5	6	7	8		10	11		9	4					45
	1	2	3		5	6	7	8		10	11		9	4					46
	1	2	3		5	6	7	8		10	11		9	4					47
	1	2	3		5	6	7	8		10	11		9	4					48
	1	2	3		5	6	7	8		10	11		9	4					49
	42	39	42	10	41	37	41	39	10	42	42	3	33	32	1	5	3		
		1		5	2	5	13	3	22	9	1	17							

	Montgomery	Irwin	Ashurst	Anderson	Hurley	McNab	Usher	Herd	Kerr	Crossan	Mulhall	Fogarty	Sharkey	Harvey	Mitchinson	Elliott	Nelson	Rooks	
	1	2	3		5	6	7	8		10	11		9	4					28
	1	2	3		5	6	7	8		10	11		9	4					31
	1	2	3		5	6	7	8		10	11		9	4					34
	1	2	3		5		7	8		10	11		9	4		6			37
	1	2	3		5		7	8		10	11		9	4		6			38
	1	2	3		5		7	8		10	11		9	4					40
	6	6	6		6	3	6	6		6	6		6	6		3			
				2	1	1	2			5	1		3						

	Montgomery	Irwin	Ashurst	Anderson	Hurley	McNab	Usher	Herd	Kerr	Crossan	Mulhall	Fogarty	Sharkey	Harvey	Mitchinson	Elliott	Nelson	Rooks	
	1	2	3	4		6	7	8	9	10	11					5			10
	1	1	1	1		1	1	1	1	1	1					1			
								1											

Charlie Hurley being chaired around ground after promotion v Charlton Athletic.

441

1964-65

Division One

Ground: Roker Park

Manager: Directors and George Hardwick

League Table

	P	W	D	L	F	A	Pts
Manchester U	42	26	9	7	89	39	61
Leeds U	42	26	9	7	83	52	61
Chelsea	42	24	8	10	89	54	56
Everton	42	17	15	10	69	60	49
Nottingham F	42	17	13	12	71	67	47
Tottenham H	42	19	7	16	87	71	45
Liverpool	42	17	10	15	67	73	44
Sheffield W	42	16	11	15	57	55	43
West Ham U	42	19	4	19	82	71	42
Blackburn R	42	16	10	16	83	79	42
Stoke C	42	16	10	16	67	66	42
Burnley	42	16	10	16	70	70	42
Arsenal	42	17	7	18	69	75	41
WBA	42	13	13	16	70	65	39
SUNDERLAND	42	14	9	19	64	74	37
Aston Villa	42	16	5	21	57	82	37
Blackpool	42	12	11	19	67	78	35
Leicester C	42	11	13	18	69	85	35
Sheffield U	42	12	11	19	50	64	35
Fulham	42	11	12	19	60	78	34
Wolver'pton W	42	13	4	25	59	89	30
Birmingham C	42	8	11	23	64	96	27

FA Cup Winners: Liverpool
League Cup Winners: Chelsea

Did you know that?

Centre-forward Brian Clough scored a hat-trick in his comeback game for Sunderland reserves; his first competitive game for 20 months.

The 7-1 win over Halifax Town reserves on 29 August 1964 was watched by five times the normal reserve attendance; 8,554 were at Roker Park that day.

Match 1: Forster made debut & first game Directors acted as Manager
Match 3: O'Hare made debut
Match 4: McLaughlan made debut
Match 6: Clough last game
Match 19: Hood made debut & Nelson last game & last game Directors acted as Manager
Match 20: Parke and Campbell made debuts & George Hardwick first game as Sunderland manager
Match 29: Crossan last game
Match 31: Hellawell made debut
Match 34: Black made debut
Match 43: Usher last game
Match 45: Moore made debut & Rooks last game
Match 46: Slack made debut
Match 47: Slack last game & Hardwick last game as Sunderland manager

Match No.	Date	Round	Venue	Opponents	Result	FT	HT	Pos.	Scorers	Attendance
1	Aug 22		H	Leicester City	D	3-3	1-2		Mulhall (2), Herd	45,465
2	26		A	West Bromwich Albion	L	1-4	1-2	18	Jones o.g.	26,172
3	29		A	Chelsea	L	1-3	0-1	20	Herd	46,710
4	Sep 2		H	West Bromwich Albion	D	2-2	1-2	18	Mulhall, Hurley	52,177
5	5		H	Leeds United	D	3-3	0-2	18	Clough, Crossan (2)	48,858
6	9		H	Aston Villa	D	2-2	1-2	18	Crossan, Hurley	44,099
7	12		A	Arsenal	L	1-3	0-1	18	Sharkey	34,291
8	14		A	Aston Villa	L	1-2	0-2	18	Sharkey	18,756
9	19		H	Blackburn Rovers	W	1-0	1-0	18	Sharkey	40,695
10	26		A	Blackpool	L	1-3	1-2	20	Hurley	31,291
12	Oct 10		A	Manchester United	L	0-1	0-0	20		48,862
13	17		H	Fulham	D	0-0	0-0	20		38,297
14	24		A	Nottingham Forest	L	2-5	1-1	20	Sharkey, Crossan	24,833
16	31		H	Stoke City	D	2-2	0-1	20	Crossan, McNab	38,213
17	Nov 7		A	Tottenham Hotspur	L	0-3	0-0	20		36,677
19	14		H	Burnley	W	3-2	2-1	20	Herd, Mulhall, Rooks (pen)	36,102
20	21		A	Sheffield United	L	0-3	0-1	20		22,335
21	28		H	Everton	W	4-0	2-0	19	Herd, Mulhall, Sharkey, Hood	41,581
22	Dec 5		A	Birmingham City	L	3-4	1-1	21	Sharkey (2), McNab	13,564
23	12		A	Leicester City	W	1-0	0-0	20	Sharkey	17,496
24	19		H	Chelsea	W	3-0	2-0	19	Sharkey, Harvey, Herd	41,236
25	26		H	Liverpool	L	2-3	0-2	20	Sharkey, Mulhall	49,902
26	28		A	Liverpool	D	0-0	0-0	20		43,528
27	Jan 2		A	Leeds United	L	1-2	0-0	20	Hood	43,808
29	16		H	Arsenal	L	0-2	0-1	21		42,158
31	Feb 6		H	Blackpool	W	1-0	0-0	20	Sharkey	36,759
32	13		A	Sheffield Wed.	L	0-2	0-0	21		17,272
33	20		H	West Ham United	W	3-2	1-0	20	Hood, Sharkey (2)	32,885
34	24		A	Manchester United	W	1-0	1-0	19	Hood	51,336
35	27		A	Fulham	L	0-1	0-1	19		16,861
36	Mar 6		H	Nottingham Forest	W	4-0	2-0	19	Sharkey (2), Hood, Hellawell	34,990
37	13		A	West Ham United	W	3-2	2-1	18	Harvey, Herd (2)	23,218
38	20		H	Tottenham Hotspur	W	2-1	1-0	16	Herd, Sharkey	44,394
39	23		A	Blackburn Rovers	L	2-3	2-1	17	Ashurst, Sharkey	10,119
40	27		A	Burnley	D	0-0	0-0	17		13,303
41	Apr 3		H	Sheffield United	W	3-1	1-0	17	Hood, Rooks (pen), Mulhall	36,573
42	10		A	Everton	D	1-1	1-0	16	Sharkey	29,455
43	16		H	Wolverhampton W.	L	1-2	1-0	16	Hellawell	43,328
44	17		H	Birmingham City	W	2-1	1-1	15	Hood, Mulhall	31,958
45	20		A	Wolverhampton W.	L	0-3	0-2	15		14,896
46	24		A	Stoke City	L	1-3	0-3	15	Slack	20,501
47	28		H	Sheffield Wed.	W	3-0	1-0	15	Ashurst, Mulhall, Hood	22,467

Appearances
Goals

FA Cup

| 28 | Jan 9 | R3 | A | Luton Town | W | 3-0 | 0-0 | | Sharkey (2), Mulhall | 16,834 |
| 30 | 30 | R4 | H | Nottingham Forest | L | 1-3 | 0-1 | | Hood | 42,957 |

Appearances
Goals

League Cup

11	Sep 30	R2	H	West Ham United	W	4-1	4-0		Mulhall, Mitchinson, Sharkey, Usher	22,382
15	Oct 26	R3	H	Blackpool	W	4-1	1-0		O'Hare (2), Herd, Crossan	20,540
18	Nov 10	R4	A	Coventry City	L	2-4	0-4		O'Hare (2)	19,227

Appearances
Goals

	Forster	Irwin	Ashurst	Harvey	Hurley	McNab	Usher	Herd	Sharkey	Crossan	Mulhall	O'Hare	McLaughlan	Mitchinson	Clough	Elliott	Rooks	Montgomery	Nelson	Hood	Parke	Campbell	Hellawell	Black	Moore	Slack	
1	2	3	4	5	6	7	8	9	10	11																	1
1	2	3	4	5	6	7	8	9	10	11																	2
1	2	3	4	5	6	7	8	9		11	10																3
	2	3	4	5	6	7			10	11		1	8	9													4
	2	3	4	5	6	7			10	11		1	8	9													5
	2	3	4	5	6	7			10	11		1	8	9													6
	2	3	4	5	6	7	8	9	10	11	1																7
	2	3	4	5	6	7	8	9	10	11	1																8
	2	3	4	5	6		8	9	10	11	1	7															9
	2	3	4	5	6		8	9	10	11	1	7															10
	2	3	4	5		7	8	9		11	1	10		6													12
	2	3	4	5			8	9	10	11	1	7		6													13
	2	3	4				8	9	10	11	1	7		6	5												14
	2	3	4	5	6			10		8	11	9		7			1										16
	2	3	4		6	7	10		8	11	9					5	1										17
		3			6	7	8			11	10				4	5	1	2	9								19
	2		4	5	6		8		10	11						1		9	3	7							20
		3	4		6	7	10	9		11						5	1		8	2							21
		3			6	7	10	9		11				4		5	1		8	2							22
		3	4		6	7	10	9		11						5	1		8	2							23
		3	4		6	7	10	9		11	1					5			8	2							24
		3	4		6	7	10	9		11						5	1		8	2							25
7		3	4		6		10	9	8	11	1					5				2							26
		3	4		6	7	10	9		11	1					5			8	2							27
		3	4		6	7	8	9	10	11	1					5				2							29
		3	4	5	6		8	10		11	1								9	2	7						31
		3	4	5	6		8	10		11	1								9	2	7						32
		3	4	5	6	7	8	10		11	1								9	2							33
			4	5	6		8	10		11	1								9	2	7	3					34
			4	5	6		8	10		11	1								9	2	7	3					35
		3	4	5	6		8	10		11	1								9	2	7						36
		3	4	5	6		8	10		11	1								9	2	7						37
		3	4	5	6		8	10		11	1								9	2	7						38
		3	4	5	6		8	10		11	1								9	2	7						39
		3	4		6		8	10		11	1					5			9	2	7						40
		3	4		6		8	10		11	1					5			9	2	7						41
		3	4	5			8	10		11	1					6			9	2	7						42
		3	4	5	6	11	8	10			1								9	2	7						43
		3		4	6		8			11	10	1				5			9	2	7						44
	2	3	4		6		8			11	1					5			10		7	9					45
	2	3	4		5		8			11		10				1		7			9	6					46
		3		5	6		8	10		11	1					9	2	7					4				47
3	19	39	38	27	38	20	39	32	16	41	5	30	10	3	5	16	9	1	24	23	3	14	2	2	2		
		2	2	3	2		8	18	5	9					1		2		8		2		1				

		3	4		6	7	10	9		11		1	8			5				2							28
		3		5	6		10	9		11		1	8			4			7	2							30
		2	1	1	2	1	2	2		2			2			2			1	2							
								2		1						1											

	2	3	4	5	6	7	8	9		11		1	10														11
	2	3	4			10			8	11	9			7		6	5	1									15
		3	4		6	7	10		8	11	9					5	1	2									18
	2	3	3	1	2	2	3	1	2	3	2	1	2	1		2	2	1									
							1	1	1	1	4		1														

George Mulhall

Mulhall missed the Good Friday game against Wolverhampton Wanderers. It was the first League game he had missed since making his debut – a run of 114 matches.

443

1965-66

Division One

Ground: Roker Park
Manager: Ian McColl

League Table

	P	W	D	L	F	A	Pts
Liverpool	42	26	9	7	79	34	61
Leeds U	42	23	9	10	79	38	55
Burnley	42	24	7	11	79	47	55
Manchester U	42	18	15	9	84	59	51
Chelsea	42	22	7	13	65	53	51
WBA	42	19	12	11	91	69	50
Leicester C	42	21	7	14	80	65	49
Tottenham H	42	16	12	14	75	66	44
Sheffield U	42	16	11	15	56	59	43
Stoke C	42	15	12	15	65	64	42
Everton	42	15	11	16	56	62	41
West Ham U	42	15	9	18	70	83	39
Blackpool	42	14	9	19	55	65	37
Arsenal	42	12	13	17	62	75	37
Newcastle U	42	14	9	19	50	63	37
Aston Villa	42	15	6	21	69	80	36
Sheffield W	42	14	8	20	56	66	36
Nottingham F	42	14	8	20	56	72	36
SUNDERLAND	42	14	8	20	51	72	36
Fulham	42	14	7	21	67	85	35
Northampton T	42	10	13	19	55	92	33
Blackburn R	42	8	4	30	57	88	20

FA Cup Winners: Everton
League Cup Winners: West Bromwich Albion

Did you know that?

Sunderland AFC Supporters' Association held their inaugural meeting on 19 July 1965 at Roker Park.

A crowd of 31,828 turned out for Brian Clough's testimonial at Roker Park against a Newcastle United Select XI on 27 October 1965.

Match 1: Baxter made debut & Ian McColl first game as Sunderland manager
Match 6: Gauden made debut
Match 16: Martin made debut
Match 19: Mitchinson last game
Match 23: McLaughlan last game
Match 30: Black last game
Match 36: Campbell last game

Match No.	Date	Round	Venue	Opponents	Result	FT	HT	Pos.	Scorers	Attendance
1	Aug 21		A	Leeds United	L	0-1	0-0			36,298
2	23		A	West Ham United	D	1-1	1-1	14	Herd	34,795
3	28		H	Sheffield United	W	4-1	2-1	10	Baxter (2), Herd, McNab	42,147
4	Sep 1		H	West Ham United	W	2-1	0-1	5	Mulhall, McNab	48,626
5	4		A	Leicester City	L	1-4	0-2	12	O'Hare	24,680
6	6		A	Aston Villa	L	1-3	0-1	14	Mulhall	25,905
7	11		H	Blackburn Rovers	W	1-0	1-0	12	Mulhall	35,357
8	15		H	Aston Villa	W	2-0	2-0	10	Sharkey, Baxter	37,961
9	18		A	Blackpool	W	2-1	1-0	6	Baxter (pen), Sharkey	28,277
11	25		H	Fulham	D	2-2	1-1	8	Sharkey, Baxter (pen)	39,092
12	Oct 6		A	Tottenham Hotspur	L	0-3	0-2	10		37,364
13	9		H	West Bromwich Albion	L	1-4	0-2	12	Baxter (pen)	19,744
15	16		H	Nottingham Forest	W	3-2	1-2	10	Mitchinson (2), Gauden	31,987
16	23		A	Sheffield Wed.	L	1-3	0-1	13	Martin	20,590
17	30		H	Northampton Town	W	3-0	2-0	13	Martin, Mulhall, Gauden	32,216
18	Nov 6		A	Stoke City	D	1-1	0-0	11	Herd	22,828
19	13		H	Burnley	L	0-4	0-2	11		38,224
20	Dec 4		A	Everton	L	0-2	0-0	15		25,393
21	11		H	Manchester United	L	2-3	1-2	16	Martin (2)	37,417
22	18		A	Nottingham Forest	D	0-0	0-0	16		16,057
23	Jan 1		H	West Bromwich Albion	L	1-5	1-2	16	Moore	34,938
24	3		H	Newcastle United	W	2-0	0-0	16	Herd, O'Hare	54,668
25	8		A	Manchester United	D	1-1	0-1	15	O'Hare	39,410
27	26		H	Sheffield Wed.	L	0-2	0-0	16		25,033
28	29		H	Leeds United	W	2-0	1-0	16	Mulhall (2)	35,942
29	Feb 5		A	Sheffield United	D	2-2	2-2	14	Gauden (2)	19,322
30	12		A	Liverpool	L	0-4	0-0	15		43,859
31	19		H	Leicester City	L	0-3	0-1	15		21,722
32	22		A	Chelsea	L	2-3	1-1	16	Mulhall, Sharkey	20,828
33	26		A	Blackburn Rovers	L	0-2	0-2	17		14,025
34	Mar 5		A	Newcastle United	L	0-2	0-1	17		52,051
35	12		H	Blackpool	W	2-1	0-0	17	O'Hare (2)	26,246
36	19		A	Fulham	L	0-3	0-3	18		20,918
37	26		H	Tottenham Hotspur	W	2-0	0-0	17	Clayton o.g., Martin	27,828
38	Apr 2		H	Stoke City	W	2-0	2-0	15	O'Hare, Mulhall (pen)	20,108
39	9		A	Burnley	L	0-1	0-1	19		15,699
40	11		H	Liverpool	D	2-2	2-2	18	Martin, Harvey	38,355
41	16		H	Chelsea	W	2-0	1-0	15	Baxter (pen), Hellawell	32,880
42	20		H	Arsenal	L	0-2	0-0	17		32,349
43	23		A	Arsenal	D	1-1	1-0	15	Hurley	25,699
44	25		A	Northampton Town	L	1-2	1-0	15	Martin	17,921
45	30		H	Everton	W	2-0	1-0	16	Martin, Herd	31,147

Appearances
Sub Appearances
Goals

FA Cup

| 26 | Jan 22 | R3 | A | Everton | L | 0-3 | 0-1 | | | 47,893 |

Appearances
Goals

League Cup

| 10 | Sep 22 | R2 | H | Sheffield United | W | 2-1 | 1-0 | | Sharkey, Mulhall | 22,303 |
| 14 | Oct 13 | R3 | H | Aston Villa | L | 1-2 | 0-1 | | McNab | 19,723 |

Appearances
Goals

	McLaughlan	Irwin	Ashurst	Harvey	Hurley	Baxter	Herd	O'Hare	Sharkey	McNab	Mulhall	Hellawell	Montgomery	Mitchinson	Gauden	Parke	Black	Moore	Martin	Campbell	Elliott	
1	1	2	3	4	5	6	7	8	9	10	11	U										1
2	1	2	3	4	5	6	8	9		10	11	7					U					2
3	1	2	3	4	5	6	8	9		10	11	7	U									3
4	1	2	3	4	5	6	8	9	U	10	11	7										4
5	1	2	3	4	5	6	8	9		10	11	7		U								5
6		2	3	4	5	6	8	9			11	7	1	10	12							6
7		2	3	5		6	8	10	9		11	7	1	U		4						7
8		2	3	5		10	8		9	6	11	7	1			4		U				8
9		2	3	5		10	8		9	6	11	7	1			4		U				9
11		2	3	5		10	8		9	6	11	7	1		U	4						11
12		2	3	5		10	8		9	6		7	1		11	4		U				12
13		2		5		10	U	9	8	6		7	1		11	4	3					13
15		2	3	5		6	8			4		7	1	10	11		12	9				15
16	1	2	3	5		6	8			4	11	7			U		9	10				16
17	1	2		4		6	8			5	11		12	7	3		9	10				17
18	1	2		4		6	8			5	11	7		U	3		9	10				18
19	1	2	U	4		6	8			5	11	7		10	3		9					19
20	1	2	3	4	5		8		9	6	11			U			10	7				20
21	1	2	3	4	5	6	8			11	7						9	10		12		21
22	1		3	4	5	6	7	9					U	11	2			10		8		22
23	1		3	4	5	6	7	9		U				11	2		10			8		23
24			3	4	5	6	7	9			11	12	1		2		10			8		24
25		2	3	4			8	9	U	5	11	7	1				10			6		25
27		2	3	5			8	9			11	7	1		U	4		10		6		27
28		2	3	5			8		9		11		1		7	4	U	10		6		28
29		2		5			8		9		11		1		7	4	3	U	10	6		29
30		2	3	5		8			9		11		1		7	4		12	10	6		30
31		2	3	5			6		9		11		1		7	4		U	10	8		31
32		2	3	5			6		9		11		1		7	4		U	10	8		32
33		2	3		5	6			9		11	7	1			4		U	10	8		33
34			3	4	5	10			9		11		1		7	2		U	8	6		34
35			3	4	5	6	8	9		10	11		1		7	2		U				35
36			3	4	5	6	8	9	U	10			1		11	2			7			36
37			3	4	5	10	8	U		6	11	7	1			2		9				37
38			3	4	5		8	9		6	11	7	1		U	2		10				38
39			3	4	5	10	8	9		6	12	7	1			2		11				39
40			3	4	5	10	8	U		6	11	7	1			2		9				40
41			3	4	5	10	8	U		6	11	7	1			2		9				41
42			3	4	5	10	8	U		6	11	7	1			2		9				42
43			3	4	5	10	8	U		6	11	7	1			2		9				43
44		2	3		5	10	8			6	11	7	1			4		9		U		44
45		2	3		5	10	8	U		6	11	7	1			4		9				45
	13	29	37	39	24	35	37	17	15	28	35	28	29	3	14	31	2	8	24	2	12	
											1	1		1	1		2				1	
		1		1	7	5	6	4	2	8	1		2	4			1	8				

| | | | 3 | 4 | | 6 | 7 | | 5 | 11 | | 1 | | 2 | | 9 | 10 | | 8 | | | 26 |
| | | 1 | 1 | | 1 | 1 | | 1 | 1 | | | 1 | | | | 1 | | 1 | 1 | | 1 | |

		2	3	5		10	8		9	6	11	7	1			4						10
			3	4	5	10	8		9	6		7	1		11	2						14
	1	2	2	1	2	2		2	2	1	2	2		1	2							
									1	1												

Jim Baxter
Baxter gained 10 Scotland caps while with Sunderland.

1966-67

Division One

Ground: Roker Park

Manager: Ian McColl

League Table

	P	W	D	L	F	A	Pts
Manchester U	42	24	12	6	84	45	60
Nottingham F	42	23	10	9	64	41	56
Tottenham H	42	24	8	10	71	48	56
Leeds U	42	22	11	9	62	42	55
Liverpool	42	19	13	10	64	47	51
Everton	42	19	10	13	65	46	48
Arsenal	42	16	14	12	58	47	46
Leicester C	42	18	8	16	78	71	44
Chelsea	42	15	14	13	67	62	44
Sheffield U	42	16	10	16	52	59	42
Sheffield W	42	14	13	15	56	47	41
Stoke C	42	17	7	18	63	58	41
WBA	42	16	7	19	77	73	39
Burnley	42	15	9	18	66	76	39
Manchester C	42	12	15	15	43	52	39
West Ham U	42	14	8	20	80	84	36
SUNDERLAND	42	14	8	20	58	72	36
Fulham	42	11	12	19	71	83	34
Southampton	42	14	6	22	74	92	34
Newcastle U	42	12	9	21	39	81	33
Aston Villa	42	11	7	24	54	85	29
Blackpool	42	6	9	27	41	76	21

FA Cup Winners:
Tottenham Hotspur

League Cup Winners:
Queens Park Rangers

Did you know that?

Sunderland reserves beat Darlington reserves 12-1 at Roker Park on 26 November 1966. This included the Black Cats scoring an incredible 6 goals in a 9 minute spell towards the end of the second half.

Match 1: Hellawell last game
Match 7: Todd made debut
Match 10: Hood last game
Match 13: Sharkey last game
Match 15: Kinnell made debut
Match 22: Gary Moore last game
Match 24: Elliott last game
Match 25: Kerr made debut
Match 26: McNab last game
Match 30: Hughes made debut
Match 33: Shoulder made debut
Match 37: Suggett made debut
Match 43: Shoulder last game
Match 49: O'Hare last game

Match No.	Date		Round	Venue	Opponents	Result	FT	HT	Pos.	Scorers	Attendance
1	Aug	20		H	Arsenal	L	1-3	1-2		Baxter	38,304
2		24		H	Southampton	W	2-0	1-0	10	Gauden, Mulhall	27,161
3		27		A	Manchester City	L	0-1	0-0	15		34,948
4		31		A	Southampton	L	1-3	0-0	18	Mulhall	24,288
5	Sep	3		H	Blackpool	W	4-0	2-0	15	Martin (3), Hood	24,941
6		7		A	Leeds United	L	1-2	1-2	17	Herd	37,646
7		10		A	Chelsea	D	1-1	0-1	17	Gauden	31,766
9		17		H	Leicester City	L	2-3	1-2	19	Martin, O'Hare	28,584
11		24		A	Liverpool	D	2-2	1-1	18	Martin, Herd	45,706
12	Oct	1		H	West Ham United	L	2-4	1-2	19	Martin, Sharkey	29,227
13		8		H	West Bromwich Albion	D	2-2	1-0	19	Herd, Martin	26,632
14		15		A	Sheffield United	L	0-2	0-1	20		19,391
15		25		H	Stoke City	W	2-1	0-0	18	O'Hare, Martin	23,320
16		29		A	Newcastle United	W	3-0	2-0	17	Mulhall, Martin, O'Hare	57,643
17	Nov	5		H	Sheffield United	W	4-1	3-0	15	Martin (2), Baxter, Moore	29,262
18		12		A	Nottingham Forest	L	1-3	0-3	15	Mulhall	24,962
19		19		H	Burnley	W	4-3	1-1	14	Martin, Mulhall (2), O'Hare	32,526
20		26		A	Manchester United	L	0-5	0-2	14		44,687
21	Dec	3		H	Tottenham Hotspur	L	0-1	0-0	17		32,733
22		17		A	Arsenal	L	0-2	0-0	19		20,482
23		26		H	Aston Villa	W	2-1	1-0	18	O'Hare, Martin	31,262
24		27		A	Aston Villa	L	1-2	0-1	19	Martin	26,612
25		31		H	Manchester City	W	1-0	0-0	17	Kerr	28,826
26	Jan	7		A	Blackpool	D	1-1	0-1	16	Herd	14,669
27		14		H	Chelsea	W	2-0	2-0	15	Martin, Kerr	35,839
28		21		A	Leicester City	W	2-1	0-1	15	Mulhall, O'Hare	25,539
30	Feb	4		H	Liverpool	D	2-2	1-2	16	Kerr, O'Hare	45,301
31		11		A	West Ham United	D	2-2	1-1	15	Mulhall, Martin	27,963
33		25		A	West Bromwich Albion	D	2-2	2-1	15	Mulhall (2)	22,296
34	Mar	4		H	Newcastle United	W	3-0	0-0	15	Kerr (2), Mulhall	50,442
37		18		A	Stoke City	L	0-3	0-0	15		17,164
39		24		H	Sheffield Wed.	W	2-0	1-0	15	Baxter, Martin	35,698
40		25		H	Everton	L	0-2	0-0	15		34,134
41		28		A	Sheffield Wed.	L	0-5	0-2	15		26,372
42	Apr	1		H	Fulham	L	1-3	1-1	16	Suggett	22,724
43		15		A	Burnley	L	0-1	0-1	17		13,765
44		19		H	Nottingham Forest	W	1-0	1-0	15	O'Hare	26,215
45		22		H	Manchester United	D	0-0	0-0	18		43,570
46	May	3		A	Tottenham Hotspur	L	0-1	0-1	18		33,936
47		6		H	Fulham	W	3-1	2-0	16	Martin (2), Mulhall	18,604
48		13		H	Leeds United	L	0-2	0-0	17		23,766
49		16		A	Everton	L	1-4	0-1	17	Martin	30,943

Appearances
Sub Appearances
Goals

FA Cup

Match No.	Date		Round	Venue	Opponents	Result	FT	HT	Scorers	Attendance
29	Jan	28	R3	H	Brentford	W	5-2	1-1	Martin (2), Mulhall, Baxter (pen), O'Hare	36,908
32	Feb	18	R4	H	Peterborough United	W	7-1	4-0	O'Hare, Martin (3), Kerr (2), Baxter (pen)	43,998
35	Mar	11	R5	H	Leeds United	D	1-1	1-1	Martin	55,763
36		15	R5r	A	Leeds United	D	1-1 (aet)	1-1	O'Hare	57,892
38		20	R5r2	N*	Leeds United	L	1-2	0-1	Gauden	40,456

* at Boothferry Park

Appearances
Sub Appearances
Goals

League Cup

Match No.	Date		Round	Venue	Opponents	Result	FT	HT	Scorers	Attendance
8	Sep	14	R2	H	Sheffield United	D	1-1	0-0	Mulhall	13,464
10		20	R2r	A	Sheffield United	L	0-1 (aet)	0-0		10,605

Appearance
Sub Appearances
Goal

Montgomery	Parke	Ashurst	Harvey	Hurley	McNab	Hellawell	Hood	Baxter	Martin	Gauden	Irwin	Herd	Mulhall	Todd	O'Hare	Elliott	Sharkey	Kinnell	Moore, G.	Kerr	Hughes	Shoulder	Suggett	Wile	#
1	2	3	4	5	6	7	8	9	10	11		U													1
1		3	U	5	6		8	10	9	7	2	4	11												2
1	4	3		5	6	U	8	10	9	11	2	7													3
1	U	3		5	6		8	10	9	7	2	4	11												4
1	12	3		5	6		8	10	9	7	2	4	11												5
1		3	4	5	6		8	10	9	11	2	7		U											6
1		3	4	5	6		8	10	9	11	2	7		12											7
1		3	5		6			10	9	7	2	4	11	12	8										9
1		3	5		6				9	7	2	10	11	12	8	4									11
1		3	5		6			10	9	7	2	4	11	U		8									12
1	4	3	6		5			10	9	U	2	7	11			8									13
1		3	6		5			10	9	2	7	11	4	8											14
1		3	6					10	9	U	2	7	11	4	8		5								15
1		3	6					10	9		2	7	11	4	8	U	5								16
1		3	6					10	9	U	2	7	11			4	5	8							17
1		3	6					10	9		2	7	11	U		4	5	8							18
1		3		5				10	9		2	7	11	4	8	U	5								19
1	12	3		5				10	9		2	7	11		8	4	5								20
1	U	3		5				10	9		2	7	11		8	4	5								21
1		3	6		12			10	9	7	2		11			4	5	8							22
1		3	6					10	9		2	7	11		8	4	5		U						23
1		3	6					10	9		2	7	11		8	4	5		U						24
1			6		3			10	9	U	2		11	4	8		5		7						25
1		6			3			10	9		2	12	11	4	8		5		7						26
1		3						6	9	12	2	10	11	4	8		5		7						27
1	U	3						6		7	2	10	11	4	9		5	8							28
1		3		U				6	9		2	10		4	8		5	7	11						30
1		3						6	9		2	10	11	4	8		5		U						31
1		6							9	U	2	10	11	4	8		5	7		3					33
1		3						6	9	U	2	10	11	4	8		5	7							34
1	10		6	5					9	7	2			4					11	3	8	U			37
1		3						6	9	7	2	10	11	4	8		5				U				39
1		3						6	9	7	2	10	11	4	8		5				12				40
1		3						6	9	7	2	8	11	4	10		5				12				41
1		3						6	9	7	2		11	4	9		5			U	10				42
1		U	6						9	7	2			4	8		5			11	3	10			43
1		3						6	9	11	2	10		4	8		5				U	7			44
1		3						6	9	11	2	10		4	8		5				U	7			45
1	12	3						6	9	7	2	4	10		8		5			11					46
	6	3							9	7	2	4	10		8		5			11	U				47
	6	3							9	7	2	4	10		8		5			11	U				48
		3						6	9	7	2	10	11	4	8		5				U				49
2	7	28	28	11	14	1	7	36	41	24	41	35	33	21	29	8	2	29	3	8	6	3	5		
	3				1				1		1		3								2				
							1	3	20	2		4	12		8		1		1	5		1			

Montgomery	Parke	Ashurst	Harvey	Hurley	McNab	Hellawell	Hood	Baxter	Martin	Gauden	Irwin	Herd	Mulhall	Todd	O'Hare	Elliott	Sharkey	Kinnell	Moore, G.	Kerr	Hughes	Shoulder	Suggett	Wile	#
		3						6	9		2	10	11	4	8		5		7		U				29
		3						6	9		2	10	11	4	8		5		7		U				32
		3						6	9	12	2	10	11	4	8		5		7						35
	U	3						6	9	7	2	10	11	4	8		5								36
		3						6	9	7	2	10	11				5				U				38
		5						5	5	2	5		5	5	5		5		3						
										1															
								2	6	1			1		3				2						

Montgomery	Parke	Ashurst	Harvey	Hurley	McNab	Hellawell	Hood	Baxter	Martin	Gauden	Irwin	Herd	Mulhall	Todd	O'Hare	Elliott	Sharkey	Kinnell	Moore, G.	Kerr	Hughes	Shoulder	Suggett	Wile	#
	3	5		6			8	10	9	7	2	4	11	U											8
	3	5		6	6	12			9	7	2	10	11	4	8										10
	2	2		2			1	1	2	2	2	2	2	1	1										
							1																		
															1										

447

1967-68

Division One
Ground: Roker Park
Managers: Ian McColl & Alan Brown

League Table

	P	W	D	L	F	A	Pts
Manchester C	42	26	6	10	86	43	58
Manchester U	42	24	8	10	89	55	56
Liverpool	42	22	11	9	71	40	55
Leeds U	42	22	9	11	71	41	53
Everton	42	23	6	13	67	40	52
Chelsea	42	18	12	12	62	68	48
Tottenham H	42	19	9	14	70	59	47
WBA	42	17	12	13	75	62	46
Arsenal	42	17	10	15	60	56	44
Newcastle U	42	13	15	14	54	67	41
Nottingham F	42	14	11	17	52	64	39
West Ham U	42	14	10	18	73	69	38
Leicester C	42	13	12	17	64	69	38
Burnley	42	14	10	18	64	71	38
SUNDERLAND	42	13	11	18	51	61	37
Southampton	42	13	11	18	66	83	37
Wolver'pton W	42	14	8	20	66	75	36
Stoke C	42	14	7	21	50	73	35
Sheffield W	42	11	12	19	51	63	34
Coventry C	42	9	15	18	51	71	33
Sheffield U	42	11	10	21	49	70	32
Fulham	42	10	7	25	56	98	27

FA Cup Winners:
West Bromwich Albion

League Cup Winners: Leeds United

Did you know that?

Malcolm Moore, on his debut, became the first substitute to score for Sunderland at Roker Park; in a 1-1 draw against Coventry City on 23 March 1968.

Match 1: Heslop and Brand made debuts
Match 21: Stuckey made debut
Match 22: Baxter last game
Match 25: Parke last game
Match 26: Porterfield made debut
Match 28: Butler made debut
Match 30: Martin last game
Match 31: Harris made debut & Ian McColl last game as Sunderland manager
Match 32: Alan Brown first game in his second spell as Sunderland manager
Match 33: Palmer made debut
Match 35: Gauden last game
Match 37: Malcolm Moore made debut

Match No.	Date		Round	Venue	Opponents	Result	FT	HT	Pos.	Scorers	Attendance
1	Aug	19		A	Leeds United	D	1-1	1-1		Kinnell	36,857
2		23		H	Fulham	W	3-0	1-0	3	Martin, Suggett, Brand	30,062
3		26		H	Everton	W	1-0	1-0	3	Suggett	37,628
4		28		A	Fulham	L	2-3	0-1	5	Suggett, Brand	19,597
5	Sep	2		A	Leicester City	W	2-0	1-0	3	Brand, Suggett	23,316
6		6		H	Manchester United	D	1-1	1-1	4	Suggett	51,527
7		9		H	West Ham United	L	1-5	1-0	6	Moore o.g.	39,772
9		16		A	Burnley	L	0-3	0-2	11		19,414
10		23		H	Sheffield Wed.	L	0-2	0-1	13		29,003
11		30		A	Tottenham Hotspur	L	0-3	0-2	19		36,017
12	Oct	7		H	Manchester City	W	1-0	1-0	16	Martin	27,885
14		14		A	Arsenal	L	1-2	0-0	16	Kinnell	30,864
15		25		H	Sheffield United	W	2-1	0-0	16	Martin, Suggett	20,464
16		28		A	Coventry City	D	2-2	1-1	16	Martin (2 pens)	30,005
17	Nov	4		H	Nottingham Forest	W	1-0	0-0	14	Barnwell o.g.	29,158
18		11		A	Stoke City	L	1-2	1-2	15	Martin	19,207
20		18		A	Liverpool	D	1-1	1-1	15	Martin	29,993
21		25		A	Southampton	L	2-3	2-1	16	Brand, Martin	22,344
22	Dec	2		H	Chelsea	L	2-3	1-2	16	Todd, Martin	26,274
23		16		H	Leeds United	D	2-2	1-1	17	Mulhall, Martin	21,189
24		23		A	Everton	L	0-3	0-2	17		38,216
25		26		A	Newcastle United	L	1-2	1-1	19	Suggett	59,579
26		30		H	Newcastle United	D	3-3	2-1	19	Suggett (2), Stuckey	46,030
27	Jan	6		A	Leicester City	L	0-2	0-2	20		24,703
28		20		A	Burnley	D	2-2	1-1	19	Suggett, Blant o.g.	27,860
31	Feb	3		A	Sheffield Wed.	W	1-0	1-0	18	Brand	24,400
32		10		H	Tottenham Hotspur	L	0-1	0-1	18		31,735
33		24		A	Manchester City	L	0-1	0-0	19		28,624
34	Mar	2		H	Southampton	L	0-3	0-0	21		23,775
35		9		A	Wolverhampton W.	L	1-2	0-1	21	Herd	31,871
36		16		A	Sheffield United	W	2-1	1-0	21	Harris, Suggett	21,701
37		23		H	Coventry City	D	1-1	0-0	21	Moore	26,286
38		30		A	Nottingham Forest	W	3-0	3-0	21	Kinnell, Palmer, Brand	24,543
39	Apr	2		A	West Bromwich Albion	D	0-0	0-0	17		15,490
40		6		H	Stoke City	W	3-1	0-0	15	Mulhall, Brand, Suggett	27,813
41		13		A	Liverpool	L	1-2	1-1	17	Suggett	40,350
42		15		H	Wolverhampton W.	W	2-0	1-0	15	Todd, Herd	34,026
43		20		H	Arsenal	W	2-0	0-0	17	Hurley, McNab o.g.	31,255
44		24		A	West Ham United	D	1-1	1-0	15	Mulhall	29,153
45		27		A	Chelsea	L	0-1	0-1	17		33,086
46	May	4		H	West Bromwich Albion	D	0-0	0-0	16		31,892
47		11		A	Manchester United	W	2-1	2-1	15	Suggett, Mulhall	62,963

Appearances
Sub Appearances
Goals

FA Cup

29	Jan	27	R3	A	Norwich City	D	1-1	0-0		Suggett	26,389
30		31	R3r	H	Norwich City	L	0-1	0-0			32,928

Appearances
Sub Appearances
Goals

League Cup

8	Sep	13	R2	H	Halifax Town	W	3-2	3-0		Kinnell (2), Martin	13,321
13	Oct	11	R3	A	Everton	W	3-2	2-2		Mulhall, Kinnell, Martin	39,918
19	Nov	15	R4	H	Leeds United	L	0-2	0-1			29,531

Appearance
Sub Appearance
Goal

448

	Montgomery	Irwin	Parke	Todd	Kinnell	Baxter	Herd	Suggett	Heslop	Brand	Mulhall	Ashurst	Martin	Gauden	Harvey	Hurley	Hughes	Stuckey	Porterfield	Forster	Butler	Harris	Palmer	Moore, M.	Brown	
1	2	3	4	5	6	7	8	9	10	11	12															1
1	2	3	4	5	6	7	8	12	10	11		9														2
1	2	3	4	5	6	7	8	10		11		9	12													3
1		2	4	5	6	7	8	10	9	11	3		U													4
1		2	4	5	6	7	8	10	9	11	3		U													5
1		2	4	5	6	7	8	10	9	11	3		U													6
1		2	4	5	6	7	8	10		11	3	9	U													7
1		2	4	5	6	7	8	11	10	12	3	9														9
1	2	3	4	5	10	7	8					9	11	4		U										10
1	2	3	4	5	6	7	8	10		11		9		U												11
1	2	3	4	8	6	U	7	10	11			9			5											12
1	2		4	8			10	7	6			9		3	5	U										14
1	2		4	8			10	7	6		U	9			5	11										15
1	2	3	4	8			10	7	6		12	9			5	11										16
1	2	3	4	8	10	U	7	6				9			5	11										17
1	2	3	4	8		6	12	7	10			9			5	11										18
1	2	3	4	6	10	U	7		8			9	11		5											20
1	2	3	4	6	10	U	7		8			9			5	11										21
1	2	3	4	U	10		7		8	11		9		6	5											22
1	2	3	4			U	8		10	11		9		6	5		7									23
1	2	3	4			U	8		10	11		9		6	5		7									24
1	2	3	4	12		7	8		10	11		9		6	5											25
1	2		4	12			8		10	11	3	9		5		7	6									26
	2		4	5		12	8		10	11	3	9				7	6	1								27
1	2		4	5			8			11	12	9		10		7	6		3							28
1	2		4	5			8		7	11	3	U		10			6			9						31
1	2		4	5			8	U	7	11	3			10			6			9						32
1	2		4	5			8	U	7	11	3			10						9	6					33
1	2		4	5		9	8	6	7	11	3						U				10					34
1	2		4	5		9	8		7	11	3		12	10							6					35
1	2		4	5			10	8	7	11	3		6								12	9				36
1	2		4	5		9	7			11	3		6							8	10	12				37
1			4	5		10	8		7	11	3		6							9	2	12				38
1			4	5		6	8		10	11			3	U						7	2	9				39
1			4	5		6	8		10	11			3	12						7	2	9				40
			6	5		8	10		9	11	3		2	4			1			7		U				41
			6	5		8	10		9	11	3		2	4			1			7		U				42
			6	5		8	10		9	11	3		2	4	U					7						43
			6	5		8	10		9	11	3		2	4	U					7						44
			6	5		8	10			11	3		2	4	9	12	7									45
				5		8	10			11	3		2	4		9	6			7		U				46
				5		8	10			11	3		2	4		9	6			7		U				47
9	27	21	42	35	16	28	42	15	28	33	22	21	2	23	20	5	8	8	3	14	7	2				
			2			2			1		2	2		2		1		1		1		2				
		2	3		2	14		7	4		10			1		1			1	1	1					

	2		4	5			8					U	9		10		11	7	6		3					29
1	2		4	5			8			11		9	U	10		7		6	3							30
	2	2	2				2		1			2		2		2	1	2	2		2					
							1																			

	2		5	6		7	8	4	10	11	3	9	12													8
1	2	3	4	8			10	7	6		11	9			5	U										13
		3	4	2	6	7	8	10		11		9	U		5											19
1	3	2	3	2	3	3	3	1	3	1	3		2													
										1																
		3							1	2																

Colin Todd.

Todd made his debut as a 17-year-old in the previous season while still an apprentice. He only missed one game in 1967-68 and was capped at England Under-23 level in May 1968 while only 19 years old.

1968-69

Division One

Ground: Roker Park
Manager: Alan Brown

League Table

	P	W	D	L	F	A	Pts
Leeds U	42	27	13	2	66	26	67
Liverpool	42	25	11	6	63	24	61
Everton	42	21	15	6	77	36	57
Arsenal	42	22	12	8	56	27	56
Chelsea	42	20	10	12	73	53	50
Tottenham H	42	14	17	11	61	51	45
Southampton	42	16	13	13	57	48	45
West Ham U	42	13	18	11	66	50	44
Newcastle U	42	15	14	13	61	55	44
WBA	42	16	11	15	64	67	43
Manchester U	42	15	12	15	57	53	42
Ipswich T	42	15	11	16	59	60	41
Manchester C	42	15	10	17	64	55	40
Burnley	42	15	9	18	55	82	39
Sheffield W	42	10	16	16	41	54	36
Wolverh'pton W	42	10	15	17	41	58	35
SUNDERLAND	42	11	12	19	43	67	34
Nottingham F	42	10	13	19	45	57	33
Stoke C	42	9	15	18	40	63	33
Coventry C	42	10	11	21	46	64	31
Leicester C	42	9	12	21	39	68	30
QPR	42	4	10	28	39	95	18

FA Cup Winners: Manchester City
League Cup Winners: Swindon Town

Did you know that?

Sunderland beat Schuttorf 10-0 on 15 May 1969 during an end of season tour of Germany. This is the last time the first team has scored double figures in a game.

Match 3: Kinnell last game
Match 11: Butler last game
Match 16: Brand last game
Match 18: Huntley only game
Match 26: Tueart made debut
Match 31: Herd last game
Match 32: Beesley made debut
Match 33: Pitt made debut
Match 34: Beesley last game
Match 38: Moore last game
Match 39: Lowrey made debut
Match 43: Hurley and Mulhall last games
Match 44: Suggett last game

Match No.	Date	Round	Venue	Opponents	Result	FT	HT	Pos.	Scorers	Attendance
1	Aug 10		A	Stoke City	L	1-2	1-1		Harris (pen)	22,478
2	14		H	Ipswich Town	W	3-0	1-0	6	Mulhall, Hughes (2)	30,037
3	17		H	Southampton	W	1-0	0-0	5	Mulhall	30,968
4	20		A	Queens Park Rangers	D	2-2	2-1	4	Harris, Keen o.g.	20,669
5	24		A	Liverpool	L	1-4	0-3	9	Suggett	46,547
6	28		A	Leeds United	D	1-1	1-1	10	Suggett	37,797
7	31		H	Newcastle United	D	1-1	0-1	10	Suggett	49,428
8	Sep 7		H	Leicester City	W	2-0	2-0	8	Porterfield, Mulhall	26,788
9	14		A	Wolverhampton W.	D	1-1	1-0	8	Hughes	27,212
10	21		H	Manchester City	L	0-4	0-0	10		31,687
11	28		A	Arsenal	D	0-0	0-0	9		35,277
12	Oct 5		A	Sheffield Wed.	D	1-1	0-0	9	Palmer	27,328
13	9		H	Leeds United	L	0-1	0-1	11		33,535
14	12		H	Nottingham Forest	W	3-1	2-1	10	Suggett, Irwin, Mulhall	25,575
15	19		A	West Ham United	L	0-8	0-4	13		24,903
16	26		H	Coventry City	W	3-0	1-0	11	Harris (2, 1 pen), Mulhall	21,981
17	Nov 2		A	Everton	L	0-2	0-2	11		40,492
18	9		H	Manchester United	D	1-1	1-0	11	Harris	33,151
19	16		A	Tottenham Hotspur	L	1-5	1-2	15	Hughes	29,072
20	23		H	Burnley	W	2-0	2-0	13	Harris, Herd	19,607
21	30		A	West Bromwich Albion	L	0-3	0-1	15		19,411
22	Dec 7		H	Chelsea	W	3-2	2-1	13	Palmer (pen), Suggett, Mulhall	21,976
23	14		A	Nottingham Forest	L	0-1	0-1	15		18,007
24	21		H	West Ham United	W	2-1	2-1	13	Palmer, Harris	23,094
25	26		H	Sheffield Wed.	D	0-0	0-0	12		26,333
26	Jan 11		H	Everton	L	1-3	1-2	14	Suggett	24,106
27	18		A	Manchester United	L	1-4	0-1	16	Mulhall	45,670
28	Feb 1		H	Tottenham Hotspur	D	0-0	0-0	15		22,251
29	22		A	Chelsea	L	1-5	0-1	17	Suggett	29,381
30	Mar 1		H	Stoke City	W	4-1	2-0	14	Suggett, Palmer, Tueart, Moore	16,092
31	4		A	Coventry City	L	1-3	0-1	14	Moore	29,546
32	8		A	Southampton	L	0-1	0-1	16		19,843
33	10		H	West Bromwich Albion	L	0-1	0-1	16		15,769
34	15		H	Liverpool	L	0-2	0-1	16		17,855
35	22		A	Newcastle United	D	1-1	0-1	17	Suggett	48,588
36	Apr 4		A	Ipswich Town	L	0-1	0-0	19		24,021
37	5		H	Arsenal	D	0-0	0-0	18		23,214
38	7		H	Queens Park Rangers	D	0-0	0-0	19		18,928
39	12		A	Manchester City	L	0-1	0-0	19		22,842
40	19		H	Wolverhampton W.	W	2-0	1-0	18	Tueart, Kerr	21,561
41	23		A	Burnley	W	2-1	2-1	17	Kerr, Lowrey	7,428
42	May 5		A	Leicester City	L	1-2	1-1	17	Kerr	32,301

Appearances
Sub Appearances
Goals

FA Cup

27	Jan 4	R3	H	Fulham	L	1-4	1-4		Kerr	27,097

Appearances
Sub Appearances
Goals

League Cup

8	Sep 4	R2	A	Arsenal	L	0-1	0-0			28,460

Appearances
Sub Appearances
Goals

Montgomery	Irwin	Harvey	Hurley	Kinnell	Todd	Herd	Harris	Brand	Suggett	Hughes	Ashurst	Mulhall	Porterfield	Kerr	Stuckey	Palmer	Butler	Huntley	Moore	Tueart	Heslop	Beesley	Pitt	Lowrey	
1	2	3	4	5	6	7	8	9	10	11			U												1
1	2		5	4	6	7	8		10	9	3	11	12												2
1		2		5	4	7	8	9	10		3	11	6	12											3
1	12	2	4		5	7	8		10		3	11	6	9											4
1		2	4		5	7	8		10	9	3	11	6	12											5
1	2	3	4		5	7	8		10	12	11	6		9											6
1		2	4		5	7	8		10	3	11	6		9	12										7
1		3	4		5	7	8		10	9		11	6	U		2									9
1		3	4		5	7	8		10	9	12	11	6			2									10
1	2	3	4		5	7	8		10	11		6	9		12										11
1	2	3	4		5	7	8		10	9	U	11	6												12
1	2	3	4		5	7	8		10	9		11	6		12										13
1	2	3	4		5	7	8		10	9		11	6		12										14
1	2	3	4		5	7	8		10	9		11	6		12										15
1	2	5	4			7	8	9	10		U	11	6		3										16
1	2	3	4		5	7	8		10	9		11	12		6										17
1	2	3			5	7	8			9		11	U		6		4	10							18
1	2	3	4		5	8	10	9	7		11	12			6										19
1	2	3	4		5	7	8		10	9		11	12		6										20
1	2		4		5	9	8		10	9	3	11	12		6										21
1	2	12	4		5				10	9	3	11	8	7	6										22
1	2	3	4		5				10	9	12	11	7	8	6										23
1	2	3	4		5				10	9	U	11	7	8	6										24
1	2	3	4		5		8		10	9		11	12	7	6										25
1	2	3	4		5		8		10	9		12	6	7					11						26
1	2	3	4		5	7	6		10	9		11	12	8											28
1	12	3	4		5	7	6		10			11		8	9	2									29
1	U	3	4		5	8	6					11		10	7	2	9								30
1	U	3	4		5	8	6		10			11		7	2		9								31
1	2	3	5		5		7		10					8			9	11	4	12					32
1	2	3			6		7		10	11				8			9		4	12	5				33
1	2	3			6		7			11			10	8			9		4	12	5				34
1		2			6		7			9	3	11	8	10					4		5	U			35
1	2				6		7		10	U	3	11		9		8			4		5				36
1		2			6		7		10	U	3		6			8		9	11	4	5				37
1		2	5		6		7		10	U	3					8		9	11	4					38
1		2	5			7	8		10		3		6			U			11	4		9			39
1		2	5		7		8		10		3		6			U		11	4			9			40
1		2			6		7		10	12	3		8					11	4	5		9			41
1		2	5		6		7		10		3	11		9		12			8	4					42
1		2	5		6		7				3	11		9		10			8	4		12			43
1	2				6		7		12		3		11	9					8	4		5			44
2	25	37	33	3	41	24	39	3	36	24	17	30	22	15	6	23	1	8	10	13		7	3		
	2	1						1	1	3	1	7	1	1	5	1				3		1			
	1				1	7		9	4		7	1	3		4		2	2				1			

	2	3	4		5		8		10	9	U		6	7					11						27
1	1	1		1			1		1	1			1	1					1						
													1												

	3	4		5	7	8		10	11		12	6		9	2										8
1	1		1	1	1	1		1	1			1	1												
								1																	

Jim Montgomery who was ever present during this season. He went on to make a record 627 first team appearances for Sunderland before leaving to join Birmingham City on 18 March 1977.

451

1969-70

Division One

Ground: Roker Park
Manager: Alan Brown

League Table

	P	W	D	L	F	A	Pts
Everton	42	29	8	5	72	34	66
Leeds U	42	21	15	6	84	49	57
Chelsea	42	21	13	8	70	50	55
Derby Co	42	22	9	11	64	37	53
Liverpool	42	20	11	11	65	42	51
Coventry C	42	19	11	12	58	48	49
Newcastle U	42	17	13	12	57	35	47
Manchester U	42	14	17	11	66	61	45
Stoke C	42	15	15	12	56	52	45
Manchester C	42	16	11	15	55	48	43
Tottenham H	42	17	9	16	54	55	43
Arsenal	42	12	18	12	51	49	42
Wolverh'pton W	42	12	16	14	55	57	40
Burnley	42	12	15	15	56	61	39
Nottingham F	42	10	18	14	50	71	38
WBA	42	14	9	19	58	66	37
West Ham U	42	12	12	18	51	60	36
Ipswich T	42	10	11	21	40	63	31
Southampton	42	6	17	19	46	67	29
Crystal Palace	42	6	15	21	34	68	27
SUNDERLAND	42	6	14	22	30	68	26
Sheffield W	42	8	9	25	40	71	25

FA Cup Winners: Chelsea
League Cup Winners: Manchester City
Anglo Italian Cup Winners: Swindon Town

Did you know that?

The Wolverhampton Wanderers v Sunderland game on 29 November 1969 was the first English League game to be broadcast live on television across Scandanavia.

Match 1: McGiven, Baker and Symm made debuts
Match 2: Park made debut
Match 10: Palmer last game
Match 22: Lathan made debut
Match 39: Ashurst last game
Match 44: Relegation confirmed
Match 47: Tones made debut
Match 48; Stuckey last game

Match No.	Date	Round	Venue	Opponents	Result	FT	HT	Pos.	Scorers	Attendance
1	Aug 9		H	Coventry City	D	0-0	0-0			20,974
2	13		A	Crystal Palace	L	0-2	0-1	19		28,897
3	16		A	Burnley	L	0-3	0-3	21		13,409
4	20		H	Crystal Palace	D	0-0	0-0	20		16,192
5	23		H	Sheffield Wed.	L	1-2	0-1	21	Todd	15,559
6	27		H	Manchester City	L	0-4	0-3	21		21,515
7	30		A	Manchester United	L	1-3	1-1	21	McGiven	50,570
8	Sep 6		H	West Bromwich Albion	D	2-2	1-1	22	Tueart, Kerr	14,410
9	9		A	Liverpool	L	0-2	0-2	22		46,370
10	13		A	Stoke City	L	2-4	2-2	22	Harris, McGiven	16,939
11	20		H	Nottingham Forest	W	2-1	1-0	22	Tueart, Harris (pen)	16,044
12	27		A	Tottenham Hotspur	W	1-0	1-0	22	England o.g.	30,523
13	Oct 4		H	Chelsea	D	0-0	0-0	22		24,216
14	8		H	Burnley	L	0-1	0-0	22		20,311
15	11		A	Everton	L	1-3	1-2	22	Tueart	47,271
16	18		H	Arsenal	D	1-1	1-0	22	Hughes	17,864
17	25		A	West Ham United	L	1-1	0-1	22	Hughes	29,191
18	Nov 1		H	Leeds United	D	0-0	0-0	22		31,842
19	8		A	Newcastle United	L	0-3	0-1	22		56,317
20	15		A	Derby County	L	0-3	0-0	22		31,918
21	19		A	Leeds United	L	0-2	0-1	22		25,890
22	22		H	Southampton	D	2-2	0-0	21	Stuckey, Lathan	15,385
23	29		A	Wolverhampton W.	L	0-1	0-1	21		21,120
24	Dec 6		A	Ipswich Town	W	2-1	2-1	21	Harris, Park	12,739
25	13		H	Stoke City	L	0-3	0-2	21		15,205
26	26		A	Sheffield Wed.	L	0-2	0-1	21		35,302
27	27		H	Manchester United	D	1-1	0-1	21	Baker	36,504
28	Jan 17		H	Tottenham Hotspur	W	2-1	1-0	20	Hughes, Harris (pen)	13,993
29	24		A	Nottingham Forest	L	1-2	0-1	20	McGiven	19,544
30	28		A	West Bromwich Albion	L	1-3	0-1	20	Kerr	19,024
31	31		H	Chelsea	L	1-3	0-2	21	Baker	38,775
32	Feb 21		H	West Ham United	L	0-1	0-1	21		16,900
33	28		A	Arsenal	L	1-3	1-1	22	Kerr	21,826
34	Mar 7		A	Southampton	D	1-1	0-0	22	Harris (pen)	19,374
35	14		A	Wolverhampton W.	W	2-1	2-1	22	McGiven, Harris (pen)	15,385
36	21		A	Ipswich Town	L	0-2	0-0	22		20,781
37	24		A	Coventry City	D	1-1	1-0	22	Hughes	24,590
38	27		H	Newcastle United	D	1-1	0-1	22	Park	51,950
39	28		H	Derby County	D	1-1	1-1	22	Harris	18,818
40	Apr 4		A	Manchester City	W	1-0	0-0	21	Tueart	22,006
41	8		H	Everton	D	0-0	0-0	21		28,774
42	15		H	Liverpool	L	0-1	0-0	21		33,001

Appearances
Sub Appearances
Goals

FA Cup

| 29 | Jan 3 | R3 | A | Leicester City | L | 0-1 | 0-1 | | | 24,870 |

Appearance
Sub Appearance
Goal

League Cup

| 8 | Sep 3 | R2 | H | Bradford City | L | 1-2 | 0-1 | | Tueart | 10,900 |

Appearance
Sub Appearance
Goal

Anglo Italian Cup

45	May 1		H	Lazio	W	3-1	2-0		Tueart, Kerr (2)	3,760
46	9		H	Fiorentina	D	2-2	2-1		McGiven, Park	5,950
47	17		A	Lazio	L	1-2	1-1		Tones	15,400
48	23		A	Fiorentina	L	0-3	0-2			6,000

Appearance
Sub Appearance
Goal

452

#	Montgomery	Harvey	Ashurst	Heslop	Pitt	McGiven	Harris	Tueart	Baker	Symm	Hughes	Palmer	Todd	Park	Lowrey	Stuckey	Kerr	Irwin	Lathan	Forster	Tones	McIver	#
1	2	3	4	5	6	7	8	9	10	11	12												1
1	3		4	5	2	7	11	9	8			10	6	12									2
1	3	12	4	5	2	7	11		10		9	6		8									3
1	2	3		5	4	7	11	9	10			6		12	8								4
1	2	3		5	4	7	11	9	10	U		6			8								5
1	2	3		5	6	7	11	9	10	12		4			8								6
1	2	3		5	6	7	11	9	12		10	4			8								7
1	2	3	4	5	6	7	11		9	10				8	12								9
1	2	3		5	6	7	8	9		11	10	4			12								10
1	2	3		5	6	7	11	9		10		4	12		8								11
1		3		5	6	7	11	9		8		4	U		10	2							12
1		3	5		6	7	11	9		8		4	12		10	2							13
1		3	5		6	7	11	9		8		4		U	10	2							14
1	12	3	6		4	7	8	10		11		5			9	2							15
1	12	3			4		8	10	7	11		5	6		9	2							16
1	U	3	5		4		11	9		8		6	7		10	2							17
1		3	5			6		11	U	8		4	7		10	2							18
1		3	5		6	7	11	9	U	8		4			10	2							19
1		3	5		6	7	11	9	U	8		4			10	2							20
1		3	5		6	7		9	12	8		4	11		10	2							21
1		3	5		6	7		9		8		4	11		10	2	12						22
1		3	5		6	7				11		4	10		8	U	2	9					23
1		3	5		6	7	11					4	10		8	12	2	9					24
1		3	5		6	10	11			12		4	7		8		2	9					25
1		3	5		6	10	11					4	7		8	U	2	9					26
1		3		5	6	10	12		11			4	7		8		2	9					27
1	3		5		6	10	8	9		11		4	7			U	2						28
1	3		5		6	10	8	9		11		4	7			U	2						30
1	3		5		6	10	8	9		11		4	7			12	2						31
1	3		5		6	10	8			11		4	7			12	2	9					32
1		3	5		6	10	8			11		4	7			U	2						33
1		3	5		6	10	8	9		11		4	7			12	2						34
1		3		5	6	10	11			9		4	7		8		2	U					35
1		3		5	6	10	11	U		9		4	7		8		2						36
1				5	6	10	11		12	9		4	7		8		2						37
		3		5	6	10	11		12	9		4	7		8		2		1				38
1		3	5		6	10	11		U	9		4	7		8		2						39
1	3		5		6	10	11		U	9		4	7		8		2						40
1	3		5		6	10	11		U	9		4	7		8		2						41
1	3		5		6	10	11		U	9		4	7		8		2						42
1	3				6	10	11		U	9		4	7		8		2						43
1	3			5	6	10	11		U	9		4	7		8		2						44
1	19	31	28	17	42	39	38	24	7	33	5	40	26	1	10	22	32	6	1				
	2	1				1		4	2	1		3	1		6		1						
					4	7	4	2		4		1	2		1	3		1					

#	Montgomery	Harvey	Ashurst	Heslop	Pitt	McGiven	Harris	Tueart	Baker	Symm	Hughes	Palmer	Todd	Park	Lowrey	Stuckey	Kerr	Irwin	Lathan	Forster	Tones	McIver	#
	6	3	5			10	8	9		11		4	7		12	2							29
	1	1	1			1	1	1		1		1	1		1								
												1											

#	Montgomery	Harvey	Ashurst	Heslop	Pitt	McGiven	Harris	Tueart	Baker	Symm	Hughes	Palmer	Todd	Park	Lowrey	Stuckey	Kerr	Irwin	Lathan	Forster	Tones	McIver	#
	2	3	4	5	6	7	11	9		12	10			8									8
	1	1	1	1	1	1	1			1				1									
											1												
						1																	

#	Montgomery	Harvey	Ashurst	Heslop	Pitt	McGiven	Harris	Tueart	Baker	Symm	Hughes	Palmer	Todd	Park	Lowrey	Stuckey	Kerr	Irwin	Lathan	Forster	Tones	McIver	#
3		5	U	6	10	11		U	9		4	7		U	8	2		U	U				45
3		5	U	6	10	11		U	9		4	7		U	8	2		U	U				46
		5	U	6	10	11		7	9		4	3			8	2		U	12	U			47
3		5	12		10	11		9			4	7		14	8	2		U	6	U			48
3		4		3	4	4		2	3		4	4			4	4			1				
			1									1				1							
				1		1						1			2								

1970-71

Division Two

Ground: Roker Park

Manager: Alan Brown

League Table

	P	W	D	L	F	A	Pts
Leicester C	42	23	13	6	57	30	59
Sheffield U	42	21	14	7	73	39	56
Cardiff C	42	20	13	9	64	41	53
Carlisle U	42	20	13	9	65	43	53
Hull C	42	19	13	10	54	41	51
Luton T	42	18	13	11	62	43	49
Middlesbrough	42	17	14	11	60	43	48
Millwall	42	19	9	14	59	42	47
Birmingham C	42	17	12	13	58	48	46
Norwich C	42	15	14	13	54	52	44
QPR	42	16	11	15	58	53	43
Swindon T	42	15	12	15	61	51	42
SUNDERLAND	42	15	12	15	52	54	42
Oxford U	42	14	14	14	41	48	42
Sheffield W	42	12	12	18	51	69	36
Portsmouth	42	10	14	18	46	61	34
Orient	42	9	16	17	29	51	34
Watford	42	10	13	19	38	60	33
Bristol C	42	10	11	21	46	64	31
Charlton A	42	8	14	20	41	65	30
Blackburn R	42	6	15	21	37	69	27
Bolton W	42	7	10	25	35	74	24

Division 1 Champions: Arsenal 65 pts

FA Cup Winners: Arsenal

League Cup Winners: Tottenham Hotspur

Did you know that?

Defender Colin Todd was transferred to Derby County on 18 February 1971. The Rams manager, Brian Clough, paid a record fee between two British clubs of £175,000.

Match 1: Heslop last game
Match 13: Malone made debut
Match 16: Chambers made debut
Match 23: Watson made debut
Match 26: Baker last game
Match 30: Todd last game
Match 40: Hepworth made debut
Match 42: Hepworth last game

Match No.	Date		Round	Venue	Opponents	Result	FT	HT	Pos.	Scorers	Attendance
1	Aug	15		A	Bristol City	L	3-4	1-2		Baker (2), Kerr	17,584
2		22		H	Watford	D	3-3	1-1	15	Park, Hughes, Kerr	16,228
3		29		A	Swindon Town	L	0-2	0-2	20		17,273
4	Sep	2		H	Charlton Athletic	W	3-0	2-0	16	Baker (3)	11,860
5		5		H	Norwich City	W	2-1	0-0	11	Hughes, McGiven	16,682
7		12		A	Orient	L	0-1	0-0	16		8,919
8		19		H	Sheffield Wed.	W	3-1	0-1	10	McGiven, Kerr, Tueart	15,328
9		26		A	Millwall	D	0-0	0-0	10		12,263
10	Oct	3		H	Bolton Wanderers	W	4-1	1-0	9	Porterfield, Harris, Park, Baker	15,972
11		7		H	Hull City	L	0-1	0-1	9		18,741
12		10		A	Leicester City	L	0-1	0-0	12		27,195
13		17		H	Bristol City	W	1-0	1-0	9	McGiven	17,335
14		20		A	Carlisle United	D	0-0	0-0	10		16,623
15		24		H	Oxford United	L	0-1	0-0	12		16,376
16		31		A	Luton Town	W	2-1	1-0	9	Baker, Kerr	19,202
17	Nov	7		H	Birmingham City	W	2-1	0-1	9	Hughes, Porterfield	16,095
18		14		A	Portsmouth	L	1-2	1-0	10	Kerr	10,474
19		21		H	Sheffield United	D	0-0	0-0	10		14,639
20		28		A	Blackburn Rovers	W	1-0	0-0	9	Kerr	7,020
21	Dec	5		H	Queens Park Rangers	W	3-1	2-0	9	Baker (2, 1 pen), Hughes	14,891
22		12		A	Cardiff City	L	1-3	0-1	10	Baker	15,619
23		19		A	Watford	D	1-1	0-0	11	Watson	12,739
24		26		H	Middlesbrough	D	2-2	1-2	10	Kerr, Hughes	42,617
25	Jan	9		A	Hull City	L	0-4	0-2	11		20,532
27		16		H	Carlisle United	W	2-0	2-0	11	Watson, Hughes	16,336
28		30		A	Blackburn Rovers	W	3-2	2-0	11	Chambers, Tueart, Pitt	10,354
29	Feb	6		A	Queens Park Rangers	L	0-2	0-1	11		11,707
30		13		A	Cardiff City	L	0-4	0-2	12		11,566
31		20		A	Sheffield United	L	0-1	0-0	12		24,944
32		27		H	Luton Town	D	0-0	0-0	11		12,471
33	Mar	6		A	Oxford United	D	0-0	0-0	11		7,747
34		13		H	Portsmouth	D	0-0	0-0	11		10,827
35		20		A	Birmingham City	L	1-3	0-3	12	Watson	34,194
36		27		A	Norwich City	L	0-3	0-0	14		10,729
37	Apr	3		H	Swindon Town	W	5-2	5-1	12	Lowrey, Kerr (2), Hughes (2)	8,596
38		9		H	Orient	W	1-0	0-0	11	Malone	15,151
39		10		A	Middlesbrough	D	2-2	2-2	11	Hughes, Watson	26,479
40		12		A	Bolton Wanderers	W	3-1	1-1	12	Lathan (2), Tueart	5,937
41		17		A	Leicester City	D	0-0	0-0	11		17,353
42		24		A	Sheffield Wed.	W	2-1	0-1	11	Tueart, Lowrey	9,462
43		27		A	Charlton Athletic	D	1-1	0-0	11	Chambers	10,520
44	May	1		H	Millwall	L	0-1	0-1	13		11,961

Appearances
Sub Appearances
Goals

FA Cup

26	Jan	11	R3	H	Orient	L	0-3	0-1			18,061

Appearances
Sub Appearances
Goals

League Cup

6	Sep	9	R2	A	Lincoln City	L	1-2	1-2		Kerr	10,631

Appearances
Sub Appearances
Goals

	Montgomery	Irwin	Harvey	Todd	Heslop	McGiven	Park	Kerr	Baker	Porterfield	Hughes	Pitt	Tueart	Malone	Chambers	Watson	Lowrey	Hepworth	Lathan	
1	1	2	3	4	5	6	7	8	9	10	11			U						1
2	1	2	3	4		6	7	8	9	10	11	5	U							2
3	1	2	3	4		6	7	8	9	10	11	5	U							3
4	1	2	3	4		6	7	8	9	10	11	5	U							4
5	1	2	3	4		6	7	8	9	10	11	5	U							5
7	1	2	3			4	7	8	9	6	11	5	10	U						7
8	1	2	3	4		6	7	8	9	10	11	5	12							8
9	1	2	3		4		7	8		6	9	5	10	11	U					9
10	1	2	3	4			7	8	12	6	9	5	10	11						10
11	1	2	3	4		12	7	8		6	9	5	10	11						11
12	1	2	3	4		12	7	8		6	9	5	10	11						12
13	1		3		4	6	12	8	9	7	11	5	10		2					13
14	1	2	3		4	6	7	8		12	9	5	10	11						14
15	1	2	3	4		6	12	8		7	9	5	10	11						15
16	1	2	3	4		6	7	10	9	8	11	5			12					16
17	1	2	3	4		7	8	9	6	11	5			12	10					17
18	1	3	7	4				8	9	6	11	5	U	2	10					18
19	1	2	3	4		7	8	9	6	11	5			U	10					19
20	1	3	6	4			8	9	7	11	5	U		2	10					20
21	1	3	7	4		8	9	6	11	5	12			2	10					21
22	1	12	3	4			8	9	6	11	5	10		2	7					22
23	1	3	12	4			8		6	11	5	10		2	7	9				23
24	1		3	4		12	8		6	11	5	10		2	7	9				24
25	1		3	4		7	8		6	11	5	10		2	12	9				25
27	1	2	3	4		12	8		6	11	5	10			7	9				27
28	1	2	3	4		12	8		6	9	5	10	11		7					28
29	1	2	3	4		12	8		6	9	5	10	11		7					29
30	1	2	3	4			U	8	6	9	5	10	11		7					30
31	1		3		4	6	8		7	9	5	10	11	2	12					31
32	1		3		4	7	8		6		5	10	11	2	U	9				32
33	1	3	4			6	7			8	5	10	11	2	U	9				33
34	1	3	4			6	7		12	8	5	10	11	2		9				34
35	1	3	4			12	7		6	8	5	10	11	2		9				35
36	1	3	4		6	8	12			11	5	10	7	2		9				36
37	1	3	4			U	7		6	11	5	10		2		9	8			37
38	1	3	4			12	7		6	11	5	10		2		9	8			38
39	1	3	4			12	7		6	11	5	10		2		9	8			39
40	1		4				7		6		10	11	2	5		9	U	3	8	40
41	1	3	4			12	7		6	11	10			2	5	9	8			41
42	1		4			12			6	11	10	7	2	5	9	8	3			42
43	1	3	4			6	7		U		10	11	2	5	9	8				43
44	1	3	4			12			6	11	10	7	2	5	9	8				44
	42	35	40	26	1	15	23	38	15	37	39	36	30	19	22	17	7	2	1	
		1	1			2	12	1	1	2		1	1	1	3					
						3	2	9	10	2	9	1	1	4	1	2	4	2	2	

	1	2	3	4			7	8	9	6	11		5	12		10				26
	1	1	1	1			1	1	1	1	1		1			1				
														1						

	1	2	3		4	7	8	9	10	11	5	6	U							6
	1	1	1		1	1	1	1	1	1	1	1								
									1											

Dick Malone.

Full-back Dick Malone made his debut in October 1970 after a £30,000 transfer from Ayr United.

1971-72

Division Two
Ground: Roker Park
Manager: Alan Brown

League Table

	P	W	D	L	F	A	Pts
Norwich C	42	21	15	6	60	36	57
Birmingham C	42	19	18	5	60	31	56
Millwall	42	19	17	6	64	46	55
QPR	42	20	14	8	57	28	54
SUNDERLAND	42	17	16	9	67	57	50
Blackpool	42	20	7	15	70	50	47
Burnley	42	20	6	16	70	55	46
Bristol C	42	18	10	14	61	49	46
Middlesbrough	42	19	8	15	50	48	46
Carlisle U	42	17	9	16	61	57	43
Swindon T	42	15	12	15	47	47	42
Hull C	42	14	10	18	49	53	38
Luton T	42	10	18	14	43	48	38
Sheffield W	42	13	12	17	51	58	38
Oxford U	42	12	14	16	43	55	38
Portsmouth	42	12	13	17	59	68	37
Orient	42	14	9	19	50	61	37
Preston NE	42	12	12	18	52	58	36
Cardiff C	42	10	14	18	56	69	34
Fulham	42	12	10	20	45	68	34
Charlton A	42	12	9	21	55	77	33
Watford	42	5	9	28	24	75	19

Division 1 Champions: Derby County 58 pts
FA Cup Winners: Leeds United
League Cup Winners: Stoke City
Anglo Italian Cup Winners: Roma

Did you know that?

Jack Ashurst made his debut in the Anglo Italian Cup tie at Atalanta. In doing so he became the first, and so far only, Sunderland player to make his debut in the month of June.

Match 1: Park last game
Match 2: Harris last game
Match 6: Irwin last game
Match 7: Coleman made debut & Symm last game
Match 8: McIver only game
Match 9: Hamilton made debut & Lowrey last game
Match 18: Taylor only game
Match 37: Harvey last game
Match 41: Horswill made debut
Match 43: Forster last game
Match 44: Bolton made debut
Match 48: Ashurst made debut & only 3 substitutes named

Matches

Match No.	Date	Round	Venue	Opponents	Result	FT	HT	Pos.	Scorers	Attendance
1	Aug 14		H	Birmingham City	D	1-1	0-1		Watson	9,749
2	21		A	Watford	D	1-1	0-1	12	Porterfield	11,283
3	28		H	Orient	W	2-0	1-0	6	Tueart, Kerr	14,544
4	Sep 1		H	Carlisle United	L	0-3	0-2	14		20,998
5	4		A	Millwall	D	1-1	0-1	12	Watson	12,446
7	11		H	Swindon Town	W	1-0	0-0	8	Chambers	12,811
8	18		A	Sheffield Wed.	L	0-3	0-0	13		13,710
9	25		H	Preston North End	W	4-3	3-1	11	Pitt, Tueart (2), Hamilton	13,102
10	29		H	Middlesbrough	W	4-1	1-0	6	Kerr, Watson, Tueart, Hughes	28,129
11	Oct 2		A	Burnley	W	1-0	0-0	4	Watson	16,432
12	9		H	Norwich City	D	1-1	0-0		Tueart	24,951
13	16		A	Birmingham City	D	1-1	1-1	6	Kerr	27,341
14	19		A	Charlton Athletic	D	2-2	2-1	7	Hughes, Warman o.g.	8,133
15	23		A	Oxford United	L	0-2	0-2	7		10,735
16	30		H	Luton Town	D	2-2	1-0		Watson, McGiven	17,979
17	Nov 6		A	Portsmouth	D	2-2	1-2	7	Watson, Tueart	14,387
18	13		H	Blackpool	D	0-0	0-0	8		17,240
19	20		A	Cardiff City	W	2-1	2-1	6	Hughes, Kerr	12,735
20	27		H	Bristol City	D	1-1	1-0	5	Pitt	15,655
21	Dec 4		A	Queens Park Rangers	L	1-2	0-2	9	Kerr	13,576
22	11		H	Fulham	W	2-1	0-1		Hughes, Tueart	11,833
23	18		H	Millwall	D	3-3	1-0	4	Pitt, Hughes, Kerr	16,484
24	27		A	Hull City	W	3-2	1-1	4	Pitt, Tueart, Hughes	26,091
25	Jan 1		H	Sheffield Wed.	W	2-0	1-0	4	Kerr, Tueart	23,228
26	8		A	Orient	L	0-5	0-2	4		6,966
28	22		A	Middlesbrough	L	0-2	0-2	5		34,846
29	29		H	Charlton Athletic	W	3-0	1-0	5	Chambers (2), Hughes	12,877
31	Feb 12		H	Oxford United	W	3-0	1-0	6	Tueart (2), Porterfield	15,368
34	19		A	Luton Town	W	2-1	1-0	5	Pitt, Tueart	10,944
35	Mar 1		H	Portsmouth	W	3-2	1-0	3	Lathan (3)	8,273
36	4		A	Blackpool	D	1-1	1-0	3	Watson	10,989
37	11		A	Norwich City	D	1-1	0-0	3	Harvey	22,143
38	25		A	Swindon Town	D	1-1	1-1	5	Lathan	12,102
39	Apr 1		H	Hull City	L	0-1	0-0	5		17,621
40	3		A	Burnley	W	4-3	1-2	5	Watson (2), Coleman, Hughes	14,034
41	4		A	Preston North End	W	3-1	2-1	5	Watson, Porterfield, Tueart	13,450
42	8		H	Cardiff City	D	1-1	0-0	4	Watson	15,224
43	15		A	Bristol City	L	1-3	1-0	5	Kerr	12,178
44	17		H	Watford	W	5-0	1-0	5	Watson (2), McGiven, Porterfield, Pitt	8,981
45	22		H	Queens Park Rangers	L	0-1	0-1	5		13,751
46	25		A	Carlisle United	W	2-1	0-1	5	Porterfield, Kerr	10,326
47	29		A	Fulham	D	0-0	0-0	5		12,360

Appearances
Sub Appearances
Goals

FA Cup

27	Jan 15	R3	H	Sheffield Wed.	W	3-0	1-0		Porterfield, Watson, Chambers	25,310
30	Feb 9	R4	A	Cardiff City	D	1-1	0-1		Chambers (pen)	28,201
32	14	R4r	H	Cardiff City	D	1-1 (aet)	1-1		Kerr	39,348
33	16	R4r2	N*	Cardiff City	L	1-3	1-1		McGiven	8,868

*at Maine Road

Appearances
Sub Appearances
Goals

League Cup

| 6 | Sep 7 | R2 | A | Bristol Rovers | L | 1-3 | 0-1 | | Hughes (pen) | 15,262 |

Appearances
Sub Appearances
Goals

Anglo Italian Cup

48	Jun 2		A	Atalanta	L	2-3	2-0		Kerr, Lathan	6,850
49	4		A	Cagliari	W	3-1	2-1		Tueart, Kerr, Lathan	1,680
50	7		H	Atalanta	D	0-0	0-0			5,798
51	10		H	Cagliari	D	3-3	2-0		McGiven, Tueart, Watson	4,010

Appearances
Sub Appearances
Goals

	Montgomery	Malone	Park	Harvey	Pitt	Porterfield	McGiven	Kerr	Watson	Harris	Hughes	Tueart	Irwin	Symm	Chambers	Coleman	McIver	Lowrey	Lathan	Hamilton	Taylor	Forster	Horswill	Bolton	Ashurst	
	1	2	3	4	5	6	7	8	9	10	11	12														1
	1	2		6	5	8	4	7	9	10	11	12	3													2
	1	2	6		5	10	4	7	9		11	8	3	12												3
	1	2		4	5	6	7	10	9		11	8	3	U												4
	1	2		4	5	10		8	9		12	11	3	6	7											5
	1	2		4	5	10		7	9		12	11		6	8	3										7
	1	2		4	5	10		8	9			11		7		3	10	12								8
	1	2		4	5	6		8	9			11		7	3		10		12							9
	1	2		4	5	6	7	8	9		12	11			3			10								10
	1	2		4	5	6	7	8	9		12	11			3			10								11
	1	2		4	5	6	7	8	9		12	11		10	3											12
	1	2		4	5	6	7	8	9			11		12	3			10								13
	1	2		4	5	6		8	9		7	11		10	3			12								14
	1	2		3	5	6	7	8	9		12	11		4				10								15
	1	2		4	5	6	7	8	9		10	11			3			12								16
	1	2		4	5		6	8	9		10	11		7	3		U									17
	1	2		4	5		6	8	9		10	11		7	3				12							18
	1	2		4	5		6	8	9		11	10		7	3		12									19
	1	2		4	5			4	8	9	10	11		7	3		U									20
	1	2		4	5			7	8	9	10	11		6	3		12									21
		2		5		10	4	8	9		7	11		6	3		12			1						22
		2		4	5	10		8	9		7	11		6	3		12			1						23
		2		4	5	6	U	8	9		10	11		7	3					1						24
		2		4	5	6	U	8	9		10	11		7	3					1						25
		2		4	5	6	12	8	9		10	11		7	3					1						26
	1	2		4	5	10	U	8	9		7	11		6	3											28
	1	2		4	5	6		8	9		10	11		7	3		U									29
	1	2		4	5	8	6		9		10	11		7	3		12									31
		2		4	5	7	6	8	9			11		U	3		10			1						34
		2		4	5	6	7	8	9			11		U	3		10			1						35
		2	12	5	6	7	8		9			11		4	3		10			1						36
	1	2		5	6	7	8	9				11		U	3		10									37
	1	2		5	6	7	8	9		U	11			4	3		10									38
	1	2		5	6	7	8	9		12	11			4	3		10									39
	1	2		5	6	7	8	9		12	11			4	3		10									40
		2		5	6	7	8	9		10	11				3		U			1	4					41
		2		5	6	7	8	9		10	11				3		12			1	4					42
		2		5	6	7	8	9		12	11				3		10			1	4					43
	1	2		5	12	7	8	9			11			6			10				4	3				44
	1			5	6	7	8	9		12	11			2			10				4	3				45
		2		5	6	7	8	9			11						10	U			4	3				46
	1	2		5	6	7	8	9		12	11						10				4	3				47
	31	41	1	31	41	36	31	41	42	2	21	40	4	2	25	32	1	2	12	4		11	7	4		
				1			1	1			11	2		1	1				7	3	1					
			1	6	5	2	9	13		8	13			3	1				4	1						

	Montgomery	Malone	Park	Harvey	Pitt	Porterfield	McGiven	Kerr	Watson	Harris	Hughes	Tueart	Irwin	Symm	Chambers	Coleman	McIver	Lowrey	Lathan	Hamilton	Taylor	Forster	Horswill	Bolton	Ashurst	
	1	2		4	5	10	U	8	9		7	11		6	3											27
	1	2		4	5	6	U	8	9		10	11		7	3											30
	1	2		4	5	6	12	8	9		10	11		7	3											32
		2		4	5	6	7	8	9		10	11		12	3					1						33
	3	4		4	4	4	1	4	4		4	4		3	4					1						
							1				1															
				1	1	1	1	1			2															

	Montgomery	Malone	Park	Harvey	Pitt	Porterfield	McGiven	Kerr	Watson	Harris	Hughes	Tueart	Irwin	Symm	Chambers	Coleman	McIver	Lowrey	Lathan	Hamilton	Taylor	Forster	Horswill	Bolton	Ashurst	
	1	2		4	5	6			8	9				11	7	3	10	12								6
	1	1		1	1	1			1	1				1	1	1	1	1								
										1								1								
																		1								

	Montgomery	Malone	Park	Harvey	Pitt	Porterfield	McGiven	Kerr	Watson	Harris	Hughes	Tueart	Irwin	Symm	Chambers	Coleman	McIver	Lowrey	Lathan	Hamilton	Taylor	Forster	Horswill	Bolton	Ashurst	
	1	2			6	7	8	9		U	11			14	12		10				4	3	5			48
	1	2		5	6	7	8	9		U	11			U	U		10				4	3	U			49
	1	2		5	6	7	8	9		14	11			12			10	U		U	4	3	U			50
	4	4		3	4	4	4	4		4	4			4			4				4	4	1			51
										1				2	1											
							1	2			2			2												

1972-73

Division One

Ground: Roker Park

Managers: Alan Brown, Billy Elliott & Bob Stokoe

League Table

	P	W	D	L	F	A	Pts
Burnley	42	24	14	4	72	35	62
QPR	42	24	13	5	81	37	61
Aston Villa	42	18	14	10	51	47	50
Middlesbrough	42	17	13	12	46	43	47
Bristol C	42	17	12	13	63	51	46
SUNDERLAND	42	17	12	13	59	49	46
Blackpool	42	18	10	14	56	51	46
Oxford U	42	19	7	16	52	43	45
Fulham	42	16	12	14	58	49	44
Sheffield W	42	17	10	15	59	55	44
Millwall	42	16	10	16	55	47	42
Luton T	42	15	11	16	44	53	41
Hull C	42	14	12	16	64	59	40
Nottingham F	42	14	12	16	47	52	40
Orient	42	12	12	18	49	53	36
Swindon T	42	10	16	16	46	60	36
Portsmouth	42	12	11	19	42	59	35
Carlisle U	42	11	12	19	50	52	34
Preston NE	42	11	12	19	37	64	34
Cardiff C	42	11	11	20	43	58	33
Huddersfield T	42	8	17	17	36	56	33
Brighton & HA	42	8	13	21	46	83	29

Division 1 Champions:
Liverpool 60 pts

FA Cup Winners: Sunderland

League Cup Winners: Tottenham Hotspur

Did you know that?

Sunderland became the first Second Division team to win the FA Cup since West Bromwich Albion in 1931.

One of Bob Stokoe's first decisions as Sunderland manager was to replace the club's white shorts with the traditional black ones.

Match 15: Alan Brown last game as Sunderland manager
Match 16: Billy Elliott first game as caretaker manager
Match 19: Billy Elliott last game as caretaker manager
Match 20: Bob Stokoe first game as Sunderland manager
Match 22: Coleman last game
Match 23: Young made debut
Match 26: Guthrie made debut
Match 27: John Hughes only game
Match 30: Halom made debut
Match 34: Ellison made debut
Match 35: Ellison last game
Match 47: Tones and Chambers last games
Match 49: Swinburne made debut

Match No.	Date		Round	Venue	Opponents	Result	FT	HT	Pos.	Scorers	Attendance
1	Aug	12		A	Middlesbrough	L	1-2	1-1		Lathan	23,853
2		19		H	Orient	W	1-0	0-0	13	Tueart	12,658
3		26		A	Brighton & Hove Albion	D	2-2	2-0	12	Lathan (2)	15,906
4		28		A	Blackpool	D	0-0	0-0	10		14,797
5	Sep	2		H	Swindon Town	W	3-2	0-0	8	Tueart, Lathan, Kerr	11,674
7		9		A	Millwall	W	1-0	1-0	7	Tueart	9,817
8		16		H	Sheffield Wed.	D	1-1	0-0	7	Tueart (pen)	16,960
9		23		A	Huddersfield Town	D	1-1	1-1	7	Porterfield	10,145
10		27		A	Aston Villa	L	0-2	0-1	10		29,895
11		30		H	Nottingham Forest	W	4-1	3-0	7	Lathan (2), Porterfield, Hughes	14,155
12	Oct	7		A	Oxford United	L	1-5	1-0	12	Kerr	8,881
13		14		H	Luton Town	L	0-2	0-2	14		13,394
14		21		A	Queens Park Rangers	L	2-3	1-1	15	Tueart, Hamilton	17,356
15		28		H	Fulham	D	0-0	0-0	14		11,618
16	Nov	4		H	Aston Villa	D	2-2	1-1	15	Hughes, Kerr	18,717
17		11		A	Carlisle United	L	3-4	1-3	17	Porterfield (2), Lathan	8,884
18		18		H	Hull City	D	1-1	1-0	17	Coleman	11,141
19		25		A	Bristol City	L	0-1	0-0	19		10,666
20	Dec	2		H	Burnley	L	0-1	0-0	19		16,812
21		9		A	Portsmouth	W	3-2	1-1	19	Watson, Hughes, Kerr	5,783
22		16		H	Preston North End	D	0-0	0-0	18		11,529
23	Jan	6		H	Brighton & Hove Albion	W	4-0	2-0	19	Hughes (2), Tueart, Bolton	12,573
26		20		A	Swindon Town	D	1-1	0-1	18	Porterfield	7,010
27		27		H	Millwall	W	2-0	0-0	17	Tueart, Kerr	22,781
30	Feb	10		A	Sheffield Wed.	L	0-1	0-0	17		16,949
31		17		H	Middlesbrough	W	4-0	1-0	17	Horswill, Halom, Hughes, Tueart	26,040
34	Mar	3		H	Oxford United	W	1-0	0-0	16	Watson	39,222
35		10		A	Luton Town	L	0-1	0-1	16		12,458
37		19		A	Preston North End	W	3-1	1-1	14	Hughes (2), Halom	7,636
38		24		A	Fulham	W	2-1	1-1	14	Tueart (pen), Halom	9,645
39		27		H	Carlisle United	W	2-1	0-1	13	Hughes, Tueart (pen)	39,930
40		31		H	Bristol City	D	2-2	1-0	13	Merrick o.g., Watson	33,265
42	Apr	10		H	Huddersfield Town	W	3-0	2-0	13	Hughes (3)	32,251
43		14		H	Portsmouth	W	2-0	1-0	11	Kerr, Tueart (pen)	31,430
44		16		A	Burnley	L	0-2	0-1	11		22,896
45		21		A	Hull City	W	2-0	0-0	11	Halom, Hughes	12,637
46		23		H	Cardiff City	W	2-1	0-1	9	Tueart (pen), Hughes	27,551
47		24		A	Nottingham Forest	L	0-1	0-0	10		10,306
48		28		H	Blackpool	W	1-0	0-0	8	Hughes	26,921
49		30		A	Orient	D	1-1	1-0	7	Young	9,157
51	May	7		A	Cardiff City	D	1-1	0-1	5	Halom	26,008
52		9		H	Queens Park Rangers	L	0-3	0-0	6		43,265

Appearances
Sub Appearances
Goals

FA Cup

24	Jan	13	R3	A	Notts County	D	1-1	0-1		Watson	15,142
25		16	R3r	H	Notts County	W	2-0	0-0		Watson, Tueart	30,033
28	Feb	3	R4	H	Reading	D	1-1	1-1		Tueart	33,913
29		7	R4r	A	Reading	W	3-1	3-0		Watson, Tueart, Kerr	19,793
32		24	R5	A	Manchester City	D	2-2	1-1		Horswill, Hughes	54,478
33		27	R5r	H	Manchester City	W	3-1	2-0		Halom, Hughes (2)	51,782
36	Mar	17	R6	H	Luton Town	W	2-0	0-0		Watson, Guthrie	53,151
41	Apr	7	S	N*	Arsenal	W	2-1	1-0		Halom, Hughes	55,000
50	May	5	F	N‡	Leeds United	W	1-0	1-0		Porterfield	100,000

*at Hillsbrough
‡at Wembley

Appearances
Sub Appearances
Goals

League Cup

6	Sep	6	R2	A	Stoke City	L	0-3	0-1			17,264

Appearances
Sub Appearances
Goals

	Montgomery	Malone	Bolton	Horswill	Pitt	Porterfield	McGiven	Kerr	Hamilton	Lathan	Tueart	Tones	Watson	Coleman	Hughes, W.	Ashurst	Chambers	Young	Guthrie	Hughes, J.	Halom	Ellison	Swinburne	Kent	
1	2	3	4	5	6	7	8	9	10	11	12														1
1	2	3	4	5	6	7	8	12	10	11		9													2
1	2		4	5	6	7	8	12	10	11		9	3												3
1	2		4	5	6	7	8		10	11		9	3	12											4
1	2		4	5	6	7	8	U	10	11		9	3												5
1	2		4		6	7	8	10		11		9	3	12	5										7
1	2		4		6	7	8	10		11		9	3	12	5										8
1	2		4		6	7	8	10		11		9	3	12	5										9
1	2		4		6		8	12	10	11		9	3	7	5										10
1	2		4		6		8	U	10	11		9	3	7	5										11
1	2		4		6		8	12	10	11		9	3	7	5										12
1	2		4		6		8	U	10	11		9	3	7	5										13
1	2	3	4	5	6	7	8	9	10	11												U			14
1	2	3	4	5	6	7	8	12	10	11		9													15
1	2		4	5	6	U	8			11		9	3	7		10									16
1	2		4		6		8	10	12	11		5	3	9		7									17
1	2		4		6		8	10	11	12		5	3	9		7									18
1	2		4	U	6		8	10	11			5	3	9		7									19
1	2		4		6		8	10	11	12		5	3	9		7									20
1	2		4		6	10	8		11	12	5	3	9		7										21
1	2		10		6	7	8			11	4	5	3	9		12									22
1	2	3	4		10	12	7	9		11		5		8			6								23
1	2		4		10		7	12		11		9		8	6		5	3							26
1	2		4	U	10		8			11		5		7			6	3	9						27
1	2		4		10		8			11		5		7	12	6		3	9						30
1	2		4	6	10		8			11		5		7	U			3	9						31
1	2		4	6	10		7			11		5		8	12				9	3					34
1		12			10		7		11	8		5			4	7	6	3		9	2				35
1	2		4	6	10		7			11		5		8		12		3	9						37
1	2	3	4	6	10		7			11		5		8		U			9						38
1	2	3	4	6	10		7			11		5		8		12			9						39
1	2		4	5	10		7			11		9		8		U	6	3							40
1	2		4	6	10		7			11		5		8		12		3	9						42
1	2		4	6	10		7			11		5		8			12	3	9						43
1	12		4	6	10		7			9		5					8	11	3						44
1	2				10	12	7			11			8	5	4	6	3		9						45
1	2	3			10	12	7			11			8	5	4	6			9						46
1	2	12	4			8	7		9	11	5				10	6	3								47
1	2		4	6	10		7			11		5		8			12	3	9						48
	2	U	4	6		10	7					5		8		11	3		9		1				49
1	2	3	4	6	10		7			11		5		8		12		9							51
1	2		4	6	10		7			11		5		8		U	3	9							52
41	41	9	39	21	40	14	41	4	20	40	2	37	17	29	11	11	15	1	15	2	1				
		3			3			5	2		4		4		6	3									
		1	1		5		6	1	7	12		3	1	15			5								

1	2	3	4			10	12	7			11	6	5		9	8									24
1	2	3	4			10	8	7		12	11	6	5		9										25
1	2		4			10		8		9	11	5		7	12		6	3							28
1	2		4	5	10		8			11		9	U	7			6	3							29
1	2		4	6	10		7			11		5		8	U			3	9						32
1	2		4	6	10		7			11		5		8	U			3	9						33
1	2		4	6	10		7			11		5		8		U	3		9						36
1	2		4	6	10		7			11		5		8		U	3		9						41
1	2		4	6	10		7			11		5		8		U	3		9						50
9	9	2	9	6	9	1	9		1	9	2	9		9	1		2	7	5						
						1		1					1												
						1							1												
										3		4		4				1	2						

1	2		4	5	6	7	8	10	11	9	3	12													
1	1		1	1	1	1		1	1	1	1														6
											1														

ROKER REVIEW
6p VOL 2
Sunderland v Manchester C. Tuesday, 27th February 1973
SUNDERLAND A.F.C. LIMITED, ROKER PARK GROUND.

459

1973-74

Division Two

Ground: Roker Park
Manager: Bob Stokoe

League Table

	P	W	D	L	F	A	Pts
Middlesbrough	42	27	11	4	77	30	65
Luton T	42	19	12	11	64	51	50
Carlisle U	42	20	9	13	61	48	49
Orient	42	15	18	9	55	42	48
Blackpool	42	17	13	12	57	40	47
SUNDERLAND	42	19	9	14	58	44	47
Nottingham F	42	15	15	12	57	43	45
WBA	42	14	16	12	48	45	44
Hull C	42	13	17	12	46	47	43
Notts Co	42	15	13	14	55	60	43
Bolton W	42	15	12	15	44	40	42
Millwall	42	14	14	14	51	51	42
Fulham	42	16	10	16	39	43	42
Aston Villa	42	13	15	14	48	45	41
Portsmouth	42	14	12	16	45	62	40
Bristol C	42	14	10	18	47	54	38
Cardiff C	42	10	16	16	49	62	36
Oxford U	42	10	16	16	35	46	36
Sheffield W	42	12	11	19	51	63	35
Crystal Palace	42	11	12	19	43	56	34
Preston NE*	42	9	14	19	40	62	31
Swindon T	42	7	11	24	36	72	25

*Preston North End had one point deducted for fielding an ineligible player

Division 1 Champions: Leeds United 62 pts
FA Cup Winners: Liverpool
League Cup Winners: Wolverhampton Wanderers
ECWC Winners: FC Magdeburg

Did you know that?

Sunderland played their only games in a European competition during this season. The 2-0 defeat at Sporting Lisbon ended a run of 15 undefeated cup games; a record for a second flight team in England.

Bob Stokoe, along with Sunderland Association Football Club Ltd, granted honorary freeman of Borough of Sunderland on 21 January 1974 to honour 1973 FA Cup win.

Match 7: Pitt last game
Match 15: Belfitt made debut
Match 18: Mitchell made debut & McGiven last game
Match 24: Hegan made debut & Lathan last game
Match 35: Hegan last game
Match 40: Longhorn made debut & Horswill last game
Match 41: Tueart last game
Match 43: Towers made debut & Young last game
Match 50: Hamilton last game

Match No.	Date	Round	Venue	Opponents	Result	FT	HT	Pos.	Scorers	Attendance
1	Aug 25		H	Orient	D	1-1	0-0		Hughes	28,211
2	Sep 1		A	Notts County	W	4-1	1-0	6	Halom (2), Tueart, Hughes	15,335
3	8		H	Cardiff City	D	1-1	0-0		Guthrie	29,495
4	11		A	Portsmouth	D	1-1	1-1	6	Halom	18,989
5	15		A	Oxford United	W	1-0	1-0	3	Tueart	9,022
7	22		H	Luton Town	L	0-1	0-1	10		27,582
8	29		A	West Bromwich Albion	D	1-1	0-0	11	Halom	17,027
10	Oct 6		H	Sheffield Wed.	W	3-1	1-0	9	Hughes, Halom, Porterfield	28,955
12	13		A	Preston North End	L	0-1	0-0	11		21,747
13	20		A	Fulham	W	2-0	1-0	10	Horswill, Mullery o.g.	14,971
15	27		H	Crystal Palace	D	0-0	0-0	12		31,935
18	Nov 3		A	Hull City	L	0-2	0-1	14		17,409
20	10		H	Swindon Town	W	4-1	1-1	13	Tueart (3), Halom	24,636
21	13		H	Bolton Wanderers	W	3-0	1-0		Halom, Tueart (pen), Porterfield	26,454
22	17		A	Bristol City	L	0-2	0-0	10		14,965
24	24		H	Nottingham Forest	D	0-0	0-0	12		22,252
25	Dec 1		A	Blackpool	W	2-0	2-0	8	Belfitt, Halom	11,000
26	5		A	Bolton Wanderers	L	0-1	0-1	8		8,425
27	8		H	Aston Villa	W	2-0	1-0	6	Tueart, Halom	20,784
28	15		A	Millwall	L	1-2	1-1		Horswill	7,570
29	22		H	West Bromwich Albion	D	1-1	1-0	8	Tueart	18,389
30	26		A	Middlesbrough	L	1-2	1-1	11	Tueart (pen)	37,038
31	29		A	Cardiff City	L	1-4	1-2	11	Halom	14,799
32	Jan 1		H	Notts County	L	1-2	1-1	12	Halom	22,578
35	12		H	Oxford United	D	0-0	0-0	11		16,509
36	19		A	Orient	L	1-2	0-0	12	Belfitt	14,533
37	Feb 2		H	Millwall	W	4-0	3-0	11	Halom (2), Hughes (2)	17,486
38	16		H	Preston North End	W	2-1	1-0	10	Belfitt, Halom	21,129
39	23		A	Sheffield Wed.	W	1-0	1-0	10	Halom	17,816
40	Mar 2		H	Middlesbrough	L	0-2	0-1	11		41,658
41	5		H	Portsmouth	W	3-0	0-0	10	Tueart (2, 1 pen), Kerr	8,142
42	9		A	Crystal Palace	L	0-3	0-1	10		16,529
43	16		H	Fulham	W	1-0	1-0	9	Longhorn	20,730
44	23		A	Swindon Town	W	2-0	2-0	9	Watson, Halom	6,178
45	30		H	Hull City	W	1-0	0-0	8	Hughes (pen)	20,418
46	Apr 6		A	Nottingham Forest	D	2-2	1-1	8	Hughes, Watson	18,044
47	12		H	Carlisle United	W	2-1	0-0	5	Halom, Hughes	34,179
48	13		H	Bristol City	L	1-2	1-1	7	Longhorn	28,884
49	16		A	Carlisle United	L	0-1	0-0	9		19,672
50	20		A	Aston Villa	W	2-1	1-1	7	McMahon o.g., Watson	17,321
51	27		H	Blackpool	W	2-1	0-0	7	Towers, Kerr	22,331
52	May 1		A	Luton Town	W	4-3	3-3	6	Hughes, Ashurst, Towers, Halom	20,285

Appearances
Sub Appearances
Goals

FA Cup

33	Jan 5	R3	A	Carlisle United	D	0-0	0-0			20,595
34	9	R3r	H	Carlisle United	L	0-1	0-0			25,712

Appearances
Sub Appearances
Goals

League Cup

11	Oct 8	R2	A	Derby County	D	2-2	0-2		Lathan (2)	29,172
16	29	R2r	H	Derby County	D	1-1 (aet)	1-0		Tueart	38,975
17	31	R2r2	H	Derby County	W	3-0	0-0		Halom (3)	38,460
23	Nov 21	R3	A	Liverpool	L	0-2	0-1			36,208

Appearances
Sub Appearances
Goals

European Cup Winners' Cup

6	Sep 19	R1leg1	A	Vasas Budapest	W	2-0	0-0		Hughes, Tueart	35,000
9	Oct 3	R1leg2	H	Vasas Budapest	W	1-0	0-0		Tueart (pen)	22,762
14	24	R2leg1	H	Sporting Lisbon	W	2-1	1-0		Kerr, Horswill	31,568
19	Nov 7	R2leg2	A	Sporting Lisbon	L	0-2	0-1			50,000

Appearances
Sub Appearances
Goals

Montgomery	Malone	Guthrie	McGiven	Watson	Young	Kerr	Hughes	Halom	Porterfield	Tueart	Bolton	Pitt	Horswill	Lathan	Ashurst	Belfitt	Mitchell	Hegan	Swinburne	Longhorn	Towers	Hamilton	Ellison	
1	2	3	4	5	6	7	8	9	10	11	12													1
1	2	3	4	5	6	7	8	9	10	11			U											2
1	2	3	4	5	U	7	8	9	10	11		6												3
1	2	3	4	5		7	8	9	10	11	U	6												4
1	2	3		5	U	7	8	9	10	11		6	4											5
1	2			5	12	7	8	9	10	11		3	6	4										7
1	2	3		5	6	7	8	9	10	11			4	U										8
1	2	3		5	6	7	8	9	10	11			4	12										10
1	2	3			6	7	8	9	10	11			4	12	5									12
1	2	3		5	6	7	8	9	10	11	12		4											13
1	2			5	6	7	8	9	10	11		3	4			12								15
1	2	10	8	5	6							3	4	7		9	11				U			18
1	2		U	5		7		9	10	11		3	4		6	8								20
1	2			5		7		9	10	11		3	4	U	6	8								21
1	2			5		7	12	9	10	11		3	4		6	8								22
1	2			5		7		9	10		3		4	11	6	8		12						24
1	2			5		7	11	9	10			3	4		6	8	U							25
1	2			5		7	11	9	10	12		3	4		6	8								26
1	2			5		7		9	10	11		3	4		6		U							27
1	2			5		7		11	10			3	4	U	6	9		8						28
1	2	3		5		7	8	9	10	11			4			6		12						29
	2	3		5	6	7	8	9	10	11				4	U		1							30
1	2	3		5		7	8	9	10	11			4	12										31
1	2			5	6	7		9	10	11	3		12		8	4								32
1	2			5	6	7			10	11	3		12	4	9		8							35
1	2			5	6	7			10	11	3		4		8	9	12							36
1	2			5	12	7	8	9	10	11	3		4			6								37
1	2			5	U	7	8	9	10	11	3		4			6								38
1	2			5		7	8	9	10	11	3		4			6		U						39
1	2			5		7	8	9	10	11	3		4			6					12			40
1	2			5		7	8	9	10	11	3				U	6					4			41
1	2			5	U	7	11	9	10		3				8	6					4			42
1	2			5	12	7		9	10		3					6					4	11		43
1	2			5		7	8	9	10		3				U	6					4	11		44
1	2			5		7	8	9	10		3				U	6					4	11		45
1	2			5		7	8	9	10		3				12	6					4	11		46
1	2			5		7	8	9	10		3				U	6					4	11		47
1	2			5		7	8	9	10		2				12	6					4	11		48
1	2	3		5		7	8	9	10				12		11	6					4			49
1	2	3		5		7	8		10		U				6	9					4	11		50
1	2	3		5		7	8	9	10						12	6					4	11		51
1	2	3		5		7	8	9			U				10	6					4	11		52
41	42	17	5	41	13	41	33	38	40	26	26	4	22	2	15	30	1	3			12	8	1	
					3			1			1		3		1	2	4		1	3	1			
		1		3		2	9	18	2	11		2			1	3					2	2		

1	2			5	6	7		9	10	11	3		4		8		12							33
1	2			5	6	7		9	10	11	3			4	8		12							34
2	2			2	2	2		2	2	2	2		1	1	2									
																	2							

1	2	3		5	6	7	8	9	10		12	4	11											11
1	2			5	6	7	8	9	10	11	3		4			12								16
1	2			5	6	7	8	9	10		3		4		U									17
1	2			5		7	8	9	10	11	3		4		6	12								23
4	4	1		4	3	4	4	4	4	3	3	1	4		1									
										1					2									
								3		1			2											

1	2	3	U	5	12	7	8	9	10	11		6	4	U			U							6
1	2	3		5	6	7	8	9	10	11	U		4	U	U		U							9
1	2		U	5	6	7	8	9	10	11	3		4	U			U		U					14
1	2	14	U	5	6	7	8	9	10	11	3		4	12			U		U					19
4	4	2		4	3	4	4	4	4	4	2	1	4											
		1			1									1										
														1			2							

1974-75

Division Two
Ground: Roker Park
Manager: Bob Stokoe

League Table

	P	W	D	L	F	A	Pts
Manchester U	42	26	9	7	66	30	61
Aston Villa	42	25	8	9	79	32	58
Norwich C	42	20	13	9	58	37	53
SUNDERLAND	42	19	13	10	65	35	51
Bristol C	42	21	8	13	47	33	50
WBA	42	18	9	15	54	42	45
Blackpool	42	14	17	11	38	33	45
Hull C	42	15	14	13	40	53	44
Fulham	42	13	16	13	44	39	42
Bolton W	42	15	12	15	45	41	42
Oxford U	42	15	12	15	41	51	42
Orient	42	11	20	11	28	39	42
Southampton	42	15	11	16	53	54	41
Notts Co	42	12	16	14	49	59	40
York C	42	14	10	18	51	55	38
Nottingham F	42	12	14	16	43	55	38
Portsmouth	42	12	13	17	44	54	37
Oldham A	42	10	15	17	40	48	35
Bristol R	42	12	11	19	42	64	35
Millwall	42	10	12	20	44	56	32
Cardiff C	42	9	14	19	36	62	32
Sheffield W	42	5	11	26	29	64	21

Division 1 Champions:
Derby County 53 pts
FA Cup Winners: West Ham Utd
League Cup Winners: Aston Villa
Texaco Cup Winners: Newcastle Utd

Did you know that?

Sunderland forward Tom Finney scored after only three minutes of his Northern Ireland debut; in Oslo against Norway on 4 September 1974 in a European Championships qualifier.

Match 1: Ternent, Moncur, Robson and Finney debuts
Match 2: Ternent last game
Match 48: Guthrie, Watson and Belfitt last games

Match No.	Date		Round	Venue	Opponents	Result	FT	HT	Pos.	Scorers	Attendance
4	Aug	17		A	Millwall	W	4-1	2-1		Kerr, Towers, Halom, Hughes	10,572
5		24		H	Southampton	W	3-1	0-1	4	Watson, Robson, Hughes	34,021
6		31		A	West Bromwich Albion	L	0-1	0-1	10		12,732
7	Sep	7		H	Bristol Rovers	W	5-1	3-0	8	Hughes (3, 1 pen), Aitken o.g., Robson	24,010
9		14		A	York City	W	1-0	0-0	3	Halom	14,964
10		21		H	Bolton Wanderers	D	0-0	0-0	4		28,453
11		24		H	Norwich City	D	0-0	0-0	3		27,737
12		28		A	Nottingham Forest	D	1-1	0-0	4	Hughes (pen)	14,885
13	Oct	2		A	Sheffield Wed.	W	2-0	1-0	2	Kerr, Hughes	11,490
14		5		H	Oxford United	W	2-0	0-0	2	Robson (2)	27,594
15		12		A	Bristol City	D	1-1	0-0	3	Halom	13,084
16		15		H	Sheffield Wed.	W	3-0	3-0	2	Hughes, Kerr, Watson	28,255
17		19		H	Aston Villa	D	0-0	0-0	2		33,232
18		26		A	Hull City	L	1-3	0-0	4	Robson	15,010
19	Nov	2		A	Cardiff City	L	0-2	0-1	3		9,883
20		9		H	Blackpool	W	1-0	0-0	3	Robson	24,939
21		16		A	Fulham	W	3-1	3-0	2	Moore o.g., Robson (2)	14,193
22		23		H	Notts County	W	3-0	1-0	2	Porterfield, Robson (2)	25,677
23		30		A	Manchester United	L	2-3	2-1	2	Hughes (2)	60,585
24	Dec	7		H	Portsmouth	W	4-1	1-0	2	Halom, Hughes (pen), Malone, Robson	25,926
25		14		H	Millwall	W	2-0	1-0	2	Robson, Kerr	26,235
26		21		A	Oldham Athletic	D	0-0	0-0	2		14,681
27		26		H	York City	W	2-0	1-0	2	Kerr (2)	35,367
28		28		A	Orient	D	1-1	1-1	2	Hughes	10,029
30	Jan	11		A	Portsmouth	L	2-4	1-0	2	Robson, Halom	14,133
31		14		A	Southampton	D	1-1	0-0	2	Hughes	16,738
32		18		H	Manchester United	D	0-0	0-0	2		45,976
34	Feb	1		A	Blackpool	L	2-3	0-2	2	Halom, Kerr	16,151
35		8		H	Cardiff City	W	3-1	0-1	2	Towers (pen), Morgan o.g., Robson	29,315
36		15		A	Notts County	D	0-0	0-0	2		15,855
37		22		H	Fulham	L	1-2	1-0	2	Towers (pen)	33,418
38	Mar	1		H	West Bromwich Albion	W	3-0	0-0	2	Halom, Robson (2)	28,867
39		8		A	Norwich City	D	0-0	0-0	2		29,285
40		15		H	Nottingham Forest	D	0-0	0-0	3		30,812
41		22		A	Bristol Rovers	L	1-2	0-2	3	Robson	13,270
42		25		A	Oldham Athletic	D	2-2	2-1	2	Robson, Watson	27,460
43		28		H	Orient	W	3-0	2-0	2	Watson, Hughes, Bolton	30,908
44		31		A	Bolton Wanderers	W	2-0	0-0	2	Hughes, Towers	18,220
45	Apr	5		H	Hull City	W	1-0	0-0	2	Halom	29,838
46		12		A	Oxford United	L	0-1	0-0	3		13,190
47		19		H	Bristol City	W	3-0	1-0	3	Bolton, Robson, Belfitt	30,530
48		26		A	Aston Villa	L	0-2	0-0	4		57,266
										Appearances	
										Sub Appearances	
										Goals	

FA Cup

Match No.	Date		Round	Venue	Opponents	Result	FT	HT		Scorers	Attendance
29	Jan	4	R3	H	Chesterfield	W	2-0	1-0		Bolton, Robson	34,268
33		24	R4	A	Middlesbrough	L	1-3	1-1		Robson	39,400
										Appearances	
										Sub Appearances	
										Goals	

League Cup

Match No.	Date		Round	Venue	Opponents	Result	FT	HT		Scorers	Attendance
8	Sep	10	R2	A	Preston North End	L	0-2	0-1			13,279
										Appearances	
										Sub Appearances	
										Goals	

Texaco Cup

Match No.	Date			Venue	Opponents	Result	FT	HT		Scorers	Attendance
1	Aug	3		H	Newcastle United	W	2-1	0-0		Halom, Kerr	28,738
2		6		H	Middlesbrough	L	0-1	0-1			22,828
3		10		A	Carlisle United	D	0-0	0-0			12,718
										Appearances	
										Sub Appearances	
										Goals	

Montgomery	Malone	Guthrie	Longhorn	Watson	Moncur	Kerr	Hughes	Halom	Robson	Towers	Belfit	Finney	Bolton	Ashurst	Porterfield	Swinburne	Tement		
1	2	3	4	5	6	7	8	9	10	11	U								4
1	2	3	4	5	6	7	8	9	10	11	12								5
1	2	3	4	5	6	7	8	9	10	11				U					6
1	2	3	4	5	6	7	8	9	10	11	U								7
1	2	3	4	5	6	7	8	9	10	11	U								9
1	2	3	4	5	6	7	8		10	11	9	12							10
1	2			4	7	8		10	11	9	U	3	5	6					11
1	2		5	4	7	8		10	11	9	U	3		6					12
1	2		5	4	7	8	9	10	11		U	3		6					13
1	2		5	4	7	8		10	11	9	12	3		6					14
1	2		5	4	7	8	9	10	11		U	3		6					15
1	2	3	5	4	7	8	9	10	11		U			6					16
1	2	3	5	4	7	8	9	10	11		U			6					17
1	2	3	5	4	7	8	9	10	11	12				6					18
1	2		5	4	7	8	9	10	11					6	U				19
1	2	3	5	4	7	8	9	10	11		U			6					20
1	2	3	5	4	7	8	9	10	11				U	6					21
1	2	3	5	4	7	8	9	10	11		U			6					22
1	2	3	5	4	7	8	9	10	11		12			6					23
1	2	3	5	4	7	8	9	10	11		U			6					24
1	2	3	6	5	4	7	8	9	10	11		U							25
1	2	3	4	5	6	7	8	9	10	11	U								26
1	2	3	6	5	4	7	8	9	10	11	12								27
1	2		6	5	4	7	8	9	10			U	3	11					28
1	2		6	5	4	7	8	9	10	11			3	12					30
	2	6			4	7	8	9	10	11	12	3	5		1				31
	2			5	4	7	8	9	10	6		11	3	12	1				32
1	2	3		5	4	7	8	9	10	11		U	6						34
1	2	6		5	4	7	8	9	10	11	U	3							35
1	2	3		5	4	7	8	9	10	11	U		6						36
1	2	3		5	4	7	8	9	10	11	12		6						37
1	2	3	6	5	4	7	8	9	10	11		U							38
1	2	3	6	5	4	7	8	9	10	11			12						39
1	2	3	4	5	4	7	8	9	10	11			12						40
1	2	3	6	5	4	7	8	9	10	11			12						41
1	2	3		5	4	7	8	9	10	11			6	U					42
1	2	3		5	4	7	8	9	10	11			6	U					43
1	2	3		5	4	7		8	9	10	11		6	12					44
1	2	3	U	5	4	7	8		10	11			6						45
1	2	3	12	5	4	7	8	9	10	11			6						46
1	2	3		5	4	7	8		10	11	9		6	U					47
1	2	3	12	5	4	7	8		10	11	9		6						48
40	42	34	15	40	42	42	36	42	42	41	6	1	20	3	14	2			
					2							2	6	3	3				
		1			4		7	15	8	19	4	1		2		1			

Montgomery	Malone	Guthrie	Longhorn	Watson	Moncur	Kerr	Hughes	Halom	Robson	Towers	Belfit	Finney	Bolton	Ashurst	Porterfield	Swinburne	Tement		
1	2			6	5	4	7	8	9	10			11	3	12				29
	2			5	4	7	8	9	10	11		U	3	6		1			33
1	2		1	2	2	2	2	2	1			1	2	1		1			
														1					
								2				1							

Montgomery	Malone	Guthrie	Longhorn	Watson	Moncur	Kerr	Hughes	Halom	Robson	Towers									
1	2	3	4	5	6	7	8	9	10	11	U								8
1	1	1	1	1	1	1	1	1	1	1	1								

Montgomery	Malone	Guthrie	Longhorn	Watson	Moncur	Kerr	Hughes	Halom	Robson	Towers	Belfit	Finney	Bolton	Ashurst	Porterfield	Swinburne	Tement		
1	2	3		5	6	7	8	9	10	11	12			U	4				1
1	2	3		5	6	7	8	9	10	11	12			U	4				2
1	2	3	4	5	6	7	8	12	10	11	9			U					3
3	3	3	1	3	3	3	3	2	3	3	1				2				
								1			1	1							
					1														

1975-76

Division Two

Ground: Roker Park

Manager: Bob Stokoe

League Table

	P	W	D	L	F	A	Pts
SUNDERLAND	42	24	8	10	67	36	56
Bristol C	42	19	15	8	59	35	53
WBA	42	20	13	9	50	33	53
Bolton W	42	20	12	10	64	38	52
Notts Co	42	19	11	12	60	41	49
Southampton	42	21	7	14	66	50	49
Luton T	42	19	10	13	61	51	48
Nottingham F	42	17	12	13	55	40	46
Charlton A	42	15	12	15	61	72	42
Blackpool	42	14	14	14	40	49	42
Chelsea	42	12	16	14	53	54	40
Fulham	42	13	14	15	45	47	40
Orient	42	13	14	15	37	39	40
Hull C	42	14	11	17	45	49	39
Blackburn R	42	12	14	16	45	50	38
Plymouth A	42	13	12	17	48	54	38
Oldham A	42	13	12	17	57	68	38
Bristol R	42	11	16	15	38	50	38
Carlisle U	42	12	13	17	45	59	37
Oxford U	42	11	11	20	39	59	33
York C	42	10	8	24	39	71	28
Portsmouth	42	9	7	26	32	61	25

Division 1 Champions: Liverpool 60 pts

FA Cup Winners: Southampton

League Cup Winners: Manchester City

Anglo Scottish Cup Winners: Middlesbrough

Did you know that?

The opening game of the season, an Anglo-Scottish cup tie at Middlesbrough, on 2 August 1975, was the earliest date that Sunderland had started a campaign.

Match 1: Clarke and Gibb made debuts
Match 3: Holden mde debut
Match 19: Henderson made debut
Match 25: Rowell made debut
Match 26: Porterfield last game
Match 27: Mitchell last game
Match 30: Greenwood made debut
Match 39: Finney last game
Match 40: Train made debut
Match 42: Halom last game
Match 49: Promotion confirmed

Match No.	Date	Round	Venue	Opponents	Result	FT	HT	Pos.	Scorers	Attendance
4	Aug 16		H	Chelsea	W	2-1	1-1		Robson, Longhorn	28,689
5	19		A	Bristol City	L	0-3	0-2	5		12,199
6	23		A	Oxford United	D	1-1	0-1	10	Moncur	9,069
7	26		H	Fulham	W	2-0	2-0	2	Holden, Gibb	25,450
8	30		H	Blackpool	W	2-0	1-0	2	Towers (2)	23,576
9	Sep 6		A	Plymouth Argyle	L	0-1	0-0	4		18,304
11	13		A	West Bromwich Albion	W	2-0	0-0	3	Halom, Hughes	25,159
12	20		A	Blackburn Rovers	W	1-0	1-0	2	Towers	15,773
13	23		A	Carlisle United	W	3-2	2-0	2	Robson, Towers (pen), Hughes	28,185
14	27		H	Notts County	W	4-0	1-0	1	Robson (2), Kerr, Halom	27,565
15	Oct 4		A	Portsmouth	D	0-0	0-0	1		13,098
16	11		H	Orient	W	3-1	1-0	1	Towers (pen), Hughes, Robson	28,327
17	18		A	Bristol Rovers	L	0-1	0-1	1		13,577
18	25		H	Luton Town	W	2-0	0-0	1	Kerr, Robson	28,338
19	Nov 1		A	York City	W	4-1	3-0	1	Hughes, Hunter o.g., Towers (2, 1 pen)	15,232
20	8		H	Nottingham Forest	W	3-0	2-0	1	Robson, Halom (2)	31,227
21	15		A	Charlton Athletic	W	2-1	1-1	1	Holden (2)	22,307
22	22		H	Bristol Rovers	D	1-1	0-1	1	Kerr	31,356
23	29		H	Oldham Athletic	W	2-0	1-0	1	Robson (2)	28,220
24	Dec 6		A	Southampton	L	0-4	0-0	1		17,598
25	13		H	Oxford United	W	1-0	0-0	1	Porterfield	22,501
26	20		A	Chelsea	L	0-1	0-0	1		22,802
27	26		H	Hull City	W	3-1	2-1	1	Holden, Finney, Henderson	35,210
28	27		A	Bolton Wanderers	L	1-2	1-0	1	Dunne o.g.	42,680
30	Jan 10		A	West Bromwich Albion	D	0-0	0-0	1		25,399
31	17		H	Plymouth Argyle	W	2-1	0-1	1	Holden, Kerr	29,737
33	Feb 7		A	Fulham	L	0-2	0-1	3		12,839
36	21		H	Charlton Athletic	W	4-1	1-1	1	Holden, Moncur, Robson, Towers	30,173
37	24		A	Carlisle United	D	2-2	2-1	2	Towers (pen), Holden	20,001
38	28		A	Luton Town	L	0-2	0-0	3		15,338
40	Mar 13		A	Orient	W	2-0	2-0	3	Kerr (2)	7,954
41	17		A	Nottingham Forest	L	1-2	1-2	3	Holden	16,995
42	20		A	Oldham Athletic	D	1-1	1-1	2	Hughes	13,704
43	23		H	Bristol City	D	1-1	0-0	2	Holden	38,395
44	27		A	Southampton	W	3-0	1-0	2	Greenwood (2), Holden	34,946
45	30		H	York City	W	1-0	1-0	2	Kerr	33,462
46	Apr 3		A	Notts County	D	0-0	0-0	2		14,811
47	10		H	Blackburn Rovers	W	3-0	1-0	1	Holden, Parkes o.g., Robson	33,523
48	17		A	Hull City	W	4-1	3-1	1	Robson, Rowell, Dobson o.g., Holden	21,296
49	19		H	Bolton Wanderers	W	2-1	2-0	1	Towers (pen), Robson	51,983
50	20		A	Blackpool	L	0-1	0-1	1		16,768
51	24		H	Portsmouth	W	2-0	2-0	1	Bolton, Hughes	40,515

Appearances
Sub Appearances
Goals

FA Cup

Match No.	Date	Round	Venue	Opponents	Result	FT	HT	Scorers	Attendance
29	Jan 3	R3	H	Oldham Athletic	W	2-0	1-0	Holden, Robson	29,226
32	Feb 3	R4	H	Hull City	W	1-0	1-0	Finney	32,320
34	14	R5	A	Stoke City	D	0-0	0-0		41,176
35	18	R5r	H	Stoke City	W	2-1	0-0	Holden, Robson	47,583
39	Mar 6	R6	H	Crystal Palace	L	0-1	0-0		50,850

Appearances
Sub Appearances
Goals

League Cup

Match No.	Date	Round	Venue	Opponents	Result	FT	HT	Scorers	Attendance
10	Sep 9	R2	A	Notts County	L	1-2	1-1	Holden	10,384

Appearances
Sub Appearances
Goals

Anglo Scottish Cup

Match No.	Date	Venue	Opponents	Result	FT	HT	Scorers	Attendance
1	Aug 2	A	Middlesbrough	L	2-3	0-0	Longhorn (pen), Gibb	12,849
2	6	A	Newcastle United	W	2-0	2-0	Robson, Halom	20,088
3	9	H	Carlisle United	L	0-1	0-0		12,673

Appearances
Sub Appearances
Goals

	Swinburne	Ashurst	Bolton	Longhorn	Clarke	Moncur	Kerr	Gibb	Halom	Robson	Porterfield	Holden	Montgomery	Malone	Towers	Hughes	Henderson	Rowell	Finney	Mitchell	Greenwood	Train	
1	2	3	4	5	6	7	8	9	10	11	12												4
1	2	3	4	5	6	7	12	9	10	11	8												5
		3		5	6	7	4	9	10	12	8	1	2	11									6
		3		5	6	7	8	12	10	11	9	1	2	4									7
		3		5	6	7	4	12	9	10	8	1	2	11									8
		3		5	6	7	4	8	10	12	9	1	2	11									9
		3	4	5	6	7		8	10	11	9	1	2		12								11
		3		5	6	7		9	10	11	U	1	2	4	8								12
		3		5	6	7		9	10	11	U	1	2	4	8								13
		3		5	6	7		9	10	11	U	1	2	4	8								14
		3		5		7		9	10	11	U	1	2	4	8								15
	6	3		5		7	U		10	11	9	1	2	4	8								16
		3		5	6	7		9	10	11	12	1	2	4	8								17
	3			5	6	7		9	10	11	12	1	2	4	8								18
				5	6	7		9	10	11	U	1	2	4	8	3							19
				5	6	7		9	10	11	U	1	2	4	8	3							20
				5	6	7		9	10	11	12	1	2	4	8	3							21
				5	6	7	U	9	10	11	8	1	2	4		3							22
			U	5	6	7		9	10	11	8	1	2	4		3							23
	12			5	6	7		9	10	11	8	1	2	4		3							24
			10	5	6	7				11	8	1	2	4		3	12						25
		3		5	6	7		9	10	11	12	1	2	4			8						26
	6	3		5		7			10		9	1	2	4		11		8	12				27
	6	3		5		7			10		9	1	2	4		11	U	8					28
		3		5	6	7			10		9	1	2	4			8	12		11			30
		3	4	5	6	7		9	10		8	1	2			12			11				31
		3	12	5	6			8	10		9	1	2	4			7		11				33
	8	3		5	6	7			10		9	1	2	4			11	12					36
	8	3		5	6	7			10		9	1	2	4			11	U					37
	8	3		5	6	7			10		9	1	2	4			11	12					38
		3	12	5	6	7			10		9	1	2	4			11	8					40
	5	3	4		6	7			10		9	1	2		12		11	8					41
	5	3			6	7		12			9	1	2	10		4		11	8				42
	5	3			6	7			10		9	1	2		8		U		11	4			43
	5	3			6	7			10		9	1	2	4		U		11	8				44
	5	3			6	7			10		9	1	2	4	12			11	8				45
	5	3			6	7			10		9	1	2	4	U			11	8				46
	5	3			6	7			10		9	1	2	4	U			11	8				47
	5	3			6	7			10		9	1	2			8		11	4				48
	5	3			6	7			10		9	1	2	4	12			11	8				49
1	5	3		6					10		9			4	11	2	7		12	8			50
1	5	3			6	7			10		9		2	8	11				U	4			51
4	20	34	6	31	39	40	5	21	40	20	31	38	39	34	14	11	3	7		13	12		
	1						1	3		2	5				3	2	1	1	3				
		1			2	1		4	13	1	12			10	6	1	1	1	2				

	Swinburne	Ashurst	Bolton	Longhorn	Clarke	Moncur	Kerr	Gibb	Halom	Robson	Porterfield	Holden	Montgomery	Malone	Towers	Hughes	Henderson	Rowell	Finney	Mitchell	Greenwood	Train	
	U	3		5	6	7			10		9	1	2	4		8		11					29
		3		5	6	7		8	10	U	9	1	2	4				11					32
	8	3		5	6	7			10		9	1	2	4	U			11					34
	8	3		5	6	7		12	10		9	1	2	4				11					35
		3	8		5	6	7			10		9	1	2	4	12			11				39
	2	5	1	5	5	5		1	5	5	5	5	5	5	1		5						
								1								1							
									2		2							1					

	Swinburne	Ashurst	Bolton	Longhorn	Clarke	Moncur	Kerr	Gibb	Halom	Robson	Porterfield	Holden	Montgomery	Malone	Towers	Hughes	Henderson	Rowell	Finney	Mitchell	Greenwood	Train	
	2	3		5	6	7		8	10	11	9	1		4	12								10
	1		1		1	1		1	1	1	1			1									
													1										
									1														

	Swinburne	Ashurst	Bolton	Longhorn	Clarke	Moncur	Kerr	Gibb	Halom	Robson	Porterfield	Holden	Montgomery	Malone	Towers	Hughes	Henderson	Rowell	Finney	Mitchell	Greenwood	Train	
J	6	3	4	5		7	12	9	10	11		1	2			8							1
1	2	3	8	5	6	7	4	9	10	11		U						12					2
1		3		5	6	7	8	U	10	11	9	U	2	4									3
2	2	3	2	3	2	3	2	2	3	3	1	2	1			1		1					
					1											1							
		1			1	1																	

1976-77

Division One

Ground: Roker Park

Managers: Bob Stokoe, Ian McFarlane & Jimmy Adamson

League Table

	P	W	D	L	F	A	Pos
Liverpool	42	23	11	8	62	33	57
Manchester C	42	21	14	7	60	34	56
Ipswich T	42	22	8	12	66	39	52
Aston Villa	42	22	7	13	76	50	51
Newcastle U	42	18	13	11	64	49	49
Manchester U	42	18	11	13	71	62	47
WBA	42	16	13	13	62	56	45
Arsenal	42	16	11	15	64	59	43
Everton	42	14	14	14	62	64	42
Leeds U	42	15	12	15	48	51	42
Leicester C	42	12	18	12	47	60	42
Middlesbrough	42	14	13	15	40	45	41
Birmingham C	42	13	12	17	63	61	38
QPR	42	13	12	17	47	52	38
Derby Co	42	9	19	14	50	55	37
Norwich C	42	14	9	19	47	64	37
West Ham U	42	11	14	17	46	65	36
Bristol C	42	11	13	18	38	48	35
Coventry C	42	10	15	17	48	59	35
SUNDERLAND	42	11	12	19	46	54	34
Stoke C	42	10	14	18	28	51	34
Tottenham H	42	12	9	21	48	72	33

FA Cup Winners: Manchester Utd
League Cup Winners: Aston Villa

Did you know that?

Sunderland had their worst goal drought in their history; 10 consecutive League games (1020 mins, 23 November to 11 February). However 17 goals were scored in the next four games.

Match 6: Swinburne and Moncur last games
Match 9: Holton and Foggon made debuts
Match 10: Lee made debut
Match 12: Montgomery last game
Match 13: Siddall made debut, Longhorn last game & Bob Stokoe last game as Sunderland manager
Match 14: Ian McFarlane first game as caretaker manager
Match 20: Ian McFarlane last game as caretaker manager
Match 21: Jimmy Adamson first game as Sunderland manager
Match 22: Brown made debut & Foggon last game
Match 23: Gilbert made debut & Malone last game
Match 25: Gibb last game
Match 26: Docherty made debut
Match 27: Train and Hughes last games
Match 28: Elliott and Arnott made debuts & Holton last game
Match 35: Waldron made debut
Match 38: Collins made debut
Match 41: Coady made debut
Match 47: Towers last game
Match 48: Relegation confirmed

Match No.	Date		Round	Venue	Opponents	Result	FT	HT	Pos.	Scorers	Attendance
1	Aug	21		A	Stoke City	D	0-0	0-0			27,424
2		24		H	Leicester City	D	0-0	0-0	13		36,668
3		28		H	Arsenal	D	2-2	2-2	16	Robson, Holden	41,111
5	Sep	4		A	Bristol City	L	1-4	1-3	17	Robson	20,865
6		11		A	Middlesbrough	L	1-2	1-0	20	Greenwood	29,000
7		18		H	Manchester City	L	0-2	0-0	22		37,395
9		25		A	West Ham United	D	1-1	0-0	22	Bolton	24,319
10	Oct	2		H	Everton	L	0-1	0-1	22		34,670
13		16		H	Aston Villa	L	0-1	0-0	22		31,578
14		23		A	Queens Park Rangers	L	0-2	0-1	22		22,408
15		30		A	Coventry City	W	2-1	1-0	21	Lee, Hughes	17,184
16	Nov	6		H	Liverpool	L	0-1	0-0	22		39,956
17		10		A	Manchester United	D	3-3	0-2	21	Lee (2), Hughes	42,685
18		20		H	Tottenham Hotspur	W	2-1	0-1	20	Train, Lee	30,324
19		23		A	Ipswich Town	L	1-3	1-3	20	Hughes (pen)	24,605
20		27		A	Derby County	L	0-1	0-1	21		25,423
21	Dec	11		A	Birmingham City	L	0-2	0-1	21		24,597
22		18		H	Norwich City	L	0-1	0-1	22		23,468
23		27		A	Newcastle United	L	0-2	0-1	22		50,048
24		29		H	Leeds United	L	0-1	0-0	22		26,999
25	Jan	1		A	Liverpool	L	0-2	0-1	22		44,687
26		3		H	Coventry City	L	0-1	0-0	22		24,942
29		15		A	Leicester City	L	0-2	0-1	22		16,051
30		22		H	Stoke City	D	0-0	0-0	22		22,901
31	Feb	5		A	Arsenal	D	0-0	0-0	22		30,925
32		11		H	Bristol City	W	1-0	0-0	22	Holden	21,407
33		19		H	Middlesbrough	W	4-0	1-0	22	Lee, Holden, Arnott, Rowell	33,205
34		22		H	West Bromwich Albion	W	6-1	3-0	21	Lee (3), Elliott, Holden, Rowell	30,317
35	Mar	5		H	West Ham United	W	6-0	3-0	18	Holden (2), Rowell (2), Kerr, Lee	35,357
36		9		A	Manchester City	L	0-1	0-1	19		44,439
37		19		H	Ipswich Town	W	1-0	0-0	19	Waldron	35,376
38		23		A	Aston Villa	L	1-4	0-2	21	Holden	34,458
39	Apr	2		H	Queens Park Rangers	W	1-0	0-0	21	Lee	27,550
40		8		H	Newcastle United	D	2-2	1-0	20	Arnott, Lee	46,056
41		9		A	Leeds United	D	1-1	0-0	20	Lee	32,966
42		11		H	Manchester United	W	2-1	2-1	16	Arnott, Towers (pen)	38,785
43		16		A	Tottenham Hotspur	D	1-1	0-0	17	Holden	34,185
44		23		H	Derby County	D	1-1	0-1	18	Towers (pen)	35,490
45		30		A	West Bromwich Albion	W	3-2	2-2	19	Towers (2, 1 pen), Lee	21,859
46	May	7		H	Birmingham City	W	1-0	0-0	16	Holden	34,193
47		14		A	Norwich City	D	2-2	0-0	16	Rowell, Kerr	27,787
48		19		A	Everton	L	0-2	0-1	20		36,075

Appearances
Sub Appearances
Goals

FA Cup

27	Jan	8	R3	H	Wrexham	D	2-2	0-1		Holton, Holden	23,356
28		12	R3r	A	Wrexham	L	0-1	0-0			16,023

Appearances
Sub Appearances
Goals

League Cup

4	Aug	31	R2	H	Luton Town	W	3-1	3-1		Hughes (2), Robson	22,390
8	Sep	22	R3	A	Manchester United	D	2-2	1-1		Train, Towers	46,170
11	Oct	4	R3r	H	Manchester United	D	2-2 (aet)	1-0		Towers (pen), Train	30,831
12		6	R3r2	A	Manchester United	L	0-1	0-0			47,689

Appearances
Sub Appearances
Goals

	Montgomery	Malone	Bolton	Towers	Clarke	Moncur	Kerr	Ashurst	Hughes	Robson	Train	Holden	Greenwood	Swinburne	Longhorn	Rowell	Holton	Foggon	Lee	Siddall	Henderson	Gibb	Brown	Gilbert	Docherty	Elliott	Arnott	Waldron	Collins	Coady	
1	2	3	4	5	6	7	8	9	10	11	U																				1
1	2	3	4	5	6	7	12	8	10	11	9																				2
1	2	3	4	5	6	7		8	10	11	9	12																			3
		3	4	5	6	7	2	9	10	8		11	1		U																5
		3		5	6	7	2		10	11	8	9	1	4	12																6
1	2	3	4	5				6	8	10	11		9		U	7															7
1		3	4	5			2	8	10	7		9			12	6	11														9
1		3	4	5			2	8	10	11	12				6	7	9														10
		3	4	5		7	2	9		12			8		6	10	11	1													13
		3	4	5			2			10	8				7	6	11	9	1	12											14
	2	3	4	5		12		8		10	11				6	7	9	1													15
	2	3	4	5		U		8		10	7				6	11	9	1													16
	2	3	4	5		7		8		10	11				6	12	9	1													17
		3	4	5		7		8		10	11		12		6		9	1	2												18
		3		5		7		8		10	11		4	6			9	1	2	12											19
		3		5		7		8		10	U		4	6			9	1	2	11											20
		3	4	5		7		8		10	11		12	6			9	1	2												21
	2	3	4	5		7		8					12	6	11		9	1		10											22
	2	3	4	5		7		8					11	6			9	1		10	12										23
		3		5		7		8		4		11	9	6			1	2	12	10											24
		3		5			4			7		11	9	6			12	1	2	8	10										25
		3		5		7	6	12		8	9	11	4				1			10	2										26
		3		5		7	4			9			8			10	1		12	2	6	11									29
		3	4	5		7	6			10			11		9	1		12	2	8											30
		3		5		7	6			9			11		10	1		12	2	4	8										31
		3	4	5		7	6			9			11		10	1	2			8	12										32
		3		5		7	6			9			11		10	1		12	2	8	4										33
		3			7	6		9		11		10	1	5	U		2	8	4											34
		3			7	6		9		11		10	1			12	2	8	4	5											35
		3			7	6		9		11		10	1		12	2	8	4	5												36
		3			7	6		10		11		9	1			2	8	4	5	U											37
		3			7	6		9				10	1	U		2	8	4	5	11											38
		3			7	6		9		11		10	1			2	8	4	5	12											39
		3			7	6		9				10	1	U		2	5	4		8											40
		3	4			6				10		9	1	U		2	8	7			5										41
		3	7			6		9		11		10	1			2	8	4	5	12											42
		3	7			6		9		11		10	1			2	8	4	5	U											43
		3	7			6		9		11		10	1			2	8	4	5	U											44
		3	4			6		9		11		10	1		U	2	7	8	5												45
		3	7		12	6		9		11		10	1			2	8	4	5												46
		3	7		12	6		9		11		10	1			2	8	4	5												47
		3	U			7	6			9			11		10	1			2	8	4	5									48
6	9	42	25	27	5	28	30	18	8	19	24	14	2	2	27	15	7	32	34	8	2	5		20	19	19	12	2	1		
			1	4			3	1	1		2				5			1	1		1	2	6	1		1		1	1		
							2			3	2	1	9	1		5		13							1	3	1				

	3		5		7	2	8		4	9			11	6			1	12		10											27
		3		5		7	2		9				11	6		10	1	4			8	12									28
	2		2		2	2	1		2				2	2		1	2	1		1											
																	1			1											
								1						1																	

1	2	3	4	5	6	7	U	8	10	11	9																				4
1	2	3	4	5			6	8	10	7		9			11						U										8
		3	4	5				2	8	10	7		9		12	6	11														11
	2	3	4	5		9		8	10	7			U	6	11																12
4	3	4	4	4	1	2	2	4	4	4	1	2			1	2	2														
			2				2	1	2						1																

When Bobby Kerr missed the game against Manchester City on 18 September 1977 it broke a run of 114 consecutive home appearances. This record will probably never be broken (92 League, 11 FA Cup, 4 League Cup, 2 ECWC, 2 Anglo Italian, 2 Texaco Cup and 1 Anglo Scottish).

467

1977-78

Division Two

Ground: Roker Park

Manager: Jimmy Adamson

League Table

	P	W	D	L	F	A	Pts
Bolton W	42	24	10	8	63	33	58
Southampton	42	22	13	7	70	39	57
Tottenham H	42	20	16	6	83	49	56
Brighton & HA	42	22	12	8	63	38	56
Blackburn R	42	16	13	13	56	60	45
SUNDERLAND	42	14	16	12	67	59	44
Stoke C	42	16	10	16	53	49	42
Oldham A	42	13	16	13	54	58	42
Crystal Palace	42	13	15	14	50	47	41
Fulham	42	14	13	15	49	49	41
Burnley	42	15	10	17	56	64	40
Sheffield U	42	16	8	18	62	73	40
Luton T	42	14	10	18	54	52	38
Orient	42	10	18	14	43	49	38
Notts Co	42	11	16	15	54	62	38
Millwall	42	12	14	16	49	57	38
Charlton A	42	13	12	17	55	68	38
Bristol R	42	13	12	17	61	77	38
Cardiff C	42	13	12	17	51	71	38
Blackpool	42	12	13	17	59	60	37
Mansfield T	42	10	11	21	49	69	31
Hull C	42	8	12	22	34	52	28

Division 1 Champions: Nottingham Forest 64 pts

FA Cup Winners: Ipswich Town

League Cup Winners: Nottingham Forest

Did you know that?

Liverpool born forward Roly Gregoire became the first black player to play for Sunderland when he made his debut in a 2-0 home victory over Hull City on 2 January 1978.

Match 1: Rostron made debut
Match 8: Stronach made debut
Match 10: Collins and Waldron last games
Match 11: Armstrong made debut
Match 20: Entwistle made debut
Match 26: Gregoire made debut
Match 28: Hindmarch made debut
Match 30: Holden last game
Match 33: Weir only game & Stronach last game
Match 42: Armstong last game

Match No.	Date	Round	Venue	Opponents	Result	FT	HT	Pos.	Scorers	Attendance
1	Aug 20		A	Hull City	L	0-3	0-0			16,189
2	23		H	Burnley	W	3-0	2-0	10	Holden (2), Stevenson o.g.	31,405
3	27		H	Orient	D	1-1	0-1	11	Ashurst (pen)	28,261
5	Sep 3		A	Sheffield United	D	1-1	0-0	12	Lee	17,994
6	10		A	Crystal Palace	D	2-2	1-2	12	Rowell, Rostron	21,305
8	17		H	Bolton Wanderers	L	0-2	0-1	15		30,342
9	24		A	Stoke City	D	0-0	0-0	15		18,820
10	Oct 1		H	Brighton & Hove Albion	L	0-2	0-2	17		24,013
11	4		H	Cardiff City	D	1-1	0-1	17	Greenwood	18,484
12	8		A	Southampton	L	2-4	2-3	18	Rowell, Lee	17,696
13	15		H	Millwall	W	2-0	0-0	17	Arnott, Rowell	22,181
14	22		A	Mansfield Town	W	2-1	1-1	14	Rostron (2)	12,827
15	29		H	Oldham Athletic	W	3-1	1-0	11	Elliott, Ashurst, Lee	24,712
16	Nov 5		A	Fulham	D	3-3	1-2	10	Greenwood, Rowell, Arnott	10,548
17	12		H	Bristol Rovers	W	5-1	2-0	8	Arnott, Greenwood, Henderson, Elliott, Lee	24,633
18	19		A	Notts County	D	2-2	2-1	7	Kerr, Rostron	12,247
19	26		H	Luton Town	D	1-1	0-1	9	Bolton	26,915
20	Dec 3		A	Charlton Athletic	L	2-3	2-1	10	Greenwood, Entwistle	12,761
21	10		H	Tottenham Hotspur	L	1-2	1-1	12	Rowell (pen)	31,960
22	17		A	Bristol Rovers	L	2-3	0-2	13	Lee, Rowell (pen)	6,516
23	26		H	Blackpool	W	2-1	1-0	12	Rowell (2, 1 pen)	30,628
24	27		A	Blackburn Rovers	D	1-1	0-0	12	Gilbert	22,860
25	31		A	Burnley	D	0-0	0-0	12		12,649
26	Jan 2		H	Hull City	W	2-0	0-0	10	Rowell (2)	29,456
28	14		H	Orient	D	2-2	2-0	11	Clarke, Rowell	6,737
29	21		H	Sheffield United	W	5-1	1-0	8	Kerr, Rostron, Elliott, Rowell (2, 1 pen)	22,634
30	28		A	Cardiff City	L	2-5	1-3	8	Clarke, Rowell (pen)	8,459
31	Feb 25		A	Brighton & Hove Albion	L	1-2	1-0	10	Clarke	25,771
32	Mar 4		H	Southampton	D	0-0	0-0	10		20,975
33	7		A	Bolton Wanderers	L	0-2	0-0	11		20,972
34	14		H	Crystal Palace	D	0-0	0-0	12		15,962
35	18		H	Mansfield Town	W	1-0	1-0	11	Lee	14,033
36	24		A	Oldham Athletic	D	1-1	1-0	11	Lee	10,086
37	25		H	Blackburn Rovers	L	0-1	0-0	12		16,900
38	27		A	Blackpool	D	1-1	0-0	11	Docherty	9,872
39	Apr 1		H	Fulham	D	2-2	1-0	11	Docherty, Lee	11,951
40	4		H	Stoke City	W	1-0	1-0	8	Kerr	11,161
41	8		A	Luton Town	W	3-1	2-0	7	Lee, Rowell, Gregoire	7,616
42	15		H	Notts County	W	3-1	3-0	7	Rostron, Kerr, Lee	14,673
43	18		A	Millwall	L	1-3	0-3	7	Rowell	7,258
44	22		A	Tottenham Hotspur	W	3-2	1-1	6	Rowell, Lee (2)	38,220
45	29		H	Charlton Athletic	W	3-0	2-0	6	Bolton (2), Rowell	16,718

Appearances
Sub Appearances
Goals

FA Cup

| 27 | Jan 7 | R3 | H | Bristol Rovers | L | 0-1 | 0-1 | | | 26,214 |

Appearances
Sub Appearances
Goals

League Cup

| 4 | Aug 30 | R2 | H | Middlesbrough | D | 2-2 | 0-1 | | Holden, Rowell | 26,597 |
| 7 | Sep 13 | R2r | A | Middlesbrough | L | 0-1 | 0-0 | | | 29,572 |

Appearances
Sub Appearances
Goals

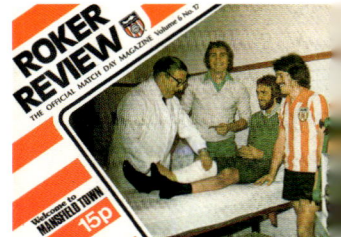

	Siddall	Docherty	Bolton	Arnott	Waldron	Ashurst	Kerr	Elliott	Holden	Lee	Rowell	Rostron	Brown	Collins	Henderson	Stronach	Greenwood	Armstrong	Entwistle	Clarke	Gilbert	Gregoire	Hindmarch	Weir	
1	2	3	4	5	6	7	8	9	10	11	12														1
1	2	3	4	5	6		8	9	10	11	7	U													2
1	2	3	4	5	6		8	10		9	7	11	12												3
1	2	3	U	5	6	7	8	9	10	4	11														5
1	2	3	U	5	6	7	8		9	10	11		4												6
1	2	3		5	6	12	8		10	11	7	9		4											8
1	2	3		5	6	12	8	9	10	4	7		11												9
1	2	3		5	6		8	9	10	11	7		4		12										10
1		3	8		6	4	5		10	11	7		2		9	12									11
1		3	8		6	4	5	12	10	11	7		2		9										12
1		3	4		6	7	5	U	10	11	8		2		9										13
1		3	8		6	4	5	U	10	11	7		2		9										14
1		3	4		6	7	5	U	10	11	8		2		9										15
1		3	4		6	7	5		10	11	8		2		9			U							16
1		3	8		6	4	5	U	10	11	7		2		9										17
1		3	8		6	4	5	10		11	7		2		9	U									18
1		3	8		6	4	5	10		11	7		2		9		U								19
1		3	8		6	4	5			11	7		2		9	10	12								20
1		3	8		6	4	12			11	7		2		9	10	5								21
1		3	8		6	4			12	11	7		2		9	10	5								22
1		3	8		6	4				12	7		2		9	10	5								23
1	5		8		6	4			12	11	7		2		9	10		3							24
1	5	3	8		6	7			12	11	10		2		9			4							25
1	5	3	8		6		12	9		11			2			10	4		7						26
1					4	8	10	9	11	7			3			5	2	U	6						28
1				6	4	8	9	10	11	7	U		2			5	3								29
1	U			4	8	9	10	11	7				2			5	3		6						30
1	11			6	4	8		10		7			2			9	5	3	12						31
1	10	2			4	6		9	11	7	8			12			5	3							32
1	10	2			4	8			11		9			7		12	5	3		6					33
1	6			7	4	8		10	11		9		2			12	5	3							34
1	6	3			7	4	12		9	11			2			8	5	10							35
1	10	3	8		6	4	U		9				2			7	5	11							36
1	11	3	8		6	7			9	12			2			10	5	4							37
1	10	3	U		6	4			9			11	2			7	5	8							38
1	10	3			6	4	U		9	8			2			7	5	11							39
1	8	3			6	4			9	11	10		2			7	5	12							40
1	10	3			6	4			9	7	11					8	5	3	12						41
1	10	3			6	4			9	8	7		2			12	5		11						42
1	10	3			6	4			9	11	7		2			U	5		8						43
1	10	3			6	4			9	11	7		2				5		8						44
1	10	3			6	4	12		9	11	7		2				5		8						44
1	10	3			6	4	12		9	11	7		2				5		8						45
42	26	36	21	8	38	36	25	11	32	38	33	6	2	32	2	15	7	7	23	14	5	2	1		
					2	4	2	4	1	1		1			1	1	4		1	1	2				
	2	3	3		2	4	3	2	12	18	6		1		4		1	3	1	1					

1	4	3	8		6				10	11	7		2			9	5		12						27
1	1	1	1		1				1	1	1		1			1	1								
																			1						

1	2	3		5	6	7	8	9		11	10	4	12												4
1	2	3	12	5	6	4	8		10	11	7		9												7
2	2	2		2	2	2	2	1	1	2	2	1	1												
		1										1													
						1			1																

Barry Siddall was ever present during 1977-78 season.

1978-79

Division Two

Ground: Roker Park

Managers: Jimmy Adamson, Dave Merrington & Billy Elliott

League Table

	P	W	D	L	F	A	Pts
Crystal Palace	42	19	19	4	51	24	57
Brighton & HA	42	23	10	9	72	39	56
Stoke C	42	20	16	6	58	31	56
SUNDERLAND	42	22	11	9	70	44	55
West Ham U	42	18	14	10	70	39	50
Notts Co	42	14	16	12	48	60	44
Preston NE	42	12	18	12	59	57	42
Newcastle U	42	17	8	17	51	55	42
Cardiff C	42	16	10	16	56	70	42
Fulham	42	13	15	14	50	47	41
Orient	42	15	10	17	51	51	40
Cambridge U	42	12	16	14	44	52	40
Burnley	42	14	12	16	51	62	40
Oldham A	42	13	13	16	52	61	39
Wrexham	42	12	14	16	45	42	38
Bristol R	42	14	10	18	48	60	38
Leicester C	42	10	17	15	43	52	37
Luton T	42	13	10	19	60	57	36
Charlton A	42	11	13	18	60	69	35
Sheffield U	42	11	12	19	52	69	34
Millwall	42	11	10	21	42	61	32
Blackburn R	42	10	10	22	41	72	30

Division 1 Champions: Liverpool 68 pts

FA Cup Winners: Arsenal

League Cup Winners: Nottingham Forest

Anglo Scottish Cup Winners: Burnley

Did you know that?

Sunderland won 2-1 at Burnley on 23 September 1978 even though they were down to nine men for the whole of the second half. Fullbacks Henderson and Bolton had been sent off in the 43rd & 45th minutes respectively.

Match 3: Watson and Chisholm debuts
Match 7: Kerr last game
Match 8: Buckley made debut
Match 15: Jimmy Adamson last game as Sunderland manager
Match 16: Dave Merrington first game as caretaker manager
Match 23: Dave Merrington last game as caretaker manager
Match 24: Greenwood last game & Billy Elliott first game of his second spell as Sunderland manager
Match 35: Watson last game
Match 39: Henderson last game
Match 40: Whitworth made debut
Match 45: Gregoire last game
Match 49: Docherty last game & Billy Elliott last game as Sunderland manager

Match No.	Date	Round	Venue	Opponents	Result	FT	HT	Pos.	Scorers	Attendance
4	Aug 19		H	Charlton Athletic	W	1-0	1-0		Rowell	20,486
5	22		A	Orient	L	0-3	0-1	12		7,373
6	26		A	Brighton & HA	L	0-2	0-1	19		19,885
8	Sep 2		H	Preston North End	W	3-1	1-0	13	Entwistle, Docherty, Greenwood	16,819
9	9		A	Crystal Palace	D	1-1	0-0	13	Entwistle	21,112
10	16		H	Fulham	D	1-1	0-0	13	Brown	17,976
11	23		A	Burnley	W	2-1	0-0	8	Rowell (2, 1 pen)	12,964
12	30		H	West Ham United	W	2-1	1-0	5	Rowell (2, 1 pen)	23,676
13	Oct 7		A	Sheffield United	L	2-3	1-0	11	Rowell, Lee	18,873
14	14		H	Newcastle United	D	1-1	0-1	10	Greenwood	35,405
15	21		H	Millwall	W	3-2	2-1	8	Rowell (2), Brown	19,962
16	28		A	Oldham Athletic	D	0-0	0-0	9		9,857
17	Nov 4		H	Stoke City	L	0-1	0-0	10		25,170
18	11		A	Charlton Athletic	W	2-1	0-0	9	Entwistle, Rowell	11,451
19	18		H	Brighton & HA	W	2-1	1-1	6	Rowell, Clarke	22,738
20	21		A	Preston North End	L	1-3	1-1	7	Entwistle	13,204
21	25		A	Luton Town	W	3-0	2-0	6	Rowell (2), Entwistle	10,249
22	Dec 2		H	Bristol Rovers	W	5-0	1-0	4	Entwistle (3), Lee, Rowell	18,864
23	9		A	Cardiff City	D	1-1	1-1	4	Rostron	7,178
24	16		H	Cambridge United	L	0-2	0-1	5		20,841
25	23		A	Notts County	D	1-1	1-0	6	Entwistle	11,281
26	26		H	Leicester City	D	1-1	0-1	5	Clarke	24,544
28	Jan 17		A	Blackburn Rovers	D	1-1	1-1	5	Rowell	8,130
29	20		A	Fulham	D	2-2	1-0	5	Bolton, Rowell (pen)	11,260
30	Feb 3		H	Burnley	W	3-1	0-1	5	Rowell (pen), Rostron, Entwistle	23,030
31	10		A	West Ham United	D	3-3	2-1	5	Lee, Rostron (2)	24,998
33	24		A	Newcastle United	W	4-1	2-0	5	Rowell (3, 1 pen), Entwistle	34,733
35	Mar 3		A	Millwall	W	1-0	0-0	5	Entwistle	8,038
36	7		H	Wrexham	W	1-0	1-0	4	Bolton	25,017
37	10		H	Oldham Athletic	W	3-0	2-0	3	Rowell (pen), Bolton, Rostron	25,090
38	14		H	Crystal Palace	L	1-2	1-2	4	Rostron	34,986
39	24		H	Orient	W	1-0	1-0	4	Rowell	21,189
40	27		A	Stoke City	W	1-0	1-0	4	Docherty	24,023
41	31		H	Luton Town	W	1-0	0-0	3	Rostron	23,358
42	Apr 7		A	Bristol Rovers	D	0-0	0-0	4		8,003
43	13		H	Notts County	W	3-0	2-0	2	Lee, Brown, Chisholm	34,027
44	14		A	Leicester City	W	2-1	0-0	2	Docherty, Brown	20,740
45	16		H	Blackburn Rovers	L	0-1	0-1	3		35,005
46	21		A	Cambridge United	W	2-0	0-0	3	Lee, Docherty	7,725
47	25		H	Sheffield United	W	6-2	2-1	1	Rostron (3, 2 pens), Lee, Brown, Gilbert	29,822
48	28		H	Cardiff City	L	1-2	0-1	3	Ashurst	36,526
49	May 5		A	Wrexham	W	2-1	0-0	4	Rostron, Brown	19,133

Appearances
Sub Appearances
Goals

FA Cup

27	Jan 10	R3	H	Everton	W	2-1	1-0		Rowell (pen), Lee	28,602
32	Feb 21	R4	A	Burnley	D	1-1	0-1		Entwistle	18,870
34	26	R4r	H	Burnley	L	0-3	0-2			37,507

Appearances
Sub Appearances
Goals

League Cup

7	Aug 30	R2	H	Stoke City	L	0-2	0-2			12,368

Appearances
Sub Appearances
Goals

Anglo Scottish Cup

1	Aug 5		H	Bolton Wanderers	W	2-0	1-0		Entwistle, Rowell	7,260
2	8		A	Oldham Athletic	L	1-2	1-1		Docherty	3,241
3	12		A	Sheffield United	L	1-2	1-1		Rowell	6,598

Appearances
Sub Appearances
Goals

Siddall	Henderson	Bolton	Chisholm	Clarke	Ashurst	Kerr	Rostron	Entwistle	Docherty	Rowell	Lee	Elliott	Gilbert	Brown	Greenwood	Buckley	Coady	Arnott	Watson	Gregoire	Whitworth	
1	2	3	4	5	6	7	8	9	10	11	12											4
1	2	3	4		6	7	10	9	8	11	12	5										5
1	2			5	6	7	10		8	11	9	4	3	12								6
1	2	3		4				9	8	11		5	6	U	7	10						8
1	2	3		5	12			9	4	11		6	10		8	7						9
1	2	3		5				9	4	11		6	10	12	8	7						10
1	2	3	7				10	9	4	11		6		8	12		5					11
1		7	5			3	9	4	11	8	6		10	U		2						12
1		3	4	5		7	9	10	11	12	6		8			2						13
1	2	3	7	5				9	4	11	10	6		8	12							14
1	2	3	7	5				9	4	11	10	6		8	12							15
1	2	3	U	5				9	4	11	10	6		8		7						16
1	2	3		5				9	4	11	10	6		8	12	7						17
1	2	3	U	5		8	9	4	11	10	6				7							18
1	2	3	4	5		8	9		11	10	6		12		7							19
1	2	3	4	5		8	9		11	10	6		12		7							20
1	2	3	4	5		8	9		11	10	6	U			7							21
1	2	3	4	5		8	9		11	10	6	U			7							22
1	2	3	4	5		8	9		11	10	6	U			7							23
1	2	3	4	5		8	9		11	10	6			12	7							24
1	2	3	U	5		8	9	4	11	10	6				7							25
1	2	3	4	5		8	9		11	10	6		12		7							26
1	2	3	U	5		8	9		11	10	6				7	4						28
1	2	3	U	5		8	9		11	10	6				7	4						29
1	2			5	U	8	9		11	10	6	3			7	4						30
1	2		7	5	U	8	9		11	10	6	3				4						31
1	2	3	7	5		8	9	12	11	10	6				4							33
	2	3	4	5		8	9	U	11		6			7	10	1						35
1	2	3	7	5		8		9		11	6			10	4		12					36
1	2	3	7	5		8	9		11		6		U		10	4						37
1	2	3	7	5		8	9		11		6		12		10	4						38
1	2	3	U	5		8	9	4	11	10	6			7								39
1		3	7	5			8	9	4		11	6		U	10				2			40
1	3		7	5			11	9	4		10	6		12	8				2			41
1		7	5				11	9	4		10	6	3	12	8				2			42
1		7		5			8	12	4		11	6	3	9	10				2			43
1		7	U	5				4		11	6	3	9		10	8			2			44
1		7		5		8		4			6	3	9		U	10		11	2			45
1			U	5		9		4		11	6	3	7		10	8			2			46
1			U	5		8		4		11	6	3	9		10	7			2			47
1		3	7	12	5		10	4		11	6		9			8			2			48
1		3			5		10	12	4		11	6		9		8	7		2			49
41	30	32	27	33	10	3	34	34	26	32	30	41	12	14	3	30	3	15	1		10	
				1	1			2	1		3			8	5			1				
		3	1	2	1		11	12	4	21	6		1	6	2							

1	2	3		5			8	9	4	11	10	6			7	U						27
1	2	3	7	5	U		8	9		11	10	6				4						32
	2	3	7	5	12		8	9		11	10	6				4	1					34
2	3	3	2	3			3	3	1	3	3	3			1	2	1					
			1																			
									1		1	1										

| 1 | 2 | 3 | | 6 | 7 | | 9 | 4 | 11 | | 5 | 10 | U | 8 | | | | | | | | 7 |
| 1 | 1 | 1 | | 1 | 1 | | 1 | 1 | 1 | | 1 | 1 | | 1 | | | | | | | | |

1	2	3		5	6	7	U	10	4	11	9			8			U					1
1		3		5	6	7	12	10	4	11	9		2	8			U					2
U		3	4	5	6	7	9	10		11			2	U			8	1				3
2	1	3	1	3	3	3	1	3	2	3	2		2	2			1	1				
							1															
							1	1	2													

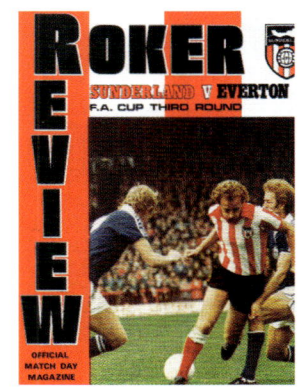

471

1979-80

Division Two

Ground: Roker Park
Manager: Ken Knighton

League Table

	P	W	D	L	F	A	Pts
Leicester C	42	21	13	8	58	38	55
SUNDERLAND	42	21	12	9	69	42	54
Birmingham C	42	21	11	10	58	38	53
Chelsea	42	23	7	12	66	52	53
QPR	42	18	13	11	75	53	49
Luton T	42	16	17	9	66	45	49
West Ham U	42	20	7	15	54	43	47
Cambridge U	42	14	16	12	61	53	44
Newcastle U	42	15	14	13	53	49	44
Preston NE	42	12	19	11	56	52	43
Oldham A	42	16	11	15	49	53	43
Swansea C	42	17	9	16	48	53	43
Shrewsbury T	42	18	5	19	60	53	41
Orient	42	12	17	13	48	54	41
Cardiff C	42	16	8	18	41	48	40
Wrexham	42	16	6	20	40	49	38
Notts Co	42	11	15	16	51	52	37
Watford	42	12	13	17	39	46	37
Bristol R	42	11	13	18	50	64	35
Fulham	42	11	7	24	42	74	29
Burnley	42	6	15	21	39	73	27
Charlton A	42	6	10	26	39	78	22

Division 1 Champions: Liverpool 60 pts
FA Cup Winners: West Ham United
League Cup Winners: Wolverhampton Wanderers
Anglo Scottish Cup Winners: St. Mirren

Did you know that?

Chris Turner became Sunderland's first goalkeeping substitute to come on in a match, at Sheffield United on 11 August 1979 in an Anglo-Scottish Cup tie. His appearance after half time was part of a pre-match arrangement.

Match 1: Ken Knighton first game as Sunderland manager
Match 3: Turner made debut
Match 8: Entwistle last game
Match 12: Ashurst last game
Match 14: Dunn made debut
Match 15: Hawley made debut
Match 16: Rostron last game
Match 21: Lee last game
Match 24: Hughes only game & Gilbert last game
Match 25: Cummins made debut
Match 26: Cooke made debut
Match 28: Marangoni made debut
Match 38: Coady last game
Match 39: Hinnigan made debut
Match 52: Promotion confirmed

Match No.	Date		Round	Venue	Opponents	Result	FT	HT	Pos.	Scorers	Attendance
4	Aug	18		A	Chelsea	D	0-0	0-0			23,500
5		22		H	Birmingham City	W	2-0	1-0	5	Robson, Brown	25,877
6		25		H	Fulham	W	2-1	0-0	5	Arnott, Robson (pen)	25,506
8	Sep	1		A	Oldham Athletic	L	0-3	0-0	11		7,830
10		8		H	Cambridge United	W	2-0	2-0	5	Buckley, Elliott	22,898
11		15		A	West Ham United	L	0-2	0-0	9		24,021
12		22		A	Burnley	D	1-1	1-0	11	Robson	8,751
14		29		H	Preston North End	D	1-1	0-0	9	Clarke	24,594
16	Oct	6		H	Charlton Athletic	W	4-0	1-0	6	Hawley (3), Robson	24,865
17		9		A	Birmingham City	L	0-1	0-0	8		18,960
18		13		A	Luton Town	L	0-2	0-1	13		13,504
19		20		H	Queens Park Rangers	W	3-0	3-0	10	Robson (2, 1 pen), Hawley	25,201
20		27		A	Leicester City	L	1-2	1-1	11	Lee	19,365
22	Nov	3		H	Chelsea	W	2-1	1-1	10	Arnott, Gilbert	24,988
24		10		A	Swansea City	L	1-3	1-1	12	Brown	15,826
25		17		H	Notts County	W	3-1	1-0	10	Robson (2, 1 pen), Cummins	21,896
26		24		A	Bristol Rovers	W	3-2	3-0	8	Elliott, Cummins, Robson	21,292
27	Dec	1		A	Orient	L	1-2	0-1	8	Robson	6,582
28		8		H	Cardiff City	W	2-1	1-0	8	Davies o.g., Robson	25,370
29		15		A	Watford	D	1-1	0-0	7	Dunn	13,965
30		21		H	Shrewsbury Town	W	2-1	1-0	7	Marangoni, Arnott	21,237
31		26		H	Wrexham	D	1-1	0-0	6	Arnott	29,567
32		29		A	Fulham	W	1-0	0-0	5	Marangoni	9,591
33	Jan	1		A	Newcastle United	L	1-3	1-1	6	Cummins	38,322
35		12		H	Oldham Athletic	W	4-2	0-1	5	Brown (3), Robson	19,456
36		19		A	Cambridge United	D	3-3	1-1	5	Marangoni, Brown, Cummins	7,107
37	Feb	9		H	Burnley	W	5-0	2-0	6	Cummins (4), Arnott	21,855
38		16		A	Preston North End	L	1-2	0-1	7	Brown	12,165
39		23		H	Luton Town	W	1-0	0-0	8	Cooke	25,387
40	Mar	1		A	Queens Park Rangers	D	0-0	0-0	8		15,613
41		8		H	Leicester City	D	0-0	0-0	8		29,487
42		15		A	Charlton Athletic	W	4-0	3-0	6	Brown, Arnott, Robson (2)	6,185
43		22		H	Swansea City	D	1-1	1-1	6	Robson	25,175
44		29		A	Notts County	W	1-0	0-0	4	Cummins	10,878
45	Apr	5		H	Newcastle United	W	1-0	0-0	5	Cummins	41,752
46		7		A	Wrexham	W	1-0	1-0	4	Brown	12,064
47		8		A	Shrewsbury Town	W	2-1	1-0	1	Robson, Cummins	12,345
48		12		H	Orient	D	1-1	1-0	1	Arnott	33,279
49		19		A	Bristol Rovers	D	2-2	1-2	3	Robson, Dunn	9,757
50		26		H	Watford	W	5-0	2-0	3	Robson (2), Buckley, Elliott (2)	32,195
51	May	3		A	Cardiff City	D	1-1	0-0	3	Robson	19,340
52		12		H	West Ham United	W	2-0	1-0	2	Arnott, Cummins	47,129

Appearances
Sub Appearances
Goals

FA Cup

| 34 | Jan | 5 | R3 | H | Bolton Wanderers | L | 0-1 | 0-1 | | | 24,464 |

Appearances
Sub Appearances
Goals

League Cup

7	Aug	29	R2L1	H	Newcastle United	D	2-2	1-0		Robson (pen), Rostron	27,658
9	Sep	5	R2L2	A	Newcastle United	W	2-2*	0-0		Brown (2)	30,553
13		26	R3	A	Manchester City	D	1-1	0-0		Chisholm	26,181
15	Oct	3	R3r	H	Manchester City	W	1-0	1-0		Robson	33,559
21		31	R4	H	West Ham United	D	1-1	1-0		Brown	30,302
23	Nov	5	R4r	A	West Ham United	L	1-2	1-1		Brown	24,454

* 7-6 penalties

Appearances
Sub Appearances
Goals

Anglo Scottish Cup

1	Aug	4		A	Bury	L	2-4	0-0		Arnott, Entwistle	3,042
2		7		A	Bolton Wanderers	L	0-2	0-0			3,924
3		11		H	Oldham Athletic	L	1-2	1-1		Rowell (pen)	7,964

Appearances
Sub Appearances
Goals

1980-81

Division One

Ground: Roker Park
Manager: Ken Knighton & Mick Docherty

League Table

	P	W	D	L	F	A	Pts
Aston Villa	42	26	8	8	72	40	60
Ipswich T	42	23	10	9	77	43	56
Arsenal	42	19	15	8	61	45	53
W.B.A.	42	20	12	10	60	42	52
Liverpool	42	17	17	8	62	42	51
Southampton	42	20	10	12	76	56	50
Nottingham F	42	19	12	11	62	44	50
Manchester U	42	15	18	9	51	36	48
Leeds U	42	17	10	15	39	47	44
Tottenham H	42	14	15	13	70	68	43
Stoke C	42	12	18	12	51	60	42
Manchester C	42	14	11	17	56	59	39
Birmingham C	42	13	12	17	50	61	38
Middlesbrough	42	16	5	21	53	61	37
Everton	42	13	10	19	55	58	36
Coventry C	42	13	10	19	48	68	36
SUNDERLAND	42	14	7	21	52	53	35
Wolverh'pton W	42	13	9	20	43	55	35
Brighton & H.A.	42	14	7	21	54	67	35
Norwich C	42	13	7	22	49	73	33
Leicester C	42	13	6	23	40	67	32
Crystal Palace	42	6	7	29	47	83	19

FA Cup Winners: Tottenham Hotspur
League Cup Winners: Liverpool

Did you know that?

After the opening two games of the season Sunderland led the top flight after winning 4-0 at Manchester City on 20 August 1980. This is the last time The Lads have been in that position.

Match 1: Allardyce made debut
Match 19: Marangoni last game
Match 21: Dunn last game
Match 31: Bowyer made debut
Match 32: Ritchie made debut
Match 35: Hawley last game
Match 42: Ken Knighton last game as Sunderland manager
Match 43: Mick Docherty first game as caretaker manager
Match 44: Vincent made debut
Match 45: Vincent last game
Match 46: Bolton and Allardyce last games & Mick Docherty last game as caretaker manager

Match No.	Date	Round	Venue	Opponents	Result	FT	HT	Pos.	Scorers	Attendance
1	Aug 16		H	Everton	W	3-1	2-0		Hawley (pen), Cummins, Wright o.g.	32,005
2	20		A	Manchester City	W	4-0	1-0	1	Cummins, Hawley (3, 1 pen)	33,271
3	23		H	Southampton	L	1-2	1-2	5	Allardyce	41,141
4	30		A	Manchester United	D	1-1	0-0	4	Brown	51,498
5	Sep 6		A	Leicester City	W	1-0	1-0	3	Hawley	20,638
6	13		H	Middlesbrough	L	0-1	0-1	7		32,745
7	20		A	Tottenham Hotspur	D	0-0	0-0	8		32,030
8	27		H	Leeds United	W	4-1	2-0	6	Robson (2), Rowell, Brown	29,619
9	Oct 4		A	Aston Villa	L	0-4	0-1	10		26,914
10	8		H	Nottingham Forest	D	2-2	2-0	10	Rowell, Brown	30,515
11	11		H	Crystal Palace	W	1-0	1-0	8	Rowell	25,444
12	18		A	Arsenal	D	2-2	0-1	8	Rowell, Cummins	32,135
13	21		H	Coventry City	L	1-2	0-1	9	Cummins	13,115
14	25		H	Ipswich Town	L	0-2	0-1	9		32,368
15	Nov 1		A	Wolverhampton W.	L	1-2	1-2	9	Allardyce	18,816
16	8		H	Stoke City	D	0-0	0-0	11		21,483
17	12		H	Manchester City	W	2-0	0-0	11	Arnott, Cooke	23,387
18	15		A	Everton	L	1-2	1-1	11	Robson	24,099
19	22		A	Norwich City	L	0-1	0-1	14		14,406
20	29		H	Liverpool	L	2-4	0-2	16	Brown, Cummins	32,340
21	Dec 6		A	Brighton & H.A.	L	1-2	0-1	18	Chisholm	13,903
22	13		H	Arsenal	W	2-0	1-0	17	Hawley, Arnott	21,595
23	20		A	Nottingham Forest	L	1-3	0-2	18	Rowell	23,151
24	26		H	West Bromwich Albion	D	0-0	0-0	17		28,296
25	27		A	Birmingham City	L	2-3	1-2	17	Hawley, Rowell	19,005
26	Jan 10		H	Norwich City	W	3-0	2-0	16	Rowell (2), Cummins	17,749
27	28		H	Manchester United	W	2-0	1-0	13	Chisholm, Rowell (pen)	31,910
28	31		A	Southampton	L	1-2	0-2	17	Chisholm	21,345
29	Feb 7		A	Middlesbrough	L	0-1	0-1	18		35,065
30	14		H	Leicester City	W	1-0	1-0	16	Cummins	22,569
31	21		A	Leeds United	L	0-1	0-0	17		23,236
32	28		H	Tottenham Hotspur	D	1-1	0-1	17	Bowyer	22,382
33	Mar 7		H	Aston Villa	L	1-2	0-2	17	Hinnigan	27,278
34	14		A	Crystal Palace	W	1-0	1-0	17	Hinnigan	16,748
35	21		H	Coventry City	W	3-0	1-0	14	Hinnigan (2), Cummins (pen)	20,622
36	28		A	Ipswich Town	L	1-4	1-1	16	Rowell	25,450
37	Apr 4		H	Wolverhampton W.	L	0-1	0-0	17		20,138
38	11		A	Stoke City	L	0-2	0-0	17		11,501
39	18		H	Birmingham City	W	3-0	2-0	16	Ritchie (3, 1 pen)	20,158
40	20		A	West Bromwich Albion	L	1-2	1-1	16	Ritchie (pen)	15,243
41	25		H	Brighton & H.A.	L	1-2	0-1	17	Brown	22,317
42	May 2		A	Liverpool	W	1-0	1-0	17	Cummins	40,337

Appearances
Sub Appearances
Goals

FA Cup

28	Jan 3	R3	A	Birmingham City	D	1-1	0-1		Chisholm	23,098
29	7	R3r	H	Birmingham City	L	1-2 (aet)	1-0		Rowell	27,793

Appearances
Sub Appearances
Goals

League Cup

4	Aug 27	R2L1	A	Stockport County	D	1-1	0-1		Arnott	6,108
6	Sep 3	R2L2	H	Stockport County	L	1-2	0-0		Cummins	17,346

Appearances
Sub Appearances
Goals

#	Turner	Whitworth	Bolton	Allardyce	Elliott	Hindmarch	Arnott	Buckley	Hawley	Brown	Cummins	Chisholm	Robson	Hinnigan	Marangoni	Rowell	Dunn	Cooke	Bowyer	Siddall	Ritchie	Vincent	West
1	1	2	3	4	5	6	7	8	9	10	11		U										
2	1	2	3	4	5	6		8	9	10	11	7	12										
3	1	2	3	4	5	6		8	9	10	11	7	12										
5	1		3	4	5		8		9	10	11	7	U	2	6								
7	1		3	4	5		8		9	10	11	7		2	6	U							
8	1		3	4	5		8		9	10	11	7		2	6	12							
9	1		3	4	5		7			10	11	6	9	2		8	12						
10	1	2	3	4	5		7			10	11	6	9			8	U						
11	1	2	3	4	5		7			9	11	6	10			8	12						
12	1	2	3	4	5		7			10	11	6	9			8	U						
13	1	2	3	4	5		7			10	11	6	9			8		U					
14	1	2	3	4	5		7			10	11	6	U			8		9					
15	1	2	3	4	5		7			10	11	6	U			8		9					
16	1	2	3	4	5		7			10	11	6	U			8		9					
17	1	2	3	4	5			7	6	10	11	U				8		9					
18	1	2	3	4	5			7	6	10	11		12			8		9					
19	1	2	3		5		4	7	6		11		10		12	8		9					
20	1	2	3	5			4	7	6		11		10	U	8			9					
21	1	2	3	4			5	7	6	12	11		10			8	9						
22	1	2	3	5	6		4	7		8	11	12	10					9					
23	1	2	3	5	6		4	7		8	11	10				12	9						
24	1	2	3	5	6		4	7	9	8	11	10						12					
25	1	2	3		5		4	7	9	8	11	10				6		12					
26	1	2	3		5	4	7		9	12	11	10				6		8					
27	1	2	3		5	4	7		9	U	11	10				6		8					
30	1	2	3		5	4	7		9	8	11	10				6		U					
31	1	2	3		5	4	7		9	12	11	10				6		8					
32		2	3		5	4	7		9		11	10				6		8	1	12			
33		2	3		5	4			9	U	11	10				6		8	1	7			
34		2			5	4			9	U	11	10	3			6		8	1	7			
35		2			5	4			9	12	11	10	3			6		8	1	7			
36		2			5	4	7			12	11	10				3		8	1	9			
37			3		5	4	7				11	10	2			6		12	1	9	8		
38			3		5	4	7	6		12	11	10	2					8	1	9			
39			3		5	4	7	6			11	10	2			U	8		1	9			
40			3		5	4	7	6		8	11		2			12			10	1	9		
41		2	3		5	4	7			8	11	6	2			12			10	1	9		
42			3	5		4	7			8	11	6	2			10				1	9	U	
43			3	5		6	4	7	8		11					2				1	9		
44			3	5		4			8		10	11	7			2				1	9	6	U
45			3		5	4			8	10	11	7				2	6			1	9	12	
46			3	12	5	4			8	10	11	7				2	6			1	9		
	27	29	39	24	38	29	34	15	16	28	42	33	9	16	3	26	1	14	9	15	14	1	
		1								6		1	3		1	5	2	3		1	1		
			2		2			2		7	5	9	3	3	4		10		1	1	4		
28	1	2	3		5	4	7		9	12	11	10				6		8					
29	1	2	3		5	4	7		9	8	11	10				6		12					
	2	2	2		2	2	2		2	1	2	2				2		1					
										1								1					
													1			1							
4	1		3	4	5	6	7		9	10	11	8	12										
6	1		3	4	5		8		9	10	11	7		2	6	12							
	2	1	2	2	2	1	2		2	2	2	2	1	1	1	1							
				1								1				1							
													1										

Rob Hindmarch

Hindmarch was Sunderland's youngest captain when he led the team at Nottingham Forest on 20 December 1980.

He was aged 19 years 247 days.

475

1981-82

Division One

Ground: Roker Park
Manager: Alan Durban

League Table

	P	W	D	L	F	A	Pts
Liverpool	42	26	9	7	80	32	87
Ipswich T	42	26	5	11	75	53	83
Manchester U	42	22	12	8	59	29	78
Tottenham H	42	20	11	11	67	48	71
Arsenal	42	20	11	11	48	37	71
Swansea C	42	21	6	15	58	51	69
Southampton	42	19	9	14	72	67	66
Everton	42	17	13	12	56	50	64
West Ham U	42	14	16	12	66	57	58
Manchester C	42	15	13	14	49	50	58
Aston Villa	42	15	12	15	55	53	57
Nottingham F	42	15	12	15	42	48	57
Brighton & H.A.	42	13	13	16	43	52	52
Coventry C	42	13	11	18	56	62	50
Notts Co	42	13	8	21	61	69	47
Birmingham C	42	10	14	18	53	61	44
W.B.A.	42	11	11	20	46	57	44
Stoke C	42	12	8	22	44	63	44
SUNDERLAND	42	11	11	20	38	58	44
Leeds U	42	10	12	20	39	61	42
Wolverh'pton W	42	10	10	22	32	63	40
Middlesbrough	42	8	15	19	34	52	39

FA Cup Winners: Tottenham Hotspur
League Cup Winners: Liverpool

Did you know that?

A 1-0 win at Heart of Midlothian in the first pre-season friendly saw Sunderland take to the field in their new 'candy' striped tops and red shorts. This unpopular kit change only lasted for two seasons.

Match 1: Munro, Pickering and McCoist made debuts & Alan Durban first game as Sunderland manager
Match 10: Venison made debut
Match 11: West made debut & Whitworth last game
Match 21: Bowyer last game
Match 24: Nicholl made debut
Match 29: McGinley made debut & Ritchie last game
Match 32: Siddall, McGinley and Brown last games
Match 37: Ursem made debut & Arnott last game
Match 41: Ursem last game
Match 47: Clarke last game

Match No.	Date	Round	Venue	Opponents	Result	FT	HT	Pos.	Scorers	Attendance
1	Aug 29		A	Ipswich Town	D	3-3	1-0		Ritchie, Buckley (2)	24,060
2	Sep 2		H	Aston Villa	W	2-1	1-1	5	Ritchie, Rowell	29,372
3	5		H	West Ham United	L	0-2	0-1	14		28,347
4	12		A	Arsenal	D	1-1	0-0	13	Rowell	26,471
5	19		H	Wolverhampton W.	D	0-0	0-0	13		22,061
6	23		A	Nottingham Forest	L	0-2	0-0	18		21,133
7	26		A	Swansea City	L	0-2	0-0	20		17,826
8	Oct 3		H	Coventry City	D	0-0	0-0	19		19,269
10	10		A	Notts County	L	0-2	0-1	20		10,683
11	17		H	Tottenham Hotspur	L	0-2	0-1	22		25,317
12	24		A	Leeds United	L	0-1	0-0	22		25,220
14	31		H	Liverpool	L	0-2	0-0	22		27,854
15	Nov 7		H	Manchester United	L	1-5	1-1	22	Cummins	27,070
17	14		A	Middlesbrough	D	0-0	0-0	22		21,019
18	21		A	Everton	W	2-1	0-0	22	Ritchie (pen), Elliott	19,759
19	25		H	Nottingham Forest	L	2-3	0-1	22	Hindmarch, McCoist	17,419
20	28		H	West Bromwich Albion	L	1-2	1-0	22	Hindmarch	15,867
21	Dec 5		A	Brighton & H.A.	L	1-2	1-1	22	Ritchie	14,251
22	19		A	Manchester City	W	3-2	1-0	21	Cummins, Rowell, Venison	29,462
26	Jan 30		A	Wolverhampton W.	W	1-0	0-0	21	Cooke	11,099
27	Feb 2		A	Aston Villa	L	0-1	0-0	21		19,916
28	6		H	Arsenal	D	0-0	0-0	21		16,345
29	10		H	Stoke City	L	0-2	0-0	21		14,317
30	16		A	Birmingham City	L	0-2	0-1	21		10,776
31	20		H	Swansea City	L	0-1	0-1	21		13,163
32	27		H	Notts County	D	1-1	0-0	21	Brown	12,910
33	Mar 10		H	Southampton	W	2-0	0-0	21	Pickering, McCoist	15,747
34	13		H	Leeds United	L	0-1	0-0	21		20,285
35	20		A	Liverpool	L	0-1	0-1	21		30,344
36	27		A	Manchester United	D	0-0	0-0	21		40,776
37	Apr 3		H	Middlesbrough	L	0-2	0-1	22		19,006
38	7		H	Ipswich Town	D	1-1	0-0	22	West	11,845
39	10		A	Stoke City	W	1-0	1-0	22	Buckley	11,399
40	12		H	Birmingham City	W	2-0	2-0	21	West (2)	14,821
41	14		A	Tottenham Hotspur	D	2-2	0-2	21	Rowell (pen), Pickering	39,898
42	17		H	Everton	W	3-1	1-1	18	Rowell (2, 1 pen), West	18,359
43	24		A	West Bromwich Albion	W	3-2	2-1	16	Cummins, Pickering, Rowell	13,268
44	27		A	Coventry City	L	1-6	1-2	16	Cummins	11,277
45	May 1		H	Brighton & H.A.	W	3-0	1-0	17	Rowell (2, 1 pen), West	16,224
46	4		A	West Ham United	D	1-1	1-0	16	West	17,130
47	8		A	Southampton	L	0-1	0-0	17		21,110
48	15		H	Manchester City	W	1-0	1-0	19	Buckley	26,167

Appearances
Sub Appearances
Goals

FA Cup

23	Jan 2	R3	A	Rotherham United	D	1-1	0-0		Rowell	11,649
24	18	R3r	H	Rotherham United	W	1-0	0-0		Buckley	14,863
25	23	R4	H	Liverpool	L	0-3	0-2			28,582

Appearances
Sub Appearances
Goals

League Cup

9	Oct 7	R2L1	H	Rotherham United	W	2-0	2-0		Rowell (pen), Ritchie	10,450
13	27	R2L2	A	Rotherham United	D	3-3	1-0		Ritchie (2), Cummins	8,179
16	Nov 11	R3	H	Crystal Palace	L	0-1	0-0			11,139

Appearances
Sub Appearances
Goals

	Turner	Himigan	Munro	Buckley	Clarke	Hindmarch	Chisholm	Ritchie	Brown	Rowell	Pickering	McCoist	Cooke	Siddall	Elliott	Arnott	Cummins	Whitworth	Venison	West	Bowyer	Nicholl	McGinley	Ursem	Dunn	
1	2	3	4	5	6	7	8	9	10	11	12															1
1	2	3	4	5	6	7	8		10	11	12	9														2
1	2	3	4	5	6	7	8		10	11	12	9														3
	2	3	4	5	6	12	9		10	11	8		1	7												4
	2	3	4	5	6		9		10	11	8		1	7						U						5
	2	3	4	5	6		9		10	11	12		1		7	8										6
	2		4	5	6		9		10	11	12		1	3	7	8										7
	2	3	4	5	6		9		10	U	8		1	7		11										8
		3			5			9	10	7	12		1	6		11	2	4								10
				5	6		9			10	8		1	3	7	11	2	4	12							11
		4		5		7	9		10	3	8		1	6		11	2	12								12
	3	4	5			7	9			10	8		1	6		11	2	12								14
		3		5				8	10	U			1	6	7	11		2	9	4						15
		3		5	4		7			10	9		1	6		11		2	U	8						17
		3	7	5	4		12			10	8		1	6		11		2		9						18
		3	7	5	4		12			10	8		1	6		11		2		9						19
		3	7	5	4		6			10	8	12	1			11		2		9						20
		3	7	5		12	6			10	8		1	4		11		2		9						21
	2		7	5	4		9		10	3	8		1	6		11	12									22
		3	7	5	4	8		12		10			9	1	6	11		2								26
		3		5	4	8	7	11		10			9	1	6			2	12							27
		3	7		4				10		12	9		1	6	11		2	5	8						28
		3	7		5		8	12	10				9	1	6			4			2	11				29
	3	10	7	5	4					12	9	5	4	1	6		11	8		2						30
	2	3	7	5	4		9			8			1	6		11		12		10						31
	2	3	7	5	4			9	10	6	12	1				11				8						32
1	2	3	7		4	5		9	10	8	U			6		11										33
1	2	3	7		4	5		9	10	8				6		11	12									34
1	2	3	7		4	5		9	10	8				6		11	12									35
1		3	7		4			9	10	8			6	5	11	2			U							36
1		3	7					9	10	8			6	5	11	2			12							37
1	2	3	7		4	5		9	10	U			6		11		8									38
1	2	3	7	4		5		9	10				6		11		8		12							39
1	2	3	7	4				9	10		5		6		11		8		12							40
1	2		7		4	5		9	10				6		11		8		12							41
1	2	3	7		4	5		9	10				6		11		8		U							42
1	2	3	7		4	5		9	10	U			6		11		8									43
1	2	3	7		4	5		9	10	12			6		11		8									44
1	2	3	7		4	5		9	10		U		6		11		8									45
1	2	3	7		4	5		9	10		U		6		11		8									46
1	2	3	7	12	4	5		9	10				6		11		8									47
1	2	3	7		4	5		9	10	U			6		11		8									48
19	30	34	37	25	36	20	18	5	30	37	19	8	23	36	6	35	2	17	13	6	3	3				
				1		2	2	2			9	2				3	5			4						
		4		2		4	1	9	3	2	1		1		4		1	6								

		2		7	5	4		9		10	3	8		1	6		11		12							23
				7	5	4		9		10	3	8		1	6		11	U		2						24
				7	5	4		9	12	10	3	8		1	6		11			2						25
		1		3	3	3		3		3	3	3		3	3		3			2						
									1								1									
			1					1																		

			3	4	5		12	9		10	7	8		1	6		11	2								9
			3		5	12	4	9		8	10			1	6	7	11	2								13
			3	12	5					8	10			1	6	7	11	2	9	4						16
			3	1	3		1	2		3	3	1		3	3	2	3	2	1	1						
			1		1	1					1					1										
								3		1				1												

Ally McCoist

Alistair Murdoch McCoist became Sunderland's record signing when he joined as a teenager from St Johnstone on 26 August 1981 for £355,000.

477

1982-83

Division One

Ground: Roker Park

Manager: Alan Durban

League Table

	P	W	D	L	F	A	Pts
Liverpool	42	24	10	8	87	37	82
Watford	42	22	5	15	74	57	71
Manchester U	42	19	13	10	56	38	70
Tottenham H	42	20	9	13	65	50	69
Nottingham F	42	20	9	13	62	50	69
Aston Villa	42	21	5	16	62	50	68
Everton	42	18	10	14	66	48	64
West Ham U	42	20	4	18	68	62	64
Ipswich T	42	15	13	14	64	50	58
Arsenal	42	16	10	16	58	56	58
W.B.A.	42	15	12	15	51	49	57
Southampton	42	15	12	15	54	58	57
Stoke C	42	16	9	17	53	64	57
Norwich C	42	14	12	16	52	58	54
Notts Co	42	15	7	20	55	71	52
SUNDERLAND	42	12	14	16	48	61	50
Birmingham C	42	12	14	16	40	55	50
Luton T	42	12	13	17	65	84	49
Coventry C	42	13	9	20	48	59	48
Manchester C	42	13	8	21	47	70	47
Swansea C	42	10	11	21	51	69	41
Brighton & H.A.	42	9	13	20	38	68	40

FA Cup Winners: Manchester United
League Cup Winners: Liverpool

Did you know that?

On 28 August 1982 Sunderland could almost call themselves Champions of Europe. Goals from Colin West, Ally McCoist and Nick Pickering gave the Black Cats a 3-1 win at European Cup holders Aston Villa in the first game of the season.

Match 1: Atkins made debut
Match 21: Worthington made debut
Match 22: Prudhoe made debut & Hinnigan last game
Match 30: James made debut
Match 37: Proctor made debut
Match 41: Nicholl last game
Match 42: Whitfield made debut & Buckley last game
Match 45: Whitfield last game
Match 48: Prudhoe, McCoist and Worthington last games

Match No.	Date	Round	Venue	Opponents	Result	FT	HT	Pos.	Scorers	Attendance
1	Aug 28		A	Aston Villa	W	3-1	0-1		West, McCoist, Pickering	22,945
2	Sep 1		H	Notts County	D	1-1	0-0	4	Rowell	18,997
3	4		H	West Ham United	W	1-0	1-0	4	Rowell	19,239
4	7		A	Coventry City	L	0-1	0-1	5		8,190
5	11		A	Brighton & H.A.	L	2-3	2-0	11	Cummins, McCoist	10,264
6	18		H	Tottenham Hotspur	L	0-1	0-1	14		21,137
7	25		A	Watford	L	0-8	0-4	18		16,744
8	Oct 2		H	Norwich City	W	4-1	0-0	15	Rowell (2), McCoist, Cooke	13,144
10	9		H	Southampton	D	1-1	0-0	16	McCoist	15,635
11	16		A	Manchester City	D	2-2	1-0	15	McCoist, Buckley	25,053
12	23		A	Everton	L	1-3	0-1	17	McCoist	20,630
14	30		H	Stoke City	D	2-2	2-1	20	Pickering, Rowell	16,406
15	Nov 6		A	Swansea City	L	0-3	0-2	20		10,034
17	13		H	Luton Town	D	1-1	0-0	20	Atkins	14,238
18	20		H	Nottingham Forest	L	0-1	0-0	21		14,716
20	27		A	Birmingham City	L	1-2	0-0	22	Rowell	12,375
21	Dec 4		H	Ipswich Town	L	2-3	1-2	22	Atkins, Worthington	15,000
22	11		A	West Bromwich Albion	L	0-3	0-2	22		11,136
23	18		H	Arsenal	W	3-0	1-0	20	Rowell (3)	11,753
24	27		A	Manchester Utd	D	0-0	0-0	22		47,783
25	28		H	Liverpool	D	0-0	0-0	22		35,041
26	Jan 1		A	Nottingham Forest	D	0-0	0-0	22		20,382
27	3		A	Notts County	W	1-0	1-0	21	Cummins	9,327
30	15		H	Aston Villa	W	2-0	1-0	19	McNaught o.g., Worthington	16,052
31	22		A	Tottenham Hotspur	D	1-1	0-1	19	Cummins (pen)	25,250
32	Feb 5		H	Coventry City	W	2-1	1-0	18	Cummins, Rowell	14,356
33	19		A	Southampton	L	0-2	0-1	18		17,326
34	26		H	Manchester City	W	3-2	0-0	17	Atkins, Rowell (2, 1 pen)	15,496
35	Mar 5		H	Everton	W	2-1	1-1	17	Rowell (2, 1 pen)	16,051
36	12		A	Stoke City	W	1-0	0-0	15	Rowell	12,806
37	19		H	Swansea City	D	1-1	0-0	16	Rowell	17,445
38	26		A	Luton Town	W	3-1	1-1	15	Pickering (2), James	11,221
39	Apr 2		A	Liverpool	L	0-1	0-0	15		35,821
40	4		H	Manchester United	D	0-0	0-0	15		31,486
41	9		H	West Ham United	L	1-2	0-0	16	Pickering	20,053
42	16		A	Norwich City	L	0-2	0-0	16		15,883
43	19		H	Brighton & H.A.	D	1-1	1-1	16	Pickering	13,414
44	23		A	Ipswich Town	L	1-4	0-2	17	Pickering	16,193
45	30		H	Birmingham City	L	1-2	1-0	18	West	14,818
46	May 2		H	Watford	D	2-2	2-1	17	Atkins, James	13,971
47	7		A	Arsenal	W	1-0	1-0	15	West	18,053
48	14		H	West Bromwich Albion	D	1-1	0-1	16	Chisholm	16,376

Appearances
Sub Appearances
Goals

FA Cup

28	Jan 8	R3	H	Manchester City	D	0-0	0-0			21,518
29	12	R3r	A	Manchester City	L	1-2	0-2		Chisholm	22,256

Appearances
Sub Appearances
Goals

Milk Marketing Board (League) Cup

9	Oct 5	R2L1	A	Wolverhampton W.	D	1-1	1-1		Rowell (pen)	13,662
13	27	R2L2	H	Wolverhampton W.	W	5-0	4-0		Chisholm (2), Hindmarch, Rowell, McCoist	11,091
16	Nov 10	R3	H	Norwich City	D	0-0	0-0			10,934
19	24	R3r	A	Norwich City	L	1-3	1-1		Cummins	10,776

Appearances
Sub Appearances
Goals

	Turner	Venison	Munro	Atkins	Chisholm	Elliott	Buckley	West	McCoist	Pickering	Cummins	Hindmarch	Rowell	Cooke	Himnigan	Nicholl	Worthington	Prudhoe	James	Proctor	Whitfield	Atkinson	
1	2	3	4	5	6	7	8	9	10	11	U												1
1	2	3	4		6	7	8	9	10	11	5	12											2
1	2	3	4		6	7		9	10	11	5	8	U										3
1	2	3	4		6	7		9	10	11	5	8	12										4
1	2	3		6		7		9	10	11	5	8	12	4									5
1	2	3		6		7		9	10	11	5	8	12	4									6
1	2	3	4			7		9	10	11	5	8	U		6								7
1	4	3		U	6	7		9	10		5	8	11		2								8
1		3	4	U	6	7		9	10		5	8	11		2								10
1	11	3	4	5	6	7		9	10	12		8			2								11
1	12	3	4	5	6	7	10	9		11		8			2								12
1	11	3	U	5		7	10	9	6		4	8			2								14
1	11	3	12	5		7	10	9	6		4	8			2								15
1	11	3	4		5		10	9	6	7		8	U		2								17
1	11	3	4		5	10	9	12	6	7		8			2								18
1		3	4	6	5	7	12	10		11		8	9		2								20
1		3	4		5	7	U	10		11	6	8			2	9							21
	2	3	4		6			U	10			8	11	5	7	9	1						22
1	7	3	4	5	6				10	11		8	U		2	9							23
1	3		4	5	6		7		10	11		8	U		2	9							24
1	7		4	5	6			12	3	11		8	10		2	9							25
1	7		4	5		6	9		3	11	U	8	10		2								26
1	7		4	5		8	9	U	3	11	6		10		2								27
1	7	3	4	5			8	12	6	11			2	9		10							30
1	7	3	4	5			8	12	6	11			2	9		10							31
1	7	3	4	5		12			6	11		8		2	9		10						32
1	7	3	4	5			12		6	11		8			2	9		10					33
1	7	3	4	5			U	6	11		8				2	9		10					34
1	7	3	4	5			12		6	11		8			2	9		10					35
1	7	3	4	5			9		6	11		8			2			10	U				36
1	7		4	5				12	3	11		8			2	9		10	6				37
1	7	3	4	5				U	11			9			2	8		10	6				38
1	7	3	4	5			12			11		8			2	9		10	6				39
1	7	3	4	5				12	11			8			2	9		10	6				40
1		3		5	4			12	11		7				2	9		10	6				41
1	7	3	4	5		12	9	11	6			8						10	2				42
	7	3	4	5			U		6			8	11			9	1	10	2				43
	2	3	4	6			8	12	11		5		7			9	1	10					44
	7	3	4	5				9	U	6	11		8				1	10	2				45
	7	3	4	5	2		9	12	6	11		8				1	10						46
	7	3	4	5	2		9	10	6	11			8			U	1						47
		3	4	5	2			9	11	8		6				12	1	10					48
5	36	37	36	32	20	18	19	19	39	29	14	34	11	3	29	18	7	18	5	3			
	1	1			2	4	9		1		1	3			1								
		4	1		1	3	6	7	4		16	1			2		2						

	7		4	6	5		9	U	3	11		8	10		2								28
	7		4	5	6			12	3	11		8	10		2	9							29
	2		2	2	2		1		2	2		2	2		2	1							
								1															
			1																				

		3	4	12	6	7		9	10		5	8	11		2								9
	11	3		5		7	10	9	6		4	8	12		2								13
	11	3	4	12	5		7	10	9	6		8			2								16
	2	3	4		5	7	9	10		11	12	8			6								19
	3	4	3	1	3	4	3	4	3	1	2	4	1		4								
			2						1		1												
			2				1			1													

Chris Turner

Chris suffered a fractured skull at Norwich City on 16 April 1983 – Nick Pickering went in goal.

1983-84

Canon Division One
Ground: Roker Park
Managers: Alan Durban, Bryan `Pop' Robson & Len Ashurst

League Table

	P	W	D	L	F	A	Pts
Liverpool	42	22	14	6	73	32	80
Southampton	42	22	11	9	66	38	77
Nottingham F	42	22	8	12	76	45	74
Manchester U	42	20	14	8	71	41	74
Q.P.R.	42	22	7	13	67	37	73
Arsenal	42	18	9	15	74	60	63
Everton	42	16	14	12	44	42	62
Tottenham H	42	17	10	15	64	65	61
West Ham U	42	17	9	16	60	55	60
Aston Villa	42	17	9	16	59	61	60
Watford	42	16	9	17	68	77	57
Ipswich T	42	15	8	19	55	57	53
SUNDERLAND	42	13	13	16	42	53	52
Norwich C	42	12	15	15	48	49	51
Leicester C	42	13	12	17	65	68	51
Luton T	42	14	9	19	53	66	51
W.B.A.	42	14	9	19	48	62	51
Stoke C	42	13	11	18	44	63	50
Coventry C	42	13	11	18	57	77	50
Birmingham C	42	12	12	18	39	50	48
Notts Co	42	10	11	21	50	72	41
Wolver'pton W	42	6	11	25	27	80	29

FA Cup Winners: Everton
League Cup Winners: Liverpool
Shirt Sponsor: Cowies

Did you know that?

Sunderland shirts first bore the name of a sponsor on 22 October 1983. Chairman Tom Cowie had his company name 'Cowies' added to the front of the shirt. The most likely reason for this was that the home game was scheduled to be shown on BBC TV's *Match of the Day* and they now allowed limited size sponsorship logos to be displayed on shirts. However an industrial dispute caused the programme to be cancelled.

Match 1: Bracewell and Atkinson made debuts
Match 16: Walker only game
Match 25: Chapman made debut
Match 34: Alan Durban last game as Sunderland manager
Match 35: Bryan `Pop' Robson only game as caretaker manager
Match 36: Len Ashurst first game as Sunderland manager
Match 38: Munro last game
Match 41: Murray only game
Match 44: Rowell last game
Match 47: Hindmarch and James last games
Match 48: Atkins & Robson last game

Match No.	Date	Round	Venue	Opponents	Result	FT	HT	Pos.	Scorers	Attendance
1	Aug 27		H	Norwich City	D	1-1	0-0		West	17,057
2	29		A	Aston Villa	L	0-1	0-0	15		20,390
3	Sep 3		A	Luton Town	L	1-4	0-0	19	West	10,846
4	7		H	Wolverhampton W.	W	3-2	1-0	16	Rowell (pen), Daniel o.g., Atkinson	12,961
5	10		H	Southampton	L	0-2	0-1	19		12,716
6	17		A	Queens Park Rangers	L	0-3	0-1	19		12,929
7	24		H	Coventry City	W	1-0	0-0	17	West	11,612
8	Oct 1		A	Liverpool	W	1-0	1-0	15	Rowell (pen)	29,534
10	15		H	Stoke City	D	2-2	1-1	16	Thomas o.g., Rowell	11,973
11	22		H	Manchester United	L	0-1	0-1	17		26,826
13	29		A	Nottingham Forest	D	1-1	0-1	17	Rowell	13,968
14	Nov 5		A	Arsenal	W	2-1	1-0	16	West, Atkins	26,064
16	12		H	Watford	W	3-0	1-0	15	West, Proctor, Chisholm	15,407
17	19		H	West Ham United	L	0-1	0-0	16		19,921
19	26		A	Birmingham City	W	1-0	0-0	14	Bracewell	11,948
20	Dec 3		H	Ipswich Town	D	1-1	1-1	14	Rowell	15,555
21	10		A	Notts County	L	1-6	1-3	15	Bracewell	7,123
22	18		H	Leicester City	D	1-1	0-0	14	Rowell	16,993
23	26		A	Everton	D	0-0	0-0	14		18,683
24	27		H	West Bromwich Albion	W	3-0	2-0	13	Robson, Bracewell (2)	17,968
25	31		H	Luton Town	W	2-0	0-0	12	Chisholm, Pickering	19,492
26	Jan 2		A	Coventry City	L	1-2	0-2	13	West	13,249
28	14		A	Norwich City	L	0-3	0-3	14		13,204
30	Feb 4		H	Liverpool	D	0-0	0-0	16		25,646
31	8		A	Tottenham Hotspur	L	0-3	0-2	16		19,327
32	11		A	Southampton	D	1-1	0-1	18	Chapman	16,958
33	18		A	Nottingham Forest	D	1-1	0-0	15	Chisholm	15,958
34	25		A	Manchester United	L	1-2	1-1	16	Chapman	40,615
35	Mar 3		H	Arsenal	D	2-2	1-1	17	Proctor, Rowell (pen)	15,370
36	7		H	Queens Park Rangers	W	1-0	0-0	16	Fenwick o.g.	13,538
37	17		A	Wolverhampton W.	D	0-0	0-0	17		9,111
38	20		A	Watford	L	1-2	0-0	17	Rowell	16,231
39	24		H	Aston Villa	L	0-1	0-1	18		11,908
40	31		A	Stoke City	L	1-2	1-2	18	Atkins	11,047
41	Apr 7		H	Tottenham Hotspur	D	1-1	1-1	18	West	15,433
42	14		A	West Ham United	W	1-0	0-0	18	Chisholm	16,558
43	21		H	Everton	W	2-1	1-1	16	Robson, West	15,876
44	23		A	West Bromwich Albion	L	1-3	1-2	18	West	11,252
45	28		H	Birmingham City	W	2-1	1-0	16	James (2 pens)	13,061
46	May 5		A	Ipswich Town	L	0-1	0-0	15		17,657
47	7		H	Notts County	D	0-0	0-0	16		14,517
48	12		A	Leicester City	W	2-0	2-0	13	Chapman, Robson	12,627

Appearances
Sub Appearances
Goals

FA Cup

Match No.	Date	Round	Venue	Opponents	Result	FT	HT	Scorers	Attendance
27	Jan 7	R3	A	Bolton Wanderers	W	3-0	1-0	West, Chapman, Rowell	14,018
29	28	R4	H	Birmingham City	L	1-2	1-0	West	21,226

Appearances
Sub Appearances
Goals

Milk Marketing Board (League) Cup

Match No.	Date	Round	Venue	Opponents	Result	FT	HT	Scorers	Attendance
9	Oct 4	R2L1	A	Cambridge United	W	3-2	0-1	Rowell (2), West	4,831
12	26	R2L2	H	Cambridge United	W	4-3	3-2	Rowell (2, 1 pen), Proctor, Cooke	9,059
15	Nov 9	R3	A	Norwich City	D	0-0	0-0		12,400
18	22	R3r	H	Norwich City	L	1-2	0-1	West	14,141

Appearance
Sub Appearance
Goals

Turner	Venison	Munro	Atkins	Chisholm	Proctor	Bracewell	Rowell	West	Pickering	Atkinson	Cooke	Elliott	James	Hindmarch	Walker	Robson	Chapman	Murray	Corner	
1	2	3	4	5	6	7	8	9	10	11	U									1
1	2	3	4	5	10	6	8	9	7	11	12									2
1	2	3	4	5	10		8	9	7	11		6	U							3
1	2	3	4	5	6		8	9	10	11		7	12							4
1	2	3	4	5	6	7	8	9	10	11		12								5
1	2		4	5	6	7	8	9	10	11	U	3								6
1	2		4	5	6	7	8	9	10		12	11	3							7
1	2		4	5	6	7	8	9	10		U	3	11							8
1	2		4	5	6	7	8	9	10		U	3	11							10
1	2		4	5	6	7	8	9	10		12	3	11							11
1	2	U		4	10	7	8	9	3		11	6		5						13
1	2		4	5	10	7	8	9	3			6	11	U						14
1	2		4	5	10	7	8	9	3				11	6	12					16
1	2		4	5	10	7	8	9	3	U			11	6						17
1	2		4	5	10	7	8	9	3	U		6	11							19
1	2		4	5	10	7	8	9	3	U		6	11							20
1	2		4	5	10	7	8	9	3	12		6	11							21
1	2		4	5	10	7	8	9	3	U		6	11							22
1	2		4	5	10	7	8	9	3	11		6	12							23
1	2		4	5	10	7		9	3	U		6	11			8				24
1	2		4	5	10	7		9	3			6	11			12	8			25
1		2	4	5	10	7	11	9	3			6				12	8			26
1	2		4		10	7	8	9	3			6		5		U	11			28
1	2		4	5	10	7	8	9	3			6	11			U				30
1	2		4		10	7	8	9	3			6	11		5	U				31
1	2	U	4		10	7	8	9	3			6	11		5					32
1	2	U	4	5	10	7	8		3			6	11			9				33
1	2		4	5	10	7	8	12	3			6	11			9				34
1	2	7	4	5	10		12	8	3			6	11			9				35
1	2	7	4	5	10		8	12	3			6	11			9				36
1	2		4	5	10	7	8		3			6	11			U	9			37
1	2	6	4	5	10	7	8		3				11			12	9			38
1	2		4	5	10	7	8		3			6	11			12	9			39
1	2		4	5	10	7	12	8	3			6	11			9				40
1	2			5	10	7	8	9	3			6	11			12	4			41
1	2		4	5		7	U	9	3			6	11	10		8				42
1	2		4		10	7	U	9	3			6	11	5		8				43
1	2		4	5	8	7	12	9	3			6	11	10						44
1	2		4		10	7		9	3			6	11	5		8	U			45
1	2		4	10	12	7		9	3			6	11	5		8				46
1	2		4		10	7		9	3			6	11	5		8	12			47
1	2		4	5	10	7		9	3	U		6				8	11			48
2	41	9	40	36	40	38	31	36	42	7	1	33	32	12		7	14	1		
						1		3	2		1	3			2	1	1	5	1	
		2	4	2	4	8	9	1	1			2				3	3			

	2	4	5	10	7	8	9	3				6	U			11				27
1	2		4	5	10	7	8	12	3			6	11			9				29
2	1	1	2	2	2	2	2	1	2			2	1			2				
							1													
					1	2							1							

	2		4	5	6	7	8	9	10		U	3	11							9
	2			5	6	7	8	9	10	U	4	3	11							12
	2		4	5	10	7	8	9	3			6	11	U						15
	2		4	5	10	7	8	9	3				11	6		12				18
	4		3	4	4	4	4	4	4	1	3	4	1							
								1												
				1		4	2		1											

Bryan 'Pop' Robson

Robson became Sunderland's oldest scorer when he put the ball in the net for the second goal at Leicester City on the final day of the season – 38 years, 183 days old. He had also been caretaker manager for one game earlier in the season.

1984-85

Canon Division One

Ground: Roker Park
Manager: Len Ashurst

League Table

	P	W	D	L	F	A	Pts
Everton	42	28	6	8	88	43	90
Liverpool	42	22	11	9	68	35	77
Tottenham H	42	23	8	11	78	51	77
Manchester U	42	22	10	10	77	47	76
Southampton	42	19	11	12	56	47	68
Chelsea	42	18	12	12	63	48	66
Arsenal	42	19	9	14	61	49	66
Sheffield W	42	17	14	11	58	45	65
Nottingham F	42	19	7	16	56	48	64
Aston Villa	42	15	11	16	60	60	56
Watford	42	14	13	15	81	71	55
W.B.A.	42	16	7	19	58	62	55
Luton T	42	15	9	18	57	61	54
Newcastle U	42	13	13	16	55	70	52
Leicester C	42	15	6	21	65	73	51
West Ham U	42	13	12	17	51	68	51
Ipswich T	42	13	11	18	46	57	50
Coventry C	42	15	5	22	47	64	50
Q.P.R.	42	13	11	18	53	72	50
Norwich C	42	13	10	19	46	64	49
SUNDERLAND	42	10	10	22	40	62	40
Stoke C	42	3	8	31	24	91	17

FA Cup Winners: Manchester United
League Cup Winners: Norwich City
Shirt Sponsor: Cowies

Did you know that?

Barry Venison became the youngest League Cup Final captain at 20 years 220 days when he deputised for the suspended Shaun Elliott against Norwich City on 24 March 1985.

Match 1: Bennett, Berry, Gayle and Walker made debuts
Match 2: Hodgson made debut
Match 3: Corner and Wylde made debuts
Match 4: Daniel made debut
Match 20: Wylde last game
Match 22: Lemon made debut
Match 31: Wallace made debut
Match 32: Agboola made debut
Match 39: West last game
Match 42: Moore made debut
Match 49: Armstrong made debut
Match 51: Cummins last game
Match 52: Relegation confirmed
Match 53: Cornforth made debut, Turner and Cooke last games & Len Ashurst last game as Sunderland manager

Match No.	Date	Round	Venue	Opponents	Result	FT	HT	Pos.	Scorers	Attendance
1	Aug 25		H	Southampton	W	3-1	2-0		Bennett, Venison, Proctor	18,152
2	27		A	Chelsea	L	0-1	0-1	9		25,554
3	Sep 1		A	Nottingham Forest	L	1-3	1-1	16	West (pen)	15,760
4	4		H	Tottenham Hotspur	W	1-0	0-0	9	West (pen)	18,895
5	8		H	West Bromwich Albion	D	1-1	0-0	12	Berry	18,206
6	15		A	Liverpool	D	1-1	1-1	14	Wylde	34,044
7	22		H	Coventry City	D	0-0	0-0	13		16,308
9	29		A	Stoke City	D	2-2	1-0	12	Gayle, Walker	8,882
10	Oct 6		A	Sheffield Wed.	D	2-2	0-2	13	Atkinson, Walker	27,766
12	13		H	Norwich City	W	2-1	1-0	9	Gayle, Berry	15,155
13	20		A	Arsenal	L	2-3	0-1	11	Walker (2)	36,987
14	27		H	Luton Town	W	3-0	1-0	8	Chisholm, Wylde (pen), Pickering	15,280
16	Nov 3		H	Queens Park Rangers	W	3-0	1-0	7	Hodgson, Wicks o.g., Wylde	16,408
18	10		A	Watford	L	1-3	0-1	9	Hodgson	18,953
19	17		A	West Ham United	L	0-1	0-0	12		15,204
21	24		H	Manchester United	W	3-2	3-2	11	Walker (3, 2 pens)	25,405
22	Dec 1		A	Aston Villa	L	0-1	0-0	13		14,669
24	8		H	Leicester City	L	0-4	0-3	14		16,441
25	15		A	Ipswich Town	W	2-0	0-0	13	Bennett, Walker	12,493
26	23		H	Nottingham Forest	L	0-2	0-1	13		21,086
27	26		H	Everton	L	1-2	0-2	14	Proctor	19,714
28	29		A	Tottenham Hotspur	L	0-2	0-1	16		26,930
29	Jan 1		A	Newcastle United	L	1-3	0-1	18	West	36,821
32	29		A	Southampton	L	0-1	0-1	18		12,423
33	Feb 2		H	Stoke City	W	1-0	0-0	18	Hodgson	14,762
35	23		A	Queens Park Rangers	L	0-1	0-0	18		10,063
36	Mar 2		A	Luton Town	L	1-2	0-2	18	Bennett	8,019
38	9		H	Arsenal	D	0-0	0-0	18		27,694
39	12		H	Watford	D	1-1	1-0	19	Walker	22,375
40	16		A	Norwich City	W	3-1	2-1	18	Downs o.g., Hodgson, Wallace	13,389
42	30		H	Chelsea	L	0-2	0-0	18		13,489
43	Apr 3		H	Liverpool	L	0-3	0-2	21		24,096
44	6		A	Everton	L	1-4	1-2	21	Wallace	35,978
45	8		H	Newcastle United	D	0-0	0-0	21		28,246
46	13		A	Coventry City	W	1-0	1-0	21	Moore	9,668
47	16		H	Sheffield Wed.	D	0-0	0-0	21		16,119
48	20		H	West Ham United	L	0-1	0-1	21		15,622
49	24		A	West Bromwich Albion	L	0-1	0-0	21		7,281
50	27		A	Manchester United	D	2-2	1-1	21	Pickering, Walker	38,979
51	May 4		H	Aston Villa	L	0-4	0-2	21		12,467
52	6		A	Leicester City	L	0-2	0-2	21		11,455
53	11		H	Ipswich Town	L	1-2	1-1	21	Wallace	9,398

Appearances
Sub Appearances
Goals

FA Cup

30	Jan 5	R3	A	Southampton	L	0-4	0-2			15,516

Appearances
Sub Appearances
Goals

Milk Marketing Board (League) Cup

8	Sep 25	R2L1	H	Crystal Palace	W	2-1	0-0		Wylde (2)	11,696
11	Oct 10	R2L2	A	Crystal Palace	D	0-0	0-0			6,871
15	31	R3	A	Nottingham Forest	D	1-1	1-1		Hodgson	14,291
17	Nov 6	R3r	H	Nottingham Forest	W 1-0 (aet)		0-0		Gayle	23,180
20	21	R4	H	Tottenham Hotspur	D	0-0	0-0			27,421
23	Dec 5	R4r	A	Tottenham Hotspur	W	2-1	1-1		Walker, Chisholm	25,835
31	Jan 23	R5	A	Watford	W	1-0	0-0		Walker	22,595
34	Feb 13	SL1	H	Chelsea	W	2-0	1-0		West (2, 1 pen)	32,440
37	Mar 4	SL2	A	Chelsea	W	3-2	1-1		Walker (2), West	38,440
41	24	F	N*	Norwich City	L	0-1	0-0			100,000

*at Wembley

Appearances
Sub Appearances
Goals

	Turner	Venison	Pickering	Bennett	Chisholm	Elliott	Berry	Gayle	West	Proctor	Walker	Hodgson	Corner	Wylde	Daniel	Atkinson	Cummins	Lemon	Cooke	Agboola	Wallace	Moore	Armstrong	Comforth	
1	2	3	4	5	6	7	8	9	10	11		U													1
1	2	3	4	5	6	7	8	9	10	11	12														2
1	2	3		6	12	8	9	10	11	4	5	7													3
1	2	3	4		6	7		9		11			8	5	10	U									4
1	2	3	4	5	6	7	8	9	U	11				10											5
1	2	3	4	5			8	9	10	11		12	7												6
1	2	3	4	5	6		8	9	10	11		12													7
1	2		4	5	6	7	8	U	10	11			9	3											9
1	2	10	4	5	6	7		9		11			8	3	12										10
1	2	3	4	5	6	10	8	12		11			9	7											12
1	2	3	4	5	4	7	10		9	11			12	8											13
1		3		5	6	4	7	12	10		11		8	2	9										14
1	2	3	4		6		8		10	11	7		9	5		12									16
1	2		5		6	4	8		10	11	7		9	3		12									18
1	2	3	5	4	6	8	12	9	10	11	7					8									19
1	2		4	5		6	8	9		11	7		3		10	U									21
1	2		4	5		6	8	9		11			3		10	12									22
1	2		5	12	6	4	8	9	10	11			3		7										24
1	2	3	5		7	6	4	8	9	10	11				U										25
1	2	3	4	5		6	8	9	10	11	7		U												26
1	2	3	4		6	8							5	12		9									27
1	2	3	5		6	4			10	11	7		8	9	12										28
1	2	3	5			6	7	9	10	11	8		4			12									29
1	2	3		5	6	12		9					10		11	7	4	8							32
1		5	6		4	8		11		10	2			12	7		9	3							33
1	2	3	4	5	6			9		11	7			10			8	12							35
1	2	3	4	5	6	10		12		11	9				7	8									36
1	2	3	10	5	6	8	12	9		11	7					4									38
1	2	3	4	5	6	10	12	9		11	7				8										39
1	2	3		5	6	10	12			11	9	4				8		7							40
1	2	3	4	5						11	9			10	7		6	8	12						42
1	2	3	4	5		12				11			10	7	6			8	9						43
1	2	3	4	5	6	8				11			7	10	12		9								44
1	2	3	4	5	6	10				11			U	7			8	9							45
1	2	3	4	5	6	10				11			12	7		8	9								46
1	2	3	4	5	6	10				11				9	7	U	8								47
1	2	3	4	5		10				11	12			9	7		6	8							48
1	2	3		5			12			11	9		6	10	7		8	4							49
1	2	3	4	5		6		12		11	9		7	10			8								50
1	2	3	4					7		11	9		5	10		6	8	12							51
1	2	3	4	5		7				11	9			12	10		8	6							52
1		3	4		12	6				9				11	10	7	8	5	2						53
2	39	37	37	31	31	31	19	20	17	38	23	3	8	25	5	13	10	4	8	14	3	3	1		
				1		1	3	6	3			2		3		4	4	1	2		1	1			
	1	2	3	1		2	2	3	2	10	4		3		1				3	1					

1	2	6	3	5		8	11	10		9	7			4		12									30
1	1	1	1	1		1	1	1		1	1			1											
																1									

1	2		4	5	6	7	8	U	10	11			9	3											8
1	2	10	4	5		7	9	12		11			8	3	6										11
	9	3		5	6	4	7	12	10		11		8	2											15
1	2		5			6	4	8		10	11		8	2		9	3								17
1	2	3	4	5		6	8	9	10	11	7		12												20
1	2		4	5	6	7	8	12	10	11	9			3											23
	2	3		5	6	4		9		11		7		10		8		12							31
	2	3	4	5	6	8		9		11			10		U										34
	2	3	4	5	6	8		9		11	7			10			12								37
	2	3	4	5		10	12			11	9	6		7			8								41
10	7	8	9	7	10	6	4	5	9	7	2	4	9	1		1	1	1							
						1	4		1					1			2								
		1				1	3			4	1		2												

483

1985-86

Canon Division Two

Ground: Roker Park

Manager: Lawrie McMenemy

League Table

	P	W	D	L	F	A	Pts
Norwich C	42	25	9	8	84	37	84
Charlton A	42	22	11	9	78	45	77
Wimbledon	42	21	13	8	58	37	76
Portsmouth	42	22	7	13	69	41	73
Crystal Palace	42	19	9	14	57	52	66
Hull C	42	17	13	12	65	55	64
Sheffield U	42	17	11	14	64	63	62
Oldham A	42	17	9	16	62	61	60
Millwall	42	17	8	17	64	65	59
Stoke C	42	14	15	13	48	50	57
Brighton & H.A.	42	16	8	18	64	64	56
Barnsley	42	14	14	14	47	50	56
Bradford C	42	16	6	20	51	63	54
Leeds U	42	15	8	19	56	72	53
Grimsby T	42	14	10	18	58	62	52
Huddersfield T	42	14	10	18	51	67	52
Shrewsbury T	42	14	9	19	52	64	51
SUNDERLAND	42	13	11	18	47	61	50
Blackburn R	42	12	13	17	53	62	49
Carlisle U	42	13	7	22	47	71	46
Middlesbrough	42	12	9	21	44	53	45
Fulham	42	10	6	26	45	69	36

Division 1 Champions: Liverpool 88 pts
FA Cup Winners: Liverpool
League Cup Winners: Oxford United
Full Members Cup Winners: Chelsea
Shirt Sponsor: Vaux

Did you know that?

This was the longest Sunderland have had to wait for their first goal in a season. The breakthrough finally came after 494 minutes when David Swindlehurst planted a header into the Fulwell End net on 7 September 1985.

Match 1: McDonagh, Gray, Swindlehurst and Gates made debuts & Lawrie McMenemy first game as Sunderland manager
Match 8: McDonagh, Chisholm and Berry last games
Match 9: Bolder made debut
Match 10: Kennedy made debut
Match 11: Burley made debut
Match 15: Daniel last game
Match 24: Walker last game
Match 34: Pickering last game
Match 37: Bolder last game
Match 38: Dibble made debut
Match 39: Hetzke made debut
Match 41: Duncan made debut
Match 42: Ford made debut
Match 43: White made debut
Match 50: Dibble, Venison, Elliott, Ford, Gayle, Wallace & Hodgson last games

Match No.	Date	Round	Venue	Opponents	Result	FT	HT	Pos.	Scorers	Attendance
1	Aug 17		H	Blackburn Rovers	L	0-2	0-0			21,202
2	20		A	Portsmouth	L	0-3	0-0	22		14,681
3	24		A	Crystal Palace	L	0-1	0-0	22		7,040
4	26		H	Oldham Athletic	L	0-3	0-2	22		16,414
5	31		A	Millwall	L	0-1	0-1	22		7,910
6	Sep 7		H	Grimsby Town	D	3-3	1-2	22	Swindlehurst (2), Gates (pen)	14,895
7	14		A	Leeds United	D	1-1	1-0	22	Gray	19,693
9	21		A	Shrewsbury Town	W	2-1	1-1	20	Pickering (2)	3,919
11	28		H	Huddersfield Town	W	1-0	0-0	20	Gates	18,980
13	Oct 5		A	Charlton Athletic	L	1-2	0-1	20	Gates	5,552
15	12		H	Hull City	D	1-1	1-1	21	Gray	16,613
16	19		A	Carlisle United	W	2-1	1-0	19	Elliott, Gayle	9,251
17	22		H	Middlesbrough	W	1-0	1-0	16	Gates	20,541
18	26		H	Norwich City	L	0-2	0-0	17		17,908
19	Nov 2		A	Fulham	W	2-1	0-1	15	Gates (pen), Bennett	5,795
21	9		H	Wimbledon	W	2-1	1-0	12	Swindlehurst (2)	15,518
22	16		A	Barnsley	D	1-1	0-1	12	Swindlehurst	9,410
23	23		H	Brighton & H.A.	W	2-1	1-0	12	Gates, Bennett	14,712
24	30		A	Stoke City	L	0-1	0-0	12		9,034
25	Dec 7		H	Portsmouth	L	1-3	0-2	15	Gates	17,229
26	14		A	Blackburn Rovers	L	0-2	0-1	15		6,045
27	22		H	Crystal Palace	D	1-1	0-1	16	Armstrong	16,710
28	26		H	Sheffield United	W	2-1	2-1	15	Gates, Bennett	17,643
29	28		A	Middlesbrough	L	0-2	0-1	15		19,774
30	Jan 1		A	Bradford City	L	0-2	0-1	15		8,369
32	11		H	Leeds United	W	4-2	1-0	15	Pickering (3, 1 pen), Wallace	15,139
33	18		H	Millwall	L	1-2	0-0	14	Gray	14,294
36	Feb 1		A	Oldham Athletic	D	2-2	1-2	17	Proctor, Hodgson (pen)	3,827
37	8		H	Carlisle United	D	2-2	0-0	16	Kennedy (2)	12,689
38	Mar 1		A	Huddersfield Town	L	0-2	0-2	18		7,150
39	8		H	Charlton Athletic	L	1-2	0-0	19	Proctor	11,885
40	15		A	Hull City	D	1-1	0-1	19	Wallace	9,295
41	22		A	Grimsby Town	D	1-1	0-1	19	Armstrong	5,339
42	29		H	Bradford City	D	1-1	0-0	19	Ford	14,870
43	31		A	Sheffield United	L	0-1	0-1	19		9,839
44	Apr 5		H	Fulham	W	4-2	3-0	19	Elliott, Proctor (2), Wallace	11,338
45	9		A	Norwich City	D	0-0	0-0	19		17,752
46	12		A	Wimbledon	L	0-3	0-0	20		6,051
47	19		H	Barnsley	W	2-0	1-0	19	Futcher o.g., Gayle	12,349
48	26		A	Brighton & H.A.	L	1-3	0-1	20	Proctor	9,189
49	29		H	Shrewsbury Town	W	2-0	0-0	18	Gates, Proctor	15,507
50	May 3		H	Stoke City	W	2-0	1-0	18	Proctor (pen), Gray	20,631

Appearances
Sub Appearances
Goals

FA Cup

Match No.	Date	Round	Venue	Opponents	Result	FT	HT	Scorers	Attendance
31	Jan 4	R3	H	Newport County	W	2-0	2-0	Burley, Corner	12,352
34	25	R4	H	Manchester United	D	0-0	0-0		35,484
35	29	R4r	A	Manchester United	L	0-3	0-2		43,402

Appearance
Sub Appearances
Goals

Milk Marketing Board (League) Cup

Match No.	Date	Round	Venue	Opponents	Result	FT	HT	Scorers	Attendance
10	Sep 24	R2L1	H	Swindon Town	W	3-2	1-1	Walker, Gates (pen), Bennett	14,20?
14	Oct 8	R2L2	A	Swindon Town	L	1-3 (aet)	0-0	Walker	9,11?

Appearance
Sub Appearance
Goals

Full Members Cup

Match No.	Date		Venue	Opponents	Result	FT	HT	Scorers	Attendance
8	Sep 17		A	Grimsby Town	L	2-3	0-0	Venison, Walker	2,43?
12	Oct 1		H	Grimsby Town	W	2-1*	1-1	Gates (pen), Hodgson	11,57?
20	Nov 4		A	Manchester City	L	0-0‡	0-0		6,64?

* 3-2 penalties
‡ 3-4 penalties

Appearance
Sub Appearance
Goals

	McDonagh	Venison	Gray	Agboola	Bennett	Elliott	Pickering	Wallace	Swindlehurst	Gates	Walker	Hodgson	Daniel	Chisholm	Berry	Gayle	Bolder	Burley	Kennedy	Atkinson	Corner	Proctor	Armstrong	Dibble	Lemon	Hetzke	Duncan	Ford	White	Moore	
1	2	3	4	5	6	7	8	9	10	11	12																				1
1	2	3	4	5	6	7	8	9	10	11	U																				2
1	2	3	4	5	6	7	8	9	10	11		12																			3
1	2	3		5	6	7	12	9	10	11	8	4																			4
1	2	3			6	7		9	10	12	8	4	5	11																	5
1	2	3		5	6	7		9	10	11	8	4		12																	6
1	2	3		5	6	7		9	10	11	8	4		U																	7
	2	3	6	5		7		9	10	11	8	4		12	1																9
	8	7		5	6			9	10	11	U	4				1	2	3													11
	8	7		5	6			9	10	11	12	4				1	2	3													13
	8	7		5	6	12			10	11	9	4				1	2	3													15
	8	7		5	6	4			10					U	9	1	2	3	11												16
	8	7	5		6	4	12		10						9	1	2	3	11												17
	8	7		5	6	4		9	10						11	1	2	3	12												18
	8	7		5	6	4		9	10						11	1	2	3	U												19
	4	7		5	6	8		9	10						11	1	2	3	U												21
	4	7		5	6		8	9	10						11	1	2	3													22
	8	7		5		4		9	10						11	1	2	3	U	6											23
	4	7		5	6	8		9	10	12					11	1	2	3													24
	8			5	6	4		9	10		11			7		1	2	3	12												25
	8						7	9	10		12					1	2	3		11											26
			4		6			9	10		12					1	2	3	7	5	11	8									27
				5	6	4		9	10	U						1	2		7	3	11	8									28
				5	6	4	12		10		9					1	2		7		11	8									29
		4	5		12			9	10							1	2	3	7	6		8									30
	8		6			4	9		10							1	2	3	7	5	11	U									32
	12	6				4	9		10							1	2	3	7	5	11										33
	8	4	6					9	10	12			7	1	2	3		5	11												36
		4	6					9	10	8					1	2	3	7	5	11	12										37
	8	12	6	5				9							2	3	7		11	4	1	10									38
	8				6			9	10					7	2	3			11	4	1	12	5								39
		8		6	12				10					7	2	3			11	4	1	9	5								40
	11	8			6		12		10					7	2			3		4		9	5	1							41
	8	11			6				10					7	2	3			4	1	9		5		12						42
	11	8		6		9			12					2	3			4	1		5		7	10							43
	2	10		6	9								8		3		11	4	1		5		7								44
	2	4		6	9		10						8		3		11	1		5		7	12								45
	2	10	6		9					12			8		3		11	4		5		7	8								46
	2	6	5		9		10						8		3	U				11		7									47
	2	4	5	6	9		10						8		3		11	U	1			7									48
	2	4	5	6	9		10						8		3	U		11	1			7									49
	2	4	5	6	9		10			12			8		3			11	1			7									50
7	36	32	12	28	32	22	14	25	38	10	9	8	1	20	22	27	32	30	9	19	13	12	4	8	1	8	2				
		2				2	5		1	2	6	1		3			3		1		1		1		1	2					
		4		3	2	5	3	5	9		1			2			2			7	2			1							

8		6			4	9		10					1	2	3	7	5	11	U												31
8		6			4	9	10					12	1	2	3	7	5	11													34
8	4	6			9	10						12	1	2	3	7	5	11													35
3	1	3		2	3	2	1					2	3	3	3	3	3														
												2																			
															1			1													

2	6	4	5		7		9	10	11	8			12	1		3															10
8	7		5	6				10	11	12	4			2		3									9						14
2	2	1	2	1	1		1	2	2	1	1		2	1	2							1									
										1			1																		
		1							1	2																					

2	3		5			7	9	10	11	8		6	12	4							U										8
8	7		5	6			9	10	12	14	4			1	2	3	11														12
8	7	U	5	6		4	9	10						11	1	2	3	12													20
3	3		3	2		2	3		1	1	1		1	2	2	2	2	2	1												
									1	1								1													
1							1	1																							

1986-87

Today Division Two

Ground: Roker Park

Manager: Lawrie McMenemy & Bob Stokoe

League Table

	P	W	D	L	F	A	Pts
Derby Co	42	25	9	8	64	38	84
Portsmouth	42	23	9	10	53	28	78
Oldham A	42	22	9	11	65	44	75
Leeds U	42	19	11	12	58	44	68
Ipswich T	42	17	13	12	59	43	64
Crystal Palace	42	19	5	18	51	53	62
Plymouth A	42	16	13	13	62	57	61
Stoke C	42	16	10	16	63	53	58
Sheffield U	42	15	13	14	50	49	58
Bradford C	42	15	10	17	62	62	55
Barnsley	42	14	13	15	49	52	55
Blackburn R	42	15	10	17	45	55	55
Reading	42	14	11	17	52	59	53
Hull C	42	13	14	15	41	55	53
W.B.A.	42	13	12	17	51	49	51
Millwall	42	14	9	19	39	45	51
Huddersfield T	42	13	12	17	54	61	51
Shrewsbury T	42	15	6	21	41	53	51
Birmingham C	42	11	17	14	47	59	50
SUNDERLAND	42	12	12	18	49	59	48
Grimsby T	42	10	14	18	39	59	44
Brighton & H.A.	42	9	12	21	37	54	39

Division 1 Champions: Everton 86 pts

FA Cup Winners: Coventry City

League Cup Winners: Arsenal

Full Members Cup Winners: Blackburn Rovers

Shirt Sponsor: Vaux

Did you know that?

Nigel Saddington played 120 minutes football on his Sunderland debut, v Barnsley 16 September 1986, in a Full Members Cup tie, and became the first, and so far only, player to take and score a penalty in a penalty shoot out on their Sunderland debut.

Match 1: Hesford and Buchanan made debuts
Match 4: Duncan last game
Match 7: Saddington made debut
Match 8: Doyle made debut
Match 19: Curran made debut
Match 23: Mimms made debut
Match 26: Mimms last game
Match 31: Saddington last game
Match 33: Curran last game
Match 36: Outterside only game
Match 37: Bertschin made debut
Match 40: Lawrie McMenemy last game as Sunderland manager
Match 41: Bob Stokoe first game, in a second spell at Sunderland, as caretaker manager
Match 48: Hetzke last game
Match 49: Kennedy and Swindlehurst last games, Bob Stokoe last game as caretaker manager & relegation confirmed

Match No.	Date		Round	Venue	Opponents	Result	FT	HT	Pos.	Scorers	Attendance
1	Aug	23		A	Huddersfield Town	W	2-0	0-0		Gray, Swindlehurst	9,937
3		30		H	Brighton & H.A.	D	1-1	1-0	8	Proctor (pen)	14,990
5	Sep	6		A	Blackburn Rovers	L	1-6	0-3	17	Swindlehurst	7,115
6		13		H	Hull City	W	1-0	1-0	12	Gray	12,911
8		20		A	Ipswich Town	D	1-1	0-0	15	Corner	12,894
9		27		H	Stoke City	W	2-0	2-0	6	Swindlehurst, Armstrong (pen)	14,394
10	Oct	1		A	Derby County	L	2-3	2-1	9	Buchanan, Lemon	12,448
11		4		H	Portsmouth	D	0-0	0-0	11		16,938
12		11		A	Oldham Athletic	D	1-1	0-1	11	Buchanan	7,088
13		18		H	Plymouth Argyle	W	4-2	2-0	8	Buchanan (2), Armstrong, Lemon	13,482
14		21		H	Reading	D	1-1	0-1	7	Swindlehurst	17,114
15		25		H	Birmingham City	W	2-0	1-0	5	Gray, Buchanan	15,553
16	Nov	1		A	Sheffield United	L	1-2	1-0	8	Bennett	12,317
18		8		H	West Bromwich Albion	L	0-3	0-1	10		16,162
19		15		A	Grimsby Town	D	1-1	1-0	10	Swindlehurst	7,065
20		22		H	Shrewsbury Town	D	1-1	0-1	10	Armstrong	12,374
21		29		A	Crystal Palace	L	0-2	0-1	11		6,930
22	Dec	6		H	Millwall	D	1-1	0-1	13	Proctor	10,665
23		13		A	Barnsley	L	0-1	0-0	16		5,535
24		21		H	Blackburn Rovers	W	3-0	2-0	12	Lemon, Gates, Buchanan	11,841
25		26		A	Leeds United	D	1-1	1-0	13	Gates	21,286
26		27		H	Grimsby Town	L	0-1	0-1	14		13,769
28	Jan	24		H	Huddersfield Town	W	2-1	1-1	15	Lemon, Buchanan	10,486
29		31		A	Reading	L	0-1	0-1	15		6,885
30	Feb	7		A	Brighton & H.A.	W	3-0	1-0	12	Gates, Curran, Bennett	7,820
31		14		H	Derby County	L	1-2	0-0	13	Bennett	16,005
32		28		A	Ipswich Town	W	1-0	0-0	14	Proctor (pen)	11,789
33	Mar	3		A	Hull City	L	0-1	0-0	14		5,713
34		14		A	Plymouth Argyle	W	2-1	1-1	15	Buchanan, Lemon	10,062
35		17		A	Stoke City	L	0-3	0-1	15		9,420
36		21		H	Oldham Athletic	L	0-2	0-1	15		10,250
37		28		A	Portsmouth	L	1-3	0-1	16	Gates	13,371
38		31		A	Birmingham City	L	0-2	0-1	17		5,563
39	Apr	4		A	West Bromwich Albion	D	2-2	2-0	17	Bertschin, Proctor (pen)	6,123
40		11		H	Sheffield United	L	1-2	1-1	17	Swindlehurst	8,544
41		18		A	Bradford City	L	2-3	1-0	21	Proctor (2, 1 pen)	11,483
42		20		H	Leeds United	D	1-1	1-0	20	Gates	14,725
43		25		A	Shrewsbury Town	W	1-0	0-0	18	Bennett	5,431
44		28		H	Bradford City	L	2-3	1-1	19	Proctor (2, 1 pen)	16,545
45	May	2		H	Crystal Palace	W	1-0	1-0	18	Armstrong	11,461
46		5		A	Millwall	D	1-1	0-1	18	Armstrong	4,211
47		9		H	Barnsley	L	2-3	1-2	20	Bertschin, Gray	19,059

Appearances
Sub Appearances
Goals

Play Offs

48	May	14		A	Gillingham	L	2-3	1-0		Proctor (2, 1 pen)	13,804
49		17		H	Gillingham	W	4-3 (aet)	2-1		Gates (2), Bennett, Bertschin	25,474

Appearances
Sub Appearances
Goals

FA Cup

27	Jan	10	R3	A	Wimbledon	L	1-2	0-1		Gates	6,231

Appearances
Sub Appearances
Goals

Littlewoods League Cup

2	Aug	26	R1L1	H	York City	L	2-4	0-2		Buchanan, Gates	9,168
4	Sep	3	R1L2	A	York City	W	3-1 (aet)	1-0		Buchanan (2), Proctor	6,481

Appearances
Sub Appearances
Goals

Full Members Cup

7	Sep	16		H	Barnsley	W	1-1*	0-0		Kennedy	6,903
17	Nov	4		A	Bradford City	L	2-3	1-1		Armstrong, Lemon	2,883

* 8-7 penalties

Appearances
Sub Appearances
Goals

Hesford	Burley	Gray	Armstrong	Hetzke	Bennett	Lemon	Proctor	Swindlehurst	Gates	Buchanan	Corner	Agboola	Kennedy	Atkinson	Doyle	Moore	Curran	Mimms	Saddington	Outterside	Bertschin	Duncan	#
1	2	3	4	5	6	7	8	9	10	11			U										1
1	2	3	4		6	7	8	9	10	11	5		U										3
		3	4		6	7	8	9	10	11	5	2	U										5
1	2	10	4		6	7	8	9		11	5		3	12									6
1	2	10	4			7		9		11	5	6	3	12	8								8
1	2	10	4		6	7		9	U	11	5		3		8								9
1	2	10	4		6	7		9	12	11	5		3		8								10
1	2	10	4		6	7		9	12	11	5		3		8								11
1	2	10	4		6	7		9	U	11			3		8								12
1	2	10	4	5	6	7		9	U	11			3		8								13
1	2	10	4	5	6	7		9	12	11			3		8								14
1	2	10	4	5	6	7		9	12	11			3		8								15
1	2	10	4	5	6	7		9	U	11			3	8									16
1	2	3	4		6	7	9		10	11	5				8	12							18
1	2	3	4	5	6	12	10	9		11					8		7						19
1	2	3	4	5	6	U	10	9		11					8		7						20
1	2	3	4	5	6	12	10	9		11					8		7						21
1	2		4	5	6	U	8	9		11			3		10		7						22
	2		4		6		10	9	12	11	5		3				7	1	8				23
	2	11	4	5	6	7	10	9	8	12			3					1					24
	2		4		6	7	8	9	11		5		3	U	10			1					25
	2		4		6	7	10		8	12	5		3		11	9		1					26
1	2	3	4		6	7	10	9	11	12					8				5				28
1	2	3	4	5	6	7	10	9		11			12		8								29
1	2	3	4	5	6	9			11	U		10			8		7						30
1		3	4	5	6	9			11	12		10			8		7	2					31
1	2	3	4		6	7	12		11		5	10			8		9						32
1		3	4	5	6	11	10	9		12		2			8		7						33
1	2	3	4	5	6	7	10	9		11			U	8									34
1		3	4	5	6	7	10	9		11	2		12	8									35
1		3	4	5	6	7	10	9		11			12	8					2				36
1	2			6	7	10		11	12	5			4	8						9			37
1		3	12		6	2	10		11	4	5		7	8						9			38
1		3	4	5	6	7	10	8	11					2	U					9			39
1		3	4	5	6	7	10	8	11	12				2						9			40
1		5	4		6	U	10	8	11		2	3		7						9			41
1		5	7		6		10	8	11		4	2	3	U						9			42
1		5	7		6		10	8	11		4	2	3	U						9			43
1		5	7		6		10		11	4	2	3		8	12					9			44
1		5	7	4	6		10	8	11	U		3	2							9			45
1		5	7	4	6		10	8	11	12		3	2							9			46
1		5	7	4	6		10	8	11	12		3	2							9			47
38	27	38	40	23	41	30	30	34	22	24	17	11	22	3	33	1	9	4	3	1	11		
			1			2	1		5	9			5		2								
	4	5		4	5	8	6	5	8	1			1						2				

Hesford	Burley	Gray	Armstrong	Hetzke	Bennett	Lemon	Proctor	Swindlehurst	Gates	Buchanan	Corner	Agboola	Kennedy	Atkinson	Doyle	Moore	Curran	Mimms	Saddington	Outterside	Bertschin	Duncan	#
1		5	7	4		6		8	10	12			2		3		11				9		48
1		5	7		6	2	8	10	11		12		3		4						9		49
2		2	2	1	2		1	2	2	1			1		2			2			2		
									1		1												
				1		2		2									1						

1	2	11	4		6		10	9	8	U	12		3		7			5					27
1	1	1	1		1		1	1	1				1		1			1					
									1				1										
											1												

	2	3	12		6	7	8	9	10	11		5	U	4				1					2
		3	4		6	7	8	9	10	11	2	5	14	12				1					4
	1	2	1		2	2	2	2	2	2	1	2	1	1				2					
			1										1	1									
						1		1	3														

	2	10	4		6	7		9	12	11	14		3	8				5					7
	2	10	4	5	6	7		9	12	11			3	8				U					17
	2	2	2	1	2	2		2	2	2			2	2				1					
								2		1													
			1		1									1									

ROKER REVIEW
MATCHDAY PROGRAMME
SUNDERLAND A.F.C.
LITTLEWOODS CHALLENGE CUP
ROUND ONE 1st LEG
50p

SUNDERLAND v.
YORK CITY
Tuesday 26th August 1986
Littlewoods Challenge Cup

1987-88

Barclays Division Three

Ground: Roker Park
Manager: Denis Smith

League Table

	P	W	D	L	F	A	Pts
SUNDERLAND	46	27	12	7	92	48	93
Brighton & H.A.	46	23	15	8	69	47	84
Walsall	46	23	13	10	68	50	82
Notts Co	46	23	12	11	82	49	81
Bristol C	46	21	12	13	77	62	75
Northampton T	46	18	19	9	70	51	73
Wigan A	46	20	12	14	70	61	72
Bristol R	46	18	12	16	68	56	66
Fulham	46	19	9	18	69	60	66
Blackpool	46	17	14	15	71	62	65
Port Vale	46	18	11	17	58	56	65
Brentford	46	16	14	16	53	59	62
Gillingham	46	14	17	15	77	61	59
Bury	46	15	14	17	58	57	59
Chester C	46	14	16	16	51	62	58
Preston N.E.	46	15	13	18	48	59	58
Southend U	46	14	13	19	65	83	55
Chesterfield	46	15	10	21	41	70	55
Mansfield T	46	14	12	20	48	59	54
Aldershot	46	15	8	23	64	74	53
Rotherham U	46	12	16	18	50	66	52
Grimsby T	46	12	14	20	48	58	50
York C	46	8	9	29	48	91	33
Doncaster R	46	8	9	29	40	84	33

Division 1 Champions: Liverpool 90 pts

FA Cup Winners: Wimbledon

League Cup Winners: Luton Town

Sherpa Van Trophy: Wolverhampton Wanderers

Shirt Sponsor: Vaux (home); Tuborg (away)

Did you know that?

Richard Ord became the youngest Sunderland player to appear at Wembley (aged 18 yrs & 44 days). The team were appearing in a 20 minute per side game against Wigan Athletic on 16 April 1988 as part of the Football League centenary celebrations. Sunderland, appearing in their third choice all yellow strip for the only time, lost this Mercantile Trophy game 2-1 on penalties.

Match 1: Hardwick, Kay, MacPhail and Owers made debuts & Denis Smith first game as Sunderland manager
Match 6: Proctor last game
Match 8: Hardwick and Buchanan last games
Match 11: Gabbiadini made debut
Match 18: White last game
Match 20: Ord and Heathcote made debuts
Match 24: Corner last game
Match 26: Burley last game
Match 45: Paul Atkinson and Moore last games
Match 46: Pascoe made debut & McGuire only game
Match 50: Carter made debut
Match 52: Promotion confirmed
Match 54: Bertschin last game and substitute Ord was substituted by Bertschin

Match No.	Date	Round	Venue	Opponents	Result	FT	HT	Pos.	Scorers	Attendance
1	Aug 15		A	Brentford	W	1-0	0-0		Bertschin	7,509
3	22		H	Bristol Rovers	D	1-1	0-0	5	Lemon	13,059
5	29		A	Doncaster Rovers	W	2-0	1-0	3	Lemon, Owers	2,740
6	31		H	Mansfield Town	W	4-1	0-1	1	Armstrong, Atkinson, MacPhail (2 pens)	13,994
7	Sep 5		A	Walsall	D	2-2	1-1	1	Bertschin (2)	6,909
8	12		H	Bury	D	1-1	1-1	3	Owers	13,227
9	15		A	Gillingham	D	0-0	0-0	5		9,184
10	19		A	Brighton & H.A.	L	1-3	0-2	10	MacPhail (pen)	8,949
11	26		H	Chester City	L	0-2	0-0	12		12,760
12	29		A	Fulham	W	2-0	1-0	10	Gabbiadini (2)	6,996
13	Oct 3		H	Aldershot	W	3-1	1-1	4	MacPhail, Gabbiadini (2)	12,542
14	10		H	Wigan Athletic	W	4-1	3-1	1	Gates (2), Gabbiadini (2)	13,974
15	17		A	Blackpool	W	2-0	0-0	2	MacPhail (2, 1 pen)	8,476
16	20		A	Bristol City	W	1-0	1-0	1	Owers	15,109
17	24		H	York City	W	4-2	3-1	1	Cornforth (2), Gabbiadini, Gates	19,314
19	31		A	Notts County	L	1-2	1-1	1	MacPhail	8,854
20	Nov 3		H	Southend United	W	7-0	3-0	1	Gates (4), Atkinson (2), Gabbiadini	15,754
21	7		H	Grimsby Town	D	1-1	0-1	1	Armstrong	18,197
23	21		A	Chesterfield	D	1-1	1-0	1	MacPhail (pen)	5,700
25	28		H	Port Vale	W	2-1	2-0	1	Gates, MacPhail (pen)	15,655
27	Dec 12		A	Northampton Town	W	2-0	0-0	1	Lemon, Gabbiadini	7,279
28	20		H	Rotherham United	W	3-0	2-0	1	Gates (3)	20,168
29	26		A	Chester City	W	2-1	2-0	1	MacPhail, Lemon	6,663
30	28		H	Preston North End	D	1-1	0-0	1	MacPhail (pen)	24,814
31	Jan 1		H	Doncaster Rovers	W	3-1	3-1	1	Gabbiadini, Lemon (2)	19,419
32	2		A	Bury	W	3-2	1-1	1	Valentine o.g., Doyle, Gates	4,883
33	16		H	Brighton & H.A.	W	1-0	1-0	1	Lemon	17,404
35	30		H	Gillingham	W	2-1	2-0	1	Bennett, Gabbiadini	16,195
36	Feb 6		H	Walsall	D	1-1	0-1	1	Bennett	18,311
38	13		A	Preston North End	D	2-2	2-2	1	MacPhail, Gates	10,852
39	20		H	Brentford	W	2-0	2-0	1	Owers, Bertschin	15,458
40	24		A	Bristol Rovers	L	0-4	0-1	1		4,501
41	27		A	Aldershot	L	2-3	2-2	2	MacPhail (pen), Gabbiadini	5,010
42	Mar 1		H	Fulham	W	2-0	2-0	1	Armstrong, Gabbiadini	11,379
43	5		A	Blackpool	D	2-2	2-1	2	Armstrong, Gates	15,513
44	12		A	Wigan Athletic	D	2-2	0-1	2	Gabbiadini, Gates	6,949
45	19		H	Notts County	D	1-1	1-0	2	Gabbiadini	24,071
46	26		A	York City	L	1-2	0-1	2	Pascoe	8,878
47	Apr 2		A	Grimsby Town	W	1-0	1-0	1	Gabbiadini	7,001
48	4		H	Chesterfield	W	3-2	2-2	1	Lemon, Pascoe, Gabbiadini	21,886
49	9		H	Southend United	W	4-1	3-1	1	MacPhail (pen), Lemon, Gabbiadini, Pascoe	8,109
50	23		A	Bristol City	L	0-1	0-1	1		18,225
51	26		A	Mansfield Town	W	4-0	2-0	1	Gates (2), Gabbiadini, Pascoe	6,930
52	30		A	Port Vale	W	1-0	0-0	1	Gates	7,569
53	May 2		H	Northampton Town	W	3-1	1-1	1	MacPhail (pen), Armstrong, Gates	29,454
54	7		A	Rotherham United	W	4-1	2-0	1	Gabbiadini (2), MacPhail (pen), Bertschin	9,374

Appearances
Sub Appearances
Goals

FA Cup

	Date	Round	Venue	Opponents	Result	FT	HT		Scorers	Attendance
22	Nov 14	R1	H	Darlington	W	2-0	1-0		Atkinson (2)	16,892
26	Dec 5	R2	A	Scunthorpe United	L	1-2	1-0		Gates	7,178

Appearances
Sub Appearances
Goals

Littlewoods League Cup

	Date	Round	Venue	Opponents	Result	FT	HT		Scorers	Attendance
2	Aug 18	R1L1	H	Middlesbrough	W	1-0	1-0		Gates	15,770
4	25	R1L2	A	Middlesbrough	L	0-2	0-1			15,571

Appearances
Sub Appearances
Goals

Sherpa Van Trophy

	Date		Venue	Opponents	Result	FT	HT		Scorers	Attendance
18	Oct 29		A	Scarborough	W	3-0	2-0		Lemon (2), Moore	3,887
24	Nov 24		H	Rotherham United	W	7-1	6-1		Corner, Burley, Lemon, Owers, Bertschin (2), Moore	6,750
34	Jan 19		H	Crewe Alexandra	W	1-0	0-0		Gabbiadini	8,881
37	Feb 9		H	Hartlepool United	L	0-1	0-0			8,976

Appearances
Sub Appearances
Goals

	Hardwick	Kay	Agboola	Bennett	MacPhail	Armstrong	Lemon	Proctor	Bertschin	Gates	Owers	Moore	Gray	Atkinson, P.	Doyle	Buchanan	Hesford	Gabbiadini	Cornforth	Corner	Ord	Heathcote	McGuire	Pascoe	Carter	Burley	White	
1	2	3	4	5	6	7	8	9	10	11	12	14																1
1	2	3	4	5	6	7	8	9	10	11	12	14																3
1	2	3	4	5	6	7	8	9		11	12	14																5
1	2	3	4	5	6	7	8	9	10		U	U	11															6
1	2	3	4	5	6	7		9	10	11	12	14	8															7
1	2	3	4	5	6	7		9		11	12	14	8	10														8
	2	3	4	5	6	7		9	10	11	U	U	8	1														9
	2	3	4	5	6	7		9	10	11		14	12	8	1													10
	2	3	4	5		7		9		6	U	12	11	8	1	10												11
	2	3	4	5		7		9		6	12	14	11	8	1	10												12
	2	3	4	5		7			9	6	12	14	11	8	1	10												13
	2	3	4	5					9	6	U	12	11	8	1	10	7											14
	2	5		4		12			9	6		14	11	8	1	10	7	3										15
	2	5		4		12			9	6		14	11	8	1	10	7	3										16
	2	3		5		U			9	6		12	11	8	1	10	7	4										17
	2	3		5	12	8			9	6		14	11		1	10	7	4										19
	2			5	8	12			9	6		3	11		1	10	7		4	14								20
	2			5	7	12		14	9	6		3	11	8	1	10			4									21
	2	3		5	7	12		10	9	6		U	11	8	1				4									23
	2	3	4	5		7		12	9	6		U	11	8	1	10												25
	2	3	4	5	11	7		U	9	6		U		8	1	10												27
	2	3	4	5	11	7		U	9	6		U			1	10	8											28
	2	3	4	5	11	7		12	9	6		U		8	1	10												29
	2	3	4	5	11	7		9		6	12	14		8	1	10												30
	2	3	4	5	11	7		12	9			14	6	8	1	10												31
	2	3	4	5	11	7		12	9	6		U		8	1	10												32
	2	3	4	5	11	7		12	9	6		14		8	1	10												33
	2	3	4	5	11	7		12	9			U	6	8	1	10												35
	2	3	4	5	11	7		U	9			U	6	8	1	10												36
	2	3	4	5	11	7			9			14	6	8	1	10	12											38
	2	3	4	5	11			10	9	7		12	6	8	1		U											39
	2	3	4	5	11			10	9	7		14	6	8	1													40
	2	3	4	5	11	12			9	7			6		1	10	8		14									41
	2	3	4	5	11	8		U	9	7			6		1	10	U											42
	2	3	4	5	11	8		14	9	7			6		1	10	12											43
	2	3	4	5	11	8		12	9	7			6	U	1	10												44
	2	3	4	5		8			9	7	12	U	11	6	1	10												45
	2	3	4	5	11			9		7		14		6	1	10					8	12						46
	2	3	4	5	11	8		9		7		14			1	10	12				6							47
	2		4	5	11			9		6		3			1	10	U	12			8							48
	2		4	5	11	7		9		6		3			1	10	U	12			8							49
	2		5		11	7		14	9	6		3	12			10		4			8	1						50
	2		4	5	11	7						3	U	6	1	10	U				8							51
	2	12	4	5	11	7			9			3	6		1	10	U				8							52
	2		4	5	11	7			9			3	6		1	10	U	U			8							53
	2		4	5	11	7		14	9			3	6		1	10		12			8							54
6	46	37	38	46	36	35	4	14	42	37		12	21	31	1	39	35	8	4	4		1	8	1				
		1			1	6		11		9	22	1	1			4		4	1	1								
		2	16	5	9			5	19	4		3	1			21	2			4								

	2	3			5	7	12			9	6		U	11	8		1	10		4								22
		3	4	5		7		12	9	6		14	11	8		1	10					2						26
	1	2	1	2	1	1			2	2			2	2			2		1			1						
						1		1		1																		
									1																			
												1		2														

1	2	3	4	5	6	7	8	9	10	11	U	U																2
1	2	3	4	5	6	7	8	9	10	11	12	14																4
2	2	2	2	2	2	2	2	2					1	1														
									1																			

	2	3		5	14	8		6	9	12	11		1		7	4				10								18
		3		5		7		10	9	6	12		11	8		1		4		14		2						24
	2	3	4	5	11	7		U	9			U	6	8		1	10											34
	3		4	5	11	7			12	9			U	6	8	1	10											37
	3	4	2	4	2	4		1	3	2	1		4	3		4	2	1	2			1	1					
				1		1		1		1	1					1												
					3		2	1		2						1			1			1						

1988-89

Barclays Division Two

Ground: Roker Park
Manager: Denis Smith

League Table

	P	W	D	L	F	A	Pts
Chelsea	46	29	12	5	96	50	99
Manchester C	46	23	13	10	77	53	82
Crystal Palace	46	23	12	11	71	49	81
Watford	46	22	12	12	74	48	78
Blackburn R	46	22	11	13	74	59	77
Swindon T	46	20	16	10	68	53	76
Barnsley	46	20	14	12	66	58	74
Ipswich T	46	22	7	17	71	61	73
W.B.A.	46	18	18	10	65	41	72
Leeds U	46	17	16	13	59	50	67
SUNDERLAND	46	16	15	15	60	60	63
Bournemouth	46	18	8	20	53	62	62
Stoke C	46	15	14	17	57	72	59
Bradford C	46	13	17	16	52	59	56
Leicester C	46	13	16	17	56	63	55
Oldham A	46	11	21	14	75	72	54
Oxford U	46	14	12	20	62	70	54
Plymouth A	46	14	12	20	55	66	54
Brighton & H.A.	46	14	9	23	57	66	51
Portsmouth	46	13	12	21	53	62	51
Hull C	46	11	14	21	52	68	47
Shrewsbury T	46	8	18	20	40	67	42
Birmingham C	46	8	11	27	31	76	35
Walsall	46	5	16	25	41	80	31

Division 1 Champions: Arsenal 76 pts
FA Cup Winners: Liverpool
League Cup Winners: Nottingham Forest
Simod Cup Winners: Nottingham Forest
Shirt Sponsor: Vaux

Did you know that?

The crowd at the first round Simod Cup tie between Charlton Athletic and Sunderland at Selhurst Park, The Addicks temporary home, was only 1,666; the lowest accurately recorded attendance for a Sunderland first team game.

Match 6: Whitehurst made debut
Match 13: Ogilvie made debut
Match 20: Lynch made debut
Match 25: Hesford last game
Match 27: Whitehurst and Ogilvie last games
Match 29: Norman made debut
Match 36: Cullen made debut
Match 37: Barnes only game
Match 38: Hauser made debut
Match 44: Hay only game
Match 46: Substitute Cullen was substituted by Hauser
Match 47: Brian Atkinson and Williams made debuts
Match 48: Hawke made debut & Wharton only game
Match 51: Gray last game
Match 53: Doyle last game

Match No.	Date		Round	Venue	Opponents	Result	FT	HT	Pos.	Scorers	Attendance
1	Aug	27		H	Bournemouth	D	1-1	1-1		Bennett	17,998
3	Sep	3		A	Ipswich Town	L	0-2	0-1	19		12,835
5		10		H	Bradford City	D	0-0	0-0	18		16,286
6		17		A	Birmingham City	L	2-3	0-1	22	Pascoe (2)	6,871
7		20		H	Crystal Palace	D	1-1	0-1	18	Pascoe	13,150
8		24		A	Shrewsbury Town	D	0-0	0-0	21		4,195
10	Oct	1		H	Oldham Athletic	W	3-2	2-2	20	Gabbiadini, MacPhail (pen), Pascoe	12,529
11		4		H	Leeds United	W	2-1	1-0	20	Gabbiadini, Whitehurst	12,671
12		8		A	Walsall	L	0-2	0-0	20		6,150
14		15		A	Hull City	D	0-0	0-0	19		8,261
15		22		H	Swindon Town	W	4-0	2-0	14	Owers, Gabbiadini (2), Whitehurst	13,520
16		25		H	Blackburn Rovers	W	2-0	2-0	14	Gabbiadini, Hendry o.g.	16,601
17		29		A	Manchester City	D	1-1	1-1	13	Armstrong	22,398
18	Nov	2		A	Oxford United	W	4-2	3-1	13	Whitehurst, Armstrong, Gabbiadini, MacPhail (pen)	6,270
19		5		H	Stoke City	D	1-1	0-1	8	Doyle	17,923
21		12		A	Chelsea	D	1-1	1-0	9	Gabbiadini	19,210
22		19		A	West Bromwich Albion	D	1-1	0-1	10	Bennett	18,141
23		26		A	Brighton & H.A.	L	0-3	0-1	12		10,039
24	Dec	3		H	Watford	D	1-1	0-1	14	MacPhail (pen)	16,330
25		10		A	Leicester City	L	1-3	0-2	16	Pascoe	11,093
26		18		A	Plymouth Argyle	W	4-1	2-0	13	Armstrong, Pascoe, Gabbiadini, Gates	13,498
28		26		H	Barnsley	W	1-0	0-0	9	Dobbin o.g.	21,994
29		31		H	Portsmouth	W	4-0	2-0	8	Gates, Ord, Armstrong, Pascoe	21,566
30	Jan	2		A	Bradford City	L	0-1	0-0	10		12,186
33		14		H	Oxford United	W	1-0	1-0	6	Owers	12,853
34		21		A	Bournemouth	W	1-0	1-0	6	Gates	8,992
35	Feb	4		A	Leeds United	L	0-2	0-1			31,985
36		11		H	Walsall	L	0-3	0-1	11		14,203
37		18		A	Swindon Town	L	1-4	1-3	13	Armstrong	7,432
38		25		H	Hull City	W	2-0	0-0	10	Pascoe, Gabbiadini	14,719
39		28		A	Blackburn Rovers	D	2-2	2-0	12	Gabbiadini (2, 1 pen)	8,288
40	Mar	1		H	Stoke City	L	0-2	0-1	14		12,489
41		14		H	Manchester City	L	2-4	1-1	14	Gabbiadini, Gates	16,167
42		18		A	Crystal Palace	L	0-1	0-0	14		9,108
43		21		H	Chelsea	L	1-2	1-1	14	Gabbiadini	14,714
44		25		H	Ipswich Town	W	4-0	1-0	13	Gabbiadini (3, 1 pen), Owers	13,359
45		27		A	Barnsley	L	0-3	0-1	14		8,070
46	Apr	1		H	Birmingham City	D	2-2	1-0	15	Lemon, Gabbiadini	10,969
47		4		H	Plymouth Argyle	W	2-1	2-0	14	Armstrong (2)	8,001
48		8		A	Portsmouth	L	0-2	0-1	14		7,724
49		15		A	Oldham Athletic	D	2-2	2-1	14	MacPhail, Hauser	5,944
50		22		H	Shrewsbury Town	W	2-1	1-0	13	Hauser, Armstrong	9,427
51		29		H	Brighton & H.A.	W	1-0	1-0	12	Pascoe	12,856
52	May	1		A	Watford	W	1-0	1-0	11	Gabbiadini	13,493
53		6		A	West Bromwich Albion	D	0-0	0-0	11		10,451
54		13		H	Leicester City	D	2-2	0-0	11	Bennett, Pascoe	15,819

Appearances
Sub Appearances
Goals

FA Cup

Match No.	Date		Round	Venue	Opponents	Result	FT	HT	Scorers	Attendance
31	Jan	7	R3	H	Oxford United	D	1-1	1-0	Ord	17,074
32		11	R3r	A	Oxford United	L	0-2	0-1		7,236

Appearances
Sub Appearances
Goals

Littlewoods League Cup

Match No.	Date		Round	Venue	Opponents	Result	FT	HT	Scorers	Attendance
2	Aug	30	R1L1	A	York City	D	0-0	0-0		4,204
4	Sep	6	R1L2	H	York City	W	4-0	2-0	Gabbiadini (2), Pascoe (2)	9,388
9		27	R2L1	H	West Ham United	L	0-3	0-1		13,691
13	Oct	12	R2L2	A	West Ham United	L	1-2	1-0	Gabbiadini	10,558

Appearances
Sub Appearances
Goals

Simod Cup

Match No.	Date		Round	Venue	Opponents	Result	FT	HT	Scorers	Attendance
20	Nov	8	R1	A	Charlton Athletic	W	1-0	1-0	Gabbiadini	1,666
27	Dec	22	R2	A	Blackburn Rovers	L	1-2	0-1	Gabbiadini	4,450

Appearances
Sub Appearances
Goals

#	Hesford	Kay	Agboola	Bennett	MacPhail	Doyle	Lemon	Armstrong	Gates	Gabbiadini	Pascoe	Owers	Ord	Gray	Cornforth	Whitehurst	Lynch	Ogilvie	Carter	Norman	Cullen	Barnes	Hauser	Hay	Atkinson, B.	Williams	Wharton	Hawke	McKenzie	#
1		2	3	4	5	6	7	8	9	10	11	12		U																1
	1	2	3	4	5	6	7	8	9	10	11			12	14															3
	1	2		4	5	6		8	9	10	11	7	U	3	12															5
	1	2	U	4	5	6		8	9		11	7		3	12	10														6
	1	2	3	4	5	6		8	9	12	11	7		14		10														7
	1	2	3	4	5	6		8	9		11	7	U	12		10														8
	1		3		5	6		8	U	9	11	7	4	2		10	U													10
	1		3		5	6		8	U	9	11	7	4	2		10	U													11
	1		3		5	6		8	12	9	11	7	4	2		10	U													12
	1		3		5	6		8	12	9	11	7	4	2		10	U													14
	1		3	12	5	6		8	U	9	11	7	4	2		10														15
	1		3	U	5	6		8	U	9	11	7	4	2		10														16
	1		3	U	5	6		8	U	9	11	7	4	2		10														17
	1		3	12	5	6		8	U	9	11	7	4	2		10														18
	1		3	12	5	6		8	U	9	11	7	4	2		10														19
	1	2		4	5	6		8	12	9	11			3		10	6	14												21
	1		U	4	5		6	8	12	9	11	7				10	3													22
	1		3	4	5	6		8	12	9	11	7	14	2		10														23
	1		3	4	5	6		8	U	9	11	7	U	2		10														24
	1		3	4	5	6		8	12	9	11	7	14	2		10														25
			U	2	5	6		8	9	10	11	7	4	3			U		1											26
			U	2	5	6		8	9	10	11	7	4	3			U		1											28
		14	2	5		6		8	9	10	11	7	4	3	12				1											29
			U	2	5	6		8	9	10			11	4	3	U			1											30
		12	2	5			7	8	9		11	6	4	3	10				1							U				33
		12	2	5				8	9	10	11	7	4	3	6				1	U										34
			U	2	5	6	12	8	9		11	7	4	3	10				1											35
		7	2	5	6			8	9				4	3	10		U		1	12										36
		12	2	5	6			8	9		11		4	3	10				1	14	7									37
			4	2	5	6		8	9	10	11			3	12				1	7	14									38
			4	2	5	6		8	9	10	11			3	U				1	7	12									39
			4	2	5	6		8	9	10	11	14		3					1	7	12									40
			4	2	5	6		8	9	10	11	7		3					1	14	12									41
			4	2	5	6	14	8	9	10		7	11	3					1		12									42
				2	5	U		11	8	U	10		7	6	3		4		1		9									43
				2	5			14	8	12	10	11	7	6	3				1		9	4								44
				2	5	4		14	8	12	10	11	7	6	3				1		9									45
		2		5			4	8	9	10	11	7	6	3					1	12	14									46
			2	5			4	8	9	10		7	6	3					1		U			11	12					47
		3	2	5		7	4	8	10					6	12				1		11		9	14						48
			2	5		7		10			8	6	3	4		11			1		9	12		U						49
		3	2	5		7	8	10			11	6	U	4					1		9			12						50
		3	2	5		4	8	12		11	7	6	14						1			9								51
			3	2	5		14	8	10	9	11	7	6	4					1						12					52
			3	2	5	8	4	11	9	10	7		6	U					1		12									53
			3	2	5		14	11	12	10	7	4	6	8					1		9									54
	20	11	25	37	45	35	12	45	27	35	39	36	31	36	10	17	4		2	24	3	1	6	1	2		1	1		
		4	3		6			10	1			2	3	4	5		1			4		7		1	1		3			
			3	4	1		1	8	4	18	10	3	1		3					2										

	U	2	5	6	12	8	9	10	11	7	4	3					1													31
		12	2	5	6		7	8	9	10	11	14	4	3				1												32
			2	2	2	1	2	2	2	2	1	2	2					2												
		1			1				1				1																	
												1																		

1	2	3	4	5	6	7	8	9	10	11	12		U																	2
	2	3	4	7		8	9	10	11	6	12	5	14																4
	2	3	4		5	6	8	9	10	11	7		12	U															9
	1		3		5	6	12	8	9	10	11	7	4	2			14													13
		3	3	3	4	4	1	4	4	4	4	3	1	2																
									1				1				1													
										3	2																			

		7		4	5	6	U	8	10	9	11			2		U	3		1											20
			5	2		6	8		10	11	7	4	3	12	9		14		1											27
	1	1	2	1	1	1	2	1		2	2	1	1	2	1	1	1	1												
														1			1													
									2																					

BARCLAYS League Division 2
SUNDERLAND AFC v LEEDS UNITED
Tuesday 4th October
50p Programme No. 7

ROKER REVIEW

1989-90

Barclays Division Two

Ground: Roker Park
Manager: Denis Smith

League Table

	P	W	D	L	F	A	Pts
Leeds U	46	24	13	9	79	52	85
Sheffield U	46	24	13	9	78	58	85
Newcastle U	46	22	14	10	80	55	80
Swindon T	46	20	14	12	79	59	74
Blackburn R	46	19	17	10	74	59	74
SUNDERLAND	46	20	14	12	70	64	74
West Ham U	46	20	12	14	80	57	72
Oldham A	46	19	14	13	70	57	71
Ipswich T	46	19	12	15	67	66	69
Wolverh'pton W	46	18	13	15	67	60	67
Port Vale	46	15	16	15	62	57	61
Portsmouth	46	15	16	15	62	65	61
Leicester C	46	15	14	17	67	79	59
Hull C	46	14	16	16	58	65	58
Watford	46	14	15	17	58	60	57
Plymouth A	46	14	13	19	58	63	55
Oxford U	46	15	9	22	57	66	54
Brighton & H.A.	46	15	9	22	56	72	54
Barnsley	46	13	15	18	49	71	54
W.B.A.	46	12	15	19	67	71	51
Middlesbrough	46	13	11	22	52	63	50
Bournemouth	46	12	12	22	57	76	48
Bradford C	46	9	14	23	44	68	41
Stoke C	46	6	19	21	35	63	37

Division 1 Champions: Liverpool 79 pts
FA Cup Winners: Manchester Utd
League Cup Winners: Nottingham Forest
Zenith Data Systems Cup Winners: Chelsea
Shirt Sponsor: Vaux

Did you know that?

Sunderland lost the Play Off Final on 28 May however were promoted on 13 June as winners Swindon Town were found guilty of breaching 36 League rules, mainly involving illegal payments to players, and were relegated to Divison 3. In addition Tranmere Rovers were promoted from Division 3.

Match 1: Hardyman made debut
Match 7: Rush made debut
Match 13: Ricardo Gabbiadini only game
Match 23: Brady made debut
Match 33: Lynch last game
Match 37: Lemon last game
Match 56: Heathcote last game
Match 59: Gates last game

Match No.	Date		Round	Venue	Opponents	Result	FT	HT	Pos.	Scorers	Attendance
1	Aug	19		A	Swindon Town	W	2-0	1-0		Gates, Hawke	10,199
2		22		H	Ipswich Town	L	2-4	0-3	9	Gates, Gabbiadini	15,965
3		27		H	Middlesbrough	W	2-1	0-1	4	Bennett, Pascoe	21,569
4	Sep	2		A	West Bromwich Albion	D	1-1	0-0	7	Gabbiadini	10,885
5		9		H	Watford	W	4-0	3-0	2	Armstrong, Gabbiadini (3)	15,042
6		16		A	Blackburn Rovers	D	1-1	0-0	3	MacPhail	10,329
7		24		H	Newcastle United	D	0-0	0-0	4		29,499
8		27		A	Leicester City	W	3-2	1-1	3	Armstrong, Hardyman (pen), Owers	10,843
9		30		H	Sheffield United	D	1-1	1-1	4	Deane o.g.	22,760
10	Oct	7		H	Bournemouth	W	3-2	1-1	2	Gates (2), Gabbiadini	15,933
11		14		A	Leeds United	L	0-2	0-2	5		27,815
12		18		A	West Ham United	L	0-5	0-3	8		20,901
13		21		H	Bradford City	W	1-0	1-0	6	MacPhail	14,849
14		28		A	Stoke City	W	2-0	0-0	5	Bracewell, Gabbiadini	12,480
15		31		H	Barnsley	W	4-2	2-0	3	Gates (2), Hardyman (pen), Bennett	14,234
16	Nov	4		A	Oldham Athletic	L	1-2	0-1	4	Owers	8,829
17		11		H	Wolverhampton W.	D	1-1	0-0	5	Hardyman (pen)	20,660
18		18		H	Plymouth Argyle	W	3-1	2-1	4	Gabbiadini, Owers, Ord	15,033
19		25		A	Brighton & H.A.	W	2-1	1-1	4	Gabbiadini, Owers	8,681
20	Dec	2		H	Swindon Town	D	2-2	0-1	4	Armstrong, Hauser	15,849
21		9		A	Ipswich Town	D	1-1	1-0	3	Owers	13,833
22		16		A	Portsmouth	D	3-3	2-1	3	Bennett, Hardyman, Gabbiadini	7,127
23		26		H	Oxford United	W	1-0	0-0	3	Gabbiadini	24,075
24		30		H	Port Vale	D	2-2	0-1	3	Gabbiadini, Hauser	21,354
25	Jan	1		A	Hull City	L	2-3	0-2	3	Hauser, Owers	9,346
26		14		A	Middlesbrough	L	0-3	0-2	5		17,698
27		20		A	West Bromwich Albion	D	1-1	1-0	5	Gabbiadini	15,583
28	Feb	4		A	Newcastle United	D	1-1	0-0	5	Gabbiadini	31,572
29		10		H	Blackburn Rovers	L	0-1	0-0	6		16,043
30		17		A	Watford	D	1-1	1-1	7	Hauser	9,093
31		24		H	Brighton & H.A.	W	2-1	2-0	5	Hauser (2)	14,528
32	Mar	3		A	Plymouth Argyle	L	0-3	0-2	7		7,299
33		10		H	Leicester City	D	2-2	0-1	8	Gabbiadini, Armstrong	13,017
34		17		A	Bournemouth	W	1-0	0-0	7	Gabbiadini	6,328
35		20		H	Leeds United	L	0-1	0-1	10		17,851
36		24		H	West Ham United	W	4-3	1-0	9	Brady, Hardyman (pen), Owers, Gabbiadini	13,896
37		31		A	Bradford City	W	1-0	0-0	7	Brady	9,826
38	Apr	3		A	Sheffield United	W	3-1	0-1	5	Bracewell, Gabbiadini (2)	20,588
39		7		H	Stoke City	W	2-1	0-0	5	Gabbiadini, Armstrong	17,119
40		10		A	Barnsley	L	0-1	0-0	5		11,141
41		14		H	Hull City	L	0-1	0-1	6		17,437
42		16		A	Oxford United	W	1-0	0-0	6	Gabbiadini	6,053
43		21		H	Portsmouth	D	2-2	1-0	6	Armstrong (2)	14,379
44		28		A	Wolverhampton W.	W	1-0	0-0	6	Hardyman	19,463
45	May	1		A	Port Vale	W	2-1	2-1	4	Owers, Hardyman	9,447
46		5		H	Oldham Athletic	L	2-3	1-1	6	Owers, Armstrong	22,243

Appearances
Sub Appearances
Goals

Play Offs

57	May 13	S1L	H	Newcastle United	D	0-0	0-0			26,641
58	16	S2L	A	Newcastle United	W	2-0	1-0		Gates, Gabbiadini	32,216
59	28	F	N*	Swindon Town	L	0-1	0-1			72,873

* at Wembley

Appearances
Sub Appearances
Goals

	Norman	Agboola	Hardyman	Bennett	MacPhail	Owers	Cullen	Armstrong	Gates	Gabbiadini, M.	Pascoe	Cornforth	Hawke	Ord	Bracewell	Carter	Hauser	Kay	Gabbiadini, R.	Atkinson	Heathcote	Brady	Williams	Lynch	Rush	Lemon	
1	1	2	3	4	5	6	7	8	9	10	11	12	14														1
2	1	2	3		5	6	7	8	9	10	11	U	4							U							2
3	1	2	3	4	5	6	U	8	9	10	11	U		7													3
4	1	2	3	4	5	6	U	8	9	10	11	12		7													4
5		2	3	4	5	6	12	8	9	10	11			7	1	U											5
6		2	3	4	5	6	12	8	9	10	11			7	1	14											6
8		2	3	4	5	6	U	8	9	10	11			7	1	U											8
9		2	3	4	5	6	U	8	9	10	11			7	1	U											9
10		2	3	4	5	6	12	8	9	10	11			7	1	14											10
12			3	4	5	6	U	8	9	10	11			7	1		2				U						12
13		2	3	4	5	6	12	8	9	10	11			7	1			14									13
14			3	4	5	6	12	8	9	10	11			7	1	14	2										14
15			3	4	5	6	U	8	9	10	11			7	1		2		U								15
17		3		4	5	6	12	8	9	10	11			7	1		2		U								17
18			3	4	5	6	12	8	9	10	11		14	7	1		2										18
19		2	3	4		6	12	8	9	10	11		5		1			7	14								19
21			3	4		6	U	8	9	10	11		5	7	1			2		U							21
23		2	3	4		6		8	9	10	11		5		1	U		7	12								23
24		3		4		6		8	9	10	11		5	7	1	U		12		2							24
26		2	3	4		6		8	9	10	11		5		1	14	12	7									26
28			2	3	4	U	6		8	9	10	11			1	U	5	7									28
29	1	2	3	4	7	6		8	9	10	11				12	5				U							29
30	1	2	3	4		6		8	9	10	11	7			12	5		U									30
31	1	2	3	4		6		8	9	10	11		14		12	5		7									31
32	1	14	3	4	5	6		8	9	10	11			7	12	2											32
34	1	3	9	4	5	6		8	U	10	11			7	12	2											34
36		12	3	4	5	6	11	8		10		14		7	1	9	2										36
38	1	4	3		5	6	12	8	9	10				7	U	2	11										38
39	1	4	3	5			8	9	10		11			7	12	2	6	U									39
40	1	4	3		5		11	8		10		12		7	9	2	6	U									40
41	1	U	3	4	5		11	8		10		U		7	9	2	6										41
42	1	12	3	4	5	11		8		10		14		7	9	2	6										42
43	1	3		4	5	6		8		10		12		7	9	2	U		11								43
44	1	3		4	5	6		8		10	12			7	9	2	14		11								44
45	1	3		4	5	6		8	9	10	11			7	12	2	U										45
46	1	12	3		5	6	U	8		10	11			7		2		4	9								46
47	1	12	3	4	5	6		8	U	10	9			7		2			11								47
48	1	U	3		5	6		8	U	10	11			7		2		4	9								48
49	1	U	3		5	6		8	12	10	9			7		2		4	11								49
50	1	U	3		5	6		8	12	10	9			7		2		4	11								50
51	1	12	3	4	5	6	14	8	9	10				7		2			11								51
52	1	11	3	4	5	6	14	8	9	10		12				2	7			4	U						52
53	1	11	3		5	6		8	9	10		U		7		2		4	U								53
54	1	11	3	4	5	6	U	8	9	10				7	U	2											54
55	1	11	3	4	5	6	U	8	9	10				7		2		12									55
56	1	11	3		5	6		8	9	10				7	12	2		4	14								56
	28	30	42	36	38	43	5	46	34	46	32	1	6	36	18	6	31	11	6	9	1						
		6				11	2			1	7	1		12	1	1	2	2	2								
			7	3	2	9		8	6	21		1	1	2		6			2								
57	1	11	3	4	5	6		8	9	10				7		U	2			U							57
58	1	3		4	5	6		8	9	10		11		7		U	2			U							58
59	1	3		4	5	6		9	10	11				7		12	2		14								59
	3	3	1	3	3	3		3	3	3		1		3			3										
												1		1					1								
									1	1																	

493

1989-90 Continued

Match No.	Date		Round	Venue	Opponents	Result	FT	HT	Pos.	Scorers	Attendance
FA Cup											
33	Jan	6	R3	A	Reading	L	1-2	1-0		Armstrong	9,344
											Appearances
											Sub Appearances
											Goals
Littlewoods League Cup											
7	Sep	19	R2L1	H	Fulham	D	1-1	1-1		Hardyman (pen)	11,416
11	Oct	4	R2L2	A	Fulham	W	3-0	2-0		Gabbiadini (2), Armstrong	6,314
16		24	R3	H	Bournemouth	D	1-1	1-1		Gabbiadini	12,595
20	Nov	7	R3r	A	Bournemouth	W	1-0	1-0		Gabbiadini	7,349
25		29	R4	A	Exeter City	D	2-2	1-0		Armstrong, Gates	8,643
27	Dec	5	R4r	H	Exeter City	W	5-2	2-1		Pascoe, Armstrong, Gates (2), Hardyman (pen)	18,130
35	Jan	17	R5	H	Coventry City	D	0-0	0-0			27,218
37		24	R5r	A	Coventry City	L	0-5	0-2			21,219
											Appearances
											Sub Appearances
											Goals
Zenith Data Systems Cup											
22	Nov	14	R1	H	Port Vale	L	1-2	1-1		Armstrong (pen)	7,035
											Appearances
											Sub Appearances
											Goals

Norman	Agboola	Hardyman	Bennett	MacPhail	Owers	Cullen	Armstrong	Gates	Gabbiadini, M.	Pascoe	Comfort	Hawke	Ord	Bracewell	Carter	Hauser	Kay	Gabbiadini, R.	Atkinson	Heathcote	Brady	Williams	Lynch	Rush	Lemon	
1	4			5	6		8	9	10	11		U	7	12	2				3							33
1	1		1	1		1	1	1	1			1							1							
							1									1										
	2	3	4	5	6	12	8	9		11	7			1	10						14					7
	3	4	5	6	U	8	9	10	11			7	1		2				12							11
	3	4	5	6	12	8	9	10	11			7	1		2		U									16
3		4		6	U	8	9	10	11					1					7		2					20
2	3	4		6		8	9	10	11		5		1	12	U			7								25
2	3	4		6		8		10	11			1		12	5		7			14						27
14	3	4	5	6		8	9	10	11			7	1	12	2											35
14	3	4		6		8	9	10		5	7	1		12	2						11					37
4	7	8	4	8		8	8	7	7	1		3	4	8	1	5		3			1			1		
	2					2							5							1		1	1			
	2									3	3	4	1													
1	2		4		6	11	8		10			5	7		9			12	U		3					22
1	1		1		1	1	1		1			1	1					1			1					
									1																	

Gordon Armstrong who was ever present during this season. His 59 appearances is the highest seasonal total by any player for Sunderland. Gordon went on to make over 400 appearances and score 60 goals during his 13 years with the club.

1990-91

Barclays Division One

Ground: Roker Park
Manager: Denis Smith

League Table

	P	W	D	L	F	A	Pts
Arsenal*	38	24	13	1	74	18	83
Liverpool	38	23	7	8	77	40	76
Crystal Palace	38	20	9	9	50	41	69
Leeds U	38	19	7	12	65	47	64
Manchester C	38	17	11	10	64	53	62
Manchester U**	38	16	12	10	58	45	59
Wimbledon	38	14	14	10	53	46	56
Nottingham F	38	14	12	12	65	50	54
Everton	38	13	12	13	50	46	51
Tottenham H	38	11	16	11	51	50	49
Chelsea	38	13	10	15	58	69	49
Q.P.R.	38	12	10	16	44	53	46
Sheffield U	38	13	7	18	36	55	46
Southampton	38	12	9	17	58	69	45
Norwich C	38	13	6	19	41	64	45
Coventry C	38	11	11	16	42	49	44
Aston Villa	38	9	14	15	46	58	41
Luton T	38	10	7	21	42	61	37
SUNDERLAND	38	8	10	20	38	60	34
Derby Co	38	5	9	24	37	75	24

*Arsenal had two points deducted for disciplinary reasons.
**Manchester United had one point deducted for disciplinary reasons.

FA Cup Winners: Tottenham Hotspur
League Cup Winners: Sheffield Wed.
Zenith Data Systems Cup Winners: Crystal Palace

Shirt Sponsor: Vaux

Did you know that?

John MacPhail played only one top flight game in a career spanning almost 600 League games; for Sunderland at Norwich City on 25 August 1990.

Match 1: Davenport made debut & MacPhail last game
Match 2: Ball made debut
Match 9: Smith made debut
Match 24: Substitute Hawke was substituted by Hardyman
Match 31: Mooney made debut
Match 36: Cornforth last game
Match 44: Relegation confirmed

Match No.	Date	Round	Venue	Opponents	Result	FT	HT	Pos.	Scorers	Attendance
1	Aug 25		A	Norwich City	L	2-3	0-2		Davenport, Gabbiadini	17,247
2	28		H	Tottenham Hotspur	D	0-0	0-0	13		30,214
3	Sep 1		H	Manchester United	W	2-1	1-0	9	Owers, Bennett	26,105
4	8		A	Chelsea	L	2-3	1-2	12	Gabbiadini, Brady	19,414
5	15		H	Everton	D	2-2	2-2	14	Davenport (pen), Gabbiadini	25,004
6	22		A	Wimbledon	D	2-2	1-0	13	Armstrong, Davenport	6,143
8	29		H	Liverpool	L	0-1	0-1	16		31,107
9	Oct 6		A	Aston Villa	L	0-3	0-1	16		26,017
11	20		H	Luton Town	W	2-0	2-0	15	Gabbiadini, Davenport	20,025
12	27		A	Arsenal	L	0-1	0-0	17		38,539
14	Nov 3		H	Manchester City	D	1-1	0-0	18	Davenport	23,137
15	10		H	Coventry City	D	0-0	0-0	18		20,101
16	17		A	Nottingham Forest	L	0-2	0-1	18		22,757
17	24		A	Sheffield United	W	2-0	0-0	14	Gabbiadini (2)	19,179
18	Dec 1		H	Derby County	L	1-2	0-1	16	Armstrong	21,212
19	8		A	Tottenham Hotspur	D	3-3	2-0	16	Pascoe (2), Davenport	30,431
21	15		H	Norwich City	L	1-2	1-0	17	Armstrong	18,693
22	23		H	Leeds United	L	0-1	0-0	17		23,773
23	26		A	Crystal Palace	L	1-2	0-0	18	Rush	15,228
24	29		H	Queens Park Rangers	L	2-3	1-1	19	Pascoe, Ball (pen)	11,072
25	Jan 1		H	Southampton	W	1-0	0-0	17	Ball (pen)	19,757
27	12		A	Manchester United	L	0-3	0-3	17		45,934
28	19		H	Chelsea	W	1-0	1-0	17	Pascoe	20,038
30	Feb 2		A	Everton	L	0-2	0-0	17		23,124
31	16		H	Nottingham Forest	W	1-0	1-0	16	Gabbiadini	20,394
32	23		A	Coventry City	D	0-0	0-0	17		10,453
33	Mar 2		A	Derby County	D	3-3	3-2	19	Armstrong, Gabbiadini, Ball	16,027
34	9		H	Sheffield United	L	0-1	0-0	19		23,238
35	16		A	Liverpool	L	1-2	1-2	19	Armstrong	37,582
36	23		H	Aston Villa	L	1-3	0-1	19	Davenport	21,099
37	30		H	Crystal Palace	W	2-1	1-0	19	Brady, Rush	19,704
38	Apr 2		A	Leeds United	L	0-5	0-3	19		28,132
39	6		H	Queens Park Rangers	L	0-0	0-0	19		17,899
40	13		A	Southampton	L	1-3	1-1	19	Hauser	16,812
41	20		A	Luton Town	L	2-1	1-1	19	Armstrong, Pascoe	11,157
42	23		H	Wimbledon	D	0-0	0-0	19		24,036
43	May 4		H	Arsenal	D	0-0	0-0	19		22,606
44	11		A	Manchester City	L	2-3	2-2	19	Gabbiadini, Bennett	39,194

Appearances
Sub Appearances
Goals

FA Cup

| 26 | Jan 5 | R3 | A | Arsenal | L | 1-2 | 0-2 | | O'Leary o.g. | 35,128 |

Appearances
Sub Appearances
Goals

Rumbelows (League) Cup

7	Sep 26	R2L1	H	Bristol City	L	0-1	0-1			10,358
10	Oct 9	R2L2	A	Bristol City	W	6-1	2-1		Hauser, Ball, Owers, Gabbiadini (2), Cullen	11,776
13	31	R3	A	Derby County	L	0-6	0-4			16,422

Appearances
Sub Appearances
Goals

Zenith Data Systems Cup

| 20 | Dec 11 | R2 | A | Notts County | W | 2-2* | 2-1 | | O'Riordan o.g., Armstrong | 3,003 |
| 29 | Jan 22 | R3 | A | Everton | L | 1-4 | 0-1 | | Ball | 4,609 |

* 3-1 penalties

Appearances
Sub Appearances
Goals

	Norman	Kay	Agboola	Bennett	MacPhail	Owers	Bracewell	Armstrong	Davenport	Gabbiadini	Atkinson	Cullen	Hauser	Ball	Hardyman	Brady	Ord	Smith	Carter	Pascoe	Hawke	Rush	Williams	Mooney	Cornforth	Gray, M.D.	Sampson	
1	2	3	4	5	6	7	8	9	10	11	12	14																1
1	2	3	4		6	7	8	9	10		12	U		5	11													2
1	2	3	4		6	7	8	9	10				14	5	11	12												3
1	2	3	4		6		8	9	10	7		U		5	11	12												4
1	2	3	4		6	7	8	9	10	U				5	11	12												5
1	2		4		6	7	8	9	10			12		5	11	U	3											6
1	2		4		6	7	8	9	10		11	12	5			3							U					8
1	2		4		6	7	8	9	10		U	11	5			U	3											9
1	2		4		6	7	8	9	10		U		5	11		3			U									11
1	2		4		6	7	8	9	10			12	5	11		U	3											12
1	2		4		6	7	8	9	10		11		5	3	12	U												14
	2		4		6	7	8	9	10				5	3		U		1	11	U								15
1	2		4		6	7	8	9	10				5	3		U			11	12								16
1	2		4		6	7	8	9	10				5	3		U			11			U						17
1	2		4		6	7	8	9	10				5	3					11	U		U						18
1	2		4		6	7	8	9	10				5	3					11	U		U						19
1	2		4		6	7	8	9	10				5	3		4			11	U			U					21
1	2		4		6	7	8		10				5	3		9			11	12			U					22
1	2		4		6	7	8		10		U		5	3		9			11	12								23
1	2		4		6	7	8	9					5	14		3			11	12	10							24
1	2		4		6	7	8						5	3					11	9	10	U						25
1			4		6	7	8		10				5	14		3			11	12	9	2						27
1			4		6	7	8	9	10	2			5	3		U			11	12								28
1	U		4		6	7	8	9	10	12			5	3		2			11									30
1	U		4		2	7	8	9	10	U			5				3		11		6							31
1	U		4		2	7	8	9	10	U			5				3		11		6							32
1			4		2	7	8	9	10				5	3		12			11	U	6							33
1			4		2	7	8						5		12	U	3		11		6							34
1	6		4		2	7	8		10				5	3	12				11	9		14						35
1	14		4		2	7	8	12						3	10	5			11	9		6						36
1	6		4		2	7		U		8				3	10	5	11			9	U							37
1	6		4		2	7	8			12				3	10	5	11			9		14						38
1	14		4		2	7	8	9					5	3	10		11	6		12								39
1	11		4		2	7	8		12				9	5	3			6		10		U						40
1	11		4		2	7	8			12			9	5	3	14		6			10							41
1			4		2	7	8	11	10				9	5	3	14	12	6										42
1	11		4		2	7			10	U			9	5	3	12		6	8									43
1	11		4		2	7			9	10				14	3	12	5	6	8									44
37	28	5	37	1	38	37	35	27	30	4	2	5	33	30	4	12	9	1	25	3	8	1	5	1				
	2							2	1	2	3	5		2	10	2			4	3		1	1					
		2		1		6	7	9			1	3	2				5		2									

1	2		4		6	7	8						5	3	12	U		11	9	10								26
1	1				1	1	1						1	1			1	1	1	1								
															1													

1	2		4		6	7	8	9	10		12		5	11	3	14												7
1	2		4		6	7	8	9	10	12	11		5		14	3												10
1	2		4		6	7	8	9	10	14			5	11	12	3												13
3	3		3		3	3	3	3	3				1	3	2	1		2										
								2	1					3														
			1				2			1	1	1																

1	2		4		6	7	8	9					5	3		12		11	10			14						20
1			4		6	7	8	9	10	2			5	3				11	12			14						29
2	1		2		2	2	2	2	1	1			2	2		1		2	1			2						
														1				1			2							
						1				1																		

Gary Owers

Gary was ever present during this season. He is one of only 16 players who have played for Sunderland in each of the top three Leagues.

497

1991-92

Barclays Division Two

Ground: Roker Park
Managers: Denis Smith & Malcolm Crosby

League Table

	P	W	D	L	F	A	Pts
Ipswich T	46	24	12	10	70	50	84
Middlesbrough	46	23	11	12	58	41	80
Derby Co	46	23	9	14	69	51	78
Leicester C	46	23	8	15	62	55	77
Cambridge U	46	19	17	10	65	47	74
Blackburn R	46	21	11	14	70	53	74
Charlton A	46	20	11	15	54	48	71
Swindon T	46	18	15	13	69	55	69
Portsmouth	46	19	12	15	65	51	69
Watford	46	18	11	17	51	48	65
Wolverh'pton W	46	18	10	18	61	54	64
Southend U	46	17	11	18	63	63	62
Bristol R	46	16	14	16	60	63	62
Tranmere R	46	14	19	13	56	56	61
Millwall	46	17	10	19	64	71	61
Barnsley	46	16	11	19	46	57	59
Bristol C	46	13	15	18	55	71	54
SUNDERLAND	46	14	11	21	61	65	53
Grimsby	46	14	11	21	47	62	53
Newcastle U	46	13	13	20	66	84	52
Oxford U	46	13	11	22	66	73	50
Plymouth A	46	13	9	24	42	64	48
Brighton & H.A.	46	12	11	23	56	77	47
Port Vale	46	10	15	21	42	59	45

Division 1 Champions: Leeds Utd 82 pts
FA Cup Winners: Liverpool
League Cup Winners: Manchester Utd
Shirt Sponsor: Vaux

Did you know that?

Sunderland became the lowest placed side in the League to appear in an FA Cup final since Leicester City (19th Division 2) in 1948-49 season.

Match 3: Sampson made debut
Match 6: Agboola last game
Match 9: Gabbiadini last game
Match 11: Beagrie made debut
Match 12: Rogan made debut
Match 14: Cullen last game
Match 16: Byrne made debut & Beagrie last game
Match 17: Russell made debut
Match 23: Goodman made debut
Match 26: Hauser last game
Match 27: Denis Smith last game as Sunderland manager
Match 28: Malcolm Crosby first game as caretaker manager
Match 47: Brady last game
Match 54: Martin Gray made debut, Pascoe last game & Malcolm Crosby first game as Sunderland manager on a permanent basis
Match 56: Hardyman last game

Match No.	Date	Round	Venue	Opponents	Result	FT	HT	Pos.	Scorers	Attendance
1	Aug 17		H	Derby County	D	1-1	0-0		Armstrong	20,509
2	20		A	Barnsley	W	3-0	2-0	1	Owers, Armstrong, Pascoe	12,454
3	24		A	Millwall	L	1-4	1-3	11	Owers (pen)	10,016
4	31		H	Oxford United	W	2-0	1-0	6	Gabbiadini, Armstrong	16,151
5	Sep 3		A	Portsmouth	L	0-1	0-0	9		9,621
6	7		H	Blackburn Rovers	D	1-1	1-1	10	Atkinson	17,043
7	14		A	Swindon Town	L	3-5	0-3	15	Owers, Gabbiadini, Armstrong	11,417
8	17		A	Charlton Athletic	W	4-1	1-1	7	Owers (pen), Gabbiadini (3)	5,807
9	21		H	Grimsby Town	L	1-2	0-1	13	Pascoe	16,535
11	28		A	Middlesbrough	L	1-2	0-2	13	Brady	19,424
12	Oct 5		H	Brighton & H.A.	W	4-2	1-2	13	Beagrie, Rush (2), Armstrong	15,119
14	12		A	Cambridge United	L	0-3	0-2	17		7,857
15	19		A	Port Vale	D	3-3	0-1	17	Brady (2), Ball	7,525
16	26		H	Bristol Rovers	D	1-1	1-1	16	Bennett	14,746
17	Nov 2		A	Watford	W	3-1	2-0	15	Byrne (2), Armstrong	12,790
18	5		A	Ipswich Town	W	1-0	1-0	13	Armstrong	9,768
19	9		A	Bristol City	L	0-1	0-1	14		10,570
20	17		H	Newcastle United	D	1-1	0-0	14	Davenport	29,224
21	23		A	Plymouth Argyle	L	0-1	0-0	15		6,007
22	30		H	Southend United	L	1-2	1-1	15	Byrne	13,575
23	Dec 7		A	Wolverhampton W.	L	0-1	0-0	19		11,922
24	14		H	Leicester City	W	1-0	0-0	16	Goodman	15,094
25	21		H	Portsmouth	W	1-0	1-0	13	Awford o.g.	14,432
26	26		A	Tranmere Rovers	L	0-1	0-1	14		13,658
27	28		A	Oxford United	L	0-3	0-0	17		6,140
28	Jan 1		H	Barnsley	W	2-0	1-0	15	Armstrong, Goodman	16,107
30	11		H	Millwall	W	6-2	1-1	11	Hardyman, Byrne, Goodman (3), Davenport	16,533
31	18		A	Derby County	W	2-1	2-0	12	Goodman, Byrne	15,384
32	Feb 1		H	Port Vale	D	1-1	1-1	12	Armstrong	19,488
34	8		A	Bristol Rovers	L	1-2	0-0	12	Byrne	6,318
35	11		H	Tranmere Rovers	D	1-1	0-1	12	Hardyman	18,060
37	22		A	Southend United	L	0-2	0-2	12		7,473
39	29		H	Wolverhampton W.	W	1-0	0-0	13	Byrne (pen)	20,106
41	Mar 14		A	Watford	L	0-1	0-1	16		8,091
43	21		H	Bristol City	L	1-3	0-3	17	Atkinson	18,933
44	29		A	Newcastle United	L	0-1	0-1	18		30,306
46	Apr 8		A	Leicester City	L	2-3	2-3	21	Bennett, Goodman	16,533
47	11		H	Charlton Athletic	L	1-2	0-0	21	Bennett	21,326
48	14		H	Ipswich Town	W	3-0	0-0	18	Goodman (2), Rush	22,131
49	16		A	Plymouth Argyle	L	0-1	0-0	18		23,813
50	18		A	Grimsby Town	L	0-2	0-0	19		8,864
51	20		H	Middlesbrough	W	1-0	1-0	18	Davenport	25,093
52	25		A	Brighton & H.A.	D	2-2	2-2	18	Goodman, Rogan	9,851
53	27		H	Swindon Town	D	0-0	0-0	18		16,716
54	29		A	Blackburn Rovers	D	2-2	0-1	18	Armstrong, Davenport	15,079
55	May 2		H	Cambridge United	D	2-2	2-1	18	Goodman, Rush	19,042

Appearances
Sub Appearances
Goals

FA Cup

Match No.	Date	Round	Venue	Opponents	Result	FT	HT	Scorers	Attendance
29	Jan 4	R3	H	Port Vale	W	3-0	2-0	Atkinson, Davenport, Byrne	15,564
33	Feb 5	R4	A	Oxford United	W	3-2	2-0	Byrne, Hardyman, Atkinson	9,968
36	15	R5	H	West Ham United	D	1-1	0-0	Byrne	25,475
38	26	R5r	A	West Ham United	W	3-2	2-1	Byrne (2), Rush	25,830
40	Mar 9	R6	A	Chelsea	D	1-1	0-1	Byrne	33,948
42	18	R6r	H	Chelsea	W	2-1	1-0	Davenport, Armstrong	26,039
45	Apr 5	S	N*	Norwich City	W	1-0	1-0	Byrne	40,102
56	May 9	F	N‡	Liverpool	L	0-2	0-0		79,544

* at Hillsborough
‡ at Wembley

Appearances
Sub Appearances
Goals

Rumblelows (League) Cup

Match No.	Date	Round	Venue	Opponents	Result	FT	HT	Scorers	Attendance
10	Sep 24	R2L1	H	Huddersfield Town	L	1-2	0-1	Hauser	8,161
13	Oct 9	R2L2	A	Huddersfield Town	L	0-4	0-0		11,177

Appearances
Sub Appearances
Goals

John Byrne scored in every round of the FA Cup except the Final.

	Norman	Williams	Hardyman	Bennett	Ord	Owers	Bracewell	Atkinson	Armstrong	Gabbiadini	Pascoe	Hauser	Sampson	Kay	Ball	Davenport	Agboola	Rush	Beagrie	Brady	Rogan	Cullen	Byrne	Russell	Goodman	Mooney	Carter	Hawke	Smith, A.	Gray, M.D.	
1	2	3	4	5	6	7	8	9	10	11	U		U																		1
1	2	3	4	5	6	7	8	9	10	12	11	U																		2
1	2	3	5	6	7	8	9	10	12	11	14																			3
1		3	4		6	7	8	9	10	U	11		2	5	12															4
1		3	4		6	7	8	9	10	12	11	U	2	5																5
1			4	U	6	7	8	9	10	12	11		2	5		3														6
1		3	4			7	8	9	10	11	14		2	5	12															7
1		3	4	U	6	7		9	10	11	U		2	5	8															8
1		3	4	U	6	7		9	10	11	2																			9
1		3	4			7	6	9				U	2	5	8		10	11	12											11
1	U			6	7		9					4	2	5	8		10	11	U	3										12
1		10		6	7		9					4	2	5	14			11	12	3	8									14
1			4		6	7	U	9					2	5	10		12	11	8	3										15
1			4			7	6	9		12	14		2	5			11	8	3		10									16
1			4			7	12	9		11			2	5	6		8		3		10	14								17
1			4			7	U	9		11			2	5	6		8	U	3		10									18
1			4		12	7		9		11			2	5	6		8		3		10	14								19
1			4		12	7				11	14	5	2		6		8		3		10									20
1			4		12	7		9		11			2	5	6		8		3		10	14								21
1			4		11	7		9		12	14		2	5	6				3		10	8								22
1	14		4		11	7		9					2	5	6		12		3		10	8								23
1			4		6	7		9		12			2	5	11	U			3		10	8								24
1		11	4		6	7			9				2	5		10		U	3			8								25
1	9	10	4		6	7				14	12		2	5	11				3			8								26
1		14	4		6	7	U	9					2	5	12			11	3		10	8								27
1		3	4		6	7	11	9					2	5	U		U		10		8									28
1		5	4		6	7	11	9				U	2		12				3		10	8								30
1		5	4			7	11	9		6			2	14	6		12		3		10	8								31
1		5	4			7	11	9					2	14	6		12		3		10	8								32
1		5	4	14		7	11						2	9	12		6		3		10	8								34
1		5	4	U				6					2	9	U	7			3		10	8								35
1	12	5				7	11	9		U			2	4	6				3		10	8								37
1		5				7	11	9				4	2		12		6		14	3	10	8								39
1	14	5				7	11	9					2	4			6		3		10		12							41
1				5			7	11	9				2	4	8		6		3		10		12	14						43
		5				7	11	9		U			2	4	8		6		3		10		12	1						44
1		5	4				11	9		U			2		8		6		3		10		7	12						46
1		5	4				11	9		U	2			8		6	12		3		10		7							47
1		5	4		14		11	9					2		12		6		3		10		8	7						48
1		5	4		14		11	9					2		12		6		3		10		8	7						49
1		5	4		14	7	11						2		12		6		3		10		8							50
1		12	4			3	7	11	9			6	2		8		14		5						10					51
1		12	4				7	11	9				2	14					5		10		8							52
1		5	12			3	7	11				6	2	4	8		9				10			14						53
1		5	4					9		6		11	2	10					8	7			14	3	12					54
		3		4	6		11	U						9			5		8	7	1	10	2	U						55
44	4	29	38	5	24	39	20	40	9	12	5	7	41	31	25	1	20	5	4	33	1	27	1	20	6	2	2	2		
	3	3	1	1	6		1		8	7	1		2	11		5	4			3	2	3	2	2	1					
		2	3		4		2	10	5	2				1	4		4	1	3	1		7		11						

1		5	4		6	7	11	9			12	2		8					14	3		10								29
1		5	4	U		7	11		12			2	9	6		8			3		10									33
1		5	4			7	11	9		12		2	8	6		U			3		10									36
1		5				7	11	9			U	2	8	6		4		12	3		10									38
1		5	4			7	11	9		12		2		8	6		14		3		10									40
1		5		12		7	11	9				2	4	8		6		U	3		10									42
1		5	12			7	11	9				2	4	8		6		U	3		10									45
1	12	4		2	7	11	9							3	8	6			5	10		14								56
8		7	5		2	8	8	7				7	6	8		6			8											
		1	1	1						2			2			3						1								
		1							2	1					2		1					7								

1		3	4	14	6	7	12	9		11	10		2	5	8															10
1		11			6	7		9				4	2	5	8		10	12	3	14										13
2		2	1		2	2	1	1		1	1	2	2	2	2		1	1	1											
			1			1														1										
								1																						

1992-93

Barclays Division One

Ground: Roker Park

Managers: Malcolm Crosby & Terry Butcher

League Table

	P	W	D	L	F	A	Pts
Newcastle U	46	29	9	8	92	38	96
West Ham U	46	26	10	10	81	41	88
Portsmouth	46	26	10	10	80	46	88
Tranmere R	46	23	10	13	72	56	79
Swindon T	46	21	13	12	74	59	76
Leicester C	46	22	10	14	71	64	76
Millwall	46	18	16	12	65	53	70
Derby Co	46	19	9	18	68	57	66
Grimsby	46	19	7	20	58	57	64
Peterborough U	46	16	14	16	55	63	62
Wolver'pton W	46	16	13	17	57	56	61
Charlton A	46	16	13	17	49	46	61
Barnsley	46	17	9	20	56	60	60
Oxford U	46	14	14	18	53	56	56
Bristol C	46	14	14	18	49	67	56
Watford	46	14	13	19	57	71	55
Notts Co	46	12	16	18	55	70	52
Southend U	46	13	13	20	54	64	52
Birmingham C	46	13	12	21	50	72	51
Luton T	46	10	21	15	48	62	51
SUNDERLAND	46	13	11	22	50	64	50
Brentford	46	13	10	23	52	71	49
Cambridge U	46	11	16	19	48	69	49
Bristol R	46	10	11	25	55	87	41

Premier League Champions:
Manchester Utd 84 pts

FA Cup Winners: Arsenal

League Cup Winners: Arsenal

Anglo Italian Cup Winners:
Cremonese

Shirt Sponsor: Vaux

Did you know that?

Sunderland celebrated becoming a city by staging a pre-season friendly with Tottenham Hotspur on 5 August 1992. Darren Anderton scored a hat-trick for the visitors who ran out 3-0 winners in front of 22,672 people at Roker Park.

Match 1: Butcher, Cunnington and Colquhoun made debuts
Match 3: Williams last game
Match 12: Byrne last game
Match 19: Carter last game
Match 21: Michael Gray made debut
Match 25: Hawke last game
Match 31: Malcolm Crosby last game as Sunderland manager
Match 32: Terry Butcher first game as player manager of Sunderland
Match 36: Mooney last game
Match 41: Harford made debut
Match 47: Rogan last game
Match 50: Howey made debut & Colquhoun last game
Match 52: Butcher, Harford and Davenport last games

Match No.	Date	Round	Venue	Opponents	Result	FT	HT	Pos.	Scorers	Attendance
1	Aug 15		A	Swindon Town	L	0-1	0-0			11,094
3	22		H	Tranmere Rovers	W	1-0	0-0	16	Cunnington	16,667
5	29		H	Bristol City	D	0-0	0-0	15		14,076
7	Sep 5		H	Charlton Athletic	L	0-2	0-0	19		17,954
8	12		A	Oxford United	W	1-0	1-0	14	Rush	6,003
10	19		A	Cambridge United	L	1-2	0-1	20	Rush	5,383
11	26		H	Bristol Rovers	D	1-1	0-1	19	Byrne	15,593
12	29		A	Watford	L	1-2	0-0	18	Goodman	6,263
13	Oct 3		H	Millwall	W	2-0	0-0	14	Goodman (2)	14,871
14	11		A	West Ham United	L	0-6	0-3	15		10,326
15	18		H	Newcastle United	L	1-2	0-0	19	Armstrong	28,098
16	24		A	Portsmouth	L	0-2	0-2	20		10,689
17	31		H	Notts County	D	2-2	1-0	21	Owers, Ball	15,473
18	Nov 3		H	Wolverhampton W.	W	2-0	1-0	20	Cunnington, Goodman	15,144
19	7		A	Peterborough United	L	2-5	0-1	20	Davenport (pen), Rush	8,193
20	15		H	Leicester City	L	1-2	1-1	21	Davenport	14,945
21	21		A	Derby County	W	1-0	1-0	20	Goodman	17,581
22	28		A	Southend United	W	1-0	0-0	18	Sampson	4,584
23	Dec 5		H	Barnsley	W	2-1	2-0	17	M. Gray, Cunnington	17,395
24	12		H	Brentford	L	1-3	1-1	17	Cunnington	16,972
25	19		A	Luton Town	D	0-0	0-0	18		8,286
26	28		H	Grimsby Town	W	2-0	1-0	17	Goodman, Rush	20,771
27	Jan 9		H	Cambridge United	D	3-3	2-1	17	Mooney, Rush, Atkinson	16,778
29	16		A	Bristol Rovers	D	2-2	2-1	16	Rush, Cunnington	6,140
31	27		H	Watford	L	1-2	0-1	17	Ball	14,703
32	Feb 6		H	Swindon Town	L	0-1	0-0	18		17,234
33	9		A	Oxford United	W	2-0	2-0	17	Goodman (pen), M. Gray	13,314
34	13		A	Charlton Athletic	W	1-0	0-0	17	Goodman (pen)	8,151
35	20		H	Bristol City	D	0-0	0-0	17		17,122
36	27		H	West Ham United	D	0-0	0-0	16		19,068
37	Mar 6		A	Millwall	D	0-0	0-0	16		8,761
38	10		A	Leicester City	L	2-3	2-2	16	Goodman, Armstrong	15,609
39	13		H	Peterborough United	W	3-0	0-0	15	Davenport, Goodman, Cunnington	18,372
40	16		A	Birmingham City	L	0-1	0-0	15		10,934
41	21		A	Barnsley	L	0-2	0-1	15		7,278
42	24		H	Derby County	W	1-0	0-0	14	Cunnington	17,246
43	27		A	Wolverhampton W.	L	1-2	1-1	14	Harford	12,731
44	Apr 3		H	Southend United	L	2-4	2-1	15	Harford, Goodman	15,071
45	6		A	Brentford	D	1-1	0-1	16	Goodman	9,302
46	10		A	Birmingham City	L	1-2	1-1	18	Davenport	16,382
47	12		A	Grimsby Town	L	0-1	0-0	20		8,090
48	17		H	Luton Town	D	2-2	1-0	18	Goodman (2)	16,493
49	25		A	Newcastle United	L	0-1	0-1	21		30,364
50	May 1		H	Portsmouth	W	4-1	1-0	18	Goodman (2 pens), M.D. Gray, Armstrong	21,309
51	4		A	Tranmere Rovers	L	1-2	1-1	18	Atkinson	9,685
52	8		A	Notts County	L	1-3	0-3	21	Ball	14,417

Appearances
Sub Appearances
Goals

FA Cup

Match No.	Date	Round	Venue	Opponents	Result	FT	HT		Scorers	Attendance
28	Jan 12	R3	A	Notts County	W	2-0	1-0		Cunnington, Goodman	8,522
30	24	R4	A	Sheffield Wed.	L	0-1	0-0			33,422

Appearances
Sub Appearances
Goals

Coca Cola (League) Cup

Match No.	Date	Round	Venue	Opponents	Result	FT	HT		Scorers	Attendance
2	Aug 18	R1L1	H	Huddersfield Town	L	2-3	0-2		Butcher, Ball	10,726
4	26	R1L2	A	Huddersfield Town	W 1-0 (aet)		0-0		Davenport	6,737

Appearances
Sub Appearances
Goals

Anglo Italian Cup

Match No.	Date	Round	Venue	Opponents	Result	FT	HT		Scorers	Attendance
6	Sep 1		A	Cambridge United	D	1-1	0-1		Armstrong	2,199
9	15		H	Birmingham City	L	0-1	0-1			5,871

Appearances
Sub Appearances
Goals

1993-94

Endsleigh Division One

Ground: Roker Park

Managers: Terry Butcher & Mick Buxton

League Table

	P	W	D	L	F	A	Pts
Crystal Palace	46	27	9	10	73	46	90
Nottingham F	46	23	14	9	74	49	83
Millwall	46	19	17	10	58	49	74
Leicester C	46	19	16	11	72	59	73
Tranmere R	46	21	9	16	69	53	72
Derby Co	46	20	11	15	73	68	71
Notts Co	46	20	8	18	65	69	68
Wolver'pton W	46	17	17	12	60	47	68
Middlesbrough	46	18	13	15	66	54	67
Stoke C	46	18	13	15	57	59	67
Charlton A	46	19	8	19	61	58	65
SUNDERLAND	46	19	8	19	54	57	65
Bristol C	46	16	16	14	47	50	64
Bolton W	46	15	14	17	63	64	59
Southend U	46	17	8	21	63	67	59
Grimsby	46	13	20	13	52	47	59
Portsmouth	46	15	13	18	52	58	58
Barnsley	46	16	7	23	55	67	55
Watford	46	15	9	22	66	80	54
Luton T	46	14	11	21	56	60	53
W.B.A.	46	13	12	21	60	69	51
Birmingham C	46	13	12	21	52	69	51
Oxford U	46	13	10	23	54	75	49
Peterborough U	46	8	13	25	48	76	37

Premier League Champions: Manchester Utd 92 pts

FA Cup Winners: Manchester Utd

League Cup Winners: Aston Villa

Anglo Italian Cup Winners: Brescia

Shirt Sponsor: Vaux

Did you know that?

Squad numbers were first used on Sunderland shirts on 17 October 1993 in televised game at Middlesbrough.

Match 1: Chamberlain, Ferguson, Melville and Power made debuts
Match 5: Phil Gray and Brodie made debuts
Match 7: Power last game
Match 15: Kay last game
Match 16: Lawrence made debut
Match 17: Martin Smith made debut
Match 22: Rodgerson made debut
Match 24: Terry Butcher last game as Sunderland manager
Match 25: Mick Buxton first game as caretaker manager
Match 39: Lawrence last game
Match 40: Sampson last game
Match 42: Kubicki made debut
Match 44: Rush last game
Match 51: Mick Buxton first game as Sunderland manager on a permanent basis

Match No.	Date	Round	Venue	Opponents	Result	FT	HT	Pos.	Scorers	Attendance
1	Aug 14		A	Derby County	L	0-5	0-3			18,027
3	21		H	Charlton Athletic	W	4-0	0-0	11	Goodman, M. Gray, Cunnington, Armstrong	17,647
5	28		A	Notts County	L	0-1	0-0	19		9,166
7	Sep 11		A	Crystal Palace	L	0-1	0-1	23		11,318
9	18		H	Wolverhampton W.	L	0-2	0-1	24		18,292
11	25		A	Watford	D	1-1	1-1	24	Owers	7,654
12	28		H	Grimsby Town	D	2-2	0-2	23	Goodman, Ord	15,468
13	Oct 2		H	Peterborough United	W	2-0	1-0	23	P. Gray, Owers	17,846
15	9		H	Birmingham City	W	1-0	1-0	17	Howey	19,265
16	17		A	Middlesbrough	L	1-4	1-3	22	Goodman	12,772
17	20		H	Luton Town	W	2-0	2-0	14	Goodman, M. Smith	13,760
18	23		H	West Bromwich Albion	W	1-0	0-0	11	Ord	19,505
20	30		A	Bristol City	L	0-2	0-0	14		8,162
21	Nov 3		A	Stoke City	L	0-1	0-0	14		13,551
22	6		H	Portsmouth	L	1-2	0-2	18	M. Smith	17,146
23	13		A	Tranmere Rovers	L	1-4	1-0	19	Goodman	8,497
24	20		H	Southend United	L	0-2	0-1	20		15,452
25	27		H	Nottingham Forest	L	2-3	1-2	22	P. Gray, M. Smith	16,968
26	Dec 4		A	Portsmouth	W	1-0	1-0	17	M. Smith	11,891
27	18		H	Derby County	W	1-0	1-0	18	P. Gray	16,001
28	27		A	Bolton Wanderers	D	0-0	0-0	17		18,496
29	28		H	Millwall	W	2-1	1-1	16	P. Gray, Russell	19,233
30	Jan 1		A	Leicester City	L	1-2	0-0	16	P. Gray (pen)	19,615
31	3		H	Barnsley	W	1-0	1-0	16	P. Gray	19,332
33	11		A	Oxford United	W	3-0	2-0	16	M. Smith (2), Goodman	5,877
34	16		H	Middlesbrough	W	2-1	0-0	14	P. Gray (pen), Howey	16,473
36	22		A	Birmingham City	D	0-0	0-0	13		15,884
38	Feb 5		A	West Bromwich Albion	L	1-2	0-2	15	Goodman	17,089
39	12		H	Bristol City	D	0-0	0-0	15		16,816
40	22		A	Charlton Athletic	D	0-0	0-0	16		7,904
41	26		H	Luton Town	L	1-2	0-2	17	Howey	9,367
42	Mar 5		H	Notts County	W	2-0	1-0	15	Russell, P. Gray	16,269
43	16		H	Crystal Palace	W	1-0	0-0	16	P. Gray	15,892
44	19		H	Watford	W	2-0	0-0	14	Russell (2)	16,479
45	26		A	Peterborough United	W	3-1	2-1	12	Russell, P. Gray (2)	8,753
46	29		A	Barnsley	L	0-4	0-2	13		10,042
47	Apr 2		H	Bolton Wanderers	W	2-0	0-0	12	Russell (2)	18,574
48	6		A	Millwall	L	1-2	0-2	13	Melville	10,244
49	9		H	Leicester City	L	2-3	1-1	15	Goodman, Melville	17,198
50	12		A	Grimsby Town	W	1-0	0-0	12	M. Smith	4,732
51	16		H	Stoke City	L	0-1	0-1	13		17,406
52	23		A	Southend United	W	1-0	0-0	12	M. Smith	4,734
53	26		H	Oxford United	L	2-3	2-1	12	P. Gray (pen), Armstrong	14,712
54	30		H	Tranmere Rovers	W	3-2	3-0	11	P. Gray (2), Russell	15,167
55	May 3		A	Wolverhampton W.	D	1-1	1-1	12	Goodman	25,079
56	8		A	Nottingham Forest	D	2-2	0-1	12	Goodman, Russell	27,010

Appearances
Sub Appearances
Goals

FA Cup

32	Jan 8	R3	H	Carlisle United	D	1-1	1-0		Ferguson	23,587
35	18	R3r	A	Carlisle United	W	1-0 (aet)	0-0		Howey	12,771
37	29	R4	A	Wimbledon	L	1-2	1-1		M. Smith	10,477

Appearances
Sub Appearances
Goals

Coca Cola (League) Cup

2	Aug 17	R1L1	H	Chester City	W	3-1	0-1		Goodman (2), Power	9,484
4	24	R1L2	A	Chester City	D	0-0	0-0			2,903
10	Sep 21	R2L1	A	Leeds United	W	2-1	1-1		Goodman, P. Gray	17,101
14	Oct 6	R2L2	A	Leeds United	W	2-1	2-0		Goodman, P. Gray	22,265
19	26	R3	H	Aston Villa	L	1-4	0-2		P. Gray	23,692

Appearances
Sub Appearances
Goals

Anglo Italian Cup

6	Aug 31		H	Tranmere Rovers	W	2-0	0-0		Goodman (2)	6,771
8	Sep 14		A	Bolton Wanderers	L	0-2	0-1			3,460

Appearances
Sub Appearances
Goals

	1 Chamberlain	2 Kay	17 Gray, M.	5 Ferguson	19 Melville	20 Sampson	7 Owers	8 Goodman	18 Howey	14 Cunnington	9 Armstrong	15 Atkinson	Power	21 Smith, A.	4 Bennett	16 Gray, M.D.	11 Russell	10 Gray, P.	23 Brodie	3 Ord	6 Ball	25 Rush	24 Lawrence	22 Smith, M.	12 Rodgerson	26 Kubicki	13 Norman	Musgrave	Preece	
1	2	3	4	5	6	7	8	9	10	11	12	14													U					1
1	2	5		6		7	8	12	9	11			10	3	4	14									U					3
1				6	2	7	8		9	11	5			4	3	10	12	14							U					5
1			5	6		2	8			11	12	14		4	7	9	10		3						U					7
1			5	6	U	7	8	12	9					4	2	11	10		3						U					9
1		12	5	6		7	8	U	9					4	2	11	10		3						U					11
1		12	5	6		7	8	U	9					4	2	11	10		3						U					12
1		12	5	6		7	8	U	9					4	2	11	10		3						U					13
1	2	U	5			7	8	9						4	10	11		3	6	12					U					15
1			5	6		7	8	9		11	10			4		12		3	2		14				U					16
1		3	5	4	14	2	8	9			11				12				6		7	11			U					17
1		12	5	4		2	8			14	9					10		3	6		7	11			U					18
1		14		4		7	8		9	5			2	3	12	10			6			11			U					20
1		12		4		2	8		9	5			2	3	U	10			6			11			U					21
1		3	5	4		2	8		9				12	U		10			6		11	7			U					22
1		5			7	8	10	9				4	2		12		3	6		11	14			U					23
1		5	6			8	U	9					4	12		10		3	2		11	7			U					24
1		5	6		7	8	12	9		U			4	2		10		3			11				U					25
1		5	6		2	8	U	7		12			4			10		3	9		11				U					26
1		5	6		2	8		7		12			4	3	U	10			9		11				U					27
1		5	6		2	8				7			4	3		10			9	U	11				U					28
1		5	6		2	8			7	11	U		4	3	12	10			9						U					29
1		5	6		2				7	11			4	3	8	10		12	9	14					U					30
1		5	6	7					11	12			4	2	8	10		3	9	14					U					31
1		5	6		2	8			11	12			4	14		10		3	9		7				U					33
1		5	6		2		14		11	12			4	8		10		3	9		7				U					34
1		5	6		2	8	14	11					4	12		10		3	9		7				U					36
1		3		6	U	2	8		5					11	10		4	9		U	7				U					38
1		3	5	6	U	2	8			9				11	10		4	12	7						U					39
1		3	5	6	12	2		8		11			4		7	10		9	14				U						40
1		3	5	6		2		8			7		4	11	10		12	9		14			U							41
1		5	6	U		8			U		7		4	11	10		3	9			7		2	U						42
1		5	6			8	U				7		4	11	10		3	9	U				2	U						43
1		5	6			8					7		4	11	10		3	9	14		12		2	U						44
		5	6							7			4	12	11	10	U	3	9		8		2	U						45
1		5	6										4	U	11	10	12	3	9		8		2	U						46
1		5	6						U	7			4	11	10	12	3	9			8		2	U						47
1		5	6		12				14	7			4	11	10		3	9			8		2		U					48
1		3	5	6		8			12	U			4	11	10			9			7		2	U						49
1		3	5	6		8			14	9			12	11	10		4				7		2	U						50
1		3	5	6		8			U	U				11	10			9			7		2	U						51
1		3	5	6					11	9			4		8	10	U	12			7		2	U						52
1		3	5	6			12		11				4	8	10	14		9			7		2	U						53
U		3	5	6			12		11	9				14	8	10		4			7		2	1						54
U		3	5	6		8			11	9				14	7	10		12					2	1						55
U		3	5	6		8				9			4		7	10		U	11				12	2	1					56
43	3	16	41	44	2	30	34	7	11	22	21	1	1	37	16	29	39		24	36		2	27	2	15	3				
		6			2			7	4	8	2		1	6	6	2	4	4		5	2	2	2							
			1		2	2	10	3	1	2					9	14	2			2	8									

1		5	6		2	8			11				4	12	U	10		3	9		7			U						32
1		5	6		2		8			11			4	U	12	10		3	9		7			U						35
1		5	6		2	8	14			11			4		12	10		3	9		7			U						37
3		3	3		3	2	1		1	2			3		3	3		3	3		3			3						
							1							1	2															
			1																		1									

1	2	5		6		7	8	12		11	9	10	3	4	14									U						2
1	2	5		6		7	8	12	9	11	14	10		4	3									U						4
1		12	5	6		7	8	U	9					4	2	11	10		3						U					10
1		14	5	6		7	8	12	9					4	2		10		3	11					U					14
1			4			7	8		9	5			12	2		10		3	6		14	11			U					19
5	2	2	2	5		5	5		1	5	2	2	1	4	4	3		3	2		1	1								
		2						3			1		1						1											
									4				1							3										

U		5	6	14	7	8		9	11	12			4	3	2	10						1								6
1		5	6	U	7	8	12		9				4	2	11	10		3			U									8
1		2	2		2	2		1	2	2			2	2	2	2		1			1	1								
				1			1																							
							2																							

503

1994-95

Endsleigh Division One

Ground: Roker Park

Managers: Mick Buxton & Peter Reid

League Table

	P	W	D	L	F	A	Pts
Middlesbrough	46	23	13	10	67	40	82
Reading	46	23	10	13	58	44	79
Bolton W	46	21	14	11	67	45	77
Wolverh'pton W	46	21	13	12	77	61	76
Tranmere R	46	22	10	14	67	58	76
Barnsley	46	20	12	14	63	52	72
Watford	46	19	13	14	52	46	70
Sheffield U	46	17	17	12	74	55	68
Derby Co	46	18	12	16	66	51	66
Grimsby	46	17	14	15	62	56	65
Stoke C	46	16	15	15	50	53	63
Millwall	46	16	14	16	60	60	62
Southend U	46	18	8	20	54	73	62
Oldham A	46	16	13	17	60	60	61
Charlton A	46	16	11	19	58	66	59
Luton T	46	15	13	18	61	64	58
Port Vale	46	15	13	18	58	64	58
Portsmouth	46	15	13	18	53	63	58
W.B.A.	46	16	10	20	51	57	58
SUNDERLAND	46	12	18	16	41	45	54
Swindon T	46	12	12	22	54	73	48
Burnley	46	11	13	22	49	74	46
Bristol C	46	11	12	23	42	63	45
Notts Co	46	9	13	24	45	66	40

Premier League Champions
Blackburn Rovers 89 pts

FA Cup Winners: Everton

League Cup Winners: Liverpool

Shirt Sponsor: Vaux Samson

Did you know that?

Alec Chamberlain became Sunderland's first goalkeeping substitute in a League game when he replaced the injured Tony Norman at home to Southend United on 1 October 1994.

Match 14: Snodin made debut
Match 18: Rodgerson last game
Match 19: Snodin last game
Match 21: Goodman last game
Match 24: Owers last game
Match 25: Scott made debut
Match 29: Agnew made debut
Match 31: Williams made debut
Match 34: Williams last game
Match 43: Cunnington last game
Match 44: Angell made debut, Matteo only game, substitute
Martin Gray substituted by Russell & Mick Buxton last game as Sunderland manager
Match 45: Ferguson last game & Peter Reid first game as Sunderland manager on a temporary basis
Match 47: Bennett last game
Match 49: Anthony Smith last game
Match 51: Norman & Brodie last games

Match No.	Date		Round	Venue	Opponents	Result	FT	HT	Pos.	Scorers	Attendance
1	Aug	13		A	Bristol City	D	0-0	0-0			11,127
2		20		H	Millwall	D	1-1	0-1	15	Goodman	17,296
3		27		A	Stoke City	W	1-0	1-0	8	P. Gray	15,159
4		30		H	Grimsby Town	D	2-2	1-1	11	Goodman (pen), P. Gray	15,788
5	Sep	3		H	Wolverhampton W.	D	1-1	1-1	11	P. Gray	15,111
6		11		A	Middlesbrough	D	2-2	1-0	11	Russell (2)	19,578
7		13		A	Sheffield United	D	0-0	0-0	12		15,239
8		17		H	Barnsley	W	2-0	0-0	9	P. Gray, Goodman	16,145
10		24		A	Tranmere Rovers	L	0-1	0-0	10		7,500
11	Oct	1		H	Southend United	L	0-1	0-1	16		15,520
13		8		A	West Bromwich Albion	W	3-1	2-0	12	M. Smith, P. Gray (2)	13,717
14		15		H	Burnley	D	0-0	0-0	10		17,700
15		22		A	Reading	W	2-0	1-0	8	Melville, P. Gray	10,757
16		29		H	Oldham Athletic	D	0-0	0-0	8		17,252
17	Nov	1		H	Charlton Athletic	D	1-1	1-0	10	M. Smith	14,085
18		5		A	Notts County	L	2-3	0-2	12	P. Gray, Owers	8,890
19		19		H	Watford	L	1-3	0-2	16	M. Smith	15,063
20		26		A	Portsmouth	W	4-1	3-0	12	Russell, Melville, P. Gray (pen), M. Smith	7,527
21		29		A	Port Vale	D	0-0	0-0	12		8,121
22	Dec	3		H	Reading	L	0-1	0-0	15		14,021
23		10		A	Millwall	L	0-2	0-0	16		7,698
24		17		H	Bristol City	W	2-0	0-0	16	Howey (2)	11,661
25		26		A	Bolton Wanderers	D	1-1	0-0	16	M. Smith	19,758
26		27		A	Luton Town	L	0-3	0-2	17		8,953
27		31		H	Derby County	D	1-1	0-0	16	P. Gray	13,979
29	Jan	14		A	Oldham Athletic	D	0-0	0-0	18		9,742
31		21		H	Notts County	L	1-2	0-1	18	Armstrong	14,334
33	Feb	4		H	Port Vale	D	1-1	1-1	21	Ball	13,377
34		11		A	Charlton Athletic	L	0-1	0-0	21		12,380
35		18		H	Portsmouth	D	2-2	2-1	21	M. Smith (2)	12,372
36		21		A	Watford	W	1-0	1-0	20	Russell	8,189
37		25		A	Southend United	W	1-0	1-0	17	Agnew	4,686
38	Mar	5		H	Tranmere Rovers	L	0-1	0-0	18		12,043
39		8		A	Wolverhampton W.	L	0-1	0-0	20		25,926
40		11		H	Stoke City	W	1-0	0-0	17	Melville	12,282
41		15		A	Swindon Town	L	0-1	0-1	19		8,233
42		19		A	Grimsby Town	L	1-3	0-2	19	Agnew	5,697
43		21		H	Middlesbrough	L	0-1	0-0	20		16,501
44		24		A	Barnsley	L	0-2	0-0	20		7,803
45	Apr	1		H	Sheffield United	W	1-0	0-0	20	Russell	17,259
46		8		A	Derby County	W	1-0	1-0	20	Ball	15,442
47		15		H	Luton Town	D	1-1	0-1	19	P. Gray	17,292
48		17		A	Bolton Wanderers	L	0-1	0-0	20		15,030
49		22		H	Swindon Town	W	1-0	1-0	20	M. Smith	16,874
50		29		A	Burnley	D	1-1	1-1	20	M. Smith	15,121
51	May	7		H	West Bromwich Albion	D	2-2	1-0	20	M. Smith, P. Gray	18,232

Appearances
Sub Appearances
Goals

Littlewoods FA Cup

Match No.	Date		Round	Venue	Opponents	Result	FT	HT	Scorers	Attendance
28	Jan	7	R3	H	Carlisle United	D	1-1	0-0	Russell	15,523
30		17	R3r	A	Carlisle United	W	3-1	2-0	Armstrong (2), P. Gray	12,201
32		29	R4	H	Tottenham Hotspur	L	1-4	0-0	P. Gray	21,135

Appearances
Sub Appearances
Goals

Coca Cola (League) Cup

Match No.	Date		Round	Venue	Opponents	Result	FT	HT	Scorers	Attendance
9	Sep	21	R2L1	A	Millwall	L	1-2	0-2	Russell	5,095
12	Oct	4	R2L2	H	Millwall	D	1-1	0-0	P. Gray	9,698

Appearances
Sub Appearances
Goals

	13 Norman	16 Gray, M.D	26 Kubicki	4 Bennett	5 Ferguson	19 Melville	7 Owers	8 Goodman	10 Gray, P.	17 Gray, M.	6 Ball	15 Atkinson	14 Cunnington	3 Ord	11 Russell	22 Smith, M.	12 Rodgerson	1 Chamberlain	25 Snodin	18 Howey	9 Armstrong	25 Scott	8 Agnew	7 Williams	23 Brodie	20 Matteo	7 Angell	21 Smith, A.	30 Musgrave	31 Preece	
1	2	3	4	5	6	7	8	9	10	11	12				U	U															1
1		3	4	5	6	2	8	9	10	11	7	12			U	U															2
1		3	4	5	6	2	8	9	10	11	7	12	U		U																3
1		3	4	5	6	2	8	9	10	11	7	12	U		U																4
1		3		5		2	8	9	10	6	7	U	4	11		U	U														5
1	2		5	6	7	8	9		12	4	11	14	3	10		U															6
1	2	12	5	6	7	8	9	U	4		11		3	10		U															7
1	2	4	5	6	7	8	9	U	11				3	10	12		U														8
1	5	2	U		6	7	8	9	U	4			3	10		11	U														10
1	5	2			6	7	8	9	U	4			3	11	10	12	13														11
	5	2	4		6		8	9		7			3	11	10	12		1		U					U						13
	5	2			6		8	9	U	7			3	11	10		12	1	4	12					U						14
	5	2			6		8	9		7			3	11	10	12	1	4	U						U						15
	5	2			6	12	8	9		7			3	11	10		1	4	14						U						16
	12	2			6	7	8	9		5			3	14	10	11	1	4							U						17
	U	2			6	7	8	9		5			3	12	10	11	1	4							U						18
U		2			6	7	8	9		5	11		3	12	10		1	4		14											19
U	5	2			6	7	U	9		4	11		3	8	10		1			U											20
U	5	2			6	7	12	9		4	11		3	8	10		1			U											21
U	5	2			6	7		9		4	11		3	8	10		1	14	12												22
U	5	2	4			7		9	U	6			3	8	10		1	12	11												23
U		3	4	7	6	2			12	5				8	10		1	9	11			U									24
U	12	2	4	7	6			9		5				8	10		1	11	U	3											25
U	5	2			6			9		4	7	11		8	10		1	12	U	3											26
U		2	4		6			9	12	5	7			8	10		1		11	3		U									27
U		2		5	6			9	12	4			U	8	10		1		11	3	7										29
U		2	4	5	6			9	U						10		1	12	11	3	7	8									31
1		2		5	6			9		4			12	10		U	U		11	3	7	8									33
1		2	6	5				9	12	11		4	8			U	14		3	7	10										34
1		2		5	U			9	8	4		6	12	10		U	11		3	7											35
1		2		7	6			9		4		5	8	10		U		12	3	11		14									36
1		2	4	7				9		6		5	8	10				12	3	11		14			U						37
1		2	4	7				9		6		5	8	10		U		12	U	3	11										38
1		2	4	7						6		5	8	10		U		9	U	3	11	12									39
1		2		5	6			U	4				8	10		U		9	11	3	7	12									40
1		2	4	5	6			9		11				10		U		8	12	3	7	14									41
1		2		5	6			9		4		12	11	8		U			10	3	7	14									42
1		2			6			9		4		7	11	8		U		12	10	3	7	14									43
1	12	2			6			9					4	14	10			11	3	7		5	8		U						44
1	12	2	4	5				9			11		6	14	10				3	7			8		U						45
1	12	2	4						5	11			6	8	10				3	7		U	9		U						46
1	7	2	4					9	14	5	11		6	12	10				3				8		U						47
1	10	2			6			9	5	7	11		4	14	12				3				8		U						48
1	7	2			6			9	5		11		4	U	10				3				8	12	U						49
1	7	2			6			9		5	11		4	12	10				3			U	8		U						50
1	5	2			6				12	4	7		11	U	10				3			9	8		U						51
9	17	46	19	23	36	18	17	41	10	42	16	3	33	28	33	3	17	6	10	24	16	3	1	1	8						
	5		1			1		1	1		1		5		10	2	3	1		9	5				7		1				
					3	1	3	12		2				5	10			2	1		2										

	2	4	5			9	12	6	7		8	10		1		U	11	3													28
	U	2	4	5	6		9		7		8	10		1		12	11	3													30
	12	2	4	7	6		9	U			8	10		1		5	11	3													32
		3	3	3	2		3		2	1		3	3		3	1	3	3													
	1							1					1																		
							2				1					2															

	2	4	5	6	7	8	9	U	11		3	10	12		U																9
5		2			6	7	8	9	14	4		3	11	10		U		12													12
1	2	1	1	2	2	2	2			2	2	1																			
							1					1																			
							2				1					1															

1995-96

Endsleigh Division One

Ground: Roker Park

Manager: Peter Reid

League Table

	P	W	D	L	F	A	Pts
SUNDERLAND	46	22	17	7	59	33	83
Derby Co	46	21	16	9	71	51	79
Crystal Palace	46	20	15	11	67	48	75
Stoke C	46	20	13	13	60	49	73
Leicester C	46	19	14	13	66	60	71
Charlton A	46	17	20	9	57	45	71
Ipswich T	46	19	12	15	79	69	69
Huddersfield T	46	17	12	17	61	58	63
Sheffield U	46	16	14	16	57	54	62
Barnsley	46	14	18	14	60	66	60
W.B.A.	46	16	12	18	60	68	60
Port Vale	46	15	15	16	59	66	60
Tranmere R	46	14	17	15	64	60	59
Southend U	46	15	14	17	52	61	59
Birmingham C	46	15	13	18	61	64	58
Norwich C	46	14	15	17	59	55	57
Grimsby	46	14	14	18	55	69	56
Oldham A	46	14	14	18	54	50	56
Reading	46	13	17	16	54	63	56
Wolverh'pton W	46	13	16	17	56	62	55
Portsmouth	46	13	13	20	61	69	52
Millwall	46	13	13	20	43	63	52
Watford	46	10	18	18	62	70	48
Luton T	46	11	12	23	40	64	45

Premiership Champions: Manchester United 82 pts

FA Cup Winners: Manchester United

League Cup Winners: Aston Villa

Shirt Sponsor: Vaux Samson

Did you know that?

Michael Bridges became Sunderland's youngest player to score a brace, at 17 years 238 days, when he netted twice against Huddersfield Town on 30 March 1996.

Match 1: Peter Reid first game as Sunderland manager on a permanent basis
Match 2: Armstrong last game
Match 3: Angell last game
Match 5: Mullin made debut
Match 6: Stewart made debut
Match 7: Aiston made debut
Match 8: Substitute Smith was substituted by Aiston
Match 12: Kelly made debut
Match 23: Atkinson last game
Match 26: Hall made debut
Match 30: Given made debut
Match 32: Cooke made debut & Martin Gray last game
Match 34: Bridges made debut
Match 37: Cooke last game
Match 42: Substitute Phil Gray last game & substituted by Hall
Match 46: Given last game & substitute Bridges was substituted by Howey
Match 50: Substitute Bridges was substituted by Hall & promotion confirmed
Match 52: Chamberlain last game

Match No.	Date	Round	Venue	Opponents	Result	FT	HT	Pos.	Scorers	Attendance
1	Aug 12		H	Leicester City	L	1-2	1-1		Agnew	18,593
3	19		A	Norwich City	D	0-0	0-0	21		16,739
5	26		H	Wolverhampton W.	W	2-0	2-0	15	Melville, P. Gray	16,816
6	30		A	Port Vale	D	1-1	0-1	14	P. Gray	7,693
7	Sep 2		A	Ipswich Town	L	0-3	0-2	19		12,390
8	9		H	Southend United	W	1-0	1-0	15	Russell	13,805
9	12		H	Portsmouth	D	1-1	1-0	15	Melville	12,282
10	16		A	Luton Town	W	2-0	0-0	9	Mullin, P. Gray	6,955
12	23		A	Millwall	W	2-1	1-0	7	Scott (pen), Smith	8,691
13	30		H	Reading	D	2-2	0-0	6	Kelly, Melville	17,503
15	Oct 7		A	Crystal Palace	W	1-0	0-0	3	Kelly	13,754
16	14		H	Watford	D	1-1	0-0	4	Scott	17,970
17	21		A	Huddersfield Town	D	1-1	0-0	5	P. Gray	16,054
18	28		H	Barnsley	W	2-1	1-0	5	Russell, Howey	17,024
19	Nov 5		A	Charlton Athletic	D	1-1	1-1	4	M. Gray	11,626
20	18		H	Sheffield United	W	2-0	0-0	4	P. Gray (2)	16,640
21	22		A	Stoke City	L	0-1	0-1	7		11,754
22	25		A	West Bromwich Albion	W	1-0	1-0	6	Howey	15,931
23	Dec 3		H	Crystal Palace	W	1-0	1-0	2	Scott (pen)	12,777
24	9		H	Millwall	W	6-0	2-0	1	Scott (pen), Russell (4), P. Gray	18,951
25	16		A	Reading	D	1-1	1-0	1	Smith	9,431
26	23		A	Derby County	L	1-3	1-1	2	M. Gray	16,882
28	Jan 14		H	Norwich City	L	0-1	0-1	8		14,983
30	21		A	Leicester City	D	0-0	0-0	7		16,130
31	24		H	Grimsby Town	W	1-0	0-0	4	Ord	14,656
32	30		H	Tranmere Rovers	D	0-0	0-0	3		17,616
33	Feb 3		A	Wolverhampton W.	L	0-3	0-2	5		26,537
34	10		H	Port Vale	D	0-0	0-0	5		15,954
35	17		A	Portsmouth	D	2-2	1-1	5	Agnew, Howey	12,241
36	20		H	Ipswich Town	W	1-0	1-0	3	Russell	14,052
37	24		H	Luton Town	W	1-0	1-0	3	James o.g.	16,693
38	27		A	Southend United	W	2-0	0-0	2	Scott (pen), Bridges	5,786
39	Mar 3		A	Grimsby Town	W	4-0	1-0	2	Ball, Russell, P. Gray, Bridges	5,318
40	9		H	Derby County	W	3-0	2-0	2	Russell (2), Agnew	21,644
41	12		A	Oldham Athletic	W	2-1	1-1	2	M. Gray, Ball	7,149
42	17		A	Birmingham City	W	2-0	1-0	1	Agnew, Melville	23,251
43	23		H	Oldham Athletic	W	1-0	0-0	1	Scott	20,631
44	30		H	Huddersfield Town	W	3-2	1-1	1	Ball, Bridges (2)	20,131
45	Apr 2		A	Watford	D	3-3	3-1	1	Agnew, Ball, Russell	11,195
46	6		A	Barnsley	W	1-0	1-0	1	Russell	13,189
47	8		H	Charlton Athletic	D	0-0	0-0	1		20,914
48	13		A	Sheffield United	D	0-0	0-0	1		20,050
49	16		H	Birmingham City	W	3-0	2-0	1	M. Gray, Stewart, Russell	19,831
50	21		H	Stoke City	D	0-0	0-0	1		21,276
51	27		H	West Bromwich Albion	D	0-0	0-0	1		22,027
52	May 5		A	Tranmere Rovers	L	0-2	0-1	1		16,193

Appearances
Sub Appearances
Goals

Littlewoods FA Cup

Match No.	Date	Round	Venue	Opponents	Result	FT	HT	Pos.	Scorers	Attendance
27	Jan 6	R3	A	Manchester United	D	2-2	0-1		Agnew, Russell	41,563
29	16	R3r	H	Manchester United	L	1-2	1-0		P. Gray	21,378

Appearances
Sub Appearances
Goals

Coca Cola (League) Cup

Match No.	Date	Round	Venue	Opponents	Result	FT	HT	Pos.	Scorers	Attendance
2	Aug 15	R1L1	A	Preston North End	D	1-1	0-0		Angell	6,327
4	23	R1L2	H	Preston North End	W	3-2	0-2		Howey (2), Kidd o.g.	7,407
11	Sep 20	R2L1	A	Liverpool	L	0-2	0-1			25,571
14	Oct 4	R2L2	H	Liverpool	L	0-1	0-1			20,565

Appearances
Sub Appearances
Goals

	Chamberlain	Kubicki	Scott	Bracewell	Ball	Ord	Gray M.	Agnew	Smith	Gray P.	Angell	Russell	Armstrong	Gray M.D.	Atkinson	Howey	Melville	Mullin	Stewart	Aiston	Kelly	Hall	Given	Cooke	Bridges	Holloway	
1	2	3	4	5	6	7	8	9	10	11	12	13		U												1
1	2		4	5	6	7		9	10	11	12		3	8	13	U										3
1	2	3	4	5		7		12	10	11		U	8	9	6	13										5
1	2	3	4	5		7		12	10	11		U	8	9	6		13									6
1	2	3	4	5	12	7			10		11			9	6	14	8	13								7
1	2	3	4	5	8	7		12	10	11			14	9	6		13									8
1	2	3	4	5	8	7		U	10	11		U		6	9		12									9
1	2	3	4	5	8	7		12	10	11			13	6	9		U									10
1	2	3	4		5	7		12	10	U		11	U	6	9			8								12
1	2	3	4	14	5	7			13	10	12		11		6	9		8								13
1	2	3	4	8	5	7		11	10		12		U	U	6			9								15
1	2	3	4	5	8	7		11	10		12			U	6	9		13								16
1	2	3	4	5	8	7	12		10		13			14	6			11	9							17
1	2	3	4	5	8	7		12		10	9	U		13	6		11									18
1	2	3	4	5	8	7	U		10	11				U	6			12	9							19
1	2	3	4	5	8	7		12	10	11				U	6			U	9							20
1	2	3	4	5	8	7		13	10	11				12	6			14	9							21
1	2	3		5	8	7	4	12	10	U				9	6	U		11								22
1	2	3		5	8	7	4	11	12				13	9	6				10			U				23
1	2	3			5	7	4	11	10		9	U	8		U	6	U									24
1	2	3			5	7	4	11	10		9	U	8		6			U								25
1	2	3			5	7	4	11	10		9		8		6		13	12	14							26
1	2	3	4		5	7	8	13	10		9				12	6		11	U							28
	2	3	4		5	7	8		10		9		12	13	6		U		11	1						30
	2	3			5	7	8		10		9		12	U	6	13		11		4	1					31
	2	3			5	7	8		10		9	12		6		U				4	1	11	U			32
	2	3	4		8	7	12		10		9			6		13				5	1	11	U			33
	2	3	4	5		7	U		10	9		U	8	6						1	11	12				34
	2		4	5		7	10		12	9			8	6	13			3	1	11	14					35
	2		4	5	8	7			U		9			10	6		U			3	1	11				36
	2	3	4	5	8	7	U			9				10	6					U	1	11	12			37
	2	3	4	5	8	7	11		10			U		9	6					U	1	12				38
	2	3	4	5	8	7	11		10		9			U	6					12	1	13				39
	2	3	4	5	8	7			12		9			6		10				13	1	U				40
	2	3	4	5		7	11		U		9					10				U	1					41
	2	3	4	5	8	7	11		12		9			6			10			13	1	14				42
	2	3	4	5	8	7	11				9			12	6		10			U	1	13				43
	2	3	4	5	8	7	11				9			U	6		10			U	1	12				44
	2	3	4	5	8	7	11				9			U	6		10			12	1	13				45
	2	3	4	5	8	7	11				9			13	6		10			U	1	12				46
1	2	3	4	5	8	7	11							12	6		10	13		U		9				47
1	2	3	4	5	8	7	11				9			U	6		10			U		12				48
1	2	3	4	5	8	7	11				9			U	6		10			U		U				49
1	2	3	4	5	8	7	11				9			10	6			13		14		12				50
1	2	3	4		8	7	11	U			9			10	6			U		5		12				51
1	2	3		5	8	7	11	12			9			6			13			4		10	U			52
29	46	43	38	35	41	46	26	9	28	2	35		4	5	17	40	5	11	4	9	8	17	6	2		
		6		4	1	4	5	2	8		13			3	4	1	1		2			4				

1	2	3	4	5		7	13	14	10		9			12	6			11								27
1	2	3	4		5	7		8	11	10		9		12		14	6	13								29
2	2	2		1	2	2	1	1	2		2			2			2			1						
							1	1					1		2		1									
									1																	

1	2	3	4	5	6	7	8	9	10	11	12	13		U												2
1	2		4	5	6		7	12	10	11		3	8	9	13	U										4
1	2	3	4	5	8	7		12	10	14		13	11		6	9										11
1	2	3	4	5		7		9	10	12			11	U	6		13	8								14
1	4	3	4	4	3	4	1	2	4	1	1		3	1	2	1		1								
								2					1	1			1									
										1						2										

n.b. Squad numbers not used during this season

1996-97

FA Carling Premiership

Ground: Roker Park

Manager: Peter Reid

League Table

	P	W	D	L	F	A	Pts
Manchester U	38	21	12	5	76	44	75
Newcastle U	38	19	11	8	73	40	68
Arsenal	38	19	11	8	62	32	68
Liverpool	38	19	11	8	62	37	68
Aston Villa	38	17	10	11	47	34	61
Chelsea	38	16	11	11	58	55	59
Sheffield W	38	14	15	9	50	51	57
Wimbledon	38	15	11	12	49	46	56
Leicester C	38	12	11	15	46	54	47
Tottenham H	38	13	7	18	44	51	46
Leeds U	38	11	13	14	28	38	46
Derby Co	38	11	13	14	45	58	46
Blackburn R	38	9	15	14	42	43	42
West Ham U	38	10	12	16	39	48	42
Everton	38	10	12	16	44	57	42
Southampton	38	10	11	17	50	56	41
Coventry C	38	9	14	15	38	54	41
SUNDERLAND	38	10	10	18	35	53	40
Middlesbrough*	38	10	12	16	51	60	39
Nottingham F	38	6	16	16	31	59	34

*Middlesbrough deducted three points

FA Cup Winners: Chelsea

League Cup Winners: Leicester City

Shirt Sponsor: Vaux Samson (Home); Scorpion Lager (away)

Did you know that?

Sunderland AFC was floated on the London Stock Market on 24 December 1996 with a share price of 585p. The two million and fifty thousand shares on offer immediately rose in value and opened at 732p each.

Match 1: Coton and Quinn made debuts
Match 4: Rae made debut
Match 12: Perez made debut & Coton last game
Match 25: Williams made debut
Match 30: Eriksson only game
Match 37: Waddle made debut
Match 38: Johnston made debut & Kelly last game
Match 39: Kubicki last game
Match 43: Howey, Waddle and Stewart last games & relegation confirmed

Match No.	Date		Round	Venue	Opponents	Result	FT	HT	Pos.	Scorers	Attendance
1	Aug	17		H	Leicester City	D	0-0	0-0			19,262
2		21		A	Nottingham Forest	W	4-1	4-1	3	Gray, Quinn (2), Ord	22,874
3		24		A	Liverpool	D	0-0	0-0	6		40,503
4	Sep	4		H	Newcastle United	L	1-2	1-0	10	Scott (pen)	22,037
5		8		H	West Ham United	D	0-0	0-0	10		18,642
6		14		A	Derby County	L	0-1	0-0	13		17,692
8		21		H	Coventry City	W	1-0	0-0	10	Agnew	19,459
10		28		A	Arsenal	L	0-2	0-0	12		38,016
11	Oct	14		H	Middlesbrough	D	2-2	1-1	13	Rae (pen), Russell	20,936
12		19		A	Southampton	L	0-3	0-1	15		15,225
14		26		H	Aston Villa	W	1-0	0-1	13	Stewart	21,059
15	Nov	2		A	Leeds United	L	0-3	0-1	17		31,667
16		16		H	Tottenham Hotspur	L	0-2	0-1	16		31,867
17		23		H	Sheffield Wed.	D	1-1	0-0	16	Melville	20,644
18		30		A	Everton	W	3-1	0-0	12	Russell, Bridges (2)	40,087
19	Dec	7		H	Wimbledon	L	1-3	0-2	15	Melville	19,672
20		15		H	Chelsea	W	3-0	1-0	14	Duberry o.g., Ball, Russell	19,683
21		21		A	Manchester United	L	0-5	0-2	14		55,081
22		26		H	Derby County	W	2-0	0-0	11	Ord, Russell	22,512
23		28		A	West Ham United	L	0-2	0-1	13		24,077
24	Jan	1		A	Coventry City	D	2-2	2-2	11	Bridges, Agnew (pen)	17,700
26		11		H	Arsenal	W	1-0	0-0	11	Adams o.g.	21,154
28		18		H	Blackburn Rovers	D	0-0	0-0	11		20,850
29		29		A	Leicester City	D	1-1	1-1	11	Williams	17,883
30	Feb	1		A	Aston Villa	L	0-1	0-1	12		32,491
31		22		H	Leeds United	L	0-1	0-1	14		21,890
32	Mar	1		A	Blackburn Rovers	L	0-1	0-0	15		24,208
33		4		A	Tottenham Hotspur	L	0-4	0-3	16		20,785
34		8		H	Manchester United	W	2-1	0-0	15	Gray, Mullin	22,225
35		12		A	Sheffield Wed.	L	1-2	1-1	15	Ball	20,294
36		16		A	Chelsea	L	2-6	0-2	15	Stewart, Rae	24,027
37		22		H	Nottingham Forest	D	1-1	0-0	16	Ball	22,120
38	Apr	5		A	Newcastle United	D	1-1	1-0	15	Gray	36,582
39		13		H	Liverpool	L	1-2	0-1	18	Stewart	21,938
40		19		A	Middlesbrough	W	1-0	1-0	16	Williams	30,106
41		22		H	Southampton	L	0-1	0-1	17		21,521
42	May	3		H	Everton	W	3-0	0-0	17	Stewart (pen), Waddle, Johnston	22,108
43		11		A	Wimbledon	L	0-1	0-0	18		21,338

Appearances
Sub Appearances
Goals

Littlewoods FA Cup

25	Jan	4	R3	A	Arsenal	D	1-1	1-1		Gray	37,793
27		15	R3r	H	Arsenal	L	0-2	0-0			15,277

Appearances
Sub Appearances
Goals

Coca Cola (League) Cup

7	Sep	17	R2L1	A	Watford	W	2-0	2-0		Quinn, Rae	9,136
9		24	R2L2	H	Watford	W	1-0	1-0		Scott	10,659
13	Oct	23	R3	A	Tottenham Hotspur	L	1-2	0-1		Ball	24,867

Appearances
Sub Appearances
Goals

Allan Johnston, scorer of the last League goal at Roker Park, against Everton on 3 May 1997.

1997-98

Nationwide Division One

Ground: Stadium of Light

Manager: Peter Reid

League Table

	P	W	D	L	F	A	Pts
Nottingham F	46	28	10	8	82	42	94
Middlesbrough	46	27	10	9	77	41	91
SUNDERLAND	46	26	12	8	86	50	90
Charlton A	46	26	10	10	80	49	88
Ipswich T	46	23	14	9	77	43	83
Sheffield U	46	19	17	10	69	54	74
Birmingham C	46	19	17	10	60	35	74
Stockport Co	46	19	8	19	71	69	65
Wolver'pton W	46	18	11	17	57	53	65
W.B.A.	46	16	13	17	50	56	61
Crewe A	46	18	5	23	58	65	59
Oxford U	46	16	10	20	60	64	58
Bradford	46	14	15	17	46	59	57
Tranmere R	46	14	14	18	54	57	56
Norwich C	46	14	13	19	52	69	55
Huddersfield T	46	14	11	21	50	72	53
Bury	46	11	19	16	42	58	52
Swindon T	46	14	10	22	42	73	52
Port Vale	46	13	10	23	56	66	49
Portsmouth	46	13	10	23	51	63	49
Q.P.R.	46	10	19	17	51	63	49
Manchester C	46	12	12	22	56	57	48
Stoke C	46	11	13	22	44	74	46
Reading	46	11	9	26	39	78	42

Premiership Champions: Arsenal 78 pts

FA Cup Winners: Arsenal

League Cup Winners: Chelsea

Shirt Sponsor: Lambtons (Vaux)

Did you know that?

Sunderland won at Portsmouth on 15 November 1997 after conceding the first goal of the game. This broke a run of 104 away games without a win after allowing the opponents to score first. The last win was 3 April 1990 at Sheffield United. The sequence saw 14 draws and 90 defeats.

Match 1: Makin, Clark & Byrne made debuts
Match 2: Phillips made debut
Match 8: Craddock made debut
Match 10: Zoetebier made debut & Bracewell and Agnew last games
Match 13: Zoetebier last game
Match 16: Holloway made debut
Match 17: Byrne and Russell last games
Match 20: Summerbee made debut
Match 32: Dichio made debut
Match 34: Lumsdon made debut & Hall last game
Match 52: Ord last game
Match 54: Perez last game

Match No.	Date	Round	Venue	Opponents	Result	FT	HT	Pos.	Scorers	Attendance
1	Aug 10		A	Sheffield United	L	0-2	0-2			17,324
2	15		H	Manchester City	W	3-1	1-0	3	Quinn, Phillips, Clark	38,827
3	23		A	Port Vale	L	1-3	0-2	15	Phillips	8,209
4	30		H	Norwich City	L	0-1	0-0	15		33,550
5	Sep 2		H	Oxford United	W	3-1	2-1	12	Phillips, Beauchamp o.g, Melville	27,643
6	5		A	Bradford City	W	4-0	0-0	6	Gray, Clark, Phillips, Johnston	16,484
7	14		A	Birmingham City	W	1-0	0-0	6	Gray	17,478
9	20		H	Wolverhampton W.	D	1-1	1-1	6	Smith	30,682
11	28		H	Middlesbrough	L	1-2	0-0	11	Ball	35,384
12	Oct 4		A	Reading	L	0-4	0-2	12		10,795
14	18		A	Huddersfield Town	W	3-1	1-1	11	Smith, Bridges, Clark	24,782
15	21		H	Swindon Town	D	0-0	0-0	13		27,553
16	25		A	Stoke City	W	2-1	1-0	9	Clark (2)	14,587
17	Nov 1		A	Stockport County	D	1-1	0-0	10	Clark	9,473
18	4		H	Charlton Athletic	D	0-0	0-0	11		25,445
19	8		H	Nottingham Forest	D	1-1	1-1	12	Phillips	33,160
20	15		A	Portsmouth	W	4-1	3-1	8	Quinn, Clark, Johnston, Summerbee	10,702
21	22		A	Bury	D	1-1	1-1	8	Phillips	7,790
22	29		H	Tranmere Rovers	W	3-0	3-0	8	Clark (2), Phillips	26,674
23	Dec 6		A	Queens Park Rangers	W	1-0	0-0	6	Quinn	15,266
24	13		H	West Bromwich Albion	W	2-0	1-0	7	Phillips, Johnston	29,231
25	20		A	Crewe Alexandra	W	3-0	2-0	6	Phillips, Summerbee, Quinn	5,404
26	26		H	Bradford City	W	2-0	1-0	5	Phillips, Johnston	40,055
27	28		A	Oxford United	D	1-1	1-1	5	Phillips	8,659
29	Jan 10		H	Sheffield United	W	4-2	1-1	4	Quinn, Rae, Phillips (2)	36,391
30	17		A	Manchester City	W	1-0	0-0	4	Phillips	31,715
32	28		A	Norwich City	L	1-2	0-1	5	Clark	15,940
33	31		H	Port Vale	W	4-2	3-1	4	Johnston, Phillips, Quinn, Carragher o.g.	39,258
34	Feb 7		H	Wolverhampton W.	W	1-0	0-0	3	Ball	27,502
35	17		H	Reading	W	4-1	2-0	3	Quinn, Rae, Phillips (2)	40,579
36	21		A	Middlesbrough	L	1-3	0-1	3	Clark	30,227
37	24		A	Huddersfield Town	W	3-2	3-0	3	Johnston (3, 1 pen)	14,615
38	28		H	Ipswich Town	D	2-2	1-2	3	Williams, Phillips	35,114
39	Mar 4		A	Nottingham Forest	W	3-0	1-0	3	Rae, Johnston, Phillips	29,009
40	7		H	Stockport County	W	4-1	1-0	2	Quinn (3), Phillips	34,870
41	10		H	Birmingham City	D	1-1	0-0	3	Johnston	37,602
42	15		A	Charlton Athletic	D	1-1	1-1	3	Phillips	15,355
43	21		H	Portsmouth	W	2-1	1-0	2	Phillips, Johnston	38,134
44	28		H	Bury	W	2-1	1-1	2	Clark, Phillips (pen)	37,425
45	Apr 3		A	Tranmere Rovers	W	2-0	2-0	2	Phillips, Summerbee	14,116
46	10		H	Queens Park Rangers	D	2-2	1-0	2	Quinn (2)	40,014
47	13		A	West Bromwich Albion	D	3-3	2-2	2	Quinn (2), Phillips	20,181
48	18		H	Crewe Alexandra	W	2-1	2-1	2	Ball, Clark	40,441
49	25		H	Stoke City	W	3-0	1-0	2	Williams, Phillips (2)	41,214
50	28		A	Ipswich Town	L	0-2	0-0	2		20,902
51	May 3		A	Swindon Town	W	2-1	2-0	3	Phillips (2)	14,861

Appearances
Sub Appearance
Goal

Play Offs

52	May 10	SL1	A	Sheffield United	L	1-2	1-0		Ball	23,80
53	13	SL2	H	Sheffield United	W	2-0	2-0		Marker o.g., Phillips	40,09
54	25	F	N*	Charlton Athletic	L	4-4‡	0-1		Quinn (2), Phillips, Summerbee	77,73

* at Wembley
‡ 6-7 penalties

Appearance
Sub Appearance
Goal

Littlewoods FA Cup

28	Jan 3	R3	A	Rotherham United	W	5-1	1-0		Phillips (4, 1 pen), Quinn	10,48
31	24	R4	A	Tranmere Rovers	L	0-1	0-0			14,05

Appearance
Sub Appearance
Goal

Coca Cola (League) Cup

8	Sep 16	R2L1	H	Bury	W	2-1	1-1		Williams, Bridges	18,77
10	23	R2L2	A	Bury	W	2-1	2-0		Smith, Rae	3,92
13	Oct 15	R3	A	Middlesbrough	L	0-2	0-0			26,45

Appearance
Sub Appearance
Goal

n.b. Squad numbers not used during this season

#	Perez	Makin	Scott	Clark	Ball	Melville	Agnew	Ord	Quinn	Rae	Gray	Bridges	Byrne	Phillips	Aiston	Williams	Mullin	Smith	Johnston	Bracewell	Russell	Craddock	Holloway	Summerbee	Hall	Dichio	Lumsdon	Zoetebier	Weaver
1	1	2	3	4	5	6	7	8	9	10	11	12	13	U															
2	1	2		4	5	6	7	8	9		3		11	10	12	13	U												
3	1	2		4	5	6		8	9		3		11	10	7		12	13		U									
4	1	2	3	4	5	6	7	8	9		11		12	10	13				U										
5	1	2	3	4	5	6		8	9		11		12	10		U		13	7										
6	1	2	3	4	5	6		8			11		U	10			12	9	7	13									
7	1	2		4	5	6		8		12	11			10		3	13	9	7	U									
9	1	2	3	4	5	6				U	11	10	12			8	9	7		13									
11	1	2	3	4	5	6		8		10	11	U	U			7		9	12										
12	1	2	3	4	5	6		8		12	11		U	13		7	10	9											
14	1	2	3	4	5			8		U	7	12	9	10			11	13		6									
15	1	2		4	5			8		11	9	U	10		3		12	7		6	U								
16	1		4	5				U	3	9			10	8	13	11	7		12	6	2								
17	1		4		U			12	3	9	8		10	6		11	7		13	5	2								
18	1		4		U				8	3	9	U	10	6		U	11	7		5	2								
19	1		4		U			12	8	3	9		U	10	6		11	7		5	2								
20	1		4		U				9	8	3	U		10	6		11	7		5	2	12							
21	1		4						9	8	3	U		10	6	12		7		5	2	11	13						
22	1		4						9	8	3	U		10	6	U		11		5	2	7	U						
23	1		4						9	8	3	U		10	6		U	11		5	2	7	U						
24	1	U	4						9	8	3	U		10	6	U		11		5	2	7	U						
25	1	U	4						9	8	3			10	6	U	12	11		5	2	7							
26	1		4					U	9	8	3			10	6	U		11		5	2	7							
27	1	U	4					U	9	8	3			10	6		12	11		5	2	7							
29	1	U	4						9	8	3			10	6	U	U	11		5	2	7							
30	1	12	4	U					9	8	3			10	6		U	11		5	2	7							
32	1	3	4	U					9	8	11			10	6			U		5	2	7	12						
33	1	2	4	8	U			12	9		3			10	6			11		5		7		U					
34	1		4	6	U			8	9		3			10			U	11		5			2	12	7				
35	1		4	6				8	9	7	3			10				11		5	2		U	12	U				
36	1	2	4	U					9	8	3			10				11		5	6	7		12					
37	1	2	4	12				U	9	8	3			10				11		5	6	7		13					
38		U	4	12					9	8	3			10				11		5	2	7		U					
39		U	4	7					9	8	3			10				11		5	2	U		U					
40		U	4	7				U	9		3			10				11		5	2	7							
41		U	4	7					12	8	3			10				11		5	2	13		9					
42		12	4	7					9	8	3			10				11		5	2	U		13					
43		2	4	7				U	9	8	3			10				11			5	12		13					
44		2	4	7				U	9	8	3			10				11		5	U	U							
45		2	4	8				U	9		3			10				6			5	7		U	U				
46		2	4	8					9	U	3			10				6		U	5	7		U					
47		2	4	8					9	12	3			10				6		13	5	7		14					
48		U	4	8					9	U	3			10				6			5	2	7						
49			4	8					9	U	3	U		10				6			5	2	7	12					
50		3	4	8				U	9	12				10				6			5	2	7	13					
51		3	4	8				U		U			12	10				6			5	2	7	9					
Apps	6	23	8	46	29	10	3	13	33	24	44	6	4	42	1	35	1	11	38		31	32	22	1	2	1			
Sub		2		2				1	2	5		3	4	1	2	1	5	5	2	1	3	1		3	1	1			
Gls			13	3	1			14	3	2	1			29		2		2	11			3							

#																													
52	3		4	8				12		13		U		10		6			11		5	2	7		9				
53			4	8				U	9	U	3			10		6			11		5	2	7		12				
54	12		4	8					9	14	3			10		6			11		5	2	7		13				
Apps	1		3	3					2		2			3		3			3		3	3	3		1				
Sub	1							1		2		1													2				
Gls			1						2					2					1										

#																													
28	U		4					U	9	8	3			10		6	U	U	11		5	2	7					U	
31	6		4	U				U	9	8	3			10			U	U	11		5	2	7			U			
Apps	1		2						2	2	2			2		1			2		2	2	2						
Sub				1				2									1	1								1		1	
Gls														1			4												

#																													
8	2	3		5		U			12	11	9			8			7	4	10		6			U					
10	2	3			13		7		10	11	U	8		5		9		4	12		6		1						
13	2	3	4	5					11	10	12			8		13	7		9	6	U		1						
Apps	3	3	1	2					1	3	2	1		3		1	2	2	2	1	2		2						
Sub					1	1			1		1					1			1		1			1					
Gls									1					1			1		1										

1998-99

Nationwide Division One

Ground: Stadium of Light
Manager: Peter Reid

League Table

	P	W	D	L	F	A	Pts
SUNDERLAND	46	31	12	3	91	28	105
Bradford C	46	26	9	11	82	47	87
Ipswich T	46	26	8	12	69	32	86
Birmingham C	46	23	12	11	66	37	81
Watford	46	21	14	11	65	56	77
Bolton W	46	20	16	10	78	59	76
Wolverhampton W	46	19	16	11	64	43	73
Sheffield U	46	18	13	15	71	66	67
Norwich C	46	15	17	14	63	61	62
Huddersfield T	46	15	16	15	62	71	61
Grimsby T	46	17	10	18	40	52	61
W.B.A.	46	16	11	19	69	76	59
Barnsley	46	14	17	15	59	56	59
Crystal P	46	14	16	16	58	71	58
Tranmere R	46	12	20	14	63	61	56
Stockport Co	46	12	17	17	49	60	53
Swindon T	46	13	11	22	59	81	50
Crewe Alex	46	12	12	22	54	78	48
Portsmouth	46	11	14	21	57	73	47
Q.P.R.	46	12	11	23	73	61	47
Port Vale	46	13	8	25	45	75	47
Bury	46	10	17	19	35	60	47
Oxford U	46	10	14	22	48	71	44
Bristol C	46	9	15	22	57	80	42

Premiership Champions: Manchester United 79 pts
FA Cup Winners: Manchester United
League Cup Winners: Tottenham Hotspur
Shirt Sponsor: Lambtons (Vaux)

Did you know that?

Sunderland's 7-0 victory over Oxford United, on 19 September 1998, is their best achieved at the Stadium of Light.
Match 1: Sorensen and Butler made debuts
Match 2: Wainwright made debut
Match 4: Maley and Thirlwell made debuts & Harrison only game
Match 12: Only 4 substitutes named
Match 21: Mullin last game
Match 22: Aiston last game
Match 23: Proctor made debut
Match 26: McCann made debut
Match 34: Scott last game
Match 48: Marriott made debut
Match 53: Promotion confirmed
Match 55: Smith last game
Match 57: Melville, Clark & Johnston last games

512

Match No.	Date		Round	Venue	Opponents	Result	FT	HT	Pos.	Scorers	Attendance
1	Aug	8		H	Queens Park Rangers	W	1-0			Phillips (pen)	40,537
3		15		A	Swindon Town	D	1-1	0-1	6	Phillips	10,207
5		22		H	Tranmere Rovers	W	5-0	2-0	6	Phillips, Dichio (2), Mullin, Butler	34,155
6		25		H	Watford	W	4-1	3-1	1	Johnston, Summerbee, Dichio, Mellville	36,587
7		29		A	Ipswich Town	W	2-0	2-0	1	Mullin, Phillips	15,813
8	Sep	8		H	Bristol City	D	1-1	1-0	2	Phillips	34,111
9		12		A	Wolverhampton W.	D	1-1	0-0	3	Phillips	26,816
11		19		H	Oxford United	W	7-0	3-0	2	Bridges (2), Gray, Dichio (2, 1 pen), Rae (2)	34,567
13		26		A	Portsmouth	D	1-1	0-1	1	Johnston	17,022
14		29		A	Norwich City	W	2-2	1-2	1	Quinn, Marshall, A. o.g.	17,504
15	Oct	3		H	Bradford City	D	0-0	0-0	2		37,828
16		18		A	West Bromwich Albion	W	3-2	0-2	2	Melville, Bridges, Ball	14,746
17		21		A	Huddersfield Town	D	1-1	1-1	2	Ball	20,741
18		24		H	Bury	W	1-0	0-0	1	Dichio	38,049
20	Nov	1		A	Bolton Wanderers	W	3-0	2-0	1	Johnston, Quinn, Bridges	21,676
21		3		A	Crewe Alexandra	W	4-1	3-0	1	Dichio, Gray, Quinn, Bridges	5,361
22		7		H	Grimsby Town	W	3-1	0-0	1	Smith (2), Quinn	40,077
24		14		A	Port Vale	W	2-0	1-0	1	Aspin o.g., Quinn	8,839
25		21		H	Barnsley	L	2-3	0-1	1	Scott (pen), Quinn	40,231
26		28		A	Sheffield United	W	4-0	3-0	1	Quinn (2), Bridges (2)	25,612
28	Dec	5		H	Stockport County	W	1-0	1-0	1	Summerbee	36,040
29		12		H	Port Vale	W	2-0	2-0	1	Smith, Butler	37,583
30		15		H	Crystal Palace	W	2-0	1-0	1	Scott (pen), Dichio	33,870
31		19		A	Birmingham City	D	0-0	0-0	1		22,095
32		26		A	Tranmere Rovers	L	0-1	0-1	1		14,248
33		28		H	Crewe Alexandra	W	2-0	1-0	1	Dichio, Bridges	41,433
35	Jan	9		A	Queens Park Rangers	D	2-2	1-1	1	Phillips, Quinn	17,444
36		17		H	Ipswich Town	W	2-1	2-1	1	Quinn (2)	39,835
39		30		A	Watford	L	1-2	1-1	1	Quinn	20,188
40	Feb	6		H	Swindon Town	W	2-0	2-0	1	Quinn, Phillips	41,304
41		13		A	Bristol City	W	1-0	0-0	1	Phillips (pen)	15,738
43		20		H	Wolverhampton W.	W	2-1	1-1	1	Johnston, Quinn	41,268
44		27		A	Oxford United	D	0-0	0-0	1		9,044
45	Mar	2		H	Portsmouth	W	2-0	1-0	1	Dichio, Phillips	37,656
46		6		H	Norwich City	W	1-0	0-0	1	Phillips	39,000
47		9		A	Bradford City	W	1-0	0-0	1	Quinn	15,124
48		13		A	Grimsby Town	W	2-0	0-0	1	Phillips, Clark	9,528
49		20		H	Bolton Wanderers	W	3-1	2-0	1	Phillips, Johnston (2)	41,505
50	Apr	3		A	West Bromwich Albion	W	3-0	2-0	1	Phillips (2), Clark	41,135
51		5		A	Crystal Palace	D	1-1	1-1	1	Phillips	22,096
52		10		H	Huddersfield Town	W	2-0	2-0	1	Quinn, Johnston	41,074
53		13		A	Bury	W	5-2	4-1	1	Phillips (4, 1 pen), Quinn	8,669
54		16		A	Barnsley	W	3-1	1-0	1	Summerbee, Clark, Phillips	17,390
55		24		H	Sheffield United	D	0-0	0-0	1		41,179
56	May	1		A	Stockport County	W	1-0	0-0	1	Phillips	10,544
57		9		H	Birmingham City	W	2-1	0-1	1	Phillips, Quinn	41,634

Appearance
Sub Appearance
Goal

AXA FA Cup

34	Jan	2	R3	A	Lincoln City	W	1-0	1-0		McCann	10,404
37		23	R4	A	Blackburn Rovers	L	0-1	0-0			30,123

Appearance
Sub Appearance
Goal

Worthington (League) Cup

2	Aug	11	R1L1	A	York City	W	2-0	2-0	Dichio (2)	6,273
4		18	R1L2	H	York City	W	2-1	0-0	Phillips, Smith	22,693
10	Sep	15	R2L1	H	Chester City	W	3-0	2-0	Scott, Phillips, Bridges	20,618
12		22	R2L2	A	Chester City	W	1-0	1-0	Johnston	2,736
19	Oct	27	R3	H	Grimsby Town	W	2-1(aet)	0-1	Bridges, Quinn	18,672
23	Nov	11	R4	H	Everton	W	1-1*	1-0	Bridges	28,132
27	Dec	1	R5	H	Luton Town	W	3-0	1-0	Johnson o.g., Bridges, Quinn	35,745
38	Jan	26	SL1	A	Leicester City	L	1-2	0-1	McCann	38,332
42	Feb	17	SL2	H	Leicester City	D	1-1	1-0	Quinn	21,232

* 5-4 penalties

Appearance
Sub Appearance
Goal

Thomas Sorensen – kept 29 clean sheets in his debut season which helped set a new Sunderland record of 30 clean sheets in a season in all competitions.

n.b. Squad numbers not used during this season

Sorensen	Gray	Scott	Clark	Craddock	Butler	Summerbee	Ball	Quinn	Phillips	Johnston	Bridges	Williams	Melville	Dichio	Mullin	Thirlwell	Smith	Wainwright	Makin	Rae	Alston	McCann	Holloway	Marriott	Maley	Harrison	Lumsdon	Proctor	Weaver	
1	2	3	4		5	6	7	8	9	10	11	12	13		U															1
1	2	3			6	7	8	9	10	11	12	4	5	13	U															3
1	3				6	7	4		10	11		2	5	9	8		12	13	14											5
1	3		U		6	7	4		10	11		2	5	9	8	U	12													6
1	3			12	6	7	4		10	11	U	2	5	9	8		U													7
1	3		U		6	7	4		10	11	U	2	5	9	8		U													8
1	3	8	U		6	7	4		10	11	12	2	5	9			U													9
1	3				6	7	4	12		11	10	2	5	9	8			13	14											11
1	3				6	7	4	12		11	10	2	5	9	8				13											13
1	3		U	6	7	4	10		11	U		5	9				U		2	8										14
1	3		U		6	7	4	10		11	U		5	9				U		2	8									15
1	3			12	6	7	4	9		11	14		5	10	13					2	8									16
1		3		U	6	7	4	9		11	10		5							2	8									17
1	3		U		6	7	4	9		11	10		5	12	U					2	8									18
1	3	12			6		4	9		11	13	14	5	10	7	8				2										20
1	3	12			6		4	9		11	13	8	5	10	7	U				2										21
1		3			6		4	9		11	10	8	5		U	7	12	2			13									22
1		3	8	U	6	7		9		11	10	4	5	13				12		2										24
1		3	8	U		7	4	12		11	10	6	5	9				U		2										25
1		3	8	12	6	7	4	9		11		5	13					2				14								26
1		3	8		6	7	4	9		11	10	12	5	13				2	14											28
1		3	8		6		4	9		10	U	5	12			11		2	7	13										29
1	12	3	4		6			9		10	14	5	13			8		2	7	11										30
1	11	3	8		6		4	9		10	13	5	12					2	7	14										31
1	11	3	8		6		4	9		10	U	5	12					2	7	13										32
1	11	3	8		6		4	9			12	13	5	10				2	7	14										33
1		8	U	6		4	9	10		12	2	5			13	3	7		11											35
1	3		8	U	6		4	9		10	11	13	5	12				2	7											36
1	3				6	7	4	9		10	11	13	5	U				2		8										39
1	3		8		6	7	4	9		10	11	12	5	13				2												40
1	3		8		6	7	4	9		10	11		5	U				2												41
1	3		8		6	7	4	9		10	11	U	U	5	U			2												43
1			U	6	7		9	10	11	U	4	5	12				2			8	3									44
1	3		8		6	7	4		9	10	11	12	13	5	U			2			U	12								45
1	3		8		6	7	4	9		10	11	U	8	5	U			2				12								46
1	3	12			6	7	4	9		10	11	U	8	5	13			2												47
	3		8		6	7	4	9		10	11	12		5	13			2			U	1								48
1	3		8	5		7	4	9		10	11	13	14	6	12			2												49
1	3		8	5	6	7	4	9		10	11	13						2				14								50
1	3		8		6	7	4	9		10	11	U		5	U			2				12								51
1	3		8		6	7	4	9		10	11		5	12				2				14								52
1	3		8		6	7	4	9		10	11	U	5	12				2				14								53
1	3		8	U	6	7	4	9		10	11			5	U			2				U								54
1	3		8	U	6	7	4				11		5	9			10	2			U	12								55
	3		8	U	6	7	U	9	10	11		5						2	4											56
1	3		8	U	6	7	4	9	10	11		5						2			U									57
5	36	14	26	3	44	36	42	36	26	40	13	16	44	16	8	1	4	37	12	5	1	1								
	1	2	1	3			3				17	9		20	1	1	4	2	1	3	1	6	5							
	2	2	3		2	3	2	3	2	18	23	7	8		2	10	2		3		2									

	11	3	8		6		4	9	U		U	7	5	10				U	2			12	U							34
	3	4			6	14	U	9	10	11			5	12			13	2	7		8	U								37
2	2	1	2		2		1	2	1	1		1	2	1				2	1		1	1								
						1											1				1									
																							1							

2	3		5	U	7	8			10	11	U	4	5	9	13			12				U								2
3			5		U			10	13	11	6	U	8	12	9	7				2	4		U							3
	3		5	12	U	U		10	U	13	6		9	8		11	7	2	4											10
	3		12	6	7	U		11	10	U	5	9	8		13		2	4												12
3	6		5			12		10			9	8	4	11		2		13			U	U	14							19
	3	14	13	6			9		11	10	8	5		4	7	U	2			U		12								23
	3	8	U	6	7	4			11	10	U	5					2			U										27
3		8	U	6	12	4	9	10	11			5	U					13		2	7	U								38
3		8		6	7	4	9	10	11	12	U	5	13			U		2	U											42
5	6	3	6	3	6	5	4	5	5	6	4	6	4	2	4	2	7	2	1	1	1	1								
		1	2	1	1		1			1	2		1	2		1	1					1	1							
	1						3	2	1	4		2		1																

1999-2000

FA Carling Premiership

Ground: Stadium of Light
Manager: Peter Reid

League Table

	P	W	D	L	F	A	Pts
Manchester U	38	28	7	3	97	45	91
Arsenal	38	22	7	9	73	43	73
Leeds U	38	21	6	11	58	43	69
Liverpool	38	19	10	9	51	30	67
Chelsea	38	18	11	9	53	34	65
Aston Villa	38	15	13	10	46	35	58
SUNDERLAND	38	16	10	12	57	56	58
Leicester C	38	16	7	15	55	55	55
West Ham U	38	15	10	13	52	53	55
Tottenham Hotspur	38	15	8	15	57	49	53
Newcastle U	38	14	10	14	63	54	52
Middlesbrough	38	14	10	14	46	52	52
Everton	38	12	14	12	59	49	50
Coventry C	38	12	8	18	47	54	44
Southampton	38	12	8	18	45	62	44
Derby Co	38	9	11	18	44	57	38
Bradford C	38	9	9	20	38	68	36
Wimbledon	38	7	12	19	46	74	33
Sheffield W	38	8	7	23	38	70	31
Watford	38	6	6	26	35	77	24

FA Cup Winners: Chelsea
League Cup Winners: Leicester City
Shirt Sponsor: Reg Vardy

Did you know that?

Kevin Phillips' 30 goal haul in this season gave him the Golden Boot Award as the highest scorer in the top flight of any of the European Leagues.

Match 1: Bould and Fredgaard made debuts
Match 2: Schwarz and Oster made debuts
Match 3: Helmer made debut
Match 4: Helmer last game
Match 7: Roy made debut
Match 8: Thomas Butler made debut & Lumsdon last game
Match 10: Marcos Di Giuseppe only game
Match 13: Reddy made debut
Match 19: Ball last game
Match 22: Kilbane made debut
Match 25: Marriott last game
Match 37: Nunez made debut
Match 43: Summerbee last game

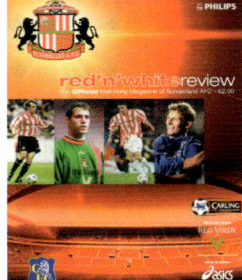

Match No.	Date	Round	Venue	Opponents	Result	FT	HT	Pos.	Scorers	Attendance
1	Aug 7		A	Chelsea	L	0-4	0-2			34,831
2	10		H	Watford	W	2-0	0-0	12	Phillips (2, 1 pen)	40,630
3	14		H	Arsenal	D	0-0	0-0	11		41,860
4	21		A	Leeds United	L	1-2	1-0	16	Phillips (pen)	39,064
5	25		A	Newcastle United	W	2-1	0-1	11	Quinn, Phillips	36,600
6	29		H	Coventry City	D	1-1	0-1	12	Phillips	39,427
7	Sep 11		H	Leicester City	W	2-0	1-0	8	P. Butler, McCann	40,105
9	18		A	Derby County	W	5-0	2-0	3	McCann, Phillips (3), Quinn	28,264
11	25		H	Sheffield Wed.	W	1-0	0-0	4	Schwarz	41,132
12	Oct 2		A	Bradford City	W	4-0	1-0	3	Rae, Quinn, Phillips (2, 1 pen)	18,204
14	18		H	Aston Villa	W	2-1	0-0	3	Phillips (2, 1 pen)	41,045
15	24		A	West Ham United	D	1-1	1-0	3	Phillips	26,022
16	31		H	Tottenham Hotspur	W	2-1	2-0	3	Quinn (2)	41,904
17	Nov 6		A	Middlesbrough	D	1-1	0-0	3	Reddy	34,793
18	20		H	Liverpool	L	0-2	0-0	4		42,015
19	27		A	Watford	W	3-2	2-1	3	Phillips (2), McCann	21,590
20	Dec 4		H	Chelsea	W	4-1	4-0	4	Quinn (2), Phillips (2)	41,199
22	18		H	Southampton	W	2-0	1-0	3	Phillips (2)	40,860
23	26		A	Everton	L	0-5	0-3	3		40,017
24	28		H	Manchester United	D	2-2	2-1	4	McCann, Quinn	42,026
25	Jan 3		A	Wimbledon	L	0-1	0-1	4		17,621
27	15		A	Arsenal	L	1-4	0-3	5	Quinn	38,039
28	23		H	Leeds United	L	1-2	0-1	5	Phillips	41,947
29	Feb 5		H	Newcastle United	D	2-2	1-2	6	Phillips (2)	42,192
30	12		A	Coventry City	L	2-3	0-3	6	Phillips, Rae	22,101
31	26		H	Derby County	D	1-1	0-0	6	Rae	41,940
32	Mar 5		A	Leicester City	L	2-5	0-2	7	Phillips, Quinn	20,432
33	11		A	Liverpool	D	1-1	0-1	9	Phillips (pen)	44,693
34	18		H	Middlesbrough	D	1-1	0-0	8	Quinn	42,013
35	25		H	Everton	W	2-1	1-1	7	Summerbee, Phillips	41,934
36	Apr 1		A	Southampton	W	2-1	1-0	6	Quinn, Phillips (pen)	15,245
37	8		H	Wimbledon	W	2-1	0-0	7	Quinn, Kilbane	41,592
38	15		A	Manchester United	L	0-4	0-1	7		61,612
39	22		A	Sheffield Wed.	W	2-0	0-0	7	Phillips (2)	28,072
40	24		H	Bradford City	L	0-1	0-0	7		40,628
41	29		A	Aston Villa	D	1-1	0-0	7	Quinn	33,949
42	May 6		H	West Ham United	W	1-0	1-0	7	Phillips	41,684
43	14		A	Tottenham Hotspur	L	1-3	1-1	7	Makin	36,070

Appearances
Sub Appearances
Goals

AXA FA Cup

21	Dec 11	R3	H	Portsmouth	W	1-0	1-0		McCann	26,535
26	Jan 8	R4	A	Tranmere Rovers	L	0-1	0-1			15,469

Appearances
Sub Appearances
Goals

Worthington (League) Cup

8	Sep 14	R2L1	H	Walsall	W	3-2	1-2		Dichio, Barras o.g., Williams	14,388
10	21	R2L2	A	Walsall	W	5-0	2-0		Dichio (2), Roy, Fredgaard (2)	5,109
13	Oct 12	R3	A	Wimbledon	L	2-3 (aet)	0-0		Dichio, Ball	4,790

Appearances
Sub Appearances
Goals

Kevin Phillips

Phillips became the first Sunderland player to score 30 goals in the top division since Raich Carter and Bobby Gurney scored 31 goals each in the last Championship winning season (1935-36). He had previously broken Sunderland's post WW2 scoring record with 35 goals in the 1997-98 season.

FA Carling Premiership

2000-01

Ground: Stadium of Light
Manager: Peter Reid

League Table

	P	W	D	L	F	A	Pts
Manchester U	38	24	8	6	79	31	80
Arsenal	38	20	10	8	63	38	70
Liverpool	38	20	9	9	71	39	69
Leeds U	38	20	8	10	64	43	68
Ipswich T	38	20	6	12	57	42	66
Chelsea	38	17	10	11	68	45	61
SUNDERLAND	38	15	12	11	46	41	57
Aston Villa	38	13	15	10	46	43	54
Charlton A	38	14	10	14	50	57	52
Southampton	38	14	10	14	40	48	52
Newcastle U	38	14	9	15	44	50	51
Tottenham Hotspur	38	13	10	15	47	54	49
Leicester C	38	14	6	18	39	51	48
Middlesbrough	38	9	15	14	44	44	42
West Ham U	38	10	12	16	45	50	42
Everton	38	11	9	18	45	59	42
Derby Co	38	10	12	16	37	59	42
Manchester C	38	8	10	20	41	65	34
Coventry C	38	8	10	20	36	63	34
Bradford C	38	5	11	22	30	70	26

FA Cup Winners: Liverpool
League Cup Winners: Liverpool
Shirt Sponsor: Reg Vardy

Did you know that?

Sunderland had their highest home attendance for a League Cup tie; 47,543 v Manchester United on 28 November 2000.

Match 1: Varga and Macho debuts
Match 2: Hutchison debut & Bould last game
Match 3: Thome and Arca debuts
Match 7: McCartney debut, Peeters only game & Maley, Holloway, Wainwright and Fredgaard last games
Match 9: Clark debut, McGill only game & Roy and Nunez last games
Match 14: Paul Butler and Reddy last games
Match 33: Substitute Thome was substituted by Makin
Match 36: Substitute McCartney was substituted by Dichio
Match 38: Makin last game
Match 39: Carteron debut
Match 40: Dichio last game
Match 45: Kyle debut
Match 47: Carteron last game

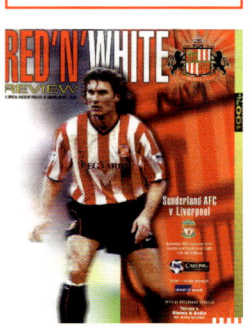

Match No.	Date		Round	Venue	Opponents	Result	FT	HT	Pos.	Scorers	Attendance
1	Aug	19		H	Arsenal	W	1-0	0-0		Quinn	47,121
2		23		A	Manchester City	L	2-4	0-2	11	Quinn, Phillips	34,410
3		26		A	Ipswich Town	L	0-1	0-0	15		21,830
4	Sep	5		H	West Ham United	D	1-1	1-1	14	Arca	46,605
5		9		A	Manchester United	L	0-3	0-1	17		67,503
6		16		H	Derby County	W	2-1	1-0	13	Kilbane, Phillips	45,343
7		23		A	Liverpool	D	1-1	1-1	13	Phillips	44,713
8	Oct	1		H	Leicester City	D	0-0	0-0	14		45,338
9		14		H	Chelsea	W	1-0	1-0	10	Phillips (pen)	45,078
10		22		A	Aston Villa	D	0-0	0-0	13		27,215
11		28		H	Coventry City	W	1-0	0-0	9	Thome	44,526
12	Nov	4		A	Tottenham Hotspur	L	1-2	0-1	12	Hutchison	36,016
13		11		H	Southampton	D	2-2	1-1	11	Quinn, Hutchison	45,064
14		18		A	Newcastle United	W	2-1	0-1	9	Hutchison, Quinn	52,030
15		25		A	Charlton Athletic	W	1-0	0-0	8	Rae	20,043
16	Dec	4		H	Everton	W	2-0	1-0	6	Rae, Phillips	46,372
17		9		H	Middlesbrough	W	1-0	0-0	4	Gray	47,742
18		16		A	Leeds United	L	0-2	0-1	5		40,053
19		23		H	Manchester City	W	1-0	1-0	6	Hutchison	47,475
20		26		A	Bradford City	W	4-1	1-0	3	Quinn, Phillips (3)	20,370
21		30		A	Arsenal	D	2-2	0-2	4	Phillips (pen), McCann	38,026
22	Jan	1		H	Ipswich Town	W	4-1	1-1	3	Arca, Phillips, Dichio, Schwarz	46,053
23		13		A	West Ham United	W	2-0	1-0	2	Varga, Hutchison	26,014
24		21		H	Bradford City	D	0-0	0-0	2		47,812
25		31		H	Manchester United	L	0-1	0-0	3		48,260
26	Feb	3		A	Derby County	L	0-1	0-1	4		29,129
27		10		H	Liverpool	D	1-1	0-0	4	Hutchison	47,553
28		24		A	Leicester City	L	0-2	0-1	4		21,086
29	Mar	5		H	Aston Villa	D	1-1	0-0	5	McCann	47,196
30		17		A	Chelsea	W	4-2	1-2	4	Hutchison (2), McCann, Phillips	34,981
31		31		H	Leeds United	L	0-2	0-1	6		48,285
32	Apr	9		A	Middlesbrough	D	0-0	0-0	6		31,284
33		14		H	Tottenham Hotspur	L	2-3	2-0	7	Kilbane, Quinn	48,029
34		16		A	Coventry City	L	0-1	0-1	7		20,946
35		21		H	Newcastle United	D	1-1	0-0	8	Carteron	48,277
36		28		A	Southampton	W	1-0	0-0	7	Kilbane	15,249
37	May	5		H	Charlton Athletic	W	3-2	2-1	7	Kilbane, Quinn, Phillips	47,671
38		19		A	Everton	D	2-2	1-1	7	Phillips (2)	37,555

Appearances
Sub Appearances
Goals

AXA FA Cup

Match No.	Date		Round	Venue	Opponents	Result	FT	HT	Scorers	Attendance
28	Jan	6	R3	H	Crystal Palace	D	0-0	0-0		30,908
30		17	R3r	A	Crystal Palace	W	4-2 (aet)	0-1	Quinn, Phillips (2), Kilbane	15,454
32		27	R4	H	Ipswich Town	W	1-0	1-0	Dichio	33,626
36	Feb	17	R5	H	West Ham United	L	0-1	0-0		36,005

Appearances
Sub Appearances
Goals

Worthington (League) Cup

Match No.	Date		Round	Venue	Opponents	Result	FT	HT	Scorers	Attendance
7	Sep	19	R2L1	H	Luton Town	W	3-0	0-0	Oster, Phillips, Thirlwell	24,668
9		26	R2L2	A	Luton Town	W	2-1	2-0	Reddy, P. Butler	5,262
14	Oct	31	R3	A	Bristol Rovers	W	2-1	1-0	Hutchison (2)	11,433
19	Nov	28	R4	H	Manchester United	W	2-1 (aet)	0-1	Arca, Phillips (pen)	47,543
23	Dec	19	R5	A	Crystal Palace	L	1-2	0-0	Rae	15,941

Appearances
Sub Appearance
Goal

Don Hutchison who was voted player of the season in his first, and only full, season with Sunderland.

2001-02

Barclaycard Premiership

Ground: Stadium of Light

Manager: Peter Reid

League Table

	P	W	D	L	F	A	Pts
Arsenal	38	26	9	3	79	36	87
Liverpool	38	24	8	6	67	30	80
Manchester U	38	24	5	9	87	45	77
Newcastle U	38	21	8	9	74	52	71
Leeds U	38	18	12	8	53	37	66
Chelsea	38	17	13	8	66	38	64
West Ham U	38	15	8	15	48	57	53
Aston Villa	38	12	14	12	46	47	50
Tottenham Hotspur	38	14	8	16	49	53	50
Blackburn R	38	12	10	16	55	51	46
Southampton	38	12	9	17	46	54	45
Middlesbrough	38	12	9	17	35	47	45
Fulham	38	10	14	14	36	44	44
Charlton A	38	10	14	14	38	49	44
Everton	38	11	10	17	45	57	43
Bolton Wanderers	38	9	13	16	44	62	40
SUNDERLAND	38	10	10	18	29	51	40
Ipswich T	38	9	9	20	41	64	36
Derby Co	38	8	6	24	33	63	30
Leicester C	38	5	13	20	30	64	28

FA Cup Winners: Arsenal

League Cup Winners: Blackburn Rovers

Shirt Sponsor: Reg Vardy

Did you know that?

The Stadium of Light's record attendance, 48,355, was set when Liverpool visited on 13 April 2002.

Match 1: Haas and Laslandes debuts
Match 2: Bellion debut
Match 3: Hutchison last game
Match 4: Rae last game
Match 5: Ingham debut
Match 11: McAteer debut
Match 18: Reyna debut & Laslandes last game
Match 27: Bjorklund debut
Match 29: Mboma debut
Match 32: Haas last game
Match 40: Mboma last game

Match No.	Date		Round	Venue	Opponents	Result	FT	HT	Pos.	Scorers	Attendance
1	Aug	18		H	Ipswich Town	W	1-0	1-0		Phillips (pen)	47,370
2		22		A	Fulham	L	0-2	0-0	10		20,197
3		26		A	Newcastle United	D	1-1	1-1	10	Phillips	52,021
4	Sep	8		H	Blackburn Rovers	W	1-0	0-0	6	Quinn	45,103
6		16		A	Aston Villa	D	0-0	0-0	7		31,688
7		19		H	Tottenham Hotspur	L	1-2	0-1	8	Phillips	47,310
8		22		H	Charlton Athletic	D	2-2	0-1	7	Quinn (2)	46,825
9		29		A	Bolton Wanderers	W	2-0	0-0	5	Phillips, Craddock	24,520
10	Oct	13		H	Manchester United	L	1-3	0-1	9	Phillips	48,305
11		22		A	Middlesbrough	L	0-2	0-2	12		28,422
12		27		H	Arsenal	D	1-1	0-1	13	Schwarz	48,029
13	Nov	3		A	Leicester City	L	0-1	0-0	15		20,573
14		18		H	Leeds United	W	2-0	0-0	13	Arca, Phillips	48,005
15		25		A	Liverpool	L	0-1	0-1	13		43,537
16	Dec	1		H	West Ham United	W	1-0	0-0	11	Phillips	47,437
17		9		H	Chelsea	D	0-0	0-0	13		48,017
18		15		A	Southampton	L	0-2	0-1	13		29,459
19		22		H	Everton	W	1-0	0-0	11	Reyna	48,013
20		26		A	Blackburn Rovers	W	3-0	2-0	9	Quinn (2), Kilbane	29,869
21		29		A	Ipswich Town	L	0-5	0-4	10		24,517
22	Jan	1		H	Aston Villa	D	1-1	0-0	10	Thome	45,324
24		12		A	Everton	L	0-1	0-1	12		30,736
25		19		H	Fulham	D	1-1	0-1	11	Phillips	45,124
26		29		H	Middlesbrough	L	0-1	0-1	13		44,579
27	Feb	2		A	Manchester United	L	1-4	1-4	15	Phillips	67,587
28		9		A	Derby County	W	1-0	0-0	11	Quinn	31,771
29		24		H	Newcastle United	L	0-1	0-0	13		48,290
30	Mar	2		A	Tottenham Hotspur	L	1-2	1-1	14	Mboma	36,062
31		5		H	Bolton Wanderers	W	1-0	1-0	14	McAteer	43,011
32		16		A	Chelsea	L	0-4	0-1	14		40,218
33		23		H	Southampton	D	1-1	0-0	15	McAteer	46,120
34		30		A	Arsenal	L	0-3	0-3	16		38,047
35	Apr	1		H	Leicester City	W	2-1	2-1	14	Reyna (2)	44,950
36		7		A	Leeds United	L	0-2	0-1	15		39,195
37		13		H	Liverpool	L	0-1	0-0	15		48,355
38		20		A	West Ham United	L	0-3	0-1	17		33,319
39		27		A	Charlton Athletic	D	2-2	2-1	17	Kilbane, Phillips	26,614
40	May	11		H	Derby County	D	1-1	1-0	17	Phillips	47,989

Appearances
Sub Appearances
Goals

AXA FA Cup

Match No.	Date		Round	Venue	Opponents	Result	FT	HT	Scorers	Attendance
23	Jan	5	R3	H	West Bromwich Albion	L	1-2	1-1	Phillips	29,133

Appearances
Sub Appearances
Goals

Worthington (League) Cup

Match No.	Date		Round	Venue	Opponents	Result	FT	HT	Scorers	Attendance
5	Sep	12	R2	A	Sheffield Wed.	L	2-4 (aet)	1-2	Phillips, Laslandes	12,037

Appearances
Sub Appearances
Goals

Claudio Reyna – joint record transfer fee when joining Sunderland from Glasgow Rangers on 7 December 2001. Captain of USA team in World Cup finals at the end of the season.

519

2002-03

Barclaycard Premiership

Ground: Stadium of Light

Managers: Peter Reid, Howard Wilkinson & Mick McCarthy

League Table

	P	W	D	L	F	A	Pts
Manchester United	38	25	8	5	74	34	83
Arsenal	38	23	9	6	85	42	78
Newcastle United	38	21	6	11	63	48	69
Chelsea	38	19	10	9	68	38	67
Liverpool	38	18	10	10	61	41	64
Blackburn Rovers	38	16	12	10	52	43	60
Everton	38	17	8	13	48	49	59
Southampton	38	13	13	12	43	46	52
Manchester City	38	15	6	17	47	54	51
Tottenham Hotspur	38	14	8	16	51	62	50
Middlesbrough	38	13	10	15	48	44	49
Charlton Athletic	38	14	7	17	45	56	49
Birmingham City	38	13	9	16	41	49	48
Fulham	38	13	9	16	41	50	48
Leeds United	38	14	5	19	58	57	47
Aston Villa	38	12	9	17	42	47	45
Bolton Wanderers	38	10	14	14	41	51	44
West Ham United	38	10	12	16	42	59	42
West Bromwich Alb.	38	6	8	24	29	65	26
SUNDERLAND	38	4	7	27	21	65	19

FA Cup Winners: Arsenal
League Cup Winners: Liverpool
Shirt Sponsor: Reg Vardy

Did you know that?

Sunderland scored all 3 goals for Charlton Athletic at the Stadium of Light on 1 February 2003. The scorers of the own goals, between 24th & 32nd minutes, were Stephen Wright and Michael Proctor (2).

Match 1: Wright and Babb debuts
Match 2: Piper debut
Match 4: Flo debut
Match 5: Stewart debut
Match 9: Myhre debut
Match 10: Peter Reid last game as Sunderland manager
Match 11: Quinn last game & Howard Wilkinson first game as Sunderland manager
Match 12: Reyna last game
Match 14: Rossiter debut
Match 19: Schwarz last game
Match 26: Macho and Rossiter last games & substitute Rossiter was substituted by Bjorklund
Match 28: Thornton debut & Medina only game
Match 34: El Karkouri debut & Thome last game
Match 37: Howard Wilkinson last game as Sunderland manager
Match 38: Mick McCarthy first game as Sunderland manager
Match 41: Poom debut & relegation confirmed
Match 42: El Karkouri last game
Match 43: Dickman only game
Match 44: Ryan debut & Bellion last game
Match 45: Black debut
Match 46: Sorensen, McCann, Craddock, Ryan and Phillips last games

Match No.	Date		Round	Venue	Opponents	Result	FT	HT	Pos.	Scorers	Attendance
1	Aug	17		A	Blackburn Rovers	D	0-0	0-0			27,122
2		24		H	Everton	L	0-1	0-1	14		37,698
3		28		A	Leeds United	W	1-0	0-0	10	McAteer	39,929
4		31		H	Manchester United	D	1-1	0-1	11	Flo	47,586
5	Sep	10		A	Middlesbrough	L	0-3	0-2	12		32,155
6		14		H	Fulham	L	0-3	0-1	18		35,432
7		21		A	Newcastle United	L	0-2	0-2	19		52,181
8		28		H	Aston Villa	W	1-0	0-0	16	Bellion	40,492
10	Oct	6		A	Arsenal	L	1-3	0-3	17	Craddock	37,902
11		19		H	West Ham United	L	0-1	0-1	19		44,352
12		28		A	Bolton Wanderers	D	1-1	1-0	19	Gray	23,036
13	Nov	3		A	Charlton Athletic	D	1-1	1-0	18	Flo	26,284
15		10		H	Tottenham Hotspur	W	2-0	0-0	16	Phillips, Flo	40,024
16		17		A	Liverpool	D	0-0	0-0	17		43,074
17		23		H	Birmingham City	L	0-1	0-1	19		38,803
18		30		A	Chelsea	L	0-3	0-0	18		38,946
20	Dec	9		H	Manchester City	L	0-3	0-1	19		36,511
21		15		H	Liverpool	W	2-1	1-0	17	McCann, Proctor	37,118
22		21		A	West Bromwich Albion	D	2-2	0-2	17	Phillips (2)	26,703
23		26		H	Leeds United	L	1-2	1-0	18	Proctor	44,029
24		28		A	Southampton	L	1-2	0-0	18	Flo	31,423
25	Jan	1		A	Manchester United	L	1-2	1-0	18	Veron o.g.	67,609
27		11		H	Blackburn Rovers	D	0-0	0-0	18		36,529
29		18		A	Everton	L	1-2	1-0	18	Kilbane	37,409
31		28		H	Southampton	L	0-1	0-0	18		34,102
32	Feb	1		H	Charlton Athletic	L	1-3	0-3	20	Phillips (pen)	36,042
34		8		A	Tottenham Hotspur	L	1-4	1-2	20	Phillips	36,075
36		22		A	Middlesbrough	L	1-3	0-2	20	Phillips	42,134
37	Mar	1		A	Fulham	L	0-1	0-0	20		16,286
38		15		H	Bolton Wanderers	L	0-2	0-0	20		42,124
39		22		A	West Ham United	L	0-2	0-1	20		35,033
40	Apr	5		H	Chelsea	L	1-2	1-0	20	Thornton	40,011
41		12		A	Birmingham City	L	0-2	0-1	20		29,132
42		19		H	West Bromwich Albion	L	1-2	0-2	20	Stewart	36,025
43		21		A	Manchester City	L	0-3	0-2	20		34,357
44		26		H	Newcastle United	L	0-1	0-2	20		45,067
45	May	3		A	Aston Villa	L	0-1	0-0	20		36,963
46		11		H	Arsenal	L	0-4	0-2	20		40,188

Appearances
Sub Appearances
Goals

FA Cup

Match No.	Date		Round	Venue	Opponents	Result	FT	HT	Scorers	Attendance
26	Jan	4	R3	A	Bolton Wanderers	D	1-1	0-1	Phillips	10,123
28		14	R3r	H	Bolton Wanderers	W	2-0 (aet)	0-0	Arca, Proctor	14,550
30		25	R4	A	Blackburn Rovers	D	3-3	1-1	Stewart, Proctor, Phillips	14,315
33	Feb	5	R4r	H	Blackburn Rovers	W	2-2*	1-0	Phillips, McCann	15,745
35		15	R5	H	Watford	L	0-1	0-0		26,916

* 3-0 penalties

Appearances
Sub Appearances
Goals

Worthington (League) Cup

Match No.	Date		Round	Venue	Opponents	Result	FT	HT	Scorers	Attendance
9	Oct	1	R2	A	Cambridge United	W	7-0	2-0	Reyna, McCann, Arca, Stewart (2), Flo (2)	8,175
14	Nov	6	R3	A	Arsenal	W	3-2	0-2	Kyle, Stewart (2)	19,059
19	Dec	3	R4	A	Sheffield United	L	0-2	0-0		27,068

Appearances
Sub Appearances
Goals

1 Sorensen	2 Wright	3 Gray	4 Reyna	12 Bjorklund	5 Babb	16 McAteer	8 McCann	10 Phillips	11 Kilbane	14 Butler	29 Quinn	19 Kyle	7 Piper	21 Thirlwell	33 Arca	9 Flo	31 Stewart	15 Bellion	18 Williams	17 Craddock	26 Myhre	30 Macho	27 McCartney	32 Proctor	28 Oster	24 Thornton	25 Clark	6 Thome	22 El Karkouri	40 Poom	37 Dickman	36 Ryan	29 Black	34 Rossiter	23 Medina	22 Varga	20 Schwarz	13 Ingham	38 Turns	35 Byrne	
1	2	3	4	5	6	7	8	9	10	11	12	U			U					U		U																			1
1	2	3	4	5	6	7	8	10		11	13	9	12		U							U	U																		2
1	2	3	4	5	6	7		9		11	U	13	10	8	12							U	U																		3
1	2	3	4	5	6	8		10		11	12	U	7	13		9					U		U																		4
1	2	3	4	5	6	8				11		U	7	U		9	10	12	U			U																			5
1	2	3	4	5	6	8	13			11	12		7			9	10	U	U			U																			6
1	2	3	4	5	6	8	10		11		12		7			9	14	U	13		U																				7
1	2		4		6		8		3		13		7	U	11	9	14	10	12	5	U																				8
1			4		6		8		3		14		12	10	11	9	U	7	2	5	13		U																		10
	2	3	4	U	6		8	10	11		13		7	14			9	12		5		1																U			11
	2	11	4	U	6		8	10	7				U	12		14		9		5	1	13	3																		12
	2	11		3	6		4	10	8				13	7		9	U		12	5		1	U															U			13
	2	11		U	6		4	10	8			13		12		9	U			5		1	3	7														U			15
		11		2	6		4	10	8			13		12		9	14		U	5		1	3	7														U			16
	2	11		U	6		4	10	8					U		9	U	12		5		1	3	7						U											17
	2	3		4	6		8	10	11					7		9	U	12	U	5		1	13							U											18
	2	11		5	6			10	8			14		4		9	13	12	U			1	3	7						U											20
	2	11		5	6		4	10	8					7		9	13	U				1	3	12				U										U			21
	2	11		U	6		4	10	8					7		9	U	12		5		1	3	U														U			22
	2	3		U	6		4	10	11			14		8		9	12			5		1	13	7														U			23
	2	11		14	6		4	10	8			9		7		13	U			5		1	3	12														U			24
U	2			U	6		4	10	8					7		9	11		12	5		1	3	13	14																25
1				U	6		4	10				U		8	12	9	13		2	5		U	3	11	7																27
1		U			6		4	10	11					8	12	9			2	5		U	3	13		7		U													29
1		3			6		4	10	11			14		13	7		8			5		U	2	9	U		12														31
1	2	3			6		4	10	8					U	11	9	12			5		U	13	7	U																32
1	2				U		4	10					14	13	11	12				5		U	3	9		7		6	8												34
1	2	3			U	8	4	10	11				12		13	9		7		5		U		14					6												36
1	2	3			U	8	4	10	11				7		U	9				5		U	13	12					6												37
1	2	11		5	U			10				14			12	9	13		4				3	7		8			6	U											38
1		11		5	U			10	8	7		12				9	14		2				3	13		4			6	U											39
1		3		5	U		4	10	11			9			U		8		2				12	U		7			6	U											40
	13	3		5			4	10	11			9			U		8		2				12	U		7			6	1									U		41
U		3					4	10	11			9			12	U	8		2	5			13	14		7			6	1											42
U		3						10	4			9			11	14	8		2	5			6	13		7	U			1	12										43
1		3		6					4			9			11	13		8	2	5			U	10		7	U			U		12									44
U		3		6			4	10	11			9				12			2	5			U	13		8				1		U	7								45
1		3		6			4	10	11			9							2	5			12	U	13	8				U		14	7								46
21	25	32	11	19	26	9	29	32	30	7		9	8	12	7	23	9	5	12	25	1	12	16	11	1	11		1	8	4			2								
	1			1			1				8	8	5	7	6	6	10	6	4		1	1	8	10	2		1				1	2									
		1				1	1	6	1							4	1	1		1				2		1															

U	2			13	6			10				9		8		14	U		4	5		1	3	11	7									12							26
1		3		5			4					9			11		10		2			U	14	13	U	7		6							8	12					28
1		3			6		4	10	11			U			7		8			5		U		9	U		2	U							U						30
1	2	3					4	10	8			14		U	11					5		U	12	9	13	7		6													33
1	2	3			6	4		10	8					U	11	9		13		5		U		14		7			12												35
4	3	4		1	3	1	3	4	3			2		1	4	1	2		2	4		1	1	3	1	3	1	2							1						
				1								1				1		1					2	2	1				1					1		1					
							1	3							1		1							2																	

U			4		6		8		3	12		U		13	11	9	10	7	2	5	1		14																		9
												9	12	7			10		4			1	3	11			U	6			U			2		5	8		U	U	14
							4					9					10	7	8			1	3	11			U	6			U			2	U	5	12		U		19
			1		1		2		1			2		1	1	1	3	2	3	1	1	2	2	2				2						2		2	1				
										1			1	1									1														1				
			1				1					1			1	2	4																								

Photo of James McClean - voted SAFC Supporters' Young Player of the Year. He made his Sunderland debut as a substitute in Martin O'Neill's first game and ended the season in Eire's European Championships squad.

2003-04

Nationwide Division One

Ground: Stadium of Light

Manager: Mick McCarthy

League Table

	P	W	D	L	F	A	Pts
Norwich C	46	28	10	8	79	39	94
W.B.A.	46	25	11	10	64	32	86
SUNDERLAND	46	22	13	11	62	45	79
West Ham U	46	19	17	10	67	45	74
Ipswich Town	46	21	10	15	84	72	73
Crystal P	46	21	10	15	72	61	73
Wigan A	46	18	17	11	60	45	71
Sheffield U	46	20	11	15	65	56	71
Reading	46	20	10	16	55	57	70
Millwall	46	18	15	13	55	48	69
Stoke C	46	18	12	16	58	55	66
Coventry C	46	17	14	15	67	54	65
Cardiff C	46	17	14	15	68	58	65
Nottingham F	46	15	14	16	61	58	60
Preston NE	46	15	14	17	69	71	59
Watford	46	15	12	19	54	68	57
Rotherham U	46	13	15	18	53	61	54
Crewe Alex	46	14	11	21	57	66	53
Burnley	46	13	14	19	60	77	53
Derby Co	46	13	13	20	53	67	52
Gillingham	46	14	9	23	48	67	51
Walsall	46	13	12	21	45	65	51
Bradford C	46	10	6	30	57	69	36
Wimbledon	46	8	5	33	41	89	29

Premiership Champions:
Arsenal 90 pts

FA Cup Winners: Manchester United

League Cup Winners:
Middlesbrough

Shirt Sponsor: Reg Vardy

Did you know that?

Mart Poom became the first Sunderland goalkeeper to score a goal when he headed in a 92nd minute corner at Pride Park, Derby County v Sunderland, 20 September 2003. He also became the first Sunderland keeper to be sent off in a first team game; v Crystal Palace, 21 April 2004.

Match 2: Whitley debut & Flo last game
Match 3: Breen debut & Gray last game
Match 4: Healy debut
Match 6: Kilbane last game
Match 8: James debut
Match 10: Leadbitter debut & James last game
Match 11: Tommy Smith debut
Match 15: Quinn debut
Match 18: Downing debut
Match 21: Black last game
Match 24: Quinn, Healy and Downing last games
Match 30: Butler and Proctor last games
Match 31: Kevin Cooper only game
Match 32: Ramsden only game
Match 33: Byfield debut
Match 42: Colin Cooper debut
Match 44: Colin Cooper last game
Match 46: Robinson debut
Match 48: Thirlwell last game
Match 54: Byfield last game
Match 56: Bjorklund, McAteer, Babb and Tommy Smith last games

Match No.	Date		Round	Venue	Opponents	Result	FT	HT	Pos.	Scorers	Attendance
1	Aug	9		A	Nottingham Forest	L	0-2	0-2			23,529
3		16		H	Millwall	L	0-1	0-1	23		24,877
4		23		A	Preston North End	W	2-0	2-0	17	Thornton, Stewart	14,018
5		25		H	Watford	W	2-0	1-0	8	Stewart (pen), Wright	23,600
6		30		A	Bradford City	W	4-0	3-0	7	Breen, Stewart, Arca, Thornton	14,116
7	Sep	13		H	Crystal Palace	W	2-1	0-0	4	Kyle, Stewart (pen)	27,324
8		16		A	Stoke City	L	1-3	0-3	8	Kyle	15,005
9		20		A	Derby County	D	1-1	0-0	9	Poom	22,535
11		27		H	Reading	W	2-0	2-0	5	Arca, Oster	22,420
12		30		H	Ipswich Town	W	3-2	1-1	5	Breen, Oster, Kyle	24,840
13	Oct	4		A	Sheffield United	W	1-0	0-0	4	Kyle	27,008
14		14		H	Cardiff City	D	0-0	0-0	4		26,835
15		18		A	Walsall	W	1-0	1-0	4	Stewart	36,278
16		21		H	Rotherham United	D	0-0	0-0	4		24,506
17		25		A	Norwich City	L	0-1	0-1	5		16,427
18	Nov	1		A	West Bromwich Albion	D	0-0	0-0	5		26,135
19		4		A	Gillingham	W	3-1	1-1	4	Downing, Oster, Stewart	9,066
20		8		H	Coventry City	D	0-0	0-0	5		27,247
21		22		A	Crewe Alexandra	L	0-3	0-0	5		9,807
22		29		H	Burnley	D	1-1	1-0	8	Kyle	29,852
23	Dec	2		H	Wigan Athletic	D	1-1	0-0	6	Downing (pen)	22,167
24		8		A	Coventry City	D	1-1	1-1	6	Downing	12,913
25		13		A	West Ham United	L	2-3	2-0	10	McAteer, Oster	30,329
26		20		H	Wimbledon	W	2-1	1-1	8	Stewart (pen), Proctor	22,334
27		26		H	Bradford City	W	3-0	1-0	6	McAteer, Smith, Kyle	29,639
28		28		A	Rotherham United	W	2-0	2-0	4	Stewart (2, 1 pen)	11,455
30	Jan	10		H	Nottingham Forest	W	1-0	1-0	4	Arca	26,340
31		17		A	Millwall	L	1-2	1-1	4	Stewart	13,048
33	Feb	7		A	Watford	D	2-2	0-1	6	Stewart, Byfield	16,798
35		21		A	Cardiff City	L	0-4	0-2	7		17,337
37	Mar	3		A	Walsall	W	3-1	1-0	9	Arca, Kyle, Stewart	7,185
39		10		H	Preston North End	D	3-3	1-1	9	Mears o.g., Thornton, Stewart (pen)	27,181
40		13		H	West Ham United	W	2-0	0-0	7	Kyle, Whitley	29,533
41		16		H	Stoke City	D	1-1	0-1	7	Byfield	24,510
42		20		A	Reading	W	2-0	0-0	6	Byfield, Smith	18,019
43		23		H	Gillingham	W	2-1	1-1	6	Thornton, Byfield	23,262
44		27		H	Derby County	W	2-1	1-0	3	Oster, Smith	30,838
46	Apr	6		A	Wimbledon	W	2-1	1-0	3	Stewart, Byfield	4,800
47		9		H	Sheffield United	W	3-0	1-0	3	Smith, Breen, Kyle	27,472
48		12		A	Ipswich Town	L	0-1	0-1	3		26,801
49		18		H	West Bromwich Albion	L	0-1	0-0	3		32,201
50		21		A	Crystal Palace	L	0-3	0-1	3		18,291
51		24		H	Wigan Athletic	D	0-0	0-0	3		11,380
52	May	1		H	Crewe Alexandra	D	1-1	1-0	4	Whitley	25,311
53		4		H	Norwich City	W	1-0	0-0	3	Robinson	35,174
54		9		A	Burnley	W	2-1	1-1	3	Breen, Kyle	18,852

Appearances
Sub Appearances
Goals

Play Offs

Match No.	Date		Round	Venue	Opponents	Result	FT	HT	Pos.	Scorers	Attendance
55	May	14	SL1	A	Crystal Palace	L	2-3	0-0		Stewart (pen), Kyle	25,287
56		17	SL2	H	Crystal Palace	W	2-1*	2-0		Kyle, Stewart	34,536

* 4-5 penalties

Appearances
Sub Appearances
Goal

Match	1 Poom	2 Wright	3 McCartney	4 McAteer	22 Bjorklund	18 Babb	12 Oster	21 Thirlwell	9 Kyle	14 Proctor	11 Kilbane	10 Stewart	20 Butler	5 Breen	6 Clark	7 Piper	15 Thornton	17 Gray	33 Arca	25 Healy	16 Williams	34 James	11 Smith, T.	8 Whitley	19 Quinn	24 Downing	23 Black	19 Cooper, K.	17 Byfield	14 Cooper, C.	24 Robinson	40 Myhre	36 Ramsden	29 Flo	13 Ingham	30 Leadbitter	41 Alnwick	42 McLean	39 Teggart	Match
1	1	2	3	4	5	6		7	8	9	10	11	12	13				U				U							U											1
3	1	2	3			13	4	9	10	11	14			5	6	7	8	12				U							U											3
4	1	2	12			U	4	9	14	11	10			5	6	7	8		3	13		U							U											4
5	1	2	6		U	7	4	9	13	11	10	U	5			8			3	12		U							U											5
6	1	2	6		U	7	4	9	14	11	10	15	5			8			3	12		U							U											6
7	1		6	7				13	4	9	14		10	11	5	U		8	3	12	2		U						U											7
8	1		6		12		7	4	9	U		10	13	5				8	11	2		3	U						U											8
9	1		6		5		7	4	9	U		10	11		U			12	3	8	2	U							U											9
11	1		6		14		7	4	9	13		10	11	5				12	3	8	2	14							U											11
12	1		6		14		7		9	13		10	11	5					3	8	2	12	4						U	U										12
13	1		6		13		7		9	U		10	11	5				12	3	8	2	U	4						U											13
14	1		6		U		7		9	14		10	11	5				13	3	8	2	12	4						U											14
15	1		3		6		7		9	U		10		5	13					8	2	12	4	11					U	U										15
16	1		6		U		7		9	12		10		5				13	3	8	2	11	4	U					U											16
17	1		6		U		7		9	12		10		5	U				3	8	2	11	4	13					U											17
18	1	U	6		U		7	13	9			10		5					3	8	2	12	4		11				U											18
19	1	U	6		U		7		9			7	U	9					3	8	2	12	4		11				U											19
20	1		6		12			13	9	U		10		5					3	8	2	14	4	7	11				U											20
21	1	2	6		5			U	12			10		U					3	8		9		7	11	13			U											21
22	1	U	6		5			13	9	10		12							3	8	2	14	4	7	11				U											22
23	1	13	6		5		7	12	9	10									3	8	2		8	14	4	U	11		U											23
24	1	13	6		5			14	9	12									3	8	2	10	4	7	11				U											24
25	1	2	6	7	5	U	8	4	12			10	13						3			9	11	U					U											25
26	1	2	3	8	5	6	7	4	12			10	13							U		9	11						U											26
27	1	2	3	8	5	6	7	4		12		13		10	U				14	9	11								U											27
28	1	2	3	4	5	6	7		12	U		10	U					11		9	8								U											28
30	1	2	3	4	5	6			12	14		10	7					11	13	9	8		U						U											30
31	1	2	3	4	5	6		7	U	9		10							U	11	8		12						U											31
33	1	2	3	4	5	6	U	8	9			12							11	U	10	7			13							U								33
35	1	2	3	4	6		7	14	9			10	5					11	U	13	8			12								U								35
37	1		6	4		5	7	8	9			12		U		U		3	2	10	11			13								U								37
39	1	2	3	7		6	11	4	9			13	5			U					14	10	8		14							U								39
40	1	2	3			6	11	4	9				5			13	7			14	10	8		U	12							U								40
41	1	2	3			6	11	4	9				5			13	7			U	10	8		U	12		U													41
42	1	2	3			6	11	4	9				5			13	7			U	12	8					10	14	U											42
43	1	2	3			6	11	4	9				5		U	7				12	13	8					10	14	U											43
44	1		3	4		6	7	8				12	5		14	U	11		2	9							10	13	U											44
46	1		3		6	U		4	9			10	5		7	13	11		2	U							12		8	U										46
47				4	U	6	11	14	12				13	5			7		3	2		9							10	8	1			U						47
48				4	U	6	11	14	9				13	5		12	7		3	2									10	8	1			U						48
49	1	3		12	6	7		13	U				5			U	11		2		9	4							10		U									49
50	1		4	U	6	13		9				14	5		7	U	3		2		11	8							10				12							50
51	1	2		4	6	4		6	3			7	9			10	5				12								14		13	U								51
52	1		3	4	13	6	7		9				10	5			14		2		11	8							12		U	U								52
53	1		3		2	6	11		9				10	5	13	7				12	4								U	8	U	U								53
54					6	3	11		13				12	5	14	7			2	9	4								10	8	1	U				U				54
	43	20	40	18	19	22	35	21	36	4	5	28	7	32	2	4	14		31	16	24	1	22	33	5	7		8	6	3										
		2		1		6		3	8	8	13		12	5	3	5	8		1	1		1	1	9	3	1		1												
	1	1	2				5		10	1		14		4		4				4	2		3			5		1												

Match	1 Poom	2 Wright	3 McCartney	4 McAteer	22 Bjorklund	18 Babb	12 Oster	21 Thirlwell	9 Kyle	14 Proctor	11 Kilbane	10 Stewart	20 Butler	5 Breen	6 Clark	7 Piper	15 Thornton	17 Gray	33 Arca	25 Healy	16 Williams	34 James	11 Smith, T.	8 Whitley	19 Quinn	24 Downing	23 Black	19 Cooper, K.	17 Byfield	14 Cooper, C.	24 Robinson	40 Myhre	36 Ramsden	29 Flo	13 Ingham	30 Leadbitter	41 Alnwick	42 McLean	39 Teggart	Match
55		3	4	13	6	7		9				10	5	U		12				2			14	11							8	U								55
56		3	4	2	6	11		9				10	5	U		7				14		13	8								12	U								56
	2	2	2	1	2	2		2				2	2			2				1		1	2	1							2									
				1																1		1	2																	
												2			2																									

523

2003-04 Continued

Mart Poom.

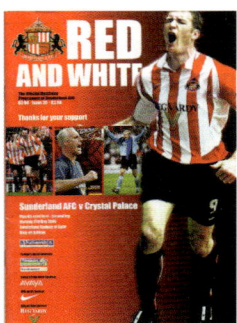

Match No.	Date		Round	Venue	Opponents	Result	FT	HT	Pos.	Scorers	Attendance
FA Cup											
29	Jan	3	R3	H	Hartlepool United	W	1-0	0-0		Arca	40,816
32		24	R4	A	Ipswich Town	W	2-1	1-0		Smith, Arca	21,406
34	Feb	14	R5	H	Birmingham City	D	1-1	1-1		Kyle	24,966
36		25	R5r	A	Birmingham City	W	2-0 (aet)	0-0		Smith (2)	25,645
38	Mar	7	R6	H	Sheffield United	W	1-0	1-0		Smith	37,115
45	Apr	4	S	N*	Millwall	L	0-1	0-1			56,112

* at Old Trafford

Appearances
Sub Appearances
Goals

Carling (League) Cup

2	Aug	13	R1	A	Mansfield Town	W	2-1	1-0		Artell o.g., Kyle	5,665
10	Sep	23	R2	H	Huddersfield Town	L	2-4	1-2		Kyle (2)	13,516

Appearances
Sub Appearances
Goals

	1 Poom	2 Wright	3 McCartney	4 McAteer	22 Björklund	18 Babb	12 Oster	21 Thirlwell	9 Kyle	14 Proctor	11 Kilbane	10 Stewart	20 Butler	5 Breen	6 Clark	7 Piper	15 Thornton	33 Gray	25 Arca	16 Healy	34 Williams	11 James	8 Smith, T.	19 Whitley	24 Quinn	23 Black	19 Downing	17 Cooper, K.	14 Byfield	24 Cooper, C.	40 Robinson	36 Myhre	29 Flo	13 Ingham	30 Leadbitter	41 Alnwick	42 McLean	39 Teggart	
	1	2	3		5	6	7		9		10	13		4				11	12			8										U		U			U		29
	1		3	4	5	6	12	8	9	U							13	11	2		10	7						14		U									32
	1	2	3	4	6		7	U	9		10		5			U		11	U		U	8										U							34
	1	2	3		6	7	4	9			10		5				13	11	U		12	8		U						U									36
	1	2	3	4		6	7	12	9		13		5				14	11	U		10	8								U									38
	1	2	3	4		6	7	8	9		12		5	13	14			11	U		10					U													45
	6	5	6	4	3	5	5	3	5	1	3			3	1		2	1			6	1		1				1			3	1	5			1			
						1		1								1					2						4												
																	1							2															

	1	13			6	14	U	12		11	10		5	7	8	3		2			4									9		U							2
	U		6		5	U	7		9	10		13	11		2		8			12	3		4										1	14					10
	1		1		1	1		1	1	1	1	1	1		2	1	2	1		1	1		2							1		1	1						
		1				1			1		1										1													1					
										1				3																									

2004-05

Coca-Cola Championship

Ground: Stadium of Light
Manager: Mick McCarthy

League Table

	P	W	D	L	F	A	Pts
SUNDERLAND	46	29	7	15	76	41	94
Wigan	46	25	12	9	79	35	87
Ipswich T	46	24	13	9	85	56	85
Derby Co	46	22	10	14	71	60	76
Preston NE	46	21	12	13	67	58	75
West Ham U	46	21	10	15	66	56	73
Reading	46	19	13	14	51	44	70
Sheffield U	46	18	13	15	57	56	67
Wolverhampton W	46	14	21	10	72	59	66
Millwall	46	18	12	16	51	45	66
Q.P.R.	46	17	11	18	54	58	62
Stoke C	46	17	10	19	36	38	61
Burnley	46	15	15	16	38	39	60
Leeds U	46	14	18	14	49	52	60
Leicester C	46	12	21	13	49	46	57
Cardiff C	46	13	15	18	48	51	54
Plymouth Argyle	46	14	11	21	52	64	53
Watford	46	12	16	18	52	59	52
Coventry C	46	13	13	20	61	73	52
Brighton & H.A.	46	13	12	21	40	65	51
Crewe Alex	46	12	14	20	66	86	50
Gillingham	46	12	14	20	45	66	50
Nottingham F	46	9	17	20	42	66	44
Rotherham	46	5	14	27	35	69	29

Premiership Champions: Chelsea 95 pts
FA Cup Winners: Arsenal
League Cup Winners: Chelsea
Shirt Sponsor: Reg Vardy

Did you know that?

Sunderland's pre-season friendly on 14 July 2004 against Carolina Select All Stars in Raleigh, North Carolina, was abandoned early in the second half due to lightning.

Match 1: Elliott, Lawrence and Whitehead debuts
Match 2: Caldwell debut
Match 3: Lynch debut
Match 7: Neill Collins debut
Match 8: Johnson debut
Match 10: Carter debut
Match 11: Brown debut & Clark and Williams last games
Match 13: Oster last game
Match 15: Johnson last game
Match 16: Poom last game
Match 17: Danny Collins debut
Match 24: Carter last game
Match 29: Welsh debut
Match 37: Lynch last game
Match 39: Bridges last game
Match 44: Deane debut & Myhre and Whitley last games
Match 45: Ingham and Thornton last games
Match 46: Alnwick debut & promotion confirmed
Match 47: Deane last game
Match 48: Stewart last game

Match No.	Date	Round	Venue	Opponents	Result	FT	HT	Pos.	Scorers	Attendance
1	Aug 7		A	Coventry City	L	0-2	0-0			16,460
2	10		H	Crewe Alexandra	W	3-1	1-1	12	Robinson, Stewart, Elliott	22,341
3	14		H	Queens Park Rangers	D	2-2	1-1	11	Stewart, Caldwell	26,063
4	21		A	Plymouth Argyle	L	1-2	0-2	16	Stewart	16,874
6	28		H	Wigan Athletic	D	1-1	0-1	16	Elliott	26,330
7	31		A	Reading	L	0-1	0-1	17		15,792
8	Sep 11		A	Gillingham	W	4-0	3-0	15	Stewart (3), Elliott	8,775
9	14		H	Nottingham Forest	W	2-0	2-0	8	Arca, Wright	23,450
10	18		A	Preston North End	W	3-1	2-1	6	Elliott (2), Carter	24,264
12	24		A	Leeds United	W	1-0	0-0	4	Robinson	28,926
13	28		A	Sheffield United	L	0-1	0-0	7		17,908
14	Oct 2		H	Derby County	D	0-0	0-0	7		29,881
15	16		H	Millwall	W	1-0	0-0	5	Muscat o.g.	23,839
16	19		A	Watford	D	1-1	1-1	6	Elliott	13,198
17	25		A	Rotherham United	W	1-0	0-0	6	Whitehead	6,026
18	30		H	Brighton & H.A.	W	2-0	0-0	5	Arca, Lawrence (pen)	25,532
19	Nov 2		H	Wolverhampton W.	W	3-1	0-1	3	Lawrence (2), Elliott	23,925
20	5		A	Millwall	L	0-2	0-2	4		10,513
21	13		A	Leicester City	W	1-0	0-0	4	Caldwell	25,817
22	21		H	Ipswich Town	W	2-0	0-0	3	Elliott, Brown	31,723
23	27		A	Stoke City	W	1-0	0-0	3	Bridges	16,980
24	Dec 4		H	West Ham United	L	0-2	0-0	3		29,510
25	11		A	Cardiff City	W	2-0	0-0	3	Whitehead, Lawrence	12,528
26	18		H	Burnley	W	2-1	1-1	3	Arca, Bridges	27,102
27	26		H	Leeds United	L	2-3	1-1	4	Lawrence (pen), Arca	43,253
28	28		A	Nottingham Forest	W	2-1	0-0	2	Elliott, Stewart	27,457
29	Jan 1		A	Preston North End	L	2-3	0-3	3	Elliott, Thornton	16,940
30	3		H	Gillingham	D	1-1	1-1	3	Brown	27,147
31	16		A	Derby County	W	2-0	0-0	3	Elliott, Whitehead	22,995
33	22		H	Sheffield United	W	1-0	1-0	3	Stewart	27,337
35	Feb 4		A	Wolverhampton W.	D	1-1	1-1	3	Elliott	26,968
36	12		H	Watford	W	4-2	2-0	3	Stewart (3, 1 pen), Brown	24,948
35	19		A	Brighton & H.A.	L	1-2	0-2	3	Arca	6,647
36	22		H	Rotherham United	W	4-1	2-0	3	Whitehead, Thornton (2), Breen	22,267
37	26		H	Cardiff City	W	2-1	2-0	2	Breen, Stewart	32,788
38	Mar 4		A	Burnley	W	2-0	1-0	1	Lawrence, Stewart	12,103
39	12		A	Crewe Alexandra	W	1-0	0-0	2	Elliott	7,949
40	15		H	Plymouth Argyle	W	5-1	3-0	2	Whitehead, Arca, Stewart (pen), Caldwell, Thornton	25,258
41	19		H	Coventry City	W	1-0	0-0	1	Brown	29,424
42	Apr 2		A	Queens Park Rangers	W	3-1	0-1	1	Welsh, Brown, Arca	18,198
43	5		A	Wigan Athletic	W	1-0	1-0	1	Stewart	20,745
44	9		H	Reading	L	1-2	0-0	1	Arca	34,237
45	17		A	Ipswich Town	D	2-2	0-1	1	Elliott, Robinson	29,230
46	23		H	Leicester City	W	2-1	1-1	1	Stewart, Caldwell	34,815
47	29		A	West Ham United	W	2-1	0-1	1	Arca, Elliott	33,482
48	May 8		H	Stoke City	W	1-0	0-0	1	Robinson	47,350

Appearances
Sub Appearances
Goals

FA Cup

Match No.	Date	Round	Venue	Opponents	Result	FT	HT	Pos.	Scorers	Attendance
31	Jan 8	R3	H	Crystal Palace	W	2-1	1-1		Welsh, Stewart (pen)	17,536
34	29	R4	A	Everton	L	0-3	0-2			33,185

Appearances
Sub Appearances
Goals

Carling (League) Cup

Match No.	Date	Round	Venue	Opponents	Result	FT	HT	Pos.	Scorers	Attendance
5	Aug 24	R1	H	Chester City	W	3-0	1-0		Hessey o.g., Kyle, Caldwell	11,450
11	Sep 21	R2	A	Crewe Alexandra	L	3-3*	1-1		Brown (2), Elliott	3,800

* 2-4 penalties

Appearances
Sub Appearances
Goals

	1 Poom	2 Wright	3 McCartney	4 Robinson	5 Breen	18 Clark	12 Oster	8 Whitley	19 Elliott	10 Stewart	33 Arca	9 Kyle	7 Lawrence	14 Whitehead	41 Myhre	6 Caldwell	15 Thornton	22 Lynch	17 Collins, N.	11 Johnson	32 Carter	20 Brown	38 Bridges	39 Collins, D.	21 Piper	11 Welsh	12 Deane	13 Ingham	30 Alnwick	16 Williams	23 Leadbitter	42 Carson	24 Teggart	
1		2	3	4	5	6	7	8	9	10	11	12	13	14	U																			1
2		2		4	5	14	11	8	12	10	3	9	7		1	6	13									U	U							2
3		2		4	5		11	8	13	10	3	9	7	U	1	6	14	12								U								3
4		2		4	5		11		14	10	3	9	7	8	1	6	13	12		12						U								4
6	1	12		4	5		7	11	14	10	3	9	U	8		6	13	2								U								6
7	1		3		5		7	8	12	10	11	9	13	4			14	U	6							U	2							7
8	1	2	3	4	5			12	8	9	10	11		7	U		14	U	13															8
9	1	2	3	4	5		13	8	9	10	11		14	7	U	6		U	12															9
10	1	2	3	4	5		U		9	10	11		12	7	U	6			13	8														10
12	1	2	3	4	5			8	10				13	7	U	6		U	U		11	9	12											12
13	1	2	3	4	5		14	8	10				7		U	6		12	U	13	11	9												13
14	1	2	3	4				8	9	10	11		13	7	U	6		U	5	U	12													14
15	1		3	4				8		U	11		12	7	U	6		2	5	10	U	9	13											15
16	1	2	3	4				8	9	10	11		13	7		6			5	U	14	12				U								16
17		2		4	5			8	9	10	3			7	1	6		U		11	13	U	12			U								17
18		2		4	5			8	9	10	11		7	13	1	6			U	14	12	3				U								18
19		2		4	5			8	9	10			7		1	6		U		14	13	12	3			U								19
20				4				8		10	11		7	13	1	6	U	2	5		14	12	9	3		U								20
21				4	5			8	9	10	3		13	14		6		2		11	12	U	14					U						21
22		2	3		5			8	9	10	11		12	7	1	6			4	13	14	U				U								22
23		2	3		5				9	10	11		7	8	1	6		14	4	12	13	U				U								23
24		2	11		5				9				7	8	1	6		U	4	12	13	3				U	U							24
25		2	3	4	5				9	13	11		7	8	1	6	U	14		10	12					U								25
26		2	3	4	5		14	12	13		11		7	8	1		6			9	10	U				U								26
27		2	3	4	5			U	12	13	11		7	8	1	6				9	10					U								27
28		2	3	4	5			12	9	10	11		7	8	1	6		14		13	U					U								28
29		2	3		5				8	9	10	11		4	1	6	13		U		12		7	14		U								29
30		2	3		5			11	9	8				4	1	6	7		13		10	14		12	U	U								30
32	U	2	3	4				8	9	10	11		7	1			U	U	5		12		6		U									32
33		2	3	4				8	9	10	11		7	1			13		5		12	14	6			U								33
35		2	3	4	5			8	9	10	11		7	1		6					13	12	14		U	U								35
36		2	3	4	5			8	9	10	11		7	1	6						12		U	U	U									36
35		2	3	4	5			8	9	10	11		7		1	6		9			12	14	U		U									35
36		2	3	4	5			8	9	10		11	7	1	6	12					13	14	U											36
37			3	4	5			8	9	10		12	7	1	6		2				14	U	13		11									37
38			3	4	5			8		10		7	2	1	6	11			U		13	9	U	12										38
39		2	3	4	5		8	12	10	13		U	7	1	6	11					14	9			U									39
40		2	3	4	5		8	9	10	11		12	7	1	6	13					14	U			U									40
41		2	3	4	5			8	9	10	11		7		1	6	13				12		U	14	U									41
42		2		4	5		8	9	10	3			7	1	6	14					12	U	13	11		U									42
43		2	3	4	5				13	10	11		7	8	1	6	U				9		12		U	U								43
44		2	3	4	5			13	U	10	11		7	8	1	6					9		U		14	12								44
45		2	3	4	5				13	10	11		7	8	1	6		14			9		U	13	12	U								45
46		2		4	5				14	10	3		7	8	1	6	U				9		12	11	13	U	1							46
47		2	3	4	5				13	10	11		7	8	1	6					9		12	U	14		1		U					47
48		2	3	4	5				12	10	11		7	8	1	6							13	9			14	U	1		U			48
	11	39	35	40	40	1	6	32	29	40	39	5	20	39	31	41	3	5	8	1	4	2	2	24	18	1	3	1	3	1				
		1			1	3	3	13	3	1	1	12	3				13	6	3	4	2	4	4	1										
		1		4	2			15	16	9		6	5		4	4				1	5	2			1									

	2	3	4				9	10				8	1	6	7	U	5		12	14		13	11		U									31
	2	3	4				9	10	11			7	1	U	8	U	5		12	13	6			U										34
	2	2				2	2	1				2	2	1	2		2				1			1										
														1							2	2		1										
								1						1								1											

	2		4	5		11		13	10	3	9	14	8	1	6	7	2	U				U											5
	14			4	11		13			7	12	1	6	10	2	5			9				U			3	8	U						11
		1	1	1	2		1	1	1		1	1	1	2	2	2	2	1					1			1	1							
	1						2						1																					
								1					1							2														

2005-06

Barclays Premiership

Ground: Stadium of Light

Managers: Mick McCarthy and Kevin Ball

League Table

	P	W	D	L	F	A	Pts
Chelsea	38	29	4	5	72	22	91
Manchester United	38	25	8	5	72	34	83
Liverpool	38	25	7	6	57	25	82
Arsenal	38	20	7	11	68	31	67
Tottenham Hotspur	38	18	11	9	53	38	65
Blackburn Rovers	38	19	6	13	51	42	63
Newcastle United	38	17	7	14	47	42	58
Bolton Wanderers	38	15	11	12	49	41	56
West Ham United	38	16	7	15	52	55	55
Wigan Athletic	38	15	6	17	45	52	51
Everton	38	14	8	16	34	49	50
Fulham	38	14	6	18	48	58	48
Charlton Athletic	38	13	8	17	41	55	47
Middlesbrough	38	12	9	17	48	58	45
Manchester City	38	13	4	21	43	48	43
Aston Villa	38	10	12	16	42	55	42
Portsmouth	38	10	8	20	37	62	38
Birmingham City	38	8	10	20	28	50	34
West Bromwich Alb.	38	7	9	22	31	58	30
SUNDERLAND	38	3	6	29	26	69	15

FA Cup Winners: Liverpool

League Cup Winners: Manchester United

Shirt Sponsor: Reg Vardy

Did you know that?

Sunderland's home game against Fulham on 8 April was abandoned after 21 mins due to snow and a waterlogged pitch.

Sunderland's total of 15 points and 3 wins were the lowest in Premiership history.

Match 1: Davis, Gray, Miller, Nosworthy and Stead debuts
Match 2: Stubbs and Woods debuts
Match 3: Le Tallec debut
Match 5: Bassila and Hoyte debuts
Match 7: Smith debut & Piper last game
Match 9: Danny Murphy debut
Match 14: Robinson last game
Match 23: Stubbs last game
Match 26: Gray last game
Match 29: Bassila last game
Match 31: Delap debut & Woods last game
Match 32: Mick McCarthy last game as Sunderland manager
Match 33: Kevin Ball first game as Sunderland caretaker manager
Match 37: Relegation confirmed
Match 39: Arca last game
Match 40: Smith last game
Match 42: Breen, Hoyte, Le Tallec and Welsh last games & Kevin Ball last game as Sunderland caretaker manager

Match No.	Date	Round	Venue	Opponents	Result	FT	HT	Pos.	Scorers	Attendance
1	Aug 13		H	Charlton Athletic	L	1-3	1-1		Gray	34,446
2	20		A	Liverpool	L	0-1	0-1	20		44,913
3	23		H	Manchester City	L	1-2	1-2	20	Le Tallec	33,356
4	27		A	Wigan Athletic	L	0-1	0-1	20		17,223
5	Sep 10		A	Chelsea	L	0-2	0-0	20		41,969
6	17		H	West Bromwich Albion	D	1-1	1-0	20	Breen	31,657
7	25		A	Middlesbrough	W	2-0	1-0	19	Miller, Arca	29,583
8	Oct 1		H	West Ham United	D	1-1	1-0	17	Miller	31,212
9	15		H	Manchester United	L	1-3	0-1	19	Elliott	39,085
10	23		A	Newcastle United	L	2-3	2-2	19	Lawrence, Elliott	52,302
11	29		H	Portsmouth	L	1-4	1-0	20	Whitehead (pen)	34,926
12	Nov 5		A	Arsenal	L	1-3	0-2	20	Stubbs	38,210
13	19		H	Aston Villa	L	1-3	0-0	20	Whitehead (pen)	39,707
14	26		H	Birmingham City	L	0-1	0-0	20		32,442
15	30		H	Liverpool	L	0-2	0-2	20		32,697
16	Dec 3		A	Tottenham Hotspur	L	2-3	1-1	20	Whitehead, Le Tallec	36,244
17	10		A	Charlton Athletic	L	0-2	0-1	20		26,065
18	26		H	Bolton Wanderers	D	0-0	0-0	20		32,232
19	31		H	Everton	L	0-1	0-0	20		30,576
20	Jan 2		A	Fulham	L	1-2	1-1	20	Lawrence	19,372
21	15		H	Chelsea	L	1-2	1-1	20	Lawrence	32,420
22	21		A	West Bromwich Albion	W	1-0	0-0	20	Watson o.g.	26,464
23	31		H	Middlesbrough	L	0-3	0-2	20		31,675
24	Feb 4		A	West Ham United	L	0-2	0-0	20		34,745
25	12		H	Tottenham Hotspur	D	1-1	0-1	20	Murphy	34,700
26	15		A	Blackburn Rovers	L	0-2	0-1	20		18,220
27	25		A	Birmingham City	L	0-1	0-1	20		29,257
28	Mar 5		A	Manchester City	L	1-2	1-2	20	Kyle	42,200
29	11		H	Wigan Athletic	L	0-1	0-1	20		31,194
30	18		A	Bolton Wanderers	L	0-2	0-0	20		23,568
31	25		H	Blackburn Rovers	L	0-1	0-1	20		29,593
32	Apr 1		A	Everton	D	2-2	1-2	20	Stead, Delap	38,093
33	14		A	Manchester United	D	0-0	0-0	20		72,519
34	17		H	Newcastle United	L	1-4	1-0	20	Hoyte	40,032
35	22		A	Portsmouth	L	1-2	0-0	20	Miller	20,078
36	May 1		H	Arsenal	L	0-3	0-3	20		44,003
37	4		H	Fulham	W	2-1	1-0	20	Le Tallec, Brown	28,226
38	7		A	Aston Villa	L	1-2	0-1	20	D. Collins	33,820

Appearances
Sub Appearances
Goals

FA Cup

23	Jan 8	R3	H	Northwich Victoria	W	3-0	2-0		N. Collins, Whitehead, Le Tallec	19,323
26	28	R4	A	Brentford	L	1-2	0-0		Arca	11,698

Appearances
Sub Appearances
Goals

Carling (League) Cup

7	Sep 20	R2	H	Cheltenham Town	W	1-0 (aet)	0-0		Le Tallec	11,969
12	Oct 25	R3	H	Arsenal	L	0-3	0-0			47,366

Appearances
Sub Appearances
Goals

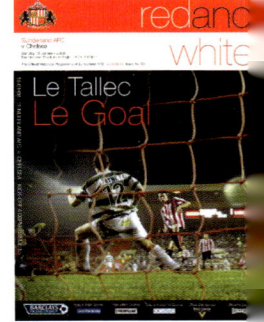

Anthony Le Tallec who became the first player on loan to Sunderland to score in all 3 major competitions.

2006-07

Coca Cola Championship

Ground: Stadium of Light
Managers: Niall Quinn and Roy Keane

League Table

	P	W	D	L	F	A	Pts
SUNDERLAND	46	27	7	12	76	45	88
Birmingham	46	26	8	12	67	42	86
Derby	46	25	9	12	62	46	84
West Brom	46	22	10	14	81	55	76
Wolves	46	22	10	14	59	56	76
Southampton	46	21	12	13	77	53	75
Preston	46	22	8	16	64	53	74
Stoke	46	19	16	11	62	41	73
Sheff Wed	46	20	11	15	70	66	71
Colchester	46	20	9	17	70	56	69
Plymouth	46	17	16	13	63	62	67
Crystal Palace	46	18	11	17	59	51	65
Cardiff	46	17	13	16	57	53	64
Ipswich	46	18	8	18	64	59	62
Burnley	46	15	12	19	52	49	57
Norwich	46	16	9	21	56	71	57
Coventry	46	16	8	22	47	62	56
QPR	46	14	11	21	54	68	53
Leicester	46	13	14	19	49	64	53
Barnsley	46	15	5	26	53	85	50
Hull	46	13	10	23	51	67	49
Southend	46	10	12	24	47	80	42
Luton	46	10	10	26	53	81	40
Leeds Utd	46	13	7	26	46	72	36

Premiership Champions: Manchester United 89 pts
FA Cup Winners: Chelsea
League Cup Winners: Chelsea
Shirt Sponsor: Reg Vardy

Did you know that?

Sunderland had their best League start to a calendar year (14 wins and 3 draws) prior to losing at Colchester United on 21 April. Also most wins in the second half of a season (17)

Marton Fulop became Sunderland's tallest player, 6ft 5in, when he made his debut v Luton Town, 9 December 2006

Match 1: Cunningham debut & Niall Quinn first game as Sunderland manager
Match 2: Clarke debut
Match 4: Arnau and Robbie Elliott debut & Kyle last game
Match 5: Arnau last game
Match 6: Hysen debut, Stead last game & Niall Quinn last game as Sunderland manager
Match 7: Connolly, Kavanagh, Liam Miller and Wallace debuts, Delap last game & Roy Keane first game as Sunderland manager
Match 8: Substitute Stephen Elliott was substituted by Leadbitter
Match 9: Yorke debut
Match 12: Alnwick last game
Match 13: Ward debut & Clarke and Robbie Elliott last games
Match 14: Nyatanga debut & Cunningham last game
Match 16: Neill Collins last game
Match 17: Lawrence last game
Match 23: Fulop debut
Match 27: Caldwell last game
Match 28: Hartley only game & Brown and Nyatanga last games
Match 29: Evans and Edwards debuts
Match 30: Stokes debut
Match 33: John and Simpson debuts & Varga last game
Match 39: Tommy Miller last game
Match 46: Stephen Elliott last game
Match 47: Simpson and Hysen last games & promotion confirmed by other results 2 days later
Match 48: Wright last game

Match Results

Match No.	Date		Round	Venue	Opponents	Result	FT	HT	Pos.	Scorers	Attendance
1	Aug	6		A	Coventry City	L	1-2	0-0		Murphy	22,366
2		9		H	Birmingham City	L	0-1	0-1	22		26,668
3		12		H	Plymouth Argyle	L	2-3	1-2	22	Murphy, S. Elliott	24,377
4		19		A	Southend United	L	1-3	0-1	21	Stead	9,848
6		28		H	West Bromwich Albion	W	2-0	1-0	23	Whitehead, N. Collins	24,242
7	Sep	9		A	Derby County	W	2-1	0-1	21	Brown, Wallace	26,502
8		13		A	Leeds United	W	3-0	2-0	14	L. Miller, Kavanagh, S. Elliott	23,037
9		16		H	Leicester City	D	1-1	0-0	14	Hysen	35,104
10		23		A	Ipswich Town	L	1-3	1-1	17	De Vos o.g.	23,311
11		30		H	Sheffield Wed.	W	1-0	0-0	14	Leadbitter	36,764
12	Oct	14		A	Preston North End	L	1-4	0-3	17	Varga	19,603
13		17		A	Stoke City	L	1-2	1-0	19	Yorke	14,482
14		21		H	Barnsley	W	2-0	0-0	17	Whitehead, Brown	27,918
15		28		A	Hull City	W	1-0	0-0	13	Wallace	21,512
16		31		H	Cardiff City	L	1-2	1-2	15	Brown	26,528
17	Nov	4		A	Norwich City	L	0-1	0-0	17		24,652
18		11		H	Southampton	D	1-1	0-0	19	Wallace	25,667
19		18		H	Colchester United	W	3-1	1-0	15	S. Elliott (2), Connolly	25,197
20		24		A	Wolverhampton W.	D	1-1	0-1	16	S. Elliott	27,203
21		28		A	Queens Park Rangers	W	2-1	2-0	14	Murphy, Leadbitter	13,108
22	Dec	2		H	Norwich City	W	1-0	0-0	13	Murphy	27,934
23		9		H	Luton Town	W	2-1	1-1	11	Murphy, Connolly	30,445
24		16		A	Burnley	D	2-2	0-1	11	Leadbitter, Connolly	14,798
25		22		A	Crystal Palace	L	0-1	0-1	11		17,439
26		26		H	Leeds United	W	2-0	0-0	11	Connolly, Leadbitter	40,116
27		30		H	Preston North End	L	0-1	0-1	12		30,460
28	Jan	1		A	Leicester City	W	2-0	1-0	10	Hysen, Connolly	21,975
30		13		H	Ipswich Town	W	1-0	1-0	9	Connolly	27,604
31		20		A	Sheffield Wed.	W	4-2	2-0	7	Yorke, Hysen, Connolly, Edwards	29,103
32		30		H	Crystal Palace	D	0-0	0-0	9		26,958
33	Feb	3		H	Coventry City	W	2-0	1-0	7	Yorke, Edwards	33,591
34		10		A	Plymouth Argyle	W	2-0	0-0	7	Stokes, Connolly	15,247
35		17		H	Southend United	W	4-0	2-0	5	Connolly, Hysen, John (2)	33,576
36		20		A	Birmingham City	D	1-1	1-0	5	Edwards	20,941
37		24		H	Derby County	W	2-1	1-0	4	Connolly (pen), L. Miller	36,049
38	Mar	3		A	West Bromwich Albion	W	2-1	1-0	4	Yorke, John	23,252
39		10		H	Barnsley	W	2-0	0-0	3	Leadbitter, Connolly	18,207
40		13		H	Stoke City	D	2-2	1-2	3	Whitehead, Murphy	31,358
41		17		H	Hull City	W	2-0	1-0	2	Evans, John	38,448
42		31		A	Cardiff City	W	1-0	0-0	2	Wallace	19,353
43	Apr	7		H	Wolverhampton W.	W	2-1	1-0	2	Murphy, Wallace	40,748
44		9		A	Southampton	W	2-1	0-0	1	Edwards, Leadbitter	25,766
45		14		H	Queens Park Rangers	W	2-1	1-0	1	Whitehead, Leadbitter	39,206
46		21		A	Colchester United	L	1-3	0-1	1	Yorke	6,042
47		27		H	Burnley	W	3-2	1-1	1	Murphy, Connolly (pen), Edwards	44,448
48	May	6		A	Luton Town	W	5-0	2-0	1	Stokes, Murphy (2), Wallace, Connolly	10,260

Appearances
Sub Appearances
Goals

E.On FA Cup

Match No.	Date		Round	Venue	Opponents	Result	FT	HT			Attendance
29	Jan	6	R3	A	Preston North End	L	0-1	0-1			10,318

Appearances
Sub Appearances
Goals

Carling (League) Cup

Match No.	Date		Round	Venue	Opponents	Result	FT	HT			Attendance
5	Aug	22	R1	A	Bury	L	0-2	0-0			2,930

Appearances
Sub Appearances
Goals

2007-08

Barclays Premier League

Ground: Stadium of Light
Manager: Roy Keane

League Table

	P	W	D	L	F	A	Pts
Manchester United	38	27	6	5	80	22	87
Chelsea	38	25	10	3	65	26	85
Arsenal	38	24	11	3	74	31	83
Liverpool	38	21	13	4	67	28	76
Everton	38	19	8	11	55	33	65
Aston Villa	38	16	12	10	71	51	60
Blackburn Rovers	38	15	13	10	50	48	58
Portsmouth	38	16	9	13	48	40	57
Manchester City	38	15	10	13	45	53	55
West Ham United	38	13	10	15	42	50	49
Tottenham Hotspur	38	11	13	14	66	61	46
Newcastle United	38	11	10	17	45	65	43
Middlesbrough	38	10	12	16	43	53	42
Wigan Athletic	38	10	10	18	34	51	40
SUNDERLAND	38	11	6	21	36	59	39
Bolton Wanderers	38	9	10	19	36	54	37
Fulham	38	8	12	18	38	60	36
Reading	38	10	6	22	41	66	36
Birmingham City	38	8	11	19	46	62	35
Derby County	38	1	8	29	20	89	11

FA Cup Winners: Portsmouth
League Cup Winners: Tottenham Hotspur
Shirt Sponsor: Boylesports

Did you know that?

Sunderland broke the British transfer record for a goalkeeper by signing Heart of Midlothian and Scotland keeper Craig Gordon for a fee that could rise to £9 million.

Match 1: Etuhu, Gordon, McShane, Richardson and Chopra debut
Match 2: Halford and O'Donovan debuts & John last game
Match 3: Anderson debut
Match 5: Anderson last game
Match 6: Higginbotham and Jones debuts
Match 10: Harte debut
Match 15: Cole debut
Match 17: Halford last game
Match 18: Ward last game
Match 20: Waghorn debut
Match 23: Kavanagh and Connolly last games
Match 25: Cole last game
Match 26: Bardsley and Prica debuts
Match 27: Substitute Prica was substituted by O'Donovan
Match 28: Reid debut
Match 29: Etuhu last game
Match 32: Prica last game
Match 37: Harte last game
Match 40: Evans, O'Donovan and Wallace last games

Match No.	Date	Round	Venue	Opponents	Result	FT	HT	Pos.	Scorers	Attendance
1	Aug 11		H	Tottenham Hotspur	W	1-0	0-0		Chopra	43,967
2	15		A	Birmingham City	D	2-2	0-1	4	Chopra, John	24,898
3	18		A	Wigan Athletic	L	0-3	0-1	7		18,639
4	25		H	Liverpool	L	0-2	0-1	14		45,645
6	Sep 1		A	Manchester United	L	0-1	0-0	17		75,648
7	15		H	Reading	W	2-1	1-0	14	Jones, Wallace	39,272
8	22		A	Middlesbrough	D	2-2	1-1	13	Leadbitter, Miller	30,675
9	29		H	Blackburn Rovers	L	1-2	0-0	15	Leadbitter	41,252
10	Oct 7		A	Arsenal	L	2-3	1-2	15	Wallace, Jones	60,098
11	21		A	West Ham United	L	1-3	0-1	16	Jones	34,913
12	27		H	Fulham	D	1-1	0-1	15	Jones	39,392
13	Nov 5		A	Manchester City	L	0-1	0-0	15		40,038
14	10		H	Newcastle United	D	1-1	0-0	15	Higginbotham	47,701
15	24		A	Everton	L	1-7	1-3	18	Yorke	38,594
16	Dec 1		H	Derby County	W	1-0	0-0	14	Stokes	42,380
17	8		A	Chelsea	L	0-2	0-1	15		41,707
18	15		H	Aston Villa	D	1-1	1-0	17	Higginbotham	43,248
19	22		A	Reading	L	1-2	0-0	18	Chopra (pen)	24,082
20	26		H	Manchester United	L	0-4	0-3	19		47,360
21	29		H	Bolton Wanderers	W	3-1	2-1	17	Richardson, Jones, Murphy	42,058
22	Jan 2		A	Blackburn Rovers	L	0-1	0-0	18		23,212
24	13		H	Portsmouth	W	2-0	2-0	18	Richardson (2)	37,369
25	19		A	Tottenham Hotspur	L	0-2	0-1	18		36,070
26	29		H	Birmingham City	W	2-0	1-0	14	Murphy, Prica	37,674
27	Feb 2		A	Liverpool	L	0-3	0-0	16		43,244
28	9		H	Wigan Athletic	W	2-0	1-0	14	Etuhu, Murphy	43,600
29	23		A	Portsmouth	L	0-1	0-0	15		20,139
30	Mar 1		A	Derby County	D	0-0	0-0	15		33,058
31	8		H	Everton	L	0-1	0-0	16		42,595
32	15		H	Chelsea	L	0-1	0-1	16		44,679
33	22		A	Aston Villa	W	1-0	0-0	16	Chopra	42,640
34	29		H	West Ham United	W	2-1	1-1	13	Jones, Reid	45,690
35	Apr 5		A	Fulham	W	3-1	1-0	13	Collins, Chopra, Jones	25,053
36	12		H	Manchester City	L	1-2	0-0	14	Whitehead	46,797
37	20		A	Newcastle United	L	0-2	0-2	15		52,305
38	26		H	Middlesbrough	W	3-2	2-1	13	Higginbotham, Chopra, Murphy	45,059
39	May 3		A	Bolton Wanderers	L	0-2	0-1	15		25,053
40	11		H	Arsenal	L	0-1	0-1	15		47,802

Appearances
Sub Appearances
Goals

E.On FA Cup

23	Jan 5	R3	H	Wigan Athletic	L	0-3	0-1			20,821

Appearances
Sub Appearances
Goals

Carling (League) Cup

5	Aug 28	R2	A	Luton Town	L	0-3	0-2			4,401

Appearances
Sub Appearances
Goals

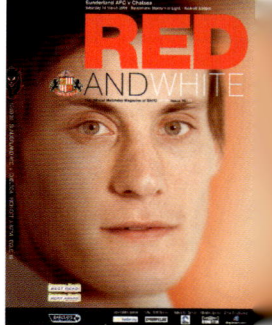

	1 Gordon	8 Whitehead	33 Wallace	4 Etuhu	5 Nosworthy	6 McShane	7 Edwards	19 Yorke	9 Stokes	11 Murphy	10 Richardson	12 Miller	15 Collins	16 Chopra	2 Halford	31 Connolly	14 John	23 O'Donovan	21 Anderson	18 Leadbitter	14 Higginbotham	17 Jones	3 Harte	20 Cole	13 Ward	39 Wagnhorn	44 Evans	26 Bardsley	45 Prica	20 Reid	32 Fulop	28 Kavanagh	35 Kay	24 Carson	36 Donoghue	
1	2	3	4	5	6	7	8	9	10	11	12	13	14		U								U													1
1	8	11	4	5	6	7					13	3	9	2	10	12	14	U					U													2
		3	4	5	6		8	10	11	7	12	13	9	2			14																			3
1		3	4	5	6		8	12	10	11	7		9	2	14			U	13				U													4
1		11	8	5	2		4	13	12		14	3	7					10	6		9		U					U								6
1		11	4	5	2		8	12	14		13	3	10	U				7	6		9		U													7
1		11	4		5		8	13			12	3	10	2			14	7	6	9	U		U													8
1		11		5	2		8		13		4	3	10		12		14	7	6	9	U		U													9
1		11	12	5	2		4	13			8	3	7				U	10	6	9	14		U													10
1		11	4	5				12			8	3	13	2	U		7	10	6	9	14		U													11
1		11	4	5				13	12		8	3	10	2	U			7	6	9	14		U													12
1		13	4	2			7	11		8	6		12	U				10	5	9	3		U				U									13
1		11	4		2	5	7				U	12	10		U			8	6	9	3		U													14
1	2	13	4		5	7	8					12	10			U		11	6	9	3	14	U													15
U	8	11			5	7		13			14	3	12	2				4	6	9	U	10	1													16
U	8	11	4		5		U	13	12		10	3		2				7	6	9		U	1													17
1	2	7	4		5	8	10	11				3	13				U		12	6	9	14	U		1											18
1	2	12	14		5		8	13	11			3	7					4	6	9	U	10	U													19
1	2	11	4		5		8			13		3	7			14		12	6	9		U	U	10												20
1	2		4		5			13	11	8	3		7			14		12	6	9		10	U	U												21
1	2	7			5	4			11	10	8	3						12	6	9		13	U	14					U							22
1	2			5	13		4	7	11	10	8	3				14		12		U		6		U												24
1	8			5	2		4	7	11		10	3	12			U			9	U	13		6				U									25
1	8			5	U		4	7	11		10	3				13			9			U	6	2	12		U									26
1	8			5	U				11	10		3	7			13			9		14	6	2	12		U										27
1	8		4	5	U				11			3	7			10		14	9				6	2	12	13	U									28
1	8		4	5	U		13		11			3	12					10	9		U		6	2	14	7										29
1	8			5	U			13	10	11			7					12	3	9			6	2	U	4	U									30
1	8			5	U			7	11	10		3	12					4	9				6	2	14	13	U									31
1	8			5	U	7	13					3				10		4	9	14			6	2	12	11	U									32
1	8			5		7	14		9	11		3	12			10		13					6	2	U	4	U									33
1	8			5	12	U		11	10			3	7					13	9				6	2		4	U									34
1	8			5		7			11	10		3	12			14		13	U	9			6	2		4	U									35
1	8			5	U	13			10	11		3	7			14		12	9				6	2		4	U									36
1	8				5	2	7		11	12	4	3	13					U	6	9	14					10	U									37
1	2			5		7			13	8	4	3	10					12	6	9		U	U	11	U	9										38
1	8		2					U	12	4	7	3	10			14		13	5	9			6			11	U									39
U	2	11		5		7	4				13	3	14					12	8	U	9		6			10	1									40
34	27	18	18	29	20	11	17	8	20	15	16	32	21	8	1		4	17	21	33	3	3	3	1	15	11		11	1							
		3	2		1	2	3		12	8	2	8	4		12		2	1	13	1	14			5	4		2			6	2					
	1	2	1				1	1	4	3	1		6					2	3	7						1	1									

1	8			2	5			9	11		3		14			7	U	13			12		10	6			U	4								23
1	1			1	1				1	1			1					1						1	1			1								
																		1		1			1													

		3	4	5				14	11	10		7		9	2	13		12	6	8				1						U	U					5
	1	1	1					1	1			1		1				1	1					1												
								1							1	1																				

Kenwyne Jones

Jones was Player of the Season and top scorer in his first year at the Stadium of Light.

533

2008-09

Barclays Premier League

Ground: Stadium of Light
Managers: Roy Keane and Ricky Sbragia

League Table

	P	W	D	L	F	A	Pts
Manchester United	38	28	6	4	68	24	90
Liverpool	38	25	11	2	77	27	86
Chelsea	38	25	8	5	68	24	83
Arsenal	38	20	12	6	68	37	72
Everton	38	17	12	9	55	37	63
Aston Villa	38	17	11	10	54	48	62
Fulham	38	14	11	13	39	34	53
Tottenham Hotspur	38	14	9	15	45	45	51
West Ham United	38	14	9	15	42	45	51
Manchester City	38	15	5	18	58	50	50
Wigan Athletic	38	12	9	17	34	45	45
Stoke City	38	12	9	17	38	55	45
Bolton Wanderers	38	11	8	19	41	53	41
Portsmouth	38	10	11	17	38	57	41
Blackburn Rovers	38	10	11	17	40	60	41
SUNDERLAND	38	9	9	20	34	54	36
Hull City	38	8	11	19	39	64	35
Newcastle United (R)	38	7	13	18	40	59	34
Middlesbrough (R)	38	7	11	20	28	57	32
West Bromwich Alb.	38	8	8	22	36	67	32

FA Cup Winners: Chelsea
League Cup Winners: Manchester United
Shirt Sponsor: Boylesports

Did you know that?

Sunderland's 2-1 victory over Newcastle United at the Stadium of Light in October was their first home victory over their near neighbours for 28 years.

Match 1: Chimbonda, Diouf, Malbranque and Tainio debuts
Match 2: Cisse debut & Higginbotham last game
Match 3: Healy debut
Match 5: Ferdinand debut
Match 8: Stokes last game
Match 13: Henderson debut
Match 18: Miller last game & Roy Keane last game as manager
Match 19: Ricky Sbragia first game as caretaker manager
Match 23: Ricky Sbragia first game as manager
Match 26: Diouf last game
Match 27: Chimbonda last game
Match 29: Chopra last game
Match 30: Kay & Luscombe only games
Match 32: Ben Haim debut
Match 36: Davenport debut
Match 37: Ben Haim last game
Match 38: McShane and Yorke last games
Match 43: Cisse last game
Match 44: Davenport and Whitehead last games & Ricky Sbragia last game as manager

Match No.	Date	Round	Venue	Opponents	Result	FT	HT	Pos.	Scorers	Attendance
1	Aug 16		H	Liverpool	L	0-1	0-0			43,259
2	23		A	Tottenham Hotspur	W	2-1	0-0	12	Richardson, Cisse	36,064
4	31		H	Manchester City	L	0-3	0-1	18		39,622
5	Sep 13		A	Wigan Athletic	D	1-1	1-0	16	Bramble o.g.	18,015
6	20		H	Middlesbrough	W	2-0	0-0	6	Chopra (2)	38,388
8	27		A	Aston Villa	L	1-2	1-2	11	Cisse	38,706
9	Oct 4		H	Arsenal	D	1-1	0-0	14	Leadbitter	40,199
10	18		A	Fulham	D	0-0	0-0	12		25,116
11	25		H	Newcastle United	W	2-1	1-1	9	Cisse, Richardson	47,936
12	29		A	Stoke City	L	0-1	0-0	10		26,731
13	Nov 1		A	Chelsea	L	0-5	0-3	14		41,693
14	8		H	Portsmouth	L	1-2	1-0	19	Cisse	37,712
16	15		A	Blackburn Rovers	W	2-1	0-1	11	Jones, Cisse	21,798
17	23		H	West Ham United	L	0-1	0-1	16		35,222
18	29		H	Bolton Wanderers	L	1-4	1-3	18	Cisse	35,457
19	Dec 6		A	Manchester United	L	0-1	0-0	18		75,400
20	13		H	West Bromwich Albion	W	4-0	3-0	17	Jones (2), Reid, Cisse (pen)	36,280
21	20		A	Hull City	W	4-1	1-1	12	Malbranque, Zayatte o.g., Jones, Cisse	24,917
22	26		H	Blackburn Rovers	D	0-0	0-0	14		44,680
23	28		A	Everton	L	0-3	0-2	15		39,146
25	Jan 10		A	Middlesbrough	D	1-1	0-1	13	Jones	29,310
26	17		H	Aston Villa	L	1-2	1-0	14	Collins	40,350
28	27		H	Fulham	W	1-0	0-0	11	Jones	36,539
29	Feb 1		A	Newcastle United	D	1-1	1-0	13	Cisse	52,084
31	7		H	Stoke City	W	2-0	0-0	11	Jones, Healy	38,350
32	21		A	Arsenal	D	0-0	0-0	10		60,104
33	Mar 3		A	Liverpool	L	0-2	0-0	12		41,587
34	7		H	Tottenham Hotspur	D	1-1	1-0	13	Richardson	37,894
35	14		H	Wigan Athletic	L	1-2	1-2	14	Leadbitter	39,266
36	22		A	Manchester City	L	0-1	0-0	14		43,017
37	Apr 4		H	West Ham United	L	0-2	0-1	17		34,761
38	11		H	Manchester United	L	1-2	0-1	17	Jones	45,408
39	18		H	Hull City	W	1-0	1-0	15	Cisse	42,855
40	25		A	West Bromwich Albion	L	0-3	0-1	15		26,256
41	May 3		H	Everton	L	0-2	0-0	16		41,313
42	9		A	Bolton Wanderers	D	0-0	0-0	16		24,005
43	18		A	Portsmouth	L	1-3	0-0	16	Jones	20,398
44	24		H	Chelsea	L	2-3	0-0	16	Richardson, Jones	42,468

Appearances
Sub Appearances
Goals

E.On FA Cup

Match No.	Date	Round	Venue	Opponents	Result	FT	HT	Scorers	Attendance
24	Jan 3	R3	H	Bolton Wanderers	W	2-1	0-0	Jones, Cisse	20,685
27	24	R4	H	Blackburn Rovers	D	0-0	0-0		22,634
30	Feb 4	R4r	A	Blackburn Rovers	L	1-2 (aet)	1-1	Healy	10,112

Appearances
Sub Appearances
Goals

Carling (League) Cup

Match No.	Date	Round	Venue	Opponents	Result	FT	HT	Scorers	Attendance
3	Aug 27	R2	A	Nottingham Forest	W	2-1 (aet)	0-0	Bardsley, Healy	9,198
7	Sep 23	R3	H	Northampton Town	W	2-2*	0-1	Stokes (2)	21,082
15	Nov 12	R4	H	Blackburn Rovers	L	1-2	0-0	Jones	18,555

* 4-3 penalties

Appearances
Sub Appearances
Goals

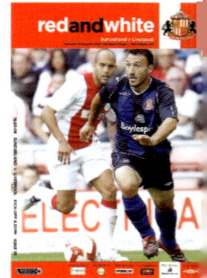

	1 Gordon	21 Chimbonda	2 Bardsley	4 Tainio	15 Collins	8 Malbranque	20 Reid	14 Murphy	11 Diouf	10 Richardson	6 Whitehead	7 Edwards	16 Chopra	22 Higginbotham	9 Cisse	12 Miller	18 Leadbitter	44 Stokes	23 Healy	3 McCartney	26 Ferdinand	19 Yorke	32 Fulop	17 Jones	39 Waghorn	42 Henderson	30 McShane	12 Ben Haim	21 Davenport	35 Kay	36 Liuscombe	13 Ward	46 Colgan	41 Meyler	34 Colback	45 Prica	
1	2	3	4	5	6	7	8	9	10	11	12	13	14	U			U	U									U										1
2	1		2		5	6	7	11	9	10	8	4		U	3	12	13	U	U	U							U										2
4	1	2	3		5	6	7	8	14	10	11			U	9	U	4	12	13		U						U										4
5	1	2	U	4	5	U	7	U	12	10	11	8			9		U		U	3	6		U														5
6	1	2	U	4	5	U	7	13	14	10	11	8	12		9		U			3	6		U														6
8	1	2			6	7	13	12	10	11	8		U	9	4		14	U	3	5		U		U													8
9	1	2	U		6	7	11	14	U	10	8		13		9		12		U	3	5	4	U														9
10	1	2	U	U		6	7	12	14	U	11	8		10	9		4		13	3	5		U														10
11		2	U	13		6	7	14		10	11	8		U	9		U			3	5	4	1	12				U									11
12			2	U	U	6	7	14		8			13		9		U			3	5	4	1	12				U									12
13		2	U	4	5		7	U		12	11	8			14					3	6		1	9	10	13		U	U								13
14		2	U	5	3	7	12	10	12	8	4				9	U	13		14		6		1		U			U									14
16		2	4	5	3	7	12	U	U	11	8				10		13				6	14	1	9		U			U								16
17		2	U	5	3	7	11	12	14	8	4	13			10						6		1	9		U			U	U							17
18	1	2	3	14	5	6	7	8	U	U	11	4			10	13	12				U		U	9					U								18
19		2	3	12	U	6	7	11	U	10		8	14		9		U				5	4	1	13					U								19
20			2	4	5	3	7	11	U	U	8		12		10	U	13				6	U	1	9					U								20
21			2	4	5	3	7	11	U		8	12	14		10		13		U		6	U	1	9					U								21
22	U	2	4	5	3	7	U	11	13	U	8	12	U		10		14				6		1	9					U								22
23		3	4	5	6	7		11		8	2		12		10				14			13	1	9		U			U	U	U						23
25		2		U	5	3	7	13	U	11	8	4	12		10			14			6	U	1	9					U								25
26		2	12	4	5	3		14		11			8	7	U	10		U		U	6		1	9		13			U								26
28		2	4		6	7	11		U		8	13	U		10		14		3		5		1	9		12			U								28
29		2			6	11	13	U		8	4	7	12		10		14		U	3	5	U	1	9					U								29
31	U	2			6	7	11	13		8	4		U		10		U	14	3	5		1	9			U	U										31
32	U		4		6	7	11	13		10	8	14					12		U	3	5		1	9		U	2	U									32
33	U	U			6	7	11	13		10	4	14			12	8			U	3	5			1	9		2	U									33
34	U	2			6	7	11	12		8	4	13			10		U		U	3			1	9			U	5	U								34
35	U	2			6	7	11	12			4	13			10		8		14	3		U	1	9			U	5	U								35
36	U	2			6	10	14	11			4	7			13	8			U	3	5	U	1	9			U		12								36
37	1	2			U	3	7	U	11		10	4	13		9	8			U		6	U		12			U	5									37
38	1	2	4		3	U	11	13				7			10	8					5	14	U	9			12	U	6				U				38
39		2	4		3	13	11	14		12		7			10	8					5	U	U				U	U	6								39
40		2	4		3	13	11	U		8	12	7			10		U		14		5		1	9			U		6				U				40
41		2	U		3	7		U		11	4	13			10		8		12		5		1	9			U	U	6				U				41
42		2	4		3	7	13	U		10	8	U			12	11	U		5		5		1	9			U		6				U				42
43		2	4		3	7	U	14		10	8	12			13		11		U		5		1	9			U		6				U				43
44		2	4		3	7	12	14		10	8				U		11		13		5		1	9			U		6				U				44
	12	13	27	18	16	35	34	20	6	11	31	30	6	1	29	1	12			16	31	4	26	25	1		5	7									
		1	3				2	12	17	3	1	4	16	5		6	2	11	2	10			3		4	1	3	1									
				1	1			4				2	10		2	1				10																	

24		2	12	5	3		13		11	8	4	7	U		10	U			U		6	U	1	9					U								24
27		5	2			3	11	8	U	U			7	9		U		4		10	12	6	U	1	13					U							27
30	1		12			6	11	8	9		U	U	7			4		10	3	5	13						2	14	U	U							30
	1	2	1		1	3	2	2	1	1	1	1	3	1		1		2	2	1	3		2	1			1										
		1	1				1				1									1			1		1			1									
																1		1																			

3	1	2	3		5	6	7	8	11	10		4	U		U	9	12	13	U	14								U									3
7	U	2		5	3		11	9		12	8	7	13		U	4	14	10		6	U								U								7
15		2	U	5	3	11	12	14	U	8	4				10		13			6		1	9		7			U	U								15
	1	1	3		3	3	2	2	2	1	1	3	1		2	1		1		2	2	1	1		1												
							1	1			1				1		2	1																			
			1												2	1					1																

Kieran Richardson — scorer of a superb free-kick to seal a 2-1 win over Newcastle United.

535

2009-10

Barclays Premier League

Ground: Stadium of Light
Manager: Steve Bruce

League Table

	P	W	D	L	F	A	Pts
Chelsea	38	27	5	6	103	32	86
Manchester United	38	27	4	7	86	28	85
Arsenal	38	23	6	9	83	41	75
Tottenham Hotspur	38	21	7	10	67	41	70
Manchester City	38	18	13	7	73	45	67
Aston Villa	38	17	13	8	52	39	64
Liverpool	38	18	9	11	61	35	63
Everton	38	16	13	9	60	49	61
Birmingham City	38	13	11	14	38	47	50
Blackburn Rovers	38	13	11	14	41	55	50
Stoke City	38	11	14	13	34	48	47
Fulham	38	12	10	16	39	46	46
SUNDERLAND	38	11	11	16	48	56	44
Bolton Wanderers	38	10	9	19	42	67	39
Wolverhampton W	8	9	11	18	32	56	38
Wigan Athletic	38	9	9	20	37	79	36
West Ham United	38	8	11	19	47	66	35
Burnley	38	8	6	24	42	82	30
Hull City	38	6	12	20	34	75	30
Portsmouth	38	7	7	24	34	66	19 †

FA Cup Winners: Chelsea
League Cup Winners: Manchester United
Shirt Sponsor: Boylesports

Did you know that?

Sunderland's winning goal at home to Liverpool, scored by Darren Bent, was deflected in off a beachball thrown onto the pitch earlier by a Liverpool fan.

Match 1: Bent, Campbell, Cana and Cattermole debuts & Steve Bruce first game as manager
Match 3: Collins last game
Match 4: Da Silva debut & Edwards, Leadbitter and Tainio last games
Match 6: Turner and Mensah debuts
Match 11: Zenden debut
Match 23: Meyler debut
Match 24: Ryan Noble debut and Liddle only game
Match 25: Fulop last game
Match 26: Healy last game
Match 27: Kilgallon debut and Nosworthy last game
Match 29: Hutton and Mwaruwari debuts
Match 43: Colback debut & Cana, Hutton, Jones and Mwaruwari last games

Match No.	Date	Round	Venue	Opponents	Result	FT	HT	Pos.	Scorers	Attendance
1	Aug 15		A	Bolton Wanderers	W	1-0	1-0		Bent	22,247
2	18		H	Chelsea	L	1-3	1-0	10	Bent	41,179
3	22		H	Blackburn Rovers	W	2-1	1-1	6	Jones (2)	37,106
5	29		A	Stoke City	L	0-1	0-1	8		27,091
6	Sep 12		H	Hull City	W	4-1	1-1	6	Bent (2, 1 pen), Reid, Zayatte o.g.	38,997
7	19		A	Burnley	L	1-3	1-1	8	Bent	20,196
9	27		H	Wolverhampton W.	W	5-2	1-0	8	Bent (pen), Jones (2, 1 pen), Turner, Mancienne o.g.	37,566
10	Oct 3		A	Manchester United	D	2-2	1-0	6	Bent, Jones	75,114
11	17		H	Liverpool	W	1-0	1-0	7	Bent	47,327
12	24		A	Birmingham City	L	1-2	0-1	7	Turner	21,723
14	31		H	West Ham United	D	2-2	1-2	8	Reid, Richardson	39,033
15	Nov 7		A	Tottenham Hotspur	L	0-2	0-1	8		35,955
16	21		H	Arsenal	W	1-0	0-0	8	Bent	44,918
17	28		A	Wigan Athletic	L	0-1	0-0	8		20,447
18	Dec 6		A	Fulham	L	0-1	0-1	10		23,168
19	12		H	Portsmouth	D	1-1	1-0	10	Bent	37,578
20	15		H	Aston Villa	L	0-2	0-1	10		34,821
21	19		A	Manchester City	L	3-4	2-3	10	Mensah, Henderson, Jones	44,735
22	26		H	Everton	D	1-1	1-0	10	Bent	46,990
23	28		A	Blackburn Rovers	D	2-2	0-0	10	Bent (2)	25,656
25	Jan 16		A	Chelsea	L	2-7	0-4	12	Zenden, Bent	41,776
27	27		A	Everton	L	0-2	0-2	13		32,163
28	Feb 1		H	Stoke City	D	0-0	0-0	13		35,078
29	6		H	Wigan Athletic	D	1-1	0-1	13	Jones	38,350
30	9		A	Portsmouth	D	1-1	1-0	13	Bent (pen)	16,242
31	20		H	Arsenal	L	0-2	0-1	14		60,083
32	28		A	Fulham	D	0-0	0-0	14		40,192
33	Mar 9		H	Bolton Wanderers	W	4-0	1-0	13	Campbell, Bent (3, 1 pen)	36,087
34	14		H	Manchester City	D	1-1	1-0	14	Jones	41,398
35	20		H	Birmingham City	W	3-1	2-0	12	Bent (2), Campbell	37,962
36	24		A	Aston Villa	D	1-1	1-1	13	Campbell	37,473
37	28		A	Liverpool	L	0-3	0-2	13		43,121
38	Apr 3		H	Tottenham Hotspur	W	3-1	2-0	13	Bent (2, 1 pen), Zenden	43,184
39	10		A	West Ham United	L	0-1	0-0	13		34,685
40	17		H	Burnley	W	2-1	2-0	13	Campbell, Bent	41,341
41	24		A	Hull City	W	1-0	1-0	13	Bent	25,012
42	May 2		H	Manchester United	L	0-1	0-1	11		47,641
43	9		A	Wolverhampton W.	L	1-2	1-1	13	Jones	28,971

Appearances
Sub Appearances
Goals

E.On FA Cup

Match No.	Date	Round	Venue	Opponents	Result	FT	HT	Scorers	Attendance
24	Jan 2	R3	H	Barrow	W	3-0	1-0	Malbranque, Campbell (2)	25,190
26	23	R4	A	Portsmouth	L	1-2	1-1	Bent	10,315

Appearances
Sub Appearances
Goals

Carling (League) Cup

Match No.	Date	Round	Venue	Opponents	Result	FT	HT	Scorers	Attendance
4	Aug 24	R2	A	Norwich City	W	4-1	3-0	Tainio, Reid (2), Tudor-Jones o.g.	12,345
8	Sep 22	R3	H	Birmingham City	W	2-0	2-0	Henderson, Campbell	20,576
13	Oct 27	R4	H	Aston Villa	L	0-0*	0-0		27,666

*1-3 penalties

Appearances
Sub Appearances
Goals

	32 Fulop	2 Bartsley	3 McCartney	39 Catermole	5 Ferdinand	15 Collins	8 Malbranque	19 Cana	17 Jones	11 Bent	10 Richardson	16 Henderson	9 Campbell	18 Leadbitter	20 Reid	6 Nosworthy	4 Turner	12 Mensah	22 Da Silva	7 Zenden	23 Healy	14 Murphy	18 Meyler	27 Kilgallon	6 Hutton	28 Mwaruwari	29 Colback	30 Noble, R.	33 Liddle	7 Edwards	24 Tainio	24 Carson	26 Reed	27 Anderson	15 Noble, L.	25 O'Donovan		
1	2	3	4	5	6		7	8	9	10	11	12	13	U		U	U				U							U									1
1	2	3	4	5	6			8	9	10	11	7	12	13	14	U	U				U							U									2
1	2	3	4	5	6	7	8	9	10	11	13	14	U	U	12	U					U																3
	2	3	4	6	U	7	8	9	10	11	14	12	U	13	5	1			U									U									5
	2		4	6		7	8	12	10	3	U	9		11	U	1	5	13	14		U							U									6
	2	3		6		7	4	12	10	8	13	9		11	U	1	5	U	U									U									7
U		14	4	13		7	8	9	10	3	12	U		11	U	1	5	6	2		U																9
U	2	14	4	6		7	8	9	10	3	12	13		11	U	1	5		U		U																10
U	2	3	4	6		7	8	9	10		12	14		11	U	1	5		U	13	U																11
U	2	13		6		7	4	9	10	3	8	12		11	U	1	5		U	14	U																12
U	U	12		U		7	4	9	10	3	8			11	5	1	6		2		U	U															14
12	2	3		13		7			9	8	4	10		11	U	1	5		6		14	U	U					U									15
1	2	3		14		7	4		9	10	8	12		11	U		5		6	13	U	U						U									16
1	2	3	U	7	4		9	10	8	12	11				5	U	6	14	13					U													17
1	2		6		7	4	9	10	3	8	13		11	12		5		U	14	U	U							U									18
1		3			13	4	9	10		8	7		11	2		5		6		U	12	U			U			U	U								19
1	14	12			U	4	9	10	8	7			2	5	13	6		U										U									20
1	U	3	4		7		12	9	13	8	10		11	2		5	6	14	U									U									21
1	2	3			7	4	9	10		8	U		11	13		5	6	12	U	U	U							U									22
1	2	3				4		10		7	9			5			6	U	U	11	8			U	U			U	U	U							23
1	2	3			7	5	9	10		4	13						6	12	U	11	8			U	U			U		U							25
U		3	8		U	4	12	9	10	7	U		13	5	1		2	14	11		U	6															27
U	U	3	8		7	4	9	10		14	13		11		1	5	2	U	12		U	6															28
U	U	3	8		U	4	9	10		7	U		11		1	5		U	12			6	2	13													29
	14	3	8		7	4	9	10			11				1	5		U	12			13	6	2	U		U										30
	14	3		4		U	8	9	11	7		10			1	5	6	U	13			U	2	12			U										31
U	14	8	3			4	9	10	11		7				1	5	6	U	12			U	2	13			U										32
12	U	8	3		11	4	9	10			7				1	5	6	U	13			U	2	14			U										33
14	U		3		11		9	10	8	12	7				1	5	6	U	13			4	U	2			U										34
12		14	3		11			10	8	13	7				1	5	6	U	U			4	U	2	9		U										35
U		4	3		11	13		9	10	8	7				1	5		U	6	12	U		U	2	U		U										36
	2		8	6		11	4	13	9	3	7				1	5		12	14				U	U	U		U										37
	14		4	2			14	13	9	3	7	10			1	5		6	12			8	U	U	U		U										38
U		4	2		11		12	9	3	7	10				1	5		6	13			8	U	U	14		U										39
U		12		11		9	10	3	8	7					1	5	6	U	13			4	U	2	14		U										40
12			13		11	14	9	10	3	8	7				1	5	U	U	U			4	6	2	U		U										41
	2	13	U		11	4	14	10	3	7		9			1	5	6	U	U			8	12				U										42
U			U		11	4	9	10	3	8	7				1	5		U	12			6	2	13	14		U										43
2	18	20	19	19	3	30	29	24	38	28	23	19		18	7	26	29	14	12	1		2	9	6	11		1										
	8	5	3	5		1	2	8			1	10	12	1	3	3			2	4	19	3	1	1		7	1										
							9	24	1	1	4		2			2	1		2																		

	2	3				7	5		10		4	9				6		13	11	8					12	14		U	U	U		U					24
	2					U	4	9	10	3	7	13		12		1	5		6	11	14	U	8			U		U									26
2	1					1	2	1	2	1	2	1			1	1		2	1		1	2	1														
										1		1								2					1	1											
								1			1									2																	

U	3		U		14		9			7	10	8	11	5	1		6			13	12					2	4	U	U		U						4
U			U		7	4	9	U	3	8	10		11	14	1	5	2	6		12	13							U			U						8
	3	13		14	4	9		7	8	10		12	5	1	6	2		U	11	U					1	1		U									13
	2			1		2	3		2	3	3	1	2	2	3	2	1	3		1			2	2		1		1	1								
			1		2								1	1							1																
										1	1			2													1										

SAFCSA Player of the Year, Darren Bent, scorer of 25 goals in his debut season for the Black Cats.

2010-11

Barclays Premier League

Ground: Stadium of Light

Manager: Steve Bruce

League Table

	P	W	D	L	F	A	Pts
Manchester United	38	23	11	4	78	37	80
Chelsea	38	21	8	9	69	33	71
Manchester City	38	21	8	9	60	33	71
Arsenal	38	19	11	8	72	43	68
Tottenham Hotspur	38	16	14	8	55	46	62
Liverpool	38	17	7	14	59	44	58
Everton	38	13	15	10	51	45	54
Fulham	38	11	16	11	49	43	49
Aston Villa	38	12	12	14	48	59	48
SUNDERLAND	38	12	11	15	45	56	47
West Bromwich Alb.	38	12	11	15	56	71	47
Newcastle United	38	11	13	14	56	57	46
Stoke City	38	13	7	18	46	48	46
Bolton Wanderers	38	12	10	16	52	56	46
Blackburn Rovers	38	11	10	17	46	59	43
Wigan Athletic	38	9	15	14	40	61	42
Wolverhampton W	38	11	7	20	46	66	40
Birmingham City	38	8	15	15	37	58	39
Blackpool	38	10	9	19	55	78	39
West Ham United	38	7	12	19	43	70	33

FA Cup Winners: Manchester City
League Cup Winners: Birmingham City
Shirt Sponsor: Tombola

Did you know that?

Sunderland played five games in London during the season; winning 2 and drawing 3. This was their best ever undefeated season in the capital.

Match 1: Mignolet, Onuoha, Bramble, Elmohamady, Riveros and Welbeck debuts
Match 3: Waghorn last game
Match 5: Gyan debut
Match 21: Cook and Angeleri debuts
Match 25: Da Silva, Angeleri and Reid last games
Match 26: Bent last game
Match 28: Sessegnon debut
Match 29: Muntari debut
Match 35: Substitute Ferdinand was substituted by Sessegnon
Match 37: Welbeck last game
Match 38: Lynch debut
Match 39: Muntari last game
Match 40: Laing debut & Mensah last game
Match 41: Henderson, Onuoha, Zenden, Malbranque, Cook and Riveros last games

Match No.	Date	Round	Venue	Opponents	Result	FT	HT	Pos.	Scorers	Attendance
1	Aug 14		H	Birmingham City	D	2-2	1-0		Bent (pen), Carr o.g.	38,390
2	21		A	West Bromwich Albion	L	0-1	0-0	15		23,624
4	29		H	Manchester City	W	1-0	0-0	10	Bent (pen)	38,610
5	Sep 11		A	Wigan Athletic	D	1-1	0-0	10	Gyan	15,844
6	18		H	Arsenal	D	1-1	0-1	10	Bent	38,950
8	25		A	Liverpool	D	2-2	1-1	10	Bent (2, 1pen)	43,626
9	Oct 2		H	Manchester United	D	0-0	0-0	10		41,709
10	18		A	Blackburn Rovers	D	0-0	0-0	13		21,894
11	23		H	Aston Villa	W	1-0	1-0	7	Dunne o.g.	41,506
12	31		A	Newcastle United	L	1-5	0-3	11	Bent	51,988
13	Nov 6		H	Stoke City	W	2-0	1-0	8	Gyan (2)	36,541
14	9		A	Tottenham Hotspur	D	1-1	0-0	7	Gyan	35,843
15	14		A	Chelsea	W	3-0	1-0	6	Onuoha, Gyan, Welbeck	41,072
16	22		H	Everton	D	2-2	1-1	7	Welbeck (2)	37,331
17	27		A	Wolverhampton W.	L	2-3	0-0	7	Bent, Welbeck	25,112
18	Dec 5		H	West Ham United	W	1-0	1-0	7	Henderson	36,940
19	11		A	Fulham	D	0-0	0-0	6		24,462
20	18		H	Bolton Wanderers	W	1-0	1-0	6	Welbeck	35,101
21	26		A	Manchester United	L	0-2	0-1	7		75,269
22	28		H	Blackpool	L	0-2	0-0	7		42,892
23	Jan 1		H	Blackburn Rovers	W	3-0	2-0	6	Welbeck, Bent, Gyan	36,242
24	5		A	Aston Villa	W	1-0	0-0	6	Bardsley	32,627
26	15		H	Newcastle United	D	1-1	0-0	6	Gyan	47,864
27	22		A	Blackpool	W	2-1	2-0	6	Richardson (2)	16,037
28	Feb 1		H	Chelsea	L	2-4	2-2	6	Bardsley, Richardson	37,855
29	5		A	Stoke City	L	2-3	1-1	6	Richardson, Gyan	26,008
30	12		H	Tottenham Hotspur	L	1-2	1-1	7	Gyan	40,986
31	26		A	Everton	L	0-2	0-2	8		37,776
32	Mar 5		A	Arsenal	D	0-0	0-0	8		60,081
33	19		H	Liverpool	L	0-2	0-1	9		47,207
34	Apr 3		A	Manchester City	L	0-5	0-2	12		44,197
35	9		H	West Bromwich Albion	L	2-3	2-1	13	Shorey o.g., Bardsley	41,586
36	16		A	Birmingham City	L	0-2	0-1	15		28,108
37	23		H	Wigan Athletic	W	4-2	0-0	10	Gyan, Henderson (2), Sessegnon (pen)	39,650
38	30		H	Fulham	L	0-3	0-1	14		39,576
39	May 7		A	Bolton Wanderers	W	2-1	1-0	11	Zenden, Muntari	22,597
40	14		A	Wolverhampton W.	L	1-3	1-1	13	Sessegnon	41,273
41	22		A	West Ham United	W	3-0	1-0	10	Zenden, Sessegnon, Riveros	32,792

Appearances
Sub Appearances
Goals

E.On FA Cup

25	Jan 8	R3	H	Notts County	L	1-2	0-1		Bent (pen)	17,582

Appearances
Sub Appearances
Goals

Carling (League) Cup

3	Aug 24	R2	H	Colchester United	W	2-0	2-0		Bent (2)	13,533
7	Sep 21	R3	H	West Ham United	L	1-2	1-1		Gyan	21,907

Appearances
Sub Appearances
Goal

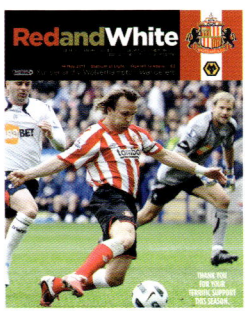

	22 Mignolet	15 Onuoha	3 Richardson	6 Cattermole	5 Mensah	19 Bramble	27 Elmohamady	10 Henderson	9 Campbell	11 Bent	8 Malbranque	16 Riveros	17 Welbeck	26 Waghorn	14 Da Silva	7 Zenden	29 Ferdinand	4 Turner	2 Bardsley	33 Gyan	20 Reid	1 Gordon	18 Meyler	26 Cook	12 Angeleri	25 Colback	28 Sessegnon	11 Muntari	31 Noble, R.	38 Lynch	40 Laing	24 Carson	34 Adams	37 Reed	30 Knott	
1	2	3	4	5	6	7	8	9	10	11	12	13	14	U	U		U									U					U					1
1	2	3			6	7	8	9	10	11	4	13	14	5	12				U					U	U					U					2
1		3	4		6	7	8	11	9	10	U	12	U		U	2	5	13							U					U					4
1	2	3	4	14	5	7	8		10	11	12	9			U	6		U	13						U					U					5
1	2	3			5	7	8		9	10	4	11		U	13	6		U	12	14					U					U					6
1	2		4		6	7	8		9	10	13	11		U	14		5	3	12	U	U				U										8
1	2		4	U	6	7	8		9	10	U			U	11	U	5	3	13	12	U														9
1	2		4	U	6	7	8		9	10	U	11		U	13	U	5	3	12		U														10
1	2		4	13	6	7	8		9	10	U	11		U	14	U	5	3	12		U														11
1	2	13	4	14	6	7	8		9	10		11		U	5	3	12	U	U																12
1	2	12	4	6		7	8			10	U	11		U	14	13	5	3	9		U		U												13
U	2	11	4		6	U	8			14	7	13		U	10	3	5	12	9		1		U												14
U	2	7	4		6	13	8			12	14	10		U	11		5	3	9		1		U							U					15
U	2	7	4			13	8		9	12	U	10		U	11	6	5	3			1		U							U					16
U	2	7	4	5		14	8		9	12	U	10		U	11	6		3	13		1		U												17
U	2	7	4	5		13	8		10	12	U	11		U	14	6		3	9		1		U												18
1	2	11	4	5		12	7		9	U		10		U	14	6		3	13	U	8		U												19
U	2	8	4	5		12	7		10	U	U	11		U	13	6		3	9		1		U												20
U	5				2	8		10	7	4				U	11	6		3	9		1	12	13	14						U	U				21
U	5	13	4		12	2	7		10	14	U	11			U	6		3	9		1	8	U												22
U		3			5	7	8		9	11	U	10			U	12	6		2	13		1	4	U	14										23
U		3			5	7	8		9	11	14	10		U	12	6		2	13		1	4			U					U					24
U	2	8			5	7	4		10	11	U			U	12	6		3	9	U	1		U	13											26
U	2	10		U	5	7	4			11	13			U	8	6		3	9	U	1		U	12											27
U	2	10			5	7	4			6						6		3	9		1	13	U	12	11				U						28
U	2	11		6	5	U	7			12	U			13	4			3	9		1	U	U	10	8										29
U	2	10			5	6	12	8		11	U			13	U			3	9		1	U	U	7	4										30
1		11		5	6	7	8			13	U			U	2			3	9		U			U	10	4	12				U				31
1		11		5	6	13	8			7	U	12			2			3	9		U			14	10	4	U				U				32
1	U	11	12	5	6	14	8			13		10			U	2		3	9		U			5	7	4									33
1			8	6		12	11				U			10		13	2	5	3	9		U			14	7	4		U		U				34
1	2	8	4	6		7	U			11		10			13	12	5	3	9		U			U	14	U									35
1	6		4			2	7			13	U	10			U		5	3	9	U	U			8	11		12	U							36
1	6		4			2	7			13	U	10			U	12	5	3	9		U			8	11	14			U						37
1	6		4	U		2	7			10	U				13	12	5	3						8	9	11		14	U	U					38
1	6			2		5	7	8		11	U				10	6		3						4	9	12	U	14		U	U				39
1	6			5		2	7			11	8				10			3					U	4	9		12	13	14	U	U		U		40
1	6					7	4			11	12				8	5		2		9			13		3	10	U	U		U	U		U		41
23	31	23	22	15	22	26	37	3	20	24	5	21		1	10	23	15	32	20		15	4			6	13	7								
		3	1	3	1	10				11	7	5	2		17	4		2	11	2			1	3	2	5	1	2	3	2	1					
		1	4				3		8		1	6			2			3	10					3	1											

1		3		U	13	12		10	7	4			5		6			14	9	11				2	8					U	U	U				25
1		1						1	1	1			1					1	1	1				1	1											
					1	1										1									1											
									1																										

	3	8		6	U	U	7	10	U		9	13		11	4	5	2		12				14							U					3
	5	3			7	8		10	13	4	11		12	14	6		2	9	U			U	U				U								7
2	1	2	1		1	1	1	1	2		1	2			1	2	1	2	1																
										1			1	1					1					1											
									2													1				1									

Player of the Year
Phil Bardsley.

2011-12

Barclays Premier League

Ground: Stadium of Light

Managers: Steve Bruce, Eric Black and Martin O'Neill

League Table

	P	W	D	L	F	A	Pts
Manchester City	38	28	5	5	93	29	89
Manchester United	38	28	5	5	89	33	89
Arsenal	38	21	7	10	74	49	70
Tottenham Hotspur	38	20	9	9	66	41	69
Newcastle United	38	19	8	11	56	51	65
Chelsea	38	18	10	10	65	46	64
Everton	38	15	11	12	50	40	56
Liverpool	38	14	10	14	47	40	52
Fulham	38	14	10	14	48	51	52
West Bromwich Alb.	38	13	8	17	45	52	47
Swansea City	38	12	11	15	44	51	47
Norwich City	38	12	11	15	52	66	47
SUNDERLAND	38	11	12	15	45	46	45
Stoke City	38	11	12	15	36	53	45
Wigan Athletic	38	11	10	17	42	62	43
Aston Villa	38	7	17	14	37	53	38
Queens Park Rangers	38	10	7	21	43	66	37
Bolton Wanderers	38	10	6	22	46	77	36
Blackburn Rovers	38	8	7	23	48	78	31
Wolverhampton W	38	5	10	23	40	82	25

FA Cup Winners: Chelsea
League Cup Winners: Liverpool
Shirt Sponsor: Tombola

Did you know that?

Martin O'Neill had the best start of any Sunderland manager; winning 9, drawing 2 and losing 2 of his first 13 competitive games.

Match 1: Brown, Larsson, Ji and Vaughan debuts
Match 2: Gardner and Wickham debuts
Match 3: Westwood debut
Match 4: O'Shea debut and Gyan Ferdinand last games
Match 5: Bendtner debut
Match 14: Steve Bruce last game as manager
Match 15: Eric Black only game as caretaker manager
Match 16: McClean debut and Martin O'Neill first game as manager
Match 26: Bridge debut
Match 35: Kyrgiakos debut
Match 38: Kyrgiakos last game
Match 43: Gordon last game
Match 44: Bendtner last game
Match 45: Bridge and Turner last game

Match No.	Date	Round	Venue	Opponents	Result	FT	HT	Pos.	Scorers	Attendance
1	Aug 13		A	Liverpool	D	1-1	0-1		Larsson	45,018
2	20		H	Newcastle United	L	0-1	0-0	14		47,751
4	27		A	Swansea City	D	0-0	0-0	13		19,938
5	Sep 10		H	Chelsea	L	1-2	0-1	16	Ji	36,699
6	18		H	Stoke City	W	4-0	3-0	12	Bramble, Woodgate o.g., Gardner, Larsson	32,296
7	26		A	Norwich City	L	1-2	0-1	14	Richardson	26,107
8	Oct 1		H	West Bromwich Albion	D	2-2	2-2	14	Bendtner, Elmohamady	34,815
9	16		A	Arsenal	L	1-2	1-1	17	Larsson	60,078
10	22		A	Bolton Wanderers	W	2-0	0-0	12	Sessegnon, Bendtner	24,349
11	29		H	Aston Villa	D	2-2	1-1	14	Wickham, Sessegnon	37,062
12	Nov 5		A	Manchester United	L	0-1	0-1	14		75,570
13	19		H	Fulham	D	0-0	0-0	15		37,688
14	26		H	Wigan Athletic	L	1-2	1-1	16	Larsson	37,883
15	Dec 4		A	Wolverhampton W.	L	1-2	0-0	17	Richardson	25,145
16	11		H	Blackburn Rovers	W	2-1	0-1	16	Vaughan, Larsson	39,863
17	18		A	Tottenham Hotspur	L	0-1	0-0	16		36,021
18	21		A	Q.P.R.	W	3-2	1-0	15	Bendtner, Sessegnon, Brown	16,167
19	26		H	Everton	D	1-1	1-0	14	Colback	43,619
20	Jan 1		H	Manchester City	W	1-0	0-0	13	Ji	40,625
21	3		A	Wigan Athletic	W	4-1	1-0	10	Gardner, McClean, Sessegnon, Vaughan	15,871
23	14		A	Chelsea	L	0-1	0-1	11		41,696
24	21		H	Swansea City	W	2-0	1-0	10	Sessegnon, Gardner	36,904
26	Feb 1		H	Norwich City	W	3-0	2-0	8	Campbell, Sessegnon, Ayala o.g.	34,476
27	4		A	Stoke City	W	1-0	0-0	8	McClean	27,717
29	11		H	Arsenal	L	1-2	0-0	9	McClean	40,312
31	25		A	West Bromwich Albion	L	0-4	0-2	9		25,311
32	Mar 4		H	Newcastle United	D	1-1	1-0	12	Bendtner (pen)	52,388
33	10		H	Liverpool	W	1-0	0-0	8	Bendtner	41,661
35	20		A	Blackburn Rovers	L	0-2	0-0	9		20,056
36	24		H	Q.P.R.	W	3-1	1-0	8	Bendtner, McClean, Sessegnon	37,128
38	31		A	Manchester City	D	3-3	2-1	9	Larsson (2), Bendtner	47,007
39	Apr 7		H	Tottenham Hotspur	D	0-0	0-0	9		39,355
40	9		A	Everton	L	0-4	0-0	10		32,249
41	14		H	Wolverhampton W.	D	0-0	0-0	9		37,476
42	21		A	Aston Villa	D	0-0	0-0	10		32,557
43	28		H	Bolton Wanderers	D	2-2	1-1	11	Bendtner, McClean	40,768
44	May 6		A	Fulham	L	1-2	1-2	11	Bardsley	25,683
45	13		H	Manchester United	L	0-1	0-1	13		46,452

Appearances
Sub Appearances
Goals

Budweiser FA Cup

Match No.	Date	Round	Venue	Opponents	Result	FT	HT	Scorers	Attendance
22	Jan 8	R3	A	Peterborough United	W	2-0	0-0	Larsson, McClean	8,954
25	29	R4	H	Middlesbrough	D	1-1	0-1	Campbell	33,275
28	Feb 8	R4r	A	Middlesbrough	W	2-1(aet)	1-0	Colback, Sessegnon	26,707
30	18	R5	H	Arsenal	W	2-0	1-0	Richardson, Oxlade-Chamberlain o.g.	26,042
34	Mar 17	R6	A	Everton	D	1-1	1-1	Bardsley	38,875
37	27	R6r	H	Everton	L	0-2	0-1		43,140

Appearances
Sub Appearances
Goals

Carling (League) Cup

Match No.	Date	Round	Venue	Opponents	Result	FT	HT	Attendance
3	Aug 23	R2	A	Brighton & Hove Albion	L	0-1(aet)	0-0	17,091

Appearance
Sub Appearances
Goal

Photo of James McClean - voted SAFC Supporters' Young Player of the Year. He made his Sunderland debut as a substitute in Martin O'Neill's first game and ended the season in Eire's European Championships squad.

SUMMARY OF SUNDERLAND'S

No.	Season	Division	Final Pos.	No. of Games	Home W	D	L	F	A	Away W	D	L	F	A	Total Goals scored	Goals conceded	Points
1	1890/91	One	7	22	7	2	2	31	13	3	3	5	20	18	51	31	23
2	1891/92	One	1	26	13	0	0	55	11	8	0	5	38	25	93	36	42
3	1892/93	One	1	30	13	2	0	58	17	9	2	4	42	19	100	36	48
4	1893/94	One	2	30	11	3	1	46	14	6	1	8	26	30	72	44	38
5	1894/95	One	1	30	13	2	0	51	14	8	3	4	29	23	80	37	47
6	1895/96	One	5	30	10	5	0	36	14	5	2	8	16	27	52	41	37
7	1896/97	One	15	30	4	6	5	21	21	3	3	9	13	26	34	47	23
8	1897/98	One	2	30	12	2	1	27	8	4	3	8	16	22	43	30	37
9	1898/99	One	7	34	11	3	3	26	10	4	3	10	15	31	41	41	36
10	1899/00	One	3	34	12	2	3	27	9	7	1	9	23	26	50	35	41
11	1900/01	One	2	34	12	3	2	43	11	3	10	4	14	15	57	26	43
12	1901/02	One	1	34	12	3	2	32	14	7	3	7	18	21	50	35	44
13	1902/03	One	3	34	10	5	2	27	11	6	4	7	24	25	51	36	41
14	1903/04	One	6	34	12	3	2	41	15	5	2	10	22	34	63	49	39
15	1904/05	One	5	34	11	3	3	37	19	5	5	7	23	25	60	44	40
16	1905/06	One	14	38	13	2	4	40	21	2	3	14	21	49	61	70	35
17	1906/07	One	10	38	10	4	5	42	31	4	5	10	23	35	65	66	37
18	1907/08	One	16	38	11	2	6	53	31	5	1	13	25	44	78	75	35
19	1908/09	One	3	38	14	0	5	41	23	7	2	10	37	40	78	63	44
20	1909/10	One	8	38	12	3	4	40	18	6	2	11	26	33	66	51	41
21	1910/11	One	3	38	10	6	3	44	22	5	9	5	23	26	67	48	45
22	1911/12	One	8	38	10	6	3	37	14	4	5	10	21	37	58	51	39
23	1912/13	One	1	38	14	2	3	47	17	11	2	6	39	26	86	43	54
24	1913/14	One	7	38	11	3	5	32	17	6	3	10	31	35	63	52	40
25	1914/15	One	8	38	11	3	5	46	30	7	2	10	35	42	81	72	41
26	1919/20	One	5	42	17	2	2	45	16	5	2	14	27	43	72	59	48
27	1920/21	One	12	42	11	4	6	34	19	3	9	9	23	41	57	60	41
28	1921/22	One	12	42	13	4	4	46	23	3	4	14	14	39	60	62	40
29	1922/23	One	2	42	15	5	1	50	25	7	5	9	22	29	72	54	54
30	1923/24	One	3	42	12	7	2	38	20	10	2	9	33	34	71	54	53
31	1924/25	One	7	42	13	6	2	39	14	6	4	11	25	37	64	51	48
32	1925/26	One	3	42	17	2	2	67	30	4	4	13	29	50	96	80	48
33	1926/27	One	3	42	15	3	3	70	28	6	4	11	28	42	98	70	49
34	1927/28	One	15	42	9	5	7	37	29	6	4	11	37	47	74	76	39
35	1928/29	One	4	42	16	2	3	67	30	4	5	12	26	45	93	75	47

SUMMARY OF SUNDERLAND'S SEASONS

LEAGUE SEASONS

No. of Players used	No. of goal-scorers	Top goalscorer	Total	% of all goals	Home Attendances Aggregate (League)	Average (League)	Comments
16	10	Campbell	16	31.37%	69000	6000	
15	8	Campbell	32	34.41%	96000	7500	
15	9	Campbell	30	30.00%	108000	7000	
19	12	Millar	19	26.39%	107000	7000	
18	11	Campbell	23	28.75%	129000	8500	
18	12	Campbell	15	28.85%	90000	6000	
23	11	Gillespie	8	23.53%	84000	5500	
20	9	Brown, Leslie & Wilson	8	18.60%	165000	11000	
25	14	Leslie	8	19.51%	198496	11676	First at Roker Park
17	10	McLatchie	11	22.00%	200490	12000	
18	11	Livingstone	12	21.05%	226465	13500	
19	12	Gemmell & W.Hogg	10	20.00%	224458	13000	
23	15	Gemmell, Hewitt & Millar	7	13.73%	239989	15000	One less home game as 'Boro, at St James' Park
23	10	Hogg	13	20.63%	223640	13000	
26	12	Holley & Watkins	9	15.00%	246000	14500	
27	15	Bridgett	17	27.87%	248000	13000	
28	12	Bridgett	25	38.46%	295000	15500	
28	13	Holley	23	29.49%	348082	18500	
24	11	Holley	19	24.36%	285993	15000	
23	8	Holley	20	30.30%	229000	12000	
26	11	Coleman	21	31.34%	312000	16500	
28	10	Holley	25	43.10%	231000	12000	
22	11	Buchan	27	31.40%	353700	18500	
25	12	Holley	15	23.81%	416700	22000	
22	8	Buchan	23	28.40%	206000	11000	
29	11	Buchan	22	30.56%	531648	25500	
32	11	Buchan	27	47.37%	566000	27000	
31	11	Buchan	21	35.00%	479035	23000	
27	6	Buchan	20	27.78%	509500	24500	
29	11	Buchan	25	35.21%	462473	22000	
25	11	Marshall	18	28.13%	452142	21500	
26	13	Halliday	38	39.58%	449409	21400	
26	13	Halliday	36	36.73%	380989	18142	
28	12	Halliday	35	47.30%	449633	21411	
27	9	Halliday	43	46.24%	529107	25196	

543

SUNDERLAND: THE COMPLETE RECORD

No.	Season	Division	Final Pos.	No. of Games	W	D	L	F	A	W	D	L	F	A	Total Goals scored	Total Goals conceded	Points
						Home					Away						
36	1929/30	One	9	42	13	3	5	50	35	5	4	12	26	45	76	80	43
37	1930/31	One	11	42	12	4	5	61	38	4	5	12	28	47	89	85	41
38	1931/32	One	13	42	11	4	6	42	29	4	6	11	25	44	67	73	40
39	1932/33	One	12	42	8	7	6	33	31	7	3	11	30	49	63	80	40
40	1933/34	One	6	42	14	6	1	57	17	2	6	13	24	39	81	56	44
41	1934/35	One	2	42	13	4	4	57	24	6	12	3	33	27	90	51	54
42	1935/36	One	1	42	17	2	2	71	33	8	4	9	38	41	109	74	56
43	1936/37	One	8	42	17	2	2	59	24	2	4	15	30	63	89	87	44
44	1937/38	One	8	42	12	6	3	32	18	2	10	9	23	39	55	57	44
45	1938/39	One	16	42	7	7	7	30	29	6	5	10	24	38	54	67	38
46	1946/47	One	9	42	11	3	7	33	27	7	5	9	32	39	65	66	44
47	1947/48	One	20	42	11	4	6	33	18	2	6	13	23	49	56	67	36
48	1948/49	One	8	42	8	10	3	27	19	5	7	9	22	39	49	58	43
49	1949/50	One	3	42	14	6	1	50	23	7	4	10	33	39	83	62	52
50	1950/51	One	12	42	8	9	4	30	21	4	7	10	33	52	63	73	40
51	1951/52	One	12	42	8	6	7	41	28	7	6	8	29	33	70	61	42
52	1952/53	One	9	42	11	9	1	42	27	4	4	13	26	55	68	82	43
53	1953/54	One	18	42	11	4	6	50	37	3	4	14	31	52	81	89	36
54	1954/55	One	4	42	8	11	2	39	27	7	7	7	25	27	64	54	48
55	1955/56	One	9	42	10	8	3	44	36	7	1	13	36	59	80	95	43
56	1956/57	One	20	42	9	5	7	40	30	3	3	15	27	58	67	88	32
57	1957/58	One	21	42	7	7	7	32	33	3	5	13	22	64	54	97	32
58	1958/59	Two	15	42	13	4	4	42	23	3	4	14	22	52	64	75	40
59	1959/60	Two	16	42	8	6	7	35	29	4	6	11	17	36	52	65	36
60	1960/61	Two	6	42	12	5	4	47	24	5	8	8	28	36	75	60	47
61	1961/62	Two	3	42	17	3	1	60	16	5	6	10	25	34	85	50	53
62	1962/63	Two	3	42	14	5	2	46	13	6	7	8	38	42	84	55	52
63	1963/64	Two	2	42	16	3	2	47	13	9	8	4	34	24	81	37	61
64	1964/65	One	15	42	12	6	3	45	26	2	3	16	19	48	64	74	37
65	1965/66	One	19	42	13	2	6	36	28	1	6	14	15	44	51	72	36
66	1966/67	One	17	42	12	3	6	39	26	2	5	14	19	46	58	72	36
67	1967/68	One	15	42	8	7	6	28	28	5	4	12	23	33	51	61	37
68	1968/69	One	17	42	10	6	5	28	18	1	6	14	15	49	43	67	34
69	1969/70	One	21	42	4	11	6	17	24	2	3	16	13	44	30	68	26
70	1970/71	Two	13	42	11	6	4	34	21	4	6	11	18	33	52	54	42
71	1971/72	Two	5	42	11	7	3	42	24	6	9	6	25	33	67	57	50
72	1972/73	Two	6	42	12	6	3	35	17	5	6	10	24	32	59	49	46
73	1973/74	Two	6	42	11	6	4	32	15	8	3	10	26	29	58	44	47
74	1974/75	Two	4	42	14	6	1	41	8	5	7	9	24	27	65	35	51
75	1975/76	Two	1	42	19	2	0	48	10	5	6	10	19	26	67	36	56

SUMMARY OF SUNDERLAND'S SEASONS

No. of Players used	No. of goal-scorers	Top goalscorer	Total	% of all goals	Home Attendances Aggregate (League)	Average (League)	Comments
31	14	Gurney	15	19.74%	515523	24549	
28	13	Gurney	30	33.71%	462306	22015	
27	14	Gurney	15	22.39%	485756	23131	
25	10	Gurney	16	25.40%	362329	17254	
20	10	Gurney	21	25.93%	383655	18269	
21	9	Gurney	30	33.33%	532968	25379	
23	10	Carter & Gurney	31	28.44%	637940	30378	
27	11	Carter	26	29.21%	602070	28670	
28	11	Carter	13	23.64%	527780	25132	
28	15	Carter	14	25.93%	456542	21740	
23	10	Robinson & Whitelum	17	26.15%	741331	35301	
26	15	Davis	12	21.43%	900653	42888	
23	12	Davis	10	20.41%	949624	45220	
20	11	Davis	25	30.12%	1003492	47785	
23	11	Ford	16	25.40%	835088	39766	
21	10	Ford & Shackleton	22	31.43%	836908	39853	
25	13	Ford	20	29.41%	835100	39767	
26	14	T.Wright	18	22.22%	897600	42743	
25	9	Chisholm	18	28.13%	903899	43043	
23	11	Fleming	29	36.25%	753641	35888	
26	12	Fleming	25	37.31%	759036	36145	
27	14	O'Neill	13	24.07%	759013	36143	
26	13	Kichenbrand	21	32.81%	583219	27772	
25	8	Lawther	17	32.69%	479447	22831	
24	16	Lawther	24	32.00%	547077	26051	
20	11	Clough	29	34.12%	692707	32986	
23	16	Clough	24	28.57%	858543	40883	
18	10	Crossan	22	27.16%	866410	41258	
26	16	Sharkey	18	28.13%	853473	40642	
21	13	Mulhall	10	19.61%	724243	34488	
24	11	Martin	20	34.48%	666347	31731	
24	12	Suggett	14	27.45%	648330	30873	
25	12	Suggett	9	20.93%	533936	25426	
21	11	Harris	7	23.33%	457585	21790	
20	14	Baker	10	19.23%	331378	15780	
25	12	Tueart & Watson	13	19.40%	332832	15849	
23	13	Hughes	15	25.42%	473877	22566	
23	13	Halom	18	31.03%	512737	24416	
18	10	Robson	19	29.23%	628570	29932	
22	14	Robson	13	19.40%	656537	31264	

SUNDERLAND: THE COMPLETE RECORD

No.	Season	Division	Final Pos.	No. of Games	W	D	L	F	A	W	D	L	F	A	Total Goals scored	Total Goals conceded	Points
					Home					**Away**							
76	1976/77	One	20	42	9	5	7	29	16	2	7	12	17	38	46	54	34
77	1977/78	Two	6	42	11	6	4	36	17	3	10	8	31	42	67	59	44
78	1978/79	Two	4	42	13	3	5	39	19	9	8	4	31	25	70	44	55
79	1979/80	Two	2	42	16	5	0	47	13	5	7	9	22	29	69	42	54
80	1980/81	One	17	42	10	4	7	32	19	4	3	14	20	34	52	53	35
81	1981/82	One	19	42	6	5	10	19	26	5	6	10	19	32	38	58	44
82	1982/83	One	16	42	7	10	4	30	22	5	4	12	18	39	48	61	50
83	1983/84	One	13	42	8	9	4	26	18	5	4	12	16	35	42	53	52
84	1984/85	One	21	42	7	6	8	20	26	3	4	14	20	36	40	62	40
85	1985/86	Two	18	42	10	5	6	33	29	3	6	12	14	32	47	61	50
86	1986/87	Two	20	42	8	6	7	25	23	4	6	11	24	36	49	59	48
87	1987/88	Three	1	46	14	7	2	51	22	13	5	5	41	26	92	48	93
88	1988/89	Two	11	46	12	8	3	40	23	4	7	12	20	37	60	60	63
89	1989/90	Two	6	46	10	8	5	41	32	10	6	7	29	32	70	64	74
90	1990/91	One	19	38	6	6	7	15	16	2	4	13	23	44	38	60	34
91	1991/92	Two	18	46	10	8	5	36	23	4	3	16	25	42	61	65	53
92	1992/93	New One	21	46	9	6	8	34	28	4	5	14	16	36	50	64	50
93	1993/94	New One	12	46	14	2	7	35	22	5	6	12	19	35	54	57	65
94	1994/95	New One	20	46	5	12	6	22	22	7	6	10	19	23	41	45	54
95	1995/96	New One	1	46	13	8	2	32	10	9	9	5	27	23	59	33	83
96	1996/97	Premier	18	38	7	6	6	20	18	3	4	12	15	35	35	53	40
97	1997/98	New One	3	46	14	7	2	49	22	12	5	6	37	28	86	50	90
98	1998/99	New One	1	46	19	3	1	50	10	12	9	2	41	18	91	28	105
99	1999/00	Premier	7	38	10	6	3	28	17	6	4	9	29	39	57	56	58
100	2000/01	Premier	7	38	9	7	3	24	16	6	5	8	22	25	46	41	57
101	2001/02	Premier	17	38	7	7	5	18	16	3	3	13	11	35	29	51	40
102	2002/03	Premier	20	38	3	2	14	11	31	1	5	13	10	34	21	65	19
103	2003/04	New One	3	46	13	8	2	33	15	9	5	9	29	30	62	45	79
104	2004/05	Championship	1	46	16	4	3	45	21	13	3	7	31	20	76	41	94
105	2005/06	Premier	20	38	1	4	14	12	37	2	2	15	14	32	26	69	15
106	2006/07	Championship	1	46	15	4	4	38	18	12	3	8	38	29	76	47	88
107	2007/08	Premier	15	38	9	3	7	23	21	2	3	14	13	38	36	59	39
108	2008/09	Premier	16	38	6	3	10	21	25	3	6	10	13	29	34	54	36
109	2009/10	Premier	13	38	9	7	3	32	19	2	4	13	16	37	48	56	44
110	2010/11	Premier	10	38	7	5	7	25	27	5	6	8	20	29	45	56	47
111	2011/12	Premier	13	38	7	7	5	26	17	4	5	10	19	29	45	46	45

SUMMARY OF SUNDERLAND'S SEASONS

No. of Players used	No. of goal-scorers	Top goalscorer	Total	% of all goals	Home Attendances Aggregate (League)	Average (League)	Comments
30	14	Lee	13	28.26%	687748	32750	
24	16	Rowell	18	26.87%	467997	22286	
22	12	Rowell	21	30.00%	534531	25454	
26	17	Robson	20	28.99%	569006	27096	
22	12	Rowell	10	19.23%	556061	26479	
24	12	Rowell	9	23.68%	411765	19608	
21	12	Rowell	16	33.33%	364771	17370	
19	12	West	9	21.43%	339788	16180	
24	14	Walker	10	25.00%	385318	18348	
30	17	Gates	9	19.15%	337067	16051	
23	11	Buchanan & Proctor	8	16.33%	285637	13602	
27	15	Gabbiadini	21	22.83%	400773	17425	
28	12	Gabbiadini	18	30.00%	342296	14882	
26	13	Gabbiadini	21	30.00%	408918	17779	
25	11	Gabbiadini	9	23.68%	428142	22534	
30	16	Goodman	11	18.03%	422566	18372	
26	15	Goodman	16	32.00%	396975	17260	
27	13	P.Gray	14	25.93%	390941	16997	
28	10	P.Gray	12	29.27%	353945	15389	
25	15	Russell	13	22.03%	402769	17512	
25	15	Russell & Stewart	4	11.43%	398497	20974	
28	12	Phillips	29	33.72%	794028	34523	First at The Stadium of Light
29	16	Phillips	23	25.27%	890662	38724	
30	15	Phillips	30	52.63%	786133	41375	
35	17	Phillips	14	30.43%	889800	46832	
27	11	Phillips	11	37.93%	888156	46745	
38	14	Phillips	6	28.57%	754267	39698	
36	15	Stewart	14	22.58%	623741	27119	
31	15	Stewart	16	21.05%	662784	28817	
30	17	Le Tallec, Miller & Whitehead 3		11.54%	644179	33904	
36	18	Connolly	13	17.11%	733406	31887	
32	16	Jones	7	19.44%	823540	43344	
32	11	Cisse & Jones	10	29.41%	763198	40168	
32	10	Bent	24	50.00%	766748	40355	
31	11	Gyan	10	22.22%	760209	40011	
28	15	Bendtner	8	17.78%	742813	39095	

Sunderland Head to Head Records

Notes: WW1 or WW2 = Guested for opposition during WW1 or WW2

Accrington

	Home					Away					Played for both
	P	W	D	L	F	A	P	W	D	L	F	A
League	3	2	1	0	10	5	3	2	0	1	12	7	Robert McDermid
FA Cup	1	1	0	0	3	0	1	1	0	0	3	1
Total	4	3	1	0	13	5	4	3	0	1	15	8

Season	H	A	Season	H	A	FA Cup	Round		
1890-91	2-2	1-4	1892-93	4-2	6-0	1891-92	2	A	3-1
1891-92	4-1	5-3				1893-94	1	H	3-0

Top scorer: Johnny Campbell 10 goals

Aldershot

Season	H	A	Played for both	
1987-88	3-1	1-2	Stephen Berry	Martin Gray
			Keith Bertschin	Denis Longhorn
			Dickie Davis (WW2)	Fred Rowell
			Len Duns (WW2)	John Smeaton (WW2)
			Patrick Gallacher (WW2)	Benny Yorston (WW2)

Top scorer: Marco Gabbiadini 3 goals

Arsenal

	Home						Away					
	P	W	D	L	F	A	P	W	D	L	F	A
League	65	29	22	14	117	78	65	15	15	35	68	127
FA Cup	4	3	0	1	10	3	4	1	1	2	4	9
L. Cup	1	0	0	1	0	3	2	1	0	1	3	3
Other	1	1	0	0	2	1	0	0	0	0	0	0
Total	71	33	22	16	129	85	70	17	16	37	75	139

Season	H	A	Season	H	A	Played for both
1904-05	1-1	0-0	1950-51	0-2	1-5	Joe Baker
1905-06	2-2	0-2	1951-52	4-1	0-3	Nicklas Bendtner
1906-07	2-3	1-0	1952-53	3-1	2-1	Steve Bould
1907-08	5-2	0-4	1953-54	7-1	4-1	Charlie Buchan
1908-09	1-0	4-0	1954-55	0-1	3-1	Brian Chambers
1909-10	6-2	2-1	1955-56	3-1	1-3	Lee Chapman
1910-11	2-2	0-0	1956-57	1-0	1-1	Andrew Cole
1911-12	1-0	0-3	1957-58	0-1	0-3	Keith Coleman
1912-13	4-1	3-1	1964-65	0-2	1-3	Tim Coleman
1919-20	1-1	2-3	1965-66	0-2	1-1	George Collin
1920-21	5-1	2-1	1966-67	1-3	0-2	Alfred Common
1921-22	1-0	2-1	1967-68	2-0	1-2	Ray Daniel
1922-23	3-3	3-2	1968-69	0-0	0-0	Fred Hall
1923-24	1-1	0-2	1969-70	1-1	1-3	David Halliday
1924-25	2-0	0-0	1976-77	2-2	0-0	David Hannah

SUNDERLAND HEAD TO HEAD RECORDS

Season	H	A	Season	H	A	Played for both
1925-26	2-1	0-2	1980-81	2-0	2-2	John Hawley
1926-27	5-1	3-2	1981-82	0-0	1-1	Justin Hoyte
1927-28	5-1	1-2	1982-83	3-0	1-0	John Kay
1928-29	5-1	1-1	1983-84	2-2	2-1	Sebastian Larsson
1929-30	0-1	1-0	1984-85	0-0	2-3	Henry Logan
1930-31	1-4	3-1	1990-91	0-0	0-1	Andy Marriott
1931-32	2-0	0-2	1996-97	1-0	0-2	Jackie Mordue
1932-33	3-2	1-6	1999-2000	0-0	1-4	George Payne
1933-34	3-0	1-2	2000-01	1-0	2-2	Richie Pitt
1934-35	2-1	0-0	2001-02	1-1	0-3	Mart Poom
1935-36	5-4	1-3	2002-03	0-4	1-3	Niall Quinn
1936-37	1-1	1-4	2005-06	0-3	1-3	Samuel Raybould
1937-38	1-1	1-4	2007-08	0-1	2-3	Dick Roose
1938-39	0-0	0-2	2008-09	1-1	0-0	Wilf Rostron
1946-47	1-4	2-2	2009-10	1-0	0-2	Stefan Schwarz
1947-48	1-1	1-3	2010-11	1-1	0-0	Len Shackleton
1948-49	1-1	0-5	2011-12	1-2	1-2	Anthony Stokes
1949-50	4-2	0-5				John Tones

FA Cup	Round				L. Cup	Round		
1892-93	1	H	6-0		1968-69	2	A	0-1
1905-06	3	A	0-5		2002-03	3	A	3-2
1960-61	3	H	2-1		2005-06	3	H	0-3
1972-73	Semi		2-1	At Hillsbrough				
1990-91	3	A	1-2					
1996-97	3	A	1-1					
1996-97	3 rep	H	0-2					
2011-12	5	H	2-0					

Top scorer: Charlie Buchan 13 goals
Sunderland won 2-1 in the Charity Shield in 1936-37 at Roker Park

Aston Villa

	Home					Away				
	P	W	D	L	F	A	P	W	D	L	F	A
League	80	38	25	17	146	101	80	15	16	49	94	151
FA Cup	1	0	1	0	2	2	8	1	0	7	9	22
L. Cup	4	0	0	4	3	9	1	0	1	0	0	0
Total	85	38	26	21	151	112	89	16	17	56	103	173

Season	H	A	Season	H	A	Played for both
1890-91	5-1	0-0	1934-35	3-3	1-1	Phil Bardsley
1891-92	2-1	3-5	1935-36	1-3	2-2	Darren Bent
1892-93	6-0	6-1	1938-39	1-5	1-1	Darren Byfield
1893-94	1-1	1-2	1946-47	4-1	0-4	Dickie Davis (WW2)
1894-95	4-4	2-1	1947-48	0-0	0-2	Stewart Downing
1895-96	2-1	1-2	1948-49	0-0	1-1	Trevor Ford
1896-97	4-2	1-2	1949-50	2-1	0-2	Craig Gardner
1897-98	0-0	3-4	1950-51	3-3	1-3	Shay Given
1898-99	4-2	0-2	1951-52	1-3	1-2	George Harper
1899-1900	0-1	2-4	1952-53	2-2	0-3	Alan Hutton
1900-01	0-0	2-2	1953-54	2-0	1-3	Harry Johnston
1901-02	1-0	1-0	1954-55	0-0	2-2	Dariusz Kubicki
1902-03	1-0	1-0	1955-56	5-1	4-1	James Logan
1903-04	6-1	0-2	1956-57	1-0	2-2	Gavin McCann
1904-05	2-3	2-2	1957-58	1-1	2-5	Thomas Mitchinson
1905-06	2-0	1-2	1959-60	1-0	0-3	Alan O'Neill
1906-07	2-1	2-2	1964-65	2-2	1-2	Kevin Phillips
1907-08	3-0	0-1	1965-66	2-0	1-3	Dick Roose

Season	H	A	Season	H	A	Played for both
1908-09	4-3	0-2	1966-67	2-1	1-2	Thomas Sozensen
1909-10	1-1	2-3	1972-73	2-2	0-2	James Stephenson
1910-11	3-2	1-2	1973-74	2-0	2-1	Mark Watkins
1911-12	2-2	3-1	1974-75	0-0	0-2	John Williamson
1912-13	3-1	1-1	1976-77	0-1	1-4	Dwight Yorke
1913-14	2-0	0-5	1980-81	1-2	0-4	
1914-15	4-0	3-1	1981-82	2-1	0-1	
1919-20	2-1	3-0	1982-83	2-0	3-1	
1920-21	0-1	5-1	1983-84	0-1	0-1	
1921-22	1-4	0-2	1984-85	0-4	0-1	
1922-23	2-0	0-1	1990-91	1-3	0-3	
1923-24	2-0	1-0	1996-97	1-0	0-1	
1924-25	1-1	4-1	1999-2000	2-1	1-1	
1925-26	3-2	2-4	2000-01	1-1	0-0	
1926-27	1-1	1-3	2001-02	1-1	0-0	
1927-28	2-3	2-4	2002-03	1-0	0-1	
1928-29	1-3	1-3	2005-06	1-3	1-2	
1929-30	4-1	1-2	2007-08	1-1	1-0	
1930-31	1-1	2-4	2008-09	1-2	1-2	
1931-32	1-1	0-2	2009-10	0-2	1-1	
1932-33	1-1	0-1	2010-11	1-0	1-0	
1933-34	5-1	1-2	2011-12	2-2	0-0	

FA Cup	Round				L. Cup	Round			
1891-92	Semi		1-4	At Bramall Lane	1962-63	Semi L1	H	1-3	
1893-94	2	H	2-2		1962-63	Semi L2	A	0-0	
1893-94	2 rep	A	1-3		1965-66	3	H	1-2	
1894-95	Semi		1-2	At Ewood Park	1993-94	3	H	1-4	
1902-03	1	A	1-4		2009-10	4	H	0-0	1-3 on pens
1912-13	Final		0-1	At Crystal Palace					
1919-20	3	A	0-1						
1932-33	4	A	3-0						
1933-34	4	A	2-7						

Top scorer: Johnny Campbell 11 goals

Atalanta

Season	H	A	
1971-72	0-0	2-3	Anglo-Italian Cup

Barnsley

	Home						Away				
	P	W	D	L	F	A	P	W	D	L	F	A
League	12	9	1	2	24	12	12	5	1	6	12	15
Other	1	1	0	0	1	1	0	0	0	0	0	0
Total	13	10	1	2	25	13	12	5	1	6	12	15

Season	H	A	Played for both	
1958-59	2-2	2-0	Steve Agnew	Andy Marriott
1985-86	2-0	1-1	Ben Alnwick	Fred Mearns
1986-87	2-3	0-1	Michael Chopra	Albert Milton
1988-89	1-0	0-3	Don Goodman	Jackie Mordue
1989-90	4-2	0-1	Andy Gray	Harry Ness
1991-92	2-0	3-0	Philip Gray	Lewin Nyatanga
1992-93	2-1	0-2	Colin Healy	John Oster
1993-94	1-0	0-4	George Henderson	Michael Reddy
1994-95	2-0	0-2	Ian Hughes	William Robinson (WW2)
1995-96	2-1	1-0	Bert Ives	Len Shackleton (WW2)

SUNDERLAND HEAD TO HEAD RECORDS

1998-99	2-3	3-1	Simon Johnson	Harry Sherwin
2006-07	2-0	2-0	John Lathan	Cliff Whitelum (WW2)
			Chris Lumsdon	Ken Willingham (WW2)
			Paul McShane	Rodger Wylde

Top scorer: 6 players with 2 goals
Sunderland won 8-7 on penalties (1-1 after full time) in a 1st Round Full Members' Cup tie in 1986-87 at Roker Park

Barrow

FA Cup	Round			Played for both		
2009-10	3	H	3-0	Michael Coady	Craig James	David Rush
				Robert Ferguson	Alan Kennedy	Rob Vincent
				Tony Ford	Brendan McGill	Neil Wainwright
				John T. Foster	Fred Mearns	George Whitelaw
				Vic Halom	Peter Meechan	Alwyne Wilks
				Fred Hall	Ted Purdon	
				Mick Horswill	Robert Robinson (b.1910)	

Birmingham City

	Home					Away				
	P	W	D	L	F	A	P	W	D	L	F	A
League	53	35	8	10	110	56	53	14	13	26	58	76
FA Cup	4	1	1	2	4	5	5	1	1	3	4	9
L. Cup	1	1	0	0	2	0	0	0	0	0	0	0
Other	1	0	0	1	0	1	0	0	0	0	0	0
Total	59	37	9	13	116	62	58	15	14	29	62	85

Season	H	A	Season	H	A	Played for both	
1894-95	7-1	1-1	1949-50	1-1	2-1	George Ainsley (WW2)	Sebastian Larsson
1895-96	2-1	1-0	1955-56	1-0	2-1	Ian Atkins	Seamus McDonagh
1901-02	1-1	3-2	1956-57	0-1	2-1	Nicklas Bendtner	Andy Marriott
1903-04	3-1	1-2	1957-58	1-6	3-2	Keith Bertschin	Jim Montgomery
1904-05	1-4	1-1	1964-65	2-1	3-4	Robert Bonthron	Thomas Myhre
1905-06	3-1	0-3	1970-71	2-1	1-3	Gary Breen	John Oliver
1906-07	4-1	0-2	1971-72	1-1	1-1	Steven Caldwell	Kevin Phillips
1907-08	1-0	2-0	1976-77	1-0	0-2	Darren Carter	Mark Prudhoe
1921-22	2-1	0-1	1979-80	2-0	0-1	Tim Carter	Ted Purdon
1922-23	5-3	2-1	1980-81	3-0	2-3	Andrew Cole	George Robinson (WW2)
1923-24	1-1	2-0	1981-82	2-0	0-2	Terry Cooke	Ian Rodgerson
1924-25	4-0	1-2	1982-83	1-2	1-2	John Cornforth	Teemu Tainio
1925-26	3-1	1-2	1983-84	2-1	1-0	Tony Coton	Colin Todd
1926-27	4-1	0-2	1986-87	2-0	0-2	John Coxford	Tony Towers
1927-28	4-2	1-1	1988-89	2-2	2-3	Kenny Cunningham	Jack Vinall
1928-29	3-4	0-1	1992-93	1-2	0-1	Thomas Daykin	Isaac Webb
1929-30	1-0	1-3	1993-94	1-0	0-0	Joseph Devine	Paul A. Williams
1930-31	1-0	0-1	1995-96	3-0	2-0	William Ellis	Frank Worthington
1931-32	2-3	0-0	1997-98	1-1	1-0	Marco Gabbiadini	Dwight Yorke
1932-33	1-0	0-2	1998-99	2-1	0-0	Craig Gardner	
1933-34	4-1	1-1	2002-03	0-1	0-2	Howard Gayle	
1934-35	5-1	2-2	2005-06	0-1	0-1	Mick Harford	
1935-36	2-1	7-2	2006-07	0-1	1-1	Michael Hellawell	
1936-37	4-0	0-2	2007-08	2-0	2-2	Harold Hooper	
1937-38	1-0	2-2	2009-10	3-1	1-2	Stern John	
1938-39	1-0	2-1	2010-11	2-2	0-2	Allan Johnston	
1948-49	1-1	0-0				Joseph Lane	

FA Cup	Round				L. Cup	Round		
1930-31	Semi		0-2	At Leeds Road	2009-10	3	H	2-0
1945-46	5 L1	H	1-0					
1945-46	5 L2	A	1-3					
1955-56	Semi		0-3	At Hillsbrough				
1980-81	3	A	1-1					
1980-81	3 rep	H	1-2					
1983-84	4	H	1-2					
2003-04	5	H	1-1					
2003-04	5 rep	A	2-0					

Top scorer: Bobby Gurney 11 goals
Sunderland lost 0-1 in an Anglo-Italian Cup group game in 1992-93 at Roker Park

Blackburn Rovers

	Home					Away				
	P	W	D	L	F	A	P	W	D	L	F	A
League	64	43	8	13	140	61	64	17	18	29	80	115
FA Cup	4	1	3	0	4	4	8	0	2	6	7	18
L. Cup	2	1	0	1	4	4	0	0	0	0	0	0
Other	0	0	0	0	0	0	1	0	0	1	1	2
Total	70	45	11	14	148	69	73	17	20	36	88	135

Season	H	A	Season	H	A	Played for both
1890-91	3-1	2-3	1926-27	2-5	2-0	Steve Agnew
1891-92	6-1	1-3	1927-28	1-0	0-0	Kevin Arnott
1892-93	5-0	2-2	1928-29	3-1	0-2	Francis Bee
1893-94	2-3	3-4	1929-30	3-1	3-5	Pascal Chimbonda
1894-95	3-2	1-1	1930-31	8-2	0-3	Andrew Cole
1895-96	2-1	4-2	1931-32	2-2	2-5	El Hadji Diouf
1896-97	0-1	2-1	1932-33	4-2	3-1	Teddy Doig
1897-98	1-1	1-2	1933-34	3-0	0-0	Dickson Etuhu
1898-99	0-1	2-3	1934-35	3-0	0-0	Howard Gayle
1899-1900	1-0	2-1	1935-36	7-2	1-1	Cyril Gilhespy
1900-01	2-0	1-0	1946-47	1-0	2-1	Shay Given
1901-02	3-2	1-0	1947-48	0-1	3-4	James Gorman
1902-03	2-2	2-0	1964-65	1-0	2-3	Michael Gray
1903-04	2-0	3-1	1965-66	1-0	0-2	Fred Hall
1904-05	2-1	1-2	1970-71	3-2	1-0	Ian Lawther
1905-06	3-0	3-0	1975-76	3-0	1-0	Jason McAteer
1906-07	1-0	1-2	1977-78	0-1	1-1	Andy Marriott
1907-08	4-0	2-4	1978-79	0-1	1-1	Dominic Matteo
1908-09	0-1	1-8	1985-86	0-2	0-2	Bobby Mimms
1909-10	0-0	0-0	1986-87	3-0	1-6	Bobby Mitchell
1910-11	2-2	1-0	1988-89	2-0	2-0	John Murray
1911-12	3-0	2-2	1989-90	0-1	1-1	Benjamin Mwaruwari
1912-13	2-4	0-4	1991-92	1-1	2-2	Mark Outterside
1913-14	2-1	1-3	1996-97	0-0	0-1	Danny Simpson
1914-15	5-1	1-3	2001-02	1-0	3-0	John Smeaton
1919-20	2-0	0-3	2002-03	0-0	0-0	Jonathan Stead
1920-21	2-0	0-2	2005-06	0-1	0-2	William Walsh (WW2)
1921-22	3-1	2-1	2007-08	1-2	0-1	Dwight Yorke
1922-23	4-3	0-0	2008-09	0-0	2-1	
1923-24	5-1	2-3	2009-10	2-1	2-2	
1924-25	1-0	1-1	2010-11	3-0	0-0	
1925-26	6-2	0-3	2011-12	2-1	0-2	

FA Cup	Round				L. Cup	Round		
1889-90	1	A	2-4		1962-63	5	H	3-2
1892-93	3	A	0-3		2008-09	4	H	1-2
1938-39	5	H	1-1					
1938-39	5 rep	A	0-0					
1938-39	5 rep 2		0-1	At Hillsbrough				
1959-60	3	H	1-1					
1959-60	3 rep	A	1-4					
1998-99	4	A	0-1					
2002-03	4	A	3-3					
2002-03	4 rep	H	2-2	Won 3-0 on pens				
2008-09	4	H	0-0					
2008-09	4 rep	A	1-2					

Top scorer: Charlie Buchan 15 goals
Sunderland lost 1-2 in a 2nd Round Full Members' Cup tie in 1988-89 at Ewood Park

Blackpool

	Home					Away				
	P	W	D	L	F	A	P	W	D	L	F	A
League	28	15	7	6	47	34	28	8	9	11	36	50
FA Cup	1	1	0	0	1	0	0	0	0	0	0	0
L. Cup	1	1	0	0	4	1	0	0	0	0	0	0
Total	30	17	7	6	52	35	28	8	9	11	36	50

Season	H	A	Season	H	A	Played for both		
1930-31	2-4	1-3	1972-73	1-0	0-0	George Ainsley (WW2)	Chris Lumsdon	
1931-32	4-0	2-3	1973-74	2-1	2-0	Jack Ashurst	Mark Maley	
1932-33	1-1	1-3	1974-75	1-0	2-3	Harry Bedford	Dick Malone	
1937-38	2-1	0-0	1975-76	2-0	0-1	Eddie Burbanks (WW2)	Hugh Morgan	
1938-39	1-2	1-1	1977-78	2-1	1-1	Thomas Bradshaw	Roy O'Donovan	
1946-47	3-2	5-0	1987-88	2-2	2-0	Darren Byfield	Colin Pascoe	
1947-48	1-0	1-0	2010-11	0-2	2-1	Steven Caldwell	Kevin Phillips	
1948-49	2-2	3-3				Tim Carter	Geoff Power	
1949-50	1-1	1-0				Shaun Elliott	Stanley Ramsay	
1950-51	0-2	2-2				Wayne Entwistle	William Read	
1951-52	1-3	0-3				John S. Foster	Andy Reid	
1952-53	1-1	0-2				Ricardo Gabbiadini	Anton Rogan	
1953-54	3-2	0-3				Charles Gladwin	Barry Siddall	
1954-55	2-0	0-0				Ian Harte	Kenneth Smith	
1955-56	0-0	3-7				Iain Hesford	Paul Stewart	
1956-57	5-2	2-1				Steve Hetzke	Ernest Taylor	
1957-58	1-4	0-7				Robert Hogg	Sean Thornton	
1964-65	1-0	1-3				Mel Holden	David Vaughan	
1965-66	2-1	2-1				Simon Johnson	Nigel Walker	
1966-67	4-0	1-1				Bobby Kerr	William Walsh (WW2)	
1971-72	0-0	1-1				Joseph Lane	Andrew Welsh	

FA Cup	Round				L. Cup	Round		
1932-33	5	H	1-0		1964-65	3	H	4-1

Top scorer: Len Shackleton 6 goals

Bolton Wanderers

	Home						Away					
	P	W	D	L	F	A	P	W	D	L	F	A
League	66	41	14	11	151	70	66	15	16	35	74	115
FA Cup	5	4	0	1	9	4	3	1	2	0	5	2
L. Cup	1	1	0	0	1	0	1	0	1	0	1	1
Other	1	1	0	0	2	0	2	0	0	2	0	4
Total	73	47	14	12	163	74	72	16	19	37	80	122

Season	H	A	Season	H	A	Played for both
1890-91	2-0	5-2	1932-33	7-4	0-0	George Ainsley
1891-92	4-1	3-4	1935-36	7-2	1-2	Sam Allardyce
1892-93	3-3	1-2	1936-37	3-0	1-1	Peter Barnes
1893-94	2-1	0-2	1937-38	3-1	1-1	Tal Ben Haim
1894-95	4-0	1-4	1938-39	2-2	1-2	John Bollands
1895-96	1-0	0-1	1946-47	3-1	1-0	Michael Bridges
1896-97	1-1	0-1	1947-48	1-2	1-3	James Davison
1897-98	2-0	0-1	1948-49	2-0	1-4	Andy Dibble
1898-99	0-0	1-6	1949-50	2-0	1-2	El Hadji Diouf
1900-01	5-1	0-0	1950-51	1-2	2-1	Alex Donaldson
1901-02	2-1	0-0	1951-52	0-2	1-1	Robbie Elliott
1902-03	3-1	0-2	1952-53	2-0	0-5	Wayne Entwistle
1905-06	3-3	2-6	1953-54	1-2	1-3	Carsten Fredgaard
1906-07	1-2	0-1	1954-55	1-1	0-3	Alan Hay
1907-08	1-2	3-2	1955-56	0-0	3-0	Joseph Hewitt
1909-10	3-0	1-2	1956-57	3-0	1-2	Darren Holloway
1911-12	0-1	0-3	1957-58	1-2	2-2	Charlie Hurley
1912-13	2-1	3-1	1970-71	4-1	3-1	Allan Johnston
1913-14	3-2	1-2	1973-74	3-0	0-1	John B. Johnston
1914-15	4-3	1-1	1974-75	0-0	2-0	James Leslie
1919-20	2-0	0-1	1975-76	2-1	1-2	Jason McAteer
1920-21	0-0	2-6	1977-78	0-2	0-2	Gavin McCann
1921-22	6-2	1-1	1993-94	2-0	0-0	Seamus McDonagh
1922-23	5-1	1-1	1994-95	1-1	0-1	Hugh Morgan
1923-24	2-2	0-1	1998-99	3-1	3-0	Barry Siddall
1924-25	1-0	2-1	2001-02	1-0	2-0	Alan Stubbs
1925-26	2-1	2-3	2002-03	0-2	1-1	Nick Summerbee
1926-27	6-2	2-2	2005-06	0-0	0-2	Emerson Thome
1927-28	1-1	2-1	2007-08	3-1	0-2	Fred Thompson
1928-29	4-0	2-2	2008-09	1-4	0-0	Ray Train
1929-30	4-1	0-3	2009-10	4-0	1-0	Stephen Whitworth
1930-31	3-1	2-2	2010-11	1-0	2-1	Frank Worthington
1931-32	3-0	1-3	2011-12	2-2	2-0	

FA Cup	Round		
1894-95	3	H	2-1
1930-31	4	A	1-1
1930-31	4 rep	H	3-1
1979-80	3	H	0-1
1983-84	3	A	3-0
2002-03	3	A	1-1
2002-03	3 rep	H	2-0
2008-09	3	H	2-1

L Cup	Round		
1961-62	1	A	1-1
1961-62	1 rep	H	1-0

Top scorer: Bobby Gurney 17 goals
Sunderland won 2-0 in an Anglo-Scottish Cup group game in 1978-79 at Roker Park
Sunderland lost 0-2 in an Anglo-Scottish Cup group game in 1979-80 at Burnden Park
Sunderland lost 0-2 in an Anglo-Italian Cup group game in 1993-94 at Burnden Park

Boston

FA Cup	Round			Played for both
1925-26	3	H	8-1	James Stephenson

Bournemouth

	Home					Away				
	P	W	D	L	F	A	P	W	D	L	F	A
League	2	1	1	0	4	3	2	2	0	0	2	0
L. Cup	1	0	1	0	1	1	1	1	0	0	1	0
Total	3	1	2	0	5	4	3	3	0	0	3	0

Season	H	A	Played for both		
1988-89	1-1	1-0	Geoff Butler	Denis Longhorn	Fred Rowell
1989-90	3-2	1-0	Brian Chambers	Thomas McInally	Bruce Stuckey
			George Collin	Thomas Mitchinson	Ray Train
			Jack Coxford	Alan O'Neill	William Watson (WW2)
			Patrick Gallacher	John O'Shea	

L. Cup	Round		
1989-90	3	H	1-1
1989-90	3 rep	A	1-0

Top scorer: Marco Gabbiadini 4 goals

Bradford City

	Home						Away					
	P	W	D	L	F	A	P	W	D	L	F	A
League	19	7	9	3	20	10	19	9	2	8	34	23
FA Cup	0	0	0	0	0	0	1	1	0	0	1	0
L. Cup	1	0	0	1	1	2	0	0	0	0	0	0
Other	0	0	0	0	0	0	1	0	0	1	2	3
Total	20	7	9	4	21	12	21	10	2	9	37	26

Season	H	A	Season	H	A	Played for both	
1908-09	2-1	2-0	2000-01	0-0	4-1	George Ainsley (WW2)	Andy Melville
1909-10	3-0	1-3	2003-04	3-0	4-0	Phil Babb	Matthew Middleton
1910-11	1-1	0-3				Peter Beagrie	William Montgomery
1911-12	1-1	1-2				Paul Butler	Jack Overfield
1912-13	1-0	5-1				Steven Caldwell	Frank Pegg
1913-14	0-1	2-0				Joe Curran	Jack Poole
1914-15	1-1	1-3				Tony Ford	Lee Power
1919-20	2-0	0-2				George Gibson	Michael Proctor
1920-21	0-0	2-2				Michael Gilhooley	Mark Prudhoe
1921-22	0-0	0-0				Don Goodman	Simon Ramsden
1985-86	1-1	0-2*				Andy Gray	Len Shackleton
1986-87	2-3	2-3				William Grimshaw	Nick Summerbee
1988-89	0-0	0-1				John Hawley	Chris Waddle
1989-90	1-0	1-0				Colin Healy	Kenneth Walshaw
1997-98	2-0	4-0				Darren Holloway	Darren Williams
1998-99	0-0	1-0				James Lawrence	Jack Young
1999-2000	0-1	4-0				Fred Mearns	

* 1985-86 away game played at Leeds Road, Huddersfield while Valley Parade rebuilt

FA Cup	Round				L. Cup	Round		
1908-09	3	A	1-0		1969-70	2	H	1-2

Top scorer: Kevin Phillips 7 goals
Sunderland lost 3-2 in a 2nd Round Full Members' Cup tie in 1986-87 at Odsal Stadium

Bradford Park Avenue

	Home					Away				
	P	W	D	L	F	A	P	W	D	L	F	A
League	3	2	1	0	10	4	3	0	2	1	4	5
FA Cup	2	2	0	0	4	1	0	0	0	0	0	0
Total	5	4	1	0	14	5	3	0	2	1	4	5

Season	H	A	Played for both		
1914-15	3-3	1-2	George Ainsley	Ricardo Gabbiadini	Henry Scott
1919-20	2-0	2-2	Harry Bedford	John Hannigan	Len Shackleton
1920-21	5-1	1-1	Jack Bell	Arthur Hawes	Robert Ward
			Ivor Broadis (WW2)	Fred Kirby	Ken Willingham (WW2)
			Ken Chisholm (WW2)	George McNestry	David Wright
			Herbert Davis	Dennis O'Donnell	
			Billy Elliott	Ronald Routledge	

FA Cup	Round		
1909-10	2	H	3-1
1937-38	5	H	1-0

Top scorer: Charlie Buchan 6 goals

Brentford

	Home						Away					
	P	W	D	L	F	A	P	W	D	L	F	A
League	7	4	1	2	12	9	7	4	2	1	16	11
FA Cup	1	1	0	0	5	2	1	0	0	1	1	2
L. Cup	0	0	0	0	0	0	1	0	0	1	3	4
Total	8	5	1	2	17	11	9	4	2	3	20	17

Season	H	A	Played for both		
1935-36	1-3	5-1	Cyril Brown	James Hartley	Thomas Stewart
1936-37	4-1	3-3	Norman Brown	James Lawrence	Trevor Swinburne
1937-38	1-0	0-4	John Curtis (WW1)	Ian Lawther	Michael Turner
1938-39	1-1	3-2	Richard Davis (WW2)	Thomas McKenzie	James Watson
1946-47	2-1	3-0	Thomas Dougall	John McPhee	Percy Whipp
1987-88	2-0	1-0	Len Duns (WW2)	John Mapson (WW2)	Leslie Wilkins
1992-93	1-3	1-1	Thomas Finney	Jamie Murray	Harry Williams
			John T. Foster	Ephraim Rhodes	Paul A Williams
			Patrick Gallacher (WW2)	Wilf Rostron	Stephen Wright
			John Haggan	Percy Saunders	Benny Yorston (WW2)
			Gareth Hall	Walter Scott (WW1)	

FA Cup	Round				L. Cup	Round		
1966-67	3	H	5-2		1960-61	2	A	3-4
2005-06	4	A	1-2					

Top scorer: Len Duns 5 goals

Brighton & Hove Albion

	Home					Away				
	P	W	D	L	F	A	P	W	D	L	F	A
League	17	11	4	2	30	13	17	3	3	11	21	33
L. Cup	0	0	0	0	0	0	1	0	0	1	0	1
Total	17	11	4	2	30	13	18	3	3	12	21	34

Season	H	A	Season	H	A	Played for both	
1958-59	4-1	0-2	1982-83	1-1	2-3	Wayne Bridge	Joseph McGhie
1959-60	0-0	1-2	1985-86	2-1	1-3	John Byrne	Paul McShane
1960-61	2-1	2-1	1986-87	1-1	3-0	Jeff Clarke	Neil Martin
1961-62	0-0	1-1	1987-88	1-0	1-3	John Dillon	Bernard Ramsden (WW2)
1972-73	4-0	2-2	1988-89	1-0	0-3	Samuel Ellison	Gary Rowell
1977-78	0-2	1-2	1989-90	2-1	2-1	Derek Forster	Thomas Stewart
1978-79	2-1	0-2	1991-92	4-2	2-2	Ricardo Gabbiadini	Clive Walker
1980-81	1-2	1-2	2004-05	2-0	1-2	John Goodchild	Reginald Wilkinson
1981-82	3-0	1-2				George Holley	Frank Worthington
						William Longair	

L. Cup	Round		
2011-12	2	A	0-1

Top scorer: 3 players with 3 goals

Bristol City

	Home						Away					
	P	W	D	L	F	A	P	W	D	L	F	A
League	20	8	8	4	33	23	20	4	5	11	18	35
FA Cup	1	1	0	0	6	1	1	1	0	0	4	2
L. Cup	1	0	0	1	0	1	1	1	0	0	6	1
Total	22	9	8	5	39	25	22	6	5	11	28	38

Season	H	A	Season	H	A	Played for both	
1906-07	3-3	1-1	1993-94	0-0	0-2	Archie Annan	Stern John
1907-08	3-3	0-3	1994-95	2-0	0-0	Gordon Armstrong	Albert Lewis
1908-09	0-2	4-2	1998-99	1-1	1-0	Philip Bach	John MacPhail
1909-10	4-0	3-2				Michael Bridges	William Maxwell
1910-11	3-1	1-1				Darren Byfield	Lewin Nyatanga
1958-59	3-1	1-4				Tim Carter	Gary Owers
1959-60	3-2	0-1				Ted Clack	Mark Prudhoe
1970-71	1-0	3-4				William Clark	Thomas Ritchie
1971-72	1-1	1-3				Andrew Cole	Richard Rooks
1972-73	2-2	0-1				John Conner	Danny Rose
1973-74	1-2	0-2				Jack Cowell	Martin Scott
1974-75	3-0	1-1				Len Duns (WW2)	Thomas Scott
1975-76	1-1	0-3				John T. Foster	Jonathan Stead
1976-77	1-0	1-4				William Fulton	Marcus Stewart
1987-88	0-1	1-0				Cyril Gilhespy	Cliff Thorley
1991-92	1-3	0-1				Mick Harford	Hugh Wilson
1992-93	0-0	0-0				Gerald Harrison	
						Alan Hay	

FA Cup	Round		
1898-99	1	A	4-2
1963-64	6	H	6-1

L. Cup	Round			
1990-91	2 L1	H	0-1
1990-91	2 L2	A	6-1

Top scorer: George Holley 5 goals

Bristol Rovers

	Home					Away				
	P	W	D	L	F	A	P	W	D	L	F	A
League	12	7	5	0	35	12	12	1	3	8	13	24
FA Cup	1	0	0	1	0	1	0	0	0	0	0	0
L. Cup	0	0	0	0	0	0	2	1	0	1	3	4
Total	13	7	5	1	35	13	14	2	3	9	16	28

Season	H	A	Season	H	A
1958-59	3-1	1-2	1979-80	3-2	2-2
1959-60	2-2	1-3	1987-88	1-1	0-4
1960-61	2-0	0-1	1991-92	1-1	1-2
1961-62	6-1	3-2	1992-93	1-1	2-2
1974-75	5-1	1-2			
1975-76	1-1	0-1			
1977-78	5-1	2-3			
1978-79	5-0	0-0			

Played for both

Thomas Becton	Gavin Jarvie
John Black	Bob Lee
Harold Buckle	Thomas Lee
Tim Carter	Robert McKay
James Chalmers	George McNestry
William Clark	Ted Purdon
James Hamilton	Marcus Stewart
Paul Hardyman	Thomas Tait

FA Cup	Round		
1977-78	3	H	0-1

L. Cup	Round		
1971-72	2	A	1-3
2000-01	3	A	2-1

Top scorers: Billy Hughes and Bryan Robson both with 4 goals

Burnley

	Home						Away					
	P	W	D	L	F	A	P	W	D	L	F	A
League	49	27	14	8	100	63	49	13	11	25	50	92
FA Cup	5	3	1	1	6	4	7	2	3	2	7	8
Total	54	30	15	9	106	67	56	15	14	27	57	100

Season	H	A	Season	H	A
1890-91	2-3	3-3	1950-51	1-1	1-1
1891-92	2-1	2-1	1951-52	0-0	1-0
1892-93	2-0	3-2	1952-53	2-1	1-5
1893-94	2-2	0-1	1953-54	2-1	1-5
1894-95	3-0	1-0	1954-55	2-2	1-0
1895-96	3-1	0-0	1955-56	4-4	0-4
1896-97	1-1	1-1	1956-57	2-1	0-2
1898-99	0-1	0-1	1957-58	2-3	0-6
1899-1900	2-1	1-3	1964-65	3-2	0-0
1913-14	1-1	1-0	1965-66	0-4	0-1
1914-15	2-1	1-2	1966-67	4-3	0-1
1919-20	3-0	1-2	1967-68	2-2	0-3
1920-21	1-0	2-2	1968-69	2-0	2-1
1921-22	3-2	0-2	1969-70	0-1	0-3
1922-23	3-1	0-2	1971-72	4-3	1-0
1923-24	0-1	3-0	1972-73	0-1	0-2
1924-25	1-1	2-1	1977-78	3-0	0-0
1925-26	2-2	2-5	1978-79	3-1	2-1
1926-27	7-1	2-4	1979-80	5-0	1-1
1927-28	2-3	0-3	1994-95	0-0	1-1
1928-29	2-1	1-3	2003-04	1-1	2-1
1929-30	3-3	0-2	2004-05	2-1	2-0
1947-48	2-0	0-4	2006-07	3-2	2-2
1948-49	0-0	1-3	2009-10	2-1	1-3
1949-50	2-1	2-2			

Played for both

Russell Anderson	Andy Marriott
Gordon Armstrong	Jack Mitton
Kevin Ball	Brian Mooney
Phil Bardsley	John Morley
Alexander Brady	John Mullin
Steven Caldwell	Tony Norman
Andrew Cole	John Oster
Doug Collins	Nick Pickering
Peter Daniel	Robert Robinson (b.1921)
Joseph Devine	Ronald Routledge
Michael Docherty	Gary Rowell
Billy Elliott	Barry Siddall
Wayne Entwistle	Paul Stewart
Steven Fletcher	Stan Ternent
Andy Gray	Stanislav Varga
Philip Gray	Dennis Tueart
William Grimshaw	Chris Waddle
Gordon Harris	Colin Waldron
Gerald Harrison	John Walker
James Hartley	Ross Wallace
William Holden	Thomas Wallace
Lee Howey	Rodger Wylde
Leighton James	
Robert Kelly	
William Longair	

FA Cup	Round			
1896-97	1	A	1-0	
1912-13	Semi		0-0	At Bramall Lane
1912-13	Semi rep		3-2	At St Andrews
1913-14	4	H	0-0	
1913-14	4 rep	A	1-2	
1919-20	2	A	1-1	
1919-20	2 rep	H	2-0	
1922-23	1	H	3-1	
1952-53	4	A	0-2	
1954-55	3	H	1-0	
1978-79	4	A	1-1	
1978-79	4 rep	H	0-3	

Top scorer: Charlie Buchan 10 goals

Bury

	Home					Away				
	P	W	D	L	F	A	P	W	D	L	F	A
League	28	20	3	5	63	26	28	10	5	13	39	48
FA Cup	1	1	0	0	3	1	2	1	0	1	7	5
L. Cup	1	1	0	0	2	1	2	1	0	1	2	3
Other	0	0	0	0	0	0	1	0	0	1	2	4
Total	30	22	3	5	68	28	33	12	5	16	50	60

Season	H	A	Season	H	A	Played for both
1895-96	0-0	2-1	1924-25	1-1	0-3	Gordon Armstrong
1896-97	0-1	1-1	1925-26	1-0	2-2	Paul Butler
1897-98	2-1	0-1	1926-27	3-0	2-1	Anthony Cullen
1898-99	3-0	2-1	1927-28	1-0	3-5	Terry Curran
1899-1900	1-0	0-2	1928-29	3-1	3-1	Wayne Entwistle
1900-01	4-1	0-0	1961-62	3-0	2-3	John Foreman
1901-02	3-0	0-1	1962-63	0-1	0-3	John Gillespie
1902-03	3-1	1-3	1963-64	4-1	1-0	Andy Gray
1903-04	6-0	1-3	1987-88	1-1	3-2	David Healy
1904-05	2-1	0-1	1997-98	2-1	1-1	William Holden
1905-06	0-3	1-3	1998-99	1-0	5-2	Leighton James
1906-07	3-5	3-2				Angus McIntosh
1907-08	6-2	1-2				Jack Maltby
1908-09	3-1	2-4				Andy Marriott
1909-10	2-3	1-0				Fred Mearns
1910-11	4-1	0-0				Jack Mitton (WW1)
1911-12	1-0	2-0				Fred Thompson
						Colin Waldron

FA Cup	Round				L. Cup	Round		
1924-25	1	A	3-0		1997-98	2 L1	H	2-1
1945-46	4 L1	H	3-1		1997-98	2 L2	A	2-1
1945-46	4 L2	A	4-5		2006-07	1	A	0-2

Top scorer: George Holley 10 goals
Sunderland lost 2-4 in an Anglo-Scottish Cup group game in 1979-80 at Gigg Lane

Cagliari

Season	H	A		Played for both
1971-72	3-3	3-1	Anglo-Italian Cup	Patrick Mboma

Cambridge United

	Home					Away				
	P	W	D	L	F	A	P	W	D	L	F	A
League	4	1	2	1	7	7	4	1	1	2	6	8
L. Cup	1	1	0	0	4	3	2	2	0	0	10	2
Other	0	0	0	0	0	0	1	0	1	0	1	1
Total	5	2	2	1	11	10	7	3	2	2	17	11

Season	H	A	Played for both	
1978-79	0-2	2-0	Darren Byfield	Alan O'Neill
1979-80	2-0	3-3	Jody Craddock	Lionel Perez
1991-92	2-2	0-3	Thomas Finney	David Rush
1992-93	3-3	1-2	Michael Heathcote	Mel Slack
			Jamie Murray	

L. Cup	Round		
1983-84	2 L1	A	3-2
1983-84	2 L1	H	4-3
2002-03	2	A	7-0

Top scorer: Gary Rowell 4 goals
Sunderland drew 1-1 in an Anglo-Italian Cup group game in 1992-93 at the Abbey Stadium

Cardiff City

	Home					Away				
	P	W	D	L	F	A	P	W	D	L	F	A
League	28	11	10	7	43	39	28	8	4	16	30	54
FA Cup	3	1	1	1	3	3	2	0	1	1	2	4
Total	31	12	11	8	46	42	30	8	5	17	32	58

Season	H	A	Season	H	A	Played for both	
1921-22	4-1	0-2	1959-60	1-1	1-2	Gary Bennett	Michael Henderson
1922-23	2-1	4-2	1962-63	2-1	2-5	Raich Carter (WW2)	Graham Kavanagh
1923-24	0-3	1-2	1963-64	3-3	2-0	Ken Chisholm	Harry Kirtley
1924-25	1-0	0-2	1970-71	0-4	1-3	Michael Chopra	Liam Lawrence
1925-26	1-3	1-0	1971-72	1-1	2-1	Kevin Cooper	John McSeveney
1926-27	2-2	0-3	1972-73	2-1	1-1	David Corner	Ian Rodgerson
1927-28	0-2	1-3	1973-74	1-1	1-4	John Cornforth	Howard Sheppeard
1929-29	1-0	1-0	1974-75	3-1	0-2	Ray Daniel	Tommy Smith
1952-52	4-2	1-4	1977-78	1-1	2-5	Andy Dibble	Arthur Welsby
1953-54	5-0	1-1	1978-79	1-2	1-1	Alan Foggon	Sean Wharton
1954-55	1-1	1-0	1979-80	2-1	1-1	Trevor Ford	Jeff Whitley
1955-56	1-1	1-3	2003-04	0-0	0-4	Tim Gilbert	Darren Williams
1956-57	1-1	0-1	2004-05	2-1	2-0	William Grimshaw	
1958-59	0-2	1-2	2006-07	1-2	1-0	Gerald Harrison	

FA Cup	Round		
1920-21	1	H	0-1
1929-30	4	H	2-1
1971-72	4	A	1-1
1971-72	4 rep	H	1-1
1971-72	4 rep2		1-3 At Maine Road

Top scorer: 7 players with 3 goals

Carlisle United

Home   Away

SUNDERLAND HEAD TO HEAD RECORDS

	P	W	D	L	F	A	P	W	D	L	F	A
League	6	4	1	1	11	9	6	2	2	2	9	9
FA Cup	3	0	2	1	2	3	3	2	1	0	4	1
Other	1	0	0	1	0	1	1	0	1	0	0	0
Total	10	4	3	3	13	13	10	4	4	2	13	10

Season	H	A	Played for both		
1970-71	2-0	0-0	Ben Alnwick	Ian Harte	Mark Prudhoe
1971-72	0-3	2-1	Jack Ashurst	Warren Hawke	Thomas Ritchie
1972-73	2-1	3-4	Brian Atkinson	Brian Heslop	Bryan Robson
1973-74	2-1	0-1	Gary Bennett	Darren Holloway	Gary Rowell
1975-76	3-2	2-2	Michael Bridges	Mick Horswill	Craig Russell
1985-86	2-2	2-1	Ivor Broadis	Billy Hughes	James Russell (WW2)
			Michael Buckley	Michael Ingham	Nigel Saddington
			Tim Carter	Joseph Kasher	Barry Siddall
			Michael Coady	Graham Kavanagh	Kenneth Smith
			John Cooke	Robert Kelly	John Spuhler (WW2)
			Anthony Cullen	Dariusz Kubicki	Paul Stannard
			Rory Delap	John Lathan	John Stoneham
			Andy Dibble	Bob Lee	Trevor Swinburne
			John Dowsey	Paul Lemon	Stan Ternent
			Wayne Entwistle	Michael Liddle	Paul Thirlwell
			Thomas Fairley	Chris Lumsdon	Harry Thompson (WW2)
			John Finlay (WW2)	Brendan McGill	Ray Train
			Ricardo Gabbiadini	Isaac McGorian	Kenneth Walshaw
			Eric Gates	Matt Middleton (WW2)	Andrew Welsh
			George Gibson (WW2)	Robert Mitchell	Keiren Westwood
			James Gorman (WW2)	Bob Moncur	George Whitelaw
			James Hamilton	Charles Parker	

FA Cup	Round		
1973-74	3	A	0-0
1973-74	3 rep	H	0-1
1993-94	3	H	1-1
1993-94	3 rep	A	1-0
1994-95	3	H	1-1
1994-95	3 rep	A	3-1

Top scorer: Billy Hughes 4 goals
Sunderland drew 0-0 in a Texaco Cup group game in 1974-75 at Brunton Park
Sunderland lost 0-1 in an Anglo-Scottish Cup group game in 1975-76 at Roker Park

Charlton Athletic

	Home						Away					
	P	W	D	L	F	A	P	W	D	L	F	A
League	37	19	9	9	70	43	37	7	11	19	47	70
Other	0	0	0	0	0	0	2	1	0	1	5	4
Total	37	19	9	9	70	43	39	8	11	20	52	74

Season	H	A	Season	H	A	Played for both	
1936-37	1-0	1-3	1963-64	2-1	0-0	Reuben Agboola	William Robinson
1937-38	1-1	1-2	1970-71	3-0	1-1	Cyril Beach	Michael Turner
1938-39	1-1	0-3	1971-72	3-0	2-2	Darren Bent	Martyn Waghorn
1946-47	1-1	0-5	1975-76	4-1	2-1	Bob Bolder	Peter Wakeham
1947-48	0-1	0-1	1977-78	3-0	2-3	Gary Breen	Paul A. Williams
1948-49	1-0	0-4	1978-79	1-0	2-1	Jordan Cook	David Young
1949-50	2-1	2-2	1979-80	4-0	4-0	Talal El Karkouri	
1950-51	4-2	0-3	1985-86	1-2	1-2	Derek Forster	
1951-52	1-1	1-2	1991-92	1-2	4-1	Patrick Gallacher (WW2)	

SUNDERLAND: THE COMPLETE RECORD

1952-53	2-1	1-3	1992-93	0-2	1-0	Andy Gray
1953-54	2-1	3-5	1993-94	4-0	0-0	Greg Halford
1954-55	1-2	3-1	1994-95	1-1	0-1	Vic Halom
1955-56	3-2	1-2	1995-96	0-0	1-1	Seamus McDonagh
1956-57	8-1	2-3	1997-98	0-0	1-1	Robert McKay
1958-59	0-3	2-3	2000-01	3-2	1-0	Samuel Morris
1959-60	1-3	1-3	2001-02	2-2	2-2	Thomas Myhre
1960-61	2-2	2-2	2002-03	1-3	1-1	Lee Power
1961-62	4-1	0-2	2005-06	1-3	0-2	Andy Reid
1962-63	1-0	2-2				George Robinson

Top scorer: Len Shackleton 8 goals
Sunderland drew 4-4, but lost 7-6 on penalties, in a Division One Play Off Final in 1997-98 at Wembley
Sunderland won 1-0 in a Simod Cup 1st Round tie in 1988-89 at Selhurst Park

Chatham Town

FA Cup	Round			Played for both
1913-14	1	H	9-0	John Conner

Chelsea

	Home					Away				
	P	W	D	L	F	A	P	W	D	L	F	A
League	55	28	9	18	105	71	55	8	11	36	55	123
FA Cup	1	1	0	0	2	1	1	0	0	1	0	1
L. Cup	1	1	0	0	2	0	1	1	0	0	3	2
Total	57	30	9	18	109	72	57	9	12	36	59	126

Season	H	A	Season	H	A	Played for both
1907-08	3-0	1-2	1954-55	3-3	1-2	Tal Ben Haim
1908-09	1-2	0-2	1955-56	4-3	3-2	Ronald Brebner
1909-10	4-0	4-1	1956-57	1-3	2-0	Wayne Bridge
1912-13	4-0	0-2	1957-58	2-2	0-0	Geoff Butler
1913-14	2-0	1-1	1962-63	0-1	0-1	Alec Chamberlain
1914-15	2-1	0-3	1964-65	3-0	1-3	Ken Chisholm (WW2)
1919-20	3-2	0-2	1965-66	2-0	2-3	Tore Andre Flo
1920-21	1-0	1-3	1966-67	2-0	1-1	Fred Hall (WW2)
1921-22	1-2	0-1	1967-68	2-3	0-1	Gareth Hall
1922-23	1-1	3-1	1968-69	3-2	1-5	Mick Harford
1923-24	2-0	1-4	1969-70	0-0	1-3	English McConnell
1930-31	2-0	0-5	1975-76	2-1	0-1	Jurgen Macho
1931-32	2-1	2-2	1979-80	2-1	0-0	William Read
1932-33	2-1	1-1	1984-85	0-2	0-1	Bryan Robson
1933-34	0-0	0-4	1988-89	1-2	1-1	Emerson Thome
1934-35	4-0	2-2	1990-91	1-0	2-3	Colin Waldron
1935-36	3-3	1-3	1996-97	3-0	2-6	Clive Walker
1936-37	2-3	3-1	1999-2000	4-1	0-4	James Watson
1937-38	1-1	0-0	2000-01	1-0	4-2	Boudewijn Zenden
1938-39	3-2	0-4	2001-02	0-0	0-4	
1946-47	1-2	1-2	2002-03	1-2	0-3	
1947-48	2-3	1-1	2005-06	1-2	0-2	
1948-49	3-0	1-2	2007-08	0-1	0-2	
1949-50	4-1	1-3	2008-09	2-3	0-5	
1950-51	1-1	0-3	2009-10	1-3	2-7	
1951-52	4-1	1-2	2010-11	2-4	3-0	
1952-53	2-1	2-3	2011-12	1-2	0-1	
1953-54	1-2	2-2				

FA Cup	Round				L. Cup	Round		
1991-92	6	A	1-1		1984-85	Semi L1	H	2-0
1991-92	6 rep	H	2-1		1984-85	Semi L2	A	3-2

Top scorer: Charlie Buchan 11 goals

Cheltenham Town

L. Cup	Round			Played for both	
2005-06	2	H	1-0	Brett Angell	Norman Case
				Philip Bach	Cliff Thorley
				Darren Carter	Clive Walker

Chester City

	Home					Away				
	P	W	D	L	F	A	P	W	D	L	F	A
League	1	0	0	1	0	2	1	1	0	0	2	1
L. Cup	3	3	0	0	9	1	2	1	1	0	1	0
Total	4	3	0	1	9	3	3	2	1	0	3	1

Season	H	A	Played for both		
1987-88	0-2	2-1	Sam Aiston	Steve Hetzke	Gary Moore
			Keith Bertschin	Joseph Hewitt	Samuel Morris
			Fred Bett (WW2)	Joe Hinnigan	Barry Siddall
			Stephen Brodie	Arthur Housam (WW2)	Alan Spence
			Paul Butler	Archibald Jackson	Harry Threadgold
			Danny Collins	Jack Jones (WW2)	Nigel Walker
			Frank Cresswell	Robert Middleton	

L. Cup	Round		
1993-94	1 L1	H	3-1
1993-94	1 L2	A	0-0
1998-99	2 L1	H	3-0
1998-99	2 L2	A	1-0
2004-05	1	H	3-0

Top scorer: Don Goodman 2 goals

Chesterfield

	Home					Away				
	P	W	D	L	F	A	P	W	D	L	F	A
League	1	1	0	0	3	2	1	0	1	0	1	1
FA Cup	1	1	0	0	2	0	1	0	0	1	1	2
Total	2	2	0	0	5	2	2	0	1	1	2	3

Season	H	A	Played for both		
1987-88	3-2	1-1	Kevin Arnott	Joseph Devine	Paul Lemon
			Harry Bedford	John Evans	Emerson Marples
			John Black	Marton Fulop	Samuel Raybould
			Eddie Burbanks (WW2)	Stephen Hardwick	Charles M. Thomson (WW2)
			John Cooke	Peter Hartley	Harry Williams
			Kevin Cooper	Warren Hawke	
			Terry Curran	Michael Henderson	

FA Cup	Round		
1946-47	3	A	1-2
1974-75	3	H	2-0

Top scorer: 7 players with 1 goal

Colchester United

	Home					Away				
	P	W	D	L	F	A	P	W	D	L	F	A
League	1	1	0	0	3	1	1	0	0	1	1	3
L. Cup	1	1	0	0	2	0	0	0	0	0	0	0
Total	2	2	0	0	5	1	1	0	0	1	1	3

Season	H	A	Played for both		
2006-07	3-1	1-3	Ian Atkins	Shaun Elliott	Andy Marriott
			Titus Bramble	Greg Halford	Gary Moore
			George Burley	Steve Hetzke	David Swindlehurst
			Alec Chamberlain	Denis Longhorn	

L. Cup	Round		
2010-11	2	H	2-0

Top scorers: Darren Bent and Stephen Elliott both with 2 goals

Corinthians

Season			Played for both
1902-03	A	3-0 Sheriff of London's Shield played at White Hart Lane	Ronald Brebner
			John Morrison
			Thomas Rowlandson

Coventry City

	Home						Away					
	P	W	D	L	F	A	P	W	D	L	F	A
League	16	8	7	1	16	4	16	2	5	9	16	29
FA Cup	1	1	0	0	2	0	2	1	0	1	3	3
L. Cup	1	0	1	0	0	0	2	0	0	2	2	9
Total	18	9	8	1	18	4	20	3	5	12	21	41

Season	H	A	Played for both	
1967-68	1-1	2-2	Sam Allardyce	James Holton
1968-69	3-0	1-3	Thomas Allen	Don Hutchison
1969-70	0-0	1-1	Phil Babb	Stern John
1976-77	0-1	2-1	Kevin Ball	Kevin Kilbane
1980-81	3-0	1-2	Peter Barnes	Kevin Kyle
1981-82	0-0	1-6	Fred Bett	Douglas McGuire
1982-83	2-1	0-1	Gary Breen	George McNestry
1983-84	1-0	1-2	Harold Buckle	Andy Marriott
1984-85	0-0	1-0	Terry Butcher	Neil Martin
1990-91	0-0	0-0	Ken Chisholm	Roy O'Donovan
1996-97	1-0	2-2	Clive Clarke	Richard Parker
1999-2000	1-1	2-3	Calum Davenport	Nick Pickering
2000-01	1-0	0-1	Thomas Dougall	Jonathan Stead
2003-04	0-0	1-1	Stephen Elliott	Jack Vinall (WW2)
2004-05	1-0	0-2	Marton Fulop	Ian Wallace
2006-07	2-0	1-2	Fred Gibson	Keiren Westwood
			Mick Harford	Stephen Wright
			Colin Healy	Andrew Yorke
			Jordan Henderson	

FA Cup	Round			L. Cup	Round		
1929-30	3	A	2-1	1964-65	4	A	2-4
1950-51	3	H	2-0	1989-90	5	H	0-0
1962-63	5	A	1-2	1989-90	5 rep	A	0-5

Top scorer: Stan Cummins 4 goals

Crewe Alexandra

	Home					Away				
	P	W	D	L	F	A	P	W	D	L	F	A
League	4	3	1	0	8	3	4	3	0	1	8	4
FA Cup	0	0	0	0	0	0	1	1	0	0	2	0
L. Cup	0	0	0	0	0	0	1	0	0	1	3	3
Other	1	1	0	0	1	0	0	0	0	0	0	0
Total	5	4	1	0	9	3	6	4	0	2	13	7

Season	H	A	Played for both		
1997-98	2-1	3-0	George Ainsley (WW2)	Cyril Gilhespy	David Vaughan
1998-99	2-0	4-1	Chris Byrne	Chris Lumsdon	Thomas Wagstaffe
2003-04	1-1	0-3	John Dillon	James McGuigan	Nigel Walker
2004-05	3-1	1-0	William Eden (WW2)	John Moore	Mark Watkins
			Wayne Entwistle	Malcolm Moore	Billy Whitehurst
			John Foreman (WW2)	Calvin Palmer	Albert Wood
			Ricardo Gabbiadini	George Robinson (WW2)	Stephen Wright

FA Cup	Round			L. Cup	Round			
1948-49	3	A	2-0	2004-05	2	A	3-3	Lost 4-2 on pens

Top scorer: Stephen Elliott 3 goals
Sunderland won 1-0 in a Sherpa Van Trophy 1st Round game in 1987-88 at Roker Park

Crystal Palace

	Home						Away					
	P	W	D	L	F	A	P	W	D	L	F	A
League	14	7	6	1	13	6	14	2	3	9	7	20
FA Cup	4	2	1	1	3	2	2	1	1	0	4	2
L. Cup	2	1	0	1	2	2	2	0	1	1	1	2
Other	1	1	0	0	2	1	1	0	0	1	2	3
Total	21	11	7	3	20	11	19	3	5	11	14	27

Season	H	A	Season	H	A	Played for both	
1969-70	0-0	0-2	1998-99	2-0	1-1	John Conner	Paul McShane
1973-74	0-0	0-3	2003-04	2-1	0-3	Stan Cummins	Neil Martin
1977-78	0-0	2-2	2006-07	0-0	0-1	Bert Davis	Bobby Mimms
1978-79	1-2	1-1				Alex Donaldson	John Oster
1980-81	1-0	1-0				Robert Ferguson	George Payne
1985-86	1-1	0-1				Marco Gabbiadini	James Russell
1986-87	1-0	0-2				Stephen Hardwick	Paul Stewart
1988-89	1-1	0-1				William Harper	Anthony Stokes
1990-91	2-1	1-2				Arthur Hudgell	David Swindlehurst
1993-94	1-0	0-1				John Hughes	Mark Watkins
1995-96	1-0	1-0				Stern John	Paul A Williams

FA Cup	Round			L. Cup	Round		
1911-12	2	A	0-0	1981-82	3	H	0-1
1911-12	2 rep	H	1-0	1984-85	2 L1	H	2-1
1975-76	6	H	0-1	1984-85	2 L2	A	0-0
2000-01	3	H	0-0	2000-01	5	A	1-2
2000-01	3 rep	A	4-2				
2004-05	3	H	2-1				

Top scorer: Marcus Stewart 4 goals
Sunderland drew 4-4, but lost 5-4 on penalties, in a two leg Division One Play-off semi-final in 2003-04; 1st leg lost 2-3 at Selhurst Park and 2nd leg won 2-1 at the Stadium of Light

Darlington

FA Cup	Round			Played for both		
1987-88	1	H	2-0	Brian Atkinson	Maurice Hepworth	Nick Pickering
				Gary Bennett	Keith Hird	Mark Prudhoe
				Ronald Brebner	Bert Hobson	Albert Quinn
				Cyril Brown	Darren Holloway	Thomas Reynolds
				Archie Brown	Arthur Hurdman	Thomas Robson
				Thomas Butler	Michael Ingham	Thomas Rowlandson
				Keith Coleman	Craig James	Craig Russell
				Jordan Cook	Simon Johnson	Thomas Scott
				David Corner	Graham Kavanagh	John Shaw
				Richard Davis	Dariusz Kubicki	Joseph Shaw
				Jonjo Dickman	Kevin Kyle	Barry Siddall
				Barry Dunn	Bob Lee	Kenneth Smith
				William Eden	Patrick Lowrey	Martin Smith
				Marco Gabbiadini	Chris Lumsdon	Alan Spence
				Allan Gauden	Jack Maltby	John Spuhler
				Tim Gilbert	Matt Middleton (WW2)	C.M. Thomson (WW2)
				John Goodchild	John Moore	Neil Wainwright
				Frank Gray	Thomas Naisby	William Walsh
				Martin Gray	James O'Neill	Derek Weddle
				Richard Healey	Mark Outterside	William Whelan

Darwen

	Home					Away				
	P	W	D	L	F	A	P	W	D	L	F	A
League	2	2	0	0	11	0	2	2	0	0	10	1
FA Cup	0	0	0	0	0	0	1	1	0	0	2	0
Total	2	2	0	0	11	0	3	3	0	0	12	1

Season	H	A	Played for both
1891-92	7-0	7-1	Leighton James
1893-94	4-0	3-0	

FA Cup	Round		
1890-91	2	A	2-0

Top scorer: Johnny Campbell 5 goals

Derby County

	Home						Away					
	P	W	D	L	F	A	P	W	D	L	F	A
League	64	41	11	12	126	56	64	15	15	34	77	125
FA Cup	2	1	0	1	3	1	2	0	2	0	6	6
L. Cup	2	1	1	0	4	1	2	0	1	1	2	8
Total	68	43	12	13	133	58	68	15	18	35	85	139

Season	H	A	Season	H	A	Played for both	
1890-91	5-1	1-3	1937-38	2-0	2-2	Russell Anderson	Tommy Smith
1891-92	7-1	1-0	1938-39	1-0	0-1	Brett Angell	Jonathan Stead
1892-93	3-1	1-1	1946-47	3-2	1-5	Harry Bedford	Alan Stubbs
1893-94	5-0	4-1	1947-48	1-1	1-5	Raich Carter	David Swindlehurst
1894-95	8-0	2-1	1948-49	2-1	2-2	George Collin	Paul Thirlwell
1895-96	2-2	0-2	1949-50	6-1	2-3	Kevin Cooper	Emerson Thome
1896-97	1-2	0-1	1950-51	1-0	5-6	James Crawford	Colin Todd
1897-98	2-1	2-2	1951-52	3-0	4-3	Terry Curran	David Watson
1898-99	1-0	2-4	1952-53	2-1	1-3	Rory Delap	Charles Yorke

Season			Season			Player
1899-1900	2-0	0-2	1958-59	3-0	0-2	Daniele Dichio
1900-01	2-1	1-1	1959-60	3-1	1-0	William Fulton
1901-02	1-0	0-1	1960-61	1-2	1-1	Marco Gabbiadini
1902-03	2-0	2-5	1961-62	2-1	1-1	George Goodchild
1903-04	0-3	2-7	1962-63	3-0	2-2	Roy Greenwood
1904-05	3-0	0-1	1963-64	3-0	3-0	John Hannigan
1905-06	2-0	0-1	1969-70	1-1	0-3	Mick Harford
1906-07	0-2	1-1	1976-77	1-1	0-1	Danny Higginbotham
1912-13	0-2	3-0	1986-87	1-2	2-3	Rob Hindmarch
1913-14	1-0	1-1	1990-91	1-2	3-3	Billy Hughes
1919-20	2-1	1-3	1991-92	1-1	2-1	Leighton James
1920-21	3-0	1-0	1992-93	1-0	1-0	Stern John
1926-27	1-2	2-4	1993-94	1-0	0-5	Kevin Kilbane
1927-28	0-1	0-1	1994-95	1-1	1-0	Sandy McAllister
1928-29	4-0	0-0	1995-96	3-0	1-3	Chris Makin
1929-30	3-1	0-3	1996-97	2-0	0-1	Ryan Noble
1930-31	1-3	1-4	1999-2000	1-1	5-0	Lewin Nyatanga
1931-32	0-0	1-3	2000-01	2-1	0-1	John O'Hare
1932-33	0-2	0-3	2001-02	1-1	1-0	Ken Oliver
1933-34	0-0	0-0	2003-04	2-1	1-1	Nick Pickering
1934-35	1-4	1-3	2004-05	0-0	2-0	Mart Poom
1935-36	3-1	0-4	2006-07	2-1	2-1	William Raisbeck
1936-37	3-2	0-3	2007-08	1-0	0-0	Samuel Raybould

FA Cup	Round				L. Cup	Round			
1899-1900	1		A	2-2	1973-74	2		A	2-2
1899-1900	1 rep		H	3-0	1973-74	2 rep		H	1-1
1932-33	6		A	4-4	1973-74	2 rep2		H	3-0
1932-33	6 rep		H	0-1	1990-91	3		A	0-6

Top scorer: Johnny Campbell 11 goals

Doncaster Rovers

	Home					Away				
	P	W	D	L	F	A	P	W	D	L	F	A
League	1	1	0	0	3	1	1	1	0	0	2	0
FA Cup	1	0	0	1	0	2	0	0	0	0	0	0
Total	2	1	0	1	3	3	1	1	0	0	2	0

Season	H	A	Played for both		
1987-88	3-1	2-0	Ben Alnwick	Brian Deane	George McNestry
			Jack Ashurst	El Hadji Diouf	John Oster
			Chris Black	Don Goodman	Mark Prudhoe
			Kieron Brady	Colin Grainger	Nigel Saddington
			Stephen Brodie	Len Hargreaves	Ian Snodin
			Alan Brown	David Healy	Trevor Swinburne
			Chris Brown	George Hunter	Sean Thornton
			Eddie Burbanks (WW2)	Michael Ingham	Brian Usher
			Darren Byfield	Simon Johnson	Billy Whitehurst
			Pascal Chimbonda	Matthew Kilgallon	Alwyne Wilks
			John Cornforth	James Lawrence	Paul L. Williams
			Anthony Cullen	Bob Lee	Martin Woods
			Terry Curran	John McGinley	

FA Cup	Round			
1953-54	3		H	0-2

Top scorer: Paul Lemon 3 goals

Elswick Rangers

FA Cup	Round			Played for both
1888-89	2 (Qual)	A	5-3	Matthew Scott

Everton

	Home					Away				
	P	W	D	L	F	A	P	W	D	L	F	A
League	77	44	14	19	153	87	77	17	11	49	93	173
FA Cup	7	3	3	1	9	7	9	1	1	7	8	24
L. Cup	0	0	0	0	0	0	2	2	0	0	4	3
Other	0	0	0	0	0	0	1	0	0	1	1	4
Total	84	47	17	20	162	94	89	20	12	57	106	204

Season	H	A	Season	H	A	Played for both
1890-91	1-0	0-1	1934-35	7-0	2-6	Brett Angell
1891-92	2-1	4-0	1935-36	3-3	3-0	Ian Atkins
1892-93	4-3	4-1	1936-37	3-1	0-3	Peter Beagrie
1893-94	1-0	1-7	1937-38	2-0	3-3	Rod Belfitt
1894-95	2-1	2-2	1938-39	1-2	2-6	Billy Bingham
1895-96	3-0	0-1	1946-47	4-1	2-4	Paul Bracewell
1896-97	1-1	2-5	1947-48	2-0	0-3	Alexander Brady
1897-98	0-0	0-2	1948-49	1-1	0-1	Michael Buckley
1898-99	2-1	0-0	1949-50	4-2	2-0	Alec Chamberlain
1899-1900	1-0	0-1	1950-51	4-0	1-3	Tim Coleman
1900-01	2-0	0-1	1954-55	3-0	0-1	Warney Cresswell
1901-02	2-4	0-2	1955-56	0-0	2-1	Charles Crossley
1902-03	2-1	3-0	1956-57	1-1	1-2	Terry Curran
1903-04	2-0	1-0	1957-58	1-1	1-3	Peter Davenport
1904-05	2-3	1-0	1964-65	4-0	1-1	Jack Hedley
1905-06	2-1	1-3	1965-66	2-0	0-2	William Holden
1906-07	1-0	1-4	1966-67	0-2	1-4	Don Hutchison
1907-08	1-2	3-0	1967-68	1-0	0-3	Jack Jones
1908-09	2-0	0-4	1968-69	1-3	0-2	Kevin Kilbane
1909-10	0-1	1-2	1969-70	0-0	1-3	Albert Lewis
1910-11	4-0	2-2	1976-77	0-1	0-2	Gavin McCann
1911-12	4-0	0-1	1980-81	3-1	1-2	Seamus McDonagh
1912-13	3-1	4-0	1981-82	3-1	2-1	Peter Meechan
1913-14	5-2	5-1	1982-83	2-1	1-3	Bobby Mimms
1914-15	0-3	1-7	1983-84	2-1	0-0	Thomas Myhre
1919-20	2-3	3-1	1984-85	1-2	1-4	John Oster
1920-21	0-2	1-1	1990-91	2-2	0-2	Dick Roose
1921-22	1-2	0-3	1996-97	3-0	3-1	Louis Saha
1922-23	3-1	1-1	1999-2000	2-1	0-5	Walter Scott
1923-24	3-0	3-2	2000-01	2-0	2-2	Ian Snodin
1924-25	4-1	3-0	2001-02	1-0	0-1	Alan Stubbs
1925-26	7-3	1-2	2002-03	0-1	1-2	Colin Todd
1926-27	3-2	4-5	2005-06	0-1	2-2	
1927-28	0-2	1-0	2007-08	0-1	1-7	
1928-29	2-2	0-0	2008-09	0-2	0-3	
1929-30	2-2	1-4	2009-10	1-1	0-2	
1931-32	2-3	2-4	2010-11	2-2	0-2	
1932-33	3-1	1-6	2011-12	1-1	0-4	
1933-34	3-2	0-1				

FA Cup	Round				L. Cup	Round			
1890-91	1	H	1-0		1967-68	3	A	3-2	
1909-10	3	A	0-2		1998-99	4	A	1-1	Won 5-4 on pens
1924-25	2	H	0-0						

SUNDERLAND HEAD TO HEAD RECORDS

1924-25	2 rep	A	1-2
1934-35	4	H	1-1
1934-35	4 rep	A	4-6
1937-38	4	A	1-0
1957-58	3	H	2-2
1957-58	3 rep	A	1-3
1958-59	3	A	0-4
1963-64	5	H	3-1
1965-66	3	A	0-3
1978-79	3	H	2-1
2004-05	4	A	0-3
2011-12	6	A	1-1
2011-12	6 rep	H	0-2

Top scorer: Charlie Buchan 15 goals
Sunderland lost 1-4 in the Zenith Data Systems Cup quarter-final in 1990-91 at Goodison Park.

Exeter City

	Home					Away				
	P	W	D	L	F	A	P	W	D	L	F	A
FA Cup	1	0	1	0	1	1	1	1	0	0	4	2
L. Cup	1	1	0	0	5	2	1	0	1	0	2	2
Total	2	1	1	0	6	3	2	1	1	0	6	4

FA Cup	Round			Played for both	
1930-31	6	H	1-1	John Cornforth	Ken Oliver
1930-31	6 rep	A	4-2	William Death	Harry Poulter
				Jock Ditchburn	Thomas Scott
L. Cup	Round			Don Goodman	Marcus Stewart
1989-90	4	A	2-2	George Hunter	Bruce Stuckey
1989-90	4 rep	H	5-2	Andy Marriott	Arthur Welsby
				Jack Mitton	

Top scorer: Jimmy Connor and Eric Gates both with 3 goals

Fairfield

FA Cup	Round		
1894-95	1	H	11-1

Fiorentina

Season	H	A		Played for both
1969-70	2-2	0-3	Anglo-Italian Cup	Stefan Schwarz

Fulham

	Home					Away					
	P	W	D	L	F	A	P	W	D	L	F	A
League	26	11	10	5	35	26	26	9	6	11	32	36
FA Cup	2	1	0	1	4	6	0	0	0	0	0	0
L. Cup	1	0	1	0	1	1	1	0	0	3	0
Total	29	12	11	6	40	33	27	10	6	11	35	36

Season	H	A	Season	H	A	Played for both	
1949-50	2-0	3-0	1979-80	2-1	1-0	Kevin Ball	Iain Hesford
1950-51	0-1	1-1	1985-86	4-2	2-1	Rod Belfitt	James Hindmarsh
1951-52	2-2	1-0	1987-88	2-0	2-0	Paul Bracewell	Arthur Hudgell (WW2)
1958-59	1-2	2-6	2001-02	1-1	0-2	Wayne Bridge	Thomas Lilley
1964-65	0-0	0-1	2002-03	0-3	0-1	Arthur Brown	Steed Malbranque

1965-66	2-2	0-3	2005-06	2-1	1-2	Lee Clark		Andy Melville
1966-67	3-1	1-3	2007-08	1-1	3-1	Andrew Cole		Kieran Richardson
1967-68	3-0	2-3	2008-09	1-0	0-0	Tim Coleman		George Robinson (WW2)
1971-72	2-1	0-0	2009-10	0-0	0-1	John Curtis		Louis Saha
1972-73	0-0	2-1	2010-11	0-3	0-0	Dickson Etuhu		James Temple
1973-74	1-0	2-0	2011-12	0-0	1-2	Patrick Gallacher (WW2)		Fred Thompson
1974-75	1-2	3-1				Howard Gayle		Barney Travers
1975-76	2-0	0-2				Martin Gray		Thomas Urwin (WW1)
1977-78	2-2	3-3				Philip Gray		Clive Walker
1978-79	1-1	2-2				Vic Halom		Paul A. Williams
						David Healy		Albert Wood

FA Cup	Round				L. Cup	Round			
1934-35	3		H	3-2	1989-90	2 L1		H	1-1
1968-69	3		H	1-4	1989-90	2 L2		A	3-0

Top scorer: Marco Gabbiadini 5 goals

Gainsborough Trinity

FA Cup	Round					Played for both	
1905-06	2		H	1-1		Alexander Brady	Robert Robinson (b.1910)
1905-06	2 rep		A	3-0	Played at Roker Park	Arthur Brown	Walter Scott
						John Curtis	Darren Williams
						Ricardo Gabbiadini	John Williamson

Gillingham

	Home					Away				
	P	W	D	L	F	A	P	W	D	L	F	A
League	3	2	1	0	5	3	3	2	1	0	7	1
FA Cup	0	0	0	0	0	0	1	0	0	1	1	3
Other	1	1	0	0	4	3	1	0	0	1	2	3
Total	4	3	1	0	9	6	5	2	1	2	10	7

Season	H	A	Played for both		
1987-88	2-1	0-0	Gary Breen	Allan Gauden	Nyron Nosworthy
2003-04	2-1	3-1	George Burley	Thomas Hall	William Raisbeck
2004-05	1-1	4-0	Darren Byfield	James Hartley	John Waugh
			William Death	Joe Hinnigan	
			William Fullarton	Seamus McDonagh	

FA Cup	Round				
1907-08	1		A	1-3	As New Brompton

Top scorer: Marcus Stewart 4 goals
Sunderland drew 6-6, but lost on away goals, in a two leg Division Two / Three Play-off semi-final in 1986-87; 1st leg lost 2-3 at the Priestfield Stadium and 2nd leg won 4-3 at Roker Park.

Glossop North End

Season	H	A	Played for both	
1899-1900	0-0	2-0	Thomas Bradshaw	Thomas McKenzie
			Joseph Butler	James Raine
			Albert Lindsay	Arthur Saxton

Top scorers: Colin McLatchie and Tommy Becton both with 1 goal

Gravesend & Northfleet

FA Cup	Round			Played for both
1962-63	4	A	1-1	Harold Johnston
1962-63	4 rep	H	5-2	

Grimsby Town

	Home					Away				
	P	W	D	L	F	A	P	W	D	L	F	A
League	24	15	6	3	59	27	24	12	6	6	37	33
FA Cup	1	1	0	0	2	1	1	1	0	0	3	1
L. Cup	1	1	0	0	2	1	0	0	0	0	0	0
Other	1	1	0	0	2	1	1	0	0	1	2	3
Total	27	18	6	3	65	30	26	13	6	7	42	37

Season	H	A	Season	H	A	Played for both	
1901-02	3-1	3-3	1985-86	3-3	1-1	Peter Beagrie	James Lawrence
1902-03	5-1	4-2	1986-87	0-1	1-1	Stephen Coglin	Stan Lloyd
1929-30	2-0	1-0	1987-88	1-1	1-0	Doug Collins	Colin McLatchie
1930-31	3-2	1-2	1991-92	1-2	0-2	Terry Cooke	Robert Mitchell
1931-32	2-0	3-1	1992-93	2-0	0-1	Robert Coverdale	Gary Moore
1934-35	3-0	0-0	1993-94	2-2	1-0	Shaun Cunnington	John Oster
1935-36	3-1	0-4	1994-95	2-2	1-3	Terry Curran	Jack Prior
1936-37	5-1	0-6	1995-96	1-0	4-0	John Finlay (WW2)	Mark Prudhoe
1937-38	2-2	2-0	1998-99	3-1	2-0	Tony Ford	Simon Ramsden
1938-39	1-1	3-1				John T. Foster	Michael Reddy
1946-47	1-2	2-1				Ricardo Gabbiadini	Raymond Robinson
1947-48	4-2	2-1				Allan Gauden	Edward Robson
1958-59	1-0	1-1				George Harper	Reginald Scotson
1962-63	6-2	2-1				Robert Hogg	Walter Scott
1963-64	3-0	2-2				Harold Johnston	Joseph Shaw

FA Cup	Round				L. Cup	Round		
1945-46	3 L1	A	3-1		1998-99	3	H	2-1
1945-46	3 L2	H	2-1					

Top scorer: Patsy Gallacher 8 goals
Sunderland drew 4-4, and won 3-2 on penalties, in a two leg 1st round Full Members' Cup tie in 1985-86; 1st leg lost 2-3 at Blundell Park and 2nd leg won 2-1 at the Roker Park.

Halifax Town

L. Cup	Round			Played for both		
1967-68	2	H	3-2	Tim Carter	Michael Heathcote	Michael Proctor
				Brian Chambers	William Holden	Kenneth Smith
				John T. Foster	Fred Kirby	Albert Snell
				Howard Gayle	Ian Lawther	Neil Wainwright
				Roland Gregoire	Bobby Mimms	William Watson
				Gerald Harrison	Lee Power	George Whitelaw

Hartlepool United

FA Cup	Round			Played for both		
2003-04	3	H	1-0	Len Ashurst	Thomas Hall (WW1)	Jackie Mordue (WW1)
				Paul Atkinson	James Hamilton	Roy O'Donovan
				Robert Best	Peter Hartley	Harry Poulter
				Clive Bircham	Alex Hastings (WW2)	Mark Proctor
				Cyril Brown (WW2)	George Herd	Michael Proctor
				Michael Buckley	Albert Heywood	Mark Prudhoe
				Thomas Butler	William Hogg (WW1)	Bernard Ramsden

Harry Carr William Hopkins George Robinson (WW2)
Raich Carter (WW2) Don Hutchison John Robinson (WW2)
Tim Carter Joseph Johnson (WW1) David Rush
Ben Clark Robert Johnston (WW2) Thomas Scott
Neill Collins Kenneth Jones Dominic Sharkey
Kelvin Davis Alan Kennedy James Shoulder
Andy Dibble Bobby Kerr Barry Siddall
Robbie Elliott Kevin Kyle Anthony Smith
Wayne Entwistle Thomas Lilley John Spuhler (WW2)
Thomas Fairley Nathan Luscombe Fred Thompson
Ambrose Fogarty Craig Lynch Nigel Walker
Alan Foggon John MacPhail Alan Weir
John Foreman John McGinley Colin West
Marco Gabbiadini Hugh McMahon Darren Williams
Ricardo Gabbiadini William McPheat Michael Whitfield
Allan Gauden Dick Malone Albert Wood
Thomas Gibb Fred Mearns Martin Woods
Harold Godbold Tommy Miller Stephen Wright
James Gorman Malcolm Moore

Sunderland lost 0-1 in a 3rd Round Sherpa Van Trophy tie in 1987-88 at Roker Park

Huddersfield Town

	Home					Away				
	P	W	D	L	F	A	P	W	D	L	F	A
League	40	24	12	4	83	40	40	11	14	15	49	60
FA Cup	1	1	0	0	6	0	1	0	0	1	1	3
L. Cup	3	0	0	3	5	9	2	1	0	1	1	4
Total	44	25	12	7	94	49	43	12	14	17	51	67

Season	H	A	Season	H	A	Played for both	
1920-21	2-1	0-0	1947-48	2-0	2-2	George Ainsley (WW2)	Seamus McDonagh
1921-22	2-2	2-1	1948-49	0-1	0-2	Sam Allardyce	George Metcalf
1922-23	1-1	1-0	1949-50	1-1	1-3	Rod Belfitt	Tommy Miller
1923-24	2-1	2-3	1950-51	0-0	4-3	Ronald Brebner	Tony Norman
1924-25	1-1	0-4	1951-52	7-1	2-2	Raich Carter (WW2)	James Richardson
1925-26	4-1	1-1	1953-54	1-1	1-2	Charles Crossley (WW1)	Dick Roose
1926-27	1-1	0-0	1954-55	1-1	1-1	Terry Curran	Daniel Smith
1927-28	3-0	2-4	1955-56	4-1	0-4	Herbert Davis (WW2)	Martin Smith
1928-29	4-1	2-1	1958-59	1-0	1-1	Andy Dibble	Jonathan Stead
1929-30	1-0	2-0	1959-60	0-0	1-1	Stephen Doyle	Marcus Stewart
1930-31	4-2	0-2	1960-61	1-2	2-4	Billy Elliott (WW2)	William Watson
1931-32	1-3	1-4	1961-62	3-1	0-0	John S. Foster	Ken Willingham
1932-33	1-2	1-2	1962-63	1-1	3-0	Roy Greenwood	Frank Worthington
1933-34	1-1	1-2	1963-64	3-2	2-0	Stephen Hardwick	
1934-35	4-1	3-0	1972-73	3-0	1-1	Gerald Harrison	
1935-36	4-3	0-1	1985-86	1-0	0-2	Michael Hellawell	
1936-37	3-2	1-2	1986-87	2-1	2-0	Robert Kelly	
1937-38	2-1	1-1	1995-96	3-2	1-1	Kevin Kilbane	
1938-39	0-0	1-0	1997-98	3-1	3-2	Kevin Kyle	
1946-47	3-0	0-0	1998-99	2-0	1-1	Thomas Lilley	

FA Cup	Round				L. Cup	Round		
1937-38	Semi		1-3	At Ewood Park	1991-92	1 L1	H	1-2
1949-50	3	H	6-0		1991-92	1 L2	A	0-4
					1992-93	1 L1	H	2-3
					1992-93	1 L2	A	1-0
					2003-04	2	H	2-4

Top scorer: Len Shackleton 7 goals

SUNDERLAND HEAD TO HEAD RECORDS

Hull City

	Home						Away				
	P	W	D	L	F	A	P	W	D	L	F	A
League	15	9	2	4	20	10	15	6	3	6	19	21
FA Cup	2	2	0	0	7	2	1	1	0	0	2	0
L. Cup	1	1	0	0	2	1	0	0	0	0	0	0
Total	18	12	2	4	29	13	16	7	3	6	21	21

Season	H	A	Played for both		
1959-60	1-3	0-0	Peter Barnes	Gerald Harrison	Robert Thomson
1970-71	0-1	0-4	Michael Bridges	John Hawley	Cliff Thorley
1971-72	0-1	3-2	Chris Brown	Iain Hesford	Michael Turner
1972-73	1-1	2-0	Eddie Burbanks	Mick Horswill	Martyn Waghorn
1973-74	1-0	0-2	Fraizer Campbell	Simon Johnson	Billy Whitehurst
1974-75	1-0	1-3	Raich Carter	Kevin Kilbane	William Wood
1975-76	3-1	4-1	Robert Coverdale	Mark Lynch	David Wright
1977-78	2-0	0-3	Terry Curran	John McSeveney	
1985-86	1-1	1-1	Peter Daniel	Paul McShane	
1986-87	1-0	0-1	Stephen Doyle	John Moore	
1988-89	2-0	0-0	Ahmed Elmohamady	Tony Norman	
1989-90	0-1	2-3	John Gibson	Michael Reddy	
2006-07	2-0	1-0	Michael Gilhooley	Don Revie	
2008-09	1-0	4-1	Roy Greenwood	Henry Scott	
2009-10	4-1	1-0	William Grimshaw (WW1)	Joseph Shaw	

FA Cup	Round			L. Cup	Round		
1919-20	1	H	6-2	1961-62	3	H	2-1
1932-33	3	A	2-0				
1975-76	4	H	1-0				

Top scorer: Charlie Buchan 4 goals

Ipswich Town

	Home						Away				
	P	W	D	L	F	A	P	W	D	L	F	A
League	23	14	3	6	39	23	23	4	4	15	19	49
FA Cup	1	1	0	0	1	0	1	1	0	0	2	1
Total	24	15	3	6	40	23	24	5	4	15	21	50

Season	H	A	Season	H	A	Played for both	
1958-59	0-2	2-0	1997-98	2-2	0-2	Ian Atkins	Eric Gates
1959-60	0-1	1-6	1998-99	2-1	2-0	Rod Belfitt	Colin Healy
1960-61	2-0	0-4	2000-01	4-1	0-1	Darren Bent	David Healy
1968-69	3-0	0-1	2001-02	1-0	0-5	Keith Bertschin	Daniel Hegan
1969-70	2-1	0-2	2003-04	3-2	0-1	Titus Bramble	Danny Higginbotham
1976-77	1-0	1-3	2004-05	2-0	2-2	George Burley	Lee Howey
1980-81	0-2	1-4	2006-07	1-0	1-3	Terry Butcher	Grant Leadbitter
1981-82	1-1	3-3				Alec Chamberlain	Chris Makin
1982-83	2-3	1-4				Lee Chapman	Tommy Miller
1983-84	1-1	0-1				Michael Chopra	Daryl Murphy
1984-85	1-2	2-0				Jack Colback	Alan Quinn
1986-87	1-0	1-1				Danny Collins	Danny Simpson
1988-89	4-0	0-2				Joe Curran	Jonathan Stead
1989-90	2-4	1-1				Kelvin Davis	Marcus Stewart
1991-92	3-0	1-0				Carlos Edwards	Robert Thomson
1995-96	1-0	0-3				Marton Fulop	Connor Wickham

FA Cup	Round		
2000-01	4	H	1-0
2003-04	4	A	2-1

Top scorers: Marco Gabbiadini and Kevin Phillips both with 4 goals

Lazio

Season	H	A	Played for both		
1969-70	3-1	1-2 Anglo-Italian Cup	Lorik Cana	Djibril Cisse	

Leeds City

FA Cup	Round			Played for both		
1909-10	1	H	1-0	James Gemmell	William B. Murray	James Stephenson (WW1)
				Thomas Hall (WW1)	Thomas Naisby	Neil Turner
				William Hopkins	Harry Sherwin (WW1)	

Leeds United

	Home					Away				
	P	W	D	L	F	A	P	W	D	L	F	A
League	41	21	6	14	68	49	41	9	10	22	46	71
FA Cup	1	0	1	0	1	1	4	1	1	2	5	6
L. Cup	2	1	0	1	2	3	1	1	0	0	2	1
Total	44	22	7	15	71	53	46	11	11	24	53	78

Season	H	A	Season	H	A	Played for both		
1924-25	2-1	1-1	1967-68	2-2	1-1	George Ainsley	David Healy	Martin Woods
1925-26	1-3	2-0	1968-69	0-1	1-1	Ben Alnwick	Cyril Hornby	Frank Worthington
1926-27	6-2	2-2	1969-70	0-0	0-2	Jack Ashurst	Matthew Kilgallon	
1928-29	2-1	3-0	1976-77	0-1	1-1	Peter Barnes	Adam Johnson	
1929-30	1-4	0-5	1980-81	4-1	0-1	Rod Belfitt	Simon Johnson	
1930-31	4-0	3-0	1981-82	0-1	0-1	Michael Bridges	George McCartney	
1932-33	0-0	3-2	1985-86	4-2	1-1	Eddie Burbanks	Jock McDougall	
1933-34	4-2	1-3	1986-87	1-1	1-1	Paul Butler	Albert McInroy	
1934-35	3-0	4-2	1988-89	2-1	0-2	Steven Caldwell	George McNestry	
1935-36	2-1	0-3	1989-90	0-1	0-2	Lee Chapman	Dominic Matteo	
1936-37	2-1	0-3	1990-91	0-1	0-5	Ken Chisholm	Liam Miller	
1937-38	0-0	3-4	1996-97	0-1	0-3	Neill Collins	John O'Hare	
1938-39	2-1	3-3	1999-2000	1-2	1-2	Brian Deane	John Oster	
1946-47	1-0	1-1	2000-01	0-2	0-2	El Hadji Diouf	Jack Overfield	
1956-57	2-0	1-3	2001-02	2-0	0-2	Robbie Elliott	Bernard Ramsden (WW2)	
1957-58	2-1	1-2	2002-03	1-2	1-0	Wayne Entwistle	Don Revie	
1960-61	2-3	4-2	2004-05	2-3	1-0	Tore Andre Flo	Danny Rose	
1961-62	2-1	0-1	2006-07	2-0	3-0	Colin Grainger	Harry Sherwin	
1962-63	2-1	0-1				Andy Gray	Ian Snodin	
1963-64	2-0	1-1				Frank Gray	Trevor Swinburne	
1964-65	3-3	1-2				Michael Gray	Chris Turner	
1965-66	2-0	0-1				Ian Harte	Percy Whipp	
1966-67	0-2	1-2				John Hawley	Ken Willingham	

FA Cup	Round				L. Cup	Round		
1926-27	3	A	2-3		1967-68	4	H	0-2
1966-67	5	H	1-1		1993-94	2 L1	H	2-1
1966-67	5 rep	A	1-1		1993-94	2 L2	A	2-1
1966-67	5 rep2		1-2 At Boothferry Park					
1972-73	Final		1-0 At Wembley					

Top scorer: Bobby Gurney 9 goals

Leicester City

	Home					Away				
	P	W	D	L	F	A	P	W	D	L	F	A
League	39	17	13	9	59	48	39	12	6	21	47	71
FA Cup	1	1	0	0	4	1	1	0	0	1	0	1
L. Cup	1	0	0	1	1	2	1	0	1	0	1	1
Total	41	18	13	10	64	51	41	12	7	22	48	73

Season	H	A	Season	H	A	Played for both	
1908-09	3-1	3-4	1970-71	0-0	0-1	Steve Agnew	Bob Lee
1925-26	3-0	1-4	1976-77	0-0	0-2	Ben Alnwick	Albert Lewis
1926-27	3-0	1-2	1978-79	1-1	2-1	Thomas Bradshaw	Chris Makin
1927-28	2-2	3-3	1979-80	0-0	1-2	Ronald Brebner	Fred Mearns
1928-29	1-2	0-1	1980-81	1-0	1-0	David Buchanan	Jock Paterson
1929-30	2-1	2-1	1983-84	1-1	2-0	Ken Chisholm	Matthew Piper
1930-31	2-5	1-1	1984-85	0-4	0-2	William Clark	Don Revie
1931-32	4-1	0-5	1988-89	2-2	1-3	Clive Clarke	Dominic Sharkey
1932-33	2-1	2-4	1989-90	2-2	3-2	David Connolly	Nick Summerbee
1933-34	2-1	0-0	1991-92	1-0	2-3	Herbert Davis	William Troughear
1934-35	2-0	2-0	1992-93	1-2	2-3	Brian Deane	Martyn Waghorn
1937-38	1-0	0-4	1993-94	2-3	1-2	Alex Donaldson (WW1)	Andrew Welsh
1938-39	2-0	2-0	1995-96	1-2	0-0	William Ellis	Stephen Whitworth
1954-55	1-1	1-1	1996-97	0-0	1-1	Marton Fulop	Frank Worthington
1957-58	3-2	1-4	1999-2000	2-0	2-5	Thomas Galbraith	
1964-65	3-3	1-0	2000-01	0-0	0-2	William George (WW1)	
1965-66	0-3	1-4	2001-02	2-1	0-1	George Gibson	
1966-67	2-3	2-1	2004-05	2-1	1-0	Billy Hughes	
1967-68	0-2	2-0	2006-07	1-1	2-0	David Kelly	
1968-69	2-0	1-2				Jamie Lawrence	

FA Cup	Round				L. Cup	Round			
1906-07	1	H	4-1	As Leicester Fosse	1998-99	Semi L1	H	1-2
1969-70	3	A	0-1		1998-99	Semi L2	A	1-1

Top scorer: David Halliday 8 goals

Leyton Orient

	Home					Away				
	P	W	D	L	F	A	P	W	D	L	F	A
League	14	10	3	1	29	11	14	3	5	6	16	27
FA Cup	2	1	0	1	6	3	0	0	0	0	0	0
Total	16	11	3	2	35	14	14	3	5	6	16	27

Season	H	A	Season	H	A	Played for both	
1958-59	4-0	0-6	1978-79	1-0	0-3	Ben Alnwick	Michael Liddle
1959-60	1-4	1-1	1979-80	1-1	1-2	Ian Bowyer	George Payne
1960-61	4-1	1-0				Peter Boyle	John Shaw
1961-62	2-1	1-1				Joe Butler	Thomas Stewart
1963-64	4-1	5-2				Norman Case	Fred Thompson
1970-71	1-0	0-1				David Corner	Sean Thornton
1971-72	2-0	0-5				Charles Crossley (WW1)	Chris Turner
1972-73	1-0	1-1				Trevor Ford (WW2)	Michael Turner
1973-74	1-1	1-2				Patrick Gallacher (WW2)	Robert Vincent
1974-75	3-0	1-1				David Halliday	Colin West
1975-76	3-1	2-0				Vic Halom	Percy Whipp
1977-78	1-1	2-2				John Hawley	

FA Cup	Round			
1912-13	1	H	6-0	As Clapton Orient
1970-71	3	H	0-3	

Top scorers: Jimmy Richardson and Billy Hughes both with 4 goals

Lincoln City

	Home					Away				
	P	W	D	L	F	A	P	W	D	L	F	A
League	3	1	1	1	6	6	3	1	1	1	3	4
FA Cup	0	0	0	0	0	0	1	1	0	0	1	0
L. Cup	0	0	0	0	0	0	1	0	0	1	1	2
Total	3	1	1	1	6	6	5	2	1	2	5	6

Season	H	A	Played for both		
1958-59	2-0	1-3	Fred Bett	Michael Ingham	Trevor Swinburne
1959-60	2-4	0-0	Joe Butler	Robert Johnston (WW2)	Colin Symm
1960-61	2-2	2-1	John Cornforth	John McGinley	Chris Turner
			Peter Daniel	Robert Mitchell	Peter Wakeham
			William Ellis	Dennis O'Donnell	Kenneth Walshaw
			William Gibson	William Pallister	Andrew Yorke
			Harold Godbold	Frank Pegg	Benny Yorston (WW2)
			Mick Harford	Jackie Robinson	
			James Hartley	William Simpson	

FA Cup	Round				L. Cup	Round		
1998-99	3	A	1-0		1970-71	2	A	1-2

Top scorers: Ian Lawther and Alan O'Neill both with 2 goals

Liverpool

	Home						Away					
	P	W	D	L	F	A	P	W	D	L	F	A
League	75	33	13	29	123	113	75	18	20	37	92	137
FA Cup	2	0	1	1	4	3	1	0	2	2	7
L. Cup	2	0	0	2	0	3	1	0	0	1	0	2
Total	79	33	14	32	124	120	79	19	20	40	94	146

Season	H	A	Season	H	A	Played for both
1894-95	3-2	3-2	1947-48	5-1	0-0	George Ainsley (WW2)
1896-97	4-3	0-3	1948-49	0-2	0-4	Len Ashurst
1897-98	1-0	2-0	1949-50	3-2	2-4	Phil Babb
1898-99	1-0	0-0	1950-51	2-1	0-4	Bob Bolder
1899-1900	1-0	2-0	1951-52	3-0	2-2	Joseph Butler (WW1)
1900-01	0-1	2-1	1952-53	3-1	0-2	Alec Chamberlain
1901-02	1-1	1-0	1953-54	3-2	3-4	Djibril Cisse
1902-03	2-1	1-1	1958-59	2-1	1-3	El Hadji Diouf
1903-04	2-1	1-2	1959-60	1-1	0-3	Teddy Doig
1905-06	1-2	0-2	1960-61	1-1	1-1	Stewart Downing
1906-07	5-5	2-1	1961-62	1-4	0-3	Howard Gayle
1907-08	1-0	0-1	1964-65	2-3	0-0	Cyril Gilhespy
1908-09	1-4	0-3	1965-66	2-2	0-4	Gordon Gunson
1909-10	2-1	4-1	1966-67	2-2	2-2	David Hannah
1910-11	4-0	2-1	1967-68	1-1	1-2	Jordan Henderson
1911-12	1-2	1-2	1968-69	0-2	1-4	Joseph Hewitt
1912-13	7-0	5-2	1969-70	0-1	0-2	David Hodgson
1913-14	1-2	3-1	1976-77	0-1	0-2	Don Hutchison
1914-15	2-2	1-2	1980-81	2-4	1-0	Jack Jones (WW2)

SUNDERLAND HEAD TO HEAD RECORDS

1919-20	0-1	2-3	1981-82	0-2	0-1
1920-21	2-1	0-0	1982-83	0-0	0-1
1921-22	3-0	1-2	1983-84	0-0	1-0
1922-23	1-0	1-5	1984-85	0-3	1-1
1923-24	0-0	2-4	1990-91	0-1	1-2
1924-25	3-0	1-3	1996-97	1-2	0-0
1925-26	3-2	2-2	1999-2000	0-2	1-1
1926-27	2-1	2-1	2000-01	1-1	1-1
1927-28	2-1	5-2	2001-02	0-1	0-1
1928-29	2-1	2-5	2002-03	2-1	0-0
1929-30	2-3	6-0	2005-06	0-2	0-1
1930-31	6-5	4-2	2007-08	0-2	0-3
1931-32	1-3	2-1	2008-09	0-1	0-2
1932-33	0-0	3-3	2009-10	1-0	0-3
1933-34	4-1	1-1	2010-11	0-2	2-2
1934-35	2-3	2-2	2011-12	1-0	1-1
1935-36	2-0	3-0			
1936-37	4-2	0-4			
1937-38	2-3	0-4			
1938-39	2-3	1-1			
1946-47	1-4	0-1			

Played for both:
Alan Kennedy
Sotirios Kyrgiakos
Anthony Le Tallec
George Livingstone
Jason McAteer
Donald McCallum
Dominic Matteo
Brian Mooney
Thomas Morrison
Reginald Pearce
Mark Prudhoe
Bernard Ramsden
Samuel Raybould
Robert S. Robinson
Thomas Scott
John Smith
Paul Stewart
Barry Venison
David Wright
Stephen Wright
Boudewijn Zenden

FA Cup	Round				L. Cup	Round		
1921-22	1	H	1-1		1973-74	3	H	0-2
1921-22	1 rep	A	0-5		1995-96	2 L1	A	0-2
1960-61	4	A	2-0		1995-96	2 L2	H	0-1
1981-82	4	H	0-3					
1991-92	Final		0-2	At Wembley				

Top scorer: Charlie Buchan 18 goals

Luton Town

	Home					Away				
	P	W	D	L	F	A	P	W	D	L	F	A
League	23	13	7	3	40	17	23	11	2	10	42	49
FA Cup	3	3	0	0	6	1	3	1	2	0	5	2
L. Cup	3	3	0	0	9	1	2	1	0	1	2	4
Total	29	19	7	3	55	19	28	13	4	11	49	55

Season	H	A	Season	H	A
1955-56	1-2	2-8	1984-85	3-0	1-2
1956-57	1-0	2-6	1990-91	2-0	2-1
1957-58	3-0	1-7	1992-93	2-2	0-0
1960-61	7-1	3-3	1993-94	2-0	1-2
1961-62	2-2	2-1	1994-95	1-1	0-3
1962-63	3-1	3-0	1995-96	1-0	2-0
1970-71	0-0	2-1	2006-07	2-1	5-0
1971-72	2-2	2-1			
1972-73	0-2	0-1			
1973-74	0-1	4-3			
1975-76	2-0	0-2			
1977-78	1-1	3-1			
1978-79	1-0	3-0			
1979-80	1-0	0-2			
1982-83	1-1	3-1			
1983-84	2-0	1-4			

Played for both:
Ben Alnwick — Len Hargreaves
Billy Bingham — William Harper
John Black — Gerald Harrison
Bob Bolder — Albert Heywood
Norman Brown — Robert Hogg
Alec Chamberlain — Don Hutchison
Brian Chambers — Albert Lindsay
Kelvin Davis — George McNestry
Andy Dibble — Daryl Murphy
Carlos Edwards — Thomas Naisby
Thomas Finney — Reginald Pearce
Patrick Gallacher (WW2) — William Robinson (WW2)
John Gibson — Arthur Saxton
Philip Gray — Fred Thompson
Vic Halom — Colin Todd
Mick Harford — Jack Vinall

FA Cup	Round				L. Cup	Round		
1906-07	2	A	0-0		1976-77	2	H	3-1
1906-07	2 rep	H	1-0		1998-99	5	H	3-0
1936-37	4	A	2-2		2000-01	2 L1	H	3-0
1936-37	4 rep	H	3-1		2000-01	2 L2	A	2-1
1964-65	3	A	3-0		2007-08	2	A	0-3
1972-73	6	H	2-0					

Top scorer: 4 players with 4 goals

Manchester City

| | Home | | | | | Away | | | | |
	P	W	D	L	F	A	P	W	D	L	F	A
League	61	33	11	17	108	88	61	12	10	39	77	124
FA Cup	4	2	1	1	6	3	4	0	1	3	5	8
L. Cup	1	1	0	0	1	0	1	0	1	0	1	1
Other	0	0	0	0	0	0	2	0	0	2	0	2
Total	66	36	12	18	115	91	68	12	12	44	83	135

Season	H	A	Season	H	A
1899-1900	3-1	1-2	1947-48	0-1	0-3
1900-01	3-0	1-1	1948-49	3-0	1-1
1901-02	1-0	3-0	1949-50	1-2	1-2
1903-04	1-1	1-2	1951-52	3-0	1-3
1904-05	0-0	2-5	1952-53	3-3	5-2
1905-06	2-0	1-5	1953-54	4-5	1-2
1906-07	1-1	3-2	1954-55	3-2	0-1
1907-08	2-5	0-0	1955-56	0-3	2-4
1908-09	2-0	0-1	1956-57	1-1	1-3
1910-11	4-0	3-3	1957-58	2-1	1-3
1911-12	1-1	0-2	1963-64	2-0	3-0
1912-13	1-0	0-1	1966-67	1-0	0-1
1913-14	0-0	1-3	1967-68	1-0	0-1
1914-15	0-2	0-2	1968-69	0-4	0-1
1919-20	2-1	0-1	1969-70	0-4	1-0
1920-21	1-0	1-3	1976-77	0-2	0-1
1921-22	2-3	0-3	1980-81	2-0	4-0
1922-23	2-0	0-1	1981-82	1-0	3-2
1923-24	5-2	1-4	1982-83	3-2	2-2
1924-25	3-2	3-1	1988-89	2-4	1-1
1925-26	5-3	1-4	1990-91	1-1	2-3
1928-29	3-1	3-5	1997-98	3-1	1-0
1929-30	5-2	2-2	2000-01	1-0	2-4
1930-31	3-3	0-2	2002-03	0-3	0-3
1931-32	2-5	1-1	2005-06	1-2	1-2
1932-33	3-2	4-2	2007-08	1-2	0-1
1933-34	0-0	1-4	2008-09	0-3	0-1
1934-35	3-2	0-1	2009-10	1-1	3-4
1935-36	2-0	1-0	2010-11	1-0	0-5
1936-37	1-3	4-2	2011-12	1-0	3-3
1937-38	3-1	0-2			

Played for both

Peter Barnes	Bobby Mimms
Peter Beagrie	Hugh Morgan
Tal Ben Haim	Benjamin Mwaruwari
Gary Bennett	Nedum Onuoha
Ian Bowyer	Thomas Porteous
Ralph Brand	Niall Quinn
Wayne Bridge	Don Revie
Ivor Broadis	Craig Russell
Ken Chisholm (WW2)	Claudio Reyna
Jeff Clarke	Barry Siddall
Andrew Cole	Paul Stewart
Terry Cooke	Nick Summerbee
Tony Coton	Tony Towers
John Crossan	Dennis Tueart
Andy Dibble	Ronald Turnbull
Michael Docherty	David Watson
Alex Donaldson	Keiren Westwood
Stephen Elliott	Jeff Whitley
Dickson Etuhu	
Marton Fulop	
Shay Given	
David Halliday	
William Harper	
James Hindmarsh	
Mick Horswill	
Adam Johnson	
Andrew Kerr	
George Livingstone	
Leslie McDowall	
Robert Marshall	
Peter Meechan	

FA Cup	Round				L. Cup	Round		
1903-04	1	A	2-3		1979-80	3	A	1-1
1912-13	2	H	2-0		1979-80	3 rep	H	1-0
1927-28	4	H	1-2					
1954-55	Semi		0-1	At Villa Park				
1972-73	5	A	2-2					
1972-73	5 rep	H	3-1					
1982-83	3	H	0-0					
1982-83	3 rep	A	1-2					

Top scorer: Bobby Gurney 10 goals
Sunderland lost 0-2 in the Charity Shield in 1937-38 at Maine Road
Sunderland drew 0-0, but lost 3-4 on penalties, in a Full Members' Cup quarter-final in 1985-86 at Maine Road

Manchester United

	Home					Away				
	P	W	D	L	F	A	P	W	D	L	F	A
League	59	26	14	19	112	80	59	11	14	34	64	121
FA Cup	4	0	3	1	6	7	5	0	2	3	7	15
L. Cup	2	1	1	0	4	3	2	0	1	1	2	3
Other	1	1	0	0	2	0	1	0	1	0	1	1
Total	66	28	18	20	124	90	67	11	18	38	74	140

Season	H	A	Season	H	A	Played for both	
1892-93	6-0	5-0	1954-55	4-3	2-2	George Ainsley (WW2)	Chris Turner
1893-94	4-1	4-2	1955-56	2-2	1-2	Phil Bardsley	Colin Waldron
1906-07	4-1	0-2	1956-57	1-3	0-4	Peter Barnes	Danny Welbeck
1907-08	1-2	0-3	1957-58	1-2	2-2	David Bellion	Harry Williams
1908-09	6-1	2-2	1964-65	1-0	0-1	Robert Bonthron	Dwight Yorke
1909-10	3-0	0-2	1965-66	2-3	1-1	Ivor Broadis (WW2)	
1910-11	1-2	1-5	1966-67	0-0	0-5	Wes Brown	
1911-12	5-0	2-2	1967-68	1-1	2-1	Fraizer Campbell	
1912-13	3-1	3-1	1968-69	1-1	1-4	Andrew Cole	
1913-14	2-0	1-3	1969-70	1-1	1-3	Terry Cooke	
1914-15	1-0	0-3	1974-75	0-0	2-3	Tony Coton	
1919-20	3-0	0-2	1976-77	2-1	3-3	Peter Davenport	
1920-21	2-3	0-3	1980-81	2-0	1-1	Jonathon Evans	
1921-22	2-1	1-3	1981-82	1-5	0-0	Alan Foggon	
1925-26	2-1	1-5	1982-83	0-0	0-0	David Healy	
1926-27	6-0	0-0	1983-84	0-1	1-2	Danny Higginbotham	
1927-28	4-1	1-2	1984-85	3-2	2-2	James Holton	
1928-29	5-1	0-3	1990-91	2-1	0-3	George Livingstone	
1929-30	2-4	1-2	1996-97	2-1	0-5	William Longair	
1930-31	1-2	1-1	1999-2000	2-2	0-4	Mark Lynch	
1936-37	1-1	1-2	2000-01	0-1	0-3	Seamus McDonagh	
1938-39	5-2	1-0	2001-02	1-3	1-4	Paul McShane	
1946-47	1-1	3-0*	2002-03	1-1	1-2	Liam Miller	
1947-48	1-0	1-3*	2005-06	1-3	0-0	Hugh Morgan	
1948-49	2-1	2-1*	2007-08	0-4	0-1	James Nicholl	
1949-50	2-2	3-1	2008-09	1-2	0-1	John O'Shea	
1950-51	2-1	5-3	2009-10	0-1	2-2	Kieran Richardson	
1951-52	1-2	1-0	2010-11	0-0	0-2	Louis Saha	
1952-53	2-2	1-0	2011-12	0-1	0-1	Danny Simpson	
1953-54	0-2	0-1				Ernest Taylor	

* = played at Maine Road because Old Trafford was closed due to bomb damage

FA Cup	Round				L. Cup	Round			
1925-26	5	H	3-3		1976-77	3	A	2-2
1925-26	5 rep	A	1-2		1976-77	3 rep	H	2-2
1963-64	6	A	3-3		1976-77	3 rep2	A	0-1
1963-64	6 rep	H	2-2		2000-01	4	H	2-1
1963-64	6 rep2		1-5	At Leeds Road				
1985-86		H	0-0					
1985-86	4 rep	A	0-3					
1995-96	3	A	2-2					
1995-96	3 rep	H	1-2					

Top scorer: David Halliday 14 goals
Sunderland drew 1-1 at Bank Street, Clayton, and won 2-0 at Newcastle Road in the end of 1896-97 Test Match Series that determined who stayed in Division One. At that time Manchester United were known as Newton Heath.

Mansfield Town

	Home					Away				
	P	W	D	L	F	A	P	W	D	L	F	A
League	2	2	0	0	5	1	2	2	0	0	6	1
L. Cup	0	0	0	0	0	0	1	1	0	0	2	1
Total	2	2	0	0	5	1	3	3	0	0	8	2

Season	H	A	Played for both		
1977-78	1-0	2-1	William Death	Denis Longhorn	Dominic Sharkey
1987-88	4-1	4-0	Ernest England	Bobby Mimms	Harry Thompson
			Tony Ford	Thomas Mitchinson	John Tones
			Cyril Gilhespy	John Moore	Neil Wainwright
			David Kelly	Colin Nelson	Darren Ward
			Samuel Kemp	Jock Paterson	Stephen Whitworth
			John Lathan	Matthew Piper	Harry Williams
			Liam Lawrence	Jack Prior	

L. Cup	Round		
2003-04	1	A	2-1

Top scorer: 3 players with 2 goals

Middlesbrough

	Home						Away				
	P	W	D	L	F	A	P	W	D	L	F	A
League	64	37	16	11	111	62	64	19	17	28	80	101
FA Cup	3	1	2	0	6	4	5	3	1	1	9	7
L. Cup	2	1	1	0	3	2	3	0	0	3	0	5
Other	1	0	0	1	0	1	1	0	0	1	2	3
Total	70	39	19	12	120	69	73	22	18	33	91	116

Season	H	A	Season	H	A	Played for both		
1902-03	2-1*	1-0	1949-50	2-0	0-2	William Agnew	Richard Jackson
1903-04	3-1	3-2	1950-51	2-1	1-1	Stan Anderson	Adam Johnson
1904-05	1-1	3-1	1951-52	3-1	2-0	Julio Arca	Allan Johnston
1905-06	2-1	1-2	1952-53	1-1	2-1	Philip Bach	Graham Kavanagh
1906-07	4-2	1-2	1953-54	0-2	0-0	Peter Beagrie	John Kay
1907-08	0-0	1-3	1958-59	0-0	0-0	Joseph Bolton	Matthew Kilgallon
1908-09	2-0	3-0	1959-60	2-2	1-1	Arthur Brown	George Kinnell
1909-10	2-2	2-3	1960-61	2-0	0-1	Jock Brown	Fred Kirby
1910-11	3-1	0-1	1961-62	2-1	1-0	Michael Buckley	Grant Leadbitter
1911-12	1-0	3-3	1962-63	3-1	3-3	Geoff Butler	James Leslie
1912-13	4-0	2-0	1963-64	0-0	0-2	Harry Carr	Donald McCallum
1913-14	4-2	4-3	1970-71	2-2	2-2	Lee Cattermole	Hugh McMahon (WW2)
1914-15	4-1	3-2	1971-72	4-1	0-2	Brian Clough	Matthew Middleton (WW2)
1919-20	1-1	2-0	1972-73	4-0	1-2	Alfred Common	Jackie Mordue
1920-21	1-2	0-2	1973-74	0-2	1-2	Colin Cooper	Mark Proctor
1921-22	1-1	0-3	1976-77	4-0	1-2	James Crawford	Richard Rooks
1922-23	2-1	0-2	1980-81	0-1	0-1	John Crossan	Gary Rowell
1923-24	3-2	3-1	1981-82	0-2	0-0	Stan Cummins	James Russell (WW2)
1927-28	1-0	3-0	1985-86	1-0	0-2	John Curtis	John Spuhler
1929-30	3-2	0-3	1989-90	2-1	0-3	Peter Davenport	Walter Tinsley
1930-31	1-1	0-1	1991-92	1-0	1-2	Brian Deane	Jack Tomlin
1931-32	0-0	1-0	1993-94	2-1	1-4	Andy Dibble	Thomas Urwin
1932-33	0-0	2-1	1994-95	0-1	2-2	Stewart Downing	James Watson
1933-34	2-0	4-0	1996-97	2-2	1-0	Robert Ferguson	Derek Weddle
1934-35	1-1	0-0	1997-98	1-2	1-3	John Finlay (WW2)	Darren Williams
1935-36	2-1	0-6	1999-2000	1-1	1-1	Alan Foggon	William Worrall

SUNDERLAND HEAD TO HEAD RECORDS

1936-37	4-1	5-5	2000-01	1-0	0-0	James Gorman (WW2)	Benny Yorston
1937-38	3-1	1-2	2001-02	0-1	0-2	Richard Healey	Boudewijn Zenden
1938-39	1-2	0-3	2002-03	1-3	0-3	Michael Heathcote	
1946-47	1-0	3-1	2005-06	0-3	2-0	Albert Heywood (WW2)	
1947-48	3-0	2-2	2007-08	3-2	2-2	David Hodgson	
1948-49	1-0	0-0	2008-09	2-0	1-1	Justin Hoyte	

* = played at St James' Park because Roker Park had been closed by the Football League for one game due to disturbances after game against Sheffield Wednesday (21 March 1903)

FA Cup	Round				L. Cup	Round		
1887-88	3	A	2-2		1977-78	2	H	2-2
1887-88	3 rep	H	4-2	Sunderland disqualified	1977-78	2 rep	A	0-1
1933-34	3	H	1-1		1987-88	1 L1	H	1-0
1933-34	3 rep	A	2-1		1987-88	1 L2	A	0-2
1938-39	4	A	2-0		1997-98	3	A	0-2
1974-75	4	A	1-3					
2011-12	4	H	1-1					
2011-12	4 rep	A	2-1					

Top scorer: George Holley 14 goals
Sunderland lost 0-1 in a Texaco Cup group game in 1974-75 at Roker Park
Sunderland lost 2-3 in an Anglo-Scottish Cup group game in 1975-76 at Ayresome Park

Millwall

	Home					Away				
	P	W	D	L	F	A	P	W	D	L	F	A
League	16	10	3	3	36	14	16	4	4	8	15	22
FA Cup	0	0	0	0	0	0	2	1	0	1	2	2
L. Cup	1	0	1	0	1	1	1	0	0	1	1	2
Total	17	10	4	3	37	15	19	5	4	10	18	26

Season	H	A	Season	H	A	Played for both	
1970-71	0-1	0-0	2003-04	0-1	1-2	Sam Allardyce	Patrick Gallacher (WW2)
1971-72	3-3	1-1	2004-05	1-0	0-2	Phil Babb	Donald Gow
1972-73	2-0	1-0				Ivor Broadis	Charlie Hurley
1973-74	4-0	1-2				Norman Brown	Don Hutchison
1974-75	2-0	4-1				Darren Byfield	Thomas Hyslop
1977-78	2-0	1-3				John Byrne	Joseph Lane
1978-79	3-2	1-0				Darren Carter	Thomas Lee
1985-86	1-2	0-1				Tim Carter	Archibald McKenzie
1986-87	1-1	1-1				Brian Chambers	William Maxwell
1991-92	6-2	1-4				John Colquhoun	Richard Parker
1992-93	2-0	0-0				John Conner	Lee Power
1993-94	2-1	1-2				Colin Cooper	Alex Rae
1994-95	1-1	0-2				Kenny Cunningham	James Richardson
1995-96	6-0	2-1				Daniele Dichio	Anton Rogan

FA Cup	Round				L. Cup	Round		
1936-37	Semi		2-1	At Leeds Road	1994-95	2 L1	A	1-2
2003-04	Semi		0-1	At Old Trafford	1994-95	2 L2	H	1-1

Top scorer: Craig Russell and Don Goodman both with 6 goals

Morpeth Harriers

FA Cup	Round		
1887-88	1	A	3-2

Newcastle United

	Home					Away				
	P	W	D	L	F	A	P	W	D	L	F	A
League	67	23	24	20	98	90	67	18	18	31	98	118
FA Cup	3	1	1	1	2	3	5	2	2	1	9	5
L. Cup	1	0	1	0	2	2	1	1	0	0	2	2
Other	2	1	1	0	2	1	2	2	0	0	4	0
Total	73	25	27	21	104	96	75	23	20	32	113	125

Season	H	A	Season	H	A
1898-99	2-3	1-0	1950-51	2-1	2-2
1899-1900	1-2	4-2	1951-52	1-4	2-2
1900-01	1-1	2-0	1952-53	0-2	2-2
1901-02	0-0	1-0	1953-54	1-1	1-2
1902-03	0-0	0-1	1954-55	4-2	2-1
1903-04	1-1	3-1	1955-56	1-6	1-3
1904-05	3-1	3-1	1956-57	1-2	2-6
1905-06	3-2	1-1	1957-58	2-0	2-2
1906-07	2-0	2-4	1961-62	3-0	2-2
1907-08	2-4	3-1	1962-63	0-0	1-1
1908-09	3-1	9-1	1963-64	2-1	0-1
1909-10	0-2	0-1	1965-66	2-0	0-2
1910-11	2-1	1-1	1966-67	3-0	3-0
1911-12	1-2	1-3	1967-68	3-3	1-2
1912-13	2-0	1-1	1968-69	1-1	1-1
1913-14	1-2	1-2	1969-70	1-1	0-3
1914-15	2-4	5-2	1976-77	2-2	0-2
1919-20	2-0	3-2	1978-79	1-1	4-1
1920-21	0-2	1-6	1979-80	1-0	1-3
1921-22	0-0	2-2	1984-85	0-0	1-3
1922-23	2-0	1-2	1989-90	0-0	1-1
1923-24	3-2	2-0	1991-92	1-1	0-1
1924-25	1-1	0-2	1992-93	1-2	0-1
1925-26	2-2	0-0	1996-97	1-2	1-1
1926-27	2-0	0-1	1999-2000	2-2	2-1
1927-28	1-1	1-3	2000-01	1-1	2-1
1928-29	5-2	3-4	2001-02	0-1	1-1
1929-30	1-0	0-3	2002-03	0-1	0-2
1930-31	5-0	0-2	2005-06	1-4	2-3
1931-32	1-4	2-1	2007-08	1-1	0-2
1932-33	0-2	1-0	2008-09	2-1	1-1
1933-34	2-0	1-2	2010-11	1-1	1-5
1948-49	1-1	1-2	2011-12	0-1	1-1
1949-50	2-2	2-1			

Played for both

William Agnew — Mick Harford
Sam Aiston — John Harvie
Stan Anderson — David Kelly
Keith Armstrong — Alan Kennedy
John Auld — Alex Lockie (WW2)
Harry Bedford — James Logan
Lyall Bolton — Andrew McCombie
Paul Bracewell — Robert McDermid
Titus Bramble — Albert McInroy
Michael Bridges — Robert McKay
Ivor Broadis — Bob Moncur
Alan Brown — Lionel Perez
Steven Caldwell — James Raine
John Campbell — Jackie Robinson (WW2)
Michael Chopra — Ray Robinson
Lee Clark — Robert Robinson (b.1921)
Jeff Clarke — Bryan Robson
Andrew Cole — Thomas Rowlandson
Anthony Cullen — Louis Saha
Joseph Devine — Len Shackleton
John Dowsey — Danny Simpson
Len Duns (WW2) — John Smith
David Elliott — John Spuhler (WW2)
Robbie Elliott — Colin Suggett
Ray Ellison — Ernest Taylor
Alan Foggon — Thomas Urwin
Patrick Gallacher (WW2) — Barry Venison
Howard Gayle — Chris Waddle
Thomas Gibb — Nigel Walker
Shay Given — Billy Whitehurst
Thomas Grey — David Willis
Ron Guthrie — David Young
Thomas Hall
Stephen Hardwick

FA Cup	Round			
1888-89	3 (Qual)	H	2-0	As Newcastle East End
1901-02	2	A	0-1	
1908-09	4	A	2-2	
1908-09	4 rep	H	0-3	
1912-13	4	H	0-0	
1912-13	4 rep	A	2-2	
1912-13	4 rep2	A	3-0	
1955-56	6	A	2-0	

L. Cup	Round			
1979-80	2 L1	H	2-2	
1979-80	2 L2	A	2-2	Won 7-6 on pens

Top scorer: George Holley 15 goals
Sunderland won 2-0 in a two leg Division One Play-off semi-final in 1989-90; 1st leg drew 0-0 at Roker Park and 2nd leg won 2-0 at St James' Park.
Sunderland won 2-1 in a Texaco Cup group game in 1974-75 at Roker Park
Sunderland won 2-0 in an Anglo-Scottish Cup group game in 1975-76 at St James' Park

Newcastle West End

FA Cup	Round			Played for both
1886-87	1	A	0-1	Len Duns
1887-88	2	H	3-1	Robert McDermid

Newport County

FA Cup	Round			Played for both		
1985-86	3	H	2-0	Keith Armstrong	David Elliott	Alexander McNab
				Stephen Berry	Trevor Ford	John McSeveney
				Tim Carter	James Hindmarsh	John Moore
				John Conner	Leighton James	Howard Sheppeard
				Kevin Cooper	Robert McKay	Ian Watson

Northampton Town

	Home				Away			
	P	W	D	L	F	A	P	W	D	L	F	A
League	3	2	0	1	6	3	3	1	0	2	4	7
FA Cup	2	1	1	0	5	3	1	1	0	0	3	0
L. Cup	1	1	0	0	2	2	0	0	0	0	0	0
Total	6	4	1	1	13	8	4	2	0	2	7	7

Season	H	A	Played for both		
1963-64	0-2	1-5	Sam Aiston	Warren Hawke	Ian Sampson
1965-66	3-0	1-2	Thomas Allen	Brian Heslop	Arthur Saxton
1987-88	3-1	2-0	Gordon Armstrong	Lee Howey	Anthony Smith
			Stephen Berry	Joseph Kiernan	Martin Smith
			Robert Bonthron	Thomas McLain	Harry Thompson
			David Buchanan	Alexander McNab (WW2)	Ray Train
			Darren Byfield	Mark Maley	William Walsh
			Tim Coleman	Maurice Marston	Mark Watkins
			John Dowsey	William B. Murray	Colin West
			Marco Gabbiadini	James Oakley	Andrew Yorke

FA Cup	Round			L. Cup	Round				
1927-28	3	H	3-3	2008-09	2	H	2-2	Won 4-3 on pens
1927-28	3 rep	A	3-0					
1963-64	3	H	2-0					

Top scorer: David Halliday 3 goals

Northwich Victoria

FA Cup	Round			Played for both		
2005-06	3	H	3-0	Peter Barnes	Brian Heslop	Alexander McNab
				Robert Ferguson	Archibald Jackson	Barry Siddall
				Gerald Harrison	Alan Kennedy	Jeff Whitley

Norwich City

	Home						Away					
	P	W	D	L	F	A	P	W	D	L	F	A
League	20	10	4	6	29	16	20	2	6	12	18	36
FA Cup	3	2	0	1	7	4	4	2	1	1	4	4
L. Cup	3	0	1	2	2	6	4	1	1	2	5	5
Total	26	12	5	9	38	26	28	5	8	15	27	45

SUNDERLAND: THE COMPLETE RECORD

Season	H	A	Season	H	A
1960-61	0-3	0-3	1997-98	0-1	1-2
1961-62	2-0	1-3	1998-99	1-0	2-2
1962-63	7-1	2-4	2003-04	1-0	0-1
1963-64	0-0	3-2	2006-07	1-0	0-1
1970-71	2-1	0-3	2011-12	3-0	1-2
1971-72	1-1	1-1			
1974-75	0-0	0-0			
1976-77	0-1	2-2			
1980-81	3-0	0-1			
1982-83	4-1	0-2			
1983-84	1-1	0-3			
1984-85	2-1	3-1			
1985-86	0-2	0-0			
1990-91	1-2	2-3			
1995-96	0-1	0-0			

Played for both

Ben Alnwick	George Martin — Reginald Wilkinson
Keith Bertschin	Frank Pegg
Alan Black	Lee Power
Chris Brown	Stanley Ramsay
Geoff Butler	Carl Robinson
James Chalmers	Robert Robinson (b.1910)
Kevin Cooper	Jack Rogers
Calum Davenport	Gary Rowell
Shaun Elliott	James Russell
Stephen Elliott	Thomas Scott
Dickson Etuhu	Colin Suggett
John Evans	Fred Thompson
Arthur Hawes	Michael Turner
David Healy	Jack Vinall
David Hodgson	Darren Ward

FA Cup	Round			
1910-11	1	A	1-3	
1950-51	5	H	3-1	
1955-56	3	H	4-2	
1960-61	5	A	1-0	
1967-68	3	A	1-1	
1967-68	3 rep	H	0-1	
1991-92	Semi		1-0	At Hillsborough

L. Cup	Round			
1961-62	5	H	1-4	
1982-83	3	H	0-0	
1982-83	3 rep	A	1-3	
1983-84	3	A	0-0	
1983-84	3 rep	H	1-2	
1984-85	Final		0-1	At Wembley
2009-10	2	A	4-1	

Top scorers: Nick Sharkey and Gary Rowell both with 5 goals

Nottingham Forest

	Home					Away				
	P	W	D	L	F	A	P	W	D	L	F	A
League	43	24	12	7	76	36	43	12	10	21	58	73
FA Cup	4	1	1	2	8	8	2	0	0	2	1	6
L. Cup	1	1	0	0	1	0	2	1	1	0	3	2
Total	48	26	13	9	85	44	47	13	11	23	62	81

Season	H	A	Season	H	A
1892-93	1-0	5-0	1964-65	4-0	2-5
1893-94	2-0	2-1	1965-66	3-2	0-0
1894-95	2-2	1-2	1966-67	1-0	1-3
1895-96	1-1	1-3	1967-68	1-0	3-0
1896-97	2-2	1-2	1968-69	3-1	0-1
1897-98	4-0	1-1	1969-70	2-1	1-2
1898-99	1-1	1-1	1972-73	4-1	0-1
1899-1900	1-0	3-1	1973-74	0-0	2-2
1900-01	0-1	0-0	1974-75	0-0	1-1
1901-02	4-0	1-2	1975-76	3-0	1-2
1902-03	0-1	2-5	1980-81	2-2	1-3
1903-04	3-1	0-3	1981-82	2-3	0-2
1904-05	1-0	3-2	1982-83	0-1	0-0
1905-06	0-1	2-1	1983-84	1-1	1-1
1907-08	7-2	1-4	1984-85	0-2	1-3
1908-09	2-1	0-4	1990-91	0-0	0-2
1909-10	2-1	3-1	1993-94	2-3	2-2
1910-11	2-2	3-1	1996-97	1-1	4-1
1922-23	0-0	0-1	1997-98	1-1	3-0
1923-24	1-0	2-1	2003-04	1-0	0-2
1924-25	3-1	1-1	2004-05	2-0	2-1
1957-58	3-0	0-2			

Played for both

Joe Baker	Andy Gray — Ian Wallace
James Baxter	Frank Gray — Darren Ward
Harry Bedford	Greg Halford
Frank Bee	Danny Higginbotham
Fred Bett (WW2)	Stern John
Ian Bowyer	William Keeton
Thomas Bradshaw	Joseph McDonald
Raich Carter (WW2)	Alexander McNab (WW2)
Lee Chapman	Andy Marriott
Michael Chopra	Harry Martin
Andrew Cole	Neil Martin
Tim Coleman	Andy Melville
Danny Collins	Jim Montgomery
Colin Cooper	John O'Hare
Jack Craggs	Calvin Palmer
Terry Curran	Jack Poole
Peter Davenport	Mark Proctor
Daniel Edgar	Andy Reid
A. Fotheringham	Martin Scott
William Fraser	Nick Summerbee
William Fullarton	Walter Tinsley
George Goodchild	Colin Todd

FA Cup	Round			L. Cup	Round		
1890-91	3	H	4-0	1984-85	3	A	1-1
1896-97	2	H	1-3	1984-85	3 rep	H	1-0
1899-1900	2	A	0-3	2008-09	2	A	2-1
1929-30	5	H	2-2				
1929-30	5 rep	A	1-3				
1964-65	4	H	1-3				

Top scorers: George Holley and Johnny Campbell both with 10 goals

Notts County

	Home					Away				
	P	W	D	L	F	A	P	W	D	L	F	A
League	37	21	10	6	85	35	37	5	12	20	36	69
FA Cup	4	3	0	1	8	2	4	1	2	1	6	6
L. Cup	0	0	0	0	0	0	1	0	0	1	1	2
Other	1	0	1	0	0	0	2	1	0	1	2	3
Total	**41**	**24**	**11**	**7**	**93**	**37**	**44**	**7**	**14**	**23**	**45**	**80**

Season	H	A	Season	H	A	Played for both	
1890-91	4-0	1-2	1914-15	3-1	1-2	Brett Angell	Bobby Mimms
1891-92	4-0	0-1	1919-20	3-1	2-2	Cyril Brown	Dennis O'Donnell
1892-93	2-2	1-3	1923-24	1-1	2-1	Raich Carter (WW2)	Gary Owers
1897-98	2-0	1-0	1924-25	0-1	1-4	James Chalmers	Simon Ramsden
1898-99	1-1	2-5	1925-26	3-1	0-2	Stephen Coglin	George Robinson (WW2)
1899-1900	5-0	1-3	1973-74	1-2	4-1	Frank Cresswell	David Rush
1900-01	1-1	2-2	1974-75	3-0	0-0	Shaun Cunnington	John Smeaton (WW2)
1901-02	2-1	0-2	1975-76	4-0	0-0	William Death	Darren Ward
1902-03	2-1	0-0	1977-78	3-1	2-2	John Dowsey	David Watson
1903-04	4-1	1-2	1978-79	3-0	1-1	Len Duns (WW2)	Jeff Whitley
1904-05	5-0	2-2	1979-80	3-1	1-0	Ernest England	
1905-06	1-3	1-4	1981-82	1-1	0-2	John Fraser	
1906-07	3-1	0-0	1982-83	1-1	1-0	Bernard Gaughran	
1907-08	4-3	0-4	1983-84	0-0	1-6	William Gibson	
1908-09	0-1	0-0	1987-88	1-1	1-2	Iain Hesford	
1909-10	0-3	1-1	1992-93	2-2	1-3	Alexander Lockie	
1910-11	1-1	1-1	1993-94	2-0	0-1	James Logan	
1911-12	5-0	1-3	1994-95	1-2	2-3	Seamus McDonagh	
1912-13	4-0	1-2				Isaac McGorian	

FA Cup	Round			L. Cup	Round		
1890-91	Semi		3-3 At Bramall Lane	1975-76	2	A	1-2
1890-91	Semi rep		0-2 At Bramall Lane				
1891-92	1	H	4-0				
1905-06	1	H	1-0				
1972-73	3	A	1-1				
1972-73	3 rep	H	2-0				
1992-93	2	A	2-0				
2010-11	3	H	1-2				

Top scorer: 4 players with 6 goals
Sunderland lost 0-1 at Trent Bridge and drew 0-0 at Newcastle Road in the end of 1896-97 Test Match Series that determined who stayed in Division One.
Sunderland drew 2-2, but won 3-1 on penalties, in a 2nd Round Zenith Data Systems Cup tie in 1990-91 at Meadow Lane.

Oldham Athletic

	Home					Away				
	P	W	D	L	F	A	P	W	D	L	F	A
League	20	12	4	4	41	23	20	2	10	8	19	31
FA Cup	1	1	0	0	2	0	1	0	0	1	1	2
L. Cup	1	1	0	0	7	1	0	0	0	0	0	0
Other	1	0	0	1	1	2	1	0	0	1	1	2
Total	23	14	4	5	51	26	22	2	10	10	21	35

Season	H	A	Season	H	A
1910-11	2-1	1-2	1975-76	2-0	1-1
1911-12	4-2	0-0	1977-78	3-1	1-1
1912-13	1-1	0-3	1978-79	3-0	0-0
1913-14	2-0	1-2	1979-80	4-2	0-3
1914-15	1-2	5-4	1985-86	0-3	2-2
1919-20	3-0	1-2	1986-87	0-2	1-1
1920-21	1-1	1-2	1988-89	3-2	2-2
1921-22	5-1	0-3	1989-90	2-3	1-2
1922-23	2-0	0-0	1994-95	0-0	0-0
1974-75	2-2	0-0	1995-96	1-0	2-1

Played for both

John Bollands	Ian Snodin
Darren Byfield	Alan Spence
Robert Carmichael	Thomas Wagstaffe
Andy Dibble	Keiren Westwood
Andy Gray	Tommy Wright
Vic Halom	Rodger Wylde
George Kinnell	
Chris Makin	
Sandy McAllister	
William Montgomery	

FA Cup	Round			L. Cup	Round		
1923-24	1	A	1-2	1962-63	2	H	7-1
1975-76	3	H	2-0				

Top scorer: Charlie Buchan 8 goals
Sunderland lost 1-2 in an Anglo-Scottish Cup group game in 1978-79 at Boundary Park
Sunderland lost 1-2 in an Anglo-Scottish Cup group game in 1979-80 at Roker Park

Oxford United

	Home					Away				
	P	W	D	L	F	A	P	W	D	L	F	A
League	13	10	1	2	25	5	13	5	4	4	13	15
FA Cup	1	0	1	0	1	1	2	1	0	1	3	4
Total	14	10	2	2	26	6	15	6	4	5	16	19

Season	H	A	Season	H	A
1970-71	0-1	0-0	1992-93	2-0	1-0
1971-72	3-0	0-2	1993-94	2-3	3-0
1972-73	1-0	1-5	1997-98	3-1	1-1
1973-74	0-0	1-0	1998-99	7-0	0-0
1974-75	2-0	0-1			
1975-76	1-0	1-1			
1988-89	1-0	4-2			
1989-90	1-0	1-0			
1991-92	2-0	0-2			

Played for both

John Byrne	David Rush
Tim Carter	Craig Russell
Robert Craig	Kenneth Smith
Marco Gabbiadini	Harry Thompson
Martin Gray	Colin Todd
Philip Gray	Ray Train
Stephen Hardwick	Dean Whitehead
Andy Melville	Billy Whitehurst
Anton Rogan	

FA Cup	Round		
1988-89	3	H	1-1
1988-89	3 rep	A	0-2
1991-92	4	A	3-2

Top scorer: Marco Gabbiadini 4 goals

Peterborough United

	Home					Away				
	P	W	D	L	F	A	P	W	D	L	F	A
League	2	2	0	0	5	0	2	1	0	1	5	6
FA Cup	1	1	0	0	7	1	1	1	0	0	2	0
Total	3	3	0	0	12	1	3	2	0	1	7	6

Season	H	A	Played for both		
1992-93	3-0	2-5	Frank Bee	Robert Ferguson	Lee Power
1993-94	2-0	3-1	Gary Breen	Len Hargreaves	Mark Prudhoe
			Cyril Brown	Michael Hellawell	Danny Rose
			David Buchanan	Lewin Nyatanga	David Rush
			Geoff Butler	Jack Overfield	David Swindlehurst
			David Corner	Reginald Pearce	Dale White
			John Cornforth		

FA Cup	Round		
1966-67	4	H	7-1
2011-12	3	A	2-0

Top scorers: Neil Martin and Phil Gray both with 3 goals

Plymouth Argyle

	Home						Away					
	P	W	D	L	F	A	P	W	D	L	F	A
League	12	9	1	2	29	11	12	3	3	6	15	16
FA Cup	3	3	0	0	8	2	0	0	0	0	0	0
Total	15	12	1	2	37	13	12	3	3	6	15	16

Season	H	A	Season	H	A	Played for both		
1959-60	4-0	0-0	1989-90	3-1	0-3	Russell Anderson	James Hindmarsh
1960-61	2-1	0-1	1991-92	0-1	0-1	Harold Buckle	Mick Horswill
1961-62	5-0	2-3	2004-05	5-1	1-2	Lee Chapman	Thomas McKenzie
1962-63	1-1	1-1	2006-07	2-3	2-0	James Clark	Matthew Middleton
1963-64	1-0	1-1				Doug Collins	Alan O'Neill
1975-76	2-1	0-1				William Fullarton	Lee Power
1986-87	2-1	4-2				James Hamilton	Ernest Taylor (WW2)
1988-89	2-1	4-1				Michael Heathcote	Nigel Walker

FA Cup	Round		
1911-12	1	H	3-1
1913-14	2	H	2-1
1938-39	3	H	3-0

Top scorers: Brian Clough and Gordon Armstrong both with 4 goals

Portsmouth

	Home						Away					
	P	W	D	L	F	A	P	W	D	L	F	A
League	49	24	16	9	98	57	49	11	16	22	72	92
FA Cup	1	1	0	0	1	0	1	0	0	1	1	2
L. Cup	1	1	0	0	2	1	1	0	1	0	0	0
Total	51	26	16	9	101	58	51	11	17	23	73	94

SUNDERLAND: THE COMPLETE RECORD

Season	H	A	Season	H	A	Played for both		
1927-28	3-3	5-3	1960-61	4-1	1-2	Steve Agnew	Edward Robson	
1928-29	5-0	0-4	1962-63	1-0	1-3	Brett Angell	Percy Saunders (WW2)	
1929-30	1-1	1-1	1963-64	3-0	4-2	Kevin Ball	Tommy Smith	
1930-31	0-0	1-1	1970-71	0-0	1-2	Tal Ben Haim	Thomas Stewart	
1931-32	5-1	0-0	1971-72	3-2	2-2	Stephen Berry	Fred Thompson	
1932-33	0-3	3-1	1972-73	2-0	3-2	Jock Brown	James Watson	
1933-34	0-2	0-0	1973-74	3-0	1-1	Harold Buckle	Derek Weddle	
1934-35	4-1	4-2	1974-75	4-1	2-4	Lee Chapman		
1935-36	5-0	2-2	1975-76	2-0	0-0	Ken Chisholm (WW2)		
1936-37	3-2	2-3	1985-86	1-3	0-3	Andrew Cole		
1937-38	0-2	0-1	1986-87	0-0	1-3	John Fraser		
1938-39	0-2	1-2	1988-89	4-0	0-2	Greg Halford		
1946-47	0-0	1-4	1989-90	2-2	3-3	Paul Hardyman		
1947-48	4-1	2-2	1991-92	1-0	0-1	Robert Hindmarch		
1948-49	1-4	0-3	1992-93	4-1	0-2	Richard Jackson		
1949-50	1-1	2-2	1993-94	1-2	1-0	John Lathan		
1950-51	0-0	0-0	1994-95	2-2	4-1	Liam Lawrence		
1951-52	3-1	2-0	1995-96	1-1	2-2	Thomas McKenzie		
1952-53	1-1	2-5	1997-98	2-1	4-1	George Martin		
1953-54	3-1	1-4	1998-99	2-0	1-1	George Metcalf		
1954-55	2-2	2-2	2005-06	1-4	1-2	Sulley Muntari		
1955-56	4-2	1-2	2007-08	2-0	0-1	Benjamin Mwaruwari		
1956-57	3-3	2-3	2008-09	1-2	1-3	Mart Poom		
1957-58	1-1	2-0	2009-10	1-1	1-1	Lee Power		
1959-60	2-0	2-1				Carl Robinson		

FA Cup	Round				L. Cup	Round		
1999-2000	3	H	1-0		1962-63	4	A	0-0
2009-10	4	A	1-2		1962-63	4 rep	H	2-1

Top scorer: David Halliday 8 goals

Port Vale

	Home					Away				
	P	W	D	L	F	A	P	W	D	L	F	A
League	7	3	4	0	12	7	7	3	3	1	10	8
FA Cup	3	1	2	0	5	2	2	0	0	2	1	5
Other	1	0	0	1	1	2	0	0	0	0	0	0
Total	11	4	6	1	18	11	9	3	3	3	11	13

Season	H	A	Played for both		
1987-88	2-1	1-0	Reuben Agboola	George Collin	Colin West
1989-90	2-2	2-1	Brett Angell	Alex Donaldson (WW1)	Jack Young
1991-92	1-1	3-3	Archie Annan	Colin Grainger	
1994-95	1-1	0-0	Paul Atkinson	David Healy	
1995-96	0-0	1-1	Peter Barnes	Craig James	
1997-98	4-2	1-3	Billy Bingham	Craig Russell	
1998-99	2-0	2-0	Arthur Bridgett	Barry Siddall	

FA Cup	Round		
1935-36	3	H	2-2
1935-36	3 rep	A	0-2
1961-62	4	H	0-0
1961-62	4 rep	A	1-3
1991-92	3	H	3-0

Top scorer: 5 players with 2 goals
Sunderland lost 1-2 in a Zenith Data Systems Cup 1st Round game in 1989-90 at Roker Park

SUNDERLAND HEAD TO HEAD RECORDS

Preston North End

	Home					Away				
	P	W	D	L	F	A	P	W	D	L	F	A
League	53	32	16	5	101	50	53	13	14	26	71	103
FA Cup	4	4	0	0	10	1	5	3	1	1	12	7
L. Cup	1	1	0	0	3	2	2	0	1	1	1	3
Total	58	37	16	5	114	53	60	16	16	28	84	113

Season	H	A	Season	H	A
1890-91	3-0	0-0	1935-36	4-2	2-3
1891-92	4-1	1-3	1936-37	3-0	0-2
1892-93	2-0	2-1	1937-38	0-2	0-0
1893-94	6-3	2-1	1938-39	1-2	1-2
1894-95	2-0	0-1	1946-47	0-2	2-2
1895-96	4-1	1-4	1947-48	0-2	2-2
1896-97	1-1	3-5	1948-49	0-0	3-1
1897-98	1-0	0-2	1951-52	0-0	2-4
1898-99	1-0	3-2	1952-53	2-2	2-3
1899-1900	1-0	1-0	1953-54	2-2	2-6
1900-01	3-1	1-1	1954-55	2-1	1-3
1904-05	3-2	1-3	1955-56	2-2	2-2
1905-06	2-0	1-1	1956-57	0-0	0-6
1906-07	1-0	0-2	1957-58	0-0	0-3
1907-08	4-1	2-3	1961-62	0-0	1-0
1908-09	2-0	0-1	1962-63	2-1	1-1
1909-10	2-1	0-1	1963-64	4-0	1-1
1910-11	1-1	2-0	1971-72	4-3	3-1
1911-12	3-0	3-0	1972-73	0-0	3-1
1913-14	3-1	2-2	1973-74	2-1	0-1
1919-20	1-0	2-5	1978-79	3-1	1-3
1920-21	2-2	1-1	1979-80	1-1	1-2
1921-22	1-0	1-1	1987-88	1-1	2-2
1922-23	2-2	0-2	2003-04	3-3	2-0
1923-24	2-1	2-1	2004-05	3-1	2-3
1924-25	2-0	2-1	2006-07	0-1	1-4
1934-35	3-1	1-1			

Played for both

Sam Allardyce	Tommy Miller
Brett Angell	Bobby Mimms
Thomas Becton	Brian Mooney
Thomas Bradshaw	John Morley
Chris Brown	John Mullin
Darren Byfield	Jock Paterson
Darren Carter	William Read
James Chalmers	Thomas Rowlandson
George Collin	Leslie Scott
Neill Collins	Thomas Scott
Alfred Common	Barry Siddall
Daniele Dichio	Marcus Stewart
Stephen Doyle	William Thompson
Barry Dunn	William Troughear (WW1)
Stephen Elliott	Ross Wallace
Dickson Etuhu	Danny Welbeck
William Fulton	Frank Worthington
Andy Gray	
David Healy	
Joe Hinnigan	
Mel Holden	
John Kay	
Robert Kelly	
Kevin Kilbane	
Colin McLatchie	
James McNab	
Chris Makin	

FA Cup	Round		
1894-95	2	H	2-0
1895-96	1	H	4-1
1908-09	2	A	2-1
1913-14	3	H	2-0
1936-37	Final		3-1 At Wembley
1954-55	4	A	3-3
1954-55	4 rep	H	2-0
1962-63	3	A	4-1
2006-07	3	A	0-1

L. Cup	Round		
1974-75	2	A	0-2
1995-96	1 L1	A	1-1
1995-96	1 L2	H	3-2

Top scorer: Johnny Campbell, Arthur Bridgett and Charlie Buchan all with 10 goals

Queens Park Rangers

	Home						Away					
	P	W	D	L	F	A	P	W	D	L	F	A
League	14	8	3	3	21	12	14	4	3	7	18	24
FA Cup	1	1	0	0	4	0	0	0	0	0	0	0
Total	15	9	3	3	25	12	14	4	3	7	18	24

Season	H	A	Played for both		
1968-69	0-0	2-2	Brett Angell	Thomas McKenzie	
1970-71	3-1	0-2	Archie Brown	Hugh McMahon	
1971-72	0-1	1-2	John Byrne	Liam Miller	
1972-73	0-3	2-3	Pascal Chimbonda	Dennis O'Donnell	
1976-77	1-0	0-2	Djibril Cisse	Nedum Onuoha	
1979-80	3-0	0-0	Joseph Devine	Richard Ord	
1983-84	1-0	0-3	Daniele Dichio	Richard Parker	
1984-85	3-0	0-1	Anton Ferdinand	Jock Paterson	
1990-91	0-1	2-3	Michael Gilhooley	Tommy Smith	
1997-98	2-2	1-0	George Goddard	James Stephenson	
1998-99	1-0	2-2	Clarence Gregory	Andrew Thompson	
2004-05	2-2	3-1	James Hannah	Clive Walker	
2006-07	2-1	2-1	Michael Hellawell	Edward Watson	
2011-12	3-1	3-2	Leighton James	Isaac Webb	
			Joseph Knowles	George Whitelaw	

FA Cup	Round			
1956-57	3	H	4-0	

Top scorer: Niall Quinn 4 goals

Reading

	Home					Away				
	P	W	D	L	F	A	P	W	D	L	F	A
League	7	3	2	2	12	8	7	2	1	4	6	9
FA Cup	1	0	1	0	1	1	2	1	0	1	4	3
Total	8	3	3	2	13	9	9	3	1	5	10	12

Season	H	A	Played for both		
1986-87	1-1	0-1	Adam Allan	Steve Hetzke	James Raine
1994-95	0-1	2-0	Philip Bach	John Huggins	William Raisbeck
1995-96	2-2	1-1	Thomas Bradshaw	Paul Lemon	Bruce Stuckey
1997-98	4-1	0-4	Jack Craggs	Chris Makin	Walter Tinsley
2003-04	2-0	2-0	James Crawford	Hugh McMahon	Billy Whitehurst
2004-05	1-2	0-1	Len Duns (WW2)	John Mapson	Alwyne Wilks
2007-08	2-1	1-2	Samuel Ellison	Thomas Naisby	David Willis
			Cyril Gilhespy	James Oakley	Charles Yorke
			Greg Halford	John Oster	Benny Yorston (WW2)
			Ian Harte	Ian Porterfield	

FA Cup	Round			
1972-73	4	H	1-1	
1972-73	4 rep	A	3-1	
1989-90	3	A	1-2	

Top scorer: 4 players with 2 goals

Redcar

FA Cup	Round		
1884-85	1	A	1-3
1885-86	1	A	0-3

Rotherham United

SUNDERLAND HEAD TO HEAD RECORDS

	Home						Away					
	P	W	D	L	F	A	P	W	D	L	F	A
League	9	5	3	1	18	5	9	5	2	2	18	8
FA Cup	1	1	0	0	1	0	2	1	1	0	6	2
L. Cup	1	1	0	0	2	0	1	0	1	0	3	3
Other	1	1	0	0	7	1	0	0	0	0	0	0
Total	12	8	3	1	28	6	12	6	4	2	27	13

Season	H	A	Played for both		
1958-59	1-1	4-0	Kevin Arnott	Mark Lynch	Michael Proctor
1959-60	1-2	0-1	Darren Byfield	Seamus McDonagh	Carl Robinson
1960-61	1-1	0-0	Doug Collins	John McGinley	Martin Scott
1961-62	4-0	3-0	Jack Cowell	Hugh McMahon	David Watson
1962-63	2-0	2-4	Anthony Cullen	Bobby Mimms	Martin Woods
1963-64	2-0	2-2	William Death	Robert Mitchell	Rodger Wylde
1987-88	3-0	4-1	John S. Foster	John Mullin	
2003-04	0-0	2-0	Vic Halom	Thomas Porteous	
2004-05	4-1	1-0	Grant Leadbitter	Ian Porterfield	

FA Cup	Round			L. Cup	Round		
1981-82	3	A	1-1	1981-82	2 L1	H	2-0
1981-82	3 rep	H	1-0	1981-82	2 L2	A	3-3
1997-98	3	A	5-1				

Top scorers: Kevin Phillips and Brian Clough both with 4 goals
Sunderland won 7-1 in a Sherpa Van Trophy Preliminary Round (North) match in 1987-88 at Roker Park.

Scarborough

Season	Round				Played for both	
1987-88	1	A	3-0	Sherpa Van Trophy	Colin Beesley	John Moore
				Preliminary Round	Gary Bennett	Geoff Power
					Stephen Brodie	Robert Robinson (b.1910)
					Ricardo Gabbiadini	James Shoulder
					Roy Greenwood	Ian Snodin
					John Kay	Andrew Yorke
					Seamus McDonagh	

Scunthorpe United

	Home						Away					
	P	W	D	L	F	A	P	W	D	L	F	A
League	6	5	1	0	11	1	6	0	3	3	9	14
FA Cup	1	0	1	0	1	1	2	1	0	1	3	3
L. Cup	1	1	0	0	2	0	0	0	0	0	0	0
Total	8	6	2	0	14	2	8	1	3	4	12	17

Season	H	A	Played for both	
1958-59	3-1	2-3	Keith Armstrong	Darren Holloway
1959-60	1-0	1-3	Peter Beagrie	George Hunter
1960-61	2-0	3-3	John Cornforth	Ian Lawther
1961-62	4-0	1-3	Wayne Entwistle	Stan Lloyd
1962-63	0-0	1-1	Tony Ford	Lionel Perez
1963-64	1-0	1-1	John Hawley	Richard Ryan

FA Cup	Round			L. Cup	Round		
1952-53	3	H	1-1	1962-63	3	H	2-0
1952-53	3 rep	A	2-1				
1987-88	2	A	1-2				

Top scorer: Ambrose Fogarty 4 goals

Sheffield United

	Home					Away				
	P	W	D	L	F	A	P	W	D	L	F	A
League	63	40	14	9	137	65	63	17	10	36	74	118
FA Cup	4	3	0	1	5	3	4	3	1	0	8	4
L. Cup	2	1	1	0	3	2	2	0	0	2	0	3
Other	1	1	0	0	2	0	2	0	0	2	2	4
Total	70	45	15	10	147	70	71	20	11	40	84	129

Season	H	A	Season	H	A
1893-94	4-1	0-1	1929-30	3-2	2-4
1894-95	2-0	0-4	1930-31	2-1	3-3
1895-96	1-1	2-1	1931-32	1-0	1-1
1896-97	0-1	0-3	1932-33	2-2	0-3
1897-98	3-1	0-1	1933-34	5-0	0-2
1898-99	1-0	0-2	1946-47	2-1	2-4
1899-1900	1-1	2-2	1947-48	1-1	2-3
1900-01	3-0	0-2	1948-49	2-0	5-2
1901-02	3-1	1-0	1953-54	2-2	3-1
1902-03	0-0	0-1	1954-55	2-2	0-1
1903-04	2-1	2-1	1955-56	3-2	3-2
1904-05	2-1	0-1	1958-59	4-1	1-3
1905-06	2-0	1-4	1959-60	5-1	2-1
1906-07	1-2	2-3	1960-61	1-1	1-0
1907-08	4-1	3-5	1964-65	3-1	0-3
1908-09	3-1	2-0	1965-66	4-1	2-2
1909-10	1-0	0-3	1966-67	4-1	0-2
1910-11	0-2	2-1	1967-68	2-1	2-1
1911-12	0-0	2-1	1970-71	0-0	0-1
1912-13	1-0	3-1	1977-78	5-1	1-1
1913-14	1-2	0-1	1978-79	6-2	2-3
1914-15	3-2	1-1	1985-86	2-1	0-1
1919-20	3-2	1-3	1986-87	1-2	1-2
1920-21	3-1	1-1	1989-90	1-1	3-1
1921-22	1-0	1-4	1990-91	0-1	2-0
1922-23	3-5	1-3	1994-95	1-0	0-0
1923-24	2-2	1-1	1995-96	2-0	0-0
1924-25	0-1	1-2	1997-98	4-2	0-2
1925-26	6-1	1-4	1998-99	0-0	4-0
1926-27	3-0	0-2	2003-04	3-0	1-0
1927-28	0-1	1-5	2004-05	1-0	0-1
1928-29	4-4	0-4			

Played for both

Brett Angell	James Raine
Archie Annan	Andy Reid
Kevin Arnott	Carl Robinson
Phil Bardsley	Wilf Rostron
Peter Beagrie	Martin Smith
Joseph Bolton	Jonathan Stead
Peter Boyle	Anthony Stokes
Arthur Brown	Trevor Swinburne
Norman Case	Paul Thirlwell
Neill Collins	Billy Whitehurst
Alfred Common	Cliff Whitelum
Jody Craddock	William Wood
Terry Curran	
Brian Deane	
Andy Dibble	
Alex Donaldson	
John Gibson	
Colin Grainger	
Andy Gray	
Greg Halford	
Michael Henderson	
Don Hutchison	
Samuel Kemp	
Matthew Kilgallon	
Albert Lewis	
Denis Longhorn	
John MacPhail	
Joseph McGhie	
John Moore	
Nyron Nosworthy	
Jack Poole (WW1)	
Alan Quinn	

FA Cup	Round		
1892-93	2	A	3-1
1900-01	1	H	1-2
1908-09	1	A	3-2
1925-26	4	A	2-1
1930-31	5	H	2-1
1955-56	5	A	0-0
1955-56	5 rep	H	1-0
2003-04	6	H	1-0

L. Cup	Round		
1965-66	2	H	2-1
1966-67	2	H	1-1
1966-67	2 rep	A	0-1
2002-03	4	A	0-2

Top scorer: Charlie Buchan 12 goals
Sunderland won 3-2 in a two leg Division One Play-off semi-final in 1997-98; 1st leg lost 1-2 at Bramall Lane and 2nd leg won 2-0 at the Stadium of Light.
Sunderland lost 1-2 in an Anglo-Scottish Cup group game in 1979-80 at Bramall Lane.

Sheffield Wednesday

	Home					Away				
	P	W	D	L	F	A	P	W	D	L	F	A
League	56	31	11	14	111	64	56	15	15	26	66	108
FA Cup	3	1	0	2	3	2	4	1	1	2	2	3
L. Cup	0	0	0	0	0	0	1	0	0	1	2	4
Total	59	32	11	16	114	66	61	16	16	29	70	115

Season	H	A	Season	H	A	Played for both	
1892-93	4-2	2-3	1931-32	3-1	2-3	Bob Bolder	Jackie Robinson
1893-94	1-1	2-2	1932-33	1-2	1-3	Alexander Brady	Wilf Rostron
1894-95	3-1	2-1	1933-34	4-0	0-2	Terry Butcher	John Smith
1895-96	2-1	0-3	1934-35	2-2	2-2	Lee Chapman	Colin Symm
1896-97	0-0	0-0	1935-36	5-1	0-0	John Cooke	Emerson Thome
1897-98	1-0	1-0	1936-37	2-1	0-2	Terry Cooke	Chris Turner
1898-99	2-0	1-0	1950-51	5-1	0-3	Terry Curran	Brian Usher
1900-01	1-0	0-1	1952-53	2-1	0-4	Michael Gray	Chris Waddle
1901-02	1-2	1-1	1953-54	2-4	2-2	Len Hargreaves	Colin West
1902-03	0-1	0-1	1954-55	2-0	2-1	Iain Hesford	Paul A. Williams
1903-04	0-1	0-0	1956-57	5-2	2-3	David Hodgson	Rodger Wylde
1904-05	3-0	1-1	1957-58	3-3	3-3	James Holton	
1905-06	2-0	3-3	1958-59	3-3	0-6	Allan Johnston	
1906-07	1-1	1-2	1964-65	3-0	0-2	Kenwyne Jones	
1907-08	1-2	3-2	1965-66	0-2	1-3	Graham Kavanagh	
1908-09	4-2	5-2	1966-67	2-0	0-5	English McConnell	
1909-10	2-0	0-1	1967-68	0-2	1-0	Fred McIver	
1910-11	1-2	1-1	1968-69	0-0	1-1	Hugh McMahon	
1911-12	0-0	0-8	1969-70	1-2	0-2	William Marsden	
1912-13	0-2	2-1	1970-71	3-1	2-1	Tommy Miller	
1913-14	0-1	1-2	1971-72	2-0	0-3	Brian Mooney	
1914-15	3-1	2-1	1972-73	1-1	0-1	Daryl Murphy	
1919-20	2-1	2-0	1973-74	3-1	1-0	Ian Porterfield	
1926-27	4-1	1-4	1974-75	3-0	2-0	Mark Proctor	
1927-28	2-3	0-0	1984-85	0-0	2-2	Mark Prudhoe	
1928-29	4-3	1-2	1996-97	1-1	1-2	Alan Quinn	
1929-30	2-4	1-1	1999-2000	1-0	2-0	Michael Reddy	
1930-31	5-1	2-7	2006-07	1-0	4-2	Carl Robinson	

FA Cup	Round		
1895-96	2	A	1-2
1897-98	1	H	0-1
1901-02	1	A	1-0
1906-07	3	A	0-0
1906-07	3 rep	H	0-1
1971-72	3	H	3-0
1992-93	4	A	0-1

L. Cup	Round		
2001-02	2	A	2-4

Top scorer: Bobby Gurney 12 goals

Shrewsbury Town

	Home						Away					
	P	W	D	L	F	A	P	W	D	L	F	A
League	4	3	1	0	7	3	4	3	1	0	5	2
Total	4	3	1	0	7	3	4	3	1	0	5	2

Season	H	A	Played for both		
1979-80	2-1	2-1	Sam Aiston	James Holton	Stanley Ramsay
1985-86	2-0	2-1	Ian Atkins	John Kay	Carl Robinson
1986-87	1-1	1-0	Alan Brown	George Lawley	Kenneth Smith
1988-89	2-1	0-0	John Cornforth	Thomas Lynch	Sean Thornton
			Michael Heathcote	John Moore	Neil Wainwright

Top scorers: Nick Pickering and Gordon Armstrong both with 2 goals

Southampton

	Home					Away				
	P	W	D	L	F	A	P	W	D	L	F	A
League	23	11	6	6	36	21	23	4	4	15	22	43
FA Cup	4	3	1	0	7	0	5	2	1	2	9	11
Total	27	14	7	6	43	21	28	6	5	17	31	54

Season	H	A	Season	H	A	Played for both		
1960-61	3-1	2-3	1981-82	2-0	0-1	Reuben Agboola	Kenwyne Jones
1961-62	3-0	0-2	1982-83	1-1	0-2	Thomas Allen	Bob Lee
1962-63	4-0	4-2	1983-84	0-2	1-1	Wayne Bridge	Chris Makin
1963-64	1-2	0-0	1984-85	3-1	0-1	David Connolly	Peter Meechan
1966-67	2-0	1-3	1990-91	1-0	1-3	Terry Curran	Jack Mitton
1967-68	0-3	2-3	1996-97	0-1	0-3	Calum Davenport	Jim Montgomery
1968-69	1-0	0-1	1999-2000	2-0	2-1	Kelvin Davis	Kevin Phillips
1969-70	2-2	1-1	2000-01	2-2	1-0	Rory Delap	John Small
1974-75	3-1	1-1	2001-02	1-1	0-2	John S. Foster	Barry Venison
1975-76	3-0	0-4	2002-03	0-1	1-2	Bernard Gaughran	David Watson
1977-78	0-0	2-4	2006-07	1-1	2-1	Danny Higginbotham	Frank Worthington
1980-81	1-2	1-2				Stern John	Charles Yorke

FA Cup	Round		
1930-31	3	H	2-0
1931-32	3	H	0-0
1931-32	3 rep	A	4-2
1936-37	3	A	3-2
1947-48	3	A	0-1
1950-51	4	H	2-0
1961-62	3	A	2-2
1961-62	3 rep	H	3-0
1984-85	3	A	0-4

Top scorer: 3 players with 4 goals

Southend United

	Home					Away					
	P	W	D	L	F	A	P	W	D	L	F	A
League	7	3	0	4	15	9	7	5	0	2	10	6
Total	7	3	0	4	15	9	7	5	0	2	10	6

Season	H	A	Played for both		
1987-88	7-0	4-1	Brett Angell	George Hunter	Mark Prudhoe
1991-92	1-2	0-2	Richard Bell (WW2)	Archibald Jackson	Arnau Riera
1992-93	2-4	1-0	Norman Brown	David Lindsay	Melvyn Slack
1993-94	0-2	1-0	Lee Chapman	Hugh McMahon	Duncan Stewart
1994-95	0-1	1-0	John Conner	Gary Moore	Harry Threadgold
1995-96	1-0	2-0	David Elliott	William Morrison	Paul A. Williams
2006-07	4-0	1-3	Alan Foggon	Daryl Murphy	William Whelan
			George Goddard	Roy O'Donovan	David Young

Top scorer: Eric Gates 4 goals

Sporting Lisbon

Season	Round					Played for both
1973-74	2 L1	H	2-1	European Cup Winners' Cup		Phil Babb
1973-74	2 L2	A	0-2	European Cup Winners' Cup		Rodger Wylde

Stockport County

	Home					Away				
	P	W	D	L	F	A	P	W	D	L	F	A
League	2	2	0	0	5	1	2	1	1	0	2	1
L. Cup	1	0	0	1	1	2	1	0	1	0	1	1
Total	3	2	0	1	6	3	3	1	2	0	3	2

Season	H	A	Played for both		
1997-98	4-1	1-1	Brett Angell	John S. Foster	William Robinson (WW2)
1998-99	1-0	1-0	Joseph Butler	James Hindmarsh	Barry Siddall
			Chris Byrne	William Holden	Arthur Welsby
			John Cooke	Michael Ingham	Andrew Welsh
			Kevin Cooper	Ian Lawther	George Whitelaw
			John Curtis	Mark Lynch	Leslie Wilkins
			Peter Davenport	James McGuigan	Frank Worthington
			Andy Dibble	James McNab	Rodger Wylde
			Wayne Entwistle	Robert Marshall	

L. Cup	Round		
1980-81	2 L1	A	1-1
1980-81	2 L2	H	1-2

Top scorer: Niall Quinn 3 goals

Stoke City

	Home						Away				
	P	W	D	L	F	A	P	W	D	L	F	A
League	64	41	16	7	125	41	64	19	13	32	63	92
FA Cup	4	2	2	0	7	2	5	0	3	2	5	8
L. Cup	1	0	0	1	0	2	1	0	0	1	0	3
Total	69	43	18	8	132	45	70	19	16	35	68	103

Season	H	A	Season	H	A	Played for both	
1891-92	4-1	3-1	1960-61	4-0	0-0	Sam Aiston	Mark Prudhoe
1892-93	3-1	1-0	1961-62	2-1	0-1	Peter Beagrie	Dick Roose
1893-94	4-0	0-2	1962-63	0-0	1-2	Keith Bertschin	Leslie Scott
1894-95	3-1	5-2	1964-65	2-2	1-3	Steve Bould	Victor Shore
1895-96	4-1	0-5	1965-66	2-0	1-1	Paul Bracewell	Barry Siddall
1896-97	4-1	1-0	1966-67	2-1	0-1	Arthur Bridgett	Thomas Sorensen
1897-98	4-0	1-0	1967-68	3-1	1-2	Lee Chapman	Victor Staley
1898-99	2-0	0-1	1968-69	4-1	1-2	Clive Clarke	Paul Stewart
1899-1900	3-0	2-1	1969-70	0-3	2-4	Danny Collins	Dennis Tueart
1900-01	6-1	0-0	1976-77	0-0	0-0	Jody Craddock	Loek Ursem
1901-02	2-0	0-3	1977-78	1-0	0-0	Rory Delap	John Walker
1902-03	0-0	1-1	1978-79	0-1	1-0	Tony Ford	Mark Watkins
1903-04	3-0	1-3	1980-81	0-2	1-0	Marton Fulop	David Watson
1904-05	3-1	3-1	1981-82	0-2	1-0	Marco Gabbiadini	Dean Whitehead
1905-06	1-0	0-1	1982-83	2-2	1-0	Patrick Gallacher	Billy Whitehurst
1906-07	3-1	2-2	1983-84	2-2	1-2	Howard Gayle	Jeff Whitley
1922-23	2-0	2-1	1984-85	1-0	2-2	James Gemmell	Stephen Wright
1933-34	4-1	0-3	1985-86	2-0	0-1	Danny Higginbotham	
1934-35	4-1	3-0	1986-87	2-0	0-3	Bert Hobson (WW1)	

1935-36	1-0	2-0	1988-89	1-1	0-2	Ernest Hodkin
1936-37	3-0	3-5	1989-90	2-1	2-0	Thomas Hyslop
1937-38	1-1	0-0	1993-94	0-1	0-1	Michael Ingham
1938-39	3-0	1-3	1994-95	1-0	1-0	Kenwyne Jones
1946-47	0-1	0-0	1995-96	0-0	0-1	Joseph Kasher
1947-48	1-0	1-3	1997-98	3-0	2-1	Graham Kavanagh
1948-49	1-1	0-0	2003-04	1-1	1-3	George Kinnell
1949-50	3-0	1-2	2004-05	1-0	1-0	Liam Lawrence
1950-51	1-1	4-2	2006-07	2-2	1-2	Dominic Matteo
1951-52	0-1	1-1	2008-09	2-0	0-1	William Maxwell
1952-53	1-1	0-3	2009-10	0-0	0-1	Iain Munro
1958-59	3-1	0-0	2010-11	2-0	2-3	Calvin Palmer
1959-60	0-2	1-3	2011-12	4-0	1-0	Charles Parker

FA Cup	Round				L. Cup	Round		
1891-92	3	A	2-2		1972-73	2	A	0-3
1891-92	3 rep	H	4-0		1978-79	2	H	0-2
1931-32	4	H	1-1					
1931-32	4 rep	A	1-1					
1931-32	4 rep 2		1-2	At Maine Road				
1951-52	3	H	0-0					
1951-52	3 rep	A	1-3					
1975-76	5	A	0-0					
1975-76	5 rep	H	2-1					

Top scorer: Johnny Campbell 12 goals

Swansea City

	Home					Away				
	P	W	D	L	F	A	P	W	D	L	F	A
League	10	7	2	1	23	8	10	3	3	4	13	22
FA Cup	2	2	0	0	4	0	1	0	1	0	2	2
L. Cup	0	0	0	0	0	0	1	0	0	1	1	3
Total	12	9	2	1	27	8	12	3	4	5	16	27

Season	H	A	Played for both		
1958-59	2-1	0-5	Reuben Agboola	Leighton James	Colin West
1959-60	4-0	2-1	Stephen Brodie	Andy Melville	Leslie Wilkins
1960-61	2-1	3-3	Thomas Butler	Gary Moore	Paul L. Williams
1961-62	7-2	1-1	Lee Chapman	Colin Pascoe	
1962-63	3-1	4-3	John Cornforth	William Read	
1963-64	1-0	2-1	Anthony Cullen	Edward Robson	
1979-80	1-1	1-3	Ray Daniel	Henry Scott	
1981-82	0-1	0-2	Trevor Ford	John Smeaton (WW2)	
1982-83	1-1	0-3	John Foreman	John Tones	
2011-12	2-0	0-0	David Hodgson	Ronald Turnbull	

FA Cup	Round				L. Cup	Round			
1936-37	5	H	3-0	As Swansea Town	1963-64	2	A	1-3	As Swansea Town
1954-55	5	A	2-2	As Swansea Town					
1954-55	5 rep	H	1-0	As Swansea Town					

Top scorer: Brian Clough 6 goals

Swindon Town

	Home					Away				
	P	W	D	L	F	A	P	W	D	L	F	A
League	12	8	3	1	28	8	12	3	3	6	13	18
FA Cup	1	1	0	0	4	2	0	0	0	0	0	0
L. Cup	1	1	0	0	3	2	1	0	0	1	1	3
Other	0	0	0	0	0	0	1	0	0	1	0	1
Total	14	10	3	1	35	12	14	3	3	8	14	22

Season	H	A	Played for both	
1963-64	6-0	0-1	Stephen Berry	Tommy Miller
1970-71	5-2	0-2	Thomas Bradshaw	Albert Milton
1971-72	1-0	1-1	James Chalmers	Michael Proctor
1972-73	3-2	1-1	Frederick Cooke	Michael Reddy
1973-74	4-1	2-0	Charles Crossley	Nick Summerbee
1988-89	4-0	1-4	Shay Given	Paul Thirlwell
1989-90	2-2	2-0	Roy Greenwood	Percy Whipp
1991-92	0-0	3-5	Gordon Gunson	Leslie Wilkins
1992-93	0-1	0-1	Fred Hall (WW2)	
1994-95	1-0	0-1	Gareth Hall	
1997-98	0-0	2-1	George Lawley	
1998-99	2-0	1-1	John Mapson	

FA Cup	Round				L. Cup	Round		
1912-13	3	H	4-2		1985-86	2 L1	H	3-2
					1985-86	2 L2	A	1-3

Top scorer: Kevin Phillips 4 goals
Sunderland lost 0-1 in a Division One Play Off Final in 1989-90 at Wembley. However Sunderland were promoted as Swindon Town were adjudged to have breached 36 League rules, mainly involving illegal payments to players.

Tottenham Hotspur

	Home					Away				
	P	W	D	L	F	A	P	W	D	L	F	A
League	49	22	14	13	75	48	49	13	13	23	57	82
FA Cup	2	0	1	1	2	5	5	1	0	4	4	14
L. Cup	1	0	1	0	0	0	2	1	0	1	3	3
Total	52	22	16	14	77	53	56	15	13	28	64	99

Season	H	A	Season	H	A	Played for both	
1909-10	3-1	1-5	1965-66	2-0	0-3	Ben Alnwick	Joseph Shaw
1910-11	4-0	1-1	1966-67	0-1	0-1	Darren Bent	Paul Stewart
1911-12	1-1	0-0	1967-68	0-1	0-3	Ivor Broadis	Teemu Tainio
1912-13	2-2	2-1	1968-69	0-0	1-5	Fraizer Campbell	Chris Waddle
1913-14	2-0	4-1	1969-70	2-1	1-0	James Chalmers	John Whitbourn
1914-15	5-0	6-0	1976-77	2-1	1-1	Pascal Chimbonda	
1920-21	0-1	0-0	1977-78	1-2	3-2	Warney Cresswell (WW1)	
1921-22	2-0	0-1	1980-81	1-1	0-0	Charles Crossley (WW1)	
1922-23	2-0	1-0	1981-82	0-2	2-2	John Curtis	
1923-24	1-0	1-1	1982-83	0-1	1-1	Calum Davenport	
1924-25	4-1	0-1	1983-84	1-1	0-3	Marton Fulop	
1925-26	3-0	0-1	1984-85	1-0	0-2	Philip Gray	
1926-27	3-2	2-0	1990-91	0-0	3-3	Fred Hall (WW2)	
1927-28	0-0	1-3	1996-97	0-4	0-2	James Hartley	
1933-34	6-0	1-3	1999-2000	2-1	1-3	Alan Hutton	
1934-35	1-2	1-1	2000-01	2-3	1-2	Joseph Knowles	
1951-51	0-0	1-1	2001-02	1-2	1-2	Steed Malbranque	

1952-53	0-1	0-2	2002-03	2-0	1-4	Fred Mearns
1953-54	1-1	2-2	2005-06	1-1	2-3	Bobby Mimms
1954-55	4-3	3-0	2007-08	1-0	0-2	William B Murray
1955-56	1-1	1-0	2008-09	1-1	2-1	George Payne
1956-57	3-2	3-2	2009-10	3-1	0-2	Andy Reid
1957-58	0-2	2-5	2010-11	1-2	1-1	Danny Rose
1958-59	1-1	1-0	2011-12	0-0	0-1	Louis Saha
1964-65	2-1	0-3				Ian Sampson

FA Cup	Round				L. Cup	Round		
1898-99	2	A	1-2		1984-85	4	H	0-0
1914-15	1	A	1-2		1984-85	4 rep	A	2-1
1937-38	6	A	1-0		1996-97	3	A	1-2
1949-50	4	A	1-5					
1960-61	6	H	1-1					
1960-61	6 rep	A	0-5					
1994-95	4	H	1-4					

Top scorer: Charlie Buchan 9 goals

Tranmere Rovers

	Home					Away				
	P	W	D	L	F	A	P	W	D	L	F	A
League	7	4	2	1	13	4	7	1	0	6	4	11
FA Cup	0	0	0	0	0	0	2	0	0	2	0	2
Other	1	1	0	0	2	0	0	0	0	0	0	0
Total	8	5	2	1	15	4	9	1	0	8	4	13

Season	H	A	Played for both		
1991-92	1-1	0-1	Sam Aiston	Michael Kay	Craig Russell
1992-93	1-0	1-2	Phil Babb	David Kelly	Barry Siddall
1993-94	3-2	1-4	Alec Chamberlain	Dariusz Kubicki	Nick Summerbee
1994-95	0-1	0-1	Kevin Cooper	Jason McAteer	Sean Thornton
1995-96	0-0	0-2	William Eden	Malcolm Moore	Ray Train
1997-98	3-0	2-0	Roy Greenwood	John Mullin	Albert Wood
1998-99	5-0	0-1	Alan Hay	Thoms Myhre	Frank Worthington
			Archibald Jackson	Mark Proctor	
			Jack Jones (WW2)	Robert S. Robinson	

FA Cup	Round			
1997-98	4	A	0-1	
1999-2000	4	A	0-1	

Top scorers: Kevin Phillips and Don Goodman both with 4 goals
Sunderland won 2-0 in an Anglo-Italian Cup group game in 1993-94 at Roker Park

Vasas Budapest

Season	Round			
1973-74	1 L1	A	2-0	European Cup Winners' Cup
1973-74	1 L2	H	1-0	European Cup Winners' Cup

Walsall

	Home						Away					
	P	W	D	L	F	A	P	W	D	L	F	A
League	5	3	1	1	10	4	5	2	1	2	11	11
L. Cup	2	2	0	0	8	4	1	1	0	0	5	0
Total	7	5	1	1	18	8	6	3	1	2	16	11

Season	H	A	Played for both		
1961-62	3-0	3-4	Brett Angell	Don Goodman	Paul McShane
1962-63	5-0	3-2	John Bell	Archibald Jackson	James O'Neill
1987-88	1-1	2-2	Keith Bertschin	David Kelly	Mark Prudhoe
1988-89	0-3	0-2	Darren Byfield	George Lawley	Carl Robinson
2003-04	1-0	3-1	Jordan Cook	James Lawrence	Robert Smellie
			Kevin Lee	Paul Lemon	Ray Train
			Charles Crossley	Albert Lewis	Jack Vinall
			Marcos Di Giuseppe	Thomas Lloyd	
			Daniel Edgar	Alexander McNab (WW2)	

L Cup	Round			
1961-62	2		H	5-2
1999-2000	2 L1		H	3-2
1999-2000	2 L2		A	5-0

Top scorer: Brian Clough 6 goals

Watford

	Home					Away				
	P	W	D	L	F	A	P	W	D	L	F	A
League	17	10	5	2	44	17	17	3	8	6	20	31
FA Cup	2	1	0	1	1	1	0	0	0	0	0	0
L. Cup	1	1	0	0	1	0	2	2	0	0	3	0
Total	20	12	5	3	46	18	19	5	8	6	23	31

Season	H	A	Season	H	A	Played for both		
1970-71	3-3	1-1	2003-04	2-0	2-2	Norman Case	Adam Johnson	Colin West
1971-72	5-0	1-1	2004-05	4-2	1-1	James Chalmers	Joseph Lane	
1979-80	5-0	1-1				Alec Chamberlain	Ryan Noble	
1982-83	2-2	0-8				Michael Chopra	Nyron Nosworthy	
1983-84	3-0	1-2				David Connolly	Richard Parker	
1984-85	1-1	1-3				Tony Coton	Kevin Phillips	
1988-89	1-1	1-0				Joseph Curran	Mart Poom	
1989-90	4-0	1-1				Calum Davenport	Edward Robson	
1991-92	3-1	0-1				John S. Foster	Danny Rose	
1992-93	1-2	1-2				John Fraser	Wilf Rostron	
1993-94	2-0	1-1				Charles Gladwin	Henry Scott	
1994-95	1-3	1-0				Andrew Hamilton	John Smeaton (WW2)	
1995-96	1-1	3-3				Gerald Harrison	Tommy Smith	
1998-99	4-1	1-2				Michael Henderson	James Stephenson	
1999-2000	2-0	3-2				James Hindmarsh	Ray Train	

FA Cup	Round				L. Cup	Round			
1937-38	3		H	1-0	1984-85	5		A	1-0
2002-03	5		H	0-1	1996-97	2 L1		A	2-0
					1996-97	2 L2		H	1-0

Top scorer: Marcus Stewart 5 goals

West Bromwich Albion

	Home						Away					
	P	W	D	L	F	A	P	W	D	L	F	A
League	71	38	22	11	152	72	71	18	18	35	98	132
FA Cup	2	0	0	2	2	4	2	0	0	2	3	6
Total	73	38	22	13	154	76	73	18	18	37	101	138

Season	H	A	Season	H	A	Played for both
1890-91	1-1	4-0	1953-54	2-1	0-2	Sam Allardyce
1891-92	4-0	5-2	1954-55	4-2	2-2	Brett Angell
1892-93	8-1	3-1	1955-56	2-1	0-3	Peter Barnes
1893-94	2-1	3-2	1956-57	1-4	0-2	Darren Carter
1894-95	3-0	2-0	1957-58	2-0	0-3	Frank Cresswell
1895-96	7-1	1-1	1964-65	2-2	1-4	Shaun Cunnington
1896-97	2-1	0-1	1965-66	1-5	1-4	Andy Dibble
1897-98	0-2	2-2	1966-67	2-2	2-2	Daniele Dichio
1898-99	2-0	0-1	1967-68	0-0	0-0	Len Duns (WW2)
1899-1900	3-1	0-1	1968-69	0-1	0-3	Tony Ford
1900-01	3-0	0-1	1969-70	2-2	1-3	Carsten Fredgaard
1902/03	0-0	3-0	1973-74	1-1	1-1	Marton Fulop
1903/04	1-1	1-1	1974-75	3-0	0-1	Don Godman
1911-12	3-2	0-1	1975-76	2-0	0-0	Bernt Haas
1912-13	3-1	1-3	1976-77	6-1	3-2	Daniel Hegan
1913-14	0-0	1-2	1980-81	0-0	1-2	James Holton
1914-15	1-2	2-1	1981-82	1-2	3-2	Kevin Kilbane
1919-20	4-1	0-4	1982-83	1-1	0-3	Albert Lewis
1920-21	3-0	1-4	1983-84	3-0	1-3	Archibald McKenzie
1921-22	5-0	1-2	1984-85	1-1	0-1	Alexander McNab
1922-23	3-2	1-1	1986-87	0-3	2-2	Paul McShane
1923-24	2-0	1-3	1988-89	1-1	0-0	Andy Marriott
1924-25	3-0	1-2	1989-90	1-1	1-1	James Millar
1925-26	4-0	5-2	1993-94	1-0	1-2	James Nicholl
1926-27	4-1	0-3	1994-95	2-2	3-1	Kevin Phillips
1931-32	2-1	0-1	1995-96	0-0	1-0	Kieran Richardson
1932-33	2-2	1-5	1997-98	2-0	3-3	Barry Siddall
1933-34	2-2	5-6	1998-99	3-0	3-2	Colin Suggett
1934-35	0-1	1-1	2002-03	1-2	2-2	Stanislav Varga
1935-36	6-1	3-1	2003-04	0-1	0-0	William Walsh (WW2)
1936-37	1-0	4-6	2005-06	1-1	1-0	Isaac Webb
1937-38	3-0	6-1	2006-07	2-0	2-1	Colin West
1949-50	2-1	2-0	2008-09	4-0	0-3	
1950-51	1-1	1-3	2010-11	2-3	0-1	
1951-52	3-3	1-1	2011-12	2-2	0-4	
1952-53	1-0	1-1				

FA Cup	Round			
1911-12	3	H	1-2	
1922-23	2	A	1-2	
1956-57	4	A	2-4	
2001-02	3	H	1-2	

Top scorer: Johnny Campbell 14 goals

West Ham United

	Home					Away				
	P	W	D	L	F	A	P	W	D	L	F	A
League	36	19	7	10	62	42	36	9	11	16	45	72
FA Cup	2	0	1	1	1	2	2	1	0	1	3	3
L. Cup	4	1	1	2	6	7	2	0	0	2	2	4
Total	42	20	9	13	69	51	40	10	11	19	50	79

Season	H	A	Season	H	A	Played for both	
1923-24	0-0	1-0	1981-82	0-2	1-1	Christian Bassila	Henry Forster
1924-25	1-1	1-4	1982-83	1-0	1-2	Richard Bell	John S. Foster
1925-26	4-1	2-3	1983-84	0-1	1-0	David Bellion	James Heyes
1926-27	2-3	2-1	1984-85	0-1	0-1	Tal Ben Haim	Harold Hooper

SUNDERLAND HEAD TO HEAD RECORDS

1927-28	3-2	4-2	1989-90	4-3	0-5	Gary Breen	Don Hutchison
1928-29	4-1	3-3	1992-93	0-0	0-6	Wayne Bridge	David Kelly
1929-30	4-2	1-1	1996-97	0-0	0-2	Lee Chapman	Matthew Kilgallon
1930-31	6-1	3-0	1999-2000	1-0	1-1	Clive Clarke	George McCartney
1931-32	2-0	2-2	2000-01	1-1	2-0	Keith Coleman	Mick McGiven
1964-65	3-2	3-2	2001-02	1-0	0-3	Danny Collins	Andy Melville
1965-66	2-1	1-1	2002-03	0-1	0-2	David Connolly	William Moore
1966-67	2-4	2-2	2003-04	2-0	2-3	Charles Crossley	George Robinson (WW2)
1967-68	1-5	1-1	2004-05	0-2	2-1	Calum Davenport	William Robinson
1968-69	2-1	0-8	2005-06	1-1	0-2	Brian Deane	Bryan Robson
1969-70	0-1	1-1	2007-08	2-1	1-3	John Dowsey	David Swindlehurst
1976-77	6-0	1-1	2008-09	0-1	0-2	Ernest England	Leslie Wilkins
1978-79	2-1	3-3	2009-10	2-2	0-1	Anton Ferdinand	Benny Yorston (WW2)
1979-80	2-0	0-2	2010-11	1-0	3-0	John Foreman	

FA Cup	Round				L Cup	Round		
1928-29	3	A	0-1		1964-65	2	H	4-1
1991-92	5	H	1-1		1979-80	4	H	1-1
1991-92	5 rep	A	3-2		1979-80	4 rep	A	1-2
2000-01	5	H	0-1		1988-89	2 L1	H	0-3
					1988-89	2 L2	A	1-2
					2010-11	3	H	1-2

Top scorer: David Halliday 11 goals

Wigan Athletic

	Home					Away				
	P	W	D	L	F	A	P	W	D	L	F	A
League	9	3	3	3	15	11	9	2	4	3	9	10
FA Cup	1	0	0	1	0	3	0	0	0	0	0	0
Total	10	3	3	4	15	14	9	2	4	3	9	10

Season	H	A	Played for both	
1987-88	4-1	2-2	Titus Bramble	Graham Kavanagh
2003-04	1-1	0-0	Steven Caldwell	Alan Kennedy
2004-05	1-1	1-0	Lee Cattermole	Kevin Kilbane
2005-06	0-1	0-1	Pascal Chimbonda	James Lawrence
2007-08	2-0	0-3	David Connolly	Chris Makin
2008-09	1-2	1-1	Terry Cooke	Andy Marriott
2009-10	1-1	0-1	Wayne Entwistle	Emerson Thome
2010-11	4-2	1-1	Joe Hinnigan	Arthur Welsby
2011-12	1-2	4-1	Jack Jones (WW2)	

FA Cup	Round			
2007-08	3	H	0-3	

Top scorers: Marco Gabbiadini and Eric Gates both with 3 goals

Wimbledon

	Home						Away					
	P	W	D	L	F	A	P	W	D	L	F	A
League	5	3	1	1	7	6	5	1	1	3	4	8
FA Cup	0	0	0	0	0	0	2	0	0	2	2	4
L. Cup	0	0	0	0	0	0	1	0	0	1	2	3
Total	5	3	1	1	7	6	8	1	1	6	8	15

Season	H	A	Played for both	
1985-86	2-1	0-3	David Connolly	Mick Harford
1990-91	0-0	2-2	Kevin Cooper	Darren Holloway
1996-97	1-3	0-1	Kenny Cunningham	John Kay
1999-2000	2-1	0-1	Kelvin Davis	David Swindlehurst
2003-04	2-1	2-1	Wayne Entwistle	

FA Cup	Round				L. Cup	Round		
1986-87	3	A	1-2		1999-2000	3	A	2-3
1993-94	4	A	1-2					

Top scorers: David Swindlehurst and Marcus Stewart both with 2 goals

Wolverhampton Wanderers

	Home					Away							
	P	W	D	L	F	A	P	W	D	L	F	A	
League	55	30	14	11	119	66	55	15	12	28	72	91	
FA Cup	4	1	3	0	6	4	4	1	1	2	6	5	
L. Cup	1	1	0	0	5	0	1	0	1	0	1	1	
Total	60	32	17	11	130	70	60	16	14	30	79	97	

Season	H	A	Season	H	A	Played for both	
1890-91	3-4	3-0	1951-52	1-1	3-0	Thomas Allen	Alex Rae
1891-92	5-2	3-1	1952-53	5-2	1-1	Len Ashurst	Carl Robinson
1892-93	5-2	0-2	1953-54	3-2	1-3	Robert Best	Henry Scott
1893-94	6-0	1-2	1954-55	0-0	0-2	Joachim Bjorklund	Harold Shaw
1894-95	2-0	4-1	1955-56	1-1	1-3	Gary Breen	Paul Stewart
1895-96	2-2	3-1	1956-57	2-3	2-2	Paul Butler	Harry Thompson
1896-97	0-3	1-0	1957-58	0-2	0-5	Michael Coady	Darren Ward
1897-98	3-2	2-4	1964-65	1-2	0-3	Neill Collins	
1898-99	3-0	0-2	1967-68	2-0	1-2	David Connolly	
1899-1900	1-2	0-1	1968-69	2-0	1-1	Kevin Cooper	
1900-01	7-2	2-2	1969-70	2-1	0-1	Jody Craddock	
1901-02	2-0	2-4	1980-81	0-1	1-2	Peter Daniel	
1902-03	3-0	3-3	1981-82	0-0	1-0	Carlos Edwards	
1903-04	2-1	1-2	1983-84	3-2	0-0	Stephen Elliott	
1904-05	3-0	0-1	1989-90	1-1	1-0	Steven Fletcher	
1905-06	7-2	2-5	1991-92	1-0	0-1	George Goddard	
1932-33	0-1	2-0	1992-93	2-0	1-2	Don Goodman	
1933-34	3-3	6-1	1993-94	0-2	1-1	Michael Gray	
1934-35	0-0	2-1	1994-95	1-1	0-1	Greg Halford	
1935-36	3-1	4-3	1995-95	2-0	0-3	George Harper	
1936-37	6-2	1-1	1997-98	1-1	1-0	Daniel Hegan	
1937-38	1-0	0-4	1998-99	2-1	1-1	Robert Hindmarch	
1938-39	1-1	0-0	2004-05	3-1	1-1	Bert Hobson (WW1)	
1946-47	0-1	1-2	2006-07	2-1	1-1	Harold Hooper	
1947-48	2-1	1-2	2009-10	5-2	1-2	David Kelly	
1948-49	3-3	1-0	2010-11	1-3	2-3	Dariusz Kubicki	
1949-50	3-1	3-1	2011-12	0-0	1-2	Kevin Kyle	
1950-51	0-0	1-2				Jack Mitton	

FA Cup	Round				L. Cup	Round		
1904-05	1	H	1-1		1982-83	2 L1	A	1-1
1904-05	1 rep	A	0-1		1982-83	2 L2	H	5-0
1936-37	6	A	1-1					
1936-37	6 rep	H	2-2					
1936-37	6 rep2		4-0	At Hillsborough				
1950-51	6	H	1-1					
1950-51	6 rep	A	1-3					
1954-55	6	H	2-0					

Top scorer: Jimmy Millar 15 goals

Wrexham

	Home					Away					
	P	W	D	L	F	A	P	W	D	L	F	A
League	2	1	1	0	2	1	2	2	0	0	3	1
FA Cup	1	0	1	0	2	2	1	0	0	1	0	1
Total	3	1	2	0	4	3	3	2	0	1	3	2

Season	H	A	Played for both		
1978-79	1-0	2-1	Sam Aiston	Joe Hinnigan	Michael Proctor
1979-80	1-1	1-0	Terry Cooke	Michael Ingham	Edward Robson
			Shaun Cunnington	Jack Jones (WW2)	Fred Rowell
			Andy Dibble	Alan Kennedy	Neil Wainwright
			Carlos Edwards	Leslie McDowall	William Watson (WW2)
			Colin Grainger	Andy Marriott	Jeff Whitley
			Gordon Gunson	Brian Mooney	

FA Cup	Round			
1976-77	3	H	2-2	
1976-77	3 rep	A	0-1	

Top scorer: Alan Brown 2 goals

Yeovil Town

FA Cup	Round			Played for both	
1948-49	4	A	1-2	Norman Case	Mark Lynch
				John Conner	Thomas Ritchie
				Kevin Cooper	Marcus Stewart
				Thomas Dougall	John Tones
				Clarence Gregory	Brian Usher
				David Halliday	Andrew Welsh
				Cecil Irwin	Leslie Wilkins
				David Lindsay	Martin Woods

York City

	Home					Away				
	P	W	D	L	F	A	P	W	D	L	F	A
League	3	3	0	0	7	2	3	2	0	1	6	3
FA Cup	1	1	0	0	2	1	1	0	1	0	0	0
L. Cup	3	2	0	1	8	5	3	2	1	0	5	1
Total	7	6	0	1	17	8	7	4	2	1	11	4

Season	H	A	Played for both		
1974-75	2-0	1-0	Steve Agnew	Michael Heathcote	Bernard Ramsden (WW2)
1975-76	1-0	4-1	David Buchanan	Michael Ingham	Michael Reddy
1987-88	4-2	1-2	John Byrne	Craig James	David Rush
			Herbert Davis (WW2)	John MacPhail	James Shoulder
			Jonjo Dickman	Hugh McMahon (WW2)	Peter Stronach
			William Ellis	Mark Maley	Richard Taylor
			Marco Gabbiadini	Matthew Middleton	Harry Thompson
			Ricardo Gabbiadini	Bobby Mimms	Derek Weddle
			John Goodchild	Richard Ord	Darren Williams
			Gerald Harrison	Michael Proctor	
			Alan Hay	Mark Prudhoe	

FA Cup	Round			L. Cup	Round			
1955-56	4	A	0-0	1986-87	1 L1	H	2-4
1955-56	4 rep	H	2-1	1986-87	1 L2	A	3-1
				1989-90	1 L1	A	0-0
				1989-90	1 L2	H	4-0
				1998-99	1 L1	A	2-0
				1998-99	1 L2	H	2-1

Top scorer: 4 players with 3 goals

Sunderland in the League 1890-2012

Position
Highest: **1st** six times – 1891-92, 1892-93, 1894-95, 1901-02, 1912-13, 1935-36
Lowest: **45th** (1st in old Division Three (= new League One)) 1987-88 – low point of 56th in September 1987 during the only season outside top two divisions

Points
Most: **61** - 1963-64 (2 points for a win), **105** – 1998-99 (3 points for a win)
Most in top flight: **56** – 1935-36 (2 points for a win), **58** – 1999-2000 (3 points for a win)
Most at home: **40** – 1975-76 (2 points for a win), **60** – 1998-99 (3 points for a win)
Most at home in top flight: **36** five times – 1919-20, 1925-26, 1935-36, 1936-37 (2 points for a win) 1999-2000 (3 points for a win)
Most away: **26** twice – 1963-64, 1978-79 (2 points for a win), **45** – 1998-99 (3 points for a win)
Most away in top flight: 24 twice – 1912-13, 1934-35 (2 points for a win), **23** – 2000-01 (3 points for a win)
Fewest: **23** twice – 1890-91, 1896-97 (2 points for a win), **15** – 2005-06 (3 points for a win)
Fewest at home: 14 – 1896-97 (2 points for a win), 7 – 2005-06 (3 points for a win)
Fewest away: 7 four times – 1890-91, 1905-06, 1964-65, 1969-70 (2 points for a win), 8 twice– 2002-03, 2005-06 (3 points for a win)

Wins
Most: 31 – 1998-99
Most in top flight: **25** twice – 1912-13, 1935-36
Most at home: **19** twice – 1975-76, 1998-99
Most at home in top flight: **17** four times – 1919-20, 1925-26, 1935-36, 1936-37
Most away: **13** – 1987-88 and 2004-05
Most away in top flight: 11 – 1912-13
Fewest: **3**– 2005-06
Fewest at home: **1** – 2005-06
Fewest away: **1** three times – 1965-66, 1968-69, 2002-03

Defeats
Fewest: **3** – 1998-99
Fewest in top flight: **4** twice – 1892-93, 1894-95
Fewest at home: **0** six times – 1891-92, 1892-93, 1894-95, 1895-96, 1975-76, 1979-80
Fewest away: **2** – 1998-99
Fewest away in top flight: **3** – 1934-35
Most: **29** – 2005-06
Most at home: **14** twice – 2002-03, 2005-06
Most away: **16** three times – 1964-65, 1969-70, 1991-92

Draws
Most: **18** twice – 1954-55, 1994-95
Most at home: **12** – 1994-95
Most at home in top flight: **11** twice – 1954-55, 1969-70
Most away: **12** – 1934-35
Fewest: **0** – 1891-92
Fewest at home: **0** twice – 1891-92, 1908-09
Fewest away: **0** – 1891-92 (1- 1955-56)

Goals in a season
Most scored: **109** – 1935-36
Most scored at home: **71** – 1935-36
Most scored away: **42** – 1892-93
Fewest scored: **21** – 2002-03
Fewest scored at home: **11** – 2002-03
Fewest scored away: **10** – 2002-03
Fewest conceded: **26** – 1900-01 (also best average in top flight 0.76. Best ever average = 0.61 in 1998-99)
Fewest conceded at home: **8** twice – 1897-98, 1974-75 (also best ever average 0.38. Best top flight average = 0.53 in 1899-1900)
Fewest conceded away: **15** – 1900-01 (also best average in top flight 0.88. Best ever average = 0.78 in 1998-99)
Most conceded: **97** – 1957-58
Most conceded at home: **38** – 1930-31
Most conceded away: **64** – 1957-58

Individual matches
Highest score for: **9** – 9-1 v Newcastle United (a) 5 Dec 1908
Highest score for at home: **8** four times – 8-1 v West Bromwich Albion, 22 Oct 1892; 8-0 v Derby County, 1 Sep 1894; 8-2 v Blackburn Rovers, 4 Feb 1931; 8-1 v Charlton Athletic, 1 Sep 1956
Highest score for away: **9** – 9-1 v Newcastle United, 5 Dec 1908
Highest score against: **8** five times (all away games) – 1-8 v Blackburn Rovers, 22 Mar 1909; 0-8 v Sheffield Wednesday, 26 Dec 1911; 2-8 v Luton Town, 19 Nov 1955; 0-8 v West Ham United, 19 Oct 1968; 0-8 v Watford, 25 Sep 1982
Highest score against at home: **6** twice – 1-6 v Newcastle United, 26 Dec 1955; 1-6 v Birmingham City 5 Apr 1958
Highest score against away: **8** five times (see highest score against above)
Biggest winning margin: **8** twice – 9-1 v Newcastle United (a) 5 Dec 1908; 8-0 v Derby County 1 Sep 1894
Biggest winning margin at home: **8** – 8-0 v Derby County, 1 Sep 1894
Biggest winning margin away: **8** – 9-1 v Newcastle United (a) 5 Dec 1908
Biggest losing margin: **8** three times – 0-8 v Sheffield Wednesday, 26 Dec 1911; 0-8 v West Ham United, 19 Oct 1968; 0-8 v Watford, 25 Sep 1982 (all away games)
Biggest losing margin at home: **5** twice – see highest score against at home
Biggest losing margin away: **8** three times – see biggest losing margin
Highest aggregate score: **11** four times – 6-5 v Liverpool (h) 6 Dec 1930, 7-4 v Bolton Wanderers (h) 29 Oct 1932; 5-6 v West Bromwich Albion (a) 24 Mar 1934; 5-6 v Derby County (a) 16 Dec 1950
Highest scoring draw: **5-5** twice – v Liverpool (h) 19 Jan 1907; v Middlesbrough (a) 17 Oct 1936

Sequences

Consecutive wins: **13** – 14 Nov 1891 to 2 Apr1892
Consecutive home wins: **19** – 20 Dec 1890 to 16 Apr 1892 (includes entire 1891-92 season)
Consecutive away wins: **5** six times: 28 Nov 1891 to 19 Mar 1892, 23 Apr 1892 to 8 Oct 1892, 20 Dec 1902 to 28 Mar 1903, 14 Dec 1912 to 26 Feb 1913, 11 May 1963 to 7 Sep 1963, 2 Apr 1988 to 7 May 1988
Consecutive games unbeaten: **19** – 3 May 1998 to 14 Nov 1998
Consecutive games unbeaten at home: **44** – 18 Oct 1890 to 6 Dec 1893
Consecutive games unbeaten away: **14** – 25 Nov 1978 to 18 Aug 1979
Best in top flight: **9** – 28 Aug 1934 to 15 Dec 1934
Consecutive defeats: **17** – 18 Jan 2003 to 16 Aug 2003
Consecutive home defeats: **9** – 28 Jan 2003 to 16 Aug 2003
Consecutive away defeats: **10** four times – 26 Aug 1964 to 5 Dec 1964, 21 Oct 1980 to 21 Feb 1981, 28 Dec 2002 to 9 Aug 2003, 7 Oct 2007 to 23 Feb 2008
Consecutive games without a win: **22** – 21 Dec 2002 to 16 Aug 2003
Consecutive home games without a win: **18** – 13 Aug 2005 to 1 May 2006
Consecutive away game without a win: **28** – 15 Nov 1952 to 2 Jan 1954 (won 4 out of 7 away games at start of 1952-53 before this run and broke sequence in 1953-54 with 4-1 win at reigning champions Arsenal - Purdon's 10 second goal)
Consecutive games without conceding a goal: **6** five times – 26 Dec 1901 to 1 Feb 1902 (run of 7 in total with one FA Cup tie which is club record for all comps), 20 Dec 1902 to 17 Jan 1903, 18 Jan 1964 to 7 Mar 1964, 18 Dec 1982 to 15 Jan 1983, 6 Apr 1996 to 27 Apr 1996
Consecutive home games without conceding a goal: **7** twice – 21 Sep 1974 to 23 Nov 1974 (Jim Montgomery 703 minutes), 24 Jan 1996 to 23 Mar 1996 (from Shay Given's home debut – he didn't concede a home goal for 729 minutes)
Consecutive away games without conceding a goal: **4** twice – 26 Dec 1901 to 1 Feb 1902, 13 Feb 1999 to 13 Mar 1999
Consecutive scoring games: **29** – 8 Nov 1997 to 25 Apr 1998
Consecutive non-scoring games: **10** – 27 Nov 1976 to 5 Feb 1977

Sunderland in the FA Cup 1884-2012

	P	W	D	L	F	A
Home	163	92	40	31	314	150
Away	177	53	40	84	240	303
Total	340	145	80	115	554	453

Note – includes one win on penalties (Blackburn Rovers (h) 2002-03)

Best performances

Winners: 1937, 1973
Finalists: 1913, 1992
Semi-finalists: 1891, 1892, 1895, 1931, 1938, 1955, 1956, 2004

Highest Winning Margins

Season	Opponents	Venue	Result
1894-95	Fairfield	Home	11-1
1913-14	Chatham Town	Home	9-0
1925-26	Boston United	Home	8-1
1966-67	Peterborough U	Home	7-1
1892-93	Woolwich Arsenal	Home	6-0
1912-13	Clapton Orient	Home	6-0
1949-50	Huddersfield T	Home	6-0
1963-64	Bristol City	Home	6-1

Highest Losing Margins

Season	Opponents	Venue	Result
1933-34	Aston Villa	Away	2-7
1905-06	Woolwich Arsenal	Away	0-5
1921-22	Liverpool	Away	0-5
1960-61	Tottenham H	Away	0-5

Highest Losing Margins at home

Season	Opponents	Result
1968-69	Fulham	1-4
1994-95	Tottenham H	1-4
1908-09	Newcastle U	0-3
1970-71	Orient	0-3
1978-79	Burnley	0-3
2007-08	Wigan A	0-3

Longest Run Without Defeat

13 – Round 3 in 1937 to Round 6 in 1938 – included longest sequence of wins (7)

Longest Run Without a Win

8 – Round 5 in 1967 to Round 3 in 1971

Leading Goal-scorers

Player	Career	Goals
Bobby Gurney	1925-1946	23
Jimmy Millar	1890-1904	19
Johnny Campbell	1889-1897	18
Charlie Buchan	1911-1925	13
Jimmy Connor	1930-1939	13
Jackie Mordue	1908-1920	11
Jimmy Richardson	1912-1914	10
Kevin Phillips	1997-2003	10

Most Appearances

Player	Career	Appearances
Jim Montgomery	1958-1977	41
Bobby Gurney	1925-1946	40
Johnny Mapson	1936-1954	36
Ted Doig	1890-1904	35
George Holley	1904-1919	35
Alex Hastings	1929-1945	34
Stan Anderson	1951-1963	34
Patsy Gallacher	1927-1938	33
Jackie Mordue	1908-1920	32
Charlie Buchan	1911-1925	32
Raich Carter	1931-1945	31

Highest Individual Scores

Player	Goals	Opponents	Venue	Season
Jimmy Millar	5	Fairfield	Home	1894-95
Jimmy Richardson	4	Clapton Orient	Home	1912-13
Jimmy Richardson	4	Chatham Town	Home	1913-14
Richardson				
Charlie Buchan	4	Hull City	Home	1919-20
Kevin Phillips	4	Rotherham United	Away	1997-98
John Breconridge	3	Elswick Rangers	Home	1888-89
Johnny Campbell	3	Accrington	Away	1891-92
Jimmy Millar	3	Woolwich Arsenal	Home	1892-93
James Hannah	3	Fairfield	Home	1894-95
Jock Paterson	3	Burnley	Home	1922-23
Bob Kelly	3	Boston United	Home	1925-26
David Halliday	3	Boston United	Home	1925-26
Bobby Gurney	3	Aston Villa	Away	1932-33
Bobby Gurney	3	Fulham	Home	1934-35
Charlie Fleming	3	Norwich City	Home	1955-56
Neil Martin	3	Peterborough U	Home	1966-67

Most Goals in One Season

Player	Goals	Season
Johnny Campbell	7	1891-92
Bobby Gurney	7	1932-33
John Byrne	7	1991-92
Jimmy Millar	6	1894-95
Jimmy Richardson	6	1912-13
Jimmy Connor	6	1930-31
Bobby Gurney	6	1936-37
Neil Martin	6	1966-67

Sunderland in the League Cup 1960-2012

	P	W	D	L	F	A
Home	76	41	12	23	139	98
Away	75	25	17	33	104	120
Total	151	66	29	56	243	218

Note – includes three wins on penalties (Newcastle United (a) 1979-80, Everton (a) 1998-99, Northampton (h) 2008-09) and two defeats (Crewe Alexandra (a) 2004-05, Aston Villa (h) 2009-10)

Best Performances

Finalists: 1985
Semi-finalists: 1963, 1999

Highest Winning Margins

Season	Opponents	Venue	Result
2002-03	Cambridge U	Away	7-0
1962-63	Oldham A	Home	7-1
1990-91	Bristol C	Away	6-1
1982-83	Wolves	Home	5-0
1999-00	Walsall	Away	5-0

Highest Losing Margins

Season	Opponents	Venue	Result
1990-91	Derby County	Away	0-6
1989-90	Coventry City	Away	0-5
1991-92	Huddersfield T	Away	0-4

Longest Run Without Defeat

9 – Round 2, 1st leg, in 1984 to Semi-final, 2nd leg, in 1985

Longest Run Without a Win

9 – Round 3 in 1976 to Round 3 in 1979

Leading Goalscorers

Player	Career	Goals
Brian Clough	1961-1964	9
Marco Gabbiadini	1987-1991	9
Gary Rowell	1972-1984	8
George Mulhall	1962-1969	6
Clive Walker	1984-1985	6
Eric Gates	1985-1990	6
Danny Dichio	1998-2001	6

Most Appearances

Player	Career	Appearances
Gary Bennett	1984-1995	35
Jim Montgomery	1958-1977	33
Gordon Armstrong	1983-1996	29
Shaun Elliott	1974-1986	28
Gary Owers	1985-1994	27
Michael Gray	1990-2004	27
Kevin Ball	1990-1999	26
Gordon Chisholm	1977-1986	24

Highest Individual Scores

Player	Goals	Venue	Opponents	Season
Brian Clough	3	Home	Walsall	1961-62
Vic Halom	3	Home	Derby C	1973-74

Most Goals in One Season

Player	Goals	Season
Brian Clough	5	1961-62
Brian Clough	4	1962-63
John O'Hare	4	1964-65
Alan Brown	4	1979-80
Gary Rowell	4	1983-84
Clive Walker	4	1984-85
Marco Gabbiadini	4	1989-90
Don Goodman	4	1993-94
Danny Dichio	4	1999-00
Marcus Stewart	4	2002-03

All statistics up to the end of 2011-12

SUNDERLAND GAMES THAT HAVE BEEN ABANDONED

Date	Venue	Opposition	Score	Time	Reason
8 April 2006	H	Fulham	0-1	21 mins	Snow and waterlogged pitch
14 July 2004	A	Carolina Select All Stars	1-2	55 mins	Lightning (friendly in Raleigh, North Carolina)
12 December 1993	A	Grimsby Town	0-0	6 mins	Waterlogged pitch (televised game)
12 January 1985	H	Liverpool	0-0	45 mins	Frozen pitch
31 March 1969	A	Burnley	0-1	45 mins	Waterlogged pitch
1 February 1913	A	Manchester City	2-0	60 mins	Crowd invasion
13 December 1890	A	Notts County	1-1	65 mins	Fog

Also

| 4 March 1970 | Roker | Engand U23 v Scotland U23 | 3-1 | 62 mins | Snow |

LANDMARKS IN SUNDERLAND AFC HISTORY

The following excludes the aborted 1939-40 season, Test Matches, Play-off games and penalty shoot-outs.

	League Game	League Goal scored	League Goal conceded
500th	14 April 1906 v Nottingham Forest (H) 0-1	11 December 1897 v Derby County (A) 2-2, first goal (Leslie)	12 December 1903 v Notts County (A) 1-2, first goal (Jock Montgomery)
1,000th	17 February 1923 v Oldham Athletic (A) 0-0	16 March 1907 v Derby County (A) 1-1 (McIntosh)	18 September 1912 v Blackburn Rovers (H) 2-4, first goal (Eddie Latheron)
1,500th	5 January 1935 v Wolves (H) 0-0	24 January 1914 v Middlesbrough (H) 4-2, second goal (Holley)	29 August 1925 v Birmingham (H) 3-1 (Joseph Bradford)
2,000th	5 December 1953 v Burnley (A) 1-5	2 September 1925 v Blackburn Rovers (H) 6-2, first goal (Coglin)	5 December 1931 v Grimsby Town (A) 3-1 (John Priestley (pen))
2,500th	6 November 1965 v Stoke City (A) 1-1	7 March 1931 v Sheffield Wednesday (H) 5-1, second goal (Andrews)	7 April 1939 v Everton (H) 1-2, second goal (Terry Gillick)
3,000th	22 October 1977 v Mansfield Town (A) 2-1	27 February 1937 v West Bromwich A (A) 4-6, fourth goal (Duns)	14 September 1953 v Aston Villa (A) 1-3, second goal (John Dixon)
3,500th	13 May 1989 v Leicester City (H) 2-2	8 March 1952 v Manchester United (H) 1-2 (Ford pen)	7 November 1959 v Charlton Athletic (A) 1-3, second goal (Dennis Edwards)
4,000th	16 December 2000 v Leeds United (A) 0-2	7 September 1959 v Sheffield United (A) 2-1, second goal (Fogarty)	26 December 1967 v Newcastle United (A) 1-2, first goal (Wyn Davies)
4,500th	4,462 games to start of 2012-13	24 September 1966 v Liverpool (A) 2-2, second goal (Herd)	8 October 1977 v Southampton (A) 2-4, first goal (Chris Nicholl)
5,000th		15 November 1975 v Charlton Athletic (A) 2-1, second goal (Holden)	8 November 1986 v West Bromwich A (H) 0-3, third goal (Garth Crooks)
5,500th		12 March 1985 v Watford (H) 1-1 (Walker)	29 April 1995 v Burnley (A) 1-1 (David Eyres (pen))
6,000th		11 January 1994 v Oxford United (A) 3-0, first goal (M. Smith)	10 December 2005 v Charlton Athletic (A) 0-2, second goal (Darren Ambrose)
6,500th		30 August 2003 v Bradford City (A) 4-0, second goal (Stewart)	6,352 goals to start of 2012-13
7,000th		6,942 goals to start of 2012-13	

SUNDERLAND: THE COMPLETE RECORD

	League Games in Top Division	**League Games outside Top Division**
500th	14 April 1906 v Nottingham Forest (H) 0-1	10 April 1976 v Blackburn Rovers (H) 3-0
1,000th	17 February 1923 v Oldham Athletic (A) 0-0	1 October 1994 v Southend United (H) 0-1
1,500th	5 January 1935 v Wolverhampton Wanderers (H) 0-0	1,312 games to start of 2012-13
2,000th	5 December 1953 v Burnley (A) 1-5	
2,500th	8 November 1980 v Stoke City (H) 0-0	
3,000th	23 August 2008 v Tottenham Hotspur (A) 2-1	
3,500th	3,150 games to start of 2012-13	

	FA Cup Games	**FA Cup goal scored**	**FA Cup goal conceded**
100th	30 January 1926 v Sheffield United (A) 2-1	4 February 1905 v Wolverhampton Wanderers (H) 1-1 (Common)	13 January 1912 v Plymouth Argyle (H) 3-1 (Freddie Burch)
200th	7 January 1961 v Arsenal (H) 2-1	14 January 1928 v Northampton Town (H) 3-3, first goal (Wright)	30 January 1937 v Luton Town (A) 2-2, second goal (Fred Roberts)
300th	15 January 1997 v Arsenal (H) 0-2	26 January 1946 v Bury (H) 3-1, third goal (Duns)	4 March 1964 v Manchester United (H) 2-2, first goal (Denis Law)
400th	340 games to start of 2012-13	4 March 1964 v Manchester United (H) 2-2, second goal (Maurice Setters own-goal)	7 January 1995 v Carlisle United (H) 1-1 (Simon Davey)
500th		29 January 1995 v Tottenham Hotspur (H) 1-4 (P. Gray)	453 goals to start of 2012-13
600th		554 goals to start of 2012-13	

	League Cup Games	**League Cup goal scored**	**League Cup goal conceded**
100th	6 October 1993 v Leeds United (A) 2-1	25 September 1985 v Crystal Palace (H) 2-1, second goal (Wylde)	4 March 1985 v Chelsea (A) 3-2, second goal (Pat Nevin)
200th	151 games to start of 2012-13	26 September 2001 v Luton Town (A) 2-1, first goal (Reddy)	21 September 2005 v Crewe Alexandra (A) 3-3, second goal (Dean Ashton)
300th		243 goals to start of 2012-13	218 goals to start of 2012-13

SUNDERLAND'S PRE-LEAGUE FRIENDLIES AND MINOR CUP GAMES

The following games were all played by Sunderland's first team. In the late Victorian era many of these games would have been seen as more prestiguous than League or FA Cup games however record books, and this one is no different, have always excluded them from players' or managers' records. This is the first time such a comprehensive list has ever been published for Sunderland AFC of these regional / minor cup games, testimonials and friendlies.

Season	Date	Opponents	Venue	Result		Comments
1880-81	Nov 13	Ferryhill	H	L	0-1	
	27	Ovingham	H	W	4-0	W. Elliott scored Sunderland's first ever goal
	Dec 11	Burnopfield	H	D	2-2	Northumberland & Durham Challenge Cup tie
	18	Burnopfield	A	W	2-0	Northumberland & Durham Challenge Cup tie
	Feb 12	The Rangers (Newcastle)	St James' Park	L	0-5	Northumberland & Durham Challenge Cup tie
	Apr 2	Ferryhill	A	D	0-0	
1881-82	Oct 1	Ferryhill	H	W	1-0	
	8	North Eastern	H	W	1-0	
	29	Sedgefield	A	L	0-4	Northumberland & Durham Challenge Cup tie
	Nov 12	Elswick Leather Works	H	W	1-0	
	19	North Eastern	A	L	1-3	
	Dec 3	Newcastle	A	L	0-1	
	31	Middlesbrough	H	L	0-1	
	Jan 14	Tyne	A	L	0-2	
	21	Derwent Rovers	H	W	1-0	
	Feb 11	North Eastern	Whitburn	W	2-0	Played at Whitburn cricket club
	18	Elswick Leather Works	A	W	1-0	
	Mar 4	East End	A	L	0-2	
1882-83	Oct 7	North Eastern	A	D	2-2	
	21	Newcastle	A	D	1-1	
	Nov 4	North Eastern	H	W	2-1	First game played at Groves Field
	11	The Rangers (Newcastle)	A	W	1-0	
	Jan 20	Stanley Star	H	W	12-1	Northumberland & Durham Challenge Cup tie
	27	Castle Eden	A	W	6-0	
	Feb 3	Haughton-le-Skerne	H	W	4-1	Northumberland & Durham Challenge Cup tie
	24	Derwent Rovers	A	W	1-0	Northumberland & Durham Challenge Cup tie

SUNDERLAND: THE COMPLETE RECORD

Season	Date	Opponents	Venue	Result		Comments
	Mar 10	Bishop Middleham	H	W	4-3	
	31	Tyne	Newcastle	L	0-2	Northumberland & Durham Challenge Cup Final
1883-84	Sep 20	Birtley	A	D	0-0	
	29	Castle Eden	H	W	8-1	First game at Horatio Street
	Oct 6	Jarrow	A	W	8-1	
	13	Whitburn	A	W	5-1	
	20	The Rangers (Newcastle)	A	L	0-1	
	27	Whitburn	H	W	3-1	
	Nov 3	Newcastle East End	A	W	3-0	
	17	Milstwell Burn	H	W	7-0	Durham Challenge Cup tie
	Jan 19	Jarrow	H	W	5-2	Durham Challenge Cup tie
	Feb 23	Hamsterley Rangers	H	W	3-1	Durham Challenge Cup tie
	Mar 15	Hobson Wanderers	Whitburn	D	0-0	Durham Challenge Cup tie
	22	Castle Eden	H	W	7-0	
	29	Hobson Wanderers	Whitburn	W	6-0	Durham Challenge Cup tie
	Apr 5	Darlington	Monkwearmouth Cricket Ground, Newcastle Rd	W	4-3	Durham Challenge Cup Final - result void after protest
	26	The District	H	L	0-1	
	May 3	Darlington	Birtley	W	2-0	Durham Challenge Cup Final - replayed
	Jun 25	Rosehill	Newcastle Town Moor	W	3-0	North of England Temperance Festival - won after extra time
	25	Newcastle East End	Newcastle Town Moor	W	3-1	North of England Temperance Festival Final
1884-85	Sep 27	Birtley	H	W	2-1	First game at Abbs Field
	Oct 4	Wearmouth	H	W	9-0	
	18	Northern Division County Colts	Durham	W	8-2	
	25	Hartlepool	A	W	3-1	
	Nov 1	Hobson Wanderers	H	W	5-1	
	8	Redcar	A	L	1-3	
	15	Jesmond	H	W	2-1	
	22	Rosehill	H	W	2-0	
	Dec 6	Whitburn	H	L	0-1	
	13	Castle Eden	H	W	8-1	
	20	Castletown	H	W	23-0	Largest ever victory and James Allan scored 12 goals
	26	Erimus (Southbank)	H	W	1-0	
	27	Heaton	H	W	2-0	
	Jan 1	St. John's Middlesbrough	H	W	2-0	
	3	Port Glasgow Athletic	H	L	1-11	First Scottish opposition
	10	Jesmond	A	L	0-1	
	24	Wearmouth	H	W	3-1	Durham Challenge Cup 2nd Round
	31	Erimus (Southbank)	H	W	4-1	
	Feb 14	5th KRV Maxwell Town	H	D	1-1	
	21	Bishop Auckland	H	W	1-0	
	Mar 7	Birtley	A	L	1-4	
	14	Birtley	H	W	1-0	Durham Challenge Cup Semi Final
	28	Darlington	A	L	0-3	Durham Challenge Cup Final

SUNDERLAND'S PRE-LEAGUE FRIENDLIES

Season	Date	Opponents	Venue	Result		Comments
	Apr 4	5th KRV Maxwell Town	A	D	2-2	
	7	Sheffield	H	D	2-2	
	18	Wearmouth	A	W	1-0	Played at Southwick
	25	Jesmond	H	D	0-0	
1885-86	Oct 3	North Eastern	H	W	4-0	
	17	Cathedral (formerly Jesmond)	H	W	9-0	
	Nov 7	Newcastle East End	A	W	1-0	
	14	Tyne	H	W	3-1	
	21	Bishop Auckland	A	L	0-2	
	28	Castle Eden	A	W	4-1	
	Dec 5	Birtley	H	W	2-1	
	12	South Bank	H	W	10-3	
	19	Heaton	H	W	5-2	
	26	North Eastern	H	W	3-0	
	Jan 1	Port Glasgow	H	L	1-2	
	2	Linthouse (Glasgow)	H	L	1-2	
	30	Hebburn	H	W	4-0	
	Feb 6	Bedlington Rovers	H	W	4-0	
	13	Newcastle West End	H	W	1-0	
	20	Newcastle East End	H	D	1-1	
	27	Heart of Midlothian	A	L	1-2	
	Mar 9	Newcastle West End	H	W	2-1	
	13	St. John's Middlesbrough	H	W	6-0	
	Apr 3	Darlington	H	W	3-1	First game at Newcastle Road ground
	10	Birtley	H	D	3-3	
	17	Darlington	A	D	1-1	
	24	Edinburgh University	H	W	1-0	
	26	Sheffield	H	L	3-4	
	27	Shankhouse Black Watch	H	W	3-0	
	May 1	Shankhouse Black Watch	H	W	3-1	
	8	Elswick Leather Works	H	W	2-1	
	15	Elswick Leather Works	H	W	3-1	
	29	Cramlington Jack Club	H	W	3-1	
1886-87	Sep 18	Notts & District	H	W	1-0	
	Oct 2	Elswick Rangers	H	W	3-2	
	9	South Bank	A	D	3-3	
	16	Morpeth Harriers	H	W	7-2	
	23	Shankhouse Black Watch	A	W	2-1	
	Nov 20	Birtley	H	W	2-0	Durham Challenge Cup tie
	27	Newcastle West End	H	W	1-0	Benefit for Oliver (broke collar bone 2 weeks earlier)
	Dec 4	Newcastle East End	H	D	1-1	
	11	Birtley	A	W	2-1	
	27	Basford Rovers (Nottingham)	H	W	2-0	
	28	Darlington	A	L	1-5	
	Jan 1	Glasgow Rangers	H	W	1-0	
	3	Dumbarton Athletic	H	L	2-5	
	4	Linthouse (Glasgow)	H	W	2-1	
	8	South Bank	H	W	2-1	
	15	Darlington St Augustine's	H	D	1-1	
	22	Gateshead	H	W	3-2	Durham Challenge Cup 2nd Round
	29	Gateshead	H	D	1-1	

Season	Date	Opponents	Venue	Result	Comments
	Feb 5	Durham University	A	W 2-0	
	19	Elswick Rangers	H	D 1-1	
	22	Durham University	H	W 8-2	
	26	District Team	H	L 2-3	
	Mar 5	Shankhouse Black Watch	H	D 2-2	
	12	Whitburn	H	W 5-3	Durham Challenge Cup Semi Final
	26	Darlington	H	W 1-0	Durham Challenge Cup Final
	Apr 2	Shankhouse Black Watch	H	D 0-0	
	9	Edinburgh St Bernard's	H	L 0-5	
	11	Sheffield Town	H	L 1-2	
	12	Nottingham Rangers	H	L 0-7	
	16	Whitburn	H	L 1-4	
	30	Accrington	H	L 1-3	
1887-88	Sep 10	Notts Mellors	H	W 8-3	
	17	Darlington	H	W 3-1	
	24	Darlington St Augustine's	H	W 1-0	First game in red & white stripes
	Oct 1	Shankhouse Black Watch	A	W 3-1	
	8	Newcastle West End	A	W 3-2	
	29	Elswick Rangers	H	W 6-2	
	Nov 12	Blackburn Rovers	H	L 0-2	
	19	Bishop Auckland Church Institute	H	W 5-2	
	Dec 10	Morpeth Harriers	H	D 2-2	
	17	Durham University	A	W 8-0	Durham Challenge Cup 2nd Round
	26	Derby Junction	H	W 4-0	
	Jan 2	Cambuslang	H	L 0-11	Worst ever defeat
	3	Partick Thistle	H	L 2-4	
	7	South Bank	H	W 5-2	
	14	Ayr	A	L 1-4	
	21	Whitburn	A	W 1-0	Durham Challenge Cup 3rd Round
	28	Elswick Rangers	A	W 1-0	
	Feb 4	Southwick	H	W 7-1	Durham Challenge Cup tie
	11	Newcastle West End	H	L 2-3	
	14	Blackburn Olympic	H	L 1-3	
	18	Sheffield Park Grange	H	W 6-0	
	25	Bishop Auckland Town	A	W 1-0	
	Mar 3	Darlington St Augustine's	A	W 6-3	
	10	Darlington	Auckland	D 1-1	Durham Challenge Cup tie
	24	Darlington	Auckland	W 2-1	Durham Challenge Cup tie replay
	31	Blackburn Olympic	H	W 4-1	
	Apr 2	Sheffield	H	W 4-0	
	3	Edinburgh St Bernard's	H	W 5-1	
	7	Bishop Auckland Church Institute	Darlington	W 2-1	Durham Challenge Cup Final
	14	Birtley	H	D 4-4	
	21	Renton	H	L 2-4	
	28	Newcastle West End	A	W 2-0	Durham & Northumberland Championship game
	May 12	Bishop Auckland Church Institute	H	W 5-1	
	19	The District	H	W 2-1	
1888-89	Sep 1	Blackburn Rovers	H	W 4-3	Sunderland's first game as a professional club

SUNDERLAND'S PRE-LEAGUE FRIENDLIES

Season	Date	Opponents	Venue	Result	Comments
	8	Cambuslang	H	D 1-1	
	15	South Bank	A	W 7-0	
	22	Canadian Touring Team	H	L 0-3	
	29	Grimsby Town	A	W 2-1	
	Oct 6	Sheffield Wednesday	H	W 2-1	
	13	Darlington	A	L 0-2	
	20	Middlesbrough	A	D 2-2	
	Nov 3	Long Eaton	H	W 5-1	
	10	Grimsby Town	H	D 1-1	
	14	Durham University	H	W 6-0	
	21	Bishop Auckland	A	W 6-1	
	24	Lincoln City	A	D 1-1	
	Dec 1	Sunderland Albion	H	W 2-0	First Sunderland local derby game
	8	Glasgow University	H	W 4-1	
	15	Bolton Wanderers	A	L 1-10	
	22	Newcastle East End	A	D 1-1	
	26	Druids	H	W 12-0	
	27	Hurlford	H	D 3-3	
	29	Dundee Harp	H	W 5-0	
	31	Mossend Swifts	H	D 2-2	
	Jan 1	Renton	H	L 0-2	
	2	Greenock Morton	H	W 4-1	
	5	Corinthians	H	D 2-2	
	12	Sunderland Albion	H	W 3-2	
	19	Paisley Abercorn	A	L 3-4	
	26	Derby St Luke's	H	W 8-0	
	30	Morpeth Harriers	A	W 6-5	
	Feb 2	Bishop Auckland Church Institute	H	W 5-2	
	9	Scottish Corinthians	H	W 7-2	
	16	Bolton Wanderers	H	W 4-3	
	23	Sheffield Wednesday	A	W 2-1	
	Mar 2	West Hartlepool	H	W 7-1	
	5	Everton	H	W 4-2	
	9	Halliwell	H	W 1-0	
	16	Middlesbrough	H	W 4-0	
	23	Glasgow Rangers	H	W 3-0	
	30	Derby County	H	W 3-1	
	Apr 6	St Mirren	H	L 1-2	
	13	Gateshead	H	W 3-0	
	20	Derby Junction	H	W 5-0	
	22	Sheffield	H	W 2-1	
	23	Wolverhampton Wanderers	H	D 1-1	
	29	Preston North End	H	W 4-1	
	May 4	Witton	H	W 4-1	
	11	Wolverhampton Wanderers	H	D 1-1	
	18	Accrington	H	W 4-0	
	27	Dumbarton	H	W 4-3	
	28	Third Lanark	H	L 2-4	
1889-90	Sep 2	Blackburn Rovers	H	W 1-0	
	7	Newcastle West End	H	W 3-0	
	9	Preston North End	H	D 1-1	

617

Season	Date	Opponents	Venue	Result		Comments
	11	Southwick	A	W	2-1	
	14	Queen of the South	H	W	5-0	
	21	Glasgow Celtic	H	L	0-1	
	28	Glasgow Celtic	A	L	2-3	
	Oct 5	Bolton Wanderers	A	W	3-2	
	12	Casuals	A	W	3-1	
	14	Wolverhampton Wanderers	A	L	0-4	
	19	South Bank	H	W	5-0	
	26	St Mirren	H	L	1-2	
	Nov 2	Middlesbrough	H	W	9-1	
	9	Birmingham St George's	H	W	3-1	
	16	Newcastle East End	A	W	4-0	
	23	Hurlford	H	W	10-2	
	30	Darlington	H	W	7-0	
	Dec 7	Middlesbrough	A	W	3-0	
	14	Bootle	H	W	3-2	
	21	Glasgow Celtic	H	L	1-2	
	26	Halliwell	H	W	10-1	
	28	Gateshead	H	W	5-0	
	Jan 1	Paisley Abercorn	H	W	3-2	
	2	Casuals	H	W	3-2	
	4	Glasgow Rangers	H	D	1-1	
	11	Darlington St Augustine's	H	W	2-1	
	25	Third Lanark	A	W	4-0	
	Feb 1	Birtley	H	W	4-0	
	8	Renton	H	W	3-2	
	15	Heart of Midlothian	A	W	4-2	
	18	Wolverhampton Wanderers	H	W	3-0	
	22	Birtley	H	W	4-0	Durham Challenge Cup 2nd Round
	Mar 1	Heart of Midlothian	H	W	3-0	
	8	Darlington St Augustine's	A	W	1-0	Durham Challenge Cup Semi Final
	15	Middlesbrough Ironopolis	H	W	7-0	
	22	Darlington	Stockton	W	2-0	Durham Challenge Cup Final
	29	Accrington	H	W	8-2	
	Apr 2	Middlesbrough Ironopolis	A	L	0-2	
	5	Aston Villa	H	W	7-2	
	7	Bolton Wanderers	H	L	0-1	
	8	Wolverhampton Wanderers	H	D	2-2	
	12	Accrington	A	L	2-3	
	19	Notts County	H	H	2-1	
	21	Everton	H	W	3-2	
	23	Stockton	A	W	5-1	
	26	Newcastle West End	A	W	4-1	
	May 3	West Bromwich Albion	H	L	3-5	
	10	Long Eaton	H	W	4-3	
	17	Glasgow Thistle	A	W	4-2	
	19	Greenock Morton	A	W	3-0	
	20	Albion Rovers	A	D	2-2	
	21	Edinburgh St Bernards	A	W	1-0	
	24	Bolton Wanderers	H	W	1-0	
	31	Glasgow Northern	H	W	6-1	

SUNDERLAND'S FRIENDLIES, TESTIMONIALS AND MINOR CUP GAMES SINCE 1890 (EXC. WARTIME)

The following games were all played by Sunderland's first team. In the late Victorian era many of these games would have been seen as more prestiguous than League or FA Cup games however record books, and this one is no different, have always excluded them from players' or managers' records. This is the first time such a comprehensive list has ever been published for Sunderland AFC of these regional / minor cup games, testimonials and friendlies.

Season	Date		Opponents	Venue	Result		Comments
1890-91	Sep	1	Renton	H	W	5-1	
		3	Middlesbrough	A	D	0-0	
		6	Preston North End	H	W	6-3	
		8	Middlesbrough Ironopolis	A	W	3-0	
		10	Rendel & Elswick Rangers	A	W	5-2	
		22	Stoke	A	L	0-1	
	Oct	2	Glasgow Celtic	A	D	2-2	
		4	Cambuslang	H	W	3-1	
	Nov	6	Nottingham Forest	H	D	1-1	
		29	Newcastle West End	H	W	5-0	
	Dec	6	Airdrieonians	H	W	4-1	
	Jan	1	Cowlairs	H	W	4-3	
		2	Glasgow Rangers	H	W	3-1	
		3	Vale of Leven	H	W	4-1	
	Mar	28	Linthouse	H	W	3-1	
		30	Corinthians	H	W	1-0	
		31	Burnley	H	W	5-0	
	Apr	4	Rendel	H	W	7-1	
		11	Notts County	H	W	6-0	
		18	Stockton	A	W	9-0	
	Apr	20	Newcastle West End	A	D	1-1	
		22	Middlesbrough	A	W	4-1	
		23	Grimsby Town	A	W	1-0	
		25	Royal Arsenal	A	W	3-1	
		27	Chatham	A	W	2-1	
		28	Millwall Athletic	A	W	3-1	
		30	Newcastle East End	A	W	3-0	
1891-92	Sep	1	Canadian Tourists	H	W	3-2	
		2	Newcastle West End	A	W	8-1	

Season	Date	Opponents	Venue	Result	Comments
	7	Newcastle East End	A	L 0-2	
	9	Middlesbrough	A	W 4-0	
	16	Spennymoor	A	W 6-0	
	23	Bishop Auckland	A	W 4-0	
	26	Newcastle East End	H	W 2-0	
	Oct 1	Queen's Park	H	L 2-4	
	10	Middlesbrough	H	W 4-1	
	Dec 14	Blackburn Rovers	A	W 5-0	
	19	Middlesbrough Ironopolis	H	W 7-1	
	28	Ardwick	A	D 0-0	
	Jan 1	Greenock Morton	H	W 4-0	
	2	Glasgow Northern	H	W 7-1	
	4	Glasgow Thistle	H	W 11-0	
	9	Newcastle East End	A	W 6-4	
	Feb 15	Sheffield United	A	D 2-2	
	Mar 7	Sheffield Wednesday	A	W 3-0	
	Apr 4	Glasgow Rangers	A	W 1-0	
	11	Newcastle East End	A	W 4-1	
	18	Sunderland Albion	H	W 6-1	
	19	Casuals	H	W 4-0	
	20	Middlesbrough Ironopolis	A	W 2-0	
	25	Everton	A	W 4-3	
	27	Sunderland Albion	A	W 8-0	
1892-93	Sep 1	Middlesbrough Ironopolis	A	W 2-1	
	5	Glasgow Celtic	H	W 1-0	
	7	Newcastle East End	A	D 2-2	
	12	Middlesbrough	A	W 4-2	
	14	Stockton	A	W 3-0	
	19	Leith Athletic	A	L 0-1	
	Oct 6	Glasgow Celtic	A	W 3-0	
	10	Dundee East End	A	W 6-2	
	Nov 12	Corinthians	A	L 2-4	
	14	Royal Arsenal	A	W 4-0	
	21	Darlington	A	W 6-0	
	Dec 10	Middlesbrough	H	W 3-2	
	27	Rotherham	A	W 2-0	
	31	Glasgow Rangers	H	W 4-0	
	Feb 11	Leith Athletic	A	W 6-0	
	25	Newcastle United	A	W 6-1	First game against them under their new name
	Mar 25	Third Lanark	A	W 4-0	
	Apr 3	Queen's Park	H	W 4-2	
	5	Middlesbrough Ironopolis	A	W 3-0	
	12	Newcastle United	A	W 4-0	
	19	Middlesbrough Ironopolis	H	L 0-1	
	22	Heart of Midlothian	A	L 2-4	
	24	King's Park, Stirling	A	W 3-2	
	26	Glasgow Rangers	A	W 6-2	
	27	Kilmarnock	A	W 7-1	
	29	Everton	A	W 3-1	
1893-94	Sep 4	Queen's Park	A	L 1-2	
	6	Newcastle United	A	W 3-1	
	11	Middlesbrough	A	W 4-2	

SUNDERLAND'S FRIENDLIES, TESTIMONIALS AND MINOR CUP GAMES SINCE 1890

Season	Date		Opponents	Venue	Result		Comments
		18	Heart of Midlothian	A	W	4-2	
		28	Glasgow Celtic	A	L	2-3	
	Oct	4	Stockton	A	W	5-1	
		9	Woolwich Arsenal	A	W	4-1	
		10	Casuals	A	W	5-1	
		23	Aston Villa	A	L	2-4	Benefit for Mr W. McGregor (founder of Football League)
	Nov	20	Darlington	A	W	4-0	
	Dec	25	Bury	A	D	1-1	First Christmas Day game played by Sunderland
		26	Everton	A	L	1-4	
	Jan	2	Glasgow Rangers	A	D	2-2	
		3	Heart of Midlothian	A	L	1-5	
	Feb	3	Moss End Swifts	H	W	6-1	
		17	Aston Villa	A	L	0-2	
		24	Everton	A	W	2-1	
	Mar	10	Cowlairs	H	W	2-1	
		14	Middlesbrough Ironopolis	A	W	3-0	Benefit for J. Oliver
		23	Bristol League	A	W	9-0	
		26	Corinthians	H	W	3-1	
		31	Glasgow Celtic	A	W	3-1	
	Apr	5	Newcastle United	A	W	2-1	
		9	Dundee	A	W	2-1	
		10	Aberdeen	A	W	7-1	
		11	East Stirling	A	W	4-0	
		14	Queen's Park	A	W	4-1	
		16	St Bernard's	A	W	4-2	
		17	Hibernian	Celtic Park, Glasgow	W	4-2	Benefit for Glasgow Thistle
		21	Newcastle United	A	L	1-4	
		24	Kilmarnock	A	D	2-2	
		25	Annbank	A	A	6-1	
		26	Scottish League	Celtic Park, Glasgow	L	0-3	Benefit for Glasgow Thistle
		28	Wishaw Thistle	A	W	1-0	
		30	Newcastle United	A	W	3-1	
1894-95	Sep	3	Glasgow Rangers	A	D	1-1	
		5	Newcastle United	A	W	4-1	
		17	Leicester Fosse	A	W	3-0	
		27	Glasgow Celtic	A	W	3-2	
	Oct	8	Dundee	A	L	0-1	
		15	Woolwich Arsenal	A	L	1-2	
		16	Casuals	A	L	3-4	
		20	Queen's Park	A	W	8-1	
	Dec	5	Rest of the League	South Shields	D	1-1	Benefit for widow of Nick Ross (Preston N.E.)
		25	Newton Heath	A	W	3-1	
	Jan	19	Newcastle United	A	W	4-1	
	Mar	30	Clyde	H	D	2-2	
	Apr	8	Dundee	A	W	2-0	
		15	Queen's Park	H	L	3-4	
		22	Newcastle United	A	L	0-1	

621

Season	Date	Opponents	Venue	Result		Comments
	27	Heart of Midlothian	A	W	5-3	English v Scottish League Champions
	29	Third Lanark	A	D	2-2	
1895-96	Sep 11	Newcastle United	H	W	5-3	
	16	Heart of Midlothian	A	W	2-1	
	26	Glasgow Celtic	A	D	1-1	
	Oct 12	Queen's Park	A	W	5-2	
	21	Burton Swifts	A	W	5-0	
	Nov 30	Newcastle United	A	W	4-0	
	Dec 7	Corinthians	A	L	1-3	
	9	Arsenal	A	W	2-1	
	10	Casuals	A	D	3-3	
	28	Corinthians	H	D	1-1	
	Jan 1	Third Lanark	H	W	5-1	
	2	Heart of Midlothian	H	W	4-2	
	Feb 29	Newcastle United	A	D	2-2	
	Mar 21	Newton Heath	A	W	1-0	
	Apr 4	Everton	A	D	1-1	
	6	Queen's Park	H	W	2-0	
	13	Dundee	A	W	2-1	
	14	St Mirren	A	D	1-1	
	15	Glasgow Celtic	A	L	2-3	
	16	Ayr Parkhouse	A	W	2-1	
	18	Heart of Midlothian	A	D	2-2	
	22	Renton	Hampden Park	D	0-0	
	23	Falkirk	A	W	5-3	
	25	Third Lanark	A	W	4-1	
	27	Belfast Distillery	A	W	1-0	
	28	Everton	Glentoran, Belfast	L	1-2	
	29	Glasgow Rangers	A	W	3-1	
	30	Newcastle United	A	D	3-3	
1896-97	Sep 2	Newcastle United	A	D	2-2	
	23	Newcastle United	H	D	1-1	Benefit for John Campbell
	28	Glasgow Celtic	A	W	3-2	
	Oct 12	Dundee	A	D	1-1	
	31	Third Lanark	H	W	4-1	
	Nov 14	Corinthians	A	L	0-2	
	Feb 6	Glasgow Celtic	H	W	4-2	
	Mar 20	Manchester City	A	L	1-2	
	31	Newcastle United	A	L	2-5	
	Apr 10	Sheffield United	H	W	1-0	
	12	Stockton	A	W	2-1	
	28	Newcastle United	A	L	0-3	
	29	Jarrow	A	L	1-3	Benefit for John Scott
	30	Stockton	A	W	3-1	
1897-98	Sep 1	Newcastle United	A	W	3-1	
	Nov 6	Belfast Distillery	H	W	4-0	
	20	Queen's Park	A	D	1-1	
	Feb 12	Aston Villa	H	W	4-1	
	26	Corinthians	A	L	0-2	
	Mar 19	Newcastle United	A	D	1-1	
	26	Tottenham Hotspur	A	W	2-0	
	Apr 9	Blackpool	A	W	4-2	

SUNDERLAND'S FRIENDLIES, TESTIMONIALS AND MINOR CUP GAMES SINCE 1890

Season	Date	Opponents	Venue	Result	Comments
	12	New Brighton Tower	A	L 1-2	
	16	Preston North End	H	W 4-2	
	18	Hibernian	A	L 2-4	
	20	Wigan County	A	W 2-1	
	21	Manchester City	A	D 0-0	
	25	Thornaby Utopians & District	A	W 4-0	
	27	South Shields	A	W 1-0	
	28	Stockton	A	W 3-1	Benefit for Rhys Daniel (Stockton)
	30	Clyde	A	D 3-3	
1898-99	Sep 1	Newcastle United	A	D 1-1	
	26	Queen's Park	A	W 3-1	
	Dec 26	Glasgow Celtic	H	L 0-1	First friendly at Roker Park
	Feb 14	Newcastle United	H	L 3-4	
	25	Middlesbrough	A	W 4-1	
	Apr 19	Bishop Auckland	A	D 2-2	
	24	Stockton	A	W 2-0	
	26	South Shields	A	D 1-1	
1899-00	Sep 6	Kaffirs (Orange Free State)	H	W 5-3	
	Dec 25	Hibernian	H	D 2-2	
	Jan 2	Tottenham Hotspur	H	L 1-3	
	Mar 17	Queens Park Rangers	A	L 1-3	
	Apr 4	West Hartlepool	A	W 7-1	
	13	Middlesbrough	A	W 1-0	
	18	Trimdon Grange	A	W 2-1	
	21	Dundee	A	D 1-1	
	25	Bishop Auckland	A	W 1-0	
1900-01	Sep 3	Glasgow Rangers	A	D 1-1	
	24	Clyde	A	W 4-2	
	Dec 15	Scarborough	A	W 10-0	
	22	Glasgow Rangers	A	W 3-0	
	Apr 15	Lincoln City	A	D 0-0	
	16	Yarmouth	A	W 7-2	
	17	Suffolk County	A	W 4-0	
	18	Lowestoft & Kirkley	A	W 5-3	
	20	Derby County	A	L 1-2	
	30	Middlesbrough	A	L 1-2	
1901-02	Sep 9	Middlesbrough	A	D 1-1	
	Dec 7	St Mirren	A	L 1-6	
	Jan 18	Preston North End	H	W 1-0	
	Mar 28	Third Lanark	H	L 2-3	
	Apr 21	St Bernard's	A	W 1-0	
	23	West Hartlepool	A	W 3-2	
	28	Middlesbrough	A	W 2-0	
	30	Glasgow Celtic	Ibrox	L 1-5	British League Cup semi-final (in aid of Ibrox Disaster Fund)
1902-03	Oct 11	Corinthians	A	W 2-1	
	Jan 2	Corinthians	H	L 2-8	
	Feb 21	Newcastle United	A	L 0-1	
	Mar 7	Blackburn Rovers	H	W 3-0	
	Apr 20	St Bernard's	A	D 2-2	
	27	West Hartlepool	A	W 7-0	
	30	Wearside League Select XI	H	L 2-3	Benefit for widow of Matthew Ferguson

SUNDERLAND: THE COMPLETE RECORD

Season	Date	Opponents	Venue	Result		Comments
1903-04	Feb 20	Darlington	A	L	6-3	
	Apr 5	Cliftonville	A	W	5-1	
	7	Derry Celtic	A	W	3-1	
	9	Distillery	A	L	1-3	
	20	North Durham	A	W	5-0	
		Wednesday League				
	23	Newcastle United	H	W	3-0	
	26	Bradford City	A	L	3-4	
	27	Leeds & District	A	W	6-2	
	30	Alnwick Percy Rovers	A	W	4-1	
1904-05	Sep 7	Hebburn Argyle	A	L	1-2	
	27	Newcastle United	A	W	2-1	
	Nov 7	Fulham	A	L	2-4	
	Feb 18	Middlesbrough	A	W	2-1	
	Apr 15	Darlington	A	W	6-0	
	21	Third Lanark	H	D	2-2	
	26	Inverness Thistle	A	W	5-0	
	27	Elgin	A	D	3-3	
	28	Raith Rovers	A	W	5-1	
	29	East Stirling	A	W	3-1	
1905-06	Sep 6	Middlesbrough	A	L	0-4	
1906-07	Apr 29	Third Lanark	A	L	2-3	
	30	Falkirk	A	W	5-2	
1907-08	Oct 9	Newcastle United	Stanley	L	0-2	For Northumberland & Durham Aged Miners' Homes fund
1908-09	Apr 13	Belfast Distillery	A	D	2-2	
	May 15	Ferencvaros	Budapest	W	3-2	First overseas tour
	16	MTK	Budapest	W	2-1	
	18	Germania FC	Vienna	W	5-0	
	19	Wien AC	Vienna	L	1-2	
	23	Deutscher Club	Prague	W	4-2	
	25	Deutscher Club	Prague	W	3-0	
	31	Bayern Club	Munich	W	5-2	
	Jun 1	Nurnberg	Nurnberg	W	6-3	
1910-11	Mar 25	Belfast Distillery	A	W	5-2	
	Apr 24	Hibernian	A	L	0-3	
1911-12	Oct 25	Newcastle United	A	L	0-1	Archibald Cup (Newcastle & Sunderland Hospitals Cup)
1912-13	Oct 23	Newcastle United	A	W	1-0	Archibald Cup (Newcastle & Sunderland Hospitals Cup)
	May 4	Fereneznurisa Torna Club	Budapest	W	9-0	
	7	Magyar FC	Budapest	W	3-2	
	11	Vienna FC	Vienna	W	7-0	
	14	Blackburn Rovers	Budapest	W	3-2	
	16	Budapest XI	Pozonoy	W	5-1	
	18	Hamburg	Hamburg	W	5-0	
	20	BFC Hertha 92	Berlin	W	7-0	
1913-14	Oct 15	Newcastle United	H	W	1-0	Archibald Cup (Newcastle & Sunderland Hospitals Cup)
1914-15	Sep 23	Newcastle United	A	W	1-0	Archibald Cup (Newcastle & Sunderland Hospitals Cup)

SUNDERLAND'S FRIENDLIES, TESTIMONIALS AND MINOR CUP GAMES SINCE 1890

Season	Date	Opponents	Venue	Result		Comments
1919-20	Apr 21	South Shields	A	W	3-1	North East Counties Cup
	28	Middlesbrough	A	W	2-0	North East Counties Cup
1920-21	Feb 19	Bolton Wanderers	H	L	2-3	
	Apr 20	South Shields	A	W	1-0	North East Counties Cup
	27	Middlesbrough	South Shields	W	3-0	North East Counties Cup
1922-23	Apr 25	South Shields	H	W	2-0	Durham Professional Cup
	May 2	Darlington	H	W	2-1	Durham Professional Cup
1923-24	Oct 10	Shildon	H	W	2-1	Durham Professional Cup
	Feb 23	Stockport County	A	W	2-0	
	Apr 9	Darlington	A	L	1-4	Durham Professional Cup
1924-25	Mar 18	West Stanley	A	W	2-1	Durham Senior Professional Cup
	Apr 27	South Shields	H	L	1-2	Durham Senior Professional Cup
1925-26	Apr 12	Dundee	A	D	1-1	Benefit game for Jimmy Irvine (Dundee)
1926-27	Apr 11	South Shields	A	W	3-2	Durham Senior Professional Cup
	27	Darlington	A	W	6-0	Durham Senior Professional Cup
1927-28	Oct 5	South Shields	H	W	3-1	Durham Senior Professional Cup
	Nov 9	Darlington	H	L	2-3	Durham Senior Professional Cup
1928-29	Oct 2	South Shields	H	W	2-0	Durham Senior Professional Cup
	Apr 1	St Mirren	H	L	0-1	Benefit game for Billy Clunas
	10	Darlington	H	W	7-3	Durham Senior Professional Cup
	30	St Mirren	A	L	1-2	
1929-30	Oct 9	Hartlepool United	A	L	0-1	Durham Senior Professional Cup
1930-31	Oct 1	Gateshead	A	L	2-5	Durham Senior Professional Cup
	Apr 29	Heart of Midlothian	A	D	1-1	
1931-32	Oct 14	Darlington	A	D	1-1	Durham Senior Professional Cup
	21	Darlington	H	W	3-2	Durham Senior Professional Cup
	Nov 18	Gateshead	H	W	4-0	Durham Senior Professional Cup
	May 4	Folkestone	A	D	2-2	
	7	Yeovil & Petters United	A	W	7-2	
1932-33	Sep 28	Darlington	A	W	2-0	Durham Senior Professional Cup
	Oct 19	Gateshead	A	W	3-2	Durham Senior Professional Cup
	Apr 26	Racing Club de Paris	H	W	5-2	
	May 1	Rest of Durham XI	A	W	4-0	
	3	Aldershot	A	L	1-5	
	10	Racing Club de Paris	A	W	3-0	
1933-34	Sep 20	Gateshead	H	W	3-1	Durham Senior Professional Cup
	Oct 4	Darlington	A	L	1-2	Durham Senior Professional Cup
	Feb 17	Corinthians	H	W	2-0	
	Apr 22	Ligue de Nord	Lille	W	3-2	
	May 13	Athletic Bilbao	A	D	3-3	
	15	Madrid XI	Madrid	D	2-2	
	20	Spanish XI	Madrid	W	3-1	
1934-35	Sep 26	Gateshead	A	D	1-1	Durham Senior Professional Cup
	Oct 17	Gateshead	H	D	3-3	Durham Senior Professional Cup
	31	Gateshead	H	W	6-5	Durham Senior Professional Cup
	May 1	Hartlepool United	H	W	2-1	Durham Senior Professional Cup
	12	Cataluna	Barcelona	W	7-1	
	15	Castille	Madrid	W	2-1	
1935-36	Sep 25	Gateshead	A	W	1-0	Durham Senior Professional Cup
	Apr 1	Hartlepool United	H	W	4-1	Durham Senior Professional Cup Final
1936-37	Sep 16	Glasgow Celtic	H	D	1-1	

SUNDERLAND: THE COMPLETE RECORD

Season	Date	Opponents	Venue	Result		Comments
	23	Gateshead	A	W	4-2	Durham Senior Professional Cup Semi Final
	30	Glasgow Celtic	A	L	2-3	
	Oct 21	Hartlepool United	H	L	0-3	Durham Senior Professional Cup Final
	Nov 15	Ligue de Nord	Lille	L	1-5	
1937-38	Sep 22	Hartlepool United	A	L	0-1	Durham Senior Professional Cup
	Oct 6	Glasgow Celtic	H	L	0-2	FA Cup and Scottish FA Cup on display at game
	Apr 25	Ipswich Town	A	W	3-0	
	May 25	Glasgow Celtic	A	D	0-0	British Empire Exhibition Cup
	26	Glasgow Celtic	A	L	1-3	British Empire Exhibition Cup
1938-39	Aug 20	Middlesbrough	H	W	4-2	
	Sep 21	Darlington	A	W	6-1	Durham Senior Professional Cup
	May 1	Hartlepool United	A	W	1-0	Durham Senior Professional Cup
1946-47	Oct 16	Hartlepool United	H	W	2-0	Durham Senior Professional Cup
	May 5	Darlington	H	L	1-2	Durham Senior Professional Cup Final
1947-48	Feb 2	Barnsley	H	W	5-1	
	Apr 4	Darlington	H	L	0-1	Durham Senior Professional Cup
	May 8	English League XI	Consett	W	5-2	In aid of Consett War Heroes Fund
1948-49	Sep 20	Hartlepool United	A	D	1-1	Durham Senior Professional Cup semi-final
	Feb 12	Blackburn Rovers	H	W	5-1	
	26	Bury	H	D	1-1	
	Apr 27	Hartlepool United	H	L	1-2	Durham Senior Professional Cup semi-final (replay)
	May 2	Crystal Palace	A	L	0-2	Jack Lewis Testimonial
	17	Glasgow Celtic	Belfast	W	6-2	Benefit game for Sam Doak at Grosvenor Park
1949-50	Sep 26	Gateshead	A	W	2-1	Durham Senior Professional Cup
	Feb 11	Motherwell	H	D	1-1	
	Apr 17	Darlington	A	L	0-1	Durham Senior Professional Cup semi-final
	May 13	Besiktas	A	W	3-0	
	16	Turkish Youths	Istanbul	W	2-1	
	20	Galatasaray	A	W	4-3	
	21	Fenerbache	A	W	3-0	
1950-51	Sep 13	Galatasaray	H	W	3-1	
	18	St Mirren	A	D	3-3	Andy Reid Testimonial
	25	Hartlepool United	H	W	4-1	Durham Senior Professional Cup semi-final
	Apr 4	Netherlands 'A'	Rotterdam	W	2-1	
	16	Aberdeen	A	L	0-1	
	May 14	Gateshead	H	L	1-3	Durham Senior Professional Cup Final
	16	Red Star Belgrade	H	W	1-0	Festival of Britain game
	Jun 6	Rapid Vienna	A	L	1-5	
	7	Austria XI	Vienna	L	4-5	
	12	Graz XI	Graz	L	1-2	
1951-52	Sep 17	Crook Town	A	W	4-3	Opening of new ground
	Apr 23	Third Lanark	H	W	6-0	
	28	Hull City	A	D	2-2	East Riding Invitation Trophy
	May 6	Netherlands 'B'	Amsterdam	W	7-3	
	8	Netherlands 'A'	Rotterdam	W	1-0	
1952-53	Dec 1	Southampton	A	D	1-1	Sunderland's first floodlit game in England
	10	Dundee	H	W	5-3	First floodlit game at Roker Park
	Mar 4	East Fife	H	L	1-3	
	11	Darlington	H	W	2-1	Durham Senior Professional Cup semi-final

SUNDERLAND'S FRIENDLIES, TESTIMONIALS AND MINOR CUP GAMES SINCE 1890

Season	Date	Opponents	Venue	Result	Comments
	18	Clyde	H	W 2-1	
	25	Racing Club de Paris	H	W 2-0	
	Apr 30	Scotland Select XI	Third Lanark	L 0-5	James Mason Testimonial at Cathkin Park
	May 4	Gateshead	H	W 3-0	Durham Senior Professional Cup Final
	6	Middlesbrough	H	L 3-4	Coronation Cup
	16	Malmo	A	W 5-3	
	19	Gothenberg	A	D 3-3	
	22	Denmark XI	Copenhagen	W 2-0	
1953-54	Oct 5	West Ham United	A	L 0-2	
	21	Racing Club de Paris	H	W 5-2	
	Nov 4	Rapid Vienna	H	L 2-3	
	23	East Fife	H	D 2-2	
	30	Darlington	H	D 1-1	Durham Senior Professional Cup semi-final
	Jan 30	Leeds United	H	W 5-2	Raich Carter last appearance at Roker Park
	Feb 8	Hibernian	H	D 2-2	
	Mar 27	Blackpool	H	L 1-2	
1954-55	Oct 13	Falkirk	H	L 2-3	
	18	Borussia Dortmund	H	W 3-2	
	Nov 3	Staevnet (Copenhagen)	H	W 4-1	
	10	Heart of Midlothian	H	D 3-3	
	24	Clyde	A	L 1-3	
	May 8	American League Stars	Brooklyn	W 7-2	
	15	Huddersfield Town	New York	W 3-2	
	17	Nurnberg	Brooklyn	D 1-1	
	22	Philadelphia Uhrik Truckers	Philadelphia	W 3-1	
	25	New York Stars	New York	W 4-1	
	29	Montreal Stars	Montreal	W 4-2	
	31	Huddersfield Town	Winnipeg	D 3-3	
	Jun 4	Huddersfield Town	Toronto	D 3-3	
	5	Huddersfield Town	Detroit	D 2-2	
1955-56	Oct 10	East Fife	A	L 0-1	
	23	Racing Club de Paris	A	W 4-3	
	Nov 2	First Vienna	H	D 4-4	
	14	Moscow Dynamo	H	L 0-1	All ticket game (att: 55,436)
	Apr 9	Darlington	H	W 5-0	Durham Senior Professional Cup semi-final
	11	Airdrieonians	H	W 1-0	
	May 3	Maccabi Petah-Tiqva	Tel Aviv	W 3-2	
	5	Haifa Maccabi	Haifa	W 4-3	
	8	Hapoel Select XI	Ramacum	D 1-1	
	13	Hapoel Haifa	Jerusalem	W 4-2	
1956-57	Sep 18	Servette	Geneva	W 2-0	
	Oct 8	Hartlepool United	H	W 2-1	Durham Senior Professional Cup Final
	17	Norwich City	A	W 3-0	Inaugural floodlit game at Carrow Road
	26	Red Banner	H	D 2-2	
	Apr 29	Darlington	A	L 1-8	Durham Senior Professional Cup semi-final
	May 6	Hull City	A	W 2-1	East Riding Invitation Trophy
1957-58	Oct 2	Maccabi Petah-Tiqva	H	W 5-2	
	16	Middlesbrough	A	L 0-2	Inaugural floodlit game at Ayresome Park
	21	Millwall	A	L 0-4	
	Dec 2	Juventus	H	L 0-2	
	Mar 5	Select X1	H	L 0-1	Jack Stelling Testimonial
	24	Hartlepool United	H	W 3-0	Durham Senior Professional Cup semi-final

Season	Date	Opponents	Venue	Result		Comments
	Apr 28	Plymouth Argyle	A	L	0-3	Jack Rowley Testimonial
	May 5	Darlington	H	W	4-0	Durham Senior Professional Cup Final
1958-59	Oct 13	Dynamo Prague	H	W	3-1	
	27	Coventry City	A	W	3-1	
	Mar 16	Gateshead	A	L	0-1	Durham Senior Professional Cup
	Apr 15	All Star XI	H	W	5-4	Len Shackleton Testimonial
	27	Middlesbrough	Kendal	L	3-4	Westmorland County Invitation Trophy
1959-60	Oct 7	Winterthur	H	W	3-0	
	21	Rapid Vienna	H	W	5-2	
	Jan 30	Glasgow Cletic	H	W	7-1	Six different Sunderland scorers
	May 5	Peterborough United	A	W	1-0	
	8	Winterthur	A	L	1-2	
	11	Cardiff City	Berne	D	0-0	
1960-61	Oct 31	England U-23	H	L	3-5	
	Apr 10	Bangu (Brazil)	H	W	3-0	
1961-62	Aug 9	Odense	H	W	5-1	
	12	Aarhus	H	W	3-0	
	Sep 6	Newcastle United	H	L	0-1	Cock of the North Tournament
	Oct 11	Middlesbrough	A	L	0-2	Cock of the North Tournament
	25	Newcastle United	A	L	1-2	Cock of the North Tournament
	Nov 1	Middlesbrough	H	D	2-2	Cock of the North Tournament
	Apr 30	Shamrock Rovers	A	W	5-2	Tommy Hamilton & Jimmy McCann Testimonial
1962-63	Aug 11	Shamrock Rovers	H	W	3-2	
	13	Linfield	A	W	5-2	
	Sep 19	Standard Liege	H	W	4-1	
	Oct 3	Standard Liege	A	W	2-1	
1963-64	Aug 10	Shamrock Rovers	H	L	1-2	
	17	Bolton Wanderers	H	L	3-4	
	Nov 14	Benfica	H	W	5-3	Filmed by Tyne Tees Television
	Apr 13	International XI	H	W	3-1	Stan Anderson Testimonial
	28	Hartlepool United	A	W	6-3	Ken Johnson & Tommy Burlison Testimonial
	May 3	Shamrock Rovers	A	W	3-1	
	4	Ards	A	W	8-3	
	6	Linfield	A	W	2-1	
1964-65	Aug 12	Middlesbrough	A	L	1-2	
	15	Huddersfield Town	H	L	2-3	
	Feb 8	ES Clydebank	A	W	5-1	Inaugural floodlit game at New Kilbowie Park
	Apr 29	Darlington	A	W	5-4	
1965-66	Aug 7	Glasgow Celtic	H	L	0-5	
	14	Sparta Rotterdam	H	W	2-1	
	Oct 27	Newcastle United	H	L	2-6	Brian Clough Testimonial
	Dec 7	Dukla Prague	H	L	0-3	
1966-67	Aug 6	Kilmarnock	H	D	3-3	
	10	Kilmarnock	A	D	0-0	
	13	Hull City	A	W	1-0	
	Sep 28	Charltons XI	H	D	6-6	Norman Clarke Testimonial
	Nov 9	Blyth Spartans	A	W	5-2	
	May 28	San Fransico Golden Gate Gales (ADO Den Haag)	San Francisco	L	1-6	US Soccer League (played as Vancouver Royal Canadians)
	Jun 4	Detroit Cougars (Glentoran)	Detroit	D	1-1	US Soccer League (played as Vancouver Royal Canadians)

SUNDERLAND'S FRIENDLIES, TESTIMONIALS AND MINOR CUP GAMES SINCE 1890

Season	Date	Opponents	Venue	Result		Comments
	7	Dallas Tornado (Dundee United)	Vancouver	W	4-1	US Soccer League (played as Vancouver Royal Canadians)
	11	Boston Rovers (Shamrock Rovers)	Vancouver	W	1-0	US Soccer League (played as Vancouver Royal Canadians)
	14	Los Angeles Wolves (Wolverhampton W)	Los Angeles	L	1-5	US Soccer League (played as Vancouver Royal Canadians)
	18	Houston Stars (Bangu)	Vancouver	L	1-4	US Soccer League (played as Vancouver Royal Canadians
	21	Toronto City (Hibernian)	Vancouver	L	2-4	US Soccer League (played as Vancouver Royal Canadians)
	25	Toronto City (Hibernian)	Toronto	D	2-2	US Soccer League (played as Vancouver Royal Canadians)
	28	Washington Whips (Aberdeen)	Washington	D	1-1	US Soccer League (played as Vancouver Royal Canadians)
	Jul 1	Chicago Mustangs (Cagliari)	Chicago	D	2-2	US Soccer League (played as Vancouver Royal Canadians)
	5	New York Skyliners (Cerro)	Vancouver	D	1-1	US Soccer League (played as Vancouver Royal Canadians)
	8	Cleveland Stokers (Stoke City)	Vancouver	W	3-1	US Soccer League (played as Vancouver Royal Canadians)
1967-68	Aug 5	Middlesbrough	H	W	1-0	
	12	Hull City	A	D	3-3	
	Sep 25	Fife Select	Dunfermline	L	2-4	In aid of the Michael Colliery Disaster Fund
	Oct 4	All Star XI	H	D	4-4	Charlie Hurley Testimonial
	Feb 17	Grimsby Town	A	W	3-2	
1968-69	Jul 30	Middlesbrough	A	W	1-0	
	Aug 3	Derby County	A	L	1-2	
	Sep 23	Heart of Midlothian	H	W	2-1	
	Dec 11	Slavia Prague	H	W	2-0	
	Mar 24	Grimsby Town	A	D	2-2	Ron Cockerill Testimonial
	Apr 28	Werder Bremen	H	D	1-1	
	May 7	Werder Bremen	A	L	0-1	
	9	Hanover 96	A	W	1-0	
	13	Koblenz	A	L	3-5	
	15	Combined Schuttorf & FC Emsdetten 05 Select XI	A	W	10-0	
	22	Napoli	H	L	0-1	
	24	Verona	H	W	2-1	
	Jun 1	Verona	A	L	2-3	
	5	Napoli	A	L	1-5	
	8	Vincenza	A	D	2-2	
1969-70	Jul 26	Middlesbrough	H	D	0-0	
	28	Millwall	H	L	0-1	
	Aug 1	Eintracht Brunswick	Hamburg	L	0-4	
	4	Aalborg	Copenhagen	W	3-1	
	Nov 12	Newcastle United	H	W	4-2	Len Ashurst Testimonial
	May 21	Perugia	A	W	2-1	
1970-71	Aug 1	Stirling Albion	A	D	1-1	
	5	Eintracht Brunswick	H	W	2-1	
	8	Hanover 96	H	W	4-3	
	Jan 23	Newcastle United	A	D	1-1	
	Apr 19	Great Britain Olympic XI	H	W	3-2	

629

SUNDERLAND: THE COMPLETE RECORD

Season	Date	Opponents	Venue	Result	Comments
1971-72	Jul 31	Aalborg	H	W 3-1	
	Aug 4	Ayr United	A	D 1-1	
	7	Rotherham United	A	D 1-1	
	May 1	Hartlepool United	A	D 3-3	
1972-73	Jul 29	Berwick Rangers	A	W 5-1	
	May 14	Newcastle United	A	L 1-2	Ollie Burton Testimonial
	22	Cannes	A	W 3-2	
1973-74	Aug 4	Aberdeen	A	L 0-3	
	6	Glasgow Celtic	A	W 2-1	
	10	Shelbourne	A	W 2-1	
	12	Cork Hibernian	A	L 1-2	
	18	Tottenham Hotspur	H	L 0-1	
	May 3	Yeovil Town	A	L 0-2	Cec Irwin Testimonial
	6	Leeds United	A	D 0-0	Billy Bremner Testimonial
	13	Newcastle United	H	L 2-3	Jimmy Montgomery Testimonial
1974-75	Jul 29	Hamilton Academicals	A	W 3-0	
	31	Berwick Rangers	A	W 2-0	
	Apr 28	Newcastle United	H	W 3-2	Martin Harvey Testimonial
	30	Newcastle United	A	L 3-5	David Craig Testimonial
1975-76	Jul 26	Hamilton Academicals	A	W 2-0	
	28	Berwick Rangers	A	W 4-1	
	30	Dunfermline Athletic	A	W 3-0	
	Nov 24	AZ 67	H	D 0-0	Richie Pitt and Bobby Park Testimonial
	Apr 26	Leeds United	H	L 1-2	Bobby Kerr Testimonial
	28	Newcastle United	A	L 3-6	Frank Clark Testimonial
	May 9	Tahiti	Papeete	W 5-1	
	11	Tahiti	Papeete	D 2-2	
	14	New Zealand	Auckland	W 3-0	
	16	Queensland	Brisbane	W 6-0	
	19	Australia	Sydney	W 4-3	
	23	Tasmania	Hobart	W 5-0	Mel Holden scored all five goals
	25	Australia	Melbourne	D 0-0	
	27	South Australia	Adelaide	W 4-0	
	30	Western Australia	Perth	W 2-1	
	Jun 2	Singapore	A	D 2-2	
1976-77	Jul 31	Berwick Rangers	A	W 2-1	
	Aug 3	IFK Eskilstuna	A	W 3-1	
	4	Vasteras SK	A	W 2-1	
	9	Norkopping	A	W 2-0	
	14	Shelbourne	H	W 3-0	
	Oct 11	Motherwell	A	L 1-3	
	Nov 15	Australian Federation	H	W 2-0	
	Jan 29	Horden CW	A	W 2-1	
	Feb 26	Kilmarnock	A	D 2-2	
	Mar 14	Charlton Athletic	A	L 2-3	Graham Tutt Testimonial
	29	International XI	H	L 3-6	Billy Hughes Testimonial
	Apr 19	Middlesbrough	A	L 1-6	John Hickton Testimonial
1977-78	Aug 9	Peterborough United	A	D 0-0	
	13	Kettering Town	A	L 0-1	
	May 20	Breweries	Nairobi	L 0-2	
	21	Gor Mahia	Nairobi	W 3-2	
	27	Ranogi	Mombasa	W 3-0	

SUNDERLAND'S FRIENDLIES, TESTIMONIALS AND MINOR CUP GAMES SINCE 1890

Season	Date	Opponents	Venue	Result	Comments
	Jun 1	Minenge	Mombasa	W 5-0	
1978-79	Jul 29	Southampton	H	L 0-1	
	Oct 25	1973 FA Cup Winners	H	L 2-6	Ian Porterfield Testimonial
1979-80	Jul 26	Lucerne	A	W 2-1	
	28	Lausanne	A	D 1-1	
	30	Berne	A	D 0-0	
	Aug 1	Neuchatel	A	W 3-2	
	6	Gateshead	A	W 1-0	
	Oct 16	Olympia Asuncion	H	W 5-2	
	Nov 7	England XI	H	L 0-2	To celebrate Centenary of Sunderland AFC
	Dec 11	Seaham Red Star	A	W 6-1	To celebrate Seaham's new floodlights
	May 5	Queens Park Rangers	H	W 3-2	Mick Docherty Testimonial
	14	Fort Lauderdale	A	W 2-1	
1980-81	27	Poskrin	A	W 2-0	
	29	Skeid	Oslo	W 3-1	
	30	Haymar	A	D 1-1	
	Aug 1	Lillestrom	A	W 3-1	
	2	Grimsby Town	A	W 2-0	
	9	Coventry City	H	W 2-1	
	Oct 15	Ashington	A	W 5-1	To celebrate Ashington's new floodlights
	Jan 22	Scunthorpe United	A	D 2-2	
	May 4	Hartlepool United	A	L 1-2	In aid of Children's Crisis Fund
	5	Hull City	A	L 0-2	Malcolm Lord Testimonial
1981-82	Aug 1	Heart of Midlothian	A	W 1-0	
	2	Hibernian	A	L 0-3	
	4	Dundee	A	D 2-2	
	5	Berwick Rangers	A	W 2-1	
	14	Panathiniakos	A	L 0-2	
	18	Newcastle United	A	D 1-1	
	22	Newcastle United	H	W 2-1	
	25	Darlington	A	D 1-1	
	Sep 8	Middlesbrough	A	W 2-1	Jim Platt Testimonial
	Dec 7	Newport, Isle of Wight	A	W 4-1	
	Mar 2	Darlington	A	W 3-1	
1982-83	Aug 5	St Mirren	Douglas	L 1-2	Match played on Isle of Man
	6	Carlisle United	A	L 0-3	
	8	St Johnstone	A	L 1-2	
	10	Dundee	A	D 2-2	
	11	Dunfermline Athletic	A	W 1-0	
	20	Derby County	A	W 0-1	
	24	Darlington	A	W 3-2	
	Jan 28	Bolton Wanderers	A	W 1-0	
	Feb 13	Hibernian	A	W 2-1	
	May 15	Glasgow Celtic	Berwick	W 3-1	Ian Cashmore Testimonial
1983-84	Aug 5	Isle of Man XI	Castletown	W 5-1	Isle of Man Tournament
	7	Burnley	Douglas	W 1-0	Isle of Man Tournament
	9	St Mirren	Douglas	W 1-0	Isle of Man Tournament Final
	15	Port Vale	A	W 1-0	
	17	Bishop Auckland	A	W 2-0	
	19	Middlesbrough	H	W 4-0	
	23	Darlington	A	D 2-2	
1984-85	Jul 21	Nissan FC	H	W 5-2	

SUNDERLAND: THE COMPLETE RECORD

Season	Date	Opponents	Venue	Result		Comments
	30	Carlisle United	Douglas	D	2-1	Isle of Man Tournament
	Aug 1	Athlone Town	Ramsey	W	1-1	Isle of Man Tournament
	4	Blackburn Rovers	Douglas	W	1-0	Isle of Man Tournament Final
	9	Huddersfield Town	Durham	D	1-1	
	14	Middlesbrough	A	W	1-0	
	17	Carlisle United	A	D	2-2	
	Oct 3	Hammarby IF, Sweden	A	L	1-2	Venison, Lemon and Walker sent off
	Dec 12	Hartlepool United	A	L	1-2	Tommy Johnson Testimonial
1985-86	Jul 31	Lincoln City	A	W	3-1	
	Aug 3	Doncaster Rovers	A	W	2-1	
	5	Hartlepool United	A	W	2-0	
	7	Darlington	A	L	0-2	
	10	Aston Villa	A	L	1-2	
	Mar 12	Scarborough	A	W	2-1	
1986-87	Jul 29	Waterford Town	A	D	1-1	
	31	Linfield	A	W	1-0	
	Aug 2	Derry City	A	L	0-1	
	5	Carlisle United	A	D	1-1	
	7	Darlington	A	W	1-0	
	9	Hartlepool United	A	D	1-1	
	15	Doncaster Rovers	A	D	0-0	
	Dec 10	Bishop Auckland	A	L	1-2	
	Feb 22	Kuwait 'B'	Kuwait	D	0-0	
1987-88	Jul 23	Gretna	A	W	3-1	
	25	Harrogate Town	A	W	2-1	
	29	Darlington	A	L	1-2	Durham Senior Cup
	Aug 1	Ryhope	A	W	5-0	Durham Senior Cup
	6	Marske	A	W	6-1	
	7	Darlington	H	W	2-1	Behind closed doors
1988-89	Aug 4	Newcastle Town	A	W	5-0	
	6	Macclesfield Town	A	D	1-1	
	10	Bishop Auckland	A	W	0-0	Won on penalties
	13	Seattle Storm	H	W	3-0	
	16	Hartlepool United	H	W	3-1	Durham Senior Cup Final
	19	Burnley	A	W	1-0	3 x 30 minute sessions behind closed doors
1989-90	Jul 27	Newcastle Town	A	D	0-0	
	29	Crewe Alexandra	A	W	2-1	
	Aug 1	Darlington	A	L	0-1	Durham Senior Cup
	5	Heart of Midlothian	A	L	0-1	
	8	Dnepr (USSR)	H	L	0-2	
1990-91	Aug 2	Anglesey XI	A	W	3-2	
	4	Bangor City	A	W	4-2	
	7	Carlisle United	A	L	0-1	
	11	Torpedo Moscow	H	L	1-4	
	14	Oldham Athletic	H	L	1-3	
	17	Kilmarnock	A	L	0-2	
	Apr 28	Berwick Rangers	A	D	1-1	Brian Marshall Testimonial
1991-92	Jul 26	Gateshead	A	D	2-2	Durham Senior Cup
	28	Bolton Wanderers	Isle of Man	D	2-2	Isle of Man Tournament (won 5-4 on penalties)
	31	Shelbourne	Isle of Man	W	3-0	Isle of Man Tournament
	Aug 3	Stoke City	Isle of Man	L	0-2	Isle of Man Tournament
	7	Limerick City	A	W	3-1	

SUNDERLAND'S FRIENDLIES, TESTIMONIALS AND MINOR CUP GAMES SINCE 1890

Season	Date	Opponents	Venue	Result		Comments
	9	Cork City	A	D	1-1	
1992-93	Jul 26	Falkirk	A	D	1-1	
	28	Ayr United	A	D	0-0	
	Aug 1	Carlisle United	A	L	2-3	
	5	Tottenham Hotspur	H	L	0-3	Match to celebrate Sunderland becoming a City
	8	Scunthorpe United	A	D	2-2	
1993-94	Jul 28	Glasgow Rangers	H	L	1-3	Gary Bennett Testimonial
	31	Glentoran	A	W	4-1	
	Aug 2	Ards	A	W	2-1	
	8	Middlesbrough	A	W	2-1	Gary Hamilton Testimonial
	May 20	Florida West Coast Select XI	Naples, Florida	W	4-0	
1994-95	Jul 19	Team Gauldal (Norway)	A	W	4-0	
	22	Averoykameratene (Norway)	A	W	2-0	
	24	Langevag (Norway)	A	D	0-0	
	26	Team Fosen / Vikingan (Norway)	A	D	2-2	
	27	Surnadal	A	W	9-0	
	29	FC Porto	H	W	2-0	Gordon Armstrong Testimonial
	Aug 2	York City	A	W	2-1	
	5	Sheffield Wednesday	H	L	1-2	
1995-96	Jul 21	St Patrick's Athletic	A	W	2-0	
	23	Drogheda United	A	W	6-0	
	25	Athlone Town	A	D	1-1	
	29	York City	A	W	2-1	Tony Canham Testimonial
	Aug 1	Darlington	A	W	3-2	
	5	Blackpool	A	W	2-1	
1996-97	Jul 24	Steaua Bucharest	H	L	0-1	Richard Ord Testimonial
	29	St Patrick's Athletic	A	W	2-0	
	31	Drogheda United	A	W	1-0	
	Aug 2	Sligo Rovers	A	W	2-0	
	4	Galway United	A	W	2-0	
	7	Bury	A	D	1-1	
	9	Chester City	A	W	2-0	
	May 13	Liverpool	H	W	1-0	Final game at Roker Park
1997-98	Jul 17	St Patrick's Athletic	A	W	4-1	
	19	Portadown	A	D	2-2	
	21	Shelbourne	A	W	2-1	
	26	Macclesfield Town	A	W	1-0	
	30	Ajax	H	D	0-0	Opening of Stadium of Light
	Aug 2	Carlisle United	A	D	0-0	
1998-99	Jul 18	Manchester City	A	D	0-0	Ian Brightwell Testimonial
	21	Plymouth Argyle	A	W	3-0	
	23	Weymouth	A	W	3-0	
	25	Yeovil Town	A	W	2-1	
	31	Hartlepool United	A	W	2-1	
	May 11	All Star XI	H	L	2-4	Jimmy McNab Testimonial
	18	Liverpool	H	L	2-3	To celebrate 100 years of Football League
1999-2000	Jul 14	Odense	A	L	0-2	
	18	Vejle	A	W	4-0	
	21	Glasgow Rangers	A	L	1-3	Ian Ferguson Testimonial
	25	Burnley	A	W	2-0	
	27	Halifax Town	A	L	0-1	George Mulhall Testimonial

Season	Date		Opponents	Venue	Result		Comments
		29	Preston North End	A	L	0-2	
		31	Sampdoria	H	D	0-0	Kevin Ball Testimonial (lost 1-0 on penalties)
2000-01	Jul	23	Le Havre	A	L	0-3	
		26	KV Mechelen	A	D	2-2	
		29	Porto	A	L	0-1	Shown live on Portuguese TV
	Aug	8	Fortuna Sittard	A	L	2-3	
		10	Apeldoornse Boys	A	W	9-0	Dutch Amateur side
		12	SC Heerenveen	A	L	1-4	
2001-02	Jul	17	Calais	A	W	1-0	
		21	Mansfield Town	A	L	1-3	
		24	Glasgow Celtic	A	L	0-1	
		28	Torquay United	A	W	5-0	
		31	Plymouth Argyle	A	W	3-0	
	Aug	2	Exeter City	A	W	5-0	
		4	West Bromwich Albion	A	W	3-0	
		8	Vitesse Arnhem	A	W	2-1	
		10	NAC Breda	A	L	0-4	
	May	14	Eire	H	L	0-3	Niall Quinn Benefit game
2002-03	Jul	20	Amiens	A	L	1-2	
		28	St Truiden	A	W	1-0	
		31	Royal Antwerp	A	D	1-1	
	Aug	3	Gent	A	L	1-2	
		8	Seville	A	L	0-1	
		10	Algeciras	A	L	0-2	
	Dec	18	Hull City	A	L	0-1	Raich Carter Trophy; Opening of KC Stadium
2003-04	Jul	12	Durham City	A	W	4-0	
		16	York City	A	W	5-0	
		19	Grimsby Town	A	D	1-1	
		23	Huddersfield Town	A	L	0-2	
		26	Hibernian	A	D	2-2	
		30	Heart of Midlothian	A	D	2-2	
	Aug	2	Kilmarnock	A	L	2-4	
2004-05	Jul	17	Charleston Battery	A	L	1-2	
		21	Wilmington Hammerheads	A	W	3-0	
		26	Barnsley	A	W	2-1	
		29	Scunthorpe United	A	D	1-1	
	Aug	1	Doncaster Rovers	A	W	3-1	
2005-06	Jul	14	British Columbia All Stars	Victoria	W	1-0	
		16	Vancouver Whitecaps	A	L	0-3	
		20	Seattle Sounders	A	W	1-0	
		23	Portland Timbers	A	D	0-0	
		27	Hull City	A	L	0-1	
		30	Sheffield United	A	L	0-1	
	Aug	6	AZ Alkmaar	A	W	1-0	
2006-07	Jul	15	Forest Green Rovers	A	W	3-0	
		19	Rotherham United	A	W	2-0	
		24	Shelbourne	A	W	2-0	
		29	Carlisle United	A	W	3-0	
2007-08	Jul	18	Darlington	A	W	2-0	
		21	Scunthorpe United	A	L	0-1	
		28	Bohemians	A	W	1-0	
		30	Cork City	A	D	1-1	

SUNDERLAND'S FRIENDLIES, TESTIMONIALS AND MINOR CUP GAMES SINCE 1890

Season	Date	Opponents	Venue	Result		Comments
	Aug 1	Galway United	A	W	4-0	
	4	Juventus	H	D	1-1	To celebrate 10th anniversary of Stadium of Light
	Nov 15	Falkirk	A	D	1-1	Alex Lawrie Testimonial
2008-09	Jul 20	Sporting Lisbon	Albufeira	W	3-1	
	23	Vitoria Setubal	Albufeira	D	1-1	
	28	Cobh Ramblers	A	W	4-0	
	30	Nottingham Forest	A	W	1-0	
	Aug 3	Ajax	H	L	0-1	
	8	Athlone Town	A	W	6-0	
2009-10	Jul 16	Darlington	A	W	4-0	
	19	Portimonese	Portimao	W	1-0	
	24	Benfica	Amsterdam	L	0-2	Amsterdam Tournament
	26	Atletico Madrid	Amsterdam	W	2-0	Amsterdam Tournament
	Aug 1	Glasgow Celtic	A	W	2-1	
	4	Peterborough United	A	W	2-0	
	8	Heart of Midlothian	A	D	1-1	
2010-11	Jul 13	Munster XI	Limerick	W	2-1	
	17	Darlington	A	W	1-0	
	21	Brighton & Hove Albion	Albufeira	D	1-1	
	24	Hull City	Albufeira	W	4-2	
	27	Benfica	Albufeira	L	0-2	
	31	Leicester City	A	W	2-1	
	Aug 8	1899 Hoffenheim	A	L	1-3	
2011-12	Jul 13	York City	A	W	2-1	
	17	Arminia Bielefeld	A	D	1-1	
	20	Hannover 96	Hamelin	L	1-3	
	23	Borussia Moenchengladbach	A	D	0-0	
	27	Kilmarnock	A	W	2-1	
	30	Burnley	A	L	0-1	
	Aug 2	Hartlepool United	A	W	3-1	Ritchie Humphreys Testimonial
	6	Hibernian	A	D	0-0	
2012-13	Jul 19	Seongnam Ilhwa Chunma	Suwon, South Korea	L	0-1	Peace Cup
	22	FC Groningen	Suwon, South Korea	W	3-2	Peace Cup
	27	Hartlepool United	A	L	0-1	
	Aug 4	Helsingborgs IF	A	L	0-2	
	8	Derby County	A	D	1-1	
	11	Leicester City	A	L	0-1	

Sunderland's Christmas and New Year Games

Season	Christmas Day Opponents	Venue	Result	Boxing Day Opponents	Venue	Result	New Year's Day Opponents	Venue	Result
1890-91				Aston Villa	A	0-0			
1891-92	Everton	A	4-0	Wolverhampton W	A	3-1			
1892-93				Wolverhampton W	A	0-2			
1893-94				West Bromwich A	A	2-0	Preston North End	H	6-3
1894-95				West Bromwich A	A	1-1	Preston North End	H	2-0
1895-96									
1896-97	Blackburn Rovers	A	2-1	Everton	A	2-5	Preston North End	H	1-1
1897-98	Blackburn Rovers	A	1-2				Preston North End	H	1-0
1898-99									
1899-1900				Wolverhampton W	A	0-1	Wolverhampton W	H	1-2
1900-01	Manchester City	A	1-1	Derby County	A	1-1	Derby County	H	2-1
1901-02				Liverpool	A	1-0	Derby County	H	1-0
1902-03	Blackburn Rovers	A	2-0				Derby County	H	2-0
1903-04				Newcastle United	A	3-1	Newcastle United	H	1-1
1904-05				Blackburn Rovers	A	1-2			
1905-06	Preston North End	A	1-1				Middlesbrough	H	2-1
1906-07	Middlesbrough	A	1-2						
1907-08	Bristol City	H	3-3	Sheffield Wed	A	3-2	Woolwich Arsenal	H	5-2
1908-09				Middlesbrough	H	2-0	Liverpool	H	1-4
1909-10	Bury	A	1-0				Bristol City	H	4-0
1910-11				Liverpool	A	2-1			
1911-12	Bury	A	2-0	Sheffield Wed	A	0-8	Sheffield Wed	H	0-0
1912-13	Sheffield Wed	A	2-1	Sheffield Wed	H	0-2	Woolwich Arsenal	H	4-1

SUNDERLAND'S CHRISTMAS AND NEW YEAR GAMES

Season	Christmas Day Opponents	Venue	Result	Boxing Day Opponents	Venue	Result	New Year's Day Opponents	Venue	Result
1913-14	Burnley	A	1-0	Burnley	H	1-1	Preston North End	H	3-1
1914-15	Newcastle United	A	5-2	Newcastle United	H	2-4	Middlesbrough	A	3-2
1919-20	Liverpool	A	2-3	West Bromwich A	A	0-4	West Bromwich A	H	4-1
1920-21	Bolton Wanderers	A	2-6				Manchester City	A	1-3
1921-22				Everton	H	1-2			
1922-23				Stoke City	A	2-1	Stoke City	H	2-0
1923-24				Everton	A	3-2	Everton	H	3-0
1924-25	Sheffield United	H	0-1	Sheffield United	A	1-2	Cardiff City	H	1-0
1925-26				Huddersfield Town	A	1-1	Leeds United	H	1-3
1926-27	Everton	A	4-5				Blackburn Rovers	H	2-5
1927-28				Birmingham	A	1-1			
1928-29	Everton	A	0-0	Arsenal	A	1-1	Arsenal	H	5-1
1929-30	Blackburn Rovers	A	3-5	Blackburn Rovers	H	3-1	Burnley	H	3-3
1930-31	Leicester City	H	2-5	Leicester City	A	1-1			
1931-32				Derby County	A	1-3	Derby County	H	0-0
1932/33				West Bromwich A	A	1-5			
1933-34				Chelsea	A	0-4	Chelsea	H	0-0
1934-35	Everton	A	2-6				Everton	H	7-0
1935-36				Leeds United	H	2-1	Aston Villa	H	1-3
1936-37	Birmingham	A	0-2	Sheffield Wed	H	2-1	Manchester United	A	1-2
1937-38	Huddersfield Town	H	2-1				Middlesbrough	A	1-2
1938-39									
1946-47	Wolverhampton W	H	0-1	Aston Villa	H	1-5			
1947-48	Everton	H	2-0	Wolverhampton W	A	1-2			
1948-49	Middlesbrough	H	1-0	Everton	A	0-3	Liverpool	H	0-2
1949-50				Stoke City	H	3-0			
1950-51	Manchester United	H	2-1	Manchester United	A	5-3			
1951-52	Newcastle United	H	1-4	Newcastle United	A	2-2	Wolverhampton W	H	1-1
1952-53				Wolverhampton W	A	1-1	Aston Villa	H	2-2
1953-54	Huddersfield Town	H	1-1	Huddersfield Town	A	1-2	Aston Villa	H	2-0

SUNDERLAND: THE COMPLETE RECORD

Season	Christmas Day Opponents	Venue	Result	Boxing Day Opponents	Venue	Result	New Year's Day Opponents	Venue	Result
1954-55	Huddersfield Town	H	1-1				Tottenham Hotspur	H	1-1
1955-56				Newcastle United	H	1-6			
1956-57	Aston Villa	H	1-0				Wolverhampton W	H	2-3
1957-58				Leeds United	H	2-1			
1958-59				Scunthorpe United	A	2-3	Leyton Orient	H	4-0
1959-60				Lincoln City	H	2-4			
1960-61				Sheffield United	H	1-1			
1961-62				Charlton Athletic	A	0-2			
1962-63				Bury	H	0-1			
1963-64				Leeds United	A	1-1			
1964-65				Liverpool	H	2-3			
1965-66				Aston Villa	H	2-1	West Bromwich A	H	1-5
1966-67				Newcastle United	A	1-2			
1967-68				Sheffield Wed	H	0-0			
1968-69				Sheffield Wed	A	0-2			
1969-70				Middlesbrough	H	2-2			
1970-71									
1971-72							Sheffield Wed	H	2-0
1972-73				Middlesbrough	A	1-2			
1973-74				York City	H	2-0	Notts County	H	1-2
1974-75				Hull City	H	3-1			
1975-76				Blackpool	H	2-1	Liverpool	A	0-2
1976-77				Leicester City	H	1-1			
1977-78				Wrexham	H	1-1	Newcastle United	A	1-3
1978-79				West Bromwich A	H	0-0			
1979-80									
1980-81				Everton	A	0-0	Nottingham Forest	A	0-0
1981-82									
1982-83									
1983-84									

SUNDERLAND'S CHRISTMAS AND NEW YEAR GAMES

Season	Opponent	H/A	Score	Opponent	H/A	Score
1984-85	Everton	H	1-2	Newcastle United	A	1-3
1985-86	Sheffield United	H	2-1	Bradford City	A	0-2
1986-87	Leeds United	A	1-1			
1987-88	Chester City	A	2-1	Doncaster Rovers	H	3-1
1988-89	Barnsley	H	1-0			
1989-90	Oxford United	H	1-0	Hull City	A	2-3
1990-91	Crystal Palace	A	1-2	Southampton	H	1-0
1991-92	Tranmere Rovers	A	0-1	Barnsley	H	2-0
1992-93						
1993-94				Leicester City	A	1-2
1994-95	Bolton Wanderers	H	1-1			
1995-96						
1996-97	Derby County	H	2-0	Coventry City	A	2-2
1997-98	Bradford City	H	2-0			
1998-99	Tranmere Rovers	A	0-1			
1999-2000	Everton	A	0-5			
2000-01	Bradford City	A	4-1	Ipswich Town	H	4-1
2001-02	Blackburn Rovers	A	3-0	Aston Villa	H	1-1
2002-03	Leeds United	H	1-2	Manchester United	A	1-2
2003-04	Bradford City	H	3-0			
2004-05	Leeds United	H	2-3	Preston North End	A	2-3
2005-06	Bolton Wanderers	H	0-0			
2006-07	Leeds United	H	2-0	Leicester City	A	2-0
2007-08	Manchester United	H	0-4			
2008-09	Blackburn Rovers	H	0-0			
2009-10	Everton	H	1-1			
2010-11	Manchester United	A	0-2	Blackburn Rovers	H	3-0
2011-12	Everton	H	1-1	Manchester City	H	1-0

SUNDERLAND'S EASTER GAMES

Season	Easter Day	Good Friday		Easter Saturday		Easter Monday		Tuesday	
1890/91	29/03/1891			Season over before Easter					
1891/92	17/04/1892			Blackburn Rovers	H 6-1				
1892/93	02/04/1893			Bolton W.	A 1-2			Newton Heath	H 6-0
1893/94	25/03/1894			Stoke	A 0-2			Darwen	H 4-0
1894/95	14/04/1895			Burnley	A 3-0				
1895/96	05/04/1896	Bury	A 2-1						
1896/97	18/04/1897	Bury	A 1-1	Notts County (test match)	A 0-1	Notts County (test match)	H 0-0		
1897/98	10/04/1898	Bury	A 0-1	Aston Villa	H 4-2	Everton	A 0-2		
1898/99	02/04/1899	Bury	A 2-1	Manchester City	H 3-1	Blackburn Rovers	H 0-1		
1899/1900	15/04/1900			Everton	A 0-1	Blackburn Rovers	H 1-0		
1900/01	07/04/1901	Newcastle Utd (Abandoned)	A			Bolton W.	H 5-1	Nottingham Forest	A 3-1
1901/02	30/03/1902			Small Heath	H 1-1	Newcastle Utd	H 0-0		
1902/03	12/04/1903	Stoke	H 0-0	Bolton W.	A 0-2	Nottingham Forest	A 2-5		
1903/04	03/04/1904	Wolverhampton W.	H 2-1	Manchester City	A 1-2	Nottingham Forest	H 3-1		
1904/05	23/04/1905			Newcastle Utd	A 3-1	Sheffield Utd	H 2-1		
1905/06	15/04/1906	Middlesbrough	A 1-2	Nottingham Forest	H 0-1	Preston N.E.	H 2-0		
1906/07	31/03/1907	Preston N.E.	A 0-2	Everton	A 1-4	Middlesbrough	H 4-2		
1907/08	19/04/1908	Sheffield Wed.	H 1-2	Newcastle Utd	A 3-1	Bristol City	A 0-3		
1908/09	11/04/1909	Manchester City	H 2-0	Newcastle Utd	H 3-1	Liverpool	A 0-3		
1909/10	27/03/1910	Tottenham H.	A 1-5	Nottingham Forest	A 3-1	Liverpool	H 2-1		
1910/11	16/04/1911	Bury	A 0-0	Preston N.E.	A 2-0				
1911/12	07/04/1912	Liverpool	A 1-2	Everton	H 4-0	Bury	H 1-0		
1912/13	23/03/1913	Sheffield Utd	H 1-0	Manchester City	H 1-0	Sheffield Utd	A 3-1		
1913/14	12/04/1914	Manchester Utd	H 2-0	Bolton W.	A 1-2				

Season	Date	Opponent	Result	Opponent	Result	Opponent	Result
1914/15	04/04/1915	Middlesbrough	H 4-1	Chelsea	A 0-3	Sheffield Utd	A 1-1
1919/20	04/04/1920	Blackburn Rovers	A 0-3	Preston N.E.	A 2-5	Blackburn Rovers	H 2-0
1920/21	27/03/1921	Derby County	H 3-0	Tottenham H.	H 0-1	Derby County	A 1-0
1921/22	16/04/1922	Bolton W.	H 6-2	Chelsea	A 0-1	Bolton W.	A 1-1
1922/23	01/04/1923	Manchester City	H 2-0	Tottenham H.	H 2-0	Manchester City	A 0-1
1923/24	20/04/1924	West Bromwich A.	H 2-0	Arsenal	H 1-1	West Bromwich A.	A 1-3
1924/25	12/04/1925			Huddersfield T.	H 1-1	Cardiff City	A 0-2
1925/26	04/04/1926			West Ham Utd	A 2-3			Leeds Utd	A 2-0
1926/27	17/04/1927			Sheffield Utd	A 0-2			Bolton W.	H 6-2
1927/28	08/04/1928	Derby County	H 0-1	Bolton W.	A 2-1	Derby County	A 0-1
1928/29	31/03/1929	Everton	H 2-2	Leicester City	H 1-2		
1929/30	20/04/1930	Bolton W.	A 0-3	Liverpool	A 6-0	Bolton W.	H 4-1
1930/31	05/04/1931	Birmingham	H 1-0	Manchester Utd	H 1-2	Birmingham	A 0-1
1931/32	27/03/1932	Aston Villa	H 1-1	Liverpool	A 2-1	Aston Villa	A 0-2
1932/33	16/04/1933	Birmingham	H 1-0	Liverpool	H 0-0	Birmingham	A 0-2
1933/34	01/04/1934	Blackburn Rovers	H 3-0	Birmingham	H 4-1	Blackburn Rovers	A 0-0
1934/35	21/04/1935	Preston N.E.	H 3-1	Birmingham	A 2-2	Preston N.E.	A 1-1
1935/36	12/04/1936	Birmingham	H 2-1	Bolton W.	A 1-2	Birmingham	A 7-2
1936/37	28/03/1937	Wolverhampton W.	H 6-2	Stoke	A 3-5	Wolverhampton W.	A 1-1
1937/38	17/04/1938	Everton	A 3-3	Leeds Utd	H 0-0	Everton	H 2-0
1938/39	09/04/1939	Everton	H 1-2	Bolton W.	A 1-2	Everton	A 2-6
1946/47	06/04/1947	Aston Villa	H 4-1	Preston N.E.	A 2-2		
1947/48	28/03/1948	Wolverhampton W.	H 2-1			Wolverhampton W.	A 1-2
1948/49	17/04/1949	Aston Villa	H 0-0	Manchester City	A 1-1	Aston Villa	A 0-4
1949/50	09/04/1950	Middlesbrough	H 2-0	Fulham	A 3-0	Middlesbrough	A 0-2
1950/51	25/03/1951	Newcastle Utd	A 2-2	Sheffield Wed.	A 0-3	Newcastle Utd	H 2-1
1951/52	13/04/1952	Huddersfield T.	H 7-1	Fulham	A 1-0			Huddersfield T.	A 1-1
1952/53	05/04/1953	Bolton W.	A 0-5	Preston N.E.	H 2-2	Bolton W.	H 2-0
1953/54	18/04/1954	Sheffield Utd	H 2-2	Middlesbrough	A 0-0	Sheffield Utd	A 3-1
1954/55	10/04/1955	Manchester Utd	H 4-3	Manchester City	A 0-1	Manchester Utd	A 2-2
1955/56	01/04/1956	Manchester City	H 0-3	Tottenham H.	H 3-2	Manchester City	A 2-4
1956/57	21/04/1957	Leeds Utd	H 2-0	Manchester Utd	A 0-4	Leeds Utd	A 1-3			Huddersfield T.	A 2-2

SUNDERLAND: THE COMPLETE RECORD

Season	Date	Opponent	Result	Opponent	Result	Extra
1957/58	06/04/1958	Manchester Utd	A 2-2	Birmingham City	H 1-2	
1958/59	29/03/1959			Middlesbrough	A 0-6	
1959/60	17/04/1960	Portsmouth	H 2-0	Hull City	A 0-0	
1960/61	02/04/1961	Norwich City	H 0-3	Scunthorpe utd	H 2-0	
1961/62	22/04/1962			Newcastle Utd	H 3-0	Rotherham Utd A 3-0
1962/63	14/04/1963	Stoke City	H 0-0	Portsmouth	H 1-0	
1963/64	29/03/1964	Rotherham Utd	H 2-0		A 2-2	
1964/65	18/04/1965	Wolverhampton W.	H 1-2	Birmingham City	H 2-1	Wolverhampton W. A 0-3
1965/66	10/04/1966			Burnley	A 0-1	
1966/67	26/03/1967	Sheffield Wed.	H 2-0	Everton	H 0-2	Sheffield Wed. A 0-5
1967/68	14/04/1968			Liverpool	H 2-2	
1968/69	06/04/1969	Ipswich Town	A 0-1	Liverpool	A 1-2	
1969/70	29/03/1970	Newcastle Utd	H 1-1	Arsenal	H 0-0	
1970/71	11/04/1971	Orient	H 1-0	Derby County	H 1-1	
1971/72	02/04/1972			Middlesbrough	A 2-2	Preston N.E. A 3-1
1972/73	22/04/1973			Hull City	H 0-1	Nottingham Forest A 0-1
1973/74	14/04/1974	Carlisle Utd	H 2-1	Hull City	A 2-0	Carlisle Utd A 0-1
1974/75	30/03/1975	Orient	H 3-0	Bristol City	H 1-2	
1975/76	18/04/1976			Hull City	A 2-0	
1976/77	10/04/1977	Newcastle Utd	H 2-2	Leeds Utd	H 2-1	Blackpool A 0-1
1977/78	26/03/1978	Oldham Ath.	A 1-1	Blackburn Rovers	A 1-1	
1978/79	15/04/1979	Notts County	H 3-0	Leicester City	H 0-1	
1979/80	06/04/1980			Newcastle Utd	A 1-0	Shrewsbury T. A 2-1
1980/81	19/04/1981			Birmingham City	A 1-2	
1981/82	11/04/1982			Stoke City	H 3-0	West Bromwich A. H 2-0
1982/83	03/04/1983			Liverpool	A 1-0	Birmingham City H 0-0
1983/84	22/04/1984			Everton	A 0-1	Manchester Utd A 1-3
1984/85	07/04/1985			Everton	H 2-1	West Bromwich A. H 0-0
1985/86	30/03/1986			Bradford City	A 1-4	Newcastle Utd A 0-1
1986/87	19/04/1987			Bradford City	H 1-1	Sheffield Utd H 1-1
1987/88	03/04/1988			Grimsby Town	A 2-3	Leeds Utd H 3-2
1988/89	26/03/1989			Ipswich Town	A 1-0	Chesterfield A 0-1; Barnsley A 0-3

SUNDERLAND'S EASTER GAMES

Season	Date	Opponent	Result	Notes
1989/90	15/04/1990	Hull City	H 0-1	
1990/91	31/03/1991	Crystal Palace	H 2-1	
1991/92	19/04/1992	Grimsby Town	A 0-2	Leeds Utd A 0-5
1992/93	11/04/1993	Birmingham City	H 1-2	
1993/94	03/04/1994	Bolton W.	H 2-0	Millwall A 1-2
1994/95	16/04/1995	Luton Town	H 1-1	
1995/96	07/04/1996	Barnsley	A 1-0	
1996/97	30/03/1997	Saturday game due to be played at Leicester City played 29/01/97 due to England v Mexico on 29/03/97		
1997/98	12/04/1998	Queens Park R.	H 2-2	West Bromwich A. A 3-3
1998/99	04/04/1999	West Bromwich A.	H 3-0	Crystal Palace A 1-1
1999/2000	23/04/2000	Sheffield Wed.	A 2-0	Bradford City H 0-1
2000/01	15/04/2001	Tottenham H.	H 2-3	Coventry City A 0-1
2001/02	31/03/2002	Arsenal	A 0-3	Leicester City H 2-1
2002/03	20/04/2003	West Bromwich A.	H 1-2	Manchester City A 0-3
2003/04	11/04/2004	Sheffield Utd	H 3-0	Ipswich Town A 0-1
2004/05	27/03/2005	No Easter Games Scheduled - internationals		
2005/06	16/04/2006	Manchester Utd	A 0-0	Newcastle Utd H 1-4
2006/07	08/04/2007	Wolves	H 2-1	Southampton A 2-1
2007/08	23/03/2008	Aston Villa	A 1-0	
2008/09	12/04/2009	Manchester Utd	H 1-2	
2009/10	04/04/2010	Tottenham H.	H 3-1	
2010/11	24/04/2011	Wigan	H 4-2	Everton A 0-4
2011/12	08/04/2012	Tottenham H.	H 0-0	

Players with 200 first team appearances

No	Player	League	Total	No	Player	League	Total
1	Jimmy Montgomery	537	627	42	Paul Bracewell	228	270
2	Len Ashurst	409	458	43	Ian Porterfield	229	268
3	Ted Doig	417	457	44	George Aitken	245	267
4	Stan Anderson	402	447	45	Charlie B. Thomson	236	264
5	Gary Bennett	369	443	46	Charlie M. Thomson	237	263
6	Bobby Kerr	368	433	47	Jimmy Millar	239	262
7	Gordon Armstrong	349	416	48	Hugh Wilson	227	256
8	Charlie Buchan	379	411	49	Charlie Parker	245	256
9	Michael Gray	363	410	50	Arthur Andrews	228	245
10	Charlie Hurley	358	401	51	Len Duns	215	245
11	Bobby Gurney	348	390	52	John Kay	199	239
12	Kevin Ball	339	388	53	Darren Williams	199	239
13	Johnny Mapson	345	383	54	Andy Melville	204	236
14	Shaun Elliott	321	368	55	Kevin Phillips	208	235
15	Martin Harvey	315	358	56	Alex Hall	206	235
16	Ernie England	336	352	57	Gordon Chisholm	197	235
17	Cecil Irwin	315	352	58	Harry Martin	213	232
18	Arthur Bridgett	320	348	59	Harry Low	203	228
19	Len Shackleton	320	348	60	Albert McInroy	215	227
20	Billy Hughes	287	335	61	Jimmy Gemmell	212	227
21	Bill Murray	304	328	62	Jimmy Watson	211	227
22	Jimmy McNab	285	323	63	Billy Bingham	206	227
23	Joe Bolton	273	325	64	Tony Norman	198	227
24	Gary Owers	268	320	65	Fred Hall	215	224
25	George Herd	278	318	66	Chris Turner	195	224
26	George Holley	280	315	67	Willie Watson	211	223
27	Patsy Gallacher	273	308	68	Sandy McAllister	210	222
28	Billy Hogg	281	303	69	Niall Quinn	203	220
29	Alex Hastings	262	297	70	Eric Gates	181	220
30	Jackie Mordue	262	294	71	Jeff Clarke	181	218
31	Gary Rowell	254	297	72	Harold Shaw	195	217
32	Jack Hedley	269	295	73	Johnny Campbell	186	215
33	George Mulhall	253	289	74	Dennis Tueart	178	214
34	Richard Ord	243	284	75	Billy Elliott	193	212
35	Jimmy Connor	254	283	76	Dave Watson	177	212
36	Dick Malone	237	282	77	Nick Pickering	179	209
37	Arthur Wright	270	281	78	Bobby Marshall	198	207
38	Raich Carter	245	278	79	Barry Venison	173	205
39	Arthur Hudgell	260	275	80	George McCartney	175	203
40	Jack Stelling	259	272	81	Billy Ellis	190	200
41	Billy Clunas	256	272	82	Dean Whitehead	185	200

Sunderland's fastest goals

Player	Seconds	Venue	Against	Date	
Ted Purdon	10	A	Arsenal	23 Jan 1954	
Billy Hughes	14	A	Orient	28 Dec 1974	
Bob Lee	25	H	West Brom	22 Feb 1977	
Daryl Murphy	28	H	Plymouth Arg.	12 Aug 2006	
Jackie Mordue	30	H	Liverpool	12 Sep 1914	Penalty
Jackie Robinson	30	A	Chesterfield	11 Jan 1947	FA Cup
Darren Bent	34	H	Tottenham H.	3 Apr 2010	Against former club
Michael Gray	40	H	Barnsley	5 Dec 1992	Home debut
Fraizer Campbell	41	H	Bolton W.	9 Mar 2010	
Niall Quinn	44	H	Chelsea	4 Dec 1999	
Marco Gabbiadini	47	A	Fulham	29 Sep 1987	
Billy Hughes	55	H	Aston Villa	4 Nov 1972	
Len Duns	60 est	H	Everton	7 Mar 1936	
Tom Wylie	60 est	H	Manchester City	14 Apr 1937	
Bobby Gurney	60 est	H	Middlesbrough	28 Aug 1937	Opening day of season
Billy Robinson	60 est	H	Chelsea	18 Mar 1939	
Mike Hellawell	72	H	Wolves	16 Apr 1965	
Phil Gray	75	H	Tranmere Rovers	30 Apr 1994	
Colin Suggett	85	H	Everton	26 Aug 1967	

Sunderland 2-0 up after 3 minutes, at home to Sheffield Wed. 3 Oct 1908
Sunderland 2-0 up after 3 minutes, at home to Chelsea 18 Mar 1939
Sunderland 2-0 up after 3 minutes, at home to Tranmere Rovers 30 Apr 1994

GOALKEEPING RECORDS

Successive Clean Sheets

Minutes	Start of Sequence	Games in between	End of Sequence	Goalkeepers (and respective time in mins)
806	21 Dec 1901 v Notts County	7	12 Feb 1902 v Newcastle United	Doig (806)
612	21 Nov 1998 v Barnsley	6	26 Dec 1998 v Tranmere Rovers	Sorensen (612)
601	13 Dec 1902 v Bolton Wanderers	6	24 Jan 1903 v Grimsby Town	Doig (601)
593	2 Apr 1996 v Watford	6	5 May 1996 v Tranmere Rovers	Given (105) and Chamberlain (488)
590	14 Mar 1979 v Crystal Palace	5	14 Apr 1979 v Leicester City	Siddall (590)
568	11 Dec 1982 v WBA	6	12 Jan 1983 v Manchester City	Prudhoe (15) and Turner (553)
566	20 Feb 1999 v Wolverhampton W.	5	20 Mar 1999 v Bolton W.	Sorensen (427), Marriott (90) and Sorensen (49)
558	22 Nov 1997 v Bury	5	28 Dec 1997 v Oxford United	Perez (558)
497	17 Feb 1996 v Portsmouth	5	12 Mar 1996 v Oldham Athletic	Given (497)
490	6 Feb 1993 v Swindon Town	5	10 Mar 1993 v Leicester City	Norman (490)

Least Goals Conceded (must have played at least 50 games)

		Apps	Average goals per game conceded
1	M. Poom	68	0.93
2	J. Butler	79	1.06
3	T. Sorensen	197	1.11
4	A. Chamberlain	108	1.13
5	T. Doig	457	1.22
6	C. Turner	224	1.25
7	S. Mignolet	61	1.26
8	J. Montgomery	627	1.28
9	I. Hesford	112	1.29
10	B. Siddall	192	1.30

Best Clean Sheet Percentage (must have played at least 50 games)

		Apps	Clean Sheets	% Clean Sheets
1	A. Chamberlain	108	53	49.1%
2	M. Poom	68	27	39.7%
3	T. Sorensen	197	72	36.5%
4	S. Mignolet	61	22	36.1%
5	J. Butler	79	27	34.2%
6	T. Doig	457	147	32.2%
7	T. Carter	50	16	32.0%
8	C. Turner	224	71	31.7%
9	J. Montgomery	627	189	30.1%
10	I. Hesford	112	32	28.6%

Goalkeeping replacements during games

Date	Venue	Opposition	Goalkeeper	Replacement	Score before change	Final score	Comments
19 Nov 1910	A	Newcastle United	Roose, Dick	Bridgett, Arthur	1-1	1-1	Roose broke wrist after 75 mins
26 Dec 1911	A	Sheffield Wednesday	Scott, Walter	Holley, George	0-8	0-8	Scott concussed and left field after 80 mins
26 Mar 1927	H	Leeds United	Bell, John	Marshall, Bobby	2-0	6-2	Bell's debut; injured after 50 mins

GOALKEEPING RECORDS

Date	Venue	Opposition	Goalkeeper	Replacement	Score before change	Final score	Comments
28 Nov 1936	A	Charlton Athletic	Mapson, John	Collin, George	0-0	1-3	Mapson injured after 12 mins
20 Apr 1957	A	Manchester United	Bollands, John	Fleming, Charlie	0-1	0-4	Bollands injured right ankle after 56 mins
12 Jan 1963	H	Aston Villa (LC)	Montgomery, Jim	Nelson, Colin	1-2	1-3	Montgomery left field injured after 70 mins
16 Oct 1965	H	Nottingham Forest	Montgomery, Jim	Harvey, Martin	3-2	3-2	Montgomery injured after 83 mins
26 Nov 1966	A	Manchester United	Montgomery, Jim	Hurley, Charlie	0-1	0-2	Montgomery injured after 35 mins, Hurley took over until half-time then Parke came on and went in goal
26 Nov 1966	A	Manchester United	Hurley, Charlie	Parke, John	0-2	0-5	
6 Apr 1968	H	Stoke City	Montgomery, Jim	Palmer, Calvin	0-0	3-1	Montgomery injured after 10 mins
4 Jan 1975	H	Chesterfield (FAC)	Montgomery, Jim	Hughes, Billy	2-0	2-0	Montgomery injured knee after 80 mins
11 Aug 1979	H	Oldham Athletic (ASC)	Siddall, Barry	Turner, Chris	1-1	1-2	Pre-arranged substitution at half-time
16 Apr 1983	A	Norwich City	Turner, Chris	Pickering, Nick	0-0	0-2	Turner fractured skull and carried off after 30 mins
1 Oct 1994	H	Southend United	Norman, Tony	Chamberlain, Alec	0-0	0-1	Norman carried off with head injury after 11 mins
19 Oct 1966	A	Southampton	Coton, Tony	Perez, Lionel	0-0	0-3	Coton broke leg after 25 mins; Perez came on to make debut
9 Mar 1999	A	Bradford City	Sorensen, Thomas	Quinn, Niall	1-0	1-0	Quinn went in goal after scoring only goal when Sorensen went off injured on 75 mins
19 Aug 2000	H	Arsenal	Sorensen, Thomas	Macho, Jurgen	0-0	1-0	Macho came on for debut at half-time
28 Nov 2000	H	Manchester United (LC)	Sorensen, Thomas	Macho, Jurgen	1-1	2-1	Sorensen injured and subbed at end of full time; Macho played 30 mins of extra-time
6 Oct 2002	A	Arsenal	Sorensen, Thomas	Myhre, Thomas	0-2	1-3	Sorensen injured after 30 mins
28 Oct 2002	A	Bolton Wanderers	Myhre, Thomas	Macho, Jurgen	0-0	1-1	Myhre had been carrying a thigh injury and could not continue past 30 mins
21 Apr 2004	A	Crystal Palace	Poom, Mart	Myhre, Thomas	0-0	0-3	Poom became first Sunderland goalkeeper to be sent off (after 18 mins); Myhre's first touch was to pick the ball out of the net after resultant Andy Johnson penalty
24 Aug 2004	H	Chester City (LC)	Myhre, Thomas	Poom, Mart	2-0	3-0	Myhre subbed due to knee injury after 61 mins
9 Apr 2005	H	Reading	Myhre, Thomas	Ingham, Michael	0-0	1-2	Ingham made his League debut coming on at half time for the injured Myhre. This was Myhre's last appearances for Sunderland
7 Nov 2009	A	Tottenham Hotspur	Gordon, Craig	Fulop, Marton	1-0	2-0	Gordon subbed after 65 mins due to broken arm
29 Oct 2011	H	Aston Villa	Mignolet, Simon	Westwood, Kieren	1-1	2-2	Mignolet subbed after 52 mins with fractured nose and eye socket. Westwood's League debut.

Sunderland's Record Signings

Player	Fee (as reported)	From	Date	Notes
Darren Bent	£16,500,000	Tottenham Hotspur	Aug 2009	
Craig Gordon	£9,000,000	Hearts	Aug 2007	National record for a goalkeeper
Tore Andre Flo	£6.750,000	Rangers	Aug 2002	
Claudio Reyna	£4,500,000	Rangers	Dec 2001	
Emerson Thome	£4,500,000	Chelsea	Sep 2000	
Stefan Schwarz	£3,750,000	Valencia	Jul 1999	
Lee Clark	£2,500,000	Newcastle United	Jun 1997	
Niall Quinn	£1,300,000	Manchester City	Aug 1996	
Alex Rae	£1,000,000	Millwall	Jun 1996	
David Kelly	£1,000,000	Wolverhampton W.	Sep 1995	Initial £900,000 rose to £1 million as a result of Sunderland's promotion
Don Goodman	£900,000	West Bromwich A.	Dec 1991	
Tony Norman	£450,000	Hull City	Dec 1988	Fee included £220,000, Billy Whitehurst and Iain Hesford
Ally McCoist	£355,000	St. Johnstone	Aug 1981	
Claudio Marangoni	£380,000	San Lorenzo	Dec 1979	Only £230,000 paid due to early sale
Stan Cummins	£300,000	Middlesbrough	Nov 1979	
Bob Lee	£200,000	Leicester City	Oct 1976	
Bryan 'Pop' Robson	£145,000	West Ham United	Jun 1974	
Tony Towers	£125,000	Manchester City	Mar 1974	Fee included £25,000 and Micky Horswill
Dave Watson	£100,000	Rotherham United	Dec 1970	
Jim Baxter	£72,500	Rangers	May 1965	
Brian Clough	£48,000	Middlesbrough	Jul 1961	

SUNDERLAND'S RECORD SIGNINGS

Player	Fee	From	Date	Notes
George Herd	£42,500	Clyde	Apr 1961	
Trevor Ford	£29,500	Aston Villa	Oct 1950	National record
Len Shackleton	£20,050	Newcastle United	Feb 1948	National Record
Ron Turnbull	£9,000	Dundee	Nov 1947	
Arthur Hudgell	£8,000	Crystal Palace	Jan 1947	
Willie Watson	£8,000	Huddersfield Town	May 1946	
Bill Murray	£8,000	St. Mirren	Apr 1927	Fee included cash and David Wright
Bob Kelly	£6.550	Burnley	Dec 1925	National record
Warney Cresswell	£5,500	South Shields	Mar 1922	National record (one day after Gilhooley signed)
Michael Gilhooley	£5,250	Hull City	Mar 1922	National record
Jock Paterson	£3,790	Leicester City	Mar 1922	Same day as Gilhooley signed
Charlie Parker	£3,500	Stoke	Oct 1920	
Joe Butler	£3,000	Glossop N. E.	Oct 1912	
Arthur Brown	£1,600	Sheffield United	Jun 1908	World record
John Foster	£800	Watford	Dec 1907	
Alf Common	£520	Sheffield United	Jun 1904	National record - fee included Albert Lewis
George Livingstone	£175	Hearts	May 1900	
Archibald McKenzie	£125	Millwall Athletic	May 1895	Paid to Everton as they held player's registration
Donald Gow	£70	Rangers	Jul 1891	

Charlie Thomson's 1908 transfer was previously thought to be a record. At the time a transfer limit of £350 had been imposed.

The transfer fee limit, set by the FA mainly as a result of 'Boro signing Alf Common for £1,000 from Sunderland in 1905, was only in place from January 1908 to April 1908. Thomson – who captained the near double winners of 1912-13 – was valued at £350. Sunderland also signed goalkeeper Thomas Allan from Hearts for £350 and he was thought to have been a 'makeweight' in the Thomson transfer. However, evidence from contemporary newspapers shows that Allan's transfer was recorded on 27th April 1908 with Thomson moving on 16th May 1908. To what extent the transfers were connected is down to conjecture especially as on the date of Thomson's transfer the £350 limit had just ended.

Sunderland's debut scorers

No	Debut Scorer	Date	Opponents	Venue	Tier	Time on pitch before scoring
94	Sebastian Larsson	13 Aug 2011	Liverpool	A	1	56
93	Asamoah Gyan (sub)	11 Sep 2010	Wigan	A	1	21
92	Darren Bent	15 Aug 2009	Bolton	A	1	5
91	David Healy (sub)	27 Aug 2008	Nottm Forest	A	LC	32
90	Djibril Cisse (sub)	23 Aug 2008	Tottenham	A	1	17
89	Rade Prica (sub)	29 Jan 2008	Birmingham	SOL	1	20
88	Michael Chopra (sub)	11 Aug 2007	Tottenham	SOL	1	22
87	Ross Wallace	9 Sep 2006	Derby	A	2	63
86	Anthony Le Tallec	20 Aug 2005	Man City	SOL	1	41
85	Andy Gray	13 Aug 2005	Charlton	SOL	1	32
84	Chris Brown (2 goals)	21 Sep 2004	Crewe	A	LC	37
83	Darren Carter	18 Sep 2004	Preston	SOL	2	45
82	Darren Byfield (sub)	7 Feb 2004	Watford	A	2	27
81	Tor Andre Flo	31 Aug 2002	Man United	SOL	1	70
80	Julio Arca	5 Sep 2000	West Ham	SOL	1	25
79	Nicky Summerbee (sub)	15 Nov 1997	Portsmouth	A	2	19
78	Kevin Phillips	15 Aug 1997	Man City	SOL	2	84
77	Martin Smith	20 Oct 1993	Luton Town	H	2	19
76	Peter Davenport	25 Aug 1990	Norwich	A	1	53
75	Colin Pascoe (sub)	26 Mar 1988	York City	A	3	37
74	Tony Ford (sub)	29 Mar 1986	Bradford	H	2	5
73	Gary Bennett	25 Aug 1984	Southampton	H	1	2
72	Frank Worthington	4 Dec 1982	Ipswich	H	1	69
71	Stan Cummins	17 Nov 1979	Notts County	H	2	56
70	Wayne Entwistle	3 Dec 1977	Charlton	A	2	39
69	Tommy Gibb	2 Aug 1975	Middlesbrough	A	ASC	27
68	Jimmy Hamilton (sub)	25 Sep 1971	Preston	H	2	5
67	Dave Watson	19 Dec 1970	Watford	A	2	48
66	John Tones (sub)	17 May 1970	Lazio	A	AIC	22
65	Malcolm Moore (sub)	23 Mar 1968	Coventry	H	1	52
64	Bobby Kerr	31 Dec 1966	Man City	H	1	89
63	Neil Martin	23 Oct 1965	Sheff Wed	A	1	57
62	Mel Slack	24 Apr 1965	Stoke	A	1	62
61	Jimmy O'Neill (2)	13 Jan 1962	Bristol Rovers	H	2	35
60	Brian Clough	19 Aug 1961	Walsall	A	2	21
59	Willie McPheat	8 Oct 1960	Leeds United	H	2	58
58	Don Kichenbrand	8 Mar 1958	Sheff Wed	H	1	70
57	John Goodchild	4 Sep 1957	Leicester	H	1	10
56	Bill Holden	27 Dec 1955	Newcastle	A	1	5
55	Ted Purdon (2)	16 Jan 1954	Cardiff	H	1	72
54	Ken Chisholm	1 Jan 1954	Aston Villa	H	1	7
53	Geoff Toseland	6 Sep 1952	Derby	H	1	20
52	Norman Case (2)	26 Dec 1949	Stoke	H	1	80
51	Ronnie Turnbull (4)	29 Nov 1947	Portsmouth	H	1	20
50	Jackie Robinson	19 Oct 1946	Grimsby	H	1	50
49	Ken Walshaw	29 Jan 1946	Bury	A	FAC	33
48	Cyril Brown	5 Jan 1946	Grimsby	H	FAC	14

SUNDERLAND'S DEBUT SCORERS

No	Debut Scorer	Date	Opponents	Venue	Tier
47	Eddie Burbanks	27 Apr 1935	Portsmouth	H	1
46	Benny Yorston	30 Jan 1932	Blackpool	A	1
45	Jimmy Temple	26 Sep 1931	Sheff United	A	1
44	Joe Devine	4 Feb 1931	Blackburn	H	1
43	James Leonard	4 Oct 1930	Leeds United	A	1
42	Bobby McKay (2)	6 Oct 1928	Man City	A	1
41	Adam McLean	29 Aug 1928	Blackburn	H	1
40	Bobby Gurney	3 Apr 1926	West Ham	A	1
39	Stan Ramsay	12 Sep 1925	Sheff United	H	1
38	David Halliday (2)	29 Aug 1925	Birmingham	H	1
37	James Hogg	19 Jan 1924	Sheff United	H	1
36	Archie Brown	21 Jan 1922	Man United	H	1
35	Arthur Hawes (2)	24 Dec 1921	West Brom	H	1
34	Bobby Marshall	23 Oct 1920	Bradford City	A	1
33	Fred Cooke	24 Apr 1920	Bradford PA	H	1
32	Victor Shore	10 Apr 1920	Preston	H	1
31	Barney Travers	30 Aug 1919	Aston Villa	H	1
30	Charlie Crossley	14 Mar 1914	Tottenham	H	1
29	Harry Martin	5 Apr 1912	Liverpool	A	1
28	Jack Young	9 Dec 1911	West Brom	H	1
27	Bobby Best	7 Oct 1911	Aston Villa	A	1
26	Tim Coleman	1 Sep 1910	Newcastle	H	1
25	Jackie Mordue	9 Sep 1908	Middlesbrough	A	1
24	John Foster	7 Dec 1907	Birmingham	A	1
23	Jack Huggins	20 Oct 1906	Man United	H	1
22	Joe Shaw	1 Jan 1906	Middlesbrough	H	1
21	Dennis O'Donnell	28 Oct 1905	Blackburn	H	1
20	George Holley	27 Dec 1904	Sheff Wed	A	1
19	Mark Watkins (2)	22 Oct 1904	Sheff Wed	H	1
18	Henry Wardle	1 Apr 1904	Wolves	H	1
17	Willie Murray	22 Mar 1902	Grimsby	H	1
16	Billy Hogg	2 Dec 1899	Notts County	H	1
15	Bobby Hogg	2 Oct 1899	Sheff United	A	1
14	Tommy Becton	16 Sep 1899	Burnley	H	1
13	Arthur Saxton	5 Feb 1898	Notts County	A	1
12	Walter Cowan	7 Sep 1895	Blackburn	H	1
11	James Gillespie (2)	15 Sep 1890	Wolves	H	1
10	John Spence	13 Sep 1890	Burnley	H	1
9	Jock Scott	18 Jan 1890	Blackburn	A	FAC
8	David Hannah	18 Jan 1890	Blackburn	A	FAC
7	Andrew Peacock (2)	27 Oct 1888	Elswick	H	FAC
6	John Breconridge (3)	27 Oct 1888	Elswick	H	FAC
5	Robert Gloag (2)	26 Nov 1887	Middlesbrough	A	FAC
4	Thomas Halliday	5 Nov 1887	Newcastle WE	H	FAC
3	Samuel Stewart	22 Oct 1887	Morpeth	A	FAC
2	G Monaghan (2)	22 Oct 1887	Morpeth	A	FAC
1	Donald McColl	8 Nov 1884	Redcar	A	FAC

Note: timings not given for pre WW2 games due to difficulty in obtaining accurate information.

Top 10s and Sunderland Miscellany

Youngest
1	Derek Forster	15 years 185 days	v Leicester City	22 August 1964
2	James Hamilton	16 years 103 days	v Preston N.E.	25 September 1971
3	Cec Irwin	16 years 166 days	v Ipswich Town	20 September 1958
4	Rob Hindmarch	16 years 262 days	v Orient	14 January 1978
5	Dominic Sharkey	16 years 341 days	v Scunthorpe Utd	9 April 1960
6	James Davison	17 years 20 days	v Scunthorpe Utd	21 November 1959
7	James Thorpe	17 years 39 days	v Huddersfield Town	25 October 1930
8	Barry Venison	17 years 55 days	v Notts County	10 October 1981
9	Joseph Bolton	17 years 75 days	v Watford	17 April 1972
10	Fred Bett	17 years 97 days	v Liverpool	12 March 1938

Oldest debutants
1	Brian Deane	37 years 58 days	v Reading	9 April 2005
2	Colin Cooper	37 years 21 days	v Reading	20 March 2004
3	Steve Bould	36 years 264 days	v Chelsea	7 August 1999
4	Chris Waddle	36 years 98 days	v Nottingham Forest	22 March 1997
5	Andrew Cole	36 years 40 days	v Everton	24 November 2007
6	Tony Coton	35 years 90 days	v Leicester City	17 August 1996
7	Kenny Cunningham	35 years 41 days	v Coventry City	6 August 2006
8	Dwight Yorke	34 years 317 days	v Leicester City	16 September 2006
9	Thomas Helmer	34 years 115 days	v Arsenal	14 August 1999
10	Mick Harford	34 years 37 days	v Barnsley	21 March 1993

Oldest
1	Thomas Urwin	39 years 76 days	v Preston N.E.	22 April 1935
2	Bryan `Pop' Robson	38 years 183 days	v Leicester City	12 May 1984
3	Steve Bould	37 years 280 days	v Manchester City	23 August 2000
4	Charlie Parker	37 years 204 days	v Leeds United	13 April 1929
5	Dwight Yorke	37 years 159 days	v Manchester United	11 April 2009
6	Teddy Doig	37 years 156 days	v Manchester City	2 April 1904
7	Brian Deane	37 years 78 days	v West Ham United	29 April 2005
8	Tony Norman	37 years 72 days	v West Bromwich A.	7 May 1995
9	Colin Cooper	37 years 28 days	v Derby County	27 March 2004
10	Charles B. Thomson	36 years 316 days	v Tottenham Hotspur	24 April 1915

Youngest Goalscorers
1	James Hamilton	16 years 103 days	v Preston N.E.	25 September 1971
2	Barry Venison	17 years 125 days	v Manchester City	19 December 1981

TOP 10S & SUNDERLAND MISCELLANY

3	Robert Marshall	17 years 203 days	v Bradford City	23 October 1920
4	Michael Bridges	17 years 206 days	v Southend United	27 February 1996
5	John Lathan	17 years 224 days	v Southampton	22 November 1969
6	Paul Atkinson	17 years 231 days	v Wolverhampton W.	7 September 1983
7	Alan Spence	17 years 261 days	v Sheffield Wed.	26 October 1957
8	John Bartley	17 years 277 days	v Birmingham	16 February 1927
9	John Cooke	17 years 304 days	v Luton Town	23 February 1980
10	Bobby Park	17 years 335 days	v Ipswich Town	6 December 1969

Oldest Goalscorers

1	Bryan 'Pop' Robson	38 years 183 days	v Leicester City	12 May 1984
2	William Grimshaw	36 years 292 days	v Birmingham	16 February 1927
3	Chris Waddle	36 years 140 days	v Everton	3 May 1997
4	Fred Hall	36 days 37 days	v Huddersfield Town	25 December 1953
5	Dwight Yorke	36 days 21 days	v Everton	24 November 2007
6	Charles B. Thomson	35 years 212 days	v Chatham Town (FA1)	10 January 1914
7	Niall Quinn	35 years 126 days	v Derby County	9 February 2002
8	Ernie Taylor	34 years 364 days	v Stoke City	31 August 1960
9	Thomas Urwin	34 years 339 days	v Southampton (FA3)	10 January 1931
10	Kevin Ball	34 years 334 days	v Wimbledon (LC3)	12 October 1999

Shortest Playing Career at Sunderland

1	Simon Ramsden	v Ipswich Town	24 January 2004 (FA Cup 4th Round)	2 minutes of injury time (90th minute substitute)
2	Peter Hartley	v Leicester City	1 January 2007	6 minutes (84th minute substitute)
3=	Nigel Walker	v Watford	12 November 1983	8 minutes (82nd minute substitute)
3=	Michael Liddle	v Barrow	2 January 2010 (FA Cup 3rd Round)	8 minutes (82nd minute substitute)
5	Kevin Cooper	v Millwall	17 January 2004	13 minutes (77th minute substitute)
6	Nathan Luscombe	v Blackburn Rovers	4 February 2009 (FA Cup 4th Round rep)	15 minutes (105th minute substitute)
7	Colin Cooper	v Reading, v Gillingham, v Derby Co.	20, 23 & 27 March 2004	20 minutes in total (3 substitute apps)
8	Alan Hay	v Ipswich Town	25 March 1989	28 minutes (substituted as injured)
9	Ricardo Gabbiadini	v Leeds United	14 October 1989	32 minutes (58th minute substitute)
9	Jordan Cook	v Manchester Utd, v Chelsea, v West Ham Utd	26 Dec 2010, 1 Feb 2011 & 22 May 2011	32 minutes in total (3 substitute apps)

Most Appearances in a Season

1	Gordon Armstrong	59	1989-90 (missed only 25 minutes playing time)
2	Marco Gabbiadini	58	1989-90
3	Thomas Sorensen	56	1998-99
4	Gary Owers	56	1989-90 (substituted in 2 games)
5	Tony Norman	54	1991-92
6	Andy Melville	54	1993-94
7	John MacPhail	54	1987-88 (substituted in 1 game)

8	Jimmy Montgomery	53	1962-63
9	Chris Turner	53	1984-85
10	Gordon Armstrong	53	1988-89 (substituted in 1 game)

Consecutive Appearances

1	Charlie Thomson	29 January 1934 – 20 March 1937	147
2	George Mulhall	17 November 1962 – 10 April 1965	124
3	Dariusz Kubicki	5 March 1994 – 8 September 1996	123
4	Dick Malone	17 March 1973 – 2 August 1975	118
5	Bobby Kerr	7 November 1974 – 3 February 1976	114
6=	Sandy McAllister	27 December 1897 – 5 January 1901	110
6=	Bert Davis	1 April 1933 – 26 October 1935	110
8=	Teddy Doig	20 September 1890 – 1 January 1894	108
8=	Jimmy Montgommery	7 April 1962 – 25 April 1964	108
10	Chris Turner	27 August 1983 – 11 May 1985	101

Most Substitute Appearances (all comps)

No	Player	Sub apps	Total apps	% sub apps
1	Michael Bridges	67	113	59%
2	Danny Dichio	62	97	64%
3	Craig Russell	56	174	32%
4	Daryl Murphy	55	124	44%
5	Grant Leadbitter	54	123	44%
6	Darren Williams	49	239	21%
7=	Thomas Hauser	39	65	60%
7=	Lee Howey	39	81	48%
9	Martin Smith	38	145	26%
10=	Bolo Zenden	37	50	74%
10=	Niall Quinn	37	220	17%

Most Substituted Players (all comps)

No	Player	Subbed	Starting apps	% replaced
1	Steed Malbranque	69	95	73%
2	Niall Quinn	66	183	36%
3	Marcus Stewart	53	91	58%
4	Michael Gray	51	383	13%
5	Eric Gates	47	199	24%
6	Julio Arca	39	165	24%
7	Daryl Murphy	37	69	52%
8	Kieran Richardson	34	137	26%
9	Michael Bridges	34	46	74%
10	Gordon Armstrong	31	393	8%

Most Goals as a Substitute (all comps)

No	Player	Goals	Sub apps	Goals per app
1	Michael Bridges	13	67	0.19
2	Stephen Elliott	7	29	0.24
3	Michael Chopra	5	18	0.28

4	Sean Thornton	5	26	0.19
5	Anthony Stokes	4	22	0.18
6	Alex Rae	4	27	0.15
7	Peter Davenport	4	31	0.13
8	Kevin Kyle	4	34	0.12
9	Chris Brown	4	35	0.11
10	Daryl Murphy	4	53	0.08

Most unused Substitutes (all comps)

No	Player	Unused	Used	Total
1	Jurgen Macho	81	3	84
2	Tony Norman	64	0	64
3	Trevor Carson	63	0	63
4	Ben Alnwick	61	0	61
5	Michael Ingham	59	1	60
6	Marton Fulop	56	1	57
7	Andy Marriott	53	0	53
8	Paul Thirlwell	52	26	78
9	Lee Howey	40	39	79
10	Paulo Da Silva	39	5	44

Three or More Goals in a Game
5 goals (4 occasions)

Jimmy Millar	v Fairfield (FA Cup)	2 February 1895
Charlie Buchan	v Liverpool	7 December 1912
Bobby Gurney	v Bolton Wanderers	7 December 1935
Nick Sharkey	v Norwich City	20 March 1963

4 goals (26 occasions)
John Campbell, Bobby Gurney, David Halliday (3 times)
Charlie Buchan, George Holley, Kevin Phillips, James Richardson (twice)
Raich Carter, Stan Cummins, Trevor Ford, Eric Gates (once)
Jimmy Hannah, Jackie Robinson, William Robinson, Craig Russell, Ron Turnbull (once)

3 goals (148 occasions)
David Halliday (12 times)
Jimmy Millar (10 times)
Bobby Gurney, George Holley (9 times)
Brian Clough (7 times)
Patrick Gallacher (6 times)
Charlie Buchan, John Campbell (5 times)
Raich Carter, Dickie Davis, Trevor Ford, Marco Gabbiadini (3 times)
Bobby Best, Ivor Broadis, John Crossan, John Goodchild, John Hawley, Billy Hogg, Billy Hughes, Don Kichenbrand, Ian Lawther, James Leonard, Bobby Marshall, Neil Martin, John Paterson, Kevin Phillips, Gary Rowell, Marcus Stewart, Barney Travers (twice)

The following 42 players all scored one hat trick for Sunderland

Joe Baker	Darren Bent	John Breconridge	Alan Brown	Ken Chisholm
Stephen Coglin	William Eden	Wayne Entwistle	Charlie Fleming	Ambrose Fogarty
Ambrose Fogarty	Eric Gates	Don Goodman	Vic Halom	Jimmy Hannah

John Hannigan	Robert Hogg	Thomas Hyslop	Allan Johnston	Robert Kelly
John Lathan	Bob Lee	Harry Low	John Mitton	Alan O'Neill
George Philip	Nick Pickering	Ted Purdon	Niall Quinn	Stanley Ramsay
Tom Ritchie	Wilf Rostron	Len Shackleton	Nick Sharkey	John Thompson
Dennis Tueart	Thomas Urwin	Clive Walker	Cliff Whitelum	Hugh Wilson
Tommy Wright	Benny Yorston			

Best Strike Rate for Players with over 50 Appearances (including substitute apps)

		Games	Goals	Goals per Game Ratio
1	David Halliday	175	165	0.943
2	Brian Clough	74	63	0.851
3	John Campbell	215	154	0.716
4	Trevor Ford	117	70	0.598
5	Bobby Gurney	390	228	0.585
6	Charlie Fleming	122	71	0.582
7	Darren Bent	63	36	0.571
8	Kevin Phillips	235	130	0.553
9	Charles Buchan	411	222	0.540
10	Ian Lawther	83	44	0.530

Quickest to score 50 goals

		Games
1	John Campbell	52
2	David Halliday	55
3	Brian Clough	57
4	James Millar	70
5	Kevin Phillips	72+1
6	Charlie Fleming	77
7	James Hannah	83
8	Trevor Ford	85
9	Nick Sharkey	87
10	Marco Gabbiadini	87+1

Penalty Shoot Outs

1 5 September 1979 v Newcastle United (League Cup 2nd Round 2nd leg) Won 7-6
   Robson, Rostron, Buckley, Ashurst, Whitworth, Chisholm, Brown

2 1 October 1985 v Grimsby Town (Full Members' Cup) Won 3-2
   Gates, Kennedy, Gray (x), Burley (x), Hodgson

3 4 November 1985 v Manchester City (Full Members' Cup) Lost 4-3
   Gates, Kennedy, Gray (x), Pickering (x), Atkinson

4 16 September 1986 v Barnsley (Full Members' Cup) Won 8-7
   Gray, Kennedy (x), Armstrong, Saddington, Atkinson (x), Gates, Lemon, Corner, Buchanan, Burley

5 11 December 1990 v Notts County (ZDS Cup Round 2) Won 3-1
   Davenport (x), Bracewell, Ball, Cornforth

6	25 May 1998	v Charlton Athletic (Play-off Final)	Lost 7-6
	Summerbee, Johnston, Ball, Makin, Rae, Quinn, Gray (x)		
7	11 November 1998	v Everton (League Cup 4th Round)	Won 5-4
	Scott, Johnston, Smith, Makin (x), Clark, Quinn,		
8	5 February 2003	v Blackburn Rovers (FA Cup 4th Round replay)	Won 3-0
	Phillips, Kilbane, Craddock (x), McCann		
9	17 May 2004	v Crystal Palace (Play-off semi-final 2nd Leg)	Lost 5-4
	Oster (x), Smith, Babb, Robinson, Breen, McAteer (x), Whitley (x)		
10	21 September 2004	v Crewe Alexandra (League Cup 2nd Round)	Lost 4-2
	Caldwell (x), Elliott, Thornton, N. Collins (x)		
11	23 September 2008	v Northampton Town (League Cup 3rd Round)	Won 4-3
	Chopra, Murphy, Stokes (x), Reid, Richardson		
12	27 October 2009	v Aston Villa (League Cup 4th Round)	Lost 3-1
	Reid (x), Cana (x), Malbranque, Henderson (x)		

Transfer Firsts (fees as reported)

Signings			Transfers	
Alfred Common	31 May 1904, Sheffield United	£500	Andy McCombie	4 Feb 1904, Newcastle United
Arthur Brown	20 Jun 1908, Sheffield United	£1,000	Alf Common	16 Feb 1905, Middlesbrough
Michael Gilhooley	2 Mar 1922, Hull City	£5,000	Warney Cresswell	3 Feb 1927, Everton
Len Shackleton	4 Feb 1948, Newcastle Utd	£10,000	Ron Turnbull	9 Sep1949, Manchester City
Jim Baxter	25 May 1965, Glasgow Rangers	£50,000	Jim Baxter	15 Dec 1967, Nottingham Forest
Dave Watson	14 Dec1970, Rotherham Utd	£100,000	Jim Baxter	15 Dec1967, Nottingham Forest
Don Goodman	5 Dec 1991, West Brom	£500,000	Marco Gabbiadini	26 Sep 1991, Crystal Palace
Alex Rae	11 June 1996, Millwall	£1,000,000	Marco Gabbiadini	26 Sep 1991, Crystal Palace
Tore Andre Flo	30 Aug 2002, Glasgow Rangers	£5,000,000	Michael Bridges	23 Jul 1999, Leeds United
Darren Bent	5 Aug 2009, Tottenham H	£10,000,000	Darren Bent	18 Jan 2011, Aston Villa
Darren Bent	5 Aug 2009, Tottenham H	£15,000,000	Darren Bent	18 Jan 2011, Aston Villa

Attendances

Attendance records have been divided into Pre and Post WW1 as many of the earlier figures are only estimates.

Pre-WW1

	Home			Away	
1	43,383	v West Bromwich Albion, 24 Feb 1912	120,081	v Aston Villa (FA), 19 April 1913
2	41,000 (est.)	v Newcastle United, 18 Sep 1909	59,740	v Aston Villa, 23 April 1913
3	40,000 (est.)	v Newcastle United, 6 Sep 1913	57,416	v Newcastle United, 19 November 1910
4	40,000 (est.)	v Blackburn Rovers, 1 Nov 1913	56,875	v Newcastle United, 1 September 1906
5	37,132	v Plymouth Argyle (FA), 31 Jan 1914	56,717	v Newcastle United (FA), 12 March 1913
**	22,000 (est.)	v Aston Villa, 23 October 1897 (probably highest at Newcastle Road Ground)		
1	1,500 (est.)	v Fairfield (FAC), 2 Feb 1895	< 1,000	v Stoke, 26 Mar 1900
2	2,000 (est.)	v Sheffield Wed, 5 Dec 1896	1,000 (est.)	v Accrington, 22 Nov 1890
3	2,000 (est.)	v Blackburn Rovers, 19 Dec 1896	1,500 (est.)	v Stoke, 28 Nov 1891
4	2,000 (est.)	v Burnley, 12 Dec 1915	1,500 (est.)	v Bolton Wanderers, 21 Jan 1899

Post-WW1

	Home			Away	
1	75,118	v Derby County (FAC), 8 Mar 1933	100,000	v Leeds United (FAC), 5 May 1973
2	68,004	v Newcastle United, 4 Mar 1950	100,000	v Norwich City (LC), 24 March 1985
3	66,654	v Newcastle United, 9 Oct 1954	93,495	v Preston North End (FAC), 1 May 1937
4	65,125	v Norwich City (FAC), 10 Feb 1951	79,544	v Liverpool (FAC), 9 May 1992
5	64,889	v Blackpool, 8 Oct 1949	77,739	v Charlton Athletic (Play-off), 25 May 1998
6	64,436	v Arsenal, 18 September 1948	75,648	v Manchester United, 1 Sep 2007
7	63,251	v Manchester United, 18 Feb 1950	75,570	v Manchester United, 5 Nov 2011
8	63,016	v Sheffield United (FAC), 14 Feb 1931	75,400	v Manchester United, 6 Dec 2008
9	62,851	v Everton (FAC), 15 February 1964	75,269	v Manchester United, 26 Dec 2010
10	62,487	v Middlesbrough , 7 April 1950	75,114	v Manchester United, 3 Oct 2009
**	48,355	v Liverpool, 13 April 2002 (highest at Stadium of Light)		
1	3,764	v Lazio (AIC), 1 May 1970	1,666	v Charlton Athletic (SC), 8 Nov 1988
2	3,841	v Manchester City, 11 Apr 1934	1,680	v Cagliari (AIC), 4 Jun 1972
3	3,911	v Portsmouth, 29 Apr 1933	2,199	v Cambridge United (AIC), 1 Sep 1992
4	4,010	v Cagliari (AIC), 10 June 1972	2,435	v Grimsby Town (FMC), 17 Sep 1985
5	4,315	v Cardiff City, 31 March 1926	2,738	v Chester City (LC), 22 Sep 1998
6	5,798	v Atalanta (AIC), 7 June 1972	2,740	v Doncaster Rovers, 29 Aug 1987
7	5,871	v Birmingham City (AIC), 15 Sep 1992	2,889	v Bradford City (FMC), 4 Nov 1986
8	5,957	v Fiorentina (AIC), 9 May 1970	2,903	v Chester City (LC), 24 Aug 1993
9	6,771	v Tranmere Rovers (AIC), 31 Aug 1993	2,930	v Bury (LC), 22 Aug 2006
10	6,904	v Barnsley (FMC), 16 Sep 1986	3,003	v Notts County (ZDS), 11 Dec 1990
**	11,450	v Chester City (LC), 24 August 2004 (lowest at Stadium of Light)		

Players sent off for Sunderland

Competitive games only

	Date	Venue	Opposition	Comp	Score	Player
1	14 Mar 1896	A	Stoke	Lge	0-5	Wilson, Hugh
2	27 Oct 1900	A	Bury	Lge	0-0	McLatchie, Colin
3	14 Nov 1903	A	Everton	Lge	1-0	Barrie, Alex
4	22 Oct 1904	H	Sheffield Wed.	Lge	3-0	Hogg, William
5	17 Mar 1906	H	Birmingham	Lge	3-1	Gemmell, James
6	07 Jan 1911	A	Aston Villa	Lge	1-2	Low, Harry
7	20 Mar 1920	A	Burnley	Lge	1-2	Coverdale, Robert
8	10 Apr 1926	H	Arsenal	Lge	2-1	Halliday, David
9	01 Oct 1927	A	Bury	Lge	3-5	Clunas, William
10	20 Apr 1929	A	Liverpool	Lge	2-5	Allan, Adam
11	23 Nov 1929	A	Grimsby Town	Lge	1-0	Allan, Adam
12	24 Jan 1931	A	Bolton W.	FAC	1-1	Urwin, Thomas
13	17 Sep 1932	A	Blackpool	Lge	1-3	Gallacher, Patsy
14	22 Sep 1934	H	Derby County	Lge	1-4	Gallacher, Patsy
15	06 Apr 1935	A	West Bromwich A.	Lge	1-1	Gallacher, Patsy
16	19 Oct 1935	A	Wolverhampton W.	Lge	4-3	Davis, Bert
17	28 Mar 1936	A	Middlesbrough	Lge	0-6	Carter, Raich
18	28 Mar 1936	A	Middlesbrough	Lge	0-6	Davis, Bert
19	07 May 1938	H	Wolverhampton W.	Lge	1-0	Hastings, Alex
20	10 Mar 1951	A	Burnley	Lge	1-1	Walsh, William
21	04 Sep 1954	H	Sheffield Wed.	Lge	2-0	Anderson, Stan
22	08 Jan 1958	A	Everton	FAC	1-3	Fogarty, Ambrose
23	09 Jan 1960	H	Blackburn Rovers	FAC	1-1	O'Neill, Alan
24	21 Aug 1965	A	Leeds Utd	Lge	0-1	Mulhall, George
25	18 Dec 1965	A	Nottingham Forest	Lge	0-0	Baxter, Jim
26	25 Oct 1966	H	Stoke City	Lge	2-1	O'Hare, John
27	20 Mar 1967	A	Leeds Utd (at Hull)	FAC	1-2	Herd, George
28	20 Mar 1967	A	Leeds Utd (at Hull)	FAC	1-2	Mulhall, George
29	23 Aug 1967	H	Fulham	Lge	3-0	Baxter, Jim
30	23 Sep 1972	A	Huddersfield Town	Lge	0-0	McGiven, Mick
31	09 May 1973	H	QPR	Lge	0-3	Horswill, Mick
32	02 Mar 1974	H	Middlesbrough	Lge	0-2	Tueart, Dennis
33	02 Mar 1974	H	Middlesbrough	Lge	0-2	Kerr, Bobby
34	08 Mar 1975	A	Norwich City	Lge	0-0	Guthrie, Ron
35	06 Sep 1975	A	Plymouth Argyle	Lge	0-1	Malone, Dick
36	09 Sep 1975	A	Notts County	LC	1-2	Towers, Tony
37	23 Mar 1977	A	Aston Villa	Lge	1-4	Waldron, Colin
38	26 Dec 1977	H	Blackpool	Lge	2-1	Bolton, Joe
39	22 Aug 1978	A	Orient	Lge	0-3	Entwistle, Wayne

SUNDERLAND: THE COMPLETE RECORD

	Date	Venue	Opposition	Comp	Score	Player
40	30 Aug 1978	H	Stoke City	LC	0-2	Ashurst, Jack
41	23 Sep 1978	A	Burnley	Lge	2-1	Henderson, Mick
42	23 Sep 1978	A	Burnley	Lge	2-1	Bolton, Joe
43	23 Dec 1978	A	Notts County	Lge	1-1	Docherty, Mick
44	07 Apr 1979	A	Bristol Rovers	Lge	0-0	Clarke, Jeff
45	07 Feb 1981	A	Middlesbrough	Lge	0-1	Bolton, Joe
46	28 Mar 1981	A	Ipswich Town	Lge	1-4	Hinnigan, Joe
47	03 Oct 1981	H	Coventry City	Lge	0-0	Munro, Iain
48	08 May 1982	A	Southampton	Lge	0-1	Hindmarch, Rob
49	26 Dec 1983	A	Everton	Lge	0-0	Chisholm, Gordon
50	28 Apr 1984	H	Birmingham City	Lge	2-1	Hindmarsh, Rob
51	24 Nov 1984	H	Manchester Utd	Lge	3-2	Hodgson, David
52	01 Jan 1985	A	Newcastle United	Lge	1-3	Gayle, Howard
53	01 Jan 1985	A	Newcastle United	Lge	1-3	Bennett, Gary
54	07 Dec 1985	H	Portsmouth	Lge	1-3	Bennett, Gary
55	29 Nov 1986	A	Crystal Palace	Lge	0-2	Doyle, Steve
56	13 Feb 1988	A	Preston N.E.	Lge	2-2	Doyle, Steve
57	11 Jan 1989	A	Oxford Utd	FAC	0-2	Gabbiadini, Marco
58	18 Mar 1989	A	Crystal Palace	Lge	0-1	Doyle, Steve
59	25 Mar 1989	H	Ipswich Town	Lge	4-0	Gabbiadini, Marco
60	19 Sep 1989	H	Fulham	LC	1-1	Hauser, Thomas
61	17 Jan 1990	H	Coventry City	LC	0-0	Bennett, Gary
62	24 Jan 1990	A	Coventry City	LC	0-5	Owers, Gary
63	13 May 1990	H	Newcastle United	Play-off	0-0	Hardyman, Paul
64	23 Dec 1990	H	Leeds Utd	Lge	0-1	Kay, John
65	09 Mar 1991	H	Sheffield Utd	Lge	0-1	Ball, Kevin
66	13 Apr 1991	A	Southampton	Lge	1-3	Armstrong, Gordon
67	23 Apr 1991	H	Wimbledon	Lge	0-0	Ball, Kevin
68	14 Sep 1991	A	Swindon Town	Lge	3-5	Owers, Gary
69	28 Sep 1991	A	Middlesbrough	Lge	1-2	Hardyman, Paul
70	09 Oct 1991	A	Huddersfield Town	LC	0-4	Owers, Gary
71	07 Dec 1991	A	Wolverhampton W.	Lge	0-1	Byrne, John
72	07 Dec 1991	A	Wolverhampton W.	Lge	0-1	Armstrong, Gordon
73	05 Sep 1992	H	Charlton Ath.	Lge	0-2	Kay, John
74	12 Apr 1993	A	Grimsby Town	Lge	0-1	Harford, Mick
75	04 May 1993	A	Tranmere Rovers	Lge	1-2	Ball, Kevin
76	25 Sep 1993	A	Watford	Lge	1-1	Gray, Phil
77	06 Apr 1994	A	Millwall	Lge	1-2	Goodman, Don (as sub)
78	24 Sep 1994	A	Tranmere Rovers	Lge	0-1	Owers, Gary
79	26 Dec 1994	H	Bolton W.	Lge	1-1	Bennett, Gary
80	29 Jan 1995	H	Tottenham H.	FAC	1-4	Bennett, Gary
81	09 Sep 1995	H	Southend Utd	Lge	1-0	Ball, Kevin
82	04 Oct 1995	H	Liverpool	LC	0-1	Smith, Martin
83	21 Jan 1996	A	Leicester City	Lge	0-0	Hall, Gareth
84	06 Apr 1996	A	Barnsley	Lge	1-0	Stewart, Paul
85	14 Sep 1996	A	Derby County	Lge	0-1	Ord, Richard
86	28 Sep 1996	A	Arsenal	Lge	0-2	Scott, Martin

PLAYERS SENT OFF FOR SUNDERLAND

	Date	Venue	Opposition	Comp	Score	Player
87	28 Sep 1996	A	Arsenal	Lge	0-2	Stewart, Paul
88	14 Oct 1996	H	Middlesbrough	Lge	2-2	Ord, Richard
89	16 Nov 1996	A	Tottenham H.	Lge	0-2	Stewart, Paul
90	04 Oct 1997	A	Reading	Lge	0-4	Williams, Darren
91	15 Mar 1998	A	Charlton Ath.	Lge	1-1	Rae, Alex
92	13 Apr 1998	A	West Bromwich A.	Lge	3-3	Gray, Michael
93	02 Jan 1999	A	Lincoln City	FAC	1-0	Williams, Darren
94	09 Jan 1999	A	QPR	Lge	2-2	Ball, Kevin
95	21 Aug 1999	A	Leeds Utd	Lge	1-2	Rae, Alex
96	24 Oct 1999	A	West Ham Utd	Lge	1-1	Bould, Steve
97	06 Nov 1999	A	Middlesbrough	Lge	1-1	Makin, Chris
98	14 May 2000	A	Tottenham H.	Lge	1-3	Rae, Alex (as sub)
99	14 Oct 2000	H	Chelsea	Lge	1-0	Kilbane, Kevin
100	06 Jan 2001	H	Crystal Palace	FAC	0-0	Varga, Stanislav
101	17 Jan 2001	A	Crystal Palace	FAC	4-2	Dichio, Daniele (as sub)
102	31 Jan 2001	H	Manchester Utd	Lge	0-1	Gray, Michael
103	31 Jan 2001	H	Manchester Utd	Lge	0-1	Rae, Alex
104	24 Feb 2001	A	Leicester City	Lge	0-2	Oster, John
105	16 Apr 2001	A	Coventry City	Lge	0-1	Varga, Stanislav
106	19 May 2001	A	Everton	Lge	2-2	Hutchison, Don (as sub)
107	13 Apr 2002	H	Liverpool	Lge	0-1	Reyna, Claudio
108	12 Apr 2003	A	Birmingham City	Lge	0-2	Stewart, Marcus
109	16 Sep 2003	A	Stoke City	Lge	1-3	Thornton, Sean
110	23 Sep 2003	H	Huddersfield Town	LC	2-4	Clark, Ben
111	04 Oct 2003	A	Sheffield Utd	Lge	1-0	Arca, Julio
112	25 Oct 2003	A	Norwich City	Lge	0-1	Oster, John
113	02 Dec 2003	H	Wigan Athletic	Lge	1-1	Arca, Julio
114	20 Dec 2003	H	Wimbledon	Lge	2-1	Kyle, Kevin (as sub)
115	21 Feb 2004	A	Cardiff City	Lge	0-4	Bjorklund, Joachim
116	10 Mar 2004	H	Preston N.E.	Lge	3-3	Whitley, Jeff
117	20 Mar 2004	A	Reading	Lge	2-0	Whitley, Jeff
118	04 Apr 2004	A	Millwall (@ Old T.)	FAC	0-1	McAteer, Jason
119	21 Apr 2004	A	Crystal Palace	Lge	0-3	Poom, Mart
120	28 Sep 2004	A	Sheffield Utd	Lge	0-1	Breen, Gary
121	04 Dec 2004	H	West Ham United	Lge	0-2	Caldwell, Stephen
122	20 Aug 2005	A	Liverpool	Lge	0-1	Welsh, Andy
123	30 Sep 2005	H	Cheltenham Town	LC	1-0	Smith, Dan (on debut)
124	02 Jan 2006	A	Fulham	Lge	1-2	Caldwell, Stephen
125	04 Feb 2006	A	West Ham United	Lge	0-2	Wright, Stephen
126	05 Mar 2006	A	Manchester City	Lge	1-2	Breen, Gary
127	22 Aug 2006	A	Bury	LC	0-2	Riera, Arnau
128	23 Sep 2006	A	Ipswich Town	Lge	1-3	Wallace, Ross
129	28 Oct 2006	A	Hull City	Lge	1-0	Wallace, Ross
130	06 Jan 2007	A	Preston N.E.	FAC	0-1	Miller, Liam
131	28 Aug 2007	A	Luton Town	LC	0-3	Halford, Greg
132	07 Oct 2007	A	Arsenal	Lge	2-3	McShane, Paul
133	27 Oct 2007	H	Fulham	Lge	1-1	Halford, Greg

	Date	Venue	Opposition	Comp	Score	Player
134	08 Dec 2007	A	Chelsea	Lge	0-2	Miller, Liam
135	02 Jan 2008	A	Blackburn Rovers	Lge	0-1	Yorke, Dwight
136	22 Mar 2009	A	Manchester City	Lge	0-1	McCartney, George
137	03 Oct 2009	A	Manchester Utd	Lge	2-2	Richardson, Kieran
138	31 Oct 2009	H	West Ham United	Lge	2-2	Jones, Kenwyne
139	15 Dec 2009	H	Aston Villa	Lge	0-2	Cana, Lorik
140	19 Dec 2009	A	Manchester City	Lge	3-4	Turner, Michael
141	09 Feb 2010	A	Portsmouth	Lge	1-1	Cattermole, Lee
142	09 Feb 2010	A	Portsmouth	Lge	1-1	Meyler, David (as sub)
143	24 Apr 2010	A	Hull City	Lge	1-0	Hutton, Alan
144	09 May 2010	A	Wolverhampton W.	Lge	1-2	Turner, Michael
145	09 May 2010	A	Wolverhampton W.	Lge	1-2	Colback, Jack (as sub & on debut)
146	14 Aug 2010	H	Birmingham City	Lge	2-2	Cattermole, Lee
147	11 Sep 2010	A	Wigan Athletic	Lge	1-1	Cattermole, Lee
148	31 Oct 2010	A	Newcastle United	Lge	1-5	Bramble, Titus
149	05 Jan 2011	A	Aston Villa	Lge	1-0	Zenden, Boudewijn (as sub)
150	20 Mar 2011	H	Liverpool	Lge	0-2	Mensah, John
151	20 Aug 2011	H	Newcastle United	Lge	0-1	Bardsley, Phil
152	04 Mar 2012	A	Newcastle United	Lge	1-1	Sessegnon, Stephane
153	04 Mar 2012	A	Newcastle United	Lge	1-1	Cattermole, Lee
154	21 Apr 2012	A	Aston Villa	Lge	0-0	Gardner, Craig

Sunderland Shirt Sponsorship

Shirt sponsorhip was approved by the FA on 3 June 1977, however, it was 1979 when Liverpool became the first club to wear a sponsored shirt in a League game. Teams could not wear sponsored shirts in televised games until 1983.

Sunderland shirts first bore the name of a sponsor for the home game against Manchester United on 22 October 1983. Chairman Tom Cowie had his company name 'Cowies' added to the front of the shirt. The most likely reason for this was that the game was scheduled to be shown on BBC TV's *Match of the Day* and they now allowed limited size sponsorhip logos to be displayed on shirts. However, an industrial dispute caused the programme to be cancelled.

From then on sponsor's names on shirts have become the norm.

Season	Sponsor	Comments
1983-84	Cowies	
1984-85	Cowies	
1985-86	Vaux	
1986-87	Vaux	
1987-88	Vaux	Tuborg on away shirts
1988-89	Vaux	
1989-90	Vaux	
1990-91	Vaux	
1991-92	Vaux	
1992-93	Vaux	
1993-94	Vaux	
1994-95	Vaux Samson	
1995-96	Vaux Samson	
1996-97	Vaux Samson	Scorpion Lager on away shirts
1997-98	Lambtons	Brand of Vaux ales
1998-99	Lambtons	
1999-2000	Reg Vardy	
2000-01	Reg Vardy	
2001-02	Reg Vardy	
2002-03	Reg Vardy	
2003-04	Reg Vardy	
2004-05	Reg Vardy	
2005-06	Reg Vardy	
2006-07	Reg Vardy	
2007-08	Boylesports	
2008-09	Boylesports	
2009-10	Boylesports	
2010-11	Tombola	
2011-12	Tombola	
2012-13	Invest In Africa	
2013-14	Invest In Africa	

ON STAGE AT SUNDERLAND

This is a list of major football events that have been held at Sunderland's home grounds.

North v South game played on 19 January 1889.

1885	7 February	Durham County	1-3	Cleveland	Abbs Field
1887	31 December	Durham County	2-4	Corinthians	Newcastle Rd
1888	22 September	Sunderland	0-3	Canadian Tourists	Newcastle Rd
1888	15 December	Durham County	0-5	Staffordshire	Newcastle Rd
1889	19 January	North	1-2	South	Newcastle Rd
1891	7 March	England	4-1	Wales	Newcastle Rd
1891	1 September	Sunderland	3-2	Canadian Tourists	Newcastle Rd
1899	18 February	England	13-2	Ireland	Roker Park
1899	6 September	Sunderland	5-3	Kaffirs (Orange Free State)	Roker Park

English Schools' Shield Final

1907	4 May	Sunderland Boys	2-2	West Ham Boys	Roker Park
1907	12 October	Football League	6-3	Irish League	Roker Park

English Schools' Shield Final replay

1910	21 May	Sunderland Boys	4-1	Walsall Boys	Roker Park
1914	21 January	England	4-3	The North	Roker Park
1920	23 October	England	2-0	Ireland	Roker Park

FA Cup first round third replay

1925	9 December	Blyth Spartans	2-1	Hartlepool United	Roker Park
1926	9 April	England Schoolboys	3-0	Scotland Schoolboys	Roker Park

FA Amateur Cup Final

1926	17 April	Northern Nomads	7-1	Stockton	Roker Park

English Schools' Shield Final

1933	6 May	Sunderland Boys	1-0	Edmonton Boys	Roker Park
1934	21 March	England	1-7	The Rest	Roker Park
1938	14 May	England Schoolboys	0-1	Scotland Schoolboys	Roker Park

FA Amateur Cup Final

1939	22 April	Bishop Auckland	3-0 (aet)	Willington	Roker Park

FA Youth County Championship Final 2nd leg

1946	11 May	Durham County	2-1	Berks & Bucks	Roker Park

Army Cadet Force International

1949	29 January	England Army Cadets	3-3 (aet)	N Ireland Army Cadets	Roker Park

FA Amateur Cup semi-final

1949	19 March	Crook Town	2-2	Romford	Roker Park
1950	15 November	England	4-2	Wales	Roker Park

ON STAGE AT SUNDERLAND

1951	15 March	England Youth	3-1	Scotland Youth	Roker Park
1953	28 March	Sunderland Boys	6-4	East of Scotland Boys	Roker Park
1954	3 March	England B	1-1	Scotland B	Roker Park
1954	15 December	England Universities	1-2	Scotland Universities	Roker Park

FA Cup semi-final replay
1955	30 March	Newcastle United	2-0	York City	Roker Park
1956	25 October	England Youth	2-1	Hungary Youth	Roker Park
1957	23 February	England Schoolboys	2-3	Scotland Schoolboys	Roker Park

FA Amateur Cup semi-final
| 1958 | 15 March | Crook Town | 1-0 | Ilford | Roker Park |

FA Amateur Cup semi-final
1959	21 March	Crook Town	2-0	Leytonstone	Roker Park
1959	13 October	Sunderland Youths	3-0	England Youths	Roker Park
1959	11 November	England Under-23	2-0	France Under-23	Roker Park

FA Amateur Cup semi-final
1961	25 March	West Auckland Town	3-1	Leytonstone	Roker Park
1961	22 April	England Under-15	2-3	Scotland Under-15	Roker Park
1961	18 October	FA XI	1-2	The Army	Roker Park
1964	18 March	Football League	2-2	Scottish League	Roker Park
1965	23 February	Sunderland Youth	3-3	England Youth	Roker Park

FA Amateur Cup semi-final
| 1965 | 27 March | Whitby Town | 2-1 | Enfield | Roker Park |
| 1965 | 10 April | England Boys' Clubs | 5-3 | Scotland Boys' Clubs | Roker Park |

FA Amateur Cup semi-final
| 1966 | 19 March | Whitley Bay | 1-2 | Hendon | Roker Park |

World Cup Finals Group Four
1966	13 July	Italy	2-0	Chile	Roker Park
1966	16 July	Italy	0-1	USSR	Roker Park
1966	20 July	Chile	1-2	USSR	Roker Park

World Cup Finals quarter-final
| 1966 | 23 July | USSR | 2-1 | Hungary | Roker Park |

FA Cup first round second replay
| 1966 | 5 December | Bishop Auckland | 3-3 (aet) | Blyth Spartans | Roker Park |

FA Cup first round third replay
| 1966 | 8 December | Bishop Auckland | 4-1 | Blyth Spartans | Roker Park |

English Schools' Trophy semi-final
| 1967 | 18 March | Seaham Boys | 2-3 | Liverpool Boys | Roker Park |
| 1967 | 20 December | Sunderland Under-19 | 0-2 | FA Youth XI | Roker Park |

English Schools' Football Association Under-18 Trophy Final 1st leg
1968	7 May	Hookergate Grammar School	4-3	SE Essex Tech College	Roker Park
1969	9 December	Sunderland Youth	0-6	England Youth	Roker Park
1970	4 March	England Under-23	3-1	Scotland Under-23	Roker Park
		(Abandoned after 62 minutes due to snow)			
1970	19 May	England Under-15	0-0	West Germany Under-15	Roker Park

| 1971 | 19 April | Sunderland | 3-2 | GB Olympic XI | Roker Park |

FA Cup first round second replay

| 1972 | 27 November | Hartlepool United | 1-2 (aet) | Scunthorpe United | Roker Park |

FA Amateur Cup semi-final

| 1974 | 23 March | Ashington | 0-0 | Bishop Stortford | Roker Park |

Sunderland Centenary Match

| 1979 | 7 November | Sunderland | 0-2 | England XI | Roker Park |
| 1980 | 26 March | England B | 1-0 | Spain B | Roker Park |

English Schools' Trophy Final 2nd leg

| 1981 | 6 May | Sunderland Boys | 0-0 | High Wycombe Boys | Roker Park |

English Schools' Trophy Final 2nd leg

1983	10 May	Sunderland Boys	2-0	Middlesbrough Boys	Roker Park
1984	11 November	England 1966 Squad	3-1	Variety Club of GB	Roker Park
1988	14 March	England Under-15	3-0	Brazil Under-15	Roker Park
1990	5 March	England Schools Under-18	0-0	Holland Schools Under-18	Roker Park
1990	24 April	England B	2-0	Czechoslovakia B	Roker Park

English Schools' Trophy Final 1st leg

1990	26 April	Sunderland Boys	1-2	Sheffield Boys	Roker Park
1990	16 October	England Under-17	0-0	Belgium Under-17	Roker Park
1994	25 February	England Under-15	5-1	Northern Ireland Under-15	Roker Park
1995	1 November	England Women	1-1	Italy Women	Roker Park
1996	23 April	England Under-21	0-1	Croatia Under-21	Roker Park

100 Years of League Football

1999	18 May	Sunderland	2-3	Liverpool	Stadium of Light
1999	10 October	England	2-1	Belgium	Stadium of Light
2000	16 July	England Under-16	1-2	Brazil Under-16	Stadium of Light

European Under-16 Championship quarter-final

| 2001 | 29 April | Spain | 1-1 (4-3 pens) | Italy | Stadium of Light |

European Under-16 Championship Final

2001	5 May	Spain	1-0	France	Stadium of Light
2002	18 November	Holland Under-16	0-3	Spain Under-16	Stadium of Light
2002	18 November	England Under-16	2-2	Germany Under-16	Stadium of Light
2002	27 November	England Under-20	3-5	Italy Under-20	Stadium of Light

European Championships qualifier

| 2003 | 2 April | England | 2-0 | Turkey | Stadium of Light |
| 2003 | 10 June | England Under-21 | 2-0 | Slovakia Under-21 | Stadium of Light |

FA Carlsberg Sunday Cup Final

| 2012 | 29 April | Hetton Lyons CC | 5-1 | Canada (Liverpool) | Stadium of Light |

English Schools' FA Premier League Under-14 Schools' Cup Final

| 2012 | 8 May | Cardinal Heenan | 1-0 | Bishop Challoner | Stadium of Light |

PLAYER OF THE YEAR

Sunderland have had a Player of the Year award since 1976-77.

Initially organised by the Sunderland AFC Supporters' Association, the club began their own official award in 1980-81 in conjunction with the local paper *The Sunderland Echo*.

For one season only in 1994-95 *The Echo* ran its own award with the official club SAFCSA awards meaning there were three Player of the Year awards in that season.

Nowadays the club provide their own award while the original SAFCSA award continues.

2011-12
Official award: Stephane Sessegnon
SAFCSA: Stephane Sessegnon

2010-11
Official award: Phil Bardsley
SAFCSA: Phil Bardsley

2009-10
Official award: Darren Bent
SAFCSA: Darren Bent

2008-09
Official award: Danny Collins
SAFCSA: Danny Collins

2007-08
Official award: Kenwyne Jones
SAFCSA: Danny Collins

2006-7
Official award: Nyron Nosworthy
SAFCSA: Nyron Nosworthy

2005-06
Official award: Dean Whitehead
SAFCSA: Not awarded

2004-05
Official award: George McCartney
SAFCSA: Julio Arca

2003-04
Official award: Julio Arca
SAFCSA: Julio Arca

2002-03
Official award: Sean Thornton
SAFCSA: Not awarded

2001-02
Official award: Jody Craddock
SAFCSA: Jody Craddock

2000-01
Official award: Don Hutchison
SAFCSA: Don Hutchison

1999-2000
Official award: Kevin Phillips
SAFCSA: Kevin Phillips

1998-99
Official award: Niall Quinn
SAFCSA: Niall Quinn

1997-98
Official award: Kevin Phillips
SAFCSA: Kevin Phillips

1996-97
Official award: Lionel Perez
SAFCSA: Kevin Ball

1995-96
Official award: Richard Ord
SAFCSA: Richard Ord

1994-95
Official award: Dariusz Kubicki
SAFCSA: Kevin Ball
Echo: Martin Smith

1993-94
Official award: Gary Bennett
SAFCSA: Phil Gray

1992-93
Official award: Don Goodman
SAFCSA: Kevin Ball

1991-92
Official award: John Byrne
SAFCSA: John Kay

1990-91
Official award: Kevin Ball
SAFCSA: Kevin Ball

1989-90
Official award: Marco Gabbiadini
SAFCSA: Marco Gabbiadini

1988-89
Official award: Marco Gabbiadini
SAFCSA: Marco Gabbiadini

1987-88
Official award: Eric Gates
SAFCSA: Eric Gates

1986-87
Official award: Gary Bennett
SAFCSA: Gary Bennett

1985-86
Official award: Mark Proctor
SAFCSA: Shaun Elliott

1984-85
Official award: Chris Turner
SAFCSA: Chris Turner

1983-84
Official award: Paul Bracewell
SAFCSA: Paul Bracewell

1982-83
Official award: Ian Atkins
SAFCSA: Ian Atkins

1981-82
Official award: Nick Pickering
SAFCSA: Nick Pickering

1980-81
Official award: Stan Cummins
SAFCSA: Stan Cummins

1979-80
SAFCSA: Jeff Clarke

1978-79
SAFCSA: Shaun Elliott

1977-78
SAFCSA: Bobby Kerr

1976-77
SAFCSA: Joe Bolton

Players on Loan to Sunderland

	Player	Signed from	Signed	Left or Signed Permanently	Position	Apps	Subs	Gls
57	Sotirios Kyrgiakos	VFL Wolfsburg	31 January 2012	14 May 2012	Central-defender	3	1	0
56	Wayne Bridge	Manchester City	31 January 2012	14 May 2012	Left-back	5	5	0
55	Nicklas Bendtner	Arsenal	31 August 2011	14 May 2012	Centre-forward	27	3	8
54	Sulley Muntari	Inter Milan	29 January 2011	13 May 2011	Midfielder	7	2	1
53	Danny Welbeck	Manchester United	12 August 2010	25 April 2011	Forward	23	5	6
52	Nedum Onuoha	Manchester City	11 August 2010	23 May 2011	Defender	32	0	1
51	John Mensah	Olympique Lyonnais	11 August 2010	23 May 2011	Central-defender	15	3	0
50	Ahmed Elmohamady	ENPPI, Cairo	1 July 2010	9 June 2011	Right-back/Midfielder	27	11	0
49	Benjamin Mwaruwari	Manchester City	1 February 2010	10 May 2010	Centre-forward	1	7	0
48	Alan Hutton	Tottenham Hotspur	1 February 2010	10 May 2010	Right-back	11	0	0
47	John Mensah	Olympique Lyonnais	28 August 2009	10 May 2010	Central-defender	15	2	1
46	Calum Davenport	West Ham United	2 February 2009	25 May 2009	Central-defender	7	1	0
45	Tal Ben Haim	Manchester City	1 February 2009	25 May 2009	Defender	5	0	0
44	Djibril Cisse	Olympique Marseille	21 August 2008	25 May 2009	Centre Forward	32	6	11
43	Jonny Evans	Manchester United	4 January 2008	12 May 2008	Central-defender	16	0	0
42	Danny Simpson	Manchester United	25 January 2007	8 May 2007	Right-back	13	1	0
41	Jonny Evans	Manchester United	4 January 2007	8 May 2007	Central-defender	19	0	1
40	Marton Fulop	Tottenham Hotspur	23 November 2006	2 January 2007	Goalkeeper	1	0	0
39	Lewin Nyatanga	Derby County	19 October 2006	2 January 2007	Central-defender	9	2	0
38	Justin Hoyte	Arsenal	31 August 2005	8 May 2006	Full-back	30	0	1
37	Anthony Le Tallec	Liverpool	2 August 2005	8 May 2006	Midfielder/Forward	15	16	5
36	Darren Carter	Birmingham City	16 September 2004	6 December 2004	Midfielder	8	2	1
35	Simon Johnson	Leeds United	10 September 2004	25 October 2004	Forward	1	4	0
34	Carl Robinson	Portsmouth	25 March 2004	10 June 2004	Midfielder	7	2	1
33	Colin Cooper	Middlesbrough	12 March 2004	6 April 2004	Central-defender	0	3	0
32	Kevin Cooper	Wolverhampton W.	7 January 2004	18 March 2004	Outside-left	0	1	0
31	Stewart Downing	Middlesbrough	29 October 2003	11 December 2003	Outside-left	9	0	3
30	Alan Quinn	Sheffield Wednesday	3 October 2003	1 January 2004	Midfielder	5	1	0
29	Talal El Karkouri	Paris St Germain	31 January 2003	12 May 2003	Central-defender	8	0	0
28	Mart Poom	Derby County	17 November 2002	10 January 2003	Goalkeeper	0	0	0
27	Patrick Mboma	Parma	13 February 2002	13 May 2002	Centre-forward	5	4	1
26	Patrice Carteron	St. Etienne	8 March 2001	21 May 2001	Right-back	8	0	1
25	Andy Marriott	Wrexham	17 August 1998	28 September 1998	Goalkeeper	0	0	0
24	Terry Cooke	Manchester United	29 January 1996	25 February 1996	Outside-right	6	0	0
23	Shay Given	Blackburn Rovers	19 January 1996	19 April 1996	Goalkeeper	17	0	0
22	Gareth Hall	Chelsea	18 December 1995	19 January 1996	Right-back/Midfielder	1	1	0
21	Paul Stewart	Liverpool	29 August 1995	4 September 1995	Forward	1	1	0
20	Dominic Matteo	Liverpool	22 March 1995	1 April 1995	Midfielder	1	0	0
19	Paul A. Williams	Crystal Palace	19 January 1995	17 February 1995	Forward	3	0	0
18	Ian Snodin	Everton	12 October 1994	19 November 1994	Midfielder	6	0	0
17	Dariusz Kubicki	Aston Villa	3 March 1994	13 July 1994	Righ-back	15	0	0
16	Lee Power	Norwich City	13 August 1993	13 September 1993	Forward	3	2	1
15	Peter Beagrie	Everton	26 September 1991	26 October 1991	Outside-left	5	0	1

	Player	Signed from	Signed	Left or Signed Permanently	Position	Apps	Subs	Gls
14	Doug McGuire	Glasgow Celtic	7 March 1988	7 April 1988	Midfielder	1	0	0
13	Steve Hardwick	Oxford United	14 August 1987	14 September 1987	Goalkeeper	8	0	0
12	Bobby Mimms	Everton	11 December 1986	3 January 1987	Goalkeeper	4	0	0
11	Iain Hesford	Sheffield Wednesday	8 August 1986	20 September 1986	Goalkeeper	6	0	0
10	Tony Ford	Grimsby Town	27 March 1986	5 May 1986	Outside-right	8	1	1
9	Andy Dibble	Luton Town	20 February 1986	5 May 1986	Goalkeeper	12	0	0
8	Bob Bolder	Liverpool	21 September 1985	16 October 1985	Goalkeeper	6	0	0
7	Seamus McDonagh	Notts County	2 August 1985	20 October 1985	Goalkeeper	8	0	0
6	Jamie Murray	Cambridge United	21 March 1984	4 May 1984	Midfielder	1	0	0
5	Mark Proctor	Nottingham Forest	15 March 1983	15 April 1983	Midfielder	5	0	0
4	Loek Ursem	Stoke City	25 March 1982	25 April 1982	Midfielder	0	4	0
3	Jimmy Nicholl	Manchester United	17 December 1981	17 February 1982	Right-back	5	0	0
2	Colin Waldron	Manchester United	28 February 1977	19 July 1977	Central-defender	12	0	1
1	Jim Holton	Manchester United	23 September 1976	28 October 1976	Central-defender	6	0	0

Sunderland's foreign-born players

No	Player	Country	Year	Apps	Goals
76	Sotirios Kyriakos	GREECE	2012	4	0
75	Nicolas Bendtner	DENMARK	2011-12	30	8
74	Ji Dong-won	SOUTH KOREA	2011-	21	2
73	Sebastian Larsson	SWEDEN	2011-	39	8
72	Sulley Muntari	GHANA	2011	9	1
71	Stephane Sessgnon	BENIN	2011-	56	11
70	Marcos Angeleri	ARGENTINA	2010-	3	0
69	Asamoah Gyan	GHANA	2010-12	37	11
68	Cristian Riveros	PARAGUAY	2010-12	14	1
67	Ahmed Elmohamady	EGYPT	2010-	59	1
66	Simon Mignolet	BELGIUM	2010-	61	0
65	Benjani Mwaruwari	ZIMBABWE	2010	3	0
64	Boudewijn Zenden	NETHERLANDS	2009-11	50	4
63	John Mensah	GHANA	2009-11	35	1
62	Paulo da Silva	PARAGUAY	2009-11	24	0
61	Lorik Cana	KOSOVO	2009-10	35	0
60	Tal Ben Haim	ISRAEL	2009	5	0
59	Djibril Cisse	FRANCE	2008-09	38	12
58	El Hadji Diouf	SENEGAL	2008-09	16	0
57	Steed Malbranque	BELGIUM	2008-11	112	2
56	Teemu Tainio	FINLAND	2008-10	23	1
55	Pascal Chimbonda	GUADELOUPE (FRANCE)	2008-09	16	0
54	Rade Prica	SWEDEN	2008-09	6	1
53	Kenwyne Jones	TRINIDAD & TOBAGO	2007-10	101	28
52	Dickson Etuhu	NIGERIA	2007-08	21	1
51	Stern John	TRINIDAD & TOBAGO	2007	16	5
50	Carlos Edwards	TRINIDAD & TOBAGO	2007-09	56	5
49	Marton Fulop	HUNGARY	2006-10	50	0
48	Dwight Yorke	TRINIDAD & TOBAGO	2006-09	62	6
47	Tobias Hysen	SWEDEN	2006-07	27	4
46	Arnau Rierra	SPAIN	2006-09	2	0
45	Christian Bassila	FRANCE	2005-06	14	0
44	Anthony Le Tallec	FRANCE	2005-06	31	5
43	Jeff Whitley	ZAMBIA	2003-05	77	2
42	Mart Poom	ESTONIA	2002-05	68	1
41	Talal El Karkouri	MOROCCO	2003	9	0
40	Nicolas Medina	ARGENTINA	2001-03	1	0
39	Tore Andre Flo	NORWAY	2002-03	33	6
38	Thomas Myhre	NORWAY	2002-05	42	0
37	Patrick Mboma	CAMEROON	2002	9	1
36	Joachim Bjorklund	SWEDEN	2002-04	65	0
35	Claudio Reyna	USA	2001-03	29	4
34	Lillian Laslandes	FRANCE	2001-03	13	1
33	Bernt Haas	AUSTRIA	2001-03	29	0
32	David Bellion	FRANCE	2001-03	24	1

SUNDERLAND: THE COMPLETE RECORD

No	Player	Country	Year	Apps	Goals
31	Patrice Carteron	FRANCE	2001	8	1
30	Stanislav Varga	SLOVAKIA	2000-03, 2006-08	54	2
29	Emerson Thome	BRAZIL	2000-03	53	2
28	Tom Peeters	BELGIUM	2000-03	1	0
27	Jurgen Macho	AUSTRIA	2000-03	27	0
26	Julio Arca	ARGENTINA	2000-06	177	23
25	Milton Nunez	HONDURAS	2000-01	2	0
24	Marcos De Giuseppe	BRAZIL	1999	1	0
23	Stefan Schwarz	SWEDEN	1999-2003	76	3
22	Eric Roy	FRANCE	1999-2001	34	1
21	Thomas Helmer	GERMANY	1999-2000	2	0
20	Carsten Fredgaard	DENMARK	1999-2001	5	2
19	Thomas Sorensen	DENMARK	1998-2006	**197**	0
18	Edwin Zoetebier	NETHERLANDS	1997-98	2	0
17	Jan Eriksson	SWEDEN	1997-98	1	0
16	Lionel Perez	FRANCE	1996-98	84	0
15	Dariusz Kubicki	POLAND	1994-97	150	0
14	Terry Butcher	SINGAPORE	1992-93	42	1
13	Thomas Hauser	GERMANY	1989-92	65	11
12	Iain Hesford	ZAMBIA	1986-88	112	0
11	Loek Ursem	NETHERLANDS	1982	4	0
10	Jimmy Nicholl	CANADA	1981-83	40	0
9	Claudio Marangoni	ARGENTINA	1979-81	22	3
8	Don Kichenbrand	SOUTH AFRICA	1958-60	54	28
7	Willie Fraser	AUSTRALIA	1954-58	143	0
6	Ted Purdon	SOUTH AFRICA	1954-57	96	**42**
5	Les McDowall	INDIA	1932-38	14	0
4	Evelyn Morrison	SOUTH AFRICA	1929-31	16	7
3	Thomas Wagstaffe	INDIA	1923-24	2	0
2	Jock Gibson	USA	1920-22	5	0
1	Fred Gibson	SOUTH AFRICA	1909-10	2	0
				2,966	260

All players born outside of United Kingdom and Republic of Ireland
38 different countries – France (9), Sweden (6), South Africa (4), Trinidad & Tobago (4) and Argentina (4) most frequent
Highest totals in bold

MOST CAPPED INDIVIDUAL PLAYERS

Player	Country	Caps
Charlie Hurley	Republic of Ireland	38
Kevin Kilbane	Republic of Ireland	37
Martin Harvey	Northern Ireland	34
Billy Bingham	Northern Ireland	33
Niall Quinn	Republic of Ireland	31
Cristian Riveros	Paraguay	30

Highest for other home countries; Andy Melville (Wales): 17, Craig Gordon (Scotland) 17, Dave Watson (England) 14

Country with Highest Number of Caps by Sunderland players

Republic of Ireland: 202 caps – John O'Shea earned the 200th cap by a Sunderland player in the Republic's second game of Euro 2012 against eventual champions Spain in Gdansk.

Most Internationals in One Game

There have been 17 occasions when three Sunderland players have appeared in one international match. 15 of these instances have occurred in games involving United Kingdom and Republic of Ireland sides and two have involved Trinidad and Tobago when Carlos Edwards, Dwight Yorke and Kenwyne Jones all played in 2010 World Cup qualifying games against Cuba and El Salvador.

In March 2011 four Sunderland players appeared in a friendly match at Wembley between England and Ghana. The visitors included Asamoah Gyan, Sunny Muntari and John Mensah while Danny Welbeck made his full international debut for England as a late substitute. Muntari (Inter Milan), Mensah (Lyon) and Welbeck (Manchester United) were all on loan to Sunderland at the time so their caps are not included in the club list. Gyan's equaliser was the fourth instance of a Sunderland player scoring at Wembley after Trevor Ford, Len Shackleton and Johnny Crossan.

Four Sunderland players would have appeared for England against Ireland in Belfast in February 1913 if George Holley, who had been the number 10 for England's previous three games (scoring in each), had not been dropped in favour of Bolton's Joe Smith. Charlie Buchan, who scored ten minutes into his debut, played alongside Jackie Mordue and Frank Cuggy on the only occasion the club has had three representatives in an England eleven.

Players capped while with Sunderland
Up to end of July 2012

No	Player	Caps with Sunderland Caps	Caps with Sunderland Goals	Date	Venue	Competition	Opponents	Result	Notes
England									
1	Tom PORTEOUS	1	0	07/03/1891	Sunderland	BC	WALES	4-1	DEBUT / First SAFC player capped
2	Phil BACH	1	0	18/02/1899	Sunderland	BC	IRELAND	13-2	DEBUT / Eng highest home win
3	Billy HOGG	3	0	03/03/1902	Wrexham	BC	WALES	0-0	DEBUT
				22/03/1902	Belfast	BC	IRELAND	1-0	
				03/05/1902	Birmingham	BC	SCOTLAND	2-2	
4	Arthur BRIDGETT	11	3	01/04/1905	Crystal Palace	BC	SCOTLAND	1-0	DEBUT
				04/04/1908	Glasgow	BC	SCOTLAND	1-1	
				06/06/1908	Vienna	F	AUSTRIA	6-1	scored / Eng's 1st overseas tour
				08/06/1908	Vienna	F	AUSTRIA	11-1	scored
				10/06/1908	Budapest	F	HUNGARY	7-0	
				13/06/1908	Prague	F	BOHEMIA	4-0	
				13/02/1909	Bradford	BC	IRELAND	4-0	
				15/03/1909	Nottingham	BC	WALES	2-0	+ Holley
				25/09/1909	Budapest	F	HUNGARY	4-2	scored
				31/05/1909	Budapest	F	HUNGARY	8-2	
				01/06/1909	Vienna	F	AUSTRIA	8-1	+ Holley
5	George HOLLEY	10	8	15/03/1909	Nottingham	BC	WALES	2-0	DEBUT / scored /+ Bridgett
				03/04/1909	Crystal Palace	BC	SCOTLAND	2-0	
				25/09/1909	Budapest	F	HUNGARY	4-2	+ Bridgett
				31/05/1909	Budapest	F	HUNGARY	8-2	scored 2 / + Bridgett
				01/06/1909	Vienna	F	AUSTRIA	8-1	scored 2 / + Bridgett
				14/03/1910	Cardiff	BC	WALES	1-0	
				10/02/1912	Dublin	BC	IRELAND	6-1	scored / + Mordue
				11/03/1912	Wrexham	BC	WALES	2-0	scored
				23/03/1912	Glasgow	BC	SCOTLAND	1-1	scored / THOMSON for SCOT
				05/04/1913	Chelsea	BC	SCOTLAND	1-0	
6	Jackie MORDUE	2	0	10/02/1912	Dublin	BC	IRELAND	6-1	DEBUT /+ Holley
				15/02/1913	Belfast	BC	IRELAND	1-2	+ Buchan, Cuggy
7	Frank CUGGY	2	0	15/02/1913	Belfast	BC	IRELAND	1-2	DEBUT / + Mordue, Buchan
				14/02/1914	Middlesbrough	BC	IRELAND	0-3	+ Martin
8	Charlie BUCHAN	6	4	15/02/1913	Belfast	BC	IRELAND	1-2	DEBUT / scored /+ Mordue, Cuggy
				15/03/1920	Arsenal	BC	WALES *	1-2	scored
				14/03/1921	Cardiff	BC	WALES	0-0	
				21/05/1921	Brussels	F	BELGIUM	2-0	scored
				10/05/1923	Paris	F	FRANCE	4-1	scored /+ Cresswell
				12/04/1924	Wembley	BC	SCOTLAND	1-1	

PLAYERS CAPPED WHILE WITH SUNDERLAND

No	Player	Caps with Sunderland Caps	Goals	Date	Venue	Competition	Opponents	Result	Notes
9	Harry MARTIN	1	0	14/02/1914	Middlesbrough	BC	IRELAND	0-3	DEBUT / + Cuggy
10	Warney CRESSWELL	5	0	10/05/1923	Paris	F	FRANCE	4-1	+ Buchan
				01/11/1923	Antwerp	F	BELGIUM	2-2	
				22/10/1924	Everton	BC	IRELAND	3-1	
				01/03/1926	Selhurst Park	BC	WALES	1-3	+ Kelly
				20/10/1926	Liverpool	BC	IRELAND	3-3	+ McInroy
11	Bob KELLY	1	0	01/03/1926	Selhurst Park	BC	WALES	1-3	+ Cresswell
12	Albert McINROY	1	0	20/10/1926	Liverpool	BC	IRELAND	3-3	DEBUT / + Cresswell
13	Raich CARTER	6	2	14/04/1934	Wembley	BC	SCOTLAND	3-0	DEBUT
				10/05/1934	Budapest	F	HUNGARY	1-2	
				04/12/1935	Tottenham	F	GERMANY	3-0	
				18/11/1936	Stoke	BC	IRELAND	3-1	scored
				02/12/1936	Arsenal	F	HUNGARY	6-2	scored
				17/04/1937	Glasgow	BC	SCOTLAND	1-3	
14	Bobby GURNEY	1	0	06/04/1935	Glasgow	BC	SCOTLAND	0-2	DEBUT
15	Len SHACKLETON	5	1	26/09/1948	Copenhagen	F	DENMARK	0-0	DEBUT
				10/11/1948	Vila Park	BC	WALES	1-0	
				15/10/1949	Cardiff	BC	WALES	4-1	
				10/11/1954	Wembley	BC	WALES	3-2	
				01/12/1954	Wembley	F	W.GERMANY	3-1	scored
16	Willie WATSON	4	0	16/11/1949	Maine Road	BC	N.IRELAND	9-2	DEBUT
				30/11/1949	Tottenham	F	ITALY	2-0	
				15/11/1950	Sunderland	BC	WALES	4-2	(selected for 1950 WCFINALS squad)
				22/11/1950	Highbury	F	YUGOSLAVIA	2-2	
17	Colin GRAINGER	1	0	06/04/1957	Wembley	BC	SCOTLAND	2-1	
18	Stan ANDERSON	2	0	04/04/1962	Wembley	F	AUSTRIA	3-1	DEBUT
				14/04/1962	Glasgow	BC	SCOTLAND	0-2	
19	Dave WATSON	14	0	03/04/1974	Lisbon	F	PORTUGAL	0-0	DEBUT
				18/05/1974	Hampden Park	BC	SCOTLAND	0-2	sub
				22/05/1974	Wembley	F	ARGENTINA	2-2	
				29/05/1974	Leipzig	F	E.GERMANY	1-1	
				01/06/1974	Sofia	F	BULGARIA	1-0	
				05/06/1974	Belgrade	F	YUGOSLAVIA	2-2	
				30/10/1974	Wembley	ECQ	CZECHOSLOVAKIA	3-0	
				20/11/1974	Wembley	ECQ	PORTUGAL	0-0	
				12/03/1975	Wembley	F	W.GERMANY	2-0	
				16/04/1975	Wembley	ECQ	CYPRUS	5-0	
				11/05/1975	Limassol	ECQ	CYPRUS	1-0	
				17/05/1975	Belfast	BC	N.IRELAND	0-0	
				21/05/1975	Wembley	BC	WALES	2-2	
				24/05/1975	Wembley	BC	SCOTLAND	5-1	
20	Tony TOWERS	3	0	08/05/1976	Cardiff	BC	WALES	1-0	DEBUT
				11/05/1976	Wembley	BC	N.IRELAND	4-0	sub
				28/05/1976	New York	F	ITALY	3-2	
21	Nick PICKERING	1	0	19/06/1983	Melbourne	F	AUSTRALIA	1-1	DEBUT
22	Kevin PHILLIPS	8	0	28/04/1999	Budapest	F	HUNGARY	1-1	DEBUT / + Gray
				10/10/1999	Sunderland	F	BELGIUM	2-1	
				23/02/2000	Wembley	F	ARGENTINA	0-0	sub
				27/05/2000	Wembley	F	BRAZIL	1-1	sub
				03/06/2000	Valetta	F	MALTA	2-1	
				15/11/2000	Turin	F	ITALY	0-1	sub
				10/11/2001	Old Trafford	F	SWEDEN	1-1	
				13/02/2002	Amsterdam	F	HOLLAND	1-1	sub
23	Michael GRAY	3	0	28/04/1999	Budapest	F	HUNGARY	1-1	sub DEBUT (for Wes Brown) / + Phillips
				05/06/1999	Wembley	ECQ	SWEDEN	0-0	sub
				09/06/1999	Sofia	ECQ	BULGARIA	1-1	

675

No	Player	Caps with Sunderland Caps	Goals	Date	Venue	Competition	Opponents	Result	Notes
24	Gavin McCANN	1	0	28/02/2001	Villa Park	F	SPAIN	3-0	DEBUT / sub
25	Darren BENT	3	1	14/11/2009	Doha	F	BRAZIL	0-1	
				30/05/2010	Graz	F	JAPAN	2-1	
				07/09/2010	Basle	ECQ	SWITZERLAND	3-1	sub/scored
26	Jordan HENDERSON	1	0	17/11/2010	Wembley	F	FRANCE	1-2	DEBUT
27	Fraizer CAMPBELL	1	0	29/02/2012	Wembley	F	HOLLAND	2-3	sub DEBUT
	Totals	98	19						

Scotland

No	Player	Caps	Goals	Date	Venue	Competition	Opponents	Result	Notes
1	Ted DOIG	3	0	04/04/1896	Celtic Park	BC	ENGLAND	2-1	
				08/04/1899	Villa Park	BC	ENGLAND	1-2	
				04/04/1903	Bramall Lane	BC	ENGLAND	2-1	+ McCombie, Watson
2	Hugh WILSON	1	0	03/04/1897	Crystal Palace	BC	ENGLAND	2-1	
3	Andy McCOMBIE	2	0	09/03/1903	Cardiff	BC	WALES	1-0	DEBUT / + Watson
				04/04/1903	Bramall Lane	BC	ENGLAND	2-1	+ Doig, Watson
4	James WATSON	4	0	09/03/1903	Cardiff	BC	WALES	1-0	DEBUT / + McCombie
				04/04/1903	Bramall Lane	BC	ENGLAND	2-1	+ Doig, McCombie
				09/04/1904	Celtic Park	BC	ENGLAND	0-1	
				01/04/1905	Crystal Palace	BC	ENGLAND	0-1	BRIDGETT for ENG
5	Charlie THOMSON	9	1	01/03/1909	Wrexham,	BC	WALES	2-3	
				02/04/1910	Hampden	BC	ENGLAND	2-0	
				18/03/1911	Celtic Park	BC	IRELAND	2-0	
				02/03/1912	Tynecastle	BC	WALES	1-0	
				23/03/1912	Hampden	BC	ENGLAND	1-1	HOLLEY for ENG
				03/03/1913	Wrexham,	BC	WALES	0-0	
				05/04/1913	Stamford Bridge	BC	ENGLAND	0-1	
				14/03/1914	Belfast	BC	IRELAND	1-1	
				04/04/1914	Hampden	BC	ENGLAND	3-1	scored
6	Tommy TAIT	1	0	06/03/1911	Cardiff	BC	WALES	2-2	DEBUT
7	Billy CLUNAS	2	1	12/04/1924	Wembley	BC	ENGLAND	1-1	DEBUT
				31/10/1925	Cardiff	BC	WALES	3-0	scored
8	Jimmy CONNOR	4	0	18/05/1930	Paris	F	FRANCE	2-0	DEBUT
				19/09/1931	Ibrox	BC	IRELAND	3-1	
				14/04/1934	Wembley	BC	ENGLAND	0-3	
				20/10/1934	Belfast	BC	IRELAND	1-2	+ Gallacher
9	Patsy GALLACHER	1	1	20/10/1934	Belfast	BC	IRELAND	1-2	DEBUT / scored / + Connor
10	Alex HASTINGS	2	0	13/11/1935	Tynecastle	BC	IRELAND	2-1	DEBUT
				10/11/1937	Aberdeen	BC	IRELAND	1-1	
11	Sandy McNAB	1	0	09/05/1937	Vienna	F	AUSTRIA	1-1	DEBUT
12	Charlie THOMSON	1	0	22/05/1937	Prague	F	CZECHOSLOVAKIA	3-1	DEBUT
13	Bert JOHNSTON	1	0	08/12/1937	Ibrox	F	CZECHOSLOVAKIA	5-0	DEBUT
14	Tommy WRIGHT	3	0	18/10/1952	Cardiff	BC	WALES	2-1	DEBUT / + Aitken (FORD goal for Wales)
				05/11/1952	Hampden	BC	N. IRELAND	1-1	+ Aitken
				18/04/1953	Wembley	BC	ENGLAND	2-2	
15	George AITKEN	3	0	18/10/1952	Cardiff	BC	WALES	2-1	+ Wright (FORD goal for Wales)
				05/11/1952	Hampden	BC	N. IRELAND	1-1	+ Wright
				03/04/1954	Hampden	BC	ENGLAND	2-4	
16	Willie FRASER	2	0	16/10/1954	Cardiff	BC	WALES	1-0	DEBUT
				03/11/1954	Hampden	BC	N. IRELAND	2-2	(BINGHAM goal for NI)
17	Joe McDONALD	2	0	08/10/1955	Belfast	BC	N. IRELAND	1-2	DEBUT (BINGHAM goal for NI)
				09/11/1955	Hampden	BC	WALES	2-0	

PLAYERS CAPPED WHILE WITH SUNDERLAND

No	Player	Caps with Sunderland Caps	Goals	Date	Venue	Competition	Opponents	Result	Notes
18	George MULHALL	2	0	07/11/1962	Hampden	BC	N. IRELAND	5-1	
				12/10/1963	Belfast	BC	N. IRELAND	1-2	
19	Neil MARTIN	1	0	09/11/1965	Hampden	WCQ	ITALY	1-0	+ Baxter
20	Jim BAXTER	10	0	02/10/1965	Belfast	BC	N. IRELAND	2-3	
				09/11/1965	Hampden	WCQ	ITALY	1-0	+ Martin
				24/11/1965	Hampden	ECQ	WALES	4-1	
				02/04/1966	Hampden	BC	ENGLAND	3-4	
				18/06/1966	Hampden	F	PORTUGAL	0-1	
				25/06/1966	Hampden	F	BRAZIL	1-1	
				22/10/1966	Cardiff	BC	WALES	1-1	
				15/04/1967	Wembley	BC	ENGLAND	3-2	
				10/05/1967	Hampden	F	USSR	0-2	
				22/11/1967	Hampden	BC	WALES	3-2	
21	Billy HUGHES	1	0	16/04/1975	Gothenburg	F	SWEDEN	1-1	sub DEBUT
22	Allan JOHNSTON	9	2	10/10/1998	Tynecastle	ECQ	ESTONIA	3-2	DEBUT
				14/10/1998	Aberdeen	ECQ	FAROES	2-1	
				31/03/1999	Celtic Park	ECQ	CZECH REPUBLIC	1-2	sub
				28/04/1999	Bremen	F	GERMANY	1-0	
				05/06/1999	Toftir	ECQ	FAROES	1-1	scored
				09/06/1999	Prague	ECQ	CZECH REPUBLIC	2-3	scored
				08/09/1999	Tallinn	ECQ	ESTONIA	0-0	
				29/03/2000	Hampden	F	FRANCE	0-2	
				30/05/2000	Dublin	F	REP OF IRELAND	2-1	KILBANE & QUINN for Rep
23	Don HUTCHISON	6	1	02/09/2000	Riga	WCQ	LATVIA	1-0	
				07/10/2000	Serravalle	WCQ	SAN MARINO	2-0	scored
				11/10/2000	Zagreb	WCQ	CROATIA	1-1	
				15/11/2000	Hampden	F	AUSTRALIA	0-2	
				24/03/2001	Hampden	WCQ	BELGIUM	2-2	
				28/03/2001	Hampden	WCQ	SAN MARINO	4-0	
24	Kevin KYLE	8	0	16/05/2002	Busan	F	SOUTH KOREA	1-4	sub DEBUT
				20/05/2002	Mongkok	F	SOUTH AFRICA	0-2	
				21/08/2002	Hampden	F	DENMARK	0-1	
				07/09/2002	Toftir	ECQ	FAROES	2-2	
				15/10/2002	Easter Road	F	CANADA	3-1	sub
				20/11/2002	Braga	F	PORTUGAL	0-2	sub
				27/05/2003	Tynecastle	F	NEW ZEALAND	1-1	
				28/04/2004	Copenhagen	F	DENMARK	0-1	
25	Stephen CALDWELL	5	0	13/11/2004	Chisinau	ECQ	MOLDOVA	1-1	with brother Gary (Hibs)
				17/08/2005	Graz	F	AUSTRIA	2-2	
				12/10/2005	Celje	WCQ	SLOVENIA	3-0	sub
				12/11/2005	Hampden	F	USA	1-1	sub
				01/03/2006	Hampden	F	SWITZERLAND	1-3	sub
26	Craig GORDON	17	0	22/08/2007	Aberdeen	F	SOUTH AFRICA	1-0	+ Anderson
				08/09/2007	Hampden	ECQ	LITHUANIA	3-1	
				12/09/2007	Paris	ECQ	FRANCE	1-0	
				13/10/2007	Hampden	ECQ	UKRAINE	3-1	
				17/10/2007	Tbilisi	ECQ	GEORGIA	0-2	
				17/11/2007	Hampden	ECQ	ITALY	1-2	
				26/03/2008	Hampden	F	CROATIA	1-1	+ Anderson
				30/05/2008	Prague	F	CZECH REPUBLIC	1-3	
				20/08/2008	Hampden	F	N. IRELAND	0-0	
				06/09/2008	Skopje	WCQ	MACEDONIA	0-1	
				10/09/2008	Rejkjavik	WCQ	ICELAND	2-1	
				11/10/2008	Hampden	WCQ	NORWAY	0-0	
				01/04/2009	Hampden	WCQ	ICELAND	2-1	
				05/09/2009	Hampden	WCQ	MACEDONIA	2-0	
				10/10/2009	Yokohama	F	JAPAN	0-2	
				03/03/2010	Hampden	F	CZECH REPUBLIC	1-0	

No	Player	Caps with Sunderland Caps	Goals	Date	Venue	Competition	Opponents	Result	Notes
				16/11/2010	Aberdeen	F	FAROES	3-0	+ Bardsley
27	Russel ANDERSON	2	0	22/08/2007	Aberdeen	F	SOUTH AFRICA	1-0	+ Gordon
				26/03/2008	Hampden	F	CROATIA	1-1	sub + Gordon
28	Phil BARDSLEY	12	0	12/10/2010	Hampden	ECQ	SPAIN	2-3	DEBUT
				16/11/2010	Aberdeen	F	FAROES	3-0	+ Gordon
				09/02/2011	Dublin	NC	N. IRELAND	3-0	
				25/05/2011	Dublin	NC	WALES	3-1	sub
				29/05/2011	Dublin	NC	REP OF IRELAND	0-1	
				10/08/2011	Hampden	F	DENMARK	2-1	
				03/09/2011	Hampden	ECQ	CZECH REPUBLIC	2-2	
				06/09/2011	Hampden	ECQ	LITHUANIA	1-0	
				08/10/2011	Vaduz	ECQ	LIECHTENSTEIN	1-0	
				11/10/2011	Alicante	ECQ	SPAIN	1-3	
				11/11/2011	Larnaca	F	CYPRUS	2-1	
				04/06/2012	Florida	F	USA	1-5	
	Totals	115	6						

Wales

No	Player	Caps	Goals	Date	Venue	Competition	Opponents	Result	Notes
1	Mark WATKINS	3	2	06/03/1905	Wrexham	BC	SCOTLAND	3-1	scored
				27/03/1905	Liverpool	BC	ENGLAND	1-3	
				08/04/1905	Belfast	BC	IRELAND	2-2	scored
2	Leigh R ROOSE	9	0	07/03/1908	Dundee	BC	SCOTLAND	1-2	
				16/03/1908	Wrexham	BC	ENGLAND	1-7	subbed
				01/03/1909	Wrexham	BC	SCOTLAND	3-2	
				15/03/1909	Nottingham	BC	ENGLAND	0-2	
				20/03/1909	Belfast	BC	IRELAND	3-2	
				05/03/1910	Kilmarnock	BC	SCOTLAND	0-1	
				14/03/1910	Cardiff	BC	ENGLAND	0-1	
				11/04/1910	Wrexham	BC	IRELAND	4-1	
				06/03/1911	Cardiff	BC	SCOTLAND	2-2	TAIT for SCOT
3	Trevor FORD	13	12	15/11/1950	Sunderland	BC	ENGLAND	2-4	scored twice / WATSON for ENG
				07/03/1951	Belfast	BC	N. IRELAND	2-1	
				12/05/1951	Cardiff	F	PORTUGAL	2-1	scored
				16/05/1951	Wrexham	F	SWITZERLAND	3-2	scored twice
				20/10/1951	Cardiff	BC	ENGLAND	1-1	
				20/11/1951	Hampden	BC	SCOTLAND	1-0	
				05/12/1951	Cardiff	F	REST OF UK	3-2	scored
				19/03/1952	Swansea	BC	N. IRELAND	3-0	
				18/10/1952	Cardiff	WCQ	SCOTLAND	1-2	scored
				12/11/1952	Wembley	BC	ENGLAND	2-5	scored twice
				15/04/1953	Belfast	BC	N. IRELAND	3-2	scored
				14/05/1953	Paris	F	FRANCE	1-6	
				21/05/1953	Belgrade	F	YUGOSLAVIA	2-5	scored twice
4	Ray DANIEL	9	0	10/10/1953	Cardiff	WCQ	ENGLAND	1-4	
				04/11/1953	Hampden	BC	SCOTLAND	3-3	
				31/03/1954	Wrexham	WCQ	N. IRELAND	1-2	
				10/11/1954	Wembley	BC	ENGLAND	2-3	
				20/04/1955	Belfast	BC	N. IRELAND	3-2	
				20/10/1956	Cardiff	BC	SCOTLAND	2-2	
				14/11/1956	Wembley	BC	ENGLAND	1-3	
				10/04/1957	Belfast	BC	N. IRELAND	0-0	
				26/05/1957	Prague	WCQ	CZECHOSLOVAKIA	0-2	
5	Leighton JAMES	1	0	23/02/1983	Wembley	HI	ENGLAND	1-2	sub
6	Colin PASCOE	8	0	19/10/1988	Swansea	WCQ	FINLAND	2-2	
				08/02/1989	Tel Aviv	F	ISRAEL	3-2	
				31/05/1989	Cardiff	WCQ	W. GERMANY	0-0	sub
				11/10/1989	Wrexham	WCQ	HOLLAND	1-2	sub

PLAYERS CAPPED WHILE WITH SUNDERLAND

Caps with Sunderland

No	Player	Caps	Goals	Date	Venue	Competition	Opponents	Result	Notes
				15/11/1989	Cologne	WCQ	W. GERMANY	1-2	sub
				06/02/1991	Wrexham	F	REP OF IRELAND	0-3	
				01/05/1991	Cardiff	F	ICELAND	1-0	sub
				11/09/1991	Cardiff	F	BRAZIL	1-0	
7	Andy MELVILLE	17	3	08/09/1993	Cardiff	WCQ	REP OF CZ & SLOV	2-2	sub
				17/11/1993	Cardiff	WCQ	ROMANIA	1-2	
				09/03/1994	Cardiff	F	NORWAY	1-3	
				20/04/1994	Wrexham	F	SWEDEN	0-2	
				23/05/1994	Tallinn	F	ESTONIA	2-1	
				07/09/1994	Cardiff	ECQ	ALBANIA	2-0	
				12/10/1994	Kishinev	ECQ	MOLDOVA	2-3	sub
				16/11/1994	Tbilisi	ECQ	GEORGIA	0-5	
				14/12/1994	Cardiff	ECQ	BULGARIA	0-3	
				11/10/1995	Cardiff	ECQ	GERMANY	1-2	
				15/11/1995	Tirana	ECQ	ALBANIA	1-1	
				02/06/1996	Serravalle	WCQ	SAN MARINO	5-0	scored
				31/08/1996	Cardiff	WCQ	SAN MARINO	6-0	scored
				05/10/1996	Cardiff	WCQ	HOLLAND	1-3	
				09/11/1996	Eindhoven	WCQ	HOLLAND	1-7	
				14/12/1996	Cardiff	WCQ	TURKEY	0-0	
				20/08/1997	Istanbul	WCQ	TURKEY	4-6	scored
8	John OSTER	10	0	09/10/1999	Wrexham	ECQ	SWITZERLAND	0-2	
				12/02/2003	Cardiff MS	F	BOSNIA	2-2	sub
				29/03/2003	Cardiff	ECQ	AZABAIJAN	4-0	
				27/05/2003	San Jose	F	USA	0-2	
				11/10/2003	Cardiff	ECQ	SERBIA-MONT.	2-3	sub
				18/02/2004	Cardiff	F	SCOTLAND	4-0	
				27/05/2004	Oslo	F	NORWAY	0-0	MYRHE for Norway
				30/05/2004	Wrexham	F	CANADA	1-0	
				04/09/2004	Baku	WCQ	AZABAIJAN	1-1	
				08/09/2004	Cardiff	WCQ	N. IRELAND	2-2	WHITLEY & McCARTNEY for N.IRE
9	Carl ROBINSON	9	1	09/10/2004	Old Trafford	WCQ	ENGLAND	0-2	sub
				09/02/2005	Cardiff	F	HUNGARY	2-0	+ Collins
				26/03/2005	Cardiff	WCQ	AUSTRIA	0-2	
				30/03/2005	Vienna	WCQ	AUSTRIA	0-1	
				17/08/2005	Swansea	F	SLOVENIA	0-0	
				03/09/2005	Cardiff	WCQ	ENGLAND	0-1	
				08/10/2005	Belfast	WCQ	N. IRELAND	3-2	scored / + Collins
				12/10/2005	Cardiff	WCQ	AZABAIJAN	2-0	+ Collins
				16/11/2005	Limassol	F	CYPRUS	0-1	+ Collins
10	Danny COLLINS	7	0	09/02/2005	Cardiff	F	HUNGARY	2-0	DEBUT / + Robinson
				08/10/2005	Belfast	WCQ	N. IRELAND	3-2	sub / + Robinson
				12/10/2005	Cardiff	WCQ	AZABAIJAN	2-0	+ Robinson
				16/11/2005	Limassol	F	CYPRUS	0-1	+ Robinson
				06/02/2007	Belfast	F	N. IRELAND	0-0	
				24/03/2007	Dublin	ECQ	REP OF IRELAND	0-1	sub
				22/08/2007	Burgas	F	BULGARIA	1-0	sub
11	David VAUGHAN	3	0	02/09/2011	Cardiff	WCQ	MONTENEGRO	2-1	
				07/10/2011	Swansea	WCQ	SWITZERLAND	2-0	sub
				29/02/2012	Cardiff	F	COSTA RICA	0-1	
	Totals	89	18						

Northern Ireland

No	Player	Caps	Goals	Date	Venue	Competition	Opponents	Result	Notes
1	Harold BUCKLE	1	0	12/03/1904	Belfast	BC	ENGLAND	1-3	DEBUT
2	English McCONNELL	4	0	17/02/1906	Belfast	BC	ENGLAND	0-5	
				16/02/1907	Liverpool	BC	ENGLAND	0-1	

SUNDERLAND: THE COMPLETE RECORD

No	Player	Caps with Sunderland		Date	Venue	Competition	Opponents	Result	Notes
		Caps	Goals						
				14/03/1908	Dublin	BC	SCOTLAND	0-5	
				11/04/1908	Aberdare	BC	WALES	1-0	
3	Billy BINGHAM	33	4	12/05/1951	Belfast	F	FRANCE	2-2	
				06/10/1951	Belfast	BC	SCOTLAND	0-3	
				20/11/1951	Villa Park	BC	ENGLAND	0-2	
				19/03/1952	Swansea	BC	WALES	0-3	
				04/10/1952	Belfast	BC	ENGLAND	2-2	
				05/11/1952	Hampden	BC	SCOTLAND	1-1	
				11/11/1952	Paris	F	FRANCE	1-3	
				15/04/1953	Belfast	BC	WALES	2-3	
				03/10/1953	Belfast	BC	SCOTLAND	1-3	
				11/11/1953	Everton	BC	ENGLAND	1-3	
				31/03/1954	Wrexham	WCQ	WALES	2-1	
				02/10/1954	Belfast	BC	ENGLAND	0-2	
				03/11/1954	Hampden	BC	SCOTLAND	2-2	scored / FRASER for SCOT
				20/04/1955	Belfast	BC	WALES	2-3	
				08/10/1955	Belfast	BC	SCOTLAND	2-1	scored / McDONALD for SCOT
				02/11/1955	Wembley	BC	ENGLAND	0-3	
				11/04/1956	Cardiff	BC	WALES	1-1	
				06/10/1956	Belfast	BC	ENGLAND	1-1	
				07/11/1956	Hampden	BC	SCOTLAND	0-1	
				16/01/1957	Lisbon	WCQ	PORTUGAL	1-1	scored
				10/04/1957	Belfast	BC	WALES	0-0	
				25/04/1957	Rome	WCQ	ITALY	0-1	
				01/05/1957	Belfast	WCQ	PORTUGAL	3-0	
				05/10/1957	Belfast	BC	SCOTLAND	1-1	scored
				06/11/1957	Wembley	BC	ENGLAND	3-2	
				04/12/1957	Belfast	F	ITALY	2-2	
				15/01/1958	Belfast	WCQ	ITALY	2-1	
				16/04/1958	Cardiff	BC	WALES	1-1	
				08/06/1958	Halmstad	WCFINALS	CZECHOSLOVAKIA	1-0	
				11/06/1958	Halmstad	WCFINALS	ARGENTINA	1-3	
				15/06/1958	Malmo	WCFINALS	W. GERMANY	2-2	
				17/06/1958	Malmo	WCFINALS	CZECHOSLOVAKIA	2-1	
				19/06/1958	Norrkoping	WCFINALS	FRANCE	0-4	
4	Ian LAWTHER	2	0	06/04/1960	Wrexham	BC	WALES	2-3	
				25/04/1961	Bologna	F	ITALY	2-3	DEBUT / + Harvey
5	Martin HARVEY	34	3	25/04/1961	Bologna	F	ITALY	2-3	DEBUT / + Lawther
				09/05/1962	Rotterdam	F	HOLLAND	0-4	
				03/04/1963	Belfast	BC	WALES	1-4	scored / + Crossan
				30/05/1963	Bilbao	F	SPAIN	1-1	+ Crossan
				12/10/1963	Belfast	BC	SCOTLAND	2-1	+ Crossan
				30/10/1963	Belfast	F	SPAIN	0-1	+ Crossan
				20/11/1963	Wembley	BC	ENGLAND	3-8	+ Crossan
				15/04/1964	Swansea	BC	WALES	3-2	scored / + Crossan
				29/04/1964	Belfast	F	URUGUAY	3-0	+ Crossan
				03/10/1964	Belfast	BC	ENGLAND	3-4	+ Crossan
				14/10/1964	Belfast	WCQ	SWITZERLAND	1-0	+ Crossan
				14/11/1964	Lausanne	WCQ	SWITZERLAND	1-2	+ Parke, Crossan
				25/11/1964	Hampden	BC	SCOTLAND	2-3	+ Parke, Crossan
				17/03/1965	Belfast	WCQ	HOLLAND	2-1	+ Parke
				31/03/1965	Belfast	BC	WALES	0-5	+ Parke
				07/04/1965	Rotterdam	WCQ	HOLLAND	0-0	+ Parke
				07/05/1965	Belfast	WCQ	ALBANIA	4-1	+ Parke
				02/10/1965	Belfast	BC	SCOTLAND	3-2	
				10/11/1965	Wembley	BC	ENGLAND	1-2	
				24/11/1965	Tirana	WCQ	ALBANIA	1-1	

PLAYERS CAPPED WHILE WITH SUNDERLAND

No	Player	Caps with Sunderland Caps	Goals	Date	Venue	Competition	Opponents	Result	Notes
				30/03/1966	Cardiff	BC	WALES	4-1	scored
				07/05/1966	Belfast	F	W. GERMANY	0-2	+ Parke
				22/06/1966	Belfast	F	MEXICO	4-1	
				22/10/1966	Belfast	ECQ	ENGLAND	0-2	+ Parke
				16/11/1966	Hampden	BC	SCOTLAND	1-2	+ Parke
				22/11/1967	Wembley	ECQ	ENGLAND	0-2	+ Parke
				28/02/1968	Wrexham	ECQ	WALES	0-2	
				10/09/1968	Jaffa	F	ISRAEL	3-2	
				23/10/1968	Belfast	WCQ	TURKEY	4-1	
				11/12/1968	Istanbul	WCQ	TURKEY	3-0	
				03/05/1969	Belfast	BC	ENGLAND	1-3	
				22/10/1969	Moscow	WCQ	USSR	0-2	
				21/04/1971	Belfast	ECQ	CYPRUS	5-0	
				22/05/1971	Belfast	BC	WALES	1-0	sub
6	Jimmy O'NEILL	1	0	11/04/1962	Cardiff	BC	WALES	0-4	
7	Johnny CROSSAN	12	5	28/11/1962	Belfast	ECQ	POLAND	2-0	scored
				03/04/1963	Belfast	BC	WALES	1-4	+ Harvey
				30/05/1963	Bilbao	F	SPAIN	1-1	+ Harvey
				12/10/1963	Belfast	BC	SCOTLAND	2-1	+ Harvey
				30/10/1963	Belfast	F	SPAIN	0-1	+ Harvey
				20/11/1963	Wembley	BC	ENGLAND	3-8	scored / + Harvey
				15/04/1964	Swansea	BC	WALES	3-2	+ Harvey
				29/04/1964	Belfast	F	URUGUAY	3-0	scored twice / + Harvey
				03/10/1964	Belfast	BC	ENGLAND	3-4	+ Harvey
				14/10/1964	Belfast	WCQ	SWITZERLAND	1-0	scored / + Harvey
				14/11/1964	Lausanne	WCQ	SWITZERLAND	1-2	+ Harvey, Parke
				25/11/1964	Hampden	BC	SCOTLAND	2-3	+ Harvey, Parke
8	John PARKE	11	0	14/11/1964	Lausanne	WCQ	SWITZERLAND	1-2	+ Harvey, Crossan
				25/11/1964	Hampden	BC	SCOTLAND	2-3	+ Harvey, Crossan
				17/03/1965	Belfast	WCQ	HOLLAND	2-1	+ Harvey
				31/03/1965	Belfast	BC	WALES	0-5	+ Harvey
				07/04/1965	Rotterdam	WCQ	HOLLAND	0-0	+ Harvey
				07/05/1965	Belfast	WCQ	ALBANIA	4-1	+ Harvey
				07/05/1966	Belfast	F	W. GERMANY	0-2	+ Harvey
				22/10/1966	Belfast	ECQ	ENGLAND	0-2	+ Harvey
				16/11/1966	Hampden	BC	SCOTLAND	1-2	+ Harvey
				21/10/1967	Belfast	BC	SCOTLAND	1-0	
				22/11/1967	Wembley	ECQ	ENGLAND	0-2	+ Harvey
9	Tom FINNEY	7	2	04/09/1974	Oslo	ECQ	NORWAY	1-2	DEBUT / scored
				17/05/1975	Belfast	BC	ENGLAND	0-0	sub
				20/05/1975	Hampden	BC	SCOTLAND	0-3	
				23/05/1975	Belfast	BC	WALES	1-0	scored
				29/10/1975	Belfast	ECQ	NORWAY	3-0	
				19/11/1975	Belgrade	ECQ	YUGOSLAVIA	0-1	
				08/05/1976	Glasgow	BC	SCOTLAND	0-3	
10	Jimmy NICHOLL	5	0	13/10/1982	Vienna	ECQ	AUSTRIA	0-2	
				17/11/1982	Belfast	ECQ	W. GERMANY	1-0	
				15/12/1982	Tirana	ECQ	ALBANIA	0-0	
				30/03/1983	Belfast	ECQ	TURKEY	2-1	
				27/04/1983	Belfast	ECQ	ALBANIA	1-0	
11	Anton ROGAN	1	0	28/04/1992	Belfast	WCQ	LITHUANIA	2-2	sub
12	Phil GRAY	13	5	08/09/1993	Belfast	WCQ	LATVIA	2-0	scored
				13/10/1993	Copenhagen	WCQ	DENMARK	0-1	
				17/11/1993	Belfast	WCQ	REP OF IRELAND	1-1	
				23/03/1994	Belfast	F	ROMANIA	2-0	scored
				20/04/1994	Belfast	F	LIECHTENSTEIN	4-1	sub
				07/09/1994	Belfast	ECQ	PORTUGAL	1-2	
				12/10/1994	Vienna	ECQ	AUSTRIA	2-1	scored

SUNDERLAND: THE COMPLETE RECORD

No	Player	Caps with Sunderland Caps	Goals	Date	Venue	Competition	Opponents	Result	Notes
				16/11/1994	Belfast	ECQ	REP OF IRELAND	0-4	
				22/05/1995	Edmonton	F	CANADA	0-2	
				26/05/1995	Edmonton	F	CHILE	1-2	sub
				03/09/1995	Oporto	ECQ	PORTUGAL	1-1	sub
				11/10/1995	Eschen	ECQ	LIECHTENSTEIN	4-0	scored
				15/11/1995	Belfast	ECQ	AUSTRIA	5-3	scored
13	George McCARTNEY	26	1	05/09/2001	Belfast	WCQ	ICELAND	3-0	DEBUT / scored
				06/10/2001	Valletta	WCQ	MALTA	1-0	
				13/02/2002	Limassol	F	POLAND	1-4	sub
				27/03/2002	Vaduz	F	LIECHTENSTEIN	0-0	
				17/04/2002	Belfast	F	SPAIN	0-5	
				21/08/2002	Belfast	F	CYPRUS	0-0	
				12/10/2002	Albarete	ECQ	SPAIN	0-3	
				16/10/2002	Belfast	ECQ	UKRAINE	0-0	
				12/02/2003	Belfast	F	FINLAND	0-1	
				02/04/2003	Belfast	ECQ	GREECE	0-2	
				03/06/2003	Campobasso	F	ITALY	0-2	
				11/06/2003	Belfast	ECQ	SPAIN	0-0	
				06/09/2003	Donetsk	ECQ	UKRAINE	0-0	
				10/09/2003	Belfast	ECQ	ARMENIA	0-1	
				11/10/2003	Athens	ECQ	GREECE	0-1	sent-off / + Whitley
				18/02/2004	Belfast	F	NORWAY	1-4	
				08/09/2004	Cardiff	WCQ	WALES	2-2	sub / + Whitley. OSTER for WALES
				13/10/2004	Belfast	WCQ	AUSTRIA	3-3	+ Whitley
				09/02/2005	Belfast	F	CANADA	0-1	+ Whitley
				04/06/2005	Belfast	F	GERMANY	1-4	+ Ingham
				06/09/2008	Bratislava	WCQ	SLOVAKIA	1-2	+ Healy
				10/09/2008	Belfast	WCQ	CZECH REPUBLIC	0-0	+ Healy
				11/10/2008	Maribor	WCQ	SLOVENIA	0-2	+ Healy
				15/10/2008	Belfast	WCQ	SAN MARINO	4-0	+ Healy
				11/02/2009	Serravalle	WCQ	SAN MARINO	3-0	+ Healy
				01/04/2009	Belfast	WCQ	SLOVENIA	1-0	+ Healy
14	Jeff WHITLEY	12	1	11/10/2003	Athens	ECQ	GREECE	0-1	+ McCartney
				31/03/2004	Tallinn	F	ESTONIA	1-0	
				28/04/2004	Belfast	F	SERBIA	1-1	
				02/06/2004	Basseterre	F	ST KITTS & NEVIS	2-0	
				06/06/2004	Barolet	F	TRINIDAD & TOB.	3-0	
				04/09/2004	Belfast	WCQ	POLAND	0-3	
				08/09/2004	Cardiff	WCQ	WALES	2-2	scored / + McCartney. OSTER for WALES
				09/10/2004	Baku	WCQ	AZABAIJAN	0-0	
				13/10/2004	Belfast	WCQ	AUSTRIA	3-3	+ McCartney
				09/02/2005	Belfast	F	CANADA	0-1	+ McCartney
				26/03/2005	Old Trafford	WCQ	ENGLAND	0-4	
				30/03/2005	Warsaw	WCQ	POLAND	0-1	
15	Michael INGHAM	1	0	04/06/2005	Belfast	F	GERMANY	1-4	sub DEBUT
16	David HEALY	19	1	06/09/2008	Bratislava	WCQ	SLOVAKIA	1-2	+ McCartney
				10/09/2008	Belfast	WCQ	CZECH REPUBLIC	0-0	+ McCartney
				11/10/2008	Maribor	WCQ	SLOVENIA	0-2	+ McCartney
				15/10/2008	Belfast	WCQ	SAN MARINO	4-0	scored / + McCartney
				19/11/2008	Belfast	F	HUNGARY	0-2	
				11/02/2009	Serravalle	WCQ	SAN MARINO	3-0	+ McCartney
				28/03/2009	Belfast	WCQ	POLAND	3-2	
				01/04/2009	Belfast	WCQ S	LOVENIA	1-0	+ McCartney
				06/06/2009	Pisa	F	ITALY	0-3	
				05/09/2009	Chorzow	WCQ	POLAND	1-1	

PLAYERS CAPPED WHILE WITH SUNDERLAND

No	Player	Caps with Sunderland Caps	Goals	Date	Venue	Competition	Opponents	Result	Notes
				09/09/2009	Belfast	WCQ	SLOVAKIA	0-2	
				14/10/2009	Prague	WCQ	CZECH REPUBLIC	0-0	
				12/08/2009	Belfast	F	ISRAEL	1-1	
				14/11/2009	Belfast	F	SERBIA	0-1	sub
				03/03/2010	Tirana	F	ALBANIA	0-1	
				03/09/2010	Maribor	ECQ	SLOVENIA	1-0	
				08/10/2010	Belfast	ECQ	ITALY	0-0	
				12/10/2010	Toftir	ECQ	FAROES	1-1	sub
				25/03/2010	Belgrade	ECQ	SERBIA	1-2	sub
	Totals	**182**	**22**						

Rep of Ireland

No	Player	Caps	Goals	Date	Venue	Competition	Opponents	Result	Notes
1	John FEENAN	2	0	17/05/1937	Berne	F	SWITZERLAND	1-0	DEBUT
				23/05/1937	Paris	F	FRANCE	2-2	
2	Charlie HURLEY	38	2	02/10/1957	Copenhagen	WCQ	DENMARK	2-0	
				11/05/1958	Katowice	F	POLAND	2-2	
				14/05/1958	Vienna	F	AUSTRIA	1-3	
				05/04/1959	Dublin	ECQ	CZECHOSLOVAKIA	2-0	
				10/05/1959	Bratislava	ECQ	CZECHOSLOVAKIA	0-4	
				01/11/1959	Dublin	F	SWEDEN	3-2	
				30/03/1960	Dublin	F	CHILE	2-0	
				11/05/1960	Dusseldorf	F	W. GERMANY	1-0	+ Fogarty
				18/05/1960	Malmo	F	SWEDEN	1-4	+ Fogarty
				28/09/1960	Dublin	F	WALES	2-3	
				06/11/1960	Dublin	F	NORWAY	3-1	
				03/05/1961	Hampden	WCQ	SCOTLAND	1-4	+ Fogarty
				07/05/1961	Dublin	WCQ	SCOTLAND	0-3	
				08/10/1961	Dublin	WCQ	CZECHOSLOVAKIA	1-3	+ Fogarty
				29/10/1961	Prague	WCQ	CZECHOSLOVAKIA	1-7	+ Fogarty
				08/04/1962	Dublin	F	AUSTRIA	2-3	
				12/08/1962	Dublin	ECR1	ICELAND	4-2	+ Fogarty
				02/09/1962	Reykjavik	ECR1	ICELAND	1-1	+ Fogarty
				09/06/1963	Dublin	F	SCOTLAND	1-0	+ Fogarty
				23/09/1963	Vienna	ECR2	AUSTRIA	0-0	+ Fogarty
				13/10/1963	Dublin	ECR2	AUSTRIA	3-2	+ Fogarty
				11/03/1964	Seville	ECQF	SPAIN	1-5	
				08/04/1964	Dublin	ECQF	SPAIN	0-2	
				10/05/1964	Krakow	F	POLAND	1-3	
				13/05/1964	Oslo	F	NORWAY	4-1	scored twice (playing no 9)
				05/05/1965	Dublin	WCQ	SPAIN	1-0	
				04/05/1966	Dublin	F	W. GERMANY	0-4	
				22/05/1966	Vienna	F	AUSTRIA	0-1	
				25/05/1966	Liege	F	BELGIUM	3-2	
				16/11/1966	Dublin	ECQ	TURKEY	2-1	
				07/12/1966	Valencia	ECQ	SPAIN	0-2	
				22/02/1967	Ankara	ECQ	TURKEY	1-2	
				21/05/1967	Dublin	ECQ	CZECHOSLOVAKIA	0-2	
				22/11/1967	Prague	ECQ	CZECHOSLOVAKIA	2-1	
				15/05/1968	Dublin	F	POLAND	2-2	
				30/10/1968	Katowice	F	POLAND	0-1	
				04/12/1968	Dublin	WCQ	DENMARK	1-1	match abandoned 51 mins (fog)
				04/05/1969	Dublin	WCQ	CZECHOSLOVAKIA	1-2	
3	Ambrose FOGARTY	10	3	11/05/1960	Dusseldorf	F	W. GERMANY	1-0	+ Hurley
				18/05/1960	Malmo	F	SWEDEN	1-4	+ Hurley
				03/05/1961	Hampden	WCQ	SCOTLAND	1-4	+ Hurley
				08/10/1961	Dublin	WCQ	CZECHOSLOVAKIA	1-3	+ Hurley

SUNDERLAND: THE COMPLETE RECORD

No	Player	Caps with Sunderland Caps	Goals	Date	Venue	Competition	Opponents	Result	Notes
				29/10/1961	Prague	WCQ	CZECHOSLOVAKIA	1-7	scored / + Hurley
				12/08/1962	Dublin	ECR1	ICELAND	4-2	scored / + Hurley
				02/09/1962	Reykjavik	ECR1	ICELAND	1-1	+ Hurley
				09/06/1963	Dublin	F	SCOTLAND	1-0	sub / + Hurley
				23/09/1963	Vienna	ECQ	AUSTRIA	0-0	+ Hurley
				13/10/1963	Dublin	ECQ	AUSTRIA	3-2	scored / + Hurley
4	John BYRNE	2	2	13/11/1991	Istanbul	ECQ	TURKEY	3-1	scored twice
				19/02/1992	Dublin	F	WALES	0-1	
5	David KELLY	4	1	11/10/1995	Dublin	ECQ	LATVIA	2-1	sub
				10/11/1996	Dublin	WCQ	ICELAND	0-0	
				11/02/1997	Cardiff	F	WALES	0-0	sub
				02/04/1997	Skopje	WCQ	MACEDONIA	2-3	scored
6	Niall QUINN	31	7	31/08/1996	Eschen	WCQ	LIECHTENSTEIN	5-0	scored twice
				20/08/1997	Dublin	WCQ	LITHUANIA	0-0	
				22/04/1998	Dublin	F	ARGENTINA	0-2	
				14/10/1998	Dublin	ECQ	MALTA	5-0	scored
				18/11/1998	Belgrade	ECQ	YUGOSLAVIA	0-1	
				10/02/1999	Dublin	F	PARAGUAY	2-0	
				28/04/1999	Dublin	F	SWEDEN	2-0	
				29/05/1999	Dublin	F	N. IRELAND	0-1	
				09/06/1999	Dublin	ECQ	MACEDONIA	1-0	scored
				01/09/1999	Dublin	ECQ	YUGOSLAVIA	2-1	
				04/09/1999	Zagreb	ECQ	CROATIA	0-1	sub
				08/09/1999	Valletta	ECQ	MALTA	3-2	
				09/10/1999	Skopje	ECQ	MACEDONIA	1-1	scored
				17/11/1999	Bursa	ECPO	TURKEY	0-0	
				23/02/2000	Dublin	F	CZECH REPUBLIC	3-2	+ P Butler, Kilbane
				30/05/2000	Dublin	F	SCOTLAND	1-2	+ Kilbane
				04/06/2000	Chicago	F	MEXICO	2-2	+ Kilbane
				06/06/2000	Foxboro	F	USA	1-1	sub / + Kilbane
				11/06/2000	East Rutherford	F	SOUTH AFRICA	2-1	scored / + Kilbane
				02/09/2000	Amsterdam	WCQ	HOLLAND	2-2	+ Kilbane
				07/10/2000	Lisbon	WCQ	PORTUGAL	1-1	+ Kilbane
				11/10/2000	Dublin	WCQ	ESTONIA	2-0	+ Kilbane
				02/06/2001	Dublin	WCQ	PORTUGAL	1-1	+ Kilbane
				06/06/2001	Tallinn	WCQ	ESTONIA	2-0	+ Kilbane
				01/09/2001	Dublin	WCQ	HOLLAND	1-0	sub / + Kilbane
				06/10/2001	Dublin	WCQ	CYPRUS	4-0	scored / + Kilbane
				10/11/2001	Dublin	WCPO	IRAN	2-0	+ Kilbane, McAteer
				13/02/2002	Dublin	F	RUSSIA	2-0	sub / + Kilbane, McAteer
				05/06/2002	Ibaraki	WCFINALS	GERMANY	1-1	sub / + Kilbane
				11/06/2002	Yokohama	WCFINALS	SAUDI ARABIA	3-0	sub / + Kilbane, McAteer
				16/06/2002	Suwon	WCFINALS	SPAIN	1-1	sub / + Kilbane
7	Kevin KILBANE	37	4	23/02/2000	Dublin	F	CZECH REPUBLIC	3-2	+ Quinn, P Butler
				26/04/2000	Dublin	F	GREECE	0-1	
				30/05/2000	Dublin	F	SCOTLAND	1-2	+ Quinn
				04/06/2000	Chicago	F	MEXICO	2-2	sub / + Quinn
				06/06/2000	Foxboro	F	USA	1-1	+ Quinn
				11/06/2000	East Rutherford	F	SOUTH AFRICA	2-1	sub / + Quinn
				02/09/2000	Amsterdam	WCQ	HOLLAND	2-2	+ Quinn
				07/10/2000	Lisbon	WCQ	PORTUGAL	1-1	+ Quinn
				11/10/2000	Dublin	WCQ	ESTONIA	2-0	+ Quinn
				15/11/2000	Dublin	F	FINLAND	3-0	scored
				24/03/2001	Nicosia	WCQ	CYPRUS	4-0	
				28/03/2001	Barcelona	WCQ	ANDORRA	3-0	scored
				25/04/2001	Dublin	WCQ	ANDORRA	3-1	scored
				02/06/2001	Dublin	WCQ	PORTUGAL	1-1	+ Quinn

PLAYERS CAPPED WHILE WITH SUNDERLAND

No	Player	Caps	Goals	Date	Venue	Competition	Opponents	Result	Notes
				06/06/2001	Tallinn	WCQ	ESTONIA	2-0	+ Quinn
				15/08/2001	Dublin	F	CROATIA	2-2	sub
				01/09/2001	Dublin	WCQ	HOLLAND	1-0	+ Quinn
				06/10/2001	Dublin	WCQ	CYPRUS	4-0	+ Quinn
				10/11/2001	Dublin	WCPO	IRAN	2-0	+ Quinn, McAteer
				15/11/2001	Tehran	WCPO	IRAN	0-1	+ McAteer
				13/02/2002	Dublin	F	RUSSIA	2-0	+ Quinn, McAteer
				17/04/2002	Dublin	F	USA	2-1	REYNA for USA
				16/05/2002	Dublin	F	NIGERIA	1-2	+ McAteer
				01/06/2002	Niigata	WCFINALS	CAMEROON	1-1	+ McAteer
				05/06/2002	Ibaraki	WCFINALS	GERMANY	1-1	+ Quinn
				11/06/2002	Yokohama	WCFINALS	SAUDI ARABIA	3-0	+ Quinn, McAteer
				16/06/2002	Suwon	WCFINALS	SPAIN	1-1	missed shoot-out pen / + Quinn
				21/08/2002	Helsinki	F	FINLAND	3-0	sub / + McAteer, T Butler
				07/09/2002	Moscow	ECQ	RUSSIA	2-4	+ McAteer / subbed by Babb
				16/10/2002	Dublin	ECQ	SWITZERLAND	1-2	+ T Butler. M McCarthy last game as manager. HAAS for Switz
				12/02/2003	Hampden	F	SCOTLAND	2-0	scored
				29/03/2003	Tbilisi	ECQ	GEORGIA	2-1	
				02/04/2003	Tirana	ECQ	ALBANIA	0-0	
				30/04/2003	Dublin	F	NORWAY	1-0	FLO for Norway
				07/06/2003	Dublin	ECQ	ALBANIA	2-1	
				11/06/2003	Dublin	ECQ	GEORGIA	2-0	
				19/08/2003	Dublin	F	AUSTRALIA	2-1	sub / + Breen, Healy
8	Paul BUTLER	1	0	23/02/2000	Dublin	F	CZECH REPUBLIC	3-2	DEBUT / + Quinn, Kilbane
9	Jason McATEER	10	0	10/11/2001	Dublin	WCPO	IRAN	2-0	+ Quinn, Kilbane
				15/11/2001	Tehran	WCPO	IRAN	0-1	+ Kilbane
				13/02/2002	Dublin	F	RUSSIA	2-0	sub / + Quinn, Kilbane
				27/03/2002	Dublin	F	DENMARK	3-0	SORENSEN for Denmark
				16/05/2002	Dublin	F	NIGERIA	1-2	+ Kilbane
				01/06/2002	Niigata	WCFINALS	CAMEROON	1-1	+ Kilbane
				11/06/2002	Yokohama	WCFINALS	SAUDI ARABIA	3-0	+ Quinn, Kilbane
				21/08/2002	Helsinki	F	FINLAND	3-0	+ Kilbane, T Butler
				07/09/2002	Moscow	ECQ	RUSSIA	2-4	+ Kilbane, Babb
				18/02/2004	Dublin	F	BRAZIL	0-0	sub
10	Thomas BUTLER	2	0	21/08/2002	Helsinki	F	FINLAND	3-0	+ Kilbane, McAteer
				16/10/2002	Dublin	ECQ	SWITZERLAND	1-2	sub / + Kilbane.
11	Phil BABB	1	0	07/09/2002	Moscow	ECQ	RUSSIA	2-4	sub for Kilbane / + McAteer
12	Gary BREEN	7	0	19/08/2003	Dublin	F	AUSTRALIA	2-1	+ Kilbane, Healy
				06/09/2003	Dublin	ECQ	RUSSIA	1-1	+ Healy
				09/09/2003	Dublin	F	TURKEY	2-2	+ Healy
				11/10/2003	Basel	ECQ	SWITZERLAND	0-2	+ Healy
				18/08/2004	Dublin	F	BULGARIA	1-1	sub
				16/11/2004	Dublin	F	CROATIA	1-0	+ Elliott
				24/05/2006	Dublin	F	CHILE	0-1	
13	Colin HEALY	4	0	19/08/2003	Dublin	F	AUSTRALIA	2-1	sub / + Kilbane, Breen
				06/09/2003	Dublin	ECQ	RUSSIA	1-1	+ Breen
				09/09/2003	Dublin	F	TURKEY	2-2	+ Breen

No	Player	Caps	Goals	Date	Venue	Competition	Opponents	Result	Notes
				11/10/2003	Basel	ECQ	SWITZERLAND	0-2	+ Breen
13	Stephen ELLIOTT	9	1	16/11/2004	Dublin	F	CROATIA	1-0	DEBUT / + Breen
				29/03/2005	Dublin	F	CHINA	1-0	
				08/06/2005	Torshavn	WCQ	FAROES	2-0	
				17/08/2005	Dublin	F	ITALY	1-2	sub
				08/10/2005	Nicosia	WCQ	CYPRUS	1-0	scored
				12/10/2005	Dublin	WCQ	SWITZERLAND	0-0	sub
				01/03/2006	Dublin	F	SWEDEN	3-0	
				18/08/2006	Dublin	F	HOLLAND	0-4	
				02/09/2006	Stuttgart	ECQ	GERMANY	0-1	sub
14	Anthony STOKES	3	0	07/02/2007	Serravalle	ECQ	SAN MARINO	2-1	sub DEBUT
				23/05/2007	New Jersey	F	ECUADOR	1-1	sub / + Murphy
				26/05/2007	Boston	F	BOLIVIA	1-1	+ Murphy
15	Daryl MURPHY	9	0	23/05/2007	New Jersey	F	ECUADOR	1-1	DEBUT / + Stokes
				26/05/2007	Boston	F	BOLIVIA	1-1	sub / + Stokes
				22/08/2007	Aarhus	F	DENMARK	4-0	sub
				08/09/2007	Bratislava	ECQ	SLOVAKIA	2-2	sub / + McShane
				13/10/2007	Dublin	ECQ	GERMANY	0-0	
				17/10/2007	Dublin	ECQ	CYPRUS	1-1	sub / + McShane, Miller
				24/05/2008	Dublin	F	SERBIA	1-1	sub / + McShane, Miller
				29/05/2008	Fulham	F	COLOMBIA	1-0	sub / + McShane, Miller
				20/08/2008	Oslo	F	NORWAY	1-1	sub
16	Paul McSHANE	12	0	08/09/2007	Bratislava	ECQ	SLOVAKIA	2-2	+ Murphy
				12/09/2007	Prague	ECQ	CZECH RE	0-1	
				17/10/2007	Dublin	ECQ	CYPRUS	1-1	+ Murphy, Miller
				17/11/2007	Cardiff	ECQ	WALES	2-2	+ Miller
				24/05/2008	Dublin	F	SERBIA	1-1	+ Murphy
				29/05/2008	Fulham	F	COLOMBIA	1-0	+ Murphy
				06/09/2008	Mainz	WCQ	GEORGIA	2-1	+ Miller
				15/10/2008	Dublin	F	CYPRUS	1-0	
				19/11/2008	Dublin	F	POLAND	2-3	
				28/03/2009	Dublin	WCQ	BULGARIA	1-1	
				01/04/2009	Bari	WCQ	ITALY	1-1	
				29/05/2009	Fulham	F	NIGERIA	1-1	sub
17	Liam MILLER	6	0	17/10/2007	Dublin	ECQ	CYPRUS	1-1	sub / + Murphy, McShane
				17/11/2007	Cardiff	ECQ	WALES	2-2	+ McShane
				06/02/2008	Dublin	F	BRAZIL	0-1	
				24/05/2008	Dublin	F	SERBIA	1-1	+ Murphy, McShane
				29/05/2008	Fulham	F	COLOMBIA	1-0	+ Murphy, McShane
				06/09/2008	Mainz	WCQ	GEORGIA	2-1	+ McShane
18	John O'SHEA	9	0	02/09/2011	Dublin	ECQ	SLOVAKIA	0-0	
				07/10/2011	Aixovall	ECQ	ANDORRA	2-0	
				11/10/2011	Dublin	ECQ	ARMENIA	2-1	
				15/11/2011	Dublin	ECPO	ESTONIA	1-1	
				29/02/2012	Dublin	F	CZECH REPUBLIC	1-1	+ McClean
				04/06/2012	Budapest	F	HUNGARY	0-0	+ Westwood
				10/06/2012	Poznan	ECF/NALS	CROATIA	1-3	
				14/06/2012	Gdansk	ECF/NALS	SPAIN	0-4	+ McClean
				18/06/2012	Poznan	ECF/NALS	ITALY	0-2	
19	James McCLEAN	3	0	29/02/2012	Dublin	F	CZECH REPUBLIC	1-1	sub DEBUT / + O'Shea
				26/05/2012	Dublin	F	BOSNIA & HERZ	1-0	+ Westwood
				14/06/2012	Gdansk	ECF/NALS	SPAIN	0-4	sub / + O'Shea

PLAYERS CAPPED WHILE WITH SUNDERLAND

No	Player	Caps with Sunderland Caps	Goals	Date	Venue	Competition	Opponents	Result	Notes
20	Kieren WESTWOOD	2	0	26/05/2012	Dublin	F	BOSNIA & HERZ	1-0	+ McClean
				04/06/2012	Bucapest	F	HUNGARY	0-0	sub / + O'Shea
	Totals	202	20						

Austria
| | Jurgen MACHO | 1 | 0 | 2002 | | | | | DEBUT 20-11-02 v Norway (F) |

Belgium
| | Simon MIGNOLET | 10 | 0 | 2010- | | | | | DEBUT 25-3-11 v Austria (ECQ) |

Benin
| | Stephane SESSEGNON | 7 | 2 | 2011- | | | | | |

Denmark
| | Carsten FREDGAARD | 1 | 0 | 1999 | | | | | DEBUT 18-8-99 v Holland (F) = only full cap |
| | Thomas SORENSEN | 27 | 0 | 2000-03 | | | | | DEBUT 17-11-99 v Israel (ECPO). WCFINALS 2002 (4 Apps) |

Egypt
| | Ahmed ELMOHAMADY | 7 | 0 | 2011- | | | | | |

Estonia
| | Mart POOM | 16 | 0 | 2003-05 | | | | | |

Finland
| | Teemu TAINIO | 9 | 0 | 2008-09 | | | | | |

Ghana
| | Asamoah GYAN | 12 | 4 | 2010-12 | | | | | |

Honduras
| | Milton NUNEZ | 14 | 7 | 2000-01 | | | | | |

Hungary
| | Marton FULOP | 19 | 0 | 2007-10 | | | | | |

Nigeria
| | Reuben AGBOOLA | 2 | 0 | 1991 | | | | | DEBUT 27-4-91 v Benin (ANCQ) |
| | Dickson ETUHU | 5 | 0 | 2007-08 | | | | | |

Norway
| | Thomas MYRHE | 12 | 0 | 2002-05 | | | | | |
| | Tore Andre FLO | 6 | 1 | 2002-03 | | | | | |

Paraguay
| | Paolo Da SILVA | 21 | 0 | 2009-11 | | | | | WCFINALS 2010 (5apps) |
| | Cristian RIVEROS | 30 | 6 | 2010-12 | | | | | WCFINALS 2010 (5apps, 1 goal) |

Senegal
| | El Hadji DIOUF | 3 | 0 | 2008-09 | | | | | |

Slovakia
| | Stanislav VARGA | 13 | 1 | 2000-01/2006 | | | | | |

South Korea
| | Ji DONG-WON | 9 | 2 | 2011- | | | | | |

Sweden
| | Stefan SCHWARZ | 7 | 0 | 1999-2001 | | | | | |
| | Sebastian LARSSON | 13 | 5 | 2011- | | | | | EC Finals 2012 (3 apps, 1 goal) |

Switzerland
| | Bernt HAAS | 14 | 2 | 2001-03 | | | | | |

Trinidad & Tobago
	Dwight YORKE	8	4	2006-09					
	Kenwyne JONES	12	1	2007-10					
	Carlos EDWARDS	16	3	2007-09					

USA
| | Claudio REYNA | 13 | 0 | 2001-03 | | | | | WCFINALS 2002 (4 apps) |

Key
BC: British Championship
F: Friendly
ECQ: European Championship Qualifier
WLQ: World Cup Qualifier
WC FINALS: World Cup Finals
EC FINALS: European Championship Finals

Sunderland: The Complete Record

Career Records

SURNAME	FORENAMES	DOB	BIRTHPLACE	DECEASED	POSITION
AGBOOLA	REUBEN OMOJOLA FOLASANJE	30/05/1962	ISLINGTON, LONDON		DEFENDER
AGNEW	DAVID GEORGE	31/03/1925	BELFAST		GOALKEEPER
AGNEW	STEPHEN MARK	09/11/1965	SHIPLEY		MIDFIELDER
AGNEW	WILLIAM BARBOUR	16/12/1880	KILMARNOCK	20/08/1936	RIGHT/LEFT BACK
AINSLEY	GEORGE EDWARD	15/04/1915	SOUTH SHIELDS	Apr 1985	INSIDE RIGHT
AISTON	SAMUEL JAMES	25/11/1976	NEWCASTLE		FORWARD
AITKEN	GEORGE GILBERT MILLER	28/05/1925	LOCHGELLY	22/01/2003	LEFT/CENTRE HALF
ALLAN	ADAM McILROY	12/09/1904	NEWARTHILL		CENTRE HALF
ALLAN	JAMES	09/10/1857	NEWTON, AYRSHIRE	18/10/1911	FORWARD
ALLAN	THOMAS E.	1883	GLASGOW		GOALKEEPER
ALLAN	WILLIAM MICHAEL	11/09/1853	SUNDERLAND	Q1 1929	HALF BACK
ALLARDYCE	SAMUEL	19/10/1954	DUDLEY		CENTRE HALF
ALLEN	ROBERT				GOALKEEPER
ALLEN	THOMAS	01/05/1897	WEDNESBURY	10/05/1968	GOALKEEPER
ALNWICK	BENJAMIN ROBERT	01/01/1987	PRUDHOE		GOALKEEPER
ANDERSON	GEORGE ALBERT	06/06/1887	HAYDON BRIDGE	28/05/1956	GOALKEEPER
ANDERSON	RUSSELL	25/10/1978	ABERDEEN		CENTRAL DEFENDER
ANDERSON	STANLEY	27/02/1934	CO.DURHAM		RIGHT HALF
ANDREWS	ARTHUR	12/01/1901	CO.DURHAM	03/05/1971	LEFT HALF
ANGELERI	MARCOS ALBERTO	07/04/1983	BUENOS AIRES, ARGENTINA		RIGHT BACK
ANGELL	BRETT ASHLEY MARK	20/08/1968	MARLBOROUGH		CENTRE FORWARD
ANNAN	WALTER ARCHIBALD (ARCHIE)	1877	CARNWATH, LANARKS.	Q1 1949	RIGHT BACK
ARCA	JULIO ANDRES	31/01/1981	QUILMES, ARGENTINA		LEFT WINGER
ARCHBOLD	ROBERT				FULL BACK
ARDLEY	GEORGE HENRY	Q4 1897	LANGLEY PARK	Q3 1927	RIGHT HALF
ARMSTRONG	GORDON IAN	15/07/1967	NEWCASTLE		MIDFIELDER
ARMSTRONG	KEITH THOMAS	11/10/1957	CORBRIDGE		FORWARD
ARNOTT	KEVIN WILLIAM	28/09/1958	BENSHAM, GATESHEAD		MIDFIELDER
ARTHUR	JOSEPH ORD	11/07/1891	SOUTH SHIELDS	Q2 1975	OUTSIDE LEFT
ASHURST	JACK	12/10/1954	COATBRIDGE		CENTRE HALF
ASHURST	LEONARD	10/03/1939	LIVERPOOL		LEFT BACK
ATKINS	IAN LESLIE	16/01/1957	SHELDON, BIRMINGHAM		MIDFIELDER
ATKINSON	BRIAN	19/01/1971	DARLINGTON		MIDFIELDER
ATKINSON	PAUL	19/01/1966	CHESTER-LE-STREET		OUTSIDE LEFT
AULD	JOHN ROBERTSON	07/01/1862	LUGAR, AYRSHIRE	29/04/1932	CENTRE HALF
BABB	PHILIP ANDREW	30/11/1970	LAMBETH		CENTRAL DEFENDER
BACH	PHILIP	29/09/1872	BITTERLEY, SHROPSHIRE	30/12/1937	FULL BACK
BAKER	JOSEPH HENRY	17/07/1940	LIVERPOOL		CENTRE FORWARD
BALL	KEVIN ANTHONY	12/11/1964	HASTINGS		CENTRE HALF / MIDFIELD
BARDSLEY	PHILIP ANTHONY	28/06/1985	ECCLES		RIGHT BACK
BARNES	PETER SIMON	10/06/1957	MANCHESTER		OUTSIDE LEFT
BARRIE	ALEXANDER	1878-82	GLASGOW	01/10/1918	CENTRE HALF
BARTLEY	JOHN (JACK)	15/05/1909	HOUGHTON-LE-SPRING	10/10/1929	LEFT HALF
BASSILA	CHRISTIAN	05/10/1977	PARIS		MIDFIELDER
BAXTER	JAMES CURRAN	29/09/1939	KIRKALDY	14/04/2001	LEFT HALF
BEACH	CYRIL HOWARD	28/03/1909	HOUNSLOW, LONDON		INSIDE RIGHT
BEAGRIE	PETER SYDNEY	28/11/1965	MIDDLESBROUGH		OUTSIDE LEFT
BECTON	THOMAS	Q1 1878	PRESTON	08/11/1957	INSIDE LEFT
BEDFORD	HENRY (HARRY)	15/10/1899	CALOW, NR.CHESTERFIELD	24/06/1976	CENTRE FORWARD
BEE	FRANCIS ERIC	23/01/1927	NOTTINGHAM		INSIDE FORWARD
BEESLEY	COLIN	06/10/1951	STOCKTON		FORWARD
BELFITT	RODERICK MICHAEL (ROD)	30/10/1945	DONCASTER		MIDFIELDER/FORWARD
BELL	EDWARD	23/12/1883	BURNOPFIELD		RIGHT BACK
BELL	JOHN CUTHBERT (JACK)	24/10/1905	SEAHAM COLLIERY		GOALKEEPER
BELL	RICHARD	1915	EAST GREENOCK		OUTSIDE LEFT

688

CAREER RECORDS

Career		League			Play Offs			FA Cup			League Cup			Other			Total		
Start	End	Apps	Sub	Gls	Apps	Sub	Gls	Apps	Sub	Gls	Apps	Sub	Gls	Apps	Sub	Gls	Apps	Sub	Gls
1985	1991	129	11	0	3	0	0	6	1	0	12	2	0	6	0	0	156	14	0
1950	1953	1	0	0	0	0	0	0	0	0	0	0	0	0	0	0	1	0	0
1995	1998	56	7	9	0	0	0	2	1	1	4	0	0	0	0	0	62	8	10
1908	1910	28	0	0	0	0	0	0	0	0	0	0	0	0	0	0	28	0	0
1932	1936	4	0	0	0	0	0	0	0	0	0	0	0	0	0	0	4	0	0
1994	2000	5	15	0	0	0	0	0	2	0	0	2	0	0	0	0	5	19	0
1951	1959	245	0	3	0	0	0	22	0	0	0	0	0	0	0	0	267	0	3
1927	1930	63	0	0	0	0	0	2	0	0	0	0	0	0	0	0	65	0	0
1879	1887	0	0	0	0	0	0	3	0	0	0	0	0	0	0	0	3	0	0
1908	1911	24	0	0	0	0	0	2	0	0	0	0	0	0	0	0	26	0	0
1881	1885	0	0	0	0	0	0	1	0	0	0	0	0	0	0	0	1	0	0
1980	1981	24	1	2	0	0	0	0	0	0	2	0	0	0	0	0	26	1	2
1907	1908	11	0	0	0	0	0	0	0	0	0	0	0	0	0	0	11	0	0
1919	1920	19	0	0	0	0	0	1	0	0	0	0	0	0	0	0	20	0	0
2001	2007	19	0	0	0	0	0	0	0	0	3	0	0	0	0	0	22	0	0
1911	1914	10	0	0	0	0	0	0	0	0	0	0	0	0	0	0	10	0	0
2007	2010	0	1	0	0	0	0	0	0	0	1	0	0	0	0	0	1	1	0
1951	1963	402	0	31	0	0	0	34	0	4	11	0	0	0	0	0	447	0	35
1922	1931	228	0	2	0	0	0	17	0	0	0	0	0	0	0	0	245	0	2
2010	2012	0	2	0	0	0	0	1	0	0	0	0	0	0	0	0	1	2	0
1995	1996	10	0	0	0	0	0	0	0	0	1	0	1	0	0	0	11	0	1
1902	1904	1	0	0	0	0	0	0	0	0	0	0	0	0	0	0	1	0	0
2000	2006	145	12	17	0	0	0	15	0	4	5	0	2	0	0	0	165	12	23
1888	1888	0	0	0	0	0	0	1	0	0	0	0	0	0	0	0	1	0	0
1920	1921	1	0	0	0	0	0	0	0	0	0	0	0	0	0	0	1	0	0
1983	1996	331	18	50	5	0	0	19	0	4	25	4	3	13	1	4	393	23	61
1974	1979	7	4	0	0	0	0	0	0	0	0	0	0	0	0	0	7	4	0
1974	1982	132	1	16	0	0	0	6	1	0	7	1	1	4	0	1	149	3	18
1910	1912	2	0	0	0	0	0	0	0	0	0	0	0	0	0	0	2	0	0
1969	1979	129	11	4	0	0	0	8	3	0	8	0	0	7	0	0	152	14	4
1957	1971	403	6	4	0	0	0	26	0	0	23	0	0	0	0	0	452	6	4
1982	1984	76	1	6	0	0	0	4	0	0	6	0	0	0	0	0	86	1	6
1987	1996	119	22	4	0	1	0	13	0	2	8	2	0	2	2	0	142	27	6
1982	1988	46	14	5	0	0	0	5	0	2	2	1	0	7	1	0	60	16	7
1889	1896	99	0	6	0	0	0	16	0	0	0	0	0	0	0	0	115	0	6
2002	2004	48	0	0	2	0	0	8	0	0	2	0	0	0	0	0	60	0	0
1897	1899	44	0	0	0	0	0	3	0	0	0	0	0	0	0	0	47	0	0
1969	1971	39	1	12	0	0	0	2	0	0	2	0	0	0	0	0	43	1	12
1990	1999	329	10	21	3	0	1	16	0	0	23	3	4	4	0	1	375	13	27
2008	2012	117	13	4	0	0	0	9	2	1	5	0	1	0	0	0	131	15	6
1989	1989	1	0	0	0	0	0	0	0	0	0	0	0	0	0	0	1	0	0
1902	1907	66	0	1	0	0	0	5	0	1	0	0	0	0	0	0	71	0	2
1926	1929	19	0	1	0	0	0	0	0	0	0	0	0	0	0	0	19	0	1
2005	2006	12	1	0	0	0	0	0	0	0	1	0	0	0	0	0	13	1	0
1965	1967	87	0	10	0	0	0	6	0	2	5	0	0	0	0	0	98	0	12
1932	1933	3	0	0	0	0	0	0	0	0	0	0	0	0	0	0	3	0	0
1991	1991	5	0	1	0	0	0	0	0	0	0	0	0	0	0	0	5	0	1
1899	1900	15	0	5	0	0	0	0	0	0	0	0	0	0	0	0	15	0	5
1932	1932	7	0	2	0	0	0	0	0	0	0	0	0	0	0	0	7	0	2
1947	1949	5	0	1	0	0	0	0	0	0	0	0	0	0	0	0	5	0	1
1966	1972	0	3	0	0	0	0	0	0	0	0	0	0	0	0	0	0	3	0
1973	1975	36	3	4	0	0	0	2	0	0	0	2	0	1	1	0	39	6	4
1905	1908	19	0	0	0	0	0	4	0	0	0	0	0	0	0	0	23	0	0
1924	1930	41	0	0	0	0	0	0	0	0	0	0	0	0	0	0	41	0	0
1935	1937	1	0	0	0	0	0	0	0	0	0	0	0	0	0	0	1	0	0

SURNAME	FORENAMES	DOB	BIRTHPLACE	DECEASED	POSITION
BELLION	DAVID	27/11/1982	PARIS		FORWARD
BEN HAIM	TAL	31/03/1982	RISHON LE TSIYON, ISRAEL		DEFENDER
BENDTNER	NICKLAS	16/01/1988	COPENHAGEN		CENTRE FORWARD
BENNETT	GARY ERNEST	04/12/1961	MANCHESTER		CENTRAL DEFENDER
BENT	DARREN ASHLEY	06/02/1984	TOOTING		CENTRE FORWARD
BERRY	STEPHEN ANDREW	04/04/1963	GOSPORT		MIDFIELDER
BERTRAM	A. ERNEST	20/01/1885	TYNEMOUTH		LEFT HALF
BERTSCHIN	KEITH EDWIN	25/08/1956	ENFIELD		CENTRE FORWARD
BEST	ROBERT	12/09/1891	MICKLEY	08/06/1947	OUTSIDE RIGHT
BETT	FREDERICK	05/12/1920	SCUNTHORPE	14/04/2005	INSIDE RIGHT
BINGHAM	WILLIAM LAURIE	05/08/1931	BELFAST		OUTSIDE RIGHT
BIRCHAM	WALTER CLIVE (CLIVE)	07/09/1939	PHILADELPHIA, CO.DURHAM		OUTSIDE RIGHT
BJORKLUND	JOACHIM	12/02/1971	VAXJO, SWEDEN		CENTRAL DEFENDER
BLACK	ALAN DOUGLAS	04/06/1943	GLASGOW		LEFT BACK
BLACK	CHRISTOPHER	07/09/1982	CRAMLINGTON		MIDFIELDER
BLACK	JOHN ROSS	26/05/1900	DENNY	Dec 1993	INSIDE RIGHT
BOE	JAMES	05/01/1891	GATESHEAD	Late 1973	GOALKEEPER
BOLDER	ROBERT JOHN	02/10/1958	DOVER		GOALKEEPER
BOLLANDS	JOHN FREDERICK	11/07/1935	MIDDLESBROUGH		GOALKEEPER
BOLTON	ARTHUR	1914-15	WHITLEY BAY		CENTRE FORWARD
BOLTON	JOSEPH	02/02/1955	BIRTLEY, CO.DURHAM		LEFT BACK
BOLTON	LYALL (LAURIE)	11/07/1932	GATESHEAD		HALF BACK
BONE	JOHN	19/12/1930	WINGATE	May 2002	CENTRE HALF
BONTHRON	ROBERT POLLOCK	14/07/1880	BURNTISLAND, FIFE	19/02/1947	RIGHT BACK
BOULD	STEPHEN ANDREW	16/11/1962	STOKE		CENTRE HALF
BOWYER	IAN	06/06/1951	ELLESMERE PORT		MIDFIELDER
BOYLE	PETER	26/04/1876	CARLINGFORD, CO.LOUTH	24/06/1939	LEFT BACK
BRACEWELL	PAUL WILLIAM	19/07/1962	HESWALL, CHESHIRE		MIDFIELDER
BRADSHAW	THOMAS DICKINSON	15/03/1876	HAMBLETON, LANCASHIRE		OUTSIDE RIGHT
BRADY	ALEXANDER	09/02/1870	CATHCART, GLASGOW	19/10/1913	FORWARD
BRADY	KIERON JOHN PAUL	17/09/1971	COATBRIDGE		OUTSIDE LEFT
BRAMBLE	TITUS MALACHI	31/07/1981	IPSWICH		CENTRAL DEFENDER
BRAND	RALPH LAIDLAW	08/12/1936	EDINBURGH		CENTRE FORWARD
BREBNER	RONALD GILCHRIST	23/09/1881	DARLINGTON	11/11/1914	GOALKEEPER
BRECONRIDGE	JOHN NISBET	05/10/1865	MAUCHLINE, AYRSHIRE	22/04/1925	FORWARD
BREEN	GARY PATRICK	12/12/1973	LONDON		CENTRE HALF
BRIDGE	WAYNE MICHAEL	05/08/1980	SOUTHAMPTON		LEFT BACK
BRIDGES	MICHAEL	05/08/1978	NORTH SHIELDS		CENTRE FORWARD
BRIDGETT	GEORGE ARTHUR (ARTHUR)	11/10/1882	FORSBROOK, STOKE	26/07/1954	OUTSIDE LEFT
BROADIS	IVAN ARTHUR (IVOR)	18/12/1922	POPLAR, LONDON		INSIDE RIGHT
BRODIE	STEPHEN ERIC	14/01/1973	SUNDERLAND		FORWARD
BROWN	ALAN	22/05/1959	EASINGTON		CENTRE FORWARD
BROWN	ARTHUR SAMUEL	06/04/1885	GAINSBOROUGH	27/06/1944	CENTRE FORWARD
BROWN	CHRISTOPHER	11/12/1984	DONCASTER		CENTRE FORWARD
BROWN	CYRIL	25/05/1918	ASHINGTON	15/04/1990	CENTRE FORWARD
BROWN	HAROLD ARCHER (ARCHIE)	Q4 1897	WITTON PARK, CO. DURHAM	Q2 1958	CENTRE FORWARD
BROWN	JOHN (JOCK)	1876	MOTHERWELL		CENTRE FORWARD
BROWN	NORMAN LIDDLE	30/01/1885	TYNEMOUTH	Jan 1938	OUTSIDE RIGHT
BROWN	THOMAS		SUNDERLAND		INSIDE RIGHT
BROWN	WESLEY MICHAEL	13/10/1979	LONGSIGHT, MANCHESTER		DEFENDER
BUCHAN	CHARLES MURRAY	22/09/1891	PLUMPSTEAD, LONDON	25/06/1960	INSIDE RIGHT/CENT.FORWARD
BUCHANAN	DAVID	23/06/1962	NEWCASTLE		FORWARD
BUCKLE	HAROLD REDMOND	06/03/1882	BELFAST	1965	OUTSIDE LEFT
BUCKLEY	MICHAEL JOHN	04/11/1953	MANCHESTER		MIDFIELDER
BURBANKS	WILLIAM EDWIN (EDDIE)	01/04/1913	BENTLEY, NR.DONCASTER	26/07/1983	OUTSIDE LEFT
BURLEY	GEORGE ELDER	03/06/1956	CUMNOCK		RIGHT BACK
BURLINSON	W.				HALF BACK
BUTCHER	TERENCE IAN	28/12/1958	SINGAPORE		CENTRE HALF

CAREER RECORDS

Career		League			Play Offs			FA Cup			League Cup			Other			Total		
Start	End	Apps	Sub	Gls	Apps	Sub	Gls	Apps	Sub	Gls	Apps	Sub	Gls	Apps	Sub	Gls	Apps	Sub	Gls
2001	2003	5	15	1	0	0	0	0	1	0	3	0	0	0	0	0	8	16	1
2009	2009	5	0	0	0	0	0	0	0	0	0	0	0	0	0	0	5	0	0
2011	2012	25	3	8	0	0	0	2	0	0	0	0	0	0	0	0	27	3	8
1984	1995	362	7	23	5	0	1	17	1	0	34	1	1	16	0	0	434	9	25
2009	2011	58	0	32	0	0	0	3	0	2	2	0	2	0	0	0	63	0	36
1984	1985	32	3	2	0	0	0	1	0	0	10	0	0	0	1	0	43	4	2
1903	1906	1	0	0	0	0	0	0	0	0	0	0	0	0	0	0	1	0	0
1987	1988	25	11	7	2	0	1	0	1	0	2	0	0	1	1	2	30	13	10
1911	1922	93	0	23	0	0	0	4	0	2	0	0	0	0	0	0	97	0	25
1937	1946	3	0	0	0	0	0	0	0	0	0	0	0	0	0	0	3	0	0
1950	1958	206	0	45	0	0	0	21	0	2	0	0	0	0	0	0	227	0	47
1956	1960	28	0	2	0	0	0	0	0	0	0	0	0	0	0	0	28	0	2
2002	2004	49	8	0	1	1	0	4	1	0	1	0	0	0	0	0	55	10	0
1964	1966	4	2	0	0	0	0	0	0	0	0	0	0	0	0	0	4	2	0
1999	2004	2	1	0	0	0	0	0	0	0	0	0	0	0	0	0	2	1	0
1921	1922	2	0	0	0	0	0	0	0	0	0	0	0	0	0	0	2	0	0
1914	1915	1	0	0	0	0	0	0	0	0	0	0	0	0	0	0	1	0	0
1985	1986	22	0	0	0	0	0	3	0	0	2	0	0	2	0	0	29	0	0
1956	1960	61	0	0	0	0	0	2	0	0	0	0	0	0	0	0	63	0	0
1938	1939	8	0	1	0	0	0	0	0	0	0	0	0	0	0	0	8	0	1
1970	1981	264	9	11	0	0	0	20	0	1	16	1	0	15	0	0	315	10	12
1950	1957	3	0	0	0	0	0	0	0	0	0	0	0	0	0	0	3	0	0
1951	1958	11	0	0	0	0	0	0	0	0	0	0	0	0	0	0	11	0	0
1907	1908	22	0	1	0	0	0	1	0	0	0	0	0	0	0	0	23	0	1
1999	2000	19	2	0	0	0	0	2	0	0	0	0	0	0	0	0	21	2	0
1981	1982	15	0	1	0	0	0	0	0	0	1	0	0	0	0	0	16	0	1
1896	1898	29	0	0	3	0	0	1	0	0	0	0	0	0	0	0	33	0	0
1983	1997	226	2	6	3	0	0	15	0	0	21	0	0	3	0	0	268	2	6
1897	1898	14	0	2	0	0	0	0	0	0	0	0	0	0	0	0	14	0	2
1888	1889	0	0	0	0	0	0	1	0	0	0	0	0	0	0	0	1	0	0
1988	1993	17	16	7	0	0	0	0	4	0	1	2	0	0	0	0	18	22	7
2010	2012	30	1	1	0	0	0	0	0	0	1	0	0	0	0	0	31	1	1
1967	1969	31	0	7	0	0	0	0	0	0	1	0	0	0	0	0	32	0	7
1905	1906	2	0	0	0	0	0	0	0	0	0	0	0	0	0	0	2	0	0
1888	1890	0	0	0	0	0	0	2	0	3	0	0	0	0	0	0	2	0	3
2003	2006	105	2	7	2	0	0	5	0	0	1	0	0	0	0	0	113	2	7
2012	2012	3	5	0	0	0	0	2	0	0	0	0	0	0	0	0	5	5	0
1995	2005	36	62	18	0	0	0	2	2	0	8	3	5	0	0	0	46	67	23
1903	1912	320	0	107	0	0	0	27	0	8	0	0	0	1	0	0	348	0	115
1949	1951	79	0	25	0	0	0	5	0	2	0	0	0	0	0	0	84	0	27
1989	1997	1	11	0	0	0	0	0	0	0	0	0	0	0	0	0	1	11	0
1975	1982	87	26	21	0	0	0	2	2	0	7	0	4	3	0	0	99	28	25
1908	1910	50	0	21	0	0	0	5	0	2	0	0	0	0	0	0	55	0	23
1999	2007	33	33	9	0	0	0	0	2	0	1	0	2	0	0	0	34	35	11
1945	1946	0	0	0	0	0	0	6	0	5	0	0	0	0	0	0	6	0	5
1922	1922	6	0	1	0	0	0	0	0	0	0	0	0	0	0	0	6	0	1
1897	1899	33	0	9	0	0	0	1	0	0	0	0	0	0	0	0	34	0	9
1904	1907	26	0	1	0	0	0	2	0	1	0	0	0	0	0	0	28	0	2
1907	1908	1	0	0	0	0	0	0	0	0	0	0	0	0	0	0	1	0	0
2011	2012	20	0	1	0	0	0	1	0	0	1	0	0	0	0	0	22	0	1
1911	1925	379	0	209	0	0	0	32	0	13	0	0	0	0	0	0	411	0	222
1986	1988	25	9	8	0	0	0	0	0	0	2	0	3	2	0	0	29	9	11
1902	1906	44	0	14	0	0	0	2	0	1	0	0	0	0	0	0	46	0	15
1978	1983	117	4	7	0	0	0	5	0	1	8	1	0	0	0	0	130	5	8
1935	1948	132	0	25	0	0	0	22	0	3	0	0	0	1	0	1	155	0	29
1985	1988	54	0	0	0	0	0	5	0	1	2	0	0	5	0	1	66	0	2
1882	1885	0	0	0	0	0	0	1	0	0	0	0	0	0	0	0	1	0	0
1992	1993	37	1	0	0	0	0	2	0	0	2	0	1	0	0	0	41	1	1

SUNDERLAND: THE COMPLETE RECORD

SURNAME	FORENAMES	DOB	BIRTHPLACE	DECEASED	POSITION
BUTLER	GEOFFREY	26/09/1946	MIDDLESBROUGH		LEFT BACK
BUTLER	JOSEPH HENRY	Q1 1879	DAWLEY BANK, SHROPSHIRE	30/11/1939	GOALKEEPER
BUTLER	PAUL JOHN	02/11/1972	MANCHESTER		CENTRE HALF
BUTLER	THOMAS ANTHONY	25/04/1981	BALLYMUN, DUBLIN		MIDFIELDER
BYFIELD	DARREN ASHERTON	29/09/1976	SUTTON COLDFIELD		CENTRE FORWARD
BYRNE	CHRIS THOMAS	09/02/1975	HULME, MANCHESTER		MIDFIELDER
BYRNE	JOHN FREDERICK	01/02/1961	WYTHENSHAWE, MANCHESTER		CENTRE FORWARD
CALDWELL	STEVEN	12/09/1980	STIRLING		CENTRAL DEFENDER
CAMPBELL	FRAIZER LEE	13/09/1987	HUDDERSFIELD		CENTRE FORWARD
CAMPBELL	JOHN MIDDLETON	19/02/1870	RENTON	08/06/1906	CENTRE FORWARD
CAMPBELL	WILLIAM GIBSON	02/07/1944	BELFAST		OUTSIDE RIGHT
CANA	LOR'K AGIM	27/07/1983	PRISTINA, YUGOSLAVIA		MIDFIELDER
CARMICHAEL	ROBERT	1886	SCOTLAND		INSIDE RIGHT
CARR	HENRY (HARRY)	Q1 1887	SOUTHBANK, MIDDLESBROUGH		CENTRE FORWARD
CARTER	DARREN ANTHONY	18/12/1983	SOLIHULL		MIDFIELDER
CARTER	HORATIO STRATTON (RAICH)	21/12/1913	HENDON, SUNDERLAND	09/10/1994	INSIDE FORWARD
CARTER	TIMOTHY DOUGLAS	05/10/1967	BRISTOL	19/06/2008	GOALKEEPER
CARTERON	PATRICE	30/07/1970	ST.BRIEUC, FRANCE		RIGHT BACK
CASE	NORMAN	01/09/1925	PRESCOT	Q1 1973	CENTRE FORWARD
CATTERMOLE	LEE BARRY	21/03/1988	STOCKTON		MIDFIELDER
CHALMERS	JAMES	03/12/1877	OLD LUCE, WIGTOWNSHIRE		OUTSIDE LEFT
CHAMBERLAIN	ALEC FRANCIS ROY	20/06/1964	MARCH		GOALKEEPER
CHAMBERS	BRIAN MARK	31/10/1949	NEWCASTLE		MIDFIELDER
CHAPMAN	LEE ROY	05/12/1959	LINCOLN		CENTRE FORWARD
CHILTON	FREDERICK	10/07/1935	WASHINGTON		LEFT BACK
CHIMBONDA	PASCAL	21/02/1979	LES ABYMES, GUADELOUPE		DEFENDER
CHISHOLM	GORDON WILLIAM	08/04/1960	GLASGOW		CENTRAL DEFENDER
CHISHOLM	KENNETH MacTAGGART	12/04/1925	GLASGOW	30/04/1990	INSIDE LEFT
CHOPRA	ROCKY MICHAEL (MICHAEL)	23/12/1983	NEWCASTLE		CENTRE FORWARD
CISSE	DJIBRIL ARUUN	12/08/1981	ARLES, FRANCE		FORWARD
CLACK	CHARLES EDWARD (TED)	04/06/1896	HIGHWORTH, WILTS.	Apr 1984	OUTSIDE RIGHT
CLARK	BENJAMIN	24/01/1983	SHOTLEY BRIDGE		CENTRE HALF / MIDFIELDER
CLARK	HENRY (HARRY)	11/09/1934	GRANGETOWN, SUNDERLAND		INSIDE LEFT
CLARK	JAMES McNICHOL CAMERON	1913	CATHCART, GLASGOW		CENTRE HALF
CLARK	LEE ROBERT	27/10/1972	WALLSEND		MIDFIELDER
CLARK	WILLIAM	1881	AIRDRIE	17/03/1937	OUTSIDE RIGHT
CLARKE	CLIVE RICHARD LUKE	14/01/1980	DUBLIN		LEFT BACK
CLARKE	JEFFREY DERRECK	18/01/1954	PONTEFRACT		CENTRE HALF
CLARKE	NORMAN SAMSON	01/04/1942	BALLYLOUGHAN, CO. ANTRIM		OUTSIDE LEFT
CLOUGH	BRIAN HOWARD	21/03/1935	MIDDLESBROUGH	20/09/2004	CENTRE FORWARD
CLUNAS	WILLIAM McLEAN	29/04/1899	JOHNSTONE, RENFREWSHIRE	01/09/1967	RIGHT HALF
COADY	MICHAEL LIAM	01/10/1958	DIPTON, CO. DURHAM		DEFENDER
COGLIN	STEPHEN	14/10/1899	WILLENHALL	Q4 1965	INSIDE LEFT
COLBACK	JACK RAYMOND	24/10/1989	KILLINGWORTH		MIDFIELDER
COLE	ANDREW ALEXANDER	15/10/1971	NOTTINGHAM		CENTRE FORWARD
COLEMAN	JOHN GEORGE (TIM)	26/10/1881	KETTERING	20/11/1940	INSIDE RIGHT
COLEMAN	KEITH	24/05/1951	WASHINGTON		LEFT BACK
COLLIN	GEORGE	13/09/1905	OXHILL, CO.DURHAM	01/02/1989	LEFT BACK
COLLINS	DANNY	06/08/1980	CHESTER		LEFT BACK/DEFENDER
COLLINS	JOHN DOUGLAS (DOUG)	28/08/1945	NEWTON, NR.DONCASTER		MIDFIELDER
COLLINS	NEILL WILLIAM	02/09/1983	IRVINE		CENTRAL DEFENDER
COLQUHOUN	JOHN MARK	14/07/1963	STIRLING		FORWARD
COMMON	ALFRED	25/05/1880	MILLFIELD, SUNDERLAND	03/04/1946	INSIDE RIGHT
CONNER	JOHN	27/12/1892	RENFREW, GLASGOW		CENTRE FORWARD
CONNOLLY	DAVID JAMES	06/06/1977	WILLESDEN		FORWARD
CONNOR	JAMES	01/06/1909	RENFREW	08/05/1980	OUTSIDE LEFT
COOK	JORDAN ALAN	20/03/1990	SUNDERLAND		MIDFIELDER
COOKE	FREDERICK ROBERT	05/07/1896	KIRKBY-IN-ASHFIELD	Q3 1976	INSIDE LEFT

CAREER RECORDS

Career		League			Play Offs			FA Cup			League Cup			Other			Total		
Start	End	Apps	Sub	Gls	Apps	Sub	Gls	Apps	Sub	Gls	Apps	Sub	Gls	Apps	Sub	Gls	Apps	Sub	Gls
1968	1968	1	2	0	0	0	0	2	0	0	0	0	0	0	0	0	3	2	0
1912	1914	65	0	0	0	0	0	14	0	0	0	0	0	0	0	0	79	0	0
1998	2001	78	1	3	0	0	0	4	0	0	11	1	1	0	0	0	93	2	4
1997	2004	16	15	0	0	0	0	0	1	0	1	3	0	0	0	0	17	19	0
2004	2004	8	9	5	0	0	0	0	0	0	0	0	0	0	0	0	8	9	
1997	1997	4	4	0	0	0	0	0	0	0	1	1	0	0	0	0	5	5	0
1991	1992	33	0	8	0	0	0	8	0	7	2	0	0	0	0	0	43	0	15
2004	2007	75	1	4	0	0	0	1	0	0	4	0	1	0	0	0	80	1	5
2009	2012	28	18	5	0	0	0	3	4	3	4	0	1	0	0	0	35	22	9
1889	1897	186	0	136	4	0	0	25	0	18	0	0	0	0	0	0	215	0	15
1964	1966	5	0	0	0	0	0	0	0	0	0	0	0	0	0	0	5	0	0
2009	2010	29	2	0	0	0	0	2	0	0	2	0	0	0	0	0	33	2	0
1907	1908	1	0	0	0	0	0	0	0	0	0	0	0	0	0	0	1	0	0
1910	1910	1	0	0	0	0	0	0	0	0	0	0	0	0	0	0	1	0	0
2004	2004	8	2	1	0	0	0	0	0	0	0	0	0	0	0	0	8	2	1
1930	1945	245	0	118	0	0	0	31	0	9	0	0	0	2	0	1	278	0	128
1987	1993	37	0	0	0	0	0	0	0	0	9	0	0	4	0	0	50	0	0
2001	2001	8	0	1	0	0	0	0	0	0	0	0	0	0	0	0	8	0	1
1949	1950	4	0	2	0	0	0	0	0	0	0	0	0	0	0	0	4	0	2
2009	2012	64	4	0	0	0	0	3	0	0	2	0	0	0	0	0	69	4	0
1897	1898	26	0	6	0	0	0	1	0	0	0	0	0	0	0	0	27	0	6
1993	1996	89	1	0	0	0	0	8	0	0	9	0	0	1	0	0	107	1	0
1965	1973	53	10	5	0	0	0	4	1	2	0	1	0	0	2	0	57	14	7
1983	1984	14	1	3	0	0	0	2	0	1	0	0	0	0	0	0	16	1	4
1953	1959	3	0	0	0	0	0	0	0	0	0	0	0	0	0	0	3	0	0
2008	2009	13	0	0	0	0	0	2	0	0	1	0	0	0	0	0	16	0	0
1977	1986	192	5	10	0	0	0	9	0	2	20	4	4	5	0	0	226	9	16
1953	1956	78	0	33	0	0	0	8	0	4	0	0	0	0	0	0	86	0	37
2007	2009	22	17	8	0	0	0	1	0	0	1	1	0	0	0	0	24	18	8
2008	2009	29	6	10	0	0	0	1	0	1	2	0	0	0	0	0	32	6	11
1921	1923	9	0	0	0	0	0	0	0	0	0	0	0	0	0	0	9	0	0
1999	2004	3	5	0	0	0	0	2	0	0	4	0	0	0	0	0	9	5	0
1956	1957	6	0	0	0	0	0	0	0	0	0	0	0	0	0	0	6	0	0
1933	1937	49	0	0	0	0	0	1	0	0	0	0	0	0	0	0	50	0	0
1997	1999	72	1	16	3	0	0	4	0	0	4	1	0	0	0	0	83	2	16
1908	1910	41	0	4	0	0	0	3	0	0	0	0	0	0	0	0	44	0	4
2006	2008	2	2	0	0	0	0	0	0	0	0	0	0	0	0	0	2	2	0
1975	1982	178	3	6	0	0	0	15	0	0	14	0	0	8	0	0	215	3	6
1962	1965	4	0	0	0	0	0	0	0	0	1	0	0	0	0	0	5	0	0
1961	1964	61	0	54	0	0	0	4	0	0	9	0	9	0	0	0	74	0	63
1923	1931	256	0	42	0	0	0	16	0	2	0	0	0	0	0	0	272	0	44
1975	1980	4	2	0	0	0	0	0	0	0	0	0	0	0	0	0	4	2	0
1924	1927	20	0	9	0	0	0	0	0	0	0	0	0	0	0	0	20	0	9
2008	2012	35	12	1	0	0	0	4	1	1	1	1	0	0	0	0	40	14	2
2007	2008	3	4	0	0	0	0	0	1	0	0	0	0	0	0	0	3	5	0
1910	1911	32	0	21	0	0	0	1	0	0	0	0	0	0	0	0	33	0	21
1966	1973	49	0	2	0	0	0	4	0	0	1	0	0	0	1	0	54	1	2
1936	1938	31	0	0	0	0	0	1	0	0	0	0	0	1	0	0	33	0	0
2004	2009	134	15	3	0	0	0	7	1	0	5	1	0	0	0	0	146	17	3
1977	1978	4	2	0	0	0	0	0	0	0	1	0	0	0	0	0	5	2	0
2004	2007	14	4	1	0	0	0	4	0	1	2	0	0	0	0	0	20	4	2
1992	1993	12	8	0	0	0	0	0	0	0	2	0	0	1	0	0	15	8	0
1900	1905	38	0	12	0	0	0	2	0	1	0	0	0	0	0	0	40	0	13
1912	1914	5	0	2	0	0	0	4	0	3	0	0	0	0	0	0	9	0	5
2006	2009	31	8	13	0	0	0	1	1	0	0	1	0	0	0	0	32	10	13
1930	1939	254	0	48	0	0	0	29	0	13	0	0	0	0	0	0	283	0	61
2007	2012	0	3	0	0	0	0	0	0	0	0	0	0	0	0	0	0	3	0
1919	1921	12	0	5	0	0	0	0	0	0	0	0	0	0	0	0	12	0	5

SURNAME	FORENAMES	DOB	BIRTHPLACE	DECEASED	POSITION
COOKE	JOHN	25/04/1962	SALFORD		FORWARD
COOKE	TERENCE JOHN	05/08/1976	MARSTON GREEN, BIRMINGHAM		OUTSIDE RIGHT
COOPER	COLIN TERENCE	28/02/1967	SEDGEFIELD		CENTRAL DEFENDER
COOPER	KEVIN LEE	08/02/1975	DERBY		OUTSIDE LEFT
CORNER	DAVID EDWARD	15/05/1966	SUNDERLAND		CENTRAL DEFENDER
CORNFORTH	JOHN MICHAEL	07/10/1967	WHITLEY BAY		MIDFIELDER
COTON	ANTHONY PHILIP	19/05/1961	TAMWORTH		GOALKEEPER
COVERDALE	WILLIAM ROBERT (BOB)	16/01/1892	WEST HARTLEPOOL	07/01/1959	WING HALF/OUTSIDE LEFT
COWAN	JAMES CLEWS	16/06/1926	PAISLEY	20/06/1968	GOALKEEPER
COWAN	WALTER GOWANS	20/01/1874	DALZIEL, LANARKSHIRE		INSIDE RIGHT
COWELL	JOHN (JACK)	09/06/1887	BLYTH		CENTRE FORWARD
COXFORD	JOHN (JACK)	25/07/1904	SEATON HIRST, NORTHUMB.	Q2 1978	LEFT HALF
CRADDOCK	JODY DARRYL	25/07/1975	REDDITCH		CENTRE HALF
CRAGGS	JOHN (JACK)	Q3 1880	TRIMDON		OUTSIDE LEFT/RIGHT
CRAIG	ROBERT	16/06/1928	CONSETT		LEFT BACK
CRAWFORD	JAMES	1877	LEITH		OUTSIDE RIGHT
CRESSWELL	FRANK	05/09/1908	SOUTH SHIELDS	02/12/1979	INSIDE LEFT
CRESSWELL	WARNEFORD (WARNEY)	05/11/1897	SOUTH SHIELDS	20/10/1973	RIGHT BACK
CRINGAN	WILLIAM	15/05/1890	MUIRKIRK, AYRSHIRE	12/05/1958	HALF BACK
CROSSAN	JOHN ANDREW	29/11/1938	LONDONDERRY		INSIDE LEFT
CROSSLEY	CHARLES ARTHUR	Q1 1892	HEDNESFORD	29/04/1965	INSIDE LEFT/RIGHT
CUGGY	FRANCIS	16/06/1889	WALKER	27/03/1965	RIGHT/CENTRE HALF
CULLEN	ANTHONY	30/09/1969	FELLING		OUTSIDE RIGHT
CUMMINS	STANLEY	06/12/1958	SEDGEFIELD		OUTSIDE LEFT/MIDFIELDER
CUNNING	ROBERT ROBERTSON I.	12/02/1930	DUNFERMLINE		OUTSIDE LEFT
CUNNINGHAM	KENNETH EDWARD	26/06/1971	DUBLIN		CENTRE BACK
CUNNINGTON	SHAUN GARY	04/01/1966	BOURNE, LINCS.		MIDFIELDER
CURRAN	EDWARD (TERRY)	20/03/1955	KINSLEY		OUTSIDE RIGHT/CENT.FORWARD
CURRAN	PATRICK JOSEPH (JOE)	13/11/1917	SUNDERLAND	17/12/2003	INSIDE RIGHT
CURTIS	JOHN JAMES	13/12/1888	SETTLE	Q1 1955	OUTSIDE RIGHT
DA SILVA	PAULO CESAR BARRIOS	01/02/1980	ASUNCION, PARAGUAY		CENTRE BACK
DALE	FRED HETHERINGTON	Q3 1864	MONKWEARMOUTH	30/07/1927	HALF BACK
DALTON	JAMES JOSEPH	1865-69	IRELAND		RIGHT BACK
DANIEL	PETER WILLIAM	12/12/1955	HULL		DEFENDER/MIDFIELDER
DANIEL	WILLIAM RAYMOND (RAY)	02/11/1928	SWANSEA	06/11/1997	CENTRE HALF
DAVENPORT	CALUM RAYMOND PAUL	01/01/1983	BEDFORD		CENTRAL DEFENDER
DAVENPORT	PETER	24/03/1961	BIRKENHEAD		FORWARD
DAVIS	HERBERT	11/08/1906	BRADFORD	17/07/1981	OUTSIDE RIGHT
DAVIS	KELVIN GEOFFREY	29/09/1976	BEDFORD		GOALKEEPER
DAVIS	RICHARD DANIEL	22/01/1922	BIRMINGHAM	11/08/1999	CENTRE FORWARD
DAVISON	ARNOLD	Q1 1864	MONKWEARMOUTH	31/08/1910	FORWARD
DAVISON	JAMES HAWKINS	01/11/1942	HENDON, SUNDERLAND	01/02/1987	OUTSIDE RIGHT
DAYKIN	THOMAS	Aug 1882	SHILDON		RIGHT HALF
DEANE	BRIAN CHRISTOPHER	07/02/1968	LEEDS		CENTRE FORWARD
DEATH	WILLIAM GEORGE	13/11/1900	ROTHERHAM	03/07/1984	OUTSIDE LEFT
DELAP	RORY JOHN	06/07/1976	SUTTON COLDFIELD		MIDFIELDER
DEMPSTER	JAMES BARCLAY	30/01/1896	NEWARTHILL, NR MOTHERWELL		GOALKEEPER
DEVINE	JOSEPH CASSIDY	09/08/1905	MOTHERWELL	09/05/1980	INSIDE LEFT
DI GIUSEPPE	MARCOS	12/03/1972	SAO PAULO, BRAZIL		CENTRE FORWARD
DIBBLE	ANDREW GERALD	08/05/1965	CWMBRAN		GOALKEEPER
DICHIO	DANIELE SALVATORE ERNEST	19/10/1974	HAMMERSMITH, LONDON		CENTRE FORWARD
DICKMAN	JONJO	22/09/1981	HEXHAM		MIDFIELDER
DILLON	JOHN	09/11/1942	COATBRIDGE		OUTSIDE LEFT
DIOUF	EL HADJI OUSSEYNOU	15/01/1981	DAKAR, SENEGAL		FORWARD
DITCHBURN	JOHN HURST (JOCK)	14/03/1897	HUNSLET	Jan 1992	CENTRE HALF
DOCHERTY	MICHAEL	29/10/1950	PRESTON		DEFENDER/MIDFIELDER
DODDS	LESLIE	12/10/1936	NEWCASTLE		GOALKEEPER
DOIG	JOHN EDWARD (TEDDY)	29/10/1866	LETHAM, FORFARSHIRE	07/11/1919	GOALKEEPER

CAREER RECORDS

Career		League			Play Offs			FA Cup			League Cup			Other			Total		
Start	End	Apps	Sub	Gls	Apps	Sub	Gls	Apps	Sub	Gls	Apps	Sub	Gls	Apps	Sub	Gls	Apps	Sub	Gls
1978	1985	42	13	4	0	0	0	3	1	0	3	1	1	0	0	0	48	15	5
1996	1996	6	0	0	0	0	0	0	0	0	0	0	0	0	0	0	6	0	0
2004	2004	0	3	0	0	0	0	0	0	0	0	0	0	0	0	0	0	3	0
2004	2004	0	1	0	0	0	0	0	0	0	0	0	0	0	0	0	0	1	0
1984	1988	33	0	1	1	1	0	3	1		3	0	0	2	1	1	42	3	3
1984	1991	21	11	2	0	0	0	0	0	0	1	1	0	1	3	0	23	15	2
1996	1998	10	0	0	0	0	0	0	0	0	2	0	0	0	0	0	12	0	0
1912	1921	21	0	0	0	0	0	1	0	0	0	0	0	0	0	0	22	0	0
1953	1955	28	0	0	0	0	0	1	0	0	0	0	0	0	0	0	29	0	0
1895	1897	17	0	7	2	0	0	0	0	0	0	0	0	0	0	0	19	0	7
1910	1911	14	0	5	0	0	0	0	0	0	0	0	0	0	0	0	14	0	5
1924	1927	10	0	0	0	0	0	0	0	0	0	0	0	0	0	0	10	0	0
1997	2003	140	6	2	3	0	0	7	2	0	8	2	0	0	0	0	158	10	2
1900	1904	42	0	13	0	0	0	1	0	1	0	0	0	0	0	0	43	0	14
1945	1951	1	0	0	0	0	0	0	0	0	0	0	0	0	0	0	1	0	0
1898	1900	55	0	4	0	0	0	2	0	1	0	0	0	0	0	0	57	0	5
1925	1929	13	0	1	0	0	0	0	0	0	0	0	0	0	0	0	13	0	1
1922	1927	182	0	0	0	0	0	8	0	0	0	0	0	0	0	0	190	0	0
1910	1917	77	0	3	0	0	0	5	0	0	0	0	0	0	0	0	82	0	3
1962	1965	82	0	39	0	0	0	10	0	8	7	0	1	0	0	0	99	0	48
1914	1920	43	0	17	0	0	0	3	0	0	0	0	0	0	0	0	46	0	17
1909	1921	164	0	4	0	0	0	23	0	0	0	0	0	0	0	0	187	0	4
1989	1992	11	18	0	0	0	0	0	0	0	5	1	1	0	0	0	12	23	1
1979	1985	145	5	29	0	0	0	8	1	0	6	0	3	0	0	0	159	6	32
1950	1951	4	0	0	0	0	0	0	0	0	0	0	0	0	0	0	4	0	0
2006	2007	11	0	0	0	0	0	0	0	0	1	0	0	0	0	0	12	0	0
1992	1995	52	6	8	0	0	0	2	0	1	3	0	0	2	0	0	59	6	9
1986	1987	9	0	1	0	0	0	0	0	0	0	0	0	0	0	0	9	0	1
1936	1938	1	0	0	0	0	0	0	0	0	0	0	0	0	0	0	1	0	0
1906	1907	1	0	0	0	0	0	0	0	0	0	0	0	0	0	0	1	0	0
2009	2011	13	4	0	0	0	0	3	0	0	3	1	0	0	0	0	19	5	0
1884	1888	0	0	0	0	0	0	6	0	0	0	0	0	0	0	0	6	0	0
1891	1894	3	0	0	0	0	0	0	0	0	0	0	0	0	0	0	3	0	0
1984	1985	33	1	0	0	0	0	1	0	0	10	0	0	1	0	0	45	1	0
1953	1957	136	0	6	0	0	0	17	0	1	0	0	0	0	0	0	153	0	7
2009	2009	7	1	0	0	0	0	0	0	0	0	0	0	0	0	0	7	1	0
1990	1993	72	27	15	0	0	0	9	1	2	5	2	1	3	1	0	89	31	18
1932	1936	150	0	38	0	0	0	12	0	2	0	0	0	0	0	0	162	0	40
2005	2006	33	0	0	0	0	0	2	0	0	0	0	0	0	0	0	35	0	0
1939	1954	144	0	73	0	0	0	10	0	7	0	0	0	0	0	0	154	0	80
1884	1889	0	0	0	0	0	0	7	0	2	0	0	0	0	0	0	7	0	2
1958	1963	62	0	10	0	0	0	3	0	1	7	0	0	0	0	0	72	0	11
1905	1908	46	0	0	0	0	0	2	0	0	0	0	0	0	0	0	48	0	0
2005	2005	0	4	0	0	0	0	0	0	0	0	0	0	0	0	0	0	4	0
1924	1928	53	0	12	0	0	0	3	0	2	0	0	0	0	0	0	56	0	14
2006	2007	11	1	1	0	0	0	0	0	0	1	0	0	0	0	0	12	1	1
1920	1922	40	0	0	0	0	0	3	0	0	0	0	0	0	0	0	43	0	0
1931	1933	68	0	7	0	0	0	9	0	0	0	0	0	0	0	0	77	0	7
1999	1999	0	0	0	0	0	0	0	0	0	0	1	0	0	0	0	0	1	0
1986	1986	12	0	0	0	0	0	0	0	0	0	0	0	0	0	0	12	0	0
1998	2001	20	56	11	1	2	0	3	3	1	11	1	6	0	0	0	35	62	18
1998	2005	0	1	0	0	0	0	0	0	0	0	0	0	0	0	0	0	1	0
1958	1962	18	0	1	0	0	0	4	0	0	1	0	0	0	0	0	23	0	1
2008	2009	11	3	0	0	0	0	1	0	0	1	0	0	0	0	0	13	3	0
1923	1926	6	0	0	0	0	0	0	0	0	0	0	0	0	0	0	6	0	0
1976	1979	72	1	6	0	0	0	2	0	0	3	0	0	2	0	1	79	1	7
1952	1960	6	0	0	0	0	0	0	0	0	0	0	0	0	0	0	6	0	0
1890	1904	417	0	0	4	0	0	35	0	0	0	0	0	1	0	0	457	0	0

SURNAME	FORENAMES	DOB	BIRTHPLACE	DECEASED	POSITION
DONALDSON	ALEXANDER POLLOCK	04/12/1890	BARRHEAD, GLASGOW		OUTSIDE RIGHT
DOUGALL	THOMAS	17/05/1921	WISHAW, NR GLASGOW	16/01/1997	OUTSIDE RIGHT
DOWNING	STEWART	22/07/1984	MIDDLESBROUGH		OUTSIDE LEFT
DOWSEY	JOHN	01/05/1905	HUNWICK, CO.DURHAM	27/10/1942	INSIDE RIGHT
DOYLE	STEPHEN CHARLES	02/06/1958	PORT TALBOT		MIDFIELDER
DUNCAN	CAMERON	04/08/1965	LANARK		GOALKEEPER
DUNLOP	WILLIAM	14/04/1871	KILMARNOCK		RIGHT HALF
DUNN	BARRY	15/02/1952	SUNDERLAND		OUTSIDE LEFT
DUNS	LEONARD	28/09/1916	NEWCASTLE	20/04/1989	OUTSIDE RIGHT
EDEN	WILLIAM	01/07/1905	STOCKTON	Nov 1993	OUTSIDE RIGHT
EDGAR	DANIEL	03/04/1910	JARROW	23/03/1991	LEFT HALF
EDGAR	JAMES	Q4 1880	BIRTLEY		OUTSIDE RIGHT
EDWARDS	AKENHATON CARLOS	24/10/1978	PATNA, TRINIDAD		MIDFIELDER
EL KARKOURI	TALAL	08/07/1976	CASABLANCA, MOROCCO		CENTRAL DEFENDER
ELLIOTT	DAVID	10/02/1945	TANTOBIE, CO.DURHAM		LEFT HALF
ELLIOTT	J.				FULL BACK
ELLIOTT	ROBERT JAMES	25/12/1973	GOSFORTH		DEFENDER
ELLIOTT	SHAUN	26/01/1958	HAYDON BRIDGE		CENTRAL DEFENDER
ELLIOTT	STEPHEN WILLIAM	06/01/1984	DUBLIN		CENTRE FORWARD
ELLIOTT	WILLIAM HENRY	20/03/1925	BRADFORD	21/01/2008	OUTSIDE LEFT/WING HALF
ELLIS	WILLIAM THOMAS	05/11/1895	WILLENHALL	18/11/1939	OUTSIDE LEFT
ELLISON	RAYMOND	31/12/1950	NEWCASTLE		FULL BACK
ELLISON	SAMUEL WALTER	27/08/1923	LEADGATE	Dec 1994	OUTSIDE RIGHT
ELMOHAMADY	AHMED EISSA	09/09/1987	EL-MAHALLA EL-KUBRA, EGYPT		RIGHT BACK / MIDFIELD
ENGLAND	ERNEST	03/02/1901	SHIREBROOK, NOTTS.	22/02/1982	LEFT BACK
ENTWISTLE	WAYNE PETER	06/08/1958	BURY		FORWARD
ERIKSSON	JAN	24/08/1967	SUNDSVALL, SWEDEN		CENTRE HALF
ERSKINE	WILLIAM				FORWARD
ETUHU	DICKSON PAUL	08/06/1982	KANO, NIGERIA		MIDFIELDER
EVANS	JOHN	21/10/1932	HETTON-LE-HOLE		INSIDE LEFT
EVANS	JONATHON	03/01/1988	BELFAST		CENTRAL DEFENDER
FAIRLEY	THOMAS	12/10/1932	PHILADELPHIA, CO. DURHAM		GOALKEEPER
FALL	WILLIAM	Q4 1900	TYNE DOCK		LEFT HALF
FARQUHAR	WILLIAM INKSTER	03/09/1877	FORDYCE	23/09/1916	INSIDE/CENTRE FORWARD
FEENAN	JOHN JOSEPH	01/07/1914	NEWRY, CO. DOWN	Oct 1994	RIGHT BACK
FERDINAND	ANTON JULIAN	18/02/1985	PECKHAM, LONDON		CENTRAL DEFENDER
FERGUSON	DEREK	31/07/1967	GLASGOW		MIDFIELDER
FERGUSON	MATTHEW	1875-76	BELLSHILL, GLASGOW	12/06/1902	RIGHT HALF
FERGUSON	ROBERT GIBSON	05/01/1902	BLYTHSWOOD, GLASGOW		RIGHT HALF
FINLAY	JOHN	16/12/1919	BIRTLEY	05/03/1985	INSIDE RIGHT
FINNEY	THOMAS	06/11/1952	BELFAST		OUTSIDE LEFT
FLEMING	CHARLES	12/07/1927	BLAIRHALL, FIFE	14/08/1997	INSIDE / CENTRE FORWARD
FLO	TORE ANDRE	15/06/1973	STRYN, NORWAY		CENTRE FORWARD
FOGARTY	AMBROSE GERALD	11/09/1933	DUBLIN		INSIDE LEFT
FOGGON	ALAN	23/02/1950	CRAGHEAD, CO.DURHAM		OUTSIDE LEFT
FORD	PETER NORMAN	30/10/1865	TRADESTON, GLASGOW	19/02/1939	FULL BACK
FORD	TONY	14/05/1959	GRIMSBY		OUTSIDE RIGHT
FORD	TREVOR	01/10/1923	SWANSEA	29/05/2003	CENTRE FORWARD
FOREMAN	JOHN JAMES	Q4 1913	TANFIELD		OUTSIDE LEFT/RIGHT
FORSTER	DEREK	19/02/1949	WALKER, NEWCASTLE		GOALKEEPER
FORSTER	HENRY (HARRY)	1884	CONSETT		FULL BACK
FOSTER	JOHN SAMUEL	19/11/1877	RAWMARSH, YORKSHIRE	05/02/1946	CENTRE FORWARD
FOSTER	JOHN THOMAS F.	21/03/1903	SOUTHWICK, SUNDERLAND		OUTSIDE RIGHT
FOTHERINGHAM	ANDREW / ALEXANDER ?		INVERNESS		LEFT BACK
FRASER	JOHN WATSON	15/09/1938	BELFAST	13/03/2011	OUTSIDE RIGHT
FRASER	WILLIAM ALEXANDER NOEL	24/02/1929	MELBOURNE, AUSTRALIA	07/03/1996	GOALKEEPER
FREDGAARD	CARSTEN	20/05/1976	BLOVSTROD, DENMARK		LEFT MIDFIELDER
FULLARTON	WILLIAM MILLWRIGHT	1882	TARDESTON, GLASGOW		CENTRE HALF

CAREER RECORDS

Career		League			Play Offs			FA Cup			League Cup			Other			Total		
Start	End	Apps	Sub	Gls	Apps	Sub	Gls	Apps	Sub	Gls	Apps	Sub	Gls	Apps	Sub	Gls	Apps	Sub	Gls
1922	1923	43	0	1	0	0	0	2	0	0	0	0	0	0	0	0	45	0	1
1948	1950	3	0	0	0	0	0	0	0	0	0	0	0	0	0	0	3	0	0
2003	2003	7	0	3	0	0	0	0	0	0	0	0	0	0	0	0	7	0	3
1927	1929	11	0	1	0	0	0	0	0	0	0	0	0	0	0	0	11	0	1
1986	1989	99	1	2	2	0	0	5	0	0	4	0	0	4	0	0	114	1	2
1983	1987	1	0	0	0	0	0	0	0	0	2	0	0	0	0	0	3	0	0
1893	1899	137	0	6	0	0	0	11	0	0	0	0	0	0	0	0	148	0	6
1979	1981	16	7	2	0	0	0	0	0	0	2	0	0	0	0	0	18	7	2
1933	1952	215	0	46	0	0	0	29	0	9	0	0	0	1	0	0	245	0	55
1929	1932	60	0	19	0	0	0	11	0	3	0	0	0	0	0	0	71	0	22
1930	1935	43	0	0	0	0	0	3	0	0	0	0	0	0	0	0	46	0	0
1905	1906	2	0	0	0	0	0	0	0	0	0	0	0	0	0	0	2	0	0
2007	2009	32	18	5	0	0	0	3	1	0	2	0	0	0	0	0	37	19	5
2003	2003	8	0	0	0	0	0	0	1	0	0	0	0	0	0	0	8	1	0
1961	1966	30	1	0	0	0	0	4	0	0	1	0	0	0	0	0	35	1	0
1883	1887	0	0	0	0	0	0	2	0	0	0	0	0	0	0	0	2	0	0
2006	2007	7	0	0	0	0	0	0	0	0	1	0	0	0	0	0	8	0	0
1974	1986	316	5	11	0	0	0	14	0	0	28	0	0	5	0	0	363	5	11
2004	2007	55	26	22	0	0	0	3	0	0	1	3	1	0	0	0	59	29	23
1953	1959	193	0	23	0	0	0	19	0	3	0	0	0	0	0	0	212	0	26
1919	1927	190	0	32	0	0	0	10	0	0	0	0	0	0	0	0	200	0	32
1973	1974	2	0	0	0	0	0	0	0	0	0	0	0	0	0	0	2	0	0
1944	1947	3	0	0	0	0	0	0	0	0	0	0	0	0	0	0	3	0	0
2010	2012	33	21	1	0	0	0	0	3	0	2	0	0	0	0	0	35	24	1
1919	1930	336	0	0	0	0	0	16	0	0	0	0	0	0	0	0	352	0	0
1977	1979	43	2	13	0	0	0	4	0	1	2	0	0	4	0	2	53	2	16
1997	1998	1	0	0	0	0	0	0	0	0	0	0	0	0	0	0	1	0	0
1885	1887	0	0	0	0	0	0	2	0	0	0	0	0	0	0	0	2	0	0
2007	2008	18	2	1	0	0	0	0	0	0	1	0	0	0	0	0	19	2	1
1954	1956	1	0	0	0	0	0	0	0	0	0	0	0	0	0	0	1	0	0
2007	2008	33	0	1	0	0	0	2	0	0	0	0	0	0	0	0	35	0	1
1951	1956	2	0	0	0	0	0	0	0	0	0	0	0	0	0	0	2	0	0
1923	1925	4	0	0	0	0	0	0	0	0	0	0	0	0	0	0	4	0	0
1899	1907	189	0	17	0	0	0	8	0	0	0	0	1	0	0	0	198	0	17
1936	1939	28	0	0	0	0	0	1	0	0	0	0	0	0	0	0	29	0	0
2008	2011	76	9	0	0	0	0	4	0	0	5	1	0	0	0	0	85	10	0
1993	1995	64	0	0	0	0	0	6	0	1	3	0	0	2	0	0	75	0	1
1896	1902	166	0	4	4	0	0	11	0	0	0	0	0	0	0	0	181	0	4
1921	1925	32	0	1	0	0	0	4	0	0	0	0	0	0	0	0	36	0	1
1938	1947	1	0	0	0	0	0	0	0	0	0	0	0	0	0	0	1	0	0
1974	1976	8	7	1	0	0	0	6	0	1	0	0	0	1	2	0	15	9	2
1955	1958	107	0	62	0	0	0	15	0	9	0	0	0	0	0	0	122	0	71
2002	2003	23	6	4	0	0	0	1	1	0	2	0	2	0	0	0	26	7	6
1957	1963	152	0	37	0	0	0	12	0	3	10	0	4	0	0	0	174	0	44
1976	1977	7	1	0	0	0	0	0	0	0	2	0	0	0	0	0	9	1	0
1887	1889	0	0	0	0	0	0	4	0	0	0	0	0	0	0	0	4	0	0
1986	1986	8	1	1	0	0	0	0	0	0	0	0	0	0	0	0	8	1	1
1950	1953	108	0	67	0	0	0	9	0	3	0	0	0	0	0	0	117	0	70
1933	1934	2	0	0	0	0	0	0	0	0	0	0	0	0	0	0	2	0	0
1964	1973	18	0	0	0	0	0	1	0	0	0	0	0	0	0	0	19	0	0
1905	1912	101	0	0	0	0	0	9	0	0	0	0	0	0	0	0	110	0	0
1907	1908	8	0	3	0	0	0	0	0	0	0	0	0	0	0	0	8	0	3
1920	1921	5	0	0	0	0	0	1	0	0	0	0	0	0	0	0	6	0	0
1899	1899	1	0	0	0	0	0	0	0	0	0	0	0	0	0	0	1	0	0
1959	1960	22	0	1	0	0	0	0	0	0	0	0	0	0	0	0	22	0	1
1954	1958	127	0	0	0	0	0	16	0	0	0	0	0	0	0	0	143	0	0
1999	2001	0	1	0	0	0	0	0	0	0	3	1	2	0	0	0	3	2	2
1903	1905	31	0	1	0	0	0	2	0	0	0	0	0	0	0	0	33	0	1

SUNDERLAND: THE COMPLETE RECORD

SURNAME	FORENAMES	DOB	BIRTHPLACE	DECEASED	POSITION
FULOP	MARTON	03/05/1983	BUDAPEST, HUNGARY		GOALKEEPER
FULTON	WILLIAM	18/11/1876	ALVA, NEAR ALLOA		INSIDE LEFT
GABBIADINI	MARCO	20/01/1968	NOTTINGHAM		CENTRE FORWARD
GABBIADINI	RICARDO	11/03/1970	NEWPORT, WALES		FORWARD
GALBRAITH	THOMAS D.	1875	BONHILL, DUMBARTONSHIRE		OUTSIDE RIGHT
GALLACHER	PATRICK	21/08/1909	BRIDGE OF WEIR, RENFREWSHIRE	04/01/1992	INSIDE FORWARD/OUTSIDE LEFT
GARDNER	CRAIG	25/11/1986	SOLIHULL		MIDFIELDER
GATES	ERIC LAZENBY	28/06/1955	FERRYHILL, CO.DURHAM		FORWARD
GAUDEN	ALLAN	20/11/1944	LANGLEY PARK, CO.DURHAM		OUTSIDE RIGHT/LEFT
GAUGHRAN	BERNARD MICHAEL (BENNY)	29/09/1915	DUBLIN	20/09/1977	CENTRE FORWARD
GAYLE	HOWARD ANTHONY	18/05/1958	LIVERPOOL		MIDFIELDER/FORWARD
GEMMELL	JAMES	17/11/1880	GLASGOW		INSIDE / CENTRE FORWARD
GEORGE	WILLIAM SAMUEL	Q3 1895	BIRMINGHAM	29/09/1962	RIGHT HALF
GIBB	THOMAS	13/12/1944	BATHGATE, GLASGOW		MIDFIELDER
GIBSON	FREDERICK THOMAS BERTRAND	08/12/1888	JOHANNESBURG, S.AFRICA	15/03/1952	OUTSIDE LEFT
GIBSON	GEORGE EARDLEY	29/08/1912	BIDDULPH	30/12/1990	CENTRE FORWARD
GIBSON	JOHN RUTHERFORD	23/03/1898	PHILADELPHIA, USA	July 1974	RIGHT BACK
GIBSON	WILLIAM	16/02/1868	LOUDOUN, AYRSHIRE	15/09/1911	FULL BACK/HALF BACK
GIBSON	WILLIAM KENNEDY	01/10/1876	GLASGOW	09/12/1949	RIGHT BACK
GILBERT	TIMOTHY HEW	28/08/1958	SOUTH SHIELDS	29/05/1995	DEFENDER/MIDFIELDER
GILHESPY	THOMAS WILLIAM CYRIL	18/02/1898	FENCE HOUSES, CO.DURHAM	Mar 1985	OUTSIDE LEFT
GILHOOLEY	MICHAEL	26/11/1896	GLENCRAIG, FIFE		CENTRE HALF
GILLESPIE	JAMES	1870	DUMBARTONSHIRE	Aug 1932	OUTSIDE RIGHT
GILLESPIE	JOHN				LEFT BACK
GIVEN	SEAMUS JOHN JAMES (SHAY)	20/04/1976	LIFFORD, COUNTY DONEGAL		GOALKEEPER
GLADWIN	CHARLES EDWARD	09/12/1887	WORKSOP	Feb 1952	RIGHT BACK
GLOAG	ROBERT				FORWARD
GODBOLD	HAROLD	31/01/1939	SPRINGWELL, GATESHEAD		OUTSIDE LEFT
GODDARD	GEORGE	20/12/1903	GOMSHALL, NR.GUILDFORD	23/04/1987	INSIDE / CENTRE FORWARD
GOODCHILD	GEORGE	Q1 1875	SEAHAM COLLIERY		OUTSIDE RIGHT
GOODCHILD	JOHN	02/01/1919	LITTLETOWN, CO. DURHAM	25/08/2011	OUTSIDE LEFT
GOODMAN	DONALD RALPH	09/05/1966	LEEDS		FORWARD
GORDON	CRAIG SINCLAIR	31/12/1982	EDINBURGH		GOALKEEPER
GORMAN	JAMES JOSEPH	03/03/1910	LIVERPOOL	01/02/1991	RIGHT BACK
GOW	DONALD ROBERTSON	08/02/1868	BLAIR ATHOLL, PERTHSHIRE	Q4 1945	FULL BACK
GRAHAM	ALLAN	23/10/1937	RYHOPE, CO.DURHAM		RIGHT BACK
GRAINGER	COLIN	10/06/1933	HAVERCROFT, WAKEFIELD		OUTSIDE LEFT
GRAY	ANDREW DAVID	15/11/1977	HARROGATE		CENTRE FORWARD
GRAY	FRANCIS TIERNEY	27/10/1954	CASTLEMILK, GLASGOW		DEFENDER/MIDFIELDER
GRAY	MARTIN DAVID	17/08/1971	SEDGEFIELD, CO.DURHAM		MIDFIELDER
GRAY	MICHAEL	03/08/1974	CASTLETOWN, SUNDERLAND		LEFT BACK/MIDFIELDER
GRAY	PHILIP	02/10/1968	BELFAST		CENTRE FORWARD
GRAYSTON	JOHN THOMAS	27/03/1862	HALIFAX	28/03/1944	FORWARD
GREENWOOD	ROY THORNTON	26/09/1952	LEEDS		OUTSIDE LEFT
GREGOIRE	ROLAND BARRY	23/11/1958	LIVERPOOL		FORWARD
GREGORY	CLARENCE	27/10/1900	ASTON, BIRMINGHAM	Q3 1975	INSIDE LEFT
GREY	THOMAS	Q1 1885	WHITLEY BAY		CENTRE HALF
GRIMSHAW	WILLIAM	30/04/1890	BURNLEY	06/05/1968	OUTSIDE RIGHT
GUNSON	JOSEPH GORDON (GORDON)	01/07/1904	CHESTER	13/09/1991	OUTSIDE LEFT
GURNEY	ROBERT	13/10/1907	SILKSWORTH, SUNDERLAND	21/04/1994	INSIDE / CENTRE FORWARD
GUTHRIE	RONALD GEORGE	19/04/1944	BURRADON, NEWCASTLE		LEFT BACK
GYAN	ASAMOAH	22/11/1985	ACCRA, GHANA		CENTRE FORWARD
HAAS	BERNT	08/04/1978	VIENNA, AUSTRIA		RIGHT BACK
HAGGAN	JOHN	16/12/1896	USWORTH	Q2 1982	FULL BACK
HAINNING	JAMES	1875	SCOTLAND		INSIDE RIGHT
HALFORD	GREGORY	08/12/1984	CHELMSFORD		RIGHT BACK
HALL	ALEXANDER WEBSTER	06/11/1908	KIRKNEWTON, MIDLOTHIAN	05/09/1991	FULL BACK
HALL	FREDERICK WILKINSON	18/11/1917	STANLEY, CO.DURHAM	08/01/1989	CENTRE HALF

CAREER RECORDS

Career		League			Play Offs			FA Cup			League Cup			Other			Total		
Start	End	Apps	Sub	Gls	Apps	Sub	Gls	Apps	Sub	Gls	Apps	Sub	Gls	Apps	Sub	Gls	Apps	Sub	Gls
2006	2010	44	1	0	0	0	0	3	0	0	2	0	0	0	0	0	49	1	0
1898	1900	26	0	3	0	0	0	5	0	3	0	0	0	0	0	0	31	0	6
1987	1991	155	2	74	3	0	1	5	0	0	14	0	9	6	0	3	183	2	87
1988	1991	0	1	0	0	0	0	0	0	0	0	0	0	0	0	0	0	1	0
1898	1898	2	0	0	0	0	0	0	0	0	0	0	0	0	0	0	2	0	0
1927	1938	273	0	100	0	0	0	33	0	7	0	0	0	2	0	0	308	0	107
2011	2012	22	8	3	0	0	0	6	0	0	1	0	0	0	0	0	29	8	3
1985	1990	163	18	43	4	1	3	7	0	2	18	0	6	7	2	1	199	21	55
1961	1968	40	4	6	0	0	0	2	1	1	3	1	0	0	0	0	45	6	7
1937	1938	2	0	0	0	0	0	0	0	0	0	0	0	0	0	0	2	0	0
1984	1986	39	9	4	0	0	0	1	2	0	6	2	1	2	0	0	48	13	5
1900	1912	212	0	46	0	0	0	15	0	0	0	0	0	0	0	0	227	0	46
1920	1921	2	0	0	0	0	0	0	0	0	0	0	0	0	0	0	2	0	0
1975	1977	7	3	1	0	0	0	0	0	0	0	0	2	1	1	9	4	2
1909	1910	2	0	0	0	0	0	0	0	0	0	0	0	0	0	0	2	0	0
1932	1934	2	0	1	0	0	0	0	0	0	0	0	0	0	0	0	2	0	1
1920	1922	4	0	0	0	0	0	1	0	0	0	0	0	0	0	0	5	0	0
1888	1896	91	0	6	0	0	0	9	0	0	0	0	0	0	0	0	100	0	6
1902	1902	1	0	0	0	0	0	0	0	0	0	0	0	0	0	0	1	0	0
1973	1981	34	2	3	0	0	0	0	0	0	5	0	0	3	0	0	42	2	3
1920	1921	15	0	1	0	0	0	0	0	0	0	0	0	0	0	0	15	0	1
1922	1924	19	0	0	0	0	0	0	0	0	0	0	0	0	0	0	19	0	0
1890	1897	129	0	50	4	0	2	13	0	2	0	0	0	0	0	0	146	0	54
1892	1893	5	0	0	0	0	0	1	0	0	0	0	0	0	0	0	6	0	0
1996	1996	17	0	0	0	0	0	0	0	0	0	0	0	0	0	0	17	0	0
1912	1915	54	0	0	0	0	0	9	0	1	0	0	0	0	0	0	63	0	1
1887	1889	0	0	0	0	0	0	2	0	2	0	0	0	0	0	0	2	0	2
1956	1961	12	0	1	0	0	0	1	0	0	0	0	0	0	0	0	13	0	1
1934	1936	14	0	5	0	0	0	0	0	0	0	0	0	0	0	0	14	0	5
1894	1896	1	0	0	0	0	0	0	0	0	0	0	0	0	0	0	1	0	0
1955	1961	44	0	21	0	0	0	1	0	0	0	0	0	0	0	0	45	0	21
1991	1994	112	4	40	0	0	0	3	0	1	9	0	4	4	0	2	128	4	47
2007	2012	88	0	0	0	0	0	3	0	0	4	0	0	0	0	0	95	0	0
1937	1944	82	0	0	0	0	0	17	0	1	0	0	0	1	0	0	100	0	1
1891	1897	98	0	1	4	0	0	13	0	0	0	0	0	0	0	0	115	0	1
1955	1958	3	0	0	0	0	0	0	0	0	0	0	0	0	0	0	3	0	0
1957	1960	120	0	14	0	0	0	4	0	0	0	0	0	0	0	0	124	0	14
2005	2006	13	8	1	0	0	0	0	0	1	0	0	0	0	0	0	13	9	1
1985	1989	118	28	8	2	0	0	4	1	0	6	2	0	7	1	0	137	32	8
1989	1996	46	18	1	0	0	0	0	3	0	6	2	0	3	1	0	55	24	1
1990	2004	341	22	16	2	0	0	17	1	1	23	4	0	0	0	0	383	27	17
1993	1996	108	7	34	0	0	0	8	0	3	9	0	4	2	0	0	127	7	41
1879	1885	0	0	0	0	0	0	1	0	0	0	0	0	0	0	0	1	0	0
1976	1979	45	11	9	0	0	0	0	0	0	3	0	0	2	0	0	50	11	9
1977	1980	6	3	1	0	0	0	0	0	1	0	0	0	0	0	0	6	4	1
1920	1922	1	0	0	0	0	0	0	0	0	0	0	0	0	0	0	1	0	0
1907	1909	1	0	0	0	0	0	0	0	0	0	0	0	0	0	0	1	0	0
1923	1927	70	0	6	0	0	0	4	0	0	0	0	0	0	0	0	74	0	6
1929	1930	19	0	11	0	0	0	4	0	1	0	0	0	0	0	0	23	0	12
1925	1946	348	0	205	0	0	0	40	0	23	0	0	0	2	0	0	390	0	228
1973	1975	66	0	1	0	0	0	7	0	1	2	0	5	1	0	0	80	1	2
2010	2012	23	11	10	0	0	0	1	0	0	1	1	1	0	0	0	25	12	11
2001	2003	27	0	0	0	0	0	1	0	0	0	1	0	0	0	0	28	1	0
1919	1922	2	0	0	0	0	0	0	0	0	0	0	0	0	0	0	2	0	0
1898	1898	1	0	0	0	0	0	0	0	0	0	0	0	0	0	0	1	0	0
2007	2009	8	0	0	0	0	0	0	0	0	1	0	0	0	0	0	9	0	0
1929	1945	206	0	1	0	0	0	27	0	0	0	0	0	2	0	0	235	0	1
1946	1955	215	0	1	0	0	0	9	0	0	0	0	0	0	0	0	224	0	1

SUNDERLAND: THE COMPLETE RECORD

SURNAME	FORENAMES	DOB	BIRTHPLACE	DECEASED	POSITION
HALL	GARETH DAVID	20/03/1969	CROYDON		RIGHT BACK / MIDFIELDER
HALL	JOHN THOMAS (JACK)				FULL BACK
HALL	MATTHEW	1884	RENFREW		INSIDE LEFT
HALL	THOMAS	04/09/1891	NEWBURN, NEWCASTLE		CENTRE FORWARD
HALLIDAY	DAVID	19/12/1901	DUMFRIES	05/01/1970	CENTRE FORWARD
HALLIDAY	THOMAS	1866	DUMFRIES		HALF BACK
HALOM	VICTOR LEWIS	03/10/1948	COTON PARK, NR BURTON		CENTRE FORWARD
HAMILTON	ANDREW	1873-74	GLASGOW	Oct 1929	OUTSIDE LEFT
HAMILTON	JAMES	14/06/1955	UDDINGSTON, GLASGOW		MIDFIELDER
HANNAH	DAVID	28/04/1867	RAFFREY, CO.DOWN	Jan 1936	INSIDE FORWARD
HANNAH	JAMES	17/03/1869	HUTCHESONTOWN, GLASGOW	01/12/1917	INSIDE/OUTSIDE FORWARD
HANNIGAN	JOHN LECKIE	17/02/1933	BARRHEAD, GLASGOW		OUTSIDE FORWARD
HARDWICK	STEPHEN	06/09/1956	MANSFIELD		GOALKEEPER
HARDYMAN	PAUL GEORGE THOMAS	11/03/1964	PORTSMOUTH		LEFT BACK/MIDFIELDER
HARFORD	MICHAEL GORDON	12/02/1959	SUNDERLAND		CENTRE FORWARD
HARGREAVES	LEONARD	07/03/1906	KIMBERWORTH	Q3 1980	OUTSIDE LEFT
HARKER	J.				INSIDE RIGHT
HARPER	GEORGE SPENCE	May 1877	BIRMINGHAM	14/07/1949	INSIDE LEFT
HARPER	WILLIAM GEORGE	15/11/1900	WISHAW, NR GLASGOW		GOALKEEPER
HARRIS	GORDON	02/06/1940	LANGOLD, NR.WORKSOP		FORWARD
HARRISON	GERALD RANDALL	15/04/1972	LAMBETH		MIDFIELDER
HARTE	IAN PATRICK	31/08/1977	DROGHEDA		LEFT BACK
HARTLEY	JAMES MILBURN	29/10/1876	DUMBARTON		INSIDE/OUTSIDE LEFT
HARTLEY	PETER	03/04/1988	HARTLEPOOL		CENTRAL DEFENDER
HARTNESS	GEORGE				INSIDE RIGHT
HARVEY	MARTIN	19/09/1941	BELFAST		FULL/HALF BACK
HARVIE	JOHN	22/01/1867	SCOTLAND	14/02/1940	INSIDE/OUTSIDE RIGHT
HASTINGS	ALEXANDER COCKBURN	17/03/1912	FALKIRK	26/12/1988	HALF BACK(LATER C.FORWARD)
HASTINGS	ANDREW STRAITEN	09/11/1865	DUMFRIES		FORWARD
HASTINGS	JOHN GEORGE	31/03/1887	THORNABY	01/04/1972	RIGHT BACK
HAUSER	THOMAS	10/04/1965	SCHOPFHEIM, W.GERMANY		CENTRE FORWARD
HAWES	ARTHUR ROBERT	02/10/1895	SWANTON MORLEY, NORFOLK	11/10/1963	INSIDE LEFT
HAWKE	WARREN ROBERT	20/09/1970	DURHAM		FORWARD
HAWLEY	JOHN EAST	08/05/1954	PATRINGTON, EAST YORKSHIRE		CENTRE FORWARD
HAY	ALAN BROWNING	28/11/1958	DUNFERMLINE		DEFENDER
HEALEY	RICHARD	20/09/1889	DARLINGTON	Q4 1974	INSIDE RIGHT
HEALY	COLIN	14/03/1980	BALLINCOLLIG, CORK		MIDFIELDER
HEALY	DAVID JONATHAN	05/08/1979	KILLYLEAGH, N. I.		FORWARD
HEATHCOTE	MICHAEL	10/09/1965	KELLOE, CO.DURHAM		CENTRE HALF
HEDLEY	JOHN ROBERT (JACK)	11/12/1923	WILLINGTON QUAY	02/06/1985	FULL BACK
HEGAN	DANIEL	14/06/1943	COATBRIDGE		MIDFIELDER
HELLAWELL	MICHAEL STEPHEN	30/06/1938	KEIGHLEY		OUTSIDE RIGHT
HELMER	THOMAS	21/04/1965	HERFORD, GERMANY		CENTRAL DEFENDER
HENDERSON	GEORGE BROWN	09/01/1902	KELTY, FIFE		CENTRE HALF
HENDERSON	JORDAN BRIAN	17/06/1990	EAST HERRINGTON		MIDFIELDER
HENDERSON	MICHAEL ROBERT	31/03/1956	GOSFORTH		FULL BACK/MIDFIELD
HEPWORTH	MAURICE	06/09/1953	BARRASFORD, NR HEXHAM		LEFT BACK
HERD	GEORGE	06/05/1936	GARTCOSH, NR COATBRIDGE		INSIDE/OUTSIDE RIGHT
HESFORD	IAIN	04/03/1960	NDOLA, ZAMBIA		GOALKEEPER
HESLOP	BRIAN	04/08/1947	CARLISLE		HALF BACK / INSIDE LEFT
HETHERINGTON	HENRY (HARRY)	07/11/1928	CHESTER-LE-STREET	Oct 1987	OUTSIDE RIGHT
HETZKE	STEPHEN EDWARD RICHARD	03/06/1955	MARLBOROUGH		CENTRE HALF
HEWITT	JOSEPH	03/05/1881	CHESTER	12/11/1971	INSIDE/OUTSIDE LEFT
HEYES	JAMES		NORTHWICH		INSIDE RIGHT
HEYWOOD	ALBERT EDWARD	12/05/1913	HARTLEPOOL	May 1989	GOALKEEPER
HIGGINBOTHAM	DANIEL JOHN	29/12/1978	MANCHESTER		DEFENDER
HINDMARCH	ROBERT	27/04/1961	STANNINGTON, NORTHUMB.	06/11/2002	CENTRE HALF
HINDMARSH	JAMES LYONS	Q2 1885	SOUTH SHIELDS	16/03/1959	INSIDE LEFT

CAREER RECORDS

Career		League			Play Offs			FA Cup			League Cup			Other			Total		
Start	End	Apps	Sub	Gls	Apps	Sub	Gls	Apps	Sub	Gls	Apps	Sub	Gls	Apps	Sub	Gls	Apps	Sub	Gls
1995	1998	41	7	0	0	0	0	2	0	0	3	0	0	0	0	0	46	7	0
1883	1886	0	0	0	0	0	0	1	0	0	0	0	0	0	0	0	1	0	0
1906	1907	8	0	0	0	0	0	0	0	0	0	0	0	0	0	0	8	0	0
1909	1913	30	0	8	0	0	0	0	0	0	0	0	0	0	0	0	30	0	8
1925	1929	166	0	156	0	0	0	9	0	9	0	0	0	0	0	0	175	0	165
1887	1888	0	0	0	0	0	0	3	0	2	0	0	0	0	0	0	3	0	2
1973	1976	110	3	35	0	0	0	10	1	2	6	0	3	8	1	2	134	5	42
1896	1897	7	0	2	0	0	0	0	0	0	0	0	0	0	0	0	7	0	2
1971	1976	9	8	2	0	0	0	0	0	0	0	0	0	0	0	0	9	8	2
1889	1894	78	0	17	0	0	0	14	0	3	0	0	0	0	0	0	92	0	20
1891	1897	152	0	68	4	0	0	15	0	7	0	0	0	0	0	0	171	0	75
1955	1958	33	0	8	0	0	0	2	0	2	0	0	0	0	0	0	35	0	10
1987	1987	6	0	0	0	0	0	0	0	0	2	0	0	0	0	0	8	0	0
1989	1992	101	5	9	1	0	0	8	1	1	11	0	2	2	0	0	123	6	12
1993	1993	10	1	2	0	0	0	0	0	0	0	0	0	0	0	0	10	1	2
1927	1929	35	0	11	0	0	0	4	0	1	0	0	0	0	0	0	39	0	12
1899	1899	1	0	0	0	0	0	0	0	0	0	0	0	0	0	0	1	0	0
1902	1904	10	0	1	0	0	0	1	0	0	0	0	0	0	0	0	11	0	1
1921	1923	28	0	0	0	0	0	0	0	0	0	0	0	0	0	0	28	0	0
1968	1972	124	1	16	0	0	0	3	0	0	3	0	0	4	0	0	134	1	16
1998	2000	0	0	0	0	0	0	0	0	0	1	0	0	0	0	0	1	0	0
2007	2008	3	5	0	0	0	0	0	0	0	0	0	0	0	0	0	3	5	0
1895	1896	11	0	1	0	0	0	0	0	0	0	0	0	0	0	0	11	0	1
2004	2008	0	1	0	0	0	0	0	0	0	0	0	0	0	0	0	0	1	0
1895	1897	2	0	0	0	0	0	0	0	0	0	0	0	0	0	0	2	0	0
1957	1973	310	5	5	0	0	0	25	0	0	15	0	0	3	0	0	353	5	5
1889	1897	95	0	12	2	0	0	12	0	3	0	0	0	0	0	0	109	0	15
1929	1945	262	0	2	0	0	0	34	0	4	0	0	0	1	0	0	297	0	6
1887	1888	0	0	0	0	0	0	3	0	0	0	0	0	0	0	0	3	0	0
1909	1913	1	0	0	0	0	0	0	0	0	0	0	0	0	0	0	1	0	0
1989	1992	22	31	9	0	1	0	0	1	0	3	6	2	1	0	0	26	39	11
1921	1927	139	0	39	0	0	0	8	0	0	0	0	0	0	0	0	147	0	39
1987	1993	7	18	1	1	0	0	1	1	0	0	0	0	1	0	0	10	19	1
1979	1981	25	0	11	0	0	0	3	0	0	3	0	0	0	0	0	31	0	11
1989	1989	1	0	0	0	0	0	0	0	0	0	0	0	0	0	0	1	0	0
1910	1912	3	0	1	0	0	0	0	0	0	0	0	0	0	0	0	3	0	1
2003	2006	16	4	0	0	0	0	0	0	0	0	0	0	0	0	0	16	4	0
2008	2010	0	13	1	0	0	0	2	2	1	1	3	1	0	0	0	3	18	3
1987	1990	6	3	0	0	0	0	0	0	0	0	0	0	1	0	0	6	4	0
1950	1959	269	0	0	0	0	0	26	0	0	0	0	0	0	0	0	295	0	0
1961	1974	3	3	0	0	0	0	0	2	0	0	0	0	0	0	0	3	5	0
1965	1966	43	1	3	0	0	0	0	0	0	2	0	0	0	0	0	45	1	3
1999	2000	1	1	0	0	0	0	0	0	0	0	0	0	0	0	0	1	1	0
1924	1929	45	0	1	0	0	0	4	0	0	0	0	0	0	0	0	49	0	1
2006	2011	60	11	4	0	0	0	2	1	0	5	0	1	0	0	0	67	12	5
1972	1979	81	3	2	0	0	0	6	1	0	2	1	0	1	0	0	90	5	2
1969	1975	2	0	0	0	0	0	0	0	0	0	0	0	0	0	0	2	0	0
1961	1970	275	3	47	0	0	0	21	0	4	19	0	4	0	0	0	315	3	55
1986	1988	97	0	0	2	0	0	3	0	0	4	0	0	6	0	0	112	0	0
1967	1971	57	1	0	0	0	0	1	0	0	4	0	0	4	0	0	66	1	0
1944	1949	2	0	0	0	0	0	0	0	0	0	0	0	0	0	0	2	0	0
1986	1987	31	0	0	1	0	0	0	0	0	0	0	0	1	0	0	33	0	0
1901	1904	36	0	9	0	0	0	0	0	0	0	0	0	1	0	1	37	0	10
1925	1927	3	0	0	0	0	0	0	0	0	0	0	0	0	0	0	3	0	0
1937	1946	4	0	0	0	0	0	0	0	0	0	0	0	0	0	0	4	0	0
2007	2008	22	0	3	0	0	0	0	0	0	0	0	0	0	0	0	22	0	3
1977	1984	114	1	2	0	0	0	5	0	0	6	2	1	0	0	0	125	3	3
1905	1906	1	0	0	0	0	0	0	0	0	0	0	0	0	0	0	1	0	0

SUNDERLAND: THE COMPLETE RECORD

SURNAME	FORENAMES	DOB	BIRTHPLACE	DECEASED	POSITION
HINNIGAN	JOSEPH PETER	03/12/1955	LIVERPOOL		FULL BACK
HIRD	ROBERT KEITH BRYAN (KEITH)	25/11/1939	ANNFIELD PLAIN	Q3 1967	GOALKEEPER
HOBSON	HERBERT BERTIE	Q1 1890	TOW LAW, CO.DURHAM	22/11/1963	RIGHT BACK
HODGSON	DAVID JAMES	06/08/1960	GATESHEAD		FORWARD
HODKIN	ERNEST	Q3 1879	CHESTERFIELD		RIGHT HALF BACK
HOGG	JAMES WILLIAM	09/08/1900	WHITBURN	Q3 1974	CENTRE FORWARD
HOGG	ROBERT	Q2 1877	WHITBURN	14/03/1963	CENTRE/INSIDE FORWARD
HOGG	WILLIAM	29/05/1879	HENDON, SUNDERLAND	30/01/1937	INSIDE/OUT.RIGHT,C.FORWARD
HOLDEN	MELVILLE GEORGE (MEL)	25/08/1954	DUNDEE	31/01/1981	CENTRE FORWARD
HOLDEN	WILLIAM	01/04/1928	BOLTON	25/01/2011	CENTRE FORWARD
HOLLEY	GEORGE	20/11/1885	SEAHAM HARBOUR	27/08/1942	INSIDE FORWARD
HOLLOWAY	DARREN	03/10/1977	BISHOP AUCKLAND		DEFENDER
HOLTON	JAMES ALLAN	11/04/1951	LESMAHAGOW, LANARKSHIRE	05/10/1993	CENTRE HALF
HOOD	HENRY ANTHONY	03/10/1944	GLASGOW		INSIDE RIGHT/CENT.FORWARD
HOOPER	HAROLD	14/06/1933	PITTINGTON, CO.DURHAM		OUTSIDE RIGHT
HOPE	JAMES WILLIAM (WILLIAM)	Q2 1885	KELLOE, CO.DURHAM		INSIDE RIGHT
HOPE (O'NEILL)	ALAN	13/11/1937	DEPTFORD, SUNDERLAND		INSIDE LEFT
HOPKINS	WILLIAM	11/11/1888	ESH WINNING, CO.DURHAM	26/01/1938	RIGHT/CENTRE HALF
HORNBY	CECIL FREDERICK (CYRIL)	25/04/1907	WEST BROMWICH	Q3 1964	CENTRE HALF/CENTRE FORWARD
HORSWILL	MICHAEL FREDERICK	06/03/1953	ANNFIELD PLAIN		MIDFIELDER
HOUSAM	ARTHUR	01/10/1917	SUNDERLAND	31/12/1975	HALF BACK
HOWEY	LEE MATTHEW	01/04/1969	SUNDERLAND		CENTRE FORWARD
HOYTE	JUSTIN RAYMOND	20/11/1984	WALTHAM FOREST		FULL BACK
HUDGELL	ARTHUR JOHN	28/12/1920	HACKNEY	Oct 2000	LEFT BACK
HUGGINS	JOHN WARWICK	02/06/1886	CROSBY RAVENSWORTH	26/04/1915	OUTSIDE LEFT
HUGHES	IAN JAMES	24/08/1961	SUNDERLAND		MIDFIELDER
HUGHES	JOHN	03/04/1943	COATBRIDGE		CENTRE FORWARD
HUGHES	WILLIAM	30/12/1948	COATBRIDGE		INSIDE FORWARD
HUNTER	GEORGE	1902	HYLTON		RIGHT HALF BACK
HUNTER	JAMES		SCOTLAND		FULL BACK
HUNTLEY	RICHARD BERNARD	05/01/1949	HETTON		RIGHT HALF
HURDMAN	ARTHUR STANLEY	Q3 1882	SUNDERLAND	20/05/1953	OUTSIDE RIGHT
HURLEY	CHARLES JOSEPH	04/10/1936	CORK, IRELAND		CENTRE HALF
HUTCHISON	DONALD OLIVER	09/05/1971	GATESHEAD		MIDFIELDER
HUTTON	ALAN	30/11/1984	PENILEE, GLASGOW		RIGHT BACK
HYSEN	GLENN TOBIAS (TOBIAS)	09/03/1982	GOTHENBURG, SWEDEN		LEFT MIDFIELDER
HYSLOP	THOMAS	22/09/1874	MAUCHLINE, AYRSHIRE	Apr 1936	INSIDE LEFT
INGHAM	MICHAEL GERARD	07/09/1980	PRESTON		GOALKEEPER
INGLIS	J.				FULL BACK
IRWIN	CECIL	08/04/1942	ELLINGTON, NORTHUMBERLAND		RIGHT BACK
IVES	ALBERT EDWARD	18/12/1908	NEWCASTLE	Q3 1980	LEFT BACK
JACKSON	ARCHIBALD	25/01/1901	PLUMPSTEAD, LONDON	11/11/1985	CENTRE HALF
JACKSON	RICHARD WILLIAM	Q1 1877	MIDDLESBROUGH		LEFT HALF BACK
JAMES	CRAIG PETER	15/11/1982	MIDDLESBROUGH		LEFT BACK
JAMES	LEIGHTON	16/02/1953	LOUGHOR, GLAMORGAN		OUTSIDE LEFT
JARVIE	GAVIN	1878	NEWTON, LANARKS.		LEFT HALF BACK
JI	DONG-WON	28/05/1991	JEJU, JEJU-DO, SOUTH KOREA		FORWARD
JOBLING	J.				FORWARD
JOHN	STERN CHRISTOPHER JAMES	30/10/1976	TUNAPUNA, TRINIDAD		FORWARD
JOHNSON	JOSEPH		FELLING		LEFT BACK
JOHNSON	SIMON AINSLEY	09/03/1983	WEST BROMWICH		FORWARD
JOHNSTON	ALLAN	14/12/1973	GLASGOW		OUTSIDE RIGHT/FORWARD
JOHNSTON	HAROLD W.	1871	GLASGOW	10/12/1936	LEFT HALF BACK/LEFT BACK
JOHNSTON	JOHN		SCOTLAND		RIGHT BACK
JOHNSTON	JOHN B.		MUIRKIRK, AYRSHIRE		LEFT BACK
JOHNSTON	ROBERT	1875-76	RENTON		INSIDE/OUTSIDE LEFT
JOHNSTON	ROBERT	02/06/1909	FALKIRK	27/09/1968	CENTRE HALF
JONES	JOHN EDWARD (JACK)	03/07/1913	BROMBOROUGH	26/01/1995	LEFT BACK

CAREER RECORDS

Career		League			Play Offs			FA Cup			League Cup			Other			Total		
Start	End	Apps	Sub	Gls	Apps	Sub	Gls	Apps	Sub	Gls	Apps	Sub	Gls	Apps	Sub	Gls	Apps	Sub	Gls
1980	1982	63	0	4	0	0	0	1	0	0	1	0	0	0	0	0	65	0	4
1957	1963	1	0	0	0	0	0	0	0	0	0	0	0	0	0	0	1	0	0
1912	1925	160	0	0	0	0	0	12	0	0	0	0	0	0	0	0	172	0	0
1984	1986	32	8	5	0	0	0	1	0	0	8	1	1	1	1	1	42	10	7
1910	1912	2	0	0	0	0	0	0	0	0	0	0	0	0	0	0	2	0	0
1923	1925	9	0	8	0	0	0	0	0	0	0	0	0	0	0	0	9	0	8
1899	1902	67	0	18	0	0	0	6	0	2	0	0	0	0	0	0	73	0	20
1899	1909	281	0	83	0	0	0	21	0	2	0	0	0	1	0	0	303	0	85
1975	1978	66	7	23	0	0	0	7	0	3	3	0	2	1	0	0	77	7	28
1955	1956	19	0	5	0	0	0	5	0	2	0	0	0	0	0	0	24	0	7
1904	1919	280	0	150	0	0	0	35	0	9	0	0	0	0	0	0	315	0	159
1997	2000	46	12	0	3	0	0	2	0	0	3	0	0	0	0	0	54	12	0
1976	1977	15	0	0	0	0	0	2	0	1	2	0	0	0	0	0	19	0	1
1964	1966	31	0	9	0	0	0	1	0	1	1	1	0	0	0	0	33	1	10
1960	1963	65	0	16	0	0	0	8	0	2	7	0	1	0	0	0	80	0	19
1908	1909	1	0	0	0	0	0	0	0	0	0	0	0	0	0	0	1	0	0
1953	1960	74	0	27	0	0	0	2	0	1	0	0	0	0	0	0	76	0	28
1912	1919	10	0	0	0	0	0	0	0	0	0	0	0	0	0	0	10	0	0
1936	1937	12	0	2	0	0	0	1	0	1	0	0	0	0	0	0	13	0	3
1968	1974	68	1	3	0	0	0	10	0	1	5	0	0	8	0	1	91	1	5
1936	1948	55	0	2	0	0	0	12	0	1	0	0	0	0	0	0	67	0	3
1993	1997	39	30	8	0	0	0	2	4	1	1	4	2	0	1	0	42	39	11
2005	2006	27	0	1	0	0	0	2	0	0	1	0	0	0	0	0	30	0	1
1947	1957	260	0	0	0	0	0	15	0	0	0	0	0	0	0	0	275	0	0
1906	1910	14	0	2	0	0	0	0	0	0	0	0	0	0	0	0	14	0	2
1977	1981	1	0	0	0	0	0	0	0	0	0	0	0	0	0	0	1	0	0
1973	1973	1	0	0	0	0	0	0	0	0	0	0	0	0	0	0	1	0	0
1964	1977	264	23	73	0	0	0	21	1	4	12	3	3	10	1	1	307	28	81
1921	1923	10	0	0	0	0	0	2	0	0	0	0	0	0	0	0	12	0	0
1885	1886	0	0	0	0	0	0	1	0	0	0	0	0	0	0	0	1	0	0
1966	1969	1	0	0	0	0	0	0	0	0	0	0	0	0	0	0	1	0	0
1906	1908	8	0	3	0	0	0	0	0	0	0	0	0	0	0	0	8	0	3
1957	1969	357	1	23	0	0	0	26	0	3	17	0	0	0	0	0	400	1	26
2000	2001	32	2	8	0	0	0	3	0	0	2	0	2	0	0	0	37	2	10
2010	2010	11	0	0	0	0	0	0	0	0	0	0	0	0	0	0	11	0	0
2006	2007	15	11	4	0	0	0	1	0	0	0	0	0	0	0	0	16	11	4
1894	1895	18	0	10	0	0	0	0	0	0	0	0	0	0	0	0	18	0	10
1999	2005	1	1	0	0	0	0	0	0	0	2	0	0	0	0	0	3	1	0
1885	1885	0	0	0	0	0	0	1	0	0	0	0	0	0	0	0	1	0	0
1958	1972	312	3	1	0	0	0	20	0	0	13	0	0	4	0	0	349	3	1
1930	1936	12	0	0	0	0	0	0	0	0	0	0	0	0	0	0	12	0	0
1922	1924	6	0	0	0	0	0	0	0	0	0	0	0	0	0	0	6	0	0
1898	1905	162	0	10	0	0	0	6	0	0	0	0	0	1	0	0	169	0	10
2000	2004	1	0	0	0	0	0	0	0	0	1	0	0	0	0	0	2	0	0
1983	1984	50	2	4	0	0	0	1	0	0	4	0	0	0	0	0	55	2	4
1907	1912	93	0	2	0	0	0	7	0	0	0	0	0	0	0	0	100	0	2
2011	2012	2	17	2	0	0	0	0	1	0	0	1	0	0	0	0	2	19	2
1887	1889	0	0	0	0	0	0	1	0	0	0	0	0	0	0	0	1	0	0
2007	2007	10	6	5	0	0	0	0	0	0	0	0	0	0	0	0	10	6	5
1919	1921	3	0	0	0	0	0	0	0	0	0	0	0	0	0	0	3	0	0
2004	2004	1	4	0	0	0	0	0	0	0	0	0	0	0	0	0	1	4	0
1997	2000	82	4	19	3	0	0	3	0	0	8	1	1	0	0	0	96	5	20
1894	1897	60	0	3	0	0	0	6	0	0	0	0	0	0	0	0	66	0	3
1907	1909	1	0	0	0	0	0	0	0	0	0	0	0	0	0	0	1	0	0
1920	1922	2	0	0	0	0	0	0	0	0	0	0	0	0	0	0	2	0	0
1896	1897	12	0	1	0	0	0	2	0	0	0	0	0	0	0	0	14	0	1
1929	1940	146	0	0	0	0	0	18	0	0	0	0	0	2	0	0	166	0	0
1945	1947	24	0	0	0	0	0	7	0	0	0	0	0	0	0	0	31	0	0

SURNAME	FORENAMES	DOB	BIRTHPLACE	DECEASED	POSITION
JONES	KENNETH	01/10/1936	EASINGTON COLLIERY		LEFT BACK
JONES	KENWYNE JOEL	05/10/1984	LA BREA, TRINIDAD		CENTRE FORWARD
KASHER	JOSEPH WILLIAM ROBINSON	14/01/1894	WILLINGTON	08/01/1992	CENTRE HALF
KAVANAGH	GRAHAM ANTHONY	02/12/1973	DUBLIN		MIDFIELDER
KAY	JOHN	29/01/1964	SUNDERLAND		RIGHT BACK
KAY	MICHAEL JOSEPH	12/09/1989	CONSETT		RIGHT BACK
KEETON	WILLIAM WALTER	30/04/1905	SHIREBROOK, DERBYSHIRE	10/10/1980	INSIDE RIGHT
KELLY	DAVID THOMAS	25/11/1965	BIRMINGHAM		CENTRE FORWARD
KELLY	PETER W.	1887	SCOTLAND		LEFT BACK
KELLY	ROBERT F.	16/11/1894	ASHTON-IN-MAKERFIELD, LANCS.	22/09/1969	INSIDE/OUTSIDE RIGHT
KELLY	THOMAS	1884-85			LEFT HALF BACK
KELSALL	JOSIAH	20/05/1892	MARYPORT, CUMBERLAND	24/04/1974	CENTRE FORWARD
KEMP	SAMUEL PATRICK	29/08/1932	STOCKTON	Aug 1987	OUTSIDE RIGHT
KENNEDY	ALAN PHILLIP	31/08/1954	SUNDERLAND		LEFT BACK
KERR	ANDREW	29/06/1931	AYR	24/12/1997	CENTRE FORWARD
KERR	ROBERT	16/11/1947	BALLOCH, STRATHCLYDE		MIDFIELDER
KICHENBRAND	DONALD BASIL	13/08/1933	GERMISTON, SOUTH AFRICA		CENTRE FORWARD
KIERNAN	JOSEPH	22/10/1942	COATBRIDGE	01/08/2006	LEFT HALF
KILBANE	KEVIN DANIEL	01/02/1977	PRESTON		FORWARD
KILGALLON	MATTHEW SHAUN	08/01/1984	YORK		DEFENDER
KINNELL	GEORGE	22/12/1937	COWDENBEATH		CENTRE HALF
KIRBY	FRED	Q2 1889	DARLINGTON		CENTRE FORWARD
KIRKLEY	WILLIAM	16/01/1863	MONKWEARMOUTH	29/05/1941	GOALKEEPER
KIRTLEY	JOHN HAROLD M. (HARRY)	23/05/1930	WASHINGTON	09/12/2007	INSIDE RIGHT/LEFT
KIRTLEY	JOHN TROTTER	Q2 1863	HYLTON, SUNDERLAND	Q4 1932	GOALKEEPER
KNOWLES	JOSEPH	Q1 1872	MONKWEARMOUTH		LEFT BACK
KUBICKI	DARIUSZ JAN	06/06/1963	KOZUCHOW, POLAND		RIGHT BACK
KYLE	KEVIN ALISTAIR	07/06/1981	STRANRAER		CENTRE FORWARD
KYRGIAKOS	SOTIRIOS	23/07/1979	MEGALOCHORI, TRIKALA, GREECE		CENTRAL DEFENDER
LAING	LOUIS	06/03/1993	NEWCASTLE		CENTRE BACK
LAIRD	J. WILLIAM (WILLIAM)	1912	LARKHALL		INSIDE LEFT/CENTRE FORWARD
LANE	JAMES CHARLES (JOSEPH)	11/07/1892	WATFORD	27/02/1959	CENTRE FORWARD
LARSSON	SEBASTIAN BENGT ULF	06/06/1985	ESKILSTUNA, SWEDEN		WINGER
LASLANDES	LILIAN	04/09/1971	PAUILLAC, FRANCE		CENTRE FORWARD
LATHAN	JOHN GEORGE	12/04/1952	SOUTHWICK, SUNDERLAND		CENTRE FORWARD
LAVERY	JAMES	Q2 1875	CHESTER-LE-STREET		OUTSIDE LEFT
LAW	JOHN	1887	SCOTLAND		OUTSIDE LEFT
LAWLEY	GEORGE HARRY	10/04/1903	WALSALL	07/04/1987	OUTSIDE LEFT/RIGHT
LAWRENCE	JAMES HUBERT	08/03/1970	BALHAM, LONDON		OUTSIDE RIGHT
LAWRENCE	LIAM	14/12/1981	WORKSOP		RIGHT WINGER / FORWARD
LAWTHER	WILLIAM IAN (IAN)	20/10/1939	BELFAST	25/04/2010	CENTRE FORWARD
LE TALLEC	ANTHONY	03/10/1984	HENNEBONT, BRITTANY, FRANCE		MIDFIELD / FORWARD
LEADBITTER	GRANT	07/01/1986	FENCEHOUSES, CO. DURHAM		MIDFIELDER
LEE	ROBERT GORDON	02/02/1953	MELTON MOWBRAY		CENTRE FORWARD
LEE	THOMAS	1872	CHOPPINGTON, NORTHUMB.		LEFT HALF BACK
LEMON	PAUL ANDREW	03/06/1966	MIDDLESBROUGH		MIDFIELDER
LEONARD	JAMES	07/10/1904	INKERMAN, PAISLEY	01/09/1959	INSIDE LEFT
LESLIE	JAMES	1873-75	BARRHEAD, GLASGOW	Sep 1920	INSIDE / CENTRE FORWARD
LEWIS	ALBERT EDWARD TALBOT	20/01/1877	BEDMINSTER, BRISTOL	22/02/1956	GOALKEEPER
LIDDLE	MICHAEL WILLIAM	25/12/1989	HOUNSLOW, LONDON		LEFT BACK
LILLEY	THOMAS	Q1 1900	NEWBOTTLE, CO.DURHAM	Q3 1964	LEFT BACK
LINDSAY	ALBERT FOWLER	26/09/1881	WEST HARTLEPOOL	Q1 1961	GOALKEEPER
LINDSAY	DAVID	29/06/1926	CAMBUSLANG		RIGHT BACK
LIVINGSTONE	GEORGE TURNER	05/05/1876	DUMBARTON	15/01/1950	INSIDE/OUTSIDE LEFT
LLOYD	THOMAS	17/11/1903	WEDNESBURY	20/01/1984	LEFT BACK
LLOYD	WILLIAM STANLEY (STAN)	01/10/1924	WEST AUCKLAND		INSIDE LEFT/RIGHT
LOCKIE	ALEXANDER JAMES	11/04/1915	SOUTH SHIELDS	25/03/1974	CENTRE HALF
LOGAN	D.				FORWARD

CAREER RECORDS

Career		League			Play Offs			FA Cup			League Cup			Other			Total		
Start	End	Apps	Sub	Gls	Apps	Sub	Gls	Apps	Sub	Gls	Apps	Sub	Gls	Apps	Sub	Gls	Apps	Sub	Gls
1953	1961	10	0	0	0	0	0	0	0	0	0	0	0	0	0	0	10	0	0
2007	2010	82	12	26	0	0	0	2	1	1	4	0	1	0	0	0	88	13	28
1919	1922	86	0	0	0	0	0	4	0	0	0	0	0	0	0	0	90	0	0
2006	2008	10	4	1	0	0	0	1	0	0	0	0	0	0	0	0	11	4	1
1987	1996	196	3	0	3	0	0	12	0	0	19	0	0	6	0	0	236	3	0
2006	2011	0	0	0	0	0	0	1	0	0	0	0	0	0	0	0	1	0	0
1930	1932	12	0	1	0	0	0	0	0	0	0	0	0	0	0	0	12	0	1
1995	1997	32	2	2	0	0	0	3	0	0	2	1	0	0	0	0	37	3	2
1908	1909	1	0	0	0	0	0	0	0	0	0	0	0	0	0	0	1	0	0
1925	1927	50	0	11	0	0	0	5	0	4	0	0	0	0	0	0	55	0	15
1905	1906	1	0	0	0	0	0	0	0	0	0	0	0	0	0	0	1	0	0
1913	1915	1	0	0	0	0	0	0	0	0	0	0	0	0	0	0	1	0	0
1951	1957	17	0	2	0	0	0	2	0	0	0	0	0	0	0	0	19	0	2
1985	1987	54	0	2	2	0	0	4	0	0	2	1	0	4	0	1	66	1	3
1963	1964	18	0	5	0	0	0	0	0	0	1	0	0	0	0	0	19	0	5
1964	1979	355	13	57	0	0	0	29	1	5	14	0	1	21	0	6	419	14	69
1958	1960	53	0	28	0	0	0	1	0	0	0	0	0	0	0	0	54	0	28
1958	1963	1	0	0	0	0	0	0	0	0	1	0	2	0	0	0	2	0	2
1999	2003	102	11	8	0	0	0	3	4	1	4	0	0	0	0	0	109	15	9
2010	2012	15	2	0	0	0	0	1	0	0	0	0	0	0	0	0	16	2	0
1966	1968	67	2	3	0	0	0	7	0	0	3	0	3	0	0	0	77	2	6
1911	1911	1	0	0	0	0	0	0	0	0	0	0	0	0	0	0	1	0	0
1885	1891	2	0	0	0	0	0	9	0	0	0	0	0	0	0	0	11	0	0
1948	1955	95	0	18	0	0	0	6	0	0	0	0	0	0	0	0	101	0	18
1883	1885	0	0	0	0	0	0	1	0	0	0	0	0	0	0	0	1	0	0
1895	1897	1	0	0	0	0	0	0	0	0	0	0	0	0	0	0	1	0	0
1994	1997	135	1	0	0	0	0	7	0	0	7	0	0	0	0	0	149	1	0
1998	2006	59	32	11	2	0	2	8	2	1	4	2	5	0	0	0	73	36	19
2012	2012	2	1	0	0	0	0	1	0	0	0	0	0	0	0	0	3	1	0
2009	2012	0	1	0	0	0	0	0	0	0	0	0	0	0	0	0	0	1	0
1931	1932	2	0	0	0	0	0	0	0	0	0	0	0	0	0	0	2	0	0
1913	1913	2	0	0	0	0	0	0	0	0	0	0	0	0	0	0	2	0	0
2011	2012	32	0	7	0	0	0	6	0	1	1	0	0	0	0	0	39	0	8
2001	2003	5	7	0	0	0	0	0	0	0	1	1	0	0	0	0	5	8	1
1967	1974	41	12	14	0	0	0	1	1	0	2	0	2	4	1	2	48	14	18
1897	1898	1	0	0	0	0	0	0	0	0	0	0	0	0	0	0	1	0	0
1906	1906	1	0	0	0	0	0	0	0	0	0	0	0	0	0	0	1	0	0
1929	1931	10	0	1	0	0	0	0	0	0	0	0	0	0	0	0	10	0	1
1993	1994	2	2	0	0	0	0	0	0	0	1	0	0	0	0	0	2	3	0
2004	2007	49	24	9	0	0	0	2	0	0	3	2	0	0	0	0	54	26	9
1958	1961	75	0	41	0	0	0	7	0	2	1	0	1	0	0	0	83	0	44
2005	2006	12	15	3	0	0	0	1	1	1	2	0	1	0	0	0	15	16	5
2000	2009	61	50	11	0	0	0	3	1	0	5	3	0	0	0	0	69	54	11
1976	1980	101	8	32	0	0	0	5	0	1	4	0	0	4	0	0	114	8	33
1897	1899	2	0	0	0	0	0	0	0	0	0	0	0	0	0	0	2	0	0
1982	1990	91	16	15	1	0	0	2	2	0	6	2	0	7	0	4	107	20	19
1930	1932	35	0	19	0	0	0	7	0	2	0	0	0	0	0	0	42	0	21
1897	1901	92	0	24	0	0	0	6	0	2	0	0	0	0	0	0	98	0	26
1904	1904	4	0	0	0	0	0	0	0	0	0	0	0	0	0	0	4	0	0
2006	2012	0	0	0	0	0	0	0	1	0	0	0	0	0	0	0	0	1	0
1926	1928	1	0	0	0	0	0	0	0	0	0	0	0	0	0	0	1	0	0
1902	1904	3	0	0	0	0	0	0	0	0	0	0	0	0	0	0	3	0	0
1946	1948	1	0	0	0	0	0	0	0	0	0	0	0	0	0	0	1	0	0
1900	1901	30	0	12	0	0	0	1	0	0	0	0	0	0	0	0	31	0	12
1925	1927	4	0	0	0	0	0	0	0	0	0	0	0	0	0	0	4	0	0
1941	1948	24	0	5	0	0	0	0	0	0	0	0	0	0	0	0	24	0	5
1935	1946	40	0	1	0	0	0	10	0	0	0	0	0	0	0	0	50	0	1
1885	1885	0	0	0	0	0	0	1	0	0	0	0	0	0	0	0	1	0	0

SURNAME	FORENAMES	DOB	BIRTHPLACE	DECEASED	POSITION
LOGAN	HENRY MORRISON	10/05/1886	SHETTLESTON, GLASGOW	04/02/1963	INSIDE RIGHT
LOGAN	JAMES	24/06/1870	TROON, AYRSHIRE	25/05/1896	OUTIDE LEFT/RIGHT
LONGAIR	WILLIAM	19/07/1870	DUNDEE	28/11/1926	CENTRE HALF
LONGHORN	DENIS	12/09/1950	HYTHE		MIDFIELDER
LORD	PETER				FORWARD
LOW	HENRY FORBES	15/08/1882	ABERDEEN	26/09/1920	HALF BACK / CENTRE FORWARD
LOWREY	PATRICK	11/10/1950	NEWCASTLE		MIDFIELDER
LUMSDON	CHRISTOPHER	15/12/1979	KILLINGWORTH		MIDFIELDER
LUSCOMBE	NATHAN JOHN	06/11/1989	NEW HARTLEY, GATESHEAD		LEFT BACK / MIDFIELD
LYNAS	JOHN	18/01/1907	BLANTYRE	Dec 1988	OUTSIDE RIGHT
LYNCH	CRAIG	25/03/1992	BOWBURN, DURHAM		FORWARD
LYNCH	MARK JOHN	02/09/1981	MANCHESTER		RIGHT BACK
LYNCH	THOMAS MICHAEL	10/10/1964	SHANNON		LEFT BACK
MACHO	JURGEN	24/08/1977	VIENNA, AUSTRIA		GOALKEEPER
MacPHAIL	JOHN	07/12/1955	DUNDEE		CENTRE HALF
MAIN	DAVID	1888	FALKIRK		CENTRE FORWARD
MAKIN	CHRISTOPHER GREGORY	08/05/1973	MANCHESTER		FULL BACK
MALBRANQUE	STEED	06/01/1980	MOUSCRON, BELGIUM		MIDFIELDER
MALEY	MARK	26/01/1981	NEWCASTLE		RIGHT BACK
MALONE	RICHARD PHILLIP	22/08/1947	CARFIN, LANARKSHIRE		RIGHT BACK
MALTBY	JOHN (JACK)	31/07/1939	LEADGATE		OUTSIDE RIGHT/CENT.FORWARD
MAPSON	JOHN	02/05/1917	BIRKENHEAD	19/08/1999	GOALKEEPER
MARANGONI	CLAUDIO OSCAR	17/11/1954	ROSARIO, ARGENTINA		MIDFIELDER
MARPLES	EMERSON ARTHUR	Q1 1879	ECKINGTON, CHESTERFIELD	Q3 1964	RIGHT BACK
MARRIOTT	ANDREW	11/10/1970	SUTTON-IN-ASHFIELD		GOALKEEPER
MARSDEN	WILLIAM	10/11/1901	SILKSWORTH, SUNDERLAND	Q3 1983	INSIDE LEFT
MARSHALL	ROBERT SAMUEL	03/04/1903	HUCKNALL	27/10/1966	INSIDE/CENTRE FORWARD
MARSHALL	W.				HALF BACK
MARSTON	MAURICE	24/03/1929	TRIMDON, CO.DURHAM	28/01/2002	RIGHT BACK
MARTIN	HENRY (HARRY)	05/12/1891	SELSTON, NOTTS.	31/12/1974	OUTSIDE LEFT
MARTIN	ISAAC GEORGE (GEORGE)	25/05/1889	GATESHEAD	06/05/1962	LEFT/RIGHT HALF BACK
MARTIN	NEIL	20/10/1940	TRANENT, EDINBURGH		CENTRE FORWARD
MATTEO	DOMINIC	28/04/1974	DUMFRIES		MIDFIELDER
MAXWELL	WILLIAM STURROCK	21/09/1876	ARBROATH	14/07/1940	INSIDE LEFT/RIGHT
MBOMA	HENRI PATRICK (PATRICK)	15/11/1970	DOULA, CAMEROON		CENTRE FORWARD
McALLISTER	ALEXANDER (SANDY)	1878	KILMARNOCK	31/01/1918	CENTRE HALF
McATEER	JASON WYNN	18/06/1971	BIRKENHEAD		MIDFIELDER
McCALLUM	DONALD	1880	ARGYLLSHIRE	1959	LEFT/RIGHT BACK
McCANN	GAVIN PETER	10/01/1978	BLACKPOOL		MIDFIELDER
McCARTNEY	GEORGE	29/04/1981	BELFAST		LEFT BACK/CENTRE BACK
McCLEAN	JAMES	22/04/1989	DERRY		LEFT WINGER
McCOIST	ALISTAIR MURDOCH (ALLY)	24/09/1962	BELLSHILL, GLASGOW		CENTRE FORWARD
McCOLL	DONALD				FORWARD
McCOMBIE	ANDREW	30/06/1876	EDINBURGH	28/03/1952	RIGHT BACK
McCONNELL	DAVID JAMES ENGLISH (ENGLISH)	14/05/1883	LARNE	13/06/1928	HALF BACK
McCREADIE	ANDREW	19/11/1870	GIRVAN, AYRSHIRE	04/04/1916	CENTRE HALF
McCULLOCH	D. ROBERT				INSIDE RIGHT
McDERMID	ROBERT	1868-70	ALEXANDRIA, DUNBARTONSHIRE		FORWARD
McDONAGH	JAMES MARTIN (SEAMUS)	06/10/1952	ROTHERHAM		GOALKEEPER
McDONALD	JOHN	1857-58	SCOTLAND	14/09/1907	FORWARD
McDONALD	JOSEPH	10/02/1929	BLANTYRE	08/09/2003	LEFT BACK
McDOUGALL	JOHN (JOCK)	21/09/1901	PORT GLASGOW	26/09/1973	CENTRE HALF
McDOWALL	LESLIE JAMES	25/10/1912	GUNGA PUR, INDIA	18/08/1991	FULL BACK / CENTRE HALF
McGHIE	JOSEPH	22/03/1884	KILBIRNIE, AYRSHIRE		CENTRE HALF
McGILL	BRENDAN	22/03/1981	DUBLIN		MIDFIELDER
McGINLEY	JOHN	11/06/1959	ROWLANDS GILL		MIDFIELDER
McGIVEN	MICHAEL	07/02/1951	NEWCASTLE		MIDFIELDER
McGORIAN	ISAAC MOOR (IKE)	19/10/1901	SILKSWORTH		LEFT/RIGHT BACK

CAREER RECORDS

Career		League			Play Offs			FA Cup			League Cup			Other			Total		
Start	End	Apps	Sub	Gls	Apps	Sub	Gls	Apps	Sub	Gls	Apps	Sub	Gls	Apps	Sub	Gls	Apps	Sub	Gls
1909	1910	1	0	0	0	0	0	1	0	0	0	0	0	0	0	0	2	0	0
1891	1891	2	0	0	0	0	0	0	0	0	0	0	0	0	0	0	2	0	0
1896	1896	2	0	0	0	0	0	0	0	0	0	0	0	0	0	0	2	0	0
1974	1976	35	5	3	0	0	0	2	0	0	1	0	0	3	0	1	41	5	4
1886	1888	0	0	0	0	0	0	1	0	0	0	0	0	0	0	0	1	0	0
1907	1919	203	0	36	0	0	0	25	0	3	0	0	0	0	0	0	228	0	39
1967	1972	13	2	3	0	0	0	0	0	0	0	0	0	0	0	0	13	2	3
1995	2001	2	0	0	0	0	0	0	0	0	1	1	0	0	0	0	3	1	0
2006	2009	0	0	0	0	0	0	0	1	0	0	0	0	0	0	0	0	1	0
1928	1929	10	0	1	0	0	0	0	0	0	0	0	0	0	0	0	10	0	1
2008	2012	0	2	0	0	0	0	0	0	0	0	0	0	0	0	0	0	2	0
2004	2005	5	6	0	0	0	0	0	0	0	2	0	0	0	0	0	7	6	0
1988	1990	4	0	0	0	0	0	1	0	0	0	0	0	1	0	0	6	0	0
2000	2003	20	2	0	0	0	0	1	0	0	3	1	0	0	0	0	24	3	0
1987	1990	130	0	22	3	0	0	5	0	0	10	0	0	5	0	0	153	0	22
1910	1911	2	0	0	0	0	0	0	0	0	0	0	0	0	0	0	2	0	0
1997	2001	115	5	1	1	1	0	7	1	0	13	0	0	0	0	0	136	7	1
2008	2011	88	14	1	0	0	0	4	0	1	3	3	0	0	0	0	95	17	2
1997	2003	0	0	0	0	0	0	0	0	0	3	0	0	0	0	0	3	0	0
1970	1977	236	1	2	0	0	0	22	0	0	10	0	0	13	0	0	281	1	2
1955	1961	22	0	4	0	0	0	1	0	0	0	0	0	0	0	0	23	0	4
1936	1954	345	0	0	0	0	0	36	0	0	0	0	0	2	0	0	383	0	0
1979	1981	19	1	3	0	0	0	1	0	0	1	0	0	0	0	0	21	1	3
1908	1910	10	0	0	0	0	0	0	0	0	0	0	0	0	0	0	10	0	0
1998	2001	2	0	0	0	0	0	0	0	0	3	0	0	0	0	0	5	0	0
1920	1924	3	0	2	0	0	0	0	0	0	0	0	0	0	0	0	3	0	2
1920	1928	198	0	69	0	0	0	9	0	5	0	0	0	0	0	0	207	0	74
1885	1887	0	0	0	0	0	0	1	0	0	0	0	0	0	0	0	1	0	0
1944	1953	9	0	0	0	0	0	0	0	0	0	0	0	0	0	0	9	0	0
1912	1922	213	0	23	0	0	0	19	0	0	0	0	0	0	0	0	232	0	23
1909	1912	16	0	0	0	0	0	0	0	0	0	0	0	0	0	0	16	0	0
1965	1968	86	0	38	0	0	0	8	0	6	5	0	2	0	0	0	99	0	46
1995	1995	1	0	0	0	0	0	0	0	0	0	0	0	0	0	0	1	0	0
1902	1903	7	0	3	0	0	0	0	0	0	0	0	0	0	0	0	7	0	3
2002	2002	5	4	1	0	0	0	0	0	0	0	0	0	0	0	0	5	4	1
1896	1904	210	0	4	1	0	0	10	0	0	0	0	0	1	0	0	222	0	4
2001	2004	53	0	5	2	0	0	6	0	0	0	0	0	0	0	0	61	0	5
1904	1904	3	0	0	0	0	0	0	0	0	0	0	0	0	0	0	3	0	0
1998	2003	106	10	8	0	0	0	11	1	3	4	3	2	0	0	0	121	14	13
1997	2012	153	22	0	2	0	0	12	4	0	8	2	0	0	0	0	175	28	0
2011	2012	20	3	5	0	0	0	6	0	1	0	0	0	0	0	0	26	3	6
1981	1983	38	18	8	0	0	0	3	1	0	5	0	1	0	0	0	46	19	9
1884	1885	0	0	0	0	0	0	1	0	1	0	0	0	0	0	0	1	0	1
1898	1904	157	0	6	0	0	0	7	0	0	0	0	0	1	0	0	165	0	6
1905	1908	39	0	0	0	0	0	6	0	0	0	0	0	0	0	0	45	0	0
1894	1896	42	0	8	0	0	0	3	0	1	0	0	0	0	0	0	45	0	9
1911	1913	1	0	0	0	0	0	0	0	0	0	0	0	0	0	0	1	0	0
1888	1889	0	0	0	0	0	0	2	0	0	0	0	0	0	0	0	2	0	0
1985	1985	7	0	0	0	0	0	0	0	0	0	0	0	1	0	0	8	0	0
1881	1885	0	0	0	0	0	0	2	0	0	0	0	0	0	0	0	2	0	0
1954	1958	137	0	1	0	0	0	18	0	0	0	0	0	0	0	0	155	0	1
1929	1934	167	0	4	0	0	0	20	0	1	0	0	0	0	0	0	187	0	5
1932	1938	13	0	0	0	0	0	1	0	0	0	0	0	0	0	0	14	0	0
1906	1908	41	0	0	0	0	0	5	0	0	0	0	0	0	0	0	46	0	0
1996	2002	0	0	0	0	0	0	0	0	0	0	1	0	0	0	0	0	1	0
1982	1982	3	0	0	0	0	0	0	0	0	0	0	0	0	0	0	3	0	0
1966	1973	107	6	9	0	0	0	2	2	1	3	0	0	7	0	2	119	8	12
1924	1929	20	0	1	0	0	0	2	0	0	0	0	0	0	0	0	22	0	1

SURNAME	FORENAMES	DOB	BIRTHPLACE	DECEASED	POSITION
McGREGOR	GEORGE W.		SALTCOATS		INSIDE RIGHT
McGUIGAN	JAMES	01/03/1924	GLASGOW	30/03/1988	OUTSIDE LEFT/RIGHT
McGUIRE	DOUGLAS JOHN	06/09/1967	BATHGATE, GLASGOW		MIDFIELDER
McINALLY	THOMAS BERNARD	18/12/1899	BARRHEAD, GLASGOW	29/12/1955	INSIDE LEFT
McINROY	ALBERT	23/04/1901	WALTON-LE-DALE, LANCS.	07/01/1985	GOALKEEPER
McINTOSH	ANGUS MUNRO	Q3 1884	BIRKENHEAD		INSIDE/CENTRE FORWARD
McINTOSH	JOHN WILLIAM	1876	TOW LAW, CO. DURHAM		CENTRE FORWARD
McIVER	FREDERICK	14/02/1952	BIRTLEY		LEFT BACK
McKAY	ROBERT	02/09/1900	GOVAN, GLASGOW	24/05/1977	INSIDE LEFT/RIGHT
McKENZIE	ARCHIBALD D.	1875	GREENOCK		INSIDE/OUTSIDE LEFT
McKENZIE	THOMAS		GLASGOW		INSIDE/CENTRE FORWARD
McLAIN	THOMAS	19/01/1922	LINTON, ROXBURGHSHIRE	Dec 1995	LEFT/RIGHT HALF
McLATCHIE	COLIN CAMPBELL	02/11/1876	NEW CUMNOCK, AYRSHIRE	07/01/1952	INSIDE/OUTSIDE LEFT
McLAUCHLAN	HUGHIE				HALF BACK
McLAUGHLAN	ALEXANDER DONALDSON (SANDY)	17/07/1936	KILWINNING		GOALKEEPER
McLEAN	ADAM	27/04/1897	COATBRIDGE	29/06/1973	INSIDE/OUTSIDE FORWARD
McMAHON	HUGH	24/09/1909	GRANGETOWN, MIDDLESBROUGH	Oct 1986	OUTSIDE LEFT
McMILLAN	JAMES	Q2 1863	ALNWICK	02/09/1930	HALF BACK
McNAB	ALEXANDER (SANDY)	27/12/1911	GLASGOW	19/09/1962	LEFT/RIGHT HALF+I./O.LEFT
McNAB	JAMES	13/04/1940	DENNY, STIRLINGSHIRE	29/06/2006	HALF BACK
McNEILL	EDWARD VINCENT	26/03/1929	WARRENPOINT, N.I.		GOALKEEPER
McNEILL	ROBERT	1868	GLASGOW		LEFT/RIGHT BACK
McNESTRY	GEORGE	07/01/1908	CHOPWELL, CO.DURHAM	16/03/1998	OUTSIDE RIGHT
McPHEAT	WILLIAM	04/09/1942	CALDERCRUIX		INSIDE LEFT
McPHEE	JOHN	1910-11	STIRLING		OUTSIDE RIGHT
McSEVENEY	JOHN HADDON	08/02/1931	SHOTTS		OUTSIDE LEFT
McSHANE	PAUL DAVID	06/01/1986	KILPEDDER, WICKLOW		DEFENDER
MEARNS	FREDERICK CHARLES	31/03/1879	SUNDERLAND	22/01/1931	GOALKEEPER
MEDINA	NICOLAS RUBEN	17/02/1982	BUENOS AIRES, ARGENTINA		MIDFIELDER
MEECHAN	PETER	28/02/1872	BROXBURN	Jun 1915	LEFT/RIGHT BACK
MELVILLE	ANDREW ROGER	29/11/1968	SWANSEA		CENTRE HALF
MENSAH	JOHN	29/11/1982	OBUASI, GHANA		DEFENDER
METCALF	GEORGE WATSON	Q3 1887	HENDON, SUNDERLAND		CENTRE HALF
MEYLER	DAVID	29/05/1989	CORK		MIDFIELDER
MIDDLETON	MATTHEW YOUNG	24/10/1907	BOLDON COLLIERY	19/04/1979	GOALKEEPER
MIDDLETON	ROBERT CONNAN	15/01/1904	BRECHIN	early 1996	GOALKEEPER
MIGNOLET	SIMON	06/08/1988	SINT TRUIDEN, BELGIUM		GOALKEEPER
MILLAR	JAMES	02/03/1870	ANNBANK, AYRSHIRE	05/02/1907	FORWARD
MILLER	LIAM WILLIAM PETER	13/02/1981	BALLINCOLLIG, CORK		MIDFIELDER
MILLER	THOMAS WILLIAM	08/01/1979	SHOTTON COLLIERY		MIDFIELDER
MILTON	ALBERT	Q4 1885	ECCLESFIELD, SHEFFIELD	11/10/1917	LEFT BACK
MIMMS	ROBERT ANDREW	12/10/1963	YORK		GOALKEEPER
MITCHELL	ROBERT	04/01/1955	HEBBURN		MIDFIELDER
MITCHINSON	THOMAS WILLIAM	24/02/1943	SUNDERLAND		INSIDE LEFT/RIGHT
MITTON	JOHN (JACK)	07/11/1895	TODMORDEN	05/08/1983	RIGHT/LEFT HALF BACK
MONAGHAN	G.		SCOTLAND		FORWARD
MONCUR	ROBERT	19/01/1945	PERTH		LEFT/RIGHT HALF
MONTGOMERY	JAMES	09/10/1943	SUNDERLAND		GOALKEEPER
MONTGOMERY	WILLIAM	02/06/1884	GOUROCK?/EGLINTON?	21/11/1953	INSIDE/OUTSIDE LEFT
MOONEY	BRIAN JOHN	02/02/1966	DUBLIN		OUTSIDE RIGHT
MOORE	GARY	04/11/1945	SOUTH HETTON		CENTRE FORWARD
MOORE	JOHN	01/10/1966	CONSETT		CENTRE FORWARD
MOORE	MALCOLM	18/12/1948	SILKSWORTH		CENTRE FORWARD
MOORE	WILLIAM GREY BRUCE	06/10/1894	NEWCASTLE	26/09/1968	INSIDE/CENTRE FORWARD
MORDUE	JOHN (JACKIE)	13/12/1886	EDMONDSLEY, CO.DURHAM	05/03/1938	INSIDE/OUTSIDE FORWARD
MORGAN	HUGH	1876	LANARKSHIRE		INSIDE/CENTRE FORWARD
MORLEY	JOHN BELL	29/01/1884	CARLISLE	26/10/1957	OUTSIDE RIGHT
MORRIS	SAMUEL WALKER	16/04/1907	PRESCOT, LIVERPOOL	10/08/1991	RIGHT/LEFT HALF

CAREER RECORDS

Career			League			Play Offs			FA Cup			League Cup			Other			Total		
Start	End	Apps	Sub	Gls	Apps	Sub	Gls	Apps	Sub	Gls	Apps	Sub	Gls	Apps	Sub	Gls	Apps	Sub	Gls
1929	1931	1	0	0	0	0	0	0	0	0	0	0	0	0	0	0	1	0	0
1947	1949	3	0	1	0	0	0	0	0	0	0	0	0	0	0	0	3	0	1
1988	1988	1	0	0	0	0	0	0	0	0	0	0	0	0	0	0	1	0	0
1928	1929	35	0	3	0	0	0	1	0	0	0	0	0	0	0	0	36	0	3
1923	1935	215	0	0	0	0	0	12	0	0	0	0	0	0	0	0	227	0	0
1905	1908	40	0	9	0	0	0	6	0	3	0	0	0	0	0	0	46	0	12
1897	1898	2	0	0	0	0	0	0	0	0	0	0	0	0	0	0	2	0	0
1968	1972	1	0	0	0	0	0	0	0	0	0	0	0	0	0	0	1	0	0
1928	1930	49	0	17	0	0	0	2	0	0	0	0	0	0	0	0	51	0	17
1895	1896	2	0	1	0	0	0	0	0	0	0	0	0	0	0	0	2	0	1
1905	1906	8	0	1	0	0	0	0	0	0	0	0	0	0	0	0	8	0	1
1946	1952	67	0	1	0	0	0	6	0	0	0	0	0	0	0	0	73	0	1
1898	1902	122	0	33	0	0	0	8	0	1	0	0	0	0	0	0	130	0	34
1888	1889	0	0	0	0	0	0	2	0	0	0	0	0	0	0	0	2	0	0
1964	1967	43	0	0	0	0	0	2	0	0	1	0	0	0	0	0	46	0	0
1928	1930	67	0	14	0	0	0	4	0	2	0	0	0	0	0	0	71	0	16
1937	1945	8	0	1	0	0	0	0	0	0	0	0	0	0	0	0	8	0	1
1883	1887	0	0	0	0	0	0	3	0	0	0	0	0	0	0	0	3	0	0
1932	1938	97	0	6	0	0	0	15	0	0	0	0	0	1	0	0	113	0	6
1956	1967	284	1	13	0	0	0	20	0	1	18	0	4	0	0	0	322	1	18
1951	1954	7	0	0	0	0	0	0	0	0	0	0	0	0	0	0	7	0	0
1894	1900	142	0	0	4	0	0	13	0	0	0	0	0	0	0	0	159	0	0
1929	1930	4	0	0	0	0	0	0	0	0	0	0	0	0	0	0	4	0	0
1959	1965	58	0	19	0	0	0	9	0	3	5	0	1	0	0	0	72	0	23
1929	1931	4	0	0	0	0	0	0	0	0	0	0	0	0	0	0	4	0	0
1951	1955	35	0	3	0	0	0	3	0	1	0	0	0	0	0	0	38	0	4
2007	2009	20	4	0	0	0	0	1	0	0	0	0	0	0	0	0	21	4	0
1901	1902	2	0	0	0	0	0	0	0	0	0	0	0	0	0	0	2	0	0
2001	2004	0	0	0	0	0	0	1	0	0	0	0	0	0	0	0	1	0	0
1893	1895	41	0	1	0	0	0	5	0	0	0	0	0	0	0	0	46	0	1
1993	1999	204	0	14	0	0	0	11	0	0	18	1	0	2	0	0	235	1	14
2009	2011	29	5	1	0	0	0	0	0	0	1	0	0	0	0	0	30	5	1
1905	1908	1	0	0	0	0	0	0	0	0	0	0	0	0	0	0	1	0	0
2008	2012	14	8	0	0	0	0	2	2	0	0	0	0	0	0	0	16	10	0
1933	1939	57	0	0	0	0	0	2	0	0	0	0	0	0	0	0	59	0	0
1930	1933	59	0	0	0	0	0	7	0	0	0	0	0	0	0	0	66	0	0
2010	2012	52	0	0	0	0	0	7	0	0	2	0	0	0	0	0	61	0	0
1890	1904	238	0	107	0	0	0	22	0	19	0	0	0	1	0	2	261	0	128
2006	2009	41	16	3	0	0	0	1	0	0	1	1	0	0	0	0	43	17	3
2005	2007	30	3	3	0	0	0	2	0	0	0	0	0	0	0	0	32	3	3
1908	1914	125	0	0	0	0	0	16	0	0	0	0	0	0	0	0	141	0	0
1986	1987	4	0	0	0	0	0	0	0	0	0	0	0	0	0	0	4	0	0
1970	1976	1	2	0	0	0	0	0	0	0	0	0	0	0	0	0	1	2	0
1958	1966	16	1	2	0	0	0	2	0	0	2	0	1	0	0	0	20	1	3
1920	1923	79	0	8	0	0	0	2	0	0	0	0	0	0	0	0	81	0	8
1887	1888	0	0	0	0	0	0	4	0	3	0	0	0	0	0	0	4	0	3
1974	1976	86	0	2	0	0	0	7	0	0	3	0	0	5	0	0	101	0	2
1958	1977	537	0	0	0	0	0	41	0	0	33	0	0	16	0	0	627	0	0
1907	1909	11	0	2	0	0	0	0	0	0	0	0	0	0	0	0	11	0	2
1991	1993	21	6	1	0	0	0	2	0	0	0	0	0	0	0	0	23	6	1
1962	1967	13	0	2	0	0	0	1	0	0	0	0	0	0	0	0	14	0	2
1983	1988	4	12	1	0	0	0	0	0	0	1	1	0	1	1	2	6	14	3
1965	1970	10	2	3	0	0	0	0	0	0	0	0	0	0	0	0	10	2	3
1912	1922	46	0	11	0	0	0	1	0	0	0	0	0	0	0	0	47	0	11
1908	1920	262	0	71	0	0	0	32	0	11	0	0	0	0	0	0	294	0	82
1896	1899	53	0	17	4	0	1	3	0	1	0	0	0	0	0	0	60	0	19
1907	1908	5	0	1	0	0	0	0	0	0	0	0	0	0	0	0	5	0	1
1928	1932	59	0	0	0	0	0	6	0	0	0	0	0	0	0	0	65	0	0

SUNDERLAND: THE COMPLETE RECORD

SURNAME	FORENAMES	DOB	BIRTHPLACE	DECEASED	POSITION
MORRISON	EVELYN SNEDDON	01/08/1902	SOUTH AFRICA (NATAL?)	15/11/1968	CENTRE FORWARD
MORRISON	JOHN STANTON FLEMING	17/04/1892	WEST JESMOND, NEWCASTLE	28/01/1961	LEFT BACK
MORRISON	THOMAS KELLY	21/01/1904	COYLTON, AYRSHIRE		RIGHT BACK
MORRISON	WILLIAM	31/03/1934	EDINBURGH	Dec 2001	RIGHT HALF
MULHALL	GEORGE	08/05/1936	STANDBURN, FALKIRK		OUTSIDE LEFT
MULLIN	JOHN MICHAEL	11/08/1975	BURY		CENTRE FORWARD
MUNRO	ALEXANDER IAIN FORDYCE	24/08/1951	UDDINGSTON, GLASGOW		LEFT BACK
MUNTARI	SULLEYMAN ALI	27/08/1984	KONONGO, GHANA		MIDFIELDER
MURDOCH	DUNCAN BELL	12/06/1860	CROYDON	03/06/1944	FORWARD
MURPHY	DARYL	15/03/1983	WATERFORD		CENTRE FORWARD
MURRAY	JAMES GERALD (JAMIE)	27/12/1958	GLASGOW		MIDFIELDER
MURRAY	JOHN WINNING	24/04/1865	STRATHBLANE, STIRLINGSHIRE	16/09/1922	LEFT BACK+L/R.HALF BACK
MURRAY	WILLIAM	10/03/1900	ABERDEEN	15/12/1961	RIGHT BACK
MURRAY	WILLIAM BRUNTON	15/11/1881	FORRES, MORAYSHIRE	21/04/1929	OUTSIDE LEFT
MWARUWARI	BENJAMIN	13/08/1978	HARARE, ZIMBABWE		FORWARD
MYHRE	THOMAS HARALD	16/10/1973	SARPSBORG, NORWAY		GOALKEEPER
NAISBY	THOMAS HENRY	12/03/1878	SUNDERLAND	03/05/1927	GOALKEEPER
NELSON	COLIN ARMSTRONG	13/03/1938	EAST BOLDON		RIGHT BACK
NESS	HARRY MARSHALL	Q3 1885	SCARBOROUGH	26/06/1957	LEFT/RIGHT BACK
NICHOLL	JAMES MICHAEL	28/02/1956	HAMILTON, ONTARIO, CANADA		RIGHT BACK
NOBLE	RYAN	06/11/1991	MILLFIELD, SUNDERLAND		FORWARD
NORMAN	ANTHONY JOSEPH	24/02/1958	MANCOT, FLINTSHIRE		GOALKEEPER
NOSWORTHY	NYRON PAUL HENRY	11/10/1980	BRIXTON, LONDON		DEFENDER
NUNEZ	MILTON OMAR GARCIA	30/10/1972	TEGUCIGALPA, HONDURAS		CENTRE FORWARD
NYATANGA	LEWIN JOHN	18/08/1988	BURTON-UPON-TRENT		CENTRE BACK
OAKLEY	JAMES ERNEST	10/11/1901	BLYTH	Q3 1972	LEFT/RIGHT BACK
O'DONNELL	DENNIS	Q1 1880	WILLINGTON QUAY		INSIDE RIGHT
O'DONOVAN	ROY SIMON	10/08/1985	CORK		CENTRE FORWARD
OGILVIE	GARY FRANCIS	16/11/1967	DUNDEE		RIGHT BACK
O'HARE	JOHN	24/09/1946	RENTON		INSIDE/CENTRE FORWARD
OLIVER	JAMES HENRY KENNETH (KEN)	10/08/1924	LOUGHBOROUGH	13/05/1994	CENTRE FORWARD/CENTRE HALF
OLIVER	JOHN SIDNEY	1867	SOUTHWICK, SUNDERLAND		LEFT BACK
O'NEILL	JAMES	24/11/1941	MAGHERAMORNE, NR.LARNE		CENTRE FORWARD
ONUOHA	CHINEDUM (NEDUM)	12/11/1986	WARRI, NIGERIA		DEFENDER
ORD	RICHARD JOHN	03/03/1970	MURTON		CENTRE HALF
O'SHEA	JOHN FRANCIS	30/04/1981	WATERFORD		DEFENDER
OSTER	JOHN MORGAN	08/12/1978	BOSTON, LINCS.		MIDFIELDER / WINGER
OUTTERSIDE	MARK JEREMY	13/01/1967	HEXHAM		RIGHT BACK
OVERFIELD	JACK	14/05/1932	OSMONDTHORPE, LEEDS		OUTSIDE LEFT
OWERS	GARY	03/10/1968	NEWCASTLE		MIDFIELDER/RIGHT BACK
PAGE	JOHN ABRAHAM	Q1 1893	SUNDERLAND		OUTSIDE RIGHT
PALLISTER	WILLIAM	Sep 1876	RYHOPE		RIGHT HALF BACK
PALMER	CALVIN IAN	21/10/1940	SKEGNESS		FULL BACK, MIDFIELDER
PARK	ROBERT	05/01/1952	COATBRIDGE		MIDFIELDER
PARKE	JOHN	06/08/1937	BANGOR, N.I.	27/08/2011	FULL BACK
PARKER	CHARLES WILLIAM	21/09/1891	SEAHAM HARBOUR	1980	RIGHT HALF BACK,CENT.HALF
PARKER	RICHARD	14/09/1894	STOCKTON	01/02/1969	CENTRE FORWARD
PASCOE	COLIN JAMES	09/04/1965	BRIDGEND		MIDFIELDER/OUTSIDE LEFT
PATERSON	JOHN WILLIAM (JOCK)	14/12/1896	DUNDEE		CENTRE FORWARD
PAYNE	GEORGE CLARK	17/02/1887	HITCHIN	21/08/1932	INSIDE LEFT
PEACOCK	ANDREW	12/09/1864	KELVINHAUGH, GLASGOW		FORWARD
PEACOCK	WILLIAM McILRAITH	23/02/1867	KELVINHAUGH, GLASGOW		FORWARD
PEARCE	REGINALD STANLEY	12/01/1930	LIVERPOOL		LEFT HALF BACK
PEETERS	TOM	25/09/1978	BORNEM, BELGIUM		MIDFIELDER
PEGG	FRANK EDWARD	02/08/1902	BEESTON, NOTTS.	09/08/1991	OUTSIDE LEFT
PEREZ	LIONEL	24/04/1967	BAGNOLS-SUR-CEZE, FRANCE		GOALKEEPER
PHILIP	GEORGE		DUNDEE		CENTRE FORWARD/INSIDE LEFT
PHILLIPS	KEVIN	25/07/1973	HITCHIN		FORWARD

CAREER RECORDS

Career		League			Play Offs			FA Cup			League Cup			Other			Total		
Start	End	Apps	Sub	Gls	Apps	Sub	Gls	Apps	Sub	Gls	Apps	Sub	Gls	Apps	Sub	Gls	Apps	Sub	Gls
1929	1931	15	0	7	0	0	0	1	0	0	0	0	0	0	0	0	16	0	7
1919	1919	1	0	0	0	0	0	0	0	0	0	0	0	0	0	0	1	0	0
1935	1936	21	0	0	0	0	0	2	0	0	0	0	0	0	0	0	23	0	0
1951	1958	19	0	0	0	0	0	0	0	0	0	0	0	0	0	0	19	0	0
1962	1969	249	4	56	0	0	0	19	0	5	16	1	6	0	0	0	284	5	67
1995	1999	23	12	4	0	0	0	2	1	0	5	1	0	0	0	0	30	14	4
1981	1984	80	0	0	0	0	0	1	0	0	7	0	0	0	0	0	88	0	0
2011	2011	7	2	1	0	0	0	0	0	0	0	0	0	0	0	0	7	2	1
1883	1885	0	0	0	0	0	0	1	0	0	0	0	0	0	0	0	1	0	0
2005	2010	60	50	15	0	0	0	4	1	0	5	4	0	0	0	0	69	55	15
1984	1984	1	0	0	0	0	0	0	0	0	0	0	0	0	0	0	1	0	0
1890	1892	41	0	0	0	0	0	10	0	0	0	0	0	0	0	0	51	0	0
1927	1937	304	0	0	0	0	0	24	0	0	0	0	0	0	0	0	328	0	0
1901	1904	8	0	3	0	0	0	0	0	0	0	0	0	0	0	0	8	0	3
2010	2010	1	7	0	0	0	0	0	0	0	0	0	0	0	0	0	1	7	0
2002	2005	35	2	0	0	0	0	2	0	0	3	0	0	0	0	0	40	2	0
1898	1907	37	0	0	0	0	0	4	0	0	0	0	0	0	0	0	41	0	0
1957	1965	145	0	2	0	0	0	12	0	0	10	0	0	0	0	0	167	0	2
1911	1920	93	0	0	0	0	0	8	0	0	0	0	0	0	0	0	101	0	0
1981	1983	32	0	0	0	0	0	4	0	0	4	0	0	0	0	0	40	0	0
2008	2012	0	5	0	0	0	0	0	1	0	0	0	0	0	0	0	0	6	0
1988	1995	198	0	0	3	0	0	14	0	0	8	0	0	4	0	0	227	0	0
2005	2011	103	11	0	0	0	0	2	0	0	8	1	0	0	0	0	113	12	0
2000	2001	0	1	0	0	0	0	0	0	0	1	0	0	0	0	0	0	2	0
2006	2007	9	2	0	0	0	0	0	0	0	0	0	0	0	0	0	9	2	0
1922	1930	84	0	0	0	0	0	6	0	0	0	0	0	0	0	0	90	0	0
1905	1906	21	0	5	0	0	0	1	0	0	0	0	0	0	0	0	22	0	5
2007	2010	4	13	0	0	0	0	1	0	0	0	1	0	0	0	0	5	14	0
1988	1989	0	1	0	0	0	0	0	0	0	0	1	0	0	1	0	0	3	0
1962	1967	51	0	14	0	0	0	5	0	3	3	0	4	0	0	0	59	0	21
1946	1949	8	0	1	0	0	0	0	0	0	0	0	0	0	0	0	8	0	1
1886	1892	22	0	0	0	0	0	12	0	0	0	0	0	0	0	0	34	0	0
1958	1962	7	0	6	0	0	0	0	0	0	0	0	0	0	0	0	7	0	6
2010	2011	31	0	1	0	0	0	0	0	0	1	0	0	0	0	0	32	0	1
1984	1998	223	20	7	0	1	0	11	1	1	17	5	0	5	1	0	256	28	8
2011	2012	29	0	0	0	0	0	5	0	0	0	0	0	0	0	0	34	0	0
1999	2005	48	20	5	2	0	0	7	3	0	9	2	1	0	0	0	66	25	6
1981	1987	1	0	0	0	0	0	0	0	0	0	0	0	0	0	0	1	0	0
1960	1963	65	0	5	0	0	0	5	0	0	4	0	0	0	0	0	74	0	5
1985	1994	259	9	25	3	0	0	10	2	0	27	1	1	8	1	1	307	13	27
1920	1921	3	0	0	0	0	0	0	0	0	0	0	0	0	0	0	3	0	0
1897	1902	1	0	0	0	0	0	0	0	0	0	0	0	0	0	0	1	0	0
1968	1970	35	6	5	0	0	0	0	0	0	2	0	0	0	0	0	37	6	5
1967	1975	50	15	4	0	0	0	2	0	0	1	0	0	4	0	1	57	15	5
1964	1968	83	3	0	0	0	0	3	0	0	5	0	0	0	0	0	91	3	0
1920	1929	245	0	12	0	0	0	11	0	0	0	0	0	0	0	0	256	0	12
1919	1920	6	0	2	0	0	0	0	0	0	0	0	0	0	0	0	6	0	2
1988	1992	116	10	22	1	0	4	4	2	0	12	0	3	4	0	0	137	12	25
1922	1924	73	0	37	0	0	0	3	0	3	0	0	0	0	0	0	76	0	40
1911	1912	2	0	0	0	0	0	0	0	0	0	0	0	0	0	0	2	0	0
1888	1889	0	0	0	0	0	0	2	0	3	0	0	0	0	0	0	2	0	3
1888	1889	0	0	0	0	0	0	1	0	0	0	0	0	0	0	0	1	0	0
1958	1961	61	0	4	0	0	0	1	0	0	0	0	0	0	0	0	62	0	4
2000	2003	0	0	0	0	0	0	0	0	0	1	0	0	0	0	0	1	0	0
1925	1926	1	0	0	0	0	0	0	0	0	0	0	0	0	0	0	1	0	0
1996	1998	74	1	0	3	0	0	4	0	0	2	0	0	0	0	0	83	1	0
1914	1915	37	0	22	0	0	0	1	0	0	0	0	0	0	0	0	38	0	22
1997	2003	207	1	113	3	0	2	14	0	10	9	1	5	0	0	0	233	2	130

SURNAME	FORENAMES	DOB	BIRTHPLACE	DECEASED	POSITION
PICKERING	NICHOLAS	04/08/1963	NEWCASTLE		MIDFIELDER/LEFT BACK
PIPER	MATTHEW JAMES	29/09/1981	LEICESTER		OUTSIDE RIGHT
PITT	RICHARD ERNEST	22/10/1951	RYHOPE, SUNDERLAND		CENTRE HALF
POOLE	JOHN SMITH (JACK)	Q3 1892	CODNOR, NR.ALFRETON	21/03/1967	LEFT HALF BACK/CENTRE HALF
POOM	MART	03/02/1972	TALLINN, ESTONIA		GOALKEEPER
PORTEOUS	THOMAS STODDART	Q4 1865	NEWCASTLE	23/02/1919	RIGHT BACK
PORTERFIELD	JOHN (IAN)	11/02/1946	DUNFERMLINE	11/09/2007	MIDFIELDER
POULTER	HENRY (HARRY)	24/04/1910	SHINEY ROW	25/02/1985	CENTRE FORWARD
POWER	GEOFFREY	07/04/1899	GRANGETOWN, MIDDLESBROUGH	Q1 1963	INSIDE RIGHT
POWER	LEE MICHAEL	30/06/1972	LEWISHAM		FORWARD
PRICA	RADE	30/06/1980	LJUNGBY, SWEDEN		CENTRE FORWARD
PRINCE	THOMAS	Q1 1897	HETTON-LE-HOLE		INSIDE/OUTSIDE LEFT
PRIOR	GEORGE		EDINBURGH		INSIDE RIGHT/CENT.FORWARD
PRIOR	JACK	02/07/1904	CHOPPINGTON, NORTHUMB.	29/08/1982	OUTSIDE RIGHT
PROCTOR	MARK GERARD	30/01/1961	MIDDLESBROUGH		MIDFIELDER
PROCTOR	MICHAEL ANTHONY	03/10/1980	MONKWEARMOUTH		CENTRE FORWARD
PRUDHOE	MARK	11/11/1963	WASHINGTON		GOALKEEPER
PURDON	EDWARD JOHN	01/03/1930	JOHANNESBURG, S.F.	29/04/2007	CENTRE FORWARD
QUINN	ALAN	13/06/1979	DUBLIN		MIDFIELDER
QUINN	ALBERT	18/04/1920	LANCHESTER, CO.DURHAM	26/06/2008	INSIDE LEFT
QUINN	NIALL JOHN	06/10/1966	DUBLIN		CENTRE FORWARD
RAE	ALEXANDER SCOTT	30/09/1969	GLASGOW		MIDFIELDER
RAINE	JAMES EDMUNDSON	03/03/1886	WINLATON, NEWCASTLE	04/09/1928	OUTSIDE RIGHT
RAISBECK	WILLIAM	22/12/1875	WALLACESTONE, POLMONT	02/11/1946	LEFT/RIGHT HALF BACK
RAMSAY	STANLEY HUNTER	10/08/1904	RYTON	19/07/1939	INSIDE FORWARD
RAMSDEN	BERNARD	08/11/1917	SHEFFIELD	Mar 1976	FULL BACK
RAMSDEN	SIMON PAUL	17/12/1981	BISHOP AUCKLAND		RIGHT BACK
RAYBOULD	SAMUEL	11/06/1875	STAVELEY	17/12/1953	CENTRE FORWARD,INSIDE LEFT
READ	WILLIAM HENRY	Q4 1885	BLACKPOOL		OUTSIDE RIGHT
REDDY	MICHAEL JASON	24/03/1980	GRAIGNAMANAGH, CO. KILKENNY		CENTRE FORWARD
REED	GRAHAM	06/02/1938	KINGS LYNN		LEFT/RIGHT HALF BACK
REID	ANDREW MATTHEW	29/07/1982	DUBLIN		LEFT WINGER
RENNIE	HENRY WILLIAM	25/03/1865	ARBROATH	1909	HALF BACK
REVIE	DONALD GEORGE	10/07/1927	MIDDLESBROUGH	26/05/1989	INSIDE/CENTRE FORWARD
REYNA	CLAUDIO	20/07/1973	LIVINGSTON, NEW JERSEY, USA		MIDFIELDER
REYNOLDS	THOMAS	02/10/1922	FELLING	13/03/1998	OUTSIDE LEFT
RHODES	EPHRAIM	16/08/1882	MIDDLESBROUGH	30/09/1960	FULL BACK
RICHARDSON	JAMES		SCOTLAND		HALF BACK
RICHARDSON	JAMES	1885-89	GLASGOW	31/08/1951	CENTRE FORWARD
RICHARDSON	KIERAN EDWARD	21/10/1984	GREENWICH		MIDFIELDER
RIERA	ARNAU CALDENTEY	01/10/1981	MANACOR, MAJORCA		LEFT MIDFIELDER
RITCHIE	THOMAS GIBB	02/01/1952	EDINBURGH		CENTRE FORWARD
RIVEROS	CRISTIAN MIGUEL NUNEZ	16/10/1982	SALDIVAR, PARAGUAY		MIDFILEDER
ROBINSON	CARL PHILIP	13/10/1976	LLANDRINDOD WELLS		MIDFIELDER
ROBINSON	GEORGE HENRY	11/01/1908	ILKESTON	14/01/1963	OUTSIDE RIGHT
ROBINSON	JOHN (JACKIE)	10/08/1917	SHIREMOOR, NORTHUMB.	30/07/1972	INSIDE RIGHT
ROBINSON	RAYMOND WILSON	Q3 1895	RYTON	06/01/1964	OUTSIDE RIGHT
ROBINSON	ROBERT	27/03/1910	RAINTON	22/01/1989	GOALKEEPER
ROBINSON	ROBERT	23/06/1921	NEWBIGGIN, NORTHUMB.	Q1 1975	GOALKEEPER
ROBINSON	ROBERT SMITH	Oct 1879	SUNDERLAND	1950	INSIDE RIGHT/CENT.FORWARD
ROBINSON	WILLIAM	04/04/1919	WHITBURN	07/10/1992	CENTRE FORWARD
ROBSON	BRYAN STANLEY (POP)	11/11/1945	SUNDERLAND		FORWARD
ROBSON	EDWARD RIDDELL	21/08/1890	HEXHAM	Q1 1977	GOALKEEPER
ROBSON	THOMAS	01/02/1936	SUNDERLAND		CENTRE HALF
RODGERSON	IAN	09/04/1966	HEREFORD		OUTSIDE RIGHT
RODGERSON	RALPH	25/12/1913	SUNDERLAND	18/04/1972	LEFT BACK
ROGAN	ANTHONY GERARD PATRICK	25/03/1966	LENADOON, BELFAST		LEFT BACK/CENTRE HALF
ROGERS	JOHN (JACK)	20/06/1895	HELSTON		INSIDE RIGHT/CENT.FORWARD

CAREER RECORDS

Career		League			Play Offs			FA Cup			League Cup			Other			Total		
Start	End	Apps	Sub	Gls	Apps	Sub	Gls	Apps	Sub	Gls	Apps	Sub	Gls	Apps	Sub	Gls	Apps	Sub	Gls
1979	1986	177	2	18	0	0	0	10	0	0	18	0	0	2	0	0	207	2	18
2002	2005	13	11	0	0	0	0	0	2	0	2	1	0	0	0	0	15	14	0
1967	1975	126	0	7	0	0	0	10	0	0	4	0	0	4	1	0	144	1	7
1919	1924	144	0	1	0	0	0	8	0	1	0	0	0	0	0	0	152	0	2
2002	2006	58	0	1	2	0	0	6	0	0	1	1	0	0	0	0	67	1	1
1889	1894	79	0	0	0	0	0	14	0	0	0	0	0	0	0	0	93	0	0
1967	1977	217	12	17	0	0	0	19	0	2	9	0	0	11	0	0	256	12	19
1931	1932	0	0	0	0	0	0	3	0	2	0	0	0	0	0	0	3	0	2
1919	1922	10	0	0	0	0	0	0	0	0	0	0	0	0	0	0	10	0	0
1993	1993	1	2	0	0	0	0	0	0	0	2	0	1	0	0	0	3	2	1
2008	2009	0	6	1	0	0	0	0	0	0	0	0	0	0	0	0	0	6	1
1897	1906	4	0	0	0	0	0	0	0	0	0	0	0	0	0	0	4	0	0
1901	1903	5	0	0	0	0	0	0	0	0	0	0	0	0	0	0	5	0	0
1923	1927	67	0	10	0	0	0	4	0	1	0	0	0	0	0	0	71	0	11
1983	1987	115	2	19	2	0	2	6	0	0	13	0	2	0	0	0	136	2	23
1996	2004	15	23	3	0	0	0	4	2	2	3	1	0	0	0	0	22	26	5
1981	1984	7	0	0	0	0	0	0	0	0	0	0	0	0	0	0	7	0	0
1954	1957	90	0	39	0	0	0	6	0	3	0	0	0	0	0	0	96	0	42
2003	2004	5	1	0	0	0	0	0	0	0	0	0	0	0	0	0	5	1	0
1946	1948	6	0	2	0	0	0	0	0	0	0	0	0	0	0	0	6	0	2
1996	2002	168	35	61	2	0	2	8	1	2	5	1	4	0	0	0	183	37	69
1996	2001	90	24	12	0	2	0	7	0	0	12	1	3	0	0	0	109	27	15
1906	1908	25	0	6	0	0	0	3	0	1	0	0	0	0	0	0	28	0	7
1898	1901	69	0	8	0	0	0	5	0	0	0	0	0	0	0	0	74	0	8
1924	1928	24	0	14	0	0	0	1	0	0	0	0	0	0	0	0	25	0	14
1948	1950	12	0	0	0	0	0	1	0	0	0	0	0	0	0	0	13	0	0
1998	2004	0	0	0	0	0	0	0	1	0	0	0	0	0	0	0	0	1	0
1907	1908	27	0	12	0	0	0	1	0	0	0	0	0	0	0	0	28	0	12
1910	1911	4	0	2	0	0	0	0	0	0	0	0	0	0	0	0	4	0	2
1999	2004	0	10	1	0	0	0	0	1	0	2	1	1	0	0	0	2	12	2
1954	1959	5	0	0	0	0	0	2	0	0	0	0	0	0	0	0	7	0	0
2008	2011	49	19	4	0	0	0	3	2	0	4	3	2	0	0	0	56	24	6
1888	1889	0	0	0	0	0	0	1	0	0	0	0	0	0	0	0	1	0	0
1956	1958	64	0	15	0	0	0	2	0	0	0	0	0	0	0	0	66	0	15
2001	2003	28	0	3	0	0	0	0	0	0	1	0	1	0	0	0	29	0	4
1946	1954	168	0	18	0	0	0	4	0	0	0	0	0	0	0	0	172	0	18
1902	1908	115	0	5	0	0	0	5	0	0	0	0	0	0	0	0	120	0	5
1887	1888	0	0	0	0	0	0	4	0	0	0	0	0	0	0	0	4	0	0
1912	1914	35	0	20	0	0	0	10	0	10	0	0	0	0	0	0	45	0	30
2007	2012	123	10	14	0	0	0	8	0	1	6	1	0	0	0	0	137	11	15
2006	2009	0	1	0	0	0	0	0	0	0	1	0	0	0	0	0	1	1	0
1981	1982	32	3	8	0	0	0	3	0	0	2	0	3	0	0	0	37	3	11
2010	2012	5	7	1	0	0	0	1	0	0	1	0	0	0	0	0	7	7	1
2004	2006	49	3	5	1	1	0	2	0	0	3	0	0	0	0	0	55	4	5
1927	1931	31	0	8	0	0	0	1	0	0	0	0	0	0	0	0	32	0	8
1946	1949	82	0	32	0	0	0	3	0	2	0	0	0	0	0	0	85	0	34
1920	1922	10	0	2	0	0	0	0	0	0	0	0	0	0	0	0	10	0	2
1926	1931	34	0	0	0	0	0	4	0	0	0	0	0	0	0	0	38	0	0
1947	1952	31	0	0	0	0	0	2	0	0	0	0	0	0	0	0	33	0	0
1902	1904	24	0	7	0	0	0	0	0	0	0	0	0	1	0	0	25	0	7
1934	1946	24	0	14	0	0	0	0	0	0	0	0	0	0	0	0	24	0	14
1974	1984	146	8	60	0	0	0	8	0	4	10	2	3	8	0	1	172	10	68
1922	1924	38	0	0	0	0	0	2	0	0	0	0	0	0	0	0	40	0	0
1953	1960	5	0	0	0	0	0	0	0	0	0	0	0	0	0	0	5	0	0
1993	1995	5	5	0	0	0	0	0	0	0	0	0	0	0	0	0	5	5	0
1935	1939	5	0	0	0	0	0	0	0	0	0	0	0	0	0	0	5	0	0
1991	1993	45	1	1	0	0	0	8	0	0	1	0	0	2	0	0	56	1	1
1923	1925	7	0	2	0	0	0	2	0	1	0	0	0	0	0	0	9	0	3

SURNAME	FORENAMES	DOB	BIRTHPLACE	DECEASED	POSITION
ROOKS	RICHARD	29/05/1940	SUNDERLAND		CENTRE HALF
ROONEY	PETER	Dec 1865	MONKWEARMOUTH	01/01/1906	FORWARD
ROOSE	LEIGH RICHMOND (DICK)	26/11/1877	HOLT, NEAR WREXHAM	07/10/1916	GOALKEEPER
ROSSITER	MARK	27/05/1983	SLIGO, IRELAND		RIGHT BACK
ROSTRON	JOHN WILFRED (WILF)	29/09/1956	SUNDERLAND		MIDFIELDER
ROUTLEDGE	RONALD WRIGHT	14/10/1937	ASHINGTON		GOALKEEPER
ROWELL	GARY	06/06/1957	SEAHAM		CENTRE FORWARD + MIDFIELDER
ROWELL	JOHN FREDERICK (FRED)	31/12/1918	SEAHAM	09/03/1988	OUTSIDE LEFT
ROWLANDSON	THOMAS SOWERBY		BARTON, NR. DARLINGTON	15/09/1916	GOALKEEPER
ROY	ERIC SERGE	26/09/1967	NICE, FRANCE		MIDFIELDER
RUSH	DAVID	15/05/1971	SUNDERLAND		CENTRE FORWARD
RUSSELL	CRAIG STEWART	04/02/1974	JARROW		CENTRE FORWARD
RUSSELL	JAMES WALKER	14/09/1916	EDINBURGH	17/08/1994	INSIDE/OUTSIDE RIGHT
RYAN	RICHARD	06/01/1985	KILKENNY, IRELAND		MIDFIELDER
SADDINGTON	NIGEL JOHN	09/12/1965	SUNDERLAND		CENTRE HALF
SAMPSON	IAN	14/11/1968	WAKEFIELD		CENTRE HALF
SAUNDERS	PERCY KITCHENER	Q3 1916	NEWHAVEN	02/03/1942	INSIDE FORWARD
SAXTON	ARTHUR WILLIAM	28/08/1874	BREASTON, DERBYSHIRE		OUTSIDE LEFT
SCHWARZ	STEFAN HANS JURGEN	18/04/1969	KULLADAL, SWEDEN		MIDFIELDER
SCOTSON	REGINALD	23/09/1919	STOCKTON	15/02/1999	HALF BACK
SCOTT	HENRY	04/08/1898	NEWBURN, NORTHUMB.		INSIDE RIGHT
SCOTT	JOHN HAMILTON (JOCK)	09/06/1867	WHIFFLET, COATBRIDGE	19/01/1932	INSIDE/OUTSIDE LEFT
SCOTT	LESLIE	Q2 1895	SUNDERLAND		GOALKEEPER
SCOTT	MARTIN	07/01/1968	SHEFFIELD		LEFT BACK
SCOTT	MATTHEW	Q3 1867	NEWCASTLE	27/12/1897	GOALKEEPER
SCOTT	THOMAS	06/04/1904	NEWCASTLE	24/12/1979	OUTSIDE RIGHT
SCOTT	WALTER	Sep 1886	WORKSOP	16/09/1955	GOALKEEPER
SESSEGNON	STEPHANE	01/06/1984	ALLAHE, BENIN		MIDFIELDER
SHACKLETON	LEONARD FRANCIS	03/05/1922	BRADFORD	28/11/2000	OUTSIDE LEFT/INSIDE FORWARD
SHARKEY	DOMINIC	04/05/1943	HELENSBURGH		CENTRE FORWARD
SHAW	HAROLD VICTOR	22/05/1905	HEDNESFORD, STAFFS.	14/06/1984	LEFT BACK
SHAW	JOHN F.				INSIDE LEFT
SHAW	JOSEPH	1882	DURHAM		CENTRE FORWARD
SHEPPEARD	HOWARD THOMAS	31/01/1933	YNYSYBWL, GLAMORGAN		INSIDE LEFT
SHERWIN	HARRY	Q4 1893	WALSALL	08/01/1953	CENTRE HALF/HALF BACK
SHORE	ALBERT VICTOR (VICTOR)	11/02/1897	DUDLEY	Q4 1981	INSIDE FORWARD
SHOULDER	JAMES	11/09/1946	ESH WINNING, CO.DURHAM		LEFT BACK
SIDDALL	BARRY ALFRED	12/09/1954	BROMBOROUGH		GOALKEEPER
SIMPSON	DANIEL PETER	04/01/1987	SALFORD		RIGHT BACK
SIMPSON	WILLIAM	1877	SUNDERLAND	20/03/1962	INSIDE RIGHT
SLACK	MELVYN	07/03/1944	COUNDON, CO. DURHAM		HALF BACK
SMALL	JOHN	29/10/1889	SOUTH BANK, MIDDLESBROUGH	09/12/1946	RIGHT HALF BACK
SMART	JOSEPH				HALF BACK
SMEATON	JOHN RAYMOND	05/08/1915	PERTH	17/02/1984	INSIDE LEFT
SMELLIE	ROBERT J.	1869-70	DALZIEL, LANARKSHIRE		LEFT BACK
SMITH	ANTHONY	21/09/1971	PENNYWELL, SUNDERLAND		LEFT BACK
SMITH	DANIEL	05/10/1963	SUNDERLAND		FULL BACK
SMITH	JOHN	1866	AYRSHIRE	03/02/1911	INSIDE/OUTSIDE RIGHT
SMITH	KENNETH	21/05/1932	SOUTH SHIELDS		CENTRE FORWARD
SMITH	MARTIN GEOFFREY	13/11/1974	SUNDERLAND		OUTSIDE LEFT
SMITH	R.				FORWARD
SMITH	THOMAS WILLIAM	22/05/1980	HEMEL HEMPSTEAD		FORWARD
SNELL	ALBERT EDWARD	07/02/1931	DUNSCROFT, YORKSHIRE	31/03/2007	LEFT HALF BACK
SNODIN	IAN	15/08/1963	ROTHERHAM		MIDFIELDER
SORENSEN	THOMAS LOVENDAHL	12/06/1976	FREDERICIA, DENMARK		GOALKEEPER
SPAIN	JACQUES				HALF BACK
SPENCE	ALAN NICHOLSON	07/02/1940	SEAHAM		CENTRE FORWARD
SPENCE	JOHN		SCOTLAND		OUTSIDE RIGHT/L. HALF BACK

CAREER RECORDS

Career		League			Play Offs			FA Cup			League Cup			Other			Total		
Start	End	Apps	Sub	Gls	Apps	Sub	Gls	Apps	Sub	Gls	Apps	Sub	Gls	Apps	Sub	Gls	Apps	Sub	Gls
1957	1965	34	0	2	0	0	0	2	0	0	4	0	1	0	0	0	40	0	3
1886	1887	0	0	0	0	0	0	2	0	0	0	0	0	0	0	0	2	0	0
1908	1911	92	0	0	0	0	0	7	0	0	0	0	0	0	0	0	99	0	0
1999	2004	0	0	0	0	0	0	0	1	0	2	0	0	0	0	0	2	1	0
1977	1979	75	1	17	0	0	0	4	0	0	5	1	1	1	2	0	85	4	18
1954	1958	2	0	0	0	0	0	0	0	0	0	0	0	0	0	0	2	0	0
1972	1984	229	25	88	0	0	0	15	1	4	19	2	8	6	0	3	269	28	103
1937	1938	0	0	0	0	0	0	0	0	0	0	0	0	1	0	0	1	0	0
1904	1904	12	0	0	0	0	0	0	0	0	0	0	0	0	0	0	12	0	0
1999	2001	20	7	0	0	0	0	2	0	0	5	0	1	0	0	0	27	7	1
1988	1994	40	19	12	0	0	0	9	0	1	1	1	0	1	1	0	51	21	13
1990	1997	103	47	31	0	0	0	6	3	2	7	6	1	2	0	0	118	56	34
1934	1938	5	0	0	0	0	0	0	0	0	0	0	0	0	0	0	5	0	0
2001	2005	0	2	0	0	0	0	0	0	0	0	0	0	0	0	0	0	2	0
1985	1988	3	0	0	0	0	0	1	0	0	0	0	0	1	0	0	5	0	0
1990	1994	13	4	1	0	0	0	0	2	0	1	0	0	0	1	0	14	7	1
1934	1939	26	0	6	0	0	0	0	0	0	0	0	0	0	0	0	26	0	6
1897	1899	19	0	2	0	0	0	0	0	0	0	0	0	0	0	0	19	0	2
1999	2003	62	5	3	0	0	0	6	0	0	2	1	0	0	0	0	70	6	3
1939	1950	61	0	1	0	0	0	0	0	0	0	0	0	0	0	0	61	0	1
1922	1925	2	0	0	0	0	0	0	0	0	0	0	0	0	0	0	2	0	0
1889	1897	96	0	25	0	0	0	15	0	5	0	0	0	0	0	0	111	0	30
1912	1922	91	0	0	0	0	0	4	0	0	0	0	0	0	0	0	95	0	0
1994	1999	104	2	9	0	0	0	6	0	0	14	0	2	0	0	0	124	2	11
1892	1897	1	0	0	0	0	0	0	0	0	0	0	0	0	0	0	1	0	0
1922	1924	2	0	0	0	0	0	0	0	0	0	0	0	0	0	0	2	0	0
1911	1912	34	0	0	0	0	0	4	0	0	0	0	0	0	0	0	38	0	0
2011	2012	49	1	10	0	0	0	5	0	1	1	0	0	0	0	0	55	1	11
1948	1957	320	0	97	0	0	0	28	0	3	0	0	0	0	0	0	348	0	100
1958	1966	99	0	51	0	0	0	12	0	8	6	0	3	0	0	0	117	0	62
1930	1936	195	0	4	0	0	0	22	0	1	0	0	0	0	0	0	217	0	5
1906	1906	1	0	0	0	0	0	0	0	0	0	0	0	0	0	0	1	0	0
1905	1907	31	0	14	0	0	0	4	0	1	0	0	0	0	0	0	35	0	15
1951	1955	1	0	0	0	0	0	0	0	0	0	0	0	0	0	0	1	0	0
1913	1921	28	0	0	0	0	0	1	0	0	0	0	0	0	0	0	29	0	0
1920	1921	5	0	1	0	0	0	0	0	0	0	0	0	0	0	0	5	0	1
1962	1969	3	0	0	0	0	0	0	0	0	0	0	0	0	0	0	3	0	0
1976	1982	167	0	0	0	0	0	9	0	0	11	0	0	5	0	0	192	0	0
2007	2007	13	1	0	0	0	0	0	0	0	0	0	0	0	0	0	13	1	0
1897	1902	3	0	1	0	0	0	0	0	0	0	0	0	0	0	0	3	0	1
1961	1965	2	0	1	0	0	0	0	0	0	0	0	0	0	0	0	2	0	1
1912	1913	1	0	0	0	0	0	0	0	0	0	0	0	0	0	0	1	0	0
1885	1888	0	0	0	0	0	0	1	0	0	0	0	0	0	0	0	1	0	0
1938	1945	28	0	4	0	0	0	5	0	1	0	0	0	0	0	0	33	0	5
1892	1893	23	0	0	0	0	0	2	0	0	0	0	0	0	0	0	25	0	0
1988	1995	19	1	0	0	0	0	0	0	0	5	0	0	0	0	0	24	1	0
2003	2006	1	2	0	0	0	0	0	0	0	1	1	0	0	0	0	2	3	0
1889	1892	24	0	2	0	0	0	8	0	2	0	0	0	0	0	0	32	0	4
1948	1953	5	0	2	0	0	0	0	0	0	0	0	0	0	0	0	5	0	2
1990	1999	90	29	25	0	0	0	7	3	1	10	6	2	0	0	0	107	38	28
1885	1888	0	0	0	0	0	0	4	0	0	0	0	0	0	0	0	4	0	0
2003	2004	22	13	4	0	2	0	3	1	4	0	0	0	0	0	0	25	16	8
1949	1955	9	0	1	0	0	0	0	0	0	0	0	0	0	0	0	9	0	1
1994	1994	6	0	0	0	0	0	0	0	0	0	0	0	0	0	0	6	0	0
1998	2003	171	0	0	0	0	0	13	0	0	13	0	0	0	0	0	197	0	0
1887	1888	0	0	0	0	0	0	1	0	0	0	0	0	0	0	0	1	0	0
1955	1960	5	0	1	0	0	0	0	0	0	0	0	0	0	0	0	5	0	1
1889	1891	5	0	2	0	0	0	0	0	0	0	0	0	0	0	0	5	0	2

SURNAME	FORENAMES	DOB	BIRTHPLACE	DECEASED	POSITION
SPUHLER	JOHN OSWALD	18/09/1917	FULWELL, SUNDERLAND	07/01/2007	OUTSIDE RIGHT/C.FORWARD
STALEY	CLIVE HOWARD VICTOR	14/05/1899	NEWHALL, DERBYSHIRE	18/03/1985	CENTRE FORWARD
STANNARD	PAUL	17/01/1895	WARWICK	24/11/1982	CENTRE FORWARD
STEAD	JONATHAN GRAEME	07/04/1983	HUDDERSFIELD		CENTRE FORWARD
STELLING	JOHN GRAHAM SURTEES (JACK)	23/05/1924	WASHINGTON	29/03/1993	RIGHT BACK
STEPHENSON	JAMES	10/02/1895	NEW DELAVAL	Feb 1958	OUTSIDE RIGHT/INSIDE FORWARD
STEVENSON	JOHN	1870	KILBIRNIE		RIGHT HALF BACK
STEWART	DUNCAN SMART	08/09/1900	DUNDEE		RIGHT BACK
STEWART	PAUL ANDREW	07/10/1964	MANCHESTER		MIDFIELD / FORWARD
STEWART	SAMUEL				FORWARD
STEWART	THOMAS WORLEY	18/02/1881	SUNDERLAND	03/11/1955	RIGHT BACK
STEWART	WILLIAM MARCUS PAUL	07/11/1972	BRISTOL		FORWARD
STOKES	ANTHONY	25/07/1988	DUBLIN		CENTRE FORWARD
STONEHAM	JOHN	15/06/1892	WITHAM, ESSEX		GOALKEEPER
STRONACH	PETER	01/09/1956	SEAHAM		MIDFIELDER
STUBBS	ALAN	06/10/1971	KIRKBY		CENTRE BACK
STUCKEY	BRUCE GEORGE	19/02/1947	TORQUAY		OUTSIDE/CENTRE FORWARD
SUGGETT	COLIN	30/12/1948	WASHINGTON		INSIDE FORWARD
SUMMERBEE	NICHOLAS JOHN	26/08/1971	ALTRINCHAM		RIGHT WINGER
SWINBURNE	TREVOR	20/06/1953	EAST RAINTON, CO.DURHAM		GOALKEEPER
SWINDLEHURST	DAVID	06/01/1956	EDGWARE, LONDON		CENTRE FORWARD
SYMM	COLIN	26/11/1946	DUNSTON		MIDFIELDER
TAINIO	TEEMU	27/11/1979	TORNIO, FINLAND		MIDFIELDER
TAIT	THOMAS SOMERVILLE	13/09/1879	CARLUKE, LANARKSHIRE		RIGHT HALF BACK
TAYLOR	ERNEST	02/09/1925	SUNDERLAND	09/04/1985	INSIDE FORWARD
TAYLOR	RICHARD WILLIAM	20/06/1951	SILKSWORTH		OUTSIDE LEFT
TEMPLE	JAMES LESLIE	16/09/1904	SCARBOROUGH	15/05/1960	OUTSIDE RIGHT
TERNENT	FRANCIS STANLEY (STAN)	16/06/1946	FELLING		MIDFIELDER
THIRLWELL	PAUL	13/02/1979	SPRINGWELL, WASHINGTON		MIDFIELDER
THOME	EMERSON AUGUSTO	30/03/1972	PORTO ALEGRE, BRAZIL		CENTRE HALF
THOMPSON					HALF BACK
THOMPSON	ANDREW	05/06/1883	SUNDERLAND		OUTSIDE RIGHT
THOMPSON	FREDERICK T.	28/04/1875	SOUTH HETTON, CO.DURHAM	13/01/1958	GOALKEEPER
THOMPSON	HARRY	29/04/1915	MANSFIELD	29/01/2000	INSIDE/CENTRE FORWARD
THOMPSON	JOHN WILLIAM (WILLIAM)	1887	ALNWICK		INSIDE/OUTSIDE RIGHT
THOMSON	CHARLES BELLANY	12/06/1878	PRESTONPANS	06/02/1936	CENTRE HALF
THOMSON	CHARLES MORGAN	11/12/1910	POLLOKSHAWS, GLASGOW	08/05/1984	RIGHT HALF BACK
THOMSON	ROBERT W.	24/10/1905	FALKIRK		LEFT BACK
THORLEY	ERNEST (CLIFF)	12/11/1913	DENABY, DONCASTER		OUTSIDE LEFT
THORNTON	SEAN	18/05/1983	DROGHEDA, IRELAND		MIDFIELDER
THORPE	JAMES HORATIO	16/09/1913	JARROW	05/02/1936	GOALKEEPER
THREADGOLD	JOSEPH HENRY (HARRY)	06/11/1924	TATTENHALL, CHESHIRE	Dec 1996	GOALKEEPER
TINSLEY	WALTER EDWARD	10/08/1891	IRONVILLE, NR.ALFRETON	07/03/1966	INSIDE LEFT
TODD	COLIN	12/12/1948	CHESTER-LE-STREET		HALF BACK
TOMLIN	JOHN (JACK)	1882-83	SEAHAM		CENTRE HALF
TONES	JOHN DAVID	03/12/1950	SILKSWORTH		CENTRE HALF
TOSELAND	GEOFFREY VINCENT	31/01/1931	KETTERING		OUTSIDE LEFT
TOWERS	MARK ANTHONY (TONY)	13/04/1952	MANCHESTER		MIDFIELDER
TRAIN	RAYMOND	10/02/1951	NUNEATON		MIDFIELDER
TRAVERS	BERNARD (BARNEY)	29/08/1894	SUNDERLAND	16/02/1955	INSIDE LEFT/CENTRE FORWARD
TROUGHEAR	WILLIAM B.	Q2 1885	COCKERMOUTH	15/10/1955	RIGHT BACK
TUEART	DENNIS	27/11/1949	NEWCASTLE		OUTSIDE LEFT
TURNBULL	RONALD WILLIAM	18/07/1922	NEWBIGGIN, NORTHUMB.	17/11/1966	CENTRE FORWARD
TURNER	CHRISTOPHER ROBERT	15/09/1958	SHEFFIELD		GOALKEEPER
TURNER	MICHAEL THOMAS	09/11/1983	LEWISHAM		CENTRAL DEFENDER
TURNER	NEIL McD.	07/10/1892	HUTCHESONTOWN, GLASGOW		OUTSIDE RIGHT
URSEM	LOEK ALOYSIUS J. MARIA	07/01/1958	AMSTERDAM, NETHERLANDS		MIDFIELDER
URWIN	THOMAS	05/02/1896	HASWELL, CO.DURHAM	07/05/1968	INSIDE/OUTSIDE RIGHT

CAREER RECORDS

Career		League			Play Offs			FA Cup			League Cup			Other			Total		
Start	End	Apps	Sub	Gls	Apps	Sub	Gls	Apps	Sub	Gls	Apps	Sub	Gls	Apps	Sub	Gls	Apps	Sub	Gls
1932	1945	35	0	4	0	0	0	0	0	0	0	0	0	1	0	0	36	0	4
1921	1922	1	0	0	0	0	0	0	0	0	0	0	0	0	0	0	1	0	0
1921	1923	13	0	2	0	0	0	1	0	1	0	0	0	0	0	0	14	0	3
2005	2007	22	13	2	0	0	0	2	0	0	2	1	0	0	0	0	26	14	2
1944	1958	259	0	8	0	0	0	13	0	0	0	0	0	0	0	0	272	0	8
1921	1922	21	0	2	0	0	0	1	0	0	0	0	0	0	0	0	22	0	2
1889	1890	0	0	0	0	0	0	1	0	0	0	0	0	0	0	0	1	0	0
1922	1924	1	0	0	0	0	0	0	0	0	0	0	0	0	0	0	1	0	0
1995	1997	31	5	5	0	0	0	0	0	0	3	0	0	0	0	0	34	5	5
1887	1889	0	0	0	0	0	0	4	0	4	0	0	0	0	0	0	4	0	4
1904	1905	3	0	0	0	0	0	2	0	0	0	0	0	0	0	0	5	0	0
2002	2005	77	25	31	2	0	2	7	2	2	5	1	4	0	0	0	91	28	39
2007	2009	15	21	3	0	0	0	0	0	0	1	1	2	0	0	0	16	22	5
1923	1927	13	0	0	0	0	0	1	0	0	0	0	0	0	0	0	14	0	0
1972	1978	2	1	0	0	0	0	0	0	0	0	0	0	0	0	0	2	1	0
2005	2006	8	2	1	0	0	0	1	0	0	0	0	0	0	0	0	9	2	1
1967	1971	24	2	2	0	0	0	1	0	0	2	0	0	0	1	0	27	3	2
1964	1969	83	3	24	0	0	0	3	0	1	4	0	0	0	0	0	90	3	25
1997	2001	87	6	7	3	0	1	4	1	0	6	1	0	0	0	0	100	8	8
1968	1977	10	0	0	0	0	0	1	0	0	0	0	0	2	0	0	13	0	0
1985	1987	59	0	11	2	0	0	3	0	0	3	0	0	5	0	0	72	0	11
1969	1972	9	5	0	0	0	0	0	0	0	1	0	0	2	0	0	12	5	0
2008	2010	18	3	0	0	0	0	0	1	0	1	0	1	0	0	0	19	4	1
1906	1912	182	0	2	0	0	0	14	0	0	0	0	0	0	0	0	196	0	2
1958	1961	68	0	11	0	0	0	3	0	0	0	0	0	0	0	0	71	0	11
1967	1972	0	1	0	0	0	0	0	0	0	0	0	0	0	0	0	0	1	0
1931	1933	31	0	12	0	0	0	3	0	0	0	0	0	0	0	0	34	0	12
1974	1976	0	0	0	0	0	0	0	0	0	0	0	0	2	0	0	2	0	0
1995	2004	55	22	0	0	0	0	5	2	0	6	2	1	0	0	0	66	26	1
2000	2003	43	1	2	0	0	0	5	0	0	4	0	0	0	0	0	52	1	2
1884	1885	0	0	0	0	0	0	1	0	0	0	0	0	0	0	0	1	0	0
1905	1905	2	0	0	0	0	0	0	0	0	0	0	0	0	0	0	2	0	0
1894	1896	2	0	0	0	0	0	0	0	0	0	0	0	0	0	0	2	0	0
1938	1945	11	0	1	0	0	0	3	0	0	0	0	0	0	0	0	14	0	1
1907	1910	34	0	15	0	0	0	0	0	0	0	0	0	0	0	0	34	0	15
1908	1919	236	0	3	0	0	0	28	0	3	0	0	0	0	0	0	264	0	6
1931	1940	237	0	7	0	0	0	24	0	1	0	0	0	2	0	0	263	0	8
1927	1928	19	0	0	0	0	0	3	0	0	0	0	0	0	0	0	22	0	0
1932	1934	4	0	0	0	0	0	0	0	0	0	0	0	0	0	0	4	0	0
2002	2005	28	21	9	1	1	0	5	4	0	4	0	0	0	0	0	38	26	9
1930	1936	123	0	0	0	0	0	16	0	0	0	0	0	0	0	0	139	0	0
1952	1953	35	0	0	0	0	0	3	0	0	0	0	0	0	0	0	38	0	0
1912	1914	10	0	3	0	0	0	0	0	0	0	0	0	0	0	0	10	0	3
1964	1971	170	3	3	0	0	0	10	0	0	4	0	0	4	0	0	188	3	3
1905	1906	13	0	1	0	0	0	0	0	0	0	0	0	0	0	0	13	0	1
1966	1973	2	4	0	0	0	0	2	0	0	0	0	0	1	1	1	5	5	1
1948	1955	6	0	1	0	0	0	0	0	0	0	0	0	0	0	0	6	0	1
1974	1977	108	0	20	0	0	0	6	0	0	6	0	2	4	0	0	124	0	22
1976	1977	31	1	1	0	0	0	1	0	0	4	0	2	0	0	0	36	1	3
1919	1921	58	0	25	0	0	0	5	0	3	0	0	0	0	0	0	63	0	28
1909	1914	100	0	0	0	0	0	8	0	0	0	0	0	0	0	0	108	0	0
1966	1974	173	5	46	0	0	0	17	1	3	6	0	2	12	0	5	208	6	56
1947	1949	40	0	16	0	0	0	3	0	2	0	0	0	0	0	0	43	0	18
1979	1985	195	0	0	0	0	0	7	0	0	21	0	0	0	0	0	223	1	0
2009	2012	67	1	2	0	0	0	5	1	0	3	0	0	0	0	0	75	2	2
1919	1920	1	0	0	0	0	0	0	0	0	0	0	0	0	0	0	1	0	0
1982	1982	0	4	0	0	0	0	0	0	0	0	0	0	0	0	0	0	4	0
1930	1936	50	0	5	0	0	0	5	0	1	0	0	0	0	0	0	55	0	6

SURNAME	FORENAMES	DOB	BIRTHPLACE	DECEASED	POSITION
USHER	BRIAN	11/03/1944	BROOMSIDE, NR.DURHAM		OUTSIDE RIGHT
VARGA	STANISLAV	08/10/1972	LIPANY, CZECHOSLOVAKIA		CENTRE HALF
VAUGHAN	DAVID OWEN	18/02/1983	ABERGELE, CONWY		MIDFIELDER
VENISON	BARRY	16/08/1964	STANLEY, CO.DURHAM		RIGHT BACK/MIDFIELDER
VINALL	EDWARD JOHN (JACK)	16/12/1910	WITTON, BIRMINGHAM	26/05/1997	CENTRE FORWARD
VINCENT	ROBERT GEORGE	23/11/1962	NEWCASTLE		MIDFIELDER
WADDLE	CHRISTOPHER ROLAND	14/12/1960	HEWORTH, GATESHEAD		OUTSIDE LEFT
WAGHORN	MARTYN THOMAS	23/01/1990	SOUTH SHIELDS		FORWARD
WAGSTAFFE	THOMAS DANIEL	18/06/1897	DINAPORE, INDIA		CENTRE FORWARD
WAINWRIGHT	NEIL	04/11/1977	WARRINGTON		MIDFIELDER
WAKEHAM	PETER FRANCIS	14/03/1936	KINGSBRIDGE, DEVON		GOALKEEPER
WALDRON	COLIN	22/06/1948	BRISTOL		CENTRE HALF
WALKER	CLIVE	26/05/1957	OXFORD		OUTSIDE LEFT
WALKER	JOHN				FULL BACK
WALKER	NIGEL STEPHEN	07/04/1959	GATESHEAD		MIDFIELDER
WALLACE	IAN ANDREW	23/05/1956	GLASGOW		FORWARD
WALLACE	ROBERT		PAISLEY		INSIDE RIGHT
WALLACE	ROSS	23/05/1985	DUNDEE		LEFT MIDFIELDER
WALLACE	THOMAS HALL	01/07/1906	JARROW	12/04/1939	CENTRE HALF
WALSH	WILLIAM	04/12/1923	EASINGTON		CENTRE HALF/HALF BACK
WALSHAW	KENNETH	28/08/1918	TYNEMOUTH	16/05/1979	INSIDE LEFT
WARD	DARREN	11/05/1974	WORKSOP		GOALKEEPER
WARD	ROBERT	1881	GREENOCK		GOALKEEPER
WARDLE	HENRY	Q4 1881	SUNDERLAND	28/02/1918	INSIDE LEFT
WATKINS	WALTER MARTIN (MARK)	Q1 1880	LLANWNOG, MONTGOMERYSHIRE	14/05/1942	CENTRE FORWARD
WATSON	DAVID VERNON	05/10/1946	STAPLEFORD, NOTTS.		CENTRE FORWARD/CENTRE HALF
WATSON	EDWARD	1899	SUNDERLAND		RIGHT BACK
WATSON	IAN	05/02/1960	NORTH SHIELDS		GOALKEEPER
WATSON	JAMES	04/10/1877	LARKHALL, LANARKSHIRE	12/06/1942	LEFT BACK
WATSON	JAMES	1883	INVERNESS		RIGHT HALF BACK/RIGHT BACK
WATSON	WILLIAM	07/03/1920	BOLTON-ON-DEARNE, YORKS	24/04/2004	RIGHT HALF BACK/FORWARD
WAUGH	JOHN		SLAMANANN, SCOTLAND		CENTRE FORWARD
WEBB	ISAAC (IKE)	10/10/1874	WORCESTER	Mar 1950	GOALKEEPER
WEDDLE	DEREK KEITH	27/12/1935	NEWCASTLE		CENTRE FORWARD
WEIR	ALAN	01/09/1959	SOUTH SHIELDS		CENTRE HALF
WELBECK	DANIEL NII TACKIE MENSAH	26/11/1990	LONGSIGHT, MANCHESTER		FORWARD
WELSBY	ARTHUR	17/11/1902	ASHTON-IN-MAKERFIELD	24/04/1980	OUTSIDE FORWARD
WELSH	ANDREW PETER DAVID	24/11/1983	MANCHESTER		OUTSIDE LEFT
WEST	COLIN	13/11/1962	WALLSEND		CENTRE FORWARD
WESTWOOD	KEIREN	23/10/1984	MANCHESTER		GOALKEEPER
WHARTON	SEAN ROBERT	31/10/1968	NEWPORT		MIDFIELDER
WHELAN	WILLIAM	20/02/1906	AIRDRIE	17/12/1982	LEFT HALF BACK/FULL BACK
WHIPP	PERCY LEONARD	28/06/1893	GLASGOW	18/10/1962	INSIDE RIGHT
WHITBOURN	JOHN GILES	Q1 1885	FARNHAM		GOALKEEPER
WHITE	DALE	17/03/1968	SUNDERLAND		FORWARD
WHITE	THOMAS	10/11/1924	HIGH HANDENHOLD, CO.DURHAM	Jun 1998	INSIDE FORWARD
WHITEHEAD	DEAN	12/01/1982	ABINGDON		MIDFIELDER
WHITEHURST	WILLIAM	10/06/1957	THURNSCOE, ROTHERHAM		CENTRE FORWARD
WHITELAW	GEORGE	01/01/1937	GLENBURN, PAISLEY	Jan 2004	CENTRE/INSIDE FORWARD
WHITELUM	CLIFFORD	02/12/1919	FARNWORTH, LANCASHIRE	29/08/2000	CENTRE/INSIDE FORWARD
WHITFIELD	MICHAEL	17/10/1962	SUNDERLAND		RIGHT BACK
WHITLEY	JEFF	28/01/1979	NDOLA, ZAMBIA		MIDFIELDER
WHITWORTH	STEPHEN	20/03/1952	ELLISTOWN, NR.COALVILLE, LEICS.		RIGHT BACK
WICKHAM	CONNOR NEIL	31/03/1993	HEREFORD		CENTRE FORWARD
WILKINS	LESLIE	21/07/1907	SWANSEA	Q4 1979	INSIDE RIGHT
WILKINSON	REGINALD GEORGE	26/03/1899	NORWICH	14/09/1946	RIGHT HALF BACK
WILKS	ALWYNE	04/09/1906	DONCASTER or CHESTERFIELD	Q3 1980	OUTSIDE RIGHT
WILLIAMS	DARREN	28/04/1977	MIDDLESBROUGH		MIDFIELDER

CAREER RECORDS

Career		League			Play Offs			FA Cup			League Cup			Other			Total		
Start	End	Apps	Sub	Gls	Apps	Sub	Gls	Apps	Sub	Gls	Apps	Sub	Gls	Apps	Sub	Gls	Apps	Sub	Gls
1959	1965	61	0	5	0	0	0	7	0	1	3	0	1	0	0	0	71	0	7
2000	2008	38	3	2	0	0	0	6	1	0	5	1	0	0	0	0	49	5	2
2011	2012	17	5	2	0	0	0	2	2	0	1	0	0	0	0	0	20	7	2
1979	1986	169	4	2	0	0	0	7	1	0	21	0	0	3	0	1	200	5	3
1931	1933	16	0	2	0	0	0	5	0	1	0	0	0	0	0	0	21	0	3
1979	1982	1	1	0	0	0	0	0	0	0	0	0	0	0	0	0	1	1	0
1997	1997	7	0	1	0	0	0	0	0	0	0	0	0	0	0	0	7	0	1
2006	2010	2	4	0	0	0	0	1	0	0	0	1	0	0	0	0	3	5	0
1923	1924	2	0	0	0	0	0	0	0	0	0	0	0	0	0	0	2	0	0
1998	2001	0	2	0	0	0	0	0	0	0	5	1	0	0	0	0	5	3	0
1958	1962	134	0	0	0	0	0	12	0	0	5	0	0	0	0	0	151	0	0
1977	1978	20	0	1	0	0	0	0	0	0	2	0	0	0	0	0	22	0	1
1984	1985	48	2	10	0	0	0	1	0	0	11	0	6	1	1	1	61	3	17
1893	1894	6	0	0	0	0	0	0	0	0	0	0	0	0	0	0	6	0	0
1983	1984	0	1	0	0	0	0	0	0	0	0	0	0	0	0	0	0	1	0
1985	1986	28	6	6	0	0	0	3	0	0	1	2	0	0	0	0	32	8	6
1928	1929	5	0	0	0	0	0	0	0	0	0	0	0	0	0	0	5	0	0
2006	2008	38	15	8	0	0	0	1	0	0	1	0	0	0	0	0	40	15	8
1931	1933	0	0	0	0	0	0	1	0	0	0	0	0	0	0	0	1	0	0
1942	1953	98	0	1	0	0	0	7	0	0	0	0	0	0	0	0	105	0	1
1944	1947	0	0	0	0	0	0	2	0	1	0	0	0	0	0	0	2	0	1
2006	2009	33	0	0	0	0	0	1	0	0	1	0	0	0	0	0	35	0	0
1906	1908	48	0	0	0	0	0	6	0	0	0	0	0	0	0	0	54	0	0
1900	1905	4	0	2	0	0	0	0	0	0	0	0	0	0	0	0	4	0	2
1904	1905	15	0	9	0	0	0	1	0	0	0	0	0	0	0	0	16	0	9
1970	1975	177	0	27	0	0	0	17	0	5	7	0	0	11	0	1	212	0	33
1920	1921	1	0	0	0	0	0	0	0	0	0	0	0	0	0	0	1	0	0
1976	1982	1	0	0	0	0	0	1	0	0	0	0	0	1	0	0	3	0	0
1900	1907	211	0	0	0	0	0	15	0	0	0	0	0	1	0	0	227	0	0
1903	1905	5	0	0	0	0	0	0	0	0	0	0	0	0	0	0	5	0	0
1946	1954	211	0	15	0	0	0	12	0	1	0	0	0	0	0	0	223	0	16
1913	1914	1	0	0	0	0	0	0	0	0	0	0	0	0	0	0	1	0	0
1904	1906	22	0	0	0	0	0	2	0	0	0	0	0	0	0	0	24	0	0
1952	1956	2	0	0	0	0	0	0	0	0	0	0	0	0	0	0	2	0	0
1977	1979	1	0	0	0	0	0	0	0	0	0	0	0	0	0	0	1	0	0
2010	2011	21	5	6	0	0	0	0	0	0	2	0	0	0	0	0	23	5	6
1931	1932	3	0	1	0	0	0	0	0	0	0	0	0	0	0	0	3	0	1
2004	2007	15	6	1	0	0	0	1	1	1	1	1	0	0	0	0	17	8	2
1978	1985	88	14	21	0	0	0	3	1	2	12	4	5	0	0	0	103	19	28
2011	2012	8	1	0	0	0	0	0	0	0	1	0	0	0	0	0	9	1	0
1985	1989	1	0	0	0	0	0	0	0	0	0	0	0	0	0	0	1	0	0
1927	1932	19	0	0	0	0	0	0	0	0	0	0	0	0	0	0	19	0	0
1922	1922	1	0	0	0	0	0	0	0	0	0	0	0	0	0	0	1	0	0
1904	1905	3	0	0	0	0	0	0	0	0	0	0	0	0	0	0	3	0	0
1983	1988	2	2	0	0	0	0	0	0	0	0	0	0	1	0	0	3	2	0
1945	1947	2	0	1	0	0	0	3	0	1	0	0	0	0	0	0	5	0	2
2004	2009	176	9	13	0	0	0	7	0	1	5	3	0	0	0	0	188	12	14
1988	1988	17	0	3	0	0	0	0	0	0	0	0	0	1	0	0	18	0	3
1958	1959	5	0	0	0	0	0	0	0	0	0	0	0	0	0	0	5	0	0
1938	1947	43	0	18	0	0	0	7	0	1	0	0	0	0	0	0	50	0	19
1979	1983	3	0	0	0	0	0	0	0	0	0	0	0	0	0	0	3	0	0
2003	2004	65	3	2	2	0	0	5	0	0	2	0	0	0	0	0	74	3	2
1979	1981	83	0	0	0	0	0	3	0	0	8	0	0	3	0	0	97	0	0
2011	2012	5	11	1	0	0	0	1	1	0	0	1	0	0	0	0	6	13	1
1929	1930	2	0	0	0	0	0	0	0	0	0	0	0	0	0	0	2	0	0
1923	1924	2	0	0	0	0	0	0	0	0	0	0	0	0	0	0	2	0	0
1927	1929	52	0	2	0	0	0	3	0	0	0	0	0	0	0	0	55	0	2
1996	2004	155	44	4	4	1	0	11	2	0	20	2	2	0	0	0	190	49	6

SUNDERLAND: THE COMPLETE RECORD

SURNAME	FORENAMES	DOB	BIRTHPLACE	DECEASED	POSITION
WILLIAMS	HARRY	1899	HUCKNALL TOKARD, NOTTS.		INSIDE LEFT
WILLIAMS	PAUL ANTHONY	16/08/1965	STRATFORD, LONDON		FORWARD
WILLIAMS	PAUL LESLIE	25/09/1970	LIVERPOOL		RIGHT BACK
WILLIAMSON	JOHN ROBERT	Q1 1887	GATESHEAD		FULL BACK
WILLINGHAM	CHARLES KENNETH (KEN)	01/12/1912	SHEFFIELD	May 1975	RIGHT HALF BACK
WILLIS	DAVID LALTY	Jul 1881	BYKER, NEWCASTLE	26/05/1949	HALF BACK
WILSON	HUGH	18/03/1869	MAUCHLINE, AYRSHIRE	07/04/1940	HALF BACK
WILSON	JOSEPH				INSIDE RIGHT
WOOD	ALBERT	25/04/1903	SEAHAM HARBOUR		INSIDE FORWARD
WOOD	NORMAN	10/08/1932	SUNDERLAND		LEFT HALF BACK
WOOD	WILLIAM	28/12/1927	BARNSLEY		LEFT BACK
WOODS	MARTIN PAUL	01/01/1986	AIRDRIE		OUTSIDE LEFT
WORRALL	WILLIAM EDWARD	Q3 1886	SHILDON		GOALKEEPER
WORTHINGTON	FRANK STUART	23/11/1948	SHELF, NR.HALIFAX		CENTRE FORWARD
WRIGHT	ARTHUR WILLIAM TEMPEST	23/09/1919	BURRADON, NORTHUMB.	27/05/1985	LEFT HALF BACK
WRIGHT	DAVID	05/10/1905	KIRKALDY, FIFESHIRE	Aug 1953	INSIDE/CENTRE FORWARD
WRIGHT	STEPHEN JOHN	08/02/1980	BOOTLE		RIGHT BACK
WRIGHT	THOMAS	20/01/1928	BLAIRHALL, NR DUNFERMLINE	05/05/2011	FORWARD
WYLDE	RODGER JAMES	08/03/1954	SHEFFIELD		CENTRE FORWARD
WYLIE	THOMAS	10/11/1907	LINWOOD, RENFREWSHIRE		INSIDE LEFT/CENTRE FORWARD
YORKE	ANDREW	14/06/1894	TYNEMOUTH	Q4 1977	LEFT BACK
YORKE	CHARLES H.	1882	EDINBURGH		INSIDE RIGHT/CENT.FORWARD
YORKE	DWIGHT EVERSLEY	03/11/1971	CANAAN, TOBAGO		MIDFIELDER
YORSTON	BENJAMIN COLLARD	14/10/1905	NIGG, NR.ABERDEEN	Nov 1977	CENTRE/INSIDE FORWARD
YOUNG	DAVID	12/11/1945	NEWCASTLE		CENTRE HALF
YOUNG	JOHN (JACK)		BURNBANK, LANARKS.		CENTRE FORWARD
YOUNG	ROBERT THORNTON	18/02/1894	BRANDON	06/09/1960	LEFT BACK
ZENDEN	BOUDEWIJN	15/08/1976	MAASTRICHT, NETHERLANDS		MIDFIELDER
ZOETEBIER	EDUARD ANDRAES D.H.J. (EDWIN)	07/05/1970	PURMEREND, NETHERLANDS		GOALKEEPER

CAREER RECORDS

Career		League			Play Offs			FA Cup			League Cup			Other			Total		
Start	End	Apps	Sub	Gls	Apps	Sub	Gls	Apps	Sub	Gls	Apps	Sub	Gls	Apps	Sub	Gls	Apps	Sub	Gls
1920	1921	1	0	0	0	0	0	0	0	0	0	0	0	0	0	0	1	0	0
1995	1995	3	0	0	0	0	0	0	0	0	0	0	0	0	0	0	3	0	0
1987	1993	6	4	0	0	0	0	0	0	0	1	0	0	2	0	0	9	4	0
1914	1915	5	0	0	0	0	0	0	0	0	0	0	0	0	0	0	5	0	0
1945	1947	14	0	0	0	0	0	6	0	0	0	0	0	0	0	0	20	0	0
1901	1907	48	0	2	0	0	0	4	0	0	0	0	0	0	0	0	52	0	2
1890	1899	227	0	42	4	0	0	25	0	5	0	0	0	0	0	0	256	0	47
1896	1897	2	0	0	0	0	0	0	0	0	0	0	0	0	0	0	2	0	0
1927	1931	30	0	11	0	0	0	2	0	0	0	0	0	0	0	0	32	0	11
1954	1957	1	0	0	0	0	0	0	0	0	0	0	0	0	0	0	1	0	0
1948	1951	1	0	0	0	0	0	0	0	0	0	0	0	0	0	0	1	0	0
2005	2006	1	6	0	0	0	0	0	0	0	1	0	0	0	0	0	2	6	0
1908	1911	12	0	0	0	0	0	0	0	0	0	0	0	0	0	0	12	0	0
1982	1983	18	1	2	0	0	0	1	0	0	0	0	0	0	0	0	19	1	2
1934	1955	270	0	13	0	0	0	11	0	1	0	0	0	0	0	0	281	0	14
1927	1930	52	0	7	0	0	0	1	0	1	0	0	0	0	0	0	53	0	8
2002	2008	88	4	2	0	0	0	10	0	0	1	2	0	0	0	0	99	6	2
1949	1955	170	0	52	0	0	0	10	0	3	0	0	0	0	0	0	180	0	55
1984	1984	8	3	3	0	0	0	0	0	0	4	1	2	0	0	0	12	4	5
1936	1938	7	0	3	0	0	0	0	0	0	0	0	0	0	0	0	7	0	3
1921	1923	1	0	0	0	0	0	0	0	0	0	0	0	0	0	0	1	0	0
1904	1904	2	0	0	0	0	0	0	0	0	0	0	0	0	0	0	2	0	0
2006	2009	49	10	6	0	0	0	0	2	0	0	1	0	0	0	0	49	13	6
1932	1934	49	0	25	0	0	0	3	0	1	0	0	0	0	0	0	52	0	26
1973	1974	24	6	1	0	0	0	4	0	0	3	0	0	3	1	0	34	7	1
1911	1913	13	0	2	0	0	0	2	0	0	0	0	0	0	0	0	15	0	2
1914	1926	50	0	0	0	0	0	6	0	0	0	0	0	0	0	0	56	0	0
2009	2011	11	36	4	0	0	0	1	0	0	1	1	0	0	0	0	13	37	4
1997	1998	0	0	0	0	0	0	0	0	0	2	0	0	0	0	0	2	0	0

Roll of Honour

Sir Bob Murray CBE
James Murray
Daniel Ethan Hourigan
Michael Gibson
Jamie Stirling Gibson
Bill Rowan Scott
Emma McGlinchey
Chris Groves
Jack Ryan Brown
Brian Robert Willey
Davey Brown
Kieron Green
Eric Nicholson
Mark Strong
Harry Joe McBeth
Peter Lynn
Ken Dixon
Craig Coates
Trevor William Selvey
Niall MacSweeney
John Hellens
Neil Milner
Malcolm Lindsey
Samantha Hillock
Stan Sharp
Simon Curle
Mark Lawson

ROLL OF HONOUR

Keith Shotton
Alan Ingram
Stephen Ingram
Chris Lindstedt
Glenn Steel
Sean Carr
Michael Lister
Russell Dunbar
Alan Howard Craggs
Michael Hunt
Jonathan Donnelly
Richard Ingman
David Oliver
Benjamin J. Maughan
Gary Soulsby
Robert Defty
Steven Archibold
Elliott Withers
Roy Dobson
Andrew J. Russell
Hazel Scott
Jim Elsdon
Roy Mills
John Dorrian
Andi Musk
Bob Green Whitby
Martin David Halcrow
David Soulsby
Craig Musk
Gary Musk
John Musk

Andrew Browell
Garry Purcell
Sel of South Shields
Conny Johanson
Gareth Hern
Mike Love (SENSSA)
Scott J. Bentley
Josh Bailey
Dick, Adrian, John Longstaff
Peter Hutchinson
Steve Ballinger
Jonas Varty
Michael Hill
Jimmy Watson
Jonathan Sager
Nick Hughes
Dave Harby. Bakewell
Paul Woodman
Michael Woodman
John Temple
David John Cox
Andrew Holland
Keith Goodwin
Barrie Richardson
J. L. Spears
Keith Charlton
Reuben Milner
Alan Scott
Richard Russo
Jeff Porter
Allan Gormley

ROLL OF HONOUR

Mal Patterson
Nigel Hugill
Glenn Hugill
Rex Hugill
Stuart Green
Colin Chapman
Alan Wood
Dale Coulthard
Ian D. Mills
Freda Robson
Andrew Clark
Dennis Crown
Benjamin Eckford
Paul Morrison
John C. Anderson
Diane Dimmock
Ron Scott
Rhoda Francombe
John Clancy
David Hetherington
Graeme Anderson
George A. McCarthy
Marc Holliday
Ian Powell
Lelanie Mattsson
John Hardy
Andrew Cockburn
Bryan Gilliland - Belfast
David Crombie
Bob Routledge
Glyn Taylor

W. K. Robinson
Simon York
Colin Dobson
Ivor Hunt
Christopher Nevin
Jon Stokoe, Whitby
Joshua James Brown
Ian Charles Butchart
Nicholas James Butchart
Richard William Butchart
Stuart Paul
Colin John Clark
Ian Blakey
John Carney
John H. Broderick
Stacey Williams
Alex Mclaughlin
Maureen Lee
Patricia Duncan
David Dixon
Janet Williams
Alan Morrison
Alan Reeks
Jack Attley
Wayne Iddon
David Warnaby
Keith Blencowe
David Ratcliffe
The Lynn Family
Jack Clark
Phil Sayers

ROLL OF HONOUR

Thomas Stronach Dodsworth
Bill Storey
David Enerson
Ted Ellis
Brian Hutchinson Greenlay
Roger Max
John Hays
Steven White
James Max Alex Ellie Stokoe
Harry Garrick
Paul Napier
Michael Jordan mjm
Margaret Rimonti
Jimmy Cairns
Jack Horrocks
Ste Gilmore (Sedgefield)
Ben Minchell
Alan Barber
Alan Fenwick
John Butler Jarrow
Jonathan Lowes
Derek Lowes
Brian Liddle
Tracy Atherton 1964-2012
David Reed
Chris Davis
Tom Davis
Gordon L. Smith
Gregory G. Smith
Adam David Theaker
Paul Jennings

Happy Father's Day - Love Andy
Stephen Coggon
Danilo 'Dan' Ronzani - Bologna
James Richard Hindmarch
John Davison
Robert Dixon
Rob Harding
Derek Edward Griffin
Brian T. Graham
Paul Williamson
Katie Williamson
Richard J. Freeman
Vincent & Carolyn Smith
Paul & Catherine Smith Hem
Jane Ivan Rachel Wigham
Gary Pickering
Philip Coulson
James Edward Thornhill
George Cook
Paul Willis
Joshua Michael Parkin
Simon & Sharon Lewis
Steven Meikle
Jordan Davison
Derek Grierson
Stuart Poole
John Docherty
Caitlin Marie McIlwraith
Richard L. Sowerby
Andrew Briggs
David Dimond

ROLL OF HONOUR

Paul Lovstad
Dave Clark
Graeme O'Keefe
Dave Brack
Alisdair Haydon Wood
Kenneth Marjoram
Stephen John Corner
Harry Cowen
Matthew Baldridge
Joanne Kumar
Michael Brett
John Stokes
Anthony Blacker
Steve Caron
James Caron
Matthew Caron
Daniel Caron
Keith Orchard
John Graham
Bryan Morrison
Colin Stuthard
Iain McLay
John Ross
Clive Booth
Graham Laverick
Martin Lancaster
Karl Whatmore
Philip Smith
William W. Robertshaw
Alan Shinkfield